The Golf Guide

KUPERARD

Where to play, Where to stay

Photos from: Cleobury Mortimer Golf Club, Shropshire · Monmouth Golf Club, Monmouth · Royal Dornoch Golf Club, Sutherland

Over 2800 courses and hundreds of hotels throughout Britain and Ireland including a selection in holiday areas abroad
PLUS Golf Tours
and Products Section

Contents page 3

2006

The Golf Guide 2006

© FHG Guides Ltd, 2006
ISBN 1 85055 375 0

Maps: ©MAPS IN MINUTES™ 2005. ©Crown Copyright, Ordnance Survey 2005.

Typeset by FHG Guides Ltd, Paisley.
Printed and bound in Singapore by Imago.

Distribution. Book Trade: ORCA Book Services, Stanley House,
3 Fleets Lane, Poole, Dorset BH15 3AJ
(Tel: 01202 665432; Fax: 01202 666219)
e-mail: mail@orcabookservices.co.uk
Published by FHG Guides Ltd., Abbey Mill Business Centre,
Seedhill, Paisley PA1 1TJ (Tel: 0141-887 0428 Fax: 0141-889 7204).
e-mail: admin@fhguides.co.uk

The Golf Guide, Where to Play, Where to Stay is published by FHG Guides Ltd,
part of Kuperard Group.

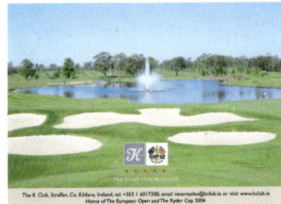

Cover design: FHG Guides
Cover Picture: courtesy of The K Club, Co. Kildare, Ireland

Acknowledgements

The Publishers wish to acknowledge the assistance of Jane Carter of GOLF MONTHLY and The Professional Golfers' Association regional golfing correspondents in the preparation of this 29th edition of **THE GOLF GUIDE : Where To Play • Where To Stay.**

For colour photographs we wish to thank Jane Carter (p4), Peter Godsiff for Bowood Park Hotel & Golf Course (p9), Thornbury Golf Centre (p18), and Burnham & Berrow Golf Club (p19), Wentworth Golf Club (p21), Alderney Golf Club (p23), John Smith for Bishops Stortford Golf Club (p27), Draycote Hotel & Whitefields Golf Course (p30), Jennifer Prentice for De Vere Bolton Woods (p34), Seaton Carew Golf Club (p36), Bingley St Ives Golf Club (p41), Builth Wells Golf Club (p44, 51), Cottrell Park Golf Club (p55), Jedburgh Golf Club (p56), Killarney Golf & Fishing Club (p78), Bowood Park Hotel & Golf Course (p153), Trevose Golf & Country Club (p160), The Dorset Golf & Country Club (p183), Tewkesbury Park Hotel, Golf & Country Club (p202), The Shropshire (p291), Royal Dornoch Golf Club (p371), Monmouth Golf Club (p453), Doonbeg Golf Club (p487), Michael Gedye for Château des Sept Tours (p99), Victoria Clube de Golfe (p101), Club de Golf Alcanada (p 103, 104, 571), Pelican's Nest Golf Club (p105), Santiburi Samui Golf Club (p106, 107, 108), Seignosse Golf Club (p544), Quinta da Ria Golf Club (p559), Palm Springs (p575), and Natural Park Resort, Chonburi (p583).

We wish to thank all our advertisers and, finally, the Club Secretaries, Professionals and others who have co-operated in the annual updating of the golf club directory entries which are the essential ingredients of **THE GOLF GUIDE : Where To Play • Where To Stay.**

Contents

Golfing Around Britain: How to Use THE GOLF GUIDE	7 / 114
Foreword: *Jane Carter* (Golf Monthly)	4
Golf in the West Country *Peter Godsiff*	9
Golf in the South *Peter Ward*	21
Golf in the East *John H. Smith*	27
Golf in the Midlands *Jennifer Prentice*	30
Golf in the North *David Birtill*	36
Golf in Wales *Chris Smart*	44
Golf in Scotland *Nick Rodger*	56
Golf in Ireland *Tony McGee*	78
Holiday Golf in France *Michael Gedye*	99
Holiday Golf in Portugal *Michael Gedye*	101
Holiday Golf in Spain *Michael Gedye*	103
Holiday Golf in the USA *Michael Gedye*	105
Holiday Golf in Thailand *Michael Gedye*	107
Golf Events 2006	117

Clubs and Courses

ENGLAND	123
SCOTLAND	371
WALES	453
IRELAND	487
THE ISLE OF MAN	539
CHANNEL ISLANDS	541
FRANCE	543
PORTUGAL	556
SPAIN and MAJORCA	565
USA	572
SOUTH AFRICA	577
DUBAI	578
THAILAND	579
Driving Ranges	586
Index of Clubs and Courses	609
Index of Advertisers/Hotels	648
Golf Tours & Golfing Products	109/113

The Golf Guide
Where to Play Where to Stay
2006

Foreword

**by Jane Carter
Editor of**

The year 2005 saw The Open return to the home of golf, St Andrews with an emotional farewell to one of the greatest golfers ever, Jack Nicklaus. It also saw a return to form of the world number one, Tiger Woods, whose performance resulted in Colin Montgomery being edged out again from that elusive Major trophy.

2006 looks like being another exciting year, with the highlight Europ's defence of the Ryder Cup in September at the K Club. There will be a 'New Venue' for the Open as it returns to Royal Liverpool for the first time since 'Hoylake' was lengthened and upgraded after the 1967 Open was staged there, won by Roberto de Vicenzo.

The massive media and television coverage these and other events continue to receive encourages newcomers to take up the game and former players to dust off their clubs. For the newly converted and regular golfers alike, there can be no better companion to the game than **The Golf Guide.**

It continues to provide comprehensive details of almost 3000 courses along with information on accommodation where golfers and their families can enjoy their golf and then relax in comfort.

Using this guide to discover areas of the country new to you and courses of different types and challenges is something no golfer should miss. Make sure you get the greatest possible enjoyment out of this marvellous game and remember to take your copy of **The Golf Guide** with you on your travels.

WHEREVER YOU'RE PLAYING

PICK UP A GUIDE MAP
TO WHAT'S BEST IN THE AREA

From all leading
Tourist Information Centres
or with the compliments of
participating hotels & golf clubs

TOURIST PUBLICATIONS
5 Eglinton Crescent, Edinburgh EH12 5DH.
Tel: 0131 225 4547. Fax: 0131 220 6789.

Golfing around Britain and Abroad

Where to Play and Where to Stay around the Golfing Regions

As anyone trying to book a space on a popular course will confirm, Golf is an increasingly popular game, not only with regular players - who are on the course every weekend come rain, hail, snow and the occasional sunshine - but also with the many who class themselves as 'Casual' golfers. These are not members of a club but play the game when on holiday, on business or simply when time permits.

Fortunately **The Golf Guide, Where to Play • Where to Stay** caters for every golfer and gives us all a chance to try out different courses and stay in the best of accommodation.

We hope the layout makes finding the courses you are interested in as easy as possible. With detailed indexes at the back of the guide it should be possible to find any of the almost 3000 courses featured in this, the most comprehensive of guides.

You may also choose to read about an area in one of the articles supplied by the PGA professionals at the front of the guide. These give a summary of what is happening in the area and highlight some of the accommodation and courses to give you a brief idea of what is available. To make this section as easy as possible to follow we have worked from the very South of the country, from the West Country to the Southern Region, following on to the East then Midlands, up to Northern England and following that with the countries of Wales, Scotland and Ireland. We finish with a selection of foreign courses in the most popular tourist destinations.

The main section of the guide consists of the detailed descriptions of the courses, all running in alphabetical order of towns within counties, within countries.

I hope that this guide gives you not only a lot of information but also a lot of pleasure as you use it during the year 2006, which looks like being another interesting year for golf enthusiasts. The Ryder Cup, always exciting viewing, comes back to Europe and is held at the K Club in Ireland. Europe has a lot to live up to, having won convincingly in 2004, but the USA team will be all out for revenge. The Open moves to Royal Liverpool ('Hoylake') in July when Tiger Woods will defend his title, but all of the UK will be hoping the time has come again for a 'Home' victory – something we have not had since Paul Lawrie in 1999 at Carnoustie.

No matter where you go in the UK or abroad, remember to take your copy of **The Golf Guide** with you and we would appreciate it if you could mention the guide when you contact Courses or Accommodation.

Golfing National Regions

Golf in the West

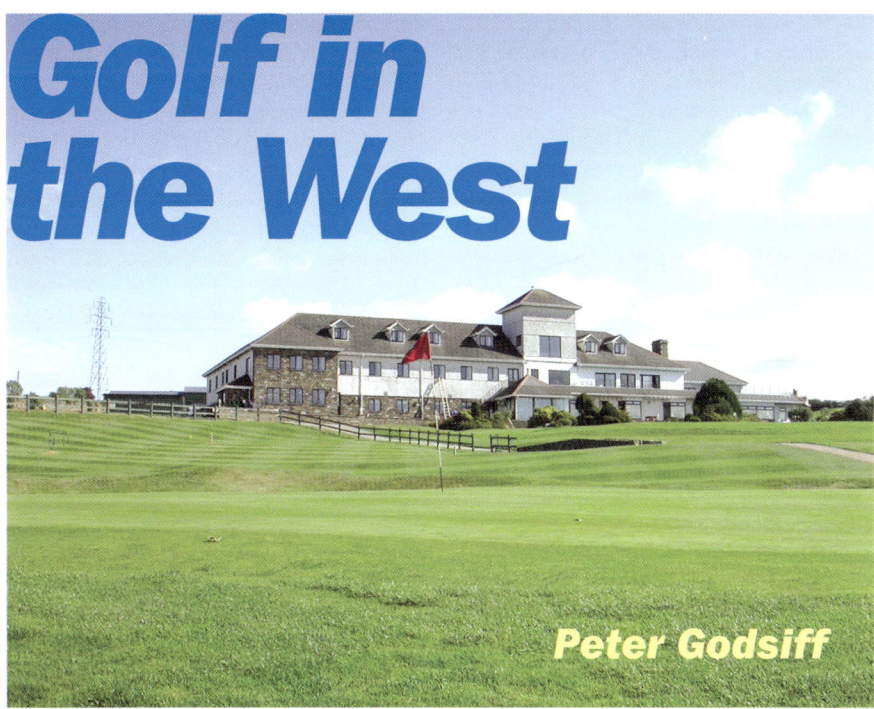

Peter Godsiff

The 18th hole at Bowood Park Hotel & Golf Course, Lanteglos, North Cornwall.

Stick a pin in the map of the West Country and there is certain to be a golf course catering for club or social golfers wishing to combine sun, surf and relaxation during a well earned holiday.

From the Cotswolds in the north to Wiltshire and Dorset in the east, and the rich golfing counties of Somerset, Devon and Cornwall to the southwest, around 300 courses beckon.

A travelling golfer could spend two dozen holidays sampling different areas and still yearn to play on dozens more links, parkland, heathland and downland courses that offer such a rich variety.

The combination of ancient monuments, important historic buildings, man-made holiday attractions for all the family, breathtaking countryside, quaint villages and towns and, of course, miles of sandy seashore and safe bathing makes the West perhaps the finest holiday destination in Britain.

Most knowledgeable golfers will be able to reel off the names of the West's championship courses. The historic links at Burnham and Berrow, St Enodoc in North Cornwall, Devon gems Saunton and Royal North Devon at Westward Ho! are all regular championship venues. They all feature on the must-play list for low handicappers.

But the region is so stimulating, where is the best place to start? Travellers from the north would appreciate the Gloucestershire hotel courses at Tewkesbury Park, the Ramada attached to Gloucester Golf Club, and the Hilton Puckrup Hall where the West Region PGA championship was played for many years.

Puckrup Hall now boasts a classic golf course measuring 6,431 yards and the number of bunkers certainly encourages play from sand.

The Ramada complex is probably more famous for its dry-ski slope visible from the M5 motorway. But the 107-bedroomed hotel and golf course in 200 acres of parkland, plus a par-three layout, offer good value.

A newish venue is Thornbury Golf Centre, again on the way west just outside Bristol, with affordable accommodation and a maturing golf course.

From the east, Lord Lansdowne's impressive Bowood course (and magnificent house) is a convenient stopover. Queenswood House, in the centre of the course, can be hired for breaks or special occasions. Wrag Barn, on the outskirts of Swindon, is another attractive venue.

Bath and Bristol, the hub of the West, offer a plentiful selection of courses. On into Somerset, Worlebury, perched high above the Bristol Channel at Weston-super-Mare, offers a challenge. Worlebury and the Weston-super-Mare clubs combine for an autumn golf festival that attracts many visitors.

Although Burnham is the premier Somerset course, the central area is well served by Wells, Taunton Vale, Mendip and the vastly improved Farrington club.

The Bournemouth-Poole area is Dorset's golf centre. As one of the favoured holiday destinations, hotels are in abundance. So are golf courses, from the long-established Ferndown, Parkstone and Broadstone, felt by many to be the best in the county, to probably the best two publicly-owned (but now privately-run) courses in the country, at Meyrick Park and Queens Park, where a round costs around £15.

There are further delights at Lyme Regis, Came Down, Weymouth and, across the Devon border at Axe Cliff, Sidmouth, the exquisite East Devon links at Budleigh Salterton and the expanding complex at Woodbury Park. Nigel Mansell became the owner in 1994 and has since

ST MELLION GOLF BREAKS offer

- Stunning Golf Course locations at or near St Mellion
- Inclusive golf packages from only £305 for two people or less than £100 for six or more in top quality accommodation
- Free pool and gym membership at St Mellion • Societies of up to 30 welcome.

We have the widest and best selection of self-catering golf breaks in and around the beautiful courses at St Mellion SE Cornwall.

OAKRIDGE COTTAGES are modern, centrally heated, two and three-bedroom stone detached houses with superb golf course views. Alternatively just two miles up the road, TREHILL COTTAGES offer relaxing lakeside accommodation in a peaceful countryside setting. There are seven cottages ranging from a one-bedroom detached cottage with its own Aga to a huge six-bedroom cottage perfect for a large golfing party.

All our golf breaks include free golf at St Mellion so two people can play these great championship courses for as little as £305 per week all inclusive.

Call us on 01579 383917 or e-mail info@stmelliongolfbreaks.co.uk   www.stmelliongolfbreaks.co.uk

HARBOUR HOLIDAYS

Quality self catering accommodation in the picturesque harbour town of Padstow and the beautiful bays surrounding.

www.harbourholidays.co.uk

tel: 01841 533402 fax: 01841 533115

e-mail: contact@harbourholidays.co.uk

Coastal and Rural Self Catering Accommodation

Trevose Golf and Country Club

- Championship Golf Course of 18 holes. 6863 yards, S.S.S.71
- 2 x 9 hole courses. One 3100 yds, par 35, the other 1369 yds par 29.
- Excellently appointed Club House with Bar and Restaurant providing à la carte catering facilities.
- Superior accommodation in 7 Chalets, 6 Bungalows, 11 Flats, 7 Dormy flats and 4 cabins. Daily rates available.
- 3 Hard Tennis Courts.
- Heated Swimming Pool open from mid May to mid September.
- Extensive Pro Shop and boutique
- Six glorious sandy bays within about a mile of the Club House, with pools, open sea and surf bathing. Lovely coastline for walking.
- Convenient for shops.
- 8 miles from Civil Airport. Daily flights to and from London Gatwick & Stansted.
- Head Professional Peter Green • Open all year • Societies welcome

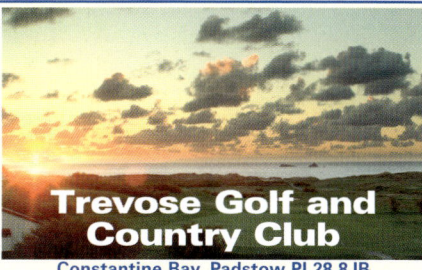

Constantine Bay, Padstow PL28 8JB
Tel: 01841 520208 • Fax: 01841 521057
e-mail: info@trevose-gc.co.uk
www.trevose-gc.co.uk

LOSTWITHIEL HOTEL, GOLF AND COUNTRY CLUB
Lower Polscoe, Lostwithiel, Cornwall PL22 0HQ
Tel: 01208 873550 • Fax: 01208 873479
e-mail: reception@golf-hotel.co.uk • website: www.golf-hotel.co.uk

Close to the Eden Project

This fine hotel and country club complex has been created from a cluster of old, mellow stone buildings. Amidst 150 acres of undulating, verdant countryside, the accommodation, cuisine and leisure facilities are truly outstanding. One may dine in style in the Black Prince Restaurant where imaginative dishes are made even more acceptable by the happy ambience of the place. Recreational diversions include a superb, 18-hole golf course with a floodlit driving range, indoor heated swimming pool, two all-weather tennis courts and gymnasium. Peaceful repose is assured by spacious and luxuriously appointed guest rooms, each one a haven of comfort. RAC ★★★.

developed it into an opulent hotel and leisure centre. It has hosted the Sunseeker Nigel Mansell Classic on the European Seniors' Tour for the past three years.

Further round the coast, the Torquay area, like Bournemouth, is an all-the-year-round destination with a balmy climate and refreshing sea breezes.

Dartmouth Golf and Country Club, which also has excellent self-catering and hotel accommodation, is a 27-hole complex offering attractive stay-and-play packages.

Further inland, a hotel was constructed last year at Padbrook Park at Cullompton while Elfordleigh, near Plymouth, has expanded into a favourite hotel, golf and leisure resort. The Manor House and Ashbury hotels at Okehampton offer great value all-the-year-round packages. There are more than enough alternative activities to keep non-golfing family members and children fully occupied.

Colebrook, Plympton, Plymouth, Devon PL7 5EB

Tel: 01752 336428
Fax: 01752 344581
e-mail: reception@elfordleigh.co.uk
website: www.elfordleigh.co.uk

Elfordleigh offers the peace, calm & tranquillity of an English Country House, to a privately owned hotel with an atmosphere of warmth, ease & charm. The acres of glorious parkland perfectly positioned for exploring the timeless elegance of Devon, yet only minutes away from the heart of Plymouth. Whether on business or taking a short break you are welcome at Elfordleigh. Only 7 miles from the centre of Plymouth and within easy reach of the sea and Dartmoor. Plymouth is on the main intercity rail network, airlink to London and totally accessible by main road links and ferry port serving connections between France, Spain and the UK.

The beauty which surrounds Elfordleigh influences the character of the hotel & its rooms. Bedrooms are light and airy with spacious bathrooms and splendid views of the green tranquillity of the golf course & beyond.

Churchill's Restaurant offers good food, excellent wines, outstanding service, exquisite conservatory, wonderful location – *need we say more!* With our growing reputation, it is advisable to book before coming. Civil wedding ceremonies are also on offer.

Our country bar serves bar meals and light snacks throughout the day and evening to cater for an impromptu visit.

- Squash Court
- Two Spas
- Sauna
- Steam Room
- Swimming Pool
- Separate Children's Pool
- Fully Equipped Gym
- Large Sun Terrace & BBQ area
- Dance Studio
- Three Tennis Courts
- Solarium
- Beauty Therapy
- Hairdresser
- Jogging Track

All this from under £1 per day.

One of the special features of Elfordleigh is our 18-hole golf course. Although the course is the home of a thriving members community it is also open to visiting golfers and hotel residents. Elfordleigh offers residential golfing breaks, society day packages (available from £20) and the unique opportunity to play golf – whatever the weather – through the smart golf indoor golf simulator, with over 33 world famous courses to choose from.

In addition we also offer practice facilities and expert tuition from PGA golf professional Scott Macaskill.

ELFORDLEIGH OFFERS A CHARMING WAY TO COMBINE BUSINESS WITH PLEASURE

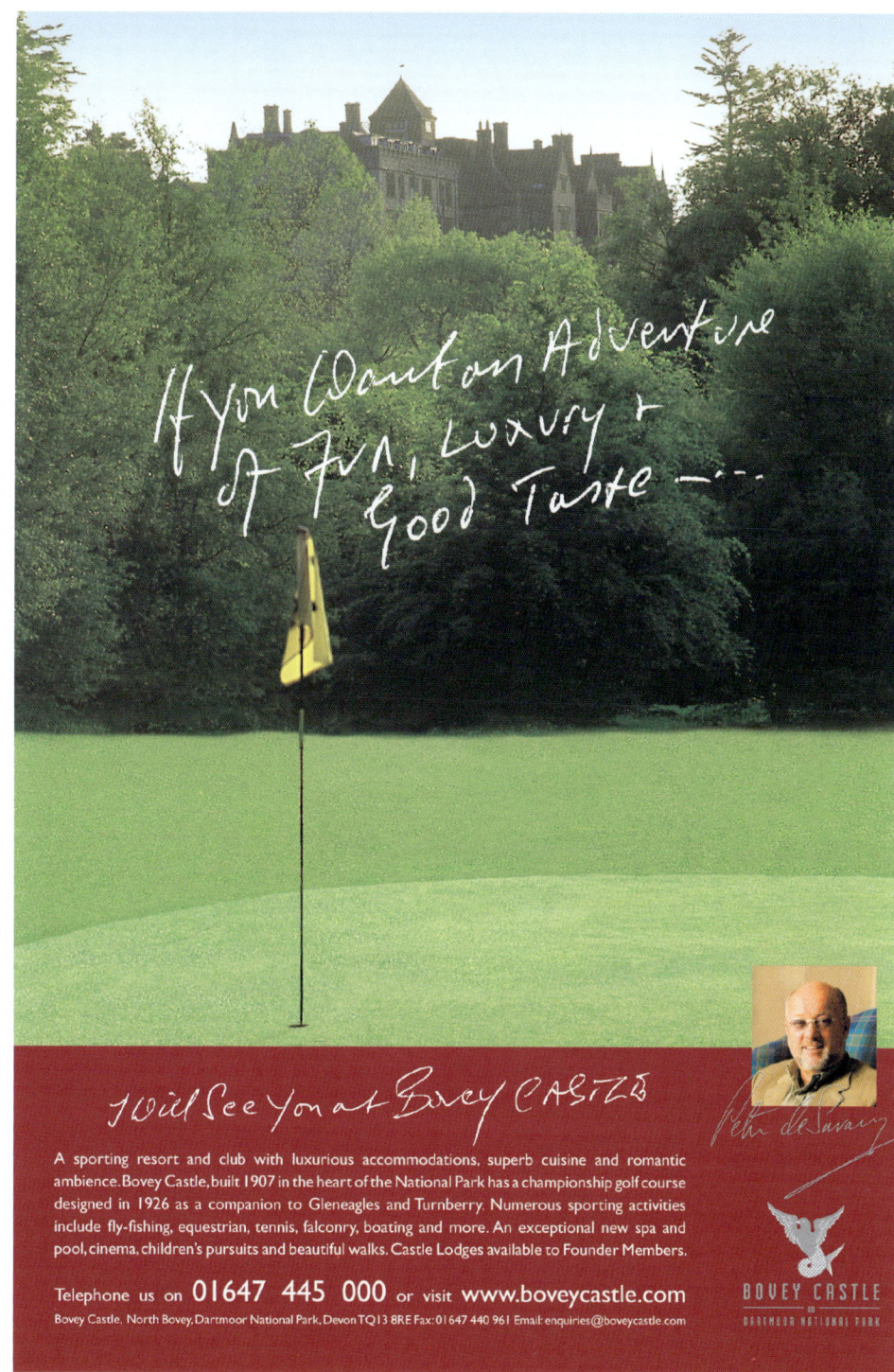

FREE GOLF ALL YEAR ROUND

27 Holes of Free Golf per night of stay
18-hole 'Oakwood' 5374 yards, Par 68
18-hole 'Pines' 5628 yards, Par 69
18-hole 'Beeches' 5351 yards, Par 68
18-hole 'Willows' Par 3 course
Buggy Roads — Buggies All Year

8-Bay Covered Range,
Practice Area, Putting Green
Golf Coaching

Golf Shop — Club and Trolley Hire
Club Locker and Drying Room

INDOOR SPORT – Bowls, Tennis, Badminton, Squash, Table Tennis, 10-Pin, Snooker – FREE

OUTDOOR SPORT – Tennis, Bowls, Pitch & Putt, Guided Walks, Crazy Golf – FREE

LEISURE – Pools, Spas, Saunas, Steam Room – FREE

CRAFT CENTRE – Pottery + 9 Tutored Crafts, including Picture Framing, Glass Engraving, Candle Making, & Enamelling – prices at cost

Available to Residents of Both Hotels

Buggy Prices £6 – £12

March	3 nts	£164/£179	4 nts	£183/£200
Mid May	3 nts	£201/£209	4 nts	£241/£250
June–mid July	3 nts	£198/£206	4 nts	£237/£247
August	3 nts	£208/£238	4 nts	£281/£318
September	3 nts	£214/£222	4 nts	£257/£268

Price per Person

All rooms en suite, TV/Video, Tea/Coffee facilities, Safe (F.O.C.) and telephone.

Full Board, Party Discounts, Bargain Breaks

Manor House & Ashbury Hotels, Okehampton, Devon EX20 4NA
Freephone 0800 781 9635
www.ashburygolfhotel.co.uk www.manorhousehotel.co.uk

3 x 18 Hole Long Courses
18-hole Par 3 • Range • Golf Buggies

There are hotel and golf course packages available in every area. Cornwall is especially rich for choice. Bude, a part-links, part-parkland course, ties in with most of the hotels to provide great value deals for golfers.

Trethorne on the Devon-North Cornwall border would be a suitable place to start a Cornish holiday. The course has improved immeasurably and accommodation is available in lodges.

The next stop is the impressive Bowood Park course at Camelford that is now well served with a new hotel. St Mellion in South Cornwall, over the Tamar Bridge from Plymouth, is perhaps the most famous resort in the county offering every type of accommodation to complement two excellent courses. The Jack Nicklaus championship course used to stage the Benson and Hedges International tournament on the European Tour.

Back on the north side, Trevose is perhaps the favourite stay-and-play complex of flats, cottages and hotel rooms in Cornwall, where the 18-hole course is augmented by nine further holes and a par-three track.

Each of the 300 courses in South West England has its own individual charm and a warm welcome for visitors.

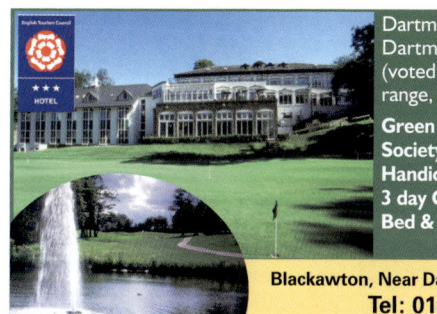

Dartmouth Golf & Country Club, situated just 5 miles from Dartmouth, offers great facilities: a 27 hole golf course (voted within the top 80 courses in Great Britain), driving range, health and leisure club, plus 35 en suite bedrooms.

Green Fees: from £35.
Society groups and visitors welcome daily.
Handicap not required. Buggies available.
3 day Golf Breaks from £110pp.
Bed & Breakfast from £40pp.

Blackawton, Near Dartmouth, Devon TQ9 7DE
Tel: 01803 712686
Website: www.dgcc.co.uk

DARTMOUTH GOLF & COUNTRY CLUB

CHARLTON KINGS HOTEL & RESTAURANT

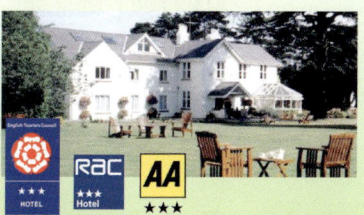

Privately owned with high standards throughout.

All rooms have en suite facilities, most have views of the Cotswold hills, and ample car parking is available. Ideally located for Cheltenham and the Cotswolds. Only 2 miles from town centre, 3 miles from racecourse. The choice is yours, whether you want the ideal base for visiting the numerous picturesque towns, villages and places of interest, or prefer the wide choice of shops and theatres, or to relax in the magnificent gardens in Cheltenham.

**London Road, Charlton Kings,
Cheltenham, Gloucestershire GL52 6UU**
Tel: 01242 231061 • Fax: 01242 241900
www.charltonkingshotel.co.uk
e-mail: enquiries@charltonkingshotel.co.uk
Condé Nast Johansens Recommended

Visit the FHG website
www.holidayguides.com
for details of the wide choice of accommodation featured in the full range of FHG titles

WEST

The Golf Guide 2006

GLOUCESTER RAMADA HOTEL and GOLF RESORT

- Set on the edge of the Cotswolds, commanding spectacular views
- Outstanding 18 Hole, par 72 championship course
- Challenging 9 Hole par 3 Golf Course, ideal for beginners and improvers
- Covered 12 Bay Golf Academy and Callaway fitting centre, open all day
- Home of the Gloucester Golf Academy, with a team of 1st Class PGA Professionals
- Professional presented grass practice area, with putting/chipping/pitching and bunker areas for you to improve the scoring side of your game
- Well stocked golf shop, Callaway, Taylormade, Ping and all other top brands
- Fully equipped clubhouse with spike bar, restaurant, and function facilities for small or large groups
- Private and Group Coaching available 7 days a week, using the V1 Golf analysis programme
- 107 bedroom Hotel with 5 suites
- Conference Centre with restaurants and bars
- Fully equipped leisure area, including indoor swimming pool, sauna, solarium, gym with qualified instructors
- Gloucester ski centre, two great slopes, ski school with qualified instructors

BOOK NOW FOR A BREAK TO REMEMBER   CALL NOW 01452 411731 or 01452 525653

E-mail: gloucester@btopenworld.com   www.gloucestergolf.com

Tewkesbury Park Hotel Golf & Country Club
Lincoln Green Lane
Tewkesbury
Gloucestershire GL20 7DN

Tewkesbury Park's scenic 18 hole, 6533 yard, par 73 course offers challenging play for both professional and amateur golfers. Designed by Frank Pennink, the course offers many interesting and testing holes, with wooded areas and water hazards early in the round opening up onto spacious fairways on the back nine holes of the undulating course.

Overlooking the Malvern Hills and the Gloucestershire Countryside, this picturesque course also offers six covered driving bays, putting and chipping greens and a 6 hole pitch and putt course.

Tel: 0870 609 6101 • 01684 295405
Fax: 01684 292386
E-mail: tewkesburypark@corushotels.com
www.tewkesburyparkgolfclub.co.uk

The Golf Guide 2006WEST

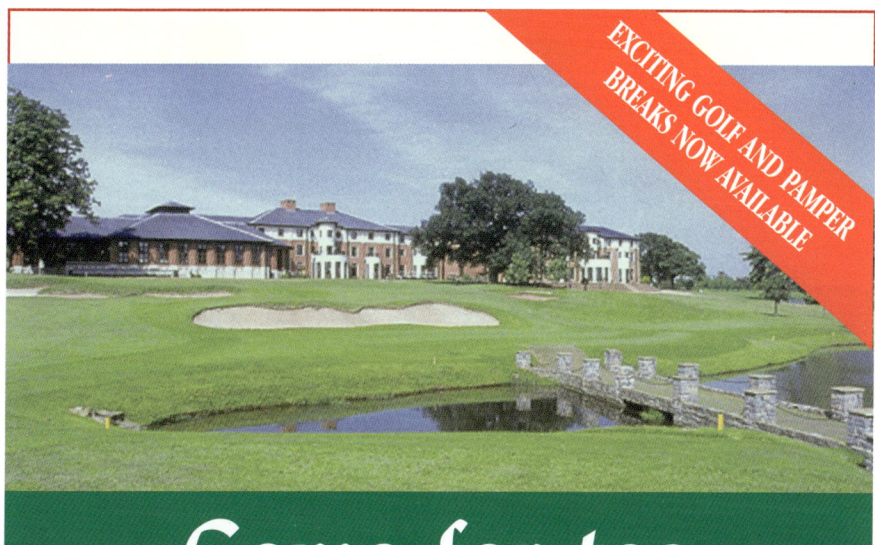

EXCITING GOLF AND PAMPER BREAKS NOW AVAILABLE

Come for tee

Do you live, breathe, eat and sleep golf? If so, we have the hotel for you.

Set in 140 acres of beautiful parkland between the Cotswolds and the Malverns, the four star Hilton Puckrup Hall has so much to enjoy, including 112 luxury bedrooms, conference facilities, a fully equipped health and leisure club, and a sumptuous restaurant, that you'll be forgiven for hardly venturing outside. That is until you see our 6219 yard, par 70 Championship Golf Course.

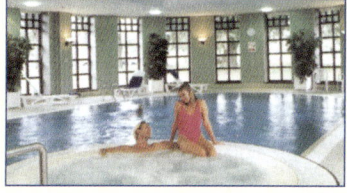

With mature trees and water hazards, and set in the lea of the Malverns, the course presents an exciting golf challenge for both the experienced and the novice golfer. Visitors are very welcome, with Green Fees starting at £25 per round weekdays, £30 for the day, and just £5 more at weekends. Society and Corporate packages start from £40.

So if you'd like the happy dilemma of the perfect golf hotel and the perfect golf course, you know where to come. For details of golf membership, to make a tee reservation, or to enquire about an appointment to view all this hotel has to offer, telephone:
01684 296200

Hilton
PUCKRUP HALL
Tewkesbury
Gloucestershire GL20 6EL
Tel 01684 296200 Fax 01684 850788
www.tewkesbury.hilton.com

WEST   **The Golf Guide 2006**

The 18th at Thornbury Golf Centre, Bristol

WHEN IN BRISTOL COME AND STAY WITH US

11 bedrooms, all en suite • Satellite TV in each room
Bar & Restaurant open all day
36 holes of Golf • 25 Bay Driving Range
Stay and Play Deals available on request

Call: 01454 281144

Thornbury Golf Centre, Bristol Road, Thornbury, Bristol BS35 3XL
www.thornburygc.co.uk
Located just 10 minutes from Junction 16 of the M5 on the A38

Room prices start from £49.50 per room per night.
Weekend rate £45 room only

AA ★★

please note

All the information in this book is given in good faith in the belief that it is correct. However, the publishers cannot guarantee the facts given in these pages, neither are they responsible for changes in policy, ownership or terms that may take place after the date of going to press. Readers should always satisfy themselves that the facilities they require are available and that the terms, if quoted, still apply.

Wells (Somerset) Golf Club

East Horrington Road, Wells,
Somerset BA5 3DS
Tel: 01749 675005 Fax: 01749 683170
e-mail: secretary@wellsgolfclub99.freeserve.co.uk

- Visitors and Societies very welcome
- 18-hole Par 70 course
- 12-bay floodlit driving range open to the public
- Buggies available for hire
- Trolleys allowed all winter

www.wellsgolfclub.co.uk

When in Somerset...

treat yourself to a stay at the Burnham & Berrow Golf Club. Championship Links golf course and accommodation at the Dormy House from £85 per night inc. Breakfast and Green Fees. Winter rate £50 per night Sundays to Thursdays.

**Burnham & Berrow Golf Club, St Christopher's Way,
Burnham on Sea TA8 2PE • Tel: 01278 785760 • Fax: 01278 795440**
e-mail: secretary@burnhamandberrowgolfclub.co.uk • www.burnhamandberrowgolfclub.co.uk

The 18th hole at Burnham & Berrow Golf Club, Burnham-on-Sea, Somerset

WEST										The Golf Guide 2006

TAUNTON VALE GOLF CLUB
Creech Heathfield, Taunton, Somerset TA3 5EY

Taunton Vale Golf Club is probably the most accessible club in the county, little more than a 5-minute drive from Junctions 24 or 25 of the M5. It comprises 27 holes of parkland course set amidst the gently rolling Somerset countryside. The Club has a 10-bay floodlit driving range, a fully stocked Pro Shop, and an excellent clubhouse offering a variety of menus. Societies are most welcome, with a package to suit all from small groups to large corporate events.

**For more details contact 01823 412220 or e-mail: tvgc@easynet.co.uk
website: www.tauntonvalegolf.co.uk**

BOWOOD GOLF & COUNTRY CLUB

Set in the heart of 'Capability' Brown's Great Park and the magnificent 2,000 acre estate of Bowood House & Gardens

The Region's finest Corporate & Society Golf Venue

- Beautifully manicured Championship Golf Course
- Expert advice by friendly hospitality staff
- PGA qualified Professional Golf Team
- Superb Clubhouse facilities with excellent cuisine
- Unique luxury accommodation in centre of course
- Visitors welcome • Signposted from M4 Junction 17

**Bowood Golf & Country Club, Derry Hill, Calne, Wiltshire SN11 9PQ
www.bowood.org
golfclub@bowood.org • Tel: 01249 822228**

WRAG BARN Golf & Country Club

**Shrivenham Road, Highworth, Swindon, Wiltshire SN6 7QQ
Telephone: 01793 861327 • Fax: 01793 861325
Professional Shop: 01793 766027**

Challenging Par 72 of 6633 yards. Friendly and welcoming. Corporate, Conference and Society Days a speciality. Golf clinic, scoring analysis, full conference facilities on request.

"THE PERFECT GOLF SOCIETY VENUE" Traditional style clubhouse with shop, locker rooms and the Spike Bar open all day for food and drink. Our Banbury and Bellingham Suite facilities offer an unrivalled combination of superb food and the perfect setting adaptable for any style of event. Our location is perfect. The Thames Valley is just 6 miles north of Swindon and only ten minutes from Junction 15 of the M4.

Set in the Vale of the White Horse, the views of the Wiltshire Countryside around the course are truly superb. For a successful and memorable occasion plan your next golf day at Wrag Barn Golf Club.

WRAG BARN

Publisher's note

While every effort is made to ensure accuracy, we regret that FHG Guides cannot accept responsibility for errors, misrepresentations or omissions in our entries or any consequences thereof. Prices in particular should be checked. We will follow up complaints but cannot act as arbiters or agents for either party.

Peter Ward

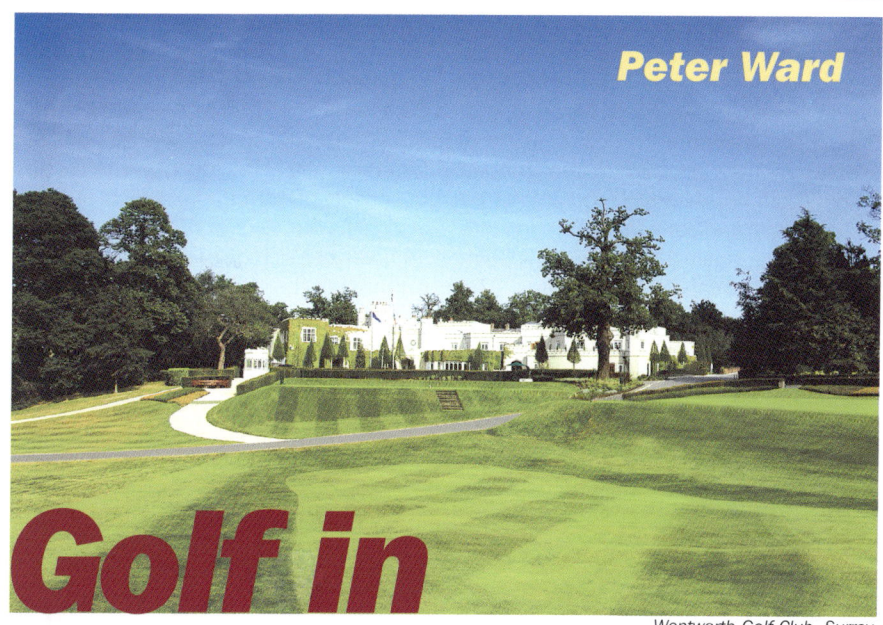

Wentworth Golf Club, Surrey

Golf in the South

The game of golf is growing in popularity week by week, and the opportunity to play courses that have stood the test of time has never been greater.

The PGA South Region encompasses the counties of Berkshire, Buckinghamshire, Oxfordshire, Hampshire including the Channel Islands, Sussex, Surrey and Kent, in which there are no less than 500 venues offering the chance to indulge in your chosen sport and recreation.

Over the years we have run tournament golf on many of the best courses in the land, both links and parkland. Opportunities exist for amateur golfers of every degree of competence to play alongside a professional under tournament conditions. So, why not select your venues and enjoy the South of England with your family over a weekend or even a full week.

The counties all have their flagship course as well as numerous established and new complexes, which will widen your choice. The TFM Networks Order of Merit was recently held at Old Thorns, which nestles 200 yards off the A3 at Liphook. With superb course and hotel facilities it provides an excellent base for visiting the many courses that are within a fifteen mile radius. The delights of Blackmoor, Hindhead and Hankley Common are within a 15 minute drive. All have been qualifying courses for The Open Championship so you will be enjoying the best along with a warm welcome.

On moving further South towards the coast, why not combine a day's racing at Goodwood with a stay at Cowdray Park. The wide variety of courses in Sussex, combined with the opportunities for evening entertainment on the Brighton coast, provides the opportunity for a really worthwhile break.

Kent, the garden of England, with its orchards and panoramic views, is a must to try your skills. The links courses at Prince's, Royal St George's, Royal Cinque Ports and Littlestone to name but four, are rivalled by another dozen venues within a half hour's drive. You will not be disappointed and continuing your trip into Surrey once again creates the problem of choosing which courses to play. The motorway system provides easy access to the Region's courses and a base at the Ramada Hotel just off M25 at Junction 9 will enable you to choose between some 50 courses within a 45 minute drive. The Drift Golf Club, just a five minute drive away, will provide you with a warm welcome and the opportunity to play the course that hosted the A-Quote Insurance PGA Southern Open won by Jon LeRoux. Boredom will never feature in your itinerary and in journeying to the northwest of the Region, drop in at Ascot and ply your wits and skill against the 18 holes of Mill Ride or Camberley Heath. Either in the Spring or Autumn, I recommend a visit to the Channel Islands, approximately 25 minutes flying time away, to sample the wonders and hospitality of these islands. You will not be disappointed in the South wherever you stay and play. Good Golfing.

Discover ALDERNEY

Leave behind the 9 to 5 and the stress of modern life. Just off the south coast of England lies the Channel Island of Alderney - so close, but a world away! Stunning scenery, mild climate, golden beaches, abundant wildlife, miles of rambling or cycling, superb cuisine, genuine hospitality, duty free and, most important of all ... total relaxation. However, for those with more energy there's a great golf course and some of the best fishing in Europe.

Getting there is fast and easy with direct flights from Bournemouth, Brighton, Southampton or Jersey and Guernsey.
For a free brochure contact: Alderney Tourism, PO Box 1, Alderney GY9 3AA Tel: 01481 822333 Email: tourism@alderney.net
Please quote this publication.

www.alderney.net
Men's Golf Open: 2-4 June
Senior Veterans Golf Open: 1-3 September

The Island for Every Season

ALDERNEY GOLF CLUB
Route des Carrieres, Alderney, Channel Islands
Tel: 01481 822835 Fax: 01481 823609

- 9 holes, 2528 yards. S.S.S. 65
- Putting green and practice range
- Green Fees: available on request
- Eating facilities: friendly lounge bar with bar meals all day
- Visitors welcome all year, tees reserved for competitions only
- Society Meetings welcome by arrangement
- Hon. Secretary: C.L. Cummings

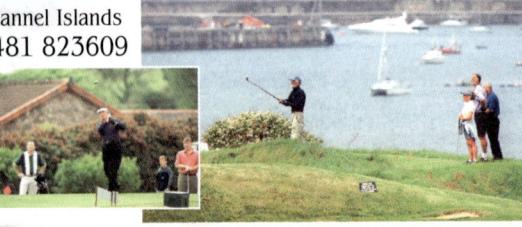

~ Located one mile east of St Annes. ~
Seaside links with sea views from every hole.

Alderney Golf Club, Channel Islands

The Royal Jersey Golf Club

Grouville, Jersey JE3 9BD
Tel: 01534 854416 • Fax: 01534 854684

- Seaside links course – 18 holes, 6100 yards, SSS 70.
- Restaurant and bar • Visitors welcome between 10am and 12 noon or 2pm to 4pm; weekends after 2.30pm. Handicap Certificate required. • Society meetings welcome by prior arrangement

Did you know that there are 3 golf courses in the Borough of Ealing ..... WHY NOT TRY ONE?

BRENT VALLEY • 18 hole course situated in a picturesque valley in the Brent River Park, Church Road, off Greenford Avenue, Hanwell W7 (020 8567 1287). Licensed bar * Food served all day * Golf shop * Changing facilities * Practice facilities * Car park*

PERIVALE PARK • 9 hole course set in Perivale Park amongst the meadows of Brent River Park, close to the A40; entrance is at Stockdove Way, Perivale (020 8575 7136). Golf shop * Food served all day * Changing facilities * Practice facilities * Car park

HORSENDEN HILL • 9 hole course situated on Horsenden Hill conservation area, off Whitton Avenue East, Greenford, Middlesex. Entrance via Woodland Rise (020 8902 4555). Licensed bar * Food served all day * Golf shop * Changing facilities *Practice facilities * Car park.

ALL 3 GOLF COURSES ARE OPEN WEEKDAYS, WEEKENDS AND BANK HOLIDAYS.

www.ealing.gov.uk

For further information on Membership/Fees contact any of the above Golf Courses or Ray Peters, Golf Course Manager, Parks and Countryside Service on 07989 343219

SEASON TICKETS ON SALE FROM ALL GOLF COURSES

The Warmest Welcome in Golf
where quality and value are standard

Situated two miles south east of Aylesbury off A41, this is an easy walking course at the foot of the Chiltern Hills. 18 holes, 6008 yards. S.S.S. 69.

Green Fees – weekdays £25.00; weekends £30.00

Visitors are truly welcome and Society Meetings are especially catered for.
Meals, snacks and visitors' bar.

Professional: Gary George
01296 425949 • Fax: 01296 395376
General Manager: David Allen
01296 424084 • Fax: 01296 395376

Weston Turville Golf Club
New Road, Weston Turville, Near Aylesbury HP22 5QT
Tel: 01296 424084 • Fax: 01296 395376

LYDD GOLF CLUB
www.lyddgolfclub.co.uk

Romney Road, Lydd, Kent
TN29 9LS
01797 320808

Lydd is a modern eighteen hole par 71 links course with nine lakes, tight lies and a consistent breeze set in the Romney Marsh, Kent.

Facilities include an Academy course and floodlight driving range.

Golfers of all abilities are made welcome

Lakes & Sky

WALMER & KINGSDOWN GOLF CLUB
The Leas • Kingsdown • Deal • Kent CT14 8EP

Open:
Monday to Friday (except Monday and Tuesday before 10.30am),
Saturday/Sunday after 12.00.

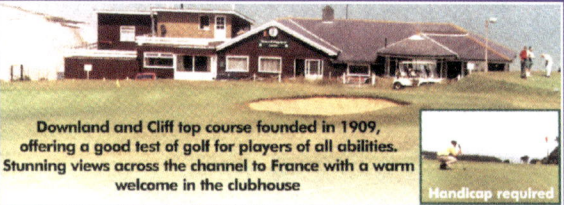
Downland and Cliff top course founded in 1909, offering a good test of golf for players of all abilities. Stunning views across the channel to France with a warm welcome in the clubhouse
Handicap required

18 Holes
Par 72
White 6471
Yellows 6291
Reds 5892

Secretary and Steward: 01304 373256 • Pro: Jude Read: 01304 363017
E-mail: info@kingsdowngolf.co.uk • Website: www.kingsdowngolf.co.uk

---

Visit the FHG website
www.holidayguides.com
for details of the wide choice of accommodation featured in the full range of FHG titles

HUNTERCOMBE

www.huntercombegolfclub.co.uk

- Famous 1901 Willie Park Jnr design, situated on the edge of the Chilterns
- Well known for its fast and true greens & its immaculate fairways
- Plays superbly well in the summer and winter

- Just 50 minutes from London
- Full catering facilities
- Societies and green fees welcome
- Winter package offer available - see website
- Fully stocked Pro shop and practice ground on-site

01491 641207 for details and bookings
or email: office@huntercombegolfclub.co.uk

Huntercombe Golf Club
Nuffield (off A4130)
Henley-on-Thames

Runnymede
★★★★ hotel&spa

Windsor Road, Egham, Surrey TW20 0AG
Tel: 01784 436171 • Fax: 01784 436340

A privately owned 4★ hotel set on the banks of the River Thames, 5 miles from Royal Windsor and minutes from Wentworth Club, the M25 and Heathrow. The hotel features 180 bedrooms, two riverside restaurants and an extensive health and fitness spa including: indoor pool, gym, tennis courts, saunas, steam room and a deluxe day package suite.

Call reservations on 01784 220980 to make a booking.

www.runnymedehotel.com • info@runnymedehotel.com

Founded in 1903 Leatherhead Golf Club celebrated its centenary in 2003.

- 18 hole parkland course
- Practice ground
- Professional's shop
- Visitors welcome

Kingston Road, Leatherhead KT22 0EE
Telephone: (01372) 843966 • Fax: (01372) 842241
E-mail: secretary@lgc-golf.co.uk
Website: www.lgc-golf.co.uk

---

publisher's note

While every effort is made to ensure accuracy, we regret that FHG Guides cannot accept responsibility for errors, misrepresentations or omissions in our entries or any consequences thereof. Prices in particular should be checked. We will follow up complaints but cannot act as arbiters or agents for either party.

FHG
K·U·P·E·R·A·R·D

SOUTH

EXPERIENCE THE DIFFERENCE!

- A Warm & Friendly welcome • Challenging 18-hole course
- Ideal society/corporate day venue • Additional practice facilities
- A la carte restaurant and bar • 18 bedroom hotel

Standon Lane, Ockley, Dorking, Surrey RH5 5PQ

Reception: 01306 627555 Pro Shop: 01306 627557

Fax: 01306 627713 E-mail: golf@gattonmanor.co.uk

GATTON MANOR

Wentworth Club, set in glorious countryside, offers one 9 and three 18-hole golf courses, Tennis and Health Club and a heated outdoor pool. Complementing its prestigious sporting reputation with comfortable and friendly ambience, the Club is charmingly informal.

Wentworth

Wentworth Club, Wentworth Drive, Virginia Water, Surrey GU25 4LS
Tel: 01344 842201 • www.wentworthclub.com

Behind the Georgian facade of the White Hart lies an historic Tudor building which has been substantially extended to create a lively county town hotel.

◆ *53 bedrooms, all en suite with colour TV, telephone, tea-making. Some rooms have views of the Downs; some with disabled access.*

◆ *Wide range of meals and snacks available daily - à la carte, carvery, bar meals, light snacks, teas and coffees.*

◆ *Leisure Centre and Health Spa with heated indoor pool, fully equipped gym, sauna, aerobics studio, beauty clinic etc.*

White Hart Hotel, High Street, Lewes BN7 1XE • Tel: 01273 476694
Fax: 01273 476695 • info@whitehartlewes.co.uk • www.whitehartlewes.co.uk

Crowborough Beacon
Golf Club

This well established 18 hole heathland course, founded in 1895, stands some 800 feet above sea level and with views on clear days of the Downs, Eastbourne and the sea, it must have arguably one of the finest panoramas in Sussex. Pine and fir trees are scattered around the course and there is plenty of heather and gorse. This course will test your accuracy rather than length off the tee!

Crowborough Beacon Golf Club, Beacon Road, Crowborough, East Sussex TN6 1UJ
Tel: 01892 661511 • Fax: 01892 667339
e-mail: secretary@cbgc.co.uk • www.crowboroughbeacongolfclub.co.uk

EAST

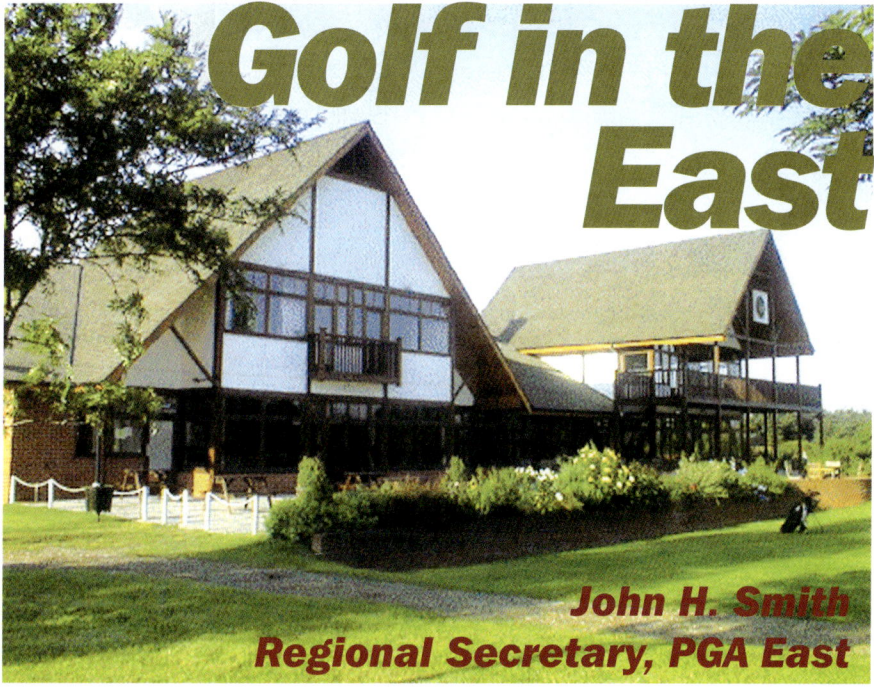

Golf in the East

John H. Smith
Regional Secretary, PGA East

Bishop's Stortford Golf Club, Hertfordshire, home of the PGA East Region.

There are countless options for a pleasant golf break in the PGA East Region where there are relatively little known gems amongst the 350 clubs in Norfolk, Suffolk, Bedfordshire, Cambridgeshire, Essex, Hertfordshire, Middlesex and Greater London.

A visit to the coast of The Wash in Norfolk is especially rewarding, and will blow a few cobwebs away. Hunstanton, the home of the Searles PGA Spring Classic, has a reputation for lightning fast greens and a seemingly ever-present wind off the sea to test golfers of all abilities.

Sheringham, with some wonderful views and fearsome rough, hosts the PGA Golf Pages Summer Classic together with Royal Cromer, which is another delightful and welcoming venue with an added bonus, the fish they serve in their restaurant is superb!

In contrast, there is the wooded King's Lynn course at Castle Rising, designed by Dave Thomas and Peter Alliss, which has been described as the "Augusta of the East". King's Lynn can be compared in many ways with Woburn.

Inland Norfolk boasts a scenic parkland course called Weston Park which, together with Eaton and Barnham Broom with its superb hotel and country club atmosphere, are always in excellent condition.

In Suffolk there are two seaside courses within three miles of one another. Aldeburgh, with gorse lining most of their fairways, is punishing for those who tend to be wayward off the tee. There are no par fives on the course, but the long par fours can be fearsome. The greens are perhaps the fastest in Suffolk.

Aldeburgh and nearby Thorpeness, a wonderful venue designed by James

EAST

The Golf Guide 2006

CAMBRIDGE NATIONAL GOLF
TOFT, CAMBRIDGE CB3 7RY
TEL: 01223 264700 • FAX: 01223 264701
www.golfsocieties.com
GOLF SOCIETIES WELCOME MIDWEEK AND WEEKEND

"A stunning test of golf"

"The area's top society venue"

"For lovers of good golf"

Cambridge National is owned by former British Women's Open Champion, Vivien Saunders OBE

Braid, host the St James's Place Autumn Classic in October. Rushmere Golf Club at Ipswich is in excellent order once again, while Fynn Valley is maturing fast.

Essex clubs host three PGA East Region Order of Merit events. The PGA East Region Championship, sponsored by Scorpion Bathroom Distribution, is set in beautiful parkland at Nazeing Golf Club, with water hazards and manicured fairways.

Braintree's course at Stisted, one of the prettiest in the region, hosts the EEIBA Charity Championship, while Stock Brook Country Club near Billericay, which hosts the Stock Brook Charity Classic, is parkland with a splendid club house and facilities. Their Charity Classic rounds off the Order of Merit events which are shown on Sky Television and on www.pgapro.tv.

Colchester, Romford and Chelmsford are other Essex courses which are both welcoming and very well established.

Cambridgeshire Moat House is the home of the prestigious PGA East Anglian Open. Situated just off the A14 it is a course which has made rapid improvement over the years. It has a par five final hole with a pond to the right of the green which can make amateurs nervous. A visit to Ely City, with lush fairways and quick greens, can double up with a visit to the magnificent cathedral.

The Links Golf Club at Newmarket provides a real test, but what better way to spend a day than golf in the morning and racing in the afternoon? Then there are the two courses at John O' Gaunt which should not be overlooked.

Bishop's Stortford, the home of the PGA East Region, is a parkland course of top quality where you are assured of superb catering and a friendly welcome. It is conveniently situated on the M11

ALDENHAM GOLF & COUNTRY CLUB

Easily accessible from M1 and M25, this picturesque 18-hole parkland course and 9-hole course are situated in the pretty village of Aldenham.
Visiting societies are always welcome and we offer excellent "value for money" golfing packages throughout the year. For details phone

01923 853929

Church Lane, Aldenham, Watford WD25 8NN
www.aldenhamgolfclub.co.uk

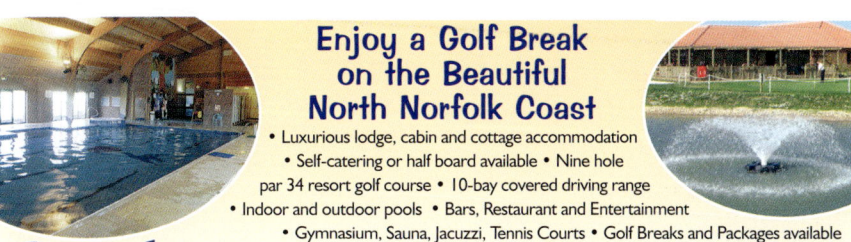

motorway and close to London Stansted International Airport. Should any readers of **'The Golf Guide 2006'** wish to play Bishop's Stortford Golf Course, the home of the PGA East Region, they should contact the Golf Club Secretary on 01279 654715 to arrange for a discounted green fee. Whilst in Hertfordshire also visit the Panshanger Golf Complex which hosts the PGA East Region Design Portfolio Plc Trainees' Championship, as well as the Powerade Assistants' Championship Regional qualifier. Fast and true greens are a feature of an interesting layout for a fine pay-and-play course.

Many of the Region's courses are within easy reach of London. Middlesex offers Old Fold Manor, Grim's Dyke, Fulwell and The Grove, a splendid new development designed for players of all abilities to have a really enjoyable round.

Courses not far from central London include Canons Brook, Wanstead, West Essex, Crews Hill, Bush Hill Park, Hendon, Enfield and Northwood. East Herts, with its huge oaks with branches that make inaccurate drives so costly, and South Herts are both enjoyable.

There is such variety in the region, with courses like Brocket Hall, where a ferry over the lake to the 18th green is a memorable experience. A golfing break in the East Region will provide great hospitality and wonderful memories for golfers of all abilities.

In conclusion, should any readers of **'The Golf Guide 2006'** like the opportunity to compete in a Professional PGA administered event/Pro-Am please contact the Regional Secretary John H Smith on 01279 652070 at PGA East Region Headquarters. **Happy Golfing!**

MIDLANDS

The Golf Guide 2006

Golf in the Midlands

Jennifer Prentice

The parkland course at Draycote Hotel & Whitefields Golf Course, near Rugby, Warwickshire

For many highly enthusiastic golfers time is often at a premium these days. This can present them with a difficult dilemma, especially if they have resolved to play as much as possible in a bid to achieve the improvements in their game that have eluded them in the past. But help could be at hand. The Midlands – stretching from the bracing east coast through to the wilder delights of the Welsh Borders – holds an accessible solution. Good transport links are another big boost.

The region offers a real chance to fulfil golfing targets without risk of disappointment as the standard of the tests varies with such a rich mix of courses – from true links, through to inland jewels, on to spectacular views from layouts on much hillier terrain. Not only keen golfers will benefit from a trip to the Midlands, but also their families of all ages. Travel by road, rail, even air, is arranged readily too. The whole family can enjoy weekend, midweek, or longer breaks, along with the addicted golfer in their midst. Leisure facilities of many different kinds are located across this vast area, ranging from top class shopping to historic houses, interesting museums, and ancient ruins, along with relaxing on-site amenities at many of the golf course and hotel complexes, or walks to test the leisurely rambler, or more strenuous hiker. Valuable family time can be integrated with a wealth of golfing aims and other activities.

A number of top international and regional golf titles were at stake on some of the Midlands best known courses again during the 2005 season. In the spring the European Tour's Daily Telegraph Dunlop Masters Championship took place over the Arden course at Marriott Forest of Arden in the heart of the Midlands. This provided plenty of drama over the four days amid the splendid, picturesque remains of a medieval woodland.

Swathes of glorious bluebells provided sharp colour contrast to rapidly emerging fresh green leaves on the many trees, some of which carry special protection on this estate. The course proved to be a true master, setting stiff challenges for the strong field of Europe's greatest professionals. Indeed, it took a three-way play-off before Thomas Bjorn of Denmark emerged as the new champion.

Marriott Forest of Arden Hotel also offers the finest facilities for those wishing to relax, or to be more active. There are two courses here – the Arden and shorter Aylesford.

Midland PGA Championships were contested on several different courses around the region too. There was a spring date for the oldest title anywhere in the world in pro golf – the De Vere Midland

Main Road, Morley, Derbyshire DE7 6DG
Tel: 01332 780480 • Fax: 01332 781094
www.morleyhayes.com • enquiries@morleyhayes.com
Golf at Morley Hayes – the ultimate golfing experience

Two courses specifically designed to accommodate all levels of expertise. The Manor Course 18 holes par 72, the Tower Course 9 holes Par 30. Both are set within parkland with water features and established trees.
• 17-bay all weather driving range • Professional tuition
• Roosters Bar • Spike Bar • Dovecote Restaurant
• Pavilion Suite • Syndicate Room
• Golf Shop • Locker & Shower Rooms
On A608 just north of M1 Junction 25

Hotel opening Summer 2005

Burghill Valley Golf Club
WELCOMES NEW MEMBERS, VISITORS & SOCIETIES

This beautiful Herefordshire course has developed into one of the leading clubs in the county, setting a challenge to players of all abilities. Situated 4 miles NW of Hereford, the course is easy walking on gently rolling fairways. Two lakes and the apple blossom of the orchards are particularly picturesque against the background of hills and woods.

With keen golfers comprising the management of the club, their enthusiasm is reflected in the excellent service provided and the condition of the course, the greens being especially praised.

The clubhouse has a warm and friendly atmosphere where visitors are made most welcome. The Club takes great pride in the catering facilities, offering a variety of packages to suit both large and small societies. All in all, **19** holes to be remembered with pleasure!

Tillington Road • Burghill • Hereford • HR4 7RW • Tel: 01432 760456
Fax 01432 761654 • Email: info@bvgc.co.uk • Web Site: www.bvgc.co.uk

THE GRANGE & LINKS HOTEL AND SANDILANDS GOLF CLUB

Our own privately owned 18 hole (Par 70, SSS 69) links golf course. Two tennis courts, 4-acre garden, gymnasium, 2 snooker tables, croquet lawn.

The Hotel is renowned for its superb cuisine in most elegant surroundings. 'Arguably the finest value we've found' *Golf Monthly*.

AA ★★★
RAC ★★★ Hotel
Dining Award Grade 1

Tel: 01507 441334
Fax: 01507 443033

Sandilands, Sutton-on-Sea, Lincs LN12 2RA
grangeandlinkshotel@btconnect.com
www.thegrangeandlinkshotel.co.uk

Lincoln Golf Club

TORKSEY • LINCOLN • LN1 2EG

- 6438 yards, SSS 71
- Venue for Lincolnshire Amateur Championship and Lincolnshire County Championships
- Putting green
- Large practice area
- 3-hole pitch and putt
- Golf shop

Founded in 1891, Lincoln is a mature, testing, championship standard course built on sandy subsoil offering a variety of holes from links-style to parkland with mature trees and some water features. We offer golfing packages in summer and winter, including a wide range of excellent snacks and meals.

Manager: Derek B. Linton
Tel/Fax: 01427 718721
Pro: Ashley Carter Tel/Fax: 01427 718723
e-mail: info@lincolngc.co.uk
www.lincolngc.co.uk

COLLINGTREE PARK GOLF COURSE LTD
Windingbrook Lane, Northampton NN4 0XN • 01604 700000 • Pro Shop: 01604 701202
Fax: 01604 702600 • enquiries@collingtreeparkgolf.com • www.collingtreeparkgolf.com

This 18-hole Johnny Miller design Championship golf course is set in lush parkland just two minutes from Junction 15 of the M1/A508, and has a host of 1st class facilities, including a 16-bay floodlit driving range, indoor video teaching room, members' bar, and 'Greens' restaurant open to the public. Collingtree Park comes with a fantastic pedigree, playing host to the British Masters in 1995 & 1996 and most recently the Euro Pro Tour and Mobile Cup Seniors' Tournament in June 2005.

Visitors, Societies and Corporate groups are all welcome, and must book in advance. Green fees are available on request.

Professional Championship. It was decided at De Vere Belton Woods, near Grantham.

The multiplicity of outdoor activities here also attracts keen interest among hotel guests, as well as the chance to visit many local beauty spots. There are also the 18-hole Woodside and 9-hole Red Arrows courses on which to develop golfing skills. Another venue for a Midland PGA Order of Merit event was Hill Valley, Whitchurch, Shropshire, where there is a hotel as well two courses – the Peter Alliss/David Thomas designed Emerald, and the shorter Sapphire.

Pro-Ams and regional tournaments were played on some other exciting courses, where there are also top class hotels and facilities, such as the De Vere Belfry, where the world famous Brabazon course is such a magnificent test; at Patshull Park, near Wolverhampton, Forest Pines in North Lincolnshire and Hawkstone Park in Shropshire.

A national tournament – the 2005 Glenmuir Club Professionals' Championship – was played at Woodhall Spa, the headquarters of the the English Golf Union in Lincolnshire, where the Hotchkin championship course was celebrating its centenary. It has been a popular golfing Mecca over all those years.

Collingtree Park in Northamptonshire and Morley Hayes, Derbyshire – where a hotel opened in 2005 – hosted national tournaments too. The Europro Tour went to both venues, with the European Seniors' Tour Mobile Cup contested at Collingtree Park at the height of the summer. Midland courses without on-site hotels have a wide choice of accommodation within easy reach, making them well placed for stays of any length for golfers, their families, friends, or groups of equally dedicated players.

Oakmere Park Golf Club

"The All Weather Course"

Admiral's Course: 18 holes, 6612 yards, SSS 72
Commander's Course: 9 holes, 6573 yards, SSS 72
◆ Full clubhouse facilities ◆ Pro Shop
◆ Practice facilities with a premier learning academy.
◆ Societies welcome ◆ Package deals available
Green Fees from £20 weekdays, £28 weekends (Admiral's);
from £6 for 9 holes weekdays (Commander's)

Professional: Daryl St John Jones
Oakmere Park Golf Club
Oaks Lane, Oxton, Nottingham NG25 0RH
Tel: 0115 965 3545 • Fax: 0115 965 5628
enquiries@oakmerepark.co.uk • www.oakmerepark.co.uk

---

27 unique holes set in 200 acres of Shropshire's most beautiful countryside

At Cleobury Mortimer Golf Club we believe that a really enjoyable game of golf takes more than just a great golf course. We make sure that your whole experience – from the friendly welcome in the golf shop to your drinks and meal in our relaxed clubhouse – is all part of a day that you'll remember.

27 holes set out in three individual 9-hole loops, covering 200 acres of Shropshire's most beautiful countryside. Each hole is designed to a very high specification, with its own character and challenge.

A Clubhouse with excellent facilities, from a full-sized antique snooker table and spike bar, – to everything a modern club must have. Choice of refreshment and dining areas to suit all tastes – open 7 days. Golf Shop with wide range of stock from all the leading brands.

Cleobury Mortimer Golf Club
Wyre Common, Cleobury Mortimer, Shropshire DY14 8HQ
Enquiries: 01299 271112 • Fax: 01299 271468
E-mail: enquiries@cleoburygolfclub.com
www.cleoburygolfclub.com

Self Catering Holiday Cottages available on site from Spring 2006

Uttoxeter Golf Club
welcomes societies and visitors

*One of the best kept secrets in the country.
A beautiful course with stunning views
across Staffordshire and Derbyshire.*

Club Secretary: 01889 566552
Club Professional: 01889 564884

MIDLANDS
The Golf Guide 2006

Welcome to Jack Barker's WORLD of GOLF!

GREENWAY HALL GOLF CENTRE — **KEELE GOLF CENTRE**

Greenway Hall		Keele Golf Centre
Weekday *Green Fees* From only £10.00	Buggy Hire *Only* £10.00 /Round Societies Welcome from *Only* £6.50	Weekday *Green Fees* From only £10.00
Weekend *Green Fees* From only £15.00	Platinum Memberships: Play 7 Courses nationwide for 1 Annual Fee - Phone for details. Annual subscriptions available at all Centres!	Weekend *Green Fees* From only £15.00

Stanley Road, Stockton Brook, Stoke-on-Trent. ST9 9LJ.
Tel: 01782 503 158 greenway@jackbarker.com   www.jackbarker.com
Keele Road, Newcastle-Under-Lyme, Staffordshire. ST5 5AB.
Tel: 01782 627 796 keele@jackbarker.com

Draycote Hotel & Whitefields Golf Course

A challenging course for all handicaps overlooking the spectacular Draycote Water Country Park. Dine and stay at the stylish Draycote Hotel, half and full day, corporate and non-golfer packages available.
• parkland course • all year round natural drainage
• floodlit driving range • practice bunker and chipping area • 18 hole putting green
Societies, corporate golf days and visitors welcome.

London Road, Thurlaston, Near Rugby, Warwickshire CV23 9LF
Tel: 01788 521 800 • Fax: 01788 521 695
www.draycotehotel.co.uk • mail@draycotehotel.co.uk

A Course Fit 'Fore' Champions

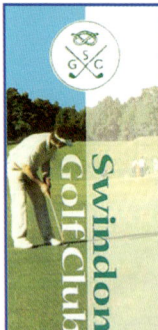

SWINDON GOLF CLUB, near Dudley in the West Midlands provides golfers with the one thing that makes the sport so great – a challenge. For at Swindon the course is littered with holes, bunkers and obstacles to test the talents of the greatest players.
Almost all holes holes are surrounded by ferns, pines and firs.
The feature hole is the 5th, a boomerang of a Par 5 flanked on both sides by towering firs. Swindon wants golfers from all over to try the course, and the experience of playing on a course with so many features will improve any player 100%.
The clubhouse has a friendly and relaxed atmosphere and you will find a selection of great food to satisfy any appetite, a snooker table and a great atmosphere. For more information telephone or visit the course.

SWINDON GOLF CLUB, BRIDGNORTH ROAD, SWINDON, DUDLEY, WEST MIDLANDS DY3 4PU
TEL: 01902 897031/895202 • FAX: 01902 326211 • www.swindongolfclub.co.uk

The 18th at De Vere Belton Woods Hotel & Country Club, near Grantham, Lincolnshire

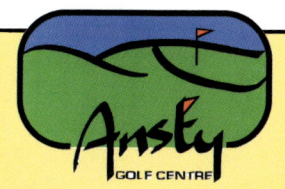

**ANSTY GOLF CENTRE IS PROUD TO SPONSOR
STEVE WEBSTER** PGA & EUROPEAN PRO.

- 18 Hole Course
- 9 Hole Academy Course
- Driving Range
- Fully Stocked Pro Shop
- PGA Tuition 7 days a week
- Tailor-made Golf Day packages
- Corporate Golf Days
- Putting Green
- Fully Licensed Club House
- Family Room
- Course always open, regardless of weather
- One mile from Junc.2 M6 and M69

**BRINKLOW ROAD, ANSTY, COVENTRY CV7 9JL
TEL: 024 7662 1341 OR 024 7660 2568**

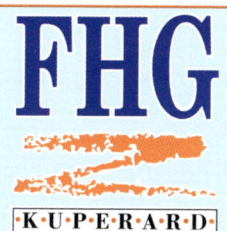

FHG Guides

publish a large range of well-known accommodation guides. We will be happy to send you details or you can use the order form at the back of this book.

Founded in 1990 the club boasts a flourishing membership and friendly staff. Our inland links-style 18-hole course offers a challenge to all golfers with some long and testing holes finished off with pacy yet accommodating greens. An 18-bay floodlit driving range offers you the chance to hit some balls with putting and chipping greens adding the finishing touches to your game. Green fees and membership rates are among the most attractive in the region with a variety of additional benefits. We always welcome new members with 5 day, 7 day, corporate, and family memberships available. Our clubhouse offers some of the best catering around in convivial surroundings that make your 'après golf' debate that much more enjoyable.

PERTON PARK GOLF CLUB
**Wrottesley Park Road, Perton, Wolverhampton WV6 7HL
Tel/Fax: 01902 380073/380103 • website: www.pertongolfclub.co.uk**

ASTON WOOD GOLF CLUB

**Blake Street, Little Aston,
Sutton Coldfield B74 4EU
Tel: 0121 580 7800 • Fax: 0121 353 0354**

An 18-hole championship course designed by Peter Alliss and Clive Clarke, constructed to USPGA standard, with well-placed bunkers, water features and fine, undulating greens. Aston Wood is easily accessible from Birmingham and the rest of the country (M6, M6 Toll, M40 and M42), and combines high standards of service with a friendly, comfortable atmosphere. Visitors welcome weekdays.

enquiries@astonwoodgolfclub.co.uk
www.astonwoodgolfclub.co.uk

NORTH

There's no place like home, especially if you're a lucky enough to live in the North of England.

It's the proverbial golfing paradise which boasts such a wide variety of courses that there's no point in looking further afield. From the great links at Hoylake, Birkdale and Lytham, to the splendid parkland settings at Prestbury, Pleasington and Ormskirk, to equally impressive locations on the other side of the Pennines such as Alwoodley, Ganton, Newbiggin and Seaton Carew, we really are spoiled for choice.

But we don't mind sharing our prized possessions!

The three Royals – Birkdale, Lytham St Annes and Liverpool – have all hosted the Open on several occasions and provided some of the event's greatest moments. In an area also noted for its fun fairs, the Open has provided many an emotional roller coaster ride for players and spectators.

And while only the privileged few can hope to kick a ball at Old Trafford or hit a six at Lord's, anyone who can play the game can follow in the spike marks of the greats such as Tiger Woods, Ernie Els and Jack Nicklaus ... and even teenage talent Michele Wie! She was the star of the the Curtis Cup match between Great Britain and Ireland and the United States at fabulous Formby last summer, where she helped to attract record attendances of 16,000 over two absorbing days.

That figure will bear no comparison alongside the multitudes who will flock to Royal Liverpool this year for the first Open at the Hoylake course since Argentina's Roberto De Vicenzo won in 1967.

Large crowds are also anticipated for the Weetabix Women's British Open this

Seaton Carew Golf Club, Hartlepool, Durham

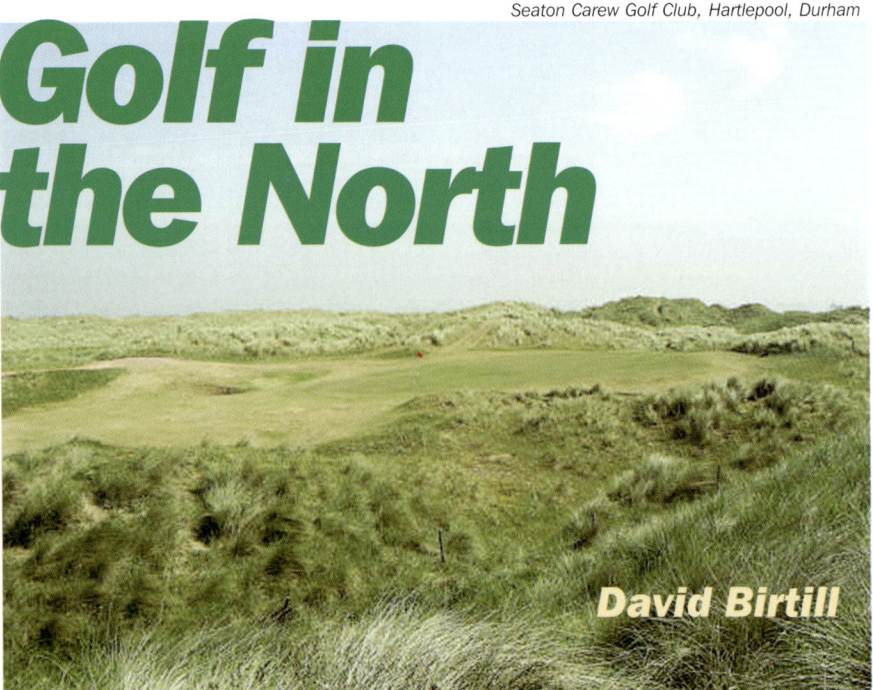

Golf in the North

David Birtill

The Eden Golf Club & Driving Range

CROSBY-ON-EDEN, CARLISLE, CUMBRIA CA6 4PZ
TEL: 01228 573003 • FAX: 01228 818435

- 18-HOLE CHAMPIONSHIP PARKLAND COURSE
- NEW FOR 2007 - ADDITIONAL 9 HOLE GOLF COURSE
- FLOODLIT COVERED DRIVING RANGE
- PITCHING GREENS AND PRACTICE BUNKERS
- EXCELLENT RESTAURANT AND LOUNGE BAR WITH OPEN FIRE

The Eden Golf Club is a hidden gem situated along the banks of the River Eden. Tight tree-lined fairways and numerous natural water hazards mark this course out as a great test of golf. Situated 5 miles from Junction 44 of M6, one hour from Newcastle. On the doorstep of the Lakes, Hadrian's Wall and Gretna Green.

e-mail: edengolf1@aol.com • www.edengolf.co.uk

Brampton Golf Club

TALKIN TARN, BRAMPTON
CUMBRIA CA8 1HN
www.bramptongolfclub.com

Consider the rest, play the best

Situated in a stunning corner of North Cumbria, the jewel of the region's crown boasts panoramic views of the Lake District, Southern Scotland and the Pennines. The undulating heathland Par 72 course offers both challenging golf and an idyllic setting which has been likened to a "mini Gleneagles".
The clubhouse provides a full range of first-class services and facilities. Visiting societies, corporate golf days and visitors most welcome, but pre-booking clearly recommended.
For societies/visiting party bookings please contact Ian Meldrum (Secretary) on 01900 827985 or e-mail: secretary@bramptongolfclub.com. Other visitor enquiries contact the Professional on 016977 2000

---

year, judging by the numbers who turned out at Royal Lytham and St Annes in 2003. And Birkdale will probably break its own record of 200,000 for Open Championship attendances in 2008 because it is generally accepted as the most popular of all the venues in the country's biggest golfing region. The Championship has been staged there on eight occasions, and it's where in 1954 Peter Thomson won the first of his five Claret Jugs. Eleven years later, back at Birkdale, he rounded off his collection with a further triumph that he described as "my greatest win." The Australian broke the final round logjam of 13 players, all of whom had a chance to win, with his second shot to the 510-yard 17th which hit the flag when he was just one stroke clear of the field. Birkdale was a great favourite of Thomson's and he lovingly described it as "man-sized but not a monster."

But above everything else, Birkdale is best remembered for Arnie Palmer's victory in 1961, which is rightly credited with starting the renaissance of the Open. It had slipped down the order of the four majors until Palmer's achievement inspired his fellow Americans to support the event and restore it to the world's biggest championship.

Hillside, which butts on to Birkdale, is regarded by some as an even better test and it's easy to see why its next door neighbour on the other side, Southport and Ainsdale, is a former Ryder Cup venue. Last year it hosted the PGA Club Professional Championship and despite the awful weather, the links stood up wonderfully well.

But if you really want to sample links golf in the raw try pegging up at West Lancs when the prevailing wind whistles across the Mersey estuary or Wallasey

SEASCALE GOLF CLUB
Play our challenging links course

Superb 6,416 yards traditional links. Reduced terms for daily parties of 8 or more. Any three consecutive days golf for £80. Bookings now being taken for 2007. Both midweek and weekend dates available. Societies and groups assured of a warm and friendly welcome.

For further details contact:
David Stobart, The Secretary, Seascale Golf Club, Seascale, Cumbria CA20 1QL
or phone 01946 728202

Seaton Carew Golf Club

The Old Course - an enjoyable challenge for golfers of all abilities, redesigned in 1925 by Dr Alister MacKenzie, who also designed Augusta, home of the US Masters.

The Brabazon Course - an extended challenge of almost 7000 yards, a tricky but rewarding course which has been chosen as a test for EGU and R&A Championships.

Visitors welcome midweek and some weekends. Societies catered for by arrangement.

Seaton Carew Golf Club, Tees Road, Seaton Carew, Hartlepool, Durham TS25 1DE
Tel: 01429 296496 • Fax: 01429 267952
www.seatoncarewgolf.co.uk

---

which has been home for many major international events. Hesketh, especially on the seaboard side, can be a real tiger, too, when the wind blows, but it does afford shelter on most of the closing holes.

Visitors to Southport can't fail to see Blackpool and its famous tower just across the water but, no matter how close it appears, don't even think about taking a short cut over the treacherous sands.

Royal Lytham needs no introduction and in addition to major pro tournaments also stages many other important ones including, at the start of May, its own Lytham Trophy, one of the county's top amateur events.

Still in the vicinity, the Alliss-Clarke designed course at Heron's Reach is a good stopping off place for the holiday golfer. It is one of many venues owned by De Vere Hotels, who sponsor the PGA North Region Championship there, and the City of Leeds Cup at the superbly-appointed Oulton Hall. Mottram Hall, near Macclesfield, is also a De Vere set-up and Dave Thomas, a former Ryder Cup player, has skilfully blended the relatively flat front nine with the contrasting, more demanding inward holes, making it a terrific venue for the Manchester Evening News Manchester Open, the PGA North Region's flagship event. De Vere also own Carden Park, home of the PGA Seniors' Championship, while nearby Northop Country Park stages the Wales Ryder Cup Challenge Tour tournament.

The Isle of Man can been reached in 90 minutes from Liverpool by catamaran, 30 minutes by plane and a little longer by the more traditional sea routes from Heysham and Fleetwood. Once you get there head straight to Castletown, and a true links with views to die for, then take in the other eight courses dotted around the island.

Back on the mainland, there are not many tracks as well kept as Stockport and Ormskirk or Prestbury and Pleasington, where the Open Championship regional qualifiers will be held for a second year in July.

Marriott Worsley Park has matured into a splendid venue since it opened six years ago and was deemed good enough to host the inaugural JJB North West Challenge last summer, which is expected to become a full European Tour event in the not-too-distant future.

On the other side of the Pennine Way, in Yorkshire, you are spoiled for choice by a vast array of courses. But few can rival Ganton, near Scarborough, one of the country's greatest inland links where Great Britain and Ireland amateurs completed a Walker Cup hat-trick over the United States in 2003.

Alwoodley, Fulford, Sand Moor, Moor Allerton, Pannal, Lindrick and Catterick are all well established clubs, complementing a host of new ones which have sprung up, including the excellent Aldwark Manor and Rudding Park, both not a million miles away from the beautiful spa town of Harrogate.

De Vere also owns the two courses at Slaley Hall, in scenic Northumberland. It is just one of many relatively new set-ups in the North East with Wynyard, Matfen Hall and Ramside among fairly recent developments which sit comfortably with well established clubs such as Newbiggin, Whitley Bay, Prudhoe in Northumberland, and Seaton Carew, South Shields, Bishop Auckland and Barnard Castle in Durham.

Matfen Hall has come a long way in a very short time since the course was opened in 1995. Set in classic parkland a short distance off the Military Road, it is home to the Northern Rock North East Masters, another PGA North Region order of merit tournament.

Darlington Golf Club
Haughton Grange, Darlington, Co. Durham. DL1 3JD

Darlington's oldest and most prestigious golf club with its lush, tree-lined fairways and unforgiving semi rough has plenty of Alistair MacKenzie inspired greens making the parkland layout a haven for putting enthusiasts.

WINTER WARMER Package
* Coffee & Bacon Sandwiches on arrival
* 18 Holes of Golf
* Meal of the Day

Only £22 per person
FOR GROUPS OF 4 OR MORE
Available Monday to Friday from 1st October to 31st March 2006

Pick & Mix Mid Week Packages for Societies and Visiting Parties
From £20 per person

For further details contact Michelle on 01325 355324 ext 2
For more information, Club News and additional Special Offers visit the Darlington Website at www.darlington-gc.co.uk

The Blue Bell Hotel
Market Place, Belford, Northumberland NE70 7NE
Tel: 01668 213543 • Fax: 01668 213787
e-mail:bluebel@globalnet.co.uk
www.bluebellhotel.com

When you arrive at the Bell at Belford you will receive a warm, genuine welcome from the friendly staff. While retaining its 250-year-old character, the hotel offers all modern comforts, the individually decorated en suite bedrooms having all the facilities expected by today's traveller. Guests can relax in the stylish hotel bar, or in the friendly Belford Tavern complete with games room. The Garden Restaurant and the more informal Bistro offer the finest local produce, some of which comes from the hotel's own garden. This unspoilt area has a wide variety of sporting and leisure activities and places of interest.

NORTH   **The Golf Guide 2006**

GOLF at LINDEN HALL

We are pleased to offer you the opportunity of playing golf on our magnificent 18 hole golf course. Our fairways run through mature woodland, rolling parkland with established burns & lakes in the serene setting of the Linden Hall estate.

Special golfing accommodation packages have been arranged representing superb value for visiting golfers, in both Hotel & Dormy House Accommodation.

LINDEN HALL

Longhorsley, Morpeth, Northumberland. NE65 8XF. Pro-Shop Tel: 01670 50 00 11
E-mail stay@lindenhall.co.uk   Take a virtual tour at www.lindenhall.co.uk

---

HAINSWORTH PARK GOLF CLUB

18-hole parkland course located 6 miles east of Beverley just off A165 to Bridlington.
- Weekdays £20-£24
- Weekends/Bank Holidays £24-£29
- Catering available
- Societies welcome by arrangement
- Accommodation at Burton Lodge Hotel on the course

For Golf • Telephone: 01964 542362
Hotel • Telephone 01964 542547
Fax: 01964 544771

**BURTON LODGE HOTEL, BRANDESBURTON
DRIFFIELD, EAST YORKSHIRE YO25 8RT**

The Oaks Golf Club & Spa

Aughton Common, Aughton, York YO42 4PW

- Excellent golf, food and drink served in a warm, friendly environment.
- Visit the Spa for a very special treat.
- Stay in beautiful accommodation.
  - Superb practice and teaching facilities incorporating Golf Monthly Top 25 UK Coach Graham Walker's:

Walker's Golf Academy

Tel: 01757 288577 • Fax: 01757 288732
www.theoaksgolfclub.co.uk • www.walkersgolfacademy.co.uk

Great golf - all year round!

A day at Romanby offers more than just great golf - it's a day to remember.

Set in 200 acres of tranquil parkland nestled between the Yorkshire Dales and the Hambleton Hills, with attractive lakes and rivers presenting excellent water hazards, Romanby provides a challenging but fair test for all categories of golfer.

**ROMANBY
GOLF & COUNTRY CLUB**
Yafforth Road, Northallerton, North Yorks.
www.romanby.com

Championship Standard
Prestigious Clubhouse
Well stocked Golf Shop
Par-3 Academy Course
Floodlit Driving Range

We're golf society specialists, focused on providing a superb day out, and we're ready and waiting to make you welcome.

To book your day at Romanby, call Grant on **01609 778855**

The Golf Guide 2006 NORTH

THE BUCK INN ETC/AA ★

Delightful Country Inn overlooking cricket green in quiet Wensleydale village. Relax in our comfortable en suite bedrooms, enjoy superb home cooked food and drink from our selection of five real ales.

Six fine courses – Bedale, Masham, Ripon, Catterick, Richmond and Romanby – within 20 minutes' drive.

GOLFING BREAKS AVAILABLE
Tel: (01677) 422461 • Fax: (01677) 422447
website: www.smoothhound.co.uk/hotels/buckinn.html

Thornton Watlass,
Near Bedale, Ripon,
North Yorkshire HG4 4AH

CALVERLEY GOLF CLUB
Woodhall Lane, Pudsey,
Leeds LS28 5QY

Halfway between Leeds and Bradford is a parkland course of distinction. Calverley's 18-hole course at 5590 yards and Par 68 may not be long by modern standards, but poses its own unique challenge in the form of tight fairways and target greens, which means accuracy is very much at a premium. The short 5th provides the course signature where a challenging tee shot down into a disused quarry is the order of the day, and haunting views out over Baildon Moors abound. Visitors and societies are welcome at this friendly club with society packages from as little as £15.

For more information call 0113 256 9244

Sandhill Golf Club

18 hole golf course. Societies welcome with various packages on request. Licensed club house providing tea, coffee, biscuits and meals at various prices.
Weekend Society Specials are available
**Middlecliffe Lane,
Little Houghton, Barnsley S72 0HW
Tel: 01226 753444**
www.sandhillgolfclub.co.uk
E-mail enquiries to:
vwistow@sandhillgolfclub.co.uk
bookings@sandhillgolfclub.co.uk

Bingley (St Ives) Golf Club, Bingley, West Yorkshire

MID YORKSHIRE GOLF CLUB

Ideally situated where the Yorkshires meet
Easily accessible all routes. M62 J33 – A1 south ½ mile.
Established 1993, incorporating existing mature woodland. Links style golf course. 18 holes, Par 72, 6424 yards. Superb clubhouse with function room. 23 bay floodlit driving range. Buggies available.

www.midyorkshiregolfclub.com
Havercroft Lane, Darrington, Pontefract WF8 3BP
Telephone: 01977 704522 • Fax: 01977 600823

Crosland Heath Golf Club
Crosland Heath, Huddersfield, West Yorkshire HD4 7AF

Designed by the renowned Dr Alister Mackenzie, before he moved on to design Royal Melbourne and then Augusta, with Bobby Jones, Crosland Heath has matured into one of the finest examples of heathland excellence, where shot making is amply rewarded. At nearly 900ft above sea level, this challenging course has easy walking, and players have fabulous views on all sides. Coupled with practice, pro shop, catering and clubhouse facilities, this makes Crosland Heath an ideal venue for a visiting party, where you are assured of a friendly welcome.
Please contact the Secretary for package details.
Tel: 01484 653216 • Fax: 01484 461079
e-mail: golf@croslandheath.wanadoo.co.uk

Hollins Hall Marriott Hotel and Country Club

The 18 hole Championship Golf Course, and host to the Sky TV – PGA Europrotour Championships, provides a great test for golfers of all abilities.
At 6671yards, Hollins Hall is a challenging course, the best defence being the huge undulating greens and well positioned bunkering. The signature hole 14th, called 'viaduct', is a tricky par four providing a masterpiece in tactical design, with the 19th century viaduct providing a fantastic backdrop.
The greens and tees are built to USGA standards providing exceptional drainage and quality surfaces.
The Marriott Hollins Hall is a fantastic Championship Golf Venue for golfing groups.
Hollins Hall Marriott Hotel and Country Club
Hollins Hill, Baildon, Shipley, Bradford, West Yorkshire BD17 7QW
Tel: 01274 530 053 • Fax: 01274 534 351 • www.marriott.com

BINGLEY ST IVES
GOLF CLUB

The Clubhouse, Harden, Bingley BD16 1AT
Superb course and facilities with magnificent views of the Aire valley. Visitors welcome, special package rates all year round.
Contact
Pro: 01274 562506
Manager:
01274 562436
for details

e-mail: bingleyst-ives@harden.freeserve.co.uk
www.bingleystivesgc.co.uk

Bradford (Hawksworth) GOLF CLUB
Hawksworth Lane, Guiseley LS20 8NP

Set in peaceful and tranquil countryside near the picturesque village of Hawksworth, this undulating parkland course enjoys magnificent views over the Yorkshire moors. The spacious greens make this a fair test of golf which must be treated with respect. Traditional-style clubhouse with two well-stocked bars and excellent catering facilities. Special packages for individuals and golfing parties. No visitors on Saturdays; by prior arrangement on Sundays and Bank Holidays.

**Enquiries to the Manager:
01943 875570**

Voted in the TOP 100 in the British Isles in 2004.

"How Mother Nature intended Golf Courses"

Castletown Golf Links
Fort Island, Derbyhaven, Isle of Man
Telephone (01624) 822220
Fax (01624) 829661
e-mail: 1sttee@manx.net
website: www.golfiom.com

For full details of clubs and courses, plus convenient accommodation

www.uk-golfguide.com

STUTELEA HOTEL & Leisure Club
ALEXANDRA ROAD
SOUTHPORT PR9 0NB

AA ★★★   Best Western

Close to Royal Birkdale

The hotel is set in picturesque gardens and all accommodation has bath and shower en suite. A 24-hour bar service is available and dining is a pleasure in our Global Restaurant where the menu, relaxed atmosphere and warm hospitality make any meal a special occasion. Golf clubs can be securely stored and we will endeavour to book your tee-off times.

The Leisure Club is second to none, providing a heated indoor swimming pool, jacuzzi, sauna, steam room and gymnasium.

Contact us now for your colour brochure on

01704 544220

or visit our website: www.stutelea.co.uk
e-mail: info@stutelea.co.uk

Golf in Wales

Chris Smart

Builth Wells Golf Club, Powys

Long, long gone are the days when reviews of Welsh golf started and finished with Royal Porthcawl and Royal St David's. Although these two stunning links still remain jewels in the Principality's crown, they have been joined by a whole plethora of new developments which have catapulted Wales to the very forefront of the sport.

You would struggle to go anywhere in Wales at the current time without hearing the words "Ryder Cup 2010" mentioned.

The magnificent Celtic Manor Resort, towering over the M4 motorway at Newport, will host the 2010 matches – the culmination of billionaire Sir Terry Matthews' dream of creating one of – if not the – finest golf and leisure complexes in the world. The Celtic Manor, certainly one of the most accessible resorts around – just minutes off the motorway, offers golf, accommodation and leisure facilities to satisfy everyone.

While the Wentwood Hills course undergoes major reconstruction ahead of 2010, the Roman Road, home to the 2005 Wales Open European Tour event, and the short Coldra Woods layout, will ensure that the standard of golf remains sky high.

And the resort also offers a variety of golf and leisure packages to suit all pockets, ensuring its popularity continues to rise.

Anyone crossing the Severn Bridge and heading to the Celtic Manor would do well to check out some of the other gems on offer in the surrounding area.

The Newport club at Rogerstone has always been regarded as one of Wales' best inland layouts and The Monmouthshire at Abergavenny and the Rolls of Monmouth offer great golf in superb settings.

Just a few big drives along the M4 from Newport lies Europe's most rapidly developing capital city, Cardiff. Now a

Gwesty Nanhoron Arms Hotel

'On the spectacular Lleyn Peninsula'

Ffordd Dewi Sant,
Nefyn, Pwllheli,
Gwynedd LL53 6EA
Telephone 01758 720203

The Nanhoron Arms Hotel provides the perfect base for your stay whether for business, holiday or sporting event.

The Bedrooms 19 en suite (bath or shower) including family rooms, suites, doubles and singles. Colour TV, hairdryer, tea & coffee facilities. Latest Z-beds and baby cots are available

Lounge Bar & Family Room Well stocked Lounge Bar. Original bar meals together with old favourites. Special children's menu and play area for younger guests.

Restaurant St David's Restaurant offers breakfast, lunch or dinner, truly "An Experience of Good Taste"

Activities Golf, pony trekking, clay shooting & walking

★ Just 1½ miles from Nefyn Golf Club ★

Clwb Golff Abersoch

Located on the Llyn Peninsula, Clwb Golff Abersoch offers a warm welcome to members and visitors alike.
- 18-hole round from £22.50
- Full catering and bar facilities
- Well-stocked Pro Shop
- Golf tuition available

Clwb Golff Abersoch, Golf Road, Abersoch, Gwynedd LL53 7EY
Tel: 01758 712622 • Fax: 01758 712777
www.abersochgolf.co.uk

---

cosmopolitan city with a string of major hotels, Cardiff is an ideal base for the holiday golfer to explore more of the country's well known - and not so well known - golf courses.

On the outskirts of the capital the Cardiff Golf Club, Whitchurch, Llanishen, Dinas Powis, Radyr and Glamorganshire are all noteworthy. And just 15 minutes east of Cardiff you can find the Vale of Glamorgan resort - which now merits a mention among the very best. The Vale is the home of both the Welsh rugby and football sides and since the arrival of the FA Cup Final in Cardiff's Millennium Stadium it has accommodated the likes of Manchester United, Arsenal and Liverpool. The Lakes course and the more recent addition, the Wales National, have both staged major events in recent years, setting a trend which looks set to continue.

Moving a few miles further west to the mid Glamorgan coast, Royal Porthcawl maintains its unique character and charm – not to mention its reputation as being one of the toughest links challenges in the world. Its neighbours, Pyle and Kenfig and Southerndown, are two more venues which will always hold a special significance in the Welsh game.

Given the shining beauty of the West Wales coastline, it is hardly surprising that links golf is so popular. The Gower, Langland Bay, Swansea Bay and Pennard are all within a stone's throw of Wales' second city, Swansea, and the tourist trade in the region means there is always

---

FHG

For full details of clubs and courses, plus convenient accommodation
www.uk-golfguide.com

affordable accommodation on offer.

To add to these, West Wales now has a new standard bearer in the Machynys Peninsula Golf Club, which boasts Wales' first course designed by that name synonymous with excellence in the sport – Nicklaus. Jack's son, Gary, headed the team which developed the spectacular layout, opened in 2005 in Carmarthenshire's coastal park.

Heading up through mid Wales there is still plenty of golf on offer, with Aberystwyth, Builth Wells and Borth and Y-nyslas just three venues to whet the appetite.

And further north Royal St David's at Harlech, home to the Wales Seniors' Open on the European Tour, heads another quality cast list which includes Aberdovey, made famous by the legendary Bernard Darwin.

Anglesey offers some rugged links golf in its most natural form and right across the A55 from Conwy through Llandudno and Prestatyn to Northop Country Park, right on the Wales-England border, the golf courses come thick and fast.

Something for everyone – that's the motto for the holiday golfer in Wales.

Aberdovey Golf Club
Tel: 01654 767210 (Club)

Clubhouse (1998) now complements famous championship links.

On-site accommodation available.

Telephone Secretary John Griffiths (01654 767493) for party concessions and hotel discounts.

Aberdovey, Gwynedd LL35 0RT
www.aberdoveygolf.co.uk

CRICCIETH GOLF CLUB
Ednyfed Hill, Criccieth LL52 0SB
Green Fees: £20 per day
Parties welcome by prior arrangement
Clubhouse: 01766 522154
Treasurer: 01766 523385

Local and Country Membership available

A pleasant undulating 18-hole course on a hilltop with magnificent views.

PLEASE MENTION THIS GUIDE WHEN YOU WRITE OR PHONE TO ENQUIRE ABOUT CLUBS OR ACCOMMODATION

TREFEDDIAN HOTEL
ABERDOVEY

FOR MORE INFORMATION OR A COLOUR BROCHURE CONTACT US

01654 767213

WWW.TREFWALES.COM

- LIFT TO ALL FLOORS
- FAMILY OWNED AND MANAGED
- NEAR ABERDOVEY GOLF CLUB
- INDOOR AND OUTDOOR PLAY AREAS

Relax in our stylish en suite bedrooms with spectacular sea views and balconies

Enjoy the spacious lounges with views over Cardigan Bay from sumptuous sofas and dine in our award-winning dining room

Leisure facilities include indoor heated swimming pool, tennis court, putting green, snooker room and beauty salon

An idyllic location, minutes away from golden sandy beaches or the many mountains and lakes of Snowdonia

Xperience it!

AND ESCAPE...

HOLYWELL GOLF CLUB
Brynford, Holywell, North Wales CH8 8LQ

The course lies on a plateau in the village of Brynford a mile-and-a-half outside Holywell.
Its position is renowned for invigorating fresh air and views of the Clwydian range and Snowdonia.
18 hole course.
Golf clubs, Societies and Visitors welcome.
For further details contact the Secretary.

6th green – 165 yards par 3

Tel/Fax: 01352 713937 • Professional: 01352 710040

CLWB GOLF TREFFYNON • ESTABLISHED 1906 • HON SECRETARY BOB FIDDAMAN

CLWB GOLFF   BETWS-Y-COED GOLF CLUB

"The Jewel of the Nines"

Situated in the heart of the Snowdonia National Park you will find something special. Visitors and societies always welcome. Packages available.

Contact Secretary: Pat Rowley
01690 710556

e-mail: info@golf-betws-y-coed.co.uk • web: www.golf-betws-y-coed.co.uk

MOSS VALLEY GOLF CLUB
Moss Road, Moss, Wrexham LL11 6HA • Fax/Tel: 01978 720518

Established in the late 1980s the 9 hole course was designed by Golf Architects in a beautiful parkland setting just 5 minutes' drive from the centre of Wrexham. The scenery can be compared with any part of North Wales and some of the views from the course are quite breathtaking. Every hole is different in character, providing a good test of golf for both beginners and the experienced. Various categories of membership are available and the club actively encourages youngsters to become involved in the club. 9/18 Holes. Twin Tees on every hole.

e-mail: info@mossvalleygolf.com
website: www.mossvalleygolf.com

The Imperial Hotel

Ideally situated overlooking Llandudno Bay. Convenient for Maesdu, North Wales and Conwy Golf Clubs. Award-winning restaurant, two bars. Use of leisure facilities during stay including 45' heated indoor pool.

The Promenade, Llandudno LL30 1AP • Tel: 01492 877466 • Fax: 01492 878043
e-mail: imphotel@btinternet.com • www.theimperial.co.uk

NORTH WALES GOLF CLUB,
West Shore, Llandudno LL30 2DZ

Join us at the North Wales • Par 71

Enjoy the infinite variety of this true links championship course with its natural beauty, undulating fairways and slick greens.

• Visitors and societies welcome •
• No entrance fee payable for membership •
• Full and Country Membership available •
(Country Membership mileage restriction now 50 miles)
• Full catering facilities available •
• Golf Shop Golf Professional •
• Buggies, trolleys and clubs for hire •

e-mail: golf@nwgc.freeserve.co.uk
website: www.northwalesgolfclub.co.uk

Office: 01492 875325 • Pro: 01492 876878

FHG
·K·U·P·E·R·A·R·D·

FHG Guides
publish a large range of well-known accommodation guides. We will be happy to send you details or you can use the order form at the back of this book.

WALES

CAERLYR HALL HOTEL

Charming Victorian country house hotel set in a natural amphitheatre with spectacular sea and mountain views. All rooms are en suite and well equipped. Excellent cuisine, fine wines and a characterful bar await you.

Ideal for walkers, golfers and enthusiasts of historic buildings. Enjoy the many attractions within easy reach and then return to the peace and quiet of Caerlyr Hall.

WTB ★★★

Conwy Old Road, Dwygyfylchi, Conwy, North Wales LL34 6SW
Tel: 01492 623518
Fax: 01492 622070
www.caerlyrhallhotel.co.uk

RHUDDLAN GOLF CLUB
Meliden Road, Rhuddlan, Denbighshire LL18 6LB

Our gently undulating and scenic parkland course is only 25 miles from Chester and less than an hour's drive from Holyhead. We offer a warm welcome, a championship quality course, and full bar and restaurant facilities. Please telephone the Secretary for our club brochure giving details of golfing breaks, our many open competitions and good local hotels.

- 18 holes, parkland course • Length 6473 yards • Par 70, SSS 71
- Green Fees £25.00 to £30.00 • Societies must book
- Secretary Mr Martin C. Jones • Professional Mr A. Carr

Tel: 01745 590217 (Secretary) • 01745 590898 (Pro) • Fax: 01745 590472
e-mail: secretary@rhuddlangolfclub.co.uk • website: www.rhuddlangolfclub.co.uk

Prestatyn Golf Club

♦ Seaside links Championship course, host to WGU Championships and many other national events.
♦ 18 holes, 6564 yards, 5959 metres. S.S.S. 72.
♦ Visitors and societies welcome.
♦ Quote ref GG8 and get £1 off your green fee.
♦ Full bar and catering service.
♦ Hire of buggy, trolley and clubs available.

Marine Road East, Prestatyn LL19 7HS ♦ Tel: 01745 854320
www.prestatyngc.co.uk ♦ e-mail: prestatyngcmanager@freenet.co.uk

please note

All the information in this book is given in good faith in the belief that it is correct. However, the publishers cannot guarantee the facts given in these pages, neither are they responsible for changes in policy, ownership or terms that may take place after the date of going to press. Readers should always satisfy themselves that the facilities they require are available and that the terms, if quoted, still apply.

FHG
KUPERARD

WALES   The Golf Guide 2006

ASHBURNHAM GOLF CLUB Cliff Terrace, Burry Port, West Wales SA16 0HN

Discover Wales' best-kept golfing secret, the course where Bernard Gallagher and Sam Torrance had their first wins as tournament professionals. You will not find Ashburnham Golf Club by chance, tucked away between Burry Port and Pembrey, just to the west of Llanelli. This course, a traditional 18 hole links, hosted the 1994 Home Internationals. You will find a warm welcome and friendly hospitality to complement superb golf.

Phone (01554) 832269 to book a tee time.
It will not remain a secret for long!

18 holes • Par 72
FOUNDED 1894

Aberystwyth Golf Club
Brynymor Road, Aberystwyth SY23 2HY

Set above the picturesque town of Aberystwyth, this championship 18-hole course was designed by Harry Vardon and was formed in 1911. It provides both exciting and challenging golf for all players, as well as offering the most picturesque and panoramic views of Cardigan Bay and the mountains of Snowdonia. It is also the ideal venue for Corporate and Society golf days and provides flexible packages to suit individual requirements.

Our resident PGA Golf Professional is on hand to assist with your golfing needs. Our friendly bar and clubhouse is managed by our resident Steward, and our restaurant caters for a variety of palates, from simple bar snacks to à la carte.

You will be sure of a friendly welcome at Aberystwyth Golf Club.

Tel: 01970 615104
e-mail: aberystwythgolf@talk21.com
www.aberystwythgolfclub.com

Cardigan Golf Club

One of the finest golf complexes in West Wales, this is a fine championship course, with outstanding views from every hole. It is a mixture of links and meadowland, with exceptional drainage making it playable all year round.

◆ Relaxed, friendly atmosphere
◆ Clubhouse with well-equipped changing rooms
◆ Three squash courts with spectator gallery
◆ Restaurant and comprehensive bar snack menu

Visitors and societies welcome every day by prior arrangement
golf@cardigan.fsnet.co.uk • www.cardigangolf.co.uk

CARDIGAN GOLF CLUB
GWBERT-ON-SEA
CARDIGAN SA43 1PR
TEL & FAX: 01239 621775

WALES

2006 GREEN FEES
• £21.00 per round, £27.00 per day weekdays •
• £25.00 per round, £30.00 per day weekends and Bank Holidays •
• Three-day ticket £55.00, Five-day ticket £90.00 •
Prices are subject to increase

The Club House
Golf Club Road, Builth Wells, Powys LD2 3NF
Tel: 01982 553296
Fax: 01982 551064
www.builthwellsgolf.co.uk
e-mail: info@builthwellsgolf.co.uk

Builth Wells Golf Club

Haverfordwest Golf Club
Arnoldstown, Haverfordwest, Pembrokeshire SA61 2XQ

Set near the Pembrokeshire National Park and boasting magnificent views of the Preseli Hills, Haverfordwest Golf Club offers a real challenge to golfers of all abilities. Easily reachable on the A40 one mile east of Haverfordwest, this course is located in majestic parkland, and despite being an easy walk, there are a few holes that test the golfer's skill. The clubhouse, built in 1994, has excellent facilities including locker rooms, lounge, bars and full catering facilities, with Teresa Davies offering a wide selection of home-cooked cuisine.

• Club founded 1904 • 18 holes • Parkland • 5986 yards • Par 70
• Societies welcome by arrangement • Green Fee Visitors Welcome • Special Winter Rate Packages
Contact: Alex Pile or Mike Le Clair on 01437 768409 or 01437 764523 • Fax: 01437 764143

Builth Wells Golf Club, Powys

TENBY GOLF CLUB
Est 1888

The Burrows, Tenby,
Pembrokeshire SA70 7NP

Telephone/Fax: 01834 842978/844447
e-mail: tenbygolfclub@uku.co.uk
website: www.tenbygolf.co.uk

Visiting Golfers and Societies are welcome to play the oldest affiliated course in Wales

Ranked 84th in Golf Monthly Magazine's UK Top 120 Courses

St Mellons Golf Club
St Mellons, Cardiff CF3 2XS
Tel: 01633 680101 • Fax: 01633 681219

First opened in 1936, St Mellons is a lovely parkland course on the eastern edge of the bustling capital city of Cardiff. Since the course was opened, some of the world's finest players have played it including Lyle, Barnes, Torrance, James, Darcy and Antonio Garrido, who held the touring Professionals' course record for many years.

Visitors are very welcome at St Mellons, which is just 15 minutes' drive from the highly rated Celtic Manor, just off Junctions 28 and 30 of the M4 and 35 minutes from the Second Severn Crossing.

BRYN MEADOWS
Golf & Country Hotel

Maesycwmmer, Near Ystrad Mynach, Caerphilly, South Wales CF82 7SN

Located in the heart of the beautiful Rhymney Valley, just 25 minutes' drive from Cardiff City Centre and 15 minutes from the M4 Junction 28. The tree-lined, mature, parkland course offers a new challenge from every tee, with receptive greens, lush fairways and water features.

Golf Break Packages
2 nights DB&B + 2 rounds golf from £117.50pp

Tel: 01495 225590 • Fax: 01495 228272
www.brynmeadows.com

The Beaufort Hotel
Chepstow, South Wales NP16 5EP

The Beaufort Hotel is ideal for St Pierre, Rolls of Monmouth and Celtic Manor Golf Clubs. A family run hotel with friendly, cheerful staff. Popular bar at pub prices and an award-winning restaurant. We can cater for all your requirements.

Tel: 01291 622497 • Fax: 01291 627389

E-mail: info@thebeauforthotel.co.uk • www.beauforthotelchepstow.com

WALES

Coed Y Mwstwr Golf Club
Coychurch, Bridgend CF35 6AF
Tel/Fax: 01656 864934
www.coed-y-mwstwr.co.uk

Just 5 minutes from the M4 in the heart of South Wales, our parkland course offers an interesting test for both low and high handicap golfers.

**With the opening of 6 new holes in June 2005, we are now a full 18-hole course.
For details of all our visitor offers, please contact our Manager on the above number.**

COED-Y-MWSTWR HOTEL
Coychurch, Bridgend, Vale of Glamorgan CF35 6AF

Perched on a Welsh hillside overlooking the picturesque Vale of Glamorgan, Coed-y-Mwstwr, "Whispering Trees", provides a cosy and secluded hideaway. Luxurious bedrooms with all modern amenities and a host of thoughtful extras. Elegant restaurant with food prepared by award-winning chefs. Enjoy a round of complimentary golf, take advantage of our heated swimming pool, Leisure Club with fully equipped gym, sauna and steamroom. An oasis of calm in a changing world, where you are always greeted with a warm Welsh welcome and assured of friendly, courteous and professional attention. *Voted top AA Hotel for Courtesy and Care. AA Award Winning Cuisine*

Tel: 01656 860621 • Fax: 01656 863122

AA ★★★★

e-mail: reservations@coed-y-mwstwr.com • www.coed-y-mwstwr.com ★★★★

GREEN ACRE PUBLIC HOUSE & MOTEL

Mike and Sue welcome you to their 17 bedroom motel, with all rooms en suite. Facilities include seasonal use of indoor swimming pool (check for availablity), squash court, Sky TV in all rooms, and bar meals served 12-2pm and 6.30-9.45pm, à la carte from 6.30-9.45pm; Sunday lunch available.
*£34 single room per night, £44 double room per night.
Weekend Specials Fri/Sat or Sat/Sun £65 single or double;
Fri/Sat/Sun £95 single or double.
All prices inclusive of breakfast and VAT.*

**111 Heol Fach, North Cornelly, Near Bridgend, South Wales CF33 4LH
Tel: 01656 743041/744707 • Fax: 01656 744208**

Caerphilly Golf Club
❖ *Established 1905* ❖

Societies and Guests always welcome. Membership available

Secretary: 029 208 63441
Professional: 029 208 69104

www.caerphillygolfclub.com
secretary@caerphillygolfclub.com

WALES   The Golf Guide 2006

Monmouth Golf Club
Leasbrook Lane, Monmouth NP25 3SN
Tel/Fax: 01600 772399
sec.mongc@barbox.net
Pro Shop: 01600 712212

Monmouth Golf Club is situated on the A40, half a mile north of the town. It was extended to an 18-hole course in 1992, when a new clubhouse was opened, offering a most comfortable location for a drink or a meal, with magnificent views of the course and the surrounding countryside. Monmouth certainly has every justification for its claim to be one of the prettiest courses in Wales, and is renowned for the warm welcome offered to its guests.

Standing on high ground above the town, the undulating parkland course plays 5698 yards off white tees, 5507 off yellow, and 5118 off red (ladies). Each aptly named hole offers a different challenge. The 8th (Cresta Run) was recently included in "Britain's 100 most extraordinary golf holes" which also nominated Monmouth as having the best value green fees in the country.

As you leave the clubhouse you become aware of the tranquillity of the verdant surroundings, mature trees, wild flowers and an abundance of wildlife.

Visit the Monmouth Golf Club- you will not be disappointed.

DEWSTOW GOLF • CLUB

Golf at its best, supported by facilities designed for your sheer enjoyment

- Two golf courses – Valley Course and Park Course
- Golf Academy with 26-bay floodlit covered driving range, coffee shop and golf shop.
- Clubhouse with lounge, bars and restaurant open every day
- Function rooms for meetings, conferences and training.
- Societies welcome weekdays; weekends by arrangement

Dewstow Golf Club, Caerwent, Monmouthshire NP26 5AH
Tel: 01291 430444 • Fax: 01291 425816
e-mail: info@dewstow.com
website: www.dewstow.com

The Monmouthshire Golf Club
Founded 1892
A superb example of a mature parkland course, popular with golfers of all ages and abilities.

♦ Comfortable lounge and dining area ♦ Friendly clubhouse
♦ Separate non-smoking bar ♦ Pro Shop with top-brand equipment ♦ Expert tuition: practice area and indoor academy ♦ Societies and visitors welcome by prior arrangement.

Please telephone R.F. Bradley 01873 852606; Fax: 01873 850470
Llanfoist, Abergavenny, Monmouthshire NP7 9HE
www.monmouthshiregolfclub.co.uk

Wenvoe Castle Golf Club
Founded 1936
Wenvoe
Cardiff CF5 6BE
Tel/Fax: 029 2059 4371
enquiries@wenvoecastlegolfclub.com
www.wenvoecastlegolfclub.com

- Exit Junction 33 M4, follow signs for Cardiff Airport.
- Parkland course founded in 1936, fairly open layout with hilly front 9, hosted first PGA Welsh Classic. Practice areas.
- 18 holes, 6458 yards. S.S.S. 71.
- Bar snacks and restaurant meals.
- Visitors welcome weekdays only.
- Society Meetings catered for weekdays only, parties of 16 or more

Cottrell Park Golf Club, Cardiff

Cottrell Park Golf Club
St Nicholas, Cardiff CF5 6JY

- Accommodation available in association with local providers
- Full Welsh Breakfast
- 18 holes on one of Cottrell's Championship golf courses.

Set in the heart of beautiful Vale of Glamorgan parkland, Cottrell Park offers the perfect Golf Break Destination

We can build the perfect Golf Getaway for you!

Mini Golf Breaks starting from £46 per person!

Cottrell Park is easily accessible from J33 of the M4 and only 15 minutes' drive from the centre of Cardiff.

www.golfwithus.com • Tel: 01446 781781 • Fax: 01446 781187 • sales@golfwithus.com

Wernddu Golf Club
Open to all visitors
18 Hole Golf Course • Driving Range
Snacks • Bar
Ring for Special Society Packages

Old Ross Road, Abergavenny, Monmouthshire NP7 8NG
Tel: 01873 856223 • Fax: 01873 852177
e-mail: info@wernddu-golf-club.co.uk
www.wernddu-golf-club.co.uk

Golf in Scotland

Nick Rodger

Jedburgh Golf Club, in the Scottish Borders

After successive Open Championships at Royal Troon and St Andrews in 2004 and 2005 respectively, the battle for the Claret Jug returns south this year to Royal Liverpool, but golf fans north of Border can still look forward to a feast of excellent competition over the coming months as the world's leading professionals and amateurs tee up at some of the country's most renowned venues.

The Barclays Scottish Open, now firmly established as one of the premier events on the European Tour, will again headline the bill as some of the game's finest players descend on Loch Lomond in July the week before the Open itself gets underway.

Last season, crowds of over 74,000 flocked to the championship to roar on Scot, Alastair Forsyth, as he led the home assault on the £400,000 top prize.

The former Scottish PGA champion from Paisley was still in the title race with ten holes to play as the event drew to an exciting conclusion, but his challenge

---

Links
Handicaps
Memberships
Bookings
Till & Stock Control
Accounts

14 Skaethorn Road, Havana Lock
Glasgow G20 0TQ • Tel: 0141 945 5501

www.linksgolf.co.uk

The Open of 2006

The Spey Valley Championship Golf Course is due to open in May 2006. Set in some of the most breathtaking scenery in the Highlands, if not the world, it's predicted to be one of Scotland's leading golf venues and destined to be in the top 5 rankings.

The spectacular course has been designed by one of Europe's leading golf architects, Dave Thomas, who has been designing courses worldwide for over 30 years. It will be kept by the former green keeper at Royal Dornoch, Bob Mackay.

The 7177 yard undulating golf course is a must-play for both amateur and professional golfers alike. As well as having the scenic backdrop of the Cairngorm mountains and the river Spey running alongside it, the course also has the longest hole in Scotland at 641 yards.

Located at Dalfaber, Aviemore, just 30 minutes south of Inverness, it's the latest in leisure activities available at the Macdonald Aviemore Highland Resort.

Be the first to receive information, updates and offers on the golf course and the resort, by emailing us at golf@ahresort.co.uk

www.AviemoreHighlandResort.com

MACDONALD AVIEMORE

HIGHLAND RESORT

Make Everyday Legendary.™

Transfers energy to the ball, so you don't have to *transfer blame* to your driver.

Standard clubs

Wilson Staff ETF Technology

Energy Transfer Frame technology, a proprietary COR-enhancement in the new Wilson Staff drivers, fairway woods and hybrids, delivers more than twice the hot zone of standard clubs. And half the excuses.

wilsonstaff.com

ETF460™
Energy Transfer Frame

Wilson Staff
Dd6 · 10°

Wilson Staff

58

SCOTLAND

The famous 18th at Gleneagles.

And the other one.

And the other one.

There is only one place in Scotland that can boast three championship golf courses. It's a place where you don't even have to stay to play; a place where there's a spa, riding, fishing, shooting and off-road driving all available amongst some of Scotland's most stunning scenery. Not to mention a choice of four restaurants including the Michelin starred 'Andrew Fairlie at Gleneagles'. That place is Gleneagles. (There is no other like it.) Book online or call us free on 0800 328 4010 for more information.

THE GLENEAGLES HOTEL
Auchterarder, Perthshire, Scotland PH3 1NF. Just 1 hour from Edinburgh/Glasgow.
Telephone +44 (0) 1764 662231 Fax +44 (0) 1764 662134 www.gleneagles.com
The GLENEAGLES word and EAGLE Device are trade marks.   A member of *The Leading Hotels of the World*   Ref: GOLF GUIDE

petered out with bogeys at the ninth and 13th and Forsyth eventually had to settle for a share of eighth place behind winner Tim Clark of South Africa, the fourth Springbok victor in the past five years.

Following last year's hugely successful staging of the Senior British Open at Royal Aberdeen, Scotland is again expected to lay out the welcome mat for the game's 'Golden Oldies' in 2006 after European Seniors' Tour chiefs announced that the event would be staying in the home of golf, with Turnberry again high on the list of possible venues.

Tom Watson, the eight-time Major winner, reigned supreme over the Balgownie links last July, following up his triumph in the 2003 championship with a sudden-death play-off win over Ryder Cup assistant captain Des Smyth, which brought four days of excellent competition in the wind-ravaged North East to a tense finale.

The impressive schedule of top level golf will continue into August this year as the European Tour bandwagon rolls back into Scotland with a stop at the Gleneagles Hotel, one of the world's leading resorts, for the £1.4 million Johnnie Walker Championship.

Barely a fortnight after that, the country's Tartan Tour players, as well as a host of Scottish professionals from the European circuit, will return to Perthshire to contest the Gleneagles Scottish PGA championship.

As ever in Scotland, amateur golf is to the fore and the season swings into action in April as West Kilbride, nestling in the great golfing heartland of Ayrshire, stages the Scottish Golf Union's traditional curtain raiser, the BP Scottish Boys' championship.

In early June, the Scottish Open Amateur Strokeplay championship, with a list of past winners that includes Colin

---

18 holes Par 69 • Parkland • 5780 yards • 2005 Green Fees: Weekday £17, Weekend £22
Craibstone Golf Centre • Bucksburn, Aberdeen AB21 9YA

Opened in 2000, the Craibstone Golf Centre offers great facilities to all levels of golfer, and is only 5 minutes from the airport and 10 minutes from the city centre. Short in length compared to most new courses, its main defences are the large sloping greens with pins that can be tucked away, making it tricky to get up and down from a missed approach shot. Excellent short game and practice area open to the public. The resident PGA Professional is always keen to help with lessons, and the shop has all the latest equipment at competitive prices. Buggy and trolley hire available. Members of the public welcome 7 days a week and catering is available for parties of any number. **e-mail: craibstonegolf@sac.co.uk • Tel: 01224 711195**

Stonehaven Golf Club
Where visitors have been welcomed for more than 100 years.

One mile north of town, signposted at mini roundabout near open-air pool
• Parkland course on cliffs overlooking North Sea with some challenging holes over natural gullies. • 18 holes, 5128 yards. S.S.S. 65.
• Full catering including bar lunches (not Mondays). • Visitors welcome, but advised to reserve tee time in advance, restricted Saturdays after 4pm.

**Tel: 01569 762124 • Fax: 01569 765973
e-mail: stonehaven.golfclub@virgin.net**

The Golf Guide 2006   SCOTLAND

Inchmarlo Royal Deeside
Inchmarlo Royal Deeside, Banchory

Inchmarlo Royal Deeside

Ponds, meandering burns and even dry stone walls, combine with the more traditional bunkers to test the skill of even the most accomplished player, at the same time rewarding the accuracy of the short game expert. The Laird's Course opened for play in July 2001 and at 6218 yards, this championship standard par 71 course is already one of Scotland's most sought after golfing venues, complementing the existing nine-hole course and the Centre's other facilities, including tuition from a team of PGA professionals.

View from 2nd Tee

Catering for all age groups, the Golf Professional's shop is stocked with all the latest in golf equipment and fashions.
Cuisine of the highest standard is available in our various bars and restaurant, and a warm and friendly welcome is assured.

Golf Professional's Shop

The Laird's, 2nd Green

Classic Golf Course design, stunning scenery, excellent facilities....
The Laird's at Inchmarlo Royal Deeside is ready for the challenge - are you?

For further details contact:
Tel: 01330 826422 (Pro-shop) or 01330 826424 (Membership/Groups)
e-mail: info@inchmarlo.com • www.inchmarlo.com

61

Carriages Hotel

1-3 Commercial Road, Insch, Aberdeenshire AB52 6JN
Tel: 01464 820604 • Fax: 01464 821408
E-mail: reservations@carriageshotel.com

A good mix of peaceful accommodation, some at ground level separate from the main building, and friendly country atmosphere with delicious food cooked to perfection by our resident Chef and served by our friendly, helpful staff.

Local golf course, open countryside next to hotel, railway station close by, easy access by train from Aberdeen, Aberdeen Airport and Inverness. Bar, Restaurant, small function room, large function room suitable for weddings, birthdays and other special occasions. Sky and Fox Children's TV.

18 Rooms, 12 en suite: £30 single, £60 twin, £60 double, £70 Executive Double Room and £80 Family Room

www.carriageshotel.com

The Moray Golf Club
founded 1889

There are 36 individual reasons to play golf at Moray - and every one is designed for enjoyment!

Moray Golf Club at Lossiemouth offers two traditional Scottish golf links 18-hole courses - Moray Old and Moray New. Like the Old Course at the "Home of Golf", St Andrews, the courses start and finish within the town boundaries.

www.moraygolf.co.uk

Stotfield Road, Lossiemouth IV31 6QS
Tel: 01343 812018 • Fax: 01343 815102 • e-mail: secretary@moraygolf.co.uk

---

Montgomerie, Andrew Coltart, Stephen Gallacher and Alastair Forsyth, makes its first trek to the impressive new links at Craigielaw in East Lothian, before the SGU's flagship event, the Scottish Amateur championship, takes place at the end of July at Nairn.

For visual splendour, Nairn, which hosted the 1999 Walker Cup, is unsurpassed, and from every hole golfers are blessed with stunning views of the Moray Firth and the golden colouring and changing lights of the Black Isle. Nineteen years after Colin Montgomerie raced to a 9 and 8 win in the Scottish championship there, the country's leading amateurs will once again return to this splendid stretch of Highlands' linksland to do battle for one of game's most prestigious honours.

While Loch Lomond will take centre stage at the height of the golf season in July with the staging of the Scottish Open, the curtain will come down on the 2006 domestic campaign with a return trip to the Bonnie Banks at the start of October.

The Bunkered Matchplay Challenge, a biennial, Ryder Cup style joust between the Scottish PGA and the Scottish Golf Union, will be held at the new Carrick on Loch Lomond, one of the country's most eagerly awaited championship golf courses.

FHG

please mention THE GOLF GUIDE
when you enquire about clubs
or accommodation

·K·U·P·E·R·A·R·D·

Designed by the award-winning Canadian architect, Doug Carrick, the Carrick on Loch Lomond will open its door to the public this year and the innovative Bunkered Matchplay Challenge – won by Bernard Gallacher's team of professionals at Cardrona in 2004 – will be the first ever tournament to be staged over Scotland's most talked about new venue.

The cut and thrust of the matchplay format always makes for exciting competition and the Bunkered Matchplay Challenge should provide a fitting conclusion to another mouth-watering year of golf north of the Border.

Visitors' Package
5 days unlimited golf £50

- Auchmill Golf Course
- Balnagask Golf Courses
- Hazlehead Golf Courses
- King's Links Golf Courses

Aberdeen City Golf

"Pay & Play" option also available

SPECIAL OFFER

01224 814772
or e-mail
golf@aberdeencity.gov.uk
for further info

ABERDEEN CITY COUNCIL

VISITORS AND SOCIETIES CATERED FOR

DUFF HOUSE ROYAL
GOLF CLUB
THE BARNYARDS, BANFF AB45 3SX
OFFICE: 01261 812062 • PRO SHOP: 01261 812075
e-mail: duff_house_royal@btinternet.com

18-HOLE PARKLAND COURSE
PRACTICE PUTTING AREA • GOLF SHOP
PGA PROFESSIONAL • PUTTING GREEN
LOUNGE BAR • CATERING FACILITIES
OPEN DAYS • CHANGING FACILITIES

Fraserburgh Golf Club FOUNDED 1779

Fraserburgh boasts a 27-hole complex with excellent practice facilities. **CORBIEHILL**, the 18-hole course is 6308 yards (Par 70) of largely unspoiled traditional Scottish links. Its main features are the tricky Par 3s together with a handful of short but very interesting Par 4s. When visiting Fraserburgh, take some time out at the third tee – the view itself is worth the trip. **ROSEHILL**, the 2400 yard 9-hole course is essentially parkland. Although short in yards, it plays its length and has two superb finishing holes.

Philorth, Fraserburgh AB43 8TL
01346 516616

The Burnett Arms Hotel

25 High Street, Banchory, Aberdeenshire AB31 5TD
Tel: 01330 824944 • Fax: 01330 825553

Situated in the centre of Banchory on Royal Deeside. "The Burnett" is an old coaching inn, fully modernised yet retaining its warm atmosphere of old. With over 20 golf courses within 45 minutes by car, the hotel is ideally situated for golf outings wishing to play on more than one course. The hotel has 16 en suite rooms with 10 channel TV, tea/coffee, hairdryer. Drying room and storage available for clubs. Two bars cater for all tastes, serving bar lunches and suppers. High teas and dinners available in the restaurant.

Special rates for golfers available on request
AMPLE PARKING • DOGS/PETS WELCOME • CREDIT CARDS ACCEPTED

Newmachar Golf Club
~ Hawkshill Course ~

Designed by Dave Thomas and Peter Alliss, Hawkshill is a challenging 6700yd, Par 72, SSS 74 course. The natural features of the pine and birch woodlands have been retained and now line the narrow fairways and surround the well-bunkered greens. Water hazards also feature on 7 holes, making Hawkshill a unique experience for golfers of all standards and one of the most demanding courses in Scotland.

Other facilities at Newmachar include Swailend 18-hole course, a floodlit driving range, two putting greens, bunkers and a pitching green. A team of PGA Professionals offer a full range of teaching packages. On an elevated site the Clubhouse enjoys spectacular views, and golfers can celebrate sinking that final putt in the lounge bar or dining room.

Newmachar Golf Club,
Swailend, Newmachar, Aberdeenshire AB21 7UU
Tel: 01651 863002 ~ Fax: 01651 863055
website: www.newmachargolfclub.co.uk
e-mail: info@newmachargolfclub.co.uk

ROTHESAY GOLF CLUB

Beautiful island in the Firth of Clyde. Frequent ferries from Wemyss Bay, 35 miles south west of Glasgow, and from Colintraive on mainland Argyll. One of Scotland's most scenic island courses, designed by Ben Sayers and James Braid. 18 holes. 5456 yards. SSS 67. Practice area. Green Fees: on request. Winter rates from 1st November to 31st March. Full catering and bar facilities. Visitors very welcome, but at weekends by prior arrangement.
All bookings: PGA Professional James M. Dougal (Tel & Fax 01700 503554)

Canada Hill, Isle of Bute PA20 9HN • www.rothesaygolfclub.com

SCOTLAND

West End Hotel
West Bay, Dunoon PA23 7HU
www.westendhotel.com

Tel: 01369 702907 • Fax: 01369 706266
e-mail: mike@westendhotel.com

Situated on the traffic-free West Bay, with private parking, the West End enjoys magnificent views of the Clyde Estuary, yet is only minutes' walk from the town centre.

- All rooms have en suite facilities • Varied menus • Licensed bar
- Live entertainment most weekends • Games room

Golf Breaks are our speciality, with 3 courses within a 15 minute drive. Experience the breathtaking scenery from the 18-hole Cowal championship course.

3-day Golf Breaks including DB&B and green fees from £150

WHITE HART Hotel
Campbeltown, Argyll PA28 6AN
Tel: 01586 552440 • Fax: 01586 554972
e-mail: whiteharthotel@amserve.net • www.whiteh.com

The White Hart is the nearest golfing hotel to Machrihanish Golf Club. If you are planning a visit to Machrihanish or Campbeltown, then the White Hart is the perfect base for your visit. While staying with us you are entitled to discounted green fees at Machrihanish. Other golf packages available.

19 stylish bedrooms, all en suite, with TV, telephone, computer outlet, and tea/coffee making facilities. Taste of Kintyre Restaurant and informal Conservatory Bistro provide a superb dining experience. Situated in the main street of Campbeltown, an ideal base for exploring the Mull of Kintyre.

THISTLE HOTELS
more than just accommodating

Just 10 minutes' transfer from Prestwick International Airport and 25 miles from Glasgow City Centre. Easy access to many world famous courses in Ayrshire including Royal Troon, host to the 133rd Open Championship. The hotel offers guests a high standard of service and comfort, with 128 large bedrooms, a choice of restaurants, a unique lagoon pool with jacuzzi and games room. On-site executive 9-hole Par 3 golf course.

Thistle Irvine, 46 Annick Road, Irvine, Ayrshire KA11 4LD
tel: 0870 333 9256 • e-mail: reservations.irvine@thistle.co.uk

2-day Golf Packages start from £150.00 • Golf Club memberships available.

LARGS GOLF CLUB
IRVINE ROAD, LARGS KA30 8EU

- £30 per round, £40 day ticket Monday - Friday
- Fourball deals available
- Package deals for 12 or more golfers
- Contact the Secretary for details

Largs Golf Club is a long-established private club with a superb 18 hole parkland course, situated in front of Kelburn Castle, one mile south of Largs town centre. From the clubhouse and course there are magnificent views of the Firth of Clyde towards the Cumbraes, Bute and the mountains of Arran.

The course is enduringly popular with visitors, who return regularly year after year. The well balanced layout offers an interesting and challenging experience to golfers across the broad spectrum of enthusiasm and ability.

Secretary/Treasurer: JIM CALLAGHAN
Tel/Fax: 01475 673754 • E-mail: secretary@largsgolfclub.co.uk • Web: www.largsgolfclub.co.uk

SCOTLAND

modern luxury

play the legend

excitement.
anticipation.
inspiration.
and that's just the view.

Pause for a moment. Breathe in that fresh sea air. Then look around you. It could only be Turnberry.

Let us reserve your stay. Call **01655 331 000**
Best rates, guaranteed at westin.com/turnberry

THE WESTIN TURNBERRY RESORT
SCOTLAND

For full details of clubs and courses, plus convenient accommodation

www.uk-golfguide.com

sportscotland
National Centre Inverclyde
Golf Practice Facility

Our course, boasting six holes, eight driving bays and clubgolf coaching bays, has been in operation since 1984 and has a fantastic outlook across the Firth of Clyde to the Isles of Cumbrae and Bute and over the hills of Arran.

The practice facility, is primarily used for members and as a clubgolf training centre, providing coach education courses, however, many other user groups can access the centre, by booking the facility, on an hourly/daily basis.

The centre can also organise tailor made tuition packages for parties of 4 or more, including accommodation and meals. If individual lessons are for you, we can contact our local Professionals, who will gladly help you improve your game.

Burnside Road, Largs KA30 8RW	Email: in.enquiries@sportscotland.org.uk Web: www.nationalcentreinverclyde.org.uk Tel: 0845 126 0664

18 holes, 6021 yards, par 69, SSS 70
• lunch • dinner • club bar • bar snacks
• tea and coffee • cart hire
• trolley hire • changing room

Situated just one mile north of Galashiels on the A7
Visitors welcome daily
Voted "The Most Visitor Friendly Golf Club" 2001

Torwoodlee GOLF CLUB
Edinburgh Road, Galashiels TD1 2NE • Tel & Fax: **01896 752260**
e-mail: thesecretary@torwoodleegolfclub.co.uk • web: www.torwoodleegolfclub.org.uk

SCOTLAND

HEATHERLIE HOUSE HOTEL

A warm welcome awaits you at this elegant Victorian Mansion situated in the heart of the Scottish Borders. Quietly located in wooded grounds. Comfortably furnished bedrooms, (8 en suite), with colour TV, tea/coffee making, direct dial telephones. Extensive menu, wine list and selection of Malts.

• 21 golf courses in the region, including new championship courses; The Roxburghe at Kelso and and Cardrona at Peebles. Special golfers' packages available in conjunction with the 'Freedom of the Fairways' passport.

Heatherlie Park, Selkirk TD7 5AL
Tel: 01750 721200 • Fax: 01750 720005
enquiries@heatherlie-house.co.uk
www.heatherlie-house.co.uk

Minto Golf Club

'A Gem of a Golf Course in one of the most beautiful corners of Scotland Located at the village of Minto, near Denholm, 6 miles east of Hawick on the A698.

All information regarding green fees, tee-bookings and available dates for visiting parties will be given by telephone and confirmed in writing. Minto Golf Club, Denholm, Hawick TD9 8SH

Tel: 01450 870 220

• 30 bedrooms (single, twin, double, triple and family) en suite; also a four-poster for that touch of luxury • B&B from £35pppn
• Bar lounge, a relaxing environment for light meals and refreshments, which are served all day, every day, from 12-9pm. • Open all year
• 20 Golf courses within 45 minutes' drive

www.georgeandabbotsford.co.uk
enquiries@georgeandabbotsford.co.uk

George & Abbotsford Hotel, High Street, Melrose, Scottish Borders TD6 9PD
Tel: 01896 822308 • Fax: 01896 823363

Jedburgh Golf Club

Situated at the gateway to the Scottish Borders, Jedburgh Golf Club is a must for any golfers to the area. Established in 1892, the parkland/moorland layout was designed by former Open Champion, Willie Park of Musselburgh.

The Dunion Course is currently in the process of being extended from 9 holes to 18 holes, with a projected opening date of Spring 2006. It will undoubtedly prove to be a real gem and a challenge to golfers of all standards. This, allied to stunning views of the surrounding countryside, will ensure that Jedburgh Golf Club will attract visitors from all corners.

5650 yards ♦ Bar Open 11am - 11pm ♦ Green fees £22 per day ♦ Buggy & trolley hire (no club hire)

Dunion Road, Jedburgh TD8 6TA • All enquiries please phone 01835 863587

SCOTLAND

The Golf Guide 2006

• HETLAND HALL HOTEL •
Golf in Dumfries & Galloway

Hetland Hall Hotel is a magnificent Country House Hotel set in 18 acres of parkland. We are within striking distance of around 30 golf clubs and other local attractions in Dumfries and Galloway, making us an ideal base for your golfing break. 30 en suite bedrooms and full leisure facilities including indoor heated pool, sauna, steam room, beauty room, toning tables, and for those of you looking for some golfing practice, we have a 9-hole Pitch 'n' Putt.

Tel: 01387 840201 • Fax: 01387 840211
www.hetlandhallhotel.co.uk
e-mail: info@hetlandhallhotel.co.uk
Carrutherstown, Dumfries DG1 4JX
*A member of Best Western Hotels
The leading chain of Independent Hotels in the World*

The Summerhill Course, Dumfries & Galloway Golf Club's championship 18-hole layout (6309 yards, Par 70) has magnificent views over the hills to the north of Dumfries. The course is maintained in excellent condition, and is a very good test of golf. Visitors are welcome on most days (limited times on competition days), and an on-line booking system is available.

• Well-stocked Pro Shop • Practice facilities
• Full catering service • Dining Room • Bar • Visitor Locker Room
Secretary: Alasdair T. Miller (Tel/Fax: 01387 263848)

Dumfries & Galloway Golf Club, Laurieston Avenue, Dumfries DG2 7NY
info@dandggolfclub.co.uk • www.dandggolfclub.co.uk

THORNHILL GOLF CLUB

The 18-hole course is a mixture of park and heathland with magnificent panoramic views. It has often been described as a 'hidden jewel'. The course is easy on the high handicapper, but offers a real challenge to the scratch golfer.
The fully licensed clubhouse offers snacks and excellent quality meals throughout the day. Situated one mile from the village cross in Thornhill which is on the main A76 Dumfries to Kilmarnock road.

Blacknest, Thornhill DG3 5DW
Tel: 01848 330546

THE MOFFAT GOLF CLUB
Moorland course designed by Ben Sayers of North Berwick

A fine, traditional Scottish moorland course with a welcoming clubhouse, making it an ideal venue for a day or weekend trip. Visitors are offered full use of the bar and catering facilities, and there are visitors' changing rooms/showers, and a games room.
Situated in the rolling hills of the southern uplands, Moffat is one hour from Glasgow, and one-and-a-half hours from Edinburgh.
Leave A74 (M) at Junction 15 and follow A701.

Special packages available for midweek and weekend parties of 8 or more.

Moffat Golf Club, Coatshill, Moffat, Dumfriesshire DG10 9SB
Tel: 01683 220020 • Fax: 01683 221802
e-mail: bookings@moffatgolfclub.co.uk • www.moffatgolfclub.co.uk

1884

The Golf Guide 2006 SCOTLAND

For full details of clubs and courses, plus convenient accommodation
www.uk-golfguide.com

Please mention
THE GOLF GUIDE
when you enquire about clubs or accommodation

Torrs Warren
Country House Hotel

Comfortable, family-run hotel, set in its own grounds, with ample parking and beer garden. Situated in south western Scotland, just 6 miles from Portpatrick. Ideally placed for exploring beautiful countryside, secluded coves, rugged cliffs, enchanted forests and long sandy beaches.

Dunskey, Portpatrick, Stranraer and Glenluce Golf Courses all within 10 minutes' drive, Newton Stewart Golf Club 25 minutes.
Bed & Breakfast from £33 double/twin room. £42 single.
Dinner, Bed & Breakfast from £49 (double/twin room)

Torrs Warren Country House Hotel
Stoneykirk, Stranraer, Scotland DG9 9DH
Tel: 01776 830204
Fax: 01776 830298
Email: TorrsWarren@hotmail.com
www.torrswarrenhotel.co.uk

Portpatrick Dunskey Golf Club
Tel: 01776 810273 • Fax: 01776 810811
enquiries@portpatrickgolfclub.com
www.portpatrickgolfclub.com

Portpatrick, Stranraer DG9 8TB

Two clifftop links courses:
Dunskey 18 holes • Dinvin 9 holes
Handicap Certificate required • Visitors advised to book in advance • Winter rates apply November to Mid-March • Eating facilities available all year except Mondays.

The Waterfront is a stylish new hotel, furnished to a very high specification and situated opposite the picturesque harbour of Portpatrick. With eight en suite bedrooms and an elegant restaurant serving a delicious selection of dishes and wines, The Waterfront is perfectly located for that Golfing Break, with Portpatrick (Dunskey) and Lagganmore Golf Clubs being within one mile and Stranraer Golf Club within 8 miles. Individual or Group Golfing packages at favourable rates available on request. 'We look forward to welcoming you."
Prices from £35 pppn (en suite, sharing).

The Waterfront Hotel & Bistro North Crescent, Portpatrick DG9 8SX
Telephone 01776 810800 • Fax 01776 810850
e-mail: WaterfrontHotel@aol.com • website: www.waterfronthotel.co.uk

SCOTLAND

The Lagganmore Hotel and Golf Club
Lagganmore, Portpatrick DG9 9AB

Special packages combining golf, dinner, a full Scottish breakfast and accommodation: two nights £120, three nights £150.

Situated just ten yards from the first tee, The Lagganmore Hotel combines traditional Scottish cuisine with comfortable, attractively furnished accommodation. The popular lounge bar remains open all day, serving lunches and suppers.

The Lagganmore course provides a great test for every golfer, combining natural valleys and contours with streams and water features. Our feature hole, the Par 5 7th, is the best in South West Scotland. **Tel: 01776 810499 or 01776 810262**

info@lagganmoregolf.co.uk • www.lagganmoregolf.co.uk

MONTROSE GOLF LINKS LTD

Medal Course (Par 71, SSS 72)
Broomfield Course (Par 66, SSS 63)

Medal course ranked fifth oldest in the world.
Open Championship Final Qualifying Course 1999 & 2007

Individual Round and Day Tickets available on both courses: All Visitors and Parties Welcome. Group Discounts offered. Special Packages available including catering and in conjunction with local hotels.

Enquiries to: Mrs M. Stewart, Secretary, Montrose Golf Links Ltd, Traill Drive, Montrose, Angus DD10 8SW

Telephone: (01674) 672932 • Fax: (01674) 671800
e-mail: Secretary@montroselinks.co.uk • www.montroselinks.co.uk

---

Located four miles from Carnoustie and ½ hour from St Andrews. Two courses offer golf for all levels with the Medal being used as an Open Championship Qualifier. These beautiful links courses also feature tree-lined fairways in many places.

Medal Course £39 Monday to Friday and £49 at weekends; Ashludie Course £19 Monday to Friday and £23 at weekends; a package includes a round of golf on each course, coffee, bacon rolls, soup and sandwiches, and high tea at the day's end **all for £59!**

For bookings call the Links Secretary on
01382 532767
The Starter's Box, Monifieth Links,
Princes Street, Monifieth DD5 4AW
monifiethgolf@freeuk.com

The hidden gem in Angus
Monifieth Golf Links

The Macdonald Marine Hotel & Spa has just undergone a multi-million pound refurbishment returning the hotel to its former glory! This Victorian building is located at the heart of East Lothian's golfing coast.

The hotel overlooks the North Berwick Championship Golf Course as well as the Firth of Forth. The well proportioned public areas and many of the bedrooms enjoy the spectacular view.

With the addition of a magnificent Spa and an 18-metre pool, the hotel will be the natural choice for golf and leisure guests. The Craigleith Restaurant offers a mix of Scottish and International cuisine, whilst the Links Bar and Sea View Lounge serves a range of light meals throughout the day.

Please call 0870 400 8129 for an introductory offer.
Cromwell Road, North Berwick EH39 4LZ
www.macdonaldhotels.co.uk/marine

MACDONALD Marine Hotel & Spa North Berwick

Edinburgh Golf

Braid Hills
"The best public course outside St. Andrews"
Business AM

- Pay and Play
- Club hire available

Edinburgh Leisure
Managing leisure and recreation facilities for the City of Edinburgh Council

Braids Hills	0131 447 6666
Princes Golf Course	0131 447 3568
Craigentinny Golf Course	0131 554 7851
Carrick Knowe Golf Course	0131 337 1096
Portobello Golf Course	0131 669 4361
Silverknowes Golf Course	0131 336 3843

Mortonhall Golf Club

Founded in 1892, this is the oldest course on which golf is still played in the city of Edinburgh. It is one of outstanding scenic beauty, emerging from a narrow valley to an open area bounded by a wood on the south and the Braid Hills in the north. At 6502 yards, it is the longest course in the city, and at 600ft above sea level, the wind can make it a formidable challenge.

The well appointed clubhouse contains many interesting photographs and golfing memorabilia. *Bar and catering facilities available.*

Vistors are welcome to play this picturesque and challenging course.

231 Braid Road, Edinburgh EH10 6PB
Tel: 0131 447 6974 •• Fax: 0131 447 8712
www.mortonhallgc.co.uk •• clubhouse@mortonhallgc.co.uk

Scotland's Premier Pay-As-You-Play Golf Course

Set in stunning parkland, 15 minutes from St Andrews, with spectacular views of the Firth of Forth.

- 18 holes, Par 72 • 9-hole pitch and putt
- Driving range
- Clubhouse with restaurant and bar.

Charleton Golf Course
Colinsburgh, Fife KY9 1HG
Tel: 01333 340505 • Fax: 01333 340583
e-mail: clubhouse@charleton.co.uk

www.charleton.co.uk

SCOTLAND

Macdonald Rusacks Hotel, St Andrews

Guests who have stayed at Rusacks include golfing and rock and roll legends. Originally opened in 1887, it has been stylishly remodelled on a golfing theme to take advantage of its prestigious location and eye-catching views over the 18th green of the Old Course.

- Golf packages available
- 68 ensuite bedrooms
- Old Course Restaurant

MACDONALD HOTELS

For Reservations or information
0870 400 8128

Pilmour Links, St Andrews, Fife KY16 9JQ
e-mail: general@macdonald-hotels.co.uk
www.macdonaldhotels.co.uk/rusacks

Advance bookings
01333 450686
www.crailgolfingsociety.co.uk

The World's 7th Oldest Golfing Society (1786) invites you to experience

Golf at Crail

Spectacular location - sea views from every hole
Balcomie Links 5922 yards • SSS 69 • Par 69
Classic Links Course
Craighead Links 6728 yards • SSS 74 • Par 72
USGA Spec Greens
Crail Golfing Society, Balcomie Clubhouse, Fifeness, Crail, Fife KY10 3XN

Leven Links, The Promenade, Leven, Fife KY8 4HS
Tel/Fax: 01333 428859
e-mail: secretary@leven-links.com

Leven Links, in part one of the oldest pieces of golfing ground in the world, is a true seaside links course. It has hosted many national and international events and is used as a final qualifying course for the Open Championship when it is held at St Andrews. The strength of Leven Links lies in its fine variety of links-type holes combined with large greens; turning into the prevailing west wind at the 13th leaves the golfer with a lot of work to do before reaching one of the finest finishing holes in golf.

Scotscraig Golf Club
Golf Road, Tayport DD6 9DZ • 01382 552515

Situated on the Tay Estuary, 10 miles north of St Andrews. With fine links turf, smooth fast greens, whin bushes and rolling fairways, this is a demanding and interesting test of golf for all levels of player.

Special Golf Packages available for parties of 12+
Meals, snacks and refreshments served daily
Well-stocked Shop with resident PGA Professional

Pro Shop: 01382 552855
e-mail: scotscraig@scottishgolf.com
www.scotscraiggolfclub.com

OPEN QUALIFYING COURSE

GOLFING PACKAGES ARE OUR SPECIALITY

The perfect location for a golfing break only minutes from the famous 'Old Course' at St Andrews, and with over 40 top courses all within an hour's drive. Only 9 miles from St Andrews and 45 minutes from Edinburgh. 21 superb en suite bedrooms, with top cuisine and traditional bars.

Ring now for brochure and Golfing Breaks

The Lundin Links Hotel
Lundin Links, Fife KY8 6AP Scotland
Tel: 01333 320207 Fax: 01333 320930
E-mail: info@lundin-links-hotel.co.uk
Website: www.lundin-links-hotel.co.uk

The Lundin Links Hotel

Balbirnie Park Golf Club
Balbirnie Park, Markinch, Glenrothes KY7 6NR
Tel: 01592 612095 • Fax: 01592 612383

Balbirnie Park is a fine example of the best in traditional parkland design – the natural contours being the inspiration behind the layout. With a par of 71 and measuring 6200 yards from the Gents' Back Tees, it is a good challenge for golfers of all abilities. It is immediately apparent to any visitor that the course is blessed with a truly superb and picturesque site, situated in the heart of the magnificent Balbirnie Park. The park has the finest collection of rhododendrons and azaleas adjacent to the golf course. Visitors and parties always welcome. Individual packages arranged. Excellent cuisine. Well stocked golf shop.

e-mail: craigfdonnelly@aol.com • website: www.balbirniegolf.co.uk

Ideally situated in 4.5 acres of grounds and gardens, a few minutes' walk from the famous Royal Dornoch Golf Course.
- 29 bedrooms, all en suite, with colour TV and tea/coffee making.
- A la carte Restaurant • Bar meals available
- Golf on Royal Dornoch and other local courses can be arranged, as well as loch and river fishing.
- Children and dogs welcome.

THE BURGHFIELD HOUSE HOTEL, DORNOCH IV25 3HN
TEL: 01862 810212 • FAX: 01862 810404
burghfield@cali.co.uk • www.burghfieldhouse.com

Royal Marine Hotel & Leisure Club
Golf Road, Brora, Sutherland KW9 6QS
Telephone: (01408) 621252 • Fax: (01408) 621181
e-mail: info@highlandescape.com
website: www.highlandescapehotels.com

Play traditional links golf and stay in a traditional Highland hotel. Adjacent to James Braid's 18-hole Brora Links, the Royal Marine Hotel combines the ambience of a bygone era with the facilities and comforts expected by the modern traveller. Choice of three restaurants and two bars. Indoor swimming pool and leisure club. AA rosette for food. A warm welcome awaits you. Luxury apartments overlooking golf course available to let.

SCOTLAND

The Golf Guide 2006

THE ROYAL DORNOCH GOLF CLUB

The Championship Course, Royal Dornoch, is rated by Golf Digest Magazine 5th in the World's top courses outside the USA. It is a classic links, providing both pleasure to the eye and a challenge to the golfer's skills. Links golf, some would argue, is the truest form of golf. Dornoch is considered the finest northerly course in the world, and offers a delicious feeling of getting away from it all.

On the Championship and the Struie Course, Royal Dornoch aims to provide traditional "links golf" of the highest quality. Golfers and their friends will be made welcome to enjoy "Highland Hospitality" in an informal relaxed style in the clubhouse where they may partake of fine Scottish beverages and food.

Green Fees 2005:
Championship Course
£72 weekdays   £82 weekends
Struie Course
£29 per round   £47 per day
Combination day ticket
(one round each course)
£85 weekdays   £95 weekends
Verification of maximum Handicap
24 men, 35 ladies – required

Tel Reservations: 01862 810219 ext 185
Fax: 01862 810792
bookings@royaldornoch.com
www.royaldornoch.com
GOLF ROAD, DORNOCH,
SUTHERLAND IV25 3LW

SCOTLAND

FORTROSE & ROSEMARKIE GOLF CLUB
NESS ROAD EAST, FORTROSE, ROSS-SHIRE IV10 8SE
Tel: 01381 620529 • Fax: 01381 621328
e-mail: secretary@fortrosegolfclub.co.uk • www.fortrosegolfclub.co.uk

This James Braid designed links has been acclaimed by golf writers as "a gem of a course" and "perhaps the brightest jewel in the Highlands' golfing crown". Small deceptive greens and strategically placed bunkers, as well as sea alongside eight holes and gorse waiting to devour the wayward shot inland, all add up to a greater golfing experience than many a longer course. This private club, established in 1888, gives a warm welcome to visitors in the knowledge that they will almost certainly wish to come back. A big off-course attraction is the bottle-nosed dolphins in the Firth in the view of the golfers. 15 miles north of Inverness – take the A832 off A9 North. Green fees £25 per round weekdays, £30 per round weekends. Buggy hire, practice area, putting green, golf shop, catering and bar.

Strathpeffer Spa Golf Club

Founded in 1888, this is arguably the most scenic course in the North of Scotland, with the drive on the first hole from tee to green featuring the longest drop on any course in the country. Visitors are welcome without reservation (although it is advisable to check in advance). Bar and catering is available daily. Clubs, trolleys and golf buggies are available for hire.

18 holes £18.00 • day ticket £23.00
Special terms for groups • 18 holes, Par 64

Golf Course Road, Strathpeffer, Ross-shire IV14 9AS
01997 421011 or 421219 • www.strathpeffergolf.co.uk
• e-mail: mail@strathpeffergolf.co.uk

NAIRN DUNBAR GOLF CLUB
LOCHLOY ROAD, NAIRN IV12 5AE
TEL: 01667 452741
FAX: 01667 456897
secretary@nairndunbar.com
www.nairndunbar.com

Situated on the shores of the Moray Firth, this is a highly rated Scottish links Championship course, renowned for its excellent condition and friendly welcome for visitors. Described by Peter Alliss as "one of Scotland's hidden gems"

Clubhouse with comfortable lounge bars, dining room, extensive locker room facilities with visitors' room and showers • Patio area with BBQ • Pro Shop

---

Ideally situated halfway between Edinburgh and Glasgow, with easy access from the M8, this 18-hole moorland course provides a challenge for all standards of golfers. Visitors should beware the notorious 4th hole, 'The Devil's Elbow', which has ruined the cards of many aspiring hopefuls. A refurbished clubhouse provides a warm and friendly welcome, with catering and bar facilities.

Shotts Golf Club
Blairhead, Shotts ML7 5BJ
Clubhouse: 01501 820431
Pro Shop: 01501 822658
E-mail: info@shottsgolfclub.co.uk
www.shottsgolfclub.co.uk

SCOTLAND

One of the Treasures of Scottish Golf, Blairgowrie Golf Club offers two eighteen hole championship courses and a classic 9 hole course. The Rosemount Course ranks among the very best of all the great inland courses in the British Isles. Alongside Rosemount, the Lansdowne Course, designed by Peter Alliss and Dave Thomas, is a testing 18 holes with a more modern layout and tighter fairways.

Within striking distance of Carnoustie, St Andrews and Gleneagles, Blairgowrie is ideally situated in the heart of beautiful Perthshire.

1889

The Blairgowrie Golf Club, Rosemount, Blairgowrie, Perthshire PH10 6LG
T: 01250 872622, F: 01250 875451, E: office@theblairgowriegolfclub.co.uk, W: www.theblairgowriegolfclub.co.uk

Royal Dunkeld Hotel

The Royal Dunkeld, a former coaching inn, is now a modern, comfortable hotel. All bedrooms have en suite facilities, colour TV, radio, hospitality tray, hairdryer, trouser press and direct-dial telephone. Located in some of the most beautiful countryside in Britain, Dunkeld is an ideal base for touring and for sporting activities such as golf, salmon fishing and trout fishing.

Atholl Street, Dunkeld, Perthshire PH8 0AR
Tel: 01350 727322 • Fax: 01350 728989 • www.royaldunkeld.co.uk

Killin, Perthshire FK21 8TX
Tel: 01567 820312

e-mail: booking@killingolfclub.co.uk
www.killingolfclub.co.uk

"A Hidden Gem"

A picturesque 9-hole course set in the beautiful scenery of the Perthshire Highlands. Food is served all day, with a bar menu available from 11am. Package deals with catering for groups of 8 or more. With a river sweeping past the first fairway, playing golf in the midst of such breathtaking scenery is a unique experience.

Buggies, trolleys and clubs for hire

LANDS OF LOYAL HOTEL
Alyth, Perthshire PH11 8JQ
Telephone: 01828 633151 • Fax: 01828 633313

Set on hillside overlooking the Vale of Strathmore lies this impressive Victorian Mansion surrounded by 10 acres of tiered gardens. Our highly acclaimed restaurant makes full use of local fish and game in a style both traditional and imaginative. For the country sportsman fishing and shooting are available, with Salmon and Trout fishing in the Loch and River. Pheasant and Grouse shooting, wild fowling and deer stalking also available as the seasons permit. The hotel makes an ideal base for the ambitious golfer with 30 courses within an hour's drive.

e-mail: info@landsofloyal.com • website: www.landsofloyal.com

SCOTLAND

FHG

K·U·P·E·R·A·R·D

FHG Guides

publish a large range of well-known accommodation guides. We will be happy to send you details or you can use the order form at the back of this book.

CRIEFF HYDRO

Scotland's leading leisure hotel welcomes all levels of golfer to the new **Culcrieff Golf Course** at Crieff Hydro Ltd. Opened in 2002, the course enjoys panoramic views over the Strathearn valley.

18 holes • Par 66 • SSS 64 • 4876 yards
6 hole pitch and putt • 8-bay driving range
Licensed clubhouse with restaurant facilities
Weekday ticket £20 • Weekend ticket £25

Reservations necessary for groups and Perthshire Green Card holders.

For further enquiries and brochure contact Andrew Downie

**Crieff Hydro Hotel
Crieff PH7 3LQ • 01764 651615
enquiries@crieffhydro.com
www.crieffhydro.com**

Why would you want to **stay** and **play** anywhere else

Just a short iron from our 46 bedroom hotel you'll find the first tees of our two scenic golf courses, **The Montgomery**, Par 71, 6438 yards and **The Bruce**, Par 73, 6256 yards. Both offer an enjoyable and stimulating challenge, whether you are a holiday golfer or low handicap player. And situated in Kinross we are well placed to reach some of Scotland's leading championship courses including; St Andrews, Gleneagles and Carnoustie. Call or email us today for a brochure and further details.

the green
HOTEL | LEISURE | BUSINESS | GOLF KINROSS

2 The Muirs, Kinross KY13 8AS, Scotland, Tel: +44 (0) 1577 863467, Email: reservations@green-hotel.com
www.green-hotel.com

---

*Relax and enjoy a meal after your round of golf.
The Red House Hotel menu is served in our Restaurant & Conservatory from 12 noon to 9.30pm. Stay in one of our 20 en suite rooms, and play some of the finest golf courses in Scotland which are only a 15- minute drive away. Also within the Red House Hotel we can provide Snooker, Squash, Sauna and Gymnasium.*

The RED HOUSE Hotel

**STATION ROAD, COUPAR ANGUS
PERTHSHIRE PH13 9AL
Tel: 01828 628500 • Fax: 01828 628574
e-mail: stay@red-house-hotel.co.uk • www.red-house-hotel.co.uk**

Tony McGee
Golf in Ireland

Killarney Golf & Fishing Club, Killarney, Co. Kerry

Golf facilities never stand still in Ireland, with more and more new courses coming on line. Some are of the top-of-the-range style, but others are for the common ordinary golfer who just wants to play a quiet round and enjoy the experience, irrespective of the score. Standards range from the likes of The K Club to the little nine-holers and driving ranges that are dotted around the country.

Among the latest top-drawer projects to reach the planning stage is Hangman's Point at Kenmare in Co Cork. Making his Irish designing debut was Ernie Els who gave his signature to the 200 million euro development. Note the name of the new club. This is an historic spot in the Rebel County and, obviously, the history goes back to the time of the stagecoaches, etc.

But, of course, most of the thousand upon thousand of visitors who come to Ireland annually for a golfing holiday are much more interested in the less exotic clubs that are dotted around the country from north to south and east to west. The visitors are also interested in the welcome on the mat and the traditional nightlife that can be experienced throughout Ireland.

Of special interest to Scots is surely the Roe Park Resort at Limavady in Co Derry. There is much history here, too. One spot on the course is unique, the mound, Mullagh Hill, where St Columba addressed the High Kings of Ireland at the Convention of Drumceatt in 575AD. He arrived from Scotland to sort out a tax argument between the Irish and Scots and a special room in the adjoining Radisson Roe Hotel is named after him.

"The Heritage Department have had discussions with us about the history of the spot, as they wanted to put a plaque there. We are not allowed to put in as much as a stake," reveals hotel manager John O'Carroll from Kerry.

IRELAND

The Golf Guide 2006

Your Plan - Your Future

NDP

EU Programme for Peace and Reconciliation

Funded by the European Union under the Programme for Peace and Reconciliation 2000-2004 (Peace 11), and part-financed by the Irish Government under the National Development Plan

Tailor-Made Holidays in Ireland and Scotland for Groups and Individuals

Saoire Fáilte
The best of Ireland north and west

Specialists in Golf & Sightseeing Holidays

- Driver Guide / Coaching Services / Self-Drive
- Extended / Short Breaks
- Guaranteed Golf Starts and Non-Golfer Sightseeing
- All types of accommodation

The Errigal Suite, Donegal Airport, Carrickfinn, Kincasslagh, Co Donegal, Ireland
Tel: 00353 74 95 48891 • Fax: 00353 74 95 48928
e-mail: info@saoirefailte.com   www.saoirefailte.com

Four scenic miles from Royal Portrush

www.bushmillsinn.com

A Best Loved Hotel of the World

the bushmills inn
HOTEL

Ireland's Golf Hotel of the Year 2003

Bushmills, Co. Antrim, N. Ireland BT57 8QG
Tel. +44 (0)28 2073 3000 mail@bushmillsinn.com

---

publisher's note

While every effort is made to ensure accuracy, we regret that FHG Guides cannot accept responsibility for errors, misrepresentations or omissions in our entries or any consequences thereof. Prices in particular should be checked. We will follow up complaints but cannot act as arbiters or agents for either party.

FHG
K·U·P·E·R·A·R·D

IRELAND

Hilton Templepatrick Hotel & Country Club

Relax with a Golf and Leisure Break

From as little as **£150** sterling per person why not spend time golfing on one of Northern Ireland's finest parkland courses?

- Enjoy 2 rounds of golf
- 2 nights bed and breakfast with dinner on the first night of your stay (3 course table d'hote)

Not a golfer? Then exchange the golf for beauty treatments or master the game under the experienced eye of our PGA professional.

An oasis of peace and tranquility Hilton Templepatrick Hotel & Country Club is the perfect destination for a relaxing break. Set in 220 acres of the Castle Upton estate in County Antrim, we have a range of facilities that will favour with the active and relaxed alike. The hotels 18 hole championship golf course meanders for over 7000 yards and will test the abilities of even the finest golfer. Make free use of LivingWell health club with its fantastic gym, 18 metre indoor swimming pool with sauna, steam room, solarium and spa. Relax in the stylish Treffners restaurant for dinner or reflect on your day in Kinahans bar brasserie.

To make your booking call **028 9443 5444** for this special deal.

Hilton Templepatrick Hotel & Country Club, Hilton Templepatrick, Castle Upton Estate, Templepatrick, BT39 0DD
Fax: **028 9443 5509** hilton.co.uk/templepatrick

Terms and conditions - Subject to availability and seasonal change.
Prices are per person for two nights, based on two people sharing a twin/double room. Terms and conditions apply.

Roe Park Resort has a lot to offer to the touring golfer. It's a parkland with links views, and each year Norman Wisdom stays at the hotel and enjoys his round of golf. "Even at his age, Norman is still a keen golfer and quite handy at the game, into the bargain," says Mr O'Carroll.

Roe Park, just over an hour from Belfast and less from Derry City, is the tail of the North Coast chain, with neighbours Castlerock, Portstewart, Royal Portrush and Ballycastle all along the line. Bushfoot, where Darren Clarke's mother Heidi was Lady Captain, is nestled in there, too, and there is Brown Trout, a few miles from Coleraine, where Darren has a big interest in the Salmon Leap Restaurant.

This web of courses, allied to the large range of accommodation, from the likes of the Radisson Roe Hotel with its leisure centre, beauty salon, restaurants and golf academy, to the popular B&Bs (bed and breakfast - not bread and bacon!) guest houses offer the holidaymaker a wide choice.

Up to three of these courses can be played in one day, if the energy allows, but pre-booking is advisable at the likes of Royal Portrush, one of the most famous clubs in the world. The British Open Championship was played there in 1951, when Max Faulkner was the winner. Ironically, Max's son-in-law Brian Barnes won the British Seniors, also on the jumbo Dunluce links that features the famous Calamity Comer - the short 14th hole.

With the north coast reasonably close to Belfast International and City Airports and Belfast Docks, it is obvious that these famed courses are busy during the height of the tourist season, but on the way north there are many more pleasant courses to visit.

Galgorm Castle at Ballymena is another spot steeped in history, and both the course and other facilities have been

DONAGHADEE GOLF CLUB • 028 9188 3624
84 Warren Road, Donaghadee, Co. Down BT21 0PQ

Located 5 miles south of Bangor on A2 on coast road. A part links and part inland course with lovely views to the Scottish coast. Well-appointed clubhouse. Visitors welcome weekdays and Sundays. Club hire and trolleys available. Special rates for Societies.
18 holes, 5561 metres, Par 71, S.S.S. 69

e-mail: deegolf@freenet.co.uk
General Manager: Mr Michael Corsar 028 9188 3624
Professional: Gordon Drew 028 9188 2392

Gregans Castle Hotel
Ballyvaughan, Co. Clare
Tel: 065 707 7005 • Fax: 065 707 7111
e-mail: stay@gregans.ie • www.gregans.ie

Gregans Castle is a family-run Country Hotel with breathtaking views across The Burren and Galway Bay. Award-winning gardens and the rural setting ensure peaceful harmony. Bedrooms have every comfort; Superior Rooms and Suites are especially recommended. The hotel is only 16 miles from Lahinch Golf Course, and there are many other activities in the area, such as hillwalking, botany and historic ruins.

Blue Ribbon

Other local courses: Gort, Galway Bay, Doonbeg, Woodstock, Dromoland

---

developed over the past few years. Hilltop Cairndhu, from where the west coast of Scotland is clearly visible – on a bright day houses can easily be seen – combines golf with climbing. One needs a good head for heights here!

Loughshore Massereene at Antrim is much, much flatter, but watch the midges in high summer. Heading towards Belfast, at Templepatrick, just a few minutes from Belfast International, is The Hilton Golf Club and Hotel. Quite a tough track where Scot Frank Ainsworth is Head Greenkeeper. Frank is also a noted course designer and was responsible for the Roe Park Resort layout.

The total number of affiliated clubs in Ireland is 414, with 123 of those in the province of Ulster – that's the nine county geographical Ulster and not the six county political Northern Ireland, often referred to as Ulster. Belfast has 14 clubs, with Shandon Park, Malone and Belvoir Park among the most famous. But don't forget suburban Dunmurry that won the AIB Club of the Year in 2003.

Trees play an important part on the Malone and Shandon Park courses and also at Belvoir Park, from where there is a superb view over the city to the Black Mountains from the elevated clubhouse.

Royal County Down, with its magnificent backdrop of the majestic Mourne Mountain, is the pride of Co Down, but it may not be the choice of the high handicap golfer. There are many tough holes here, with the deep gorse and heather gobbling up balls constantly. However, the par four ninth hole must be one of the most spectacular of any in the land. Here the drive disappears over a hill and drops into an angled valley about 80 feet below.

Ardglass, Kirkistown Castle, Bangor, Clandeboye, the third northern 'Royal' – Royal Belfast – and Holywood are other Co Down courses, that attract much holiday traffic.

Deeper into the province one finds the likes of up-market Slieve Russell at Ballyconnell in Co Cavan. The Sean Quinn Complex – a non-golfer himself, Sean recently bought The Belfry! – was created out of the Breffni Drumlin country. The plush hotel is attached to an excellent course where PGA events are staged annually. Liam McCool wears two hats, as he is head golf pro and Golf Director. His sister Lynn is the Golf Director at The Hilton, making a rare brother-sister act.

Castle Hume, outside Enniskillen, is only 12 miles away. It's poised on the shores of Lough Erne where a sister course and hotel is being built. The PGA Ulster Championship has been held at Castle Hume for the past couple of years.

Further west, Donegal has 17 clubs, from Ireland's most northerly course at Ballyliffin to Bundoran at the bottom end of the county. Celtic captain Jackie McNamara held a tournament at Ballyliffin as part of his Benefit Year. This is the club that Nick Faldo wanted to buy but the members refused to sell. Faldo still keeps in touch with the Glashedy and Old Course links and has made some bunker adjustments on the latter.

Co Donegal at Murvagh, between sea and mountains, will test the best, as players in both the men's Irish Close and the Ladies' Irish Championship found over the past couple of years. Incidentally, this is one of the courses used during the Carlsberg West Coast Challenge Tournament during the first week in September. The others are Bundoran, Enniscrone and Strandhill. Visitors are very welcome to enter.

Co Sligo, at Rosses Point, hosts the West of Ireland Championship every Easter and in 2005 history was made there when Holywood's 15-year-old Rory McIlroy became the youngest ever winner of the competition. This is one of those courses that leaves the clubhouse and doesn't return until the 18th hole.

Cork Golf Club was founded in 1888 and designed in 1927 by Alister MacKenzie. It has matured to become one of the finest courses in the country.
Many Amateur and Professional championships have been hosted here.
The course is always in immaculate condition and playable all year round.
For further information regarding green fees, please contact Matt Sands, General Manager, at:

CORK GOLF CLUB

Little Island, Co. Cork, Ireland
Tel: 00 353 21 4353451 • Fax: 00 353 21 4353410
e-mail: corkgolfclub@eircom.net
www.corkgolfclub.ie

Fernhill Golf & Country Club lies just 10km from the city of Cork, beautifully situated overlooking the scenic Owenabue Valley near the south coast. It is close to the ferry terminal at Ringaskiddy, offering the first and last opportunity for a game for those visiting Ireland by ferry. It offers a good challenge to players of all handicaps.

18-hole Parkland course • Visitors welcome.
40 rooms en suite • 10 holiday homes on site
Indoor swimming pool, sauna and tennis court
Fernhill Golf & Country Club, Carrigaline, Co. Cork, Ireland
Tel: 353 21 4372226 • Fax: 353 21 4371011
e-mail: fernhill@iol.ie • www.fernhillcountryclub.com

The Silver Tassie Hotel

The Silver Tassie Hotel nestles in the beautiful 'Hills of Donegal' near the heritage town of Ramelton, and just 5 minutes' drive from a championship golf course. Unwind in comfort and style in our luxurious bedrooms, all en suite, with multi-channel TV and tea/coffee making facilities. The hotel has a great reputation for food, served in both the oak-panelled restaurant and the lively bar and lounge. The bustling town of Letterkenny is only five minutes away, and is an ideal base to explore Donegal and the spectacular Glenveagh National Park.

Silver Tassie Hotel
Ramelton Road, Letterkenny, Co. Donegal
Tel: 074 9125619 • Fax: 074 9124473
info@theblaneygroup.com
www.theblaneygroup.com

Milford Inn Hotel

Situated 10 miles from Letterkenny, this luxurious family hotel is ideally placed for exploring Donegal's rugged Atlantic coast. Relax in luxury and style in a choice of en suite bedrooms, all with satellite TV and tea/coffee making facilities. Carvery lunches are available, as well as an extensive bar menu, while 'The Arches' Restaurant offers both à la carte and table d'hôte menus. There is live entertainment every weekend and most nights during the holiday season, and a hair and beauty salon offering a variety of specialist treatments. Local attractions include a choice of golf courses, fishing and horse riding.

Milford Inn Hotel
Milford, Co. Donegal
Tel: 074 9153313 • Fax: 074 9153388
milfordinnhotel@eircom.net
www.milfordinnhotel.com

Set among sand dunes on cliffs overlooking three beaches, the wind factor plays a big part on Rosses Point, while a burn meanders through the course and comes into play at a number of holes. The famous Benbulben, close to the grave of William B. Yeats at Drumcliffe, towers in the distance to the north, with the Ox Mountains to the west giving a panoramic view to relax golfers who may be having a bad day.

Westport Town and the local golf club are among the busiest and friendliest in the country. This is a tourists' paradise, where sport and entertainment mingle daily. Traditional music pumps out from Matt Molloy's pub on the main street, and if you don't know who Matt Molloy is, I'll tell you. He's the celebrated flute player with the Chieftains.

The Westport Club hosted the Irish Close Championship in 2005. The course commands a superb view of Clew Bay and is overshadowed by famous Croagh Patrick, the holy mountain to which visitors flock in their thousands throughout the year. The 15th hole, a jumbo par five of 580 yards, is played over an inlet of Clew Bay.

Christy O'Connor Junior, was the architect of the Galway Bay course on the Renville Peninsula where one needs to ignore the beautiful scenery if a good score is to be carded. When visiting this rugged area of Ireland, no self-respecting tourist could miss out on playing Connemara, a remote course on the western seaboard, nine miles from Clifden, famous for its Pony Show, and past the old Marconi Wireless Station where Alcock and Brown landed after their trans-Atlantic flight in 1919. Big hitters will enjoy the Connemara Course.

The Links of Heaven, as the North & West Coast Links is dubbed, join a number of courses in Connacht and Ulster from Connemara to Royal Portrush, and by contacting the offices at Galway

Golf Centre in Salthill a tour can be arranged.

The south-west corner of the country is littered with up-market clubs and courses but one that most visitors like to play is Lahinch. Nestling on the Co Clare coast beside the Shannon, as with many clubs, there are two courses to choose from. Sand dunes are the norm and one superb hole on the Old Course is 'The Dell', a great par three with the hidden hole in a basin well below the tee. 'The Klondyke' is another aptly named hole.

Doonbeg is, of course, world famous as well, with its created village and US attachment. Fota Island, a few miles from Cork City, was re-launched in recent years and then there is the lavish Old Head at Kinsale, poised on an Atlantic promontory rising hundreds of feet above serious cliffs and surrounded by the ocean on all sides. Every hole has at least six tees to suit all

---

Where the Water meets the Wild
ROSAPENNA HOTEL & GOLF LINKS
DOWNINGS, CO DONEGAL
TEL: +353 (0)74 55301 FAX: +353 (0)74 55128
e-mail: rosapenna@eircom.net • www.rosapenna.ie

A unique experience awaits you at Rosapenna Hotel & Golf Links, where four-star luxury nestles amidst the rolling Donegal landscape. Tranquil lounges and elegant dining areas overlook the bay, and a choice of bedrooms, including standard, de luxe with sea views, and spacious junior suites, provide the comforts and style one would expect from a hotel with such history. This is a haven of tranquillity where you can recharge after a day on the links or simply escape from the pressures of modern-day living.

Links course, designed by old Tom Morris • 18 holes 6271 yards, SSS 71
• New 18 hole Sandy Hills Links Course designed by Pat Ruddy due to open June 2003
• Visitors welcome at all times • Golfers welcome with Club Handicaps.

INISHOWEN GATEWAY HOTEL
RAILWAY ROAD, BUNCRANA, INISHOWEN, CO. DONEGAL
TEL: (00353) 74 93 61144
FAX: (00353) 74 93 62278

Elegant Hotel with 79 luxurious bedrooms, situated on the sandy shores of Lough Swilly. Close to Ballyliffin and North West Golf Clubs; ideal location for links golf enthusiasts. Gateway Health and Fitness Club with pool, steam, sauna, spa bath and gym on site. Fabulous Health and Beauty Spa now open for relaxing treatments. Groups and societies welcome.

website: www.inishowengateway.com
e-mail: info@inishowengateway.com

Malahide Golf Club

Set on Dublin's golden North Coast in the beautiful seaside resort of Malahide, this superb 27-hole course is one of Ireland's oldest golf clubs, established in 1892. The Eddie Hackett design offers a challenge for all on a course in play all year through.

Each hole presents its own test with trees and water a frequent feature. Located close to Dublin City and Airport. The fine clubhouse, with a panoramic view across to the Dublin Mountains, has full catering facilities.

Our motto is "a light heart and cheerful spirit", play, dine and relax with friends in this charming venue. Societies are always welcome.

Beechwood • The Grange • Malahide • Co. Dublin
Tel: (01) 846 1611 • Fax: (01) 846 1270
E-mail: manager@malahidegolfclub.ie
Web: www.malahidegolfclub.ie

IRELAND

Fáilte Ireland • Les Routiers Ireland • RAC • Irish Hotels Federation

THE RED BANK
Restaurant & Guesthouse
5-7 Church Street, Skerries, Co. Dublin
Tel: +353 1 8490439 • Fax: +353 1 8491598
E-mail: info@redbank.ie • www.redbank.ie

The area around this fine Bed & Breakfast, located in the sea fishing village of Skerries, just 18 miles north of Dublin, is particularly rich in golf clubs, with as many as 25 championship courses just a short drive away. Three of our links courses, situated right on the sea, are rated as belonging to the Top 100 Golf Courses in the World. So why not try some real *'Gourmet Golf'*.

• *Fantastic Offer!* • *Gourmet Golf Package*
Have dinner at the award-winning Redbank with one night accommodation and full Irish breakfast the following morning.
Then on to a round of links golf at Corballis Golf Course – all for only €125.00pp.

In a very short space of time, The South County Golf Club has established itself as one of Dublin's 'must play' venues. The combination of a challenging course, exquisite cuisine, panoramic views, and close proximity to Dublin and the M50 have made it a real favourite.

The South County Golf Club
Lisheen Road, Brittas Village, Co. Dublin
Tel: +353 1 458 2965 • Fax: +353 1 458 2842
e-mail: info@southcountygolf.ie
www.southcountygolf.com

The split-level design clubhouse has a spacious reception area, well appointed changing facilities and an excellent Pro Shop. On the upper level, which has spectacular views of the 'Seat of Kings', are a bar, function room, restaurant and terrace. Immediately adjacent are four acres of practice area including a driving range and putting green. Society Packages available - details on request.

---

categories of golfers, but even the 260 euro green fee is no guarantee of anyone gaining admittance.

Over in Kerry the famed Killarney and Waterville courses are backed up by many lesser lights such as Tralee and Killorglin while inland at Dundrum House is Co Tipperary Golf Club where Willie Crowe will make you especially welcome. Tramore and Faithlegg in Waterford are also courses suited to the traveller.

Indeed, it has been said that in the northeast corner of Ireland there are too many golf clubs. Could that be possible? Anyhow, there is a wide selection of courses for visitors to play. Mount Juliet in Co Kilkenny and sister clubs Druid's Glen and Druid's Heath up the coast in Co Wicklow, are, of course, the doyens, but maybe not for the high handicapper.

There are many, many more, like the European Club, Courtown and St Helen's Bay to name just a few that attract much attention. Further inland in Leinster there is a big selection like Glasson, Headfort that won the AIB Club of the Year plaque in 2004, and Mullingar. Close to Maynooth is The K Club, venue for the 2006 Ryder Cup, and Carlton House where the headquarters of the GUI are situated, and Colin Montgomerie and Mark O'Meara designed two different styles of course.

In South Dublin City is Hermitage, and north of the city are the older Portmarnock and the newer Portmarnock Links. In between there are over 20 other courses to choose from and further out from Portmarnock is Malahide. Par 73 Co Louth, the scene of many big tournaments, is further north.

It would be totally impossible to give even a reasonable glimpse of the golf scene in Ireland, a country famed for its links courses. The attraction is the variety, with tracks to suit every taste and capability. Travel in the Emerald Isle is not exhausting either, with uncluttered roads once clear of the cities and big towns.

IRELAND

The Golf Guide 2006

Deer Park Hotel & Golf Courses

Deer Park Hotel incorporates Ireland's largest golf complex, with four courses to choose from, ranging from a testing 12-hole par 36 course to a par 72, 6830 yard 18 hole course.

Deer Park is just 9 miles from Dublin City and Airport. The hillside location offers spectacular views of Dublin Bay and the Northeastern coastline. 80 superb en suite rooms, 17m swimming pool complex and all weather tennis courts, bar, bistro and the elegant "Four Earls" Restaurant.

Deer Park Hotel & Golf Courses, Howth, Co. Dublin
Tel: (01) 832 2624 • Fax: (01) 839 2405
E-Mail: sales@deerpark.iol.ie • Web: www.deerpark-hotel.ie

★★★
AA / Bord Failte

THE ISLAND Golf Club
Tel: +353 (0)1843 6205
Fax: +353 (0)1843 6460
Established 1890 — Corballis, Donabate, Co. Dublin, Ireland

OPEN QUALIFYING COURSE FOR 2005-2010

For sheer awe — the kind inspired by 25 foot-high dunes, vaguely lunar crevasses running through the terrain and challenging greens — the best choice is The Island Golf Club. This classic championship links course is less than 15 minutes from Dublin airport, yet the members have kept it a great secret since 1890. It is one of the best courses in Ireland and is definitely the best golf course you have never heard of.
Par 71, SSS 73, 6,857 yds. €110 (£75 approx) visitor green fee. All visitors ensured of warm and friendly welcome.

Motorways are common and car hire is on a par with anywhere else in Europe.

By the way, what should interest many people is that the holidaymaker can travel by water from Lough Erne in Fermanagh to the mouth of the Shannon River in Co Clare. Along the route there are plenty of stopping off places where the traveller can have a game of golf and also enjoy a night's craic.

Designed by Christy O'Connor Jnr and Peter McEvoy, the golf course at **Rathsallagh** has rapidly taken its place as one of the top golf courses in Ireland.

Home to important domestic tournaments, many regard Rathsallagh as the best parkland course in Ireland. Measuring 7200 yards from the Medal Tees, Rathsallagh is one of the best laid out courses you could play. Several lakes and small streams meander their way across the fairways, and the undulating countryside creates the perfect golf terrain which proves a great test for golfers, but is fair to all.

For full details of clubs and courses, plus convenient accommodation
www.uk-golfguide.com

The Golf Guide 2006　　　　　　　　　　　　　　　　　IRELAND

Fingal Tourism
Mainscourt
Main Street
Swords
Fingal
Co. Dublin

fingal
Dublin | Ireland

Tel: +353 1 840 0077
Fax: + 353 1 840 4988
email: info@fingaltourism.ie
web: www.fingal-dublin.com

Fingal – Dublin – Ireland

Located minutes from Dublin City and home to Dublin International Airport, Fingal is arguably the golfing capital of Europe. A picturesque open countryside and magnificent coastline provide the essential ingredients for over 27 superb parkland and links courses. Both experienced and novice golfers will find a course to suit their ability, taste and pocket.

**Request The Golfer's Guide to Fingal online at
www.fingal-dublin.com or by e-mail: info@fingaltourism.ie**

Tee Time in Fingal
Dublin | Ireland

The picturesque open countryside and magnificent coastline of Fingal are ideal environments against which to fashion great golf courses. Fingal is arguably the golfing capital of Ireland, offering the golfer everything from superb parkland courses to excellent links courses.

There are 25 golf courses in total, many of which are of championship standard, some have already hosted major tournaments. Both novice and experienced golfers will find a course to suit their ability, taste and pocket. A number of 9-hole courses, driving ranges and pitch and putt courses complement this feast of superb golfing challenges.

Public golf courses include fine parkland courses at Elmgreen Golf Centre, Castleknock and Sillogue Golf Course, Ballymun, as well as a fine links course at Corballis, near Donabate.

Fingal Golf Classic

Fingal Tourism hosts the Fingal Golf Classic annually. To date the event has taken place at four of Fingal's top golf courses; Luttrellstown Castle, Portmarnock, Hollystown, and St Margaret's Golf Clubs. The Classic is run over a period of four days and prizes are awarded at a Gala Dinner on the evening of day four.

IRELAND

The Golf Guide 2006

There's no mistaking the authentic charm of the Lucan Spa Hotel. From the unique copper tower on the roof to the cheerful familiarity of the staff, there's nothing quite like it. Situated on the Road to the West (N4), in close proximity to the M50, this elegant hotel offers guests comfort and convenience in a rural setting.
The exceptionally well appointed en suite rooms are equipped to 3* standard. Guests may choose to dine in The Earl Bistro or the award-winning Honora D Restaurant. This an ideal location for many events, especially as it is in close proximity (five miles) to the venue of the 2006 Ryder Cup at The K Club.

Special Offer on round of golf at The K Club available to residents • Carton House Golf Club, Hermitage Golf Club and the Liffey Valley Golf Club are nearby

The Lucan Spa Hotel, Lucan, Co Dublin
Tel: +353 (0)1 628 0494　Fax: +353 (0)1 628 0841
info@lucanspahotel.ie　www.lucanspahotel.ie

Donabate Golf Club
Balcarrick, Donabate, Co. Dublin

A challenging 27-hole, mature tree lined parkland course only fifteen minutes drive north of Dublin airport, just off the M1 motorway. The greens, built to USGA standards, have the reputation as being amongst the best in the country. A relatively flat course where good course management is required, water comes into play on 8 holes. Ultra modern clubhouse with top-class facilities that are second to none. Excellent hotels, guest houses and restaurants nearby.
Food available all day, pro-shop, golf clinics, buggies for hire.
Tel: 353 1 843 7266
Fax: 353 1 843 4488
e-mail: info@donabategolfclub.com
web: www.donabategolfclub.com

The Royal Dublin Golf Club
DOLLYMOUNT, DUBLIN 3, IRELAND

Situated 3½ miles north-east of the city centre on the coast road to Howth.
Seaside links. 18 hole Championship Links: Championship 6309 metres. SSS 73; Medal Course 6002 metres, SSS 71. Grill room, restaurant, bars. Visitors welcome; Society meetings catered for.

Clubhouse: 833 7153 • Secretary/Manager: 833 6346
Professional: 833 6477 • Caterer: 833 3370 • Fax: 353-1-833 6504
e-mail: info@theroyaldublingolfclub.com • website: www.theroyaldublingolfclub.com

Connemara Golf Club
Ballyconneely, Clifden, Co. Galway
Tel: 095 23502/23602 • Fax: 095 23662
E-mail: links@iol.ie
website: www.connemaragolflinks.com

Opened in 1973, the links course is bounded on three sides by the Atlantic Ocean, with, on the inland side, superb views of the Twelve Bens.
27 holes • practice range • pitching green • putting green
Green Fees: weekdays 50 euros, weekends 55 euros
Clubs, caddie cars, golf carts and caddies for hire.

Darby O'Gills
❖ Country House Hotel ❖
Lissivigeen, Mallow Road, Killarney, Co Kerry, Ireland

Traditional Irish food with full à la carte menu, extensive wine list and 2 licensed bars. Evening music and live session throughout the weekends. Information on all golf courses within the area. Tour arrangements and collections organised. Conveniently located for Cork and Kerry courses. Tea/coffee, direct dial telephones, colour television, all rooms en suite.

Tel: 064 34168/30016 • Fax: 064 36794
E-mail: darbyogill@eircom.net • www.darbyogillskillarney.com

Céad mile Fáilte

DINGLE GOLF LINKS
CEANN SIBÉAL

Experience the Magic! 6,696 yards, Par 72 Traditional Championship Links. Each hole on this magnificent links is carved from the natural landscape of one of the most unspoiled parts of Europe, with hazards laid down long before the game of golf was dreamt of, including a winding "burn" that twists and turns through the entire course. As you play, the whole panorama of the Dingle Peninsula is revealed - hidden bays with small fishing villages, glorious hills and mountains and the Blasket Islands out in the wild Atlantic. This area abounds in archaeological treasures, wild flora and fauna, arts and crafts and ancient Gaelic culture. The Irish language is still spoken here. Thank you for visiting us!

Dingle Golf Club, Ceann Sibéal, Ballyferriter, Dingle, Co Kerry, Ireland
Tel +353 66 915 62 55 • Fax +353 66 915 64 09
E-mail: dinglegc@iol.ie • www.dinglelinks.com

Europe's most westerly Golf Course

Individual & Group rates available on request

KILLARNEY
Golf & Fishing Club
Mahony's Point, Killarney, Co. Kerry

Ireland's Golfing Mecca for over 100 years.
3 Magnificent Lakeside Courses.
For Reservations
Phone: 00 353 64 31034
Fax: 00 353 64 33065
E-mail: reservations@killarney-golf.com
www.killarney-golf.com

Waterville Golf Links,
Waterville, Co Kerry

Tel: 066-9474102
Fax: 066-9474482
wvgolf@iol.ie
www.watervillegolflinks.ie

Heaven Sent

Location: 55 miles from Killarney and Tralee, half way round the Ring of Kerry. Links Course established in 1889.
Awards: Golf Monthly Top 5 British Isles, Golf Digest Top 100 World, Golf Digest No.1 Ireland, Golf Magazine - Best International Resorts.
7309 yards - SSS 74. Green Fees 2006: 150 euros per person. Early/Late Green Fees: 105 euros per person. Visitors welcome every day. Bar and Restaurant facilities available, carts and caddies available on request. Secretary/Manager: Noel Cronin.

WATERVILLE
Golf Links

IRELAND   The Golf Guide 2006

County Kildare
Nowhere else has so many great courses

Sensational golf courses, legendary race courses and delicious main courses, historic buildings and gardens, breathtaking scenery and the warmest of Irish welcomes.

Welcome to County Kildare.

KILDARE
THE THOROUGHBRED
COUNTY

FOR FURTHER INFORMATION
County Kildare Fáilte
38 South Main Street, Naas,
County Kildare, Ireland

Tel: + 353 45 898888,
Fax: + 353 45 898887,
Email: info@rydercupcounty.com
www.visitkildare.ie
www.rydercupcounty.com

The Ryder Cup County

Check out the County Kildare Quality Golf Passport at www.rydercupcounty.com

The finest club in Ireland

At the K Club we pride ourselves on the style and comfort we afford our guests. Nestled amid lush green woodlands, just 17 miles from Dublin, The K Club is the most rewarding place to stay. Already acclaimed as one of the finest in the world, this magnificent 5 star Hotel offers you the highest standards of accommodation and service, without losing the elegance and unique charm of an Irish country house.

For incredible relaxation, guests can enjoy our extensive facilities including the K Spa, where with its mix of the very best treatments from around the world you can be lavishly pampered. Or indulge in any of the quality leisure activities available including our two championship golf courses, both designed by Arnold Palmer.

Be it for business or pleasure, at The K Club you can expect the warmest of welcomes in the most luxurious of surroundings.

For further information and reservations:
Hotel Tel: 353 (0)1 601 7200 Fax: 353 (0)1 601 7299
Golf Tel: 353 (0)1 601 7300 Fax: (0)1601 7399
e-mail: golf@kclub.ie e-mail: sales@kclub.ie
The K Club, Straffan, Co. Kildare, Ireland.
Home of The European Open and The Ryder Cup 2006

IRELAND   The Golf Guide 2006

Beaufort
GOLF COURSE
KILLARNEY

18 HOLE PARKLAND CHAMPIONSHIP GOLF COURSE – PAR 71

★ Stone built clubhouse offers a traditional and warm atmosphere
★ Societies, Groups and Visitors welcome 7 days
★ Electric buggies, trolleys, clubs and caddies for hire
★ Golf Professional   ★ Golf shop
★ Bar food and snacks all day

Killarney:10km • Kerry Airport: 20km • Cork Airport: 90km

Tel: 00353 64 44440 • Fax: 00353 64 44752
E-mail: beaufortgc@eircom.net
www.beaufortgolfclub.com

CHURCHTOWN • BEAUFORT • KILLARNEY • Co KERRY

Gowran Park
Gowran, Co Kilkenny

A wonderful Jeff Howes-designed golf course set in traditional parkland of the old Annally Estate. Only 1½ hours from Dublin, this Par 71, 18-hole course provides an exciting playing experience for golfers of all abilities. Our newly developed clubhouse, with stunning views of the course, offers full restaurant and bar facilities in a relaxed atmosphere. The Golf Shop offers an excellent product range. We guarantee a warm welcome to visitors, societies and corporate groups. For full details contact Michael O'Sullivan, Secretary/Manager.

Tel: 056 77 26699 Fax: 056 77 26173
E-mail: gowranpk@eircom.net
www.gowranpark.ie

Located in the picturesque village of Adare, the 4 Star Dunraven Arms Hotel offers the ambience of a country house, along with first-class service and friendly, efficient staff.
• 86 rooms incl. 24 Junior Suites and 6 Executive Suites, with antique furniture, four-poster bed and separate dressing room and bathroom.
• Leisure Centre with 17m pool, steam room, gym and massage and beauty therapy rooms.
• 30 minutes from Shannon Airport.
• Two 18-hole courses in Adare incl. Adare Manor. Other courses nearby incl. Ballybunion, Lahinch, Doonbeg, Old Head and Tralee.

The Dunraven Arms Hotel, Adare, Co Limerick
00353 61 396633 • Fax: 00353 61 396541
E-mail: reservations@dunravenhotel.com • www.dunravenhotel.com

Marriott
JOHNSTOWN HOUSE HOTEL & SPA ENFIELD

Set on 120 acres of stunning parkland landscape, along with its own riverside walks, this 126 bedroom luxury four star hotel is developed around a magnificent 1750s Georgian rural residence.

Located on the main Dublin to Galway Road, just 40 minutes from Dublin Airport and 45 minutes from Dublin City Centre.

Relax and enjoy a choice of dining experiences — Pavilion Restaurant, Atrium Brasserie and Coach House Bar with live music every Saturday night.

Unwind after a game of golf in our 30,000 sq ft Spa and leisure facility.

Golf, fishing, horseracing and shopping are all located nearby. A courtesy car is available for free booking in the immediate locality and at reduced rates for airport transfers.

Special offers of 2 nights Bed & Breakfast and 1 Evening Meal from €150 pps.

Golf Escape — Carton House resident rates available on request.

Special Group Rates available on request.

**Marriott Johnstown House Hotel & Spa
Enfield, Co. Meath
Ireland
Tel: 046 9540000**
e-mail: reservations@johnstownhouse.com
www.marriottjohnstownhouse.com

IRELAND						The Golf Guide 2006

Seapoint Golf Club
Termonfeckin, Drogheda, Co. Louth
Tel: +353 (0)41 9822333 • Fax: +353 (0)41 9822331
e-mail: info@seapointgolfclub.com
www.seapointgolfclub.com
Voted into Ireland's Top 25 Golf Courses 2003/4

Opened in 1993, Seapoint Golf Club lies by the mouth of the River Boyne, near the historic town of Drogheda which is just under one hour from Dublin. The 260-acre course is designed to accommodate all standards of golfer – our aim is that you enjoy the challenge. Being a links course, it is playable all year. Mature trees border the course on the west, with water hazards coming into play on six of the first nine holes, and the closing holes have magnificent views of the Mountains of Mourne and the Irish Sea.

Secretary: Kevin Carrie • Professional: David Carroll

A Christy O'Connor Jnr designed masterpiece built on unique terrain where no two holes are remotely alike. Esker Hills is located just over an hour from Dublin, Galway and Limerick, and only 45 minutes from the K Club, the 2006 Ryder Cup venue.

◆ Parkland course with excellent natural drainage and distinct links feel
◆ 18 holes, par 71.
◆ Visitors welcome daily.
◆ Golf buggies, power caddies and pull trolleys for hire.

"If you are a golfer, never, ever pass this place"
DAVID WALSHE, SUNDAY TIMES

**Esker Hills Golf Club, Tullamore, Offaly • Tel: +353 (0) 506 55999
Fax: +353 (0) 506 55021 • info@eskerhillsgolf.com • www.eskerhillsgolf.com**

- 70 Deluxe Rooms & Suites, The Springs Leisure Club & Wellness Suites with 20m Pool, Sauna, SteamRoom, Jacuzzi, Hydrotherapy Suite, Gym & Exotic Elemis Spa Treatments.
- Discounts available for Golfing Groups of all sizes.
- Less than 90 minutes from Galway, Limerick, Shannon or the M50.
- Golf at **Birr, Roscrea, Portumna, Nenagh, Esker Hills, Tullamore, Glasson.**
- Golf from €10 (Midweek) €25 (weekend).

Check our Website for Special Offers

County Arms HOTEL

Roscrea Road, Birr, Co. Offaly
Tel: +353 (0)509 20791
Fax: +353 (0)509 21234
www.countyarmshotel.com
Completely Refurbished in 2005

An island dream!... .that is **Waterford Castle Hotel & Golf Club**

Waterford Castle Hotel & Golf Club is Ireland's only true island golf course resort. Detached from the mainland and the only golf course in Ireland, Europe and possibly the world to be accessed by private ferry. This privately owned 320-acre island, home of the renowned Waterford Castle Hotel, is the site for a wonderful parkland golf course. Designed by Des Smith, this 18-hole Par 72 championship golf course leads you through mature woodland and parkland. The course itself runs to 6814 yards, and covers an area of 200 acres.

**Waterford Castle Hotel & Golf Club
The Island, Ballinakill, Waterford, Ireland
Tel: 00 353 51 871633 • Fax: 00 353 51 871634
e-mail: golf@waterfordcastle.com • www.waterfordcastle.com/golf**

The Golf Guide 2006 — IRELAND

Ireland's Ryder Cup Region

The K Club, Co. Kildare

Ireland's East Coast & Midlands region will host one of the world's most prestigious golfing events, the **Ryder Cup, in 2006**.

We invite you to come and experience the magnificent range of links, heath and parkland courses all within an hour of Ireland's Ryder Cup venue.

Want to play the K Club, Carton House & PGA National Ireland for just €300? Now you can using the Quality Golf Passport.

For your **FREE** Ryder Cup Region Golf Guide and other great golf offers log onto:

www.eastcoastmidlands.ie

East Coast and Midlands Tourism, Dublin Road, Mullingar, Co. Westmeath, Ireland
Tel: +353 (0) 44 48650   Fax: +353 (0) 44 40613
email: info@eastcoastmidlands.ie   web: www.eastcoastmidlands.ie

Kildare - Laois - Longford - Louth - Meath
Offaly - Westmeath - Wicklow

Ireland | Fáilte Ireland | RYDER CUP 2006 IRELAND | East Coast & Midlands Tourism

IRELAND   The Golf Guide 2006

Welcome to Ashdown Park Hotel....

Ashdown Park Hotel ★★★★

Where your time is our pleasure.....

Luxurious, superbly appointed hotel, located in its own private grounds, just a three minute stroll from Gorey Town. Eighty splendid bedrooms incorporating Executive Suites, all are modern classical in style, offering the highest level of comfort, with all conveniences.

CONFERENCE & LEISURE CENTRE
THE COACH ROAD - GOREY TOWN
COUNTY WEXFORD - IRELAND
Tel: 00 353 5394 80500
Fax: 00 353 5394 80777
E-mail: info@ashdownparkhotel.com
www.ashdownparkhotel.com

For full details of clubs and courses, plus convenient accommodation

www.uk-golfguide.com

Kilrane, Rosslare Harbour Co. Wexford

Tel: (053) 33234 • Fax: (053) 32263
E-mail: info@sthelensbay.com

18 hole championship seaside parkland and links course, with several water features, 10 miles south of Wexford. Newly refurbished fully licensed bar and restaurant. Visitors always welcome with no restrictions. Society stay and play specialists. **Self-catering cottage & B&B acccommodation on site.**

web: www.sthelensbay.com

St Helens Bay Golf Resort

The Chester Beatty Inn • Ashford • Co. Wicklow

(on main N11 40km from Dublin)

With 12 superbly appointed bedrooms and a renowned reputation for hospitality, the hotel is ideally suited for small groups. All rooms are 5* standard, with spacious en suite facilities, TV, telephone etc. A fine range of food and wine is available in the Restaurant, and the traditional Irish Bar and Lounge with open log fires offer an authentic Irish atmosphere. Wicklow is a golfers' paradise, with many courses within a short distance of the hotel, and there are many visitor attractions, as well as fishing, horse riding, hillwalking and sailing.

Tel: 0404 40206 • Fax: 0404 49003
e-mail: hotelchesterbeatty@eircom.net • www.hotelchesterbeatty.ie

Rathsallagh House Hotel & Golf Club
County Wicklow • Tel: +353 45 403112

Rathsallagh is a large 4-star Grade A country house set in peaceful parkland and surrounded by the magnificent Rathsallagh Golf Club. Dublin is less than one hour's drive away. The atmosphere is happy and relaxed, with log and turf fires, central heating throughout, and luxurious en suite bathrooms. The food is country house cooking at its best – game in season and fresh fish are specialities.

Other leisure facilities include the Brendan McDaid Golf Academy, sauna, tennis, croquet, snooker, clay pigeon shooting, archery. Fishing and horse riding can be arranged. Nearby courses include the K Club, Mount Juliet and Portmarnock.

www.rathsallaghhousehotel.com

Druids Glen Golf Club

Venue for the Seve Trophy 2002
European Golf Course of the Year 2000
Home of the Irish Open 1996, '97, '98 & '99

Druids Glen Golf Club – although nestling in the beauty of the Wicklow County, this golfers' dream is only 30 minutes from Dublin City Centre.

Newtownmountkennedy
Co. Wicklow, Ireland
Tel: 00353 1287 3600
Fax: 00353 1287 3699
e-mail: druids@indigo.ie
website: www.druidsglen.ie

Glenview Hotel & Leisure Club
AA/RAC ★★★★

- 70 De luxe en suite bedrooms
- 5 ★ Leisure Centre with indoor pool
- Beauty treatments and therapies
- Award-winning Woodlands Restaurant
- Conservatory Bar
- Snooker room
- Woodland walks and gardens. Golf nearby

e-mail: sales@glenviewhotel.com
www.glenviewhotel.com

GLEN OF THE DOWNS, DELGANY, CO. WICKLOW
TEL: 00353 1287 3399

Tranquil luxury and indulgent relaxation.
A convivial Irish experience.

Championship Golf Resort
• Druids Glen – host to four Irish Open Championships and the Seve Trophy; Voted 'European Golf Course of the Year 2000' by Hertz International Travel Awards;
• Druids Heath scheduled to open in September 2003. A stunning Championship golf course carved from the natural landscape of Ireland's Garden County.

Magnificent Spa and Health Club
Journey on the pathway of rediscovery to soothe the mind, nourish the soul, calm the spirit, and escape the challenges of a modern lifestyle.

thinking of you...

DRUIDS GLEN Marriott
HOTEL & COUNTRY CLUB

• 20 minutes from South Dublin in County Wicklow, "The Garden of Ireland"

Newtownmountkennedy, Co. Wicklow, Ireland.
Tel: +353 1 2870800 Fax: +353 1 2870801
email: events.druids@marriotthotels.co.uk
www.marriotthotels.com/dubgs

IRELAND
The Golf Guide 2006

At Powerscourt you get a choice of courses.

With two of Ireland's finest golf courses and a new clubhouse located just half-an-hour south of Dublin, isn't it time you paid a visit to Powerscourt. Both our courses are open to visitors every day of the week, so why not find out for yourself what makes us one of the country's leading golf locations. Come and shoot a round here, it's always open season.

West Course

POWERSCOURT
GOLF CLUB

East Course

Powerscourt Estate, Enniskerry, Co. Wicklow Tel: +353 1 204 6033 Fax: +353 1 276 1303
email: golfclub@powerscourt.ie www.powerscourt.ie/golfclub

Wicklow Golf Club

Situated on cliffs overlooking Wicklow Bay, on the coast road to Brittas Bay, this is a challenging test of golf, each hole having its own individual features. The new clubhouse, with stunning views of the course and coastline, offers full bar, snacks, lunch and dinner facilities.

Caddy car and buggy hire • Green Fees: 40 Euros weekdays and weekends.
• Group rates available on request •

Dunbur Road, Wicklow Town, Co Wicklow
Tel: 00353 (0) 404 67379 • www.wicklowgolfclub.ie
e-mail: info@wicklowgolfclub.ie

Holiday Golf in France

Michael Gedye

Château des Sept Tours in the Loire Valley

One of Britain's most far-reaching and influential exports made its overseas debut in a city deep in Pyrenean south-west France, not far from the pilgrimage destination of Lourdes. A group of expatriates, led by one Bernard Ducuing, created the early rustic holes at Pau in 1856 and introduced golf for the first time outside the British Isles. France became the world's first destination for holiday golf, with coastal courses following either side of the end of the nineteenth century at Dinard, Biarritz, Cannes Mandelieu, Dieppe-Pourville, Le Touquet, Wimereux and Monte Carlo. These seaside gems, often allied to casinos and horse racing, attracted royalty, the wealthy and well-connected and gave golf the social status that remains in France to this day. They also provide an intriguing and time-honoured contrast to some modern marvels where power and length rather than accuracy and finesse are major requirements.

Just as golf itself has spread to the far corners of the globe, nudging 30,000 courses worldwide, so the game has grown in France. There are just under 540 courses across the country, many created over the last twenty years by some of the world's most famous course designers, with a large number in easily accessible, highly attractive resort locations. While the number of licensed French golfers is increasing, up thirty per cent in the last decade, this is mostly due to greater involvement by wives and children. Holiday courses remain very accessible to visitors (with the possible exception of the national holiday month of August),

FRANCE

with surprisingly low rates. In fact, some clubs a little away from key resorts, offer bargain prices over the summer months. Over half of all the golf courses in France are found in the eight most popular holiday regions, yet less than a quarter of French players live there. Despite domestic growth, holiday golf for the visiting player has never offered greater opportunities. New courses continue to apppear, including the ultra-luxurious charms of the new 36 holes and spa resort of the Four Seasons Golf Club in Provence.

Despite the improving success of French professionals like Thomas Levet and Jean- Francois Remesy, the game itself languishes in public popularity. A recent survey put golf twenty-fourth amongst participant sports, behind such alternatives as petanque, table tennis, gymnastics, dancing and water skiing. More good news for the golfing visitor, especially as a large number of the newer players will be found on the practice ground rather than the course.

Golfing in France has many charms. With few exceptions, the visitor will find a warm welcome and relaxed ambience wherever he chooses to play. Such a large country has much to offer in terms of varying terrain – from coastal dunes to serene parkland graced by an ancient chateau; from modern fairways snaking past lakes and tall ranks of pine to alpine courses where dramatic views of permanently snow-capped peaks can seriously distract you from your game. Expect to find excellent facilities, moderate prices and a certain quality that only the French can bring to the sport.

Recent research confirms national priorities about what is seen as essentially a family activity – that the social aspects of a club such as the restaurant, bar and swimming pool were more important than the difficulty of the course or the number of holes. Equally, proximity to the course and natural beauty outweighed a competition programme. Be that as it may, the attractive legacy of these preferences tends to be clubhouse restaurants offering gourmet dining with affordable fine wines and excellent facilities with style. It also creates some novel facets to the game itself. Where else could you find courses with each hole dedicated to a grand cru, outsize bottles as distance markers and all the holes replicated on the clubhouse wine list. There are competitions combining golf and cooking, golf and winetasting, even an 18-hole marathon where players sample the creations of 18 chefs by each green en route. Another involves a sumptuous evening clubhouse feast to be followed by 18-holes in the dark using luminous balls. Play in a competition in France for a new experience. You may also enjoy complimentary champagne, wine, pate and oysters as part of the prizegiving ceremony. Golfing à la France can be something to truly savour and cherish.

Victoria Clube de Golfe, Vilamoura, Algarve

Michael Gedye

Holiday Golf in Portugal

Think of winter golf in the sun and many people automatically turn to Portugal (or its near neighbour Spain). Tucked away in the most southwesterly corner of Europe, only a couple of hours flight away, this country of great charm, history and cultural influence has become a golfing magnet during the peak winter holiday season from September to April. The vacation destination with the fastest recent growth of places to play, Portugal is a mirror of the rising demand for relaxing sunshine golf by winter-bound countries in northern Europe. Forty years ago it could boast nine courses, many of them traditional members' clubs catering to an international elite near the main cities. Now there are seventy-five courses, mostly in holiday areas along the Algarve and near Lisbon, and this development is gathering pace.

The game owes its origins to pioneering expatriate Brits, starting with a seaside links near Oporto in 1890. The more recent rapid expansion has also been led by British influence, both in ownership, design and most importantly visiting players, sixty percent of whom come from the British Isles. The locals have never really taken to the game in great numbers. Even today less than 18,000 Portuguese are registered players. This compares with more than 1.5 million in Great Britain & Ireland, 554,293 in Sweden, 483,172 in Germany and 251,000 in the Netherlands – the four northern European countries providing the most golfing visitors, as well as owners of second homes and retirees, especially along the southern coast of the Algarve.

Such strong influences have shaped the game in Portugal, entirely in the favour of visiting players. You can be reassured that wherever you choose to visit, you will feel instantly at home. Originally introduced by the British, there is still a strong Anglo-Saxon feel about clubs and their facilities, especially in resort areas. After all, most players will be European visitors, English is the common language and everything has been designed to suit a holiday player's requirements.

Most winter-season golf is played along the Algarve coast, which currently offers thirty-two courses in play and more on the way. Players are lured by the promise of lush, well watered green fairways, winding past umbrella pines under warm, welcoming sunshine. The most recent courses have been designed by world-famous names in golf architecture, including Robert Trent Jones, Arnold Palmer, Rocky Roquemore, Cabell Robinson, Ronald Fream and Donald Steel. All have the most up-to-date construction and automatic watering, keeping fairways and greens in excellent condition.

Among the newcomers, six are in the Algarve. From westerly Boavista, with its deceptive design, sub-tropical garden setting and stunning clifftop views, Golfe do Morgado, near Portimao, to the new Arnold-Palmer designed Victoria course at Vilamoura, a links-style layout with much strategic water, which hosts the World Cup in November 2005. Further east past Faro, one comes to the beautifully conditioned and much praised layouts of Quinta de Cima and Quinta da Ria, where ancient olive trees frame superb sea views in a protected nature reserve, and Castro Marim near the border with Spain. Further north outside Lisbon are the gloriously natural holes of Oitavos amid the coastal dunes at Quinta da Marinha, which hosted the 2005 Portuguese Open, and inland, Quinta do Brincal, as well as the two courses of Ribagolf and Santo Estevao. Finally, on the Madeiran island of Porto Santo, twenty-seven holes have opened, some along cliff tops with dramatic sea views, designed by Spanish master Severiano Ballesteros.

A wealth of new courses on offer, excellent weather where the sun is tempered by Atlantic breezes and a wide choice of outstanding locations. Be prepared for fairly high fees and busy fairways in the peak season but in a country with so much to enjoy, from history and colourful culture, fresh seafood and very drinkable wines, backed by boundless local charm, Portugal has much in its favour.

Hotel Berry A Colina •• Algarve

Your host, Keith Lloyd, and his staff welcome you to this country inn hotel which specialises in all-inclusive golfing packages, winter breaks, birdwatching and summer holidays. They offer a friendly and personal service, a refreshing change from the often impersonal attitudes of larger hotels. The hotel is located in the peaceful Ludo Valley near Almancil and the Ria Formosa Natural Park. It is just 15 minutes from Faro International Airport and a short drive from many golf courses – 12 within 15 minutes' drive.

SPECIAL GOLFING PACKAGES from a weekend break to a comprehensive golf holiday. All we need to know is numbers, dates and courses – just bring your clubs and we will do the rest!

Keith Lloyd, Hotel Berry A Colina, Apartado 3761, Almancil, Algarve, Portugal
Tel/Fax: ++00351 289 395422 • www.acolina.com

Holiday Golf in Spain

Michael Gedye

Club de Golf Alcanada, Majorca

Fifty years ago, few would have considered Spain as a holiday destination. Access was limited, there were few coastal resorts and a complete lack of holiday infrastructure in what was essentially an agricultural and fishing economy. How it has all changed. Cheap charter flights, package holidays and the promise of warm sunshine, lured the northern Europeans and a new travel destination blossomed. Spain became and remains a focal point for summer holiday travel to a burgeoning mass market. Inevitably, developers realised the commercial value of Spain's coasts as winter retreats for ice-bound golfers, as well as the potential sale of fairway plots for second or retirement homes. This winter market provided the stimulus for an explosion of golf courses and upmarket resorts, in complete contrast to the country's popular summer holiday image.

Although golf had been played in Spain by a select few in the major cities since 1896, the new winter market created golfing locations around the southern and eastern coasts which were purely designed to cater to holiday visitors. Top international architects built modern, verdant, well-irrigated golf courses, green oases in an essentially bare and arid landscape, with sophisticated resorts and hotels to match. In the early 1960s there were seven golf courses along the holiday coasts and islands. Now Spain has 267 in total, many of genuine world class, with more on the way.

In contrast to Portugal, where holiday golf development has grown without much impact or participation by the local population, the game has, in recent years, taken a hold with Spaniards and new courses have sprung up throughout the country. There are now nearly a quarter of a million national players, virtually the same number as in Scotland, Ireland or the Netherlands. Much of the new golf development has been to satisfy this burgeoning local demand

SPAIN

The Golf Guide 2006

La Costa Golf & Beach Resort ★★★★
...for Pals Beach
...for Pals Golf

With its magnificent location at the heart of the Costa Brava, the **Hotel La Costa** offers a huge range of activities on land and sea in addition to its own health and leisure facilities.

Adjoining Platja de Pals Golf, one of the best golf courses in Spain, five minutes from Serres de Pals course, and convenient for the other courses in the region, the Hotel naturally attracts golfers and their families.

50% discount on green fees at Platja de Pals and Serres de Pals.

Fine cuisine and wines, a choice of bars and restaurants, large and exotic pool and tennis make the **Hotel La Costa** an obvious choice for golfing holidays in Spain.

Hotel La Costa, 17256 Playa de Pals, Pals (Costa Brava), Girona, Spain
Tel: +34 972 667 740   Fax: +34 972 667 736
e-mail: info@lacostahotel.com   website: www.lacostahotel.com

---

across the country rather than in the expansion of places to play in tourist resorts. However, eighteen further new courses in holiday areas in the last five years have added to the rich choice available to the off-season visitor. In the five prime vacation areas – Andalucia, Catalonia, Majorca, Valencia and Murcia – there are now 172 golf courses, 65% of the national total. Notable among these new offerings are the subtle, strategic holes of Sherry Golf, just outside Jerez, and the Trent-Jones layout of Alcanada with its sea views on the eastern coast of Majorca.

Club de Golf Alcanada, Majorca

The most popular region for holiday golf is along the southerly Costa del Sol. If one expands this coastline west to Cadiz and east past Malaga to Almeria, it forms a verdant golfing strip of 69 courses, a clear rival to the world-famous golfing resorts of Myrtle Beach and Palm Springs in the U.S.A. A popular sunshine family playground in the summer months, this coast becomes a magnet for golfers from colder northern climes in the winter. Predominantly from Great Britain, Ireland, Scandinavia, Germany and the Netherlands, they migrate south for warm sun, superb playing conditions and immaculate courses designed by such world-class names as Robert Trent Jones, Jack Nicklaus, Cabell Robinson, Gary Player and Perry Dye, plus home-grown stars Javier Arana, Pepe Gancedo, Manuel Pinero, Severiano Ballesteros and Jose Maria Olazabal.

Other popular golf resort areas are the craggy Costa Brava, the eastern coastline running down from Valencia through Alicante to Murcia and the golden Mediterranean island of Majorca. In a country famous for vibrant music, colourful dance, rich history and exciting cuisine and wines, there is now the largest offering of winter sunshine golf in Europe.

Holiday Golf in USA

Michael Gedye

Like so many other aspects of life in America, golfing in the popular vacation resorts is a totally different experience for players brought up on this 'side of the pond'. There are many positive benefits to be gained from visiting a nation positively bulging with record statistics – the most registered players of any country in the world (26,700,000), the most courses (17,108) and the widest geographical choice of locations and topography anywhere. One result of this surfeit of riches is the fact that most Americans take their holidays on home soil (the majority do not even own a passport) and this in turn has generated a competitive, highly efficient and very commercial system of domestic resort golf. The market is primarily American, many of them infrequent, high-handicap players but they know what they want and expect to find the same standard and range of facilities wherever they choose to go. This may lead to a certain uniformity and relatively modest level of difficulty in some resort courses but you can be confident of superb service, excellent facilities and a genuine welcome. Playing the game in America is an experience like no other. Look forward to enjoying standards of efficiency, course maintenance and clubhouse benefits well above the norm anywhere else and, given the competitive situation between resort destinations, reasonable prices.

Generally, when you arrive at a golf club, your clubs will be taken from your car and, after your progress through a welcoming and fully-stocked pro shop, you will find your clubs mounted on an obligatory golf cart. Often this will be replete with scorecard, pencil, tees, even

Pelican's Nest Golf Club, Fort Myers, Florida

a full ice bucket, lined up for progress to the appropriate tee. The golf courses may tend to be fairly wide open and relatively undemanding, catering to the broad spectrum of ability of the visitors, but the fairways and greens will be manicured to perfection. In case you find the pace of play a touch slower than you are used to, there will be regular stops every few holes for drinks and hot snacks. A couple of holes from home, you may even find a telephone to place your clubhouse bar or restaurant order to await your arrival. The American golfer on holiday wants to enjoy his day from the first tee rather than leave the socialising to the bar afterwards. Go with the flow, enjoy the sunshine and the scenery, and discover a new approach to the Royal & Ancient game.

From the wide range of holiday opportunities available, we have chosen three areas where vacation golf has a priority and there is an excellent choice of places to play. All can offer guaranteed sunshine and a full selection of resort facilities American style.

We have selected some of the best from both the east and west coasts of the sunshine state of Florida, the holiday golfing peninsula with more courses than any other. Further up the east coast you will find the Carolinas, including the comprehensive yet highly contrasting resort areas of Myrtle Beach and Hilton Head. Finally, for a touch of class, visit the incredible man-made oasis of Palm Springs, sprouting in green magnificence out of the Californian desert. Plenty of choice in some of the most popular American golfing holiday playgrounds, where facilities and weather combine to make any visit truly memorable.

Michael Gedye

*Above and opposite:
17th and 13th holes,
Santiburi Samui course, Thailand*

Everyone has their own dream of golfing heaven – the opportunity to play on a fine selection of world-class courses, where lush green fairways wind past tall palms gently waving in a coastal breeze; where the sun shines daily on manicured perfection and colourful flowers blaze at every turn; where the surrounding views are holiday postcards reflected in the clear crystal lakes; where courses are uncrowded, charges are modest and cool drinks and snacks are on offer every three holes; where charming young lady caddies treat you like royalty and help you play like a pro. Every golfer's dream yet, hard to believe, it actually exists in fabled, exotic Thailand. No further away by air than California or South Africa, the myriad courses of Thailand wait to make your golfing dreams come true.

Thailand has a wide variety of locations to visit, from the relatively cool,

Holiday Golf in Thailand

mountainous north, bordering Laos, Myanmar and access to China, down to Bangkok and the popular holiday areas around the Gulf of Thailand and then south through the long tail of land which connects the Kingdom to Malaysia. The ideal season to visit runs from November to March, a time of relatively little rain, superb sunshine and more moderate temperatures, especially in the north. Best known and best-served with a fine selection of holiday golf are the beachside vacation areas of Pattaya and Rayong south east of the central capital, Bangkok, and the holiday islands of Phuket and Koh Samui, the latter now offering one of the world's truly spectacular resort courses – the new Santiburi Golf Club, whose challenging, palm-fringed fairways rise and plunge over the mountainside above dramatic sea views. Other destinations with good golfing choice are northern Chiang Mai, western Kanchanaburi and the peaceful coastline of Cha-Am/Hua Hin.

Two hundred golf courses are spread around this colourful, charming country, with a high proportion of them in purpose-built luxury resorts around the most popular holiday areas. Most have been built in the last fifteen years, using the very latest construction and design techniques. Many bear the name of such leading international architects as Jack Nicklaus, Pete Dye, Peter Thomson, Ronald Fream, Greg Norman, Gary Player, Nick Faldo and Dennis Griffiths. Another feature of Thai golf are the magnificent clubhouses, many built like palaces, with excellent facilities, great service and panoramic restaurants overlooking the course, offering Thai, Chinese, Japanese and international menus. Despite a long history (the first nine-hole golf course dates from 1898), the game really exploded into life in the early 1990s, further fuelled by the emergence of one Tiger Woods, whose mother is a Thai. More than 300,000 locals play the game, more than the individual golfing populations of such established European golfing countries as Scotland, Ireland, the Netherlands and Spain. Although you would probably be well advised to avoid the inevitably crowded courses around Bangkok at the weekend, the wealth of holiday resort courses remain attractively underplayed at quite moderate prices.

Wherever golf is played, each country lends some memorable local touch to the game. In Thailand, it is most definitely the caddies. At every club, you will find a virtual army of smiling lady caddies, dressed in distinctive colourful uniforms and highly trained in their craft. For around the price of a top-class golf ball, she will pull your bag, give you exact yardage, mark and clean your ball on the green, know the correct putting line and, throughout, do her best to make sure you enjoy your game. After the round, she will clean your clubs, even your golf shoes if you ask her. Playing in Thailand has a great deal to offer the visitor; the caddies are the icing on the cake.

However, one should never consider a holiday in Thailand for golf alone. There is so much more. This ancient, exotic kingdom has a wealth of elegant Bhuddist temples, graceful classical dancers, colourful flora, shimmering silks and spicy, complex cuisine. From the distinctive northern hilltribes, with their unique culture and handicrafts, elephant treks and jungle trails to the shimmering beaches, curving in white magnificence under tall coconut palms, this a photographers' paradise. With ever-cheaper air travel and world-class hotels, Thailand is still waiting to be discovered by discerning travelling golfers. It offers wide choice, superb escapist weather, golf of the highest quality at bargain prices and a truly colourful holiday experience. The Land of Smiles, with its gentle, delightful people, is a wonderful and refreshing addition to the world of vacation golf.

16th hole, Santiburi Samui course, Thailand

The Golf Guide 2006 **TOURS & PRODUCTS**

Golf Tours & Golfing Products

Golf Around Scotland is a well established, Scottish-based golf tour company specialising in golf tours, golf short breaks and golf vacations – all in Scotland. Our expert knowledge of Scottish golf courses and accommodation providers means that we are able to deliver tailor-made vacations and tours to suit all budgets and group sizes. Call us today **01350 727059**

www.golfaroundscotland.com

THINK OF IT!!
- think of a golfing tour in Scotland, the USA, Asia or Africa
- everything provided for your leisure • clubs, trolleys, buggies, accommodation, transport • no lugging bags around
- your own guided escort • intelligence on each course

Don't just dream! Do it!
GLOBAL GOLF TOURS • tee up at www.ggtours.org

TOURS & PRODUCTS   The Golf Guide 2006

Golf Insurance

Lowest Prices Guarantee®

Why Golf Insurance?
Golf is becoming an increasingly popular hobby in the UK. Some people wrongly believe their household contents insurance will cover their golfing equipment. For just 8p a day you can relax knowing you and your equipment are protected by E&L® Insurance.

FREE 10% Nevada Bob's discount voucher
Details available on request

E&L INSURANCE™

Call **08704 022 103** for instant cover
or visit **www.eandl.org.uk/golfguide**

Entertainment & Leisure Ins. Services Ltd. Appointed representative of the Equine & Livestock Insurance Co. Ltd. which is authorised and regulated by the Financial Services Authority (FSA register No. 202748).

Make Everyday Legendary.

Transfers energy to the ball, so you don't have to *transfer blame* to your driver.

Standard clubs

Wilson Staff ETF Technology

Energy Transfer Frame technology, a proprietary COR-enhancement in the new Wilson Staff drivers, fairway woods and hybrids, delivers more than twice the hot zone of standard clubs. And half the excuses.

wilsonstaff.com

ETF460™
Energy Transfer Frame

Wilson Staff Dd6 ·10°

Wilson and Staff are registered trademarks of Wilson Sporting Goods Co.

Wilson WS Staff

TOURS & PRODUCTS
The Golf Guide 2006

Golf Tee-Time Service

Golf Tee-Time Service offers the complete range of golfing services. From tee-time bookings, Brittany Ferries golf breaks in France/Northern Spain, Golf breaks in Wales and Portugal, through to large corporate golf days. Please phone **01822 618181** for more information on any of our services or visit **www.golfteetimeservice.com** (e-mail info@golfteetimeservice.com).

- **Tournaments:** For competitive golf with a friendly atmosphere played on superb courses. We have a tournament programme.
- **Corporate Management:** A total solution-why waste time, money and precious resources organising your golf day.
- **Tee-Time Booking:** We specialise in organising pre-reserved tee-times in Portugal, Spain, France, Mallorca, UK and Ireland.
- **UK Specials:** Offering superb value for short breaks at some great locations.
- **World-Wide Golf:** Golf holidays in Madeira, Barbados, Bermuda, USA and other exotic locations.
- **Brittany Ferries Golf Desk 0870-9021818.** We manage the Brittany Ferries Golf Desk and can offer superb golf in France.
- **Greens of Southern Wales 0870-600608.** Golf breaks in Wales.
- **Golf in Portugal 01822-610035.** Golf breaks in Portugal.

UNBEATABLE VALUE — SUNDAY/MONDAY GOLF BREAKS

PLAY & STAY AT SOME OF THE UK'S BEST GOLF RESORTS

- The Belfry • Woodhall Spa • Marriott Hanbury Manor • De Vere Slaley Hall
- Trevose, Cornwall • De Vere Mottram Hall • Forest Pines • Marriott Forest of Arden
- Marriott Meon Valley • Marriott St Pierre • Marriott Tudor Park • Hawkstone Park

Prices from only £89.00 *(per person based on a twin or double share)* **including:**
- 2 rounds of golf • Dinner, Bed & Breakfast in the 4/5 Star Hotel • Full use of leisure facilities

To book call or fax **GMM Ltd on 01492 877123** or e-mail breaks@gmmltd.co.uk

visit www.foretour.co.uk for details

---

golf breaks

carnoustie st andrews
islay campbeltown
isle of man
cork

for reservations and useful information:
0141 305 5006
golf@scotiatravel.com • www.scotiatravel.com

scotia golf

For full details of clubs and courses, plus convenient accommodation

www.uk-golfguide.com

Make Everyday Legendary.

Perfect best-ball foursome.

The superior forgings of the Fi5. The tour-proven performance of the Pi5. And now, with the new Ci6's enhanced control and the new Di6's maximum distance, Wilson Staff is proud to present an unrivalled line of irons that will meet the needs of any player. Or any four players.

wilsonstaff.com

Fi5
Timeless
Classic Forgings

Pi5
Tour-Proven
Cavity-Back Blades

Ci6
Classic Shape
Control and Forgiveness

Di6
Maximum Forgiveness
and Playability

Wilson Staff

How to use the Golf Guide

THE GOLF GUIDE Where to Play • Where to Stay contains up to date basic information on every course (as far as we know) in Britain and Northern Ireland. Details are provided by the clubs themselves. You will also find sections on the Irish Republic plus holiday golf in Spain and Majorca, Portugal, France, the USA, South Africa, Dubai and Thailand.

The guide carries entries from hotels, guest houses and other accommodation convenient to specific courses or areas. These are generally 'paid' entries and usually follow a recommendation from a club.

THE GOLF GUIDE, in association with *Golf Monthly,* is usually available for sale in golf clubs through the Professional and/or the Secretary, as well as bookshops etc.

• Golf Course Information

For virtually every course you will find the following details, updated annually:
1. Name, address and telephone number.   2. Location.   3. Brief description.
4. Number of holes, length and Standard Scratch Score.   5. Green fees.
6. Details of facilities for visitors – individuals, groups and societies.
7. Name and telephone number of the Professional and the Secretary.

The accuracy of details published depends on the response of the clubs and to our best knowledge is correct at the time of going to press (October 2005). Where entry details have not been confirmed an asterisk (*) is shown.

• Choosing a Course

The golf clubs and courses are listed alphabetically by nearest town or village within the appropriate county section for England, Scotland, Wales, Ireland, the Isle of Man and the Channel Islands. Courses overseas are also listed by region. We have chosen to classify by place-name rather than club or course name since this seems more straightforward and recognisable to the majority.

If you want to find a club or course by its name, you should simply refer to the Index where you will see the page number of the listing. In each entry the name of the club or course is always shown in bold type after the place-name heading.

• Accommodation

Accommodation entries are placed as near a particular club or course as possible and there are also hotel displays in the front colour section. Most of the accommodation advertised has been recommended by the local golf club. A full index is provided.

The location details supplied with each entry should get you there and if you are in any doubt at all you should ask directions from the club itself.

Please mention **THE GOLF GUIDE Where to Play • Where to Stay** when you make a hotel booking or play at courses after using our guide.

Publisher's Note

With the addition of new courses and ones not previously covered, the 29th edition of **THE GOLF GUIDE Where to Play • Where to Stay** now features over 2,800 UK and Irish courses, along with a small taster of golf available in other countries including France, Spain, Portugal, South Africa, Thailand and the USA.

Golf is a game which is increasing in popularity and is attracting a wider range of people than ever. It is a game for all ages with juniors trying to be the next Tiger Woods while senior members still try to emulate Ben Hogan or Arnold Palmer.

With so many courses to choose from it is difficult for a new golfer to know where to start. Each course has its own character and each hole presents its own unique challenge and this, the definitive guide to courses, gives you the opportunity to try, and enjoy, as many as possible. As usual, we offer the following advice to readers.

Enquiries and Bookings. It is quite normal to confirm a booking in writing and also to receive written confirmation – and a receipt for any advance payment. You should check prices and also any special requirements.

Cancellations. Any booking is a form of contract for both parties. If you have to cancel, try to give maximum notice. With reasonable notice the hotel should normally refund any advance payment but on short notice a full refund is not necessarily a legal entitlement.

Complaints. Most owners/managers are anxious to sort out problems on the spot so that you are a satisfied customer. If a problem persists you can get advice from a Citizens' Advice Bureau, Consumers' Association, Trading Standards Office, Tourist Board or indeed your own solicitor.

Serious complaints are unlikely to arise with the kind of accommodation you'll find on our pages. FHG Guides Ltd. do not inspect accommodation and an entry does not imply a firm recommendation. However, most of the advertisers have been recommended or proposed by local golf clubs and have standards which satisfy and in many cases far exceed those expected by inspecting authorities. In addition we will be pleased to hear from you if you have a serious complaint and although we cannot act as intermediaries or accept responsibility for our advertisers, we will record the complaint and follow it up with the advertiser in question.

We are grateful to all Club Secretaries and Club Professionals who assist in the supply and revision of entries and to the PGA for editorial support. We are happy to hear from any Club which for some reason does not already have an entry. We also thank our advertisers for the wide range of accommodation choices available in this edition for golfers, their families, friends and colleagues, and welcome suggestions for the future. We are particularly keen to receive accommodation recommendations from clubs and golfers themselves.

When you make enquiries and bookings for golf, accommodation or both, please mention this latest edition of **THE GOLF GUIDE: Where to Play • Where to Stay.**

George Pratt

Publishing Director

ENGLAND and WALES Counties

NORTH WALES
1. Denbighshire
2. Flintshire
3. Wrexham

SOUTH WALES
4. Swansea
5. Neath and Port Talbot
6. Bridgend
7. Rhondda Cynon Taff
8. Merthyr Tydfil
9. Vale of Glamorgan
10. Cardiff
11. Caerphilly
12. Blaenau Gwent
13. Torfaen
14. Newport
15. Monmouthshire

©MAPS IN MINUTES™ 2005

A selection of Golf Events in 2006

• APRIL

DUNCAN PUTTER
Southerndown
April 15-16

PETER MCEVOY TROPHY
Copt Heath
April 19-20

HELEN HOLM SCOTTISH OPEN STROKE PLAY CHAMPIONSHIP
Troon/Portland
April 22-23

TRUBSHAW CUP
Ashburnham/Tenby
April 22-23

• MAY

LYTHAM TROPHY
Royal Lytham & St Annes
May 5-7

IRISH OPEN STROKE PLAY CHAMPIONSHIP
Royal Dublin
May 12-14

CLWYD OPEN
Prestatyn/Wrexham
May 13-14

SCOTTISH LADIES' CLOSE AMATEUR CHAMPIONSHIP
Dunbar
May 16-20

ENGLISH MEN'S STROKE PLAY CHAMPIONSHIP (BRABAZON TROPHY)
Ganton Golf Club
May 19-21

ENGLISH LADIES' CLOSE AMATEUR CHAMPIONSHIP
West Lancashire
May 23-27

WELSH OPEN STROKE PLAY CHAMPIONSHIP
Southerndown
May 26-28

• JUNE

SCOTTISH OPEN STROKE PLAY CHAMPIONSHIP
Craigielaw
June 2-4

ST RULE TROPHY
St Andrews
June 3-4

WELSH OPEN YOUTHS' CHAMPIONSHIP
Monmouthshire
June 3-4

ST ANDREWS LINKS TROPHY
St Andrews
June 9

ENGLISH SENIORS' CHAMPIONSHIP
Yelverton
June 7-9

ABERCONWY TROPHY
Maesdu/Conwy
June 10-11

WELSH SENIORS' CHAMPIONSHIP
Aberdovey
June 13-15

LADIES' BRITISH OPEN AMATEUR CHAMPIONSHIP
Royal County Down
June 13-17

BRITISH AMATEUR CHAMPIONSHIP
Royal St George's
June 19-24

SCOTTISH YOUTHS' OPEN CHAMPIONSHIP
Morton Hall
June 23-25

WALES SENIORS OPEN
Tenby
June 27-29

FHG
For full details of clubs and courses, plus convenient accommodation
www.uk-golfguide.com

•JULY

LADIES' BRITISH OPEN MID-AMATEUR CHAMPIONSHIP
Nairn
July 7-9

JUNIOR OPEN
Heswall Golf Club
July 17-19

OPEN CHAMPIONSHIP
Royal Liverpool Golf Club,
July 20-23

ENGLISH LADIES' CLOSE AMATEUR STROKE PLAY CHAMPIONSHIP
Little Aston
July 25-27

WELSH BOYS' OPEN CHAMPIONSHIP
Pennard
July 26-28

SENIOR BRITISH OPEN CHAMPIONSHIP
Turnberry
July 27-30

•AUGUST

ENGLISH GIRLS' CHAMPIONSHIP
King's Norton
August 1-5

WELSH AMATEUR CHAMPIONSHIPS
Pyle & Kenfig
August 1-5

WEETABIX WOMEN'S BRITISH OPEN
Royal Lytham & St Anne's
August 3-6

BOYS' HOME INTERNATIONALS
Moray
August 8-10

GIRLS' HOME INTERNATIONALS
Portstewart
August 9-11

BRITISH SENIORS' OPEN AMATEUR CHAMPIONSHIP
Saunton
August 9-11

GIRLS' BRITISH OPEN AMATEUR CHAMPIONSHIP
Portstewart
August 14-18

BOYS' AMATEUR CHAMPIONSHIP
Royal Aberdeen
August 14-19

ENGLISH LADIES' OPEN MID-AMATEUR CHAMPIONSHIP
Cotswold Hills
August 15-18

BRITISH MID-AMATEUR CHAMPIONSHIP
Southport & Ainsdale
August 16-20

WELSH TEAM CHAMPIONSHIP
Llandudno Maesdu
August 18-20

LADIES' BRITISH OPEN AMATEUR STROKE PLAY CHAMPIONSHIP
The Prince's,
August 23-25

•SEPTEMBER

WELSH BOYS' INTER COUNTIES CHAMPIONSHIP
Wrexham
September 1

LADIES' HOME INTERNATIONALS
Frilford Heath
September 13-15

WELSH INTER COUNTIES CHAMPIONSHIP
Borth & Ynyslas
September 17

SENIOR LADIES' BRITISH OPEN AMATEUR CHAMPIONSHIP
Dumfries & County,
September 19-21

SCOTTISH LADIES' COUNTY FINALS
The Hirsel
September 22-24

Ryder Cup, K Club
September 22-24

•OCTOBER

LADIES' SENIOR HOME INTERNATIONAL MATCHES
Hamilton Golf Club
October 3-5

Make Everyday Legendary.

Transfers energy to the ball, so you don't have to *transfer blame* to your driver.

Standard clubs

Wilson Staff ETF Technology

Energy Transfer Frame technology, a proprietary COR-enhancement in the new Wilson Staff drivers, fairway woods and hybrids, delivers more than twice the hot zone of standard clubs. And half the excuses.

wilsonstaff.com

ETF460™
Energy Transfer Frame

Wilson Staff Dd6·10°

Wilson and Staff are registered trademarks of Wilson Sporting Goods Co.

Wilson Staff

Golf Tee-Time Service

Golf Tee-Time Service offers the complete range of golfing services. From tee-time bookings, Brittany Ferries golf breaks in France/Northern Spain, Golf breaks in Wales and Portugal, through to large corporate golf days. Please phone **01822 618181** for more information on any of our services or visit **www.golfteetimeservice.co.uk** (e-mail info@golfteetimeservice.co.uk).

- **Tournaments:** For competitive golf with a friendly atmosphere played on superb courses. We have a tournament programme.
- **Corporate Management:** A total solution-why waste time, money and precious resources organising your golf day.
- **Tee-Time Booking:** We specialise in organising pre-reserved tee-times in Portugal, Spain, France, Mallorca, UK and Ireland.
- **UK Specials:** Offering superb value for short breaks at some great locations.
- **World-Wide Golf:** Golf holidays in Madeira, Barbados, Bermuda, USA and other exotic locations.
- **Brittany Ferries Golf Desk 0870-9021818.** We manage the Brittany Ferries Golf Desk and can offer superb golf in France.
- **Greens of Southern Wales 0870-600608.** Golf breaks in Wales.
- **Golf in Portugal 01822-610035.** Golf breaks in Portugal.

THINK OF IT!!

- think of a golfing tour in Scotland, the USA, Asia or Africa
- everything provided for your leisure • clubs, trolleys, buggies, accommodation, transport • no lugging bags around
- your own guided escort • intelligence on each course

Don't just dream! Do it!

GLOBAL GOLF TOURS • tee up at **www.ggtours.org**

FHG Guides 2006

October Edition

- Recommended COUNTRY HOTELS
- Recommended COUNTRY INNS & PUBS
- BED & BREAKFAST STOPS • CHILDREN WELCOME!
- The Original FHG Guide to COAST & COUNTRY HOLIDAYS
- CARAVAN & CAMPING HOLIDAYS, England, Scotland, Wales & Ireland
- BRITAIN'S BEST HOLIDAYS
- THE GOLF GUIDE Where to Play / Where to Stay
- PETS WELCOME!
- Recommended SHORT BREAK HOLIDAYS in Britain
- SELF CATERING HOLIDAYS in Britain

Available from bookshops or larger newsagents

April Edition

FHG Guides LTD
Abbey Mill Business Centre,
Seedhill, Paisley PAI ITJ
www.holidayguides.com

Make Everyday Legendary.

Perfect best-ball foursome.

The superior forgings of the Fi5. The tour-proven performance of the Pi5. And now, with the new Ci6's enhanced control and the new Di6's maximum distance, Wilson Staff is proud to present an unrivalled line of irons that will meet the needs of any player. Or any four players.

wilsonstaff.com

Fi5
Timeless
Classic Forgings

Pi5
Tour-Proven
Cavity-Back Blades

Ci6
Classic Shape
Control and Forgiveness

Di6
Maximum Forgiveness
and Playability

Wilson and Staff are registered trademarks of Wilson Sporting Goods Co.

Wilson W/S Staff®

Golf Insurance

Lowest Prices Guarantee*

Why Golf Insurance?
Golf is becoming an increasingly popular hobby in the UK. Some people wrongly believe their household contents insurance will cover their golfing equipment. For just 8p a day you can relax knowing you and your equipment are protected by E&L® Insurance.

FREE 10% Nevada Bob's discount voucher*

*Details available on request

E&L INSURANCE™

Call **08704 022 103** for instant cover
or visit www.eandl.org.uk/golfguide

Entertainment & Leisure Ins. Services Ltd. Appointed representative of the Equine & Livestock Insurance Co. Ltd. which is authorised and regulated by the Financial Services Authority (FSA register No. 202748).

London (Central & Greater)

ASHFORD. **Ashford Manor Golf Club,** Fordbridge Road, Ashford, Middlesex TW15 3RT (01784 424644; Fax: 01784 424649). Parkland course, flat with narrow fairways. 18 holes, 6352 yards. S.S.S. 71. *Green Fees:* weekdays £40.00 per round, £50.00 per day. *Eating facilities:* dining room and snacks. *Visitors:* welcome weekdays; it is advisable to ring in advance, Handicap Certificate required. May not play at weekends other than with a member. *Society Meetings:* welcome. Professional: (01784 255940). Manager: Gina Rivett (01784 424644; Fax: 01784 424649). e-mail: secretary@ashfordmanorgolfclub.fsnet.co.uk

BARNET. **North Middlesex Golf Club,** The Manor House, Friern Barnet Lane, Whetstone N20 0NL (020 8445 1732; Fax: 020 8445 5023). *Location:* five miles south of Junction 23 of M25. 18 holes, 5594 yards. S.S.S. 67. *Green Fees:* information not available. *Eating facilities:* luncheons, snacks and dining facilities. *Visitors:* welcome (with Official Handicap), weekends after 12 noon. Advisable to telephone Professional to book time. *Society Meetings:* catered for. Professional: Freddy George (020 8445 3060). General Manager: Miss Alex McDonald (020 8445 1604; Fax: 020 8445 5023). *

BARNET. **Old Fold Manor Golf Club,** Old Fold Lane, Hadley Green, Barnet, Herts EN5 4QN (020 8449 1650). *Location:* Junction 23 M25 - A1000 one mile north of Barnet. Heathland course. 18 holes, 6447 yards. S.S.S. 71. Practice ground and putting green. *Green Fees:* information not available. *Eating facilities:* restaurant and bar except Mondays and Wednesdays when cafeteria/snack bar is available. *Visitors:* welcome weekdays, public days Monday/ Wednesday; special visitors' concessions at weekends by arrangement. *Society Meetings:* catered for Thursdays and Fridays. Professional: Peter McEvoy (020 8440 7488). Manager: Brian Cullen (020 8440 9185; Fax: 020 8441 4863).* website: www.oldfoldmanor.co.uk

BEXLEYHEATH. **Barnehurst Public Pay and Play Golf Course,** Mayplace Road East, Bexleyheath, Kent DA7 6JU (01322 523746; Fax: 01322 523860). *Location:* 10 minutes from M25, follow signs for Erith. Mature inland course in traditional woodland setting. 9 holes, 2737 yards. S.S.S. 68 (for 18 holes). Designed by five times Open Champion James Braid in 1903. Practice ground. *Green Fees:* information not available. *Eating facilities:* fully licensed bar with catering facilities. *Visitors:* welcome, no restrictions. Newly refurbished club house. *Society Meetings:* catered for. Large function rooms. Golf Manager: Freda Sunley.*

BROMLEY. **Bromley Golf Club,** Magpie Hall Lane, Bromley, Kent BR2 8JF. *Location:* off A21 Bromley to Farnborough road. Open course with many trees and water. 9 holes, 2397 yards. S.S.S. 67. Putting green and teaching facilities. *Green Fees:* information not available. *Eating facilities:* food available. *Visitors:* no booking required as this is a public course. Professional: Alan Hodgson (0208 462 7014).*

CHINGFORD. **Chingford Golf Club,** 158 Station Road, Chingford E4 (020 8529 2107). 18 holes, 6342 yards. S.S.S. 70. *Green Fees:* information not available. *Visitors:* welcome weekdays only, an article of red must be worn. Pro shop: 020 8529 5708. Professional: Andy Traynor. Secretary: Bryan Sinden.*

CHINGFORD. **Royal Epping Forest Golf Club,** Forest Approach, Chingford, London E4 7AZ (020 8529 2195). *Location:* 200 yards east of Chingford (BR) Station. A private club on a public course. Wooded. 18 holes, 6342 yards. S.S.S. 71. *Green Fees:* weekdays £14.00; weekends £18.00. *Eating facilities:* public snack bar. *Visitors:* may play course but may not use clubhouse. Must wear red garment (trousers or shirt/sweater). Professional: Andy Traynor (020 8529 5708). Secretary: Mr D Bright - Thomas (020 8529 2195).

CHINGFORD. **West Essex Golf Club,** Bury Road, Sewardstonebury, Chingford, London E4 7QL (020 8529 7558; Fax: 020 8524 7870). *Location:* two miles north of Chingford BR Station. M25 (Junction 26) and Waltham Abbey follow directions to Chingford (Daws Hill on left). Parkland, wooded, hilly. 18 holes, 6289 yards. S.S.S. 70. Driving range (for members, members' guests and societies). *Green Fees:* weekdays £40.00 per round, £45.00 per day; weekends with member only. *Eating facilities:* restaurant and bar facilities. *Visitors:* welcome weekdays except Tuesday mornings. Phone first. *Society Meetings:* catered for by arrangement Mondays, Wednesdays and Fridays. Professional: Robert Joyce (Tel & Fax: 020 8529 4367). Secretary: (020 8529 7558; Fax: 020 8524 7870). e-mail: sec@westessexgolfclub.co.uk website: www.westessexgolfclub.co.uk

DULWICH. **Dulwich and Sydenham Hill Golf Club,** Grange Lane, College Road, London SE21 7LH (020 8693 3961). *Location:* off South Circular, Dulwich Common. 18 holes, 6051 yards. S.S.S. 69. *Green Fees:* information not available. *Eating facilities:* lunch every day. *Visitors:* welcome, prior arrangement advised. *Society Meetings:* catered for. Professional: David Baillie. Secretary: Mr Brian O'Farrell.*

FHG
For full details of clubs and courses, plus convenient accommodation
www.uk-golfguide.com

EDMONTON. Leaside Golf Club, Lee Valley Leisure Centre, Pickett's Lock Lane, Edmonton N9 0AS (020 8803 3611; Fax: 020 8884 4975). *Location:* M25 Juntion 25, nearest town Enfield. Flat parkland course, lake on first 9 holes, good drainage; short but challenging course. 18 holes, 4811 yards (yellow). S.S.S. 64 (yellow). 20 bay driving range, practice ground. *Green Fees:* information not available. *Eating facilities:* cafe and bar. *Visitors:* welcome everyday. Trolleys available. Professional: Richard Gerken (020 8803 3611). Membership/Secretary: David Campbell (020 8364 7782).*

EDMONTON. Lee Valley Leisure Golf Course, Picketts Lock Lane, Edmonton N9 0AS. (020 8803 3611). *Location:* off Meridian Way between north Circular Road and Ponders End. Flat parkland course with lake and River Lea as water hazards. Short but challenging. 18 holes, 4902 yards. S.S.S. 66. *Green Fees:* information not available. Senior Citizens/Junior weekday concessions. *Visitors:* welcome, pay and play everyday. *Society Meetings:* small societies welcome, prior booking. Professional: R.G. Gerken (020 8803 3611). *

ELTHAM. Eltham Warren Golf Club, Bexley Road, Eltham SE9 2PE (020 8850 1166). *Location:* off East Rochester Way (A2) at Falconwood, then onto A210 Bexley Road. Parkland course, narrow fairways. 9 holes, 5840 yards. S.S.S. 68. Practice ground. *Green Fees:* £28.00 per day; with member £14.00. *Eating facilities:* dining room and bar. *Visitors:* welcome weekdays only, weekends with member only. *Society Meetings:* welcome Thursdays only. Professional: Gary Brett (020 8859 7909). Secretary: D.J. Clare (020 8850 4477).

ELTHAM. Royal Blackheath Golf Club, The Clubhouse, Court Road, Eltham SE9 5AF. *Location:* M25, A20 exit London bound, second set of traffic lights turn right, 600 yards up hill on right. Parkland, wooded with water. 18 holes, 6219 yards. S.S.S. 70. Practice area. *Green Fees:* £50.00 per round, £70.00 per day. *Eating facilities:* excellent dining room and two bars. *Visitors:* welcome weekdays, weekends only if introduced by and playing with member. Museum. *Society Meetings:* catered for midweek, prior booking essential. Professional: Richard Harrison (020 8850 1763). Secretary: (020 8850 1795; Fax: 020 8859 0150).
e-mail: info@rbgc.com
website: www.rbgc.com

ENFIELD. Crews Hill Golf Club, Cattlegate Road, Crews Hill, Enfield EN2 8AZ (020 8363 6674). *Location:* off Junction 24 M25, follow directions to Enfield. Parkland. 18 holes, 6230 yards. S.S.S. 70. Practice area. *Green Fees:* on application. *Eating facilities:* full bar and snacks available, restaurant by arrangement. No catering Mondays. *Visitors:* welcome weekdays. Handicap Certificate required. Weekends by invitation of member. *Society Meetings:* by arrangement. Professional: N. Wichelow (020 8366 7422). Club Manager: R. Williams (020 8363 6674; Fax: 020 8363 2343).

ENFIELD. Enfield Golf Club, Old Park Road South, Enfield, Middlesex EN2 7DA (020 8363 3970; Fax: 020 8342 0381). *Location:* off Junction 24, M25; follow directions to Enfield. Parkland; designed by James Braid. 18 holes, 6154 yards. S.S.S. 70. *Green Fees:* on request. *Eating facilities:* full bar and catering facilities. *Visitors:* welcome weekdays, limited availability at weekends. Please telephone Professional Shop before travelling. *Society Meetings:* welcome weekdays by prior arrangement. Professional: Martin Porter (020 8366 4492). Secretary: Peter Monument (020 8363 3970; Fax: 020 8342 0381).
e-mail: secretary@enfieldgolfclub.co.uk
website: www.enfieldgolfclub.co.uk

ENFIELD. Whitewebbs Golf Club, Clay Hill, Beggars Hollow, Enfield EN2 9JN (020 8363 2951). *Location:* A10 off M25, north of Enfield. Parkland course. 18 holes, 5863 yards. S.S.S. 68. Practice area, separate 9 hole pitch and putt. *Green Fees:* information not available. *Eating facilities:* public cafe on site. *Visitors:* welcome, public course, no restrictions. *Society Meetings:* contact the Secretary. Professional: Gary Sherrif (020 8363 4454). Secretary: Stephen Pyke (020 8363 2951). *

FINCHLEY. Finchley Golf Club, Nether Court, Frith Lane, Mill Hill NW7 1PU (020 8346 2436; Fax: 020 8343 4205). *Location:* close A1/M1, near Mill Hill East underground station. Parkland course, tree lined, designed by James Braid. 18 holes, 6411 yards. S.S.S. 71. *Green Fees:* weekdays £30.00 per round, £40.00 per day; weekends £40.00 per round. *Eating facilities:* two bars and catering. *Visitors:* welcome weekdays except Tuesdays, Thursdays and weekend mornings. Clubs, shoes, trolleys and carts for hire. Excellent 19th century Manor House. *Society Meetings:* catered for Mondays, Wednesdays and Fridays. Professional: David Brown (020 8346 5086). Secretary: J. Seatter (020 8346 2436).
e-mail: secretary@finchleygolfclub.co.uk

GREENFORD. Ealing Golf Club, Perivale Lane, Greenford, Middlesex UB6 8TS. *Location:* on Western Avenue A40 half a mile from Hanger Lane Gyratory System. Flat parkland. 18 holes, 6216 yards. S.S.S. 70. *Green Fees:* information not provided. *Eating facilities:* spike bar, mixed lounge, restaurant - lunch, dinner and bar snacks. Conference room. *Visitors:* welcome weekdays with reservation through Professional Shop. *Society Meetings:* catered for on Monday, Wednesday and Thursday only. Professional: Ricky Willison (020 8997 3959). General Manager: June Mackison (020 8997 0937; Fax: 020 8998 0756).

GREENFORD. Horsenden Hill Golf Club, Greenford, Middlesex UB6 0RD. *Location:* two miles from A40; off Whitton Avenue East, next door to Sudbury Golf Course. Situated on Horsenden Hill Conservation Area. Undulating parkland course, eight Par 3, one Par 4. 9 holes, 1632 yards. S.S.S. 28. Practice area, nets and putting green. *Green Fees:* £4.50 for 9 holes weekdays, £7.00 weekends. *Eating facilities:* bar/cafe. *Visitors:* welcome at all times, public course. Membership available. Trolley hire. *Society Meetings:* welcome. Professional: Jeff Quarshie (020 8902 4555). Golf Course Manager: Ray Peters (07989 243219).

THE GOLF GUIDE 2006　　ENGLAND / London (Central & Greater)

GREENFORD. **Perivale Park Golf Club,** Stockdove Way, Argyle Road, Greenford, Middlesex. *Location:* A40, turn off at sign for Ealing and Perivale. Entrance to golf club is at Stockdove Way, Perivale. Flat, riverside course set amongst the meadows of Brent River Park. Internal out of bounds areas. 9 holes (18 holes), 2733 yards (white tees). S.S.S. 65. Practice area. *Green Fees:* information not available. *Eating facilities:* cafeteria. *Visitors:* welcome at all times. Public course. Membership available. Professional: P. Bryant (020 8575 7116). Golf Course Manager: Ray Peters: (07989 243219).*

HAMPSTEAD. **Hampstead Golf Club,** Winnington Road, London N2 0TU (020 8455 6420). *Location:* off Hampstead Lane adjacent to Spaniards Inn. Undulating parkland with mature trees. 9 holes, 5812 yards. S.S.S. 68. *Green Fees:* information not provided. *Eating facilities:* bar meals/snacks and afternoon teas. *Visitors:* welcome weekdays (not Tuesdays); limited at weekends, telephone Professional. Professional: P J. Brown (020 8455 7089). Secretary: (020 8455 0203; Fax: 020 8731 6194).

HAMPTON. **The Fulwell Golf Club,** Wellington Road, Hampton Hill, Middlesex TW12 1JY. *Location:* opposite Fulwell Railway Station and bus garage. Stunning parkland course. 18 holes, 6544 yards. S.S.S. 71. Practice ground. *Green Fees:* weekdays £36.00 per round, £45.00 per day; weekends £50.00, £18.00 with member. *Eating facilities:* bar lunches and teas. *Visitors:* welcome weekdays, weekends by prior arrangement. *Society Meetings:* welcome Monday, Thursday and Friday. Professional: Nigel Turner (Tel & Fax: 020 8977 3844). Secretary: Mark Walden (020 8977 2733; Fax: 020 8977 7732).
e-mail: secretary@fulwellgolfclub.org.uk
website: www.fulwellgolfclub.org.uk

HAMPTON WICK. **Hampton Court Palace Golf Club,** Hampton Wick, Kingston-upon-Thames KT1 4AD (020 8977 2658). *Location:* between Hampton Court and Kingston Bridge, entrance at Kingston Bridge roundabout. Flat parkland. 18 holes, 6513 yards. S.S.S. 71. *Green Fees:* information not available. *Eating facilities:* full bar and dining facilities. *Visitors:* welcome; booking one week in advance through Pro Shop. *Society Meetings:* catered for by arrangement. Professional: Adam Smith (020 8977 2658).*

HANWELL. **Brent Valley Golf Club,** Church Road, Hanwell, London W7. *Location*: one mile from Uxbridge Road, off Greenford Avenue, entrance at Church Road. Situated in a picturesque valley in the Brent River Park, 18 holes, 5446 yards. S.S.S. 67. Pay and Play. Nets and practice area. *Green Fees*: information not available. *Eating facilities*: bar/cafe. *Visitors* :welcome at all times. Membership available Public course. *Society Meetings*: welcome. Professional: V. Santos (020 8567 1287). Golf Course Manager: Ray Peters (07989 243219).*

HENDON. **Hendon Golf Club,** Ashley Walk, Devonshire Road, Mill Hill, London NW7 1DG (020 8346 6023) *Location:* leave M1 southbound at Junction 2. Turn off A1 into Holders Hill Road, first circle , take first left into Devonshire Road, golf club approx. 50 metres on the left. 10 miles north of London. Parkland, wooded, well bunkered. 18 holes, 6289 yards. S.S.S. 70. *Green Fees:* weekdays £32.00 per round, £40.00 per day; weekends £40.00 per round. *Eating facilities:* full bar and catering facilities. *Visitors:* welcome weekdays (limited at weekends and Bank Holidays), book through Pro Shop. *Society Meetings:* catered for by arrangement Tuesdays to Fridays, book through Secretary's office. Professional: Matt Deal (020 8346 8990). Secretary: David Ryan (020 8346 6023; Fax: 020 8343 1974). e-mail: hendongolfclub@globalnet.co.uk

HIGHGATE. **Highgate Golf Club,** Denewood Road, Highgate, London N6 4AH (020 8340 1906). Founded 1904. *Location:* near A1, turn down Sheldon Avenue, opposite Kenwood House and first left. Parkland. 18 holes, 5985 yards. S.S.S. 69. *Green Fees:* £32.00. *Eating facilities:* bar, restaurant. *Visitors:* welcome weekdays except Wednesdays from 9.30 am. *Society Meetings:* catered for Thursdays/Fridays. Professional: Robin Turner (020 8340 5467). Secretary: Nigel Challis (020 8340 3745).

For full details of clubs and courses, plus convenient accommodation

www.uk-golfguide.com

Did you know that there are 3 golf courses in the Borough of Ealing ….. WHY NOT TRY ONE?

BRENT VALLEY • 18 hole course situated in a picturesque valley in the Brent River Park, Church Road, off Greenford Avenue, Hanwell W7 (020 8567 1287). Licensed bar * Food served all day * Golf shop * Changing facilities * Practice facilities * Car park*

PERIVALE PARK • 9 hole course set in Perivale Park amongst the meadows of Brent River Park, close to the A40; entrance is at Stockdove Way, Perivale (020 8575 7116). Golf shop * Food served all day * Changing facilities * Practice facilities * Car park

HORSENDEN HILL • 9 hole course situated on Horsenden Hill conservation area, off Whitton Avenue East, Greenford, Middlesex. Entrance via Woodland Rise (020 8902 4555). Licensed bar * Food served all day * Golf shop * Changing facilities * Practice facilities * Car park.

ALL 3 GOLF COURSES ARE OPEN WEEKDAYS, WEEKENDS AND BANK HOLIDAYS.

Ealing
www.ealing.gov.uk

For further information on Membership/Fees contact any of the above Golf Courses or Ray Peters, Golf Course Manager, Parks and Countryside Service on 07989 343219

SEASON TICKETS ON SALE FROM ALL GOLF COURSES

See also Colour Advertisement on page 23

London (Central & Greater) / ENGLAND — THE GOLF GUIDE 2006

HILLINGDON. **Hillingdon Golf Club,** 18 Dorset Way, Hillingdon, Uxbridge, Middlesex UB10 0JR (01895 239810). *Location:* near A40, adjacent to RAF Uxbridge. Gently undulating wooded parkland course sloping down to river. 9 holes, 5490 yards, 5068 metres. S.S.S. 67. *Green Fees:* information not available. *Eating facilities:* bar meals available Tuesday to Friday. *Visitors:* welcome Mondays, Tuesdays and Fridays; Thursdays - Ladies' Day. *Society Meetings:* catered for by special arrangement only with Committee through Club Secretary. Professional: Phil Smith (01895 460035). Secretary: B.L. Russell (01895 233956).*

HOUNSLOW. **Airlinks Golf Club,** Southall Lane, Hounslow, Middlesex TW5 9PE (020 8561 1418; Fax: 020 8813 6284). *Location:* Junction 3 on M4, A312 to Hayes. Same entrance as D. Lloyd Tennis Centre. Parkland course with water holes and doglegs. 18 holes, 6000 yards. S.S.S. 68. Floodlit driving range. *Green Fees:* information not available. *Eating facilities:* full catering and bar facilities/restaurant area. *Visitors:* weekdays no restrictions, some restrictions weekends, bookings advised seven days in advance. Membership, including 5 and 7 day, now open. *Society Meetings:* catered for all week. Professional: Tony Martin. Secretary: Stefan Brewster.*

HOUNSLOW. **Hounslow Heath Municipal Golf Course,** Staines Road, Hounslow TW4 5DS (020 8570 5271). *Location:* Staines Road A315 between Hounslow and Bedfont. Heathland course with water hazards, tight fairways. 18 holes, 5901 yards. S.S.S. 68. Practice area. *Green Fees:* information not provided. *Eating facilities:* snacks; teas and coffee. *Visitors:* welcome at all times, bookings seven days in advance for weekends and Bank Holidays. *Society Meetings:* by arrangement.

ISLEWORTH. **Wyke Green Golf Club,** Syon Lane, Osterley, Isleworth, Middlesex TW7 5PT (020 8560 8777). *Location:* situated half-a-mile north of A4 near Gillettes Corner. Fairly flat parkland. 18 holes, 6182 yards. S.S.S. 70. *Green Fees:* Monday to Thursday £40.00 per day, £30.00 per round, £20.00 after 5pm Monday to Friday £18.00 with a member. *Eating facilities:* full catering restaurant and halfway house. *Visitors:* welcome; weekends only with member until after 4pm. *Society Meetings:* catered for on Tuesdays and Thursdays by arrangement, minimum 12. Professional: Neil Smith (020 8847 0685) Secretary: David Pearson (020 8560 8777; Fax: 020 8569 8392).

LONDON. **Dukes Meadows Golf Club,** Dukes Meadows, Great Chertsey Road, London W4 2SH (020 8995 0537 Fax: 020 8995 5326). *Location:* next to Chiswick Bridge on the A316, one mile south Hogarth roundabout. Parkland course, greens to USGA standard. 50 bay floodlit driving range.6 hole Academy Course for young players acccompanied by adult golfers. *Green Fees:* information not available. *Eating facilities:* bar/restaurant area available. *Visitors:* welcome, tee times up to 48 hours advance booking. 12 teaching PGA professionals, trolleys available. *Society Meetings:* welcome by arrangement. Professional: Malcolm Henbery (020 8995 0537). General Manager/PGA Professional: Scott Margetts. (020 8994 3314). *

LONDON. **London Scottish Golf Club,** Windmill Enclosure, Wimbledon Common SW19 5NQ (020 8788 0135). *Location:* just off A3 – Tibbetts Corner – just south of Putney SW15. Wooded commonland. 18 holes, 5458 yards. S.S.S. 66. *Green Fees:*information not available. *Eating facilities:* bar and catering. *Visitors:* welcome weekdays only. Check with Professional recommended. Red top must be worn, no jeans or sweatshirts. *Society Meetings:* welcome. Professional/Secretary: Stephen Barr (020 8789 1207/7517).*

LONDON. **Mill Hill Golf Club,** 100 Barnet Way, Mill Hill, London NW7 3AL (020 8959 2339). Est. 1925. *Location:* A1, south half a mile before Apex Corner left into clubhouse car park – signposted. Wooded parkland. 18 holes, 6247 yards, 5697 metres. S.S.S. 70. Practice ground. *Green Fees:* weekdays £28.00; weekends £35.00. *Eating facilities:* restaurant and bar. *Visitors:* welcome Monday to Friday; weekends and Bank Holidays prior bookings recommended. Two snooker tables. *Society Meetings:* welcome weekdays with prior booking. For green fees ring the Pro Shop (020 8959 7261); for society and membership enquiries ring Club Office (020 8959 2339). Professional: D. Beal. Secretary: R. Haslehurst.

LONDON. **Richmond Park Golf Club,** Roehampton Gate, Richmond Park, London SW15 5JR (020 8876 1795; Fax: 020 8878 1354). *Location:* set within parkland in Richmond. Two courses (36 holes), 6036 yards and 5868 yards. S.S.S. 68/68/67. Driving range. *Green Fees:* information not provided. *Visitors:* welcome every day. *Society Meetings:* all welcome. Secretary: Tony Gourvish (020 8876 3205).

LONDON. **Thamesview Golf Centre,** Fairway Drive (off Summerton Way), Thamesmead North, London SE28 8PP (020 8310 7975; Fax: 020 8312 0546). Delightful, undulating Public Pay & Play Course, founded 1991. Water hazards and a mixture of new and mature trees. The 4th hole is a challenging 515 yards down a narrow fairway. 9 holes, 5462 yards, par 70. S.S.S. 67. Floodlit 30 bay driving range, putting green. *Green Fees:* information not available. *Eating facilities*: restaurant, bars and function room. *Visitors:*

Wyke Green Golf Club *Probably the most convenient course to Central London*

Situated between Heathrow Airport and Marble Arch, this flat, parkland course, built in 1926 (designed by Hawtree and Taylor), offers a good challenge to every calibre of golfer, particularly the seven par 4 holes in excess of 420 yards. Enjoy the warm, friendly surroundings of the clubhouse as well as enjoying a 'quick bite' at our famous 'Halfway House'. Societies and Corporate days welcome between Mondays & Fridays.

e-mail: office@wykegreengolfclub.org • *website: www.wykegreengolfclub.co.uk*

TEL: 020 8560 8777
FAX: 020 8569 8392

Wyke Green Golf Club, SYON LANE, ISLEWORTH, MIDDLESEX TW7 5PT

THE GOLF GUIDE 2006　　ENGLAND / London (Central & Greater)　**127**

no restriction. Fully stocked Pro Shop, club hire. *Society Meetings*: welcome, book by telephone or in writing. Professional: Graeme Wilson. Club Secretary: Sarah Springham.*
e-mail: enquiries@thamesview-golf.fsnet.co.uk
website: www.thamesview-golf.fsnet.co.uk

LONDON. **Trent Park Public Golf Course,** Bramley Road, Southgate, London N14 (020 8367 4653). *Location:* opposite Oakwood Tube Station. Undulating parkland. 18 holes, 6176 yards. S.S.S. 69. Modern heated, floodlit 36 bay driving range. *Green Fees:* information not available. *Eating facilities:* restaurant and snacks. *Visitors:* open to public at all times. Bookings advised on weekdays and necessary at weekends. Golf superstore. *Society Meetings:* welcome any day. Professional: Ray Stocker. Secretary: Richard Flint. *

NORTHWOOD. **Northwood Golf Club Ltd,** Rickmansworth Road, Northwood, Middlesex HA6 2QW (01923 821384; 01923 840150). *Location:* on A404 between Pinner and Rickmansworth. Parkland/wooded course. 18 holes, 6535 yards. S.S.S. 71. *Green Fees:* information not available. *Eating facilities:* restaurant and bar snacks, lounge bar. *Visitors:* welcome weekdays, except Tuesdays; with members only at weekends. *Society Meetings:* by arrangement, details from the Secretary. Professional: C.J. Holdsworth (01923 820112). Secretary: T. N. Collingwood (01923 821384).*

NORTHWOOD. **Sandy Lodge Golf Club,** Sandy Lodge Lane, Northwood, Middlesex HA6 2JD. *Location:* adjacent to Moor Park Underground Station. Sandy Lodge Golf Club is a member of the Hertfordshire Golf Union and situated on the Moor Park Estate close to Moor Park, Batchworth Park, Chorleywood and Rickmansworth. Inland links. 18 holes, 6328 yards. S.S.S. 71 (white). *Green Fees:* on application. *Eating facilities:* full catering and bar service available. *Visitors:* weekdays only, please telephone in advance. Handicap Certificate required. *Society Meetings:* by prior written arrangement. Professional: Jeff Pinsent (01923 825321). Secretary: John C. Coombes (01923 825429; Fax: 01923 824319).

PINNER. **Grim's Dyke Golf Club,** Oxhey Lane, Hatch End, Pinner, Middlesex HA5 4AL (020 8421 1286). *Location:* on A4008 Watford to Harrow (2 miles west of Harrow). Undulating parkland, tree lined, testing greens. 18 holes, 5600 yards. S.S.S. 67. Practice area. *Green Fees:* information not available. *Eating facilities:* bar snacks, lunches available on request. *Visitors:* must produce Certificate of Handicap. Buggies available. *Society Meetings:* catered for Mondays to Fridays. Professional: Lee Curling. Office & Pro: (020 8428 4539; Fax: 020 8421 5494).*

PINNER. **Pinner Hill Golf Club,** Southview Road, Pinner Hill HA5 3YA (020 8866 0963; Fax: 020 8868 4817). *Location:* one mile west Pinner Green. Parkland course with magnificent views over London. 18 holes, 6392 yards. S.S.S. 71. *Green Fees:* inmformation not available. *Eating facilities:* bar and catering available at all times; parties by prior arrangement please. *Visitors:* welcome with Handicap Certificate. *Society Meetings:* weekdays. Professional: Mr Mark Grieve (020 8866 2109). General Manager: Jeremy Duffy (020 8866 0963). *
e-mail: pinnerhillgc@uk2.net
website: www.pinnerhillgc.co.uk

ROEHAMPTON. **Roehampton Club Ltd,** Roehampton Lane, London SW15 5LR (020 8480 4200; Fax: 020 8480 4265). *Location:* just off South Circular Road between Sheen and Putney. Parkland. 18 holes, 6065 yards. S.S.S. 69. *Green Fees:* information not provided. *Eating facilities:* restaurant, club café, juice bar. *Visitors:* welcome as members' guest only, Handicap Certificate required at weekends. *Society Meetings:* catered for by arrangement. Professional: Alan L. Scott (020 8876 3858). Chief Executive: Mark Wilson (020 8480 4205). Sports Manager: Alistair Cook (020 8480 4200).

RUISLIP. **Ruislip Golf Club**, King's End, Ickenham Road, Ruislip, Middlesex HA4 7OQ (01895 638081). *Location:* two and a half miles from Junction 1, M40, first left after M40/A40 merge, onto B467, then left at T-Junction onto B466. Parkland course. 18 holes, 5571 yards. S.S.S. 67. Driving range (40 bays). *Green Fees:* information not provided. *Eating facilities:* full restaurant facilities. *Visitors:* welcome, booking system at all times. *Society Meetings:* welcome by arrangement. Professional: Paul Glozier (01895 638835). Secretary: P.C. Thornton (01895 638081).

SHEPPERTON. **Sunbury Golf Club,** Charlton Lane, Shepperton TW17 8QA (01932 772898). *Location:* two miles south-west of M3 Junction 1; south-east of Queen Mary Reservoir between villages of Charlton and Upper Halliford. Two parkland courses. 18 holes, 5103 yards. S.S.S. 65, Par 68. 9 holes, 2444 yards, Par 33. 32 bay floodlit driving range (8am to 10pm), practice puttting green. *Green Fees:* 18 hole course £21.00 weekends, £16.50 weekdays; 9 hole course £11.00 weekends, £9.00 weekdays. *Eating facilities:* snacks, meals and bar. *Visitors:* welcome, no restrictions. Booking up to one week in advance essential. Buggies and trolleys for hire. *Society Meetings*: welcome at all times; advance booking required; special packages available. Professional: Adrian McColgan. General Manager: Patrick Dawson (01932 771414; Fax: 01932 789300).

SHOOTERS HILL. **Shooters Hill Golf Club Ltd,** "Lowood", Eaglesfield Road, Shooters Hill, London SE18 3DA (020 8854 6368; Fax: 020 8854 0469). *Location:* off A207 between Blackheath and Welling. Hilly wooded course with fine views. 18 holes, 5721 yards. S.S.S. 68. *Green Fees:* weekdays £25.00 per round, £30.00 per day; weekends with a member only, £16.00 per round or day. *Eating facilities:* bar and diningroom; jacket and tie required. *Visitors:* members of other clubs welcome weekdays on production of letter of introduction, or official Handicap Certificate. Buggies available. *Society Meetings:* catered for Tuesdays and Thursdays only. Professional: David Brotherton (020 8854 0073). Secretary: Sharon Deadman (020 8854 6368).

London (Central & Greater) / ENGLAND

SOUTHALL. **West Middlesex Golf Club,** Greenford Road, Southall, Middlesex UB1 3EE (020 8574 3450). *Location:* junction of Uxbridge Road (A4020) and Greenford Road. 18 holes, 6119 yards. S.S.S. 69. *Green Fees:* please telephone the Pro Shop on 020 8574 1800. *Visitors:* welcome weekdays and at weekends after 2.00pm, except on competition days. *Society Meetings:* catered for by prior arrangement. Professional: T. Talbot. Secretary: Miss R. Khanna (020 8574 3450; Fax: 020 8574 2383).

SOUTHWARK. **Aquarius Golf Club,** Beachcroft Reservoir, Marmora Road, Honor Oak SE22 0RY (020 8693 1626). *Location:* nearest main road - Forest Hill Road. The course is situated on and around a reservoir, testing first and eighth holes. 9 holes, 5246 yards. S.S.S. 66. *Green Fees:* information not available. *Eating facilities:* limited. *Visitors:* welcome with member only. Professional: F. Private. Secretary: Jim Halliday*.
e-mail: aquariusgolfclub@btopenworld.com

STANMORE. **Brockley Hill Golf Park,** Brockley Hill, Stanmore HA7 4LR (020 8420 6222; Fax: 020 8420 6333). *Location:* Junction 4 M1, A41. Parkland course. 9 holes, 1102 yards, 1007 metres. S.S.S. 27. Covered and floodlit 2 tier driving range. *Green Fees:* information not available. *Visitors:* welcome anytime - pay as you play. *Society Meetings:* welcome on application. Professionals: Cranfield Golf Academy.*

STANMORE. **Stanmore Golf Club,** 29 Gordon Avenue, Stanmore, Middlesex HA7 2RL (Tel & Fax: 020 8954 2599). *Location:* turn off A410 by church to Old Church Lane, Gordon Avenue is to the right. Wooded, parkland course. 18 holes, 5879 yards. S.S.S. 68. Practice and putting areas. *Green Fees:* from £17.00. *Eating facilities:* restaurant facilities available *Visitors:* welcome. No jeans or trainers. Jacket and tie after 7pm. *Society Meetings:* catered for Wednesday and Thursday by prior booking only. Professional: James Reynolds. Secretary: Maria Bateman. Caterer: (020 8954 4661).
e-mail: secretary@stanmoregolfclub.co.uk
website: www.stanmoregolfclub.co.uk

SUNBURY ON THAMES. **Hazelwood Golf Club,** Croysdale Avenue, Sunbury on Thames TW16 6QU (01932 770932; Fax: 01932 770933). *Location:* Junction 1 of M3. Parkland course. 9 holes, 2785 yards. Practice putting green, 36 bay driving range, bunker and chipping practice. *Green Fees:* information not available. *Eating facilities:* Bunkers Cafe/Bar. *Visitors:* welcome every day. *Society Meetings* welcome. Professional: Francis Sheridan.*

TOTTERIDGE. **South Herts Golf Club,** Links Drive, Totteridge N20 8QU (020 8445 2035). *Location:* off Totteridge Lane N20, one mile from Whetstone, nearest underground station Totteridge & Whetstone. Parkland. 18 holes, 6432 yards. S.S.S. 71. *Green Fees:* on request. *Eating facilities:* lunch, high tea (breakfast and dinner by arrangement). *Visitors:* welcome with reservation Monday to Friday and Sunday pm. *Society & Corporate Meetings:* welcome Monday to Friday. Professional: R.Y. Mitchell (020 8445 4633). Secretary: B. Weeds (020 8445 2035; Fax: 020 8445 7569).
website: www.southhertsgolfclub.co.uk

TWICKENHAM. **Amida Golf Course and Teaching Academy,** Staines Road, Twickenham TW2 5JD (020 8783 1698: Fax: 020 8941 9134). *Location:* at end of M3, on A305 near its junction with 35. Golf teaching academy. *Green Fees:* information not available. *Eating facilities:* Golfers' Bar and Indoor Virtual Golf. *Visitors:* welcome, play and pay. Function room available. *Society Meetings:* welcome. Professional: Suzy Watt (020 8783 1698; Fax: 020 8941 9134)*
website: www.amidaclubs.com

TWICKENHAM. **Strawberry Hill Golf Club,** Wellesley Road, Strawberry Hill, Twickenham TW2 5SD (020 8894 0165). *Location:* near Twickenham Green, 200 yards Strawberry Hill Station. Flat parkland. 9 holes, 4762 yards. S.S.S. 63. *Green Fees:* 18 holes £18.00; with a member £11.00. 9 holes £14.00, with a member £8.00. *Eating facilities:* restaurant and bar. *Visitors:* welcome, restrictions weekends and competition days. *Society Meetings:* welcome weekdays, small parties only. Professional: Peter Buchan (020 8898 2082). Secretary: Paul Astbury (020 8894 0165; Fax: 020 8898 0786).

UXBRIDGE. **Stockley Park Golf Club,** Stockley Park, Uxbridge UB11 1AQ (020 8813 5700; Fax: 020 8813 5655). *Location:* Junction 4 M4, Heathrow Airport turnoff, A408 to Uxbridge. Parkland course, designed by Robert Trent Jones Snr. 18 holes, 6754 yards. S.S.S. 71. Practice nets, chipping and putting greens. *Green Fees:* on application. *Eating facilities:* balcony restaurant and bar. *Visitors:* all welcome. Trolleys available all year round. *Society Meetings:* welcome. Professional: Stuart Birch. Adminstration: Jackie Hickey.
website: www.stockleyparkgolf.com

UXBRIDGE. **Uxbridge Golf Course,** The Drive, Harefield Place, Uxbridge UB10 8AQ (01895 237287; Fax: 01895 810262). *Location:* off Swalkelys Junction - M40. Undulating parkland. 18 holes, 5753 yards. S.S.S. 68. *Green Fees*: information not available. *Eating facilities*: bars, carvery restaurant. *Visitors*: welcome anytime, booking required at weekends. Function suite. *Society Meetings*: welcome. Professional: Phil Howard (01895 237287). Secretary: Tom Atkins (01895 272457).*

WANDSWORTH. **Central London Golf Centre,** Burntwood Lane, Wandsworth SW17 0AT (020 8871 2468; Fax: 020 8874 7447). *Location:* turn right through the Wandsworth town centre into Garrat Lane, Burntwood Lane is off Garrat Lane. Short course with three good Par 3s and several good Par 4s. 9 holes, 2223 yards. S.S.S. 31. Large practice putting green. 14 bay driving range. *Green Fees:* information not available. *Eating facilities:* full bar and restaurant; function room. *Visitors:* welcome, no restrictions. Special disabled putting green. Trolleys for hire. *Society Meetings:* welcome, special terms on request. Professional: Jeremy Robson (020 8871 2468).*
e-mail: golf@clgc.co.uk website: www.clgc.co.uk

ENGLAND / London (Central & Greater)

WANSTEAD. **Wanstead Golf Club,** Overton Drive, Wanstead E11 2LW (020 8989 3938; Fax: 020 8532 9138). *Location:* one mile from junction of A12 and A406. Parkland bordering Epping Forest with featured lake. 18 holes, 6109 yards. S.S.S. 69. *Green Fees:* information not available. *Eating facilities:* dining room and bars. *Visitors:* welcome Mondays, Tuesdays and Fridays by prior arrangement with the Secretary. Handicap Certificate required. Weekends with member only. *Society Meetings:* welcome, apply Secretary. Professional: David Hawkins (020 8989 9876). Secretary: Keith Jones (020 8989 3938; Fax: 020 8532 9138).*

WEMBLEY. **Sudbury Golf Club Ltd,** Bridgewater Road, Wembley, Middlesex HA0 1AL (020 8902 3713). *Location:* junction of A4005 (Bridgewater Road) and A4090 (Whitton Ave East). Undulating parkland. 18 holes, 6282 yards. S.S.S. 70. Practice ground. *Green Fees:* information not available. *Eating facilities:* dining room and bars. *Visitors:* welcome weekdays with Handicap Certificate. *Society Meetings:* catered for. Professional: Neil Jordan (020 8902 7910). General Manager: Neil Cropley.*

WEST DRAYTON. **Heathpark Golf Club,** Stockley Road, West Drayton, Middlesex UB7 9NA (01895 444232). *Location:* in grounds of Crown Plaza Hotel, Junction 4 M40. Undulating parkland course. 9 holes, 2275 yards. S.S.S. 64. *Green Fees:* information not available. *Eating facilities:* catering and bars. *Visitors:* welcome, dress code. *Society Meetings:* welcome at all times. Contact: B. Sharma.

WIMBLEDON. **Royal Wimbledon Golf Club,** 29 Camp Road, Wimbledon SW19 4UW. *Location:* one mile west of War Memorial in Wimbledon Village. 18 holes, 6348 yards. S.S.S. 70. *Visitors:* weekdays by prior arrangement. *Society Meetings:* Wednesdays and Thursdays only, by arrangement. Professional: David Jones. Secretary: Norman Smith (020 8946 2125; Fax: 020 8944 8652).
e-mail: secretary@rwgc.co.uk
website: www.rwgc.co.uk

WIMBLEDON. **Wimbledon Common Golf Club,** 19 Camp Road, Wimbledon Common, Wimbledon SW19 4UW (020 8946 0294; Fax: 020 8947 8697). *Location:* Wimbledon Common. Wooded course. 18 holes, 5438 yards. S.S.S. 66. Par 68. *Green Fees:* Monday £10.00, Tuesday to Friday £16.00. Four or more £13.00. *Eating facilities:* bar, full catering every day except Mondays. *Visitors:* welcome weekdays, only with a member at weekends. Dress code – pillar box red upper garment must be worn. *Society Meetings:* welcome, groups of up to 50 catered for. Professional: J.S. Jukes (020 8946 0294; Fax: 020 8947 8697). Secretary: Ray Pierce (020 8946 7571).

WIMBLEDON. **Wimbledon Park Golf Club,** Home Park Road, Wimbledon, London SW19 7HR (020 8946 1002; Fax: 020 8944 8688). *Location:* Church Road, Arthur Road and Home Park Road from Wimbledon High Street, or by District Line to Wimbledon Park Station where signposted. Parkland, wooded around a lake. 18 holes, 5492 yards. S.S.S. 66. *Green Fees:* £50.00. *Eating facilities:* dining room and bar snacks each day. *Visitors:* welcome on production of letter of introduction or Handicap Certificate. *Society Meetings:* welcome. Special rate 36 holes, morning coffee, Ploughmans, three-course meal £65.00; Winter Package – bacon roll, 18 holes, three-course meal £35.00. Professional: Dean Wingrove (020 8946 4053). Secretary: Eileen Inwood (020 8946 1250; 020 8944 8688).
e-mail: secretary@wpgc.co.uk
website: www.wpgc.co.uk

WINCHMORE HILL. **Bush Hill Park Golf Club,** Bush Hill, Winchmore Hill, London N21 2BU (020 8360 5738; Fax: 020 8360 5583). *Location:* half a mile south of Enfield town (off London Road). Parkland. 18 holes, 5825 yards. S.S.S. 68. Practice ground and nets. *Green Fees:* weekdays £28.50 per round, weekends only with member. *Eating facilities:* restaurant, bar, bar snacks. *Visitors:* welcome weekdays except Wednesday mornings, Handicap Certificate required. *Society Meetings:* catered for Tuesdays, Thursdays and Fridays. Professional: Lee Fickling (020 8360 4103). Secretary: Rachael Meade (020 8360 5738; Fax: 020 8360 5583).

WOOD GREEN. **Muswell Hill Golf Club,** Rhodes Avenue, Wood Green, London N22 7UT (020 8888 2044; Fax: 020 8889 9380). *Location:* North Circular/Bounds Green tube station one mile. Mature parkland. 18 holes, 6438 yards. S.S.S. 71. Practice ground. *Green Fees:* information not available. *Eating facilities:* restaurant open seven days. *Visitors:* welcome weekdays, weekends pre-booked with Professional. *Society Meetings:* welcome weekdays; terms on request. Professional: D. Wilton (020 8888 8046). Secretary: Mrs J. Underhill (020 8888 1764).*

THE APPEARANCE OF AN ASTERISK (*) AT THE END OF A CLUB OR COURSE ENTRY INDICATES THAT UP-TO-DATE INFORMATION HAS NOT BEEN SUPPLIED

For full details of clubs and courses, plus convenient accommodation

www.uk-golfguide.com

Bedfordshire

AMPTHILL. **The Millbrook Golf Club,** Millbrook, Ampthill MK45 2JB (01525 840252; Fax: 01525 406249). *Location:* just off A507 Ampthill to Woburn Road, near Junction 13 of M1. Rolling links situated on the Greensand Ridge overlooking Bedfordshire. 18 holes, 7021 yards. S.S.S. 73. Two practice areas. *Green Fees:* weekdays £25.00 18 holes; weekends only after 12 noon £35.00. *Eating facilities:* bar/restaurant, breakfasts, lunches, dinners. *Visitors:* welcome midweek. *Society Meetings:* by invitation only. Professional & Tee Time bookings: Geraint W. Dixon (01525 402269). Manager: Derek Cooke (01525 840252; Fax: 01525 406249).
e-mail: info@themillbrook.com
website: www.themillbrook.com

ASPLEY GUISE. **Aspley Guise and Woburn Sands Golf Club,** West Hill, Aspley Guise MK17 8DX (Tel & Fax: 01908 583596). *Location:* two miles west of Junction 13 M1, between Aspley Guise and Woburn Sands. Undulating parkland, 18 holes, 6079 yards. S.S.S. 70. *Green Fees:* weekdays £30.00 per round, £40.00 per day; weekends by prior arrangement. *Eating facilities:* catering service, bar. *Visitors:* welcome weekdays with bona fide handicaps - check with Secretary. *Society Meetings:* Wednesdays and Fridays. Professional: Colin Clingan (01908 582974). Secretary: Richard Norris (Tel & Fax: 01908 583596).

BEADLOW. **Beadlow Manor Hotel, Golf and Country Club,** Beadlow, Near Shefford SG17 5PH (01525 860800). *Location:* from M1 (J12) take A5120 east to Ampthill, then A507 to Shefford. From A1 (J10) take A507 west to Ampthill. Challenging, rolling parkland with water hazards. Two courses (Baron and Baroness): 18 holes, 6819 yards. S.S.S. 72; 18 holes, 6072 yards. S.S.S 69. Covered 25 bay floodlit driving range, practice area. *Green Fees:* information not available. *Eating facilities:* restaurant, three bars, snacks, refreshments, two function rooms. *Visitors:* welcome at all times. Residential Golf Breaks available. Professional academy and shop. Special mid-week and weekend Breaks for Society and Company Groups. All reservations through Sales and Marketing Office. General Manager: Graham Wilson.*

BEDFORD. **The Bedford Golf Club,** Great Denham Golf Village, Biddenham, Bedford MK40 4FF (01234 320022; Fax: 01234 320023). *Location:* two miles west of Bedford on A428. American-style course with 90 bunkers and eight water features, built on free-draining sandy soil. 18 holes, 6478 yards. S.S.S. 72. Practice range. *Green Fees:* midweek £30.00, weekends £40.00. *Eating facilities:* restaurant and bar meals; course refreshments. *Visitors:* always welcome - excellent rates. Buggies for hire. Part of the Kolven Golf Group. *Society Meetings:* welcome. Manager: Simon Pepper.
e-mail: thebedford@btopenworld.com
website: www.kolvengolf.com

BEDFORD. **Bedford and County Golf Club,** Green Lane, Clapham, Bedford MK41 6ET (01234 354010). *Location:* off A6 north of Bedford before Clapham Village. Parkland. 18 holes, 6420 yards. S.S.S. 70. *Green Fees:* information not available. *Eating facilities:* full catering facilities and bar. *Visitors:* welcome without reservation except weekends. *Society Meetings:* catered for Mondays, Tuesdays, Thursdays and Fridays. Professional: Mr R Tattersall (01234 359189). Manager: Mr R Walker (01234 352617; Fax: 01234 357195).*
website: www.bedfordandcountygolfclub.co.uk

BEDFORD. **Bedfordshire Golf Club,** Spring Lane, Stagsden, Bedford MK43 8SR (01234 822555; Fax: 01234 825052). *Location:* one mile west of Bedford town centre on the A422. Wooded parkland, flat. 18 holes, 6565 yards. S.S.S. 72. 9-hole course. 24-bay driving range. *Green Fees:* information not available. *Eating facilities:* bar and catering; evening meals by arrangement. *Visitors:* welcome on weekdays, must be with members at weekends. *Society Meetings:* catered for weekdays. Professional: Peter Saunders (01234 826100). Manager: D.E. Romans (01234 822555).*

BEDFORD. **Mowsbury Golf Club,** Cleat Hill, Kimbolton Road, Bedford MK41 8DQ (01234 771493). *Location:* on B660 at northern limit of city boundary. 18 holes, 6510 yards. S.S.S. 71. Driving range. *Green Fees:* on request. *Eating facilities:* meals and bar snacks until 2pm; evening meals if booked in advance. *Visitors:* welcome. Squash courts. *Society Meetings:* by arrangement with the Professional. Professional: Malcolm Summers (01234 772700), for tee reservations and fees. Secretary: C. H. Spencer (01234 771041).

BEDFORD. **Pavenham Park Golf Club,** Pavenham, Bedford MK43 7PE (01234 822202; Fax: 01234 826602). *Location:* take the A6 out of North Bedford, from Clapham follow signs to Pavenham. Parkland course with fast and contoured greens. 18 holes, 6400 yards. S.S.S. 71. Practice ground. *Green Fees:* information not available. *Eating facilities:* bar and catering available. *Visitors:* welcome midweek only, must adhere to dress code. Buggies and carts available. Part of the Kolven Golf Group. *Society Meetings:* welcome, excellent rates. Professional: Zac Thompson. Secretary: Lee Pepper.*
e-mail: kolvengolf@ukonline.co.uk
website: www.kolvengolf.com

www.uk-golfguide.com

THE GOLF GUIDE 2006   ENGLAND / Bedfordshire   131

CADDINGTON. **Griffin Golf Club,** Chaul End Road, Caddington LU1 4AX (01582 415573 Fax: 01582 415314). *Location:* Ten minutes from Junctions 9 or 11 M1. Gently undulating parkland. 18 holes, 6240 yards. S.S.S.70. *Green Fees:* information not available. *Eating facilities:* bar with catering available. *Visitors:* welcome anytime midweek; weekends by arrangement. *Society Meetings:* welcome, special deals available. Secretary: Alan Sigee.*
e-mail: griffin@griffingolfclub.fsbusiness.co.uk

COLMWORTH. **Colmworth and North Bedfordshire Golf Club,** New Road, Colmworth MK44 2NN (01234 378181; Fax: 01234 376678). *Location:* north of Bedford just off B660 and only 10 minutes from the A1 at Wyboston. Fast maturing, well drained course in its 13th year offering easy walking yet challenging golf all year round. 18 holes, 6459 yards. S.S.S. 71. 9-hole Par 3 course. 8 bay driving range. *Green Fees:* weekdays £14.00; weekends and Bank Holidays £23.00. *Eating facilities:* licensed clubhouse with bar. *Visitors:* no restrictions. Self-catering cottages offer base to play numerous courses in the area, play this well-maintained course, or for "learn to play golf or swim' holidays.

DUNSTABLE. **Dunstable Downs Golf Club,** Whipsnade Road, Dunstable LU6 2NB (01582 604472; Fax: 01582 478700). *Location:* on B4541; one and a half miles from town centre. Downland course with exceptional views. 18 holes, 5903 yards. S.S.S. 70. Practice ground. *Green Fees:* information not available. *Eating facilities:* bar and restaurant. *Visitors:* welcome weekdays, weekends with member only. Handicap Certificate required. Carts for hire. *Society Meetings:* Mondays, Tuesdays and Thursdays, limited availability on Fridays. Professional: Michael Weldon (01582 662806). Secretary/Manager: Alan Sigee (01582 604472; Fax: 01582 478700).

DUNSTABLE. **Tilsworth Golf Centre,** Dunstable Road, Tilsworth, Leighton Buzzard LU7 9PU (01525 210721; Fax: 01525 210465). *Location:* two miles north of Dunstable off the A5, Tilsworth turn-off. Parkland course, water hazards on three holes! 18 holes, 5306 yards. S.S.S. 67, Par 69. 30 bay floodlit driving range. *Green Fees:* information not available. *Eating facilities:* bar snacks and restaurant available. *Visitors:* welcome any time except Sundays before 10am. Bookings taken up to seven days in advance. *Society Meetings:* welcome by prior arrangement. Professional: Nick Webb.*

HENLOW. **Mount Pleasant Golf Course,** Station Road, Lower Stondon, Henlow SG16 6JL (01462 850999). *Location:* three-quarters of a mile west of A600 (Hitchin to Bedford) at Henlow Camp roundabout. Undulating meadowland. 9 holes (alternative tees for second 9 holes), 6185 yards, 5656 metres. S.S.S. 70. Practice chipping, putting and nets. *Green Fees:* weekdays £8.50 for 9 holes, £15.00 for 18 holes; weekends £11.00 for 9 holes, £19.00 for 18 holes. Reductions for Senior Citizens and Juniors. *Eating facilities:* spike bar, dining room. Group catering by prior arrangement. *Visitors:* welcome anytime, booking required for weekends and summer evenings. *Society Meetings:* welcome on weekdays. Professional: Mike Roberts. Proprietor: David Simkins.
website: www.mountpleasantgolfclub.co.uk

LEIGHTON BUZZARD. **Aylesbury Vale Golf Club,** Stewkley Road, Wing, Leighton Buzzard LU7 0UJ (01525 240196). *Location:* four miles west of Leighton Buzzard on Stewkley to Wing road. Gently undulating course with water hazards. 18 holes, 6622 yards, S.S.S. 72. 9-bay driving range. *Green Fees:* weekdays £20.00; weekends £27.00 up to 11am, £21.00 after 11am. Please telephone for availability. Senior Citizens £9.00 Tuesdays. *Eating facilities:* first floor bar and balcony, ground floor bar and restaurant. *Visitors:* welcome any time, no restrictions apart from correct dress. Telephone in advance. Individual lessons from £15.00. *Society Meetings:* welcome, competitive rates, Monday to Friday only. Professional: Terry Bunyan (07731 966749). Secretary: Chris Wright (01525 240196).

LEIGHTON BUZZARD. **Leighton Buzzard Golf Club,** Plantation Road, Leighton Buzzard LU7 3JF (01525 244800). *Location:* off A5 between Dunstable and Milton Keynes at village of Heath and Reach. Wooded parkland course. 18 holes, 6101 yards. S.S.S. 70. Practice ground. *Green Fees:* weekdays, please call for current prices; weekends with members only. *Eating facilities:* available - dining room and three bars. *Visitors:* welcome weekdays. (Tuesday Ladies' Day). Weekends and Bank Holidays with member only. *Society Meetings:* catered for weekdays only, except Tuesdays. Professional: M. Campbell (01525 244815). Secretary: D. Mutton (01525 244800; Fax: 01525 244801).
e-mail: secretary@leightonbuzzardgolf.net
website: www.leightonbuzzardgolf.net

LEIGHTON BUZZARD near. **Ivinghoe Golf Club,** Wellcroft, Ivinghoe, Near Leighton Buzzard LU7 9EF (01296 668696; Fax: 01296 662755). *Location:* leave A41 at Tring and take B488 to Ivinghoe. When approaching the village, the church is on the left, and Vicarage Lane is on the right. Go down the lane to the Rose & Crown pub and turn right up to the club. Gently rolling parkland course in lee of Ivinghoe Beacon. 9 holes, 4508 yards. S.S.S. 62. Pro shop, tuition available. *Green Fees:* 9 holes £6.50 (not before 12 noon Sundays), 18 holes £10.00. *Eating facilities:* bar meals anytime. *Visitors:* welcome except before 8am Monday to Saturday and 9am Sundays; dress code in operation. *Society Meetings:* catered for. Professional: Mark Flitney (01296 668696). Secretary: Mrs S.E. Garrad (01296 668696). Steward: Mr B. Burton (01296 661186).

For full details of clubs and courses, plus convenient accommodation
www.uk-golfguide.com

132 Bedfordshire / ENGLAND

LEIGHTON BUZZARD near. **Mentmore Golf and Country Club,** Mentmore, Near Leighton Buzzard LU7 0UA (01296 662020; Fax: 01296 662592). *Location:* between Leighton Buzzard and Aylesbury in village of Mentmore. Rolling parkland, mature trees and with many water features. Two courses - Rothschild and Rosebery. 36 holes, 6777 and 6763 yards. S.S.S. 72. Driving range. *Green Fees:* information not available. *Eating facilities:* restaurant, two bars, spike bar; function room. *Visitors:* welcome. Also available swimming pool, sauna, jacuzzi and steam room, two tennis courts, full gymnasium and aerobics studio. *Society Meetings:* welcome everyday, please telephone for details. General Manager: Kevin Whitehouse. Sales Manager: Matthew Darley. Professional: Robert Davies. *

LUTON. **South Beds Golf Club,** Warden Hill Road, Luton LU2 7AE (01582 591500). *Location:* on east side A6, two and a half miles north of Luton. Undulating downland course. 18 holes, 6438 yards. S.S.S. 71. Also 9 holes, 4784 yards. S.S.S. 63. Practice fairway and chipping area. *Green Fees:* weekdays 9 hole course £10.00 for 18 holes, 18 hole course £24.00; weekends 9 hole course £13.00 for 18 holes, 18 hole course £36.00. *Eating facilities:* three-course meals (must be booked), snacks at all times. *Visitors:* welcome anytime on 9-hole course, weekdays and limited weekends on 18-hole course. Handicap Certificate essential for 18-hole course. Tuesday is Ladies' Day. *Society Meetings:* catered for by arrangement on Mondays, Wednesdays and Thursdays. Professional: Eddie Cogle (01582 591209). Secretary: Ray Wright (01582 591500; Fax: 01582 495381).

LUTON. **Stockwood Park Golf Club,** London Road, Luton LU1 4LX (01582 431788). *Location:* adjacent Exit 10 of M1 exit Luton Airport. Parkland. 18 holes, 6049 yards. S.S.S. 69. Driving range, mini golf course and pitch and putt. *Green Fees:* information not available. *Eating facilities:* two bars and restaurant. *Visitors:* always welcome, municipal club. *Society Meetings:* catered for Mondays, Tuesdays and Thursdays by prior arrangement. Professional: G. McCarthy (01582 413704). Secretary: Roy Fay (01582 431788).*

SANDY. **John O'Gaunt Golf Club,** Sutton Park, Sandy SG19 2LY (01767 260360; Fax: 01767 262834). *Location:* on B1040 off A1 two miles north of Biggleswade. Parkland courses. Two 18 hole courses: John O'Gaunt Course 6513 yards S.S.S. 71 and Carthagena Course 5869 yards S.S.S. 69. Small practice area. *Green Fees:* weekdays £35.00 per round, £50.00 per day; weekends £60.00 (subject to review). *Eating facilities:* restaurant and bar. *Visitors:* welcome weekdays, Handicap Certificate required. *Society Meetings:* welcome weekdays. Professional: Lee Scarbrow (01767 260094). Secretary: Stephen Anthony (01767 260360).

THE GOLF GUIDE 2006

SHARNBROOK. **Colworth Golf Club,** Colworth House, Sharnbrook MK44 1LQ (01933 353269). *Location:* off A6 between Bedford and Rushden through Sharnbrook village. Parkland course, narrow fairways, tree lined. 9 holes, 5210 yards. S.S.S. 66. *Green Fees:* information not available. *Eating facilities:* none. *Visitors:* with members only. Secretary: E.W. Thompson (01933 353269).

TODDINGTON. **Chalgrave Manor Golf Club,** Dunstable Road, Toddington, Near Dunstable LU5 6JN (Tel & Fax: 01525 876556). *Location:* two minutes from Junction 12 M1 (Toddington Services), on main A5120 between Toddington and Houghton Regis. Rolling, open course with many natural undulations; four holes with water features. 18 holes, 6417 yards, 5892 metres. S.S.S. 71. Practice areas. *Green Fees:* weekdays £20.00 per round, weekends and Bank Holidays £30.00 per round. Day tickets available. *Eating facilities:* meals available Tuesday to Sundays inclusive, licensed bar. *Visitors:* booking not required. No starting times before 1pm weekends and Bank Holidays, no restrictions midweek. *Society Meetings:* welcome weekdays by prior arrangement. Secretary: Steve Rumball (01525 876554). e-mail: steve@chalgravegolf.co.uk website: www.chalgravegolf.co.uk

WYBOSTON. **Wyboston Lakes Golf Course,** Great North Road, Wyboston Lakes, Wyboston MK44 3AL (01480 223004). *Location:* one mile south of St Neots at the junction of the A1 and the A428 east. Flat parkland with five lakes. 18 holes, 5955 yards. S.S.S. 69. Driving range. Putting green. *Green Fees:* phone for details. *Eating facilities:* available. *Visitors:* welcome, bookings required for weekends and Bank Holidays. Motel on site. *Society Meetings:* catered for seven days. Professional: P.G. Ashwell (01480 223004; Fax: 01480 407330). Secretary: D. Little (01480 212625; Fax: 01480 223000).

FHG
·K·U·P·E·R·A·R·D·

FHG Guides

publish a large range of well-known accommodation guides. We will be happy to send you details or you can use the order form at the back of this book.

THE APPEARANCE OF AN ASTERISK (*) AT THE END OF A CLUB OR COURSE ENTRY INDICATES THAT UP-TO-DATE INFORMATION HAS NOT BEEN SUPPLIED

Berkshire

ASCOT. **The Berkshire Golf Club,** Swinley Road, Ascot SL5 8AY (01344 621495). *Location:* on A332 between Bagshot and Ascot. Heathland (wooded) course. 36 holes. Blue Course: 6260 yards, S.S.S. 71, Par 71. Red Course: 6369 yards, S.S.S. 71, Par 72. Practice facilities. *Green Fees:* information not available. *Eating facilities:* dining room open daily except Monday, snack bar open daily; bar open every day. *Visitors:* welcome weekdays only by application to the Secretary. *Society Meetings:* catered for by prior bookings. Professional: P. Anderson (01344 622351). Secretary: Lt. Col. J.C.F. Hunt (01344 621496).

ASCOT. **Lavender Park Golf Centre,** Swinley Road, Ascot SL5 8BD (01344 893344). *Location:* Ascot to Bracknell Road, half a mile from racecourse. Very pleasant flat 9 hole, Executive course, 8 Par 3s and one Par 4. 9 holes, 1104 yards. S.S.S. 28. 23-bay driving range. *Green Fees:* information not available. *Eating facilities:* bar snacks. *Visitors:* welcome at all times; pay and play. 8 table snooker hall. *Society Meetings:* welcome. Director of Golf/Senior Professional: David Johnson (01344 893344).

ASCOT. **Mill Ride Golf Club,** Mill Ride Estate, Ascot SL5 8LT (01344 891494; Fax: 01344 886820). *Location*: off Junction 3 of M3 or Junction 6 of M4, one mile west Ascot Racecourse. Parkland, links course, seven lakes in play on 11 holes; designed by Donald Steel. 18 holes, 6807 yards. S.S.S. 72. Driving range. *Green Fees:* information not provided. *Eating facilities:* bar food. *Visitors:* welcome on application. Accommodation available. *Society Meetings:* individual and corporate membership available; contact Carey Sheffield. Professional: Terry Wild (01344 886777; Fax: 01344 886820). Manager: Wayne Sheffield (01344 891494; Fax: 01344 886820). e-mail: golf@mill-ride.com
website: www.mill-ride.com

ASCOT. **Royal Ascot Golf Club,** Winkfield Road, Ascot SL5 7LJ (01344 625228; Fax: 01344 872330). *Location:* Winkfield Road is off Ascot High Street (A329). Parkland; new 18-hole course. 18 holes, 6293 yards. S.S.S. 70. Par 70. *Green Fees:* weekdays £25.00 as member's guest; weekends £30.00 as member's guest. *Eating facilities:* full catering available. *Visitors:* welcome only as guests of members. *Society Meetings:* catered for Wednesdays and Thursdays, maximum 40. Professional: Alistair White (01344 624656). Secretary: Mrs Sheila Thompson (01344 625175). e-mail: secretaries@royalascotgolfclub.co.uk

Please mention
THE GOLF GUIDE
when you enquire about clubs
or accommodation

ASCOT. **Swinley Forest Golf Club,** Coronation Road, Ascot SL5 9LE (01344 620197). *Location:* between Ascot and Bagshot. Wooded heathland course. 18 holes, 6001 yards. S.S.S. 69. *Green Fees:* information not provided. *Eating facilities:* lunches served. *Visitors:* welcome only with a member. *Society Meetings:* catered for. Professional: Stuart Hill (01344 874811). Secretary: I.L. Pearce (01344 874979; Fax: 01344 874733).

BINFIELD. **Blue Mountain Golf Centre,** Wood Lane, Binfield, Bracknell RG42 4EX (01344 300220; Fax: 01344 360960). *Location:* two miles from M4 near Bracknell/Wokingham. Parkland course with numerous lakes. 18 holes, 6097 yards. S.S.S 70. 33 bay covered floodlit range. *Green Fees:* £18.00 Monday to Thursday, £20.00 Friday, £25.00 weekends. *Eating facilities:* fully licensed restaurant/ bar, Blues Bar with live jazz and food. *Visitors:* welcome any time. *Society Meetings:* always welcome, please call for details. Professional: Chris Lilleystone (01344 300220).

BURNHAM. **Huntswood Golf Club,** Taplow Common Road, Burnham SL1 8LS (01628 667144). *Location:* Junction 7 of M4, at roundabout turn left onto A4, then at Sainsburys roundabout turn right. Go straight over next two roundabouts, Huntswood Golf Club is quarter of a mile on the left. Only 18 hole Pay & Play course in Burnham. 18 holes, Par 68. *Green Fees:* information not available. *Eating facilities:* bar and dining facilities after 7am. Professional: Neil Pagett.*

CROWTHORNE. **East Berkshire Golf Club,** Ravenswood Avenue, Crowthorne RG45 6BD (01344 772041; Fax: 01344 777378). *Location:* M3 Junction 3 - Bracknell turn off, follow signs to Crowthorne, Ravenswood Avenue opposite Railway Station. Heathland course. 18 holes, 6344 yards. S.S.S. 70. *Green Fees:* information not provided. *Eating facilities:* bar snacks. *Visitors:* welcome weekdays by prior notification. *Society Meetings:* Thursdays and Fridays only. Professional: Jason Brant (01344 774112). Secretary: David Kelly (01344 772041; Fax: 01344 777378).

MAIDENHEAD. **Maidenhead Golf Club,** Shoppenhangers Road, Maidenhead SL6 2PZ (01628 624693; Fax: 01628 780758). *Location:* adjacent to Maidenhead Station (south side), one mile from M4. Parkland course. 18 holes, 6364 yards. S.S.S. 70. *Green Fees:* weekdays £40.00. *Eating facilities:* restaurant and bar meals Monday to Friday. *Visitors:* welcome weekdays, no visitors after 12 noon Fridays. Handicap Certificate required. *Society Meetings:* welcome, main days Wednesdays and Thursdays. Professional: Steve Geary (01628 624067). Secretary: N.J. Randall.
e-mail: manager@maidenheadgolf.co.uk
website: www.maidenheadgolf.co.uk

MAIDENHEAD. **Temple Golf Club,** Henley Road, Hurley, Near Maidenhead SL6 5LH (01628 824248; Fax: 01628 828119). *Location:* exit M4 Junction 8/9 or M40 at Junction 4. From M4 or M40 take A404 then A4130 signposted Henley. Chalk Downland course - exceptional drainage. 18 holes, 6266 yards. S.S.S. 70. Excellent practice area, putting and chipping green. *Green Fees:* weekdays £40.00 per round, £52.00 per day; weekends and Public Holidays £50.00 per round, £60.00 per day. *Eating facilities:* bar and bar snacks available daily; lunch and dinner available by prior arrangement. *Visitors:* welcome by prior arrangement. Handicap Certificate required. *Society Meetings:* welcome weekdays by prior arrangement; booking accepted one year in advance; minimum number 12, maximum 40. Professional: James Whiteley (01628 824254; Fax: 01628 828119). Secretary: Keith G.M. Adderley (01628 824795; Fax: 01628 828119).
e-mail: templegolfclub@btconnect.com

MAIDENHEAD. **Winter Hill Golf Club,** Grange Lane, Cookham SL6 9RP (01628 527613). *Location:* M4 Junction 8/9, four miles from Maidenhead. Parkland with extensive views of the Thames. 18 holes, 6408 yards - white tees, 6228 yards - yellow tees. S.S.S. 71. Large practice area. *Green Fees:* information not available. *Eating facilities:* lunches and snacks available every day. *Visitors:* welcome weekdays; preliminary enquiries advisable, and with member at weekends. *Society Meetings:* may be accepted by application to the Secretary; minimum number 16, maximum 40. Dress rules: strictly no jeans, trainers on course or in clubhouse. PGA Club and Teaching Professional: Mr Roger Frost (01628 527610). Secretary: Mr Mick Goodenough (01628 527613).*

MAIDENHEAD near. **Bird Hills (UK) Ltd.,** Drift Road, Hawthorn Hill, Near Maidenhead SL6 3ST (01628 771030; Fax: 01628 31023). *Location*: M4 Junction 8/9, take A308 then A330 to Bracknell. Flat parkland course. 18 holes, 6176 yards. S.S.S. 69. 36 bay driving range. *Green Fees:* information not available. Juniors/Senior Citizens concessionary rates. *Eating facilities:* club bar, restaurant, members bar, barbecue, private function hall. *Visitors:* always welcome, open every day except Christmas Day. Large Pro shop, Conference facilities. *Society Meetings:* always welcome. Professional: Mr Nick Slimming. Secretary: Mrs Eve Lane. *

NEWBURY. **Deanwood Park Golf Club,** Stockcross, Newbury RG20 8JS (Tel & Fax: 01635 48772). *Location*: 200 yards off the A4 west of Newbury towards Stockcross village. Two miles from Newbury town centre. Undulating parkland/wooded course. 9 holes, 2114 yards, 1932 metres. S.S.S. 60 (18 holes). 7 bay driving range, practice net, practice bunker and putting green. *Green Fees:* information not available. *Eating facilities:* Lounge/ bar/restaurant facilities; food served all day. *Visitors:* welcome at all times but must book in advance. Standard golf dress code applies, no jeans allowed on the course. Trolley/club hire available. *Society Meetings:* Society/Company groups welcome at all times - mix and match price structuring for golf and catering. Professional: James Purton. Secretary: John Bowness (Tel & Fax: 01635 48772).*
e-mail: deanwood@newburyweb.net
website: www.newbury.net//deanwood

NEWBURY. **Donnington Grove Country Club,** Grove Road, Newbury RG14 2LA (01635 581000; Fax: 01635 552259). *Location:* northwestern outskirts of Newbury 3 miles from M4 J13. From the A4 running through Newbury take the B4494 (signposted Wantage) at Waitrose roundabout. After 600 yards turn left at mini roundabout. Dave Thomas designed, USGA specification greens, championship standard course. Parkland with lakes and other features; 18 holes, 7108 yards. Practice range for members, guests and visitors only. *Green Fees:* contact Pro Shop for current rate. *Eating facilities:* hotel with bar snacks and restaurant. *Visitors:* welcome anytime weekdays, after 11am weekends. *Society Meetings:* catered for; several packages available - phone for information. Professional: Gareth Williams (01635 551975). Secretary: Elfed Davies (01635 581000).
e-mail: enquiries@donnington-grove.com
website: www.donnington-grove.com

NEWBURY. **Donnington Valley Hotel & Golf Club,** Snelsmore House, Snelsmore Common, Newbury RG14 3BG (01635 568140; Fax: 01635 568141). *Location:* Junction 13 of M4, then A34 towards Newbury. Take first exit off A34, follow signs to Donnington Castle, entrance on the right. 18 holes, 6353 metres. Practice net, computer analysis of swing. *Green Fees:* information not available. *Eating facilities:* two bars and a restaurant. *Visitors:* welcome, must have own shoes. Accommodation in 4-star 58-bedroom hotel. *Society Meetings:* welcome. Professional: Martin Balfour (01635 568142; Fax: 01635 568141). Secretary: Lorraine Storey (01635 568140; Fax: 01635 568141).*
e-mail: golf@donningtonvalley.co.uk
website: www.donningtonvalley.co.uk

NEWBURY. **Newbury and Crookham Golf Club Ltd,** Bury's Bank Road, Greenham, Newbury RG19 8BZ (01635 40035; Fax: 01635 40045). *Location:* on south side of Newbury; Junction 13 on M4. Varied and interesting with woods or trees on almost every hole. 18 holes, 5949 yards. S.S.S. 69. *Green Fees:* weekdays £35.00 per round, £40.00 per day. *Eating facilities:* restaurant/bar. *Visitors:* welcome, except weekends and Bank Holidays unless with a member. *Society Meetings:* welcome Wednesdays, Thursdays and Fridays. Professional: Mr David Harris (01635 31201). Club Manager: Mr Stephen Myers M.B.E (01635 40035).

NEWBURY. **Newbury Racecourse Golf Centre,** The Racecourse, Newbury RG14 7NZ (01635 551464; Fax: 01635 528354). *Location:* one mile south east of Newbury. Challenging flat links course for all standards. Good conditions throughout the year. 18 holes, 6500 yards, S.S.S. 71. Pro Shop, Driving range, practice area and green. *Green Fees:* information not available. *Eating facilities:* bar food. *Visitors:* welcome to pay and play. *Society Meetings:* all welcome. Professional: Nick Mitchell (01635 551464). Manager: N. Mitchell (01635 40015; Fax: 01635 528354).*

ENGLAND / Berkshire

NEWBURY. **The West Berkshire Golf Course,** Chaddleworth, Newbury RG20 7DU (01488 638574). *Location:* M4 Junction 14. A338 towards Wantage, then follow signposts to RAF Welford. Downland. 18 holes, 7001 yards. S.S.S. 74. Two practice grounds, tuition available. *Green Fees:* information not provided. *Eating facilities:* full catering available. *Visitors:* welcome weekdays; restricted to afternoons weekends, reservation required. Trolleys and buggies available. *Society Meetings:* welcome by arrangement. Professional: Paul Simpson (01488 638851). Secretary: Mrs C.M. Clayton (01488 638574; Fax: 01488 638781).

READING. **Calcot Park Golf Club,** Bath Road, Calcot, Reading RG31 7RN (0118 9427124; Fax: 0118 945 3373). *Location:* off Exit 12, M4 along A4 towards Reading, approximately one and a half miles. Undulating wooded parkland. 18 holes, 6216 yards. S.S.S. 70. Limited practice areas. *Green Fees*: weekdays £50.00 per day, £35.00 after 2pm. *Eating facilities:* fully licensed restaurant, snacks available, three bars. *Visitors*: welcome on provision of Handicap Certificate. Not weekends or Bank Holidays. Advisable to ring first to check availability. *Society Meetings:* catered for midweek. Professional: Mark Grieve (0118 942 7797; Fax: 0118 945 3373). Secretary: Kim Brake (0118 942 7124; Fax: 0118 945 3373).
e-mail: info@calcotpark.com
website: www.calcotpark.com

READING. **Castle Royle Golf and Country Club,** Knowl Hill, Reading RG10 9XA (01628 820700; Fax: 01628 829299). *Location*: alongside A4 between Maidenhead and Reading. Junction 8/9 M4. Parkland, links course. 18 holes, 6828 yards. S.S.S. 73. Practice ground. *Green Fees:* information not available. *Visitors*: members' guests only. Health and fitness club, 20x10m swimming pool, jacuzzi, sauna, gym, health and beauty and dance studio. *Eating facilities:* Full restaurant facilities and spike bar. Professional: Robert Watts. Golf Operations Manager: Nick Roberts. General Manager: Simon Jones.*

READING. **Hurst Golf Club,** Sandford Lane, Hurst, Reading RG10 0SU (01189 344355). *Location:* five miles Reading towards Wokingham. Parkland by the side of a large lake. 9 holes, 3154 yards. S.S.S. 70. *Green Fees:* information not available. *Eating facilities:* bar and restaurant seating for 30. *Visitors:* unrestricted, bookings accepted. *Society Meetings:* welcome. Manager: Mr P. Priddle.*

READING. **Pincents Manor Golf,** Pincents Lane, Calcot, Reading RG31 4UQ (01734 323511; Fax: 01734 323503). *Location:* Junction 12 M4 behind Savacentre. Parkland. Two courses: Manor Course - 18 holes, 6028 yards. S.S.S. 69; Lodge Course - 9 holes, 2600 yards. S.S.S. 68. Par 3 course. *Green Fees:* information not available. *Eating facilities:* Orchard Restaurant, Oak Bar, cruck barn. *Visitors:* welcome on Lodge Course, members only on Manor Course. Accommodation available in three bedrooms. *Society Meetings:* welcome. Professional: Alistair Thatcher.*

READING. **Reading Golf Club,** 17 Kidmore End Road, Emmer Green, Reading RG4 8SG (0118 947 2909). *Location:* two miles north of Reading off the Peppard Road (B481). Parkland. 18 holes, 6212 yards. S.S.S. 70. Practice facilities. *Green Fees:* information not provided. *Eating facilities:* available. *Visitors:* welcome Monday to Thursday if member of recognised club, with handicap of 28 or less. Friday to Sunday with member only. *Society Meetings:* catered for by arrangement Tuesdays, Wednesdays and Thursdays. Professional: Scott Fotheringham (0118 947 6115). Secretary: Andrew Chaundy (0118 947 2909).
website: www.readinggolfclub.com

READING. **Sonning Golf Club,** Duffield Road, Sonning RG4 6GJ (01189 693332; Fax: 01189 448409). *Location*: left off A4 at Sonning Roundabout, then left again. Parkland. 18 holes, 6366 yards. S.S.S. 70. *Green Fees:* on application. *Eating facilities:* new restaurant - phone for booking 01189 272055. *Visitors:* welcome, must be member of a recognised golf club with an official handicap; weekends with members only. *Society Meetings:* catered for Wednesdays. Professional: R. McDougall (01189 692910). Secretary: A.J. Tanner.

READING. **Wokefield Park Golf Club,** Mortimer, Reading RG7 3AE (0118 9334018; Fax: 0118 9334031). *Location:* 10 minutes Junction 11 M4, 20 minutes Junction 5 M3. Championship parkland course with winding streams, 9 lakes and large bunkers. 18 holes, 6961 yards. S.S.S. 73. Practice facilities. *Green Fees:* call 0118 9334078. Seasonal special offers. *Eating facilities:* bar and two restaurants. *Visitors:* welcome at all times. Hotel with 322 en suite bedrooms; leisure facilities. *Society Meetings:* contact Golf Sales Team (0118 933 4018). Professional: Gary Smith (0118 9334078; Fax: 0118 9334162). Secretary: Norman West.*
website: www.golf-isc.co.uk.

Visit the FHG website
www.holidayguides.com
for details of the wide choice of accommodation featured in the full range of FHG titles

136 Berkshire / ENGLAND

SINDLESHAM. **Bearwood Golf Club,** Mole Road, Sindlesham RG41 5DB (0118 976 0060). *Location*: on B3030 from Winnersh to Arborfield. Flat, wooded course. 9 holes, 2802 yards. S.S.S. 68 (18 holes). Driving range 7.30am to 7.30pm every day. *Green Fees:* information not available. *Eating facilities:* food available all day. *Visitors:* welcome weekdays and weekends after 3pm. *Society Meetings:* maximum of 21 catered for. Thursday only. Professional: Bayley Tustin; Manager: Barry Tustin (0118 976 0060). Shop: 0118 976 0156.*

SLOUGH. **Datchet Golf Club,** Buccleuch Road, Datchet SL3 9BP (Tel & Fax: 01753 541872; Clubhouse: 01753 543887). *Location:* within two miles of both Windsor and Slough. 9 holes, 6087 yards. S.S.S. 69. *Green Fees:* £25.00 per round, £35.00 per day. Subject to review. *Visitors:* welcome weekdays until 3pm. *Society Meetings:* small societies welcome, maximum 24 players. Professional: Ian Godleman (01753 545222) Secretary/Manager: Keith Smith (Tel & Fax: 01753 541872).
e-mail: secretary@datchetgolfclub.org.uk
website: www.datchetgolfclub.co.uk

STREATLEY ON THAMES. **Goring and Streatley Golf Club,** Rectory Road, Streatley on Thames RG8 9QA (01491 873229; Fax: 01491 875224). *Location:* 10 miles north west of Reading off A417 Wantage Road. Downland course on Berkshire Downs. 18 holes, 6355 yards. S.S.S. 70. *Green Fees:* £32.00 per round, £42.00 per day. *Eating facilities:* full restaurant and bar meals. Restaurant (01491 875122). *Visitors:* welcome on weekdays by telephone booking. *Society Meetings:* catered for. Professional: Jason Hadland (01491 873715). Secretary: Mr A.B.W. James (01491 873229).
website: www.goringgc.org

SUNNINGDALE. **Sunningdale Ladies' Golf Club,** Cross Road, Sunningdale SL5 9RX (01344 620507). *Location:* second left going west on A30, past Sunningdale level crossing. Heathland. 18 holes, 3622 yards. (Designed for Ladies' Golf). S.S.S. 60. *Green Fees:* £25 per round weekdays, £30 per round weekends/Bank Holidays. *Eating facilities:* light lunches available except Sundays. *Visitors:* welcome, telephone first. Must have Handicap Certificate. *Society Meetings:* catered for. Secretary: Stephen Harris.
e-mail: slgolfclub@tiscali.co.uk
website: www.sunningdaleladies.co.uk

THE GOLF GUIDE 2006

WARGRAVE. **Hennerton Golf Club,** Crazies Hill Road, Wargrave RG10 8LT (0118 940 1000; Fax: 0118 940 1042). *Location:* halfway between Maidenhead and Reading off the A321 to Henley, follow "Golf Club" signs from Wargrave High Street. Scenic course overlooking the Thames Valley. 18 holes, 4430 yards. Par 65. Driving range. *Green Fees:* on application. *Eating facilities:* clubhouse with full facilities. *Visitors:* welcome most times, phone Pro Shop. *Society Meetings:* telephone for details. Professional/Manager: William Farrow (0118 940 4778; Fax: 0118 940 1402).

WOKINGHAM. **Bearwood Lakes Golf Club,** Bearwood Road, near Sindlesham, Wokingham RG41 4SJ (0118 979 7900; Fax: 0118 979 2911). *Location:* just off M4 at Reading. Wooded 18 hole golf course. 6800 yards, S.S.S. 72. *Green Fees:* information not available. *Eating facilities:* restaurant, bar, function room, dining club. *Visitors:* must be the guest of a member. Practice ground available. Professional: Tim Waldron (0118 978 3030). General Manager: Scott Evans (0118 979 7900).*

WOKINGHAM. **Downshire Golf Course,** Easthampstead Park, Wokingham RG40 3DH (01344 302030; Fax: 01344 301020). *Location*: off Nine Mile Ride/Easthampstead Road Bracknell. Parkland course, water on 14 holes. 18 holes, 5988 yards. S.S.S. 69. 9 hole pitch and putt, 30 bay floodlit driving range. *Green Fees:* weekdays £17.00, weekends £21.00. *Eating facilities:* new clubhouse. Function room available. *Visitors:* welcome. *Society Meetings:* welcome. Large Pro Shop. Professional: Wayne Owers (01344 302030; Fax: 01344 301020). Golf Manager: Paul Stanwick.*
e-mail: downshiregc@bracknell-forest.gov.uk
website: bracknell-forest.gov.uk/downshiregc/

WOKINGHAM. **Sand Martins Golf Club,** Finchampstead Road, Wokingham RG40 3RQ (0118 9792711; Fax: 0118 9770282). *Location:* off Nine Mile Ride, two miles from Wokingham town centre. Parkland, links/wooded course. 18 holes, 6204 yards. S.S.S. 70. Practice area including bunker/pitching area. *Green Fees:* £35.00. *Eating facilities:* bar, bar food and restaurant. *Visitors:* welcome weekdays' weekends with a member. *Society Meetings:* welcome weekdays, except Friday afternoons. Professional: Andrew Hall (0118 9770265). Club Secretary: James McDonald (0118 9792711; Fax: 0118 9770282).

FHG GUIDES publish a large range of well-known accommodation guides. We will be happy to send you details or you can use the order form at the back of this book.

FHG

·K·U·P·E·R·A·R·D·

Buckinghamshire

AMERSHAM. **Harewood Downs Golf Club,** Cokes Lane, Chalfont St Giles HP8 4TA (01494 762308; Fax: 01494 766869). *Location:* off A413, two miles east of Amersham. Rolling, tree lined. 18 holes, 5958 yards, 5448 metres. S.S.S. 69. Practice ground. *Green Fees:* weekdays £33.00 per round, £38.00 per day; weekends £38.00 per round, £45.00 per day. Special rates, winter golf. *Eating facilities:* full restaurant and bar. *Visitors:* welcome on weekdays with current Handicap, weekends by prior arrangement only. *Society Meetings:* welcome, mainly Thursdays and Fridays. Professional: G. Morris (01494 764102). Secretary: S.J. Thornton (01494 762184).

AYLESBURY. **Aylesbury Golf Centre,** Hulcott Lane, Bierton, Aylesbury HP22 5GA (01296 393644). *Location:* north of Aylesbury on the A418 Leighton Buzzard road. 18 holes. 30 bay covered floodlit driving range. *Green Fees:* 18 holes £10.00 midweek, £15.00 weekends. *Eating facilities:* bar, bar snacks 11am to 11pm. *Visitors:* welcome. *Society Meetings:* catered for. Professional coaching available. General Manager: Kevin Partington. Professional: R. Wooster

AYLESBURY. **Aylesbury Park Golf Club,** Oxford Road, Aylesbury HP17 8QQ (01296 399196; Fax: 01296 336830). *Location:* Just outside Aylesbury town centre off the A418. Historic parkland course. 18 holes, 6146 yards. S.S.S. 69. New 9 hole short course now open. *Green Fees:* £18.00 midweek, £23.00 weekends. 9 hole short course £5.00 per round. Numerous green fee special offers take place throughout the year - call for details. *Visitors:* welcome at all times. No Handicap Certificate required. *Society Meetings:* please call for details.

AYLESBURY. **Chiltern Forest Golf Club,** Aston Hill, Halton, Aylesbury HP22 5NQ (01296 631267; Fax: 01296 632709). *Location:* five miles south-east of Aylesbury, signposted St. Leonards. Wooded, hilly course. 18 holes, 5765 yards. S.S.S. 69. *Green Fees:* £34.00 weekdays; £17.00 with a member weekends. *Visitors:* weekdays unrestricted, weekends with a member. *Society Meetings:* welcome, preferably Wednesdays. Professional: Andy Lavers (01296 631817). Secretary: Bob Clift (01296 631267; Fax: 01296 632709). e-mail: secretary@chilternforest.co.uk website: www.chilternforest.co.uk.

AYLESBURY. **Ellesborough Golf Club,** Butlers Cross, Aylesbury HP17 0TZ (01296 622375). *Location:* on B4010 one-and-a-half miles from Wendover. Chiltern Hills course. Undulating links. 18 holes, 6360 yards, 5815 metres. S.S.S. 71. Practice net/ground. *Green Fees:* £30.00 per round, £50.00 per day. *Eating facilities:* full catering available. *Visitors:* welcome except Tuesday mornings and competition days, weekends with a member only. Must provide Handicap Certificate. *Society Meetings:* catered for Wednesdays and Thursdays only by arrangement. Professional: Mark Squire (Tel & Fax: 01296 623126). General Manager: (Tel & Fax: 01296 622114).

AYLESBURY. **Weston Turville Golf Club,** New Road, Weston Turville, Near Aylesbury HP22 5QT (01296 424084; Fax: 01296 395376). *Location:* two miles south east of Aylesbury off A41. Easy walking course at the foot of the Chiltern Hills. 18 holes, 6008 yards. S.S.S. 69. *Green Fees:* information not provided. *Eating facilities:* meals, snacks and visitors' bar. *Visitors:* truly welcome. *Society Meetings:* especially catered for. Professional: Gary George (01296 425949; Fax: 01296 395376). General Manager: David Allen (01296 424084; Fax: 01296 395376).

BEACONSFIELD. **Beaconsfield Golf Club,** Seer Green, Near Beaconsfield HP9 2UR (01494 676545; Fax: 01494 681148). *Location:* from A40 at Beaconsfield, A355 Amersham Road, one mile turn right to Jordans, one mile signposted. Parkland course. 18 holes, 6508 yards, Par 72. Large practice ground, driving range. *Green Fees:* £50.00 per round, £60.00 per day. Subject to review. *Eating facilities:* dining room or bar menu; two bars. *Visitors:* welcome weekdays with accredited introduction – check with Pro. Handicap Certificate required. *Society Meetings:* catered for Tuesdays and Wednesdays. Professional: Mike Brothers (01494 676616). Secretary: K.R. Wilcox (01494 676545). e-mail: secretary@beaconsfieldgolfclub.co.uk website: www.beaconsfieldgolfclub.co.uk

The Warmest Welcome in Golf
where quality and value are standard

Situated two miles south east of Aylesbury off A41, this is an easy walking course at the foot of the Chiltern Hills. 18 holes, 6008 yards. S.S.S. 69.

Green Fees – weekdays £25.00; weekends £30.00

Visitors are truly welcome and squash courts are available. Society Meetings are especially catered for. Meals, snacks and visitors' bar.

Professional: Gary George
01296 425949 • Fax: 01296 395376
General Manager: David Allen
01296 424084 • Fax: 01296 395376

Weston Turville Golf & Squash Club,
New Road, Weston Turville, Near Aylesbury HP22 5QT
Tel: 01296 424084 • Fax: 01296 395376

See also Colour Advertisement on page 24

138 Buckinghamshire / ENGLAND

BUCKINGHAM. **Buckingham Golf Club,** Tingewick Road, Buckingham MK18 4AE (01280 815566; Fax: 01280 821812). *Location*: two miles south west of Buckingham on A421. Undulating parkland - eight holes affected by river. 18 holes, 6162 yards. S.S.S. 70. Practice ground. *Green Fees:* weekdays £30.00; weekends as members' guests only. (2006 under review.) *Eating facilities:* seven day catering - bars, lunch and evening. (01280 813282) *Visitors:* welcome weekdays only. Pro shop (01280 815210). *Society Meetings:* pre-booked on Tuesdays or Thursdays. Secretary Manager: Gerald L. Pearce M. Inst. GCM (01280 815566; Fax: 01280 821812). Professional: Gregor Hannah (01280 815210). e-mail: admin@buckinghamgolfclub.co.uk website: www.buckinghamgolfclub.co.uk

BURNHAM. **Burnham Beeches Golf Club,** Green Lane, Burnham, Slough SL1 8EG (01628 661448; Fax: 01628 668968). *Location*: Junction 7 on M4. Parkland/wooded course. 18 holes, 6449 yards. S.S.S. 71. *Green Fees:* weekdays 18 holes £40.00, 36 holes £60.00. *Eating facilities:* bar and restaurant. *Visitors:* welcome weekdays, Handicap Certificate required. *Society Meetings:* welcome Wednesdays to Fridays April to October. Professional: R. Bolton (01628 661661). Secretary: T.P. Jackson (01628 661448).

BURNHAM. **The Lambourne Golf Club,** Dropmore Road, Burnham SL1 8NF (01628 666755; Fax: 01628 663301). *Location:* take M4 to Exit 7; take M40 to Exit 2. Parkland course, six lakes. 18 holes, 6771 yards. S.S.S. 73. Practice facilities available. *Green Fees:* Monday to Friday £60.00. *Eating facilities:* snack bar, half-way hatch, restaurant. *Visitors:* welcome. Handicap Certificate required. Golf Director: (01628 606717). Professional: David Hart (01628 606717; Fax: 01628 663301). General Manager: Brian Sparks.

CHALFONT ST GILES. **Oakland Park Golf Club,** Bowles Farm, Threehouseholds, Chalfont St Giles HP8 4LW (01494 871277 Office). *Location*: off main A413 towards Amersham, 10 minutes from J2, M40. Parkland course. 18 holes, 5246 yards. S.S.S. 66. Practice range, green and bunkers. *Green Fees*: weekdays £25.50, £30.50 weekends. Twilight fees during Winter. *Eating facilities*: clubhouse bar, full catering all week. *Visitors*: welcome 7 days (after midday at weekends and Bank Holidays). *Society Meetings:* welcome. Professional: Alistair Thatcher (01494 877333; Fax: 01494 874692). General Manager: Ian Donnelly.

CHESHAM. **Chartridge Park Golf Club,** Chartridge, Chesham HP5 2TF (01494 791772). *Location*: M25 Junction 18, Amersham, Chesham, three miles from roundabout by pond. Flat parkland course with wooded areas, two water holes and views over the Chiltern Valley. 18 holes, 5510 yards, 5061 metres. S.S.S. 68. Small chipping and putting area, driving nets. *Green Fees*: weekdays £30.00; weekends £40.00. *Eating facilities*: snacks and cooked food available seven days a week; bar. *Visitors*: always welcome, please ring to book tee times. *Society Meetings*: always welcome but please book in advance. Professional: Peter Gibbins. Secretary: Anita Gibbins.

THE GOLF GUIDE 2006

CHESHAM. **Chesham and Ley Hill Golf Club,** Ley Hill, Chesham HP5 1UZ (01494 784541). *Location:* off A41 on B4504 to Ley Hill, nearest town - Chesham. Wooded parkland. 9 holes, 5296 yards. S.S.S. 65. *Green Fees:* weekdays £15.00. *Eating facilities:* licensed bar, food available at certain times. *Visitors:* welcome Mondays and Thursdays all day; Wednesdays after 12 noon; Fridays up to 4pm. *Society Meetings:* Thursdays only by prior arrangement. Secretary: B.E. Durand (01494 784541).

DENHAM. **Buckinghamshire Golf Club,** Denham Court, Denham Court Drive, Denham UB9 5PG (01895 835777; Fax: 01895 835210). *Location:* Junction 1 M40 off Denham roundabout, follow signs to Denham Country Park. Gently undulating parkland, River Colne and River Misbourne run through course. 18 holes, 6880 yards. S.S.S. 73. Practice range with ball dispenser and collection. *Green Fees:* weekdays £90.00; weekends £100.00. *Eating facilities:* Heron Restaurant, spike bar; food served all day. *Visitors:* welcome Mondays to Thursdays; advance bookings only. *Society Meetings:* welcome, golf company days up to 80 – details on application. Professional: John O'Leary. Enquiries: Dubravka Barancek.
website: www.buckinghamshiregc.com

DENHAM. **Denham Golf Club,** Tilehouse Lane, Denham UB9 5DE (01895 832022; Fax: 01895 835340). *Location:* off A412 near Uxbridge. Parkland - undulating. 18 holes, 6462 yards, 5903 metres. S.S.S. 71. Practice ground. *Green Fees:* information not available. *Eating facilities:* diningroom, bar snacks. *Visitors:* welcome Monday to Thursday by prior arrangement only. Handicap Certificate. *Society Meetings:* catered for Tuesdays, Wednesdays and Thursdays. Professional: Stuart Campbell (01895 832801). Secretary: J. W. Tucker (01895 832022; Fax: 01895 835340).*
e-mail: club.secretary@denhamgolfclub.co.uk
website: www.denhamgolfclub.co.uk

GERRARDS CROSS. **Gerrards Cross Golf Club,** Chalfont Park, Gerrards Cross SL9 0QA (01753 278500; Fax: 01753 883593). *Location:* alongside A413 (to Amersham) about three miles from junction with A40 (London to Oxford road). Wooded parkland course. 18 holes, 6295 yards. S.S.S. 70. Practice nets and putting green. *Green Fees:* weekdays £40.00 per round, £53.00 per day. Subject to review. *Eating facilities:* lunch, bar snacks, afternoon tea always available, evening meals to order. *Visitors:* welcome except at weekends and Public Holidays but must produce a letter of introduction or current Handicap Certificate. Tuesday is Ladies' Day. *Society Meetings:* catered for Thursdays and Fridays, maximum number 100. Professional: M. Barr (01753 885300). Secretary/Manager: B.F. Cable MBE (01753 883263).

HIGH WYCOMBE. **Flackwell Heath Golf Club Limited,** Treadaway Road, Flackwell Heath, High Wycombe HP10 9PE (01628 520929; Fax: 01628 530040). *Location:* M40 Exit 3 from London, Exit 4 from Oxford. 2 miles High Wycombe. Undulating heath and woodland. 18 holes, 6211 yards. S.S.S. 70. *Green Fees:* weekdays £30.00 per round, £40.00 per day; weekends with member only – £16.00. *Eating*

ENGLAND / Buckinghamshire

facilities: restaurant and bars daily. *Visitors:* welcome weekdays with Handicap Certificate, weekends with member only. *Society Meetings:* catered for by arrangement Wednesdays and Thursdays – contact the Secretary. Professional: Paul Watson (01628 523017). Secretary: S. J. Chandler (01628 520929). e-mail: info@flackwellheathgolfclub.co.uk website: www.flackwellheathgolfclub.co.uk

HIGH WYCOMBE. **Hazlemere Golf Club,** Penn Road, Hazlemere, Near High Wycombe HP15 7LR (01494 719300; Fax: 01494 713914). *Location*: from M40 North: Junction 2, via Beaconsfield and Penn on B474; from M40 South; Junction 4, through High Wycombe on A404. Undulating parkland course with a number of feature water holes. Practice area. 18 holes, 5810 yards. S.S.S. 69. *Green Fees:* weekdays £30.00; weekends £45.00. *Eating facilities:* coffee shop and bar. *Visitors:* welcome 7 days a week (after midday weekends). *Society Meetings:* welcome weekdays. Professional: Paul Harrison (01494 719306). Secretary: (01494 719300).

HIGH WYCOMBE. **Wycombe Heights Golf Centre,** Rayners Avenue, Loudwater, High Wycombe HP10 9SW (01494 816686; Fax: 01494 816728). *Location:* one mile south-east of High Wycombe off A40. Impressive tree-lined parkland course with panoramic views of Chilterns. Challenging final loop from 15th to 18th. 18 holes, 6265 yards, Par 70, S.S.S. 72. 18-hole, Par 3 course, practice green and bunker, 24-bay floodlit driving range. *Green Fees:* information not available. *Eating facilities:* full clubhouse facilities. *Visitors:* welcome, booking in advance advisable. *Society Meetings:* welcome 7 days, telephone or write for details. Professional: Cranfield Golf Academy. Manager: Christopher Benson.*

IVER. **Iver Golf Club,** Hollow Hill Lane, Off Langley Park Road, Iver SL0 0JJ (01753 655615; Fax: 01753 654225). *Location:* near Slough. Situated on the right off Langley Park Road leaving the town of Langley and heading towards Iver. Flat parkland, easy walking with natural ditches and ponds. 9 holes, 5628 yards. S.S.S. 67. 18 bay driving range, practice area, putting green, bunker area onto a green. Plus NEW 9 hole short course. *Green Fees:* weekdays £8.50 for 9 holes, £15.00 for 18; weekends £9.50 for 9 holes, £17.00 for 18. Special rates available, please enquire. *Eating facilities:* bar lunches 11:30am until 2:30pm seven days. *Visitors:* always welcome, best to phone on day of play for booking. We have a new Junior section, a vet society every Tuesday and are willing to accommodate most requests. Senior Members' competitions Thursday mornings. *Society Meetings:* always welcome. Professional: Jim Lynch (01753 655615; Fax: 01753 654225).

IVER. **Richings Park Golf and Country Club,** North Park, Iver SL0 9DL (01753 655370; Fax: 01753 655409). *Location:* M4 Junction 5. Flat parkland. 18 holes, 6209 yards. S.S.S. 70. Practice area, two putting greens, bunker and chipping area. *Green Fees:* information not provided. *Eating facilities:* bar, restaurant, and spike bar. *Visitors:* welcome with restrictions at weekend. *Society Meetings:* welcome, minimum 12. Professional/Secretary/General Manager: Robert Mullane (01753 655352).

LITTLE CHALFONT. **Little Chalfont Golf Club,** Lodge Lane, Little Chalfont HP8 4AJ (01494 764877; Fax: 01494 762860). *Location:* Junction 18 M25, two miles towards Amersham on A404, first left past garden centre. Undulating parkland. 9 holes, 5752 yards S.S.S. 68. *Green Fees:* information not available. *Eating facilities:* full bar and restaurant. *Visitors:* always welcome. *Society Meetings:* welcome mid-week. Professional: J.M. Dunne (01494 762942). Secretary: Michael Dunne. *

MARLOW. **Harleyford Golf Club,** Harleyford Estate, Henley Road, Marlow SL7 2SP (01628 816161; Fax: 01628 816160). *Location:* two miles from Marlow on the A4155 to Henley. Parkland course designed by Donald Steel. 18 holes, 6809 yards, S.S.S. 72. *Green fees:* information not available. *Eating facilities:* restaurant, lounge and bar. *Visitors:* book via Pro Shop. Handicap certificate required. *Society Meetings:* welcome by arrangement Tuesday, Wednesday and Friday - contact events office (01628 816164). Excellent practice range and green available. Soft spikes only, no metal spikes allowed. Professional: Darren Brewer (01628 816162). General Manager: Gary Ivory (01628 816164).*
e-mail: info@harleyfordgolf.co.uk
website: www.harleyfordgolf.co.uk

MILTON KEYNES. **Abbey Hill Golf Centre,** Monks Way, Two Mile Ash, Milton Keynes MK8 8AA (01908 563845; Fax: 01908 569538). *Location:* 2 miles west of town centre, just off the A5 on the H3. Undulating parkland course with mature trees and impressive backdrops. Water comes into play on seven holes. 18 holes, 6025 yards. S.S.S. 69, Par 71. Additional Par 3 course, putting green, 21 bay floodlit driving range. *Green Fees:* information not available. *Eating facilities:* full clubhouse facilities. *Visitors:* welcome, booking in advance advisable. *Society Meetings:* welcome, telephone or write for details. Professional: Cranfield Golf Academy. Manager: Jonathan Gale.*

MILTON KEYNES. **Kingfisher Country Club,** Buckingham Road, Deanshanger, Milton Keynes MK19 6DG (01908 560354; Fax: 01908 260857). *Location*: twixt Milton Keynes/Buckingham on A422. Mature course setting - wooded - lakes and ponds major feature. 9 holes, 5471 yards. S.S.S. 67. Full 9 hole floodlit. 10 bay covered range. *Green Fees:* information not available. *Eating facilities:* full club house and separate spike lodge both overlooking lake. *Visitors:* welcome, some weekend restrictions on Sundays and Public Holidays. *Society Meetings:* welcome. Director: D.M. Barraclough. *

THE APPEARANCE OF AN ASTERISK (*) AT THE END OF A CLUB OR COURSE ENTRY INDICATES THAT UP-TO-DATE INFORMATION HAS NOT BEEN SUPPLIED

140 Buckinghamshire / ENGLAND THE GOLF GUIDE 2006

MILTON KEYNES. **Three Locks Golf Club,** Great Brickhill, Milton Keynes MK17 9BH (01525 270050 golf; Tel & Fax: 01525 270470 accommodation). *Location:* A4146 Bletchley to Leighton Buzzard. Parkland with lakes and water hazards. 18 holes, 6400 yards. S.S.S. 71. Practice ground. *Green Fees:* weekdays £18.50 per round, £28.00 per day; weekends £23.00 per round. After 3.30pm twilight fees £12.00. *Eating facilities:* hot bar food. *Visitors:* welcome every day. Golf buggies for hire. *Society Meetings:* all welcome. Professional: Visiting Professional. Secretary: Julia Faid (01525 270470).

MILTON KEYNES. **Wavendon Golf Centre,** Lower End Road, Wavendon, Milton Keynes MK17 8DA (01908 281811; Fax: 01908 281257). *Location:* from Junction 13 M1, A421, follow signs to Woburn Sands. Parkland with six small lakes as hazards. Three courses: 18 holes, 5608 yards. S.S.S. 69. 9 holes, 1424 yards. S.S.S. 27, pitch and putt course, Par 26, 536 yards. 36 bay driving range, practice, putting and bunker. *Green Fees:* weekdays £14.50, weekends £20.00, Friday rate £15.00. *Eating facilities:* fully licensed bar and carvery restaurant. *Visitors:* always welcome. Buggies. *Society Meetings:* welcome. Professional/ Secretary: Greg Iron (01908 281811).

MILTON KEYNES. **Windmill Hill Golf Centre,** Tattenhoe Lane, Bletchley, Milton Keynes MK3 7RB (01908 630660; Fax: 01908 630034; Tee reservations 01908 631113. 7 days in advance). *Location:* M1 South Junction 14/M1 North Junction 13 A421 towards Buckingham. 32 bay covered floodlit driving range, seven grassed bays. Two putting greens; practice area. *Green Fees:* information not available. *Eating facilities:* restaurant, cafeteria, bars, function room; pool and games room. *Opening hours:* 7.30am till 11pm. *Society Meetings:* welcome (after 11am weekends and Bank Holidays); weekday and weekend packages. Three teaching Professionals, tuition, Pro shop. Professional: Colin Clingan (01908 378623). Secretary: Brian Smith (Tel & Fax: 01908 366457).*

MILTON KEYNES. **Woburn Golf Club,** Little Brickhill, Milton Keynes MK17 9LJ (01908 370756; Fax: 01908 378436). *Location:* four miles west of Junction 13 M1. Three courses, 54 holes: Duke's Course 6976 yards, S.S.S. 74; Duchess' Course 6651 yards, S.S.S. 72; Marquess Course 7214 yards, S.S.S. 74. Practice facilities. *Green Fees:* by request. *Eating facilities:* restaurant; breakfasts and lunches; dinner by prior arrangement. *Visitors:* welcome weekdays by prior arrangement. Weekends restricted to members and their guests only. *Society Meetings:* catered for, details on application. Secretary: Mrs G. Beasley (01908 370756). Professional: L. Blacklock (01908 626600).

PRINCES RISBOROUGH. **Princes Risborough Golf Club,** Lee Road, Saunderton Lee, Princes Risborough HP27 9NX (01844 346989. Fax: 01844 274938). *Location:* A4010, Princes Risborough, turn off at Rose and Crown Inn, one mile on right. Parkland course, slightly undulating, water hazards and has beautiful views. 9 holes, 5552 yards. S.S.S. 67. Practice area and nets. *Green Fees:* 9 holes weekdays £12.00; weekends £14.00, 18 holes weekdays £16.50; weekends £21.50. *Eating facilities:* restaurant and bar. *Visitors:* always welcome properly attired. *Society Meetings:* welcome. Outside functions, wedding receptions, parties and Christmas dinners catered for. Professional: Simon Lowry (01844 274567). Secretary/Proprietor: J.F. Tubb.

PRINCES RISBOROUGH. **Whiteleaf Golf Club Ltd,** Upper Icknield Way, Whiteleaf HP27 0LY (01844 274058/343097). *Location:* A4010 from Princes Risborough turn off at signpost for Whiteleaf into Upper Icknield Way. Hilly course with beautiful Chiltern views. 9 holes, 5391 yards. S.S.S. 66. Practice area. *Green Fees:* information not available. *Eating facilities:* full catering facilities, except Mondays. *Visitors:* always welcome; probably better to phone Secretary in case of disappointment. *Society Meetings:* on Thursdays – apply to Secretary. Professional: Ken Ward (01844 345472). Secretary: Derek Hill (01844 274058). *

SLOUGH. **Farnham Park Pay and Play Golf Course,** Park Road, Stoke Poges, Slough SL2 4PJ (Tel & Fax: 01753 643332). *Location:* just off A355, two miles north of A4. Challenging parkland course with water. 18 holes, 6172 yards. S.S.S. 71. Short game practice facilities, 20 bay driving range at our nearby golfing academy (one mile away). *Green Fees:* weekdays £13.00, weekends £20.00. Reductions for juniors and seniors. *Eating facilities:* hot and cold food always available. *Visitors:* welcome, hire facilities available. Pro shop with hire facilities. *Society Meetings:* welcome, special packages available, from as little as £20.00 per person. Professional: David Green (01753 643332). Operated by South Bucks District Council. Secretary: Mrs M Brooker, M. Inst. GCM (01753 647065).

For full details of clubs and courses, plus convenient accommodation
www.uk-golfguide.com

WAVENDON GOLF CENTRE Lower End Road, Wavendon, Milton Keynes MK17 8DA
Tel: **01908 281811** • Fax: **01908 281257** • E-mail: wavendon-jackbarker@btinternet.com
• Three courses over parkland with six small lakes • Pitch and putt; 36-bay driving range, practice, putting and bunker • Fees: weekdays £14.50, weekends £20.00, Friday rate £15.00. Half price twilight fees • Fully licensed bar and carvery restaurant • Visitors and societies welcome.
CONTACT SECRETARY/PROFESSIONAL GREG IRON: **01908 281811**

ENGLAND / Buckinghamshire

STOKE POGES. **Lanes Golfing Academy,** Stoke Road, Stoke Poges SL2 4NL (01753 554840). *Location:* half-a-mile from Slough Railway Station in direction of Stoke Poges. Parkland course ideal for the less experienced player. 9 holes. 2400 yds. S.S.S. 62 (18 holes). 18 bay driving range. *Green Fees:* information not available. *Eating facilities:* small lounge area with snack facilities. *Visitors:* open to the public seven days a week. Clubs for hire. Expert tuition available. The Tiger Club for under 12's with 12 monthly competitions held. *Society Meetings:* ideal for company tuition days. A Golf Foundation starter centre. Professional: Paul Warner (01753 554840). Operated by South Bucks District Council Contact: Mr K Simpkins (01753 533333).*

STOKE POGES. **Stoke Park Club,** North Drive, Park Road, Stoke Poges SL2 4PG (01753 717171; Fax: 01753 717181). *Location:* one mile north of Slough, eight miles from Heathrow. Parkland course. 27 holes, 6670 yards. S.S.S. 72. Practice ground (tokens available from Club Shop). *Green Fees:* information not provided. *Eating facilities:* Orangery, dining room, President's Bar and Park Restaurant. *Visitors:* welcome weekdays with Handicap Certificate or letter of introduction; weekends subject to availability. 21 bedrooms now available, conference facilities. *Society Meetings:* catered for. Club Director: Mark Fagan (01753 717171; Fax: 01753 717181). Professional: Stuart Collier. Club Shop: 01753 717184.
website: www.stokeparkclub.com

THE APPEARANCE OF AN ASTERISK (*) AT THE END OF A CLUB OR COURSE ENTRY INDICATES THAT UP-TO-DATE INFORMATION HAS NOT BEEN SUPPLIED

STOWE. **Silverstone Golf Club,** Silverstone Road, Stowe MK18 5LH (01280 850005; Fax: 01280 850156). *Location:* A43 half mile south of Silverstone Grand Prix Circuit. Flat, maturing copses bordered by woodland. 18 holes, Par 72. 6558 yards. S.S.S. 71. Putting area, covered driving range. *Green Fees:* information not provided. *Eating facilities:* meals at all times, licensed bar. *Visitors*: welcome, booking seven days in advance. Conference facilities. Coporate days with motorsport activities and golf. *Society Meetings:* welcome. Professional: Rodney Holt. Manager: Bryan Major.

STOWE. **Stowe Golf Club,** Stowe, Buckingham MK18 5EH (01280 816264). *Location:* situated at Stowe School, four miles north of Buckingham. Parkland course with follies and lakes. 9 holes, 2189 yards. S.S.S. 63. *Green Fees:* information not available. *Visitors:* only as a guest of a member. *Society Meetings:* catered for by appointment. Secretary: Bill Kemp (01280 818282). *

WEXHAM. **Wexham Park Golf Course,** Wexham Street, Wexham, Slough SL3 6ND (01753 663271; Fax: 01753 663318). *Location:* M40 to Beaconsfield, A40 to Gerrards Cross, direction Fulmer on right hand side, near Wexham Park Hospital. Undulating parkland courses. 18 holes, 5251 yards. S.S.S. 66. Also 9 hole course, 2727 yards, par 34; and 9 hole course, 2219 yards, par 32. Driving range and short game practice area. *Green Fees:* information not available. *Eating facilities:* clubhouse bar and full kitchen facilities. *Visitors:* welcome, Pay and Play, open to all. *Society Meetings:* 7 days a week by prior arrangement. Professional: John Kennedy (01753 663271). Secretary: J. Dunne.*

WOOBURN COMMON. **Hedsor Golf Course,** Pay & Play, Broad Lane, Wooburn Common HP10 0JW (01628 851285). *Location:* from Junction 2 of M40, take A355 to Slough, turn right at Hedsor Golf Course sign, then follow golf arrows to course. Easy walking course in mature parkland; many water hazards. 9 holes. Par 34. 18 holes S.S.S 64. *Green Fees:* special rates for senior citizens. *Eating facilities:* bar and catering available. Professional: Stuart Cannon.

Visit the FHG website
www.holidayguides.com
for details of the wide choice of accommodation featured in the full range of FHG titles

Cambridgeshire

CAMBRIDGE. **Cambridge Golf Club,** Station Road, Longstanton, Cambridge CB4 5DR (01954 789388). *Location:* 10 minutes from city, off A14 at Bar Hill, turn right to Longstanton B1050. Parkland course. 18 holes, 6736 yards, S.S.S. 73. 9 bay floodlit grassed driving range, 9 holes pitch and putt. *Green Fees:* information not available. *Eating facilities:* clubhouse; 50-seat function room available for hire. *Visitors:* welcome, may need to book on competition days. Coaching by appointment. *Society Meetings:* catered for. Professionals: Adrienne Engleman, Geoff Hugget.*

CAMBRIDGE. **Cambridge National Golf (Home of Cambridge Meridian Golf Club),** Comberton Road, Toft, Cambridge CB3 7RY (01223 264700; Fax: 01223 264701). *Location:* 5 minutes from Junction 12 of M11 onto B1046. Heavily landscaped championship design set in 250 acres with six lakes and 108 bunkers. 18 holes, 6707 yards. S.S.S. 72. Practice ground and putting green. *Green Fees*: weekdays £20.00 round, £36.00 day; weekends £27.00 round, £46.00 day. Subject to review. *Eating facilities:* available all day. *Visitors:* welcome at all times (subject to availability). Buggies and trolleys for hire. *Society Meetings:* corporate and society golf days catered for. Professional: Jamie Donaldson (01223 264702). Golf Administrator: Chatelle Martine.
e-mail: meridian@golfsocieties.com

CAMBRIDGE. **Cambridgeshire Moat House Hotel Golf Club,** Bar Hill, Cambridge CB3 8EU (01954 249988). *Location:* five miles north from Cambridge on A14 Huntingdon Road, Junction 29. Well established parkland course with many mature trees. 18 holes, 6750 yards (newly extended 18th tee). S.S.S. 73. Practice grounds. *Green Fees:* information not available. *Eating facilities:* two restaurants and three bars (Mon-Fri lunch). *Visitors:* welcome anytime by prior phone call. 134 Bedroom Hotel including 35 air-conditioned executive bedrooms. Full leisure facilities including gym, heated pool, sauna, solarium, steam rooms and tennis courts. *Society Meetings:* welcome weekdays. Professional: Paul Simpson (01954 780098). Golf Co-ordinator: (01954 249971; Fax: 01954 780010).*

CAMBRIDGE. **Girton Golf Club,** Dodford Lane, Girton, Cambridge CB3 0QE (01223 276169; Fax: 01223 277150). *Location:* two miles north of Cambridge. Flat parkland. 18 holes, 6012 yards. S.S.S. 69. Large practice area. *Green Fees:* Monday to Friday £22.00. *Eating facilities:* diningroom, lounge and bar. *Visitors:* weekdays only. *Society Meetings:* welcome Tuesdays to Fridays. Professional: S. Thomson (01223 276991). Secretary: Miss V. Webb (01223 276169; Fax: 01223 277150). website: www.club-noticeboard.co.uk /girton

CAMBRIDGE. **Gog Magog Golf Club,** Shelford Bottom, Cambridge CB2 4AB (01223 247626; Fax: 01223 414990). *Location:* Two miles from the A11-A1307 roundabout, Colchester - Cambridge Road A604. Open, undulating chalkland hill course. Old Course - 18 holes, 6400 yards, S.S.S. 70. Wandlebury Course - 18 holes, 6750 yards, S.S.S. 72. Large driving range and practice areas, with ball hire available. *Green Fees:* weekdays £40.00 per round. *Eating facilities:* diningroom, bar meals, large bar area with lounge and spike bar. *Visitors:* welcome, only with members at weekends and Bank Holidays, Handicap Certificate required. *Society Meetings:* catered for Tuesdays and Thursdays. Professional: I. Bamborough (01223 246058). Secretary: I.M. Simpson (01223 247626).
e-mail: secretary@gogmagog.co.uk
website: www.gogmagog.co.uk

CAMBRIDGE NATIONAL GOLF
TOFT, CAMBRIDGE CB3 7RY
Tel: 01223 264700 • Fax: 01223 264701
Shop: 01223 264702
www.golfsocieties.com
e-mail: meridian@golfsocieties.com

GOLF SOCIETIES WELCOME WEEKDAY AND WEEKEND

"For lovers of good golf"

See also Colour Advertisement on page 28

As Peter Alliss said of the National "It offers a level of playing and social facilities which most can only dream of enjoying at such a realistic price."
Magical, Peter Alliss designed course – 6,700 yards from championship tees in a rolling 210-acre site. Home of Cambridge Meridian Golf Club. Water, wildlife, stunning greens and real ale! A truly enjoyable day's golf. The course is just outside the city of Cambridge, to the South West, with the very easy access from Junction 12 of the M11. "*The area's number one corporate and society golf venue*".

THE APPEARANCE OF AN ASTERISK (*) AT THE END OF A CLUB OR COURSE ENTRY INDICATES THAT UP-TO-DATE INFORMATION HAS NOT BEEN SUPPLIED

ENGLAND / Cambridgeshire 143

ELY. **Ely City Golf Course Ltd,** 107 Cambridge Road, Ely CB7 4HX (01353 662751). *Location:* on southern outskirts of city on A10 if heading towards Cambridge. Parkland course, undulating, magnificent views of the 12th century cathedral. 18 holes, 6627 yards. S.S.S. 72. Practice area. *Green Fees:* information not provided. *Eating facilities:* full bar, catering and restaurant facilities. *Visitors:* welcome anytime with a member or if in possession of a valid Handicap Certificate. Jeans, T-shirts and trainers not allowed. Well equipped Pro Shop. Snooker. *Society Meetings:* welcome Tuesday to Friday inclusive by arrangement. Professional: Andrew George (01353 663317). General Manager: Michael Hoare (01353 662751;Fax:01353 668636)
e-mail: elygolf@lineone.net
website: www.elygolf.com

HUNTINGDON. **Brampton Park Golf Club,** Buckden Road, Brampton, Huntingdon PE28 4NF (01480 434705). *Location*: three-quarters of a mile off A1, travelling north take first Huntingdon turn, south take second sign for "RAF Brampton". Picturesque with many water hazards, wooded areas and prolific wildlife – swans, badgers, muntjac deer, Canada geese, water fowl, etc. 18 holes, 6300 yards. S.S.S. 72. 10 bay driving range. *Green Fees*: weekdays £28.00 per round £35.00 per day; weekends £35.00 per round. £45.00 per day. *Eating facilities*: bar snacks, restaurant, two bars. *Visitors*: welcome at all times, no restrictions save telephone for tee reservations prior to arrival. Accommodation and business conference facilities and banqueting for up to 120 available. Buggies now available. *Society Meetings*: welcome. Professional: Alisdair Currie (Tel & Fax: 01480 434705). Secretary: Richard Oakes (01480 434700; Fax: 01480 411145).

HUNTINGDON. **Hemingford Abbots Golf Club,** Cambridge Road, Hemingford Abbots, Huntingdon PE28 9HQ (01480 495000; Fax: 01480 496000). *Location:* two miles south of Huntingdon on the A14. Gently undulating parkland with trees. 9 holes, 2680 yards. S.S.S.68. *Green Fees:* weekdays £10.00 for 9 holes, £14.00 for 18 holes; weekends £12.00 for 9 holes, £17.00 for 18 holes. *Eating facilities:* comfortable clubhouse with bar. *Visitors:* welcome, no restrictions. New conference facility for meetings and private functions. *Society Meetings:* welcome. 'The Friendly One', all standards welcome. Alternative tee positions on back nine. Secretary: Sonja McCabe. Proprietor: R. D. Paton.

HUNTINGDON. **Lakeside Lodge Golf Centre,** Fen Road, Pidley, Huntingdon PE28 3DF (01487 740540; Fax: 01487 740852). *Location*: on the B1040 St Ives to Warboys Road. Course has 8 lakes and considerable landscaping. Three courses - Lodge Course: 18 holes, 6437 yards. S.S.S. 73; Manor Course: 9 holes, 2601 yards; Church Course: 6 holes, 1645 yards. Driving range and Teaching Academy. *Green Fees:* weekdays £16.00 for 18 holes, £9.00 for 9 holes; weekends £25.00 for 18 holes, £13.00 for 9 holes. After 12 noon weekends £18.00. *Eating facilities:* full bar serving all day snacks and meals. *Visitors:* welcome but best to book. Ten Pin Bowling. Accommodation available in 46 twin en suite bedrooms adjoining the course. *Society Meetings:* all welcome. Professional: Scott Waterman PGA (01487 741541). Secretary: Mrs Jane Hopkins (01487 740540; Fax: 01487 740852).
e-mail: info@lakeside-lodge.co.uk
website: www.lakeside-lodge.co.uk

HUNTINGDON. **Ramsey Golf and Bowls Club,** 4 Abbey Terrace, Ramsey, Huntingdon PE26 1DD (01487 812600; Fax: 01487 815746). *Location:* 20 minutes from A1, 12 miles south of Peterborough, 10 miles north of Huntingdon. Flat parkland with a river running full length which comes into play on many holes. 18 holes, 6163 yards. S.S.S. 70. Two practice grounds, chipping area. *Green Fees:* information not available. *Eating facilities:* bar and full catering service available. *Visitors:* welcome weekdays, with member weekends. Six rink county standard bowling green. *Society Meetings:* welcome by prior arrangement. Professional: Stuart Scott (01487 813022). Secretary/Administrator: M. Kjenstad (01487 812600; Fax: 01487 815746).
e-mail: admin@ramseyclub.co.uk
website: www.ramseyclub.co.uk

MARCH. **March Golf Club,** Frogs Abbey, Grange Road, March PE15 0YH (01354 652364). *Location:* quarter of a mile west of March bypass (A141). Flat parkland. 9 holes, 6204 yards. S.S.S. 70. Six acre practice area. *Green Fees:* £20.00 per day midweek. *Eating facilities:* bar, bar meals (Saturday). *Visitors:* welcome. *Society Meetings:* welcome mid week only. Professional: Alex Oldham. Secretary: Mrs M.A. Simpson.
website: www.marchgolfclub.co.uk

ELY CITY GOLF CLUB, 107 Cambridge Road, Ely CB7 4HX
18 hole 'family' course used extensively for County Competitions and Regional Finals.
Practice ground and putting green. Pleasant Clubhouse.
Full bar and restaurant service. Well-stocked Professional's shop.
For lessons, coaching and equipment contact: Andrew George (Head Professional) on 01353 663317.
Tel: 01353 662751 • Fax: 01353 668635 • E-mail: elygolf@lineone.net • website: www.elygolf.co.uk

---

For full details of clubs and courses, plus convenient accommodation
www.uk-golfguide.com

PETERBOROUGH. **Elton Furze Golf Club,** Bullock Road, Haddon, Peterborough PE7 3TT (01832 280189; Fax: 01832 280299). *Location*: four miles west of Peterborough on old A605 Oundle to Peterborough road. Opened April 1993. Scenic parkland, wooded. 18 holes, 6279 yards, 5715 metres. S.S.S. 70. Driving range. *Green Fees:* weekdays £32.00 per round; weekends £36.00 per round. Subject to review. *Eating facilities:* new spacious bar and restaurant (holds 120). *Visitors:* welcome any time. Buggies available for hire £14.00 for 18 holes, £20.00 all day. *Society Meetings:* welcome Monday to Friday - small groups only on Friday - need to pre-book. Contact: Helen Barron. Bar/Restaurant (01832 280118). Professional: Glyn Krause (01832 280614).

PETERBOROUGH. **Orton Meadows Golf Course,** Ham Lane, Orton Waterville, Peterborough PE2 5UU (01733 237478). *Location*: three miles west of Peterborough on A605, at entrance to Nene Park. Parkland, lakes. 18 holes, 5613 yards. S.S.S. 68. with 12 hole pitch and putt course adjoining. *Green Fees*: weekdays £12.30, Concessions; £7.30, Juniors; £5.30. Weekends and Bank Holidays £16.20, Juniors £5.30. Pitch and Putt weekends £3.60, Juniors £2.70; weekdays £3.00, Juniors £2.40. *Visitors*: welcome; unrestricted – Pay as you Play course. Catering at adjoining pub/restaurant. Bookings taken seven days in advance. *Society Meetings*: Golf Societies welcome, contact Pro Shop (01733 237478). Head Professional: Ashley Howard (01733 237478). Director of Golf: Roger Fitton.
e-mail: enquiries@ortonmeadowsgolfcourse.co.uk
website: www.ortonmeadowsgolfcourse.co.uk

PETERBOROUGH. **Peterborough Milton Golf Club,** Milton Ferry, Peterborough PE6 7AG. *Location*: on A47 west of Peterborough, three miles east of A1. Parkland. 18 holes, 6505 yards. S.S.S. 72. *Green Fees:* £35.00 per round, £45.00 per day. Societies £40.00 per day. *Eating facilities:* available daily except Mondays. *Society Meetings:* available by arrangement with Secretary. Professional: Mike Gallagher (01733 380793). Secretary: Andy Izod (01733 380489).

PETERBOROUGH. **Thorney Golf Centre,** English Drove, Thorney, Peterborough PE6 0TJ (01733 270570). *Location*: left at traffic lights in Thorney off A47 Peterborough to Wisbech road out of village. Fen Course - flat, ideal for beginners; Lakes Course - challenging links with lakes. 36 holes: Fen 18 holes, 6104 yards, S.S.S. 69; Lakes 18 holes, 6399 yards, S.S.S. 71. Driving range. *Green Fees:* weekdays Fen £8.75, Lakes £15.00; weekends Fen £10.75, Lakes £23.50. *Eating facilities:* three bars and restaurant. *Visitors:* welcome, no restrictions on Fen Course, Lakes Course contact in advance at weekends. *Society Meetings:* all welcome. Professional: Mark Templeman. Secretary: Jane Hind.

PETERBOROUGH. **Thorpe Wood Golf Course,** Thorpe Wood, Peterborough PE3 6SE (01733 267701). *Location*: two miles west of Peterborough on A47. Parkland. 18 holes, 7086 yards. S.S.S. 74. Practice ground. *Green Fees*: weekdays £13.00; Concessions; £8.00; Juniors £5.30. Weekends and Bank Holidays £17.50, no concessions, Juniors £5.30. *Visitors*: welcome, unrestricted - Pay-as-you-Play course. Catering at adjoining pub/restaurant. Bookings taken 7 days in advance. *Society Meetings*: Golf societies welcome – contact Jenny Walters (01733 267701). Head Coach: Gary Casey (01733 267701). Director of Golf: Roger Fitton.
e-mail: enquiries@thorpewoodgolfcourse.co.uk
website: www.thorpewoodgolfcourse.co.uk

RAMSEY. **Old Nene Golf Club,** Muchwood Lane, Bodsey, Ramsey PE26 2XQ (01487 813519 or 815622). *Location:* three-quarters of a mile north of Ramsey towards Peterborough, halfway between Ramsey and Ramsey Mereside and half mile from Rainbow Superstore. Easy walking course with water hazards, quiet with wildlife – herons, swans, pheasants, partridges. 1996 Eastern Area Environmental Winner. 9 holes, 5605 yards, S.S.S. 68. Edrich driving range on site. *Green Fees:* information not available. *Eating facilities:* in clubhouse, open to all, fully licensed bar; bar snacks always available, meals to order.. *Visitors:* welcome, telephone to avoid club tee closures. *Society Meetings:* welcome. Professional: Neil Grant. Secretary: G. Stoneman (01487 815622).*

Two Great Courses – Two Great Choices

Orton Meadows
Golf Course
Orton Waterville, Peterborough PE2 5UU
Tel: 01733 237478
www.ortonmeadowsgolfcourse.co.uk

Thorpe Wood
Golf Course
Thorpe Wood, Peterborough PE3 6SE
Tel: 01733 267701
www.thorpewoodgolfcourse.co.uk

☑ Pay as you play at affordable prices ☑ Club and Trolley Hire available
☐ You do not have to be a member or have a Handicap to play
☑ Large well-stocked Golf Shops ☑ 12-hole Pitch and Putt Course at Orton Meadows
☑ Golf Societies welcome ☑ Catering available at adjoining pub restaurants

ST IVES. **St Ives (Hunts) Golf Club,** Westwood Road, St Ives PE27 6DH (01480 464459). *Location:* B1040 off A14. 9 holes, 6180 yards. S.S.S. 70. *Green Fees:* information not available. *Eating facilities:* full catering. *Visitors:* welcome weekdays. *Society Meetings:* welcome. Professional: Mark Pond (Tel & Fax: 01480 466067). Manager: Vince Benson (Tel & Fax: 01480 468392).*

ST NEOTS. **Abbotsley Golf Club and Hotel,** Eynesbury Hardwicke, St Neots PE19 6XN (01480 474000; Fax: 01480 471018). *Location:* A428 St Neots bypass, turn towards St. Neots at Tesco's follow signs to Eynesbury Hardwicke and Abbotsley. Pleasantly undulating, parkland course with several water features. Two courses, 36 holes - Abbotsley 6311 yards, S.S.S. 72; Cromwell 6087 yards, S.S.S. 69. Floodlit covered driving range, 300 yard grass practice area. 9 hole Par 3 course. *Green Fees:* available on request. *Eating facilities:* 80 cover restaurant, three bars. *Visitors:* always welcome. 42 bedroom hotel. *Society Meetings:* welcome. General Manager: Jonathan Tubb. Professional: Steve Connolly. Sales Manager: Heather Tubb (01480 474000; Fax: 01480 471018).

ST NEOTS. **St Neots Golf Club,** Crosshall Road, St Neots PE19 7GE (01480 472363). *Location:* just off the A1, Junction B1048 heading for St Neots. Picturesque, undulating parkland course with water hazards and challenging greens. 18 holes, 6033 yards. S.S.S. 69. Practice ground, putting green. *Green Fees:* weekdays £35.00. *Eating facilities:* full catering and bar. *Visitors:* welcome, with Handicap Certificates; weekends with a member only. *Society Meetings:* welcome weekdays. Club Secretary: (01480 472363; Pro shop: 01480 476513).
e-mail: office@stneots-golfclub.co.uk
website: www.stneots-golfclub.co.uk

WISBECH. **Tydd St Giles Golf Centre,** Kirkgate, Tydd St Giles, Wisbech PE13 5NZ (01945 871007; Fax: 01945 870566). *Location:* A1101 from Wisbech to Long Sutton to Tydd Gate and follow the river to Tydd St Giles, one mile from this junction on right hand side. Slightly undulating course, fenland Grade 1 silt/loam free draining. Course always open. 18 holes, 6264 yards, S.S.S. 70. Indoor/outdoor floodlit driving range. *Green Fees*: Midweek £16, weekends £20, prices for all day golf. *Eating facilities*: all day snacks/grills. Full Pub licence - everyone welcome. *Visitors*: welcome, please ring for a tee off time, dress code applies. Tuition available daily. *Society Meetings*: welcome, packages available. Professionals: John Ronson (07841 402024); Alison Johns (07887 594313).
e-mail: enquiries@tyddgolf.co.uk
website: www.tyddgolf.co.uk

For full details of clubs and courses, plus convenient accommodation
www.uk-golfguide.com

FHG
K·U·P·E·R·A·R·D

Other specialised FHG Guides
Published annually: available in all good bookshops or direct from the publisher.

Recommended **COUNTRY INNS & PUBS OF BRITAIN** £7.99
Recommended **COUNTRY HOTELS** OF BRITAIN £7.99
Recommended **SHORT BREAK HOLIDAYS IN BRITAIN** £7.99
The bestselling **PETS WELCOME!** £8.99

FHG Guides • Abbey Mill Business Centre, Seedhill, Paisley, Renfrewshire PAI ITJ
Tel: 0141-887 0428 • Fax: 0141-889 7204
e-mail: admin@fhguides.co.uk
www.holidayguides.com

Cheshire

ADLINGTON. **Adlington Golf Centre,** Sandy Hey Farm, Adlington, Macclesfield SK10 4NG (01625 850660). *Location*: 2 miles south of Poynton off A523, via Adlington Industrial Estate. 24 bay covered, floodlit driving range. *Fees*: information not provided. *Eating facilities:* tea and coffee available. *Opening hours*: 9am to 10.00pm Monday to Friday, 8.30am to 9.00pm weekends. 9 hole Par 3 course plus 9 hole Academy Course. Reductions for Senior Citizens/Juniors. Tuition available all the time. Professionals: Chad Goldstraw, John Watson and Dave Jeffery. Proprietor: David Moss (01625 850660).

ALDERLEY EDGE. **Alderley Edge Golf Club,** Brook Lane, Alderley Edge SK9 7RU (01625 586200). *Location*: off A34. 9 holes, 5836 yards. S.S.S. 68. *Green Fees:* weekdays £12.00 9 holes, £22.00 18 holes, weekends £15.00 9 holes, £27.50 18 holes. 2-fore-1 vouchers accepted. *Eating facilities:* meals served in clubhouse. *Visitors:* subject to restrictions on Tuesday mornings, Wednesday afternoons and weekends. *Society Meetings:* welcome on Thursdays. Professional: P. Bowring (01625 584493). Secretary: R.C. Harrison.

ALSAGER. **Alsager Golf and Country Club,** Audley Road, Alsager, Stoke-on-Trent ST7 2UR (01270 875700; Fax: 01270 882207). *Location*: off M6 at Junction 16 onto A500 to Stoke, first left to Alsager, course is one and a half miles on right. Parkland. 18 holes, 6201 yards. S.S.S. 70. *Green Fees:* information not available. *Eating facilities:* restaurant and bar snacks. *Visitors:* welcome Mondays, to Thursdays and Fridays 8am to 12pm, without reservation. Wedding, conference and banqueting facilities. Bowls. *Society Meetings:* welcome Mondays, Wednesdays and Thursdays, packages arranged. Professional: Richard Brown (01270 877432; Fax: 01270 882207). Administration Manager: Margaret Davenport (01270 875700).*
e-mail: business@alsagergolfclub.com

APPLETON. **Warrington Golf Club,** Hill Warren, London Road, Appleton, Near Warrington WA4 5HR (01925 261620). *Location:* M56 Junction 10, A49 Warrington one and a half miles on left. Parkland course. 18 holes, 6210 yards. S.S.S. 70. Practice ground. *Green Fees:* weekdays £27.00 per round, £35.00 per day; weekends £30.00 per round. *Eating facilities:* available every day. *Visitors:* welcome with booking through Professional. *Society Meetings:* Wednesdays only, booked through Secretary. Professional: R. MacKay (01925 265431). Secretary: S. Higham (01925 261775; Fax: 01925 265933).
e-mail: secretary@warrington-golf-club.co.uk

CHEADLE. **Cheadle Golf Club,** Cheadle Road, Cheadle SK8 1HW (0161-428 2160). *Location:* one-and-a-half miles Junction 11 M63. Parkland. 9 holes, 5006 yards. S.S.S. 65. *Green Fees:* on application. *Eating facilities:* by arrangement with the Steward. *Visitors:* welcome, must be members of a bona fide golf club; current Handicap Certificate to be produced; no visitors on Tuesdays or Saturdays. *Society Meetings:* catered for by arrangement with the Secretary. Professional: D. Cain (0161-428 9878). Secretary: C.T. Openshaw (0161-491 4452).

Alderley Edge Golf Club
www.aegc.co.uk

Set beneath the "Edge", a steeply wooded escarpment rising above the Cheshire Plain **ALDERLEY EDGE GOLF CLUB** offers both a challenging course and a warm welcome to visitors - phone club to check for availability. The attractive clubhouse serves a full range of meals and snacks, and there is a popular Spike Bar. Societies are welcome by prior arrangement on Thursdays - packages including meals available - please call the Professional **01625 584493**.

Brook Lane, Alderley Edge, Cheshire SK9 7RU • Tel: 01625 586200

Alsager Golf & Country Club
A day's golf to remember & Much More!
Golf Societies Welcome. Visit this lovely 18 hole parkland course. Large and small function rooms available for private parties, weddings, conferences, etc. Excellent facilities including dance floor, stage and bar. Large car park. Business functions and conferences arranged for you by the Administration Manager. Menus to cover all tastes and pockets.
Audley Road, Alsager, Cheshire ST7 2UR. Tel: 01270 875700 e-mail: business@alsagergolfclub.uk
(Just 2 miles from Junction 16 on M6)

ENGLAND / Cheshire 147

CHEADLE. **Gatley Golf Club Ltd,** Waterfall Farm, Styal Road, Heald Green, Cheadle SK8 3TW (0161-437 2091). *Location:* from Gatley village to South down Styal Road and follow directions into Yew Tree Grove, then Motcombe Grove to Club entrance. Parkland course. 9 holes, 5934 yards. S.S.S. 68. *Green Fees:* information not provided. Special rates by arrangement. *Eating facilities:* available except Monday, bar. *Visitors:* welcome Mondays, Wednesdays and Thursdays. *Society Meetings:* welcome Thursdays. Professional: James Matterson (0161-436 2830). Secretary: R.W.R. Salt (0161-437 2091).

CHESTER. **Aldersey Green Golf Club,** Aldersey, Near Chester CH3 9EH (01829 782157). *Location:* on A41 Chester to Whitchurch road five minutes from Broxton roundabout. Flat wooded parkland. 18 holes, 6159 yards. S.S.S. 69. Practice area. *Green Fees:* information not available. *Eating facilities:* bar with meals available. *Visitors:* welcome. *Society meetings:* welcome. Professional and Secretary: Stephen Bradbury. *

CHESTER. **Carden Park Hotel Golf Resort & Spa,** Carden, near Chester CH3 9DQ (01829 731000; Fax: 01829 731032). *Location:* take A41 from Chester to Broxton roundabout, turn right onto A534 (Wrexham). Parkland courses with trees and superb views over the Cheshire countryside. Cheshire Course, 18 holes, 6824 yards. Par 72. Nicklaus Course, 18 holes, 7045 yards, Par 72. Par 3 Azalea Course. Driving range. *Green Fees:* information not available. *Eating facilities:* Clubhouse; brasserie within hotel. *Visitors:* welcome, some restriction on certain competition and members' days. No metal spikes allowed. Accommodation in 192 bedroom hotel. *Society Meetings:* welcome. Professional: Paul Hodgson.*
e-mail: enquiries.carden@devere-hotels.com

CHESTER. **Chester Golf Club,** Curzon Park, Chester CH4 8AR (01244 675130). *Location:* one mile south west of city centre. From Chester Castle take A483 (Wrexham) to first roundabout over Grovesnor Bridge. Turn right into Curzon Park North and follow signs. Parkland on two levels overlooking the River Dee. 18 holes, 6508 yards. S.S.S. 71. *Green Fees:* weekdays £30.00 per day; weekends £35.00. Reductions if playing with a member. *Eating facilities:* full restaurant and bar facilities. *Visitors:* welcome most days but advisable to telephone first. *Society Meetings:* catered for by prior arrangement. Professional: Scott Booth (01244 671185). Secretary: V.F.C. Wood (01244 677760).

CHESTER. **Eaton Golf Club,** Guy Lane, Waverton, Chester CH3 7PH (01244 335885). *Location*: three miles south east of Chester off A41. 18 holes, 6580 yards. S.S.S. 72. Substantial practice area. *Green Fees*: weekdays £30.00, weekends £35.00. *Eating facilities*: catering available seven days. *Visitors:* welcome at all times but with Handicap Certificate and prior checking with either Secretary or Professional. *Society Meetings*: welcome except Wednesdays. Society rates available on request. Professional: Bill Tye (01244 335826). Secretary: Kerry Brown (01244 335885; Fax: 01244 335782).

CHESTER. **Mollington Grange Golf Club,** Townfield Lane, Mollington, Chester CH1 6NJ (01244 851185; Fax: 01244 851349). *Location:* A 540, 5 minutes from end of M56 and two miles from Chester City. A superb undulating course with five lakes, 16 ponds and a Par 3 island green, providing a challenge for the advanced player while remaining friendly to the average player or beginner. 18 holes, 6400 yards. Par 71. Driving range. *Green Fees:* information not available. *Eating facilities:* club house with warm and friendly atmosphere, lounge and bar area, restaurant and sports lounge/bar situated on the first floor. *Visitors:* welcome. Membership open, details on request. Fully stocked golf shop and comfortable changing facilities. *Society Meetings:* welcome. Corporate days and corporate membership catered for. Details available on request. Director of Golf: Ben Keegan. Secretary: Gail Matthews.*

CHESTER. **Pryors Hayes Golf Club,** Willington Road, Oscroft, Near Tarvin CH3 8NL (01829 741250; Fax: 01829 749077). *Location:* signposted; situated just off A54 between Kelsall and Tarvin. Flat, parkland course. 18 holes, 6054 yards. S.S.S. 69. Practice area. *Green Fees:* £20.00 weekdays, £30.00 weekends. *Eating facilities:* restaurant and bar. *Visitors:* welcome every day subject to availability. *Society Meetings:* Societies/Companies/Groups all welcome. Professional: Martin Redrup (01829 740140; Fax: 01829 749077). Secretary: Joan Quinn (01829 741250; Fax: 01829 749077).

CHESTER. **Upton-by-Chester Golf Club,** Upton Lane, Chester CH2 1EE (01244 381183; Fax: 01244 376955). *Location:* off A41, near Zoo turn-off traffic lights. Flat parkland course. 18 holes, 5807 yards. S.S.S. 68. *Green Fees:* £30.00 per day, £20.00 per round. *Eating facilities:* large restaurant and bar. *Visitors:* no restrictions except Competition Days. *Society Meetings:* welcome except Mondays, Tuesdays and weekends. Minimum number 16. All day packages £39.00. Professional: Stephen Dewhurst (01244 381183). Secretary: Fred Hopley (01244 381183; Fax: 01244 376955).

Eaton
GOLF CLUB
Tel: 01244 335885
Fax: 01244 335782

Guy Lane, Waverton, Chester CH3 7PH
e-mail: office@eatongolfclub.co.uk • www.eatongolfclub.co.uk
♦ Three miles south east of Chester off the A41 ♦ 18 holes, 6580 yards. S.S.S. 72. ♦ Visitors welcome at all times but with Handicap Certificate and prior checking with either Secretary or Professional ♦ Catering available seven days a week
Professional: 01244 335826 ♦ *Secretary: 01244 335885*

CHESTER. **Vicars Cross Golf Club,** Tarvin Road, Great Barrow, Chester CH3 7HN (01244 335174; Fax: 01244 335686). *Location:* four miles east of Chester on the A51. Undulating parkland course, wooded. 18 holes, 6446 yards. S.S.S. 71. Practice grounds/ covered bays. *Green Fees:* £30.00 weekdays, £35.00 weekends and Bank Holidays, £20.00 after 3pm every day. Subject to review. *Eating facilities:* restaurant and bar snacks. *Visitors:* welcome every day except competition days - phone Secretary or Professional beforehand. *Society Meetings:* welcome Tuesday/Thursday. Conference facilities, lounge/dining rooms available for hire. Professional: John Forsythe (01244 335595). Secretary: Mrs Katrina Hunt.
e-mail: manager@vicarscrossgolf.co.uk

CONGLETON. **Astbury Golf Club,** Peel Lane, Astbury, Near Congleton CW12 4RE (01260 272772). *Location:* on outskirts south of Congleton, leave A34 Congleton to Newcastle Road at Astbury Village. Parkland/meadowland, water feature on four holes. 18 holes, 6178 yards. S.S.S. 69. Large practice area. *Green Fees:* information not available. *Eating facilities:* dining room and bar. *Visitors:* welcome weekdays, weekend with a member only. Must be members of recognised golf club with bona fide Handicap. Smart casual dress in clubhouse, jackets expected when meal/presentation held. *Society Meetings:* Thursdays only April to November £27.50 per player. Professional: Ashley Salt (01260 272772). Secretary: Fred Reed (01260 272772). Caterer: (01260 272772).*

CONGLETON. **Congleton Golf Club,** Biddulph Road, Congleton CW12 3LZ (01260 273540). *Location:* one mile south of Congleton Railway Station on Biddulph Road. Parkland. 9 holes, 5119 yards. S.S.S. 65. *Green Fees:* weekdays £21.00, weekends £31.00. *Eating facilities:* lunches and evening meals served if ordered in advance. Snacks available. *Visitors:* welcome. *Society Meetings:* welcome Mondays and Thursdays by prior arrangement. Professional: John Colclough (01260 273540). Secretary: D. Lancake (01260 273540).

CREWE. **Crewe Golf Club Ltd,** Fields Road, Haslington, Crewe CW1 5TB (01270 584099). *Location:* off A534 between Crewe and Sandbach in the village of Haslington. Parkland course. 18 holes, 6424 yards. S.S.S. 71. *Green Fees:* available on request. *Eating facilities:* bar, diningroom. *Visitors:* welcome weekdays only, not Bank Holidays. Snooker room. *Society Meetings:* Tuesdays only. Catering (01270 584227). Professional: David Wheeler (01270 585032). Secretary: Steve Dunlop (01270 584099; Fax: 01270 256482).
e-mail: secretary@crewegolfclub.co.uk
website: www.crewegolfclub.co.uk

CREWE. **Onneley Golf Club,** Barr Hill Road, Onneley, Near Crewe CW3 5QF (01782 750577). *Location:* one mile from Woore on A525, 12 miles from Stoke-on-Trent. Parkland on gentle slope. 18 holes, 5728 yards. S.S.S. 68. Par 70. *Green Fees:* weekdays £20.00 (£10.00 with member); Saturdays and Bank Holidays with member only. Juniors half normal price. *Eating facilities:* dining room and bar snacks. *Visitors:* welcome weekdays unrestricted. *Society Meetings:* welcome, except Tuesdays and Fridays (weekdays £22.50 per round including meal; Saturdays £27.50 per round including meal). Secretary: Peter Ball (01782 846759).

CREWE. **Queens Park Golf Course,** Queens Park Drive, Crewe CW2 7SB (01270 662378). *Location:* next to Queens Park, one mile from Crewe Station. Parkland. 9 holes x 2, 4920 yards. S.S.S. 64. *Green Fees:* information not available. *Eating facilities:* bar with excellent bar snacks. *Visitors:* welcome, restrictions Sunday mornings to 11am. *Society Meetings:* welcome. Professional: Jamie Lowe (01270 666724). Secretary: Tom Weston (01270 662887).*

DISLEY. **Disley Golf Club Ltd,** Stanley Hall Lane, Disley, Stockport SK12 2JX (01663 764001). *Location:* off A6 at Disley Village. Open hillside/parkland course. 18 holes, 6015 yards, 5832 metres. S.S.S. 69. *Green Fees:* £25.00 weekdays, £30.00 weekends. *Eating facilities:* available. *Visitors:* welcome. *Society Meetings:* catered for by arrangement. Professional: A.G. Esplin (01663 764001). Secretary: Mr Paul Smallwood (01663 764001).

FRODSHAM. **Frodsham Golf Club,** Simons Lane, Frodsham WA6 6HE (01928 732159; Fax: 01928 734070). *Location:* 10 minutes from Junction 12 M56. Parkland with views over Mersey estuary. 18 holes, 6328 yards. S.S.S. 70 (gents), 70 (ladies). Two practice areas, putting green, bunker and net. *Green Fees:* information not available. *Eating facilities*: clubhouse: dining room, lounge bar, spike bar, snooker room. *Visitors:* welcome weekdays only, guests of members only at weekends. *Society Meetings:* welcome weekdays. Professional: Graham Tonge (01928 739442; Fax: 01928 739037). Secretary: Mr E.I Roylance (01928 732159; Fax: 01928 734070).*
e-mail: office@frodshamgc.golfagent.co.uk
website: www.frodshamgolfclub.co.uk

HELSBY. **Helsby Golf Club,** Towers Lane, Helsby WA6 0JB (01928 722021; Fax: 01928 725384). *Location:* 7 miles south of Chester. M56 Junction 14 take B5117 to Helsby. Through traffic lights one mile, first right into Primrose Lane, then first right into Towers Lane (400 yards). James Braid designed parkland course. 18 holes, 6229 yards. S.S.S. 70. Practice area available. *Green Fees:* £27.50 weekdays; £17.00 with a member weekends. Subject to review. *Eating facilities:* full restaurant facilities. *Visitors:* welcome weekdays, weekends must play with a member. Snooker facilities. *Society Meetings:* welcome Tuesdays and Thursdays by arrangement. Professional: M. Jones (Tel & Fax: 01928 725457). Secretary: L.J. Norbury (01928 722021).

KNUTSFORD. **Heyrose Golf Club,** Budworth Road, Tabley, Knutsford WA16 0HZ (Tel & Fax: 01565 733664). *Location:* Junction 19 on M6 right at Windmill Pub to Pickmere, three-quarters of a mile right fork, half a mile further on right. Undulating parkland, wooded course. 18 holes, 6513 yards. S.S.S. 71. New 12 bay driving range, net and bunker, putting green, indoor teaching room. *Green Fees:* weekdays £25.00 per round; weekends £30.00 per round. Subject to review. *Eating facilities:* bar and restaurant. *Visitors:* no visitors on Saturdays before

THE GOLF GUIDE 2006　　　　　　　　　　　ENGLAND / Cheshire　149

3.30pm, Ladies priority Wednesdays, Seniors priority Thursdays. *Society Meetings:* welcome weekdays. Professional: Mike Grantham and Mark Davies (Tel & Fax: 01565 734267). General Manager: Mrs Elizabeth Bridge (Tel & Fax: 01565 733664).
e-mail: secretary@heyrosegolfclub.com
website: www.heyrosegolfclub.com

KNUTSFORD. **Mere Golf and Country Club,** Chester Road, Mere, Knutsford WA16 6LJ (01565 830155; Fax: 01565 830713). *Location:* one mile east of Junction 19 M6 and two miles west of Junction 7 M56. Parkland Championship course. 18 holes, 6817 yards. S.S.S. 73. Short game practice area, one 18 hole putting green, driving range (April to October). *Green Fees:* information not available. *Eating facilities:* informal atrium spike bar and brasserie. *Visitors:* welcome by prior arrangement only. *Society Meetings:* Mondays, Tuesdays and Thursdays only by arrangement. Professional: Peter Eyre (01565 830219). Golf Bookings: Karen Gallagher (01565 830155). Secretary: S. Janvier.*

KNUTSFORD. **Knutsford Golf Club,** Mereheath Lane, Knutsford WA16 6HS (01565 633355). *Location:* quarter of a mile from town centre. 9 holes, 6200 yards. S.S.S. 70. *Green Fees:* information not available. *Eating facilities:* bar snacks, other meals by prior arrangement. *Visitors:* welcome with reservation except Wednesdays and Saturdays and Sundays before 10:00am. *Society Meetings:* catered for by prior arrangement. Professional: Granville Ogden. Secretary: Danny Burgess. *

KNUTSFORD. **Mobberley Golf Club,** Burleyhurst Lane, Mobberley, Knutsford WA16 7JZ (01565 880188; Fax: 01565 880178). *Location:* exit 6 M56 to A538 Wilmslow, turn right at Mobberley Road. 9 hole course set in rolling Cheshire countryside. 5542 yards, S.S.S. 67. *Green Fees*: information not available. *Eating facilities*: fully licensed facilities available. *Visitors*: welcome at all times. Dress code must be adhered to. No denims, tracksuits, collarless shirts. Golf shoes must be worn. *Society Meetings*: welcome at all times. Professional: John Cheetham. Secretary: Nicholas Donaghy (Tel & Fax: 01565 880178).*

KNUTSFORD near. **Peover Golf Club,** Plumley Moor Road, Lower Peover, Near Knutsford WA16 9SE (01565 723337; Fax: 01565 723311). *Location:* Junction 19 of M6, A556, Knutsford. Parkland course, 18 holes, 6702 yards. S.S.S. 72. Practice area, putting green. *Green Fees:* £23.00 weekdays, £30.00 weekends. Subject to change. *Eating facilities:* bar food and function room. *Visitors:* always welcome. Please ring for a tee time. Buggy and trolley hire. *Society Meetings:* welcome.
e-mail: mail@peovergolfclub.co.uk
website: www.peovergolfclub.co.uk

KNUTSFORD. **The Wilmslow Golf Club,** Great Warford, Mobberley, Knutsford WA16 7AY (01565 873620). *Location:* two miles from Wilmslow off the Knutsford Road. Parkland course. 18 holes, 6607 yards. S.S.S. 72. Practice facility. *Green Fees:* weekdays £45.00 per round, £55.00 per day; weekends £55.00 per round, £65.00 per day. *Eating facilities:* full catering, two bars. *Visitors:* welcome, Ladies' Day Wednesday. *Society Meetings:* Tuesdays and Thursdays only. Professional: L. J. Nowicki (01565 873620). Secretary: Mrs M. I. Padfield (01565 872148; Fax: 01565 872712).
e-mail: info@wilmslowgolfclub.co.uk
website: www.wilmslowgolfclub.co.uk

LYMM. **Lymm Golf Club,** Whitbarrow Road, Lymm WA13 9AN (Tel & Fax: 01925 755020). *Location:* five miles south east of Warrington, two and a half miles from Junction 20 on M6 and Junction 9 on M56. Parkland. 18 holes, 6304 yards. S.S.S. 70. Practice ground. *Green Fees:* weekdays £28.00. *Eating facilities:* coffee, bar snacks, lunches and dinner, bar. *Visitors:* welcome with Handicap Certificates, no visitors at weekends, Bank Holidays or Thursdays until 2.30pm. *Society Meetings:* catered for with reservation. Professional: Steve McCarthy (01925 755054). Secretary: T.H.Glover (Tel & Fax: 01925 755020). Clubhouse (01925 752177).
website: www.lymm-golf-club.co.uk

MACCLESFIELD. **Macclesfield Golf Club,** The Hollins, Macclesfield SK11 7EA (01625 423227). *Location:* turn off A523 Leek Road into Windmill Street, half a mile fork right. Hillside course with extensive views. 18 holes, 5769 yards. S.S.S. 68. *Green Fees:* £30.00 weekdays; £40.00 weekends and Bank Holidays. *Eating facilities:* full catering and bars. *Visitors:* welcome by arrangement. *Society Meetings:* welcome weekdays except Thursdays. Professional: Tony Taylor (01625 616952). Secretary: David English (01625 615845; Fax: 01625 260061).
e-mail: secretary@Maccgolfclub.co.uk
website: www.Maccgolfclub.co.uk

MACCLESFIELD. **The Tytherington Club,** Dorchester Way, Tytherington, Macclesfield SK10 2JP (01625 506000; Fax: 01625 506040). *Location:* one mile north of Macclesfield off A523. Undulating parkland with numerous water features and ample woodland. 18 holes, 6765 yards. S.S.S. 70. Driving range, short game area. *Green Fees:* information not available. *Eating facilities:* bar with brasserie-style food and private function rooms available. *Visitors:* welcome, by prior arrangement. Buggies available. *Society Meetings:* welcome weekdays only. Highly competitive packages available. Professional: Gavin Beddow (01625 506013). General Manager: Daniel Sheratte.*
e-mail: tytherington.events@clubhaus.com

PEOVER GOLF CLUB

Situated in the heart of Cheshire, close to the historic town of Knutsford, which makes it ideally accessible to golfers. Close to Junction 19 M6. Peover's 18-hole par 72 parkland course measures 6,702 yards off the back tees. One of its most attractive features is the Peover Eye River which winds its way through the centre of the course, coming into play on three of the holes, while the tees and greens are situated to maximise the benefits of the natural contours. Clubhouse facilities available. Bar/food. Function room. Locker rooms. **Visitors Most Welcome**
Plumley Moor Road, Lower Peover, Near Knutsford WA16 9SE • Tel: 01565 723337
• Fax: 01565 723311 • e-mail: mail@peovergolfclub.co.uk • www.peovergolfclub.co.uk

NANTWICH. **Alvaston Hall Golf Club,** Alvaston Hall Hotel, Middlewich Road, Nantwich CW5 6PD (01270 628473; Fax: 01270 623395). *Location*: A530 Middlewich Road. Parkland course. 9 holes. S.S.S. 59. *Green Fees*: 9 holes £8.00; £10.00 per day. Professional: Kevin Valentine. Secretary: John Walkington.

NANTWICH. **Reaseheath Golf Club,** Reaseheath College, Nantwich CW5 6DF. *Location:* B5074 just north of Nantwich. Flat parkland. 9 holes, 1866 yards. S.S.S. 58. Short challenging course (4 par 4s, 5 par 3s) with narrow fairways and well guarded greens. Two tee positions for most holes. Also used for training greenkeepers. *Green Fees:* £8.00. *Visitors:* with a member or by prior approval. *Society Meetings:* subject to approval. Secretary: Chris Bishop (01270 625131; Fax: 01270 625665).

NORTHWICH. **Antrobus Golf Club,** Foggs Lane, Antrobus, Northwich (01925 730890; Fax: 01925 730100). *Location:* two minutes from Junction 10 of M56 between Northwich and Warrington. Parkland course with lakes. 18 holes, 6220 yards. S.S.S. 72. Putting green and driving range. *Green Fees:* information not available. *Eating facilities:* available. *Visitors:* welcome every day, except Saturdays. *Society Meetings:* welcome any day except Saturday. Ring for discounted rates. Professional: Paul Farrance (01925 730900). Secretary: Celia Axford (01925 730890; Fax: 01925 730100).*

NORTHWICH. **Delamere Forest Golf Club,** Station Road, Delamere, Northwich CW8 2JE (01606 883264). *Location:* opposite Delamere Station on the B5152 Tarporley to Frodsham road. Undulating heathland course suitable for play winter or summer. 18 holes, 6305 yards. S.S.S. 71. Two practice grounds. *Green Fees:* weekdays £40.00 18 holes; £55.00 per day, weekends £55.00 *Eating facilities:* bar meals, diningroom. *Visitors:* welcome most weekdays if no large parties booked. Some restrictions on four balls on Sundays. Prior booking with Pro advisable. *Society Meetings:* societies, corporate days, parties and small groups catered for. Professional: E.B. Jones (01606 883307). Secretary: J.J Mulder (01606 883800; Fax: 01606 889444). e-mail: info@delameregolf.co.uk
website: www.delameregolf.co.uk

NORTHWICH. **Hartford Golf Club,** Burrows Hill, Hartford, Northwich CW8 3AP (01606 871162; Fax: 01606 872182). *Location:* Just off A49 and A556 near ICI at Winnington. Undulating parkland course with numerous water hazards. 9 holes, 2780 yards, Par 35. 26 bay driving range. *Green Fees:* weekdays £7.00, weekends £9.00. *Eating facilities:* available. Large golf shop, tuition available. *Society Meetings:* welcome. Professional: L. Percival (01606 871162; Fax: 01606 872182). Secretary: C. Maddock.

NORTHWICH. **Sandiway Golf Club,** Chester Road, Sandiway, Northwich CW8 2DJ (01606 883247). *Location:* off A556, Northwich by-pass. Undulating heavily wooded parkland. 18 holes, 6404 yards. S.S.S. 71. *Green Fees:* information not available. *Eating facilities:* lunches and teas served daily, full restaurant facilities. *Visitors:* welcome on weekdays with Handicap Certificate from home club. *Society Meetings:* restricted to Tuesdays, parties up to 90; Wednesday and Friday; parties up to 20. Professional: William Laird (01606 883180). Secretary: R.H. Owens (01606 883247; Fax: 01606 888548). Caterer: (01606 882606).*

NORTHWICH. **Vale Royal Abbey Golf Club,** Whitegate, Northwich CW8 2BA (01606 301291; Fax: 01606 301414). Parkland championship course. 18 holes, 6463 yards, S.S.S. 71. Short game practice area, putting green, chipping green, practice range. *Green Fees:* information not provided. *Eating facilities:* informal spike bar. *Society Meetings:* welcome by arrangement. Professional: David Ingman.

POYNTON. **Davenport Golf Club,** Worth Hall, Middlewood Road, Poynton SK12 1TS (01625 876951: Fax: 01625 877489). *Location:* A6 from Stockport, Macclesfield Road at Hazel Grove, left at Poynton Church. Undulating parkland course. 18 holes, 6027 yards. S.S.S. 69. Putting green and practice ground. *Green Fees:* weekdays £30.00 (£12.50 with member), weekends £40.00 (£15.00 with a member). *Eating facilities:* bar snacks daily except Mondays, full meals by arrangement. *Visitors:* welcome, advisable to check with the Professional for availability of first tee. *Society Meetings:* catered for Tuesdays and Thursdays only. Professional: Gary Norcott (01625 877319). Secretary: Chris Souter (01625 876951; Fax: 01625 877489).

POYNTON. **Shrigley Hall Hotel, Golf & Country Club,** Shrigley Park, Pott Shrigley, Near Macclesfield SK10 5SB (01625 575757; Fax: 01625 575437). *Location:* easily accessible from the M56, M62,M60, M6,A523 and A6, only 10 minutes from Manchester Airport. Parkland course with magnificent views. 18 holes, 6305 yards. S.S.S 71. *Green Fees:* information not provided. *Eating facilities:* private rooms catering 16-250 people plus hotel Orangery Restaurant. *Visitors:* corporate, society and resident golfers welcome. 156 bedroomed four star hotel. Professional: Tony A. Stevens (01625 575626). Secretary: Alex Brannigan (01625 576681).

PRESTBURY. **De Vere Mottram Hall Golf Course,** Wilmslow Road, Mottram St. Andrew, Prestbury SK10 4QT (01625 820064). *Location*: M56 and M6. Flat parkland/woodland course. 18 holes, 7006 yards, 6250 metres. S.S.S. 72. Practice area. *Green Fees*: information not available. *Eating facilities*: Golf Brasserie. *Visitors*: no restrictions. Accommodation in 132 bedrooms. *Society Meetings*: no restrictions except at weekends. Professional: Tim Rastall. Golf Manager: Gordon Burniston.*

PRESTBURY. **Prestbury Golf Club,** Macclesfield Road, Prestbury, SK10 4BJ (01625 828241). *Location*: between Wilmslow and Macclesfield. 18 holes, 6359 yards, 5812 metres. S.S.S. 71. Practice ground. *Green Fees:* to be arranged. *Eating facilities:* snacks, lunches, teas and dinners. *Visitors:* welcome on weekdays 9.30am to 11.30am and after 2.30pm;

THE GOLF GUIDE 2006   ENGLAND / Cheshire   151

Tuesdays Ladies' Day until 2.30pm. Wednesdays Gentlemen members only until 3pm. Bank Holidays and weekends only with a member. *Society Meetings:* Thursdays only. Professional: Nick Summerfield (01625 828242). Secretary: (Tel & Fax: 01625 828241).
e-mail: office@prestburygolfclub.com
website: www.prestburygolfclub.com

RUNCORN. **Runcorn Golf Club,** Clifton Road, Runcorn WA7 4SU (01928 572093). *Location:* signposted The Heath, A557; M56 Junction 12. High parkland, easy walking course. 18 holes, 6035 yards, 5514 metres. S.S.S. 69. *Green Fees:* information not available. *Eating facilities:* bar snacks, lunches; dinner by arrangement. *Visitors:* welcome weekdays, Tuesday is Ladies' Day. No visitors weekends or Bank Holidays except with a member. Handicap Certificate required. *Society Meetings:* by arrangement Mondays and Fridays. Professional: K.Hartley (01928 564791). Secretary: A. Booth (Tel & Fax: 01928 574214).*

SANDBACH. **Malkins Bank Municipal Golf Course,** Betchton Road, Malkins Bank, Sandbach CW11 4XN (01270 765931). *Location:* M6, Junction 17 west on A534 for one mile, south on A533 for 400 metres, turn into Hassall Road (signposted). Parkland course. 18 holes, 5971 yards, S.S.S. 69. Practice area. *Green Fees:* information not available. All rates subject to review. *Eating facilities:* bar and food available. *Visitors:* welcome at all times, please pre-book (01270 765931). *Society Meetings:* welcome, please pre-book (01270 765931). Professional: Davron Hackney (01270 765931; Fax: 01270 764730)*

SANDBACH. **Sandbach Golf Club,** 117 Middlewich Road, Sandbach CW11 1FH (01270 762117). *Location:* two miles from Junction 17 of M6 on Middlewich Road. Meadowland course. 9 holes, 5397 yards. S.S.S. 67. Practice field. *Green Fees:* information not provided. *Eating facilities:* available except Mondays and Thursdays. *Visitors:* welcome weekdays, weekends by invitation only. *Society Meetings:* catered for only by advance arrangement with Hon. Secretary. Secretary: H. Buckley.

SOUTH WIRRAL. **Ellesmere Port Golf Centre,** Chester Road, Childer, Thornton, South Wirral CH66 1QF (0151-339 7689). *Location:* approximately six miles north of Chester on main A41 trunk road to Birkenhead. Wooded parkland with a lot of ponds. 18 holes, 6296 yards. S.S.S. 70. Practice ground with green and Smart Golf Simulator. *Green fees*: information not available. Eating facilities: bar and catering facilities. *Visitors*: welcome anytime. *Society Meetings*: by arrangement with Professional. Professional: Danny Youd (0151-339 7689); Secretary: Colin Craggs (0151-334 6579).*

STALYBRIDGE. **Stamford (Stalybridge) Golf Club,** Oakfield House, Huddersfield Road, Carrbrook, Stalybridge SK15 3PY (01457 835266). *Location:* on B6175 off A6018. Moorland course. 18 holes, 5701 yards. S.S.S. 68. *Green Fees:* weekdays £20.00; weekends after 3pm £25.00. Special rates for golf societies. *Eating facilities:* full meals except

Monday (bar available). *Visitors:* welcome without restrictions. *Society Meetings:* catered for by appointment only. Golf Shop: (01457 834829). Secretary: Mr B.D. Matthews (0161-633 5721)
e-mail: stamford.golfclub@totalise.co.uk

STYAL. **Styal Golf Club,** Station Road, Styal SK9 4JN. (01625 530063). *Location:* Station Road, Styal, five minutes from Manchester Airport, Junction 5 M56, five minutes from Wilmslow. Flat, parkland course with many water hazards and interesting features. 18 holes, 6194 yards, 5760 metres. S.S.S. 70. 9 hole, par 3 course, 1242 yards, Par 27. 24 bay deluxe driving range and short game academy. New 12 bay outdoor range. *Green Fees:* information not available. *Eating facilities:* fully equipped restaurant and bar. *Visitors:* welcome. *Society Meetings:* welcome; packages available. Professional: Simon Forrest (01625 528910). Director of Golf: Glynn Traynor (01625 530063). Golf booking line (01625 531359).*
e-mail: gtraynor@styalgolf.co.uk
website: www.styalgolf.co.uk

SUTTON WEAVER (NEAR RUNCORN). **Sutton Hall Golf Club,** Aston Lane, Sutton Weaver WA7 3ED (01928 790747; Fax: 01928 759174). *Location:* M56, Junction 12 signposted Frodsham. Wooded, parkland course. 18 holes, 6608 yards. S.S.S. 71. Full practice ground, putting green. *Green Fees:* weekdays £20, weekends £25 (subject to review). *Eating facilities:* Club catering available all day. *Visitors:* welcome weekdays; by arrangement only at weekends. *Society Meetings:* welcome. Professional: Jamie Hope (01928 714872; Fax: 01928 759174). Secretary: Maxwell Faulkner.

TARPORLEY. **Portal Golf and Country Club,** The Championship Course, Cobblers Cross Lane, Tarporley CW6 0DJ (01829 733933; Fax: 01829 733928). *Location:* half-a-mile from Tarporley on A49. Near Oulton Park. Donald Steel Championship course set in scenic parkland in the heartland of Cheshire with breathtaking panoramic views – lots of water! 18 holes, 7037 yards. S.S.S. 74. Driving range, practice facilities, putting green. Indoor golf academy. *Green Fees:* information not available. *Eating facilities:* excellent facilities with large banquet suite and bar area. *Visitors:* all visitors are required to book tee times in advance - seven day availability. Golf Shop, locker rooms, buggies. *Society Meetings:* welcome. Professional: Adrian Hill. Director of Golf: David Wills.*

TARPORLEY. **Portal, The Premier Course,** Forest Road, Tarporley CW6 0JA (01829 733884). *Location:* half a mile from Tarporley on A49. Undulating parkland with scenic views of Cheshire Plains. 18 holes, 6600 yards. S.S.S. 71. Practice area and putting green. *Green Fees:* information not available. *Eating facilities:* bar and restaurant. *Visitors:* welcome. *Society Meetings:* welcome, except weekends. Professional: Judy Statham (01829 733703). Director of Golf: David Wills.*

Please mention THE GOLF GUIDE when you enquire about clubs or accommodation

WARRINGTON. **Alder Root Golf Club,** Alder Root Lane, Winwick, Warrington WA2 8RZ (Tel & Fax: 01925 291919). *Location*: M6 Junction 22, A49 2 miles north of Warrington. Flat, parkland course. 10 holes, 5834 yards. S.S.S. 68. Putting green. Practice ground. Lessons available. *Green Fees:* £15.00 weekdays; £20.00 weekends. Two "Fore" one rates available. *Eating facilities:* available. *Visitors:* no restrictions weekdays, ring at weekends for details. *Society Meetings:* welcome. Professional: C. McKevitt (Tel & Fax: 01925 291932). Secretary: Mr E. Lander (Tel & Fax: 01925 291919).

WARRINGTON. **Birchwood Golf Club,** Kelvin Close, Science Park North, Birchwood, Warrington WA3 7PB (01925 818819; Fax: 01925 822403). *Location*: Junction 11 off M62, follow A574 signs for Risley then Science Park North signs. Flat parkland course with numerous natural ponds and streams. 18 holes, 6727 yards. S.S.S. 73. Practice ground, putting green. *Green Fees:* information not provided. *Eating facilities:* bar snacks throughout the day; restaurant facilities on request. *Visitors:* welcome on weekdays. Conference and banqueting facilities. Trolleys for hire. *Society Meetings:* Societies, companies and groups are welcome Mondays and Wednesdays if booked in advance. Professional: Paul McEwan (01925 825216; Fax: 01925 822403). Secretary: Mike Cullen (01925 818819; Fax: 01925 822403).

WARRINGTON. **Leigh Golf Club,** Kenyon Hall, Broseley Lane, Culcheth, Warrington WA3 4BG (01925 762943). *Location:* off A580 East Lancs Road to Culcheth Village. Parkland with tree-lined fairways. 18 holes, 5876 yards. S.S.S. 69. Three practice areas, practice nets. *Green Fees:* £32.00. *Eating facilities:* two bars and restaurant. *Visitors:* check with Professional. *Society Meetings:* catered for Mondays (except Bank Holidays), Tuesdays and Fridays. Professional: Andrew Baguley (01925 762013). Secretary: D.A. Taylor.

WARRINGTON. **Poulton Park Golf Club Ltd,** Dig Lane, Cinnamon Brow, Warrington WA2 0SH (01925 812034). *Location*: M6 (Junction 21), off A574 (Warrington/Leigh) Crab Lane. 9 holes, 5048 metres. S.S.S. 69. Practice ground. *Green Fees:* on application. *Eating facilities:* available except Mondays. *Visitors:* welcome most days, restricted at weekends. *Society Meetings*: catered for except weekends. Golf Society Packages available. PGA Professional: Ian Orrell (01925 825220). Secretary: J.K.Perkin (01925 822802).

WARRINGTON. **Walton Hall Golf Club,** Warrington Road, Higher Walton, Warrington WA4 5LU (01925 266775). *Location*: two miles south of Warrington off A56. Wooded parkland. 18 holes, 6801 yards. S.S.S. 73, Par 72. Practice ground. *Green Fees:* information not provided. *Eating facilities:* licensed clubhouse, meals and bar snacks. *Visitors*: unrestricted. *Society Meetings:* welcome, weekends after 1pm. Professional: J. Jackson (01925 263061). Secretary: Dave Johnson (01925 266775 or 01925 230860). e-mail: dave@waltonhallgolf.wanadoo.co.uk website: www.waltonhallgolfclub.co.uk

WESTON. **Wychwood Park Golf Club,** Weston CW2 5PG (01270 829200; Fax: 01270 820596). Location: 5 minutes from Junction 16 of M6 towards Nantwich. European PGA tour-standard course opened in 2002. 7191 yards off the championship tees. Water features throughout with a number of protected wildlife areas. Practice range, chipping and putting green. *Green Fees*: contact the Professional Shop (01270 820955). *Eating facilities:* superb modern clubhouse facility to cater for up to 150 people. *Visitors:* always welcome, handicap certificate requested. 108 en suite twin and double bedrooms, fitness suite. Meeting rooms for up to 160. *Society Meetings:* society and corporate welcome. Professional: Frank Kiddie (01270 820955). Secretary Pete Keena (01270 761696).*
website: www.golf-isc.co.uk

WIDNES. **Mersey Valley Golf & Country Club,** Warrington Road, Bold Heath, Widnes WA8 3XL (0151-424 6060; Fax: 0151 257 9097). *Location*: two miles from Junction 7 off M62, on the A57 towards Warrington. Flat parkland course. 18 holes, 6511 yards. S.S.S. 71, Par 72. *Green Fees:* weekdays £22.00; weekends £25.00. *Eating facilities*: full facilities available. *Visitors*: welcome at all times. Tuition available. Non members welcome. Buggies available. *Society Meetings*: very welcome, special rates apply. Contact General Manager. Professional: Andy Stevenson PGA. General Manager: Chris Gerrard.

WIDNES. **St Michaels Jubilee Golf Club,** Dundalk Road, Widnes WA8 8BS (0151-424 6230). Parkland course. 18 holes, 5638 yards. S.S.S. 67, Par 69. *Visitors*: unrestricted. Professional: D.Chapman (0151-424 6230). Secretary: A.J. Woodall (01695 726953).*

WIDNES. **Widnes Golf Club,** Highfield Road, Widnes WA8 7DT (0151-424 2440; Fax: 0151-495 2849). *Location:* near town centre, five miles from M56 and M62. Parkland course. 18 holes, 5729 yards. S.S.S. 68 White, 69 Ladies. *Green Fees:* weekdays £22.00; weekends £30.00. *Eating facilities:* two bars and full catering service. *Visitors:* welcome weekdays; weekends by arrangement. *Society Meetings:* very welcome, special rates apply, contact Secretary (0151-424 2995). Professional: Jason O'Brien (0151-420 7647).

WINSFORD. **Knights Grange Sports Complex,** Grange Lane, Winsford CW7 2PT (01606 552780). *Location:* signposted "Outdoor Sports Complex" from traffic lights Winsford Town Centre. 6 miles from M6, 16 miles from Chester. Set in beautiful Cheshire countryside on the outskirts of Winsford. A challenging course for golfers of all abilities. 18 holes - front 9 mainly flat but with water, ditches and other hazards. Back 9 take players deep into the countryside with many tees giving panoramic views of the course. There is also a lake and many mature woodland areas. Red Tees 5137 yards, S.S.S. 70; yellow tees 5270 yards, S.S.S. 66; white tees 5921 yards, S.S.S. 70. *Green Fees:* information available from Reception. *Eating facilities:* snacks and hot drinks available from Complex. Public house adjacent. *Visitors:* unrestricted, advance booking (01606 552780). Tennis, football, athletics. *Society Meetings:* welcomed - booking in writing in advance to Manager. Manager: Mrs P. Littler (01606 552780).

Cornwall

BODMIN. **Lanhydrock Golf Club,** Lostwithiel Road, Bodmin PL30 5AQ (01208 73600; Fax: 01208 77325). *Location:* one-and-a-half miles outside Bodmin on B3269. Parkland with generous tees and greens, easy walking, with many natural water features. 18 holes, 6100 yards, 5600 metres, Par 70, S.S.S. 70. Practice range. *Green Fees:* on application. One week unlimited golf pass available. *Eating facilities:* full catering facilities available, two bars. *Visitors:* welcome all week, booking advised. New hotel opening June 2006. Large Pro shop, golf buggies available. *Society Meetings:* welcome by arrangement, private suite available. Professional: Phillip Brookes. Manager: Graham Bond.
e-mail: golfing@lanhydrock-golf.co.uk
website: www.lanhydrock-golf.co.uk

BUDE. **Bude and North Cornwall Golf Club,** Burn View, Bude EX23 8DA (01288 352006; Fax: 01288 356855). *Location:* seaside links course situated in the centre of the town adjacent to beaches. 18 holes, 6205 yards. S.S.S. 70. Practice net and grounds. *Green Fees:* weekdays £27.00 per day; weekends £27.00 per round. *Eating facilities:* restaurant and bar snacks. *Visitors:* welcome without reservation. Snooker, billiards and pool. *Society Meetings:* catered for by bookings. Professional: John Yeo (01288 353635). Secretary: Mrs Pauline Ralph (01288 352006).

CAMBORNE. **Tehidy Park Golf Club,** Camborne TR14 0HH (Tel & Fax: 01209 842208). *Location:* A30 via Blackwater and Camborne by-passes to sign for Portreath. Parkland, wooded, 3 new lakes. 18 holes, 6241 yards. S.S.S. 71. *Green Fees:* information not available. *Eating facilities:* bar snacks, à la carte restaurant except Mondays. *Visitors:* welcome with Handicap Certificate. *Society Meetings:* by arrangement; early booking essential. Catering Manager: (01209 842557). Professional: J. Dumbreck (01209 842914). Secretary/Manager Ian Veale (Tel & Fax: 01209 842208).
e-mail:secretary-manager@tehidyparkgolfclub.co.uk
website: www.tehidyparkgolfclub.co.uk

The 15th hole at Bowood Park, Camelford

www.uk-golfguide.com

CAMELFORD. **Bowood Park Hotel & Golf Course,** Lanteglos, Camelford PL32 9RF (01840 213017; Fax: 01840 212622). *Location:* M4, M5, A30, A39 through Camelford, turn right to Boscastle/Tintagel before BP garage, then left after Park Lane Motors. Well groomed, parkland course set in 230 acres of rolling hills and woodland with 26 ponds and lakes. 18 hole, par 72. Covered driving range and Golf School. *Green Fees:* price on application. *Eating facilities:* full restaurant and bar facilities. *Visitors:* welcome. Large, well-stocked Pro Shop. Buggies for hire. Hotel accommodation available in 31 spacious en suite rooms, most with golf views, from £50.00 per person per night dinner, bed, breakfast and Golf. *Society Meetings:* society and corporate days welcome by arrangement. Professional: John Phillips. Hotel Manager: Verity Blake.
e-mail: golf@bowoodpark.com
website: www.bowoodpark.com

FALMOUTH. **Budock Vean Golf and Country House Hotel,** Near Mawnan Smith, Falmouth TR11 5LG (01326 250288; Fax: 01326 250892). *Location:* near Mawnan Smith, Falmouth – area of Helford River. 9 holes/18 tees, 5227 yards. Par 68. S.S.S. 65. *Green Fees:* weekdays £20.00, weekends £25.00. *Eating facilities:* two bars, two restaurants, lunchtime bar menu. *Visitors:* daily only for outside visitors who are most welcome, but must have Handicap Certificate and book start time. Hotel accommodation. Secretary: D. McFarlane (01326 252102). Golf Manager: A. Ramsden.

FALMOUTH. **Falmouth Golf Club,** Swanpool Road, Falmouth TR11 5BQ (01326 311262 / 314296; Fax: 01326 317783). *Location:* quarter of a mile west of Swanpool Beach, Falmouth, on the road to Maenporth. Under new ownership since July 2004, magnificent course with stunning sea and coastal views. 18 holes, 6037 yards. S.S.S. 70, Par 71. Driving range. *Green Fees:* £30.00 per 18 holes. *Eating facilities:* catering and bar all year round. *Visitors:* welcome at all times, except during major competitions. *Society Meetings:* always welcome. Professional: Nick Rogers.

HELSTON. **Helston Golf and Leisure,** Redruth Road, Wendron, Helston TR13 0LX (Golf: 01326 572228; Restaurant: 01326 565103). *Location:* one mile out of Helston on B3297 Redruth Road. Parkland course. 18 holes, 2000 yards. S.S.S. 54. Nets and practice green. *Green Fees:* £7.00 per 18 holes, day card £10.00. *Eating facilities:* licensed bar with meals and snacks. *Visitors:* welcome; family course, all ages welcome, pay and play; playable all weather. Club and ball hire £1. *Society Meetings:* all welcome, please book. Secretary/Owner: J.M.Othen.

HELSTON. **Mullion Golf Club,** Cury, Helston TR12 7BP (01326 241176). *Location:* from Helston on the A3083 past Culdrose Air Station, take first right past roundabout; signposted three miles. Cliff top and links. Indoor Golf Teaching Academy. 18 holes, 6037 yards. S.S.S. 70. *Green Fees:* information not available. *Eating facilities:* bar and catering available each day. Caterers: (01326 241231). *Visitors:* welcome, with Handicap only. *Society Meetings:* by prior arrangement. Professional: Ian Harris (01326 241176). Secretary/Treasurer: G. Fitter (01326 240685).

HELSTON. **RNAS Culdrose Golf Club,** Royal Naval Air Station, Helston TR12 7RH (01326 552413). *Location:* A3083 one mile from Helston towards Lizard. Flat parkland course built around part of the airfield. 18 holes, 6132 yards. S.S.S. 70. Large practice area. *Visitors:* members only. President: RNAS Culdrose.

LAUNCESTON. **Launceston Golf Club,** St Stephens, Launceston PL15 8HF (01556 773442). *Location:* one mile north of town on Bude road (B3254). Parkland. 18 holes, 6407 yards. S.S.S. 71. *Green Fees:* weekdays £25.00 per round, £30.00 per day. *Eating facilities:* available. *Visitors:* welcome. *Society Meetings:* catered for. Professional: J. Tozer (01566 775359). Secretary: P. M. Jones (01566 773442; Fax: 01566 777506).

LAUNCESTON. **Trethorne Golf Club,** Kennards House, Launceston PL15 8QE (01566 86903). *Location:* 200 yards off A30. Set in a picturesque valley with mature trees and water. 18 holes, 6432 yards. S.S.S. 68/69/71. Driving range, putting green. *Green Fees:* £28.00 weekdays; £32.00 weekends. Winter and twilight rates on application. *Eating facilities:* bar, lounge bar and restaurant seating 150. *Visitors:* welcome, please ring for tee times. Non-handicap players welcome after 1pm. Accommodation available in 35 en suite bedrooms at the Club. Driving range available. Voted by "Fore" magazine as the best 2 fore 1 course in 2000. *Society Meetings:* welcome, rates on application. Professional/ Secretary/Golf Manager: Mark Boundy.

LOOE. **Looe Golf Club,** Bindown, Looe PL13 1PX (01503 240239; Fax: 01503 240864). *Location:* three miles east of Looe on A387. Downland/parkland, panoramic views over countryside to sea; designed by Harry Vardon. 18 holes, 5940 yards. S.S.S. 69. Large practice ground. *Green Fees:* on application. *Eating facilities:* catering available. *Visitors:* most welcome, phone for tee reservations. Clubs, buggies and electric trolleys for hire. Golf tuition available. *Society Meetings:* welcome by arrangement. Professional: Jason Bowen. Secretary: Tony Day.

Visit the FHG Website
www.holidayguides.com
for details of the wide choice of accommodation featured in the full range of FHG titles

ENGLAND / Cornwall

CHIMNEYS • Port Gaverne, Port Isaac, Cornwall PL29 3SQ
Tel & Fax: 01208 880254
A charming 18th Century Cottage just 10 metres from the beach making it a wonderful venue for pets and their owners. Four bedrooms, two bathrooms, lounge, dining room and kitchen. Good size garden. Close to Eden Project and many golf courses. Brochure available from **Mrs Holmes**.

BOWOOD PARK
HOTEL & GOLF COURSE

"If you do nothing else in Cornwall, you MUST visit Bowood Park" – Golf Monthly

- Winner of Golf Monthly's Gold Award
- Par 72 6,700 yard championship course
- Visitors welcome
- Free draining USGA greens open all year round
- 3 star hotel with 31 luxury en-suite rooms
- Breaks start at just £90 for two nights half board INCLUDING golf

01840 213017
Call for further details

Bowood Park, Lanteglos, North Cornwall PL32 9RF
E: golf@bowoodpark.com www.bowoodpark.com

See also Inside Front Cover

The perfect venue for your golfing break, only 30 minutes from Exeter. With mature trees, lakes and streams, it is a real test of golf – 6432 yards, Par 71.

Trethorne's Professional Golf Shop offers the full range of golf equipment, lessons, repairs and advice on all your golfing needs.

Accommodation is available in 4 luxury lodges, plus new cottages at the club entrance; all built to the highest standard, with en suite bedrooms, TV, coffee-making facilities, and private gardens.

Trethorne Golf Club
Kennards House, Launceston PL15 8QE • 01566 86903
Fax: 01566 86929 • gen@trethornegolfclub.com
www.trethornegolfclub.com

FHG
PLEASE MENTION THIS GUIDE WHEN YOU WRITE OR PHONE TO ENQUIRE ABOUT CLUBS OR ACCOMMODATION

LOSTWITHIEL. **Lostwithiel Hotel, Golf and Country Club,** Lower Polscoe, Lostwithiel PL22 0HQ (01208 873550; Fax: 01208 873479). *Location:* off A390, Lostwithiel. Parkland course. 18 holes, 5984 yards. S.S.S. 71. Driving range and practice area. *Green Fees:* information not available. *Eating facilities:* bar and restaurant. Visitors: welcome by prior arrangement. 21 bedroomed 3 Star Hotel. *Society Meetings:* welcome by prior arrangement. Professional: Tony Nash (01208 873822).*
e-mail: reception@golf-hotel.co.uk
website: www.golf-hotel.co.uk

NEWQUAY. **Merlin Golf Club and Driving Range,** Mawgan Porth, Newquay TR8 4DN (01841 540222; Fax: 01841 541031). *Location:* on coast road between Newquay and Padstow, after Mawgan Porth take St. Eval Road, golf course on right. Heathland, fairly flat course. 18 holes, 6210 yards. S.S.S. 71. Covered driving range. *Green Fees:* information not available. *Eating facilities:* catering and bar all year round. *Visitors:* very welcome, some restrictions during club competitions. Buggies, carts and clubs for hire. *Society meetings:* very welcome. Proprietor: Mr Ross Oliver. Secretary: Mrs Margaret Oliver.*

NEWQUAY. **Newquay Golf Club,** Tower Road, Newquay TR7 1LT (01637 874354). *Location:* 400 yards from Newquay Town Centre. Gently undulating seaside course running parallel to the beach and open to wind. Breathtaking views. 18 holes, 6155 yards, S.S.S. 69. *Green Fees:* information not available. *Eating facilities:* lunches and bar snacks, evening meal by arrangement with the caterer on 01637 872091. *Visitors:* welcome at all times, please telephone. *Society Meetings:* catered for except Saturdays and Sundays. Professional: Mark Bevan (01637 874830). Secretary: G. Binney (01637 874354; Fax: 01637 874066).

NEWQUAY. **Treloy Golf Club,** Newquay TR7 4JN (01637 878554). *Location:* five minutes' drive from Newquay on the A3059 Newquay to St. Columb Major road. Parkland. 9 hole Executive golf course. First of its kind in Cornwall – sculptured greens, American Pencross grass, extensive mouldings and bunkers. 9 holes, 2143 yards, 1955 metres. Par 32. Practice green. *Green Fees:* information not available. *Eating facilities:* available, bar. *Visitors:* welcome. *Society Meetings:* welcome. Changing facilities, golf shop, club hire and buggy hire. Secretary: Jane Paull. *

NEWQUAY near. **Carvynick Golf and Country Club,** Carvynick, Summercourt, Near Newquay (01872 510716; Fax: 01872 510172). *Location:* turn off the A30 at Summercourt then take B3058 towards Newquay. Half a mile on left. Parkland and wooded course. 9 holes, 1246 yards. S.S.S. 27. *Green Fees:* information not available. *Eating facilities:* at 16th century village inn and restaurant. *Visitors:* welcome all year. Sauna, gym, indoor swimming pool and badminton court. Luxury holiday cottages available.*
e-mail: info@carvynick.co.uk
website: www.carvynick.co.uk

NEWQUAY near. **Holywell Bay Golf Club,** Holywell Bay, Near Newquay TR8 5PW (01637 830095; Fax: 01637 831000). *Location:* take A3075 out of Newquay then follow signs to Holywell Bay and Cubert. Par 3 Links course. 18 holes, 2755 yards. Pitch and putt. Open 7 days a week, all year round. *Green Fees:* £12.50. *Eating facilities:* bar and club house open April to October. *Visitors:* welcome at all times. Excellent value, no dress code and no Handicap. Fun Park with go-karts, boats etc. Tourist Park. *Society Meetings:* all welcome, ring for special prices. Secretary: R. Hartley (01637 830095).

PADSTOW. **Trevose Golf and Country Club,** Constantine Bay, Padstow PL28 8JB (01841 520208; Fax: 01841 521057). *Location:* M5 to A30 to A39 to B3274. At St Merryn turn right for golf club. Links course, superb test of golf in lovely coastal setting. H. Colt designed Championship course 18 holes, 6863 yards. S.S.S. 73. 9 hole full length course (Par 35) and one 9 hole short course (Par 29). *Green Fees:* information not available. *Eating facilities:* Club house with bar and restaurant providing à la carte catering facilities. *Visitors:* welcome if arranged by telephone beforehand; Handicap Certificate required. Accommodation, three tennis courts, heated swimming pool in summer. *Society Meetings:* welcome if arrangements have been made. Head Professional: Peter Green (01841 520261). Secretary: Nick Gammon (01841 520733).*
e-mail: admin@trevose-gc.co.uk
website: www.trevose-gc.co.uk

Please mention THE GOLF GUIDE when you enquire about clubs or accommodation

LOSTWITHIEL HOTEL, GOLF AND COUNTRY CLUB
Lower Polscoe, Lostwithiel, Cornwall PL22 0HQ
Tel: 01208 873550 • Fax: 01208 873479
e-mail: reception@golf-hotel.co.uk • website: www.golf-hotel.co.uk
Close to the Eden Project
This fine hotel and country club complex has been created from a cluster of old, mellow stone buildings. Amidst 150 acres of undulating, verdant countryside, the accommodation, cuisine and leisure facilities are truly outstanding. One may dine in style in the Black Prince Restaurant where imaginative dishes are made even more acceptable by the happy ambience of the place. Recreational diversions include a superb, 18-hole golf course with a floodlit driving range, indoor heated swimming pool, two all-weather tennis courts and gymnasium. Peaceful repose is assured by spacious and luxuriously appointed guest rooms, each one a haven of comfort. RAC ★★★.

See also Colour Advertisement on page 10

FHG Guides

publish a large range of well-known accommodation guides. We will be happy to send you details or you can use the order form at the back of this book.

stayplay

www.treglos hotel.com   www.merlingolfcourse.co.uk

TREGLOS
CONSTANTINE BAY
CORNWALL
Tel: 01841 520727

MERLIN
GOLF & COUNTRY CLUB
MAWGAN PORTH
CORNWALL
Tel: 01841 540222

See also Colour Advertisement on page 11

HARBOUR HOLIDAYS

Quality self catering accommodation in the picturesque harbour town of Padstow and the beautiful bays surrounding. tel: 01841 533402 fax: 01841 533115
e-mail: contact@harbourholidays.co.uk   **www.harbourholidays.co.uk**

See also Colour Advertisement on page 10

- Championship Golf Course of 18 holes. 6863 yards, S.S.S.71
- 2 x 9 hole courses. One 3100 yds, par 35, the other 1369 yds par 29.
- Excellently appointed Club House with Bar and Restaurant providing à la carte catering facilities.
- Superior accommodation in 7 Chalets, 6 Bungalows, 11 Flats, 7 Dormy flats and 4 cabins. Daily rates available.
- 3 Hard Tennis Courts.
- Heated Swimming Pool open from mid May to mid September.
- Extensive Pro Shop and boutique
- Six glorious sandy bays within about a mile of the Club House, with pools, open sea and surf bathing. Lovely coastline for walking.
- Convenient for shops.
- 8 miles from Civil Airport. Daily flights to and from London Gatwick & Stansted.
- Head Professional Peter Green • Open all year • Societies welcome

Trevose Golf and Country Club
Constantine Bay, Padstow PL28 8JB
Tel: 01841 520208 • Fax: 01841 521057
e-mail: info@trevose-gc.co.uk
www.trevose-gc.co.uk

See also Colour Advertisement on page 11

THE APPEARANCE OF AN ASTERISK (*) AT THE END OF A CLUB OR COURSE ENTRY INDICATES THAT UP-TO-DATE INFORMATION HAS NOT BEEN SUPPLIED

PENZANCE. **Cape Cornwall Golf & Country Club,** Cape Cornwall, St Just, Penzance TR19 7NL (Tel & Fax: 01736 788611). *Location:* A30 to Land's End, A3071 from Penzance to St Just, turn left at clock tower to Cape Cornwall. Cliff top course with spectacular coastal views. 18 holes, 5650 yards. S.S.S. 68, Par 70. Practice putting green and golf area. *Green Fees:* adults from £22.00 for 18 holes. *Eating facilities:* restaurant open daily; extensive à la carte evening menu Wed-Sat evenings incl. *Visitors:* welcome anytime. Accommodation available on site. Leisure facilities: gymnasium, indoor heated swimming pool, sauna, tanning suite. Golf shop now permanantly on site. *Society Meetings:* welcome; prior booking advisable. PGA Professional: Jonathan Lamb. Club Managers: E. Keddie, U. Handley.
e-mail: info@capecornwall.com
website: www.capecornwall.com

PENZANCE. **Praa Sands Golf Club,** Germoe Crossroads, Near Penzance TR20 9TQ (01736 763445; Fax: 01736 763399). *Location:* midway between Helston and Penzance on A394. Parkland - beautiful sea views from all holes. 9 holes, 4122 yards. S.S.S. 60 men, 63 ladies, Par 62. Putting green and net. *Green Fees:* information not available. *Eating facilities:* restaurant, bar snacks. *Visitors:* welcome at all times without Handicap Certificate except Sunday mornings. Clubs and trolleys for hire. *Society Meetings:* catered for by arrangement. Secretary: Simon Edwards. Proprietors: Kate and David Phillips. *
e-mail: praasandsgolf@aol.com

PERRANPORTH. **Perranporth Golf Club,** Budnic Hill, Perranporth TR6 0AB. Seaside links course overlooking Perranporth and beach. 18 holes, 6252 yards. S.S.S. 72. Par 72. Practice green. *Green Fees:* £25.00 to £35.00. *Eating facilities:* lunch and dinner. *Visitors:* welcome without reservation. Concessionary rates from selected holiday accommodation. *Society Meetings:* catered for with advance notice; concessionary rates. Professional: D. Michell (01872 572317). Secretary: David Mugford (01872 573701).
website: www.perranporthgolfclub.com

REDRUTH. **Radnor Golf and Ski Centre,** Radnor Road, Treleigh, Redruth TR16 5EL (01209 211059). *Location:* two miles north east of Redruth, signposted from A3047 at Treleigh and North Country crossroads. Purpose-built Par 3 - interesting layout. 9 holes, 1312 yards. S.S.S. 52. Covered driving range. *Green Fees:* information not available. *Eating facilities:* coffee, tea etc. *Visitors:* welcome. Indoor ski training machine. Small touring caravan site. Professional: Gordon Wallbank.

ST AUSTELL. **Carlyon Bay Hotel Golf Course,** Beach Road, Carlyon Bay, St Austell PL25 3RD (Hotel: 01726 812304; Golf Club: 01726 814250). *Location:* St Austell A390. Clifftop course running into parkland. 18 holes, 6597 yards. S.S.S. 71. Six acre practice ground. *Green Fees:* £25.00 to £42.00 depending on season. *Eating facilities:* bar open 11am to 11pm, food available during high season 10am to 9pm Tuesday to Friday, 10am to 6pm Saturday to Monday. *Visitors:* welcome, must phone Professional for starting times. Accommodation available in 4 star hotel. *Society Meetings:* catered for by arrangement. Professional: Mark Rowe (01726 814228). Manager: Peter Clemo (01726 814250).
e-mail: golf@carlyonbay.com
website: www.carlyonbay.com

ST AUSTELL. **St Austell Golf Club,** Tregongeeves, Tregongeeves Lane, St Austell PL26 7DS (01726 74756; Fax: 01726 71978). *Location:* one mile west of St Austell on A390 St Austell to Truro road. Parkland course. 18 holes, 6091 yards. S.S.S. 69. Floodlit driving range. *Green Fees:* information not available. *Eating facilities:* bar and restaurant – meals can be arranged. *Visitors:* welcome with reservation, must be club members and hold Handicap Certificate. *Society Meetings:* catered for weekdays by arrangement. Professional: Tony Pitts (01726 62681). Secretary: K. Trahair (01726 74756; Fax: 01726 71978).*

ST IVES. **Tregenna Castle Hotel Golf and Country Club,** St Ives TR26 2DE (01736 797381). *Location:* on the main road between Carbis Bay and St Ives, half a mile from town centre. Parkland, 73 acres of grounds with beautiful sea views overlooking St Ives Harbour and Atlantic coast – a very tricky course. 14 holes, 1846 yards. Par 42. *Green Fees:* £15.00 per round. *Visitors:* welcome. Accommodation available in the hotel if booked. *Society Meetings:* welcome. Golf Supervisor: Simon Davey.

THE APPEARANCE OF AN ASTERISK (*) AT THE END OF A CLUB OR COURSE ENTRY INDICATES THAT UP-TO-DATE INFORMATION HAS NOT BEEN SUPPLIED

FAIRWAYS CARAVANS
Perranporth Golf Club
Luxury 6 & 8 berth caravans sited in Cornwall's finest links course.
Families and Societies equally well catered for. **Free Golf Available.**
Contact: **Perranporth G.C., Budnic Hill, Perranporth, Cornwall TR6 0AB**
Telephone 01872 573701 • Website: www.perranporthgolfclub.com

ST IVES. **West Cornwall Golf Club,** Church Lane, Lelant, St Ives TR26 3DZ (Tel & Fax: 01736 753401). *Location:* two miles from St Ives - in village of Lelant - take Church Road, course situated approximately quarter of a mile past Lelant Church. True links course - wonderful coastal views. 18 holes, 5884 yards. S.S.S. 69. Practice ground, putting green. *Green Fees:* weekdays £28.00 per day; weekends £33.00. Five Day ticket £100.00, Seven Day ticket £125.00. *Eating facilities:* bar with bar menus and à la carte dining room. *Visitors:* must be golf club members with Handicap Certificate. Trolleys for hire. Snooker table. Home of "Long" Jim Barnes - first American Professional Champ 1916, Open Champion USA 1921, British Open Champion 1925 and World Champion of Golf 1921–1925. *Society Meetings:* welcome, written application required. Professional: Jason Broadway (01736 753177). Secretary: Ian Veale (01736 753401). e-mail: ian@westcornwallgolfclub.fsnet.co.uk website: www.westcornwallgolfclub.co.uk

SALTASH. **China Fleet Country Club,** Saltash PL12 6LJ (01752 848668). *Location:* one mile from Tamar Bridge. Parkland course with beautiful river views. 18 holes, 6551 yards, S.S.S. 72. 28 bay floodlit driving range. *Green Fees:* information on request. *Eating facilities:* bars and bar meals, full restaurant facilities, coffee shop. *Visitors:* welcome, Handicap Certificate required. Other facilities include large Pro Shop, full leisure facilities and 42 self contained apartments. *Society Meetings:* welcome, minimum number 12 persons. Professional: Nick Cook (01752 854665; Fax: 01752 848456). Golf Manager: Linda Goddard (01752 854657; Fax: 01752 848456).

SALTASH. **St Mellion Hotel, Golf and Country Club,** Near Saltash PL12 6SD (01579 351351; Fax: 01579 350537). *Location:* A38 to Saltash, A388 from Saltash to Callington. Parkland. Nicklaus Course: 18 holes, 6651 yards, par 72, S.S.S. 72 - designer Jack Nicklaus. Venue of the Benson & Hedges International Open 1990-1995. Old Course: 18 holes, 5782 yards, par 68. S.S.S. 68 - designer J. Hamilton-Stutt. Practice range. *Green Fees:* information not available. *Eating facilities:* full restaurant (awarded AA Rosette) and The Gallery Brasserie. *Visitors:* welcome at all times. Leisure club includes two indoor swimming pools, gymnasium, dance studio, sauna, steam room, spa pool, sports hall, creche. Skincare and spa centre. Founder member of the Premier Golf Clubs of Great Britain. *Society Meetings:* welcome. Accommodation available in Hotel overlooking 18th fairway, and in Fairway Lodges in the grounds. Head Professional: David Moon (01579 352002).*

TORPOINT. **Whitsand Bay Hotel Golf Club,** Portwrinkle, Torpoint PL11 3BU (01503 30276). *Location:* on coast six miles from Torpoint. Clifftop course. 18 holes, 5953 yards. S.S.S. 69. *Green Fees:* information not available. *Eating facilities:* hotel. *Visitors:* welcome at all times with Handicap Certificate. Swimming/leisure complex. *Society Meetings:* catered for and hotel accommodation arranged on application to hotel. Professional: D.S. Poole (01503 30778). Acting Secretary: B. Cranch (01752 829173). Hotel: (Tel & Fax: 01503 230276).*

TRURO. **Killiow Golf Club & Driving Range,** Kea, Near Truro TR3 6AG (01872 270246; Fax: 01872 240915). *Location:* take A39 Truro to Falmouth road, turn right into club at first Playing Place roundabout (2½ miles). 18 holes, Par 72. All-weather floodlit driving range open 8am to 9pm weekdays (weekends until 6pm). *Green Fees:* information on request. *Eating facilities:* bar and restaurant. *Visitors:* only restricted by competitions; phone for availability. Secretary: John Crowson (01872 266876).

TRURO. **Truro Golf Club,** Treliske, Truro TR1 3LG (01872 272640). *Location:* two miles west of Truro on A390 to Redruth. Undulating parkland with magnificent views. 18 holes, 5357 yards. S.S.S. 66. *Green Fees:* weekdays £25.00 per day or round, weekends and Bank Holidays £30.00 per day or round. *Eating facilities:* restaurant and bar snacks available. *Visitors:* welcome with Handicap Certificates. Buggies and carts available. *Society Meetings:* welcome – special rates on application. Professional: N. Bicknell (01872 276595). Secretary: H.W.D. Leicester (01872 278684; Fax: 01872 225972).

ST MELLION GOLF BREAKS offer

- Stunning Golf Course locations at or near St Mellion
- Inclusive golf packages from only £305 for two people or less than £100 for six or more in top quality accommodation
- Free pool and gym membership at St Mellion • Societies of up to 30 welcome.

We have the widest and best selection of self-catering golf breaks in and around the beautiful courses at St Mellion SE Cornwall.

OAKRIDGE COTTAGES are modern, centrally heated, two and three-bedroom stone detached houses with superb golf course views. Alternatively just two miles up the road, **TREHILL COTTAGES** offer relaxing lakeside accommodation in a peaceful countryside setting. There are seven cottages ranging from a one-bedroom detached cottage with its own Aga to a huge six-bedroom cottage perfect for a large golfing party.

All our golf breaks include free golf at St Mellion so two people can play these great championship courses for as little as £305 per week fully inclusive.

Call us on **01579 383917** or e-mail **info@stmelliongolfbreaks.co.uk**   www.stmelliongolfbreaks.co.uk

See also Colour Advertisement on page 10

WADEBRIDGE. **Roserrow Golf and Country Club,** Roserrow, St Minver, Near Wadebridge PL27 6QT. *Location:* between Wadebridge and Polzeath off the B3314. Undulating wooded valley. 18 holes, 6507 yards, 5951 metres. S.S.S. 71. 15 bay driving range with indoor swing-analysis studio, practice putting green. *Green Fees:* £25.00 July and August, £20.00 rest of year. Discounts for groups of 8+. *Eating facilities:* restaurant, bar food available. *Visitors:* always welcome, phone for tee times. Luxury self-catering accommodation on site. Indoor swimming pool, fitness suite, sauna, jacuzzi, steam room, solarium, outdoor tennis courts. Buggies, electric trolleys, carts for hire. *Society Meetings:* welcome by arrangement. Club Manager: Simon Welch (01208 863000; Fax: 01208 863002).
e-mail: roserrow@aol.com
website: www.roserrow.co.uk

WADEBRIDGE. **St Enodoc Golf Club,** Rock, Wadebridge PL27 6LD (01208 863216; Fax: 01208 862976). *Location:* take the B3314 from Wadebridge, signposted Rock (three miles). Seaside links. Two courses: Church Course 18 holes, 6243 yards. S.S.S. 69; Holywell Course 18 holes, 4103 yards. S.S.S. 61. Practice range, putting greens, etc. *Green Fees:* information not available. *Eating facilities:* restaurant and bar snacks. *Visitors:* Handicap Certificates (24 and below) required for Church Course; no restrictions for Holywell Course. *Society Meetings:* all welcome by arrangement with the Secretary. Professional: Nick Williams (01208 862402*

WADEBRIDGE. **St Kew Golf Club,** St Kew Highway, Near Wadebridge, Bodmin PL30 3EF (Tel & Fax: 01208 841500). *Location:* on the main A39, two-and-a-half miles from Wadebridge towards Camelford. Parkland course, 9 holes (18 tees), 4543 yards. S.S.S. 62. Covered driving range, practice chipping/bunker area. *Green Fees:* information not available. *Eating facilities:* coffee shop and restaurant; licensed bar. *Visitors:* welcome. No restrictions. *Society Meetings:* discounts for eight or more. Professional: Nick Rogers (Tel & Fax: 01208 841500). Secretary: John Brown.*

ISLES OF SCILLY

ST MARY'S. **Isles Of Scilly Golf Club,** St Mary's, Isles of Scilly (01720 422692). *Location*: one mile from Hugh Town, St Mary's. Heathland links course with magnificent views. 9 holes, 18 tees, 5898 yards. S.S.S. 69. Par 73. *Green Fees:* £23.50 per day. *Eating facilities*: lunches and evening meals available. *Visitors*: welcome. Secretary: Sam Ellis (01720 423899).

Trevose Golf & Country Club, Padstow

PLEASE MENTION THE GOLF GUIDE WHEN YOU WRITE OR PHONE TO ENQUIRE ABOUT CLUBS OR ACCOMMODATION

Cumbria

ALSTON. **Alston Moor Golf Club,** The Hermitage, Middleton in Teesdale Road, Alston CA9 3DB (Tel & Fax: 01434 381675; Fax: 01434 381675). *Location:* one and three quarter miles from Alston on B6277 to Barnard Castle. Penrith, Hexham, Carlisle all within 30 miles. Parkland with panoramic views (highest golf course in England). 10 holes (18 tees), 5456 yards. S.S.S. 66. Practice ground. *Green Fees:* information not available. *Eating facilities:* 19th Hole bar, catering at weekends May to October. *Visitors:* welcome anytime, prior notice required for groups. Competitions most Sundays, tee reserved 9am to 10am and 1pm to 2.30pm. *Society Meetings:* welcome by arrangement. Secretary: Mr H. Robinson (01434 381354).*

APPLEBY. **Appleby Golf Club,** Brackenber Moor, Appleby-in-Westmorland CA16 6LP (017683 51432). *Location:* off A66 at Coupland Beck, two miles east of Appleby. Moorland course. 18 holes, 5901 yards. S.S.S. 68. *Green Fees:* weekdays £20.00 per round, £25.00 per day; weekends and Bank Holidays £24.00 per round, £30.00 per day. *Eating facilities:* meals available each day. *Visitors:* welcome with Handicap Certificate without reservation. *Society Meetings:* 12 or more catered for by prior arrangement. Handicap Certificate required. Professional: James Taylor (017683 52922). Secretary: J.M.F. Doig.

ASKAM-IN-FURNESS. **Dunnerholme Golf Club,** Duddon Road, Askam-in-Furness LA16 7AW (01229 462675/467421). *Location:* A595 Askam-in-Furness, over level crossing. Seaside links with stream on four holes, spectacular views from elevated 6th green. 10 holes (18 tees), 6154 yards. S.S.S. 70 White, 70 Red, 69 Yellow. Practice ground. *Green Fees:* £15.00 per day. *Eating facilities:* bar in evenings; meals not available. *Visitors:* welcome without reservation, excluding competition days. Competitions Saturday mornings and Sundays May to October. *Society Meetings:* catered for by prior arrangement. Secretary: Mr A. Haines (01229 462675 day, 01229 826198 evenings).

ASPATRIA. **Brayton Park Golf Club,** Lakeside Inn, Brayton, Aspatria CA7 3TD (016973 20840). *Location:* one mile east of Aspatria. Parkland course. 9 holes. S.S.S. 65 (18 holes). *Green Fees:* information not available. *Eating facilities:* available at Lakeside Inn. *Visitors:* always welcome. *Society Meetings:* welcome. Coarse fishing pond. Secretary: David Warwick (016973 71708).*

BARROW-IN-FURNESS. **Barrow Golf Club,** Rakesmoor Lane, Hawcoat, Barrow-in-Furness LA14 4QB (01229 825444). *Location:* one mile from Barrow town centre, approach via Dalton bypass, turn left at Bank Lane opposite "Kimberley Clarke" paper mill. Clubhouse at top of hill on left hand side. 18 holes, 6184 yards, 5679 metres. S.S.S. 70. *Green Fees:* Monday to Friday £25.00; Saturdays, Sundays and Bank Holidays £30.00. County Cards/2 for 1 accepted. Ladies' Day Fridays. *Eating facilities:* catering available by prior arrangement. *Visitors:* welcome without formal reservation. *Society Meetings:* welcome by prior arrangement, call Club Administrator or Secretary. Club Administrator: E. Payne (01229 825444). Secretary: W. R. Edwards (01229 835406)
e-mail: barrowgolf@supanet.com

BARROW-IN-FURNESS. **Furness Golf Club,** Central Drive, Walney Island, Barrow-in-Furness LA14 3LN (01229 471232). *Location*: A590 into Barrow via Dalton by-pass, follow sign to Walney Island, over bridge, straight on at lights. Clubhouse half-a-mile on right hand side. Seaside links. 18 holes, 6363 yards. S.S.S. 71. Practice area. *Green Fees*: information not available. *Eating facilities*: full catering (except Mondays), licensed bar. *Visitors*: parties by prior arrangement, others without reservation; must hold current Handicap Certificate. Ladies' Day - Wednesdays; Competition Days - Saturdays or Sundays in summer. *Society Meetings*: welcome (tee reservation by prior arrangement). Secretary: J.W. Anderson.*
e-mail: jimanderson@talkgas.net

Visit the FHG website
www.holidayguides.com
for details of the wide choice of accommodation featured in the full range of FHG titles

·K·U·P·E·R·A·R·D·

BRAMPTON. **Brampton Golf Club,** Talkin Tarn, Brampton CA8 1HN (016977 2255). *Location*: situated on the Brampton-Castle Carrock road (B6413), approximately one and a half miles from Brampton. Rolling fell countryside, excellent views. 18 holes, 6407 yards. S.S.S. 71. Driving range/practice facilities available plus snooker and pool tables. *Green Fees:* information not available. *Eating facilities:* catering available every day during playing season and on most days during winter period. *Visitors:* welcome without reservation but pre-booking is advisable. *Society Meetings:* very much catered for, limited numbers at weekends. Secretary and contact for visiting societies/party bookings: I.J. Meldrum (01900 827985). Professional: S. Wilkinson (016977 2000; Fax: 016977 41487).*
e-mail: secretary@bramptongolfclub.com
website: www.bramptongolfclub.com

CARLISLE. **Carlisle Golf Club,** Aglionby, Carlisle CA4 8AG (01228 513029). *Location*: on A69 Newcastle Road, half a mile from Junction 43 of M6. Parkland course with wide variety of trees, strategic hazards, etc. 18 holes, 6278 yards. S.S.S. 70. Practice area. *Green Fees*: weekdays £35.00 per round, £45.00 per day; £40.00 per round Sundays only; Saturdays with member only. Subject to review. Package deals for parties of 12 or more. *Eating facilities*: bar meals, restaurant, two bars, etc. *Visitors*: welcome except on a Saturday (unless with a member), unless tee is reserved; visitor bookings (01228 513029). Trolley hire. *Society Meetings*: catered for Mondays, Wednesdays and Fridays. Professional: Mr G. Lisle (01228 513241). Secretary: Roger Johnson (01228 513029; Fax: 01228 513303).
website: www.carlislegolfclub.org

CARLISLE. **Dalston Hall Golf Club,** (aka Caldow Golf Club) Dalston Hall, Dalston, Carlisle CA5 7JX (01228 710165). *Location:* leave M6 at Exit 42, take road to Dalston; at Dalston take B5299, Carlisle road, course on the right after one mile. Scenic parkland course. 10 holes, (18 Tees) 5294 yards. S.S.S. 67. Practice area. *Green Fees*: £15.00 to £20.00 for 18 holes. *Eating facilities:* full catering and bar facilities *Visitors:* welcome, tee reservation is required at Bank Holidays and weekends and after 4pm during the week. Pool table. *Society Meetings:* welcome by prior arrangement. Secretary: Nigel Farthing (01228 710165).
e-mail: nigel@etmanco.fsnet.co.uk
website: www.dalstonhall.co.uk

CARLISLE. **The Eden Golf Course,** Crosby-on-Eden, Carlisle CA6 4RA (01228 573003). *Location*: M6 Junction 44, A689 to Low Crosby. Parkland course incorporating lakes, streams and River Eden. 18 holes, 6368 yards. S.S.S. 72. 9-hole course. *Green Fees*: weekdays £28.00, weekends £32.00. *Eating facilities*: full restaurant and bar meals. *Visitors*: welcome at all times, telephone booking requested. *Society Meetings*: welcome at all times, telephone booking requested. 16 bay floodlit driving range and practice facilities. Professional: Steven Harrison.
website: www.edengolf.co.uk

CARLISLE. **Stoney Holme Municipal Golf Course,** St Aidans Road, Carlisle (01228 33208). *Location:* off A69 between M6 Junction 42 and town. Parkland course, 18 holes, 6000 yards. S.S.S. 68. Large practice area, changing rooms. *Green Fees:* information not available. *Eating facilities:* bar and restaurant. *Visitors:* welcome without reservation, but booking advisable weekends and Bank Holidays. *Society Meetings:* welcome by prior arrangement. Professional: Stephen Ling (01228 625511). *

EMBLETON. **Cockermouth Golf Club,** The Clubhouse, Embleton, Near Cockermouth CA13 9SG (017687 76223/76941; Fax: 017687 76941). *Location:* three miles east of Cockermouth. Scenic fell land course. 18 holes, 5496 yards, S.S.S. 67. *Green Fees:* weekdays £20.00; weekends and Bank Holidays £25.00. Concessionary rates parties of 10 or more (includes food): £25.00 weekdays, £30.00 weekends. *Eating facilities:* bar, meals by arrangement with Secretary. *Visitors:* welcome except Wednesdays between 3.30pm and 6pm, some restrictions at weekends. Some trolleys for hire. *Society Meetings:* welcome as per visitors. Secretary: R.S.Wimpress (Tel & Fax: 017687 76941 mornings only weekdays).

GRANGE-OVER-SANDS. **Grange Fell Golf Club,** Fell Road, Grange-over-Sands LA11 6HB (015395 32536). *Location:* Cartmel Road from Grange one mile. Hillside course with panoramic views. 9 holes, 4840 metres. S.S.S. 66. *Green Fees:* weekdays £15.00, weekends and Bank Holidays £20.00. *Eating facilities:* bar. *Visitors:* welcome without reservation, closed most Sundays until 4pm during season. *Society Meetings:* not catered for. Secretary: Mr J. G. Park (015395 58513).

GRANGE-OVER-SANDS. **Grange-over-Sands Golf Club,** Meathop Road, Grange-over-Sands LA11 6QX (015395 33180; Fax: 015395 33754). *Location:* leave the A590 at roundabout signposted Grange, take the B5277 for approximately three miles. Flat parkland. 18 holes, 5958 yards, 5422 metres. S.S.S. 69. Practice area, bunker, green. *Green Fees:* weekdays £25.00 per round, £30.00 per day; weekends and Bank Holidays £30.00 per round, £35.00 per day. *Eating facilities:* dining room open every day; bar snacks and bar every day. *Visitors:* welcome without reservation weekdays and most weekends. *Society Meetings:* by arrangement with Secretary. Professional: Andrew J. Pickering (015395 35937). Secretary: S.D. Wright (015395 33754).

KENDAL. **Carus Green Golf Club,** Burneside Road, Kendal LA9 6EB (Tel & Fax: 01539 721097). *Location*: one mile north-east of Kendal on Burneside Road. Flat parkland course. 18 holes, 5716 yards, S.S.S. 68. 160 yard practice ground, putting green, net. *Green Fees*: information not available. *Eating facilities*: light snacks available, licensed. *Visitors*: welcome anytime, restrictions on competition days. Tuition available. Clubs, buggy and trolley hire. *Society Meetings*: welcome anytime, please call for details. Professional: David Turner (Tel & Fax: 01539 721097). Secretary: Bryan Lumsden.*

ENGLAND / Cumbria 163

Brampton Golf Club
**TALKIN TARN, BRAMPTON
CUMBRIA CA8 1HN**
www.bramptongolfclub.com

Consider the rest, play the best

Situated in a stunning corner of North Cumbria, the jewel of the region's crown boasts panoramic views of the Lake District, Southern Scotland and the Pennines. The undulating heathland Par 72 course offers both challenging golf and an idyllic setting which has been likened to a "mini Gleneagles".
The clubhouse provides a full range of first-class services and facilities. Visiting societies, corporate golf days and visitors most welcome, but pre-booking clearly recommended.
For societies/visiting party bookings please contact Ian Meldrum (Secretary) on 01900 827985 or e-mail: secretary@bramptongolfclub.com. Other visitor enquiries contact the Professional on 016977 2000

See also Colour Advertisement on page 37

Stony Holme Golf Course, Carlisle
Where Great Golfing Costs Less

With the magnificent backdrop of the Lakeland Fells, this mature, flat, easy walking parkland course with abundant water hazards is a challenge to any golfer. Delicious food is served in the Riverside Restaurant & Bar. A fully stocked shop and golf professional are available. Tailored golf packages for visiting groups and a pay-as-you-play system is also in operation.

BBC GOLF MAGAZINE RECOMMENDED

St Aidans Road, Carlisle, Cumbria CA7 1LS • 01228 625511
e-mail: StephenL.@Carlisle-City.gov.uk

The Eden Golf Club & Driving Range

**CROSBY-ON-EDEN, CARLISLE,
CUMBRIA CA6 4PZ
TEL: 01228 573003 • FAX: 01228 818435**

* 18-HOLE CHAMPIONSHIP PARKLAND COURSE
* NEW FOR 2007 - ADDITIONAL 9 HOLE GOLF COURSE
* FLOODLIT COVERED DRIVING RANGE • 18-HOLE PUTTING GREENS
* PITCHING GREENS AND PRACTICE BUNKERS
* EXCELLENT RESTAURANT AND LOUNGE BAR WITH OPEN FIRE

*The Eden Golf Club is a hidden gem situated along the banks of the River Eden. Tight tree-lined fairways and numerous natural water hazards mark this course out as a great test of golf.
Situated 5 miles from Junction 44 of M6, one hour from Newcastle. On the doorstep of the Lakes, Hadrian's Wall and Gretna Green.*

e-mail: edengolf1@aol.com • www.edengolf.co.uk

See also Colour Advertisement on page 37

COCKERMOUTH GOLF CLUB

MIDWEEK: ONLY £25. Midweek Tee reservations available most days • Coffee and biscuits on arrival • 9 holes of golf - Soup and Sandwiches • 18 holes of golf - 2 course evening meal
SATURDAYS: ONLY £30. First Tee available 10.30am - 12.00pm • Coffee and biscuits on arrival • 18 holes of golf - 2 course meal on completion.

VISITING PARTIES MINIMUM OF 10 GOLFERS
The Club House, Embleton, Near Cockermouth, Cumbria CA13 9SG
Tel: 01768 776223 • Tel & Fax: 017687 76941• www.cockermouthgolf.co.uk

---

**PLEASE MENTION THE GOLF GUIDE WHEN YOU WRITE
OR PHONE TO ENQUIRE ABOUT CLUBS OR ACCOMMODATION**

164 Cumbria / ENGLAND　　　THE GOLF GUIDE 2006

KENDAL. **Kendal Golf Club**, The Heights, Kendal LA9 4PQ (01539 723499). *Location:* off A6 at Town Hall, signposted. Undulating parkland course with magnificent views in all directions. 18 holes, 5769 yards. S.S.S. 68. *Green Fees:* weekdays £22.00 per round, £26.00 per day; weekends £27.50 per round, £32.50 per day. *Eating facilities:* meals available all day; bar. *Visitors:* welcome with reservation. Buggy hire available. Professional: Peter Scott (01539 723499). website: www.kendalgolfclub.co.uk

KESWICK. **Keswick Golf Club,** Threlkeld Hall, Threlkeld, Keswick CA12 4SX (017687 79324; Fax: 017687 79861). *Location:* four miles from Keswick on A66 road to Penrith. Scenic fell and parkland course. 18 holes, 6225 yards. S.S.S. 72, Par 71. Extensive practice area. *Green Fees:* weekdays £20.00; weekends and Bank Holidays £25.00. *Eating facilities:* bar and restaurant. *Visitors:* welcome, Ladies' Day Thursdays 11am to 2pm. *Society Meetings:* welcome by arrangement. Professional: Gary Watson. Administration Manager: Lesley Roberts

KIRKBY LONSDALE. **Kirkby Lonsdale Golf Club,** Scaleber Lane, Barbon, Kirkby Lonsdale, Carnforth, Lancs LA6 2LJ (015242 76265). *Location:* three and a half miles from Kirkby Lonsdale on the A683 Sedbergh Road. Parkland course in Lune Valley crossing Barbon Beck and along the banks of the River Lune. 18 holes, 6538 yards. S.S.S. 72. Par 72. Practice area, lessons. *Green Fees:* weekdays £28.00; weekends £33.00. Subject to review. *Eating facilities:* full facilities. *Visitors:* welcome, no restrictions except on competition days. Handicap Certificate required or certificate of competence. *Society Meetings:* welcome by arrangement. Package deals available for groups of eight or more. Professional: Chris Barrett (015242 76366). Secretary: Geoffrey Hall (015242 76365).
e-mail: KLGolf@Dial.Pipex.com
website: www.klgolf.dial.pipex.com

THE APPEARANCE OF AN ASTERISK (*) AT THE END OF A CLUB OR COURSE ENTRY INDICATES THAT UP-TO-DATE INFORMATION HAS NOT BEEN SUPPLIED

KIRKBY LONSDALE near. **Casterton Golf Course,** Sedbergh Road, Casterton, Near Kirkby Lonsdale, Cumbria LA6 2LA (015242 71592; Fax: 015242 74387). *Location:* from Junction 36 of M6 take A65 to Skipton, five miles to Kirkby Lonsdale, one mile north on A683. Undulating parkland course, scenic with wonderful views. 9 holes, 5726 yards. S.S.S. 68. Practice area and driving net. *Green Fees:* weekdays £12.00; weekends and Bank Holidays £15.00. *Eating facilities:* light refreshments and shop in clubhouse (licensed). *Visitors:* always welcome. Booking advisable. Clubhouse has well-stocked Pro Shop, changing facilities and toilets. Clubs and trolleys available for hire. Two holiday flats sleeping four/five. *Society Meetings:* parties of under 32 persons only. Professional: Roy Williamson. Secretary: Elizabeth Makinson. Course Manager: John Makinson.
e-mail: castertongc@hotmail.com
website: www.castertongolf.co.uk

MARYPORT. **Maryport Golf Club Ltd,** Bankend, Maryport (01900 812605). *Location:* approximately one mile north of Maryport on B5300 towards Silloth. 9 holes links extended to 18 with new holes parkland type, exposed, relatively flat. 18 holes, 6088 yards. S.S.S. 69. *Green Fees:* weekdays £23.00, weekends £28.00. *Eating facilities:* available. *Visitors:* welcome, no restrictions. *Society Meetings:* catered for by prior arrangement. Secretary: Mrs L. Hayton.

PENRITH. **Penrith Golf Club,** Salkeld Road, Penrith CA11 8SG (01768 891919). *Location:* off Junction 41 M6 motorway, towards Penrith, golf course signposted. Parkland course. 18 holes, 6026 yards. S.S.S. 69. Range facilities. *Green Fees:* weekdays £26.00/£31.00; weekends £31.00/£36.00. *Eating facilities:* all day catering seven days a week. *Visitors:* welcome, book through Professional shop, tee times required at weekends. *Society Meetings:* by appointment with Secretary. Professional: Mr Garry Key (Tel & Fax: 01768 891919). Secretary: Mr David Noble (Tel & Fax: 01768 891919).

ST BEES. **St Bees Golf Club**, Peckmill, Beach Road, St Bees (01946 824300). *Location:* four miles south of Whitehaven off A595. Hilly, seaside course. 9 holes, 5307 yards. S.S.S. 66. *Green Fees:* £12.00. *Visitors:* welcome weekdays (except after 4pm Wednesdays). Only after 3pm weekends. Bar available April to September between 12 noon and 8pm. Secretary: B. G. Ritson.*

KIRKBY LONSDALE GOLF CLUB
GOLF SOCIETIES & VISITING PARTIES

*Golfing packages from £38.00 to include:
Coffee & Biscuits on arrival, Full Day's
Golf, Lunch and Evening Meal.*

Telephone: 015242 76365

Scaleber Lane, Barbon, Kirkby Lonsdale, Carnforth LA6 2LJ
Telephone: Secretary 015242 76365 – Pro Shop 015242 76366 - Caterer 015242 76367
e-mail: klgolf@dial.pipex.com   website: www.klgolf.dial.pipex.com

THE GOLF GUIDE 2006　　　　　　　　ENGLAND / Cumbria　165

SEASCALE. **Seascale Golf Club,** Seascale CA20 1QL (Tel & Fax: 019467 28202). *Location:* B5344 off A595 to north of village. Links. 18 holes, 6416 yards. S.S.S. 71. 16-acre practice ground. *Green Fees:* information not available. *Eating facilities:* catering available every day. *Visitors:* welcome when no tee reservations in force. *Society Meetings:* catered for by arrangement with Secretary. Professional: Sean Rudd (019467 21799). Secretary: David Stobart (019467 28202).*

SEDBERGH. **Sedbergh Golf Club,** Sedbergh LA10 5SS (015396 21551). *Location:* five miles J37, M6, one mile out of Sedbergh on road to Dent, well signposted. Superbly scenic course in Yorkshire Dales National Park. 9 holes, 5588 yards. S.S.S. 69. *Green Fees:* weekdays and weekends £20.00 per round. *Eating facilities:* full bar and catering facilities. *Visitors:* welcome, but prior booking advisable (essential at weekends). Various packages available. Golf shop; hire trolleys. *Society Meetings:* very welcome by prior arrangement. Manager: Craig Gardner (015396 21551).

SILECROFT. **Silecroft Golf Club,** Silecroft, Near Millom LA18 4NX (01229 774250). *Location:* three miles north of Millom on the coast. Near junction of A595 and A5093, eight miles west of Broughton-in-Furness. Seaside links course with good greens. 9 holes (18 tees), 5877 yards. S.S.S. 68 (67 off Yellow tees). *Green Fees:* £15.00 per day Monday to Friday, £20.00 per day weekends and Bank Holidays. *Eating facilities:* catering available at nearby public house (Silecroft Miners Arms), bar at club. *Visitors:* welcome, although access to the course may be restricted on Bank Holidays or on competition days. Secretary: Mr D.L.A. MacLardie (01229 774342).

SILLOTH. **Silloth on Solway Golf Club,** The Clubhouse, Silloth, Carlisle CA7 4BL (016973 31304). *Location:* from south - M6 Junction 41 B5305 Wigton, B5302 Silloth. From north and east - M6 Junction 43 A69 Carlisle, A595/596 Wigton, B5302 Silloth. Seaside links, rated in the best five links courses in England. 18 holes, 6618 yards. S.S.S. 73. Practice facilities. *Green Fees:* weekdays £33.00 per day, weekends and Bank Holidays £45.00 per round. Subject to review. Restriction, only one round allowed per day at weekends. *Eating facilities:* full bar and catering. *Visitors:* welcome without reservation. *Society Meetings:* welcome midweek, weekend times available on request. Professional: J. Graham (016973 32404; Fax: 016973 31782). Secretary: John Rich (016973 31304; Fax: 016973 31782).

ULVERSTON. **Ulverston Golf Club Ltd,** Bardsea Park, Ulverston LA12 9QJ (01229 582824). *Location:* Exit 36, M6. A590 to Barrow then A5087 to Bardsea village. Wooded parkland. 18 holes, 6201 yards. S.S.S. 70. *Green Fees:* information not available. *Eating facilities:* lunch and bar snacks. *Visitors:* welcome except Saturdays (competition day), and Tuesdays (Ladies' Day). Must be members of accredited golf club and have a Handicap. *Society Meetings:* welcome, write with reservation to the Secretary. Professional: M.R. Smith (01229 582806). Secretary: R. Rushforth.

WHITEHAVEN. **Whitehaven Golf Club,** Red Lonning, Whitehaven CA28 8UD (01946 591177). *Location:* set in parkland above Whitehaven. Parkland course with spectacular views of the Lakeland fells. 18 holes, 6079 yards, par 70. *Green Fees:* information not available. *Eating facilities:* clubhouse and bar. *Visitors:* always welcome. Tee booking system in operation from May 25th, phone 01946 591144. Professional: Craig Hamilton. *
e-mail: whitehavengolf@freeuk.com
website: www.whitehavengolf.freeuk.com

WINDERMERE. **Windermere Golf Club,** Cleabarrow, Windermere LA23 3NB (015394 43123). *Location:* one mile from Bowness-on-Windermere on Crook road, B5284. Idyllic National Park setting. 18 holes, 5122 yards, S.S.S. 65. Practice ground. *Green Fees:* Monday to Friday £30.00 per round (2005), weekends and Bank Holidays £37.00 per round (2005). *Eating facilities:* Restaurant. *Visitors:* made most welcome. *Society Meetings:* catered for by prior arrangement with the Secretary, numbers from 12 to 50, corporate days by arrangement. Professional: W.S.M. Rooke (015394 43550). Secretary: R.M.Cox (015394 43123).
website: www.windermeregolfclub.net

WORKINGTON. **Workington Golf Club Ltd,** Branthwaite Road, Workington CA14 4SS (01900 603460). *Location:* on A596, two miles east of town. Meadowland. 18 holes, 6252 yards. S.S.S. 70. *Green Fees:* information not available. *Eating facilities:* available seven days a week. *Visitors:* welcome without reservation; must have own insurance and must be members of recognised golf club. Buggies only by prior arrangement with Pro. *Society Meetings:* welcome by prior arrangement. Professional: A. Drabble (01900 67828). Secretary: T.F. Stout (01900 603460).*

SEASCALE GOLF CLUB
Play our challenging links course

Superb 6,416 yards traditional links. Reduced terms for daily parties of 8 or more. Any three consecutive days golf for £80. Bookings now being taken for 2007. Both midweek and weekend dates available. Societies and groups assured of a warm and friendly welcome.
For further details contact: David Stobart, The Secretary, Seascale Golf Club, Seascale, Cumbria or phone 01946 728202

See also Colour Advertisement on page 38

Derbyshire

ALFRETON. **Alfreton Golf Club,** Wingfield Road, Alfreton DE55 7LH (01773 832070). *Location:* B6024 (Matlock Road) one mile from Alfreton. Parkland course. 11holes, 5121 yards. S.S.S. 66. *Green Fees:* £19.00 per round, £28.00 per day. *Eating facilities:* bar snacks except Mondays. *Visitors:* welcome Monday to Friday with reservation. *Society Meetings:* catered for. Professional: (01773 831901). Secretary: S. Bradley.

ASHBOURNE. **Ashbourne Golf Club Ltd,** Off Wyaston Road, Ashbourne DE6 1NB (01335 342078; Fax: 01335 347937). *Location:* Wyaston Road, Ashbourne, one and a half miles out of Ashbourne. Undulating parkland. 18 holes, 6402 yards. S.S.S. 71. Practice area. *Green Fees:* information on request. *Eating facilities:* available daily; parties must make prior arrangement. *Visitors:* welcome by arrangement with Professional. *Society Meetings:* welcome weekdays. Professional: Andrew Smith (01335 347960). Secretary: J.W. Hammond (01335 342078).

BAKEWELL. **Bakewell Golf Club,** Station Road, Bakewell DE45 1GB (01629 812307). *Location:* Sheffield Road out of Bakewell, turn right over River Bridge. Parkland, scenic hillside course. 9 holes, 5240 yards. S.S.S. 68. *Green Fees:* information not available. *Eating facilities:* bar meals, formal catering except Mondays. *Visitors:* welcome weekdays, occasional weekends by prior arrangement. *Society Meetings:* welcome by arrangement. Secretary: Mrs P. Moody.*

BRAILSFORD. **Brailsford Golf Club,** Pools Head Lane, Brailsford, Near Ashbourne DE6 3BU (01335 360096). *Location*: on the main A52 Derby to Ashbourne road, Derby 6 miles, Ashbourne 5 miles. Parkland course. 9 holes, 6219 yards (18 holes), S.S.S. 70. Practice facilities and driving range. *Green Fees*: weekdays 9 holes £10.00, 18 holes £13.50; weekends 9 holes £12.00, 18 holes £16.50. Special rates for juniors, Senior Citizens (weekdays only). *Eating facilities*: available. *Visitors:* welcome at any time except Sunday mornings. Tuition available - two teaching Professionals. *Society Meetings*: welcome except Sunday mornings. Special rates available. Professional: David McCarthy (01335 360096). Secretary: Mr K. Wilson (01332 553703).*

BURTON-ON-TRENT. **Burton-on-Trent Golf Club,** 43 Ashby Road East, Burton-on-Trent DE15 0PS *Location:* three miles east of Burton-on-Trent on the A511 towards Ashby de la Zouch. Undulating parkland course with many trees, testing finishing hole. 18 holes, 6579 yards. S.S.S. 71. Practice ground. *Green Fees:* weekdays £28.00 per round, £38.00 per day; weekends and Bank Holidays £32.00 per round, £40.00 per day. Special rates by arrangement. *Eating facilities:* dining room, lounge bar. *Visitors:* welcome weekdays, restrictions at weekends and Bank Holidays. *Society Meetings:* welcome, apply in writing for terms. Professional:

Gary Stafford (01283 562240). Secretary: W. Nicholson (Tel & Fax: 01283 544551).
e-mail: TheSecretary@BurtonGolfClub.co.uk
website: www.burtongolfclub.co.uk

BUXTON. **Buxton and High Peak Golf Club,** Town End, Waterswallows Road, Buxton SK17 7EN (01298 23453; Fax: 01298 26333; Office: 01298 26263). *Location:* A6 one mile north of Buxton. Parkland, good positional play required. 18 holes, 5966 yards. S.S.S. 69. Practice facilities. *Green Fees:* weekdays £24.00 per round, £30.00 per day; weekends £30.00 per round, £36.00 per day. *Eating facilities:* full catering facilities. *Visitors:* welcome without reservation, ring at weekends. *Society Meetings:* welcome. Professional: Mr Gary Brown (01298 23112). Secretary: Helen Smith.
e-mail: sec@bhpgc.co.uk
website: www.buxtonandhighpeakgolfclub.co.uk

BUXTON. **The Cavendish Golf Club Ltd,** Gadley Lane, Buxton SK17 6XD (01298 79708). *Location*: three quarters of a mile from town centre, on Leek Road A53, signposted. Parkland/moorland course, designed by Dr Alister Mackenzie who designed Augusta. Parkland/moorland course. 18 holes, 5833 yards. S.S.S. 68. Practice ground. *Green Fees:* £30.00 per round weekdays; £40.00 per round weekends. Juniors half price and visitors £15.00 if playing with a member. Visiting parties £28.00. *Eating facilities:* restaurant, usual bar hours, snacks, meals available at all times. *Visitors:* apply to Professional. Snooker. *Society Meetings:* catered for weekdays only except Thursdays, apply to the Professional for booking arrangements. Professional: Paul Hunstone (01298 79708). Secretary: E. G. Thompson (01298 79708; Fax: 01298 23127).

CHAPEL-EN-LE-FRITH. **Chapel-en-le-Frith Golf Club,** The Cockyard, Manchester Road, Chapel-en-le-Frith SK23 9UH (01298 812118). *Location:* midway between Sheffield and Manchester, 25 miles from each on the B5470. Parkland, scenic. 18 holes, 6434 yards. S.S.S. 71. Practice ground. *Green Fees:* weekdays £28.00 per round, £38.00 per day; weekends £38.00 per round. *Eating facilities:* all meals daily. *Visitors:* welcome, small numbers without reservation. *Society Meetings:* catered for by arrangement. Professional: D. Cullen (01298 812118). Secretary: S. Smith (01298 813943; Fax: 01298 814990).
e-mail: info@chapelgolf.co.uk

CHESTERFIELD. **Birch Hall Golf Club,** Sheffield Road, Unstone, Near Chesterfield S18 5DH (01246 291979). *Location:* off A61 between Sheffield and Chesterfield. Moorland course with outstanding views. 18 holes, 6409 yards, 5860 metres. S.S.S. 71. Practice area. *Green Fees:* information not available. *Eating facilities:* bar with meals available. *Visitors:* welcome but prior booking essential. *Society Meetings:* welcome but prior booking essential. Hon. Gen. Secretary: E. Gallagher.

ENGLAND / Derbyshire

CHESTERFIELD. **Chesterfield Golf Club Ltd,** Matlock Road, Walton, Chesterfield S42 7LA (01246 279256; Fax: 01246 276622). *Location:* two miles from Chesterfield town centre on Matlock road (A632); Junction 29 M1. Parkland with natural hazards. 18 holes, 6281 yards. S.S.S. 70. Practice ground, putting green. *Green Fees:* weekdays £32.00 per round, £40.00 per day; Sundays £40.00 per round after 1.30pm. Subject to review. *Eating facilities:* full catering (dining room), two bars. *Visitors:* welcome weekdays, and Sundays after 1.30pm; other times at weekend as members' guests only. Trolleys. Snooker. *Society Meetings:* catered for on application. Professional: Michael McLean (01246 276297). Secretary: Brian Broughton.

CHESTERFIELD. **Grassmoor Golf Centre,** North Wingfield Road, Grassmoor, Chesterfield S42 5EA (01246 856044; Fax: 01246 853486). *Location:* 4 miles M1 Junction 29 or A61 near Chesterfield. Heathland course incorporating water hazards, testing greens, testing par 3's for distance. 18 holes, 5723 yards, S.S.S. 68. 25 bay covered, floodlit range. 9 hole practice putting area and a practice area. *Green Fees:* weekdays £12.00, weekends £15.00. County Cards reduction. *Eating facilities:* Excellent bar and restaurant facilities available 8am to 10pm. *Visitors:* welcome, weekends included, 6 days' advance booking system by phone. *Society Meetings:* group bookings and societies welcome, including at weekends. Lessons available with Senior PGA Professional. Open daily 8am to 10 pm, everyone welcome. Professional: Gary Hagues. Club Manager: Helen Hagues (01246 856044). website: www.grassmoorgolf.co.uk

CHESTERFIELD. **Stanedge Golf Club,** Walton Hay Farm, Chesterfield S45 0LW (01246 566156). *Location:* five miles south-west of Chesterfield, off B5057 near "Red Lion" public house. Course 1000ft above sea level, views of four counties. 9 holes, 5786 yards. S.S.S. 68. *Green Fees:* weekdays £15.00, £10.00 with member; Saturdays and Bank Holidays £15.00, must be playing with member. *Visitors:* welcome by prior arrangement. Must book in by 2pm Monday to Fridays. No visitors on Sundays until 4pm and they must be with member. *Society Meetings:* catered for by prior arrangement. Secretary: W.C. Tyzack (01246 276568).

CHESTERFIELD. **Tapton Park Golf & Leisure Centre,** Crow Lane, Chesterfield S41 0EQ (01246 239500; Fax: 01246 555140). *Location:* behind railway station. Wooded parkland course. 18 hole course, 9 hole course and pitch and putt course. 18 hole course - 6025 yards. S.S.S. 69; 9 hole course - 2595 yards, Par 34. Putting and pitching greens. *Green Fees:* information not available. *Eating facilities:* bar and restaurant open to the public. *Visitors:* welcome at all times, booking for 18 hole course taken six days in advance. Club/Trolley/Locker hire. *Society Meetings:* welcome on written application. Professional: Andrew Carnall. Secretary: (01246 273887; Fax: 01246 558024). *

CODNOR. **Ormonde Fields Golf Club,** Nottingham Road, Codnor, Ripley DE5 9RG (01773 744157). *Location:* five miles M1 Junction 26 towards Ripley on A610. Parkland. 18 holes, 6504 yards. S.S.S. 72. Practice area, putting green. *Green Fees:* information not available. *Eating facilities:* full restaurant available. *Visitors:* unrestricted. *Society Meetings:* catered for; book through Secretary. Professional: M. Myford (01773 742987). Secretary: Mr K. Constable (01773 570043).

DERBY. **Allestree Park Golf Club,** Allestree Hall, Duffield Road, Allestree, Derby DE22 2EU (01332 552971). Location: 3 miles north of city centre on A6. Municipal course - hilly parkland with outstanding views. 18 holes, 5774 yards. S.S.S. 68. Practice ground. *Green Fees:* information not available. *Eating facilities:* full bar, catering arranged with Steward. *Visitors:* welcome anytime except Sundays morning (club competitions). *Society Meetings:* welcome, details on request. Professional: Steve Lamb (01332 550616; Fax: 01332 541195). Secretary: Mr A.R. Maguire (01283 703702).*

DERBY. **Derby Golf Club,** Shakespeare Street, Sinfin, Derby DE24 9HD (01332 766323). *Location:* two miles city centre, access via Wilmore Road. Parkland. 18 holes, 6185 yards, 5653 metres. S.S.S. 70. Practice area. *Green Fees:* £12.80. *Eating facilities:* bar and catering available. *Visitors:* welcome weekdays. *Society Meetings:* welcome weekdays. Professional: Dan Delaney (01332 766462; Fax: 01332 769004). Secretary: M. J. Fowler (01332 766323).

DERBY. **Marriott Breadsall Priory Hotel and Country Club,** Moor Road, Morley DE7 6DL (01332 836080; Fax: 01332 836036). *Location:* turn off the A61 towards Breadsall, proceed on Croft Lane, turn left into Rectory Lane, then bear right onto Moor Road, continue past the Church for approximately one mile. Two courses - Priory is a parkland course and Moorland is a contrast of open moorland. Priory - 18 holes, 5871 yards. S.S.S. 68 off yellow tees; Moorland - 18 holes, 5820 yards. S.S.S. 68 off yellow tees. Practice area and putting green; floodlit driving range. *Green Fees:* starting from £18. *Eating facilities:* Hotel - Priory Restaurant and cocktail bar; leisure club - Longweekends bar, Longweekend restaurant. *Visitors:* welcome any time subject to availability. *Society Meetings:* welcome at any time subject to availability. Hotel has 112 bedrooms, leisure club and conference facilities. Buggies. Professional: Darren Steels. Golf Operations Manager: J. Winterbottom.

For full details of clubs and courses, plus convenient accommodation www.uk-golfguide.com

DUFFIELD. **Chevin Golf Club,** Golf Lane, Duffield DE56 4EE (01332 841864). *Location:* five miles north of Derby on A6 at Duffield village. Hilly course, part parkland, part moorland with superb views. 18 holes, 6057 yards, 5451 metres. S.S.S. 69. Two practice areas. *Green Fees:* information not available. *Eating facilities:* bar snacks and diningroom. *Visitors:* welcome weekdays, Handicap Certificates required. Snooker. *Society Meetings:* welcome weekdays, but never weekends. Professional: W. Bird (01332 841112). Secretary: J.A. Milner (Tel: 01332 841864; Fax: 01332 844028).*

GLOSSOP. **Glossop and District Golf Club,** Sheffield Road, Glossop SK13 9PU (01457 865247). *Location:* off A57, one mile from town centre. Moorland course. 11 holes, 5800 yards. S.S.S. 68. *Green Fees:* information on request. *Eating facilities:* full catering facilities available. *Visitors:* welcome with reservation through Professional, except Saturdays during playing season. *Society Meetings:* welcome, same restrictions as visitors. Professional: Daniel Marsh (01457 853117). Secretary: R. Hargreaves (01457 861977).

HORSLEY. **Horsley Lodge Golf Club,** Smalley Mill Road, Horsley DE21 5BL (01332 780838; Fax: 01332 781118). *Location:* north of Derby on A61, past Little Eaton, right turn to Horsley - signposted. Meadowland. 18 holes, 6381 yards. S.S.S. 70. Par 71. Driving range. *Green Fees:* £30.00; £17.50 as members' guests, weekends by arrangement. *Eating facilities:* two bars, bar meals, à la carte restaurant; function room seats 140. *Visitors:* welcome weekdays and some weekends but not on competition days. Four-star accommodation available. *Society Meetings:* by appointment. Professional: Graham Lyall (01332 780838; Fax: 01332 781118). Company Secretary: Richard Salt. Hon. Secretary (club): George Johnson (01332 880599).

ILKESTON. **Erewash Valley Golf Club Ltd,** Stanton-by-Dale, Near Ilkeston DE7 4QR (0115 932 3258). *Location:* Junction 25 of the M1, Stanton-by-Dale village. Parkland with two holes in an old quarry. 18 holes, 6557 yards, 5996 metres. S.S.S. 71. Driving, pitching and putting practice area. *Green Fees:* weekdays £30.50 per round, £40.50 per day; weekends and Bank Holidays £40.50 per round.

DUGC Card reduced rate. *Eating facilities:* bar snacks available at all times, diningroom service on request. *Visitors:* welcome at all times subject to club events and society bookings. *Society Meetings:* welcome Monday, Wednesday and Friday only. Professional: Mike Ronan (0115 932 4667). Secretary: C. Huckle (0115 932 2984).
e-mail: secretary@erewashvalley.co.uk
website: www.erewashvalley.co.uk

ILKESTON. **Ilkeston Borough Golf Club,** Peewit Municipal Golf Course, West End Drive, Ilkeston DE7 5GH (01602 304550). *Location:* one mile west of Ilkeston market place. Slightly hilly meadowland. 9 holes, 4116 yards. S.S.S. 60. *Green Fees:* information not available. *Eating facilities:* not available. *Visitors:* welcome, no restrictions. Secretary: B. Smith (01602 302114).*

ILKESTON. **Morley Hayes Golf Club,** Main Road, Morley, Ilkeston (01332 782000). *Location:* just north of Junction 25 of M1, on A608 between Derby and Heanor. Parkland with water features and established trees, surrounded by mature woodland and deer park. Manor course, 18 holes, 6891 yards. Par 72. Tower course, 9 holes, 1614 yards, Par 30. 17 bay driving range. Pay and Play course. *Green Fees:* Manor course weekdays: £19.00, weekends/Bank Holidays: £26.00. Tower course weekdays: £9.00, weekends/Bank Holidays £11.00. *Eating facilities:* two bars, bar meals, à la carte restaurant, function suites. Hotel now open, 32 bedrooms. *Society Meetings:* company and society days welcome seven days a week. Professional: Mark Marriott. Golf Manager: Debby Hollis (01332 782000).

MATLOCK. **Matlock Golf Club,** Chesterfield Road, Matlock Moor, Matlock DE4 5LZ (01629 582191). *Location*: Matlock-Chesterfield road, A632, one mile out of Matlock, left hand side main road. Moorland with extensive views. 18 holes, yellow tees, 5808 yards. S.S.S. 68. *Green Fees:* information not available. *Eating facilities:* snacks available, luncheons and evening meals by arrangement (except on Mondays). *Visitors:* welcome weekdays. *Society Meetings:* catered for Tuesday to Friday. Professional: M.A. Whithorn (01629 584934). Secretary: J. Odell.

Main Road, Morley, Derbyshire DE7 6DG
Tel: 01332 780480 • Fax: 01332 781094
www.morleyhayes.com • enquiries@morleyhayes.com

Golf at Morley Hayes - the ultimate golfing experience

Two courses specifically designed to accommodate all levels of expertise. The Manor Course 18 holes par 72, the Tower Course 9 holes Par 30. Both are set within parkland with water features and established trees.

- 17-bay all weather driving range • Professional tuition
  - Roosters Bar • Spike Bar • Dovecote Restaurant
    - Pavilion Suite • Syndicate Room
  - Golf Shop • Locker & Shower Rooms

On A608 just north of M1 Junction 25
See also Colour Advertisement on page 31

Hotel opening Summer 2005

ENGLAND / Derbyshire

MICKLEOVER. Mickleover Golf Club, Uttoxeter Road, Mickleover, Derby DE3 9AD (Tel & Fax: 01332 516011). *Location:* three miles west of Derby on the A516/B5020 to Uttoxeter. Undulating course. 18 holes, 5702 yards, 5222 metres. S.S.S. 68. *Green Fees:* £30.00 per round, £40.00 per day Monday - Sunday. Societies £25.00 (no restriction on holes to be played). *Eating facilities:* full restaurant facilities. *Visitors:* welcome, no restrictions; telephone Professional before arrival. *Society Meetings:* Tuesdays and Thursdays. Company days Fridays. Professional: Tim Coxon (01332 518662). Secretary: Graham Finney (Tel & Fax: 01332 516011).

MICKLEOVER. Pastures Golf Club, Social Centre, Off Merlin Way, Mickleover DE3 0DQ (01332 516700). *Location:* four miles west of Derby, A516, half a mile past Mickleover Court Hotel. Undulating meadowland. 9 holes, 5014 yards. S.S.S. 64. Practice area, putting area. *Green Fees:* information not available. *Eating facilities:* snacks; bar/lounge bar. *Visitors:* welcome, DUGC Card holders welcome. *Society Meetings:* welcome any weekday by arrangement, catering available. Secretary: S. McWilliams (01332 516700).

QUARNDON. Kedleston Park Golf Club, Kedleston, Quarndon, Derby DE22 5JD (Tel & Fax: 01332 840035). *Location:* Derby, follow signs to Kedleston Hall. Parkland with lakes. 18 holes, 6675 yards. S.S.S. 72. *Green Fees:* weekdays £45.00 per round, £55.00 per day. *Eating facilities:* full catering, bars. *Visitors:* welcome Monday and Friday; weekends with member. Carts available. *Society Meetings:* welcome Monday and Friday. Professional: Paul Wesselingh. Secretary: G. Duckmanton (01332 840035).

RISLEY. Maywood Golf Club, Off Rushy Lane, Risley, Draycott DE72 3SW (0115 939 2306). *Location:* between Derby and Nottingham at Risley, two minutes from Junction 25 M1. Parkland course. 18 holes, 6424 yards. S.S.S. 71. Practice area. *Green Fees:* information not available. *Eating facilities:* licensed bar and bar meals. *Visitors:* welcome, please phone to check availability. *Society Meetings:* rates on request. Professional: Simon Purcell-Jackson (0115 949 0029). Manager: Miss Tory Moon. Proprietors: P. and B. Moon.

SHEFFIELD. Renishaw Park Golf Club, Golf House, Mill Lane, Renishaw, Sheffield S21 3UZ (01246 432044). *Location:* A6135 Barlborough (Junction 30 M1) to Sheffield. Parkland/meadowland. 18 holes, 6262 yards. S.S.S. 70. Practice area. *Green Fees:* weekdays £28.00 per round, £37.50 per day; weekends £42.00 per round/day. *Eating facilities:* bar meals, full restaurant. *Visitors:* welcome without reservation (advisable to ring Pro prior to arrival). *Society Meetings:* by prior arrangement. Full day package available. Professional: J. Oates (01246 435484). Secretary: T.J. Childs (01246 432044).

SHEFFIELD. Sickleholme Golf Club, Bamford, Hope Valley S33 0BN (01433 651306). *Location:* 3A625 west of Sheffield, right at Marquis of Granby, Bamford. Scenic wooded course in the Peak District. 18 holes, 6064 yards. S.S.S. 69. Practice ground, putting green. *Green Fees:* information not available. *Eating facilities:* bar snacks and restaurants. *Visitors:* no visitors Wednesday mornings; must be members of a recognised Golf Club; advance booking required. *Society Meetings:* welcome by prior arrangement. Professional/ Secretary: P. H. Taylor (01433 651306).*

SHIRLAND. Shirland Golf Club, Lower Delves, Shirland, Alfreton DE55 6AU (01773 834969). *Location*: one mile north of Alfreton off A61, three miles from M1 Junction 28 via A38. Tree-lined rolling parkland, 18 holes, 6072 yards. S.S.S. 69. Par 71. Two practice grounds. *Green Fees:* £24.00 per round, £38.00 per day weekdays; £30.00 per round weekends. 241 vouchers accepted throughout the week and after 1.00pm at weekends. *Eating facilities:* bar meals. Conference and banquet rooms. *Visitors:* unrestricted weekdays, but must book through Professional at weekends. *Society Meetings:* welcome. Professional: Neville Hallam (01773 834935). Secretary: Mrs C.S. Fincham (01773 832515).

STOCKPORT. The New Mills Golf Club, Shaw Marsh, New Mills, High Peak SK22 4QE (01663 743485). *Location:* signposted off the B6101 from Marple to New Mills, between Buxton and Stockport. Relatively flat upland course, magnificent views, excellent greens. 18 holes, 5604 yards. S.S.S. 69. Large practice area and driving range. New members accepted. *Green Fees:* information not available. *Eating facilities:* full catering, very good value; wide range of food. *Visitors:* welcome any day but not competition days, contact the Professional for these dates. *Society Meetings:* welcome. Professional: Carl Cross (01663 746161). Secretary: Philip Jenkinson (01663 744305).*

www.uk-golfguide.com

Devon

AXMOUTH. **Axe Cliff Golf Club,** Squires Lane, Axmouth, Seaton EX12 4AB (01297 21754; Fax: 01297 24371). *Location:* A35 from Sidmouth to Lyme Regis, turn right on to B3172 at junction with A358 Seaton. Clifftop course. 18 holes, 5969 yards, 5460 metres. S.S.S. 70. *Green Fees:* weekdays £17.00 per day, weekends £22.00 per day. *Eating facilities:* bar and small restaurant. *Visitors:* welcome without reservation, course closed until 11am on Sundays, Wednesdays till 10.30am and Fridays till 9.30am. Handicap Certificate not required. Electric cart hire, pull trolleys and clubs for hire. *Society Meetings:* societies very welcome, prices start from £18.00. More details on website. Secretary: (01297 21754). website: www.axecliff.co.uk

BARNSTAPLE. **Portmore Golf Park,** Landkey Road, Barnstaple EX32 9LB (01271 378378). *Location*: A361 just east of Barnstaple, turn right to Landkey 200 yards, turn right Newport, turn right again after a mile. Two parkland courses. The Landkey, Par 3. The Barum, Par 71. 24 bay floodlit golf range, chipping green, bunker, putting green. *Green Fees*: information not available. *Eating facilities:* full catering available. *Visitors*: welcome at all times, must telephone for tee times. Full dress code applies for Barum course. Tuition available. *Society Meetings*: welcome with prior booking, group rates available. Professionals: Steve Gould, Darren Everet.*
e-mail: colin@portmoregolfpark.freeserve.co.uk
website: www.portmoregolf.co.uk

BIDEFORD Near. **Hartland Forest Golf Club,** Near Clovelly, Bideford EX39 5RA (01237 431442; Fax: 01237 431734). *Location:* between Bideford and Bude A39, signposted from main A39 road. Parkland with water hazards. 18 holes, 5870 yards. S.S.S. 68. Par 70. *Green Fees:* from £30.00 all day, from £21.00 for 18 holes, from £13.00 for 9 holes. *Visitors:* welcome at all times. Buggies for hire. Luxury accommodation, indoor pool, spa, sauna, tennis and fishing. *Society Meetings:* welcome. Secretary: Kevin Murphy (01271 343160).
e-mail: hartlandgolfsec@hotmail.com

BIGBURY. **Bigbury Golf Club Ltd,** Bigbury-on-Sea, TQ7 4BB. *Location*: off main Plymouth to Kingsbridge road, turn right at Harraton Cross. Undulating cliff top course. 18 holes, 5896 yards. S.S.S. 68. *Green Fees*: currently under review; see website. *Eating facilities*: catering facilities available every day. *Visitors*: welcome, Handicap Certificate preferred. *Society Meetings*: catered for by prior arrangement. Professional: Simon Lloyd (01548 810412). Secretary: Martin Lowry (01548 810557). website: www.Bigburygolfclub.com

BRIXHAM. **Churston Golf Club Ltd,** Dartmouth Road, Churston, Near Brixham TQ5 0LA (01803 842751; Fax: 01803 845738). *Location:* A379 from Torquay to Brixham. At Windy Corner take A3022 to Brixham. Club situated half-a-mile on. Downland/parkland course stretching westward along the cliffs towards Brixham. 18 holes, 6219 yards. S.S.S. 70. *Green Fees*: please phone for information. *Eating facilities:* restaurant, bar and separate function room. *Visitors*: welcome, must be members of recognised club. Conference facilities available. Handicap Certificate preferred. *Society Meetings*: catered for by arrangement. Mondays, Thursdays and Fridays only. Professional: Rob Butterworth (01803 843442; Fax: 01803 845738). Manager: S.R. Bawden (01803 842751; Fax: 01803 845738).

BUDLEIGH SALTERTON. **East Devon Golf Club,** Links Road, Budleigh Salterton EX9 6DG (01395 445195). *Location:* exit M5 Junction 30; follow A376 and B3179 for Exmouth/Budleigh Salterton. Cliff top and heathland; special features: Superb greens, spectacular views over English Channel. 18 holes, 6239 yards. S.S.S. 70. *Green Fees:* information not available. *Eating facilities:* full bar and restaurant. *Visitors:* anytime by prior arrangement. Handicap Certificate required. Ladies' Day Tuesdays. *Society Meetings:* catered for Thursdays only by arrangement. Professional: T. Underwood (01395 445195). Secretary: Robert Burley (01395 443370).*

CHITTLEHAMHOLT. **Highbullen Hotel Golf & Country Club,** Chittlehamholt, Umberleigh EX37 9HD (01769 540561; Fax: 01769 540492). *Location*: M5 Tiverton Exit 27, A361 to South Molton, B3226 five miles. Right uphill following tourist signs through Chittlehamholt. Undulating parkland setting amongst mature specimen trees and water hazards, spectacular views to Exmoor and Dartmoor. 18 holes, 5562 yards. S.S.S. 67. Practice ground, golf simulator, indoor putting green. *Green Fees:* information not available. *Eating facilities:* restaurant, brasserie and bars. *Visitors:* welcome, check availability. Accommodation on site at Highbullen Hotel. New leisure complex and healthspa with full shower and changing facilities. *Society Meetings:* golf societies welcome subject to availablilty. Professional: Paul Weston (01769 540530). Secretary: Julian Reynolds (01769 540664).

CHULMLEIGH. **Chulmleigh Golf Course,** Leigh Road, Chulmleigh EX18 7BL (Tel & Fax: 01769 580519). *Location:* approximately midway between Barnstaple and Crediton on A377. North Devon's only tailor-made short game course. Undulating parkland course. 18 holes, 1450 yards Summer, 2353 yards Winter for 18 holes. S.S.S. 54. *Green Fees:* from £7.50. *Eating facilities:* licensed bar, bar snacks. *Visitors:* welcome. No Handicap Certificate required. Suitable for experienced golfers to improve short game, ideal for beginners, Juniors and retired golfers. Teaching available for beginners, juniors and adults by arrangement. Holiday cottage available. *Society Meetings:* welcome by prior arrangement. Secretary: Roy Dow. Proprietors: Mr and Mrs R.W Dow.
e-mail: chulmleighgolf@aol.com
website: www.chulmleighgolf.co.uk

CREDITON. **Downes Crediton Golf Club,** Hookway, Crediton EX17 3PT (01363 773025; Fax: 01363 775060). *Location:* off Crediton-Exeter road. Part flat, part hilly course featuring woods and water. 18 holes, 5951 yards. S.S.S. 69. *Green Fees:* £28.00 per day weekdays; £32.00 per day weekends. Special rates on application. *Eating facilities:* available from 11.30am to one hour before bar closes. *Visitors:* welcome, advisable to phone first and must produce Handicap Certificate. *Society Meetings:* by arrangement. Professional: Barry Austin (01363 774464). Managing Secretary: Philip Lee.

CREDITON near. **Waterbridge Golf Course,** Down St Mary, Near Crediton EX17 5LG (01363 85111). *Location:* on the A377 north of Crediton (one mile north of Copplestone). Attractive, gentle parkland course in a beautiful setting. 9 holes (18 tees), 3910 yards, S.S.S. 64. *Green Fees:* weekdays £7.50 9 holes, £12.50 18 holes; weekends £8.50 9 holes, £14.50 18 holes. 12.5% discount on parties of 10 and over. *Eating facilities:* café bar, lunches. *Visitors:* welcome. Club and trolley hire available. *Society Meetings:* welcome. Professional: David Ridyard. Secretary: Mrs A. Wren.

CULLOMPTON. **Padbrook Park Golf Club,** Padbrook Park, Cullompton EX15 1RU (01884 836100; Fax: 01884 34359). *Location:* one mile from Junction 28 M5. Parkland. 9 holes (18 tees), 6108 yards. S.S.S. 70. Nets, driving range. *Green Fees:* weekdays £13.00 9 holes, £18.00 18 holes; weekends £17.00 9 holes, £22.00 18 holes. Juniors half price. *Eating facilities:* two bars and restaurant. *Visitors:* always welcome. Indoor bowls, fishing; full conference and meeting facilities. Health and Fitness studio. 40 bedroom hotel, crazy golf. *Society Packages:* welcome by prior arrangement. Golf Manager: Cary Rawlings. Directors: Susan and Garry Scargill.
e-mail: info@padbrookpark.co.uk
website: www.padbrookpark.co.uk

DARTMOUTH. **Dartmouth Golf and Country Club,** Blackawton, Near Dartmouth TQ9 7DE (01803 712686; Fax: 01803 712628). *Location:* five miles from Dartmouth on the A3122. Undulating inland course with lakes, rock faces and multiple tees. Dartmouth Course: 9 holes, 2583 yards. S.S.S. 33. Championship Course: 18 holes, 7191 yards. S.S.S. 74. 15-bay driving range. *Green Fees:* £35.00 weekdays, £45.00 weekends. *Eating facilities:* full restaurant and lounge bar. *Visitors:* welcome daily, Handicap Certificate not essential. 3 Star hotel accommodation in 35 en suite bedrooms; 3 stone self-catering cottages. Leisure suite with pool, gym and beauty therapy etc. Buggies available £25.00 per round. *Society Meetings:* welcome daily. Professional: Richard Stevenson (01803 712650). Secretary: Bob Clark (01803 712016).
e-mail: info@dgcc.co.uk
golfoperations@dgcc.co.uk
website: www.dgcc.co.uk

For full details of clubs and courses, plus convenient accommodation
www.uk-golfguide.com

Dartmouth Golf & Country Club, situated just 5 miles from Dartmouth, offers great facilities: a 27 hole golf course (voted within the top 80 courses in Great Britain), driving range, health and leisure club, plus 35 en suite bedrooms.

Green Fees: from £35.
Society groups and visitors welcome daily.
Handicap not required. Buggies available.
3 day Golf Breaks from £110pp.
Bed & Breakfast from £40pp.

Blackawton, Near Dartmouth, Devon TQ9 7DE
Tel: 01803 712686
www.dgcc.co.uk

DARTMOUTH GOLF & COUNTRY CLUB

See also Colour Advertisement on page 15

PLEASE MENTION THE GOLF GUIDE WHEN YOU WRITE OR PHONE TO ENQUIRE ABOUT CLUBS OR ACCOMMODATION

DAWLISH. Warren Golf Club, Dawlish Warren EX7 0NF (01626 862255; Fax: 01626 888005). *Location:* 12 miles south of Exeter off A379. Links golf course lying on a spit of land between the sea and Exe Estuary. A challenging course situated in an internationally renowned conservation area. 18 holes, 5912 yards. S.S.S. 68. *Green Fees:* weekdays £31.00, weekends and Bank Holidays £36.00 (half price with a member). *Eating facilities:* bar and full catering available. *Visitors:* members of other bona fide golf clubs welcome. *Society Meetings:* welcome by arrangement, Special Packages available. Professional: D. Prowse (01626 864002). Club Secretary: Tim Aggett (01626 862255).
e-mail: secretary@dwgc.co.uk
website: www.dwgc.co.uk

EXETER. **Exeter Golf and Country Club,** Countess Wear, Exeter EX2 7AE (Tel & Fax: 01392 874139; Course Information: 01392 876413). *Location:* near M5, exit Junction 30, take main Plymouth/Torquay Road. Turn left Topsham, 300 yards left. Flat parkland course, many trees. 18 holes, 6000 yards. S.S.S. 69. Large practice ground. *Green Fees:* on application. *Eating facilities:* sports bar, lounge bar, diningroom. *Visitors:* welcome except Tuesdays (Ladies' Day) and Saturdays very busy course, booking sheet in operation, Bookings taken one week prior subject to availability. Booking number 01392 876303. Function suite. *Society Meetings:* catered for Thursdays only. Professional: Gary Milne (01392 875028; Fax: 01392 874914). Secretary: Keith Ham (01392 874639; Fax: 01392 874914).

EXETER. **Woodbury Park Golf and Country Club,** Woodbury Castle, Woodbury, Near Exeter EX5 1JJ (01395 233382; Fax: 01395 233384). *Location:* six miles east of Exeter between Sidmouth and Exmouth. Parkland with many water hazards. 18 hole championship course and 9 hole course. 18 holes, 6905 yards. S.S.S. 73. 18 bay driving range, practice green. *Green Fees:* on request. *Eating facilities:* two restaurants, two bars. *Visitors*: welcome at all times. Buggies for hire. Leisure Centre, Hydrotherapy Centre and conference facilities. Five chalet-style luxury lodges ideal for four/six golfers in each. 57-bedroom hotel. *Society Meetings:* welcome, Golf Packages available. Bookings please ring (01395 233500). Professional: Allan Perry. Golf Manager: Alan Richards.*
e-mail: enquiries@woodburypark.co.uk

EXETER near. **Fingle Glen Hotel, Golf and Country Club,** Tedburn St. Mary, Near Exeter EX6 6AF (01647 61817; Fax: 01647 61135). *Location*: A30 five miles from Exeter on the Okehampton Road. Parkland with streams and lakes. 9 holes, 2475 yards. S.S.S. 63 (18 holes). Golf academy, 12 bay floodlit driving range. *Green Fees:* information not available. *Eating facilities:* restaurant, bar snacks, sun terrace. *Visitors:* welcome at all times. En suite accommodation available. *Society Meetings:* welcome at all times. Pro Shop: Mervyn Kemp. Teaching Professional: Stephen Gould. Secretary: Peter Miliffe. Manager: A. Bridgeman. *

EXETER near. **Teign Valley Golf Club,** Christow, Near Exeter EX6 7PA. (01647 253026). *Location:* Four miles off the A38 Devon Expressway between Exeter and Plymouth. Varied and interesting course set in beautiful valleys in the Dartmoor National Park. Probably the best value golf in Devon,18 holes, 6000 yards. *Green Fees:* information not available. *Eating facilities:* a welcoming spirit in the friendly clubhouse offering tasty bar snacks and a choice of real ales. *Visitors:* welcome. *Society Meetings:* welcome. Conference facilities for 40 available.*

HOLSWORTHY. **Holsworthy Golf Club,** Kilatree, Holsworthy EX22 6LP (Tel & Fax: 01409 253177). *Location:* leave Holsworthy on Bude road, A3072; one and a half miles on left. Parkland - gentle undulating hills. 18 holes, 6062 yards. S.S.S. 69. Practice area. *Green Fees:* £25.00. Twilight after 6 pm £10.00. *Eating facilities:* bar, dining room. *Visitors:* welcome anytime. *Society Meetings:* welcome, special reductions for parties of 12 or more. Professional: Alan Johnston (01409 254771; Fax: 01409 253177). Secretary: Barry Megson (Tel & Fax: 01409 253177).
e-mail: hgcsecretary@aol.com
website: www.holsworthygolfclub.com

For full details of clubs and courses, plus convenient accommodation
www.uk-golfguide.com

WARREN GOLF CLUB

Visitors and Societies most welcome!
Enjoy an easy walking links course with fantastic sea and Exe Estuary views. All usual clubhouse facilities are available.
Dawlish Warren, Devon EX7 0NF
e-mail: secretary@dwgc.co.uk • www.dwgc.co.uk

For bookings and further details contact the Secretary
Tel: 01626 862255
Fax: 01626 888005

ENGLAND / Devon

HONITON. **Honiton Golf Club,** Middlehills, Honiton EX14 9TR (01404 44422). *Location*: one mile south of town proceed from A35 at Tower Cross to Farway. Flat parkland. 18 holes, 5859 yards. S.S.S. 68. Small practice ground. *Green Fees:* weekdays £25.00 per day, weekends and Bank Holidays £30.00. *Eating facilities:* bar and restaurant. *Visitors:* bona fide members of other clubs welcome, with restrictions on Wednesdays (Ladies' day) and weekends (club competitions). Facilities for 10 touring caravans during summer months with electrics. *Society Meetings:* bookable on Thursdays only. Professional: Adrian Cave (01404 42943). Secretary: Brian Young (01404 44422; Fax: 01404 46383).

HONITON. **Otter Valley Golf Centre,** Upottery, Honiton EX14 9QP (Tel & Fax: 01404 861266). *Location*: Take the A303 from Honiton, continue one and a half miles, turn off left at Upottery and Rawridge. Rolling parkland course. 9 holes, 1500 yards. Par 29. Four indoor practice bays, large putting green, eight tees on the driving range, chipping green. *Green Fees*: information not provided. *Eating facilities*: snacks and refreshments, hot and cold drinks. Lounge with TV. *Visitors*: welcome, no restrictions. Holiday cottages, video analysis, lessons. *Society Meetings*: Societies and Company Days very welcome. Please phone for information. Professional: Andrew Thompson. Manager: Ryan Eaton. e-mail: andrewthompson@otter-golf.co.uk
website: www.otter-golf.co.uk

ILFRACOMBE. **Ilfracombe Golf Club,** Hele Bay, Ilfracombe EX34 9RT. *Location*: on main coastal road between Ilfracombe and Combe Martin. Undulating parkland with spectacular views of sea and moors from every tee and green. 18 holes, 5893 yards. S.S.S. 68. 9 hole practice area and driving range. *Green Fees*: information not available. *Eating facilities*: catering available all day. *Visitors*: welcome (Handicap/ membership Certificate preferred). Members only before 10am weekends. *Society Meetings*: welcome, but book in advance. Bookings: (01271 863328). Catering: (01271 862675). Professional: Mark Davies (01271 863328). Club Secretary: Arnie Williams (01271 862176; Fax: 01271 867731).

ILFRACOMBE. **Ilfracombe and Woolacombe Golf Range,** Woolacombe Road, Ilfracombe EX34 7HF (01271 866222; Fax: 01271 342939). *Location*: on main road between Ilfracombe and Woolacombe. Flat course. 9 holes, 695 yards. 300 yard driving range with covered bays, 18 hole putting course, golf shop. *Green Fees:* information not available. *Eating facilities:* pre-packed snacks and drinks available. *Visitors:* everyone is welcome. Tennis court. Lessons and custom built clubs provided. Professional: Jimmy McGhee. Secretary: David Crocker-White.*

IVYBRIDGE. **McCaulay's Fitness and Golf,** Dinnaton Golf Club, Ivybridge PL21 9HU (01752 892512; Fax: 01752 698334). *Location:* from the Ivybridge turn off on A38, we are just two minutes drive, please follow the brown tourist signs. 9 holes, 2028 yards. Par 32. *Green Fees:* 9 holes from £8.00, 18 holes from £10.00. *Eating facilities*: Coffee Bar. *Visitors:* always welcome. No Handicap Certificate required. Other facilities offered include gym, 25m heated swimming pool, aerobics studio, tennis, squash, sauna, solarium and steam room. Contact: Jamie Phillips.
website: www.mccaulays.com

Honiton Golf Club

DEVON

A flat elevated parkland golf course
Telephone: 01404 44422
GREEN FEES FOR VISITORS
(Members of a recognised Golf Club)
Midweek -£25, Weekend - £30 per day

Weekly Rate £90
Men 5859 yds, Par 69, SSS 68
Ladies 5385 yds, Par 71, SSS 73
Caravan Site - 10 pitches.
Rent £12.00 per night for 2 persons.
Contact Mrs G. Lynes for brochures and bookings

Honiton Golf Club, Middlehills, Honiton, Devon EX14 9TR

FHG

Visit the **FHG** website
www.holidayguides.com
for details of the wide choice of accommodation featured in the full range of FHG titles

MORETONHAMPSTEAD. **Bovey Castle,** Moretonhampstead TQ13 8RE (01647 445000; Fax: 01647 440961). *Location:* Junction 31 from M5, B3212 for two miles. Parkland with rivers and narrow fairways. 18 holes, 6303 yards, 5450 metres. S.S.S. 70. Golf academy. *Green Fees:* £117.50. *Eating facilities:* brunch service, bar. *Visitors:* welcome. Please book in advance, golf shoes must be worn. Accommodation in 5 star Hotel, tennis courts; carts available. *Society Meetings:* by prior arrangement. Professional/Secretary: Richard Lewis (01647 445009; Fax: 01647 440961).

MORTEHOE. **Mortehoe and Woolacombe Golf Club,** Easewell, Mortehoe EX34 7EH (01271 870225). *Location:* just outside Mortehoe village. Parkland course with superb sea views. 9 holes (18 tees), 4690 yards, S.S.S. 63. Practice nets. *Green Fees:* information not available. *Eating facilities:* clubhouse; restaurant and bar snacks. *Visitors:* welcome at all times. Cafeteria and golf shop with extensive range of equipment. Touring campsite facilities. Indoor bowls, short mat bowls, table tennis, indoor heated pool; trolleys available. *Society Meetings:* welcome by prior booking. Secretary: Malcolm Wilkinson (01271 870745).*

NEWTON ABBOT. **Dainton Park Golf Club,** Totnes Road, Ipplepen, Newton Abbot TQ12 5TN (01803 815000). *Location:* on A381 between Newton Abbot and Totnes. Undulating parkland course. 18 holes, 6400 yards. S.S.S. 70. Driving range and practice area. *Green Fees:* weekdays £23.00; weekends £26.00. *Eating facilities:* full catering and licensed bar. *Visitors:* unrestricted. *Society Meetings:* welcome by arrangement. Secretary: Mike Penlington. website: www.daintonparkgolf.co.uk

NEWTON ABBOT. **Hele Park Golf Club,** Ashburton Road, Newton Abbot TQ12 6JN (01626 336060; Fax: 01626 332661). *Location:* A383 on Newton Abbot to Ashburton road, one and a half miles from Newton Abbot town centre. Parkland course. 9 holes, 5168 yards. S.S.S. 65 (for 18 holes). Floodlit driving range. *Green Fees:* from £11.50 for 9 holes and £17.50 for 18 holes. *Eating facilities:* bar and restaurant. *Visitors:* welcome. Booking advised. Normal dress rules apply. Pay as you play and members' club. *Society Meetings:* welcome, special rates on application. Professionals: James Langmead, Sarah Burnell, Duncan Arnold, David Jeffs. Secretary: A.J. Taylor. Manager: W. Stanbury.
e-mail: info@heleparkgolf.co.uk
website: www.heleparkgolf.co.uk

NEWTON ABBOT. **Newton Abbot (Stover) Golf Club,** Bovey Road, Newton Abbot TQ12 6QQ (01626 352460; Fax: 01626 330210). *Location:* A382 three miles north of Newton Abbot. Tight wooded parkland course with river in play on 8 holes. 18 holes, 5764 yards, 5271 metres. S.S.S. 68. *Green Fees:* £32.00 per round/day; half price with a member. *Eating facilities:* full catering daily from 11am. *Visitors:* welcome on production of Handicap Certificate or membership card of county affiliated golf club. Must telephone in advance. *Society Meetings:* catered for on Thursdays. Professional: Malcolm Craig (01626 362078). Secretary: G.W. Rees (01626 352460).

FHG Guides

Visit the FHG website
www.holidayguides.com
for details of the wide choice of accommodation featured in the full range of FHG titles

www.uk-golfguide.com

THE GOLF GUIDE 2006　　　　　　　　　　　　　　　　ENGLAND / Devon **175**

If you want an Adventure of Fun, Luxury + Good Taste —...

I will see you at Bovey Castle

Peter de Savary

A sporting resort and club with luxurious accommodations, superb cuisine and romantic ambience. Bovey Castle, built 1907 in the heart of the National Park has a championship golf course designed in 1926 as a companion to Gleneagles and Turnberry. Numerous sporting activities include fly-fishing, equestrian, tennis, falconry, boating and more. An exceptional new spa and pool, cinema, children's pursuits and beautiful walks. Castle Lodges available to Founder Members.

Telephone us on **01647 445 000** or visit **www.boveycastle.com**
Bovey Castle, North Bovey, Dartmoor National Park, Devon TQ13 8RE Fax: 01647 440 961 Email: enquiries@boveycastle.com

BOVEY CASTLE
DARTMOOR NATIONAL PARK

See also Colour Advertisement on page 13

OKEHAMPTON. **Okehampton Golf Club,** Off Tors Road, Okehampton EX20 1EF (01837 52113). *Location:* from A30 take turning from centre of Okehampton then follow the signposts. Parkland. 18 holes, 5286 yards. S.S.S. 65. *Green Fees:* £25.00. *Eating facilities:* bar and dining room. *Visitors:* welcome; contact by telephone or letter. *Society Meetings:* welcome by prior arrangement. Professional: Ashley Moon (01837 53541). Secretary: Clive Yeo.
e-mail: okehamptongc@btconnect.com

OKEHAMPTON near. **Ashbury Hotel,** Higher Maddaford, Ashbury, Near Okehampton EX20 4NL (01837 55453; Fax: 01837 55468). *Location:* signposted "Ashbury" off the B3079, three miles west of Okehampton. Hilly, wooded courses. Ashbury, three courses: Pines 18 holes, 5628 yards, Par 69; Beeches 18 holes, 5351 yards, Par 68; Willows 18 holes, Par 3. Oakwood Course 18 holes, 5374 yards, Par 68. Practice area, putting green and 8-bay covered driving range. *Green Fees:* information not available. *Eating facilities:* fully licensed bar, bar snacks 12 noon to 5pm. *Visitors:* welcome, after midday, please telephone to arrange a tee time. Buggies, clubs and trolleys for hire. Coaching available. Accommodation in 2 star hotel, tennis, bowls, swimming (01837 53053). Secretary: Ian Gill.

PLYMOUTH. **Elfordleigh Hotel, Golf and Leisure Club,** Colebrook, Plympton, Plymouth PL7 5EB (01752 336428; Fax: 01752 344581). *Location:* one mile from Plympton. Woodland course in picturesque countryside. 18 holes, S.S.S. 67. Practice area. *Green Fees:* information not available. *Eating facilities:* Churchill Restaurant, bar meals available from Brasserie. *Visitors:* welcome. Hotel accommodation available. *Society Meetings:* catered for, contact Golf Manager. Professional/Director of Golf: Dominik Naughton (01752 348425).
website: www.elfordleigh.co.uk

PLYMOUTH. **Sparkwell Golf Club,** Sparkwell, Plympton, Plymouth PL7 5DF (Tel & Fax: 01752 837219). *Location:* Sparkwell village centre. Parkland course. 9 holes, 5772 yards, S.S.S. 68. Practice area, pitch and putt. *Green Fees:* information not available. *Eating facilities:* restaurant and bar. *Visitors:* all welcome – pay-as-you-play course. *Society Meetings:* all welcome. Secretary: J. M. Sandiford.*

PLYMOUTH. **Staddon Heights Golf Club,** Staddon Heights, Plymstock, Plymouth PL9 9SP (01752 402475). *Location:* from city centre follow signs to Kingsbridge, then Turnchapel then Bouvisand. Cliff tops course overlooking Plymouth Sound. 18 holes, 5807 yards. S.S.S. 68. Practice area. *Green Fees:* weekdays £22.00, weekends and Bank Holidays £26.00. Reductions for members' guests; twilight golf (April - Oct). Subject to review. *Visitors:* welcome. *Eating facilities:* full bar and restaurant facilities. *Society Meetings:* welcome. Professional: Ian Marshall (Tel & Fax: 01752 492630). Secretary: R. W. Brown (01752 402475).
e-mail: golfclub@btopenworld.com
website: www.staddon-heights.co.uk

SAUNTON. **Saunton Golf Club,** Saunton, Braunton EX33 1LG (01271 812436; Fax: 01271 814241). *Location:* eight miles west of Barnstaple. Two traditional links courses. East course 18 holes, 6779 yards. S.S.S. 72. West course 18 holes, 6403 yards. S.S.S. 71. Practice ground and covered practice range. *Green Fees:* £55.00 per 18 holes, £75.00 per day. All green fees inclusive of meal voucher. *Eating facilities:* full catering available. *Visitors:* welcome, no play before 9.30am, Handicap Certificate required. Prior booking recommended. *Society Meetings:* welcome with prior booking. Professional: A.T. MacKenzie (01271 812013; Fax: 01271 812126). Secretary: T.C. Reynolds (01271 812436; Fax: 01271 814241).
e-mail: info@sauntongolf.co.uk
website: www.sauntongolf.co.uk

SIDMOUTH. **Sidmouth Golf Club,** Cotmaton Road, Peak Hill, Sidmouth EX10 8SX (01395 513451; Fax: 01395 514661). *Location:* half a mile from town centre, 12 miles south east of M5 Junction 30. Parkland with breathtaking views over Sid Valley and Lyme Bay. 18 holes, 5068 yards. S.S.S. 65. *Green Fees:* weekdays £24.00 per round, £30.00 per day; weekends £29.00 per round. Summer and winter packages available. Society packages on request. *Eating facilities:* catering available everyday. *Visitors:* welcome anytime depending on tee reservations. *Society Meetings:* by arrangement with Professional: (01395 516407). Club Manager: Ian M. Smith (01395 513451; Fax: 01395 514661).
e-mail: secretary@sidmouthgolfclub.co.uk

Saunton Golf Club
Two Championship Links Courses
Visitors and societies welcome (handicap certificates are required)
Excellent bar and restaurant facilities (prior booking is recommended).

2005 Green Fees (inclusive of lunch)
Weekdays • Single round £55 • All day: £75
2006 green fees on application

(reductions and all inclusive packages available for party bookings)

WINTER SPECIALS available November to March at £35
(Coffee, 18 holes of golf and 2-course meal)

Tel: 01271 812436 • www.sauntongolf.co.uk • e-mail: info@sauntongolf.co.uk

FREE GOLF ALL YEAR ROUND

INDOOR SPORT - Bowls, Tennis, Badminton, Squash, Table Tennis, 10-Pin, Snooker - FREE

OUTDOOR SPORT - 4x18 hole Golf Courses, Tennis, Bowls, Pitch & Putt, Guided Walks, Crazy Golf - FREE

LEISURE - Pools, Spas, Saunas, Steam Room - FREE

CRAFT CENTRE - Pottery + 9 Tutored Crafts, including Picture Framing, Glass Engraving, Candle Making & Enamelling - prices at cost

Buggy Prices £6 – £12

March	3 nts	£164/£179	4 nts	£183/£200
Mid May	3 nts	£201/£209	4 nts	£241/£250
June–mid July	3 nts	£198/£206	4 nts	£237/£247
August	3 nts	£208/£238	4 nts	£281/£318
September	3 nts	£214/£222	4 nts	£257/£268

Price per Person – *Full Board*

All rooms en suite, TV/Video, Safe (F.O.C.) and telephone.

Party Discounts ~ Bargain Breaks

Manor House & Ashbury Hotels, Okehampton, Devon EX20 4NA
Freephone 0800 781 9635
AA www.ashburygolfhotel.co.uk   www.manorhousehotel.co.uk **AA**

See also Colour Advertisement on page 14

ELFORDLEIGH
HOTEL : GOLF : LEISURE

Elfordleigh offers peace, calm and tranquillity in acres of glorious parkland, minutes from the heart of Plymouth. Our 18 hole golf course offers residential golfing breaks, society packages, practice facilities and expert tuition from **PGA Golf Professional Scott Macaskill**.

Our Oasis Leisure facilities include:
SQUASH COURT • 2 SPAS • SAUNA • STEAM ROOM
• SWIMMING POOL • SEPARATE CHILDREN'S POOL • FULLY EQUIPPED GYMNASIUM • SUN TERRACE • DANCE STUDIO
• 3 TENNIS COURTS • SOLARIUM • BEAUTY THERAPY
• HAIRDRESSER • JOGGING TRACK

Churchills Restaurant offers fine wine and cuisine and excellent service-(need we say more!). Elfordleigh has 2 function suites, ideal for civil weddings or wedding receptions.

ELFORDLEIGH HOTEL
COLEBROOK, PLYMPTON, PLYMOUTH, DEVON PL7 5EB
Tel: 01752 336428 • Fax: 01752 344581
E-mail: reception@elfordleigh.co.uk
Website: www.elfordleigh.co.uk

See also Colour Advertisement on page 12

SOUTH BRENT. **Wrangaton Golf Club,** Golf Links Road, Wrangaton, South Brent TQ10 9HJ (01364 73001). *Location:* A38 from Exeter (Wrangaton Cross turn off), from Plymouth A38 Ivybridge turn off via Bittaford. Parkland course, first 9 holes on Dartmoor. 18 holes, 6063 yards. S.S.S 69. Practice ground, putting green and net. *Green Fees:* weekdays £23.00; weekends and Bank Holidays £25.00. *Eating facilities:* full catering and bar facilities available. *Visitors:* welcome at all times but telephone first in case of club competition. *Society Meetings:* all welcome, written notice required. Professional: Glenn Richards (01364 72161). Secretary: Mike Daniels (Tel & Fax: 01364 73229).

TAVISTOCK. **Hurdwick Golf Club,** Tavistock Hamlets, Tavistock PL19 0LL (01822 612746). *Location:* one mile north of Tavistock on the Brentor Road. Parkland. 18 holes, 5300 yards. S.S.S. 67. *Green Fees:* information not available. *Eating facilities:* fresh sandwiches, licensed bar. *Visitors:* welcome anytime. *Society Meetings:* (10 or more) 36 holes and buffet for £20 a head. Professional: available. Secretary: Roger Cullen and R. Hurle.*

TAVISTOCK. **Tavistock Golf Club,** Down Road, Tavistock PL19 9AQ (Tel & Fax: 01822 612344). *Location:* Whitchurch Down one mile from Tavistock. Moorland course with spectacular views. 18 holes, 6495 yards. S.S.S. 71. Practice ground. *Green Fees:* weekdays £28.00 per day, weekends and Bank Holidays £35.00 per day. *Eating facilities:* all day catering and bar. *Visitors:* welcome, telephone first. *Society Meetings:* by prior arrangement, fees negotiable. Professional: D. Rehaag (01822 612316). Secretary: J. Coe (Tel & Fax: 01822 612344).
e-mail: tavygolf@hotmail.com
website: www.tavistockgolfclub.org.uk

TEIGNMOUTH. **Teignmouth Golf Club,** Haldon Moor, Teignmouth TQ14 9NY (01626 777070). *Location:* two miles north of Teignmouth on the Exeter Road - B3192. Level heathland course, designed by Dr Mackenzie (also designed Augusta National USA), with panoramic views. 18 holes, 6090 yards. S.S.S. 69. *Green Fees:* On application. *Eating facilities:* catering from 9 am to 6 pm. *Visitors:* welcome with reservation if members of another club with Handicap Certificate. *Society Meetings:* catered for Thursdays. Professional: Robert Selley (01626 772894). General Manager: Andy Stubbs (01626 777070; Fax: 01626 777304).

THURLESTONE. **Thurlestone Golf Club,** Thurlestone, Kingsbridge TQ7 3NZ (01548 560405). *Location:* turn off A379 near Kingsbridge. Undulating beside sandy beaches and over cliff tops, with superb coastal views. 18 holes, 6340 yards. S.S.S. 70. Practice area. *Green Fees:* £36.00 per day. Weekly and fortnightly tickets available. *Eating facilities:* catering available from 10.00am until 5.30pm daily. *Visitors:* must produce Handicap Certificate, please telephone in advance. *Society Meetings:* not catered for. Professional: Peter Laugher (Tel & Fax: 01548 560715). Secretary: Terry Gibbons (01548 560405; Fax: 01548 562149).

TIVERTON. **Tiverton Golf Club,** Post Hill, Tiverton EX16 4NE (01884 252187; Fax: 01884 251607). *Location:* three miles east of Tiverton, Junction 27 of M5, proceed through Sampford Peverell and Halberton. Parkland, tree-lined fairways. 18 holes, 6346 yards. S.S.S. 71. *Green Fees:* on application. *Eating facilities:* snacks, lunches, teas and evening meals. *Visitors:* welcome, must ring Pro Shop in advance. Handicap Certificate or introduction required. *Society Meetings:* by arrangement with General Manager. Professional: Mike Hawton (01884 254836). General Manager: Richard Jessop (01884 252187).

TORQUAY. **Torquay Golf Club,** Petitor Road, St Marychurch, Torquay TQ1 4QF (01803 314591; Fax: 01803 316116). *Location:* north east of Torquay at St. Marychurch. Parkland. 18 holes, 6192 yards. S.S.S. 69. *Green Fees:* £29.00 - £35.00. *Eating facilities:* lunches, teas and evening meals available. *Visitors:* welcome if members of a golf club with Handicap Certificate. *Society Meetings:* ring for rates. Professional: M. Ruth (01803 329113). Secretary: A. R. Gravestock (01803 314591).

TORRINGTON. **Great Torrington Golf Club,** Weare Trees, Torrington EX38 7EZ (01805 622229; Fax: 01805 623878). *Location:* one mile north of Torrington on Weare Giffard road. Heathland course with excellent views. 9 holes, 4419 yards. S.S.S. 62. Small practice area. *Green Fees:* £15.00 per day. *Eating facilities:* full meals and bar snacks available during bar hours. *Visitors:* welcome except on Tuesdays, Wednesdays, Saturdays and Sundays before noon and during club and open competitions. *Society Meetings:* catered for by arrangement. Secretary: Mrs J.M. Cudmore (01271 375927).

UMBERLEIGH. **Libbaton Golf Club Ltd.,** High Bickington, Umberleigh EX37 9BS (01769 560269; Fax: 01769 560342). *Location:* A377 Exeter to Barnstaple, turn off on B3227 to Torrington, at Atherington, turn off B3217 to High Bickington. Parkland with many lakes. 18 holes, 6481 yards. S.S.S. 71. Driving range, teaching centre. *Green Fees:* weekdays £20.00; weekends £26.00. *Eating facilities:* bar, bar meals and first class restaurant. *Visitors:* always welcome, seven days a week. Dress code must be observed. *Society Meetings:* welcome by prior arrangement. Special Society Packages. Fully stocked golf shop. Secretary: Anne Fenge (01769 560269).

THE APPEARANCE OF AN ASTERISK (*) AT THE END OF A CLUB OR COURSE ENTRY INDICATES THAT UP-TO-DATE INFORMATION HAS NOT BEEN SUPPLIED

ENGLAND / Devon

WESTWARD HO!. Royal North Devon Golf Club, Golf Links Road, Westward Ho!, Bideford EX39 1HD (01237 473817). *Location:* two miles North Bideford. Oldest links course in England. 18 holes, 6653 yards. S.S.S. 72. Practice area. *Green Fees:* £38.00 per round weekdays; £44.00 per round weekends. Society discounts and winter rates available. *Eating facilities:* full catering available. *Visitors:* welcome with Handicap Certificate. Tee reservations should be made in advance. *Society Meetings:* catered for. Professional: Iain Parker (01237 477598; Fax: 01237 475347). Secretary: Bob Fowler (01237 473817; Fax: 01237 423456).
e-mail: info@royalnorthdevongolfclub.co.uk
website: www.royalnorthdevongolfclub.co.uk

YELVERTON. **Yelverton Golf Club,** Golf Links Road, Yelverton PL20 6BN (01822 852824). *Location*: eight miles north of Plymouth on A386 road. Testing moorland course with views across Dartmoor. 18 holes, 6363 yards. S.S.S. 71. Practice ground. *Green Fees:* weekdays £30.00 per day or part day; weekends and Bank Holidays £40.00 per day or part day. *Eating facilities:* full catering and bar facilities available. *Visitors:* welcome if member of a recognised golf club or golf society. Handicap Certificate required. Snooker. *Society Meetings:* catered for, welcome by arrangement with Secretary. Professional: T. McSherry (01822 853593). Secretary: S. M. J. Barnes (01822 852824; Fax: 01822 854869).

Royal North Devon Golf Club

Championship Course: 6984 yards. White 6665 yards par 72; Yellow 6424 yards par 71; Ladies 5703 yards par 75.
Play England's oldest Golf Course (1864) and afterwards visit the Golf Museum.
e-mail: info@royalnorthdevongolfclub.co.uk   website: www.royalnorthdevongolfclub.co.uk
Westward Ho!, Bideford, Devon EX39 1HD   Tel: 01237 473817 (Secretary)   01237 477598 (Professional)

FHG Guides 2006
October Edition

- Recommended COUNTRY HOTELS
- Recommended COUNTRY INNS & PUBS
- BED & BREAKFAST STOPS • CHILDREN WELCOME!
- The Original FHG Guide to COAST & COUNTRY HOLIDAYS
- CARAVAN & CAMPING HOLIDAYS, England, Scotland, Wales & Ireland
- BRITAIN'S BEST HOLIDAYS
- THE GOLF GUIDE Where to Play / Where to Stay
- PETS WELCOME!
- Recommended SHORT BREAK HOLIDAYS in Britain
- SELF CATERING HOLIDAYS in Britain

Available from bookshops or larger newsagents

FHG Guides LTD
Abbey Mill Business Centre,
Seedhill, Paisley PA1 1TJ
www.holidayguides.com

Dorset

BLANDFORD. **The Ashley Wood Golf Club,** Wimborne Road, Blandford Forum DT11 9HN (01258 452253; Fax: 01258 450590). *Location:* half a mile south of Blandford on B3082. Downland with magnificent views over Tarrant and Stour valleys. 18 holes, 6270 yards. S.S.S. 70. Practice ground, putting green. *Green Fees:* weekdays £25.00; weekends £30.00 after 1pm. *Eating facilities:* hot and cold snacks all day. *Visitors:* welcome during week; after 12 noon Saturday and Sundays with Handicap Certificate or with member only. Ladies only Tuesday mornings. *Society Meetings:* welcome by arrangement with Secretary. Professional: Jon Shimmons (01258 480379). Manager: Yvonne Brown (01258 452253).
e-mail: officemanager@ashleywoodgolfclub.com
website: www.ashleywoodgolfclub.com

BOURNEMOUTH. **Knighton Heath Golf Club,** Francis Avenue, Bournemouth BH11 8NX (01202 572633; Fax: 01202 590774). *Location:* A348 and A3049 roundabout exit Francis Avenue. Undulating heathland, 18 holes, 6094 yards. S.S.S. 69. *Green Fees:* weekdays £30.00 per round, £35.00 per day. *Eating facilities:* meals and bar snacks available daily. *Visitors:* welcome with reservation, after 9.30am weekdays. Restrictions on competition days. Not at weekends unless with a member. Handicap Certificate required. *Society Meetings:* catered for if arranged in advance. Professional: Paul Brown (01202 578275). Club Manager: P. Bodle (01202 572633; Fax: 01202 590774).
e-mail: khgc@btinternet.com

BOURNEMOUTH. **Meyrick Park Golf Club,** Central Drive, Bournemouth BH2 6LH (01202 786040). *Location:* one mile from Bournemouth town centre. Beautiful and challenging woodland course. 18 holes, 5802 yards. S.S.S. 68. Practice area. *Green Fees:* from £14.00. *Eating facilities:* Pulse Cafe Bar and Summer Terrace. *Visitors:* welcome. Lodge on site offering 17 en suite bedrooms – golf breaks available. *Society Meetings:* welcome by prior arrangement. Professional: Andrew Britton (01202 786040).
website: www.theclubcompany.com

BOURNEMOUTH. **Queens Park (Bournemouth) Golf Club,** Queens Park West Drive, Bournemouth BH8 9BY (01202 396198). *Location:* off Wessex Way. Parkland course in centre of Bournemouth. 18 holes, 6090 yards. S.S.S. 69. Small practice area. *Green Fees:* information on application. *Eating facilities:* restaurant and bar. *Visitors:* welcome anytime, last tee off times Sundays 12 noon. *Society Meetings:* welcome by prior arrangement. Secretary: Tony Cleasby (01202 302611).

BOURNEMOUTH. **Solent Meads Golf Centre,** Rolls Drive, Hengistbury Head, Bournemouth BH6 4NA (01202 420795). *Location:* south of Christchurch, 2 miles from Bournemouth town centre. Seaside course. 18 holes, 2182 yards. S.S.S. 54. Driving range, 9 hole `Snag' pitch and putt. Lessons available. *Green Fees:* £7.50 for 18 holes, concessions available. *Eating facilities:* cafe. *Visitors:* no restrictions. Professional: Warren Butcher (01202 420795).
e-mail: solentmeads@yahoo.co.uk
website: www.solentmeads.co.uk

BOURTON. **Bullpits Golf Club,** Bourton, Near Gillingham SP8 5AX (01747 840084; Fax: 01747 840090). *Location:* off the A303 at Bourton and follow sign in village. Wooded parkland with streams and water, and River Stour. 9 holes, 18 tees, 3362 yards. S.S.S. 55. Putting/croquet green. *Green Fees:* £10.00; reductions for students and juniors; 2 fore 1 welcome. *Eating facilities:* Bar; light refreshments by prior arrangement. *Visitors:* welcome at all times except early Sunday mornings. *Society Meetings:* welcome by appointment. Owners: Simon & Kay Bull.

BRIDPORT. **Bridport and West Dorset Golf Club,** Burton Road, Bridport DT6 4PS (01308 421095). *Location*: one mile east of Bridport on B3157. Clifftop links course. 18 holes, 5729 yards. Par 70. Driving range and 9-hole pitch and putt course, 18 hole putting green May to September. *Green Fees*: £24.00, £18.00 after 12pm weekdays, (2pm weekends), £12.00 after 5pm. *Eating facilities*: lounge and dining room, spikes bar. *Visitors*: welcome, but not before 9.30am Mondays, Wednesdays, Fridays and Saturdays, and after 12.30pm Tuesdays, Thursdays and Sundays. Members only 8am – 9.30am daily and 12pm – 2pm weekends. Please check with Professional in advance. *Society Meetings*: catered for by prior arrangement. Clubhouse: (01308 422597). Caterer: (01308 421998). Professional: David Parsons (01308 421491). Secretary: Peter Ridler (Tel & Fax: 01308 421095).
e-mail: secretary@bridportgolfclub.org.uk
website: www.bridportgolfclub.org.uk

BROADSTONE. **Broadstone (Dorset) Golf Club,** Wentworth Drive, Broadstone BH18 8DQ (01202 692595). *Location:* off A349 to B3072 to Broadstone. Heathland. 18 holes, 6315 yards. S.S.S. 70. Practice area. *Green Fees:* weekdays £45.00 per round, £70.00 per day. Weekend/Bank Holidays one round £55.00 (very limited). *Eating facilities:* full catering service. *Visitors:* welcome weekdays, weekends by prior arrangement, current Handicap Certificate required. *Society Meetings:* welcome by arrangement except weekends. Professional: Nigel Tokely (Tel & Fax: 01202 692835). Secretary: Colin Robinson (Tel & Fax: 01202 692595).
e-mail: admin@broadstonegolfclub.com
website: www.broadstonegolfclub.com

Please mention THE GOLF GUIDE when you enquire about clubs or accommodation

CHRISTCHURCH. **Dudmoor Farm Golf Course,** Dudmoor Farm Road, Christchurch BH23 6AQ. *Location:* off Fairmile road, near Christchurch Hospital. Wooded course. 9 holes. Longest hole 280 yards. *Green Fees:* £8.50 for 18 holes. *Eating facilities:* tea, coffee, crisps, chocolate, ice cream. *Visitors:* welcome, no need to book. Riding instruction and trekking also available. (01202 473826; Fax: 01202 480207).

CHRISTCHURCH. **Highcliffe Castle Golf Club,** 107 Lymington Road, Highcliffe BH23 4LA (01425 272953). *Location:* on the coastal road linking Lymington and Christchurch. Flat, wooded course. 18 holes, 4776 yards, 4347 metres. S.S.S. 63. Two practice nets. *Green Fees:* weekdays £26.00; weekends £36.00. Reductions during winter months and after 4pm in summer. Must be in possession of Handicap Certificate. *Eating facilities:* full bar/catering facilities. *Visitors:* welcome after 9.30am if member of recognised golf club. Please phone to check tee reservations. *Society Meetings:* catered for by prior arrangement. Secretary: Graham Fisher (01425 272210).

CHRISTCHURCH. **Parley Court Golf Club,** Parley Green Lane, Hurn, Christchurch BH23 6BB (01202 591600). *Location:* opposite Bournemouth International Airport. Flat and challenging course. 9 holes, 2469 yards. S.S.S. 64, Par 68. Putting and chipping areas. *Green Fees:* weekdays £11.00 18 holes, £8.00 9 holes; weekends (no booking required) £12.00 18 holes, £9.50 9 holes. *Eating facilities:* licensed bar; catering available. *Visitors:* welcome. No booking or Handicap Certificate required. Membership available. *Society Meetings:* welcome. Professional: Richard Hill. Secretary: S.D. Mitchell (01202 591600).

DORCHESTER. **Came Down Golf Club,** Came Down, Dorchester DT2 8NR (01305 813494). *Location*: two miles south of Dorchester. Downland course on chalk downs with excellent drainage and magnificent views. Birthplace of the Ryder Cup. Designed by Harry S. Colt. 18 holes, 6255 yards, 5720 metres. S.S.S. 70. Practice area and nets. *Green Fees*: weekdays £26.00; weekends £30.00 plus VAT. *Eating facilities*: full catering facilities. *Visitors*: welcome without reservation except Sunday mornings - phone in advance. All visitors must have Handicap Certificate. Buggies for hire. Established in 1896. *Society Meetings*: Wednesdays only. Package (around £30) includes golf (36 holes), morning coffee, lunch and evening meal. Professional: Nick Rodgers (01305 812670). Manager: (Tel & Fax: 01305 813494). e-mail: manager@camedowngolfclub.co.uk website: www.camedowngolfclub.co.uk

DORCHESTER. **Charminster Golf Club,** Wolfedale Golf Course, Dorchester DT2 7SG (01305 260186; Fax: 01305 257074). *Location:* Dorchester. Parkland course. 18 holes, 5467 yards. S.S.S. 67. 6 hole practice area. *Green Fees:* information not available. *Eating facilities:* Caddy Shack bar and restaurant. *Visitors:* welcome anytime. Sundays mainly competition days. *Society Meetings:* welcome. Professional: Tim Lovegrove (01305 260186; Fax: 01305 833668).

FERNDOWN. **Dudsbury Golf Club,** Christchurch Road, Ferndown BH22 8ST (01202 593499; Fax: 01202 594555). *Location:* Ferndown town centre. Follow signs for Poole on A348, turn left at first mini roundabout, turn left to Hurn Airport, 200 yards. Club on right hand side. Parkland course designed by Donald Steel, featuring six lakes in beautiful Dorset countryside rolling gently down to the River Stour. 18 holes, 6904 yards. S.S.S 73. 6 hole academy course, driving range. *Green Fees:* information not available. *Eating facilities:* two bars, spike bar, food served all day. *Visitors:* welcome at all times. Buggies and trolleys available. *Society Meetings:* welcome, phone Secretary for details. Professional: Kevin Spurgeon (01202 594488). Secretary: Giles Legg.*

FERNDOWN. **Ferndown Forest Golf Club,** Forest Links Road, Ferndown BH22 9QE (01202 876096; Fax: 01202 894095). *Location:* off main A31 trunk road. Flat, wooded parkland. 18 holes, 5200 yards, Par 68. Covered, floodlit driving range; large practice putting green. *Green Fees:* £15.00/£13.00. *Eating facilities:* licensed bar and patio serving breakfast, lunch, dinner. *Visitors*: all welcome. *Society Meetings*: welcome. Professional/Secretary: Mike Dodd (01202 876477).

FERNDOWN. **Ferndown Golf Club,** 119 Golf Links Road, Ferndown BH22 8BU (01202 872022). *Location*: off A31. Wooded heathland. 18 holes, 6501 yards. S.S.S. 71. 9 holes, 5604 yards. S.S.S. 68. Practice ground. *Green Fees:* £60.00 per round, £80.00 per day weekdays. *Eating facilities*: available. *Visitors:* welcome but prior permission recommended. Handicap Certificate required from a recognised golf club. Professional: Neil Pike (01202 873825). Secretary: M.C. Davies (01202 874602; Fax: 01202 873926).

For full details of clubs and courses, plus convenient accommodation
www.uk-golfguide.com

PARLEY COURT GOLF CLUB An easy walking 9-hole layout and an enjoyable test of golf. Clubs, trolleys and buggies available for hire. The friendly clubhouse provides meals from a sandwich to a full Sunday lunch. Pay and Play club - no booking required.
Parley Green Lane, Hurn, Christchurch Dorset BH23 6BB
01202 591600 • info@parleygolf.co.uk • www.parleygolf.com

HALSTOCK. **Halstock Golf Club,** Common Lane, Halstock BA22 9SF (01935 891689; Fax: 01935 891839). *Location:* six miles south of Yeovil near Sutton Bingham Reservoir, signposted in village. Flat parkland course, short, tight but challenging. 18 holes, 4481 yards. S.S.S. 63. 12 bay driving range. *Green Fees:* £15.00 per round weekdays; £18.00 per round weekends. *Eating facilities:* light refreshments available, bar, restaurant (01935 891747). *Visitors:* welcome at all times. Please telephone for booking. *Society Meetings:* catered for by prior arrangement. Secretary: John Page.

LYME REGIS. **Lyme Regis Golf Club,** Timber Hill, Lyme Regis DT7 3HQ (01297 442043). *Location:* between Lyme Regis and Charmouth (A35). Cliff top course (not hilly) with fine coastal views. 18 holes, 6283 yards. S.S.S. 70. Practice ground, chipping area and bunker. *Green Fees:* information not available. *Eating facilities:* bars (normal hours) and catering every day. *Visitors:* welcome, but not before 9.30am weekdays and Saturdays, Thursdays after 2.15pm and Sundays after 12 noon. Best to check with Professional. Handicap Certificate or proof of membership of a golf club required. *Society Meetings:* minimum for Tee Booking 14. Professional: Duncan Driver (01297 443822). Secretary: Stephen Wright (01297 442963).

POOLE. **Parkstone Golf Club,** 49a Links Road, Parkstone, Poole BH14 9QS (01202 707138). *Location*: off A35 Bournemouth to Poole. Wooded heathland. 18 holes, 6250 yards. S.S.S. 70. *Green Fees:* £50.00 per round, £75.00 per day weekdays; £60.00 per round, £85.00 per day weekends and Bank Holidays (subject to review). *Eating facilities:* comprehensive. *Visitors:* welcome with booking and Handicap Certificate. *Society Meetings:* catered for as above. Professional: Martyn Thompson (01202 708092). General Manager: Christine Radford (01202 707138); Fax: 01202 706027).

POOLE near. **Bulbury Woods Golf Club,** Bulbury Lane, Lytchett Minster, Poole BH16 6HP (01929 459574; Fax: 01929 459000). *Location:* just off A35 , one mile after the Bakers Arms roundabout, three miles from Poole centre. Excellent woodland course, superbly manicured, panoramic views across Poole harbour and the Purbeck Hills. 18 holes, 6000 yards, par 71. Practice ground. *Green Fees:* information not available. *Eating facilities:* fully licensed bar and restaurant. *Visitors:* welcome anytime subject to availability. *Society Meetings:* societies and corporate days by prior arrangement.

SHERBORNE. **Sherborne Golf Club,** Higher Clatcombe, Sherborne DT9 4RN (01935 814431; Fax: 01935 814218). *Location:* one mile north of Sherborne off the B3145 to Wincanton. Parkland with extensive views. 18 holes, 6414 yards. Par 72. S.S.S. 71. Practice ground. *Green Fees:* information not available. *Eating facilities:* snacks, lunches, suppers, teas; dinners to order. *Visitors:* as commitment allows, telephone in advance. Handicap Certificates required. Thursday is Ladies' Day. *Society Meetings:* catered for Tuesdays and Wednesdays. Professional: Alistair Tresidder (Tel & Fax: 01935 812274). Secretary/ Manager: Phil Gamble (01935 814431; Fax: 01935 814218).*

SOUTH PERROTT. **Chedington Court Golf Club,** South Perrott DT8 3HU (01935 891413). *Location:* three miles south east of Crewkerne on A356. Parkland course surrounded by woods, very picturesque, several ponds. 18 holes, 5924 yards, S.S.S. 70. 5-acre practice area. *Green Fees:* weekdays £20.00, weekends £25.00. *Eating facilities:* restaurant and bar open all day; new dining facility. *Visitors:* all welcome. Dress restrictions. Trolleys, buggies and clubs for hire. *Society Meetings:* all welcome, special rates available.
e-mail: admincgc@tiscali.co.uk
website: www.chedingtongolf.co.uk

STUDLAND. **Isle of Purbeck Golf Club,** Studland, Swanage BH19 3AB (01929 450361). *Location:* A351 towards Swanage, at Corfe Castle turn onto B3351 to Studland. Heathland courses with wonderful views. Purbeck - 18 holes, 6295 yards. S.S.S. 70. Dene - 9 holes, 2022 yards. S.S.S. 30. *Green Fees:* information not available. *Eating facilities:* bar and restaurant. *Visitors:* welcome. Buggies available. *Society Meetings:* catered for by arrangement, minimum 8. Professional: Ian Brake (01929 450354). Secretary: Mrs J. Robinson (01929 450361; Fax: 01929 450501).*
e-mail: bookings@purbeckgolf.co.uk
website: www.purbeckgolf.co.uk

VERWOOD. **Crane Valley Golf Club,** The Clubhouse, Verwood BH31 7LE (01202 814088; Fax: 01202 813407). *Location:* on B3081 Verwood to Cranborne Road. Parkland featuring lakes and River Crane. 18 holes, 6400 yards. S.S.S. 71. 9 hole woodland course, 2100 yards. Covered driving range. *Green Fees:* 18 hole course weekdays £30.00, weekends £40.00; 9 hole course weekdays £7.00; weekends £10.00. *Eating facilities:* restaurant and spikes bar. *Visitors:* welcome at all times. Accommodation adjoining course at West Farm. *Society Meetings*: by appointment. Secretary/ Manager: Darrel Ranson

WAREHAM. **The Dorset Golf & Country Club,** Bere Regis, Near Poole BH20 7NT (01929 472244; Fax: 01929 471294). *Location*: take A352 off Wareham by-pass, enter Puddletown Road, Worgret Heath or the Wool road from Bere Regis. After 4 miles, the Club is clearly signposted. A fantastic Golfing Complex. The courses have 27 holes with mixes of the three 9 holes. From 7027 yards Lakeland and Parkland, to 5901 yards Parkland and Woodland courses. Par 72 and Par 69. Driving range and Pro Shop. *Green Fees*: weekdays £36.00; weekends £40.00. *Eating facilities*: excellent bar and restaurant. *Visitors*: welcome anytime with prior tee reservation. *Society Meetings*: welcome by advance booking. The Dorset Golf Hotel overlooks course – 16 en suite bedrooms and luxury Scandinavian log homes for rent. Professional: Scott Porter (01929 472244). Secretary: Graham Packer (01929 472244; Fax: 01929 471294).
e-mail: admin@dorsetgolfresort.com
website: www.dorsetgolfresort.com

ENGLAND / Dorset

WAREHAM. **Wareham Golf Club,** Sandford Road, Wareham BH20 4DH (01929 554156; Fax: 01929 557993). *Location*: adjoining A351 north of Wareham. Partly wooded course with splendid views over Purbeck Hills and Poole Harbour. 18 holes, 5753 yards, S.S.S. 68. Practice ground, putting green. *Green Fees*: £22.00 per round, £28.00 per day; weekends £25.00 per round. *Eating facilities*: excellent bar and restaurant. *Visitors*: welcome, after 9.30am weekdays and after 1pm weekends. Handicap Certificate preferred. *Society Meetings*: very welcome, special packages available.
e-mail: warehamgolf@tiscali.co.uk
website: www.warehamgolfclub.com

WEYMOUTH. **Wessex Golf Centre,** Radipole Lane, Weymouth DT4 9HX (01305 784737). *Location:* Wessex roundabout off Weymouth by pass, behind football stadium. Flat public course. 9 holes, 1432 yards. Par 3. Large driving range, putting green, practice bunker. *Green Fees:* information not available. *Visitors:* welcome; public course. Shop. Professional: Jon Bevan.*

WEYMOUTH. **Weymouth Golf Club Ltd,** Links Road, Weymouth DT4 0PF (01305 773981; Fax: 01305 773981). *Location:* A354 from Dorchester, take last exit at Manor roundabout then second left at Chafeys roundabout. Undulating parkland. 18 holes, 5981 yards. S.S.S. 69. Practice area. *Green Fees:* weekdays £26.00 per day, weekends and Bank Holidays £32.00. £16.00 after 4pm. Half price playing with a member. Juniors half price. Green fees are subject to review. *Eating facilities:* full restaurant and bar. *Visitors:* welcome, but only with EGU or Club Handicap Certificate. *Society Meetings:* welcome by prior arrangement except weekends. Special rates for Society, Company/ Corporate Days. Conference facilities and local transport arranged. Professional: Des Lochrie (01305 773997). Manager: Stuart Elliott (01305 773981; Fax: 01305 788029).
e-mail: weymouthgolfclub@aol.com
website: www.weymouthgolfclub.co.uk

WIMBORNE. **Canford Magna Golf Club,** Knighton Lane, Wimborne BH21 3AS (01202 592552; Fax: 01202 592550). *Location*: off A341, near Bear Cross roundabout on the main A348 Ringwood Road. Three courses: Parkland – 18 holes, 6495 yards; Riverside – 18 holes, 6231 yards; Knighton – 9 holes, 2754 yards, Par 3. 6-hole academy course and driving range, practice area. *Green Fees*: Knighton – weekdays £7.00 for 9 holes, £10.00 for 18 holes, weekends £8.00 for 9 holes, £12.00 for 18 holes. Riverside – weekdays £10.00 for 9 holes, £18.00 for 18 holes, weekends £13.00 for 9 holes, £21.00 for 18 holes. Parkland – weekdays £12.00 for 9 holes, £22.50 for 18 holes, weekends £15.00 for 9 holes, £26.00 for 18 holes. Under 18s £12.00. *Eating facilities*: two bars, meals served throughout day; restaurant. *Visitors*: welcome. Prior booking advisable (one week in advance). Club hire and lessons; Pro Shop. Handicap Certificate not required. Conference facilities. Professionals: 6 full-time professionals headed by PGA Pro Martin Cummins. General Manager: Stuart Hudson.
e-mail: admin@canfordmagnagc.co.uk
website: www.canfordmagnagc.co.uk

WIMBORNE. **Canford School Golf Club,** Canford School. Wimborne BH21 3AD (01202 841254; Fax: 01202 881009). *Location*: close to Wimborne, Poole and Bournemouth. Flat Parkland course. 9 (x2) holes, 5934 yards. S.S.S. 69. *Green Fees*: information not available. *Society Meetings*: Contact Secretary. Secretary: Mark Burley (01202 841254; Fax: 01202 881009).*

WIMBORNE. **Sturminster Marshall Golf Club,** Moor Lane, Sturminster Marshall, Wimborne BH21 4AH (01258 858444; Fax: 01258 858262). *Location:* Poole to Blandford Forum road, A350 signposted at village. Flat parkland course, suits golfers of all abilities. 9/18 holes, 5028 yards. S.S.S. 65. Practice net. *Green Fees:* information not available. *Eating facilities:* fully licensed snack bar. *Visitors:* welcome, no restrictions. *Society Meetings:* welcome. Professional: Graham Howell. Secretary: D.R. Holdsworth.*

The Dorset Golf & Country Club, Bere Regis, Near Poole

Durham

BARNARD CASTLE. **Barnard Castle Golf Club,** Harmire Road, Barnard Castle DL12 8QN (01833 638355 or 637237). *Location:* one mile north of Barnard Castle Town Centre on the B6278. Open parkland with a number of streams to be crossed and with maturing copses. 18 holes, 6406 yards. S.S.S. 71. Practice area. *Green Fees:* weekdays £20.00 per round, £24.00 per 27 holes; weekends and Bank Holidays £30.00 per round, £35.00 27 holes. Reduced rates playing with member. *Eating facilities:* full catering. *Visitors:* welcome, but formal booking system applies at weekends and Bank Holidays. *Society Meetings:* catered for by prior arrangement. Professional: Darren Pearce (01833 631980). Secretary: J. Kilgarriff (01833 638355).

BEAMISH. **Beamish Park Golf Club,** Beamish, Stanley DH9 0RH (0191-370 1382; Fax: 0191-370 2937). *Location:* follow directions to Beamish Museum. Parkland, 18 holes, 6183 yards (white markers). S.S.S. 70. 5963 yards (yellow markers). S.S.S. 69. Two practice areas. *Green Fees:* information not available. *Eating facilities:* bar and à la carte menu. *Visitors:* welcome weekdays. Carts for hire. *Society Meetings:* welcome. Professional: Chris Cole (0191-370 1984). Hon. Secretary: Les Howes.

BILLINGHAM. **Billingham Golf Club**, Sandy Lane, Billingham TS22 5NA (01642 554494). *Location:* off A19 trunk road, one mile west of Billingham town centre. Undulating parkland. 18 holes, 6346 yards. S.S.S. 70. Practice area including pitching green and putting greens. *Green Fees:* weekdays £25.00, £15.00 with member; weekends £40.00, £20.00 with member. *Eating facilities:* full catering. *Visitors*: welcome weekdays, prior booking advised. *Society Meetings:* catered for by prior arrangement with Secretary. Caterer (01642 554494). Professional: M. Ure (01642 557060). Secretary: P.B. Hodgson (Tel & Fax: 01642 533816).
e-mail: billinghamgc@onetel.com
website: www.billinghamgolfclub.com

BISHOP AUCKLAND. **Bishop Auckland Golf Club,** High Plains, Durham Road, Bishop Auckland DL14 8DL (01388 661618). *Location:* leave Bishop Auckland Market Place on route to Spennymoor/ Durham, half a mile on left. Parkland, 18 holes, 6379 yards. S.S.S. 70 (Par 72). Practice fairways. *Green Fees:* £25.00 per round. *Eating facilities:* bar, full catering facilities. *Visitors:* welcome mid-week only. Ladies' Day Tuesday. Two snooker tables. *Society Meetings:* catered for on application, not weekends and Christmas period, and official Handicap required. Special package £33.00 for parties of 4 or more, includes catering. Professional: D. Skiffington (01388 661618). Secretary: F. Cohoon (01388 661618).
e-mail: enquiries@bagc.co.uk
website: www.bagc.co.uk

BRANCEPETH. **Brancepeth Castle Golf Club,** The Clubhouse, Brancepeth DH7 8EA (0191-378 0075; Fax: 0191-378 3835). *Location:* A690 Durham to Crook, turn left at crossroads in Brancepeth village, take immediate left at the castle gates, 200 yards down lane. Parkland course undulating in parts. 18 holes, 6285 yards, S.S.S. 70. Practice field, putting green. *Green Fees:* information not available. *Eating facilities:* full bar and restaurant facilities. *Visitors:* parties welcome weekdays, individuals only at weekends. Changing rooms and showers, lessons by arrangement. *Society Meetings:* welcome weekdays, good rates available. Tee available 9.30am and 1.30pm. Professional: D. Howdon (0191-378 0183). Secretary: I.B. Murray (0191-378 0075; Fax: 0191-378 3835).

CHESTER-LE-STREET. **Chester-le-Street Golf Club,** Lumley Park, Chester-le-Street DH3 4NS (0191 3883218). *Location:* half a mile east of Chester-le-Street adjacent to Lumley Castle. Fairly flat parkland. 18 holes, 6457 yards, 5535 metres. S.S.S. 71. Practice area. *Green Fees:* midweek £25.00 per round, £30.00 per day; weekends and public holidays £30.00 per round, £35.00 per day. *Eating facilities:* snacks, lunches, dinners. *Visitors:* welcome 9.30am to 12 noon, 1.30pm to 4.30pm weekdays; 10.30am to 12 noon, 2pm onwards weekends. Must be members of a golf club and have a Handicap. Hotel adjacent. *Society Meetings:* welcome except weekends and Public Holidays. Professional: D. Fletcher (0191 3890157; Fax: 0191 3881220). Secretary: Bill Routledge (0191 3883218).

CHESTER-LE-STREET. **Roseberry Grange Golf Club,** Grange Villa, Chester-le-Street DH2 3NF (0191-370 0670). *Location:* three miles west of Chester-le-Street on A693. Parkland course. 18 holes, 5809 yards. S.S.S. 68. Driving range. *Green Fees:* weekdays £14.50; weekends £18.50; visiting party packages. *Eating facilities:* bar meals 12 noon to 2pm and 7pm to 9.30pm. *Visitors:* welcome, no restrictions weekdays, Saturdays 7am to 10.30am, Sundays 7am to 11.30am. Professional: C. Jones (0191-370 0660). Secretary: Raymond McDermott (0191-370 2047).

CONSETT. **Consett and District Golf Club Ltd,** Elmfield Road, Consett DH8 5NN (01207 502186; Fax: 01207 505060). *Location:* 14 miles north of Durham on A691 (hidden turning on steep hill). 18 holes, 6023 yards. S.S.S. 69. Parkland, undulating, excellent views over Derwent Valley. *Green Fees:* weekdays £20.00; weekends £26.00, half fees with member. *Eating facilities*: full catering available (limited on Mondays). *Visitors:* welcome most times, phone Secretary. *Society Meetings:* catered for by arrangement, enquiries welcomed through Secretary. Secretary: P. Crinnion (01207 505060 Fax/Answer machine)

CROOK. **Crook Golf Club,** Low Jobs Hill, Crook DL15 9AA (01388 762429). *Location:* eleven miles west of Durham City on A690. Scenic views; excellently conditioned course. 18 holes, 6102 yards, 5902 metres. S.S.S. 69. Practice area. *Green Fees:* information not available. *Eating facilities:* available, limited Mondays. *Visitors:* welcome but limited times at weekends. *Society Meetings:* welcome by arrangement with Secretary. Special packages available. Hon Secretary: Les Shaw (01388 762429).*

DARLINGTON. **Blackwell Grange Golf Club,** Briar Close, Blackwell, Darlington DL3 8QX (01325 464464). *Location:* one mile south of Darlington on A66 turn into Blackwell. Signposts to Club. Parkland course. 18 holes, 5621 yards. S.S.S. 68. *Green Fees:* weekdays £20.00 per round, £25.00 per day; weekends and Bank Holidays £30.00 per round. *Eating facilities:* full menu except Sundays and Mondays. *Visitors:* welcome without reservation except weekends. *Society Meetings:* catered for except Wednesdays and weekends. Professional: Joanne Furby (01325 462088). Secretary: Peter Burkill (Tel & Fax: 01325 464458).

DARLINGTON. **The Darlington Golf Club (Members) Ltd,** Haughton Grange, Darlington DL1 3JD (01325 355324; Fax: 01325 480668). *Location:* northern outskirts of town, A1150 off A167, easy access from A1(M) or A19. Flat wooded parkland course designed by Dr Alister Mackenzie. 18 holes, 6181 yards. S.S.S. 69. 10 acre practice ground, chipping area and net. *Green Fees*: information not available. *Eating facilities*: dining room, lounge and bar. *Visitors:* welcome weekdays and selected weekends with reservation. Must be members of recognised golf club. Buggies available for hire. *Society Meetings:* package deals by arrangement weekdays. Professional: Craig Dilley (01325 484198). Secretary: George W. Storey (01325 355324 Ext. 1 or 2).*
e-mail: darlington.golfclub@virgin.net
website: www.darlington-gc.co.uk

DARLINGTON. **Dinsdale Spa Golf Club,** Neasham Road, Middleton-St-George, Darlington DL2 1DW (01325 332222). *Location:* near Teesside Airport. Parkland. 18 holes, 6090 yards. S.S.S. 69. Large practice ground. New course layout (3 holes) in May 2006. *Green Fees:* £25.00 per day. Playing with a member £12.50 weekdays, £15.00 weekends. *Eating facilities:* bar, catering. *Visitors:* welcome weekdays, weekends with a member only. *Society Meetings:* catered for Monday, Wednesday, Thursday and Friday by advance booking. Professional: Martyn Stubbings (Tel & Fax: 01325 332515). Secretary: P. Davison (01325 332297).

DARLINGTON. **Hall Garth Golf and Country Club Hotel,** Coatham, Mundeville, Darlington DL1 3LU (01325 300400; Fax: 01325 310083). *Location:* A1 J59, follow the A167 toward Darlington, after 300 yards turn left at Brafferton, entrance after 200 yards on right. Parkland course. 9 holes, 6621 yards. S.S.S. 72. *Green Fees:* information not available. *Eating facilities:* Stables Country Pub. *Visitors:* always welcome. *Society Meetings:* welcome; prices on request.*

DARLINGTON. **Stressholme Golf Club,** Snipe Lane, Darlington DL2 2SA (01325 461002; Fax: 01325 461002). *Location:* signposted off the A66 Teesside to Scotch Corner outside of Darlington. Parkland course with water features. 18 holes, 6431 yards. S.S.S. 71. 25 bay driving range with nets, chipping greens, distance markers, etc. *Green Fees:* information not available. *Eating facilities:* bar in clubhouse with extensive catering facilities. *Visitors:* welcome all week. Professional/Secretary: Ralph Givens (Tel & Fax: 01325 461002).

www.uk-golfguide.com

Darlington Golf Club
Haughton Grange, Darlington, Co. Durham. DL1 3JD
Darlington's oldest and most prestigious golf club with its lush, tree-lined fairways and unforgiving semi rough has plenty of Alister MacKenzie inspired greens making the parkland layout a haven for putting enthusiasts.

WINTER WARMER Package
* Coffee & Bacon Sandwiches on arrival
* 18 Holes of Golf
* Meal of the Day

Only £22 per person
FOR GROUPS OF 4 OR MORE
Available Monday to Friday from
1st October to 31st March 2006

Pick & Mix
Mid Week Packages
for Societies and Visiting Parties
From £20 per person

For further details contact Michelle on 01325 355324 ext 2
For more information, Club News and additional Special Offers visit the Darlington Website at www.darlington-gc.co.uk

See also Colour Advertisement on page 39

BLACKWELL GRANGE GOLF CLUB BRIAR CLOSE, BLACKWELL, DARLINGTON DL3 8QX

Established 1930. 5,584 yards, Par 68.
Beautiful, picturesque course with tree-lined fairways.
VISITORS AND SOCIETIES WELCOME **Call 01325 464458**
or Professional on 01325 462088 for latest Green Fee offers

DURHAM. **Durham City Golf Club,** Littleburn, Langley Moor, Durham DH7 8HL (0191-378 0806). *Location:* from Durham City take A690 to Crook - course signposted in Langley Moor. Parkland, bordered by the River Browney. 18 holes, 6326 yards. S.S.S. 70. Large practice area. *Green Fees:* weekdays £25.00, weekends £35.00. Half fees if playing with a member. Substantial discounts for parties of 20 or more. *Eating facilities:* no catering Mondays or Thursday evenings. *Visitors:* welcome at all times, only restrictions when club competitions are being held – ring Professional for details. *Society Meetings:* welcome, but restricted to weekdays. Professional: S. Corbally (0191-378 0029). Hon. Secretary: Ian Wilson (0191-386 4434).

DURHAM. **Mount Oswald Manor and Golf Course,** South Road, Durham DH1 3TQ (0191-386 7527; Fax: 0191-386 0975; *Location:* A1(M) Junction marked Bowburn, A177 Durham City follow signs for Darlington. Parkland, partially wooded. 18 holes, 6101 yards. S.S.S. 69. *Green Fees:* information not available. *Eating facilities:* bar meals, Sunday lunches, set meals, etc. *Visitors:* welcome except Sunday mornings before 10am (members only). Bookings only at weekends and Bank Holidays. *Society Meetings:* welcome, same restrictions as visitors. Must order food. General Manager: Mr N. P. Galvin (0191-386 7527).
e-mail: information@mountoswald.co.uk
website: www.mountoswald.co.uk

DURHAM. **Ramside Hall Hotel and Golf Club,** Carrville DH1 1TD (0191-386 9514; Fax: 0191- 386 9519). *Location:* two miles north-east of Durham on A690. A1 (M) Junction 62. 27 holes, 6217/6851 yards. S.S.S. 70/73. Driving range and golf academy. *Green Fees:* please telephone for information. *Eating facilities:* choice of three eating areas. *Visitors:* welcome. Professional: R. Lister (0191-386 9514). Secretary: M. J. Davis.*

EAGLESCLIFFE. **Eaglescliffe Golf Club Ltd,** Yarm Road, Eaglescliffe, Stockton-on-Tees TS16 0DQ (01642 780098; Office: 01642 780238). *Location:* on A135 one mile north of Yarm and three miles south of Stockton. Hilly parkland course, sloping to River Tees. 18 holes, 6245 yards. S.S.S. 70. Practice area and putting green. *Green Fees:* weekdays £30.00 per round, £40.00 per day.; weekends and Bank Holidays £36.00 per round, £50.00 per day. *Eating facilities*: two bars, meals available, separate diningroom. *Visitors:* welcome weekdays, restriction on Tuesdays and Fridays. *Society Meetings*: societies and visiting parties catered for weekdays, some restrictions Tuesdays and Fridays. Professional: Graeme Bell (01642 790122). Secretary: M.R. Sample (01642 780238).

HARTLEPOOL. **Castle Eden Golf Club,** Castle Eden, Hartlepool TS27 4SS (01429 836220). *Location*: two miles south of Peerlee, use exits from A19. Picturesque parkland course. 18 holes, 6262 yards. S.S.S. 70. Practice ground. *Green Fees:* information not available. *Eating facilities:* restaurant, lounge and bar and snooker room. *Visitors:* welcome weekdays 9.30am–11.30am, 1.45pm– 3.30pm. Tuesday Ladies' day. No visiting parties weekends or Bank Holidays. *Society Meetings:* weekdays only with reservation. Professional: Peter Jackson (01429 836689). Secretary: Derek Livingston (01429 836510).

HARTLEPOOL. **Hartlepool Golf Club Ltd,** Hart Warren, Hartlepool TS24 9QF (01429 274398; Fax: 01429 274129). *Location:* turn right off A1086 at Hart Station – north of town, signposted. Seaside links course. 18 holes, 6125 yards. S.S.S. 70. *Green Fees:* midweek £30.00, weekends £42.00. *Eating facilities:* full catering available except Mondays. *Visitors:* welcome (excluding Sunday) without reservation. Caddy carts. *Society Meetings:* catered for by prior arrangement. Professional: G. Laidlaw (01429 267473). Hon. Secretary: L.G. Gordon (01429 261723).
website: www.hartlepoolgolfclub.co.uk

HARTLEPOOL. **High Throston Golf Club,** Hart Lane, Hartlepool TS26 0UG (01429 275325). *Location:* two miles from A19. Course designed by Jonathan Gaunt (USGA specification) with natural banks, rolling countryside with sea views - 7000 trees planted. 18 holes, 6247 yards, S.S.S. 71. Practice nets, putting green. *Green Fees:* information not available. *Eating facilities:* only light refreshments available at present. *Visitors:* welcome usually at all times. Secretary: Mrs J. Sturrock (01429 268071). *

HARTLEPOOL. **Seaton Carew Golf Club,** Tees Road, Seaton Carew, Hartlepool TS25 1DE (01429 266249). *Location:* two miles south of Hartlepool on A178. Championship seaside links. 22 holes. Old Course: 6658 yards. S.S.S. 72. Brabazon Course: 6900 yards. S.S.S. 73. Micklem Course: 6574 yards. S.S.S. 71. *Green Fees:* information not available. *Eating facilities:* bar snacks, full catering to order. *Visitors:* welcome midweek and some weekends. Advance booking recommended. Buggies for hire. *Society Meetings:* catered for by arrangement. Professional: Mark Rogers (01429 890660). Secretary: J. Hall (01429 296496; Fax: 01429 267952).
e-mail: enquiries@seatoncarewgolf.co.uk
website: www.seatoncarewgolf.co.uk

www.uk-golfguide.com

Ramside Hall Hotel and Golf Club is the North East's largest privately owned hotel with Golf, and it's BRILLIANT!
27 holes of golf, fabulous clubhouse, superb range and academy, 80 beautiful bedrooms, choice of three eating areas and a bar that never shuts - its no wonder that "EVERYONE'S TALKING ABOUT US!".
Ramside Hall Hotel & Golf Club, Carrville, Durham DH1 1TD
Hotel: 0191 3865282 • Fax: 0191 3860399 • Golf: 0191 3869514 • Fax: 0191 3869519
e-mail: info@ramsidehallhotel.co.uk   web: www.ramsidehallhotel.co.uk

THE GOLF GUIDE 2006　　　　　　　　　　　　　　　　ENGLAND / Durham　187

MIDDLESBROUGH. **Middlesbrough Municipal Golf Centre,** Ladgate Lane, Middlesbrough TS5 7YZ (01642 315533; Fax: 01642 300726). *Location*: three miles south of Middlesbrough on A174. Parkland course with featured streams. 18 holes, 6333 yards. S.S.S. 71. Floodlit driving range, practice area and putting green. *Green Fees*: information not available. *Eating facilities*: lunches available seven days, snacks at all other times. *Visitors*: welcome anytime, but starting times must be booked in advance. *Society Meetings*: by prior arrangement, special golf packages available. Professional: Alan Hope (01642 300720). Manager: Mr M. Gormley (01642 315533). Secretary: J. C. Taylor (01642 590910).

NEWTON AYCLIFFE. **Oak Leaf Golf Complex,** School Aycliffe Lane, Newton Aycliffe DL5 6QZ (01325 310820). Location: three miles from A1(M) and A68 on the outskirts of Newton Aycliffe. Rolling parkland. 18 holes, 5568 yards. S.S.S. 67. Driving range (floodlit), chipping and bunker practice. *Green Fees*: information not available. *Eating facilities*: bar and catering available at Oakleaf Golf Complex. Contact (01325 300600). *Visitors*: public course. Visiting parties by appointment. Showers/toilets/changing facilities. Squash/Indoor Bowls at Oakleaf Golf Complex. *Society Meetings*: all welcome by prior arrangement. Professional: Ernie Wilson (01325 310820) Secretary: Mr R. Mitchie (Club) (01325 316040).*

NEWTON AYCLIFFE. **Woodham Golf and Country Club,** Burnhill Way, Newton Aycliffe DL5 4PN (01325 320574; Fax: 01325 315254). *Location*: A167, one mile north of Newton Aycliffe on the Shildon road. Parkland, wooded with lakes. 18 holes, 6771 yards. S.S.S. 72. Practice grounds, putting green. *Green Fees*: information not available. *Eating facilities*: bar/restaurant. *Visitors*: welcome Monday Friday between 10.30am and 12 noon, and from 2pm to 3pm. Weekends 11.30am to 12.30pm & 2pm to 3pm. Buggies, trolleys available. *Society Meetings*: all welcome. Professional: Peter Kelly (01325 315257; Fax: 01325 315254). Secretary: John D. Jenkinson. Steward: (01325 301551).

SALTBURN BY THE SEA. **Saltburn by the Sea Golf Club Ltd,** Hob Hill, Saltburn by the Sea TS12 1NJ (01287 622812). *Location*: from Saltburn take Guisborough Road, one mile out of town on left. parkland course. 18 holes, 5846 yards. S.S.S. 68. *Green Fees*: information not available. *Eating facilities*: available. *Visitors*: welcome, limited Sundays and Thursdays and no visitors Saturdays. *Society Meetings*: catered for by arrangement. Professional: (01287 624653). Secretary: Mike Murtha (01287 622812).

SEAHAM. **Seaham Golf Club,** Shrewsbury Street, Seaham SR7 7RD (0191-581 2354). *Location*: Dawdon, two miles north east of A19 leave for Seaham. Heathland. 18 holes, 6017 yards. S.S.S. 69. Practice area. *Green Fees*: weekdays £21.00 (£14.00 playing with a member); weekends and Bank Holidays £26.00 (£16.00 playing with a member). *Eating facilities*: snacks available, meals on request. *Visitors*: welcome, unrestricted weekdays, booking for weekends. *Society Meetings*: welcome on application. Professional: Andrew Blunt (0191-513 0837). Secretary: Alan Bowmaker (0191-581 1268).

STANLEY. **South Moor Golf Club,** The Middles, Craghead, Stanley DH9 6AG (01207 232848; Fax: 01207 284616). *Location*: eight miles north-west of Durham, seven miles west of A1 (M) from Chester-le-Street. Parkland and moorland. 18 holes, 6307 yards. S.S.S. 70. *Green Fees*: weekdays £18.00 per round, £25.00 per day; with a member £12.00 per round, £18.00 per day; weekends and Bank Holidays £30.00 per day; with a member £15.00 per round, £20.00 per day. *Eating facilities*: available. *Visitors*: visiting parties between 10am and 11.30am and 2pm to 3.30pm. *Society Meetings*: catered for except Sundays. Professional: Shaun Cowell (01207 283525). Secretary: B. Davison (01207 232848).

FHG Guides

Seaton Carew Golf Club

www.seatoncarewgolf.co.uk

The Old Course - an enjoyable challenge for golfers of all abilities, redesigned in 1925 by Dr Alister MacKenzie, who also designed Augusta, home of the US Masters.
The Brabazon Course - an extended challenge of almost 7000 yards, a tricky but rewarding course which has been chosen as a test for EGU and R&A Championships.

Visitors welcome midweek and some weekends
Societies catered for by arrangement.

**Seaton Carew Golf Club, Tees Road,
Seaton Carew, Hartlepool, Durham TS25 1DE
Tel: 01429 296496 • Fax: 01429 267952**

See also Colour Advertisement on page 38

THE APPEARANCE OF AN ASTERISK (*) AT THE END OF A CLUB OR COURSE ENTRY INDICATES THAT UP-TO-DATE INFORMATION HAS NOT BEEN SUPPLIED

STOCKTON-ON-TEES. Knotty Hill Golf Centre, Sedgefield, Stockton-on-Tees TS21 2BB (01740 620320; Fax: 01740 622227). *Location:* A1 (M) Junction 60, one mile north of Sedgefield A177. Princes Course set in rolling parkland with many holes routed through shallow valleys. Bishops Course, a developing course with varied water features laid out within attractive rolling terrain. Princes Course – 18 holes, 6433 yards, 5882 metres, S.S.S. 71, par 72; Bishops Course – 18 holes, 5915 yards, 5406 metres, par 70. Indoor Golf Academy, video and tuition range, high quality floodlit driving range, open grass tee area, chipping and putting greens, practice bunker. *Green Fees:* 9 holes £8.00, 18 holes £13.00. *Eating facilities:* restaurant, coffee shop. *Visitors:* welcome at all times. Buggy and cart hire. *Society Meetings*: welcome, information on request. Secretary: Mrs J. Reynolds (01740 620320).

STOCKTON-ON-TEES. Norton Golf Course, Junction Road, Norton, Stockton-on-Tees TS20 2SU (01642 676385; Fax: 01642 608467). *Location:* turn into Junction Road to Norton from A177 at Horse and Jockey, two miles north of Stockton roundabout. Slightly hilly course with five lakes. 18 holes, 5393 yards. S.S.S. 70. *Green Fees:* weekdays £11.50 for 18 holes, weekends and Bank Holidays £13.50. Subject to review. E*ating facilities:* catering and bar available (Bar 01642 612452). *Visitors:* must have golf shoes and own clubs; no jeans. Parties welcome weekdays. *Society Meetings:* rates on application. Secretary: Mrs Dianne Harper (01642 674636).

STOCKTON-ON-TEES. Teesside Golf Club, Acklam Road, Thornaby, Stockton-on-Tees TS17 7JS (01642 676249; Fax: 01642 676252). *Location*: A19 - A1130 to Thornaby, 0.7 miles on right hand side. Flat parkland. 18 holes, 6535 yards. S.S.S. 71. Practice ground, putting green. *Green Fees:* weekdays £26.00, weekends £30.00. *Eating facilities:* catering except Mondays, bar 11am to 11pm. *Visitors:* welcome midweek up to 4.30pm, weekends after 11am by arrangement. *Society Meetings:* Monday - Friday. Special rates and conditions for parties and guests. Professional: K.W. Hall (01642 673822). Secretary: M. Fleming (01642 616516). e-mail: teessidegolfclub@btconnect.com website: www.teessidegolfclub.com

THE APPEARANCE OF AN ASTERISK (*) AT THE END OF A CLUB OR COURSE ENTRY INDICATES THAT UP-TO-DATE INFORMATION HAS NOT BEEN SUPPLIED

FHG
K·U·P·E·R·A·R·D

Other specialised FHG Guides
Published annually: available in all good bookshops or direct from the publisher.

£7.99 £7.99

Recommended **COUNTRY INNS & PUBS** OF BRITAIN

Recommended **COUNTRY HOTELS** OF BRITAIN

Recommended **SHORT BREAK HOLIDAYS** IN BRITAIN

The bestselling **PETS WELCOME!**

£7.99

FHG Guides • Abbey Mill Business Centre, Seedhill, Paisley, Renfrewshire PA1 1TJ
Tel: 0141-887 0428 • Fax: 0141-889 7204
e-mail: admin@fhguides.co.uk
www.holidayguides.com

£8.99

Essex

BASILDON. **Basildon Golf Club,** Clay Hill Lane, Basildon SS16 5JP (01268 533297). *Location:* off A13 or A127 on A176 – Kingswood Roundabout. Undulating woodland. 18 holes, 6236 yards. S.S.S. 70. Practice area. *Green Fees:* information not available. *Eating facilities:* snacks, full meals, bar. *Visitors:* welcome anytime, booking system at weekends and Bank Holidays. *Society Meetings:* welcome, booking through Professional. Professional: Mike Oliver (01268 533532). Secretary: A.M. Merrington (01268 533297; Fax: 01268 284163).

BILLERICAY. **Stock Brook Golf & Country Club,** Queens Park Avenue, Stock, Near Billericay CM12 0SP (01277 653616; Fax: 01277 633063). *Location:* nearest main roads A12 and A127, Billericay. Parkland - gently undulating with featured lakes. 18 hole championship course, 6905 yards. S.S.S. 73. Manor - 9 holes, 2997 yards. Driving range, putting green and three par 3 practice holes. *Green Fees:* information not available. *Eating facilities:* bar meals available. *Visitors:* welcome. Handicap Certificate required. Extensive conference and banqueting facilities. Country club, swimming pool, tennis courts, gym. *Society Meetings:* welcome. Professional: Craig Laurence (01277 653616). Membership, Corporate and Society enquiries: Caron Morton.*

BRAINTREE. **Braintree Golf Club,** Kings Lane, Stisted, Braintree CM77 8DD (01376 346079; Fax: 01376 348677). *Location:* A120 to Colchester, 300 yards east of Braintree by-pass, signposted Stisted and Golf Club. Parkland, with slopes down to the river, many specimen trees. 18 holes, 6228 yards, S.S.S. 70. Practice ground, pitching area. *Green Fees:* weekdays £38.00 per day, £30.00 per round; £42.00 Saturdays only. *Eating facilities:* available. *Visitors:* welcome Monday to Fridays (weekends must have Handicap Certificate). *Society Meetings:* catered for Wednesdays, Thursdays and Friday pm. Professional: A.K. Parcell (01376 343465). Secretary: Mrs N. Wells (01376 346079; Fax: 01376 348677).

BRAINTREE. **Towerlands Golf Club,** Panfield Road, Braintree CM7 5BJ (01376 326802; Fax: 01376 552487). *Location:* off A120 into Braintree, then B1053. Undulating course. 9 holes, 2749 yards. S.S.S. 66. Practice area. *Green Fees:* information not available. *Eating facilities:* bars and restaurants. *Visitors:* welcome. We have equestrian facilities, no accommodation. *Society Meetings:* by arrangement. Secretary: B. Clark (01376 326802; Fax: 01376 552487).

BRENTWOOD. **Bentley Golf Club,** Ongar Road, Brentwood CM15 9SS (01277 373179). *Location:* situated on A128 approximately five miles from Junction 28 of M25. Flat parkland course. 18 holes, 6709 yards, 6136 metres. S.S.S. 72. Practice field. *Green Fees:* 18 holes £27.50. *Eating facilities:* food and bar available all day. *Visitors:* welcome weekdays; Bank Holidays after 11am. *Society Meetings:* welcome by prior arrangement. Professional: Nick Garrett (01277 372933). Secretary: Geoff Scott (01277 373179).

BRENTWOOD. **Hartswood Golf Club,** (Play on Brentwood Municipal), King George's Playing Fields, Ingrave Road, Brentwood CM15 8AY (01277 218850). *Location:* one mile south of Brentwood on A128. Parkland, 18 holes, 6238 yards. S.S.S 70. *Green Fees:* information not available. *Eating facilities:* full catering available. *Visitors:* welcome without reservation. Tee Reservation – 01277 214830. *Society Meetings:* unlimited weekdays. Professional: Stephen Cole (01277 218714). Secretary:J Gander (01277 218850)

BRENTWOOD. **South Essex Golf and Country Club,** Brentwood Road, Herongate, Brentwood CM13 3LW (01277 811006; Fax: 01277 811304). *Location:* Halfway House Exit (A128) from A127 (Junction 29 - M25). Gently rolling countryside incorporating established woodland. 27 holes, 6851 yards. S.S.S. 73. Covered 14 bay driving range. *Green Fees:* Monday to Thursday £19.00, Fridays £21.00; weekends £25.00. Twilight and Early Bird rates available. *Eating facilities:* restaurant and fully licensed bar. *Visitors:* welcome with appropriate dress. Buggies available. *Society Meetings:* welcome, including weekends. General Manager: Olly Wooster (01277 811289; Fax: 01277 811304).

BRENTWOOD. **Thorndon Park Golf Club Ltd,** Thorndon Park, Ingrave, Brentwood CM13 3RH (01277 811666). *Location:* three miles south of Brentwood on A128. 18 holes, 6492 yards. S.S.S. 71. *Green Fees:* £60.00 per day, £45.00 per round weekdays, £50.00 per round after 1pm Sundays. Saturday and Sunday morning with members only. Subject to review. *Eating facilities:* lunches served at club. *Visitors:* welcome with reservation, weekdays subject to prior permission. *Society Meetings:* catered for. Professional: Brian White (01277 810736). Secretary: Lt Col R.M. Estcourt (01277 810345). website: www.thorndonparkgolfclub.com

FHG please mention THE GOLF GUIDE when you enquire about clubs or accommodation

·K·U·P·E·R·A·R·D·

BRENTWOOD. **The Warley Park Golf Club,** Magpie Lane, Little Warley, Brentwood CM13 3DX (01277 224891). *Location:* leave M25 at Intersection 29. A127 towards Southend. Turn left three-quarters-of-a-mile Little Warley, Hall Lane. Turn left into Magpie Lane. Parkland, 3 Courses, (27 holes). S.S.S. 70-70-69. Large practice area, putting greens. *Green Fees:* weekdays £50.00 per round, £70.00 per day. *Eating facilities:* lounge bar and restaurant/spike bar. *Visitors:* welcome Monday to Friday, must produce club Handicap Certificate. *Society Meetings:* catered for. Professional: K. Smith (01277 200441). Golf Manager: S. Young (01277 224891).

BRENTWOOD. **Weald Park Golf Club,** Coxtie Green Road, South Weald, Brentwood CM14 5RJ (01277 375101). *Location:* M25 and A12 junction (map available). Parkland course surrounded by countryside. 18 holes, 6612 yards. S.S.S. 72/70. *Green Fees:* information not available. *Eating facilities:* bar and restaurant. *Visitors:* welcome. *Society Meetings:* welcome Monday to Friday. Professional: Dean Vickerman (01277 375101; Fax: 01277 374888). General Manager: Darcy Tallon (01277 375101; Fax: 01277 374888).*

BULPHAN. **The Langdon Hills Golf & Country Club,** Lower Dunton Road, Bulphan RM14 3TY (01268 548444; Fax: 01268 490084). *Location:* eight miles from M25, Dartford River crossing, Basildon three miles between A127 and A13. Gently undulating parkland. Three loops of 9 holes – 27 holes: 6760 yards S.S.S. 72, 6537 yards S.S.S. 72, 6279 yards S.S.S. 71. 22 bay floodlit driving range, practice area and two putting greens. *Green Fees:* information not available. *Eating facilities:* brasserie restaurant, spike bar, Function Suite available. *Visitors:* welcome at all times subject to availablity. Hotel accommodaton and function suite available. *Society Meetings:* welcome. Professional: Terry Moncur (01268 544300; Fax: 01268 490084). Secretary: Brian Hardie (01268 548444; Fax: 01268 490084). Manager: Colin Phillips. *

BURNHAM-ON-CROUCH. **Burnham-on-Crouch Golf Club Ltd,** Ferry Road, Creaksea CM0 8PQ (01621 782282). *Location:* Burnham-on-Crouch, one and a half miles before Burnham town. Undulating meadowland rolling alongside River Crouch. 18 holes, 6056 yards. S.S.S. 69. Par 70. Practice ground. *Green Fees:* information not available. *Eating facilities:* bar, full catering. *Visitors:* welcome weekdays, and weekend afternoons, with Handicap Certificate. *Society Meetings:* welcome Mondays, Tuesdays, Wednesdays and Fridays only. Secretary: (01621 782282). Private members club.*

CANVEY ISLAND. **Castle Point Golf Club,** Somnes Avenue, Canvey Island SS8 9FG (01268 696298). *Location:* A13 towards Southend, A130 to Canvey Island, opposite sports centre. Links course, with views of Hadleigh Downs and Castle. 18 holes, 6176 yards. S.S.S. 69. Floodlit driving range. *Green Fees:* information not available. *Eating facilities:* clubhouse open to public – full catering. *Visitors:* welcome anytime, booking required at weekends. Changing room and showers; buggies available. Pro Shop (01268 510830). *Society Meetings:* welcome. Professional: Steve Richardson (01268 510830). Secretary: Belinda de Kuster (01268 692899).*

CHELMSFORD. **Channels Golf Club,** Belsteads Farm Lane, Little Waltham, Chelmsford CM3 3PT (01245 440005). *Location:* three miles north east of Chelmsford on A130. Reclaimed gravel workings, many lakes, hazards and an abundance of wild life. Two courses – Channels 6402 yards, S.S.S. 71; Belsteads 4779 yards, S.S.S. 63. *Green Fees:* Channels Course – weekdays only £36.50 per 18 holes; members and guests only at weekends. Belsteads Course – £15.00 9 holes, £22.00 18 holes, no restrictions weekends. *Eating facilities:* excellent restaurant in 13th century clubhouse. *Visitors:* welcome. *Society Meetings:* catered for weekdays. Professional: I.B. Sinclair (01245 441056). Secretary: Mrs S. Stubbings-Larner (01245 440005; Fax: 01245 442032).
e-mail: info@channelsgolf.co.uk
website: www.channelsgolf.co.uk

CHELMSFORD. **Chelmsford Golf Club,** Widford Road, Chelmsford CM2 9AP (Tel & Fax: 01245 256483). *Location:* A12–A414 to Chelmsford, first roundabout turn right. Parkland course. 18 holes, 5996 yards. S.S.S. 69. *Green Fees:* weekdays £40.00. *Eating facilities:* dining room and bar. *Visitors:* welcome Monday to Friday with reservation. *Society Meetings:* welcome, discounts available. Professional: Mark Welch (01245 257079). Secretary: G. Winckless.
e-mail: office@chelmsfordgc.co.uk
website: www.chelmsfordgc.co.uk

CHELMSFORD. **The Regiment Way Golf Centre,** Pratts Farm Lane, Little Waltham, Chelmsford CM3 3PR (01245 361100). *Location:* three miles north east of Chelmsford off A130. Flat parkland, ideal novice course. 9 holes, 2500 yards. S.S.S. 64. 22 bay floodlit driving range. *Green Fees:* weekdays £11.00 9 holes, £15.00 18 holes; weekends £12.00 9 holes, £17.00 18 holes. Student and Senior discount £2.00 9 holes, £3.00 18 holes. *Visitors:* pay as you play. *Society Meetings:* welcome. Professionals: David March. Secretary: Roger Pamphilon.

CHELMSFORD. **Three Rivers Golf and Country Club,** Stow Road, Cold Norton, Purleigh, Near Chelmsford CM3 6RR (01621 828631; Fax: 01621 828060). *Location:* four miles from South Woodham Ferrers, six miles from Maldon. Parkland with lakes and wooded copses; spectacular views. Two courses: 36 holes, 6403 yards Kings Course, 4501 Jubilee Course. Kings par 72/Jubilee par 64. *Green Fees:* price on application. *Eating facilities:* bar meals available all day, carvery available Sunday lunchtime. *Visitors:* welcome. Function suites available. Buggies available. *Society meetings:* very welcome. Specialists in looking after companies and groups. Professional: Kevin Clark, individual and group lessons available. (01621 829781).*

ENGLAND / Essex

CHIGWELL. **Chigwell Golf Club,** The Clubhouse, High Road, Chigwell IG7 5BH (020 8500 2059; Fax: 020 8501 3410). *Location:* on A113, 14 miles from London, seven miles from Exit 26 on the M25. Testing undulating parkland course. 18 holes, 6279 yards. S.S.S. 70. Practice bays and ground. *Green Fees:* weekdays £35.00 per round (£25.00 per 2.30pm), £50.00 per day; weekends with introduction by member only. *Eating facilities:* restaurant and bars available. *Visitors:* weekdays by prior arrangement, Handicap Certificate required and membership of authorised Golf Club. *Society Meetings:* weekdays by arrangement. Professional: R. Beard (020 8500 2384). Secretary: Richard Danzey (020 8500 2059; Fax: 020 8501 3410).
e-mail: info@chigwellgolfclub.co.uk
website: www.chigwellgolfclub.co.uk

CHIGWELL. **Hainault Forest Golf Club,** Romford Road, Chigwell IG7 4QW (020 8500 2097). *Location:* off A12 towards Hainault/Chigwell. Undulating parkland with tree-lined fairways. 36 holes: Lower 6545 yards. S.S.S. 72; Upper 5886 yards. S.S.S. 69. Driving range, practice hole and putting green. *Green Fees:* information not available. *Eating facilities:* fully licensed bar and restaurant, cafe. *Visitors:* welcome any time, all week. *Society Meetings:* welcome all week, enquiries welcome. Head Professional: Chris Hope. Secretary: Ben Jones.*

CHIGWELL. **Woolston Manor Golf Club,** Woolston Manor, Abridge Road, Chigwell IG7 6BX (020 8500 2549; Fax: 020 8501 5452). Private exclusive members' club - for membership enquiries call membership secretary on 020 8500 2549. *Location:* Junction 5, M11 one mile. Parkland, Neil Coles Championship design, 18 holes, 6435 yards. S.S.S. 71. Top golf driving range. *Green Fees:* information not available. *Eating facilities:* full catering available. *Visitors:* welcome weekdays after 10.30am and after 11.30am weekends. Handicap Certificate required. *Society Meetings:* welcome weekdays only. Professional: Paul Eady (020 8559 8272; Fax: 020 8501 5452). Secretary: Peter Spargo.*

CLACTON-ON-SEA. **Clacton-on-Sea Golf Club,** West Road, Clacton-on-Sea CO15 1AJ (01255 421919). *Location:* A12 then A120 to Clacton-on-Sea, follow signs for promenade/pier then turn right along promenade to sharp right hand bend. 250 metres on left. Seaside course. 18 holes, 6448 yards. S.S.S. 71. *Green Fees:* weekdays £25.00 per round, £35.00 per day; weekends £30.00 per round, £45.00 per day. *Eating facilities:* full bar and catering facilities available from 11am. *Visitors:* welcome with reservation and current Handicap Certificate. Please check with Pro Shop prior to visit. *Society Meetings:* Monday to Friday catered for by arrangement. Professional: Stuart Levermore (01255 426304). Secretary: Helen Woodrow (Tel: 01255 421919).
e-mail: secretary@clactongolfclub.com
website: www.clactongolfclub.com

COLCHESTER. **Birch Grove Golf Club,** Layer Road, Colchester CO2 0HS (01206 734276). *Location:* on B1026, two miles south of town. Parkland - small but challenging. 9 holes, 4500 yards. Par 66. *Green Fees:* £10.00 per 9 holes, £13.00 per 18 holes. *Eating facilities:* hot meals and snacks are available during opening hours. *Visitors:* welcome without reservation Monday to Saturday and after 1pm Sundays. *Society Meetings:* catered for weekdays. Secretary: Mrs M. Marston.

COLCHESTER. **Colchester Golf Club,** Braiswick, Colchester CO4 5AU (01206 853396). *Location:* one mile north-west of Colchester North Station, on B1508. Parkland course with wooded areas. 18 holes, 6347 yards. S.S.S. 70. *Green Fees:* information not available. *Eating facilities:* catering available all day. *Visitors:* welcome except Saturday and Sunday mornings, must have Handicap Certificates. *Society Meetings:* catered for by prior arrangement. Professional: Mark Angel (01206 853920). Secretary: Mr J. H. Wiggam (01206 853396; Fax: 01206 852698).
e-mail: colchester.golf@btinternet.com

COLCHESTER. **Colne Valley Golf Club,** Station Road, Earls Colne, Colchester CO6 2LT (01787 224343; Fax: 01787 224126). *Location:* off the A1124, 10 miles from Colchester. Parkland course in the Valley of the River Colne. 18 holes, 6286 yards. S.S.S. 71. Practice ground. *Green Fees:* weekdays £25.00 per round; weekends £30.00 per round. *Eating facilities:* two bars and restaurant facilities open all day. *Visitors:* welcome anytime but weekends only after 11am and please phone in advance to confirm. Carts for rental. *Society Meetings:* midweek anytime, weekends after 11am, packages available. Head Professional: Peter Garlick.

COLCHESTER. **Lexden Wood Golf Club,** Colchester and Lexden Golf Centre, Bakers Lane, Colchester CO3 4AU (01206 843333; Fax: 01206 854775). *Location:* one mile north west of Colchester, two minutes on the A12 northbound on A133. Undulating parkland with many water features. 27 holes –18 hole and 9 hole short course. 5300 yards. S.S.S. 67. *Green Fees:* information not provided. *Eating facilities:* home cooked food always available during opening hours. *Visitors:* always welcome, please phone to book tee time. Floodlit covered driving range/putting green. *Society Meetings:* always welcome by prior arrangement. Professional: Phil Grice (01206 843333; Fax: 01206 854775).

THE APPEARANCE OF AN ASTERISK (*) AT THE END OF A CLUB OR COURSE ENTRY INDICATES THAT UP-TO-DATE INFORMATION HAS NOT BEEN SUPPLIED

www.uk-golfguide.com

Essex / ENGLAND

COLCHESTER. The Essex Golf and Country Club, Earls Colne, Colchester CO6 2NS (01787 224466; Fax: 01787 224410). *Location:* B1024 off the A120 opposite Coggeshall. Flat parkland 18 hole/9 hole courses. 18 holes, 6900 yards. S.S.S. 73. Floodlit driving range. *Green Fees:* information not available. *Eating facilities:* Poolside Grill, sports brasserie, restaurant. *Visitors:* all welcome, no restrictions. Buggies and trolleys available. Full leisure facilities, indoor pool, sauna, steam room, gym, tennis courts. Full day nursery facilities available, conference and entertainment facilities. On site 42 bedroom hotel including two suites. *Society Meetings:* welcome. Professional: Lee Cocker. Secretary: David Clark.*
website: www.clubhaus.com

ELSENHAM. Elsenham Golf Centre, Hall Road, Elsenham CM22 6DH (01279 812865; Fax: 01279 816970). *Location:* A120 Takley, turn towards Elsenham. Just past the "Jam Factory". Parkland, part wooded course. 9 holes, 3000 yards. S.S.S. 68. 18 bay driving range, 3 hole Academy Course. *Green Fees:* information not available. *Eating facilities:* bar, food. Open to non-members, children welcome. *Visitors:* always welcome. Changing facilities. Pro Shop. Teaching facility. *Society Meetings:* all welcome. Professional: Owen McKenna (01279 812865; Fax: 01279 816970).

EPPING. North Weald Golf Club, Rayley Lane, North Weald, Epping CM16 6AR (01992 522118; Fax: 01992 522881). *Location:* from M11 Junction 7 take A414 to Chelmsford, two miles to first roundabout, turn right. Club is 200 yards on left. Parkland and lakes. 18 holes, 6377 yards. S.S.S. 71. Driving range, putting green, chipping green and practice bunker. *Green Fees:* weekdays £20.00; weekends £30.00. *Eating facilities:* available. *Visitors:* welcome by arrangement. *Society Meetings:* welcome by arrangement. Professional: Ben Goodey (01992 525737). Secretary: Andrew Lloyd-Skinner (01992 522118; Fax: 01992 522881).
website: www.northwealdgolfclub.co.uk

EPPING. Theydon Bois Golf Club, Theydon Road, Epping CM16 4EH. *Location:* M25 Waltham Abbey/Epping A121 London to Cambridge, turn right at Bell Motel. Wooded course. 18 holes, 5480 yards. S.S.S. 68. Practice area. *Green Fees:* £30.00 per round, £20.00 after 5pm weekdays. *Eating facilities:* restaurant and bar. *Visitors:* welcome except Wednesday and Thursday morning. *Society Meetings:* Monday, Tuesday and Friday. Professional: R. Hall (01992 812460). Manager: M.C. Slatter (01992 813054).

FRINTON-ON-SEA. Frinton Golf Club, 1 Esplanade, Frinton-on-Sea CO13 9EP. *Location:* 17 miles east of Colchester, A12 - A133, B1033. Flat seaside links course, strength of wind always a feature. 18 holes, 6265 yards. S.S.S. 70. Short Course 3062 yards, no Handicap Certificate required. Practice facilities. *Green Fees:* weekdays £36.00 per round. Short course, 18, 27 or 36 holes £16.00. Weekends £42.00 per round. Cheaper green fees during winter period. *Eating facilities:* snack and restaurant facilities. *Visitors:* welcome, check with Secretary. Handicap Certificate required. *Society Meetings:* catering by arrangement. Professional: Peter Taggart (Tel & Fax: 01255 671618). Secretary: P. H. Jones (01255 674618).
e-mail: frintongolf@lineone.net
website: www.frintongolfclub.com

HALSTEAD. Gosfield Lake Golf Club, The Manor House, Gosfield, Halstead CO9 1SE. *Location:* off the A1017 four miles north of Braintree. Gently undulating parkland course with lakes and woods; designed by Sir Henry Cotton. Two courses: Lakes Course 18 holes, 6615 yards. S.S.S. 72; Meadows Course 9 holes (double teed to 18), 4990 yards S.S.S. 64. Practice facilities including putting, chipping, bunkers. *Green Fees:* please contact Pro Shop for information (01787 474488). *Eating facilities:* bar and catering facilities from 11am; bar menu. *Visitors:* welcome. Weekdays booking advisable, weekends from 12 noon (booking necessary). Handicap Certificate required for Lakes Course, Meadows Course ideal for beginners/improvers. Trolley hire. Buggy hire (summer only). *Society Meetings:* welcome by prior arrangement. Professional: Richard Wheeler (01787 474488) Secretary: J.A. O'Shea (01787 474747; Fax: 01787 476044).
e-mail: gosfieldlakegc@btconnect.com.
website: www.gosfield-lake-golf-club.co.uk

HARLOW. Canons Brook Golf Club, Elizabeth Way, Harlow CM19 5BE (01279 425142). *Location*: Turn onto Elizabeth Way at Harlow Town Station on A414 from M11. Parkland course. 18 holes, 6745 yards. S.S.S. 73. *Green Fees*: £27.00 per round. *Eating facilities*: available, open all day. *Visitors*: welcome weekdays, weekends with a member. *Society Meetings:* catered for Mondays, Wednesdays and Fridays. Professional: Alan McGinn (01279 418357). Secretary: Mrs S. Langton (01279 421482; Fax: 01279 626393).

HARWICH. Harwich and Dovercourt Golf Club, Station Road, Parkeston, Harwich CO12 4NZ (01255 503616; Fax: 01255 503323). *Location:* A120 then to Parkeston Quay, course marked on left hand side of Station Road. Flat course. 9 holes, 5742 yards. S.S.S. 68. *Green Fees:* information not available. *Eating facilities:* licensed clubhouse, catering available to order (not Thursdays). *Visitors:* welcome with Handicap Certificates. No visitors Saturdays, Sundays and Bank Holidays unless with a member. *Society Meetings:* small groups welcome by arrangement. Hon. Secretary: Mr A. Boddy (01255 503616).

ILFORD. Fairlop Waters, Forest Road, Barkingside, Ilford IG6 3JA (020 8500 9911). *Location:* two miles north of Ilford, half a mile from A12, one and a half miles from southern end of M11. Covered, floodlit range, 36 bays. 18 hole golf course, 9 hole Par 3 course. Individual or group tuition available. *Green Fees:* information not available. Opening hours: 9am to 10pm. *Eating facilities:* bars and diner. Banqueting facilities and conferences. 38 acre sailing lake, 25 acre country park, children's play area. Professional: Paul Davies (020 8501 1881). General Manager: Mr F. Taylor.*

ILFORD. **Ilford Golf Club,** 291 Wanstead Park Road, Ilford IG1 3TR (020 8554 2930). *Location:* at end of M11, off A406. Parkland with winding river. 18 holes, 5299 yards. S.S.S. 66. *Green Fees:* weekdays £17.00 plus special offers, weekends £22.00. *Eating facilities:* restaurant and bar. *Visitors:* welcome weekdays, restricted times at weekends. *Society Meetings:* welcome. Professional: S. Jackson (020 8554 0094). General Manager (020 8554 2930; Fax: 020 8554 0822).

INGATESTONE. **Hylands Golf Complex,** Main Road, Margaretting, Ingatestone CM4 0ET (01277 356016; Fax: 01277 356056). *Location*: off A12. Parkland course. 9 holes 2445 yards, 18 holes 6604 yards. Driving range, practice bunker. *Green Fees:* information not available. *Eating facilities:* coffee and soft drinks available. *Visitors:* all welcome. New complex, pay and play only; no membership. Accommodation at Ivy Hill Hotel, Margaretting. Professional: Lee Porter (01277 356016; Fax: 01277 356056).*

LEIGH-ON-SEA. **Belfairs Golf Club,** Eastwood Road North, Leigh-on-Sea SS9 4LR (01702 526911). Park front 9, heavy woodland back 9; easy walking but challenging golf. Play over Belfairs Municipal course, 18 holes, 5857 yards. S.S.S. 68. *Green Fees:* information not available. *Visitors:* unrestricted on the course but no clubhouse facilities available. Bookings required (01702 525345). Secretary: B. J. Harvey (01702 714567).

LITTLE BURSTEAD. **The Burstead Golf Club,** Tye Common Road, Little Burstead CM12 9ST (01277 631171; Fax: 01277 632766). Parkland course. 18 holes, 6275 yards, S.S.S. 70. Practice field, chipping area, putting green. *Green Fees*: information not available. *Eating facilities*: restaurant, bar and spike bar. *Visitors:* welcome Monday to Friday except Bank Holidays, weekends after 1pm. Tuiton available. *Society Meetings*: welcome Monday to Friday, except Bank Holidays. Professional: Keith Bridges. Secretary: Lee Mence. *

LOUGHTON. **Loughton Golf Club,** Clay's Lane, Debden Green, Loughton IG10 2RZ (020 8502 2923). *Location*: just north of Loughton, on edge of Epping Forest. Parkland, wooded. 9 holes, 4700 yards. S.S.S. 63. Practice range. *Green Fees:* weekdays £8.00 9 holes, £13.00 18 holes; weekends £9.00 for 9 holes, £15.00 for 18 holes. *Eating facilities:* bar, snacks available. *Visitors:* welcome, telephone to book. *Society Meetings:* welcome. Manager: Alan Day.

MALDON. **Bunsay Downs Golf Club,** Little Baddow Road, Woodham Walter, Maldon CM9 6RW (01245 222648; Fax: 01245 223989). *Location:* 7 miles east of Chelmsford off A414 at Woodham Walter, left onto Little Baddow Road. Undulating landscaped partly wooded course. 9 holes, 2932 yards. S.S.S. 68. Par 3 course. *Green Fees:* information not available. *Eating facilities:* bar/grill restaurant. *Visitors:* welcome at all times. Gift shop. *Society Meetings:* small societies welcome. Professional: Mickey Walker. Secretary: Mr M. Durham (01245 223258).*

THE ESSEX GOLF & COUNTRY CLUB

THE LODGE AT THE ESSEX

Also see Meyrick Park, Dorset

Discover one of the finest Clubs in the Heart of the Essex Countryside!

Full English Breakfast and complimentary use of the health & fitness club throughout your stay

- 18 Hole Championship Golf Course
- 9 Hole Executive Course
- 42 Room Lodge
- Café Bar & Brasserie
- Gym
- 3 Aerobics Studios
- Indoor Pool, Spa, Sauna, Steam Room
- aura Health & Beauty

01787 22 44 66

Earls Colne, Colchester, Essex CO6 2NS
email: essex.hotel@clubhaus.com
www.clubhaus.com

MALDON. **Five Lakes Resort,** Colchester Road, Tolleshunt Knights, Maldon CM9 8HX (01621 868888; Fax: 01621 869696). *Location:* seven miles from A12 on B1026 north of Maldon and south of Colchester. Parkland. Two courses: Links Course - 18 holes, 6181 yards, S.S.S. 70; Lakes Course - 18 holes, 6751 yards, S.S.S. 72. Driving range, three putting greens. *Green Fees:* information not available. *Eating facilities:* three restaurants and two bars. *Visitors:* welcome at most times except before 10am weekend mornings. 194 en suite bedrooms, conference and banqueting facilities, indoor pool, air conditioned gym, health club, sauna, steam room and spa bath, tennis, squash and badminton. *Society Meetings:* catered for by appointment. Professional: Gary Carter (01621 862326; Fax: 01621 862320). Golf Consultant: James Taylor (01621 862307; Fax: 01621 862320).*

MALDON. **Forrester Park Golf and Tennis Club,** Beckingham Road, Great Totham, Near Maldon CM9 8EA (Tel & Fax: 01621 891406). *Location:* three miles off A12 Rivenhall turn-off, on B1022 in Great Totham, near Maldon between Compasses and Bull. Parkland course. 18 holes, 6073 yards. S.S.S. 69. Practice ground. *Green Fees:* weekdays £21.00 per round, £26.00 per day; weekends £22.00 after 12 noon only. *Eating facilities:* full catering and bar facilities. *Visitors:* welcome subject to prior booking, but not before 12 noon Tuesdays, Wednesdays and weekends. Trolley hire. Buggy hire (summer only). *Society Meetings:* welcome subject to prior booking. Professional: Gary Pike (01621 893456). Manager: Tim Forrester-Muir (Tel & Fax: 01621 891406).

MALDON. **Maldon Golf Club,** Beeleigh, Langford, Maldon CM9 6LL (01621 853212). *Location:* B1019 two miles northwest of Maldon, turn off by the Museum of Power. Flat parkland. 9 holes, 6253 yards, 5718 metres. S.S.S. 70. *Green Fees:* 18 holes £18.00, all day £25.00 weekdays; weekends 18 holes £15.00, all day £20.00 with a member only. *Eating facilities:* full catering service, bar. *Visitors:* welcome weekdays. *Society Meetings:* catered for by arrangement. Secretary: D. Kelly.

MALDON. **Warren Golf Club,** Woodham Walter, Maldon CM9 6RW (01245 223198/223258; Fax: 01245 223989). *Location*: close to Chelmsford. A414 turn off to Maldon. Undulating wooded course. 18 holes, 6263 yards. S.S.S. 70. Large practice area. *Green Fees:* information not available. *Eating facilities:* restaurant, bar, bar snack menu. *Visitors:* welcome with reservation weekdays except Wednesday mornings. Handicap Certificate required. Golf Academy. *Society Meetings:* catered for weekdays - up to 40 players. Professional: David Brooks (01245 224662). Managing Director: M.F.L. Durham.

NAZEING. **Nazeing Golf Club,** Middle Street, Nazeing EN9 2LW (01992 893915; Fax: 01992 893882). *Location:* from Waltham Abbey Town Centre - signposted. Parkland course, American design (sand based greens and tees). 18 holes, 6617 yards. S.S.S. 72. Continental style driving range. *Green Fees:* information not available. *Eating facilities:* available. *Visitors:* welcome anytime except weekend mornings, must ring and book through Pro shop. Buggies, trolleys available. *Society Meetings:* welcome. Professional: Robert Green (01992 893798; Fax: 01992 893882).

OCKENDON. **Belhus Park Golf Club,** Belhus Park, Aveley By-Pass, South Ockendon RM15 4QR (01708 852240 complex, 01708 854748 office). *Location:* on A13 London - Southend Road, approximately one mile from Dartford Tunnel. Parkland. 18 holes, 5350 yards. S.S.S. 69. Driving range. *Green Fees:* information not available. *Eating facilities:* cafe and bar. *Visitors:* welcome anytime (municipal course), but booking essential weekends and Bank Holidays. Swimming pool. *Society Meetings:* by arrangement, telephone complex. Professional: Jamie Gowan (01708 854260). Secretary: J. Cleary (01708 865645).*

ONGAR. **Toot Hill Golf Club,** School Road, Toot Hill, Near Ongar CM5 9PU (01277 365523; Fax: 01277 364509). *Location:* A128 to Ongar, A414 to Harlow, two miles left at Blake Hall Road. Parkland course, lakes and brook. 18 holes, 6197 yards, Par 70, S.S.S. 69. Practice range, putting and chipping green. *Green Fees:* midweek £25.00 per round, £35.00 per day. *Eating facilities:* available, clubhouse and spike bar. *Visitors:* welcome. *Society Meetings:* welcome Tuesdays and Thursdays, various packages. Professional: Mark Bishop (01277 365747). Secretary: Mrs C. Cameron.

ORSETT. **Orsett Golf Club,** Brentwood Road, Orsett RM16 3DS (01375 891352). *Location:* A13 Junction roundabout with A128. South towards Chadwell St Mary on A128. Heathland course. 18 holes, 6693 yards. S.S.S. 72. *Green Fees:* weekdays £40.00 per round, £55.00 all day. *Eating facilities:* full catering available. *Visitors:* welcome on weekdays only by arrangement. Must be members of a club and have Handicap. Proof must be produced. *Society Meetings:* welcome on Mondays and Tuesdays. Professional: R. Herring (01375 891797). Secretary: Office (01375 891352; Fax: 01375 892471).

RAYLEIGH. **Hanover Golf and Country Club,** Hullbridge Road, Rayleigh SS6 9QS (01702 232377; Fax: 01702 231811). *Location:* A130, A127 Rayleigh. Parkland course, seven lakes. 18 holes, 6669 yards. S.S.S. 72. Par 73. Putting green. *Green Fees:* information not available. *Eating facilities:* two bars, restaurant, bar meals, function rooms. *Visitors:* welcome weekdays, Club Handicap required. *Society Meetings:* welcome weekdays. Professional: A. Blackburn (01702 230033). Secretary: T. Harrold.*

ROCHFORD. **Rochford Hundred Golf Club,** Hall Road, Rochford SS4 1NW (01702 544302; Fax: 01702 541343). *Location:* A127 towards Southend on Sea, turning for Rochford. Flat parkland course, ancient clubhouse, course surrounds church. 18 holes, 6176 yards (white boxes). S.S.S. 71. *Green Fees:* information not available. *Eating facilities:* full restaurant and snack facilities; bars. *Visitors:* welcome, Tuesday mornings ladies only. Handicap Certificate necessary. *Society Meetings:* catered for except Tuesday mornings, Fridays and weekends. Professional: G. Hill (01702 548510). Secretary: W. J. Collantine.

ROCHFORD near. **Ballards Gore Golf and Country Club,** Gore Road, Canewdon, Near Rochford SS4 2DA (01702 258917). *Location*: Southend Airport three miles, London via A127, club two miles from Rochford. Parkland with lakes. 18 holes, 6845 yards. S.S.S. 73. Practice area. *Green Fees:* information not available. *Eating facilities:* diningroom (100 covers). *Visitors:* welcome weekdays, except Tuesday mornings. *Society Meetings:* catered for by arrangement. Professional: Gary McCarthy (01702 258924; Fax: 01702 258924 Secretary: Mr A. S. Hall (01702 258917; Fax: 01702 258571).

ROMFORD. Maylands Golf and Country Club, Harold Park, Romford RM3 0AZ (01708 341777). *Location:* turn off Junction 28 M25, directly on A12 between Romford and Brentwood. 18 holes, 6182 yards. S.S.S. 70. Driving Range and putting green. *Green Fees:* information not available. *Eating facilities:* bar, spike bar, restaurant and bar snacks. *Visitors:* welcome midweek if members of recognised clubs with Handicap Certificates. *Society Meetings:* catered for Mondays, Wednesdays and Fridays. Professional: Darren Parker (01708 346466). Secretary/Proprietor: R. Fraser (Tel & Fax: 01708 341777).*

ROMFORD. Risebridge Golf Centre, Risebridge Chase, Romford RM1 4DG (01708 741429). Location: off Lower Bedfords Road, between Collier Row and Harold Hill, signposted from Gallows Corner (A12). Mature parkland course with some long tough holes. 18 holes, 6342 yards. S.S.S. 70. 9 hole Par 3 course, driving range, practice green. *Green Fees:* midweek £13.00, weekend £18.00. Off peak rates apply every day. *Eating facilities:* cafe and spike bar. *Visitors:* welcome at all times. *Society Meetings:* all welcome, for details contact the Professional. Professional/Manager: Mr P. Jennings (Tel & Fax: 01708 741429).

SAFFRON WALDEN. Saffron Walden Golf Club, Windmill Hill, Saffron Walden CB10 1BX (01799 522786). *Location:* end of town on A130 to Cambridge. 18 holes, 6606 yards. S.S.S. 72. *Green Fees:* on application. *Eating facilities:* snacks, lunches and evening meals (by prior arrangement). *Visitors:* welcome with current Handicap Certificate Monday to Friday. *Society Meetings:* catered for Mondays, Wednesdays and Thursdays. Professional: Philip Davis. General Manager: Chris Charlton. e-mail: office@swgc.com website: www.swgc.com

SOUTH BENFLEET. Boyce Hill Golf Club Ltd, Vicarage Hill, South Benfleet SS7 1PD (01268 793625). *Location*: one-and-a-half-miles south of A13/A127. Hilly course, 18 holes, 6003 yards, 5489 metres. S.S.S. 69. *Green Fees*: £35.00 18 holes, £45.00 36 holes. *Eating facilities*: full bar and dining facilities daily. *Visitors*: welcome, except Tuesday mornings and weekends. 24 hours notice of booking and Handicap Certificate required. *Society Meetings*: catered for Thursdays only. Professional: G. Burroughs (01268 752565). Secretary: P.D. Keeble (01268 793625; Fax: 01268 750497).

SOUTHEND-ON-SEA. Southend-on-Sea Golf Club, Belfairs Lodge, Belfairs Park, Leigh-on-Sea SS9 4LR (01702 524836). *Location*: A127 London to Southend Road. Parkland/wooded course (Belfairs Municipal course). 18 holes, 5877 yards. S.S.S. 68. *Green Fees:* information not available. *Eating facilities:* restaurant in the park near Starter's Hut. *Visitors:* welcome, unrestricted, but bookings required by phone to Starter's Hut (01702 525345). Professional: Martin Foreman (01702 520202). Secretary: Alan Wood (01702 474737).*

SOUTHEND-ON-SEA. **Thorpe Hall Golf Club,** Thorpe Hall Avenue, Thorpe Bay, Southend-on-Sea SS1 3AT (Tel & Fax: 01702 582205). *Location:* one mile east of Southend-on-Sea. Parkland. 18 holes, 6421 yards. S.S.S. 71. *Green Fees:* information not available. *Eating facilities:* Two restaurants and bars. *Visitors:* welcome weekdays with Handicap Certificate, weekends with members only. Squash, snooker and sauna available. *Society Meetings:* welcome Fridays only. Professional: Bill McColl (01702 588195). Secretary: G.H. Smith (01702 582205; Fax: 01702 584498).*

STANFORD LE HOPE. **St. Cleres Hall Golf Club,** St. Cleres Hall, London Road, Stanford le Hope SS17 0LX (Tel & Fax: 01375 361565). *Location:* from M25, A13 Stanford turnoff, Linford exit on roundabout, course half mile on left. Parkland course with Thames Estuary views, sand based, year round play. 18 holes, 6474 yards. S.S.S. 71. 15 bay floodlit driving range, chipping and putting greens. *Green Fees:* information not available. *Eating facilities:* bar; restaurant. *Visitors:* welcome, enquire about tee closures. *Society Meetings:* welcome anytime weekdays; weekends afternoons only. Please telephone for details. Professional/Secretary: David Wood.

STAPLEFORD ABBOTTS. **Stapleford Abbotts Golf Club,** Horseman's Side, Tysea Hill, Stapleford Abbotts, Romford RM4 1JU (01708 381108; Fax: 01708 386345). *Location:* three miles from Junctions 28 and 29 of the M25, off main Ongar Road B175 at Stapleford Abbotts. Parkland course with many mature trees, large bunkers and water hazards. 18 holes, 6501 yards, S.S.S. 72. Par 3 9-hole course. Two practice grounds and practice nets. Also The Priors 18 hole pay-and-play course, 5878 yards, S.S.S 70. *Green Fees:* from £15, please call for more information. *Eating facilities:* fully licensed bar, extensive menu. *Visitors:* welcome weekdays, weekends after 12 noon; welcome all week on 9-hole course. Correct golfing attire must be worn. *Society Meetings:* welcome, call 01708 381108 for more information. Pro Shop: 01708 381278 .

For full details of clubs and courses, plus convenient accommodation
www.uk-golfguide.com

STAPLEFORD TAWNEY. **Abridge Golf and Country Club,** Epping Lane, Stapleford Tawney RM4 1ST (01708 688396). *Location:* A113 from London through Chigwell to Abridge, left at The Rodings, right after 300 yards. Two miles on. Parkland. 18 holes, 6704 yards. S.S.S. 72. *Green Fees:* on application. *Eating facilities:* bar lunches, drinks, snacks available all week. *Visitors:* welcome but must be a member of a recognised golf club and produce evidence of current Handicap, weekdays and weekend afternoons. *Society Meetings:* catered for on Mondays, Wednesdays and Fridays only by arrangement. Professional: Stuart Layton (01708 688333). Secretary: Mr M Gottlieb (Fax: 01708 688550).
e-mail:info@abridgegolf.com
website: www.abridgegolf.com

STOCK. **Crondon Park Golf Club,** Stock Road, Stock CM4 9DP (01277 841115; Fax: 01277 841356). *Location:* off the A12, on to B1007 towards Billericay. Set in parkland valley with trees, lakes and magnificent greens, longest hole in the country (18th 655yds). 18 holes, 6250 yards (Club). S.S.S. 70. 9-hole Par 3 course. Driving range and putting green. Academy Lessons. *Green Fees:* information not available. *Eating facilities:* bar, restaurant. *Visitors:* welcome weekdays; weekend afternoons only. Modern changing rooms, showers, etc. *Society Meetings:* welcome weekdays (Monday to Friday). Professional: Fred Sunderland (Head Pro), Chris Woods (01277 841887). Secretary: Paul Cranwell (01277 841115).

STOKE BY NAYLAND. **Stoke by Nayland Golf Club,** Keepers Lane, Leavenheath, Colchester CO6 4PZ (01206 262836; Fax: 01206 263356). *Location:* just off A134 Colchester to Sudbury on B1068 towards Stoke by Nayland. Undulating parkland with water hazards. Two courses (1) Gainsborough - 18 holes, 6516 yards. S.S.S. 71. (2) Constable - 18 holes, 6544 yards. S.S.S. 71. 20 bay covered range, practice area. *Green Fees:* please enquire for prices. *Eating facilities:* full catering and bars. *Visitors:* welcome, please ring for availability and tee bookings. *Society Meetings:* welcome weekdays, book well in advance. Seasonal packages offered. Excellent golf and spa breaks. Extensive Health and Leisure Facility including gymnasium, pool, sauna, jacuzzi and spa; modern, spacious, en suite hotel rooms overlooking lake and fairways. Professional: Kevin Lovelock (01206 262769). Golf Secretary: Peter Barfield (01206 265815).
e-mail: sales@stokebynayland.com
website: www.stokebynaylandclub.co.uk

UPMINSTER. **Top Meadow Golf Club and Hotel,** Fen Lane, North Ockendon, Upminster RM14 3PR (01708 852239; Fax: 01708 852598) *Location*: M25, A127, B186 towards North Ockendon - Fen Lane. Parkland course with panoramic views of Essex countryside. 18 holes, 6227 yards. S.S.S. 72. Practice range. On site hotel. *Green Fees:* information not available. *Eating facilities:* fully licensed bar and à la carte restaurant. *Visitors*: Visitors and Societies welcome Monday to Friday. Golfing holidays available midweek and weekends. Professional: Roy Porter (01708 859545). Secretary: Daniel Stock (01708 852239). *

UPMINSTER. **Upminster Golf Club,** 114 Hall Lane, Upminster RM14 1AU (01708 222788). *Location:* one mile (north) Upminster Station, one and a half miles west M25/A127 junction. Parkland/wooded – River Ingrebourne runs through the course. Beautiful Grade II Listed Clubhouse, rebuilt in 1654, with an official ghost – listed in the British Book of Ghosts. 18 holes, 6076 yards. S.S.S. 69. *Green Fees:* information not available. *Eating facilities:* full catering service every day. *Visitors:* welcome weekdays by arrangement except Tuesday mornings. *Society Meetings:* catered for Wednesdays, Thursdays and Fridays (max 60). Professional: Steven Cipa (01708 220000). Secretary: Russell Winmill (01708 222788; Fax: 01708 222484).
e-mail: secretary@upminstergolfclub.co.uk
website: www.upminstergolfclub.co.uk

WITHAM. **Benton Hall Golf Club,** Wickham Hill, Witham CM8 3LH (01376 502454 Fax: 01376 521050). *Location:* one mile from A12 between Chelmsford and Colchester. Wooded course with natural lakes. 18 holes 6495 yards. S.S.S. 72. 9 hole executive par three course. *Green Fees:* information not provided. *Eating facilities:* Blackwater Suite function room, Waterside Bar and Restaurant. *Visitors:* welcome, not before 12 noon at weekends. *Society Meetings:* welcome. Director of Golf: Colin Fairweather. General Manager: James Gathercole.

WITHAM. **Braxted Park Golf Club,** Braxted Park, Witham CM8 3EN (01376 572372; Fax: 01621 892840). *Location:* A12 south of Witham; from Chelmsford take Rivenhall turn-off, if travelling towards Colchester take Silver End turn-off. Established 50 years, set in 18th century parkland. 9 holes, 5880 yards. Par 35, S.S.S. 34. Practice ground. *Green Fees:* information not available. *Eating facilities:* clubhouse (licensed), snacks. *Visitors:* welcome. Corporate entertainment available, activity days, wedding receptions. *Society Meetings:* welcome. Professional: John Hudson. *

WOODFORD GREEN. **Woodford Golf Club,** Sunset Avenue, Woodford Green (020 8504 3330). *Location*: near The Harvester (formerly The Castle Public House), Woodford High Road. Forest land. 9 holes, 5867 yards. S.S.S. 68. *Green Fees:* £15.00 per 18 holes. *Eating facilities:* bar. *Visitors:* no green fees Tuesday mornings, Saturdays all day, Sundays before 11.30pm. Red (scarlet) clothing must be worn - trousers or top. *Society Meetings:* welcome. Professional: Jon Robson (020 8504 4254). Hon Secretary: F. R. Wolstenholme (020 8504 3330; Fax: 020 8559 0504).
e-mail: office@woodfordgolfclub.fsnet.co.uk

For full details of clubs and courses, plus convenient accommodation

www.uk-golfguide.com

Gloucestershire

BRISTOL. **Bristol and Clifton Golf Club,** Beggar Bush Lane, Failand, Bristol BS8 3TH (01275 393474). *Location:* M5 Junction 19 - A369 towards Clifton, turn right at A.T.S. into Beggar Bush Lane. Parkland course. 18 holes, 6294 yards. S.S.S. 70. Practice ground. *Green Fees:* weekdays £38.00; weekends £45.00. *Eating facilities:* available. *Visitors:* welcome weekdays without reservation, must have current golf club Handicap. *Society Meetings:* most welcome, Thursdays. Professional: Paul Mitchell (Tel & Fax: 01275 393031). Secretary: Charles Vane Percy (01275 393474; Fax: 01275 394611).
e-mail: mansec@bristolgolf.co.uk
website: www.bristolgolf.co.uk

BRISTOL. **Chipping Sodbury Golf Club,** Chipping Sodbury, Bristol BS37 6PU (01454 319042). *Location:* 12 miles north of Bristol, nine miles from Junction 14 on M5 and three miles from Junction 18 on M4. Parkland course. 6786 yards. *Green Fees:* 18-hole course weekdays £25.00; weekends £30.00. *Eating facilities:* full catering available. *Visitors:* welcome except Saturday/Sunday morning and Bank Holidays. Must have Handicap Certificate. *Society Meetings:* catered for by prior arrangement weekdays only. Professional: Mike Watts (01454 314087). Secretary: S.P. Mowbray.

BRISTOL. **Filton Golf Club,** Golf Course Lane, Filton, Bristol BS34 7QS (0117 969 4169; Fax: 0117 931 4359). *Location:* off A38 north of Bristol and only 3 miles from J15 of M5. Interesting, undulating and challenging mature parkland course on high ground to the north of the City. Established 1909 and regular host to County Championships and events. 18 holes, 6174 yards, Par 70, S.S.S 70. Excellent practice facilities. *Green Fees:* (2005) weekdays £28.00 per round, £35.00 per day. Weekends only as guest of member. Buggies and trolleys for hire. *Eating Facilities:* excellent menu of bar and main meals. *Visitors:* welcome weekdays with a Handicap Certificate or letter of competence. *Society Meetings:* welcome subject to programme of club events - usually available Monday, Wednesday and Friday - information pack on request. Advance booking essential. Professional: Daryl Kelley (0117 969 6968) Secretary: Rob East (0117 969 4169; Fax: 0117 931 4359).
e-mail: thesecretary@filtongolfclub.co.uk
website: www.filtongolfclub.co.uk

THE APPEARANCE OF AN ASTERISK (*) AT THE END OF A CLUB OR COURSE ENTRY INDICATES THAT UP-TO-DATE INFORMATION HAS NOT BEEN SUPPLIED

BRISTOL **"The Gloucestershire",** Tracy Park Estate, Bath Road, Wick, Near Bristol BS30 5RN (0117 937 2251; Fax: 0117 937 4288). *Location*: M4 Junction 18, A46 towards Bath, A420 towards Bristol. Turn left at bottom of steep hill for Lansdown/Bath. Wooded parkland, 400-year-old trees with water hazards and magnificent views of surrounding countryside. Two courses: Crown Course - 18 holes, 6252 yards, Par 69; Cromwell Course - 18 holes, 6246 yards, Par 71. 13 bay driving range. *Green Fees:* information not available. *Eating facilities:* full catering available all day. *Visitors:* welcome - telephone ahead. *Society Meetings:* welcome. 18 en suite bedrooms. Professional: David Morgan. Tee reservations (0117 937 2251; Fax: 0117 937 4288). Secretary: David Knipe. *
e-mail: info@thegloucestershire.com
website: www.thegloucestershire.com

BRISTOL. **Henbury Golf Club,** Henbury Road, Westbury-on-Trym, Bristol BS10 7QB (0117 9500044). *Location:* north M5 Junction 17 A4018 to Westbury-on-Trym; right to Blaise Castle, top of hill turn left. Wooded parkland, very pretty; easily accessible from City Centre and M5. 18 holes, 6007 yards. S.S.S. 70. Practice ground. *Green Fees:* information not available. *Eating facilities*: bars and dining room. *Visitors*: welcome weekdays, Handicap required. Clubs and trolleys for hire. *Society Meetings:* Tuesdays and Fridays only, minimum number 20. Professional: Nick Riley (Tel & Fax: 0117 9502121) Secretary: John Keight (0117 9500044; Fax: 0117 9591928).*
e-mail: thesecretary@henburygolfclub.co.uk

BRISTOL. **The Kendleshire Golf Club,** Henfield Road, Coalpit Heath, Bristol BS36 2UY (0117 956 7007; Fax: 0117 957 3433). *Location:* Henfield Road, off Westerleigh Road from New Avon Ring Road, five minutes from Junction 1 M32. Parkland with water features. 27 holes, from 6001 to 6507 yards. S.S.S. 71. Practice range. *Green Fees:* weekdays £32.00, weekends £35.00, after 3pm £25.00. *Eating facilities:* two bars, restaurant, and function room. *Visitors:* welcome but prior booking essential. *Society Meetings:* welcome weekdays, packages available. Professional: Tony Mealing. Secretary: Patrick Murphy.

BRISTOL. **Knowle Bristol Golf Club,** Fairway, West Town Lane, Brislington, Bristol BS4 5DF (0117 977 0660). *Location:* three miles south of city centre, left off Wells Road. A4 - Bath. Parkland course. 18 holes, 6006 yards. S.S.S. 69. Practice field, putting green. *Green Fees:* weekdays £28.00 for 18 holes, £35.00 for 27 holes; weekends £33.00 for 18 holes, £40.00 for 27 holes. *Eating facilities:* bar/dining room, dinners by arrangement with Steward. *Visitors:* welcome with Handicap Certificate. *Society Meetings:* Thursdays only. Professional: Mr Rob Hayward (0117 977 9193). Secretary: Mr Mike Harrington (0117 977 0660; Fax: 0117 972 0615).
website: www.knowlegolfclub.co.uk

BRISTOL. **Long Ashton Golf Club,** Clarken Coombe, Long Ashton, Bristol BS41 9DW (01275 392229; Fax: 01275 394395). *Location:* three miles south-west of Bristol on the B3128 Clevedon/Bristol Road. Wooded parkland. 18 holes, 6193 yards. S.S.S. 70. Practice ground. *Green Fees:* weekdays £30.00 18 holes, £35.00 36 holes; weekends £35.00 18 holes. *Eating facilities:* full catering daily, bar open Monday to Sunday (11am to 10.30pm). *Visitors:* welcome, must have current Handicap Certificate. *Society Meetings:* by arrangement with Secretary. Professional: Mike Hart (01275 392229). Secretary: Bob Williams (01275 392229).
e-mail: info@longashtongolfclub.org.uk
website: www.longashtongolfclub.org.uk

BRISTOL. **Shirehampton Park Golf Club,** Park Hill, Shirehampton, Bristol BS11 0UL (0117 982 2083). *Location:* two miles from Junction 18 on M5 on B4054 to Shirehampton. Parkland course with spectacular views across Avon Gorge. 18 holes, 5430 yards. S.S.S. 66. *Green Fees:* weekdays £22.00, weekends £20.00 only with member. *Eating facilities:* lunches, snacks, teas, etc available daily. *Visitors:* welcome. *Society Meetings:* catered for by prior arrangement. Professional: Brent Ellis (0117 982 2488). Managing Secretary: Adrian Hobbs (0117 982 2083).

BRISTOL. **Shortwood Lodge Golf Club,** Carsons Road, Mangotsfield, Bristol BS16 9LW (0117 9565501). *Location:* four miles M32 via Downend, one mile Warmley A420. Parkland, hilly course. 18 holes, 5337 yards, 4877 metres. S.S.S. 66. Small practice area. *Green Fees:* information not available. *Eating facilities:* no restriction on food and drink. *Visitors:* welcome anytime, no restrictions. *Society Meetings:* catered for weekdays only. Professional/Secretary: Craig Trewin.*

BRISTOL. **Thornbury Golf Centre,** Bristol Road, Thornbury, Bristol BS35 3XL (01454 281144; Fax: 01454 281177). *Location:* five miles A38 north from Junctions M4/M5 at Almondsbury. Parkland course overlooking River Severn. 18 holes, 6308 yards. S.S.S. 70. Floodlit driving range, video bay, Par 3 course. *Green Fees*: £19.00 weekdays; £23.00 weekends. *Eating facilities*: restaurant and licensed bar. *Visitors*: welcome. Smart casual clothing desirable. Golf Lodge available with 11 rooms. Conference facilities. *Society Meetings:* welcome. Professional: Paul Middleton. Secretary/Manager: Kevin Pickett.

www.uk-golfguide.com

BRISTOL. **Woodlands Golf and Country Club,** Trench Lane, Almondsbury, Bristol BS32 4JZ (01454 619319). *Location:* Junction 16 M5 - A38 towards Bristol. Left off AZTEC roundabout, first left Woodlands Lane. Attractive parkland course with five lakes and ponds, elevated tees and two drop holes. 18 holes, 6068 yards. S.S.S. 69. Practice area. *Green Fees:* weekdays £14.00 per round, weekends £16.00 per round. *Eating facilities:* bar/lounge, bar snacks. *Visitors:* welcome, no restrictions and hire of clubs available. Trolleys and buggies available £12.00 per round. *Society Meetings:* bookable in advance. Large well stocked Pro shop. Professional: Leigh Riddiford. Secretary: David Knipe (Fax: 01454 619397; Shop: 01454 619319; Bar: 01454 618121).
website: www.woodlands-golf.com

BROADWAY. **Broadway Golf Club,** Willersey Hill, Broadway WR12 7LG (01386 853683; Fax: 01386 858643). *Location:* 1½-miles east Broadway (A44). 18 holes, 6211 yards. S.S.S. 70 *Green Fees:* on application. *Eating facilities:* available daily (except Mondays during Winter). *Visitors:* welcome; reservation advised. Handicap Certificates required. Saturdays (April/September) with member only before 3pm. October/March no restrictions. Affiliated to the "Gloucestershire Golf Union". Society Meetings: by arrangement (Wednesday, Thursday and Friday). Professional: Martyn Freeman (01386 853275). Managing Secretary: K. Hodgson (01386 853683).

CHELTENHAM. **Cleeve Cloud Golf Club,** Cleeve Hill, Near Cheltenham GL52 3PW (01242 672025). *Location:* three miles north of Cheltenham on B4632. Hilltop inland links with gorse and natural quarries. Outstanding views from the highest point in the Cotswolds. 18 holes, 6411 yards. S.S.S. 72. *Green Fees:* weekdays £15.00; weekends £18.00. *Eating facilities:* full restaurant and bar facilities. *Visitors:* welcome with prior booking. *Society Meetings:* welcome with prior booking (01242 672025). Professional: Dave Finch (01242 672592). Secretary: Hugh Fitzsimons (01242 672025).

CHELTENHAM. **Cotswold Hills Golf Club,** Ullenwood, Near Cheltenham GL53 9QT (01242 515264). *Location:* at Ullenwood, off the A436 south of Cheltenham (two miles from town). Undulating Cotswold country course, excellent drainage. 18 holes, 6565 yards. S.S.S. 71. Large practice ground. *Green Fees:* weekdays £34.00 18 holes; weekends £39.00 18 holes. *Eating facilities:* full restaurant and bars. *Visitors:* no restrictions as a rule, but it is wise to telephone. *Society Meetings:* catered for on Wednesdays and Fridays only by arrangement with Secretary. Professional: James Latham (01242 515263). Secretary: Annie Hale (01242 515264).
e-mail: golf@chgc.freeserve.co.uk
website: www.cotswoldhills-golfclub.com

THORNBURY GOLF CENTRE AND LODGE
When in Bristol come and stay with us
Call us on **01454 281144** or see for yourself @
www.thornburygc.co.uk

See also Colour Advertisement on page 18

ENGLAND / Gloucestershire 199

CHELTENHAM. **Lilley Brook Golf Club,** Cirencester Road, Charlton Kings, Cheltenham GL53 8EG (01242 526785). *Location:* two miles south-east of Cheltenham on main Cirencester road (A435). Parkland, 18 holes, 6212 yards. S.S.S. 70. Practice field. *Green Fees:* weekdays £25.00 per round, £30.00 per day; weekends £30.00 per round, £35.00 per day. *Eating facilities:* full catering available. *Visitors:* welcome weekdays, weekends subject to availability. Handicap Certificates required. *Society Meetings:* by arrangement. Professional: Karl Hayler (01242 525201). Secretary: M.F. Jordan (01242 526785; Fax: 01242 256880).

CHELTENHAM. **Naunton Downs Golf Club Ltd,** Naunton, Cheltenham GL54 3AE (01451 850092; Fax: 01451 850091). Rolling Cotswold countryside with a valley running through course. 18 holes, 6135 yards. S.S.S. 70. Practice ground. *Green Fees:* Mondays £19.00, Tuesday - Friday £22.00, weekends and Bank Holidays £28.00. *Eating facilities:* available. *Visitors:* welcome midweek only, must book at all times. *Society Meetings:* welcome. Professional: Nick Ellis (01451 850092); Golf Manager: Nick Ellis (01451 850090); Club Steward: Phil Clark (01451 850093).

CHELTENHAM. **Ullenwood Manor Golf Course,** National Star College, Ullenwood, Cheltenham GL53 9QU (01242 527631). *Location*: turn off A436 past junction with A417. Parkland course, 18 holes (using 9 fairways). 2980 yards S.S.S. 54. Designed by Norm Allen, opened 1975. *Green Fees:* £10.00 all day. *Eating facilities*: catering available at Air Balloon pub half mile away. *Visitors:* welcome anytime. Society Meetings: welcome anytime. Secretary: Richard Greenwell.

CHURCHDOWN. **Brickhampton Court Golf Complex,** Cheltenham Road, Churchdown GL2 9QF (01452 859444; Fax: 01452 859333). *Location:* midway between Cheltenham and Gloucester on B4063; 5 minutes from Junction 11 of M5. Rolling parkland courses featuring lakes, streams, strategic white sand bunkers, tree plantations and no steep hills. Two courses: Spa Course - 18 holes, 6449 yards. S.S.S. 71; Glevum Course – 9 holes, 1859 yards. Par 31. 26 bay floodlit covered driving range with Ping custom fitting centre. *Green Fees:* Spa Course – Monday to Thursday £23.00 per round, Friday £25.00, weekends and Bank Holidays £30.00. Glevum Course – weekdays £8.00; weekends and Bank Holidays £10.00. *Eating facilities:* spike bar and restaurant offering varied menu and Sunday lunches. *Visitors:* welcome although pre-booking advised. Buggies and trolleys for hire. Two fully stocked Pro shops. Corporate and Society Golf days available, call for details. Professional: Bruce Wilson.
e-mail: info@brickhampton.co.uk
website: www.brickhampton.co.uk

FHG Guides

CHARLTON KINGS HOTEL & RESTAURANT

Privately owned with high standards throughout.
All rooms have en suite facilities, most have views of the Cotswold hills, and ample car parking is available. Ideally located for Cheltenham and the Cotswolds. Only 2 miles from town centre, 3 miles from racecourse. The choice is yours, whether you want the ideal base for visiting the numerous picturesque towns, villages and places of interest, or prefer the wide choice of shops and theatres, or to relax in the magnificent gardens in Cheltenham.

London Road, Charlton Kings, Cheltenham, Gloucestershire GL52 6UU
Tel: 01242 231061 • Fax: 01242 241900
www.charltonkingshotel.co.uk
e-mail: enquiries@charltonkingshotel.co.uk
Condé Nast Johansens Recommended

See also Colour Advertisement on page 15

BEAUTIFUL PARKLAND COURSES IN THE HEART OF GLOUCESTERSHIRE AND ONLY MINUTES FROM J11 OF THE M5

18 HOLE SPA COURSE (PAR 71)
9 HOLE GLEVUM COURSE (PAR 31)
26 BAY FLOODLIT DRIVING RANGE
2 GOLF SHOPS (SALES, SERVICE, REPAIRS, BUGGY HIRE)
PING CUSTOM FIT CENTRE
SUPERB CLUBHOUSE, RESTAURANT AND BAR
CONFERENCE ROOM
VISITORS - CORPORATE- SOCIETIES
TAILOR MADE GOLF PACKAGES

'EXCITING STIMULATING CHALLENGING GOLF'

Brickhampton Court Golf Complex
CHELTENHAM RD
CHURCHDOWN
GLOUCESTERSHIRE
GL2 9QF
TEL 01452 859444
FAX 01452 859333
EMAIL info@brickhampton.co.uk WEB www.brickhampton.co.uk

Gloucestershire / ENGLAND

CIRENCESTER. **Cirencester Golf Club,** Cheltenham Road, Bagendon, Cirencester GL7 7BH (01285 652465; Fax: 01285 650665). *Location:* two miles north of Cirencester on A435 Cheltenham road. Scenic and free-draining Cotswold course. 18 holes, 6055 yards. S.S.S. 69. Driving range, par-3 course. *Green Fees:* information not available. *Eating facilities:* bar and restaurant - snacks available 10am to 6pm. *Visitors:* welcome, Handicap Certificate required. Buggies for hire. *Society Meetings:* catered for Wednesday and Friday only. Professional: Ed Goodwin (01285 656124). General Manager: Robert Caldecott (01285 652465).
website: www.cirencestergolfclub.co.uk

COLEFORD. **Forest Hills Golf Club Ltd,** Mile End Road, Coleford GL16 7BY (01594 810620; Fax: 01594 810823). *Location:* 10 miles from Severn Bridge, six miles from Monmouth M5, M50. Coleford town centre on Gloucester Road. Parkland with panoramic views to Welsh hills. 18 holes, 6300 yards. Par 72. Practice ground, driving range. *Green Fees:* information not available. *Eating facilities:* bar, restaurant. *Visitors:* welcome, no restrictions. Buggies available. *Society Meetings:* very welcome. Professional: Richard Ballard. Secretary: Colin Revill.*

COLEFORD. **Forest of Dean Golf Club,** Lords Hill, Coleford GL16 8BD (01594 832583; Fax: 01594 832584). *Location:* quarter of a mile from Coleford town centre on B4431 Coleford to Parkend Road, 10 miles from Severn Bridge, M4, M5 and M50. Parkland course in Forest of Dean. 18 holes, 6033 yards. S.S.S. 69. Practice area. *Green Fees:* information not available. *Eating facilities:* food available all day - breakfast, coffee, lunches, teas and dinner. Table d'hôte restaurant, bar open all day. *Visitors:* always welcome, please book teeing-off times with Professional. Own 52 bedroom Hotel, the regions largest golf shop on site, tennis court, bowling green, golf cars available. *Society Meetings:* welcome. Professional: Andy Grey (01594 833689). Secretary: Mrs J. Sandalls (01594 832583).*

DURSLEY. **Stinchcombe Hill Golf Club,** Stinchcombe Hill, Dursley GL11 6AQ (01453 542015; Fax: 01453 549545). *Location*: M5 between Junctions 13 and 14, A38 to Dursley. At traffic lights in centre of Dursley turn right to enter May Lane, continue to top of Hill and turn right onto Golf Course. A gently undulating course situated on a hilltop at the southern edge of the Cotswolds, spectacular views. 18 holes, 5734 yards. S.S.S. 68. Practice and teaching areas. *Green Fees*: £26.00 per round, £32.00 per day weekdays (£13.00 with member); £36.00 per round, £42.00 per day weekends and Bank Holidays (£20.00 with member). *Eating facilities*: full catering and bar service available. *Visitors*: welcome, please call the Professional in advance for availability. *Society Meetings*: Monday, Wednesday and Friday; other days by arrangement. Professional: Paul Bushell (01453 543878). Secretary: I. Crowther (01453 542015).
e-mail: secretary@stinchcombehill.plus.com

GLOUCESTER. **Ramada Hotel and Golf Resort,** Matson Lane, Gloucester GL4 9EA (01452 411331; Fax: 01452 302212). *Location:* follow signs off B4073. Stunning 18 hole, par 72 championship golf course, with breathtaking views of the surrounding countryside, complemented by challenging Par 3, 9-hole course, ideal for beginners and improvers, but a test to better players. Floodlit covered 12 bay golf academy with Callaway custom fit centre open 9.00am to 9.00pm, 7 days a week. Grass practice area with putting, chipping, pitching and bunker areas. *Green Fees:* Championship Course: Monday-Thursday £27.50; guest fee £17.50. Friday-Sunday and Bank Holidays £35.00; guest fee £20.00. Junior fee £10.00. 9-hole course: £6.00 plus club hire. *Eating facilities:* full catering and bar services available. *Visitors:* very welcome, please call for availability. Well-stocked and priced golf shop with all the leading brands, including Callaway, Ping and Taylormade. Hotel with 107 rooms with 5 suites. Extensive leisure complex with indoor swimming pool, gymnasium, sauna and solarium, health and beauty centre. Gloucester Ski Centre with qualified ski instructors. Golf breaks available, golf school with 2, 3 or 5 day programmes. Gloucester Golf Academy with team of registered PGA Golf Professionals. Pro-shop: (01452 411331/01452 874807)
e-mail: gloucester@btopenworld.com
website: www.gloucestergolf.com

GLOUCESTER. **Rodway Hill Golf Course,** Highnam, Gloucester GL2 8DN (01452 384222). 18 holes, 6040 yards. S.S.S. 69. Practice area. *Green Fees:* £14.00 weekdays, £16.00 weekends. *Eating facilities:* Cosy bar and restaurant. *Visitors:* all welcome - pay as you play. *Society Meetings:* special rates available. Professional: not yet appointed.

LYDNEY. **Lydney Golf Club,** The Links, off Lakeside Avenue, Lydney GL15 5QA (01594 842614). *Location:* between by-pass and the town, note - no access off by-pass, enter the town and take Hams Road off the main thoroughfare of Newerne Street. Lakeside Avenue is the 7th road on the left hand side. Flat meadowland with views over the River Severn. 9 holes, 5298 yards. S.S.S. 66. Small practice area. *Green Fees:* information not available. *Eating facilities:* snack meals only. *Visitors:* welcome weekdays, only with a member at weekends/Bank Holidays. *Society Meetings:* welcome by prior arrangement (maximum 36). Hon. Secretary: D.A. Barnard (01594 843940).*

MINCHINHAMPTON. **Minchinhampton Golf Club (Old Course),** Minchinhampton, Stroud GL6 9AQ (01453 832642). *Location*: three miles east of Stroud. Easy walking course. 18 holes, 6019 yards. S.S.S. 69. Practice area. *Green Fees:* weekdays £15.00, weekends and Bank Holidays £18.00. *Eating facilities:* bar and restaurant available. *Visitors:* welcome. *Society Meetings:* most welcome by arrangement. Admin Manager: A.P. Dangerfield (01453 832642). Shop: (01453 836382).
e-mail: mail@mincholdcourse.co.uk
website: www.mincholdcourse.co.uk

MINCHINHAMPTON. **Minchinhampton Golf Club (New Courses),** Minchinhampton, Stroud GL6 9BE (01453 833866; Fax: 01453 837360). *Location:* five miles east of Stroud. Reasonably level, set in typical Cotswold countryside. Avening is cleverly bunkered, Cherington has large undulating greens of superb quality. A members' club with two fine and challenging courses and a fine Cotswold stone clubhouse, all set in lovely countryside. Two courses: both 18 holes, Cherington 6434 yards S.S.S. 71, Avening 6263 yards. S.S.S. 70. Practice area. *Green Fees:* information not available. *Eating facilities:* dining room and bar. *Visitors:* welcome, telephone booking essential on 01453 833840. Handicap Certificate required. *Society Meetings:* welcome weekdays, details on application. Professional: Chris Steele (Tel & Fax: 01453 837351). Secretary: David Calvert (01453 833866; Fax: 01453 837360).*

PAINSWICK. **Painswick Golf Club,** Painswick, Near Stroud GL6 6TL (01452 812180). *Location:* one mile north of Painswick village on A46 turn left. Hilltop, wooded course. 18 holes, 4900 yards. S.S.S. 65. *Green Fees:* weekdays £17.50; Saturdays and Bank Holidays £20.00 but reduced if with a member and/or in the winter. *Eating facilities:* lunches at clubhouse bar Tuesday to Sunday, evening meals in restaurant Tuesday to Saturday subject to availability of tables. *Visitors:* welcome weekdays and Saturday mornings. Saturday afternoons, Sunday mornings and Public Holidays only with member. *Society Meetings:* welcome weekdays. Secretary: Ann Smith.

TETBURY. **Westonbirt Golf Course,** c/o Bursar, Westonbirt School Ltd, Westonbirt, Near Tetbury GL8 8QG (01666 880 242). *Location:* three miles south from Tetbury on A433 to Bath. Parkland. 9 holes, 4504 yards. S.S.S. 61. Practice area and green. *Green Fees:* information not available. *Eating facilities:* tea and refreshments from seasonal caravan. *Visitors:* welcome without reservation. *Society Meetings:* welcome. Enquiries: Bursar's Office, Westonbirt School.*

For full details of clubs and courses, plus convenient accommodation
www.uk-golfguide.com

GLOUCESTER RAMADA HOTEL and GOLF RESORT

- Set on the edge of the Cotswolds, commanding spectacular views
- Outstanding 18 Hole, par 72 championship course
- Challenging 9 Hole par 3 Golf Course, ideal for beginners and improvers
- Covered 12 Bay Golf Academy and Callaway fitting centre, open all day
- Home of the Gloucester Golf Academy, with a team of 1st Class PGA Professionals
- Professional presented grass practice area, with putting/chipping/pitching and bunker areas for you to improve the scoring side of your game
- Well stocked golf shop, Callaway, Taylormade, Ping and all other top brands
- Fully equipped clubhouse with spike bar, restaurant, and function facilities for small or large groups
- Private and Group Coaching available 7 days a week, using the V1 Golf analysis programme
- 107 bedroom Hotel with 5 suites
- Conference Centre with restaurants and bars
- Fully equipped leisure area, including indoor swimming pool, sauna, solarium, gym with qualified instructors
- Gloucester ski centre, two great slopes, ski school with qualified instructors

BOOK NOW FOR A BREAK TO REMEMBER   CALL NOW 01452 411331 or 01452 525653

e-mail: gloucester@btopenworld.com   www.gloucestergolf.com

See also Colour Advertisement on page 16

TEWKESBURY. **Hilton Puckrup Hall,** Puckrup, Tewkesbury GL20 6EL (01684 296200; Fax: 01684 850788). *Location*: leave M5 at Junction 8. Take M50 one mile to Junction 1, leave and bear left taking A38 towards Tewkesbury, Puckrup is half a mile along on the right. Undulating parkland with water hazards, spectacular views of the Malverns. 18 holes, 6219 yards. S.S.S. 70. Practice ground. *Green Fees:* weekdays £25.00; weekends £30.00. Day ticket £30.00 weekdays, £35.00 weekends. *Eating facilities:* choice of bars and restaurants. *Visitors:* welcome, subject to golfing ability and course availability. Buggies available. 112 bedroomed hotel with full leisure facilities. Golfing Breaks available. *Society Meetings:* welcome, packages available from £19.50. Professional: Mark Fenning (01684 271591). Secretary: Janet Stuart (01684 274961).

TEWKESBURY. **Sherdons Golf Centre,** Tredington, Tewkesbury GL0 7BP (01684 274782; Fax: 01684 275358). *Location:* follow brown sign directions from A38 two miles south of Tewkesbury or A46 two miles east. Countryside course with gentle slopes and new plantations. 9 holes, 5308 yards. S.S.S. 66. 26 bay floodlit driving range. *Green Fees:* weekdays 9 holes £7.00, 18 holes £12.00; weekends 9 holes £8.00, 18 holes £15.00. *Eating facilities:* bar, coffee and light snacks available. *Visitors:* welcome at all times. *Society Meetings:* by arrangement, weekdays only. Professionals: Philip Clark and John Parker (01684 274782). Secretary: Richard Chatham (01684 274782; Fax: 01684 275358).

TEWKESBURY. **Tewkesbury Park Hotel Golf and Country Club,** Lincoln Green Lane, Tewkesbury GL20 7DN (01684 295405; Fax: 01684 292386). *Location:* off Junction 9 of M5 through Tewkesbury on A38 - signposted. Parkland. 18 holes, 6533 yards. S.S.S. 71. Golf range, and pitching and chipping greens. *Green Fees:* information not available. *Eating facilities:* full Hotel facilities. *Visitors:* welcome, reservation required. Valid Handicap Certificate required. 80-bedroom hotel plus leisure section. *Society Meetings:* all welcome by prior arrangement. Professional: Charlie Boast (01684 272320; Fax: 01684 292386).*

WOTTON-UNDER-EDGE. **Cotswold Edge Golf Club,** Upper Rushmire, Wotton-under-Edge GL12 7PT (01453 844167). *Location:* eight miles from Junction 14 M5, on B4058 Tetbury road. Fairly flat course with magnificent views. 18 holes, White Tees - 6170 yards. S.S.S. 70; Yellow Tees - 5816 yards. S.S.S. 69. *Green Fees:* information not available. *Eating facilities:* good lunch time catering service, usual bar facilities. *Visitors:* welcome weekdays. Telephone call in advance advisable. *Society Meetings:* by arrangement with Secretary. Professional: Rod Hibbitt (01453 844398). Secretary: E. Johnson (01453 844167; Fax: 01453 845120).

www.uk-golfguide.com

Floodlit Driving Range & Golf Course

- 2 PGA Professionals
- Tuition for groups and individuals at all levels
- Full practice facilities.
- Open 7 days a week

at Tredington, Tewkesbury Tel: 01684 274782

SHERDONS GOLF CENTRE

Tewkesbury Park Hotel, Golf & Country Club

ENGLAND / Gloucestershire

Tewkesbury Park Hotel Golf & Country Club

Lincoln Green Lane
Tewkesbury
Gloucestershire GL20 7DN

Tel: 0870 609 6101 • 01684 295405
Fax: 01684 292386
E-mail: tewkesburypark@corushotels.com
www.tewkesburyparkgolfclub.co.uk

Tewkesbury Park's scenic 18 hole, 6533 yard, par 73 course offers challenging play for both professional and amateur golfers. Designed by Frank Pennick, the course offers many interesting and testing holes, with wooded areas and water hazards early in the round opening up onto spacious fairways on the back nine holes of the undulating course.

Overlooking the Malvern Hills and the Gloucestershire Countryside, this picturesque course also offers six covered driving bays, putting and chipping greens and a 6 hole pitch and putt course.

Hilton Puckrup Hall
★★★★
Hotel & Golf Club

Tewkesbury
Gloucestershire GL20 6EL
Tel: 01684 296200
Fax: 01684 850788
www.tewkesbury.hilton.com

Hilton Puckrup Hall Hotel is the perfect choice for your golfing break. Mature trees, lakes and parkland play host to a challenging and beautifully tended Par 70 Championship course, situated between the Malverns and the Cotswold Hills. Phone now for a brochure on **01684 296200**

See also Colour Advertisement on page 17

Hampshire

ALDERSHOT. **Army Golf Club,** Laffan's Road, Aldershot GU11 2HF (01252 337272; Fax: 01252 337562). *Location:* access from Eelmoor Bridge off A323 Aldershot Fleet Road - second oldest course in Hampshire. 18 holes, 6550 yards. S.S.S. 71. *Green Fees:* special rates for servicemen. *Eating facilities:* bar snacks, restaurant/dining room. *Visitors:* weekdays only, members' guests anytime. *Society Meetings:* catered for. Professional: G. Cowley (01252 336722; Fax: 01252 336686). Manager: John Hiscock (01252 337272; Fax: 01252 337562). e-mail: secretary@armygolfclub.com

ALRESFORD. **Alresford Golf Club,** Cheriton Road, Tichborne Down, Alresford SO24 0PN (01962 733746; Fax: 01962 736040). *Location*: on B3046 south of A31, two miles north A272. Rolling downland, wooded. 18 holes, 5905 yards, 5397 metres. S.S.S. 69. Practice area. *Green Fees:* weekdays £28.00 per round; weekends and Bank Holidays £35.00 per round. *Eating facilities:* full catering. *Visitors:* welcome but not before 12 noon weekends/Bank Holidays. *Society Meetings*: welcome weekdays only, by arrangement. Professional: Malcolm Scott (Tel & Fax: 01962 733998). Secretary: David Maskery (01962 733746; Fax: 01962 736040).
e-mail: secretary@alresford-golf.demon.co.uk
website: www.alresfordgolf.co.uk

ALTON. **Alton Golf Club,** Old Odiham Road, Alton GU34 4BU (01420 82042). *Location:* off B3349 (turn off at Golden Pot). Undulating meadowland, wooded course. 9 holes, 5744 yards. S.S.S. 68. Practice area, putting green. *Green Fees:* information not available. *Eating facilities:* bar, hot and cold snacks all day. *Visitors:* weekdays welcome without reservation. Weekends and Bank Holidays with Handicap Certificate. Trolleys for hire. *Society Meetings:* welcome weekdays only. Professional/Secretary: Richard Keeling (01420 86518). *

ALTON. **Blacknest Golf & Country Club,** Blacknest Road, Blacknest, Alton GU34 4QL (01420 22888). *Location*: Bently exit of A31, between Farnham and Alton. Parkland course with several water features. 18 holes, Par 69; also Par 3 course. *Green Fees:* weekdays £20.00 18 holes, weekends £25.00. *Eating facilities:* bar and dining available from 8am to 5pm. *Visitors:* welcome by arrangement. *Society Meetings:* welcome. Professionals: Darren Burgess, Steve Cowle.

Please mention
THE GOLF GUIDE
when you enquire about clubs or accommodation

ALTON. **Worldham Park Golf Club,** Caker Lane, Worldham, Alton GU34 3BF (01420 543151). *Location:* B3004 Alton to Bordon road, one mile from Alton. Parkland course with views of the Wey Valley. 18 holes, 6199 yards. S.S.S. 70. 14 bay driving range. *Green Fees:* weekdays £12.50; weekends £16.00. *Eating facilities:* spike bar with hot and cold food, lounge area. *Visitors:* welcome - pay and play. Booking required at weekends. Professional shop. *Society Meetings:* welcome any day. Professional: Tony Cook (01420 543151). Secretary: Neil Harvey (01420 544606).

AMPFIELD. **Ampfield Par Three Golf and Country Club,** Winchester Road, Ampfield, Near Romsey SO51 9BQ (01794 368480). *Location:* A31 Winchester to Romsey road, next door to White Horse Public House. Parkland course designed by Henry Cotton. All holes par 3. 18 holes, 2478 yards. S.S.S. 53. *Green Fees:* see website. *Eating facilities:* restaurant meals and snacks, bar facilities. *Visitors:* welcome, but best to phone first. Recognised golf shoes must be worn. *Society Meetings:* catered for by prior arrangement. Professional: Richard Benfield (01794 368750). Secretary: Miss J. Johnston.
website: www.ampfieldpar3.co.uk

ANDOVER. **Andover Golf Club,** 51 Winchester Road, Andover SP10 2EF (01264 323980). *Location:* Stockbridge Exit from A303, left towards Andover, quarter of a mile on right. Gently sloping downland course with views over town and country. 9 holes, 6096 yards. S.S.S. 69. *Green Fees:* weekdays £21.00 per round, £11.00 with a member; £26.00 weekends and Bank Holidays, £16.00 with a member. *Eating facilities:* full catering available. *Visitors:* welcome, check tee reservations with Professional. *Society Meetings:* welcome, please phone for availability. Professional: D. Lawrence (01264 324151). Secretary: Guy Davis (01264 358040). Clubhouse Manager: (01264 323980).

ANDOVER. **The Hampshire Golf Club,** Winchester Road, Goodworth Clatford, Andover SP11 7TB (01264 357555; Fax: 01264 356606). *Location:* one mile south of Andover on A3057 Stockbridge Road. Downland with new trees and lakes. 18 holes, 6382 yards. S.S.S. 71. 10 bay covered driving range. *Green Fees:* weekdays £20.00, weekends £27.00. 9 hole, par 3 course £5.00 weekdays, £6.00 weekends. *Eating facilities:* full catering facilities, bar seven days a week. *Visitors:* always welcome. *Society Meetings:* welcome weekdays only. Professional: Ian Powell (01264 357555). Secretary: Jan Miles (01264 356462; Fax: 01264 356606).

BARTON-ON-SEA. **Barton-on-Sea Golf Club,** Milford Road, New Milton BH25 5PP (01425 615308; Fax: 01425 621457). *Location:* one mile from centre of New Milton on B3058 towards Milford-on-Sea. Cliff top links with easy walking; superb views of Isle of Wight and Christchurch. 27 holes. S.S.S. 72 any 18

THE GOLF GUIDE 2006　　　ENGLAND / Hampshire 205

holes. *Green Fees:* £40.00 per day weekdays; £45.00 weekends and Bank Holidays. Subject to review. *Eating facilities:* lunch, snacks and teas daily, full bar service. *Visitors:* welcome after 8.30am weekdays; weekends and Bank Holidays after 8:45am; evening green fees after 5pm. Handicap Certificate required. Buggies for hire. *Society Meetings:* welcome by arrangement Mondays, Wednesdays and Fridays. Professional: P. Rodgers (01425 611210). Secretary/Manager: Gary Prince (01425 615308). website: www.barton-on-sea-golf.co.uk

BASINGSTOKE. **Basingstoke Golf Club,** Kempshott Park, Basingstoke RG23 7LL (01256 465990; Fax: 01256 331793). *Location:* M3 Junction 7, A30 three miles west of town. Parkland course - easy walking. 18 holes, 6350 yards. S.S.S. 70. Small practice ground. *Green Fees:* information not available. *Eating facilities:* dining room, lounge and back bar. *Visitors:* welcome weekdays. Buggies, trolleys for hire. *Society Meetings:* catered for Wednesdays and Thursdays. Professional: G. Shoesmith (01256 351332). Secretary: W.A. Jefford (01256 465990; Fax: 01256 331793).*

BASINGSTOKE. **Bishopswood Golf Club,** Bishopswood Lane, Tadley, Basingstoke RG26 4AT (0118-981 2200; Fax: 0118-940 8606). *Location:* six miles north of Basingstoke off the A340. Parkland/wooded course. 9 holes, 6474 yards. S.S.S. 71. 12 bay floodlit driving range open seven days a week. *Green Fees:* information not available. *Eating facilities:* lounge and spike bars - snacks, bar meals and 50 seater restaurant facility. *Visitors:* welcome weekdays only by prior booking. *Society Meetings:* welcome by arrangement. Listed in the CAMRA Good Beer Guide 2005. Professional: S. Ward (Tel & Fax: 0118-981 5213; Fax: 0118-940 8602). Manager: D. Goss (0118-981 2200).* website: www.bishopswoodgolfcourse.co.uk

BASINGSTOKE. **Sandford Springs Golf Club,** Sandford Springs, Wolverton, Tadley RG26 5RT (01635 296800; Fax: 01635 296801). *Location:* on north side of A339 Basingstoke to Newbury road at Kingsclere. Three scenic loops of 9 holes combines woodland, parkland and lakes quite beautifully. 27 holes. S.S.S. 69/70/69. Driving range and putting green. *Green Fees:* information not available. *Eating facilities:* available all day; also conference and banqueting facilities. *Visitors:* welcome every day, subject to availability. *Society Meetings:* welcome, subject to availability. Professionals: G. Edmunds, J Barnes, C. Duffy (01635 296808).*

BASINGSTOKE. **Test Valley Golf Club,** Micheldever Road, Overton, Near Basingstoke RG25 3DS (01256 771737; Fax: 01256 771285). *Location*: on the C79, one mile north of A303 signposted Overton. Downland course; easy walking; beautiful countryside views; excellent drainage, playable all year. 18 holes, 6663 yards. S.S.S. 72. Full practice facilities. *Green Fees:* weekdays £24.00, weekends £30.00. *Eating facilities:* spike bar; main bar, full dining facility. *Visitors:* welcome weekdays, or weekends after 11.30am. *Society Meetings:* welcome weekdays. Professional/Secretary: Alistair Briggs (01256 771737). Venue for Hippo Tour, Hampshire Open and Lombard Top Club Trophy.

BASINGSTOKE. **Tylney Park Golf Club,** Rotherwick, near Hook RG27 9AY (01256 762079; Fax: 01256 763079). *Location*: M3 Junction 5 one-and-a-half miles. Parkland course with mature trees. 18 holes, 6135 yards. S.S.S. 69, Par 70. Good practice ground. *Green Fees:* information not available. *Eating facilities:* catering and bar available. *Visitors:* weekdays unrestricted, weekends with Handicap Certificate or as a guest of a member. *Society Meetings*: welcome Mondays to Thursdays. Secretary: M.R. Alcock.*

BASINGSTOKE. **Weybrook Park Golf Club,** Rooksdown Lane, Basingstoke RG24 9NT (01256 320347; Fax: 01256 812973). *Location:* two miles north west of Basingstoke town centre, A339 Newbury Road, turn at first crossroads on A339. Parkland course with magnificent views, pleasantly undulating and picturesque landscape, excellent chalk drainage ensures continuous play. 18 holes, 6468 yards, 5914 metres. S.S.S. 71. Driving range, practice area. *Green Fees:* information not available. *Eating facilities:* bar with restaurant and spike bar. *Visitors:* welcome, advisable to telephone in case of competitions. All players must have their own clubs, suitable casual/smart attire must be worn. *Society Meetings:* welcome, telephone for booking and costs. Professional: Mr Anthony Dillon (01256 333232; Fax: 01256 334242). Secretary: Mr G.E. Carpenter (01256 320347; Fax: 01256 812973).*

BASINGSTOKE Near. **Dummer Golf Club,** Dummer Village, Near Basingstoke RG25 2AF (01256 397888; Fax: 01256 397889). *Location:* at Junction 7 of M3. A downland course designed by Peter Alliss – easy walking, panoramic views, free draining; genuine all-year-round course. Par 72, 6500 yards. S.S.S. 71. 10 bay covered driving range plus teaching studios and practice facilities. *Green Fees*: information not available. *Eating facilities*: Spike Bar, conservatory and dining room. *Visitors*: welcome weekdays and after midday at weekends, 25% off for a four ball. *Society Meetings*: welcome. Professionals: Andrew Fannon, Scott Watson and David Holman. website: www.dummergolfclub.com

BORDON. **Blackmoor Golf Club,** Firgrove Road, Whitehill, Bordon GU35 9EH (01420 472775; Fax: 01420 487666). *Location:* lies midway between Petersfield and Farnham on A325. Parkland, wooded course. 18 holes, 6164 yards. S.S.S. 69. *Green Fees:* weekdays £38.00 per round, £49.00 36 holes. *Eating facilities:* dining room. *Visitors:* welcome weekdays, Handicaps necessary, Sat/Sun no visitors for golf but open for catering. Suitable dress code - no jeans in club or on course. Trolleys available. *Society Meetings:* catered for weekdays: Monday, Wednesday, Thursday and Friday. Morning coffee, lunch, evening meal. Professional: Stephen Clay (01420 472345). Secretary: Mr Tony Harris (01420 472775; Fax: 01420 487666). e-mail: admin@blackmoorgolf.co.uk

www.uk-golfguide.com

Hampshire / ENGLAND

BORDON near. **Kingsley Golf Club,** Main Road, Kingsley, Near Bordon GU35 9NG (01420 489478). *Location*: B3004 off A325 Farnham to Petersfield road. Ideal beginners' course. 9 holes. *Green Fees*: information not provided. Trolleys available. Professional/Acting Secretary: C. Howard.

BROCKENHURST. **Brokenhurst Manor Golf Club,** Sway Road, Brockenhurst SO42 7SG (01590 623332; Fax: 01590 624140). *Location:* one mile from Brockenhurst. Beautiful New Forest forest course. 18 holes, 6222 yards. S.S.S. 70. Practice ground. *Green Fees:* information not available. *Eating facilities:* restaurant and bar. *Visitors:* welcome by arrangement. Handicap Certificate required. *Society Meetings:* welcome Thursdays by arrangement. Professional: Bruce Parker (01590 623092). Secretary: Paul E. Clifford (01590 623332; Fax: 01590 624140).*

CRONDALL. **Oak Park Golfing Complex,** Heath Lane, Crondall, Near Farnham, Surrey GU10 5PB (01252 850880; Fax: 01252 850851). *Location:* one and a half miles off A287 Farnham-Odiham road, five miles from Junctions 4, 4a and 5 of M3 motorway. Gently undulating parkland course. Woodland Course - 18 holes, 6247 yards. S.S.S. 70; Village Course - 9 holes, 3279 yards. Par 36. 16 bay covered driving range, putting green, chipping green and practice bunker. *Green Fees:* Monday - Thursday £25.00; Friday £28.00; Saturday/Sunday pm only £28.00. *Eating facilities:* Restaurant: available for private hire and special occasions. Bar snacks available. V*isitors:* welcome; must book through Professional; reserved tee system at all times. *Society Meetings:* by arrangement. Professional: Paul Archer (01252 850066; Fax: 01252 850851). Manager: Mr. Robert Brewer (01252 850850).

DENMEAD. **Furzeley Golf Club,** Furzeley Road, Denmead PO7 6TX (023 9223 1180). *Location:* A3(M) Exit for Waterlooville, follow the B2150 to Denmead. Parkland course. 18 holes, 4611 yards. S.S.S. 62. *Green Fees:* £7.70 weekdays, £8.50 weekends for 9 holes. £13.00 weekdays, £14.50 weekends for 18 holes. Concessions for Senior Citizens and Juniors. *Eating facilities:* restaurant. *Visitors:* welcome anytime - Pay and Play and membership available. *Society Meetings:* always welcome. Professional: Derek Brown (023 9223 1180). Secretary: Lorna Brown.

DIBDEN. **Dibden Golf Centre,** Main Road, Dibden, Hythe, Southampton SO45 5TB Bookings: (023 8020 7508). *Location:* half-mile off A326 Totton to Fawley road, on the road to Hythe. Parkland course with views over Southampton Water. 18 holes, 5965 yards, 5455 metres. S.S.S. 69. 9 hole course, 24 bay floodlit driving range. *Green Fees:* information not available. *Eating facilities:* full catering facilities available. *Visitors:* welcome. *Society Meetings:* welcome by prior booking. Catering: Clare Flowers (02380 845060) Professionals: John Slade/ Paul Smith (023 8084 5596). *
website: www.nfdc.gov.uk/golf

EASTLEIGH. **Fleming Park Golf Course,** The New Club House, Passfield Avenue, Eastleigh SO50 9HL (023 8061 2797). *Location*: two miles off M27 Eastleigh Airport turning. Parkland. 18 holes, 4524 yards. S.S.S. 62. *Green Fees:* information not available. *Eating facilities:* bar. *Visitors:* welcome, book on day or one week in advance. *Society Meetings:* all welcome. Professional: I. Warwick (023 8061 2797). Secretary: A. Wheavil (023 8061 2797).*

FAREHAM. **Cams Hall Estate Golf Club,** Fareham PO16 8UP (01329 827732; Fax: 01329 827111). *Location:* Junction 11 M27 follow signs to Fareham/Portchester, take A27 to Portchester. 18 hole creek course links, 9 hole parkland course; five lakes, 99 bunkers, Fareham Creek, Creek course 18 holes, 6244 yards. S.S.S. 71; Park Course 9 holes, 3247 yards. S.S.S. 36. Practice ground, putting green, chipping green. *Green Fees:* weekdays from £26.00; weekends from £35.50. 50% reduction at off-peak times. One free in every four ball subject to availability. *Eating facilities*: Bar food. *Visitors*: welcome. Luxurious clubhouse, spacious locker rooms, sauna. *Society Meetings:* Societies/Groups welcome. Professional: Jason Neve (01329 827732; Fax: 01329 827111). Sales Manager: Janet Bell (01329 827222; Fax: 01329 827111). General Manager: Robert Climas.
e-mail: camshall@crown-golf.co.uk

FAREHAM. **Southwick Park Golf Club,** Pinsley Drive, Southwick, Fareham PO17 6EL (023 9237 0683; Fax: 023 9221 0289). Location: near Southwick village, adjacent to P144, HMS Dryad (B2177). Parkland. 18 holes, 5884 yards. S.S.S. 69. Practice area, pitch and putt. *Green Fees:* weekdays £22.00 per round, weekends after 2pm £25.00. Subject to review. *Eating facilities:* bar and snacks available. *Visitors:* weekdays. *Society Meetings:* book through Manager. Professional: J. Green (023 9238 0442). Manager: N.W. Price (023 9238 0131).

FAREHAM. **Wickham Park Golf Club,** Titchfield Lane, Wickham, Fareham PO17 5PJ (01329 833342; Fax: 01329 834798). *Location:* 2 miles north of Fareham, J10 of M27. Undulating parkland course. 18 holes, 5733 yards. S.S.S. 67. 12-bay covered driving range and dedicated short game area. *Green Fees:* weekdays £14.00, weekends £18.00. Special rates for Juniors and Senior Citizens. *Eating facilities:* full menu. *Visitors:* welcome at all times but must pre-book. *Society Meetings:* welcome Monday to Friday - please telephone to book in advance. Professional: James Pitcher. Manager: Rob Gumbrell.

FARNBOROUGH. **Southwood Golf Course,** Ively Road, Cove, Farnborough GU14 0LJ (01252 548700). *Location:* approximately half a mile west of A325. Flat parkland. 18 holes, 5738 yards. S.S.S. 68. Putting green. *Green Fees:* information not available. *Eating facilities:* bar and diningroom available. *Visitors:* welcome, bookable at all times. *Society Meetings:* catered for by arrangement. Professional: Chris Hudson. Secretary: Mike Pettifor.

FHG GUIDES

THE GOLF GUIDE 2006 ENGLAND / Hampshire

FLEET. **North Hants Golf Club,** Minley Road, Fleet GU51 1RF (01252 616443). *Location:* B3013 off A30, M3 Junction 4a. 400 yards from railway station. Heathland. 18 holes, 6472 yards. S.S.S. 72, Par 70. Practice ground. *Green Fees:* information not available. *Eating facilities:* lunch daily, evening meals by prior arrangement. *Visitors:* welcome weekdays only by prior arrangement, Handicap Certificates required, Thursdays Ladies' Day. *Society Meetings:* Tuesdays and Wednesdays only. Professional: Steve Porter (01252 616655). Secretary: G. Hogg (01252 616443; Fax: 01252 811627)
e-mail: secretary@north-hants-fleetgc.co.uk
website: www.northhantsgolf.co.uk

FOUR MARKS. **Four Marks Golf Club,** Headmore Lane, Fourmarks GU34 3ES (01420 587214; Fax: 01420 587313). *Location*: A31 to Four marks follow brown signs to golf course. Parkland course. 9 holes, 2300 yards, S.S.S 62. Practice nets. *Green Fees:* information not available. *Eating facilities:* bar snacks and drinks available. *Visitors*: welcome at all times. Tuition by Professional available. *Society Meetings*: welcome at any time. Professional: Peter Chapman (01420 587214).

GOSPORT. **Fleetlands Golf Club,** DARA Fleetlands, Fareham Road, Gosport PO13 0AW (023 9254 4492). *Location*: two miles south of Fareham on Fareham/Gosport Road. Flat/wooded Course. 9 holes, 4852 yards. S.S.S. 64. *Green Fees:* information not available. *Eating facilities:* bar/clubhouse. *Visitors:* by appointment with member only. *Society Meetings:* by appointment with member only. Secretary: Mr R. Sheehan (023 9254 4903). *

GOSPORT. **Gosport and Stokes Golf Club,** off Fort Road, Haslar, Gosport PO12 2AT (023 9258 1625). *Location:* A32 to Gosport, course is one mile east of Stokes Bay, near Gilkicker Point. Water course, natural hazards. 9 holes, 5957 yards. S.S.S. 70. Nets and putting green. *Green Fees:* information not available. *Eating facilities:* full catering service, fully licensed bar. *Visitors:* welcome all week, restricted Sundays and Thursdays. *Society Meetings:* by arrangement. Secretary/Manager: M. Chivers (Tel & Fax: 023 9252 7941). Tee Shop (023 9258 7423).

HARTLEY WINTNEY. **Hartley Wintney Golf Club,** London Road, Hartley Wintney, Hook RG27 8PT (01252 844211; Fax: 01252 844211). *Location:* on A30 between Camberley and Basingstoke. Parkland, wooded. 18 holes, 6240 yards. S.S.S. 71. Practice area, indoor teaching studio. *Green Fees:* £30.00 per round, £45.00 per day. *Eating facilities:* full catering facilities available. *Visitors:* restricted Wednesdays (Ladies' Day). *Society Meetings:* catered for Mondays, Tuesdays, Thursdays and Fridays on application. Professional: Martin Smith (01252 844211). Secretary: (Tel & Fax: 01252 844211).

HAVANT. **Rowlands Castle Golf Club,** 31 Links Lane, Rowlands Castle PO9 6AE (023 9241 2216). *Location:* four miles north of Havant or Horndean/ Rowlands Castle Junction from A3M. Flat parkland, wooded course. 18 holes, 6612 yards White Tees, 6386 yards Yellow Tees. S.S.S. 72 (White), 70 (Yellow). *Green Fees:* weekdays £34.00 per round/day; weekends £38.00. Subject to review. *Eating facilities:* full catering and bar facilities. *Visitors:* welcome, except Saturdays unless playing with a member, maximum 12 visitors on a Sunday and Bank Holidays. *Society Meetings:* catered for Tuesdays and Thursdays, bookings through Secretary. Professional: Peter Klepacz (023 9241 2785). Secretary: Mr K.D. Fisher (023 9241 2784).

HAYLING ISLAND. **The Hayling Golf Club,** Links Lane, Hayling Island PO11 0BX (023 9246 4491). *Location:* A3023 five miles south of Havant. Seaside links. 18 holes, 6531 yards, 5965 metres. S.S.S. 71. *Green Fees:* weekdays £45.00 per round; weekends £60.00 per round. Concessions for Juniors. Subject to review. *Eating facilities:* breakfasts, lunches and afternoon teas available and dinners by arrangement. *Visitors:* welcome with current Handicap Certificate and must be members of recognised clubs. *Society Meetings:* Tuesdays and Wednesdays only by arrangement with the Secretary. Professional: Ray Gadd (023 9246 4491). General Manager: Carole A Davison (023 9246 4446; Fax: 02392 461119).
e-mail: generaloffice@haylinggolf.co.uk
website: www.haylinggolf.co.uk

LEE-ON-THE-SOLENT. **Lee-On-The-Solent Golf Club,** Brune Lane, Lee-on-the-Solent PO13 9PB (023 9255 0207). *Location:* M27 Exit 9 eastbound, Exit 11 westbound, three miles south of Fareham. Flat parkland course. 18 holes, 5962 yards. S.S.S. 69. Practice range. *Green Fees:* weekdays £34.00; weekends £39.00. *Eating facilities:* full catering, extensive bar snack menu, lounge bar. *Visitors:* welcome weekdays, Handicap Certificate required. *Society Meetings:* welcome Thursdays, other days by special arrangement. Professional: Rob Edwards (023 9255 1181). Manager: Ian Walton (023 9255 1170; Fax: 023 9255 4233).

LIPHOOK. **Liphook Golf Club,** Wheatsheaf Enclosure, Liphook GU30 7EH (01428 723271; Fax: 01428 724853). *Location:* one mile south of Liphook on B2070 (old A3). Heathland. 18 holes, 6167 yards. S.S.S. 69. *Green Fees:* contact Club for details. *Eating facilities:* bar and restaurant. *Visitors:* welcome, Handicap Certificate required, check with Secretary. Buggy available for hire. *Society Meetings:* catered for Wednesdays to Fridays. Professional: Ian Mowbray (01428 723271). Secretary: Major J.B. Morgan MBE (01428 723785; Fax: 01428 724853).
e-mail: liphookgolfclub@btconnect.com
website: www.liphookgolfclub.com

THE APPEARANCE OF AN ASTERISK (*) AT THE END OF A CLUB OR COURSE ENTRY INDICATES THAT UP-TO-DATE INFORMATION HAS NOT BEEN SUPPLIED

208 Hampshire / ENGLAND — THE GOLF GUIDE 2006

LIPHOOK. **Old Thorns Hotel, Golf & Country Club,** Longmoor Road, Liphook GU30 7PE (01428 724555). *Location:* A3 to Griggs Green then 500 yards on right. Parkland, wooded, with natural streams and lakes. 18 holes, 6529 yards. S.S.S. 72. Practice range, putting green, buggies, Pro shop. *Green Fees*: information not available. *Eating facilities*: choice of Sands Brasserie or award-winning Japanese Restaurant. *Visitors*: welcome at all times. *Society Meetings:* a range of golf days available for booking. Range of individual and corporate membership available. Facilities: 32 en suite bedrooms, indoor swimming pool, sauna, solarium, steam room, massage, fitness centre, treatment rooms, two tennis courts, conference and banqueting rooms. General Manager: Ken Flockhart.*
website: www.oldthorns.com

LYNDHURST. **Bramshaw Golf Club,** Brook, Lyndhurst SO43 7HE (023 8081 3433). *Location:* M27 (Interchange 1) one mile from M27 (north) at Brook. Two courses: one parkland, one woodland. Both 18 holes. Forest Course 5774 yards. S.S.S. 68. Manor Course 6517 yards. S.S.S. 71. Practice facilities. *Green Fees:* contact club or check website for current rates. *Eating facilities:* clubhouse and restaurant, also Bell Inn close by. *Visitors:* welcome. Accommodation in 22 bedroomed hotel. *Society Meetings:* catered for by arrangement. Professional: Clive Bonner (023 8081 3434). General Manager: Ian Baker (023 8081 3433).
e-mail: golf@bramshaw.co.uk
website: www.bramshaw.co.uk

LYNDHURST. **New Forest Golf Club Ltd,** Southampton Road, Lyndhurst SO43 7BU (023 8028 2752; Fax: 023 8028 4030). *Location:* on the A35 between Ashurst and Lyndhurst. Forest heathland course. 18 holes, 5772 yards. S.S.S. 67. Practice ground. *Green Fees:* weekdays £15.00 per round, £20.00 per day. Weekends £20.00 per round, £26.00 per day. *Eating facilities:* bar, dining room. *Visitors:* welcome, weekdays after 9am, Saturdays after 10am and Sunday afternoons. *Society Meetings:* advance booking only. Professional: Colin Murray (07884 333613). Secretary: Mrs Barbara Shaw (023 8028 2484; Fax: 023 8028 4030).

PETERSFIELD. **Petersfield Golf Club (New Course),** Tankerdale Lane, Liss GU33 7QY. *Location:* from the north, first turning left past the Liss exit on the Petersfield by-pass; from the south, leave by-pass at the Liss turn off (B3006), join the Southern dual carriage way then take the first turning left. Members club in Area of Outstanding Natural Beauty, gently undulating and wooded. 18 holes. White, 6450 yards, S.S.S. 71, Par 72. Yellow, 6000 yards, S.S.S. 69, Par 69. Red, 5447 yards, S.S.S. 71, Par 72. Practice ground, nets and putting green. *Green Fees:* weekdays £28.00 per round, weekends £35.00. Booking required at weekends. *Eating facilities:* full bar and catering service. *Visitors:* welcome, Handicap Certificate or proof of club membership required. Booking required for weekends via Professional. *Society Meetings:* welcome, see our website for details of packages. Professional: Greg Hughes (01730 895216). General Manager: Richard Hine (01730 261675; Fax: 01730 894713).
website: www.petersfieldgolfclub.co.uk

PETERSFIELD. **Petersfield Golf Club (Pay & Play Course),** Sussex Road, Petersfield. *Location*: from Petersfield, take the B2146 (Sussex Road), the club is situated on the right hand side, just past the car park for Heath Lake. 9 hole pay & play course (to be extended to 12 holes). Level wooded course. *Green Fees*: information not available. *Eating facilities*: limited, tea, coffee and cold drinks available. *Visitors*: welcome, booking advisable, especially at weekends (01730 267732). Equipment hire available. General Manager: Richard Hine (01730 261675; Fax: 01730 894713).*
website: www.petersfieldgolfclub.co.uk

PORTSMOUTH. **Great Salterns Golf Course,** Burrfields Road, Portsmouth PO3 5HH (023 9266 4549). *Location:* public golf course and home of Southsea Golf Club. South on A2030 off M27 signposted "Southsea". Flat meadow land course. 18 holes, 5620 yards. S.S.S. 67. Floodlit driving range. *Green Fees:* information not available. *Eating facilities:* full bar and catering service at Farmhouse Pub next door. *Visitors:* always welcome, tee time booking required one week ahead. Innlodge Hotel overlooks 18th green (73 bedrooms). *Society Meetings:* welcome, administered by Noreen Jefferies. Professional: Terry Healy (023 9266 4549; Fax: 023 9265 0525). Secretary (Southsea Golf Club): Roger Collinson (023 9269 9110)
e-mail: roger.collinson@ntlworld.com

PORTSMOUTH. **Portsmouth Golf Club (1926),** Crookhorn Lane, Widley, Waterlooville PO7 5QL (023 9237 2210). *Location:* two thirds of a mile from junction of B2177 and A3. Hilly course with views of harbour; outstanding 6th hole. 18 holes, 6139 yards. S.S.S. 70. Practice ground, putting green. *Green Fees:* information not available. Reduced rates for Juniors and over 60s. *Eating facilities:* full restaurant and bar. *Visitors:* welcome, tee bookings required. *Society Meetings:* welcome by prior arrangement with Pro Shop. Professional: (023 9237 2210 ext. 24; Fax: 023 9220 0766). Secretary: D. Houlihan (023 9220 1827 ext. 21).*

PORTSMOUTH. **Waterlooville Golf Club,** Cherry Tree Avenue, Cowplain, Waterlooville PO8 8AP (023 9226 3388; Fax: 023 9224 2980). *Location:* off A3 or A3 (M), 10 miles north of Portsmouth. Parkland course. 18 holes, 6602 yards. S.S.S. 72. *Green Fees:* £30.00 per round, £40.00 per day, weekdays only. *Eating facilities:* full catering service available, bar facilities. *Visitors:* welcome weekdays, weekends as members' guests; weekends also after 2.30pm by prior arrangement with Professional. *Society Meetings:* Thursdays only by prior arrangement, limited availablility other days by prior arrangement with Secretary. Professional: John Hay (Tel & Fax: 023 9225 6911). Secretary: David Nairne.

RINGWOOD. **Burley Golf Club,** Cott Lane, Burley, Ringwood BH24 4BB (01425 402431/403737; Fax: 01425 404168). *Location:* A31 from Ringwood and turn right at Picket Post and on through Burley Street. Open heathland course in the New Forest. 9 holes, 6151 yards. S.S.S. 69, Par 71. *Green Fees:* weekdays £16.00 per round (£10.00 with member),

£20.00 per day; weekends and Bank Holidays £20.00 per round (£15.00 with member), £25.00 per day. Under 18s £8.00 per round weekdays, £9.00 per round weekends. Weekly ticket £75.00. *Eating facilities:* bar open, food available lunchtimes most days. *Visitors:* welcome, but not before 4pm Saturdays, 8am Sundays, and 1.45pm Wednesdays. Handicap Certificates preferred. *Society Meetings:* limited to 14 players Tuesdays or Fridays. Secretary: Mr G.J. Stride (01425 402431; Fax: 01425 404168). e-mail: secretary@burleygolfclub.fsnet.co.uk

RINGWOOD. **Moors Valley Golf Course,** Horton Road, Ashley Heath, Ringwood BH24 2ET (01425 479776). *Location*: signposted from A338/A31 roundabout. Heathland course set in the valley of the Moors River. 18 holes, 6337 yards. S.S.S. 70. 4 hole short course, full size pitching green and practice nets. *Green Fees:* £20.00. *Eating facilities:* spikes bar and bar. *Visitors:* welcome. *Society Meetings:* welcome by arrangement. Professional: James Daniels (Tel & Fax: 01425 479776). Manager: Desmond Meharg (01425 479776).

ROMSEY. **Dunwood Manor Golf Club,** Danes Road, Awbridge, Near Romsey SO51 0GF (01794 340549; Fax: 01794 341215). *Location:* four miles from Romsey off A27. Undulating parkland. 18 holes, 5767 yards. S.S.S. 68. Practice area. *Green Fees:* £30.00 per round, £45.00 per day weekdays; £35.00 per round weekends after 2pm. Society rates from £32.50. *Eating facilities:* full catering, all day bar. *Visitors:* welcome by prior arrangement. Self-catering accommodation for up to 32 people available. *Society Meetings:* welcome by prior arrangement. Professional: Heath Teschner (01794 340663; Fax: 01794 341215). Secretary: Hazel Johnson (01794 340549; Fax: 01794 341215). e-mail: admin@dunwood-golf.co.uk

ROMSEY. **Paultons Golf Centre,** Old Salisbury Road, Ower, Near Romsey SO51 6AN (023 8081 3345; Fax: 023 8081 3993). *Location:* off M27 at Junction 2, A36 towards Salisbury, at first roundabout take first exit, then first right at the Vine Public House. Parkland/woodland laid out within the original grounds of Paulton House, landscaped by Capability Brown. 18 holes, 6200 yards, 5670 metres. S.S.S. 71. 9-hole academy course. 24-bay floodlit driving range. *Green Fees:* information not available. *Visitors:* welcome anytime. *Society Meetings:* welcome anytime with prior booking. Professional/ Secretary: R. Park.*

ROMSEY. **Wellow Golf Club,** Ryedown Lane, East Wellow, Romsey SO51 6BD (01794 322872; Fax: 01794 323832). *Location:* M27 Junction 2 - A36 Salisbury, one mile right to East Wellow, one mile right Ryedown Lane. Parkland. 27 holes (three loops of 9 holes). S.S.S. 69, 70, 68. Large practice ground. *Green Fees:* weekdays £20.00; weekends £25.00. *Eating facilities:* full catering and bar facilities available all day. *Visitors:* welcome – advise phone to confirm availability. Correct dress code must be observed. *Society Meetings:* all welcome. Professional: Neil Bratley (01794 323833). Secretary: Mrs C. Gurd.

SHEDFIELD. **Marriott Meon Valley Hotel and Country Club Resort,** Sandy Lane, Shedfield, Southampton SO32 2HQ (01329 833455; Fax: 01329 834411). *Location:* leave M27 at Exit 7, take A334 to Botley then towards Wickham. Sandy Lane is 2 miles on the left. Wooded course. 18 holes, 6520 yards. S.S.S. 71. 9 holes, 2714 yards. S.S.S. 34. Covered practice area. *Green Fees:* weekdays £42.00; weekends £50.00. *Eating facilities:* Treetops Restaurant, The Long Weekend Restaurant and three bars. *Visitors:* welcome, no restrictions. Handicap Certificates required to play. 113 bedroomed 4 Star Hotel. *Society Meetings:* welcome, arranged in advance. Professional: Rod Cameron (01329 832184; Fax: 01329 834411). Director of Golf: George McMenemy (01329 833455; Fax: 01329 834411).

SOUTHAMPTON. **Botley Park Golf Club,** Winchester Road, Botley, Southampton SO3 2UA (01489 780888; Fax: 01489 789242). *Location*: approximately two miles from Junction 7 on M27. Parkland. 18 holes, 6341 yards. S.S.S. 70. Driving range. *Green Fees:* information not available. *Eating facilities:* two bars, main restaurant and club lounge. *Visitors:* welcome by prior booking by phone. Handicap Certificate required. 100 bedroomed hotel on site; tennis, squash, swimming, sauna, solarium, steam room, fitness suite, beauty spa. Dance studio. *Society Meetings:* weekdays only. Professional: Kevin Caplehorn (01489 789771; Fax: 01489 789242). Secretary/Golf Manager: Phil Hanks (01489 796000)*

SOUTHAMPTON. **Chilworth Golf Club,** Main Road, Chilworth, Southampton SO16 7JP (02380 740544; Fax: 02380 733166). *Location*: situated off the A27. Parkland course. 18 holes, 5837 yards, S.S.S. 68. Covered driving range. *Green Fees*: information not available. *Eating facilities*: bar. *Visitors:* welcome, must follow dress code, please telephone for details. Pro shop. Tuition available. Professional: Darren Newing. Secretary: Fred Bendal. *

SOUTHAMPTON. **Corhampton Golf Club,** Shepherds Farm Lane, Corhampton, Southampton SO32 3GZ (01489 877279; Fax: 01489 877680). *Location:* one mile from Corhampton on Bishops Waltham–Corhampton road (B3135). Free draining downland course. 18 holes, 6444 yards. S.S.S. 71. Large practice ground. *Green Fees:* weekdays £30.00 per round, £40.00 per day; weekends £15.00 with a member only. *Eating facilities:* full catering. *Visitors:* welcome Monday to Friday; weekends and Bank Holidays with a member. Buggies and trolleys for hire. *Society Meetings:* Mondays and Thursdays. Professional: Ian Roper (01489 877638; Fax: 01489 877680). Secretary: Margaret Middleton (01489 877279). e-mail: secretary@corhamptongc.co.uk

Visit the FHG website
www.holidayguides.com
for details of the wide choice of accommodation featured in the full range of FHG titles

SOUTHAMPTON. **Romsey Golf Club Ltd,** Nursling, Southampton SO16 0XW (023 8073 4637; Fax: 023 8074 1036). *Location:* two miles south east of Romsey on A3057, M27/M271 Junction 3. Well wooded, undulating course with extremely good views. 18 holes, 5718 yards. S.S.S. 68. *Green Fees:* weekdays £30.00 per round, £36.00 per day; weekends with a member only. *Eating facilities:* bar and restaurant. *Visitors:* welcome weekdays only. *Society Meetings:* welcome Mondays, Tuesdays or Thursdays only. Professional: Mark Desmond (023 8073 6673). Secretary: Michael Batty.

SOUTHAMPTON. **Southampton Golf Club** (Play over the Municipal Golf Course), Golf Course Road, Bassett, Southampton SO18 3NG (023 8076 7942). *Location:* off Bassett Avenue. Parkland course. 18 holes, 6218 yards, S.S.S. 70. 9 hole Par 32. Practice area and putting greens. *Green Fees:* information not available. *Eating facilities:* bar and full catering (023 8076 7996). *Visitors:* welcome but must book at weekends - three and four ball play only at weekends. Professional: E. Rawlings, M. Williamson (01489 893 020). Secretary: E. Hemsley (023 8047 6582). Bookings: (023 8076 0546).

SOUTHAMPTON. **Stoneham Golf Club,** Monks Wood Close, Bassett, Southampton SO16 3TT (023 8076 9272). *Location:* A33/M27 north of Southampton find Chilworth roundabout, take road to Airport (A27), half mile on left. Undulating parkland course, used for Brabazon Trophy 1993, English County Finals 1998 and English Ladies' Championship 2001. 18 holes, 6387 yards. S.S.S. 70. *Green Fees:* weekdays £40.00 per round, £45.00 per day; weekends £50.00 per round, £60.00 per day. *Eating facilities:* full catering, bar open all day. *Visitors:* welcome, except competition days. *Society Meetings:* catered for Monday, Thursday and Friday by arrangement. Professional: Ian Young (023 8076 8397). Manager: Richard Penley-Martin (023 8076 9272; Fax: 023 8076 6320).

WINCHESTER. **Hockley Golf Club,** Twyford, Near Winchester SO21 1PL (01962 713165; Fax: 01962 713612). *Location:* 100 yards Junction 11 M3 motorway. Downland with excellent views of Winchester and surrounding areas. James Braid designed course, long vistas. 18 holes, 6381 yards. S.S.S. 71. Large practice ground. *Green Fees:* April to September £35.00 per 18 holes, £45.00 per day; October to March £45.00 per 18 holes, £48.00 per 36 holes. *Eating facilities:* full catering and bar facilities. *Visitors:* welcome. Handicap Certificate preferred. *Society Meetings:* welcome by prior arrangement. Professional: (01962 713678). Secretary: Mrs Lyn Dyer. e-mail: secretary@hockleygolfclub.com website: www.hockleygolfclub.com

WINCHESTER. **Otterbourne Golf Centre,** Poles Lane, Otterbourne, Winchester SO21 1DZ (Tel & Fax: 01962 775225). Parkland course. 9 holes, 1939 yards, S.S.S. 30. 10 bay uncovered driving range. *Green Fees:* information not available. *Visitors:* welcome, pay as you play. Tuition available. *Society Meetings:* open to discussion. Professional: Garry Stubbington.*

WINCHESTER. **The Park Golf Course,** Avington, Winchester SO21 1DA (01962 779945; Fax: 01962 779530). *Location:* 5 miles east of Winchester. Mature parkland course. 9 holes, 1907 yards, S.S.S. 58. *Green Fees:* information not available. *Visitors:* always welcome, please telephone to book.

WINCHESTER. **Royal Winchester Golf Club,** Sarum Road, Winchester SO22 5QE (01962 852462). *Location:* from Junction 11 M3 follow signs to Oliver's Battery. At Pitt roundabout follow signs to Winchester then left into Kilham Lane. At end turn right into Sarum Road. Traditional downland course. 18 holes, 6216 yards, 5685 metres. S.S.S. 70. *Green Fees:* weekdays 18 holes £36.00, 36 holes £60.00; weekends with member only. *Eating facilities:* full catering and bar facilities available. *Visitors:* welcome weekdays, Handicap Certificate required. *Society Meetings:* by prior arrangement. Professional: Steven Hunter (01962 862473). Secretary: Andrew Buck (01962 852462; Fax: 01962 865048). e-mail: manager@royalwinchestergolfclub.com website: www.royalwinchestergolfclub.com

WINCHESTER. **South Winchester Golf Club,** Romsey Road, Pitt, Winchester SO22 5QX (01962 877800; Fax: 01962 877900). *Location:* situated between Winchester and Hursley in the village of Pitt. Championship links-style course - home of the Hampshire PGA. 18 holes, 7086 yards. S.S.S. 74. Driving range. Chipping green, practice bunker and practice green. *Green Fees:* information not available. *Eating facilities:* two bars, one dining room, one conservatory/dining room, food available all day. *Visitors:* visiting golfers welcome. Golf days for non members by arrangement with the Professional. Professional: Richard Adams (01962 840469). General Manager: Laurence Ross.*
website: www.crown-golf.co.uk

THE APPEARANCE OF AN ASTERISK (*) AT THE END OF A CLUB OR COURSE ENTRY INDICATES THAT UP-TO-DATE INFORMATION HAS NOT BEEN SUPPLIED

PLEASE MENTION THIS GUIDE WHEN YOU ENQUIRE ABOUT CLUBS OR ACCOMMODATION

Herefordshire

BELMONT. **Belmont Lodge and Golf,** Belmont, Hereford HR2 9SA (01432 352666; Fax: 01432 358090). *Location:* one and a half miles south of Hereford, off A465 to Abergavenny. Parkland running alongside the River Wye offering tremendous views. 18 holes, 6511 yards. S.S.S. 72. *Green Fees:* information not available. *Eating facilities:* restaurant meals and bar snacks. *Visitors:* welcome at all times, advisable to check availability first. Other facilities available include a 30 bedroom hotel, bowls, tennis, fishing and walking; buggies and trolleys for hire. *Society Meetings:* catered for, special packages available. Professional: Mike Welsh (01432 352717). Reception/Reservations: (01432 352666; Fax: 01432 358090).*
e-mail: info@belmont-hereford.co.uk
website: www.belmont-hereford.co.uk

HAY-ON-WYE. **Summerhill Golf Course,** Clifford, Near Hay-on-Wye HR3 5EW (01497 820451). *Location:* half a mile out of Hay on B4350 for Clifford and Whitney Toll Bridge and Hereford Road A438. Parkland. 9 holes 2929 yards (18 holes, 5858 off white tees). S.S.S. 68. *Green Fees:* informaiton not available. *Eating facilities:* restaurant, two bars and large function room. *Visitors:* welcome, not on Thursday evening or Sunday mornings. *Society Meetings:* welcome Monday, Wednesday and Friday. Professional: Andy Gealy. Secretary: Mike Tom.*

HEREFORD. **Burghill Valley Golf Club,** Tillington Road, Burghill, Hereford HR4 7RW (01432 760456; Fax: 01432 761654). *Location:* three miles north-west of Hereford. From Worcester and North (avoiding Hereford city), take A4103 for two miles, first right after traffic lights. From south (via Hereford city) take A4110, turn left at traffic lights after Three Elms Inn and then first right. Follow signs to club. Pleasantly undulating parkland including two lakes, and easy walking with some interesting holes through mature cider orchards. 18 holes, 6204 yards. S.S.S. 70. Large practice area. *Green Fees:* on application. *Eating facilities:* bar and dining room with full catering available every day. *Visitors:* welcome at any time, must book tee time with Professional. *Society Meetings:* by prior arrangement with the Manager. Special rates available, please enquire. Professionals: Keith Preece PGA, Andy Cameron PGA (01432 760808; Fax: 01432 761654). General Manager: Keith Smith.
e-mail: golf@bvgc.co.uk
website: www.bvgc.co.uk

HEREFORD. **Hereford Municipal Golf Course,** Hereford Leisure Centre, Holmer Road, Hereford HR4 9UD (01432 344376; Fax: 01432 266281). *Location:* follow A49 Leominster to Hereford road; north of city centre next to Leisure Centre. Flat parkland course with excellent greens all year round. 9 holes, 3060 yards. S.S.S. 69 for 18 holes. Large practice area, bunker and practice green. *Green Fees:* please ring for details. *Eating facilities:* full catering and bar in Leisure Centre. *Visitors:* welcome at all times. *Society Meetings:* welcome, prices on application. Professional: Gary Morgan (01432 344376; Fax: 01432 266281).

HEREFORD. **The Herefordshire Golf Club,** Ravens Causeway, Wormsley, Hereford HR4 8LY (01432 830219). *Location:* six miles north-west of Hereford on a B road to Weobley. Undulating parkland course. 18 holes, 6031 yards. S.S.S. 69. *Green Fees:* information available on request. *Eating facilities:* catering available at all times. *Visitors:* welcome. *Society Meetings:* welcome, packages arranged through Secretary (01432 830219).
e-mail: herefordshiregolf@breathe.co.uk
website: www.herefordshiregolfclub.co.uk

Burghill Valley Golf Club
WELCOMES NEW MEMBERS, VISITORS & SOCIETIES

This beautiful Herefordshire course has developed into one of the leading clubs in the county, setting a challenge to players of all abilities. Situated 4 miles NW of Hereford, the course is easy walking on gently rolling fairways. Two lakes and the apple blossom of the orchards are particularly picturesque against the background of hills and woods.

With keen golfers comprising the management of the club, their enthusiasm is reflected in the excellent service provided and the condition of the course, the greens being especially praised.

The clubhouse has a warm and friendly atmosphere where visitors are made most welcome. The Club takes great pride in the catering facilities, offering a variety of packages to suit both large and small societies. All in all, **19** holes to be remembered with pleasure!

Tillington Road • Burghill • Hereford • HR4 7RW • Tel: 01432 760456
Fax 01432 761654 • Email: info@bvgc.co.uk • Web Site: www.bvgc.co.uk

See also Colour Advertisement on page 31

KINGTON. **Kington Golf Club,** Bradnor Hill, Kington HR5 3RE (01544 230340). *Location*: one mile out of Kington, on B4355 to Presteigne. Easy walking hill course with superb greens and views over seven counties. Highest 18 hole course in England. 18 holes, 5966 yards. S.S.S. 69. *Green Fees:* weekdays £20.00 per round, £24.00 per day; weekends and Bank Holidays £26.00 per round, £30.00 per day. *Eating facilities:* full catering and bar facilities. *Visitors:* welcome. Please contact Professional to ensure course is available. *Society Meetings:* by arrangement with the Professional. Professional: Andy Gealy (01544 231320). Secretary: Glyn R. Wictome (Tel & Fax: 01544 340270).

LEOMINSTER. **Grove Golf Centre,** Fordbridge, Leominster HR6 0LE (01568 610602). *Location:* three miles south of Leominster on A49. Challenging wooded course with many water features, U.S.G.A. spec greens. 9 holes, 1780 yards. S.S.S. 60. New 9 holes opening 2004, S.S.S.72. Floodlit, covered driving range. Golf shop. *Green Fees:* information not available. *Eating facilities:* full catering and bar. *Visitors:* welcome anytime. Professional: Phil Brookes (01568 615333).*

LEOMINSTER. **Leominster Golf Club,** Ford Bridge, Leominster HR6 0LE (01568 610055). *Location:* three miles south of Leominster on A49 bypass, clearly signed. Undulating parkland with some holes alongside River Lugg and extensive views over Herefordshire countryside. 18 holes, 6026 yards. S.S.S. 69. Driving range adjacent to course. *Green Fees:* weekdays £15.00 per round, £20.00 per day; Mondays and Fridays £10.00 after 9.30am; weekends £25.00 per round, £30.00 per day. *Eating facilities:* bar open daily, full catering daily. *Visitors:* welcome every day; please telephone to check availability. Trolley and buggy hire available. *Society Meetings:* most welcome. Full weekday £29.00, weekends £36.00 golf and catering. Professional: Nigel Clarke (01568 611402). Secretary: Les Green (Tel & Fax: 01568 610055). Manager: Jessica Kingswood.
e-mail: contact@leominstergolfclub.co.uk
website: www.leominstergolfclub.co.uk

ROSS-ON-WYE. **The Ross-on-Wye Golf Club,** Gorsley, Ross-on-Wye HR9 7UT (01989 720267; Fax: 01989 720212). *Location:* adjacent Junction 3 M50, five miles east of Ross-on-Wye. Tree lined, undulating parkland course. 18 holes, 6451 yards. S.S.S. 71. Driving range, practice area. *Green Fees:* £40.00 per round. £50.00 per day. Societies: £34.00 for 18 holes, £40.00 for 27 holes. *Eating facilities:* full restaurant catering, excluding Mondays. *Visitors:* welcome any day if prior arrangement made with Professional or Secretary. Snooker tables (2). *Society Meetings:* welcome, minimum 16. Tee reservations Wednesdays to Fridays. Professional: (01989 720439). Secretary: P.H. Plumb (01989 720267; Fax: 01989 720212).
e-mail: secretary@therossonwyegolfclub.co.uk
website: www.therossonwyegolfclub.co.uk

ROSS-ON-WYE. **South Herefordshire Golf Club,** Twin Lakes, Upton Bishop, Ross-on-Wye HR9 7UA (01989 780535; Fax: 01989 740611). *Location:* end roundabout of M50 at Ross take B4221 to Upton Bishop, in Upton Bishop turn right, club half a mile. Good test of golf for all standards with variety of holes. Superb views. Rarely on temporary greens in Winter. 18 holes S.S.S. 72. 16 bay covered, floodlit driving range. *Green Fees*: weekdays £18.00 per round; weekends £22.50 per round. *Eating facilities:* fully licensed bar serving snacks and full meals. *Visitors*: always welcome, no restrictions. Ring to reserve tee time. Buggies and trolleys available. Fully qualified PGA Professional, club fitting centre, Pro shop. Free junior training Saturday mornings, group lessons available. *Society Meetings:* always welcome; weekend prices from £20.00 for day's golf.
e-mail: shgc.golf@clara.co.uk

www.uk-golfguide.com

Visit the FHG website
www.holidayguides.com
for details of the wide choice of accommodation featured in the full range of FHG titles

PLEASE MENTION THE GOLF GUIDE WHEN YOU WRITE OR PHONE TO ENQUIRE ABOUT CLUBS OR ACCOMMODATION

Hertfordshire

BARKWAY. **Barkway Park Golf Club,** Nuthampstead Road, Barkway SG8 8EN (01763 849070). *Location:* A10 north from M25 for 15 miles, B1368 to Barkway 8 miles. Inland links. 18 holes, 6997 yards. S.S.S. 74. Practice areas. *Green Fees:* information not available. *Eating facilities:* bar, restaurant. *Visitors:* welcome at all times. *Society Meetings:* always welcome. Professional: Jamie Bates. Secretary: Val Sadler. *

BARNET. **Arkley Golf Club,** Rowley Green Road, Barnet EN5 3HL (Fax: 020 8440 5214). *Location*: follow A411 from A1 Stirling Corner towards Barnet, left into Rowley Lane. Wooded parkland. 9 holes, 18 tees, 6046 yards. S.S.S. 69. Practice ground. *Green Fees:* weekdays £25.00 per round, £32.00 per day; weekends with a member only £15.00. *Eating facilities:* available, no catering Mondays. *Visitors:* welcome weekdays, please phone Professional. *Society Meetings:* catered for Wednesdays and Fridays; special rates available. Professional: Andrew Hurley (020 8440 8473). Secretary: R. Campbell (020 8449 0394). website: www.arkleygolfclub.co.uk

BARNET. **Hadley Wood Golf Club,** Beech Hill, Near Barnet EN4 0JJ (020 8449 4328). *Location:* off the exit from M25 at Junction 24 on to A111 Cockfosters. Down hill, third turning on the right. Very attractive undulating parkland with lakes. Regional Open qualifying venue 2000 - 2005. 18 holes, 6514 yards. S.S.S. 71. Practice range open to members and green fees only. Chipping and putting areas. *Green Fees:* £50.00 weekdays, £70.00 weekends. *Eating facilities:* available weekdays. *Visitors:* welcome weekdays, (not Tuesday a.m.), with club Handicap Certificate or letter of introduction. *Society Meetings:* corporate and society days catered for weekdays except Tuesday mornings and Wednesdays. Professional: Peter Jones (020 8449 3285). General Manager: Bill Beckett (020 8449 4328; Fax: 020 8364 8633).
e-mail: gen.mgr@hadleywoodgc.com
website: www.hadleywoodgc.com

BERKHAMSTED. **Ashridge Golf Club,** Little Gaddesden, Berkhamsted HP4 1LY (01442 842379). *Location:* on B450, five miles north west of Berkhamsted. Parkland. 18 holes, 6625 yards. Par 72. Practice area, putting green. *Green Fees:* on application. *Eating facilities:* dining room and spike bar, two lounges. *Visitors:* welcome with reservation weekdays only. *Society Meetings:* catered for. Professional: Andrew Ainsworth (01442 842307). Secretary: Martin S. Silver (01442 842244; Fax: 01442 843770).
e-mail: info@ashridgegolfclub.ltd.uk
website: www.ashridgegolfclub.ltd.uk

BERKHAMSTED. **Berkhamsted Golf Club,** The Common, Berkhamsted HP4 2QB (01442 865832; Fax: 01442 863730). *Location*: A41 to Berkhamsted, up past the castle to the common. Heathland, wooded, grass bunkers. 18 holes, 6605 yards. S.S.S. 72. Two practice grounds. *Green Fees:* weekdays £37.00 per round, £50.00 per day; weekends £45.00 per round after 11.30am. (2006 prices subject to review). *Eating facilities:* bar and restaurant. *Visitors:* welcome, best to phone first. Handicap Certificate required. *Society Meetings:* catered for Mondays, Wednesdays and Fridays. Professional: John Clarke (01442 865851). General Manager: Barry Hill (01442 865832)
e-mail: barryh@berkhamstedgc.co.uk
website: www.berkhamstedgolfclub.co.uk

BISHOP'S STORTFORD. Bishop's Stortford Golf Club, Dunmow Road, Bishop's Stortford CM23 5HP (01279 654715). *Location*: M11 Junction 8, follow signs for Bishop's Stortford, entrance quarter of a mile on left. Undulating parkland, fairly flat: well-established course and a true test of golf. 18 holes, 6404 yards. S.S.S. 71. *Green Fees*: weekdays £32.00 per round, £40.00 per day, 27 holes £36.00; weekends as guest of member. *Eating facilities:* restaurant and bar service. *Visitors*: welcome weekdays; weekends with member only. Valid Handicap Certificate required. *Society Meetings*: catered for weekdays except Tuesdays (minimum 12). Special rates available. Professional: Simon Sheppard (01279 651324). Secretary: Judy Barker (01279 654715; Fax: 01279 655215).
e-mail: office@bsgc.co.uk
website: www.bsgc.co.uk

BISHOP'S STORTFORD. **Great Hadham Golf and Country Club,** Great Hadham Road, Much Hadham, Near Bishop's Stortford SG10 6JE (01279 843558; Fax: 01279 842122). *Location:* two miles west of Bishop's Stortford on the B1004, four miles west of Junction 8 M11 motorway. Rolling meadowland course. 18 holes, 6854 yards. S.S.S. 73. Three Par 3 practice tees, practice bunker, 18 bay driving range. *Green Fees:* information not available. *Eating facilities:* well stocked bar, comfortable lounge and dining room/spike bar. *Visitors:* welcome weekdays (Ladies' Day Wednesday mornings), weekends after 12 noon. Health Club with fitness centre facilities. *Society Meetings:* welcome weekdays. Professional: Kevin Lunt. Secretary: Ian Bailey.*

HADLEY WOOD GOLF CLUB

★ Visitors and Societies Welcome ★ Renowned for Catering
★ Beautiful 18-Hole Course ★ Large Practice Range
★ Splendid Georgian Club House ★ Professional Shop/Coaching
Beech Hill, Near Barnet, Hertfordshire EN4 0JJ Tel: 020 8449 4328
See entry under BARNET for full details

BROXBOURNE. **The Hertfordshire Golf & Country Club,** Broxbournebury Mansion EN10 7PY (01992 466666; Fax: 01992 470326). *Location:* 10 minutes north on A10 from Junction 25 of M25 take Broxbourne exit, third left Bell Lane, over A10 right hand side. 18 hole "Nicklaus" design set around a Grade II Listed clubhouse, full USGA Specifications - irrigated and drained. 18 holes, 6388 yards. S.S.S. 70. 30 bay floodlit driving range. *Green Fees:* information not available. *Eating facilities:* Spike Bar, Cocktail Bar. Health club, golf academy, indoor and outdoor tennis courts, indoor swimming pool. *Visitors:* welcome weekdays, weekends restricted. *Society Meetings:* welcome. Head Teaching Professional: David Smith. Head Professional: Russell Hind. Pro Shop: (01992 441268). General Manager: James Hetherington.*

BUNTINGFORD. **East Herts Golf Club Ltd,** Hamels Park, Buntingford SG9 9NA (01920 821923). *Location:* one mile north of Puckeridge on A10. 18 holes, 6456 yards. S.S.S. 71. *Green Fees:* details on application. *Eating facilities:* separate restaurant. *Visitors:* welcome, with members only at weekends. *Society Meetings:* catered for weekdays. Professional: G. Culmer (01920 821922). Secretary:Colin Day (01920 821978; Fax: 01920 823700).
e-mail: secretary@ehgc.fsnet.co.uk
website: www.ehgc.co.uk

BUSHEY. **Bushey Country Club,** High Street, Bushey WD23 1TT (020 8950 2215). *Location:* Junction 5 of M1 onto A41, south to second roundabout, turn right to Bushey Heath; take A411 towards Watford, entrance down hill on left. 9 holes. Par 70. Driving range. *Green Fees:* information not available. *Eating facilities:* bar and dining facilities open from 8am to 11pm. *Visitors:* welcome. *Society Meetings:* welcome. Professional: Martin Siggins.

BUSHEY. **Bushey Hall Golf Club,** Bushey Hall Drive, Bushey WD23 2EP (01923 222253; Fax: 01923 229759). *Location:* one mile from M1 Junction 5, off Aldenham Road roundabout. Undulating parkland. 18 holes, 6099 yards, 6670 metres. S.S.S. 69. Practice nets, putting green. *Green Fees:* weekdays £26.00, weekends £35.00. *Eating facilities:* full catering available, two bars. *Visitors:* welcome, no restrictions. *Society Meetings:* catered for weekdays. Secretary/Manager: Gordon Forster (01923 222253).
e-mail: info@golfclubuk.co.uk
website: www.busheyhallgolfclub.co.uk

BUSHEY HEATH. **Hartsbourne Golf and Country Club,** Hartsbourne Avenue, Bushey Heath WD2 1JW (020 8421 7272; Fax: 020 8950 5357). *Location*: five miles south east of Watford. Parkland. 18 holes, 6385 yards. S.S.S. 70. 9 holes, 5773 yards. S.S.S. 68. *Green Fees:* information not available. *Eating facilities:* restaurant and snack bar available. *Visitors:* guests of members only. *Society Meetings:* catered for Mondays and Fridays. Professional: Reeves Weedon (020 8421 7266). General Manager: Ian Thomas (020 8421 7272; Fax: 020 8950 5357).

CHORLEYWOOD. **Chorleywood Golf Club Ltd,** Common Road, Chorleywood WD3 5LN (01923 282009; Fax: 01923 286739). *Location:* half a mile from Junction 18 of M25 via A404, three miles from Rickmansworth. A challenging mix of heath and woodland with natural hazards. 9 holes, 5686 yards. S.S.S. 67. *Green Fees:* £20.00 weekdays, £25.00 weekends. *Eating facilities:* meals available at most times. *Visitors:* welcome weekdays except Tuesday mornings, restricted at weekends. *Society Meetings:* contact Secretary for details. Secretary: Rod Botham (01923 282009; Fax: 01923 286739).
e-mail: chorleywood.gc@btclick.com

DAGNALL. **Whipsnade Park Golf Club,** Studham Lane, Dagnall HP4 1RH (0144-284 2330/2331; Fax: 0144-284 2090). *Location:* between Dagnall and Studham. Junction 11 M1 (from north), Junction 9 (from south). Parkland. 18 holes, 6800 yards. S.S.S. 72. Large practice area. *Green Fees:* £29.00 per round, £40.00 two rounds weekdays, weekends after 1pm visitors welcome, (without member) £35.00. *Eating facilities:* restaurant open daily, two bars. *Visitors:* welcome weekdays with reservation. *Society Meetings:* welcome with reservation. Professional: Mark Day (0144-284 2310). Secretary: Ruth Whalley (0144-284 2330).
e-mail: whipsnadeparkgolfc@btopenworld.com
website: www.whipsnadeparkgolf.co.uk

ELSTREE. **Elstree Golf and Country Club,** Watling Street, Elstree WD6 3AA (020 8953 6115; Fax: 020 8207 6390). *Location*: between Radlett and Elstree. Watling Street is also known as A5 (A5183) road. Close to M1, M25, A41, A1 (map available on request). Parkland course - undulating with ponds and ditches. 18 holes, 6556 yards. S.S.S. 72. 60 bay driving range. *Green Fees*: weekdays £37.00, weekends £45.00, 2 for 1. Please check for special offers. *Eating facilities*: bar, restaurant, conservatory available all day. *Visitors*: welcome weekdays anytime, weekends after 10.30am. Buggy and trolley hire, lockers/showers; large car park. Conference and function facilities. *Society Meetings*: welcome, information pack sent on request. Professionals: Marc Warwick, Mark Wood. Managing Director: Dean Cottrell. Secretary: Kathy Roberts (020 8238 6942).
e-mail: admin@elstree-golf.co.uk
website: www.elstree-golfclub.co.uk

Please mention **THE GOLF GUIDE** when you enquire about clubs or accommodation

---

Bushey Hall GOLF CLUB

Membership now available at Hertfordshire's oldest Golf Club.
Book your Society or Corporate Golf Day Now. Visitors welcome.
Green Fees Midweek £26.00; Weekend £35.00.
For further information & tee bookings:
**Tel: 01923 222253 • Fax 01923 229759 • www.busheyhallgolfclub.co.uk
Bushey Hall Golf Club, Bushey Hall Drive, Bushey, Hertfordshire WD23 2EP**

HARPENDEN. Aldwickbury Park Golf Club, Piggottshill Lane, Harpenden AL5 1AB (01582 760112; Fax: 01582 760113). *Location:* east of Harpenden on the Wheathampstead Road, Luton and St. Albans 10 minutes' drive. Rolling parkland with mature woodland. Two courses. Park Course – 18 holes, 6350 yards. S.S.S. 70. Manor Course – 9 holes, 1000 yards. Par 3. Practice area. *Green Fees:* weekdays £29.00; weekends £34.00 afternoons only. Twilight ticket £15.00. *Eating facilities:* licensed bar/restaurant and all day snack menu available. *Visitors:* welcome, call first; no weekend mornings play. PGA tuition, buggies and trolleys for hire. *Society Meetings:* welcome weekdays, please call for further details/prices. Professional: Robin Turley (01582 760112; Fax: 01582 760113). Secretary: Allan Knott (01582 765112; Fax: 01582 760113). website: www.aldwickburyparkgolfclub.com

HARPENDEN. Harpenden Common Golf Club, East Common, Harpenden AL5 1BL (01582 711320). *Location:* on A1081 between Harpenden and St. Albans. Flat heathland. 18 holes, 6214 yards. S.S.S. 70. *Green Fees:* weekdays and weekends £40.00 per round, weekdays £45 per day. *Eating facilities:* bar and restaurant daily. *Visitors:* welcome weekdays (not Tuesdays) and weekends. *Society Meetings:* Thursday and Friday only. Professional: D. Fitzsimmons (01582 460655). Manager: Clive Bailey (01582 711320; Fax: 01582 711321) e-mail: admin@hcgc.co.uk

HARPENDEN. Harpenden Golf Club, Hammonds End, Redbourn Lane, Harpenden AL5 2AX (01582 712580; Fax: 01582 712725). *Location:* turn off A1081, four miles after St. Albans on B487. Parkland course. 18 holes, 6377 yards. S.S.S. 70. *Green Fees:* weekdays £30.00 per round, £40.00 per day; weekends £40.00 per round. *Eating facilities:* snacks and lunches, order in advance. *Visitors:* welcome weekdays and weekends strictly by arrangement. *Society Meetings:* by arrangement only. Professional: Peter Cherry (01582 767124; Fax: 01582 712725). General Manager: Frank Clapp.

HATFIELD. Brookmans Park Golf Club, Golf Club Road, Brookmans Park, Hatfield AL9 7AT (01707 652459; Fax: 01707 661851). *Location:* A1000, just north of Potters Bar; M25 Junction 24. Parkland, two lakes. 18 holes, 6249 yards. S.S.S. 71. Practice ground and putting green. *Green Fees:* weekdays £32.00 per round, £42.00 per day; weekends with a member only. Handicap Certificate required. *Eating facilities:* bar snacks and lunches weekdays. *Visitors:* welcome weekdays; weekends with member only. *Society Meetings:* catered for Wednesdays and Thursdays. Professional: Ian Jelley (01707 652468). General Manager: Peter A. Gill (01707 652487; Fax: 01707 661851).

THE APPEARANCE OF AN ASTERISK (*) AT THE END OF A CLUB OR COURSE ENTRY INDICATES THAT UP-TO-DATE INFORMATION HAS NOT BEEN SUPPLIED

HATFIELD. Hatfield London Country Club, Bedwell Park, Essendon, Hatfield AL9 6HN (01707 260360; Fax: 01707 278475). *Location:* four miles south of Junction 4 A1(M), five miles north east of Junction 24 M25 Potters Bar. 9 holes Pitch and Putt. 36 holes (Old Course, 18 holes, 6808 yards, Par 72; New Course, 18 holes, 6938 yards, Par 72). Practice ground. *Green Fees:* information not available. *Eating facilities:* bar and restaurant with full catering available. *Visitors:* welcome, advance bookings only. *Society Meetings:* always welcome.

HEMEL HEMPSTEAD. Boxmoor Golf Club, 18 Box Lane, Boxmoor, Hemel Hempstead HP3 0DJ (01442 242434). *Location:* two miles from Hemel Hempstead, three-quarters of a mile from Hemel Hempstead Station on A41. Hilly/moorland course, 9 holes, 4112 yards. S.S.S. 62. *Green Fees:* weekdays £8.00, weekends (after 11.30am) £10.00. *Eating facilities:* ring Steward. *Visitors:* welcome without reservation, except on Sundays. *Society Meetings:* catered for on application. Secretary: Brian Swann.

HEMEL HEMPSTEAD. Little Hay Golf Complex, Box Lane, Bovingdon, Hemel Hempstead HP3 0DQ (01442 833798). *Location*: just off A41, along Chesham Road from Hemel Hempstead. Parkland. 18 holes, 6678 yards. S.S.S. 72. 6 hole pitch and putt course, short game practice area, floodlit driving range. *Green Fees:* information not available. *Eating facilities:* available, open all day. *Visitors:* welcome. *Society Meetings:* welcome by arrangement. Professionals: Nick Allen and Michael Perry (01442 833798). Complex Manager: Chris Gordon (01442 833798).

HEMEL HEMPSTEAD. Shendish Manor Golf Club, London Road, Apsley, Hemel Hempstead HP3 0AA (01442 251806; Fax: 01442 230683). *Location:* Two miles from J20 M25 on the west side of A4251 London Road (ex A41) between Kings Langley and Hemel Hempstead. Mature parkland course. 18 holes, 5660 yards. S.S.S. 67 (Par 70). 9 hole pitch and putt course. *Green Fees:* information not available. *Eating facilities:* Sportsman's bar and Brasserie. *Visitors:* no restrictions, please telephone to ensure tee time. Conference and full banqueting facilities, health club and putting green. *Society Meetings:* welcome seven days a week. Professional: Murray White (01442 251806). Secretary: Ralph Thornberry.*

HERTFORD. Brickendon Grange Golf Club, Brickendon, Near Hertford SG13 8PD (01992 511258; Fax: 01992 511411). *Location:* three miles south of Hertford, one mile from Bayford Railway Station. Undulating parkland with specimen trees. 18 holes, 6458 yards. S.S.S. 71. Excellent practice area. *Green Fees:* £36.00 per round, £45.00 per day. *Eating facilities:* bar and restaurant, snack meals available lunchtimes. *Visitors:* welcome weekdays only, Handicap Certificate required. *Society Meetings:* catered for by arrangement. Professional: G. Tippett (01992 511218). General Manager: Martin Bennet (01992 511258; Fax: 01992 511411).
e-mail: play@brickendongrangegc.co.uk
website: www.brickendongrangegc.co.uk

HITCHIN. **Chesfield Downs Golf Club,** Jack's Hill, Graveley, Near Hitchin SG4 7EQ (01462 482929). *Location*: just off Junction 8 of the A1(M), approximately two miles along the B197. Parkland. Two Courses: Chesfield Downs–18 holes, 6646 yards. S.S.S. 72. Par 71. Lannock Links–Par 3. 9 holes, 975 yards. S.S.S. 27. 27 bay floodlit driving range/practice bunker, putting green. *Green Fees:* information not available. *Eating facilities*: "Chesfields Restaurant and Bar". *Visitors*: welcome, advance booking system available to reserve tee-off times. Geoff Budds Golf Emporium, Learn Golf Academy, changing facilities. Part of the Leisure Links International Group. *Society Meetings*: catered for by arrangement. Head Professional: Keith Bond. General Manager: Paul Barnfather.*

KNEBWORTH. **Knebworth Golf Club,** Deards End Lane, Knebworth SG3 6NL (01438 812752). *Location:* one mile south of Stevenage, off B197 (A1(M)) turnoff no. 7. Undulating parkland. 18 holes, 6492 yards. S.S.S. 71. *Green Fees:* weekdays £35.00. *Eating facilities:* full facilities available. *Visitors:* welcome weekdays, with members only at weekends. *Society Meetings:* welcome Mondays, Tuesdays and Thursdays only. Professional: G. Parker (01438 812757). General Manager: A. S. Hobbs (01438 812752).
e-mail: knebworth@btconnect.com
website: www.knebworthgolfclub.com

LETCHWORTH. **Letchworth Golf Club,** Letchworth Lane, Letchworth SG6 3NQ. *Location:* two miles from A1 (M) near village of Willian, adjacent to Letchworth Hall Hotel. Parkland course. 18 holes, recently extended to 6420 yards. S.S.S. 71. Large practice ground with 9 hole pitch and putt course. *Green Fees:* weekdays (except Mondays) £32.00 per round, £37.00 for 27 holes, £42.00 per day; Mondays £18.00 per round, £27.00 per day; weekend accompanied only. *Eating facilities:* bars and restaurant (limited menu Monday lunchtime only). *Visitors:* Handicap Certificate required. *Society Meetings:* catered for Wednesdays, Thursdays and Fridays. Professional: Karl Teshner (01462 682713). Secretary: Michael Jordan (01462 683203; Fax: 01462 484567).

POTTERS BAR. **Potters Bar Golf Club,** Darkes Lane, Potters Bar EN6 1DE (01707 652020; Fax: 01707 655051). *Location:* one mile north of M25 exit 24 signposted Potters Bar, turn right at third traffic lights, club on left at end of shopping centre. Parkland course, well wooded, undulating, with streams. 18 holes, 6279 yards. S.S.S. 70. Small practice ground. *Green Fees:* weekdays £26.00 per round, £36.00 per day; weekends with member only. *Eating facilities:* luncheons and bar available from 11.30am. *Visitors:* weekdays only, must produce valid Handicap Certificate. *Society Meetings:* welcome weekdays, Wednesday afternoons only. Professional: Gary A'ris (01707 652987; Fax: 01707 655051). Secretary: Peter Watson (01707 652020; Fax: 01707 655051).
e-mail: info@pottersbargolfclub.com

RADLETT. **Porters Park Golf Club,** Shenley Hill, Radlett WD7 7AZ (01923 854127; Fax: 01923 855475). *Location*: approximately 3 miles south west of Junction 22 (M25), three miles north-east Junction 5 (M1), half a mile north of Radlett Station on Shenley Hill. Undulating parkland with fine trees and a brook. 18 holes, 6313 yards. S.S.S. 70. Open and Regional qualifying course. Three practice areas, putting. *Green Fees:* information not available. *Visitors:* welcome Monday to Friday. Handicap Certificate required. *Society Meetings:* catered for Wednesday and Thursday. Professional: David Gleeson (01923 854366). Managing Secretary: P.A. Marshall (01923 854127; Fax: 01923 855475).*
e-mail: info@porterspark.fsnet.co.uk

REDBOURN. **Redbourn Golf Club,** Kinsbourne, Green Lane, Redbourn AL3 7QA (01582 793493; Fax: 01582 794362). *Location:* one mile east of M1 Junction 9, four miles north of St. Albans, four miles south of Luton. Parkland course on which water comes into play on several holes. Two courses - Ver 18 holes. 6506 yards. S.S.S. 71. Kinsbourne Course - challenging Par 3, 9 holes, 1361 yards. S.S.S. 27. Driving range. *Green Fees:* information not available. *Eating facilities:* licensed bar, restaurant, snacks and hot meals readily available. *Visitors:* welcome weekdays, weekends and Bank Holidays after 12 noon. *Society Meetings:* welcome weekdays only. Professional: Stephen Hunter. Golf Secretary: Stuart Hatch (01582 794888).
email: golfclubsecretary@redbourngolfclub.com
website: www.redbourngolfclub.com

RICKMANSWORTH. **Batchworth Park Golf Club,** London Road, Rickmansworth WD3 1JS (01923 711400; Fax: 01923 710200). *Location:* situated five miles from Junction 17 M25 on the A404. Undulating parkland course. 18 holes, 6723 yards. S.S.S. 72. Practice range, putting green and chipping area. *Green Fees:* information not available. *Eating facilities:* bar, dining room - food served all day. *Visitors:* guests of members only. Professional: Stephen Proudfoot (01923 714922).*

RICKMANSWORTH. **Moor Park Golf Club,** Moor Park, Rickmansworth WD3 1QN (01923 773146; Fax: 01923 777109). *Location*: Junction 18 of M25 and follow A404, signs to Moor Park Golf Club. Parkland course with rolling fairways. High Course: 18 holes, 6713 yards (white), 6370 (yellow). S.S.S. 72 (white), 70 (yellow). West Course: 18 holes, 5815 yards (white), 5516 yards (yellow). S.S.S. 68 (white), 67 (yellow). Practice ground. *Green Fees:* weekdays High Course £82.50, West Course £52.50. *Eating facilities:* full catering available. *Visitors:* welcome on weekdays only by prior arrangement. *Society Meetings:* welcome weekdays only. Professional: L. Farmer (Tel & Fax: 01923 774113). Secretary: J. Moore.
e-mail: enquiries@moorparkgc.co.uk
website: www.moorparkgc.co.uk

THE APPEARANCE OF AN ASTERISK (*) AT THE END OF A CLUB OR COURSE ENTRY INDICATES THAT UP-TO-DATE INFORMATION HAS NOT BEEN SUPPLIED

ENGLAND / Hertfordshire

RICKMANSWORTH. **Rickmansworth Public Golf Course,** Moor Lane, Rickmansworth WD3 1QL (01923 775278). *Location*: from town centre along A404 to Waterworks, left along B4504, then first right. Testing, undulating parkland course. 18 holes, 4557 yards, Par 65. *Green Fees:* information not available. *Eating facilities:* bars, restaurant. *Visitors:* welcome. *Society Meetings:* catered for, contact Professional. Professional: Alan Dobbins (01923 775278). Secretary: Andre de Bruin (01895 270453).*

ROYSTON. **Heydon Grange Golf and Country Club,** Heydon, Royston SG8 7NS (01763 208988; Fax: 01763 208926). *Location*: A505 10 minutes drive east of Royston and minutes from M11 Duxford. Parkland course, gently rolling countryside. 27 holes, 6512 yards. S.S.S. 71. Covered range. *Green Fees:* information not available. *Eating facilities:* bar menu, bar, patio. *Visitors:* welcome all times. Buggies available. *Society Meetings:* welcome. Professional: J. O'Leary.

ROYSTON. **Malton Golf,** Meldreth, Royston SG8 6PE (01763 262200; Fax: 01763 262209). *Location*: Junction 12 of M11, A603 West to Orwell, through village, right to Malton. 230 acres beautiful landscaped countryside, lightly wooded with River Cam running through the course. 18 holes, 6708 yards, 6134 metres. S.S.S. 72. Driving range. *Green Fees*: information not available. *Eating facilities:* clubhouse (seats 50 diners) providing bar, snacks and hot meals. *Visitors:* all welcome, no restrictions. *Society Meetings*: all welcome (Handicap not required) Packages from £12.00 (18 holes, including food). Secretary: A.R. Boyce (01638 751222; Fax: 01638 751821).*
website: www.maltongolf.co.uk

ROYSTON. **Royston Golf Club (Founded 1892),** Baldock Road, Royston SG8 5BG (01763 242696). *Location*: alongside the A505 on right hand side when approaching from Baldock, clubhouse at top of hill before entering town. Links - undulating heathland. 18 holes, 6086 yards. S.S.S. 69 yellow, 70 white. Practice fairway. *Green Fees:* information not available. *Eating facilities:* lounge bar – 19th hole bar, diningroom and bar meals. *Visitors:* welcome weekdays; weekends only with member. *Society Meetings:* weekdays only, book through Secretary. Professional: S. Clark (01763 243476). Secretary: J Beech (Tel & Fax: 01763 242696).*
e-mail: roystongolf@btconnect.com
website: www.roystongolfclub.co.uk

www.uk-golfguide.com

ST ALBANS. **Batchwood Golf and Tennis Centre,** Batchwood Drive, St Albans AL3 5XA (01727 844250; Fax: 01727 858506). *Location*: near City Hospital, close to St Albans town centre. Flat, parkland, wooded course. 18 holes, 6463 yards. S.S.S. 71. *Green Fees*: information not available. *Eating facilities*: bar and restaurant. *Visitors*: welcome. *Society Meetings*: welcome with reservation. Bookings: (01727 844250) PGA Professional: Mark Flitton (07797 386003). Secretary: Bernard Hudson (01582 833530).*

ST ALBANS. **Mid-Herts Golf Club,** Gustard Wood, Lamer Lane, Wheathampstead, Near St Albans AL4 8RS (01582 832242). *Location*: B651, six miles north of St Albans. Flat heathland, short and tight course. 18 holes, 6060 yards. S.S.S. 69. Course record 63. *Green Fees:* information not available. *Eating facilities:* by arrangement. *Visitors:* welcome weekdays with reservation; Handicap Certificate required. *Society Meetings:* catered for by arrangement. Professional: Barney Puttick (01582 832788). Secretary: R.J.H. Jourdan (01582 832242; Fax: 01582 834834).*
e-mail: secretary@mid-hertsgolfclub.co.uk
website: www.midhertsgolfclub.co.uk

ST ALBANS. **Verulam Golf Club,** 226 London Road, St Albans AL1 1JG (01727 839016). *Location*: M25 Junction 22a or 22 to A1081 to St. Albans, course is off London Road (A1081) near railway bridge. Easy walking parkland course designed by James Braid. 18 holes, 6457 yards. S.S.S. 71. Practice ground, nets, putting and chipping green, bunker and driving tee. *Green Fees:* Monday £24.00, Tuesday - Friday £32.00, weekends O/A. *Eating facilities:* bar snacks from 11am to 4.30pm, other dining by prior arrangement. *Visitors:* welcome weekdays except Wednesday mornings. *Society Meetings:* welcome by prior arrangement with Secretary - deposit required. Professional: Nick Burch (01727 861401). General Manager: David Cliffe (01727 853327; Fax: 01727 812201).
e-mail: gm@verulamgolf.co.uk
website: www.verulamgolf.co.uk

SAWBRIDGEWORTH. **Manor of Groves,** High Wych, Sawbridgeworth CM21 0JU (0870 4108833; Fax: 0870 4178833). *Location:* Junction 7 off M11 follow A414 to High Wych. Parkland/woodland course with water features. 18 holes, 6237 yards. S.S.S. 71. Practice ground. Soft spikes only. *Green Fees:* please call. *Eating facilities:* hotel and golf club facilities, bar. *Visitors:* welcome anytime weekdays, advise phoning; weekends after 12 noon only. Accommodation available in our 80 bedroomed Hotel. Leisure facilities including pool, gym, aerobics studio, E'spa beauty salon. *Society Meetings:* most welcome, special packages available. General Manager: James Jude.

MALTON GOLF

Great value golf in tranquil surroundings
welcomes all Golfers and Societies
Clubhouse • 18 holes • Driving Range
www.maltongolf.co.uk • Tel: 01763 262200
8 miles SW of Cambridge, 4 miles N of Royston

218 Hertfordshire / ENGLAND   THE GOLF GUIDE 2006

STEVENAGE. **Stevenage Golf Centre,** Aston Lane, Stevenage SG2 7EL (01438 880322). *Location*: turn off A1(M) at Stevenage South Junction onto A602 to Hertford, course signposted at Van Hagues Garden Centre. Water hazards on course. 18 holes, 6451 yards. S.S.S. 71. Par 72. 20 bay driving range. *Green Fees*: information not available. *Eating facilities:* restaurant and bar. *Visitors:* welcome. Municipal course, advance booking system available to reserve tee-off times. Shower facilities. *Society Meetings*: catered for by arrangement. Professional: Pat Winston (01438 880424). Secretary: Mrs S. Elwin (01438 880322).

TRING near. **Stocks,** Stocks Road, Aldbury, Near Tring HP23 5RX (01442 851341; Fax: 01442 851253). *Location:* M1 Junction 11 or 9, A41 (Tring) follow signs to Tring B.R. Parkland course, feature lake second and 10th holes, a test of length and accuracy. 18 holes, 6988 yards. S.S.S. 74. Practice range, practice green, chipping green. *Green Fees:* information not available. *Eating facilities:* Club house bar snack menu. *Visitors:* welcome, after 12pm weekends. *Society Meetings:* welcome weekdays only. Director of Golf: Peter Lane (01442 852511). Golf Manager: Robin Darling (01442 852504).*
e-mail: plane@stocksgolf.co.uk
          rdarling@stocksgolf.co.uk
website: www.stocksgolf.co.uk

WALTHAM CROSS. **The Cheshunt Golf Club,** The Clubhouse, Park Lane, Cheshunt EN7 6QD (01992 629777). *Location:* M25 Junction 25 to Hertford, A10 left at second set of traffic lights, turn right at mini roundabout then approximately quarter of a mile. Flat parkland course. 18 holes, 6608 yards. S.S.S. 71. Practice area. *Green Fees:* information not available. *Eating facilities:* public cafe. *Visitors:* welcome anytime. For tee-off times phone Pro Shop (01992 624009). Professional: D. Banks (01992 624009). Secretary: B. Furne (01992 629777).*

WARE. **Briggens House Golf Club,** Briggens Park, Stanstead Road, Stanstead Abbotts, Ware SG12 8LD (01279 793742; Fax: 01279 793685). *Location:* A414 near Harlow, Essex. Parkland course. 9 holes, 5582 yards. S.S.S. 69. Practice area. *Green Fees:* information not available. *Eating facilities*: hotel restaurant and coffee shop with snacks, both with bars. *Visitors:* welcome anytime except Sunday mornings. *Society Meetings:* very welcome. Professional: Alan McGinn. Secretary: Alan Battle.

WARE. **Chadwell Springs Golf Club,** Hertford Road, Ware SG12 9LE (01920 461447). *Location*: just off A10 Hertford to Ware. Heathland. 9 holes, 6418 yards, S.S.S. 71. Practice area. *Green Fees:* information not provided. *Eating facilities:* bar, bar meals; function room. *Visitors*: welcome weekdays except Tuesday and Thursday mornings; weekends with member only. Carts available. *Society Meetings*: welcome weekdays by arrangement. Professional: David Smith. Secretary: David Robertson (01920 462075).

WARE. **Hanbury Manor Golf and Country Club,** Ware SG12 0SD (01920 487722; Fax: 01920 487692). *Location:* leave the M25 at Junction 25 and take the A10 towards Hertford, continue for 12 miles and Hanbury Manor is located on the left. Parkland and Championship course designed by Jack Nicklaus II. Host to 1997, 1998 and 1999 English Open. 18 holes, 7052 yards. S.S.S. 74 (blue tees). Putting green, practice ground. *Green Fees:* information not available. *Eating facilities:* two award-winning restaurants in five star Marriott Hotel which overlooks course. *Visitors:* golf available only to Club members or hotel guests. Club and buggy hire, golf shop. *Society Meetings:* Corporate Golf Days are available. Director of Golf: Jason O'Malley.
website: www.hanbury-manor.com

WARE. **Whitehill Golf Club,** Whitehill Golf Centre, Dane End, Ware SG12 0JS (01920 438495; Fax: 01920 438891). *Location:* turn off A10 at Raj Villa, High Cross. Undulating course. 18 holes, 6618 yards. S.S.S 72. 25 bay floodlit driving range. *Green Fees:* information not available. *Eating facilities:* bar, restaurants and function room. *Visitors:* welcome. Snooker room. *Society Meetings:* welcome, groups of 12 or more. Professional: Matt Belsham. Secretary: Andrew Smith.*
e-mail: whitehillgolfcentre@btinternet.com

WATFORD. **Aldenham Golf and Country Club,** Church Lane, Aldenham, Watford WD25 8NN (01923 853929; Fax: 01923 858472). *Location:* three minutes from M1 Junction 5, off B462 to Radlett. Flat parkland course. 18 holes, 6500 yards. S.S.S. 71. 9 holes, 2350 yards. Practice area. *Green Fees:* weekdays £28.00, weekends £36.00. *Eating facilities*: full catering and bar facilities. *Visitors:* welcome, weekends after 1pm. Buggy cars for hire. *Society Meetings:* welcome by prior arrangement. Professional: Tim Dunstan (01923 857889). Secretary: (01923 853929).
e-mail: info@aldenhamgolfclub.co.uk
website: www.aldenhamgolfclub.co.uk

WATFORD. **West Herts Golf Club,** Cassiobury Park, Watford WD3 3GG (01923 236484). *Location:* off Rousebarn Lane from Links Way, A412 at Croxley Green. Parkland. 18 holes, 6488 yards. S.S.S. 71. *Green Fees:* weekdays £38.00 per round; weekends £52.00. *Eating facilities:* catering (including breakfast) available seven days a week. *Visitors:* welcome. *Society Meetings:* catered for. Professional: Charles Gough (01923 220352). General Manager: Clive Dodman (01923 236484; Fax: 01923 222300).

WELWYN GARDEN CITY. **Brocket Hall Golf Club,** Welwyn Garden City AL8 7XG (01707 335241; Fax: 01707 390052). *Location*: A1(M) two minutes from Junction 4. Parkland course and woodland course. 36 holes, 6600 yards and 7050 yards, S.S.S. 72 and 73 respectively. Par 3 course, Faldo Golf Institute. *Eating facilities*: available all day. *Visitors*: must be a member's guest. *Society Meetings:* corporate days welcome. Professional: Keith Wood.
e-mail: info@brocket-hall.co.uk
website: www.brocket-hall.co.uk

THE APPEARANCE OF AN ASTERISK (*) AT THE END OF A CLUB OR COURSE ENTRY INDICATES THAT UP-TO-DATE INFORMATION HAS NOT BEEN SUPPLIED

WELWYN GARDEN CITY. Mill Green Golf Club, Gypsy Lane, Welwyn Garden City AL7 4TY (01707 276900; Fax: 01707 276898). *Location:* from A1 North exit 4 (Hatfield) A414 to Hertford, take first slip road on left to A1000, left at lights, second right Ascots Lane, mini roundabout turn right into Gypsy Lane. Parkland course. Peter Alliss and Clive Clarke designed. 18 holes, 6615 yards. S.S.S. 72. Two contrasting loops of 9 holes. Front 9 open and elevated, back 9 long narrow fairways through woodland. Par 3 course, driving range, putting green. *Green Fees:* weekdays £27.50, weekends £32.50. *Eating facilities:* full bar menu available and extensive conference and banqueting facilities. *Visitors:* Monday to Friday all day, after midday at weekends. *Society Meetings:* welcome Monday to Friday. Professional: Ian Parker. General Manager: Tim Hudson
e-mail: millgreen@crown-golf.co.uk

WELWYN GARDEN CITY. Panshanger Golf Complex, Old Herns Lane, Panshanger, Welwyn Garden City AL7 2ED (01707 333312; Fax: 01707 390010). *Location*: just off Junction 6 A1(M), 10 minutes from M25. Parkland set in the Mimram Valley. 18 holes, 6347 yards. S.S.S. 70. Practice ground, 9 hole pitch and putt. *Green Fees:* information not available. *Eating facilities:* Fairway Tavern and cafe. *Visitors:* municipal course, pay as you play, all welcome, dress conditions. *Society Meetings:* welcome weekdays. Professionals: Bryan Lewis and Michael Corlass (01707 333350; Fax: 01707 339507). Secretary: Trish Skinner (01707 332837). General Manager: Michael Corlass.

WELWYN GARDEN CITY. Welwyn Garden City Golf Club Ltd, Mannicotts, High Oaks Road, Welwyn Garden City AL8 7BP (01707 325243). *Location*: from north Junction 5 on A1M and take B197 to Valley Road. From south Junction 4 on A1M to Lemsford Lane and Valley Road. Undulating parkland. 18 holes, 6200 yards. S.S.S. 69. Practice ground. *Green Fees:* £35.00 weekdays. *Eating facilities*: by order for lunches; sandwiches available. *Visitors:* welcome weekdays with Handicap Certificate; weekends with member only. *Society Meetings*: Mondays, Wednesdays and Thursdays only (£60.00 per person per day). Professional: R. May (01707 325525). General Manager: (01707 325243; Fax: 01707 393213)

WHEATHAMPSTEAD. Lamerwood Country Club, Codicote Road, Wheathampstead AL4 8GB (01582 833013; Fax: 01582 832604). *Location:* from London take A1(M) exit at Junction 4. After Hatfield Tunnel take B653 towards Wheathampstead. Set in 240 acres of mature wood and parkland. 18 holes, 6953 yards. S.S.S. 73. 9 hole short course and practice facilities available. *Green Fees:* information not available. *Eating facilities:* full bar and restaurant, private function rooms. *Visitors:* always welcome. *Society Meetings:* always welcome. Accommodation available at Sopwellhouse Hotel and Country Club, St. Albans (01727 864477; Fax: 01727 844741). Professional: Matthew Masters (01582 833013). Director: Mr. S. Takabatake. *

ALDENHAM GOLF & COUNTRY CLUB

Easily accessible from M1 and M25, this picturesque 18-hole parkland course and 9-hole course are situated in the pretty village of Aldenham.
Visiting societies are always welcome and we offer excellent "value for money" golfing packages throughout the year.

For details phone 01923 853929
Church Lane, Aldenham, Watford WD25 8NN
www.aldenhamgolfclub.co.uk

See also Colour Advertisement on page 28

FHG

Visit the **KUPERARD** website
www.holidayguides.com
for details of the wide choice of accommodation featured in the full range of FHG titles

Isle of Wight

COWES. **Cowes Golf Club,** Crossfield Avenue, Cowes, Isle of Wight PO31 8HN (Tel & Fax: 01983 292303). *Location:* entrance adjacent Cowes High School. Parkland with sea views. 9 holes, 5934 yards. S.S.S. 68. *Green Fees:* weekdays £16.00; weekends £20.00. *Eating facilities:* snack meals available in bar in summer. Bar open 11am to 2pm summer months. *Visitors:* welcome except Sunday before 1pm and Thursday, Ladies' Day (11.30am to 3pm). *Society Meetings:* welcome Mondays to Wednesdays by arrangement with Secretary. Society rates by arrangement. Secretary: D.C. Weaver (01983 292303) Steward (01983 280135)

EAST COWES. **Osborne Golf Club,** Osborne House Estate, East Cowes PO32 6JX (01983 295421). *Location:* off A3021 south-east of East Cowes. One mile from Southampton/East Cowes ferry terminal; 4 miles from Portsmouth/Fishbourne ferry terminal. Parkland. 9 holes, 6372 yards. S.S.S. 70. Practice area. *Green Fees:* weekdays £20.00; weekends and Bank Holidays £25.00. Subject to review. *Eating facilities:* catering available each day, bar facilities. *Visitors:* welcome except Tuesday, Saturday and Sunday before noon. Telephone for tee availability. *Society Meetings:* catered for (24 maximum). e-mail: info@osbornegolfclub.wanadoo.co.uk website: www.osbornegolfclub.co.uk

FRESHWATER. **Freshwater Bay Golf Club,** Afton Down, Freshwater (Tel & Fax: 01983 752955). *Location:* western end of Island, approximately half-a-mile east of Freshwater Bay on coast road to Ventnor. Links type course on chalk uplands. 18 holes, 5725 yards. S.S.S. 68. *Green Fees:* information not available. *Eating facilities:* licensed bar, catering. *Visitors:* welcome. *Society Meetings:* welcome by arrangement. Secretary: Terry Riddett.*
e-mail: tr.fbgc@btopenworld.com

NEWPORT. **Newport (Isle of Wight) Golf Club,** St Georges Down, Near Shide, Newport PO30 2JB Founded 1895. *Location*: one mile south east of Newport, taking Sandown road. Testing downland course. 9 holes, 5704 yards. S.S.S. 68. Driving range available to visitors. *Green Fees*: weekdays £20.00, weekends £25.00. *Eating facilities*: full catering available- breakfast, lunches, evening dinners. *Visitors*: welcome anytime except Wednesday 12pm-3pm, Saturday before 3pm and Sunday before noon. *Society Meetings*: groups of 12 plus welcome by arrangement weekdays except Wednesdays and not before 3pm on Saturdays or noon on Sundays. Secretary: Dave Boon (01983 525076).

RYDE. **Ryde Golf Club,** Binstead Road, Ryde, Isle of Wight PO33 3NF. *Location:* on A3054 Ryde to Newport Road, just outside Ryde. Parkland course. 9 holes, extended June 2002 to 5772 yards. Par 70. S.S.S. 69. *Green Fees:* weekdays £20.00; weekends and Bank Holidays £23.00. *Eating facilities:* Bar and catering available all day April to September; lunchtime only October to March. *Visitors:* welcome, restrictions Wednesdays and Sundays. *Society Meetings:* catered for. Limited Pro Shop on site. Secretary: Richard Dean (01983 614809; Fax: 01983 567418).
e-mail: secretary@rydegolfclub.freeserve.co.uk
website: www.rydegolf.co.uk

SANDOWN. **Shanklin and Sandown Golf Club,** The Fairway, Lake, Sandown PO36 9PR (01983 404424/403217). *Location:* from Sandown travel towards Shanklin. Soon after Heights Leisure Centre turn right into The Fairway. One mile to Club. A traditional, beautiful heathland County Championship course. The 13th hole is one of the best in Southern England. 18 holes, 6062 yards. S.S.S. 69. Practice ground. *Green Fees:* £29.50 weekdays; £35.00 weekends. Three day ticket weekdays £66.00. *Eating facilities:* full catering and bar facilities. *Visitors:* welcome. Handicap Certificate preferred. *Society Meetings:* welcome by arrangement. Professional: Peter Hammond (01983 404424). Secretary: A. Creed (01983 403217).

UPPER VENTNOR. **Ventnor Golf Club,** Steephill Down Road, Upper Ventnor PO38 1BP (01983 853326). *Location:* northwest boundary of Ventnor. Downland undulating with side slopes overlooking the sea. 12 holes, 5767 yards. S.S.S. 68. *Green Fees:* information not available. *Eating facilities:* bar snacks only. *Visitors:* welcome, Sundays after 1pm, Ladies' Day Monday tee closed 11am till 1pm. Secretary: Stewart Blackmore. *

For full details of clubs and courses, plus convenient accommodation
www.uk-golfguide.com

FHG please mention **THE GOLF GUIDE** when you enquire about clubs or accommodation
KUPERARD

Kent

ASH. **The London Golf Club,** South Ash Manor Estate, Ash TN15 7EN (01474 879899; Fax: 01474 879912). *Location*: 1 mile east of Brands Hatch on A20, turn left after motorway underpass when leaving West Kingsdown. 36 holes Heritage Course: Nicklaus design 7208 yards, S.S.S. 74. International course: 7005 yards, S.S.S. 73. Practice range (350 yards), covered bays and grass tees; practice chipping and bunker facilities, 2x practice putting greens. *Green Fees:* Heritage Course: members guest only; International Course £80.00/£90.00. *Eating facilities*: restaurant, terrace bar, spike bar, plus private rooms, full changing facilities. *Visitors:* Heritage Course: members and guests only. International Course: visitors and corporate days by prior arrangement. General Manager: Mr Scott Evans. Director of Golf: Alasdair Robertson. Head Professional: Paul Stuart. Marketing: Heath Harvey. Golf Events: Gordon Frost. Events Co-ordinator: Debbie Nash. Membership Secretary: Philip Watts. e-mail: golf@londongolf.co.uk
website: www.londongolf.co.uk

ASH. **Redlibbets Golf Club,** Manor Lane, West Yoke, Ash TN15 7HT (01474 879190). Undulating woodland 18 hole course. Practice range, practice short game area, putting green and indoor net room. *Green Fees*: information not available. *Eating facilities*: Bar and restaurant. Secretary: J. Potter.

ASHFORD. **Ashford Great Chart Golf & Leisure,** Great Chart, Ashford (01233 645858). *Location*: Junction 9 off M20; A28 to Great Chart, follow signs. 9 hole main course, family pitch and putt course. 26 bay floodlit covered driving range. *Green Fees*: information not available. *Eating facilities*: bar/cafe. *Visitors*: welcome, juniors and families welcome. Video tuition, shop, practice bunkers. Volley ball/beach soccer sand pitch. Professional: Cameron Cowie. Secretary: Grant Kay/ John Kay.*

ASHFORD. **Ashford (Kent) Golf Club,** Sandyhurst Lane, Ashford TN25 4NT (01233 620180). *Location:* just off A20, one and a half miles west of Ashford. Parkland - stream cutting through course. 18 holes, 6261 yards. S.S.S. 70. *Green Fees:* information not available. *Eating facilities:* available every day. *Visitors:* welcome. Handicap Certificate required. *Society Meetings:* catered for Tuesdays and Thursdays by arrangement. Professional: Hugh Sherman (01233 629644). Secretary: A.H. Story (Tel & Fax: 01233 622655). *

www.uk-golfguide.com
For full details of clubs and courses, plus convenient accommodation

ASHFORD. **Chart Hills Golf Club,** Weeks Lane, Biddenden, Ashford TN27 8JX (01580 292222; Fax: 01580 292233). *Location:* M25, M20 Leeds Castle turn off (B2163), A274 to Tenterden. Parkland course designed by Nick Faldo. 18 holes, 7119 yards. S.S.S. 74. Short game area, golf academy. *Green Fees:* weekdays £45.00 per person summer, weekends £68.00 per person summer. Winter special offers every year. *Eating facilities:* restaurant, bar snacks, bar, conference facilities. *Visitors:* welcome, limited at weekends, members only on Mondays and Wednesdays. Gymnasium, fitness centre. *Society Meetings:* mid-week only, contact Events Co-ordinator.
e-mail: info@charthills.co.uk
website: www.charthills.co.uk

ASHFORD. **The Homelands Bettergolf Centre,** Ashford Road, Kingsnorth, Ashford TN26 1NJ (01233 661620; Fax: 01233 720553). *Location:* take exit 10 off M20, follow A2070 course signposted from second roundabout to Kingsnorth. 9 hole parkland course. 2250 yards, S.S.S. 62. *Green Fees:* information not available. *Visitors:* welcome at all times. Buggies, trolleys and clubs available for hire. *Society Meetings:* welcome with prior notice. Short breaks organised. Professional: Tony Bowers. Secretary: Ian S. Johnson. *

BECKENHAM. **Beckenham Place Park Golf Club,** Beckenham Hill Road, Beckenham. *Location:* on A222 north of Bromley. Parkland. 18 holes, 5722 yards. S.S.S. 68. Practice ground, nets, putting green. *Green Fees:* information not available. *Eating facilities:* bar and cafeteria. *Visitors:* welcome but must book in advance. *Society Meetings:* catered for. Other facilities include tennis courts and putting green. Professional: H. Davies-Thomas (020 8650-2292). Secretary: T. A. Moorcroft.*

BECKENHAM. **Braeside Golf Club,** Beckenham Place Park, Beckenham Hill, Beckenham (020 8650 2292). Parkland course. 18 holes, 5722 yards, 5230 metres. S.S.S. 69. Practice area, putting green and nets. *Green Fees:* information not available. *Eating facilities:* cafe and bar. *Visitors:* welcome, will need to book weekends. Secretary: Mr Nicholas Wilkins.*

BECKENHAM. **Langley Park Golf Club,** Barnfield Wood Road, Beckenham BR3 6SZ (020 8658 6849). *Location:* one mile from Bromley South station. Flat wooded parkland. 18 holes, 6469 yards, 5916 metres, S.S.S. 71. Practice areas and nets. *Green Fees:* information not available. *Eating facilities:* bar snacks, restaurant/dining room. *Visitors:* welcome weekdays by arrangement with Pro Shop. Handicap Certificate required. *Society Meetings:* Wednesdays and Thursdays by arrangement with the Club Manager. Other days considered. Professional: Colin Staff (020 8650 1663). Club Manager: Rodger Pollard (020 8658 6849).

BEXLEYHEATH. **Bexley Heath Golf Club,** Mount Road, Bexley Heath DA6 8JS (020 8303 6951). *Location:* adjacent to A2. Hilly parkland. 9 holes, 5239 yards, 4788 metres. S.S.S. 66. *Green Fees:* £20.00 (approximately). Weekends with member only. *Eating facilities:* catering available. *Visitors:* weekdays only. Professional: To be appointed. Secretary: Mrs J. Smith.

BIGGIN HILL. **Cherry Lodge Golf Club,** Jail Lane, Biggin Hill TN16 3AX (01959 572250; Fax: 01959 540672). *Location:* A233 to M25 Junction 5, Bromley, eight miles. Undulating Parkland 600 ft. above sea level with panoramic views of surrounding countryside. 18 holes, 6652 yards, 6084 metres. S.S.S. 73. Extensive practice ground. *Green Fees:* £40.00 weekdays only. *Eating facilities:* bar snacks all day, Sunday lunches. *Visitors:* welcome weekdays except Bank Holidays. *Society Meetings:* welcome weekdays (except Bank Holidays) by arrangement. Professional: Nigel Child (01959 572989; Fax: 01959 540672). Secretary: A. Salter (Assistant) (01959 572250; Fax: 01959 540672).
e-mail: info@cherrylodgegc.co.uk
website: www.cherrylodgegc.co.uk

BRENCHLEY. **The Kent National Golf and Country Club,** Waterman's Lane, Brenchley TN12 6ND (01892 724400; Fax: 01892 723300). *Location:* from A21 take the B2160 to Matfield/Paddock Wood. Drive through Matfield and continue downhill through double bends until road flattens, turn right at post box into Chantlers Hill and then right again into Watermans Lane. Take the train from Charing Cross Station (London) to Paddock Wood (approximately 45 minutes). Parkland course built on the slopes of the Kentish High Wealds, full advantage has been taken of the individual contours and environmental features found on the Moatland Estate. Developed to the highest standards and specifications, Kent National is an all year round championship course. 18 holes, 7111 yards (Blue tees), 6738 (white tees), 6260 (yellow tees), 5516 (black tees), 5440 (red tees). S.S.S. 72. Full practice facilities. *Green Fees:* information not available. *Eating facilities:* bars, private room. *Visitors:* welcome, but subject to availability of tee times. *Society Meetings:* welcome by arrangement (01892 724400; Fax: 01892 723300).
e-mail: info@kentnational.com
website: www.kentnational.com

BROADSTAIRS. **North Foreland Golf Club,** The Clubhouse, Convent Road, Broadstairs CT10 3PU (01843 862140). *Location:* Broadstairs Station, A2, M2, A299, A253, A256, B2052. Cliff top, chalk based, free draining. 18 holes, 6382 yards. S.S.S. 71. Short Course: 18 holes, 1752 yards. Par 3. *Green Fees:* main course: weekdays £38.00 per round, £50.00 per day; weekends £50.00 per round. Par 3 course: weekdays £7.00 per day; weekends £8.50 per day. *Eating facilities:* bar, dining room and "Halfway House". *Visitors:* welcome weekdays and weekend afternoons with current Handicap Certificate. Tennis. *Society Meetings:* Wednesdays and Fridays by prior arrangement with Secretary. Professional: Darren Parris (01843 604471; Fax: 01843 862663). Secretary: Tony Adams (01843 862140).
website: www.northforeland.co.uk

BROMLEY. **Magpie Hall Lane Municipal Golf Club,** Magpie Hall Lane, Bromley. *Location:* off Bromley Common on A21. 9 holes, 5490 yards, 5014 metres. S.S.S. 67. *Green Fees:* weekdays £6.80, weekends £9.20. *Eating facilities:* Food available. *Visitors:* welcome anytime without reservation. *Society Meetings:* phone the Professional for details. Professional: Alan Hodgson (020 8462 7014).*

BROMLEY. **Shortlands Golf Club,** Meadow Road, Shortlands, Bromley BR2 0DX (020 8460 2471; Fax: 020 8460 8828). *Location:* car park and entrance in Ravensbourne Avenue, off the main Beckenham to Bromley Road, adjacent Shortlands B.R. Station. 9 holes, 5261 yards. S.S.S. 66. *Green Fees:* £20.00 for 18 holes, £15.00 for 9 holes. *Eating facilities:* available. *Visitors:* restricted to playing with a member. *Society Meetings:* only when member involved. Professional: (020 8464 6182). Manager: P.S. May (020 8460 8828).

BROMLEY. **Sundridge Park Golf Club,** Garden Road, off Plaistow Lane, Bromley BR1 3NE (020 8460 0278). *Location:* five minutes' walk from Sundridge Park station. Wooded parkland. 36 holes. East 6493 yards. West 5973 yards. S.S.S. 71 and 69. Two practice grounds. *Green Fees:* £55.00 per round, £85.00 per day weekdays. *Eating facilities:* restaurant, spike bar, lounge bar, members' bar and snack bar. *Visitors*: welcome weekdays only, with Handicap Certificate. *Society Meetings:* catered for by arrangement. Professional: Stuart Dowsett (020 8460 5540). General Manager: Richard Browne (020 8460 0278; Fax: 020 8289 3050).

CANTERBURY. **Broome Park Golf Club,** Broome Park Estate, Barham, Near Canterbury CT4 6QX (01227 830728; Fax: 01227 832591). *Location:* off the A2 at the A260 in the direction of Folkestone, half a mile on right. Undulating parkland, lake in front of 18th green. 18 holes, 6580 yards, S.S.S. 71. Driving range and practice ground. *Green Fees:* weekdays £40.00; weekends £50.00. *Eating facilities:* available all week. *Visitors:* welcome. Handicap Certificate required. *Society Meetings:* welcome weekdays by arrangement. Professional: Tienie Britz (01227 831126). Golf Manager: Graeme Robins (01227 830728; Fax: 01227 832591).
e-mail: golf@broomepark.co.uk
website: www.broomepark.co.uk

CANTERBURY. **Canterbury Golf Club,** Scotland Hills, Littlebourne Road, Canterbury CT1 1TW (01227 453532; Fax: 01227 784277). *Location:* one mile from centre of Canterbury on the A257 road to Sandwich. Parkland and wooded course. 18 holes, 6249 yards. S.S.S. 70. Practice ground. *Green Fees:* weekdays £45.00 per round, £70.00 per day; weekends £50.00 per round (after 11.30am only). *Eating facilities:* full bar and catering service (snacks, sandwiches, lunches, dinners). *Visitors:* welcome without reservation but Handicap Certificate necessary (or evidence that visitor is bona fide playing member of another club). *Society Meetings:* catered for Tuesday, Thursday and Friday. Professional: Paul Everard (01227 462865). Secretary: John Morgan (01227 453532).

THE GOLF GUIDE 2006   ENGLAND / Kent 223

CHISLEHURST. **Chislehurst Golf Club,** Camden Park Road, Chislehurst BR7 5HJ (020 8467 3055). *Location:* between Bromley and junction of A222 and Sidcup bypass. Parkland. 18 holes, 5128 yards. S.S.S. 65. *Green Fees:* information not available. *Eating facilities:* catering available. Large parties by prior arrangement. *Visitors:* welcome but restricted to weekdays (except Wednesday mornings) and only with a member at weekends. *Society Meetings:* catered for by arrangement. Professional: Jonathan Bird (020 8467 6798). Secretary: Peter Foord (020 8467 2782; Fax: 020 8295 0874). Caterers: Mr & Mrs L. de Bruyn.*

CHISLEHURST. **World of Golf,** A20 Sidcup Bypass, Chislehurst BR7 6RP (020 8309 0181; Fax: 020 8308 1691). *Location:* six miles from Junction 3 on M25 heading towards London on A20. Parkland. Short game practice area, 54-bay driving range, adventure putting. *Eating facilities:* licensed cafe/bar. *Visitors:* welcome, no restrictions. Tennis courts. *Society Meetings:* welcome. Head Golf Professional: David Young. Centre Manager: Colin Payne.*

CRANBROOK. **Hemsted Forest Golf Club,** Golford Road, Cranbrook TN17 4AL (01580 712833; Fax: 01580 714274). *Location:* two miles south of Sissinghurst. Parkland, a beautiful tree lined course in superb condition. 18 holes, 6305 yards. S.S.S. 71. *Green Fees:* weekdays £28.00 per round, weekends £40.00 per round. *Eating facilities:* open all day, special menus catered for. *Visitors:* welcome weekdays after 8.30am and weekends after 11am. *Society Meetings:* available weekdays. Professional: Chris Weston (01580 712833; Fax: 01580 714274). Secretary: Karl Stevenson (01580 712833; Fax: 01580 714274).

DARTFORD. **Birchwood Park Golf Centre,** Birchwood Road, Wilmington, Dartford DA2 7HJ (01322 662038; Fax: 01322 667283). *Location:* from Junction 3 of M25, B2173 towards Sidcup. Turn right into Birchwood Road at Vauxhall Garage. Attractive undulating course surrounded by ancient woodland. Two courses - Main Course: 18 holes, 6364 yards, S.S.S. 70; Orchard Course: 9 holes, 1274 yards. 41 bay floodlit driving range. *Green Fees:* information not available. *Eating facilities:* snacks and bar food always available, dining/function room. *Visitors*: very welcome but advised to book tee times in advance. London Golf Centre Superstore, health and fitness facilities. *Society Meetings*: welcome, a variety of packages available. Teaching Professionals available. Manager: Scott Morley (01322 662038; Fax: 01322 667283).*

DARTFORD. **Dartford Golf Club Ltd.,** The Clubhouse, Heath Lane (Upper), Dartford DA1 2TN (01322 223616). *Location:* backing on to A2, one mile from Dartford Tunnel and M25. Flat parkland. 18 holes, 5914 yards. S.S.S. 69. *Green Fees:* weekdays £23.00 per round, £22.00 per day; weekends (accompanied by member): one round £15.00, two rounds £22.50. *Eating facilities:* catering available. *Visitors:* welcome on weekdays with reservation, must be member of another golf club. *Society Meetings:* welcome on Mondays and Fridays by prior arrangement with Secretary. Professional: John Gregory (01322 226409). Secretary: Amanda Malas (Tel & Fax: 01322 226455).
e-mail: dartfordgolf@hotmail.com

DARTFORD. **Fawkham Valley Golf Club,** Fawkham Valley Road, Fawkham, Longfield DA3 8LY (01474 707144). *Location:* off the A2 East of Dartford/off A20 North of Brands Hatch. Wooded course (tree lined), special feature being lakes in front of the 3rd and 6th greens. 9 holes, 6547 yards. S.S.S. 72. Practice area and putting green. *Green Fees:* information not available. *Eating facilities:* members' bar. *Visitors:* welcome anytime. *Society Meetings:* welcome Mondays, Wednesdays and Fridays. Professional: Nigel Willis. Secretary: Jo Marchant.*
e-mail: info@fawkhamvalleygolf.co.uk
website: www.fawkhamvalleygolf.co.uk.

DEAL. **Royal Cinque Ports Golf Club,** Golf Road, Deal CT14 6RF (01304 374007; Fax: 01304 379530). *Location:* A258 from Sandwich. In Upper Deal leave for Middle Deal Road, left turn into Albert Road, Western Road, on to Golf Road (or from Dover, A258 via Sea front and Godwin Road). Championship 18 hole links course. 18 holes, 6899 yards. S.S.S. 73. Par 72. Large practice area. *Green Fees:* weekdays £80.00 per round, £95.00 per day; weekends and Bank Holidays, £85.00 per round, £105.00 per day. *Eating facilities:* hot and cold comprehensive bar snack menu. *Visitors:* welcome, 4 ball rounds may be played on Tuesdays and Thursdays. Special packages available. Handicap Certificate required (max 22); times must be pre-booked. Buggies; cart and caddies by arrangement. *Society Meetings:* by arrangement. Professional: Andrew Reynolds (01304 374170; Fax: 01304 379530). Secretary: Ian Symington (01304 374007; Fax: 01304 379530).
e-mail: rcpgcsec@aol.com
website: www.royalcinqueports.com

PLEASE NOTE

All the information regarding Golf Clubs in this guide is given in good faith in the belief that it is correct. However, the publishers cannot guarantee the facts given in these pages, neither are they responsible for changes in ownership or facilities, such as green fees, that may take place after the date of going to press. Readers should always satisfy themselves that the facilities they require are available and that the terms, if quoted, still apply.

224 Kent / ENGLAND   THE GOLF GUIDE 2006

DEAL. **Walmer and Kingsdown Golf Club,** The Leas, Kingsdown, Deal CT14 8EP (01304 373256). *Location:* take A258 from Dover (A2) to Deal, Kingsdown club signposted at village of Ringwould. Downland course on the White Cliffs of Dover overlooking the English Channel. 18 holes, 6444 yards. S.S.S. 71. Practice ground. *Green Fees:* information not available. *Eating facilities:* full catering and bar service. *Visitors:* welcome after 9.30am weekdays and 12 noon at weekends. *Society Meetings:* catered for by arrangement. Professional: Jude Read (01304 363017). Secretary: Reg Harrison (01304 373256; Fax: 01304 382336).
e-mail: info@kingsdowngolf.co.uk
website: www.kingsdowngolf.co.uk

DEANGATE. **Deangate Ridge Golf Club,** Duxcourt Road, Hoo, Rochester ME3 8RZ (01634 250537). *Location*: three miles from Rochester off A228 towards Isle of Grain. Municipal course – wooded. 18 holes, 6300 yards. S.S.S. 70. 18 hole Pitch and Putt; 11-bay driving range. *Green Fees:* information not available. Special rates for Senior Citizens. *Eating facilities:* available. *Visitors:* welcome without reservation, bookings required for weekends. *Society Meetings:* catered for, book through Professional. Professional: Richard Fox (01634 251180). Secretary: C.J. Williams (01634 251950). General Manager: Steve Hillman (01634 250537).*

EDENBRIDGE. **Edenbridge Golf Club and Country Club,** Crouch House Road, Edenbridge TN8 5LQ (01732 867381; Fax: 01732 867167). *Location:* from M25 take A25, at Limpsfield take B2026 to Edenbridge. Parkland. Old Course 18 holes, 6577 yards. S.S.S. 72. 20 bay floodlit driving range. *Green Fees:* (2005) £16.00 weekdays, £22.00 weekends. *Eating facilities:* bar and restaurant. *Visitors:* welcome, call for start time. Buggies and carts available. Five tennis courts. *Society Meetings:* societies welcome weekdays and weekends. Conference facility seats up to 65. General Manager: Chris Foreman (01732 867381).
e-mail: info@edenbridgegolf.co.uk
website: www.edenbridgegolf.co.uk

ETCHINGHILL. **Etchinghill Golf Club,** Canterbury Road, Etchinghill CT18 8FA (01303 863863; Fax: 01303 863210). *Location:* one mile north of M20 Junction 12 on B2065. 27 holes, 6121 yards. S.S.S. 69. 9 hole Par 3 course. Covered and floodlit driving range. *Green Fees:* information not available. *Eating facilities:* full range of catering facilities available. *Visitors:* welcome. Professional: C. Hodgson (01303 863966).*

EYNSFORD. **Austin Lodge Golf Club,** Upper Austin Lodge Road, Eynsford DA4 0HU (01322 863000; Fax: 01322 862406). *Location:* Eynsford - 10 minutes' drive from Junction 3 of M25, M20, A20. Secluded rolling countryside with lakes. 18 holes, 6575 yards Yellow Tees, 7118 yards White Tees. S.S.S. 73. Practice ground. *Green Fees:* information not available. *Eating facilities:* bar, restaurant with light meals all day. *Visitors:* welcome weekdays, and after 12noon weekends. Buggies available. *Society Meetings:* welcome, telephone booking only. Professional/Manager: Greg Haenan.*

FARNBOROUGH. **High Elms Golf Club,** High Elms Road, Downe BR6 7SL (01689 853232). *Location:* two miles from Farnborough Hospital on A21, turn right at Shire Lane, second on left. Beautiful parkland. 18 holes, 6210 metres. S.S.S. 70. *Green Fees:* weekdays £13.50; weekends £18.50. Subject to review. *Eating facilities:* food available every day. *Visitors:* welcome, no restriction but should phone in advance. *Society Meetings:* apply to Catering Manageress - Mrs Griggs. Professional: Peter Remy (01689 858175). Secretary: Mrs P. O'Keeffe.

FAVERSHAM. **Boughton Golf Club,** Brickfield Lane, Boughton, Faversham ME13 9AJ (01227 752277; Fax: 01227 7523610. *Location:* north-east of Boughton, near M2/A2 interchange; six miles west of Canterbury 18 holes, 6452 yards. S.S.S. 71. Driving range. *Green Fees*: information not available. *Eating facilities:* available. *Visitors:* welcome. Professional: T. Dungate.*

WALMER & KINGSDOWN GOLF CLUB
The Leas, Kingsdown, Deal, Kent CT14 8EP

Downland and Cliff top course founded in 1909, offering a good test of golf for players of all abilities. Stunning views across the English Channel to France with a warm welcome in the clubhouse. Handicap required. 18 Holes Par 72

• White 6471 • Yellows 6291 • Reds 5892 • Open Monday to Friday *(except Monday and Tuesday before 10.30 am)*, Saturday/ Sunday after 12.00.

Secretary and Steward: **01304 373256** • Pro: Jude Read: **01304 363017**
e-mail: **info@kingsdowngolf.co.uk** • website: **www.kingsdowngolf.co.uk**

See also Colour Advertisement on page 24

FAVERSHAM. **Faversham Golf Club Ltd.,** Belmont Park, Faversham ME13 0HB (01795 890561). *Location:* M2 Faversham Exit (A251) to A2 junction, left to Brogdale Road, left to Belmont. Long established (1902) very attractive parkland course in rural surroundings. 18 holes, 5965 yards. S.S.S. 69. *Green Fees:* £35.00 per round, £45.00 per day. *Eating facilities:* full catering. *Visitors:* welcome weekdays (Handicap Certificate required); weekends with member only. *Society Meetings:* catered for Mondays, Wednesdays and Fridays only. Professional: S. Rokes (01795 890275). Secretary: J. Edgington (01795 890561; Fax: 01795 890760).

FOLKESTONE. **Sene Valley Golf Club,** Sene, Folkestone CT18 8BL (01303 268513; Fax: 01303 237513). *Location:* M20 Junction 12, take A20 to Ashford turn left at first roundabout. Downland course with magnificent views over English Channel. 18 holes, 6271 yards. S.S.S. 70. Practice area. *Green Fees:* weekdays £25.00; weekends £30.00. *Eating facilities:* snacks, meals on request. *Visitors:* welcome, Handicap Certificate required. Preferable to book in advance. *Society Meetings:* welcome by prior arrangements. Professional: Nick Watson (Tel & Fax: 01303 268514). Manager: Stuart More.
e-mail: svgc@svgc.freeserve.co.uk
website: www.sceneatsene.co.uk

GILLINGHAM. **Gillingham Golf Club Ltd.,** Woodlands Road, Gillingham ME7 2AP (01634 850999). *Location*: on old A2 Gillingham. Flat parkland. 18 holes, 5557 yards, 5077 metres. S.S.S. 69. Practice nets. *Green Fees:* available weekdays, rates on application. *Eating facilities:* available. *Visitors:* welcome at all times except weekends. Must have proof of Handicap or membership of another club. *Society Meetings:* welcome by prior arrangement. Professional: (01634 855862). Office (01634 853017; Fax: 01634 574749).

GRAVESEND. **Mid-Kent Golf Club,** Singlewell Road, Gravesend DA11 7RB (01474 352387). *Location:* A227 off A2. Parkland. 18 holes, 6106 yards. S.S.S. 70. *Green Fees:* weekdays £30.00 per round, £35.00 per day; weekends with member only. *Eating facilities:* breakfast, dinner by arrangement, lunch every day, bar 11am to 11pm. *Visitors:* welcome weekdays except competition days with Handicap Certificate. *Society Meetings:* catered for Tuesdays only. Professional: Mark Foreman (01474 332810). Secretary: P. Gleeson (01474 568035; Fax: 01474 564218).

GRAVESEND. **Southern Valley Golf Course,** Thong Lane, Shorne, Gravesend DA12 4LF (01474 568568; Fax: 01474 360366). *Location:* take J4 off A2 (not M2), signposted "Inn on the Lake/Thong", at top of slip road turn left into Thong Lane at T-junction. Golf course is approx. one mile along on right-hand side. Undulating greens and rolling fairways. 18 holes, 6100 yards. Par 69. Practice area, putting green. *Green Fees:* Monday to Thursday £18.50, weekends £24.00. *Eating facilities:* fully licensed bar and restaurant. *Visitors:* all welcome. No jeans or tracksuits; golf shoes must be worn. Tuition available; golf shop; buggies for hire April to October. *Society Meetings:* welcome, telephone in advance. Professional: Larry Batchelor. Club Administrator: Mrs Anne Green (01474 740026).

HALSTEAD. **Broke Hill Golf Club,** Sevenoaks Road, Halstead, Kent TN14 7HR (01959 533225; Fax: 01959 532680). *Location:* four minutes from M25 Junction 4, A21, four miles from Bromley and two miles from Orpington. Parkland course, with strategically placed bunkers and 5 holes where water comes into play. 18 holes, 6415 yards. S.S.S. 71. Two practice grounds. *Green Fees:* information not available. *Eating facilities:* lounge bar, restaurant and banqueting facilities. *Visitors:* welcome weekdays only, strict dress code applies. Soft spikes or dimple shoes preferred. Golf buggies and carts available. *Society Meetings:* weekdays only. Professional: Cameron McKillop (01959 533810; Fax: 01959 532680). General Manager: Bill Thompson (01959 533225; Fax: 01959 532680).*

HAWKHURST. **Hawkhurst Golf Club,** High Street, Hawkhurst TN18 4JS (01580 754074/752396; Fax: 01580 754074). *Location:* on A268 from Flimwell to Hawkhurst. Undulating parkland. 9 holes, 5751 yards. S.S.S. 68. Practice ground. *Green Fees:* £20.00 per round weekdays; £24.00 weekends with member only. *Eating facilities:* bar, spike bar, dining room. *Visitors:* welcome weekdays, weekends with member only. Handicap Certificate recommended. Squash courts. Clubs, trolleys and buggies are available for hire. *Society Meetings:* welcome Wednesdays and Fridays. Professional: James Walpole (Tel & Fax: 01580 754088). Secretary: Brian Morrison (Tel & Fax: 01580 754074).

HEADCORN. **Weald of Kent Golf Course,** Maidstone Road, Headcorn TN27 9PT (01622 890866; Fax: 01622 890070). *Location*: Junction 8 M20, five miles south of Maidstone on A274. Scenic undulating parkland course featuring a range of natural hazards, including waterways, lakes and ditches. 18 holes, 6289 yards. S.S.S. 70. *Green Fees:* Mon – Thurs £17.00pp, Friday £19.00pp, Weekends £22.50pp. *Eating facilities:* spacious architect designed clubhouse, extensive bar menu available 7.00am till 9.30pm. Banqueting and conference facilities also available (30 to 200 delegates). *Visitors:* welcome anytime, bookings available seven days in advance (01622 890866). Hotel accommodation. Golf Breaks available (01622 890866). *Society Meetings:* welcome midweek and generally after 12pm, weekends subject to availability; booking required in advance, minimum 12. Director of Golf: Keith Brown.

HERNE BAY. **Herne Bay Golf Club,** Eddington, Herne Bay CT6 7PG (01227 373964). *Location:* off the New Thanet Way. Parkland/links course. 18 holes, 5567 yards. S.S.S. 68. Practice ground. *Green Fees:* information not available. Twilight fee after 3pm. *Eating facilities:* bar meals, restaurant by arrangement. *Visitors:* welcome weekdays unrestricted, weekends and Bank Holidays after 12 noon only. Handicap Certificate required. *Society Meetings:* welcome by prior arrangement. Professional: D. Ledingham (01227 374727).*

HEVER. **Hever Castle Golf Club,** Hever, Edenbridge TN8 7NP (01732 700771; Fax: 01732 700775). *Location:* at Junction 6 take A22 turning to Godstone, then turn left onto the A25 to Sevenoaks, after three and a half miles take the Edenbridge road. Adjacent to Hever Castle. Go past the entrance to castle and the club is one mile further on the right. Parkland, wooded. 27 holes. Kings and Queens course: 18 holes, 7002 yards. S.S.S. 74. Princes course: 9 holes, 2784 yards. S.S.S. 67 (for 18 holes). Large practice range, chipping and pitching areas, practice bunker, putting green. *Green Fees:* weekdays £40.00 18 holes, £60.00 per day; weekends £60.00 18 holes, £80.00 per day. *Eating facilities:* restaurant and bars. *Visitors:* welcome by appointment, or with a member; limited weekends. *Society Meetings:* welcome by prior arrangement; competitive rates available. Head PGA Professional: Peter Parks. General Manager: Mark Hickson.

HYTHE. **Hythe Imperial Golf Club,** Princes Parade, Hythe CT21 6AE (01303 267441). *Location:* come off M20 Junction 11, directions for Hythe A261. Flat seaside course. 9 holes, 5533 yards. S.S.S. 67. Practice ground. *Green Fees:* information not available. *Eating facilities:* available at the hotel. *Visitors:* welcome weekdays, no green fees weekends up to 1pm. *Society Meetings:* welcome weekdays only. Professional: J. Leaver (01303 233745). Professional Shop: (01303 233745). Secretary: Mr R. Duncan (Tel & Fax: 01303 267554).

LYDD. **Lydd Golf Club and Driving Range,** Romney Road, Lydd, Romney Marsh TN29 9LS (01797 320808; Fax: 01797 321482). *Location:* B2075 within half a mile of Lydd Airport. Traditional links course with added water hazards. 18 holes, 6517 yards. S.S.S. 71. 24 bay floodlit driving range. *Green Fees:*information not available. *Eating facilities:* bar and restaurant. *Visitors:* no restrictions. Pull trolleys, electric trolleys and golf carts. *Society Meetings:* welcome, discount rates available. Professional: Richard Perkins (01797 321201). Secretary: Brian Evans (01797 320808; Fax: 01797 321482).

MAIDSTONE. **Bearsted Golf Club,** Ware Street, Bearsted ME14 4PQ (01622 738389). *Location:* Junction 7 off M20, turn right to Bearsted and follow signs. Undulating parkland course with view of North Downs. 18 holes, 6320 yards, 5739 metres. S.S.S. 70. Practice area, putting green, net. *Green Fees:* £32.00/£42.00 weekdays; weekends with a member. *Eating facilities:* bar/restaurant, open all day. *Visitors:* welcome weekdays, weekends must be with members. Current Handicap Certificates required. *Society Meetings:* catered for Tuesdays to Fridays by prior arrangement. Professional: Tim Simpson (01622 738024). Secretary: Mrs L.M. Siems (01622 738198; Fax: 01622 735608).

LYDD GOLF CLUB
www.lyddgolfclub.co.uk

Romney Road, Lydd, Kent
TN29 9LS
01797 320808

Lydd is a modern eighteen hole par 71 links course with nine lakes, tight lies and a consistent breeze set in the Romney Marsh, Kent.

Facilities include an Academy course and floodlight driving range.

Golfers of all abilities are made welcome

Lakes & Sky

See also Colour Advertisement on page 24

---

www.uk-golfguide.com

THE APPEARANCE OF AN ASTERISK (*) AT THE END OF A CLUB OR COURSE ENTRY INDICATES THAT UP-TO-DATE INFORMATION HAS NOT BEEN SUPPLIED

MAIDSTONE. **Cobtree Manor Park Golf Club,** Chatham Road, Sandling, Maidstone ME14 3AZ (01662 753276). *Location:* M20, A229 Chatham (not Maidstone). Undulating course with trees, and interesting 12th hole over lake. 18 holes, 5611 yards. S.S.S. 69. Tuition, practice, putting. *Green Fees:* information on request. *Eating facilities:* restaurant and bar. *Visitors:* welcome, book four days in advance through Professional. *Society Meetings:* welcome phone (01622 751881). Professional: Paul Foston (01622 753276).

MAIDSTONE. **Leeds Castle Golf Course,** Leeds Castle, Near Maidstone ME17 1PL (01622 767828). *Location:* M20 Junction 8, A20 near Maidstone. Situated in the grounds of Leeds Castle, parkland. 9 holes, 2681 yards. S.S.S. 33. Putting green and practice nets. *Green Fees:* (2005 rates) weekdays £11.00 9 holes, £18.50 18 holes; Juniors / Senior Citizens £8.00 / £15.50; weekends and Bank Holidays £13.00 9 holes, £26.00 18 holes. *Eating facilities:* Leeds Castle Restaurant on Leeds Castle Estate. *Visitors:* welcome anytime, bookings taken from six days in advance. Correct dress must be worn - no denim jeans allowed, golf shoes preferred. *Society Meetings:* welcome weekdays. Professional: Steve Purves. Secretary: Ann Bishop.

MAIDSTONE. **Marriott Tudor Park Hotel and Country Club,** Ashford Road, Bearsted, Maidstone ME14 4NQ (01622 734334). *Location:* east of Maidstone, on A20 at Bearsted. Off Junction 8 of M20. Parkland. 18 holes, 6085 yards. S.S.S. 69. Practice area. *Green Fees:* weekdays £35.00; weekends £40.00. *Eating facilities:* restaurants and bars. *Visitors:* Hotel with 120 bedrooms, leisure and conference facilities. *Society Meetings:* Societies and Company Days catered for. Professional: Nick McNally (01622 739412). Secretary: John Ladbrooke (01622 737119). Golf Operations Manager: Jason King.

MAIDSTONE. **The Ridge Golf Club,** Chartway Street, East Sutton, Maidstone ME17 3JB (01622 844243; Fax: 01622 844168). *Location:* Junction 8 M20, past Leeds Castle on Sutton Valence Road to A274 turn left and first turning on left. 18 holes, 6254 yards. S.S.S. 71. Driving range. *Green Fees:* information not available. *Eating facilities:* two bars, bar snack menu and full menu. *Visitors:* welcome. *Society Meetings:* welcome Monday to Sunday. (01622 844243).

MAIDSTONE. **West Malling Golf Club,** London Road, Addington, West Malling ME19 5AR (01732 844785; Fax: 01732 844795). *Location:* M20, A228 turn off. Parkland/wooded course. Spitfire Course - 18 holes, 6142 yards. S.S.S. 70. Hurricane Course - 18 holes, 6300 yards. S.S.S. 70. Practice ground. *Green Fees:* weekdays £25.00 per round, £40.00 per day; weekends £30.00 per round after 12 noon. *Eating facilities*: restaurant available. *Visitors:* welcome weekdays anytime, weekends after 12 noon. Conference/function facilities available. Buggies available. *Society Meetings:* catered for by prior arragement. Professional: Duncan Lambert (01732 844022). Secretary: Mike Ellis (01732 844785; Fax: 01732 844795).

NEW ROMNEY. **Littlestone Golf Club,** St Andrews Road, Littlestone, New Romney TN28 8RB (01797 362231; Fax: 01797 362740). *Location:* M20 Junction 10 (Ashford), B2070 to Brenzett - New Romney, one mile from New Romney. Seaside Championship links course. 18 holes, Blue tees 6676 yards, S.S.S. 73, White tees 6486 yards, S.S.S 72. Driving range, practice ground, chipping and putting greens. *Green Fees:* £60.00 per day weekdays; £75.00 per day weekends. *Eating facilities:* full dining room and bar. *Visitors:* Handicap Certificate required. Visitors restricted at weekends. Singles and foursomes only. Caddie cars available. *Society Meetings:* welcome. Professional: Andrew Jones (01797 362231). Secretary: Col. Charles Moorhouse (01797 363355; Fax: 01797 362740). e-mail: secretary@littlestonegolfclub.org.uk website: www.littlestonegolfclub.org.uk

NEW ROMNEY. **Romney Warren Golf Club,** St Andrews Road, Littlestone, New Romney TN28 8RB (01797 362231; Fax: 01797 362740). *Location:* one mile from New Romney off A259, down B2070; 20 minutes from J10 on M20. Undulating seaside links crisscrossed with dykes. 18 holes, 5126 yards. S.S.S. 67. Practice range. *Green Fees:* weekdays £18.00 per round, £30.00 per day; weekends £23.00 per round, £36.00 per day. *Eating facilities:* bar and restaurant. *Visitors:* welcome. *Society Meetings:* welcome by arrangement. Professional: Andrew Jones. Hon. Secretary: Mr J. Purkiss (01797 362768). website: www.romneywarrengolfclub.org

ORPINGTON. **Chelsfield Lakes Golf Centre,** Court Road, Orpington BR6 9BX (01689 896266; Fax: 01689 824577). *Location:* M25 Junction 4, A224 Court Road. Gently undulating course with hazards and sandtraps; played through some orchards. 18 holes, 6077 yards. S.S.S. 69. 9 holes, 1188 yards. Par 3. 40 bay floodlit driving range, practice area. *Green Fees:* information not available. *Eating facilities:* bar and restaurant. *Visitors:* welcome, pay as you play facility, non members can book 7 days in advance. Pro shop. *Society Meetings:* welcome. Professionals: Nigel Lee, Bill Hodkin.*

ORPINGTON. **Cray Valley Golf Club,** Sandy Lane, St. Paul's Cray, Orpington BR5 3HY. *Location:* Ruxley roundabout A20; turn off into Sandy Lane, half a mile on left. Parkland. 18 holes, 5624 yards. S.S.S. 67. Also 9 hole course. *Green Fees:* information not available. *Eating facilities:* hot meals available lunchtimes, also bar. *Visitors:* welcome all week. *Society Meetings:* welcome. Professional: Gary Stewart (01689 837909). General Manager: Tom Ashman (01689 839677). *

ORPINGTON. **Lullingstone Park Golf Club,** Park Gate Road, Chelsfield, Near Orpington, Kent BR6 7PX (01959 533794). *Location:* two miles from Junction 4 off M25, fifth exit on left (signposted). Undulating parkland. 18 holes, 6779 yards. S.S.S. 72. 9 holes, 2432 yards. Par 33. 22 bay driving range, pitch and putt course, putting green. *Green Fees:* information not available. *Eating facilities:* cafeteria and bar. *Visitors:* bookings welcome. *Society Meetings:* very welcome, telephone Professional for package details. Professional: Mark Watt (01959 533793; Fax: 01959 534129). Secretary: Chris Pocock. *

228 Kent / ENGLAND | THE GOLF GUIDE 2006

ORPINGTON. **Ruxley Park Golf Centre,** Sandy Lane, St. Pauls Cray, Orpington BR5 3HY (01689 871490; Fax: 01689 891428). *Location:* off old A20 at Ruxley Corner. 18 holes, Par 71. 9 hole Academy course. 24 bays, covered, floodlit, grassed. *Green Fees:* information not available. *Eating facilities:* breakfast, lunch available, bar open all day. *Society Meetings:* welcome all week. Head Professional: Mike Worley. General Manager: Tom Ashman.*

ORPINGTON. **West Kent Golf Club,** Milking Lane, Downe, Near Orpington BR6 7LD (01689 851323). *Location:* from Downe village south along Luxted Lane, 600 yards turn right into West Hill. 18 holes, 6426 yards. S.S.S. 70. *Green Fees:* £40.00 per round, £55.00 per day. *Eating facilities:* meals by arrangement. *Visitors:* welcome weekdays only with recognised Handicap. Casual golfers should phone at least 24 hours in advance. *Society Meetings:* catered for. Professional: C.W. Forsyth (Tel & Fax: 01689 856863). Secretary: Tony Barclay (01689 851323).

RAMSGATE. **Manston Golf Centre,** Manston Road, Manston, Ramsgate CT12 5BE (01843 590005). *Location:* a quarter mile east of Manston village on the B2050. Flat seaside course with superb views across the English Channel. 9 holes, 2479 yards. Par 33. *Green Fees:* weekdays £6.00 9 holes; weekends £8.00 for 9 holes. 20 bay floodlit covered driving range. Grass tees and shortgame area with bunkers and two putting greens. Five PGA qualified coaches. *Eating facilities:* Snack bar with burgers and sandwiches etc. *Visitors:* unrestricted. *Society Meetings:* groups of 8 or more. 18 holes and breakfast bap, tea or coffee £12.00 inclusive midweek. Secretary. Professional: Philip Sparks (01843 590005).*
website:www.manstongolf.co.uk

RAMSGATE. **St Augustine's Golf Club,** Cottington Road, Cliffsend, Ramsgate CT12 5JN (01843 590333; Fax: 01843 590444). *Location:* two miles south-west of Ramsgate – approaching from A253 or A256 follow signs to St Augustine's Cross. Entrance 75 yards beyond Cross by railway bridge. Mainly parkland, flat - tight and challenging course. 18 holes, 5129 yards. S.S.S. 65. *Green Fees:* weekdays £21.00 per round, £25.00 per day. Weekends and Bank Holidays £23.00 per day, £30.00 per day. *Eating facilities:* usual bar facilties; catering available 9.00am to 3.30pm daily; Fridays also 6.30pm to 10.30pm. *Visitors:* welcome, advisable to ring Professional the day before to check periods booked for matches; booking necessary Saturdays and Sundays (Sundays visitors only after 1pm). *Society Meetings:* catered for, book through Secretary. Dormy flat available for 7 nights stay - ring Secretary. Professional: D. Scott (01843 590222). Secretary: R. F. Tranckle (01843 590333).
e-mail: sagc@ic24.net

RAMSGATE. **Stonelees Golf Centre,** Ebbsfleet Lane, Near Ramsgate CT12 5DJ (01843 823133; Fax: 01843 850569). *Location:* near junction of A256 and B2048 (Ebbsfleet Lane). Undulating seaside/ parkland courses. Executive course - 9 holes, 1510 yards, 1393 metres, S.S.S. 29; Par 3 course - 9 holes, 1159 yards, 1393 metres, S.S.S. 27. Excellent teaching facilities, 20 bay driving range, Smart Golf simulator, practice putting green, chipping area, miniature putting course. *Green Fees:* Executive - weekdays £6.30 9 holes, £9.60 18 holes; weekends £6.90 9 holes, £10.30 18 holes. Par 3 - weekdays £4.80 9 holes, £7.90 18 holes; weekends £5.70 9 holes, £9.00 18 holes. Prices subject to review. Junior rates and membership discounts available. A full length 9-hole course (3400 yards) is under construction and 8 holes are in play as an academy course. Day ticket £9.00 weekdays, £14.00 weekends. *Eating facilities:* licensed bar, restaurant. *Visitors:* always welcome, no restrictions. *Society Meetings:* small societies/groups welcome. Professional: David Bonthron. Manager: Dr Peter Nicholson.

ROCHESTER. **Rochester and Cobham Park Golf Club,** Park Pale, by Rochester ME2 3UL (01474 823411; Fax: 01474 824446). *Location:* on A2, two miles east of Gravesend East turn-off. Open championship regional qualifying course. Undulating parkland. 18 holes, 6597 yards. S.S.S. 72. Extensive practice facilities. *Green Fees:* weekdays £35.00 per round, £45.00 per day. *Eating facilities:* morning coffee, lunch, tea, dinner available, two bars. *Visitors:* welcome midweek only with Handicap Certificate. *Society Meetings:* welcome Tuesdays and Thursdays, must be pre-booked. Professional: Iain Higgins (01474 823658). Manager: David Smith (01474 823411; Fax: 01474 824446).

SANDWICH. **Royal St. George's Golf Club,** Sandwich CT13 9PB (01304 613090; Fax: 01304 611245). *Location:* one mile from Sandwich on the road to Sandwich Bay. From Canterbury A257, from Dover A258. Links. 18 holes, Championship 7102 yards, Medal 6607 yards. S.S.S. Championship 74, Medal 72. Practice ground. *Green Fees:* £115.00 for one round, £150.00 for two rounds weekdays. Subject to review. *Eating facilities:* snack bar and dining room. *Visitors:* welcome weekdays only, must be pre-booked. No visitors at weekends or on Public Holidays. Must have Handicap Certificate (under 18) to be member of club affiliated to E.G.U. Caddies to be booked in advance, trolleys available. *Society Meetings:* catered for by arrangement. All players must meet requirements for visitors. Professional: A. Brooks (01304 615236). Secretary: H.C.G. Gabbey (01304 613090; Fax: 01304 611245). Caddiemaster: (01304 626931).

SANDWICH BAY. **Prince's Golf Club,** Prince's Drive, Sandwich Bay, Sandwich CT14 7LN (01304 611118; Fax: 01304 612000). *Location:* four miles from Sandwich through the Sandwich Bay Estate. Seaside links. 27 holes arranged as 3 loops of 9 holes named "Dunes", "Himalayas", "Shore". D & H 6262 - 6776 yards, Par 71, S.S.S. 70-73. H & S 6238 - 6813 yards, Par 71, S.S.S. 70-73. S & D 6466-7145 yards, Par 72, S.S.S. 71-73. Championship 7145 yards. Driving range, full practice facilities. *Green Fees:* £40.00 to £80.00 depending on season. Packages available. *Eating facilities:* breakfast, lunch, dinner available every day (pre-booking advisable); bar; light snacks throughout the day. *Visitors & Societies:*

ENGLAND / Kent

welcome without restriction, Company days and private parties catered for. Brochure available on request. Professional: Derek Barbour (01304 613797). Information & Bookings: Richard Kimber (01304 611118). General Manager: W.M. Howie (01304 626909; Fax: 01304 612000).
e-mail: office@princesgolfclub.co.uk
website: www.princesgolfclub.co.uk

SEVENOAKS. **Darenth Valley Golf Course Ltd**, Station Road, Shoreham, Near Sevenoaks TN14 7SA (01959 522944; Fax: 01959 525089). *Location:* A225 between Otford and Eynsford, approximately four miles north of Sevenoaks. Pay and play parkland course. 18 holes, 6258 yards. S.S.S. 72. Practice area, putting green. *Green Fees:* weekdays £18.75; weekends £25.00, four-ball £92.00 (subject to review). *Eating facilities:* bar snacks and meals; diningroom, functions up to 150 covers. *Visitors:* welcome with reservation through Pro shop. *Society Meetings:* welcome by arrangement. Professional: Ashley Weller (01959 522922). General Manager: Jonathan Cooper (01959 522944; Fax: 01959 525089).
website: www.dvgc.co.uk

SEVENOAKS. **Knole Park Golf Club**, Seal Hollow Road, Sevenoaks TN15 0HJ (01732 452150; Fax: 01732 463159). *Location:* one mile north-east of Sevenoaks town centre. Deer Park; beautiful, natural course. Second to none in the South East. 18 holes, 6246 yards. S.S.S. 70. Practice ground and nets. *Green Fees:* weekdays only, £35.00 per round, £46.00 per day. Subject to review. *Eating facilities:* full bar and catering. *Visitors:* welcome by appointment, Handicap Certificate required. Squash courts. Society Meetings: catered for by arrangement only. Professional: (01732 451740). Secretary: Peter Mitchell (01732 452150; Fax: 01732 463159).
website: www.knoleparkgolfclub.co.uk

www.uk-golfguide.com
For full details of clubs and courses, plus convenient accommodation

SEVENOAKS. **Wildernesse Club**, Park Lane, Seal, Sevenoaks TN15 0JE (01732 761199). *Location:* A25 between Sevenoaks and Borough Green. Park and woodland. 18 holes, 6501 yards. S.S.S. 71. Large practice ground. *Green Fees:* £46.00 per round. *Eating facilities:* by arrangement. *Visitors:* welcome weekdays only by prior arrangement; Handicap Certificate required. *Society Meetings:* catered for Mondays, Thursdays and Fridays. Professional: Craig Walker (01732 761527). Secretary: Robin Foster (01732 761199).

SEVENOAKS. **Woodlands Manor Golf Club**, Tinkerpot Lane, Woodlands, Near Otford, Sevenoaks TN15 6AB (01959 523806). *Location*: Junction 3, M25 take "Brands Hatch" sign on A20, seven miles. Parkland, designated Area of Outstanding Natural Beauty. 18 holes, 6100 yards. S.S.S. 69. Six acre practice ground. *Green Fees:* on application. *Eating facilities:* bar daily. *Visitors:* welcome weekdays, weekends after 1pm. Buggies for hire. *Society Meetings:* welcome by arrangement Monday to Friday. Professional: Philip Womack. Secretary: C.G. Robins (01959 523806).

SEVENOAKS. **Wrotham Heath Golf Club**, Seven Mile Lane, Comp, Sevenoaks TN15 8QZ (01732 884800). *Location:* on B2016 half-a-mile south of junction with A20. Woodland/heathland. 18 holes, 5954 yards. S.S.S. 69. *Green Fees:* information not available. *Eating facilities:* bar and snacks, meals by arrangement, except Mondays. *Visitors:* welcome on weekdays with Handicap Certificate, but not Bank Holidays. *Society Meetings:* catered for Thursdays and Fridays only, no more than 30 people. Professional: H. Dearden (01732 883854). Secretary: L.J. Byrne (01732 884700). *

SHEERNESS. **Sheerness Golf Club**, Power Station Road, Sheerness ME12 3AE (01795 662585). *Location:* follow A249 then A250 towards Sheerness. Flat marshland/meadowland; numerous water hazards. 18 holes, 6460 yards. S.S.S. 71. Practice area. *Green Fees*: weekdays £20.00 per round, £28.00 per day; weekends £25.00 per round (by appointment only). *Eating facilities:* available. *Visitors:* weekdays only except with member. *Society Meetings:* catered for weekdays, except Mondays, by previous arrangement. Secretary: A. Jones.

the bell hotel
sandwich

Renowned for its warm hospitality and stylish accommodation, this newly renamed, restyled and decorated hotel has stood on its present site since the early 17th century. The spacious bedrooms have en suite facilities and views over the ancient town or across the river. At the Place Brasserie we use local free range and organic products whenever possible, including seafood straight from Sandwich Bay and lamb from nearby Romney Marsh, changing the menu according to the seasons.

Sandwich has become known as Kent's "Home of Golf", boasting two magnificent courses both of which have hosted the Open Championship. Many other excellent courses are within easy driving distance. Please send for our brochure giving further details and full tariff including golf breaks.

the quay, sandwich, kent CT13 9EF tel: 01304 613388 fax: 01304 615308
reservations@bellhotelsandwich.co.uk   www.bellhotelsandwich.co.uk

230 Kent / ENGLAND — THE GOLF GUIDE 2006

SIDCUP. **Sidcup Golf Club (1926) Ltd,** 7 Hurst Road, Sidcup DA15 9AE (020 8300 2150). *Location:* three minutes' walk from Sidcup Station. Parkland. 9 holes, 5571 yards. S.S.S. 68. Practice area. *Green Fees:* weekdays £18.00. *Eating facilities:* restaurant and bar. *Visitors:* welcome weekdays except Bank Holidays. *Society Meetings:* (up to 30 members) catered for by arrangement. Secretary: John Aughterlony (020 8300 2150).

SITTINGBOURNE. **The Oast Golf Centre Ltd,** Church Road, Tonge, Sittingbourne ME9 9AR (01795 473527). *Location*: one mile north A2 between Faversham and Sittingbourne, take the turning to Tonge at Bapchild. 17 bay covered floodlit driving range. *Green Fees*: 9 holes £5.50, 18 holes £7.50. *Eating facilities*: sandwiches, rolls available. *Opening hours:* Range 8.30am to 10pm; Par 3 Course 8.30am to dusk. Par 3 approach course, 9 holes £5.00, 18 holes £7.00. Tuition available, golf shop. Two short mat bowls facility. *Society Meetings*: welcome. Professional: David Chambers. Secretary: Sally Chambers.
e-mail: mail@oastgolf.co.uk

SITTINGBOURNE. **Sittingbourne and Milton Regis,** Wormdale, Newington, Sittingbourne ME9 7PX (01795 842261; Fax: 01795 844117). *Location:* Junction 5 M2, follow signs to Danaway Chestnut Street, three quarters of a mile, first left over Bridge to Wormdale. Undulating course with trees. 18 holes, 6291 yards, 5771 metres. S.S.S. 70. *Green Fees:* 18 holes £30.00, 36 holes £40.00. No visitors weekends. *Eating facilities:* available. *Visitors:* welcome weekdays. *Society Meetings:* catered for Tuesdays and Thursdays by arrangement. Professional: J. Hearn (01795 842775). Manager: Charles Maxted.

SITTINGBOURNE near. **Upchurch River Valley Golf Courses,** Oak Lane, Upchurch, near Sittingbourne ME9 7AY (01634 360626; Fax: 01634 387784). *Location:* M2, Junction 4 (A278) or Junction 5 (A249) onto A2 between Rainham and Newington, Oak Lane (opposite Little Chef). Undulating parkland with ponds and panoramic views. 18 holes, 6237 yards, 5701 metres. S.S.S. 70. 9 holes, 1596 yards, Par 30. Driving range. *Green Fees:* information not available. *Eating facilities:* 120 seater à la carte restaurant, all day food and drinks lounge. *Visitors:* unrestricted. Swimming pool. *Society Meetings:* welcome weekdays. Professional: Roger Cornwell (01634 379592). Secretary: (Members only) D. Candy (01634 260594). Course Controller: URVGC Ltd.*

SNODLAND. **Oastpark Golf Course,** Malling Road, Snodland ME6 5LG (01634 242661). *Location:* half a mile from M20, two miles from M2; five miles from Maidstone. Easy walking, good test of golf, lots of water/sand/trees. 9 holes, 3150 yards. S.S.S. 70. Extensive practice facilities. Floodlit driving range. *Green Fees:* information not available. *Eating facilities:* full bar and catering service. *Visitors:* welcome, no restrictions. No jeans, tracksuits; golf shoes must be worn. *Society Meetings:* all welcome weekdays, and weekends after 11am. Professional: David Porthouse (01634 242661). Secretary: Mrs Lesley Murrock (01634 242818; Fax: 01634 240744).

SWANLEY. **Pedham Place Golf Centre,** London Road, Swanley BR8 8PP (01322 867000; Fax: 01322 861646). *Location:* 300 yards east of Junction 3 M25, on A20 towards Brands Hatch. Two elevated links-style courses. 18 holes, 6444 yards. S.S.S. 71, Par 72; 9 holes, 1165 yards, Par 3. 40-bay floodlit driving range, putting green, practice facilities. *Green Fees:* information not available. *Eating facilities:* bar snacks to full meals; licensed bar. Modern marquee for larger groups. *Visitors:* all welcome. Thursday morning Ladies' day, Wednesday morning Veterans. Appropriate clothing/footwear must be worn. Buggy hire available. *Societies:* welcome, special rates available. Secretary: Laurence Goodwin. Professionals: Fred Hanlon, Ron Mitchell.*
e-mail: golf@ppgc.co.uk
website: www.ppgc.co.uk

TATSFIELD. **Park Wood Golf Club,** Chestnut Avenue, Tatsfield, Near Westerham TN16 2EG (01959 577744). *Location:* on B2024 Croydon road which becomes Clarks Lane. At Church Hill junction join Chestnut Avenue. In an area of natural beauty, flanked by an ancient woodland, with superb views across Kent and Surrey. Undulating course, tree-lined and with some interesting water features. Playable in all weather. 18 holes, 6835 yards. Par 72. S.S.S. 72. Course record 66. *Green Fees:* on application. *Visitors:* telephone in advance. May not play on Bank Holidays. *Societies:* apply in writing/telephone. Professional: Nick Terry. Assistant Professional: Robert Parkhouse.
e-mail: mail@parkwoodgolf.co.uk
website: www.parkwoodgolf.co.uk

TENTERDEN. **Tenterden Golf Club,** Woodchurch Road, Tenterden TN30 7DR (Tel & Fax: 01580 763987). *Location:* 30 minutes from Channel Tunnel and west of Ashford International Station, on B2067 Woodchurch Road, Tenterden. Parkland course set in beautiful undulating Wealden countryside. 18 holes, 6152 yards. S.S.S. 70. Practice ground. *Green Fees:* information not available. *Eating facilities:* available, breakfast on request, lunch, snacks and dinner, all day bar. *Society Meetings:* dedicated society days Wednesday and Thursday. Professional: (01580 762409). Secretary: Norman Taylor (01580 763987).*
website: www.tenterdengolfclub.co.uk

TONBRIDGE. **Hilden Golf Centre,** Hilden Park, Rings Hill, Hildenborough, Tonbridge TN11 8LX (01732 833607; Fax: 01732 834484). *Location*: take exit off A21 for Tonbridge North/Hildenborough; take second turning right (Watts Cross Road), follow road past station to bottom of the hill, golf centre is on the left. 36 bay covered, floodlit and grassed driving range. *Green Fees:* information not available. *Eating facilities:* fully licensed cafe bar open 8am to 10pm. all year round. Opening hours: weekdays 8am to 10pm, weekends 7.30am to 8pm. Three PGA professionals (tuition available), large golf shop, 9 hole golf course and putting green. Leisure centre and creche. Teaching academy and large golf discount store stocking all the top brands at discount prices. Professionals: Nicky Way, Rupert Hunter and Matt Jarvis. Secretary: Vicki Brett (01732 834404; Fax: 01732 834484).*

THE GOLF GUIDE 2006   ENGLAND / Kent   231

TONBRIDGE. **Nizels Golf Club,** Nizels Lane, Hildenborough, Near Tonbridge TN11 8NU (01732 833833; Fax: 01732 833492). *Location:* M25 B245 off A21. Take signs to Tonbridge North, Club 1 mile, Nizels Lane. Undulating parkland, several holes where water comes into play, many mature trees. 18 holes, 6297 yards off white tees. S.S.S. 71. Par 72. Limited practice area. *Green Fees:* information not available. *Eating facilities:* bar snacks and fine dining available. *Visitors:* welcome Monday - Friday after 9.30am, Saturday - Sunday after 12.30pm. *Society Meetings:* weekdays only after 9.30am. Professional: Neil Thirkell (01732 838926).*

TONBRIDGE. **Poult Wood Public Golf Centre,** Higham Lane, Tonbridge TN11 9QR (01732 364039). *Location:* signposted from the A26 between Hadlow and Tonbridge. Parkland, very wooded. 18 holes, 5569 yards. S.S.S. 67. 9 hole course, practice ground. *Green Fees:* information not available. *Eating facilities:* restaurant, bar, snack bar. *Visitors:* welcome every day. *Society Meetings:* welcome by booking only (01732 366180). Squash court. Professional: Chris Miller (01732 364039). *

TUNBRIDGE WELLS. **Lamberhurst Golf Club,** Church Road, Lamberhurst TN3 8DT (01892 890241; Fax: 01892 891140). *Location:* A21 from Tunbridge Wells to Hastings, take 3rd exit on roundabout towards Lamberhurst village, turn left prior to descending hill to Lamberhurst then first right. Attractive parkland course. 18 holes, 6409 yards. S.S.S. 71. Small practice ground. *Green Fees:* available from website. *Eating facilities:* full catering by arrangement. *Visitors:* welcome after 8am weekdays, 12 noon weekends and Bank Holidays. Handicap Certificate required. *Society Meetings:* catered for Tuesdays, Wednesdays and Thursdays by arrangement. Professional: Brain Impett (01892 890552). Secretary: P. M. Jeynes (01892 890591; Fax: 01892 891140).
e-mail: secretary@lamberhurstgolfclub.com
website: www.lamberhurstgolfclub.com

TUNBRIDGE WELLS. **Nevill Golf Club,** Benhall Mill Road, Tunbridge Wells TN2 5JW (01892 527820; Fax: 01892 517861). *Location:* off Forest Road, south of Tunbridge Wells. Parkland course with trees. 18 holes, 6349 yards. S.S.S. 70. Practice ground. *Green Fees:* weekdays £25.00 per round, £33.00 two rounds; weekends and Bank Holidays £46.00. *Eating facilities:* lunches at club by prior arrangement. *Visitors:* welcome with 48 hours notice. Handicap Certificate required. Trolley hire. *Society Meetings:* welcome with previous booking. Professional: Paul Huggett (01892 532941). Secretary: Mr T.J. Fenson (01892 525818; Fax: 01892 517861).
website: www.nevillgolfclub.co.uk

TUNBRIDGE WELLS. **Tunbridge Wells Golf Club,** Langton Road, Tunbridge Wells TN4 8XH (01892 523034). *Location:* adjoining Spa Hotel on A264. Parkland. 9 holes, 4725 yards. S.S.S. 62. *Green Fees:* information not available. *Eating facilities:* menu choices available daily but best to check requirements in advance. *Visitors:* welcome anytime subject to availability. *Society Meetings:* welcome, contact the Secretary for details. Professional: M. Barton (01892 541386). Secretary: R.F. Mealing (01892 536918).*

WESTERHAM. **Westerham Golf Club,** Valence Park, Brasted Road, Westerham TN16 1LJ (01959 567100; Fax: 01959 567101). *Location:* midway between Westerham and Brasted on the A25. Mainly wooded with some parkland. 18 holes, 6329 yards. S.S.S. 72. Driving range. *Green Fees:* Monday to Thursday £32.00 per round, £50.00 per day; Friday £35.00 per round, £55.00 per day; weekends and Bank Holidays £40.00 after 12 noon; £25.00 after 3pm. *Eating facilities:* bar and catering facilities available. *Visitors:* welcome weekdays and weekends (at restricted times). Buggies and carts available for hire. *Society Meetings:* welcome weekdays only. Professional: James Marshall. General Manager: Rob Sturgeon.
e-mail: terri.willison@westerhamgc.co.uk
website: www. westerhamgc.co.uk

WESTGATE ON SEA. **Westgate and Birchington Golf Club,** 176 Canterbury Road, Westgate on Sea CT8 8LT. *Location:* seaside course between Westgate on Sea and Birchington (A28). Seaside links course. 18 holes, 4926 yards, 4547 metres. S.S.S. 64. *Green Fees:* weekdays £17.00, weekends and Bank Holidays £20.00 (includes £1.00 compulsory insurance). *Eating facilities:* available by prior arrangement with Steward. *Visitors:* welcome after 10am. *Society Meetings:* by arrangement with Secretary. Professional: R. Game (01843 831115). Secretary: T.J. Sharp (01843 831115).

WEST MALLING. **King's Hill Golf Club,** Discovery Drive, King's Hill, West Malling ME19 4AG (01732 875040; Fax: 01732 875019). *Location:* Junction 4 of M20. Heathland course. 18 holes, 6622 yards. S.S.S. 72. *Green Fees:* information not available. *Eating facilities:* restaurant and bar open all day. *Visitors:* welcome Monday to Friday. Tuition available. *Society Meetings:* welcome Monday to Friday. Professional: David Hudspith (01732 842121). Secretary: Margaret Gilbert (01732 875040; Fax: 01732 875019).
e-mail: khatkhgolf@aol.com
website: www.kingshillgolf.co.uk

WHITSTABLE. **Chestfield (Whitstable) Golf Club,** 103 Chestfield Road, Chestfield, Whitstable CT5 3LU (01227 794411). *Location:* half a mile south of Old Thanet Way (A2990). Parkland with sea views. 18 holes, 6208 yards. S.S.S. 70. *Green Fees:* information not available. *Eating facilities:* lunchtime snacks, bar 11am to 11 pm. *Visitors:* welcome. *Society Meetings:* welcome and catered for weekdays. Professional: John Brotherton (01227 793563).
e-mail: secretary@chestfield-golfclub.co.uk
website: www.chestfield-golfclub.co.uk

WHITSTABLE. **Whitstable and Seasalter Golf Club,** Collingwood Road, Whitstable CT5 1EB (01227 272020). *Location:* course adjoins town centre, take Nelson Road turning off main street. Flat seaside links. 9 holes, 5357 yards. S.S.S. 65. Practice net. *Green Fees:* 18 holes £15.00, 9 holes £10.00. *Eating facilities:* bar snacks. Secretary: M.D. Moore.

Lancashire

ACCRINGTON. **Accrington and District Golf Club,** New Barn Farm, West End, Oswaldtwistle, Accrington (01254 231091). *Location*: on A679, 2 miles from Blackburn. 18 holes, 6060 yards. S.S.S. 69. *Green Fees*: Monday to Thursday £25.00, Friday to Sunday £30.00. (2006 fees not yet approved). *Eating facilities*: lunches and evening meals. *Visitors*: welcome by prior arrangement. *Society Meetings*: prior bookings catered for. Professional: Bill Harling (01254 231091). Secretary: S. Bradbury (01254 350112).
e-mail: info@accrington-golf-club.co.uk

ACCRINGTON. **Green Haworth Golf Club,** Green Haworth, Accrington BB5 3SL (01254 237580). *Location*: off A679, one mile Town Centre, via Willows Lane, turn left 300 yards beyond Red Lion Inn. Moorland. 9 holes, 5557 yards. S.S.S. 67. *Green Fees:* information not available. *Eating facilities:* full catering and bar facilities. *Visitors:* welcome, no visitors on Saturdays or Sundays March to October. *Society Meetings:* catered for weekdays only. Packages available. Secretary: Mike Shorroch (01254 237580; Fax: 01254 396176).*

BACUP. **Bacup Golf Club,** Bankside Lane, Bacup OL13 1HY (01706 873170; Fax: 01706 87726). *Location:* one mile from Bacup centre. Moorland. 9 holes, 6018 yards. S.S.S. 69. *Green Fees:* information not available. *Eating facilities:* by arrangement except Mondays. *Visitors:* welcome without reservation except Mondays and Saturdays. Secretary: T. Leyland (01706 879644).*

BAXENDEN. **Baxenden and District Golf Club,** Wooley Lane, Baxenden BB5 2EA (01254 234555). *Location*: towards Accrington from M65, past Hollands Pies right, signposted. Golf course has fantastic views as far as the Fylde Coast and Ingleborough. 9 holes, 5702 yards. S.S.S. 68. *Green Fees*: weekdays only £20.00, with member £10.00. Society package £28.00 includes 27 holes of golf and meals. Details on request. *Eating facilities*: available. *Visitors*: welcome weekdays only. *Society Meetings*: welcome by arrangement with Secretary. Secretary: N. Turner (01254 234555).
e-mail: baxgolf@hotmail.com
website: www.baxendengolf.co.uk

BLACKBURN. **Blackburn Golf Club,** Beardwood Brow, Blackburn BB2 7AX (01254 51122; Fax: 01254 665578). *Location:* off A677 within easy reach of M6 (Junction 31), M61 and M65; west end of Blackburn. Parkland with superb views of Lancashire coast and Pennine Hills. 18 holes, 6144 yards. S.S.S. 70. Par 71. Practice area. *Green Fees:* weekdays £26.00 (£10.00 with a member); weekends and Bank Holidays £30.00 (£10.00 with a member). *Eating facilities:* full catering and bar facilities (restricted Mondays). *Visitors:* welcome without reservation except on competition days. *Society Meetings:* catered for by arrangement. Professional: Alan Rodwell (01254 55942). Secretary: K. Taylor (01254 51122; Fax: 01254 665578).

BLACKBURN. **Great Harwood Golf Club,** Harwood Bar, Great Harwood, Blackburn BB6 7TE (01254 884391). Flat wooded course. 9 holes, 6411 yards, 5862 metres. S.S.S. 71. *Green Fees:* information not available. *Eating facilities:* all meals catered for, bar hours 12-2pm, 4-11pm. *Visitors:* welcome Wednesday - Friday. *Society Meetings:* catered for by advance bookings. Secretary: J. Spibey (01254 884391).

BLACKBURN. **Mytton Fold Hotel & Golf Complex,** Whalley Road, Langho, Blackburn BB6 8AB (01254 245392/240662). *Location*: from Junction 31 of M6, follow A59 towards Whalley/Clitheroe for 10 miles. At second roundabout follow Whalley sign, entrance 500 yards on right. Undulating parkland with panoramic views over the Ribble Valley. 18 holes. Par 70. *Green Fees:* information not available. *Eating facilities*: bar open all day, food till 9.30pm. *Visitors:* prior booking essential. Buggies available. Professional: Gary Coope. *
e-mail: mytton_fold.hotel@virgin.net

BLACKBURN. **Pleasington Golf Club,** Pleasington, Near Blackburn BB2 5JF (01254 202177). *Location:* M6 north to Junction 31. Blackburn eight miles. Undulating woodland. 18 holes, 6445 yards. S.S.S. 71. *Green Fees:* weekdays from £45.00, weekends and Bank Holidays £55.00. *Eating facilities:* full catering available. *Visitors:* welcome by prior arrangement. *Society Meetings:* Mondays, Wednesdays, Fridays by arrangement. Professional: G.J. Furey (01254 201630). Secretary: T. Ashton (01254 202177). Caterer: D. Whittam (01254 207346).
e-mail: secretary-manager@pleasington-golf.co.uk
website: www.pleasington-golf.co.uk

BLACKBURN. **Rishton Golf Club,** Eachill Links, Rishton BB1 4HG (01254 884442; Fax: 01254 887701). *Location:* between Junctions 6 and 7 M65 signposted from Rishton village centre. Moorland course. 9 holes, 6094 yards. S.S.S. 69. *Green Fees:* weekdays £12.00 with a member, £20.00 without a member. Weekends £15.00 with member only. *Eating facilities:* full catering by prior arrangement. *Visitors:* welcome on weekdays and with a member at weekends and on Bank Holidays. *Society Meetings:* visiting parties welcome by prior arrangement, special rates can be obtained. Secretary: T. Charnock (0771 0371118).

THE APPEARANCE OF AN ASTERISK (*) AT THE END OF A CLUB OR COURSE ENTRY INDICATES THAT UP-TO-DATE INFORMATION HAS NOT BEEN SUPPLIED

THE GOLF GUIDE 2006   ENGLAND / Lancashire 233

BLACKBURN. **Wilpshire Golf Club Ltd,** 72 Whalley Road, Wilpshire, Blackburn BB1 9LF (01254 248260; Fax: 01254 246745). *Location:* A666 three miles north of Blackburn on Blackburn to Whalley road. Parkland/moorland. 18 holes, 5961 yards. S.S.S. 69. Practice ground. *Green Fees:* information not available. *Eating facilities:* lunch, high tea, dinner except Mondays. *Visitors:* welcome, no restrictions except competition days. Clubs and trolley hire. *Society Meetings:* catered for by prior booking through the Secretary. Professional: Walter Slaven (01254 249558; Fax: 01254 246745). Secretary: S. H. Tart. e-mail: admin@wilpshiregolfclub.co.uk website: www.wilpshiregolfclub.co.uk

BLACKPOOL. **Blackpool North Shore Golf Club,** Devonshire Road, Blackpool FY2 0RD (01253 352054; Fax: 01253 591240). *Location:* north Blackpool on A587 behind North Prom. Undulating parkland. 18 holes, 6431 yards. S.S.S. 71. *Green Fees:* weekdays £32.00 day; weekends £38.00 day. Society Package £45.00, *Eating facilities:* full catering and bar facilities. *Visitors:* welcome except Thursdays and Saturdays. Professional: Brendan Ward (01253 354640). Secretary: John Morris (01253 352054).

BLACKPOOL. **Blackpool Park Golf Club,** North Park Drive, Blackpool FY3 8LS (Tel & Fax: 01253 397916). *Location:* one mile east of Tower. Parkland course. 18 holes, 6089 yards. S.S.S. 69. *Green Fees:* information not available. *Eating facilities:* full restaurant facilities. *Visitors:* welcome (bookings for tee reservations must be made to Blackpool Borough Council). *Society Meetings:* Apply to Blackpool Borough Council in writing. Professional: B. Purdie (01253 391004). Secretary: Mr David Stones (Tel & Fax: 01253 397916).*

BLACKPOOL. **De Vere Herons' Reach Golf Club,** East Park Drive, Blackpool FY3 8LL (01253 766156; Fax: 01253 798800). *Location:* leave M55 at Junction 4, follow signs for Stanley Park and Victoria Hospital. Designed by Peter Alliss & Clive Clark. Testing championship course with 10 man-made lakes- all year round play course. Heron's Reach Course -18 holes, 6461 yards, S.S.S. 72. 18 bay floodlit driving range, putting and chipping green. *Green Fees:* information not available. *Eating facilities*: Nineteen Bar serving from 7am daily, leisure bar and Brasserie open seven days. *Visitors*: welcome. 164 bedroomed hotel with extensive conference and banqueting facilities for up to 600 plus leisure complex. *Society Meetings*: welcome. Golf Centre: (01253 766156; Fax: 01253 798800).

BLACKPOOL. **Knott End Golf Club Ltd,** Wyre Side, Knott End-on-Sea, Poulton-le-Fylde FY6 0AA (01253 810576). *Location:* M55 Exit 3, A585 Fleetwood Road then A588 to Knott End. Scenic riverside course, slight undulations. 18 holes, 5843 yards. S.S.S. 68. Practice ground. *Green Fees:* £29.00 18 holes weekdays, weekends £37.00. *Eating facilities:* full catering and bar. *Visitors:* welcome, time sheet in use, contact Professional with 24 hours notice. Buggies for hire. *Society Meetings:* by arrangement weekdays and Sundays. Professional: Paul Walker (01253 811365). Manager: Louise Freeman (01253 810576; Fax: 01253 813446). website: www.knottendgolfclub.co.uk

BLACKPOOL. **Poulton-le-Fylde Golf Club,** Myrtle Farm, Breck Road, Poulton-le-Fylde, Blackpool FY6 7HJ (01253 893150; Fax: 01253 892444). *Location:* from M55 follow Poulton/Thornton/Cleveleys, roundabout with River Wyre pub on left, turn left and follow signs. Parkland/wooded course. 9 holes, 3260 yards. Par 36. Practice and putting facilities. *Green Fees:* weekdays £8.50 for 9 holes (£7.00 Seniors/Juniors), £13.00 day ticket, weekends 9 holes for £10.00, £15.00 day ticket. *Eating facilities:* breakfast and lunch served, all day bar in summer. *Visitors:* welcome anytime, bookings taken up to one week in advance (01253 892444). Snooker. *Society Meetings:* welcome by prior booking. Professional: John Greenwood (Tel & Fax: 01253 892444). Secretary: Victoria Taylor (01253 893150; Fax: 01253 892444).

BOLTON. **Bolton Open Golf Course,** Longsight Park, Longsight Lane, Harwood, Bolton (01204 597659). *Location:* one and a half miles from Bolton town centre. Parkland, mature wooded, superb layout. 18 holes, 6000 yards. S.S.S. 68. 20 bay floodlit driving range. *Green Fees:* information not available. *Eating facilities:* one bar, all day catering. *Visitors:* no restrictions, everyone welcome at all times. *Society Meetings:* welcome anytime, discounts available.*

BOLTON. **Douglas Valley Golf Club,** A6 Blackrod By-Pass, Blackrod, Bolton BL6 5HX. *Location:* M61 Junction 6, off A6. Parkland greens. 9 holes, 2190 yards, 2004 metres. 22 bay floodlit driving range. *Green Fees:* Weekdays - 9 holes £8.00, 18 holes £10.00, weekends - 9 holes £9.00, 18 holes £12.00. 18 holes, breakfast/lunch £12.00 (all day every day), 9 holes, soup and sandwich (Mon-Thur). *Visitors:* welcome anytime. Bookings two days in advance. Dress code at all times on the golf course, collared shirt, tailored trousers. Fully stocked pro shop and A-Star teaching academy. *Society Meetings:* society and corporate days available, ring for brochure. *Eating facilities:* Bistro Bar menu available all day in Willows Restaurant, all types of function available in Willows Function Suite, ring for menu and price list or visit website. Head Professional: Mr Andrew Green. Manager: Monique Parry. Head Chef: Stuart Roscoe. Company Secretary: Mrs Julie Downes (01257 474844).
website: www.GolfDealsToday.co.uk

Cotswold

The flats are situated in a quieter, select area on the edge of town adjoining the promenade with acres of grass and level walking.
Our famous trams pass by frequently for the town centre, Cleveleys and Fleetwood. The Fylde is well known by golf and bowls enthusiasts.
Our ground floor flat is spacious, fully self-contained and centrally heated. Sleeps up to four adults.
Midweek/Weekend Short Breaks can be arranged. Phone or send SAE for brochure.

2a Haddon Road, Norbreck, Blackpool FY2 9AH   Telephone: 01253 352227

234 Lancashire / ENGLAND

BURNLEY. **Burnley Golf Club,** Glen View, Burnley BB11 3RW (01282 421045). *Location:* 300 yards from junction of A56 and A646. Moorland. 18 holes, 5939 yards, 5430 metres. S.S.S. 69. *Green Fees:* weekdays £20.00; weekends and Bank Holidays £25.00. *Eating facilities:* available except Mondays and Tuesdays. *Visitors:* welcome except Saturdays. *Society Meetings:* catered for. Professional: Matthew Baker (01282 455266). Secretary: R.D.M. Wills (Tel & Fax: 01282 451281).

BURNLEY. **Towneley Golf Club,** Towneley Park, Todmorden Road, Burnley BB11 3ED (01282 415636). *Location:* Todmorden Road, Burnley, Top Gates to Towneley Park. Guarded greens (ie. bunkered) and internal O.B.B. 18 holes, 5811 yards. S.S.S. 68. Practice ground. *Green Fees:* information not available. *Eating facilities*: full licensed bar and catering (full meals). *Visitors*: welcome but make tee reservations in advance. *Society Meetings:* welcome, apply to course booking shop. Professional: James Major (01282 438473) Secretary: Chris Gilbert (01282 703912).

CHORLEY. **Charnock Richard Golf Club,** Preston Road, Charnock Richard, Chorley PR7 5LE (01257 470707). *Location:* on A49 between M6 turn-offs for Standish and Leyland, five minutes from Camelot Theme Park. Parkland with water features. 18 holes. Par 71. Buggy hire. *Green Fees:* information not available. *Eating facilities*: restaurant. Professional: L. Taylor.*

CHORLEY. **Chorley Golf Club,** Hall o' the Hill, Heath Charnock, Chorley PR6 9HX (01257 480263; Fax: 01257 480722). *Location:* south of Chorley, just off the A673 at the junction with the A6. Scenic course with some of the finest views in Lancashire. 18 holes, 6269 yards. S.S.S. 70. *Green Fees:* weekdays £32.00. *Eating facilities:* restaurant and lounge bar. *Visitors:* welcome by prior arrangement except Bank Holidays or weekends. Two buggies and carts for hire. *Society Meetings:* catered for by arrangement. Professional: M.N. Bradley (01257 481245). Secretary: Mrs A. Green (01257 480263). Catering: (01257 474664).

CHORLEY. **Duxbury Park Golf Club (Municipal),** Duxbury Hall Road, Duxbury Park, Chorley PR7 4AS (01257 265380, 01257 241634). *Location:* one mile south of town centre off A6. Wooded parkland with water hazards on several holes. 18 holes, 6390 yards, 5843 metres. S.S.S. 70. Practice area. *Green Fees:* information not available. *Eating facilities:* Golf Cafe open 7 days a week, very reasonable prices. For details contact Paul (01257 277049). *Visitors:* welcome, book seven days in advance. *Society Meetings:* book in advance. Professional: (01257 265380). Secretary: F. Holding (01257 262209). Membership available, contact Secretary.

CHORLEY. **Euxton Park Golf Centre,** Euxton Lane, Chorley PR7 6DL (01257 261601; Fax: 01257 261601). *Location:* Euxton Lane, between A6 and A49, next to Royal Ordnance factory. A short, yet challenging Par 3 course, ideal for beginners. 9 holes, Par 3. 40 bay driving range, practice bunkers.

THE GOLF GUIDE 2006

Green Fees: information not available. *Eating facilities:* fully licensed bar. *Visitors:* welcome every day, no need to book, pay and play course. *Society Meetings:* welcome, professionally catered for. Virtual golf indoor simulator. Professional: Jon Haines (01257 233500). Secretary: T.R. Evans (Tel & Fax: 01257 261601). *

CHORLEY. **Shaw Hill Hotel Golf and Country Club,** Preston Road, Whittle-le-Woods, Chorley PR6 7PP (01257 269221; Fax: 01257 261223). *Location:* A6 between Chorley and Preston. (Near M6 J28 & M61 J8) Parkland course with many water hazards. 18 holes, 6109 yards. S.S.S. 69 yellow. Practice area. *Green Fees:* information not available. *Eating facilities:* spike bar and formal bar, à la carte restaurant. *Visitors:* welcome weekdays only, must hold current Handicap Certificate. Hotel with 30 bedrooms available. Golf trolleys and buggies also available. *Society Meetings:* catered for midweek only. Professional: D. Clarke (01257 279222). General Manager: Mrs K. Tyrer. Secretary: L. Bateson.

CLITHEROE. **Clitheroe Golf Club,** Whalley Road, Pendleton, Clitheroe BB7 1PP (Tel & Fax: 01200 422292). *Location:* A59, junction A671 (south of Clitheroe); 300m turn left (signposted Barrow) clubhouse 100m on right. Parkland with extensive countryside views. 18 holes, 6326 yards, 5785 metres. S.S.S. 71. Practice ground and range. *Green Fees:* weekdays from £32.00; weekends and Bank Holidays £45.00. With a member £12.00. Subject to review. *Eating facilities:* full service available. *Visitors:* welcome but restricted to times available. No jeans, trainers, track/shell suits. *Society Meetings:* catered for, maximum 48 Friday; maximum 24 Thursday. No parties weekends. Professional: Paul McEvoy (01200 424242). General Manager: Christopher Spencer (Tel & Fax: 01200 422292). e-mail: secretary@clitheroegolfclub.com website: www.clitheroegolfclub.com

CLITHEROE. **Whalley Golf Club,** Clerk Hill Rd, Whalley, Clitheroe BB7 9DR (01254 822236). *Location:* seven miles east of Blackburn on A59. Parkland. 9 holes, 6258 yards, 5727 metres. S.S.S. 71. *Green Fees:* information not available. *Eating facilities:* full catering and bar facilities. *Visitors:* welcome except Thursday afternoons and Saturdays April to September. *Society Meetings:* welcome by appointment. Professional: Jamie Hunt (01254 822236).*

COLNE. **Colne Golf Club,** Law Farm, Skipton Old Road, Colne BB8 7EB (01282 863391). *Location:* come off eastern end of M65. Carry on one mile to next roundabout and take first exit on left, Goup Hill. Flat scenic moorland course with trees. 9 holes, 6053 yards, 5535 metres. S.S.S. 69. Full practice facilities. *Green Fees:* £20.00 weekdays, £25.00 weekends and Bank Holidays (subject to review). Parties of 12 or more £19.00 per person (not weekends, Thursdays or competition days). *Eating facilities:* available daily except Mondays. *Visitors:* welcome except on competition days; two-balls only on Thursdays. *Society Meetings:* welcome except weekends, Thursdays and competition days. Secretary: A. Turpin.

ENGLAND / Lancashire

DARWEN. Darwen Golf Club, Winter Hill, Darwen BB3 0LB (01254 704367). *Location:* one-and-a-half miles from Darwen centre. Moorland. 18 holes, 6354 yards. S.S.S. 71. Large practice area. *Green Fees:* £25.00 per round. *Eating facilities:* full catering. *Visitors:* welcome, not Tuesdays (Ladies' Day) or Saturdays. *Society Meetings:* welcome, except Saturdays. Professional: W. Lennon (01254 776370). Secretary: J.R. Lawson (01254 704367).

FLEETWOOD. Fleetwood Golf Club Ltd., The Golf House, Princes Way, Fleetwood FY7 8AF (Tel & Fax: 01253 773573). *Location:* on Fylde Coast, eight miles from Blackpool, Coast Road Blackpool to Fleetwood, two miles west of Fleetwood Centre. Seaside, true links. White course 18 holes, 6557 yards, S.S.S. 71; Yellow course 18 holes, 6308 yards, S.S.S. 70. *Green Fees:* weekdays £30.00; weekends £40.00. Special rates available on request. *Eating facilities:* full catering and bar service. *Visitors:* welcome weekdays, certain Saturdays and Sundays. *Society Meetings:* welcome by arrangement. Professional: S. McLaughlin (01253 873661). Secretary/Manager: N. Robinson (01253 773573).
e-mail: fleetwoodgc@aol.com

HEYSHAM. Heysham Golf Club, Trumacar Park, Middleton Road, Heysham LA3 3JH (01524 851011; Fax: 01524 853030). *Location:* five miles from M6 via Lancaster and Morecambe. Parkland, flat, part-wooded. 18 holes, 6338 yards. S.S.S. 70. Driving range and chipping green. *Green Fees:* weekdays £30.00 per round, £35.00 per day; weekends and Bank Holidays £40.00. Subject to review. Special rates for parties on application. *Eating facilities:* full catering seven days, closed Mondays October to March. *Visitors:* welcome with Handicap Certificates. Tee reserved for members 1pm to 1.45pm. Buggy hire available. *Society Meetings:* catered for by arrangement with Secretary. Professional: R. Done (01524 852000). Secretary: F.A. Bland (01524 851011).

LANCASTER. Lancaster Golf Club Ltd, Ashton Hall, Ashton-with-Stodday, Lancaster LA2 0AJ (01524 752090). *Location:* three miles south of Lancaster on A588. Parkland. 18 holes, 6288 yards. S.S.S. 71. *Green Fees:* £35 per round, £42 per day (subject to review for 2006). *Eating facilities:* available (Caterer: 01524 751105). *Visitors:* welcome weekdays only unless staying in the Dormy House. Club has a Dormy House (part of Ashton Hall), single and double rooms with en suite facilities, 2 nights minimum stay. *Society Meetings:* catered for weekdays only. Professional: David Sutcliffe (01524 751802). Secretary: P.J. Irvine (01524 751247; Fax: 01524 752742).
e-mail: secretary@lancastergc.co.uk

LANCASTER. Lansil Golf Club, Caton Road, Lancaster LA1 3PE (01524 39269/61233). *Location:* A683, towards Lancaster from Junction 34 M6. Parkland. 9 holes, 5608 yards. S.S.S. 67. *Green Fees:* information not available. *Eating facilities:* bar meals available - contact Steward. *Visitors:* welcome weekdays, not before 1pm Sundays. *Society Meetings:* groups of 12 plus welcome weekdays by prior arrangement. Steward: 01524 39269.*

LEYLAND. Leyland Golf Club Ltd., Wigan Road, Leyland, Preston PR25 5UD (01772 436457). *Location:* leave M6 at Exit 28, turn right to traffic lights, (200 yards) turn right onto the A49, course located one mile on left. Flat parkland. 18 holes, 6298 yards. S.S.S. 70. *Green Fees:* £30.00 weekdays. *Eating facilities:* full catering except Mondays. *Visitors:* welcome weekdays; weekends only with a member. *Society Meetings:* welcome by arrangement with Secretary. Professional: C. Burgess (01772 423425). Administration Manager: Stephanie Drinkall (01772 436457).
e-mail: manager@leylandgolfclub.com
website: www.leylandgolfclub.com

LYTHAM ST ANNES. Fairhaven Golf Club Ltd., Lytham Hall Park, Lytham St Annes FY8 4JU (01253 736741). *Location:* on B5261, two miles from Lytham, eight miles from Blackpool. 18 holes, 6880 yards. S.S.S. 73. Practice ground and net. *Green Fees:* information not available. *Eating facilities:* full catering. *Visitors:* welcome with reservation. Handicap Certificate required.*Society Meetings:* catered for by arrangement Mondays, Tuesdays, Wednesdays and Fridays. Professional: B. Plucknett (01253 736976). Secretary: Stephen Last (Tel & Fax:01253 736741).*

LYTHAM ST ANNES. Lytham Green Drive Golf Club, Ballam Road, Lytham St Annes FY8 4LE (01253 737390; Fax: 01253 731350). *Location:* one mile from town centre. Flat parkland course. 18 holes, 6363 yards. S.S.S. 70. *Green Fees:* under review. *Eating facilities:* catering available daily. *Visitors:* welcome. *Society Meetings:* welcome by prior arrangement. Professional: A. Lancaster (01253 737379). Secretary: M. Caunce (01253 737390; Fax: 01253 731350).
e-mail: mark@lythamgreendrive.co.uk
website: www.lythamgreendrive.co.uk

Please mention THE GOLF GUIDE when you enquire about clubs or accommodation

Fleetwood Golf Course is the only true links course on the **Fylde Coast**. It was opened in 1932 and designed to perfection by **James Steer**. It is a definite must for keen golfers, and those willing to travel from inland courses have the option to stay overnight in any of the hundreds of hotels in the area, if they can bear to leave the course.
Princes Way, Fleetwood, Lancashire FY7 8AF   Tel: 01253 773573
e-mail: fleetwoodgc@aol.com   www.fleetwoodgolfclub.org.uk

236 Lancashire / ENGLAND — THE GOLF GUIDE 2006

LYTHAM ST ANNES. **Royal Lytham and St Annes Golf Club,** Links Gate, Lytham St Annes FY8 3LQ (01253 724206; Fax: 01253 780946). *Location:* within one mile of the centre of St Annes on Sea. Seaside Championship links course. 18 holes, 6334 yards. S.S.S. 71. Practice ground. *Green Fees:* Mondays and Thursdays £110.00, limited availability on Sundays £165.00. 2005 rates, subject to review. *Eating facilities:* restaurant and bar. *Visitors:* welcome, times by arrangement. Dormy House accommodation available. *Society Meetings:* by arrangement. Professional: Eddie Birchenough (01253 720094). Secretary: R.J.G Cochrane. e-mail: bookings@royallytham.org

LYTHAM ST ANNES. **St Annes Old Links Golf Club,** Highbury Road, Lytham St Annes FY8 2LD (01253 723597). *Location:* M55 via Blackpool South Shore, following airport signs. Past airport down to coast road, turn left and first left at next real traffic lights. The only true links course in Lancashire. 18 holes, 6616 yards. S.S.S. 72. Practice ground, putting and chipping greens. *Green Fees:* weekdays £55.00 per day, £40.00 for 18 holes after 1.30pm; weekends £50.00. *Eating facilities:* restaurant and snack facilities, bar. *Visitors:* welcome, not Saturdays, restricted Sundays. Tuesday is Ladies' Day. *Society Meetings:* restricted to those with Handicaps and membership of other clubs. Professional: D. Webster (01253 722432). General Manager: S. Mainwaring (01253 723597; Fax: 01253 781506). e-mail: secretary@coastalgolf.co.uk website: www.coastalgolf.co.uk

MORECAMBE. **Morecambe Golf Club Ltd.,** The Club House, Bare, Morecambe LA4 6AJ (01524 418050). *Location:* on A589 leaving Morecambe towards Carnforth. Parkland course affected by sea breezes and offering superb views. 18 holes, 5770 yards. S.S.S. 69. *Green Fees:* weekdays £25.00 per round, £30.00 per day; weekends and Bank Holidays £30.00 per round, £35.00 per day. Subject to review. Special rates for visiting parties, package deals. *Eating facilities:* diningroom and bar snacks. *Visitors:* welcome at all times, tee reserved for members up to 9.30am and from 12 noon to 1.30pm. *Society Meetings:* welcome at all times. Professional: Simon Fletcher (Tel & Fax: 01524 415596). Secretary: Mrs Judith Atkinson (01524 412841; Fax: 01524 400088). e-mail: secretary@morecambegolfclub.com website: www.morecambegolfclub.com

NELSON. **Nelson Golf Club,** King's Causeway, Brierfield, Nelson BB9 0EU (01282 614583). *Location:* leave M65 at Junction 12, take A682 for Brierfield, turn left at Brierfield centre traffic lights, course on the right at top of the hill. Wooded moorland, good views of the surrounding Pendle Area. 18 holes, 6007 yards. S.S.S. 69. Large practice area. *Green Fees:* weekdays £30.00, weekends and Bank Holidays £35.00. *Eating facilities:* lunches, dinners by arrangement except Mondays. *Visitors:* weekdays except Thursdays (Ladies' Day), or Saturdays during Competition season. Carts. *Society Meetings:* daily except Monday, Thursday and Saturday. Professional: Neil Reeves (01282 617000). Secretary: B.R. Thomason (01282 611834).

ORMSKIRK. **Mossock Hall Golf Club,** Liverpool Road, Bickerstaffe, Ormskirk L39 0EE (01695 421717). *Location:* one mile from Junction 3 of M58 or two miles from Junction 1 of M57, between Kirby and Ormskirk. Parkland course; USGA greens with water in play on four holes. 18 holes. Par 71. *Green Fees:* information available on (01695 421717). *Eating facilities:* licensed bar and restaurant. *Society Meetings:* catered for - advance bookings only, contact manager Jackie Fray (01695 421717). Professional: Phil Atkiss.

ORMSKIRK. **Ormskirk Golf Club,** Cranes Lane, Lathom L40 5UJ (01695 572112). *Location:* two miles east of Ormskirk. Parkland course. 18 holes, 6358 yards. S.S.S. 70. *Green Fees:* weekdays (not Wednesday) £40.00 per round, £50.00 per day, weekends and Wednesdays £45.00 per round, £55.00 per day. *Eating facilities:* available except Monday. *Visitors:* welcome, Handicap Certificates required, notice advised with reservation. *Society Meetings:* catered for, book in advance. Professional: J. Hammond (01695 572074). Secretary: R.D.J. Lawrence (01695 572227).

PRESTON. **Ashton and Lea Golf Club Ltd,** Tudor Avenue, off Blackpool Road, Lea, Preston PR4 0XA (01772 735282; Fax: 01772 735762). *Location:* on A5085, three miles west of Preston, turn opposite Toby Carvery. Parkland with water features. 18 holes, 6334 yards. S.S.S. 70. Small practice ground. *Green Fees:* weekdays £26.00; weekends and Bank Holidays £30.00. Reduced rates if playing with member. *Eating facilities:* full catering every day. *Visitors:* welcome but please telephone the Professional to reserve tee time. Conference and function facilities available. *Society Meetings:* catered for weekdays only, contact the Secretary. Professional: Mike Greenough (01772 720374). Secretary: Ian Hulley (01772 735282). e-mail: secretary@ashtonleagolfclub.co.uk website: www.ashtonleagolfclub.co.uk

PRESTON. **Fishwick Hall Golf Club,** Glenluce Drive, Farringdon Park, Preston PR1 5TD (01772 798300). *Location*: two minutes from Junction 31 M6, off A59 Blackburn to Preston Road. Parkland, part wooded, bounded by river. 18 holes, 6045 yards. S.S.S. 69. Small practice area. *Green Fees:* weekdays £28.00; weekends and Public Holidays £32.00. Reductions if playing with members. *Eating facilities:* bar, full catering available except Mondays. *Visitors:* welcome unless club competition on. *Society Meetings:* welcome weekdays, including Mondays. Professional: M. Watson (01772 795870). Secretary: J.P. Davis (01772 798300; Fax: 01772 704600).

PRESTON. **Ingol Golf Club,** Tanterton Hall Road, Ingol, Preston PR2 7BY (01772 734556; Fax: 01772 729815). *Location:* two miles from Junction 32 M6 (joins M55). Parkland. 18 holes, 6294 yards, Par 72. Chipping and putting practice areas. *Green Fees:* information not available. *Eating facilities:* bar/restaurant. *Visitors:* welcome anytime, please telephone to check tee reservations. Buggies and trolleys available. Squash courts. Meeting room available. Stay and play packages. *Society Meetings:* welcome by arrangement. Professional: Ryan Grimshaw (01772 769646). Secretary: Marjorie Kenny (01772 734556; Fax: 01772 729815).

PRESTON. **Longridge Golf Club,** Fell Barn, Jeffrey Hill, Longridge, Preston PR3 2TU (01772 783291; Fax: 01772 783022). *Location:* eight miles north-east of Preston off B6243. Moorland with extensive spectacular views. One of the oldest clubs in England (Est. 1877). 18 holes, 5975 yards. S.S.S. 69. *Green Fees:* weekdays £30.00 per day, £20.00 per round; weekends £35.00. *Eating facilities:* full catering and bars. *Visitors:* welcome. *Society Meetings:* welcome by prior arrangement. Professional: Stephen Taylor. Secretary: David Simpson.
e-mail: secretary@longridgegolfclub.fsnet.co.uk
website: www.longridgegolfclub.com

PRESTON. **Penwortham Golf Club Ltd.,** Blundell Lane, Penwortham, Preston PR1 0AX (01772 744630; Fax: 01772 740172). *Location:* one mile west of Preston on main Southport to Liverpool road. Parkland. 18 holes, 5877 yards. S.S.S. 69. *Green Fees:* £25.00 weekdays; £33.00 weekends. *Eating facilities:* lunches and dinners served at Club. *Visitors:* welcome. *Society Meetings:* by arrangement Monday, Wednesday, Thursday, Friday only. Professional: Darren Hopwood (01772 742345). Secretary: Neil Annandale (01772 744630; Fax: 01772 740172).

PRESTON. **Preston Golf Club,** Fulwood Hall Lane, Fulwood, Preston PR2 8DD (01772 700011; Fax: 01772 794234). *Location:* exit 32 on M6 marked Preston & Garstang, partway to Preston turning at Watling Street Road. Parkland course. 18 holes, 6312 yards. S.S.S. 71. *Green Fees:* information not available. *Eating facilities:* first class dining room, bars. *Visitors:* welcome weekdays, weekends or Bank Holidays must be accompanied by a member. *Society Meetings:* welcome except Tuesdays, weekends or Bank Holidays. Handicap Certificate required. Professional: Andrew Greenbank (01772 700022). Secretary: S.H. Newland (01772 700011).*

ROCHDALE. **Tunshill Golf Club Ltd,** Kiln Lane, Milnrow, Rochdale OL16 3TS (01706 342095). *Location:* two miles east of Rochdale, M62 J21. Hillside course adjacent to M62 motorway. 9 holes/18 tees, 5743 yards. S.S.S. 68. *Green Fees:* £16.00. *Visitors:* welcome during the week. *Society Meetings:* welcome.

ROSSENDALE. **Rossendale Golf Club Ltd.,** Ewood Lane Head, Haslingden, Rossendale BB4 6LH (01706 831686). *Location:* 14 miles north of Manchester, easy access from M66 and A56. 18 holes, 6293 yards. S.S.S. 71. *Green Fees:* information not available. *Eating facilities:* full catering except Mondays; bar. *Visitors:* welcome except Saturdays during season. *Society Meetings:* welcome. Professional: S.J. Nicholls (01706 213616). Hon. Secretary: K. Wilson (01706 831339; Fax: 01706 228669).
e-mail: rgc@golfers.net
website: www.rossendalegolfclub.net

ST HELENS. **Houghwood,** Billinge Hill, Crank Road, Crank, St Helens WA11 8RL (Tel & Fax: 01744 894754). *Location*: ten minutes from M6. Parkland. 18 holes, 6268 yards. S.S.S. 69. Practice ground. Snooker table. *Green Fees:* weekdays £25.00, weekends £35.00. Special rates - 4 ball £65.00 Mon/Tue/Thur or £85.00 with bar meal. *Eating facilities*: spike bar open 11am to 11pm every day. First floor public restaurant with quality food, reasonable prices and superb views, soft spikes required by all. *Visitors*: always welcome. *Society Meetings*: welcome Mondays, Tuesdays and Thursdays. Professional: Paul Dickenson (01744 894444; Fax: 01744 894754). Secretary: Julie Melling (Tel & Fax: 01744 894754).

SCARISBRICK. **Hurlston Hall Golf Club,** Hurlston Lane, Scarisbrick L40 8JD (01704 840400; Fax: 01704 841404). *Location:* six miles from Southport and two miles from Ormskirk along A570 trunk road; eight miles from M58. Parkland with several lakes and streams. 18 holes, 6746 yards. S.S.S. 72. Golf centre with 18-bay driving range, putting green. Flood-lit driving range. *Green Fees:* weekdays £35.00, weekends £40.00. For winter fees please telephone Golf Shop (01704 841120). *Eating facilities:* three bars; à la carte restaurant. *Visitors:* welcome, must book in advance. Handicap Certificate or letter of introduction preferred. *Society Meetings:* Golf Societies welcome. Golf centre and driving range (01704 841120; Fax: 01704 841404). General Manager: Malcolm Atherton (01704 840400; Fax: 01704 841404).
e-mail: info@hurlstonhall.co.uk
website: www.HurlstonHall.co.uk

INGOL GOLF CLUB
www.ingolgolfclub.com

**Tanterton Hall Road, Ingol, Preston PR2 7BY
Tel: 01772 734556 • Fax: 01772 729815**
• Visitors welcome anytime, please telephone Pro Shop 01772 769646 for tee times. Buggies and trolleys available.
• Bar/restaurant • Society Meetings welcome by arrangement.
• 18 holes, 6294 yards, Par 72. • Chipping and putting practice areas.

FHG

PLEASE MENTION THIS GUIDE WHEN YOU WRITE OR PHONE TO ENQUIRE ABOUT CLUBS OR ACCOMMODATION

·K·U·P·E·R·A·R·D·

SILVERDALE. **Silverdale Golf Club,** Redbridge Lane, Silverdale, Carnforth LA5 0SP (01524 701300). *Location:* M6 to Carnforth, then two miles west, adjacent to railway station and RSPB nature reserve. Testing heathland course with rock outcrops and excellent views. 18 holes, 5535 yards. S.S.S. 68. *Green Fees:* weekdays from £20.00, weekends and Bank Holidays from £25.00. *Eating facilities:* full catering and bar facilities. *Visitors:* welcome except Sundays a.m. in the summer unless with a member. *Society Meetings:* welcome by arrangement with Secretary. Secretary: K. Smith (Tel & Fax: 01524 702074). website: www.silverdalegolfclub.org.uk

UPHOLLAND. **Beacon Park Golf & Country Club,** Beacon Lane, Dalton WN8 7RU (01695 625551). *Location:* ten minutes from J26 of M6. Follow signs for A577 Upholland. Undulating parkland course. Designed by Donald Steel. 18 holes, 6151 yards. S.S.S. 70. Driving range, practice ground. *Green Fees:* (2005) midweek £10.50, weekends £14.00. *Eating facilities:* fully licensed restaurant as part of the complex. *Visitors:* welcome, no restrictions, a six day advance booking system applies. Tuition available. *Society Meetings:* welcome, special deals on offer that include food and golf. Professional: Gary Nelson (01695 622700). Secretary: Mark Prosser (01695 625551)
e-mail: info@beaconparkgolf.com
website: www.beaconparkgolf.com

THE APPEARANCE OF AN ASTERISK (*) AT THE END OF A CLUB OR COURSE ENTRY INDICATES THAT UP-TO-DATE INFORMATION HAS NOT BEEN SUPPLIED

UPHOLLAND. **Dean Wood Golf Club,** Lafford Lane, Upholland, Skelmersdale WN8 0QZ (01695 622219). *Location:* Exit 26 from M6 signposted for Wigan. Follow A577 to Upholland, first right after church. Wooded parkland course. 18 holes, 6137 yards. S.S.S. 70. *Green Fees:* weekdays £30.00; weekends £33.00. *Eating facilities:* daily catering available, bar. *Visitors:* welcome with reservation, not before 10.30am weekends and Bank Holidays. *Society Meetings:* catered for by prior arrangement. Professional: Stuart Danchin. Secretary: A.S. McGregor (01695 622219).
e-mail: dwgc1922secretary@freenet.co.uk

WIGAN. **Standish Court Golf Club,** Rectory Lane, Standish, Wigan WN6 0XD (Tel & Fax: 01257 425777). *Location:* one mile off M6 Junction 27, on A5209 through Standish. Undulating parkland, back nine holes through picturesque woodland. 18 holes, 4860 yards, S.S.S. 68. Large putting green. *Green Fees:* Monday and Tuesday £9.50, Wednesday through Friday £12.00, weekends and Bank Holidays £16.00. *Eating facilities:* food available all day in bistro; spike bar. *Visitors:* welcome all week, phone in advance to reserve tee times. *Society Meetings:* welcome all week by prior arrangement. Professional/General Manager: Blake Toone.
e-mail: info@standishgolf.co.uk
website: www.standishgolf.co.uk

WIGAN. **Wigan Golf Club,** Arley Hall Haigh, Wigan WN1 2UH (01257 421360). Location: M6 Exit 27, two miles on B5329, east of Standish. Parkland. 18 holes, 6026 yards. Par 70. Green Fees: £30.00. Eating facilities: meals and bar snacks available. *Visitors*: welcome anytime except Tuesdays, Saturdays and Sundays. Society Meetings: catered for on Wednesdays, Thursdays and Fridays. Secretary: E. Walmsley.
e-mail: info@wigangolfclub.co.uk

Silverdale Golf Club
Redbridge Lane, Silverdale, Lancs LA5 0SP
Tel: 01524 702074/701300
e-mail: silverdalegolfclub@ecosse.net
www.silverdalegolfclub.co.uk

The jewel in the crown of North Lancashire's golf clubs
- Centenary Year 2006 -

SILVERDALE GOLF CLUB WELCOMES VISITORS TO ITS SCENIC 18-HOLE COURSE.
♦ Licensed bar & catering facilities ♦ Golf shop ♦ Discounts for parties
♦ Membership now available ♦ Tuition available from PGA Golf Pro ♦ Many golfing competitions and social activities
Find us just off M6/A6 Junction 35, follow RSPB Leighton Moss, opposite Silverdale Station

---

FHG

FHG Guides publish a large range of well-known accommodation guides. We will be happy to send you details or you can use the order form at the back of this book.

·K·U·P·E·R·A·R·D·

Leicestershire & Rutland

ASHBY DE LA ZOUCH. **Willesley Park Golf Club,** Measham Road, Ashby de la Zouch LE65 2PF (01530 411532). *Location:* on B5006 towards Tamworth, one mile from centre of Ashby. Wooded parkland, semi-heathland. 18 holes, 6304 yards. S.S.S. 70. *Green Fees:* weekdays £30.00, weekends £35.00. *Eating facilities:* dining room and bar, no catering Mondays. *Visitors:* welcome with reservation. *Society Meetings:* catered for Wednesday, Thursday and Friday. Professional: B.J. Hill (01530 414820). Secretary: A.M. Sanders (01530 414596).

BIRSTALL. **Birstall Golf Club,** Station Road, Birstall LE4 3BB (0116 267 4322). *Location:* three miles north of Leicester on A6, adjacent to Great Central Steam Railway. Parkland. 18 holes, 6213 yards. S.S.S. 70. Practice ground. *Green Fees:* £30.00 per round; £35.00 per day (weekdays). *Eating facilities:* bar, diningroom. *Visitors:* welcome Mondays, Wednesdays and Fridays. *Society Meetings:* minimum 15, catered for by prior arrangement from £25.00 per person. Professional: D. Clark (0116 267 5245). Secretary: Mrs S.E. Chilton (0116 267 4322).

BLABY. **Blaby Golf Centre,** Lutterworth Road, Blaby LE8 4DP (0116 278 4804). Flat parkland. 9 holes, S.S.S. 68, Par 4. *Green Fees:* £7.00 per 9 holes, £10.00 for 18 holes. *Eating facilities:* available. *Visitors:* welcome. 9 hole pitch and putt opening May 2005.
website: www.blabygolfcourse.com

THE APPEARANCE OF AN ASTERISK (*) AT THE END OF A CLUB OR COURSE ENTRY INDICATES THAT UP-TO-DATE INFORMATION HAS NOT BEEN SUPPLIED

BOTCHESTON. **Forest Hill Golf Club,** Markfield Lane, Near Botcheston LE9 9FJ (01455 824800; Fax: 01455 828522). *Location:* M1 junction 22, take Leicester exit on A50, at first roundabout turn right towards Desford, golf course 3 miles on left. Parkland course with trees, easy walking. 18 holes, 6126 yards. S.S.S. 69, Par 71. Floodlit driving range. *Green Fees:* please telephone for details. *Eating facilities:* available. *Visitors:* welcome Monday to Thursday. Professional tuition available. Conference facilities. *Society Meetings:* welcome by prior arrangement Monday to Thursday. Professional: Glyn Quilter (01455 824800). Secretary: Gerry Hyde (01455 824800).*
e-mail: gerry@hyde14.fsnet.co.uk

COSBY. **Cosby Golf Club,** Chapel Lane, off Broughton Road, Cosby, Leicester LE9 1RG (0116 2864759; Fax: 0116 2864484). *Location:* eight miles south of Leicester, four miles from Junction 21 M1. Undulating parkland. 18 holes, 6410 yards. S.S.S. 71. *Green Fees:* £25.00 per round, £35.00 per day. Special rates for societies over 20 in number. *Eating facilities:* bar and food available, wide range of meals by arrangement. *Visitors:* most welcome before 4pm weekdays. Handicap Certificates may be required for all visitors. *Society Meetings:* welcome, prior booking essential. Professional: Martin Wing (0116 2848275). Secretary: D. Jones (0116 2864759; Fax: 0116 864484).
e-mail: secretary@cosby-golf-club.co.uk
website: www.cosby-golf-club.co.uk

EAST GOSCOTE. **Beedles Lake Golf Centre,** 170 Broome Lane, East Goscote LE7 3WQ (0116 2607086). *Location:* off A46 just north of Leicester, through village of Ratcliffe on the Wreake. Fairly flat course in river valley, adjoining lake. 18 holes, 6732 yards, 6156 metres. S.S.S. 72. 17 bay floodlit driving range. *Green Fees:* weekdays £13.00, weekends £18.00. Twilight fees £11.00. *Eating facilities:* restaurant and bar available. *Visitors:* always very welcome. *Society Meetings:* welcome but with restricted tee-times at weekends. Steward: (0116 260 7086). Professional: Sean Byrne (0116 260 6759). Manager: Ian Needham (0116 260 4414).

• Private Members' Club with attractive 18-Hole Parkland Course.
• Welcomes Society Bookings and Visitors. • Full catering facilities.
• Fully stocked Professional Shop with all leading brands available.
• Lessons anytime. • 24-hour repair service. • Clubhouse/Secretary: 0116 286 4759
• Professional/shop: 0116 284 8275 • Fax: 0116 286 4484
• E-mail: secretary@cosby-golf-club.co.uk • Website: www.cosby-golf-club.co.uk

COSBY GOLF CLUB
**Chapel Lane, off Broughton Road
Cosby, Leicester LE9 1RG**

ENDERBY. **Enderby Golf Course,** Mill Lane, Enderby (0116 2849388) *Location:* two miles from M1/M69 Junction 21 roundabout. Gently undulating course with lakes and ditches. 9 holes. 2856/5712 yards. S.S.S. 61. Par 36/72. *Green Fees:* weekdays £6.30/£7.80; weekend £7.80/£10.00. *Eating facilities*: two bars, restaurants, open 9.30am to 10.30pm. *Visitors*: welcome at all times, no booking required. Leisure centre, bowls, squash, badminton, sauna, solarium, fitness suite, etc. Professional/Secretary: Chris d'Araujo.

HINCKLEY. **Hinckley Golf Club,** Leicester Road, Hinckley LE10 3DR (01455 615124; Fax: 01455 890841). *Location:* situated one mile from Hinckley, just off Hinckley's A47 perimeter road. Parkland with lakeside features. 18 holes, 6517 yards, 5959 metres. S.S.S. 71. Practice area for members. *Green Fees:* weekdays £30.00 per round, £40.00 per day; weekends with a member only. *Eating facilities:* bar meals daily except Sundays. *Visitors:* welcome except Tuesdays and weekends. *Society Meetings:* Mondays and Wednesdays by appointment. Professional: R. Jones (01455 615014). Finance and Administration Manager: Y. Watts (01455 615124).

KIRBY MUXLOE. **Kirby Muxloe Golf Club,** Station Road, Kirby Muxloe LE9 2EP (0116 2393457). *Location:* Junction 21a M1, just off A47 heading to Hinckley, towards Kirby Muxloe village. Parkland, fourth tee is set outside the course. 18 holes, 6351 yards. S.S.S. 71. Driving range, practice area and tuition from Professional. *Green Fees:* information not available. *Eating facilities:* full restaurant and bar. *Visitors:* welcome weekdays except Tuesdays and Thursday 12 noon to 2pm. Advisable to phone in advance. Snooker room. *Society Meetings:* by arrangement with Manager. Professional: Mr B. Whipham (Tel & Fax: 0116 2392813). Club Manager: Mr B. Woodcock (Tel & Fax: 0116 2393457).*

THE APPEARANCE OF AN ASTERISK (*) AT THE END OF A CLUB OR COURSE ENTRY INDICATES THAT UP-TO-DATE INFORMATION HAS NOT BEEN SUPPLIED

LEICESTER. **Humberstone Heights Golf Club,** Gipsy Lane, Leicester LE5 0TB (0116 276 1905). *Location:* A563 ring road, Uppingham side of Leicester. Parkland. 18 holes, 6343 yards. S.S.S. 70. 30 bay driving range, 9 hole pitch and putt course. *Green Fees:* weekdays £13.00 per round; weekends £16.00. 9 holes £10.00, Twilight £13.00, Juniors £5.00. Subject to review. *Eating facilities:* bar, snacks; clubhouse closed Mondays. *Visitors:* welcome (Municipal Golf Course). Green Fee ticket gains entry to Clubhouse. *Society Meetings:* welcome. Professional: P. Highfield (0116 229 5570). Secretary: Brian Tuttle (0116 276 3680).

LEICESTER. **Kibworth Golf Club,** Weir Road, Kibworth Beauchamp, Leicester LE8 0LP (0116 2796172). *Location:* A6, four miles Market Harborough, 12 miles Leicester. Flat wooded course. 18 holes, 6354 yards. S.S.S. 71. 8 bay golf range. *Green Fees:* information not available. *Eating facilities:* Contact Catering (0116 2796560). *Visitors:* welcome, Handicap Certificate required or introduction from club member. *Society Meetings:* welcome, prior booking essential; reductions for large societies. Professional: Bob Larratt (0116 2792283). Secretary: J. Noble (0116 2792301; Fax: 0116 2796434).
e-mail: secretary@kibworthgolfclub.freeserve.co.uk

LEICESTER. **The Leicestershire Golf Club,** Evington Lane, Leicester LE5 6DJ (Tel & Fax: 0116 2738825). *Location:* Evington Village, two miles from city centre off A6 road. Parkland. 18 holes, 6329 yards. S.S.S. 71. Practice area. *Green Fees:* information not available. *Eating facilities:* available. *Visitors:* welcome but not normally weekends or Tuesdays. Handicap Certificate required. *Society Meetings:* welcome. Professional: D. Jones (Tel & Fax: 0116 2736730) Secretary: C.R. Chapman (0116 2738825; Fax: 0116 2498799).
e-mail: secretary@thelgc.co.uk

LEICESTER. **Scraptoft Golf Club,** Beeby Road, Scraptoft, Leicester LE7 9SJ (0116 241 9000). *Location:* off A47 Scraptoft. Undulating. 18 holes, 6235 yards. S.S.S. 70. *Green Fees:* information not available. *Eating facilities:* full restaurant service seven days a week from April to October. *Visitors:* welcome, proof of Handicap required. *Society Meetings:* catered for on application weekdays only (contact Secretary). Professional: Simon Wood (0116 2419138).*

Forget "Par for the Course" - Go First Class!

• Centrally located, within a few miles of the M69, M1 and M6. • Extensive supervised car parking. • Competitively priced. • Flexibility, with packages to suit all requirements.

Hinckley Golf Club

Leicester Road, Hinckley LE10 3DR Tel: 01455 615124 • Fax: 01455 890841
Club Professional: Richard Jones 01455 615014
E-mail: rjones@hinckleygolfclub.com • Website: www.hinckleygolfclub.com

THE GOLF GUIDE 2006   ENGLAND / Leicestershire & Rutland 241

LEICESTER. **Western Park Golf Club,** Scudamore Road, Braunstone Frith, Leicester LE3 1UQ. *Location:* four miles west of Junction 21 (M1) and M69. Flat, wooded course. 18 holes, 6518 yards. S.S.S. 71. Practice area. *Green Fees:* currently being reviewed. *Eating facilities:* full catering facilities. *Visitors:* welcome, book weekends - Tuesdays at 8am for Saturdays and Wednesdays at 8am for Sundays. Indoor school; carts for hire. *Society Meetings:* all welcome, contact Professional. Professional: Mr Dave Butler (01162 995566; Fax: 01162 995567). Secretary: Lee Preston (0116 291 3644).

LEICESTER. **Whetstone Golf Club and Driving Range,** Cambridge Road, Cosby LE9 5SH (Tel & Fax: 0116 286 1424). *Location:* 10 minutes off Junction 21 M1, between Cosby and Whetstone. Flat parkland. 18 holes, 5795 yards. S.S.S. 68. Driving range, putting green. *Green Fees:* information not available. *Eating facilities:* bar/lounge serving full range of meals. Smart casual dress please. *Visitors:* Handicap not required. Welcome by prior arrangement. Dress code to be observed. *Society Meetings:* welcome by prior arrangement. Professional: D. Raitt. Secretary: J. Fisher.*

LOUGHBOROUGH. **Charnwood Forest Golf Club,** Breakback Road, Woodhouse Eaves, Near Loughborough LE12 8TA (01509 890259; Fax: 01509 890925). *Location:* A6 to B591 or M1 Junction 23 - A512 - Snells Nook Lane. Heather, gorse and bracken - no bunkers. Oldest golf club in Leicestershire played around volcanic rocks. 9 holes, 5960 yards. S.S.S. 69. *Green Fees:* weekdays £23.00 per 18 holes, £28.00 per day; weekends £28.00 per 18 holes. *Eating facilities:* full catering. *Visitors:* welcome Wednesdays and Thursdays, Mondays and Fridays by special arrangement, not Tuesdays (Ladies' Day). *Society Meetings:* welcome by prior arrangement on Wednesdays, Thursdays and Fridays only. Secretary: Mr A. Flamson (01509 890259).
e-mail: secretary@charnwoodforestgc.co.uk
website: www.charnwoodforestgc.co.uk

LOUGHBOROUGH. **Longcliffe Golf Club,** Snell's Nook Lane, Nanpantan, Loughborough LE11 3YA (01509 239129; Fax: 01509 216321). *Location:* M1 Junction 23 – A512 Loughborough, first right, Snells Nook Lane. Wooded heathland, EGU Championship course. 18 holes, 6672 yards. S.S.S. 73. Practice ground. *Green Fees:* weekdays £30.00 per round, £40.00 per day. *Eating facilities:* bar and restaurant. *Visitors:* welcome weekdays and weekends. Handicap Certificate required. *Society Meetings:* welcome by arrangement Mondays, Tuesdays, Wednesdays, Thursdays and Fridays. Professional: D.C. Mee (01509 231450). Secretary: Mrs E. Mackenzie (01509 239129; Fax: 01509 216321).
e-mail: longcliffe@btconnect.com
website: www.longcliffegolf.co.uk

LOUGHBOROUGH. **Park Hill Golf Club,** Park Hill, Seagrave, Loughborough LE12 7NG (01509 815454; Fax: 01509 816062). *Location:* 5 miles from J21a of M1 northbound. Just off the A46 northbound. Undulating parkland course with rolling tree-lined fairways and excellent views – the closing hole is a challenging par 5 with water protecting both sides of the green. Excellent playing conditions all year round! 18 holes, 7219 yards. S.S.S. 74. Large practice area and putting green. 20 bay fully covered floodlit driving range, including grass bays. *Green Fees:* weekdays £25.00, with a member £14.00; weekends and Bank Holidays £30.00, with a member £16.00. Seniors (55 years and over) Monday to Wednesday. Students half price. weekdays and weekends. *Eating facilities:* lunch/dinner/ bar snacks, fully licensed bar. *Visitors:* welcome at all times Monday to Friday, after 9am at weekends. Conference room for up to 120 people (function room). *Society Meetings:* all welcome by prior arrangement. Special rates for societies over 12 people. Professional: Matt Ulyett (01509 815775; Fax: 01509 816062). Secretary: Jonathan Hutson (01509 815454; Fax: 01509 816062).
e-mail: mail@parkhillgolf.co.uk
website: www.parkhillgolf.co.uk

LUTTERWORTH. **Lutterworth Golf Club,** Rugby Road, Lutterworth LE17 4HN. *Location:* Junction 20 M1; Junction 1 M6. Parkland course. 18 holes, 6226 yards. S.S.S. 70. Practice area, computerised indoor teaching academy. *Green Fees:* £22.00 per round, £30.00 per day. *Eating facilities:* catering available and bar facilities. *Visitors:* welcome all day Monday to Thursday, and Friday till noon. *Society Meetings:* welcome Monday to Thursday all day, and Friday mornings. Secretary: John Faulks (01455 552532). Professional: Roland Tisdall (01455 557199). Bar/Catering (01455 557141).

LUTTERWORTH near. **Ullesthorpe Court Golf Club,** Frolesworth Road, Ullesthorpe, Near Lutterworth LE17 5BZ. *Location:* 10 minutes M1, M6, M69, A5; near Lutterworth between Leicester and Coventry. Open parkland course, with interesting greens, a fair test for all abilities; lakes on three holes. 18 holes, 6662 yards. S.S.S. 72. *Green Fees:* information not available. *Eating facilities:* à la carte restaurant, bar meals, club bar. *Visitors:* welcome weekdays, except Bank Holidays, and must book in advance. Hotel with 38 en suite bedrooms and full leisure centre. *Society Meetings:* five packages available, bookable in advance. Tel: Golf Office 01455 209023. Professional: David Bowring (01455 209150; Fax: 01455 202537).*
e-mail: bookings@ullesthorpecourt.co.uk

MARKET HARBOROUGH. **Market Harborough Golf Club,** Great Oxendon Road, Market Harborough LE16 9HB (01858 463684). *Location:* one mile south of Market Harborough on A508. Parkland. An excellent testing course, lovely views and lakes a feature of the course. 18 holes, 6070 yards. S.S.S. 69. Practice ground. *Green Fees:* information not available. *Eating facilities:* bar snacks and full meals available. *Visitors:* welcome weekdays; weekends only with a member. *Society Meetings:* welcome on application. Professional: F. Baxter. Secretary: Mr A.P. Price-Jones (01858 525688).*

www.uk-golfguide.com

242 Leicestershire & Rutland / ENGLAND   THE GOLF GUIDE 2006

MELTON MOWBRAY. **Melton Mowbray Golf Club,** Waltham Road, Thorpe Arnold, Melton Mowbray LE14 4SD (01664 562118). *Location:* A607 road two miles north-east of Melton Mowbray. Undulating parkland, course established in 1925. A private members club. 18 holes, 6222 yards, S.S.S. 70. Practice ground. 7 bay driving range. *Green Fees:* weekdays £25.00; weekends £30.00; Juniors £5.00. *Eating facilities:* full catering and bar facilities. *Visitors:* welcome before 3pm. *Society Meetings:* by prior arrangement weekdays only. Professional: Neil Curtis (01664 569629). Office: (01664 562118). website: www.mmgc.org

MELTON MOWBRAY. **Six Hills Golf Club,** Six Hills, Melton Mowbray LE14 3PR (01509 881225). *Location:* On B676, half way between Melton Mowbray and Loughborough. Flat course. 18 holes, 5758 yards, S.S.S. 69. Practice green and ground. Driving range. *Green Fees:* £13.00 weekdays, £16.00 weekends. *Eating facilities:* Cafe style; new restaurant and bar. *Visitors:* No restrictions. Professional: James Hawley. Secretary: Mrs J. Showler.

NORTH KILWORTH. **Kilworth Springs Golf Club,** South Kilworth Road, North Kilworth LE17 6HJ (Clubhouse/office: 01858 575082; Pro-shop: 01858 575974; Fax: 01858 575078). *Location:* six miles from Junction 20, four miles M6 - A14 Junction. Links type, parkland course. 18 holes, 6718 yards. S.S.S. 72. Driving range. *Green Fees:* weekdays £13.00 9 holes, £22.00 18 holes; weekends £15.00 9 holes, £25.00 18 holes. Day rate £40.00. Special society rates for 12 people or over. *Eating facilities:* restaurant, bar, bar snacks. *Visitors:* welcome at all times subject to tee times being available. Buggies available. *Society Meetings:* welcome. Professional: Anders Mankert. Secretary: Ann Vicary.

OADBY. **Glen Gorse Golf Club,** Glen Road, Oadby LE2 4RF (0116 271 4159). *Location:* on A6, four and a half miles south of Leicester between Oadby and Great Glen. Fairly flat parkland course, some ridge and furrow. 18 holes, 6648 yards, 6079 metres. S.S.S. 72. *Green Fees:* weekdays £25.00 per round, £30.00 per day (£12.50 with member); weekends £12.50 with member only. *Eating facilities:* bar and meals/snacks. *Visitors:* welcome weekdays, weekends with members only. Snooker room. *Society Meetings:* welcome Monday to Friday by prior arrangement. Professional: Dominic Fitzpatrick (0116 271 3748). Secretary: Mrs J. James (Tel & Fax: 0116 271 4159). e-mail: secretary@gggc.co.uk
website: www.gggc.org

OADBY. **Oadby Golf Course,** Leicester Road, Oadby, Leicester LE2 4AB (0116 270 0215). *Location:* on A6 south of Leicester, one mile from City boundary, at Leicester Racecourse. Parkland. 18 holes, 6376 yards, 5827 metres. S.S.S. 70. Practice ground, coaching, driving bays. *Green Fees:* (2005) weekdays £11.00, weekends £14.00. Subject to review. *Eating facilities:* snacks always available, bar with meals on prior notice. *Visitors:* welcome, booking is advised at weekends and Bank Holidays. Please contact Professional. *Society Meetings:* welcome, bookings taken through Golf Shop (0116 270 9052).Caterers (0116 270 0215).

ROTHLEY. **Rothley Park Golf Club,** Westfield Lane, Rothley, Leicester LE7 7LH (0116 2302019). *Location:* off A6, north of Leicester. Parkland. 18 holes, 6481 yards. S.S.S. 71. *Green Fees:* £30.00 per round, £35.00 per day (mid-week). *Eating facilities:* available daily. *Visitors:* welcome except Tuesdays, weekends and Bank Holidays, must be members of recognised golf club with Handicap. *Society Meetings:* As visitors' restrictions and by prior arrangement only. Professional: Danny Spillane (Tel & Fax: 0116 2303023). Secretary: S.G. Winterton (Tel & Fax: 0116 2302809). e-mail: secretary@rothleypark.co.uk
website: www.rothleypark.com

RUTLAND. **Greetham Valley Golf and Country Club,** Wood Lane, Greetham, Near Oakham, Rutland LE15 7NP (01780 460444; Fax: 01780 460623). *Location:* one mile off A1 between Stamford and Grantham on the B668. Four miles from Rutland Water. Parkland, gently undulating with many water features. Many holes playing over natural valley. 45 holes. "The Lakes" 6736 yards, S.S.S 72; "The Valley" 5595 yards, S.S.S. 68; Academy Course 9 holes, 1263 yards, S.S.S. 27. 14 bay floodlit driving range. *Green Fees:* please contact for seasonal rates. *Eating facilities:* excellent clubhouse, lounge, bar and restaurants. *Visitors:* welcome, please phone first for tee availability. Bowls green, conference rooms, banqueting suite, pool table, quad biking, 4x4 off-roading, mud buggies, fishing and bowls. Buggies and electric trolleys for hire. Hotel with 35 en-suite bedrooms, hair, beauty and spa massage suite. *Society Meetings:* welcome except weekends and Bank Holidays. Professional: John Pengelly (01780 460666; Fax: 01780 460623). Secretary: Maggie Davidson (01780 460444; Fax: 01780 460623). e-mail: info@gvgc.co.uk
website: www.gvgc.co.uk

STAMFORD. **Luffenham Heath Golf Club,** Ketton, Stamford, Lincolnshire PE9 3UU (01780 720205). *Location:* one-and-a-half miles south-west of Ketton on A6121. Undulating heathland, in conservation area for flora and fauna. 18 holes, 6315 yards. S.S.S. 70. Practice ground. *Green Fees:* £40.00 per round, £50.00 per day. *Eating facilities:* snacks available daily, full meals by arrangement. *Visitors:* welcome, advisable to contact Secretary first. Handicap Certificate required. *Society Meetings:* by arrangement through the Secretary. Professional: Ian Burnett (Tel & Fax: 01780 720298). Secretary: John R. Ingleby (01780 720205; Fax: 01780 722146). e-mail: jringleby@theluffenhamheathgc.co.uk
website: www.luffenhamheath.co.uk

WOODHOUSE EAVES. **Lingdale Golf Club,** Joe Moore's Lane, Woodhouse Eaves, Near Loughborough LE12 8TF (01509 890035). *Location:* on B5300, Anstey – Shepshed road, three miles from Exit 23 on M1. Woodland and parkland – set in Charnwood Forest. 18 holes, 6545 yards. S.S.S. 71. Practice ground. *Green Fees:* weekdays £26.00 per round, £33.00 per day; weekends £32.00 per round, £46.00 per day. Societies £25.00 per 18 holes, £30.00 per 27/36 holes. *Eating facilities:* full catering available. *Visitors:* welcome, but please telephone first. *Society Meetings:* catered for Tuesdays to Fridays. (one month's notice required). Professional: P. Sellears (01509 890684). Managing Secretary: Neil Cathill (01509 890703).

Lincolnshire

ALFORD. **Woodthorpe Hall Golf Club,** Woodthorpe, Alford LN13 0DD (01507 450294). *Location:* on the B1373, 3 miles north of Alford, 8 miles SE of Louth. Undulating parkland. 18 holes, 5140 yards. S.S.S. 65. *Green Fees:* information not available. *Eating facilities:* at Woodthorpe Country Inn on site; conference rooms also available (01507 450079). *Visitors:* welcome, unrestricted. *Society Meetings:* by prior arrangement with the Secretary. Secretary: Mrs J. Smith. (Tel & Fax: 01507 450000).*

BLANKNEY. **Blankney Golf Club,** near Metheringham, Lincoln LN4 3AZ (01526 320263; Fax: 01526 322521). *Location:* near Metheringham on B1188 Lincoln to Sleaford Road. Parkland, slightly undulating. 18 holes, 6638 yards. Par 72. Centenary Year 2004, host to Midland PGA Tournament. Practice area, putting green and snooker. *Green Fees:* weekdays £27.00; weekends £34.00. Special rates available Tuesday/Thursday. *Eating facilities:* dining room and bar meals. *Visitors:* welcome except Wednesday mornings, limited numbers at weekends. *Society Meetings:* welcome with prior booking. Professional/Club Manager: G. Bradley (01526 320202). Admin Office (01526 320263; Fax: 01526 322521). website: www.blankneygolf.co.uk

BOSTON. **Boston Golf Club,** Cowbridge, Horncastle Road, Boston PE22 7EL (01205 350589; Fax: 01205 367526). *Location:* two miles north of Boston on B1183. Look for sign to right if travelling north. Parkland with featured water. 18 holes, 6490 yards, 5930 metres. S.S.S. 71. *Green Fees:* midweek and weekends £30.00 round and day. *Eating facilities:* daily by arrangement with resident Steward (01205 352533). *Visitors:* welcome without reservation. *Society Meetings:* small groups catered for midweek. Professional: N. Hiom (01205 362306). Secretary: S.P. Shaw (Tel & Fax: 01205 350589).

BOSTON. **Boston West Golf Club,** Hubberts Bridge, Boston PE20 3QX (01205 290670; Fax: 01205 290725). *Location:* Junction of A1121 and B1392, one-and-a-half miles west of Boston. Parkland course with 25,000 trees and shrubs planted, with water in play on five holes. 18 holes, 6411 yards. S.S.S. 71. 6 hole short course, putting greens, practice bunker. 20 bay floodlit driving range. *Green Fees:* weekdays £16.00; weekends £18.00. *Eating facilities:* catering available all day in newly extended Clubhouse, with restaurant overlooking the course. *Visitors:* no restrictions but must book in advance. Lessons available from Simon Collingwood. VI Digital Coaching System available. Large discount store with custom fitting on site. *Society Meetings:* welcome at all times, including weekends. Special rates on request. Secretary: Mike Couture (01205 290670).
e-mail: info@bostonwestgolfclub.co.uk
website: www.bostonwestgolfclub.co.uk

BOSTON. **Kirton Holme Golf Club,** Holme Road, Kirton Holme, Boston PE20 1SY (01205 290669). *Location:* four miles west of Boston, signposted off A52. Flat parkland. 9 holes, 2884 yards. S.S.S. 34. Small practice area includes net. *Green Fees:* weekdays £5.50 per 9 holes, £9.00 per day; weekends and Bank Holidays £6.50 per 9 holes, £10.00 per day. *Eating facilities:* bar open 11am to dusk, snack meals available. *Visitors:* always welcome - smart dress required. *Society Meetings:* by arrangement. Secretary: T. Welberry (01205 290669).

BOURNE. **The Toft Hotel Golf Club,** Toft, Near Bourne PE10 0JT (01778 590614; Fax: 01778 590264). *Location:* in Toft village on A6121 Stamford to Bourne road. Undulating course with natural lake. 18 holes, 6486 yards. S.S.S. 71. Practice area. *Green Fees:* information not available. *Eating facilities:* bar open all day; bar snacks and restaurant. *Visitors:* welcome at all times, prior booking essential. Hotel has 22 bedrooms. *Society Meetings:* welcome, prior booking essential. Professional: Mark Jackson (01778 590616). Secretary: Robin Morris (01778 590616).*
website: www.thetofthotelgolfclub.com

BRIGG. **Elsham Golf Club,** Barton Road, Elsham, Brigg DN20 0LS (01652 680291; Fax: 01652 680308). *Location:* off M180 at J5 or A15 through Brigg to Barton. Wooded parkland course. 18 holes, 6428 yards. S.S.S. 71. Outdoor practice ground. *Green Fees:* weekdays only £25.00 for 18 holes, £33.00 for 36 holes. £12.00 with a member both during the week and at weekends. Special rates for societies of 12 or more. *Eating facilities:* full catering. *Visitors:* welcome weekdays. *Society Meetings:* catered for on weekdays. Steward (01652 688382). Professional: Stuart Brewer (01652 680432). Secretary: T. Hartley (01652 680291).
e-mail: manager@elshamgolfclub.co.uk
website: www.elshamgolfclub.co.uk

Blankney Golf Club
Blankney
Lincolnshire LN4 3AZ
Tel: 01526 320263
Fax: 01526 322521
www.blankneygolf.co.uk

Established in 1904, this superb 18 hole, Par 72 championship course is now considered to be one of the most challenging courses in Lincolnshire. Societies and visitors are welcome by prior arrangement.

244 Lincolnshire / ENGLAND   THE GOLF GUIDE 2006

BRIGG. **Forest Pines Golf Club,** The Forest Pines Hotel, Ermine Street, Broughton, Near Brigg DN20 0AQ (01652 650770; Fax: 01652 650495). *Location:* 200 yards from Junction 4 M180 towards Scunthorpe. Three 9 hole courses – Forest, Pines, Beeches. Forest/Pines Championship Course: 6882 yards, S.S.S. 73. Pines/Beeches: 6693 yards, S.S.S. 72. Forest/Beeches: 6393 yards, S.S.S. 70. Practice range, practice green, bunkers. *Green Fees:* information not available. *Eating facilities:* clubhouse. *Visitors:* welcome; telephone in advance. Compulsory 'soft spikes' or dimples, no steel spikes. All facilities of The Forest Pines Hotel, golf course and spa available - 114 bedrooms. Buggies, carts, caddies for hire; residential golf schools, leisure club (swimming, gym, sauna and jacuzzi). *Society Meetings:* welcome. Various packages available from £49.95, residential Golfing Breaks available. Professional/Director of Golf: David M. Edwards (01652 650756; Fax: 01652 650495).*

CLEETHORPES. **Cleethorpes Golf Club Ltd,** Golf House, Kings Road, Cleethorpes DN35 0PN (01472 816110). *Location:* approximately one mile south of Cleethorpes Leisure Centre. Mature coastal course, slight undulations give variation but local topography makes for easy walking. Presented to the highest standards the course provides a challenge to all level of players. 18 holes, 6349 yards. S.S.S. 70. Large and small practice areas. *Green Fees:* weekdays £20.00, £10.00 with member, weekends £25.00, £15.00 with member. Handicap Certificate required. *Eating facilities:* bar lunches, evening meals by arrangement. *Visitors:* welcome anytime except Wednesdays, but must be member of another golf club. *Society Meetings:* only by arrangement with the Secretary. Attractive packages available Monday, Thursday, Friday and Sunday. Professional: P. Davies (01472 814060). Secretary: Andrew Thompson (01472 816110).
e-mail: secretary@cleethorpesgolfclub.co.uk
website: www.cleethorpesgolfclub.co.uk

GAINSBOROUGH. **Gainsborough Golf Club,** Thonock, Gainsborough DN21 1PZ (01427 613088; Fax: 01427 810172). *Location:* signposted from A631 Gainsborough to Grimsby Road. Thonock Park Course is a parkland course with many deciduous trees, Karsten Lakes Course is a Championship Course designed by Neil Coles (opened 1.4.97). Thonock Park Course - 18 holes, 6620 yards. Par 70, S.S.S. 70. Karsten Lakes Course - 18 holes, 6724 yards. Par 72, S.S.S. 72. 20 bay floodlit driving range. *Green Fees:* Thonock Park Course - weekdays £25.00 per round, £40.00 per day, weekends with a member only; Karsten Lakes Course - £30.00 per round, £40.00 per day. *Eating facilities:* restaurant and coffee shop, two bars. *Visitors:* welcome, seven days on both courses (tee time bookings available). *Society Meetings:* welcome (booking in advance necessary). Professional: Stephen Cooper. Secretary: J.D. Bowers.

GRANTHAM. **Belton Park Golf Club,** Belton Lane, Londonthorpe Road, Grantham NG31 9SH (01476 567399; Fax: 01476 592078). *Location:* two miles from Grantham. 250 acre Deer Park adjacent to the historical Belton House. Three loops of 9 holes each beginning and ending at the clubhouse: Brownlow Course 6472 yards (Championship). S.S.S. 71. Ancaster Course 6325 yards. S.S.S. 70. Belmont Course 6075 yards. S.S.S. 69. Two large practice areas. *Green Fees:* weekdays £30.00 per round, £36.00 per day; weekends and Bank Holidays £36.00 per round, £42.00 per day. Special winter rates November to March. *Eating facilities:* full restaurant facilities every day except Mondays. *Visitors:* welcome without reservation. *Society Meetings:* catered for by arrangement weekdays only (except Tuesday). Special day package. Professional: S. Williams. General Manager: S Rowley.
e-mail: greatgolf@beltonpark.co.uk

GRANTHAM. **Stoke Rochford Golf Club,** Stoke Rochford, Near Grantham NG33 5EW (01476 530275). *Location:* five miles south of Grantham on A1. Entrance at BP petrol station. Parkland. 18 holes, 6313 yards. S.S.S. 70. Small practice ground. *Green Fees:* £24.00 per round, £33.00 per day. *Eating facilities:* meals available daily, to be booked before playing. *Visitors:* cannot commence play before 10.30am at weekends or on Public Holidays. No visitors on Sundays November, December and January. Buggies and numerous trolleys for hire. Snooker room. *Society Meetings:* by prior arrangement. Professional: A.E. Dow (01476 530218). Secretary: J.Martindale (01572 756305).

GRANTHAM. **Sudbrook Moor Golf Club,** Charity Street, Carlton Scroop, Grantham NG32 3AT (01400 250796). *Location:* A607 Lincoln to Grantham, six miles north-east of Grantham. Private course in picturesque valley; easy walking parkland/meadowland. 9 holes, 4827 yards. S.S.S. 63/64/64. Covered driving range bays. *Green Fees:* winter weekdays £7.00, winter weekend £9.00; summer weekdays £9.00, summer weekend £12.00. *Eating facilities:* Spike Bar and dining room (alcohol-free). *Visitors:* welcome by appointment. Professionals: Tim Hutton/Ben Hutton. Club Secretary: Judith M. Hutton (01400 250796). Catering: (01400 250876).

GRANTHAM near. **De Vere Belton Woods Hotel and Country Club,** Belton, Near Grantham NG32 2LN (01476 593200; Fax: 01476 574547). *Location:* three miles from Grantham, two miles from the A1. Parkland course. Belton Woods Hotel, the golfers' paradise, offers not only one but three challenges, two 18 hole courses: the Championship Course, the Lakes, 6774 yards and the Championship length the Woodside: 6834 yards and the Red Arrows a 9 hole par 3 course, 1184 yards. 20 bay floodlit driving range. *Green Fees:* information not available. *Eating facilities:* Spikes Bar, food all day choice of two restaurants and three bars in hotel. *Visitors:* welcome at all times, check in advance for availability. Accommodation in Hotel – 136 luxurious bedrooms and suites, with extensive leisure and conference facilities. Golfing Breaks and society meetings a speciality. *Society Meetings:* welcome, ring for society offers/golf breaks. Golf and Leisure Manager: Andrew Cameron. Golf Professional: Steve Sayers. Golf Sales: Rina Ozolins (01476 514308).*

THE GOLF GUIDE 2006   ENGLAND / Lincolnshire   245

GRIMSBY. **Grimsby Golf Club Ltd,** Littlecoates Road, Grimsby DN34 4LU (01472 342823). *Location:* two miles west of town centre, one mile from A180 and A46. Undulating parkland course. 18 holes, 6098 yards. S.S.S. 69. Practice ground, chipping area. *Green Fees:* information not available. *Eating facilities:* quality food available at all times and bar facilities. *Visitors:* welcome weekdays, must be members of golf clubs. *Society Meetings:* catered for Mondays and Fridays by arrangement with Secretary (Club Ladies' Day Tuesday, club ladies have priority in the afternoons). Professional: Richard Smith (01472 356981). Secretary: Mr K. Skingle (Tel & Fax: 01472 342630).

GRIMSBY. **Manor Golf Club,** Laceby Manor, Laceby, Grimsby DN37 7EA (01472 873468; Fax: 01472 871266). *Location:* A18, half a mile on left hand side from Oaklands Hotel, situated at Laceby roundabout. Parkland - tree lined fairways, many water features including green surrounded by water. 18 holes, 6343 yards. S.S.S. 70. Netted driving area, putting green, chipping area. *Green Fees:* £18.00 weekdays, £20.00 weekends. Twilight £12.00 (not feasible to complete 18 holes at this time). Subject to review. *Eating facilities:* bar, lounge bar, dining area. *Visitors:* welcome any day. Booked tee system operated all days, non-members may book up to six days in advance. *Society Meetings:* welcome by prior arrangement. Professional: Neil Lambourne (01472 873468). Secretary: Judith MacKay (01472 873469).

GRIMSBY. **Waltham Windmill Golf Club,** Cheapside, Waltham, Grimsby DN37 0HT (01472 824109). *Location:* off A16 main Louth to Grimsby road. Parkland course incorporating seven lakes. 18 holes, 6442 yards. S.S.S. 71. Practice ground. *Green Fees:* weekdays £25.00, with member £14.00; weekends £30.00, with member £20.00. Reductions for societies; minimum 12. *Eating facilities:* bar and restaurant. *Visitors:* welcome, telephone booking. *Society Meetings:* welcome, contact the Secretary. Professional: Stephen Bennett (01472 823963). Secretary: George W. Fielding (01472 824109; Fax: 01472 828391).

HORNCASTLE near. **Horncastle Golf Club,** West Ashby, Near Horncastle LN9 5PP (01507 526800). *Location:* just off A158 between Horncastle and Baumber. Parkland course - water features on 14 holes. 18 holes, 5800 yards. S.S.S. 70. *Green Fees:* information not available. *Eating facilities:* bars, restaurant. *Visitors:* welcome anytime but helpful to phone. Special package available golf range, golf course, food and drink. Ballroom and conference facilities. Accommodation available, caravan site. Carts. Fishing lakes. *Society Meetings:* please phone in advance. Professional: Alison Johns. Secretary: Chris Redfearn.

IMMINGHAM. **Immingham Golf Club,** St Andrew's Lane, Church Lane, Immingham DN40 2EU (01469 575298; Fax: 01469 577636). *Location:* two miles off A180, behind St Andrew's Church, Immingham. Undulating parkland with water hazards. Drainage dyke comes into play for over half the holes. Excellent greens. 18 holes, 6215 yards, 5682 metres. S.S.S. 70. Small practice area. *Green Fees:* weekdays £18.00 per round, £10 with member; weekends £20.00 per round; £12.00 with member. *Eating facilities:* snacks; full catering (book in advance). *Visitors:* welcome anytime except Thursday pm, Saturday pm and Sunday am. Handicap Certificate preferred. *Society Meetings:* welcome midweek during the day, limited availability at weekends. Professional: Nick Harding (01469 575493). Manager: D. McCully (01469 575298). e-mail: admin@immgc.com
website: www.immgc.com

LINCOLN. **Canwick Park Golf Club,** Canwick Park, Washingborough Road, Lincoln LN4 1EF (01522 522166). *Location*: two miles east of Lincoln on B1190. Parkland, wooded course - two testing Par 3s (5th & 13th). 18 holes, 6160 yards, 5600 metres, S.S.S. 69. Practice ground. *Green Fees:* £20.00, Special rate 10am - noon and 2pm - 4pm, £12.00. £21.00 weekends. *Eating facilities:* bar snacks and meals to order. *Visitors*: welcome weekdays; weekends after 2:30pm without a member. Locker rooms. *Society Meetings*: welcome by prior arrangement. Professional: S.J. Williamson (Tel & Fax: 01522 536870). Office Manager: M. Hooks (01522 542912; Fax: 01522 526997).
e-mail: manager@canwickpark.co.uk
website: www.canwickpark.org

LINCOLN. **Carholme Golf Club,** Carholme Road, Lincoln LN1 1SE (01522 523725). *Location:* one mile from city centre on A57 to Worksop. Flat parkland. 18 holes, 6215 yards. S.S.S. 70. *Green Fees:* £18.00 per round, £22.00 per day. *Eating facilities:* full service. *Visitors:* welcome most days subject to restrictions regarding starting times, information available on request. *Society Meetings:* by prior arrangement only. Office: Tel/Fax: 01522 533733. Secretary: J. Lammin (01522 523725).
e-mail: info@carholme-golf-club.co.uk
website: www.carholme-golf-club.co.uk

LINCOLN. **Pottergate Golf Club,** Moor Lane, Branston, Lincoln (01522 794867). *Location:* south of Lincoln on B1188 to Branston. Turn left at Moor Lodge Hotel into Moor Lane. Parkland course. 9 holes. Par 34. Indoor golf simulator with 17 golf courses and driving range. Putting green. *Green Fees:* information not available. *Eating facilities:* bar and food from 11am to 10pm (light snacks available). Food by prior arrangement. *Society Meetings:* welcome. Professional: Lee Tasker. Proprietor: Robert Mawer.*

LINCOLN. **RAF Coningsby Golf Club,** Coningsby, Lincoln LN4 4JT (01526 342581). *Location:* on the B1192 halfway between Tattershall Thorpe and Woodhall Spa, signposted RAF Woodhall. Parkland course. 9 holes (18 tees), 5354 yards, S.S.S. 66. *Green Fees:* £8.00, with member £6.00, Juniors £4.00. Day ticket £10.00, Juniors £4.00. *Visitors:* welcome weekdays except Monday am (Ladies). *Society Meetings*: welcome weekdays by appointment. Secretary: Nick Parsons (01526 347946; Fax: 01526 347413).

LINCOLN. Lincoln Golf Club, Torksey, Lincoln LN1 2EG (Tel & Fax: 01427 718721). *Location*: A156 approximately 6 miles south of Gainsborough. Mature, testing championship standard course built on sandy subsoil. 18 holes, 6438 yards. S.S.S. 71. *Green Fees:* £30.00 per round, £38.00 per day. Subject to review. Winter packages available. *Eating facilities*: full facilities available. *Visitors*: welcome anytime except Tuesday mornings (Ladies' Day). *Society Meetings*: welcome by prior arrangement (not weekends). Professional: Ashley Carter (Tel & Fax: 01427 718273). Secretary: Derek B. Linton (Tel & Fax: 01427 718721). e-mail: info@lincolngc.co.uk
website: www.lincolngc.co.uk

LINCOLN. **Welton Manor Golf Centre,** Hackthorn Road, Welton, Lincoln LN2 3PD (01673 862827). *Location:* six miles north of Lincoln. Off A46 to Welton village, through Welton, turn left at mini roundabout signposted Spridlington, entrance half-a-mile on left. Undulating parkland with streams, ponds and tree-lined fairways. 18 holes, Par 70/71. *Green Fees:* information not available. *Eating facilities:* bar and dining from 8am to 11pm. Caravan club site, fishing lake. Professional: Gary Leslie*

LOUTH. **Louth Golf Club,** 59 Crowtree Lane, Louth LN11 9LJ (01507 603681; Fax: 01507 608501). *Location:* western outskirts of Louth. Undulating parkland course in an Area of Outstanding Natural Beauty. 18 holes, 6430yards. S.S.S. 71. Practice ground, putting green. *Green Fees:* information not available. *Eating facilities:* full catering 11am to 9pm (earlier to order). *Visitors:* welcome without reservation other than notification and dress rules. Squash court. *Society Meetings:* catered for. Professional: A.J. Blundell (01507 604648). Secretary: Robert Perkins (01507 603681; Fax: 01507 608501).*
website: louthgolfclub.com

LOUTH. **Kenwick Park Golf Club,** Kenwick Park, Louth LN11 8NY (01507 605134; Fax: 01507 606556). *Location:* one mile south of Louth. Undulating parkland, wooded course. 18 holes, 6815 yards. S.S.S. 73. Driving range, teaching facilities. *Green Fees:* information not available. *Eating facilities:* contact 01507 608210. *Visitors:* welcome but please telephone in advance. Buggies available. Hotel (01507 608806). *Society Meetings:* welcome, contact Secretary. Professional: Eric Sharp (Tel & Fax: 01507 607161). Secretary: Shelley Storr (01507 605134; Fax: 01507 606556).
e-mail: golfatkenwick@nascr.net
website: www.louthnet.co.uk

LOUTH. **Louth Golf Club,** 59 Crowtree Lane, Louth LN11 9LJ (01507 603681; Fax: 01507 608501). *Location:* western outskirts of Louth. Undulating parkland course in an Area of Outstanding Natural Beauty. 18 holes, 6430yards. S.S.S. 71. Practice ground, putting green. *Green Fees:* weekdays £24.00 per round, day £30.00, Sundays £30.00 per round, day £35.00. *Eating facilities:* full catering 11am to 9pm (earlier to order). *Visitors:* welcome without reservation other than notification and dress rules. Squash court. *Society Meetings:* catered for. Professional: A.J. Blundell (01507 604648). Golf Administration Manager: Lesley Elliott (01507 603681; Fax: 01507 608501). Golf Development Manager: Trevor Moody.
e-mail: enquiries@louthgolfclub.com
website: louthgolfclub.com

MABLETHORPE. **Sandilands Golf Club,** Roman Bank, Sandilands, Sutton-on-Sea LN12 2RJ (01507 441432). *Location:* A52 one mile south of Sutton-on-Sea. Seaside links adjacent to sea and sand. 18 holes, 6021 yards. S.S.S. 69. 40 acre practice area. *Green Fees:* information not available. *Eating facilities:* Bar and restaurant. *Visitors:* welcome. *Society Meetings:* welcome with reductions for numbers, catered for weekdays. Professional/Manager: Simon Sherratt. Secretary: Philip Ross (01507 441432).*

MARKET RASEN. **Market Rasen and District Golf Club,** Legsby Road, Market Rasen LN8 3DZ (01673 842319). *Location:* A46 to Market Rasen - one mile east of town. Wooded heathland course. 18 holes, 6239 yards. S.S.S. 70. Practice ground. *Green Fees:* weekdays £33.00 per day, £22.00 per round; weekends only with member. Under review for 2006. *Eating facilities:* available every day. *Visitors:* welcome weekdays with prior booking, must be members of a bona fide golf club, weekends with members only. *Society Meetings:* welcome weekdays with prior booking. Professional: A.M. Chester (01673 842416). Secretary: J.P. Smith (01673 842319).

- 6438 yards, SSS 71
- Venue for Lincolnshire Amateur Championship and Lincolnshire County Championships
- Putting green
- Large practice area
- 3-hole pitch and putt
- Golf shop

Lincoln Golf Club
TORKSEY • LINCOLN • LN1 2EG

Founded in 1891, Lincoln is a mature, testing, championship standard course built on sandy subsoil offering a variety of holes from links-style to parkland with mature trees and some water features.
We offer golfing packages in summer and winter, including a wide range of excellent snacks and meals.

**Manager: Derek B Linton Tel/Fax: 01427 718721
Pro: Ashley Carter Tel/Fax: 01427 718273.
e-mail: info@lincolngc.co.uk • website: www.lincolngc.co.uk**

See also Colour Advertisement on page 32

ENGLAND / Lincolnshire

MARKET RASEN. **Market Rasen Racecourse 9-Hole Pay and Play Course,** Legsby Road, Market Rasen LN8 3EA (01673 843434; Fax: 01673 844532). *Location:* on A631 Market Rasen to Louth road, midway between Lincoln and Grimsby. Course is in centre of picturesque National Hunt racecourse. 9 holes, 2532 yards. S.S.S. 33. *Green Fees:* information not available. *Eating facilities:* hot and cold drinks and sweet shop available April to October. *Visitors:* no restrictions. Golf course is closed on race days. *Society Meetings:* welcome on application to Secretary. Secretary: Pip Adams*

METHERINGHAM. **Martin Moor Golf Club,** Martin Road, Blankney LN4 3BE (01526 378243). *Location:* B1189 between Martin and Metheringham. Flat wooded course. 9 holes (yellow Tees), 18 tees including three Par 5s, 6132 yards. S.S.S. 69. Large practice area. *Green Fees:* 9 holes £6.50, 18 holes £9.00. (subject to review 2006.) *Eating facilities:* bar and snacks; meals available. *Visitors:* welcome. Lessons by arrangement. *Society Meetings:* welcome. Rates negotiable. Catering on request. Secretary: Mrs C. Roberts (01526 378243).

SCUNTHORPE. **Ashby Decoy Golf Club,** Burringham Road, Scunthorpe, North Lincolnshire DN17 2AB (01724 866561; Fax: 01724 271708). *Location:* leave M181 Scunthorpe South, turn right, right again, third right by ASDA Superstore. Flat wooded, parkland course. 18 holes, 6281 yards. S.S.S. 70. Large practice area. *Green Fees:* information not available. *Eating facilities:* full catering and bar available. *Visitors:* welcome weekdays only, not Tuesdays. *Society Meetings:* by arrangement weekdays, except Tuesdays. Professional: Andrew Miller (01724 868972). Secretary: Mrs J.A. Harrison (01724 866561; Fax: 01724 271708).
e-mail: ashby@eur-isp.com
website: www.ashbydecoy.co.uk

SCUNTHORPE. **Grange Park Golf Club,** Butterwick Road, Messingham, Scunthorpe DN17 3PP (01724 762945). *Location:* five miles south of Scunthorpe between Messingham and East Butterwick, four miles south of Junction 3 of M180.

New parkland course with interesting water features. 18 holes, 6146 yards. S.S.S. 69. Second 9 hole course – flat parkland course, 1300 yards. S.S.S 27. Floodlit driving range. Clubhouse offering full facilities. *Green Fees:* weekdays £15.00, weekends £17.00, Juniors 50% reduction. Memberships available. *Eating facilities:* full catering facilities available. *Visitors:* welcome at all times. Pro shop. Caravan site also available. *Society Meetings:* welcome, ring for details. Golf Professional: Jonathan Drury. Manager: Ian Cannon.

SCUNTHORPE. **Holme Hall Golf Club,** Holme Lane, Bottesford, Scunthorpe DN16 3RF (Tel & Fax: 01724 862078). *Location:* M180 Exit 4 (Scunthorpe East). Heathland with sandy subsoil. 18 holes, 6404 yards. S.S.S. 71. *Green Fees:* £25.00 per round, £35.00 per day. *Eating facilities:* full catering and restaurant facilities available. *Visitors:* welcome Monday to Friday. *Society Meetings:* society and corporate packages available by arrangement. Professional: R. McKiernan (01724 851816). Secretary/Manager: R.B. Bickley (01724 862078).
e-mail: secretary@holmehallgolf.co.uk

SCUNTHORPE. **The Lincolnshire Golf Course,** Crowle, Scunthorpe DN17 4BU (01724 711619). *Location:* M180 Junction 2, A161 to Crowle Goole, course 800 yards on left. Flat parkland. 18 holes, 6430 yards. S.S.S.70. Practice green. *Green Fees:* information not available. *Eating facilities:* bar and restaurant. *Visitors:* welcome, no restrictions. *Society Meetings:* welcome, no restrictions. Proprietor: A. York. Secretary: J. Middlehurst.*

SCUNTHORPE. **Normanby Hall Golf Club,** Normanby Park, Near Scunthorpe DN15 9HU (01724 720226). *Location:* five miles north of Scunthorpe on B1130. Follow signs for Normanby Hall Country Park. Parkland. 18 holes, 6561 yards. S.S.S. 71. Practice area. *Green Fees*: information not available. *Eating facilities*: fully licensed Clubhouse, restaurant; meals most times. *Visitors*: welcome, check times in advance with Professional. *Society Meetings*: bookings taken for weekdays. Professional: Chris Mann (01724 720226). Manager: Susan Hopkinson (01724 720588).*

THE GRANGE & LINKS HOTEL AND SANDILANDS GOLF CLUB

Our own privately owned 18 hole (Par 70, SSS 69) links golf course. Two tennis courts, 4-acre garden, gymnasium, 2 snooker tables, croquet lawn.

The Hotel is renowned for its superb cuisine in most elegant surroundings. 'Arguably the finest value we've found' *Golf Monthly*.

AA ★★★
RAC ★★★ Hotel
Dining Award Grade 1

Tel: 01507 441334
Fax: 01507 443033

Sandilands, Sutton-on-Sea, Lincs LN12 2RA
grangeandlinkshotel@btconnect.com
www.thegrangeandlinkshotel.co.uk

See also Colour Advertisement on page 31

248 Lincolnshire / ENGLAND   THE GOLF GUIDE 2006

SKEGNESS. **North Shore Hotel and Golf Club,** North Shore Road, Skegness PE25 1DN (01754 763298; Fax: 01754 761902). *Location:* north of town one mile. Part links, part parkland, challenging course situated overlooking the sea. 18 holes, 6134 yards. S.S.S. 71. Putting green. *Green Fees:* information not available. *Eating facilities:* formal restaurant, spike bar serving home cooked bar food 10am to 9 pm. Hotel accommodation on course 36 en suite bedroomed hotel. Special winter deals available. *Visitors:* welcome, prior notice required. Golf schools and instruction provided by professional; juniors welcome. *Society Meetings:* welcome, catering from between 4 and 200. Professional: John Cornelius (01754 764822). General Manager: N. Wardle*
e-mail: golf@north-shore.co.uk

SKEGNESS. **Seacroft Golf Club,** Drummond Road, Seacroft, Skegness PE25 3AU (Tel & Fax: 01754 763020). *Location:* towards Gibraltar Nature Reserve. Seaside links course. 18 holes, 6490 yards. S.S.S. 71. *Green Fees:* weekdays £35.00 per round, £45.00 per day; weekends and Bank Holidays £40.00 per round, £50.00 per day. *Eating facilities:* available all day/evenings. *Visitors:* welcome after 9.30am if members of recognised club or society, Handicap Certificate required. *Society Meetings:* societies/ company golf days and groups catered for. Professional: R. Lawie (01754 769624). Secretary: Richard England (Tel & Fax: 01754 763020).
e-mail: richard@seacroft-golfclub.co.uk
website: www.seacroft-golfclub.co.uk

SKEGNESS. **Southview Golf Club,** Southview Leisure Park, Burgh Road, Skegness PE25 2LA (01754 760589; Fax: 01754 768455). *Location:* half a mile from Skegness towards Burgh Le Marsh A158. Flat parkland. 9/18 holes, 5126 yards. S.S.S. *Green Fees:* information not available. *Eating facilities:* full bar and meals service. *Visitors:* welcome. *Society Meetings:* welcome weekdays. Golf Manager: P. Cole.

SLEAFORD. **Sleaford Golf Club,** Willoughby Road, South Rauceby, Sleaford NG34 8PL (01529 488273). *Location:* off A153, two miles west of Sleaford. Inland links-type course, fairly flat and lightly wooded. 18 holes, 6503 yards. S.S.S. 71. Practice field, 6 hole pitch and putt. *Green Fees:* weekdays £25.00 per round, £32.00 per day, £13.00 with a member, Juniors £8.00 per round or day; weekends £36.00 per round or day. Subject to review. *Eating facilities:* full catering except Mondays. Bar open seven days. *Visitors:* welcome without reservation, except winter weekends. Handicap Certificate required and must be members of a recognised club. *Society Meetings:* catered for weekdays only by prior arrangement. Professional: J.N. Wilson (01529 488644). Secretary: Ms E.N. Downey (01529 488273; Fax: 01529 488326).

SOUTH KYME. **South Kyme Golf Club,** Skinners Lane, South Kyme LN4 4AT (01526 861113; Fax: 01526 861080)). *Location:* approximately four miles off A153 road from Sleaford to Horncastle, turn right before North Kyme. Four miles off A17 from Sleaford to Boston, turn left before East Heckington. An interesting "inland links" with excellent greens all year round. 18 holes, 6482 yards White, 6122 yards Yellow, 5395 yards Red. S.S.S. White 71, Yellow 69, Red 70. 6 hole Par 3 course, practice ground. *Green Fees:* from £15.00 per round. Check for seasonal 'special offers'. Society discount for 8 players or more. Expert golf instruction available, send for brochure. *Eating facilities:* bar and restaurant. Snacks available all day. Lunch menu available. *Visitors:* no restrictions at present but advisable to check at weekends in case of competitions. *Society Meetings:* welcome with prior booking. PGA Director of Golf/Secretary: Peter Chamberlain.
e-mail: southkymegc@hotmail.com
website: www.skgc.co.uk

SPALDING. **The Spalding Golf Club,** Surfleet, Spalding PE11 4EA (01775 680234). *Location:* four miles from Spalding on A16 to Boston. Parkland course, water features on many of the holes with the drive on the second over the River Glen. 18 holes, 6433 yards. S.S.S. 71. Driving range and practice area. *Green Fees:* weekdays £25.00 per round, £30.00 per day, £12.00 with a member; weekends £30.00, £15.00 with a member. *Eating facilities:* full catering and bar facilities except Tuesdays when there is a bar and filled rolls only. *Visitors:* welcome, advisable to telephone in advance. Handicap Certificates required. *Society Meetings:* large groups on Thursdays, smaller groups of up to 16, any weekday April to October. Professional: John Spencer (01775 680474). Secretary: Barrie Walker (Tel & Fax: 01775 680988).

SPALDING. **Sutton Bridge Golf Club,** New Road, Sutton Bridge, Spalding PE12 9RQ (01406 350323). *Location:* off A17 between Long Sutton and King's Lynn, New Road leads off Sutton Bridge main street (Bridge Road), almost opposite church. Parkland course built around former Victorian dock basin. 9 holes. Small practice ground, new driving range from June 2002. *Green Fees:* April to September £20.00; October to March £15.00. £10.00 with a member. *Eating facilities:* bar and catering open Tuesday to Sunday. *Visitors:* welcome weekdays except Tuesday after 3pm, and Wednesday mornings. *Society Meetings:* welcome weekdays by arrangement; some restrictions, contact club for details. Special concessions for groups of 8 or more; package available. Professional: Antony Lowther (01406 351422). Secretary: N. E. Davis (01945 582447).

SPALDING near. **Gedney Hill Golf Course,** West Drove, Gedney Hill, Near Spalding PE12 0NT (01406 330183). *Location:* six miles from Radar Tower near Crowland, off B1073 follow signs or follow 1066 off A47. Testing interesting course, Guinness Book of Records for longest hole in Britain (671 yards). 18 holes, 5357 yards. S.S.S. 66. 10 bay driving range, practice/putting area. *Green Fees:* £8.50 per round, £15.00 per days weekdays, £13.50 per round, £22.00 per days weekends. *Eating facilities:* two bars (one casual spike bar), restaurant (80 seater). *Visitors:* welcome, no restrictions. Full snooker room/snookerette table, new restaurant conservatory. *Society Meetings:* all very welcome. Discount Golf shop: Austin Curtis (01406 330922). Secretary: R. Newns.

STAMFORD. **Burghley Park (Stamford) Golf Club,** St. Martins Without, Stamford PE9 3JX (Tel & Fax: 01780 753789). *Location:* leave A1 at roundabout on B1081 south of Stamford, club one mile on right. Flat parkland. 18 holes, 6236 yards. S.S.S. 70. *Green Fees:* weekdays £30.00, weekends as members' guests only. Half price after 5pm May to September. *Eating facilities:* restaurant and bar. *Visitors:* welcome weekdays. Handicap Certificates required. Visit Burghley House, the greatest of Elizabethan mansions. *Society Meetings:* Wednesdays and Thursdays only. Professional: Glenn Davies (Tel & Fax: 01780 762100). Secretary: Howard Mulligan (Tel & Fax: 01780 753789). e-mail: burghley.golf@lineone.net

STAMFORD. **Rutland County Golf Club,** Great Casterton, Stamford PE9 4AQ (Tel & Fax: 01780 460330). *Location:* head north on A1 from Stamford roundabout, take Pickworth turn, follow golf signs. Inland links, easy walking. 18 holes, 6401 yards. S.S.S. 71. 9 holes short course. 20 bay driving range, practice bunker, chipping green, putting green. *Green Fees:* weekdays £25.00 to £30.00 per day; weekends £30.00 to £35.00 per day. *Eating facilities:* bar meals, lounge bar, dining room. *Visitors:* welcome. *Society Meetings:* welcome on application. Professional: Fred Fearn (01780 460239). Secretary: Steve Lowe.

WOODHALL SPA. **The National Golf Centre,** Woodhall Spa LN10 6PU (01526 352511; Fax: 01526 351817). *Location:* 19 miles from Lincoln, Boston, Sleaford; 23 miles from Skegness; 50 miles from Nottingham. Hotchkin is a flat heathland course and Bracken is a flat parkland course. Hotchkin Course: 18 holes, 7080 yards. S.S.S. 75; Bracken Course: 18 holes, 6735 yards S.S.S. 74. Driving range, practice and pitch and putt course. *Green Fees:* Hotchkin – £65.00 per round, £95.00 per day; Bracken – £50.00 per round, £75.00 per day. Reduced rates for Juniors and EGU members. *Eating facilities:* clubroom with bar, dining room with all facilities. *Visitors:* welcome at all times by prior arrangement. Handicap Certificates required. *Society Meetings:* catered for if booked in advance. Director of Golf: R.A. Latham.

AA/RAC ★★★ • PETWOOD HOTEL • ETC ★★★
WOODHALL SPA, LINCOLNSHIRE LN10 6QF

After an enjoyable day's golf at the Woodhall Spa Golf Course, Petwood is the ideal setting in which to relax. A unique hotel famous for its beautiful gardens and woodland, with 5 excellent golf courses within 30 minutes drive.

Tel: 01526 352411   Website: www.petwood.co.uk   Fax: 01526 353473

WOODHALL SPA
THE NATIONAL GOLF CENTRE

Summer Green Fees
The Hotchkin
Visitor £65 · EGU Member £55
The Bracken
Visitor £50 · EGU Member £40

For further information or to make golf reservations contact:
Telephone: 01526 352511
Email: booking@englishgolfunion.org
Web: www.woodhallspagolf.com

The National Golf Centre,
The Broadway, Woodhall Spa,
Lincs LN10 6PU

THE HOME OF ENGLISH GOLF
Play the 47th best course in the world as ranked by GOLF Magazine

Greater Manchester

ALTRINCHAM. **Altrincham Golf Club,** Stockport Road, Timperley, Altrincham, Cheshire WA15 7LP (0161-928 0761). *Location:* one mile east of Altrincham on A560. Parkland. 18 holes, 6190 yards, 5659 metres. S.S.S. 69. Driving range. *Green Fees:* weekdays £10.50, weekends £14.00. *Eating facilities:* Old Hall Hotel attached to course. *Visitors:* welcome any time, book one week in advance. Public course. Professional: Scott Partington Secretary: C. Golding.

ALTRINCHAM. **Dunham Forest Golf and Country Club,** Oldfield Lane, Altrincham WA14 4TY (0161-928 2605; Fax: 0161-929 8975). *Location:* approximately 9 miles south of Manchester off A56. Wooded parkland. 18 holes, 6772 yards. S.S.S. 72. *Green Fees:* weekdays £42.50; weekends and Bank Holidays £55.00. *Eating facilities:* clubhouse restaurant and bar open daily. *Visitors:* welcome, but should telephone to check availability. *Society Meetings:* welcome by prior arrangement. Professional: I. Wrigley (0161-928 2727). Secretary: Mrs J. Burgess (0161-928 2605).

ALTRINCHAM. **Hale Golf Club,** Rappax Road, Hale, Altrincham WA15 0NU (0161-980 4225). *Location*: off Bankhall Lane near Altrincham Priory Hospital. Undulating parkland with River Bollin featuring on 3 holes. 9 hole course (played twice for a round), 5780 yards, S.S.S. 68. Practice ground. *Green Fees:* £25 per day. *Eating facilities:* by arrangement with Steward; lunches available, dinner; two bars. *Visitors:* welcome weekdays (except Thursday), weekends with a member only. Meetings: by arrangement with Hon. Secretary. Professional: Alec Bickerdike (0161-904 0835). Hon. Secretary: John Savin (0161-980 4225).

ALTRINCHAM. **The Ringway Golf Club Ltd,** Hale Road, Hale Barns, Altrincham WA15 8SW (0161-980 2630). *Location:* Junction 6, M56 then A538 signposted Hale and Altrincham, one mile. Parkland. 18 holes, 6482 yards. S.S.S. 71. Putting green, short game area and practice ground. *Green Fees:* weekdays £40.00, weekends and Bank Holidays £50.00. Subject to review. *Eating facilities:* full service except Mondays (snacks only). *Visitors:* generally not on Tuesdays, Fridays or Saturdays. *Society Meetings:* catered for by arrangement. Professional: Nick Ryan (0161-980 8432). Secretary: A. Scully (0161-980 2630; Fax: 0161-980 4414).

www.uk-golfguide.com

ASHTON-IN-MAKERFIELD. **Ashton-in-Makerfield Golf Club Ltd,** Garswood Park, Liverpool Road, Ashton-in-Makerfield, Wigan WN4 0YT (01942 727267). *Location:* M6, Junction 23 from south, Junction 24 from north. Parkland course. 18 holes, 6205 yards. S.S.S. 70. *Green Fees:* information not available. *Eating facilities:* available. *Visitors:* welcome mid-week (except Wednesday) with reservation but not before 9.45am. *Society Meetings:* catered for Mondays, Tuesdays, Thursdays and Fridays by prior appointment. Professional: P. Allan (01942 724229). Secretary: H. G. Williams (01942 719330).*

ASHTON-UNDER-LYNE. **Ashton-under-Lyne Golf Club,** Gorsey Way, Ashton-under-Lyne OL6 9HT (0161-330 1537; Fax: 0161-330 6673). *Location*: three miles from town centre, Mossley Road, left at Queens Road, right at Nook Lane, Clubhouse top of St. Christopher's Road. Wooded course. 18 holes, 6209 yards. S.S.S. 70. Practice ground. *Green Fees:* £27.00; weekends £27.00 with member only. *Eating facilities*: full catering except Mondays. *Visitors:* welcome weekdays except Wednesdays; members of recognised golf clubs welcome without reservation. *Society Meetings*: catered for on application: special daily rates. Professional: Mr Colin Boyle (0161-308 2095). Secretary: Mr A.H. Jackson.
e-mail: info@ashtongolfclub.co.uk
website: www.ashtongolfclub.co.uk

BOLTON. **Bolton Golf Club Ltd,** Lostock Park, Chorley New Road, Bolton BL6 4AJ (01204 843067). *Location:* off main road half-way between Bolton and Horwich. 18 holes, 6237 yards. S.S.S. 70. *Green Fees:* winter: (1 Nov - 4 April) £20.00, summer (5 April - 31 Oct) £25.00. Fourball £90.00. *Eating facilities:* luncheons and evening meals. *Visitors:* welcome. *Society Meetings:* catered for weekdays except Tuesdays. Professional: R. Longworth (01204 843073). Secretary: Mrs H.M. Stuart (Tel & Fax: 01204 843067)

BOLTON. **Bolton Old Links Golf Club Ltd,** Chorley Old Road, Montserrat, Bolton BL1 5SU (01204 840050). *Location:* on B6226, 400 yards north of roundabout on ring road. Championship course, moorland. 18 holes, 6469 yards. S.S.S. 71. Practice facilities, Indoor net. *Green Fees:* information not available. *Eating facilities:* available. *Visitors:* welcome except weekends. *Society Meetings:* catered for weekdays. Professional: P. Horridge (01204 843089). Secretary: Mrs J. Boardman (01204 842307).*

Ashton Under Lyne Golf Club
An enjoyable day's golf. A challenge for golfers of all abilities.
Green fees £27, weekends £27 with member only.
Visiting Societies welcome by arrangement. **Telephone: 0161 330 1537**
e-mail: info@ashtongolfclub.co.uk • www.ashtongolfclub.co.uk

BOLTON. **Breightmet Golf Club,** Red Bridge, Ainsworth, Bolton BL2 5PA (01204 527381). *Location*: leave Bolton on main road to Bury, turn left two miles on Milnthorpe road for the bridge. 9 holes, 6418 yards. S.S.S. 71. *Green Fees*: information not available. *Eating facilities*: lunches and light refreshments. *Visitors:* welcome, preliminary phone call advisable. *Society Meetings*: catered for on application. Secretary: I.D. Cooke.*

BOLTON. **Deane Golf Club,** Broadford Road, Deane, Bolton (01204 61944). *Location:* one mile east of Junction 5 of M61 towards Bolton Centre. Rolling parkland with number of small ravines to cross. 18 holes, 5652 yards, 5168 metres. S.S.S. 67. *Green Fees:* weekdays £24.00; weekends £28.00. *Eating facilities:* lunches and evening meals by arrangement. *Visitors:* welcome. *Society Meetings:* Tuesdays, Thursdays and Fridays only. Professional: David Martindale. Secretary: P. Parry (01204 651808; Fax: 01204 652047).

BOLTON. **Dunscar Golf Club Ltd,** Longworth Lane, Bromley Cross, Bolton BL7 9QY (01204 598228). *Location:* one and a half miles north of Bolton on A666. Parkland, moorland course. 18 holes, 5982 yards. S.S.S. 69. Practice ground available. *Green Fees:* weekdays £25.00, weekends £35.00. *Eating facilities:* available. *Visitors:* welcome, on Sunday by arrangement. Carts available. *Society Meetings:* catered for by arrangement with the Secretary. Professional: Gary Treadgold (01204 592992). Secretary: Alison Jennings (01204 303321). e-mail: secretary@dunscargolfclub.fsnet.co.uk

BOLTON. **Great Lever and Farnworth Golf Club Ltd,** Plodder Lane, Farnworth, Bolton BL4 0LQ (01204 656650; Fax: 01204 656137). *Location:* A666 or M61 (Junction 4), two miles from Bolton town centre. Parkland. 18 holes, 5833 yards. S.S.S. 68. Practice ground. *Green Fees:* weekdays £25.00; weekends £30.00. *Eating facilities:* restaurant and bar every day except Monday. *Visitors:* welcome, preferably by appointment. *Society Meetings:* welcome weekdays. Professional: Tony Howarth (01204 656650). Secretary: Mrs J. Ivill (Tel & Fax: 01204 656137).

BOLTON. **Harwood Golf Club,** Roading Brook Road, Harwood, Bolton BL2 4JD (01204 522878). *Location:* situated just off the B6196 three miles east of Bolton – A58 from Bury, turn right through Ainsworth village. Parkland/meadowland course. 18 holes, 5813 yards. S.S.S. 68. Par 70. Large practice area. *Green Fees:* weekdays £12.00 weekdays and weekends, without a member £20.00 weekdays only. *Eating facilities:* catering available Tuesday to Sunday (Monday by arrangement). *Visitors:* welcome weekdays only, weekends only with a member. Should be members of recognised golf club or society. Carts allowed. *Society Meetings:* welcome Monday, Tuesday, Thursday and Friday by arrangement with the Secretary. Professional: Colin Maroney (01204 362834). Secretary: Ian W. Lund (01204 524233).
e-mail: secretary@harwoodgolfclub.co.uk
website: www.harwoodgolfclub.co.uk

BOLTON. **Regent Park Golf Club Ltd,** Links Road, off Chorley New Road, Lostock, Bolton BL6 4AF (01204 495421). *Location:* midway between Bolton and Horwich, A763. Parkland, stream and ditches cross five fairways, tough par 4 to start with, out of bounds to the left;18 holes, 6217 yards. S.S.S. 69. Driving range and practice chipping to green; floodlit, automated golf driving range. *Green Fees:* £10 weekdays, £12.50 weekends and Bank Holidays. *Eating facilities:* meals/bar available. *Visitors:* welcome seven days, telephone Professional to book time slot. Buggies and club hire. *Society Meetings:* welcome every day. Book in advance. Professional: Neil Brazzel (01204 842336/495420). Secretary: K. J. Taylor (01204 652882).

BOLTON. **Turton Golf Club,** Wood End Farm, Bromley Cross, Bolton BL7 9QH (01204 852235). *Location:* three miles north of Bolton off the A666; near Last Drop Hotel, Hospital Road, Bromley Cross, Bolton. Moorland course with extensive views. 18 holes, 6124 yards. S.S.S. 69. Practice area. Buggy hire also available. *Green Fees:* weekdays £20.00 per day; weekends £25.00 per day. *Eating facilities:* to order except Mondays. *Visitors:* welcome weekdays, Sundays by arrangement, restrictions Wednesdays (Ladies' Day) 10.30am to 3.00pm. *Society Meetings:* welcome on Tuesdays to Fridays by arrangement. Secretary: M.J. McNeill (01204 852235).
e-mail: turtongolfclub@btconnect.com
website: www.turtongolfclub.com

BURY. **Bury Golf Club,** Unsworth Hall, Blackford Bridge, Bury BL9 9TJ (0161-766 4897; Fax: 0161-766 3480). *Location:* A56 between Whitefield and Bury. Semi-moorland course, tight fairways, good greens. 18 holes, 5927 yards. S.S.S. 69. Small practice area. *Green Fees:* weekdays £30.00, with a member £15.00; weekends £35.00, with a member £18.00. *Eating facilities:* restaurant and bar. *Visitors:* welcome, Tuesday is Ladies' Day. Handicap Certificate will be required prior to play. *Society Meetings:* welcome except weekends (£40.00 per person including meal). Professional: Mr G. Coope (0161-766 2213). Secretary: Mr R. Adams.

TURTON GOLF CLUB 01204 852235 / turtongolfclub.com

Wood End Farm, Chapeltown Road, Bromley Cross, Bolton BL7 9QH

Challenging mixture of moorland and parkland. 18 holes, 6124 yards, Par 70. Green Fees: April to October £24 round, £28 day; weekends & BHs £30 round, £34 day. November to March £20 round/day. Golf society packages. Places of interest list. Call Asst Sec Val Hinchley

BURY. **Greenmount Golf Club,** Greenhalgh Fold Farm, Greenmount, Bury BL8 4EH (01204 883712). *Location:* three miles north of Bury. Undulating parkland. 9 holes, 6214 yards. S.S.S. 70. *Green Fees:* £20.00, £10.00 with member. *Eating facilities:* available, clubhouse closed all day Monday. *Visitors:* welcome, weekends with members only, Tuesday – Ladies' Day. *Society Meetings:* welcome, £15.00 per player. Secretary: Martin Barron (Tel & Fax: 01204 882576).

BURY. **Lowes Park Golf Club Ltd,** Hill Top, Lowes Road, Bury BL9 6SU (0161-764 1231). *Location:* take A56 north from Bury, turn right at Sundial Inn into Lowes Road. Moorland course, exposed, easy walking. 9 holes, 6009 yards. S.S.S. 69. Small practice area. *Green Fees:* £15.00, £10.00 with member. *Eating facilities:* full catering except Mondays. *Visitors:* welcome weekdays except Wednesdays (Ladies' Day); weekends, Sunday by appointment. *Society Meetings:* catered for by appointment. Secretary: John Entwistle (0161-764 1231; Fax: 0161-763 9503).
e-mail: lowes@parkgc.fsnet.co.uk

BURY. **Pike Fold Golf Club,** Hills Lane, Unsworth, Bury BL9 8QP (0161-766 3561). *Location:* just off the Whitfield turn off on the M60. New course with an abundance of water and USA specification greens. 9 holes, 6312 yards. S.S.S. 72. *Green Fees:* weekdays £22 per round; weekends £25 per round. *Eating facilities:* restaurant and bar facilities available at all times. *Visitors:* welcome weekdays without reservation. *Society Meetings:* catered for Tuesday to Friday. Professional: Andrew Cory.

BURY. **Walmersley Golf Club,** Garretts Close, Walmersley, Bury BL9 6TE (0161-764 1429). *Location:* leave A56 approximately two miles north of Bury at Walmersley Post Office into Old Road, right at Masons Arms Inn. Moorland course. 18 holes, 5341 yards, 4872 metres. S.S.S. 67. *Green Fees:* £22.00 per day, £11.00 with a member. *Eating facilities:* lunches and evening meals served except Mondays. *Visitors:* welcome weekdays except Tuesdays 1pm to 4.30pm. *Society Meetings:* catered for weekdays. Professional: P. Thorpe (0161-763 9050). Secretary: D.L. Thomas (0161-764 7770).

DAVYHULME. **Davyhulme Park Golf Club,** Gleneagles Road, Davyhulme, Urmston M41 8SA (0161-748 2260). *Location:* one mile from M60/M62. Wooded parkland, flat course. 18 holes, 6237 yards. S.S.S. 70. *Green Fees:* variable depending on season. *Eating facilities:* lunches and dinners. *Visitors:* welcome Tuesdays and Thursdays. *Society Meetings:* catered for Tuesdays and Thursdays. Professional: Dean Butler (0161-748 3931). Secretary: G.R. Swarbrick (0161-748 2260).

DENTON. **Denton Golf Club,** Manchester Road, Denton M34 2GG (0161-336 3218; Fax: 0161-336 4751). *Location:* M60 Junction 24 to Manchester (A57), after quarter of a mile turn right at traffic lights. Parkland. 18 holes, 6443 yards, 5891 metres. S.S.S. 71. Practice area and putting green. *Green Fees:* weekdays £28.00; weekends and Bank Holidays £35.00. £15.00 with a member. *Eating facilities:* catering by arrangement. *Visitors:* welcome with Club Handicap. *Society Meetings:* catered for on Wednesday to Friday. Professional: Michael Hollingworth (0161-336 2070; Fax: 0161-336 4751). Secretary (0161-336 3218; Fax: 0161-336 4751).

DUKINFIELD. **Dukinfield Golf Club,** Lyne Edge, Yew Tree Lane, Dukinfield SK16 5DB (0161-338 2340). *Location:* six miles east of Manchester via Ashton-under-Lyne. Parkland. 18 holes, 5303 yards. S.S.S. 66. *Green Fees:* £20 visitor, £10 visitor with member. *Eating facilities:* full catering and bar facilities. *Visitors:* welcome except Wednesdays noon to 2pm and 4pm to 6pm and weekends. Times may be booked in advance by phoning Pro Shop. *Society Meetings:* catered for by prior arrangement; special package rates available. Professional: Mr David Green. Secretary: Mr Pat O'Keeffe (0161-338 5032).

ECCLES. **Worsley Golf Club,** Stableford Avenue, Monton, Eccles M30 8AP (0161-789 4202). *Location:* A580 East Lancs Road, one mile from Junction 13 M62. Parkland. 18 holes, 6200 yards. S.S.S. 70. *Green Fees:* information not available. *Eating facilities:* snacks, lunches and evening meals. *Visitors:* welcome, if past or present members of recognised golf clubs. *Society Meetings:* catered for Mondays, Wednesdays and Thursdays. Professional: Ceri Cousins. Hon. Secretary: M. Heath.

FLIXTON. **Acre Gate Golf Club,** Pennybridge Lane, Flixton, Manchester M41 3DN (0161 748 1226 (Sat/Sun). *Location:* off Flixton Road downside of Bird in the Hand public house. Flat parkland course. 18 holes, Par 64. Chipping area, putting green, practice net and bunkers. *Green Fees:* information not available. *Eating facilities:* food and drink available at clubhouse by prior arrangement. *Visitors:* course is Municipal (William Wroe Golf Course) and bookings, in advance, with Golf Shop. William Wroe Golf Course Shop/Professional: (0161-748 8680).*

HORWICH. **Horwich Golf Club,** Victoria Road, Horwich, Bolton BL6 5PH (01204 696980). *Location:* Junction 6 M61 - Chorley New Road - Victoria Road, Horwich. Tight tricky course, hilly with fast greens. 9 holes, 5286 yards, 4832 metres. S.S.S. 66. *Green Fees:* information not available. *Eating facilities:* dining and bar. *Visitors:* Wednesday Ladies' Day but tee times still available. Snooker room. *Society Meetings:* by arrangement. Professional: B. Sharrock. Secretary: R. Swift.*

HYDE. **Werneth Low Golf Club Ltd,** Werneth Low Road, Hyde, Cheshire SK14 3AF (0161-368 2503). *Location:* M67 to Hyde, through town to Gee Cross turn left to NLQC. Scenic, hilly course with excellent views, postage stamp greens, terrific test of golf. 18 holes,(7,4,7) 6550 yards. S.S.S. 70. *Green Fees:* information not available. *Eating facilities:* bar snacks daily, à la carte by arrangement. *Visitors:* welcome any time except Sunday before 4pm and Tuesday mornings and after 4pm. *Society Meetings:* catered for by prior arrangement. Professional: Tony Bacchus (0161-367 9376). Secretary: M. Gregg (0161-336 9496; Fax: 0161-320 0053).*
e-mail: mel.gregg@btinternet.com

LEIGH. Pennington Golf Club (Municipal), Pennington Golf Course, Pennington Country Park, off St Helens Road, Leigh WN7 3PA. *Location:* Junction 23 on M6 follow A580 towards Manchester, then follow signs for Pennington Flash. Flat parkland with water coursing through. 9 holes, 5516 yards. S.S.S. 68. *Green Fees:* 9 holes: weekdays £4.00, weekends and Bank Holidays £5.00. *Eating facilities:* snack facilities. *Visitors:* welcome, no restrictions. Professional: T. Kershaw (01942 682852). Secretary: Mrs A. Lythgoe (01942 741873).

LITTLEBOROUGH. **Whittaker Golf Club,** Whittaker Lane, Littleborough OL15 0LH (01706 378310). *Location:* one mile from town centre along Blackstone Edge Old Road. Moorland course. 9 holes, 5632 yards. S.S.S. 67. *Green Fees:* information not available. *Eating facilities:* bar only. *Visitors:* welcome without reservation, except Tuesday afternoons and Sundays. *Society Meetings:* weekdays and Saturdays only by prior arrangement with Secretary. Secretary: Mr S. Noblett (01706 842541).

MANCHESTER. **Blackley Golf Club,** Victoria Avenue East, Blackley, Manchester M9 7HW (0161-643 2980). *Location:* five miles north from City Centre. Parkland. 18 holes, 6217 yards, 5708 metres. S.S.S. 69. *Green Fees:* £24.00. *Eating facilities:* diningroom/bar. *Visitors:* welcome, Thursdays and weekends with member only. *Society Meetings:* catered for. Professional: Craig Gould (0161-643 3912). Secretary: Brenda Beddoes (0161-654 7770; Fax: 0161 653 8300).

MANCHESTER. **Brookdale Golf Club Ltd,** Medlock Road, Woodhouses, Failsworth, Manchester M35 9WQ (Tel & Fax: 0161-681 4534). *Location:* five miles north of Manchester. Parkland course, hilly with river running through. 18 holes, 5874 yards. S.S.S. 68. Small practice ground. *Green Fees:* information not available. *Eating facilities:* bar snacks available; evening meal by prior arrangement. *Visitors:* welcome, only with a member weekends. *Society Meetings:* welcome except Tuesdays (Ladies' Day). Package Deal £35.00 by arrangement. Professional: Tony Cuppello (0161-681 2655). Secretary: M.J. Chadwick (Tel & Fax: 0161-681 4534). website: www.brookdalegolfclub.co.uk

MANCHESTER. **Chorlton-cum-Hardy Golf Club,** Barlow Hall Road, Chorlton-cum-Hardy M21 7JX (0161-881 3139; Fax: 0161-881 4532). *Location:* near junction of A5145 and A5103 (M60) Barlow Moor Road, South Cemetery. Meadowland. 18 holes, 5980 yards. S.S.S. 69. *Green Fees:* weekdays £27.00, weekends £32.00. *Eating facilities:* catering provided 7 days a week. *Visitors:* welcome without reservation, except on Competition days, must provide proof of recognised Handicap. *Society Meetings:* catered for Thursdays and Fridays by arrangement with Secretary. Professional: D.R. Valentine (0161-881 9911). Secretary: I.R. Booth (0161-881 5830).

MANCHESTER. **Didsbury Golf Club Ltd,** Ford Lane, Northenden, Manchester M22 4NQ (0161-998 2743). *Location:* Junction 5 on M60 to Palatine Road, to Church Road, to Ford Lane. Riverside parkland. 18 holes, 6276 yards. S.S.S. 70. Good practice facilities. *Green Fees:* weekdays £28.00, weekends £32.00. 'Two for One' scheme available. *Eating facilities:* fully equipped bar and restaurant. *Visitors:* welcome 10am to 12 noon and 1.30pm to 4pm except competition times and match days. *Society Meetings:* catered for Thursdays and Fridays. Professional: P. Barber (Tel & Fax: 0161-998 2811). Manager: A.L. Watson (0161-998 9278; Fax: 0161-902 3060).
e-mail: golf@didsburygolfclub.com
website: www.didsburygolfclub.com

MANCHESTER. **Ellesmere Golf Club,** Old Clough Lane, Worsley, Manchester M28 7HZ (0161-790 2122; Fax: 0161-790 7322). *Location:* off A580 East Lancs Road, adjacent to M60 (clockwise) northbound, (eastbound) access. Wooded parkland. 18 holes, 6247 yards. S.S.S. 70. *Green Fees:* weekdays £25.00 per round, £28.00 per day; weekends £30.00 per day. *Eating facilities:* bar; catering available, with or without reservation. *Visitors:* members of recognised golf clubs welcome, but not during club competitions or Bank Holidays, contact Professional for restrictions. *Society Meetings:* catered for by appointment. Professional: Simon Wakefield (0161-790 8591). Secretary: A. Chapman (0161-799 0554).
e-mail: honsec@ellesmeregolf.fsnet.co.uk

MANCHESTER. **Fairfield Golf and Sailing Club,** "Boothdale", Booth Road, Audenshaw, Manchester M34 5GA *Location:* off A635, five miles east of Manchester. Parkland bounded in part by reservoir. 18 holes, 4956 yards. S.S.S. 68. *Green Fees:* information not available. *Eating facilities:* available. *Visitors:* welcome, restrictions Wednesdays, Thursdays and weekends. *Society Meetings:* catered for by prior arrangement mid-week. Professional: Steven Pownell (0161-370 2292). Manager: H. Jagger (0161-301 4528; Fax: 0161 301 4254).*
e-mail: manager@fairfieldgolf.co.uk

MANCHESTER. **Flixton Golf Club,** Church Road, Flixton, Urmston M41 6EP (Tel & Fax: 0161-748 2116). *Location:* five miles from Manchester on B5213. Parkland. 9 holes, 6410 yards. S.S.S. 71. *Green Fees:* £8.00 weekdays, Bank Holidays and Christmas and New Year holiday period - playing with a member. £22.00 weekdays without a member. *Eating facilities:* daily. *Visitors:* welcome, please contact Professional. Hand pulled golf carts for hire from Professional. *Society Meetings:* catered for by arrangement. Professional: I. Singleton (Tel & Fax: 0161-746 7160). Hon. Secretary: F. Baker (Tel & Fax: 0161-748 2116). Catering: (0161-749 8834).

THE APPEARANCE OF AN ASTERISK (*) AT THE END OF A CLUB OR COURSE ENTRY INDICATES THAT UP-TO-DATE INFORMATION HAS NOT BEEN SUPPLIED

254 Greater Manchester / ENGLAND   THE GOLF GUIDE 2006

MANCHESTER. **Heaton Park Golf Centre,** Middleton Road, Prestwich, Manchester M25 2SW (0161-654 9899; Fax: 0161-653 2003). *Location:* Junction 19 M60. Undulating mature parkland, J.H. Taylor designed. 18 holes, 5755 yards. S.S.S. 70. 18-hole Par 3 course. *Green Fees:* information not available. *Eating facilities:* two bars; range of meals and bar snacks. *Visitors:* welcome at all times. PlayGolf Teaching Academy, practice range, Pro Shop. *Society Meetings:* catered for; society teaching and clinics. Professional: Gary Dermott. Manager: John Mort.*

MANCHESTER. **Houldsworth Golf Club Ltd,** Houldsworth Street, Reddish, Stockport SK5 6BN (0161-442 1712). *Location:* off A6 between Manchester and Stockport, close to M60. Flat parkland with water hazards. 18 holes, 6209 yards. S.S.S. 70, Par 71. Practice area. *Green Fees:* weekdays £30.00 per day; weekends £36.00 per day. Half price with member. *Eating facilities:* bar snacks, or full restaurant service. *Visitors:* must be pre-arranged with Professional or Hon. Secretary. *Society Meetings:* Monday, Thursday and Friday, catered for on application (0161-442 1712). Professional: Steven McLean (0161-442 1714). Secretary: K. Smith (0161-442 1712).
e-mail: secretary@houldsworthgolfclub.org.uk
website: www.houldsworthgolfclub.org.uk

MANCHESTER. **Manchester Golf Club,** Hopwood Cottage, Rochdale Road, Middleton, Manchester M24 6QP (0161-643 3202; Fax: 0161-643 9174). *Location:* M62 Junction 20 to Middleton. Moorland/parkland. 18 holes, 6454 yards, 5895 metres. S.S.S. 72. Large practice ground. Driving range. *Green Fees:* weekdays £25.00 per round, £35.00 per day; weekends £45.00 per round. *Eating facilities:* two bars; restaurant booking by arrangement. *Visitors:* welcome weekdays. *Society Meetings:* parties up to 120 catered for by arrangement. Professional: B. Connor (0161-643 2638). Secretary: S. Armstead (0161-643 3202; Fax: 0161-643 9174).

MANCHESTER. **New North Manchester Golf Club Ltd,** Rhodes House, Manchester Old Road, Middleton, Manchester M24 4PE (0161-643 2941). *Location:* A576, less than one mile from Junction 19 on M60. Rolling parkland including lakes. 18 holes, 6527 yards, 5987 metres. S.S.S. 72. Large practice area. *Green Fees:* £30.00 per day. Weekends £35.00. *Eating facilities:* catering every day except Tuesdays. *Visitors:* welcome most days, please telephone for course availability. *Society Meetings:* welcome, contact Professional for details. Reductions available for societies over 12. Professional: J. Peel (0161-643 7094). Secretary: D. Parkinson (0161-643 9033; Fax: 0161-643 7775).
e-mail: secretary@nmgc.co.uk

MANCHESTER. **Northenden Golf Club,** Palatine Road, Northenden, Manchester M22 4FR (0161-998 4738; Fax: 0161-945 5592). *Location:* half a mile off Junction 2 M56, half a mile off Junction 5 M60. Parkland with plenty of trees, first six tees on bank of river. 18 holes, 6432 yards. S.S.S. 71. Practice net. *Green Fees:* available on request. *Eating facilities:* available (0161-998 4079). *Visitors:* welcome most days, preferably with reservation. Restrictions 11.30am to 1.30pm Tuesdays and Fridays. Carts available. *Society Meetings:* catered for Tuesdays and Fridays only. Professional: James Curtis (0161-945 3386; Fax: 0161-945 5592). Manager: P. Powell (0161-998 4738; Fax: 0161-945 5592). Steward: R. Singleton (0161-998 4079).

MANCHESTER. **Prestwich Golf Club,** Hilton Lane, Prestwich, Manchester M25 9XB (0161-772 0700). *Location:* 1 mile from Junction 17 of the M60 on the A6044. Parkland. 18 holes, 4757 yards. S.S.S. 64. *Green Fees:* information not available. *Eating facilities:* by arrangement. *Visitors:* welcome weekdays. *Society Meetings:* catered for weekdays, special rates for parties of 16 and over. Professional: Simon Wakefield (Tel & Fax: 0161-773 1404). Secretary: Ron Mason (0161-772 0700).
website: www.prestwichgolf.co.uk

MANCHESTER. **Stand Golf Club,** The Dales, Ashbourne Grove, Whitefield, Bury, Manchester M45 7NL (0161-766 2388). *Location:* M62 Exit 17, A56/A665 one mile. Undulating parkland with sandy subsoil, playable all year round. 18 holes, 6426 yards. S.S.S. 71. *Green Fees:* weekdays £30.00; weekends £35.00. Various Society packages; information on request. *Eating facilities:* meals served daily and bar except Mondays, order in advance. *Visitors:* welcome Monday to Friday; weekends by prior arrangement. *Society Meetings:* welcome Wednesday/Friday by prior arrangement. Professional: Mark Dance (0161-766 2214). Hon. Secretary: Trevor E. Thacker (0161-766 3197; Fax: 0161-796 3234).

MANCHESTER. **Swinton Park Golf Club,** East Lancashire Road, Swinton, Manchester M27 5LX (0161-794 1785). *Location:* on the A580 Manchester to Liverpool Road, five miles from Manchester centre. Parkland course. 18 holes. White tees 6726 yards – Yellow tees 6519 yards. Practice area. *Green Fees:* on application. *Eating facilities:* full catering facilities available. *Visitors:* welcome, please ring for details. *Society meetings:* welcome, please ring for details. Conferencing, meetings and banqueting facilities. Private hire also available Corporate golf days catered for. Professional: J. Wilson (0161-793 8077). General Manager: Barbara Wood (0161-794 0861; Fax: 0161-281 0698).

MANCHESTER. **Withington Golf Club,** 243 Palatine Road, West Didsbury, Manchester M20 2UE (0161-445 3912). *Location:* three miles from Manchester city centre, adjacent M56 and M63. Flat parkland. 18 holes, 6410 yards. S.S.S. 70. *Green Fees:* weekdays only (except Thursdays) £28.00 per round, £32.00 per day; weekends by prior arrangement only (£30.00 per round, £35.00 per day). *Eating facilities:* lunches and evening meals to order. Snacks available at all times. *Visitors:* welcome except Thursdays, and weekends which are by prior arrangement. Ring Professional for times. *Society Meetings:* catered for by arrangement with the Secretary. Professional: S. Marr (0161-445 4861). Secretary/Manager: B. Grundy (0161-445 9544).

MARPLE. **Marple Golf Club,** Barnsfold Road, Marple, Stockport SK6 7EL (0161-427 2311). *Location:* off A6 at Hawk Green sign. Parkland. 18 holes, 5565 yards. S.S.S. 67. Practice area. *Green Fees:* (including liability insurance) Mon to Fri £30.00 per day, if playing with a member £12.50. Sat, Sun and Bank Holidays £40.00 per day, £15.00 if playing with a member. *Eating facilities:* full meals available every day along with bar snacks. *Visitors:* welcome, not competition days or Tuesdays between 10am and midday or Thursdays between 11am and 3.30pm. *Society Meetings:* all welcome by arrangement with Professional. Professional: D. Myers (0161-427 1195). Secretary: R. Hough (Tel & Fax: 0161-427 2311). e-mail: marple.golfclub@virgin.net

OLDHAM. **Crompton and Royton Golf Club Ltd,** High Barn, Royton, Oldham OL2 6RW (0161-624 0986; Fax: 0161-652 4711). *Location:* near Junction 20 follow signs to Oldham/Royton. Heathland. 18 holes, 6186 yards. S.S.S. 70. Nets. *Green Fees:* information not available. *Eating facilities:* lunches and meals served, except Mondays. *Visitors:* welcome without reservation, not at weekends. *Society Meetings:* catered for by arrangement with Steward. Professional: D.A. Melling (0161-624 2154). Hon. Secretary (0161-624 0986). Steward: (0161-624 9867).*

OLDHAM. **Oldham Golf Club,** Lees New Road, Oldham OL4 5PN (0161-624 4986). *Location:* B6194 between Ashton-under-Lyne and Oldham. Moorland course. 18 holes, 5122 yards. S.S.S. 65. *Green Fees:* information not available. *Eating facilities:* full catering. *Visitors:* welcome, telephone to check for competitions, especially weekends. *Society Meetings:* catered for by prior arrangement with Secretary. Professional: R. Heginbotham (0161-626 8346). Secretary: J. Brooks (0161-624 4986).*

OLDHAM. **Saddleworth Golf Club,** Mountain Ash, Ladcastle Road, Uppermill, Near Oldham OL3 6LT (01457 873653). *Location:* five miles from Oldham – M62. A moorland course with superb views of the Pennines. 18 holes, 6118 yards. S.S.S. 69. Practice area. *Green Fees:* weekdays £25.00 per day (£10.00 per day with member), weekends and Bank Holidays £35.00 per day (£15.00 per day with member); weekends after 4.30pm with member £8.00. *Eating facilities:* snacks and meals available. *Visitors:* welcome weekdays. Ladies' Day Thursdays. Buggies available. *Society Meetings:* groups of 12 or more catered for except weekends. Professional: R.I. Johnson (01457 810412; Fax: 01457 820647). Secretary: A.E. Gleave (01457 873653).

OLDHAM. **Werneth Golf Club,** 124 Green Lane, Garden Suburb, Oldham OL8 3AZ (0161-624 1190). Semi moorland. 18 holes, 5363 yards. S.S.S. 66. Practice ground. *Green Fees:* £16.00 weekdays only. *Eating facilities:* full catering service available. *Visitors:* welcome, ring for details. *Society Meetings:* catered for, ring for details. Professional: Roy Penney (Tel & Fax: 0161-628 7136). Secretary: John Barlow.

ROCHDALE. **Castle Hawk Golf Club,** Chadwick Lane, Castleton, Rochdale OL11 3BY (01706 640841; Fax: 01706 860587). *Location:* five minutes from exit 20 M62. Parkland course. 18 holes, 2699 yards. S.S.S. 55. 9 holes, 5398 yards, S.S.S. 66. Driving range. *Green Fees:* information not available. *Eating facilities:* fully licensed bar and restaurant. *Visitors:* welcome. Trolley and equipment hire. Tuition available, fully stocked Pro shop. *Society Meetings:* welcome. Professional: Andy Duncan. Secretary: Louise Entwistle.*
e-mail: teeoff@castlehawk.co.uk
website: www.castlehawk.co.uk

HEATON PARK GOLF CENTRE

Manchester's premier public golfing facility
• 18 Hole Golf Course • Fun Par 3 Course
• Catering Service & Bar • Equipment Hire
• Function Room for Hire
Find us just off Junction 19 - M60

Tel: 0161 - 654 9899
Middleton Road, Prestwich, Manchester M25 2SW

playgolf heaton park

MANCHESTER
CITY COUNCIL

Why not take this opportunity to play **Withington Golf Club.** Enjoy our wonderful parkland course with its beautiful greens. Full catering available. Spring/Summer Society Golf Packages.

For information & bookings telephone: 0161 445 9544

Withington Golf Club, West Didsbury, Manchester M20 2UE

ROCHDALE. **Lobden Golf Club,** Whitworth, Near Rochdale OL12 8XJ (Tel & Fax: 01706 343228). *Location:* take A671 from Rochdale, turn right at Dog and Partridge Pub in Whitworth. Moorland. 9 holes, 5697 yards, 5212 metres. S.S.S. 68. *Green Fees:* weekdays £12.00; weekends £15.00, £10.00 at all times with a member. Subject to review. *Eating facilities:* by prior arrangement with Secretary. *Visitors:* welcome all week except Saturday. *Society Meetings:* catered for by arrangement. Secretary: John A. Keate (01706 345598).

ROCHDALE. **Rochdale Golf Club,** The Clubhouse, Edenfield Road, Rochdale OL11 5YR (01706 643818; Fax: 01706 861113). *Location:* three miles from M62, Junction 20, on A680. Parkland. 18 holes, 6034 yards. S.S.S. 69. Practice ground, putting green. *Green Fees:* per round or day – weekdays £22.00, £15.00 with a member; weekends £27.00, £17.00 with a member. *Eating facilities:* meals and bar snacks available. *Visitors:* welcome, please check for tee closures. *Society Meetings:* catered for by prior arrangement Mondays, and Wednesdays. Professional: A. Laverty (01706 522104). Manager: John Nolan (01706 643818).

ROCHDALE. **Springfield Park Golf Club,** Springfield Park, Bolton Road, Marland, Rochdale OL11 4RE (01706 56401 weekends only). *Location:* A58 out of Rochdale, along Bolton Road on right. Parkland. 18 holes, 5237 yards. S.S.S. 66. *Green Fees:* information not available. *Visitors:* welcome, no restrictions weekdays, booking in advance weekends. Professional: Mr D. Wills (01706 49801). Secretary: Mr J. Wallis (01706 623570).*

SALE. **Ashton-on-Mersey Golf Club,** Church Lane, Ashton-on-Mersey, Sale M33 5QQ (0161-973 3220). *Location:* M60 Junction 7; 1½ miles, off Glebelands Road. Parkland course. 9 holes, 6242 yards. S.S.S. 69. *Green Fees:* £20.50 weekdays, £10.00 with a member. *Eating facilities:* available weekdays except Mondays. *Visitors:* welcome on weekdays. Saturdays, Sundays and Bank Holidays only with member. *Society Meetings:* Thursdays. Professional: M.J. Williams (0161-962 3727). Secretary: R. Tomlinson (0161-976 4390).

SALE. **Sale Golf Club,** Sale Lodge, Golf Road, Sale M33 2XU (0161-973 1638; Fax: 0161-962 4217). *Location:* M60 Junction 6, A6144. Flat parkland course. 18 holes, 6368 yards. S.S.S. 70. Practice ground. *Green Fees:* weekdays £30.00, weekends £35.00. *Eating facilities:* catering and bar facilities 7 days. *Visitors:* welcome Mondays, Tuesdays, Wednesdays and Sundays. Carts available for hire. *Society Meetings:* welcome by arrangement with Professional. Professional: Mike Stewart (0161-973 1730). Hon. Secretary: P. Sykes (0161-973 1638; Fax: 0161-962 4217).

SALFORD. **Brackley Golf Club,** Bullows Road, Little Hulton, Worsley M38 9TR (0161-790 6076). *Location:* off Captain Fold Lane. M61 to Junction 4 onto A6, left at roundabout onto A6 (Walkden), half a mile turn left at White Lion pub. Flat parkland course. 9 holes, 3003 yards, 2747 metres. S.S.S. 69. *Green Fees:* information not available. *Visitors:* welcome anytime. *Society Meetings:* welcome. Secretary: Gary Jones (0161-790 6076).

STOCKPORT. **Bramhall Golf Club,** The Clubhouse, Ladythorn Road, Bramhall, Stockport SK7 2EY (0161-439 6092). *Location:* half-a-mile from Bramhall Railway Station off Bramhall Lane South. Parkland with views of Pennines and Lyme Park. 18 holes, 6347 yards, 5801 metres. S.S.S 70. Practice ground. *Green Fees:* information available on request. *Eating facilities:* full bar and dining facilities and bar snacks. *Visitors*: welcome except Thursdays and Competition Days. *Society Meetings*: catered for Wednesdays, minimum 30; Fridays maximum 30. Professional: R. Green (0161-439 1171; Fax: 0161-439 0789). Secretary: (0161-439 6092).

STOCKPORT. **Bramall Park Golf Club,** 20 Manor Road, Bramhall, Stockport SK7 3LY (0161-485 3119). *Location*: 10 miles south of Manchester, one mile from Cheadle Hulme. Parkland. 18 holes, 6224 yards. S.S.S. 70. *Green Fees*: weekdays £34.00; weekends and Bank Holidays £40.00. *Eating facilities:* full eating facilities except Mondays. *Visitors:* welcome, apply to Professional. *Society Meetings:* welcome, please contact Secretary's office. Professional: M. Proffitt (0161-485 2205). Secretary: C.J. Shallcross (Tel & Fax: 0161-485 7101).

STOCKPORT. **Hazel Grove Golf Club,** Buxton Road, Hazel Grove, Stockport SK7 6LU (0161-483 3217 clubhouse). *Location*: A6 to Buxton out of Hazel Grove, three miles south of Stockport. Parkland with tree-lined fairways. 18 holes, 6310 yards. S.S.S. 71. *Green Fees*: weekdays £35.00 per round; weekends and Public Holidays £40.00 per round. Subject to review. Society booking £38.00 for parties of 12 or more. *Eating facilities*: available daily. *Visitors*: welcome, ring Professional for booking of tee times. *Society Meetings*: catered for on Mondays, Thursdays and Fridays. Professional: James Hopley (0161-483 7272). Secretary: David J. Billington (0161-483 3978).

STOCKPORT. **Heaton Moor Golf Club,** Mauldeth Road, Heaton Mersey, Stockport SK4 3NX (0161-432 2134). *Location:* M56 to A34 or M60 Junction 1; near Glass Pyramid – Didsbury Road. Flat parkland course, tree lined fairways. 18 holes, 5968 yards. S.S.S. 69. Practice ground. *Green Fees:* weekdays £30.00 per day, £26.00 per round; weekends £38.00 per day, £34.00 per round; winter: £28.00 per day, £21.00 per round weekdays, £36.00 per day, £29 per round weekends. *Eating facilities:* lunches and evening meals available; bar. *Visitors:* welcome all times. Trolley hire. *Society Meetings:* catered for by arrangement. Professional: Simon Marsh (0161-432 0846). Secretary: J. Whiston (0161-432 2134).

STOCKPORT. **Mellor and Townscliffe Golf Club Ltd,** Gibb Lane, Mellor, Tarden, Stockport SK6 5NA (0161-427 9700 – Clubhouse/Steward). *Location:* seven miles south-east of Stockport off A626. Parkland with trees/moorland. 18 holes, 5925 yards. S.S.S. 69. *Green Fees:* weekdays £24.00 per day, £11.00 with a member; weekends and Bank Holidays

£32.00, with a member £13.00. *Eating facilities:* available daily except Tuesdays. *Visitors:* welcome weekdays, no casual visitors weekends. *Society Meetings:* catered for by prior arrangement. Professional: Gary R. Broadley (0161-427 5759). Secretary: G. Lee (0161-427 2208). website: www.mellorgolf.co.uk

STOCKPORT. **Reddish Vale Golf Club,** Southcliffe Road, Reddish, Stockport SK5 7EE (0161-480 2359). *Location:* one mile north east of Stockport. Varied undulating heathland course, designed by Dr Alister MacKenzie. 18 holes, 6086 yards. S.S.S. 69. *Green Fees:* information not available. *Eating facilities:* bar and catering. *Visitors:* welcome on weekdays (not 12.30-1.30pm). *Society Meetings:* catered for by arrangement, groups of eight or more. Professional: Bob Freeman (0161-480 3824). Secretary: S. Mellor. (0161-480 2359).*

STOCKPORT. **Romiley Golf Club Ltd,** Goosehouse Green, Romiley, Stockport SK6 4LJ (0161-430 2392). *Location:* B6104 off A560, signposted from Romiley village. Parkland. 18 holes, 6454 yards. S.S.S. 71. *Green Fees:* information not available. *Eating facilities:* full catering by arrangement. *Visitors:* welcome all week except Saturdays. *Society Meetings:* catered for by prior arrangement with Secretary. Professional: Lee Paul Sulliivan (0161-430 7122). Secretary: P.R. Trafford (0161-430 2392).*

STOCKPORT. **Stockport Golf Club Ltd,** Offerton Road, Offerton, Stockport, Cheshire SK2 5HL (Tel & Fax: 0161 427 8369). *Location:* one mile from lights at Hazel Grove, along Torkington Road. Parkland. 18 holes, 6326 yards. S.S.S. 71. *Green Fees:* weekdays £40.00 per round, weekends £50.00 per round. *Eating facilities:* available, excellent. *Visitors:* welcome weekdays, contact Professional at weekends. *Society Meetings:* catered for. Professional: M. Peel (0161 427 8369). Secretary: Mr D.R.G. Mitchell (0161 427 8369).

TRAFFORD. **William Wroe Municipal Golf Course,** Pennybridge Lane, off Flixton Road, Flixton, Trafford M41 5DC (0161-748 8680). Course and shop managed by Trafford Borough Council, Acre Gate Golf Club play over the course. *Location:* from M60 follow Urmston, Flixton Road to Bird i'th Hand pub. Flat parkland course. 18 holes, 4395 yards. S.S.S. 61. Driving range two miles from course. *Green Fees:* information not available. *Eating facilities:* at Bird i'th Hand Public House. *Visitors:* public course - book seven days in advance, weekend mornings some restrictions. *Society Meetings:* booking accepted in writing. Professional: Mr Scott Partington (0161-928 0761).*

WESTHOUGHTON. **Westhoughton Golf Club,** Long Island, School Street, Westhoughton, Bolton BL5 2BR (01942 811085). *Location:* four miles south west of Bolton on A58. Parkland. 18 holes, 5918 yards. S.S.S. 69. *Green Fees:* £20.00 weekdays only, except Tuesdays. *Eating facilities:* bar meals and home cooking. *Visitors:* welcome weekdays except Tuesdays. Snooker room. *Society Meetings:* welcome weekdays except Tuesdays and Saturdays, maximum 32. Secretary: B. Axon (01942 811085).

WHITEFIELD. **Whitefield Golf Club,** Higher Lane, Whitefield, Manchester M45 7EZ (0161-351 2700; Fax: 0161-351 2712). *Location:* Exit 17, off M60 then take road to Radcliffe for half a mile. 18 holes, 6063 yards. S.S.S. 69. *Green Fees:* on application. *Eating facilities:* restaurant facilities every day. *Visitors:* welcome. *Society Meetings:* catered for. Professional: P. Reeves (0161-351 2709). Secretary: Mrs M. Rothwell (0161-351 2700; Fax: 0161-351 2712). e-mail: enquiries@whitefieldgolfclub.com

WIGAN. **Gathurst Golf Club,** Miles Lane, Shevington, Wigan WN6 8EW (01257 252861). *Location:* one mile south of Junction 27 M6. Parkland course. 18 holes, 6016 yards (from men's tee). S.S.S.69. *Green Fees:* £30.00; weekends with a member only. *Eating facilities:* available bar hours daily. *Visitors:* welcome Monday, Tuesday, Thursday and Friday with reservation. *Society Meetings:* catered for by appointment with Secretary. Professional: David Clarke (01257 255882). Secretary: Mrs. I. Fyffe (01257 255235).

WIGAN. **Haigh Hall Golf Club,** Haigh Country Park, Aspull, Near Wigan WN2 1PE (01942 831107). *Location:* well signposted from M6, Junction 27 and M61, Junction 5. Balcarres 18 hole course, 6358 yards. Par 70. Crawford course 9 holes, 1446 yards. Par 28. 18 hole Himalayan putting green and golf academy practice facilities. All U.S.G.A specification greens and tees. Brand new golf complex in the superb surroundings of Haigh Country Park. *Green Fees:* information not available. *Eating facilities:* full catering available, bar facilities and function rooms in The Stables Golf & Visitor Centre. *Visitors:* welcome at all times. *Society Meetings:* welcome at all times - packages available. Professional: Ian Lee (01942 831107). Members' Secretary: William Fleetwood (01942 833337).*
e-mail: hgen@wiganmbc.gov.uk
website: www.Haighhall.net

WIGAN. **Hindley Hall Golf Club,** Hall Lane, Hindley, Wigan WN2 2SQ (01942 525020). *Location:* two miles east of Wigan, Junction 6 M61, or A58 to Ladies Lane/Hall Lane. 18 holes, 5913 yards. S.S.S. 68. *Green Fees:* information not available. *Eating facilities:* book before playing. *Visitors:* welcome without reservation if members of a recognised golf club. *Society Meetings:* catered for by arrangement with the Secretary. Professional: D. Clarke (01942 255991). Secretary: L. Hedley (01942 255131).

WORSLEY. **Marriott Worsley Park Hotel & Country Club,** Worsley Park, Worsley, Manchester (0161 975 2043). *Location:* Junction 13 off M60, follow A575 to Worsley. Challenging new parkland course. 18 holes. Par 79. *Green Fees:* information not available. *Eating facilities:* bar and dining facilities 8am to 10pm. *Visitors:* welcome. Handicap Certificate is required. *Society Meetings:* details of golf and leisure breaks on request. Conference and banqueting facilities available. Superbly equipped country club, including 20-metre pool, spa bath, sauna, steam room and health and beauty salons. Professional: David Screeton.*
website: www.marriott.com/marriot/mangs

Merseyside

BIDSTON. **Bidston Golf Club Ltd,** Bidston Link Road, Wallasey, Wirral CH44 2HR (0151-638 3412). *Location:* M53 Junction 1 (from Chester direction) turn right at roundabout, course entrance 200 yards on dual carriageway. Mixture of links and parkland. 18 holes, 6140 yards. S.S.S. 70. Practice ground and nets. *Green Fees:* information not available. *Eating facilities:* restaurant, snacks, lounge bar. *Visitors:* welcomed weekdays and weekends. *Society Meetings:* welcome weekdays and weekends. Professional: Mark Eagles (0151-638 3412). Secretary:J. Whitton.*

BIRKENHEAD. **Arrowe Park Golf Course,** Arrowe Park, Birkenhead CH49 5LW. *Location:* Mersey Tunnel into Brough Road, then Woodchurch Road, head for Arrowe Park roundabout, bear left approximately 400 yards, turn right into Arrowe Park. Flat tree-lined parkland. 18 holes, 6396 yards, 5885 metres. S.S.S. 71. 9 hole pitch and putt, putting green. *Green Fees:* information not available. *Eating facilities:* restaurant/cafe - bar. *Visitors:* welcome except weekends before noon. *Society Meetings:* by arrangement through Professional. Professional: Colin Disbury (0151-677 1527). Secretary: P. Hickey (0151-678 3296).*

BIRKENHEAD. **Prenton Golf Club,** Golf Links Road, Prenton, Birkenhead CH42 8LW (0151-609 3426). *Location:* M53 Junction 3, off A552 towards Birkenhead. Parkland course. 18 holes, 6411 yards. S.S.S. 71. *Green Fees:* prices on application. *Eating facilities:* full catering facilities available. *Visitors:* welcome, reservation advisable. *Society Meetings:* catered for Mondays, Wednesdays and Fridays. Professional: Robin Thompson (0151-608 1636). Secretary: N. Brown.

BIRKENHEAD. **The Wirral Ladies' Golf Club Ltd,** 93 Bidston Road, Oxton, Birkenhead CH43 6TS (0151-652 5797). *Location:* off the M53 Junction 1 or 3. Acid heath/gorse and heather course. 18 holes, 4948 yards (Ladies), 5182 yards (Men). S.S.S. 69 (Ladies), S.S.S. 65 (Men). Practice ground. *Green Fees:* £25.50 per round, £35.00 per day. *Eating facilities:* dining room, meals during day to order. *Visitors:* welcome weekdays; weekends after 11am Club Competitions permitting. Trolleys. *Society Meetings:* welcome weekdays only. Professional: Angus Law (0151-652 2468). Secretary: S.A. Headford (0151-652 1255; Fax: 0151-653 4323).

For full details of clubs and courses, plus convenient accommodation
www.ukgolfguide.com

BLUNDELLSANDS. **West Lancashire Golf Club,** Hall Road West, Blundellsands, Merseyside L23 8SZ (0151-924 1076; Fax: 0151-931 4448). *Location:* A565 Liverpool - Southport to Crosby, follow signs to West Lancashire Golf Club from Crosby. Links Course. 18 holes, 6767 yards. S.S.S. 73. Substantial practice ground. *Green Fees:* weekdays £60.00 per round, £75.00 per day; weekends £80.00 per round. *Eating facilities:* full bar and catering available. *Visitors:* welcome on weekdays except Tuesdays. All subject to availability. *Society Meetings:* booking in advance with Secretary. Professional: Gary Edge (0151-924 5662). Secretary: Stewart King (0151-924 1076; Fax: 0151-931 4448).
e-mail: golf@westlancashiregolf.co.uk
website: www.westlancashiregolf.co.uk

BOOTLE. **Bootle Golf Club,** 3 Dunnings Bridge Road, Bootle L30 2PP (0151-928 6196). *Location:* five miles north of Liverpool, one mile from M57 and M58. Links course. 18 holes, 6362 yards. S.S.S. 70. *Green Fees:* information not available. *Eating facilities:* full catering as required by arrangement. *Visitors:* welcome weekdays and by arrangement at weekends. *Society Meetings:* by arrangement. Professional: Alan Bradshaw (0151-928 1371). Secretary: John Morgan (07966 208972).*

BROMBOROUGH. **Bromborough Golf Club,** Raby Hall Road, Bromborough, Wirral, Merseyside CH63 0NW(0151-334 2155). *Location:* Exit 4 Wirral Motorway M53. Parkland. 18 holes, 6547 yards. S.S.S. 72. *Green Fees:* £45.00. *Eating facilities:* bar and full catering facilities. *Visitors:* welcome weekdays, but essential to ring in advance for weekends and Bank Holidays. *Society Meetings:* catered for by prior arrangement. Professional: G. Berry (0151-334 4499). Secretary: P. Mather (0151-334 2155; Fax: 0151-334 7300).

CALDY. **The Caldy Golf Club Ltd,** Links Hey Road, Caldy, Wirral CH48 1NB. *Location:* one mile south of West Kirby on the River Dee, 10 miles from Chester. Undulating heathland with cliff top, links, open aspect with views across the Dee to the North Wales hills. 18 holes, 6651 yards, 6082 metres. S.S.S. 72. Practice ground and putting green. *Green Fees:* weekdays £70.00 per round, £80.00 per day; weekends with member only. *Eating facilities:* bars and restaurant throughout the day. *Visitors:* welcome weekdays with advance booking and Handicap Certificate. Restrictions Tuesdays and Wednesdays. Jeans not allowed on course or in Clubhouse. *Society Meetings:* Thursdays by prior arrangement. Professional: Alan Gibbons (Tel & Fax: 0151-625 1818). Secretary/ Manager: G.M. Copple (0151-625 5660; Fax: 0151-625 7394).
e-mail: secretarycaldygc@btconnect.com
website: www.caldygolfclub.co.uk

ENGLAND / Merseyside

EASTHAM. **Eastham Lodge Golf Club,** 117 Ferry Road, Eastham, Wirral, Merseyside CH62 0AP (0151-327 3003). *Location:* exit Junction 5 M53 into Eastham village from A41, follow signs for Eastham Country Park. Flat pleasant parkland course with many trees. 18 holes, 5706 yards. S.S.S. 68. *Green Fees:* weekdays £23.50; weekends with a member only £12.50. *Eating facilities:* bar snacks, full restaurant (book in advance). *Visitors:* welcome weekdays, with member weekends. *Society Meetings:* welcome mainly Tuesdays, some Mondays/Fridays by special arrangement; £22.50 per day, £18.50 per round. Professional: Nick Sargent (0151-327 3008). Secretary: Mrs J.L. Lyon (0151-327 3003).

FORMBY. **Formby Golf Centre,** Moss Side, Formby L37 0AF (01704 875952). *Location*: off Formby bypass A565 (Liverpool to Southport road). 20 bay driving range, 9 hole pitch and putt. *Green Fees:* £4.00 for 18 holes (twice round). *Eating facilities:* small cafe. *Visitors:* welcome anytime. Golf shop. Professional: Michael Mawdsley. Proprietors: Mike and Caroline Mawdsley.

FORMBY. **Formby Golf Club,** Golf Road, Formby, Liverpool L37 1LQ (01704 872164). *Location:* one mile west of A565 by Freshfield Station. Seaside links, wooded. 18 holes, 6701 yards. S.S.S. 73. *Green Fees:* information not available. *Eating facilities:* available. *Visitors:* welcome by arrangement with the Secretary, except before 10am Wednesdays, 3.30pm weekends or Bank Holidays. Handicap Certificate/introduction required. "Dormy" accommodation available. *Society Meetings:* catered for Tuesdays, Thursdays and Fridays. Professional: G.H Butler (01704 873090). Secretary: (01704 872164; Fax: 01704 833028).*
e-mail: info@formbygolfclub.co.uk

FORMBY. **Formby Ladies' Golf Club,** Golf Road, Formby, Liverpool L37 1YH (01704 873493). *Location:* A565 (Southport Bypass) to Formby. Seaside links. 18 holes, 5374 yards, 4914 metres. S.S.S. 71. Practice area. *Green Fees:* information not available. *Eating facilities:* light lunches, afternoon teas. *Visitors:* by prior reservation. *Society Meetings:* catered for with prior reservation. Professional: Mr Gary Butler (01704 873090). Secretary: Mrs A. Bromley (Tel & Fax: 01704 873493).

HESWALL. **Heswall Golf Club,** Cottage Lane, Gayton, Wirral CH60 8PB (0151-342 1237). *Location:* off A540, eight miles north-west of Chester. Parkland on the banks of River Dee estuary overlooking Welsh coast and hills. 18 holes, 6556 yards, 5993 metres. S.S.S. 72. Large practice area. *Green Fees:* weekdays £50.00, weekends £60.00. *Eating facilities:* bar snacks, full meals by arrangement. *Visitors:* welcome, subject to availability. Must have accredited Handicaps. *Society Meetings:* catered for fully on Wednesdays and Fridays only. Winter packages available October/March. Professional: Alan Thompson (0151-342 7431). Secretary: (0151-342 1237).
e-mail: dawn@heswallgolfclub.com

The West Lancashire Golf Club
Hall Road West, Blundellsands L23 8SZ
founded 1873

Visitors are welcome to use the facilities of Lancashire's oldest club. This true links course has hosted numerous championships.

"Only in Britain can one sample the true flavour of seaside golf of which West Lancashire is a perfect example" **Donald Steel**

Tel: 0151 924 1076 • www.westlancashiregolf.co.uk
e-mail: sec@westlancashiregolf.co.uk

Corporate days a speciality

HOYLAKE. **Royal Liverpool Golf Club,** Meols Drive, Hoylake, Wirral, Merseyside CH47 4AL (0151-632 3101 *Location:* 10 miles southwest of Liverpool on Wirral Peninsula. Approach from M6, M56 and M53 Junction 2. Championship links. Host to The Open Championship in 2006. 18 holes, 6847 yards. S.S.S. 74. Large practice area. *Green Fees:* weekdays £100.00 per round, £150.00 per day; weekends and Public Holidays £150.00 per round, after 2pm only. Subject to review. *Eating facilities:* buffet lunch included in green fee. *Visitors:* welcome weekdays except Thursday mornings (Ladies' Day) and very limited at weekends. Proof of handicap required. Caddies available. *Society Meetings:* catered for Wednesdays and Fridays. Professional: John Heggarty (0151-632 5868). Secretary: Group Captain C.T. Moore CB (0151-632 3101).
e-mail: sec@royal-liverpool-golf.com
website: www.royal-liverpool-golf.com

HUYTON. **Bowring Municipal,** Bowring Park, Roby Road, Knowsley L36 4HD (0151-489 1901). *Location:* Junction 5, M62 signposted. 200 metres. Parkland. 18 holes, S.S.S. 73. *Green Fees:* information not available. *Eating facilities:* limited. Private club facilities on site, bar. *Visitors:* no restrictions. *Society Meetings:* bookings required.*

HUYTON. **Huyton and Prescot Golf Club Ltd,** Hurst Park, Huyton Lane, Huyton, Liverpool L36 1UA (0151-489 3948). *Location:* from M57 Junction 2 follow B5199 signposted Huyton. Parkland. 18 holes, 5779 yards. S.S.S. 68 white, 67 yellow. *Green Fees:* information not provided. *Eating facilities:* bar snacks and restaurant area 9am to 5pm; normal bar hours. *Visitors:* welcome, midweek days 9.30am to 12.00pm, 2pm to 4pm, except Tuesdays. Snooker table. *Society Meetings:* catered for Mondays, Wednesdays, Thursdays and Fridays. Summer and Winter packages available. Professional: John Fisher (0151-489 2022). Secretary: David Hughes (0151-489 3948; Fax: 0151-489 0797).

LIVERPOOL. **Allerton Park Golf Club,** Allerton Municipal Golf Course, Allerton Road, Liverpool L18 3JT (0151-428 8510). *Location:* end of M62, two miles to Allerton Road, one and a half miles along Allerton Road. Undulating parkland course. 18 holes, 5494 yards, 5023 metres. S.S.S. 67. 9 hole course 1685 metres. S.S.S. 34. *Green Fees:* information not available. *Eating facilities:* in clubhouse, (bar snacks only), licensed bar. *Visitors:* welcome anytime, booking system for all games. *Society Meetings:* welcome by prior arrangement with the Professional. Professional: Barry Large (0151-428 7490). Secretary: H. O'Neill.*

LIVERPOOL. **The Childwall Golf Club Ltd.,** Naylors Road, Gateacre, Liverpool L27 2YB (0151-487 9982). *Location:* Exit 6 M62 to Liverpool, follow Huyton A5080 to second set of traffic lights, turn left into Wheathill Road. Parkland, flat, designed by James Braid. 18 holes, 6425 yards. S.S.S. 72. Practice area. *Green Fees:* information not available. *Eating facilities:* bar, snacks and restaurant. *Visitors:* no visitors weekends and Tuesdays. *Society Meetings:* catered for on weekdays, contact the Manager. Professional: Mr N.M. Parr (0151-487 9871). Manager: Mr P. Bowen (0151-487 0654; Fax: 0151-487 0882). website: www.childwallgolfclub.co.uk

LIVERPOOL. **Dudley Golf Club,** Allerton Municipal Golf Course, Menlove Avenue, Allerton, Liverpool L18 3EE (0151-428 8510). *Location:* end of M62, then two miles on Allerton road, five miles from city centre. Wooded parkland. Two courses. (1) 18 holes, 5459 metres. S.S.S. 67. (2) 9 holes, 1685 metres. S.S.S. 34. *Green Fees:* information not available. *Eating facilities:* licensed bar, bar snacks. *Visitors:* welcome at any time, please book in advance. *Society Meetings:* welcome by advance booking. Professional: Barry Large (0151-428 1046). Secretary: Brian L. Harris (01244 661511).

LIVERPOOL. **Lee Park Golf Club,** Childwall Valley Road, Liverpool L27 3YA (0151-487 9861). *Location:* Childwall Valley Road. Parkland. 18 holes, 6074 yards. Medal tees: 5569 yards. Front tees: S.S.S. 68. Ladies' tee: 5650 yards. S.S.S. 72. *Green Fees:* information not available. *Eating facilities:* restaurant and bar snacks daily. *Visitors:* welcome anytime except between 12.15pm and 2.15pm daily (reserved for members). *Society Meetings:* catered for. Secretary: Angela Fagan (0151-487 3882).*

LIVERPOOL. **West Derby Golf Club,** Yew Tree Lane, West Derby, Liverpool L12 9HQ (0151-254 1034). Flat parkland course. 18 holes, 6277 yards. S.S.S. 70. *Green Fees:* weekdays £29.50 per round; weekends £37.00 after 2pm. *Eating facilities:* soup and sandwiches, light meals available at lunch. Evening meals by prior arrangement. *Visitors:* welcome if members of a recognised golf club. *Society Meetings:* catered for only by arrangement with Secretary. Professional: Andrew Witherup (0151-254 1034). Secretary: A.P. Milne (0151-254 1034; Fax: 0151-259 0505).

Please mention THE GOLF GUIDE when you enquire about clubs or accommodation

---

ROYAL LIVERPOOL GOLF CLUB, HOYLAKE Founded 1869
Visitors are welcome to use the full facilities of this long established Club, the home of the first Amateur Championship in 1885, venue for 10 Open Championships, and venue for the Open Championship in 2006. Hoylake offers the challenge of a magnificent Championship Links as well as the chance to experience the history of a traditional Clubhouse with its impressive displays of golfing memorabilia. Green fees on application. Full dining facilities by prior arrangement.

Meols Drive, Hoylake, Wirral CH47 4AL • Tel: 01516 323101 • e-mail: bookings@royal-liverpool-golf.com

THE GOLF GUIDE 2006 ENGLAND / Merseyside

LIVERPOOL. **Woolton Golf Club,** Doe Park, Speke Road, Woolton, Liverpool L25 7TZ (0151 486 2298). *Location:* South Liverpool, one mile from Woolton Village. Parkland, rolling terrain, excellent springy fairways affording inviting lies. 18 holes, 5747 yards. S.S.S. 68. *Green Fees:* weekdays £30.00, weekends £40.00. *Eating facilities:* bar snacks daily, evening dining by arrangement. *Visitors:* welcome; very few restrictions. *Society Meetings:* catered for by arrangement with the Secretary; various packages - information pack on request. Professional: D. Thompson (0151-486 1298). Secretary: K. Hamilton (0151-486 2298; Fax: 0151-486 1664).

MORETON. **Leasowe Golf Club,** Leasowe Road, Moreton, Wirral, Merseyside CH46 3RD (0151-677 5852; Fax: 0151-641 8519). *Location:* Exit 1 from M53, one mile towards Hoylake. Flat seaside links. 18 holes, 6263 yards, S.S.S. 71. Practice area. *Green Fees:* information not available. *Eating facilities:* dining room and bar snacks. *Visitors:* welcome anytime except Saturdays and Sunday mornings. Phone first. *Society Meetings:* available at discount, catered for except Saturdays , must book in advance. Professional: Andrew Ayre (0151-678 5460). Secretary/Manager: L. Jukes (0151-677 5852).

NEWTON-LE-WILLOWS. **Haydock Park Golf Club,** Newton Lane, Newton-le-Willows WA12 0HX (01925 228525). *Location:* off East Lancs Road (A580) and M6, three quarters of a mile from Newton-le-Willows High Street. Flat, wooded parkland course in beautiful setting. 18 holes, 6058 yards. S.S.S. 69. Large practice ground. *Green Fees:* weekdays £35.00; weekends £10.00 with member only. *Eating facilities:* restaurant and two bars. *Visitors:* welcome weekdays except Tuesdays, identification (club membership card) or letter of introduction required. *Society Meetings:* catered for by arrangement. Professional: P. Kenwright (01925 226944). Secretary: Mr S. Dale (01925 228525).

RAINHILL. **Blundells Hill Golf Club,** Blundells Lane, Rainhill L35 6NA (0151-426 9040; Fax: 0151-426 5256). *Location:* three minutes from Junction 7 of M62, course lies adjacent to eastbound M62. Built on a gently sloping hill, created from some 120 acres of parkland surroundings with wide fairways, big bunkers and large undulating greens, several ponds, ditches and a beautifully landscaped lake. 18 holes, 6256 yards. S.S.S. 71. Practice ground, putting green. *Green Fees:* information not available. *Eating facilities:* licensed bar, restaurant, snooker room, function room, Sky TV. *Visitors:* all welcome, call 0151-430 0100 to pre-book tee times. No jeans, tracksuits, tee shirts, trainers, short socks, etc. Expert tuition. *Society Meetings:* welcome, packages available; call 0151-430 9551 for brochure. Professional: Richard Burbidge (0151-430 0100). Hon. Secretary: Andy Roberts (0151-430 9551; Fax: 0151-426 5256). *

RAINHILL. **Eccleston Park Golf Club,** Rainhill Road, Rainhill, Prescot L35 4PG (0151 493 0033). *Location:* Junction 7 of M62, follow A57 towards Prescot; at traffic lights after humpback bridge, turn right into Rainhill. Gently undulating open parkland layout. 18 holes. Par 70. *Green Fees:* information not available. *Eating facilities:* bar and dining from 8am to 11pm (9am to 6pm during winter). *Visitors:* Handicap Certificate required at weekends.*
e-mail: eccleston-sales@crown-golf.co.uk

ST HELENS. **Grange Park Golf Club,** Prescot Road, St. Helens WA10 3AD (Tel & Fax: 01744 26318). *Location:* one and a half miles south west of St. Helens on A58. Wooded parkland. 18 holes, 6422 yards. S.S.S. 71. Practice area. *Green Fees:* weekdays £30.00, weekends £35.00. *Eating facilities:* full catering and bar facilities. *Visitors:* welcome anytime except Tuesdays and times are often not available at weekends/Bank Holidays; reservation through Professional recommended. *Society Meetings:* welcome except Tuesdays, Bank Holidays and weekends. Professional: Paul Roberts (01744 28785; Fax: 01744 26318). Secretary: Gavin R Brown (Tel & Fax: 01744 26318).
e-mail: secretary@grangeparkgolfclub.co.uk
website: www.grangeparkgolfclub.co.uk

ST HELENS. **Sherdley Park Municipal Golf Course and Driving Range,** Off Elton Road, Sutton, St Helens WA9 5DE (01744 813149). *Location:* Exit 7 off M62, follow St Helens Linkway to second island, turn right for 300 yards, course on left hand side. Undulating parkland course. 18 holes, 5974 yards. S.S.S. 71. Driving range. *Green Fees:* for information and bookings phone (01744 813149). *Eating facilities:* Licensed bar and Hot Putt Cafe open most times, phone Karen on (01744 815518) for more information. *Visitors/Society Meetings:* welcome mid-week and weekends (book early). Booking system operates up to six days in advance. Golf Professional: Danny Jones. Manager: Jeff Barston (01744 817967). *

For full details of clubs and courses, plus convenient accommodation
www.uk-golfguide.com

THE APPEARANCE OF AN ASTERISK (*) AT THE END OF A CLUB OR COURSE ENTRY INDICATES THAT UP-TO-DATE INFORMATION HAS NOT BEEN SUPPLIED

STUTELEA HOTEL & Leisure Club

ALEXANDRA ROAD
SOUTHPORT PR9 0NB

AA ★★★   Best Western

Close to Royal Birkdale

The hotel is set in picturesque gardens and all accommodation has bath and shower en suite. A 24-hour bar service is available and dining is a pleasure in our Global Restaurant where the menu, relaxed atmosphere and warm hospitality make any meal a special occasion. Golf clubs can be securely stored and we will endeavour to book your tee-off times.

The Leisure Club is second to none, providing a heated indoor swimming pool, jacuzzi, sauna, steam room and gymnasium.

Contact us now for your colour brochure on

01704 544220

or visit our website: www.stutelea.co.uk
e-mail: info@stutelea.co.uk

See also Colour Advertisement on page 43

SOUTHPORT. **Hesketh Golf Club,** Cockle Dicks Lane, Cambridge Road, Southport PR9 9QQ (01704 536897). *Location:* one mile north of town centre. Seaside links Championship course. 18 holes, 6655 yards. S.S.S. 72. Practice ground. *Green Fees:* weekdays £50.00 per round, £60.00 per day; weekends and Bank Holidays £60.00 per round. *Eating facilities:* bar snacks and dining room; three bars. *Visitors:* welcome by prior arrangement with Secretary. *Society Meetings:* catered for by arrangement with Secretary; special rates for parties over 12 in number. Professional: Scott Astin (01704 530050). Secretary: Martyn G. Senior (01704 536897; Fax: 01704 539250).
e-mail: secretary@heskethgolfclub.co.uk
website: www.heskethgolfclub.co.uk

SOUTHPORT. **Hillside Golf Club,** Hastings Road, Hillside, Southport PR8 2LU (01704 567169; Fax: 01704 563192). *Location:* three miles south of town centre on A565, Hillside station one mile. Championship links course. 18 holes, 6850 yards. S.S.S. 74. Practice ground. *Green Fees:* Monday to Friday £65.00 per round, £85.00 per day; Saturday and Sunday £85.00 per round (2005). *Eating facilities:* bar and restaurant. *Visitors:* welcome, book through Office. Tuesday up to 2pm Ladies' Day; no visitors Saturdays, limited Sundays. Buggies and carts for hire. *Society Meetings:* welcome with prior reservations. Professional: B. Seddon (01704 568360). Secretary: John G. Graham (01704 567169; Fax: 01704 563192).

SOUTHPORT. **Royal Birkdale Golf Club,** Waterloo Road, Birkdale, Southport PR8 2LX (01704 567920; Fax: 01704 562327). *Location:* one mile south of Southport town centre. Classic Links on the Open Championship rota. 18 holes, 6703 yards. S.S.S. 73. *Green Fees:* contact the Secretary. *Visitors:* welcome but it is essential to make prior arrangements with the Secretary's office, official golf Handicap required. *Society Meetings:* catered for, dining room facilities. Professional: Brian Hodgkinson (01704 568857). Secretary: M.C. Gilyeat (01704 567920).
e-mail: secretary@royalbirkdale.com
website: www.royalbirkdale.com

SOUTHPORT. **Southport and Ainsdale Golf Club,** Bradshaw's Lane, Off Liverpool Road, Ainsdale, Southport PR8 3LG (01704 578000; Fax: 01704 570896). *Location:* south of Southport on A565. Links course. 18 holes, 6705 yards. S.S.S. 73. *Green Fees:* weekdays £65.00 per round, £80.00 per day; weekends £80.00 per round. *Eating facilities:* full catering available. *Visitors:* welcome at all times; by arrangement at weekends. *Society Meetings:* catered for by arrangement. Professional: J. Payne (01704 577316). Secretary: Mrs C.A. Birrell (01704 578000; Fax: 01704 570896).
e-mail: secretary@sandagolfclub.co.uk
website: www.sandagolfclub.co.uk

SOUTHPORT. **Southport Municipal Golf Club,** Park Road West, Southport PR9 0JR (01704 55130). *Location:* Park Road West, north end of Promenade, near Marine Lake, Southport. Flat seaside links. 18 holes, 6139 yards. S.S.S. 70. *Green Fees:* information not available. *Eating facilities:* licensed cafe. *Visitors:* booking system operates up to seven days in advance (visitors unrestricted). *Society Meetings:* welcome, book in advance. Professional: William Fletcher (01704 35286)*

THE APPEARANCE OF AN ASTERISK (*) AT THE END OF A CLUB OR COURSE ENTRY INDICATES THAT UP-TO-DATE INFORMATION HAS NOT BEEN SUPPLIED

Metropole Hotel

Portland Street, Southport PR8 1LL
Tel: 01704 536836 • Fax: 01704 549041
e-mail: metropole.southport@btinternet.com
www.btinternet.com/~metropole.southport
AA ★★ RAC   Fully Licensed

Within five minutes of Royal Birkdale and four championship courses. Fully licensed, privately owned family hotel run by golfing proprietors who can make golfing arrangements if required. All 23 bedrooms are en suite with colour TV, tea/coffee makers and direct-dial telephones. Full-sized snooker table available in the hotel. Late bar facilities for residents. Party reductions. Phone now for your full colour brochure.

ENGLAND / Merseyside

SOUTHPORT. **Southport Old Links Golf Club,** Moss Lane, Churchtown, Southport PR9 7QS (01704 228207). *Location:* end of Roe Lane, Churchtown, at the rear of Meols Hall. Tree lined links course. 9 holes, (x2), 6371 yards. S.S.S. 71. *Green Fees:* information not available. *Eating facilities:* available daily except Mondays. *Visitors:* welcome except Wednesdays, Sundays and Bank Holidays. *Society Meetings:* catered for by arrangement, letter of application required. Secretary: B. Kenyon (01704 228207; Fax: 01704 505353).

WALLASEY. **Wallasey Golf Club,** Bayswater Road, Wallasey CH45 8LA (0151-691 1024; Fax: 0151-638 8988). *Location:* via M53 through Wirral or 15 minutes from Liverpool centre via Wallasey Tunnel. Championship seaside links. 18 holes, 6503 yards. S.S.S. 72. *Green Fees:* weekdays £70.00 per round, £80.00 per day; weekends and Bank Holidays £75.00 per round, £85.00 per day. *Eating facilities:* snacks and full catering facilities. *Visitors:* welcome with reservation. *Society Meetings:* catered for by arrangement. Professional: Mike Adams (0151-638 3888). Secretary: Trevor Barraclough (0151-691 1024).

WALLASEY. **Warren Golf Club,** The Grange, Grove Road, Wallasey CH45 0JA (0151-639 8323). *Location:* 300 yards Grove Road Station. Seaside links course, wonderful view over Mersey. 9 holes, 5914 yards. S.S.S. 68. *Green Fees:* information not available.

Visitors: welcome Mondays to Saturdays. Course closed to public Sundays 7am to 11am. *Society Meetings:* welcome. Professional: Mark Eagles (0151-639 5730). Secretary: Kevin McCormack (0151-678 0330-).
e-mail: golfer@warrengc.freeserve.co.uk

WIRRAL. **Brackenwood Golf Club,** Bracken Lane, Bebington, Wirral L63 2LY (0151-608 5394). *Location:* M53 Clatterbridge roundabout Junction 4. Flat parkland. 18 holes, 5745 yards. S.S.S. 70. *Green Fees:* £10.00 per round. *Visitors:* welcome, weekends must be booked through Professional one week in advance. *Society Meetings:* welcome, book through Professional. Professional: Ken Lamb (0151-608 3093). Secretary: G.W. Brogan (0151-339 9817).

WIRRAL. **Hoylake Golf Club,** Carr Lane, Hoylake, Wirral CH47 4BG (0151 632 2956). *Location:* turn at roundabout Hoylake town centre, over railway. Part flat semi links. 18 holes, 6313 yards, 5780 metres. S.S.S. 70. *Green Fees:* information not available. *Eating facilities:* cafe and bar. Phone in advance (0151 632 4883). *Visitors:* welcome, booking fee required in advance. *Society Meetings:* society bookings weekdays and after 1.30pm Saturday; after 12 midday Sunday. Professional: S.N. Hooton (0151-632 2956). Secretary: Peter Davies (0151 632 0523).

FHG Guides 2006

October Edition

- Recommended COUNTRY HOTELS
- Recommended COUNTRY INNS & PUBS
- BED & BREAKFAST STOPS • CHILDREN WELCOME!
- The Original FHG Guide to COAST & COUNTRY HOLIDAYS
- CARAVAN & CAMPING HOLIDAYS, England, Scotland, Wales & Ireland
- BRITAIN'S BEST HOLIDAYS
- THE GOLF GUIDE Where to Play / Where to Stay
- PETS WELCOME!
- Recommended SHORT BREAK HOLIDAYS in Britain
- SELF CATERING HOLIDAYS in Britain

April Edition

Available from bookshops or larger newsagents

FHG Guides LTD
Abbey Mill Business Centre,
Seedhill, Paisley PA1 ITJ
www.holidayguides.com

Norfolk

CROMER. **Links Country Park Hotel and Golf Club,** Sandy Lane, West Runton, Cromer NR27 9QH (01263 838383). *Location:* midway between Cromer and Sheringham on the A149, turn left opposite the village inn. Undulating parkland with narrow fairways and tricky greens. 9 holes, 4814 yards, S.S.S. 64. *Green Fees:* information not available. *Eating facilities:* grill room, snacks, hotel restaurant table d'hôte and à la carte. *Visitors:* welcome weekdays, restrictions weekends. Adjoining Hotel offers free golf to residents; gym, sauna, solarium, swimming pool etc. *Society Meetings:* welcome. Professional: Nick Catchpole (01263 838215; Fax: 01263 838264). Hon. Secretary: Carl Abbott (01263 838383; Fax: 01263 838264).*

CROMER. **Royal Cromer Golf Club,** 145 Overstrand Road, Cromer NR27 0JH (01263 512884; Fax: 01263 512430). *Location:* one mile east of Cromer on B1159 Coast Road. Undulating cliff top course. 18 holes, 6280 yards. S.S.S. 72. Large practice ground. *Green Fees:* £45.00 weekdays, £55.00 weekends; weekly tickets available, also joint tickets with Sheringham. *Eating facilities:* full catering and bar snacks. *Visitors:* welcome, booking essential from 1st April to 31st October, Handicap Certificates required. *Society Meetings:* welcome. Professsional: Lee Patterson (Tel & Fax: 01263 512267). Secretary/ Manager: Mrs Diane Hopkins (01263 512884).

DEREHAM. **Dereham Golf Club,** Quebec Road, Dereham NR19 2DS (01362 695900; Fax: 01362 695904). *Location:* three-quarters of a mile from town centre on B1110. Wooded parkland. 9 holes (double tees), 6225 yards. S.S.S. 70. Practice nets, practice ground. *Green Fees:* information not available. *Eating facilities:* full restaurant (except Mondays). *Visitors:* welcome with prior notice. Handicap Certificates required. *Society Meetings:* catered for with advance booking. Professional: Neil Allsebrook (01362 695631). Secretary: S. Kaye (01362 695900; Fax: 01362 695904).*

DISS. **Diss Golf Club,** Stuston Common, Diss IP21 4AA (01379 641025). *Location:* B1077 off A140, half-a-mile from Diss railway station, one mile from town centre. The course with its natural hazards provides a good test of golf. 18 holes, 6206 yards. S.S.S. 70. Par 70. 15 bay driving range one mile from clubhouse adjacent to 15th hole. *Green Fees:* £28.00 per round, £36.00 per day. *Eating facilities:* are excellent. *Visitors:* welcome weekends with a member. *Society Meetings:* Golf Societies and groups welcome, contact the Secretary for further details. There is a well stocked shop and lessons are available from the Professional. Special deals on membership packages, contact the Secretary for details. Professional: Nigel Taylor (01379 644399). Secretary: Chris Wellstead (01379 641025; Fax: 01379 644586). Steward: J.W. Mackrell (01379 642847).
e-mail: sec.dissgolf@virgin.net
website: www.club-noticeboard.co.uk/diss

DOWNHAM MARKET. **Ryston Park Golf Club,** Ely Road, Denver, Downham Market PE38 0HH (01366 382133; Fax: 01366 383834). *Location:* one mile south Downham Market on A10. 36 miles north Cambridge. Parkland with mature trees and water on three holes. 9 holes, 6310 yards, 5774 metres. S.S.S. 70. Practice ground, practice putting green, practice bunker. *Green Fees:* weekdays £20.00, weekends restricted – contact Club. *Eating facilities:* restaurant and bar. *Visitors:* welcome weekdays, weekends by prior arrangement. *Society Meetings:* welcome (up to 50 members). Secretary: Joe Flogdell (01366 382133).

FAKENHAM. **Fakenham Golf Club,** Gallow Sports Centre, Hempton Road, Fakenham NR21 7LA (01328 862867). *Location:* half-a-mile town centre on Swaffham Road. Parkland. 9 holes, 6245 yards. S.S.S. 70. Large practice area. *Green Fees:* information not available. *Eating facilities:* available in Sports Centre. *Visitors:* welcome by appointment. *Society Meetings:* welcome, reduced rates. Professional: Colin Williams (01328 863534). Secretary: G.G. Cocker (01328 855678).

GREAT YARMOUTH. **Caldecott Hall Golf Club and Hotel,** Beccles Road, Fritton, Great Yarmouth NR31 9EY (01493 488488; Fax: 01493 488561). *Location:* on the A143 just north of the village of Fritton. Parkland. 18 holes, 6685 yards, S.S.S. 73. 18-hole short course. Floodlit driving range, putting and pitching practice area. *Green Fees:* weekdays £20.00 per round, £35.00 per day; weekends £26.00 per round, £40.00 per day. *Eating facilities:* bar, restaurant. *Visitors:* welcome at all times, starting sheets weekends and Bank Holidays. Luxury en suite rooms. Packages available. The Barnworks Leisure Spa; massage treatments. *Society Meetings:* welcome by arrangement. Professional: (01493 488488; Fax: 01493 488561).
website: www.caldecotthall.co.uk

GREAT YARMOUTH. **Gorleston Golf Club,** Warren Road, Gorleston, Great Yarmouth NR31 6JT (01493 661082). *Location:* A12 Lowestoft to Great Yarmouth. Seaside links, seventh green is the most easterly green in the British Isles. 18 holes, 6400 yards. S.S.S. 71. *Green Fees:* weekdays £25.00 per person, weekends £30.00 per person. *Eating facilities:* restaurant/bars open seven days. *Visitors:* welcome, advisable to check in advance for details of restrictions. *Society Meetings:* catered for by prior arrangement (membership of recognised club required). Professional: Nick Brown (01493 662103). Secretary: J.E. Woodhouse (01493 661911).

Please mention THE GOLF GUIDE when you enquire about clubs or accommodation

GREAT YARMOUTH. Great Yarmouth and Caister Golf Club, Beach House, Caister-on-Sea, Great Yarmouth NR30 5TD (01493 728699). *Location:* A149 coast road, two miles north of Great Yarmouth. Links. 18 holes, 6330 yards. S.S.S. 70. Practice ground. *Green Fees:* £35.00 per day, £20.00 after 3pm weekdays; £45.00 per day, £30.00 after 3pm weekends. (2005/6) Members' guests 50%. *Eating facilities:* full range of catering; bar. *Visitors:* welcome, not before 11.30am Saturdays, Sundays and Bank Holidays. *Society Meetings:* catered for. Clubhouse Catering (01493 720214). Professional: Martyn Clarke (01493 720421). Secretary: R. Peck. e-mail: office@caistergolf.co.uk
website: www.caistergolf.co.uk

HUNSTANTON. Hunstanton Golf Club, Golf Course Road, Old Hunstanton PE36 6JQ (01485 532811; Fax: 01485 532319). *Location:* off A149. Adjoins Old Hunstanton village, approximately half a mile north east of Hunstanton. Championship links course with excellent fast greens. 18 holes, 6735 yards. S.S.S. 72. Practice ground. *Green Fees:* (2005) weekdays £65.00 per day; weekends £75.00 per day. Special rates in winter, also after 4pm all year. Subject to review. *Eating facilities:* catering and bar facilities. *Visitors:* welcome but limited times available at weekends. Prior booking advisable. Visitors must be member of recognised golf club and hold a current Handicap. Play in two-ball format only. *Society Meetings:* welcome. Professional: Jim Dodds (01485 532751). Secretary: Derek Thomson (01485 532811).

Great Yarmouth & Caister Golf Club
Beach House, Caister-on-Sea, Great Yarmouth NR30 5TD

Founded in 1882, Great Yarmouth & Caister Golf Club is a traditional-style links course, set along the coast north of Great Yarmouth. Partly set among sand dunes, it is always well-drained and has challenging fairways and excellent greens. Golfers of all abilities will find something to test themselves here.

SOCIETIES AND VISITORS ARE MOST WELCOME. Various packages are available to societies from Monday to Friday. For details and bookings please call **01493 728699 (Secretary)** or **01493 729421 (Professional).**
For more information see our website or e-mail your enquiry.

Tel: 01493 728699 • Fax: 01493 728831
www.caistergolf.co.uk • office@caistergolf.co.uk

Visit North Norfolk's Greens

Near to **Hunstanton Golf Club,** a course renowned for having the slickest greens in the country, is the Best Western Le Strange Arms Hotel. The many golf courses that are within reach of the hotel include Brancaster and Kings Lynn.

The hotel overlooks the sea and offers many attractions.
- Excellent restaurant
- Private dining available
- On-site pub
- Range of bedroom styles

Le Strange Arms Hotel
Golf Course Road, Old Hunstanton, Norfolk PE36 6JJ
Tel: 01485 534411 email: reception@lestrangearms.co.uk
www.bw-lestrangearmshotel.co.uk

See also Colour Advertisement on page 29

Bed & Breakfast at Grove Farm

Grove Farm, Roughton, is a delightful mix of 17th Century farmhouse and recently converted barn nestling round a secluded courtyard. The B&B accommodation is in a magnificent vaulted room, with four-poster double (private bathroom), or a double with its own little sitting area (en suite shower).

Self-catering barn accommodation (2 double/twin plus 2 bathrooms) with 40 foot living room on the first floor. Exposed beams and wood-burning stoves. Well located between the coast and the Broads, Grove Farm is an ideal place to enjoy so much of what Norfolk has to offer. Homemade breads and conserves, produce from garden or local farm shop.

Grove Farm, Back Lane, Roughton, Norfolk NR11 8QR
Tel: 01263 761594 • Fax: 01263 761505
e-mail: grovefarm@homestay.co.uk • www.grove-farm.com

Rogue's Barn & Rascal's Barn

HUNSTANTON. Searles Resort Golf Course, Searles Leisure Resort, South Beach Road, Hunstanton PE36 5BB (01485 536010; Fax: 01485 533815). *Location:* A149 from King's Lynn to Hunstanton; at roundabout on hill at Hunstanton take 2nd left down Oasis Way; at mini-roundabout straight over and immediate left into Leisure Resort; follow signs. Seaside links-style course. 9 holes, 2850 yards. S.S.S. 34. 10-bay covered driving range. Putting. *Green Fees:* £8.50 adults, £6.50 under-18s (add £1.00 for weekends). *Eating facilities:* new clubhouse with bar, restaurant, shop, changing facilities etc. *Visitors:* welcome at all times. Lodges and cabin on site available for hire. Club hire. Fishing lake and bowling green. *Society Meetings:* all welcome. Secretary/Manager: Paul Searle.
e-mail: golf@searles.co.uk

KING'S LYNN. Eagles Golf Club, 39 School Road, Tilney All Saints, King's Lynn PE34 4RS (01553 827147). *Location:* off A47 between King's Lynn and Wisbech. Parkland. 9 holes, 4284 yards. S.S.S. 61. Par 3 course, driving range, practice bunkers and putting green. *Green Fees:* weekdays £10.50 9 holes, £14.50 18 holes; weekends and Bank Holidays £11.50 9 holes, £17.50 18 holes. Weekday special Seniors/ Juniors £6.75 9 holes, £10.00 18 holes. *Eating facilities:* bar/restaurant. *Visitors:* welcome, restrictions at weekends; no visitors before 10am. Dress code must be adhered to at all times. *Society Meetings:* apply to Secretary. Professional: Nigel Pickerell. Secretary: R. K. Shipman (Tel & Fax: 01553 829777).

KING'S LYNN. King's Lynn Golf Club, Castle Rising, King's Lynn PE31 6BD (01553 631654; Fax: 01553 631036). *Location:* four miles north-east of King's Lynn. Undulating wooded course. 18 holes, 6609 yards. Par 72, S.S.S. 73. Practice areas. *Green Fees:* information not available. *Eating facilities:* snacks, lunches, teas available; dinners by arrangement; two bars. *Visitors:* welcome on production of Handicap Certificate. *Society Meetings:* catered for by prior arrangement. Professional: J. Reynolds (01553 631655). General Manager: M.P. Sackree.

KING'S LYNN. Middleton Hall Golf Club, Middleton, King's Lynn PE32 1RH (Tel & Fax: 01553 841800). *Location:* on A47 King's Lynn to Norwich, 3 miles from King's Lynn. Undulating parkland. 18 holes, 6004 yards. Par 71. Floodlit driving range, practice greens. *Green Fees:* weekdays £25.00, weekends £30.00. *Eating facilities:* full restaurant services. *Visitors:* welcome. *Society Meetings:* welcome, special rates available. Professional: Steve White (01553 841801). Secretary: J. Holland (Tel & Fax: 01553 841800).

KING'S LYNN. Royal West Norfolk Golf Club, Brancaster, Near King's Lynn PE31 8AX (01485 210223). *Location:* one mile off A149, Beach Road junction, seven miles east of Hunstanton. Seaside links. 18 holes, 6458 yards. S.S.S. 71. *Green Fees:* weekdays £70.00 per day; weekends £80.00 per day. *Eating facilities:* available. *Visitors:* all visitors must be members of a recognised Golf Club, hold an official Handicap and must make prior arrangements with the Secretary to play. No visitors prior to 10am Sundays and no visitors in August. Maximum numbers in party 24. Professional: S. Rayner (01485 210616). Secretary: Major N.A. Carrington Smith (Tel & Fax: 01485 210087).

MATTISHALL. Mattishall Golf Club, South Green, Mattishall, Dereham NR20 3JZ (01362 850111). *Location:* Signposted from Mattishall Church. 9 hole (18 tees), flat course, 6170 yards, SSS 69. *Green Fees:* £8.00 for 9 holes. *Eating facilities:* small bar only. *Visitors:* welcome seven days, no restrictions. Secretary: Mrs Bridgette Hall.

NORWICH. Barnham Broom Hotel & Golf Club, Barnham Broom, Norwich NR9 4DD (01603 759393 (Hotel); 01603 759552 (Golf Shop); Fax: 01603 758224). *Location:* situated 10 miles west of Norwich off A47 and A11 trunk routes; follow brown tourist signs. Two 18 hole courses in 250 acres of the beautiful River Yare Valley. The Valley Course: 6483 yards, S.S.S. 71; The Hill Course: 6495 yards, S.S.S. 71. Exceptional practice facilities including 5 acre practice ground and three full length academy holes. GPS buggies available. Group and individual tuition

---

Searles Resort Golf Course

9 hole par 34 Golf course with 10 bay covered driving range. Designed in a Links Style with good large greens and the **Heacham River** winding through the 3rd & 4th holes.
The par 5 8th hole follows the ancient reed bed to finish with the par 3 9th in front of the Clubhouse. Bowling green and fishing lake now open. Societies and groups are welcome. Accommodation available on Park.

£8.50 Adults   £6.50 U18   Add £1 for weekends.

Societies & Groups very welcome.   Tel: 01485 536010
E-mail: golf@searles.co.uk   Website: www.searles.co.uk
Access via Searles of Hunstanton, South Beach Rd, Hunstanton

Searles LEISURE RESORT · HUNSTANTON ·

See also Colour Advertisement on page 29

at the Barnham Broom Golf School. *Green Fees:* information not provided. *Eating facilities:* Flints Restaurant, Sports Bar and Cafe (serving light meals and drinks throughout the day).Conference and private dining for up to 200 people. *Visitors:* welcome anytime. Hotel with 52 en suite bedrooms. Leisure Club. *Society Meetings:* welcome all year; corporate Golf Events. PGA Professional: Ian Rollett, PGA Golf Manager: James Hill (01603 757504).
e-mail: golfschool@barnham-broom.co.uk
golfmanager@barnham-broom.co.uk
website: www.barnham-broom.co.uk

NORWICH. **Bawburgh Golf Club,** Glen Lodge, Marlingford Road, Bawburgh, Norwich NR9 3LU (01603 740404; Fax: 01603 740403). *Location*: directly off Norwich Southern Bypass – exit follow Royal Norfolk Showground/Bawburgh. Rolling landscape mixture of heath and parkland. 18 holes, 6231 yards. S.S.S. 70. Driving range covered and floodlit, group tuition. *Green Fees:* weekdays £28.00; weekends £34.00 on application. *Eating facilities:* restaurant and bar, snacks. *Visitors:* welcome, advisable to ring in advance. *Society Meetings:* welcome on application, Corporate Days arranged. Professional: Chris Potter (01603 742323). Director of Golf: Ian Ladbrooke.
e-mail: info@bawburgh.com
website: www.bawburgh.com

NORWICH. **Costessey Park Golf Course,** Old Costessey, Norwich NR8 5AL (01603 746333). *Location:* off the A47 Norwich to King's Lynn road, in the village of Old Costessey (adjacent to Norwich). Set in river valley with some parkland. 18 holes, 5900 yards. S.S.S. 69. Par 71. Practice area. *Green Fees:* information not available. *Eating facilities:* bar and bar snacks; set meals available. *Visitors:* welcome anytime except weekends when visitors allowed only after 11am. Handicap Certificates required weekends only. Golf carts available for hire. *Society Meetings:* catered for by arrangement. Professional: Andrew Young (01603 747085).*

NORWICH. **De Vere Dunston Hall,** Ipswich Road, Norwich NR14 8PQ (Hotel: 01508 470444; Fax: 01508 470689; Shop: 01508 470178). *Location:* on A140 Ipswich Road. Parkland, wooded, with many water features. USGA spec. greens. 18 holes, 6319 yards. Par 71. 22 bay covered driving range, putting green. *Green Fees:* information not available. *Eating facilities:* three restaurants, two bars. *Visitors:* pay and play course, all welcome at any time. Golfing weekends; accommodation available in 130-bedroom Hotel; tennis courts; leisure centre with indoor pool, sauna, steam room and jacuzzi. *Society Meetings:* special packages available. Professional: Peter Briggs.*

NORWICH. **Eaton (Norwich) Golf Club,** Newmarket Road, Norwich NR4 6SF (01603 451686; Fax: 01603 457539). *Location:* off A11, one and a half miles from city centre. Parkland course – "the hidden gem". 18 holes, 6114 yards. S.S.S. 70. Practice areas available. *Green Fees:* information not available. *Eating facilities:* full bar, snacks, lunches, dinners by arrangement. *Visitors:* welcome; only after 11.30am

weekends. Handicap Certificate required. *Society Meetings:* welcome, fees by arrangement. Professional: Mark Allen (01603 251 394). Secretary: Mrs L. Bovill (01603 451686; Fax: 01603 457539).
e-mail: administrator@eatongc.co.uk
website: www.eatongc.co.uk

NORWICH. **Marriott Sprowston Manor Hotel and Country Club,** Wroxham Road, Norwich NR7 8RP (0870 400 7229; Fax: 0870 400 7329). *Location:* off A1151 Norwich to Wroxham. £1.6 million Championship course set in mature parkland. Host to Sky Televised PGA Europro Tour 2004 & 2005. Full USGA specification greens and tees. Designed by Ross McMurray (European Golf Design), who has also designed the Marquess at Woburn and improvements at Celtic Manor for 2010 Ryder Cup. 18 holes, 6547 yards. S.S.S. 71. Putting green, chipping and bunker practice area. 27 bay floodlit driving range, PGA tuition including Explanar and GASP video analysis. *Green Fees:* weekdays £39.00 per round; weekends £48.00 per round. *Eating facilities:* Zest café bar and grill. Four-star hotel on site. *Visitors:* always welcome. Bookings 10 days in advance. *Society Meetings:* special packages available - must be pre-booked. Preferential green fee rates and group packages available for residents. Professional: Guy Ireson (0870 400 7229). Secretary: Mr A. Moule (0870 400 7229).
website: www.marriott.co.uk/nwigs

NORWICH. **Mundesley Golf Club,** Links Road, Mundesley, Norwich NR11 8ES (Tel & Fax: 01263 720279). *Location:* one mile from village centre. Undulating, testing downland course with fine panoramic views. 9 holes, 5377 yards. S.S.S. 66. Covered driving range, small practice area. *Green Fees:* £25.00 per round weekdays, £30.00 per round weekends. *Eating facilities:* full catering facilities. *Visitors:* welcome, but course reserved for members until 11.30am at weekends and Bank Holidays and 11.00am to 3.30pm Wednesdays. *Society Meetings:* catered for, restrictions as for visitors. Professional: T.G. Symmons (01263 720279). Manager: T.E. Duke (01263 720095; Fax: 01263 720279).

NORWICH. **Royal Norwich Golf Club,** Drayton High Road, Hellesdon, Norwich NR6 5AH (01603 429928; Fax: 01603 417945). *Location:* centre of city and thence by A1067 Fakenham or via Ring Road, then 500 yards along A1067. Mature parkland. 18 holes, 6506 yards. S.S.S. 72. Large practice ground. *Green Fees:* weekdays and weekends £40.00 per day, £25.00 per round. Discounted rates for groups of 12 and over £30.00 per day, £22.00 per round. Reduction if playing with a member, special winter rates available on request. *Eating facilities:* two bars, restaurant plus bar menu. Prior booking required for evening meals. *Visitors:* welcome weekdays after 9am, weekends by prior booking only. Handicap Certificate required. *Society Meetings:* welcome weekdays except Wednesday by prior arrangement. Golf Manager: Simon Youd (01603 408459). General Manager: John Meggy.
e-mail: mail@royalnorwichgolf.co.uk
website: www.royalnorwichgolf.co.uk

Norfolk / ENGLAND

NORWICH. Wensum Valley Hotel, Golf and Country Club, Beech Avenue, Taverham, Norwich NR8 6HP (01603 261012; Fax: 01603 261664). *Location:* five miles out of Norwich on the A1067 to Fakenham. Two courses. Parkland and very picturesque set in the valley. Wensum Course: 18 holes, 6037 yards S.S.S. 69. Valley Course: 18 holes, 6223 yards. S.S.S. 70. Covered, floodlit driving range. *Green Fees:* information not available. *Eating facilities:* full catering and bar facilities. *Visitors:* always welcome. Hotel on site with en suite twin bedrooms. Special golf, fishing and leisure breaks available. *Society Meetings:* all welcome; package available. Professional: Peter Whittle. Secretary: Bridgette Hall (01603 261012).*
e-mail: enqs@wensumvalley.freeserve.co.uk
website: www.wensumvalley.freeserve.co.uk

NORWICH. Weston Park Golf Club, Weston Longville, Norwich (01603 872998; Fax: 01603 873040). *Location:* nine miles north west of Norwich off the A1067 Norwich to Fakenham road. Parkland, wooded course. 18 holes, 6606 yards. S.S.S. 72. Practice ground and net. *Green Fees:* weekdays £35.00; weekends £45.00 (subject to review). *Eating facilities:* available. *Visitors:* welcome. Must book teeing off times. Handicap Certificate required. Two tennis courts and croquet lawn. *Society Meetings:* welcome. Professional: Michael Few (01603 872998). Administrator: C. E. Ashmore (01603 872363).
e-mail: info@weston-park.co.uk

REYMERSTON. The Norfolk Golf and Country Club, Hingham Road, Reymerston NR9 4QQ (01362 850297; Fax: 01362 850614). *Location:* Dereham B1135 five miles, Wymondham 10 miles. Parkland course. 18 holes, 6609 yards. S.S.S. 69. *Green Fees:* information not available. *Eating facilities:* clubhouse, bar, function room. *Visitors:* welcome subject to availability. Advisable to check in advance. Full Leisure facilities in Leisure Centre; swimming pool, sauna, gym, spa bath. *Society Meetings:* society and conference packages available. Professional: Tony Varney (01362 850297; Fax: 01362 850614). Secretary: Mike de Boltz.
e-mail: suzy@the-norfolk.co.uk
website: www.the-norfolk.co.uk

SHERINGHAM. Sheringham Golf Club, Weybourne Road, Sheringham NR26 8HG (01263 823488). *Location:* one mile west of town on Weybourne Road (A149). Clifftop course. 18 holes, 6456 yards. S.S.S. 71. Large practice area. *Green Fees:* Sunday to Friday per day £45.00 (April to Sept), £30.00 (Nov to Feb). Saturday per day £60.00 (April to Sept), £40.00 (Nov to Feb), £45.00 (Oct and March). subject to review. Twilight and 3-day tickets available. *Eating facilities:* full catering to order. *Visitors:* welcome, telephone first, with reservation for members of other clubs, Handicap Certificate required. *Society Meetings:* catered for by prior arrangement with Secretary. Professional: M.W. Jubb (01263 822980). Secretary: P.J. Mounfield (01263 823488).

SWAFFHAM. Dunham Golf Club, Canister Hall, Little Dunham near Swaffham PE32 2DF (Tel. & Fax: 01328 701906). *Location:* off A47 four miles from Swaffham at Necton Q8 garage. Follow Tourist Board golf flags. Parkland with lakes. 9 holes, 4986 yards. S.S.S. 64. *Green Fees:* information not available. *Eating facilities:* restaurant and bar. *Visitors:* welcome with dress restrictions. Accommodation and swimming pool. *Society Meetings:* welcome, telephone for details. Professional: Gary Potter (01328 701906). Secretary: F. Reid (01328 701718).*

SWAFFHAM. Swaffham Golf Club, Cley Road, Swaffham PE37 8AE (01760 721611/721621). *Location:* two miles south-west of Swaffham Market Place (signposted) on Cley Road. Heathland course. 18 holes, 6533 yards. S.S.S. 71. Practice ground. *Green Fees:* Please call (01760 721611) for Summer/Winter deals. *Eating facilities:* full catering now available every day. *Visitors:* welcome without reservation weekdays, weekends only if playing with member. *Society Meetings:* catered for subject to prior notice being given. Professional: Peter Field. Secretary: M. Rust.

THETFORD. Feltwell Golf Club, Thor Avenue, off Wilton Road, Feltwell, Thetford IP26 4AY (01842 827644). *Location:* take the B1386 off the A10 at Southery (five miles south of Downham Market). Inland links – can be windy! 9 holes, 6488 yards, 6197 metres. S.S.S. 71. Practice range and nets. *Green Fees:* weekdays £16.00 per day, £10.00 with a member; weekends £25.00, per day, £16.00 with a member. *Eating facilities:* bar, hot and cold food available Tuesday through Sunday from noon. *Visitors:* welcome at all times but check with Secretary. *Society Meetings:* welcome, packages available. Professional: Christian Puttock (01842 829089). Secretary: Linda Ball (01842 827644).

THETFORD. Richmond Park Golf Club, Saham Road, Watton, Thetford IP25 6EA (01953 881803; Fax: 01953 881817). *Location:* half a mile north west of Watton town centre. Parkland. 18 holes, 6289 yards. S.S.S. 70. Driving range. *Green Fees:* information not available. *Eating facilities:* bar, bar food, restaurant. *Visitors:* always welcome. Accommodation available on site. *Society Meetings:* welcome, excellent facilities available. Professional/Secretary: Alan Hemsley.*

THETFORD. Thetford Golf Club, Brandon Road, Thetford IP24 3NE (01842 752258). *Location:* one mile west of Thetford on B1107 Brandon Road. Wooded breckland course. 18 holes, 6849 yards. S.S.S. 73. Practice ground. *Green Fees:* £40.00 weekdays. *Eating facilities:* catering and bar service. *Visitors:* welcome weekdays. *Society Meetings:* catered for Wednesdays, Thursdays and Fridays – Handicap Certificate needed. Professional: Gary Kitley (01842 752662). Secretary: Mrs S.A. Redpath (01842 752169; Fax: 01842 766212).

THE APPEARANCE OF AN ASTERISK (*) AT THE END OF A CLUB OR COURSE ENTRY INDICATES THAT UP-TO-DATE INFORMATION HAS NOT BEEN SUPPLIED

Northamptonshire

CORBY near. **Priors Hall Golf Club,** Stamford Road, Weldon, Near Corby NN17 3JH (01536 260756). *Location:* on the A43, four miles from Corby on the Stamford Road. Parkland course. 18 holes, 6631 yards, 6063 metres. S.S.S. 72. Practice nets and ground. *Green Fees:* weekdays £15.00; weekends £18.00. Certain concessions apply to local residents. *Eating facilities:* bar meals. *Visitors:* welcome at all times; pre-booking advisable; starting sheet in operation. *Society Meetings:* welcome by prior arrangement. Professional: Jeff Bradbrook. Secretary: Phill Ackroyd.

DAVENTRY. **Daventry and District Golf Club,** Norton Road, Daventry NN11 2LS (01327 702829). *Location:* on Borough Hill, site of Iron Age Fort and Roman Camp. 9 holes, 5812 yards. S.S.S. 68. *Green Fees:* weekdays £12.00; weekends and Bank Holidays £20.00. *Visitors:* welcome weekdays and weekends except Sunday before 11.30am. *Society Meetings*: welcome with prior booking. Secretary: R. Lattaway.

DAVENTRY. **Staverton Park Golf Club,** Daventry Road, Staverton, Near Daventry NN11 6JT (01327 302000; Fax: 01327 311428). *Location:* one mile from Daventry on A425 to Leamington Spa. Easy access from M1 Junctions 16 or 18. Undulating parkland. Championship course – 18 holes, 6609 yards. S.S.S. 73. Practice range, two putting greens. *Green Fees:* summer £36.00 per round, winter £30.00 per round. *Eating facilities:* full catering available at all times. *Visitors:* always welcome. Handicap Certificate required at weekends. Advance Tee Time (visitors) booking (01327 705506). 245 bedroomed hotel with leisure and conference facilities. Residential golf packages available. Buggies, trolleys and clubs for hire. *Society Meetings:* welcome, for details please contact Lindi Rawden (01327 302000). Professional: Richard Mudge (01327 311119; Fax: 01327 312787). Secretary: Roy Patrick (01327 876020).
e-mail: staverton@initialstyle.co.uk
website: www.golf-isc.co.uk

HELLIDON. **Hellidon Lakes Golf Club,** Hellidon Lakes Hotel, Hellidon, Daventry NN11 6GG (01327 262550; Fax: 01327 262559). *Location:* one and a half miles from A361, six miles from Daventry, 12 miles from Banbury. Parkland. 27 hole championship course, putting green. *Green Fees*; information not available. *Eating facilities*: themed 100 seater casual bar and restaurant. AA rosette restaurant. *Visitors*: always welcome. 110 en suite bedrooms, leisure centre, tennis, health and beauty centre with salon, gym, sunbed, steam room, whirlpool bath and heated indoor swimming pool. Indoor golf simulator, 4-lane tenpin bowling. *Society Meetings:* all welcome. Professional: Joe Kingston (01327 262551).*
e-mail: hellidon@marstonhotels.com
website: www.hellidon@marstonhotels.com

KETTERING. **Kettering Golf Club,** Headlands, Kettering NN15 6XA (01536 511104). *Location:* off A14 (Junction 8) A43 to Kettering, right at 1st roundabout and follow signs for golf club. Flat parkland. 18 holes, 6035 yards, 5515 metres. S.S.S. 69. *Green Fees:* information not available. *Eating facilities:* by prior arrangement. *Visitors:* welcome weekdays only. *Society Meetings:* catered for Wednesdays and Fridays only by arrangement. Professional: K. Theobald (01536 481014). Secretary: N. Sandell (Tel & Fax: 01536 511104).

MARKET HARBOROUGH near. **Stoke Albany Golf Club,** Ashley Road, Stoke Albany, Market Harborough LE16 8PL (01858 535208; Fax: 01858 535505). *Location:* A427, A14 five minutes away, Market Harborough 10 minutes. Undulating parkland. 18 holes, 6175 yards. S.S.S. 70. Practice area, putting green. *Green Fees:* weekdays £17.00; weekends £21.00 per round. *Eating facilities:* restaurant, bar and spike bar. *Visitors:* welcome, no restrictions. *Society Meetings:* all welcome, but booking is essential. Professional: Adrian Clifford. Secretary: R. Want.
e-mail: info@stokealbanygolfclub.co.uk
website: www.stokealbanygolfclub.co.uk

NORTHAMPTON. **Brampton Heath Golf Centre,** Sandy Lane, Church Brampton, Northampton NN6 8AX (01604 843939; Fax: 01604 843885). *Location:* signposted off A5099 five miles north of Northampton town centre. Undulating heathland course, very dry winter conditions. 18 holes, 6533 yards. S.S.S 71, par 72. 18 bay covered, floodlit driving range, PGA Short Course British Championships par 3 course. *Green Fees:* information not available. *Eating facilities:* full facilities available from 7.30am. *Visitors:* welcome, no restrictions, advisable to book. Buggies and carts available all year round. Short course available - ideal for beginners. Golf superstore. *Society Meetings:* welcome seven days. Professional: Richard Hudson. Manager: David Coulson.*
website: www.bhgc.co.uk

NORTHAMPTON. **Cold Ashby Golf Club,** Stanford Road, Cold Ashby, Northampton NN6 6EP (Tel & Fax: 01604 740548). *Location:* midway between Rugby, Leicester and Northampton, close to Junction 1 A14 and Junction 18 M1. Undulating parkland. 27 holes, 6308 yards. S.S.S. 71. Good practice area. Driving range. *Green Fees:* midweek £16.00 per round, £25.00 per day; weekends £18.50 per round, £28.50 per day. *Eating facilities:* meals and bar snacks available daily. *Visitors:* welcome midweek anytime, weekends must reserve a starting time. *Society Meetings:* catered for weekdays and some weekends. Professional: Shane Rose (01604 740099; Fax: 01604 740548). Secretary: David Croxton.
e-mail: coldashby.golfclub@virgin.net
website: www.coldashbygolfclub.com

NORTHAMPTON. **Collingtree Park Golf Course Ltd,** Windingbrook Lane, Northampton NN4 0XN (01604 700000; Fax: 01604 702600). *Location:* 2 minutes from Junction 15 off M1-A508. Johnny Miller design Championship Course with its signature 18th hole set on a stunning island green. Host to The British Masters 1995/96 and Europro Challenge Tour, and Mobile Cup Seniors Tournament 2005. 18 holes, 6692 yards. S.S.S. 72. Floodlit, covered 16 bay driving range, academy practice holes. *Green Fees:* information not available. *Eating facilities:* members bar, Greens restaurant open to the public. *Visitors:* welcome - advised to book in advance. Handicap Certificates required. Indoor teaching facilities. *Society Meetings:* welcome, advisable to book in advance; discount for group bookings. Professionals: Geoff Pook and Henry Bareham (01604 701202/ 700000). General Manager: Jamie Hammond (01604 700000).
e-mail: kmundy@collingtreeparkgolf.com

NORTHAMPTON. **Delapre Golf Centre,** Eagle Drive, Nene Valley Way, Northampton NN4 7DU (01604 764036; Fax: 01604 706378). *Location:* two miles from Junction 15 M1 on A45 towards Wellingborough. Parkland. Five courses: 18 hole main course; 9 holes course; two Par 3 courses; pitch and putt course and putting greens. 40 bay covered floodlit range. *Green Fees:* please visit website for information. *Eating facilities:* licensed bar and restaurant, coffee shop. Opening hours: 7am to 10pm daily. Digicards and meal deals available. *Visitors:* PGA qualified coaches available for private or group tuition; golf schools, video etc. Buggies for hire. *Society Meetings:* welcome. Professional: Greg Iron. Secretary/General Manager: Julie Howes (01604 764036).
website: www.jackbarker.com

NORTHAMPTON. **Kingsthorpe Golf Club,** Kingsley Road, Northampton NN2 7BU. *Location:* off M1 and A43. Undulating parkland. 18 holes, 5918 yards. S.S.S. 69. *Green Fees:* weekdays - £30.00 per round/day April - October, £20.00 per round/day Nov - March; weekends - members and guests only. *Eating facilities:* full catering. *Visitors:* welcome weekdays; weekends must be guest of member. *Society Meetings:* catered for by arrangement normally Thursdays and Fridays only; brochure available. Professional: Paul Armstrong (01604 719602). Secretary: John Harris (Tel & Fax: 01604 710610).
e-mail: secretary@kingsthorpe-golf.co.uk
website: www.kingsthorpe-golf.co.uk

NORTHAMPTON. **Northampton Golf Club,** Harlestone, Northampton NN7 4EF (01604 845102; Fax: 01604 820262). *Location:* on A428 north-west of Northampton in the village of Harlestone. Parkland with a lake coming into play 16th and 18th holes. 18 holes, 6615 yards. S.S.S. 72. Practice ground. *Green Fees:* £40.00 weekdays, weekends must play with a member. *Eating facilities:* restaurant and bar snacks. *Visitors:* welcome weekdays but must have a Certificate of Handicap. *Society Meetings:* weekdays except Wednesdays. Inclusive packages available. Professional: Barry Randall (01604 845167). Secretary/Manager: Mr Sean Malherbe (01604 845155; Fax: 01604 820262).
e-mail: golf@northamptongolfclub.co.uk
website: www.northamptongolfclub.co.uk

NORTHAMPTON. **Northamptonshire County Golf Club,** Sandy Lane, Church Brampton, Northampton NN6 8AZ (01604 842951). *Location:* four miles north west of Northampton between A50 and A428. Heathland with woods, gorse and stream. 18 holes, 6505 yards, 5948 metres. S.S.S. 72. Practice ground. *Green Fees:* 18 holes £40.00, 27 holes £50.00, 36 holes £60.00. *Eating facilities:* restaurant and bar. *Visitors:* by prior arrangement, must have Club Handicap. *Society Meetings:* catered for Wednesdays, small groups on Thursdays. Professional: T. Rouse (Tel & Fax: 01604 842226). Secretary: (01604 843025; Fax: 01604 843463).

NORTHAMPTON. **Overstone Park Golf and Country Club,** Billing Lane, Northampton NN6 0AP (01604 647666; Fax: 01604 642635). *Location:* seven miles from Junction 15 M1 A508 merges with A45. Follow signs for Overstone from Billing turn off Undulating parkland with some water features. 18 holes, 6602 yards. S.S.S. 72. Practice ground. *Green Fees:* telephone for up to date prices. *Eating facilities:* bar, brasserie/restaurant and spike bar. *Visitors:* welcome seven days - must pre book at weekends. *Society Meetings:* welcome Monday to Friday, special packages available. Accommodation consisting 30 en suite rooms. Leisure Club. Professional: Brian Mudge (01604 643555). General Manager: Allan McLundie.

COLLINGTREE PARK GOLF COURSE LTD
Windingbrook Lane, Northampton NN4 0XN • 01604 700000 • Pro Shop: 01604 701202
Fax: 01604 702600 • enquiries@collingtreeparkgolf.com • www.collingtreeparkgolf.com

This 18-hole Johnny Miller design Championship golf course is set in lush parkland just two minutes from Junction 15 of the M1/A508, and has a host of 1st class facilities, including a 16-bay floodlit driving range, indoor video teaching room, members' bar, and 'Greens' restaurant open to the public. Collingtree Park comes with a fantastic pedigree, playing host to the British Masters in 1995 & 1996 and most recently the Euro Pro Tour and Mobile Cup Seniors' Tournament in June 2005.

Collingtree Park
Visitors, Societies and Corporate groups are all welcome, and must book in advance. Green fees are available on request.

OUNDLE. **Oundle Golf Club,** Benefield Road, Oundle, Peterborough PE8 4EZ (01832 273267). *Location:* one mile from Oundle on Corby Road A447. Parkland course. Home of "The Oundle Putter".18 holes, 6265 yards. Par 72 S.S.S. 70. *Green Fees:* weekdays £25.50 per round, £34.00 per day; weekends £44.00 per round/day. *Eating facilities:* bar meals/restaurant. *Visitors:* welcome, check with Professional. No visitors before 10.30am at weekends. *Society Meetings:* welcome by arrangement. Professional: R. Keys (01832 272273). Secretary: D Foley (Tel & Fax: 01832 273267). e-mail: oundlegc@btopenworld.com website: www.oundlegolfclub.com

RUSHDEN. **Rushden Golf Club,** Kimbolton Road, Chelveston, Wellingborough NN9 6AN (01933 418511). *Location:* on B645 two miles east of Higham Ferrers. Undulating meadowland. 10 holes, 6249 yards. S.S.S. 70. Small practice area. *Green Fees:* weekdays £18.00, weekends restricted. *Eating facilities:* bar and dining area - no catering Mondays. *Visitors:* welcome except Wednesday afternoons, weekends must play with member. *Society Meetings:* small societies catered for weekdays. Secretary: D.L. Waite (01933 418511).

TOWCESTER near. **Whittlebury Park Golf and Country Club,** Whittlebury, Near Towcester NN12 8WP (01327 858092; Fax: 01327 858009). *Location*: on A413 south of Whittlebury village, 10 minutes from M1, J 15a (Northampton), 15 minutes from M1, J14 (Milton Keynes), 20 minutes M40, J10 (Banbury/Oxford). 36 hole Championship course in 4 loops of 9, each with its own distinctive character. Two tier driving range with extensive practice facilities. *Green Fees*: from £10.00 to £40.00. *Eating facilities*: bar/bistro within clubhouse plus special function suites. *Visitors*: individual golfers, societies and corporate guests welcome seven days. Other sports and activities offered. Indoor Golf Centre with astro turfed putting green and private teaching bays. *Society Meetings*: welcome seven days, by arrangement. Bookings: please contact Golf Shop on (01327 858588).
e-mail: enquiries@whittlebury.com
website: www.whittlebury.com

Please mention **THE GOLF GUIDE** when you enquire about clubs or accommodation

Whittlebury Park Golf & Country Club

36 Hole Championship Course set in Historic Oak Parkland with numerous lakes and copses.

'When it's wet play dry in our unique indoor golf centre'

ANNUAL HOST TO THE EUROPRO TOUR   COURSES RANKED IN THE UK TOP 100

36 Hole Championship Golf Course: in four loops of 9, each with its own distinctive character. 2 tier driving range: 300 yards long with extensive practice facilities.
Indoor Golf Centre: containing the latest in golfing technology, state of the art simulators, x-golf machine, 420 sq ft indoor astro-turfed putting green & private teaching bays.
Green fees: from £15. To reserve a tee time call the Golf Shop direct on Tel: 01327 85 85 88.
Bar/Bistro: Extensive menus & room for functions, meetings, banquets and parties from 12 to 500.
Sunday Carvery: 12pm to 3pm, dine overlooking the terrace, patio and gardens.
Gift Gallery: an Aladdin's Cave of exquisite gifts.
Visitors Welcome: Individual golfers, Societies or Corporate Guest and non-members, seven days.
Memberships: 7 day/5 day/Lifestyle/Student.
Activities: a wide range including clay shooting, 4x4, team building.
Location: on A413 south of Whittlebury village. 10 minutes from M1, Junction 15a (Northampton). 15 minutes M1, Junction 14 (Milton Keynes) & 20 minutes M40, Junction 10 (Banbury/Oxford).

Whittlebury, Near Towcester, Northants NN12 8WP • Tel: 01327 850000 • Fax: 01327 850001
e-mail: enquiries@whittlebury.com • www.whittlebury.com

THE APPEARANCE OF AN ASTERISK (*) AT THE END OF A CLUB OR COURSE ENTRY INDICATES THAT UP-TO-DATE INFORMATION HAS NOT BEEN SUPPLIED

TOWCESTER near. **Farthingstone Golf Club and Hotel,** Farthingstone, Near Towcester NN12 8NA (01327 361291; Fax: 01327 361645). *Location:* just a few minutes from Junction 16 of the M1, close to A5 and A45. Major towns within easy reach include Milton Keynes, Banbury, Oxford, Rugby and Northampton. Undulating wooded countryside. 18 holes, 6299 yards. S.S.S. 70 (Par). Practice area. *Green Fees:* information not available. *Eating facilities:* bar snacks and restaurant. *Visitors:* welcome, advance bookings available. Rental of golf buggies. Hotel, squash court. *Society Meetings:* bookings welcome. Professional: Luke Brockway (01327 361533). Secretary: Christian Donaldson.

WELLINGBOROUGH. **Wellingborough Golf Club,** Harrowden Hall, Great Harrowden, Wellingborough NN9 5AD (01933 677234; Fax: 01933 679379). *Location:* one mile out of Wellingborough on A509, turn right at crossroads by Great Harrowden Church. Undulating parkland. 18 holes, 6651yards, 6079 metres. S.S.S. 72. Practice ground. *Green Fees:* £48.00 weekdays; weekends as member's guest only £20.00. *Eating facilities:* bar with casual lunch or dinner menu, restaurant. *Visitors:* weekdays only. Buggies available. *Society Meetings:* welcome by appointment. Conference facilities available. Professional: David Clifford (01933 678752). Secretary: Roy Tomlin (01933 677234; Fax: 01933 679379).

WELLINGBOROUGH
GOLF CLUB

Harrowden Hall, Great Harrowden
Wellingborough, Northamptonshire NN9 5AD

TELEPHONE 01933 677234
FACSIMILE 01933 679379

The house, rebuilt in 1719, has been in recent years restored and is now home to Wellingborough Golf Club, a private members' club and one of the best in the country. Wellingborough Golf Club, situated at Harrowden Hall in the heart of the English countryside, presents a magnificent golf course with facilities for conferences, business meetings and private functions.
We cater for numbers from 4 to 80 at competitive inclusive rates.

★ All facilities within a short distance of the main motorway network.

★ Telephone and fax available. ★ Easy parking available.

★ Coffee on arrival. ★ Snacks available throughout the day. ★ Full lunch and dinner menus daily.

*Situated 2 miles from Wellingborough on the A509,
68 miles from London and 3 miles from A1/M1 link.*

– For further details contact: The Secretary/Manager on 01933 677234 –

PLEASE NOTE

All the information regarding Golf Clubs in this guide is given in good faith in the belief that it is correct. However, the publishers cannot guarantee the facts given in these pages, neither are they responsible for changes in ownership or facilities, such as green fees, that may take place after the date of going to press. Readers should always satisfy themselves that the facilities they require are available and that the terms, if quoted, still apply.

Northumberland

ALLENDALE. **Allendale Golf Club,** High Studdon, Allenheads Road, Allendale, Hexham NE47 9DH (0870 1614728). *Location:* B6295 Allendale to Allenheads Road, 10 miles south of Hexham. Parkland course, hilly but not too severe. 9 holes, 16 tees. 4501 yards. S.S.S. 64. Driving net and putting green. *Green Fees:* £12.00 weekdays, £15.00 weekends. £2.00 reduction if playing with a member. Special rates after 6pm weekdays, and for visiting parties. *Eating facilities:* new clubhouse with licensed bar, catering by arrangement. *Visitors:* welcome anytime other than August Bank Holiday Monday before 3pm. *Society Meetings:* welcome, contact Secretary. Secretary: Ian Robinson (01434 683438). e-mail: ianr@sandhill27.fsnet.co.uk

ALNMOUTH. **Alnmouth Golf Club Ltd,** Foxton Hall, Lesbury, Alnwick NE66 3BE (01665 830231). *Location:* four miles east of Alnwick. 18 holes, 6414 yards, 5855 metres. S.S.S. 71. *Green Fees:* £33.00 per person per day, £27.50 after 2pm. Juniors £12.00. *Eating facilities:* diningroom and bars. *Visitors:* welcome Monday to Thursday and Sundays. Packages available. Handicap Certificate required. Dormy House accommodation available. *Society Meetings:* welcome Monday to Thursday and Sundays. Secretary: Peter Simpson (01665 830231; Fax: 01665 830922).

ALNMOUTH. **Alnmouth Village Golf Club,** Marine Road, Alnmouth NE66 2RZ (01665 830370). *Location:* leave A1 from Alnwick to Alnmouth. Seaside links course. 9 holes, 6090 yards, 5572 metres. Par 71. S.S.S. 70. *Green Fees:* weekdays £16.00 per 18 holes; weekends and Bank Holidays £20.00 per 18 holes, weekly ticket £60.00. *Eating facilities:* available. *Visitors:* welcome, restrictions on club competition days. *Society Meetings:* must book in advance and only with official Golf Club Handicaps. Secretary: Mr J. E. Clark (01665 603797). e-mail: golf@alnmouth-village.fsnet.co.uk

THE APPEARANCE OF AN ASTERISK (*) AT THE END OF A CLUB OR COURSE ENTRY INDICATES THAT UP-TO-DATE INFORMATION HAS NOT BEEN SUPPLIED

ALNWICK. **Alnwick Golf Club,** Swansfield Park, Alnwick NE66 2AB (01665 602632). *Location:* signposted from the south A1 slip road. A friendly welcome awaits you at Alnwick Golf Club. Established in 1907, extended to 18 holes in 1995. Superb layout set in mature parkland, open grassland and gorse with panoramic views out to sea. 18 holes, 6250 yards. S.S.S. 70. *Green Fees:* weekdays, weekends and Bank Holidays £20.00 per round; £25.00 per day. Subject to review. *Eating facilities*: catering and bar facilities available most times. *Visitors:* welcome most times, part restrictions during competitions. Buggies available. Packages available. *Society Meetings:* welcome by prior arrangement with the Secretary. Secretary: Lawrie E. Stewart (01665 602499).
e-mail: mail@alnwickgolfclub.co.uk
website: www.alnwickgolfclub.co.uk

BAMBURGH. **Bamburgh Castle Golf Club,** The Club House, Bamburgh NE69 7DE (01668 214378). *Location:* midway between Alnwick and Berwick upon Tweed on A1, take B1341 or B1342 to Bamburgh village. Seaside course with outstanding views of Farne Islands, Holy Island and magnificent coastal area. 18 holes, 5621 yards, 5132 metres. S.S.S. 67. Practice area. *Green Fees:* weekdays £33.00 per round, £40.00 per day; weekends and Bank Holidays £38.00 per round, £50.00 per day. Five-day weekday ticket £95.00. Juniors £20.00. Restricted play at weekends. *Eating facilities:* bar snacks, lunch, high tea, beverages, etc. *Visitors:* welcome except on competition days and Bank Holidays. Buggy hire. *Society Meetings:* welcome, by written application. Secretary: R.A. Patterson (01668 214321).

BEDLINGTON. **Bedlingtonshire Golf Club,** Acorn Bank, Bedlington NE22 6AA (01670 822457). *Location:* one mile south west of Bedlington on A1068. Parkland. 18 holes, 6813 yards, 6230 metres. S.S.S. 73. Practice ground and putting green. *Green Fees:* £22.00 per round midweek; £27.00 per round weekends and Bank Holidays. *Eating facilities:* catering, bar services, open all day. *Visitors:* welcome, but not before 9.00am weekdays and 10.00am weekends. *Society Meetings:* welcome, contact the Secretary. Professional: Marcus Webb (01670 822457). Secretary: (01670 822457).

ALNWICK GOLF CLUB

GREEN FEES (Subject to review for 2005/6):
Weekdays, Weekends and Bank Holidays £20 per round, £25 per day.
2 fore 1 vouchers accepted. Golf passport & special packages available.
CONTACT THE CLUBHOUSE: 01665 602632
Or apply in writing to: Lawrie Stewart, 4 Ravensmede, Alnwick NE66 2PX
e-mail: mail@alnwickgolfclub.co.uk website: www.alnwickgolfclub.co.uk

BELFORD. **The Belford,** South Road, Belford NE70 7DP (01668 213232; Fax: 01668 213282). *Location:* turn off A1 sign-posted Belford, first turning on right. Parkland course. 9 holes, 18 tee box, 6225 yards. S.S.S. 70, Par 72. Floodlit driving range. *Green Fees:* weekdays £12.00 for 9 holes, £18.00 for 18 holes; weekends £14.00 for 9 holes, £20.00 for 18 holes. *Eating facilities:* catering available 9am - 9pm, 7 days a week. *Visitors:* welcome all year. Buggies available. *Society Meetings:* open all year round to non-members, visitors and societies. Secretary: A.M. Gilhome (01668 213433). website: www.thebelford.com

BELLINGHAM. **Bellingham Golf Club,** Boggle Hole, Bellingham, Hexham NE48 2DT (01434 220152). *Location:* 15 miles north of Hexham on B6320. Situated in the picturesque North Tyne Valley between Hadrian's Wall and the Scottish Border. Rolling parkland course with an abundance of natural hazards. 18 holes, 6077 yards, 5557 metres. S.S.S. 70. Driving range. *Green Fees:* weekdays £24.00; weekends and Bank Holidays £29.00. Subject to review. *Eating facilities:* full bar and catering available throughout the golf season. *Visitors:* welcome at all times, daily starting sheet, casual visitors advised to book in advance. Buggies for hire. *Society Meetings:* welcome by advance booking. Secretary: Peter Cordiner (01434 220152/220530; Fax: 01434 220160).

BERWICK-UPON-TWEED. **Berwick-upon-Tweed (Goswick) Golf Club,** Goswick, Berwick-upon-Tweed TD15 2RW (01289 387256; Fax: 01289 387392). *Location:* signposted off A1, five miles south of Berwick-upon-Tweed. Seaside links, undulating fairways, elevated tees. 18 holes, 6686 yards. S.S.S. 72. Driving range, practice ground. *Green Fees:* weekdays £30.00 per round, £37.00 per day; weekends £35.00 per round, £45.00 per day. *Eating facilities:* full catering available. *Visitors:* welcome, restricted at weekends. Buggies and carts for hire. *Society Meetings:* welcome midweek and weekends. Professional: Paul Terras (01289 387380). Secretary: (01289 387256; Fax: 01289 387392). e-mail: goswickgc@btconnect.com
website: www.goswicklinksgc.co.uk

BERWICK-UPON-TWEED. **Magdalene Fields Golf Club,** Magdalene Fields, Berwick-upon-Tweed TD15 1NE (01289 306130). *Location:* five minutes' walk from town centre and railway station. Seaside, parkland course with stunning scenic views. 18 holes, 6407 yards. S.S.S. 71. Practice area and putting area. *Green Fees:* weekdays £20.00 per round; weekends £22.00 per round. Reductions for Senior Citizens, Ladies, Juniors, parties. Fees subject to review. *Eating facilities:* bar and dining area - first class meals. *Visitors:* welcome Monday to Saturday, restrictions on Sundays. Member of Parsport to Scenic Northumberland. *Society Meetings:* all welcome. Club Manager: M. Lynch (01289 306130). Secretary: M.J. Lynch (01289 306130).
website: www.magdalene-fields.co.uk

BLYTH. **Blyth Golf Club Ltd,** New Delaval, Blyth NE24 4DB. *Location:* 12 miles north of Newcastle near the coast. Flat parkland, water hazards. 18 holes, 6424 yards. S.S.S. 71. Large practice area and putting green. Host to Northumberland County Championships 2005. *Green Fees:* weekdays £24.00 per round, £30.00 per day; weekends £28.00 per round. *Eating facilities:* full catering and bar. *Visitors:* welcome weekdays up to 4pm and weekends after 2pm. Starting times available three days in advance; please ring Professional. *Society Meetings:* welcome, packages available. Professional: Mr Andrew Brown (01670 356514). Manager: Mr Jim Wright (01670 540110).
e-mail: clubmanager@blythgolf.com
website: www.blythgolf.co.uk

CARLISLE. **Haltwhistle Golf Course,** Wallend Farm, Greenhead, Via Carlisle CA8 7HN (016977 47367). *Location*: off the A69 at the village of Greenhead on Gilsland Road, two and a half miles west of Haltwhistle. Undulating parkland course with wooded areas. 18 holes, 5532 yards. S.S.S. 67. Practice Area. *Green Fees*: information not available. *Eating facilities*: clubhouse bar, catering by prior arrangement. *Visitors*: welcome, no restrictions except Sundays 8am to 11am competition days. *Society Meetings*: welcome by prior arrangement. Secretary: Mr K.L. Dickinson (01434 320708).

EMBLETON. **Dunstanburgh Castle Golf Club,** Embleton NE66 3XQ (01665 576562). *Location:* seven miles off A1, to the north-east of Alnwick. Seaside links course in area of outstanding natural beauty. Designed by James Braid. 18 holes, 6298 yards. S.S.S. 70. *Green Fees:* weekdays £22.00 per day; weekends £26.00 per round, £32.00 per day. *Eating facilities:* snacks, lunches, high teas; bar. *Visitors:* welcome without reservation. *Society Meetings:* welcome anytime. Secretary: P F. C. Gilbert.
e-mail: enquiries@dunstanburgh.com
website: www.dunstanburgh.com

HEXHAM. **Hexham Golf Club,** Spital Park, Hexham NE46 3RZ (01434 603072; Fax: 01434 601865). *Location:* 20 miles west of Newcastle upon Tyne, one mile west of Hexham town centre. An undulating parkland course, one of the driest in the area, with superb views of the north and south Tyne valleys. 18 holes, 6294 yards. S.S.S. 70. *Green Fees:* weekdays £30.00 per round, £40.00 per day; weekends and Bank Holidays £40.00 per round only. Special packages available. *Eating facilities:* lunches and evening meals. *Visitors:* welcome without reservation. Preliminary booking advisable. *Society Meetings:* catered for Monday to Friday by arrangement. Professional: M.W. Forster (01434 604904). Secretary: Dawn Wylie (01434 603072; Fax: 01434 601865).

THE APPEARANCE OF AN ASTERISK (*) AT THE END OF A CLUB OR COURSE ENTRY INDICATES THAT UP-TO-DATE INFORMATION HAS NOT BEEN SUPPLIED

The Blue Bell Hotel
Market Place, Belford, Northumberland NE70 7NE
Tel: 01668 213543 • Fax: 01668 213787
e-mail:bluebel@globalnet.co.uk
www.bluebellhotel.com

When you arrive at the Bell at Belford you will receive a warm, genuine welcome from the friendly staff. While retaining its 250-year-old character, the hotel offers all modern comforts, the individually decorated en suite bedrooms having all the facilities expected by today's traveller. Guests can relax in the stylish hotel bar, or in the friendly Belford Tavern complete with games room. The Garden Restaurant and the more informal Bistro offer the finest local produce, some of which comes from the hotel's own garden. This unspoilt area has a wide variety of sporting and leisure activities and places of interest.

RIVERDALE HALL HOTEL
AA ★★ RAC ★★

Opposite Bellingham Golf Course – host to county events and one of the most highly rated moorland courses in the north. Indoor pool and sauna and the only hotel in the north with Les Routiers Gold Plate Award for its restaurant. 28 bedrooms all en suite plus 8 self-catering cottages and apartments. Nearby courses include Minto and Roxburgh (Scotland), Slaley Hall, Hexham and Matfen Hall.

GOLF, BED AND BREAKFAST AND DINNER FROM £72.00 PER PERSON (TWIN ROOM).
Bellingham, Northumberland • Telephone 01434 220254
e-mail: iben@riverdalehall.demon.co.uk   **ETC ★★**

2 The Courtyard, Church Street, Berwick-upon-Tweed TD15 1EE
Golfers can expect 2, The Courtyard to be an ideal base for their holiday, as it is situated within a few minutes' walk of the lovely Magdalene Fields clifftop course, shops, restaurants and numerous interesting historic sites. Furthermore, it's only a short drive from the excellent Goswick Links, and many beautiful beaches and castles. J. Morton, 1, The Courtyard, Church Street, Berwick-upon-Tweed TD15 1EE
Tel: 01289 308737   *please see www.berwickselfcatering.co.uk*

Magdalene Fields Golf Club, Berwick-upon-Tweed, Northumberland TD15 1NE
Welcomes visitors and societies.
◆ *For enquiries and bookings Telephone (01289) 306130* ◆
www.magdalene-fields.co.uk

Visitors are welcomed at **BERWICK-UPON-TWEED GOSWICK GOLF CLUB**
Signposted off the A1, south of Berwick, only 15 minutes from the centre. The club is open all year to non-members. * Anytime weekdays * Bookings weekends * Bar service * Catering * Resident Pro
Secretary M.D. Rowell (01289 387256)   Pro Shop Mr Paul Terras (01289 387380)
e-mail: goswickgc@btconnect.com   e-mail: paul@pterras.freeserve.co.uk
www.goswicklinksgc.co.uk   ◆ *Please book via Professional*
                                         Full and Country Membership Available

Blyth Golf Club • Blyth, Northumberland NE24 4DB • 01670 540110

Enjoy our superb 18 hole parkland course, host to the Northumberland County Championships 2005. Added to this, superb catering from our Stewardess, Christine, will ensure that you have a day to remember. Genuine hospitality awaits you, here in Blyth!

Excellent package deals for Golf Societies & Company days. Ring Club Manager Jim Wright on the above number for details or e-mail clubmaster@blythgolf.com
Website: www.blythgolf.co.uk

FHG
please mention THE GOLF GUIDE when you enquire about clubs or accommodation

HEXHAM. **Tynedale Golf Club,** Tynegreen, Hexham NE46 3HQ (01434 608154). *Location:* off A69 towards Hexham over Tyne Bridge, first roundabout turn right - golf course at the end of road. Flat, parkland course along the banks of the river. 9 holes, 5403 yards. S.S.S. 67. *Green Fees:* information not available. *Eating facilities:* full catering available. *Visitors:* welcome, restricted Sunday mornings 11.30am members only. *Society Meetings:* welcome, discounts for parties over 10 people. Secretary: Trevor Hodge.

MATFEN. **Matfen Hall Golf Club,** Matfen, Newcastle-upon-Tyne NE20 0RH (01661 886400; Fax: 01661 886055). *Location:* 15 miles west of Newcastle, five miles north of Corbridge, off B6318 (Military Road). Lovely parkland setting directly in front of Matfen Hall, with natural and added water hazards. 18 holes, 6516 yards. S.S.S. 71. 9 hole, Par 3 course. Range-type practice ground. *Green Fees:* information not available. *Eating facilities:* bar, dining room. *Visitors:* very welcome any day; after 11am weekends. Good locker room facilities. 'Stay and Play' packages available at Matfen Hall Country House Hotel. *Society Meetings:* very welcome. Professional: John Harrison; Golf Manager: David Burton.*

MORPETH. **Burgham Park Golf and Leisure Club,** Near Felton, Morpeth NE65 9QP (01670 787898; Fax: 01670 787164). *Location:* 5½ miles north of Morpeth, one mile west of A1 on Longhorsley Road. 18 holes, 6751 yards, 6173 metres. S.S.S. 72. Practice area. *Green Fees:* on application. *Eating facilities:* catering and bar available daily. *Visitors:* welcome; special rates for parties by arrangement. Professional: David Mather. Secretary/Golf Manager: Terry Minett.

For full details of clubs and courses, plus convenient accommodation

www.uk-golfguide.com

MORPETH. **Longhirst Hall Golf Course,** Longhirst, Morpeth NE61 3LL (Tee Reservations: 01670 791505; Fax: 01670 818309). *Location:* on A1 3 miles north from Morpeth take B1337 Hebron road. Florida style course with two 18 hole layouts during the summer, and one layout in winter, with water featuring on many holes. Greens built to U.S.G.A. specifications. Astro Turf driving range. Full spec chipping and putting green. *Green Fees:* £20.00, £30.00 and £14.00 twilight rate depending on time of day. All prices subject to change without notice. *Eating facilities:* bar and restaurant. *Visitors:* welcome (advisable to pre-book). *Society Meetings:* welcome (any day of the week). 75 bedroom hotel on site with sports village. Sports Club Manager: (01670 791505). Bookings Administrator: Ian Brodie (01670 858519). e-mail: enquiries@longhirstgolf.co.uk
website: www.longhirstgolf.co.uk

MORPETH. **Macdonald Linden Hall,** Longhorsley, Morpeth NE65 8XF (01670 500011; Fax: 01670 500001). *Location:* A697 from A1, half a mile from Longhorsley. Mature woodland parkland and rolling countryside with many water features. 18 holes, 6846 yards. S.S.S. 73. Driving range, pitching green, putting green. *Green Fees:* weekdays £30.00, weekends £35.00. Handicap Certificate required. *Eating facilities:* Linden Tree (traditional country pub), Dobson Restaurant, function suites. *Visitors:* welcome, prior booking essential, packages available. *Society Meetings:* welcome, telephone for enquiries. Professional/Golf Manager: David Curry.

MORPETH. **The Morpeth Golf Club Ltd.,** The Clubhouse, Morpeth NE61 2BT (01670 515675). *Location:* turn off A1 for Morpeth, A167 south side of town. Easy walking parkland. 18 holes, 6206 yards. S.S.S. 69. Practice area. *Green Fees:* weekdays £25.00 per round, £30.00 per day; weekends £30.00 per round, £40.00 per day. *Eating facilities:* restaurant/bar meals/snacks etc. *Visitors:* welcome, weekdays after 9.30am, Handicap Certificates may be asked for. Venue for 1997 County Strokeplay and 2000 County Matchplay Championships. *Society Meetings:* catered for weekdays by prior arrangement; discounts available for large parties. Professional: M.R. Jackson (01670 515675). Secretary: K.D. Cazaly (01670 504942; Fax: 01670 504918).

GOLF at LINDEN HALL

We are pleased to offer you the opportunity of playing golf on our magnificent 18 hole golf course. Our fairways run through mature woodland, rolling parkland with established burns & lakes in the serene setting of the Linden Hall estate.

Special golfing accommodation packages have been arranged representing superb value for visiting golfers, in both Hotel & Dormy House Accommodation.

LINDEN HALL

Longhorsley, Morpeth, Northumberland. NE65 8XF. Pro-Shop Tel: 01670 50 00 11
E-mail stay@lindenhall.co.uk   Take a virtual tour at www.lindenhall.co.uk

See also Colour Advertisement on page 40

NEWBIGGIN-BY-THE-SEA. **Newbiggin-by-the-Sea Golf Club,** Clubhouse, Prospect Place, Newbiggin-by-the-Sea NE64 6DW (01670 817344; Fax: 01670 520236). *Location:* take signpost for Newbiggin off A189 (spine road from Tyne Tunnel). Clubhouse at most easterly point of village, adjacent to Church Point Caravan Park. Links course. 18 holes, 6452 yards, 5900 metres. S.S.S. 71. Practice area. *Green Fees:* information not available. *Eating facilities:* restaurant, bar and lounge. *Visitors:* welcome, not before 10am or on competition days. *Society Meetings:* catered for by prior arrangement with Secretary. Secretary: George Beattie (01670 817344).

NEWCASTLE UPON TYNE. **Arcot Hall Golf Club Ltd,** Arcot Hall, Dudley, Cramlington NE23 7QP (0191-236 2794). *Location:* seven miles north of Newcastle. Turn off A1 for Cramlington and then signposted. Flat, parkland – mostly tree lined. 18 holes, 6389 yards, 5840 metres. S.S.S. 70. Practice ground, chipping area, putting green. *Green Fees:* weekdays £28.00 (£23.00); weekends £32.00. *Eating facilities:* good restaurant, bar. *Visitors:* welcome, booking is essential due to popularity of the course. *Society Meetings:* catered for on application to Secretary. Professional: (0191-236 2794). Secretary: Frank Elliott (0191-236 2794).

NEWCASTLE UPON TYNE. **De Vere Slaley Hall Hotel, Golf Resort and Spa,** Hexham NE47 0BY (01434 673350; Fax: 01434 673152). *Location:* 20 miles west of Newcastle upon Tyne, seven miles south of Corbridge, signposted off A68. Set in parkland and moorland with an abundance of lakes and streams, woodland and heather. PGA European Tour Venue 2000. Hunting Course:- Championship Standard, home of the Compaq European Grand Prix: 18 holes, 7088 yards (5903 yards - ladies). S.S.S. 74, 72. Priestman Course: Championship Standard, 18 holes, 6951 yards (5755 yards - ladies). S.S.S 72, 73. Golf academy and driving Range. *Green Fees:* information not available. *Eating facilities:* clubhouse bar and restaurant; hotel bar and restaurant. *Visitors:* welcome, prior booking essential. 4-star hotel. Buggy hire. *Society Meetings:* welcome anytime, book through Golf Co-ordinator. Pro Shop (01434 673154) Manager: Mark Stancer (01434 673350; Fax: 01434 673152).*
e-mail: slaley@dircon.co.uk

NEWCASTLE UPON TYNE. **Ponteland Golf Club,** Bell Villas, Ponteland, Newcastle upon Tyne NE20 9BD (01661 822689). *Location:* A696, one and a half miles north of Newcastle Airport. Parkland. 18 holes, 6524 yards. S.S.S. 71. Large practice area. *Green Fees:* £30.00 per day or round (inclusive VAT). *Eating facilities:* full menu in restaurant and bar. *Visitors:* welcome Monday to Thursday, must be member's guest Friday, weekends and Bank Holidays. Handicap Certificate required. *Society Meetings:* Tuesdays or Thursdays, catered for with pre-booking agreed by Secretary. Professional: Alan Robson-Crosby (01661 822689). Secretary: Mrs P.M. Spong (01661 822689). e-mail: secretary@thepontelandgolfclub.co.uk
website: www.thepontelandgolfclub.co.uk

PRUDHOE. **Prudhoe Golf Club,** Eastwood Park, Prudhoe NE42 5DX (01661 832466; Fax: 01661 830710). *Location:* 10 miles west of Newcastle upon Tyne, off A695 to Hexham. Wooded parkland with scenic views of the Tyne Valley. 18 holes, 5839 yards. S.S.S. 69. Practice area. *Green Fees:* £24.00 weekdays; £32.00 weekends. £11.00 with a member, parties £20.00. *Eating facilities:* bar facilities and bar meals available. *Visitors:* welcome midweek and after 4pm weekends. *Society Meetings:* welcome. Professional: John Crawford (01661 836188). Secretary: Ian Pauw (01661 835168).

ROTHBURY. **Rothbury Golf Club**, Old Race Course, Thropton Road, Rothbury, Morpeth NE65 7TR (01669 621271). *Location:* 15 miles north of Morpeth, take A697 turn off at Weldon Bridge for Rothbury. Flat course on Haugh alongside river. 9 holes, 5779 yards. S.S.S. 67. 18 holes planned for 2006. *Green Fees:* £13.00 per round weekdays, £18.00 per round weekends. Visiting parties welcome; packages from £14.00 by arrangement with the Secretary. *Eating facilities*: catering and bar facilities available (April to November). *Visitors:* welcome weekdays except Wednesday mornings and weekends by arrangement. New Clubhouse planned for 2006. *Society Meetings:* welcome by arrangement. Secretary: D. Woolley (01669 630378).
website: www.rothburygolfclub.com

ROTHBURY GOLF CLUB • Old Race Course, Rothbury, Morpeth NE65 7TR
Tel: 01669 621271 • www.rothburygolfclub.com

NEW FOR 2006! Picturesque 18-hole course within easy walking distance of the historic village of Rothbury, with spectacular views of the Coquet Valley and the Cheviot Hills. NEW clubhouse offers bar, catering, function room, changing rooms with showers, ample car parking, driving range and practice green.
Visiting parties and societies welcome by arrangement with the Secretary.

SEAHOUSES. **Seahouses Golf Club,** Beadnell Road, Seahouses NE68 7XT (01665 720794; Fax: 01665 721994). *Location:* 15 miles north of Alnwick, turn off A1 for B1340. Flat seaside links with water hazards. 18 holes, 5542 yards. S.S.S. 67. Practice ground. *Green Fees:* weekdays £18.00 per round, £25.00 per day; weekends £25.00 per round, £30.00 per day. Juniors under 16 half rates. *Eating facilities:* full catering and bar. *Visitors:* welcome with no restrictions, please telephone clubhouse. *Society Meetings:* by arrangement. Secretary: John A. Gray (01665 720794; Fax: 01665 721994).
e-mail: secretary@seahousesgolf.co.uk
website: www.seahousesgolf.co.uk

STOCKSFIELD. **Stocksfield Golf Club,** New Ridley, Stocksfield NE43 7RE (01661 843041; Fax: 01661 843046). *Location:* 15 miles west of Newcastle on A69, and three miles east of A68. Half woodland, half parkland, slight hillside. 18 holes, 5991 yards. S.S.S. 69. Small practice areas. *Green Fees:* weekdays £18.00 per round, £24.00 per day; Saturday £30.00 per round, Sunday and Bank Holidays £25.00 per round. Subject to review. Reduced rates for parties of over 10 and 20. *Eating facilities:* available, also bar. 2-fore-1 tickets accepted. *Visitors:* welcome except Wednesday mornings and not until 4pm Saturdays. Full size snooker table. Buggies, trolleys and clubs for hire. *Society Meetings:* catered for by prior arrangement. Professional: (01661 843041; Fax: 01661 843046). Secretary: B. Garrow (01661 843041; Fax: 01661 843046).

SWARLAND. **Percy Wood Golf & Country Retreat,** Coast View, Swarland, Morpeth NE65 9JG (01670 787940). *Location:* approximately one mile west of A1 trunk road, eight miles south of Alnwick. Undulating parkland course within mature woodland. 18 holes, 6628 yards, 6060 metres. S.S.S. 72. *Green Fees:* weekdays £15.00 per round, weekends £20.00 per round. *Eating facilities:* full dining facilities, bar meals, licensed bar. *Visitors:* welcome any day, but suggest telephoning to avoid club competitions on Sundays. Accommodation available on site. *Society Meetings:* welcome. Golf Shop: (01670 787010). Secretary: Keith Rutter (01670 787010).

WARKWORTH. **Warkworth Golf Club,** The Links, Warkworth, Morpeth NE65 0SW (01665 711596). *Location:* off A1068 at Warkworth. Seaside links orginally designed by "Old Tom Morris" in 1891. 9 holes, 5986 yards, S.S.S. 69. Practice area. *Green Fees:* weekdays £12.00 per day, weekends £20.00 per day. *Eating facilities:* bar open 11.30am to 2.30pm and from 7.30pm to 11pm during season. *Visitors:* welcome except Tuesdays and Saturdays. *Society Meetings:* welcome by arrangement. Secretary: M. Rowe (01665 711596).

WOOLER. **Wooler Golf Club,** Dod Law, Doddington, Wooler NE71 6EA. *Location:* situated on the high ground named Dod Law to the east of the B6525 Wooler–Berwick road. The route is signposted from Doddington village. Hillside course with exceptional panoramic views. 9 holes (18 tees), 6411 yards. S.S.S. 71. Limited practice area. *Green Fees:* weekdays £15.00 per day, weekends and Bank Holidays £20.00 per day. *Eating facilities:* bar open evenings (operated voluntarily). *Visitors:* always welcome except during all day competitions, check with Secretary. Buggies available. *Society Meetings:* welcome by arrangement with Secretary. Secretary: S. Lowrey (01668 281631).

For full details of clubs and courses, plus convenient accommodation
www.uk-golfguide.com

SEAHOUSES GOLF CLUB 18 HOLES, 5542 YARDS, S.S.S. 67.
Green Fees: £18 per round/£25 per day (weekdays), £25 per round/£30 per day (weekends & Bank Holidays). Full catering and bar. Visitors, Society meetings by arrangement.
For details Tel: Secretary 01665 720794 or Fax: 01665 721994
Beadnell Road, Seahouses, Northumberland NE68 7XT
e-mail: secretary@seahousesgolf.co.uk • website:www.seahousesgolf.co.uk

---

PLEASE MENTION THIS GUIDE WHEN YOU ENQUIRE ABOUT CLUBS OR ACCOMMODATION

Nottinghamshire

BRAMCOTE. **Bramcote Hills Golf Course,** Thoresby Road, off Derby Road, Bramcote NG9 3EP (0115 928 1880). *Location:* A52 Nottingham to Derby road, close to Bramcote Leisure Centre, turn off A52 at Bramcote into Thoresby Road, half a mile on left hand side. Mainly flat parkland but some slightly hilly areas. 18 holes, 1500 yards. Par 3. *Green Fees:* information not available. *Eating facilities:* refreshments available. *Visitors:* always welcome anytime, pay and play course. *Society Meetings:* welcome.*
website: www.bramcotehillsgolf.com

BULWELL. **Bulwell Forest Golf Club,** Hucknall Road, Bulwell NG6 9LQ (0115 977 0576) *Location:* A610 north of Nottingham, M1 Junction 26, three miles from course. Heathland or links type course, very tight. 18 holes, 5616 yards. S.S.S. 67. *Green Fees:* £13.00 per round weekdays; £16.00 per round weekends. Visitors 4 ball £44.00. *Eating facilities:* bar snacks available, societies or parties catered to order. *Visitors:* welcome weekdays except Tuesday mornings (Ladies' Day) and limited times weekends. Flat green bowls, hard tennis court and children's play ground all on site. *Society Meetings:* catered for, but book well in advance. Secretary: David Nehra (0115 9770576; Fax: 0115 9671734).
e-mail: david@dnehra.co.uk

CALVERTON. **Ramsdale Park Golf Centre,** Oxton Road, Calverton NG14 6NU (0115 965 5600). *Location:* north east of Nottingham city, on B6386 Oxton Road. 25 bay covered floodlit range. 18 hole main course and 18 hole Par 3 course. *Fees:* information not available. *Eating facilities:* bar, restaurants. Food all day. Function room. *Opening hours:* 7.30am to 11pm. Professional tuition, PGA video teaching bay and custom-fit centre. Manager: N. R. Birch.*

www.uk-golfguide.com

CALVERTON. **Springwater Golf Club,** Moor Lane, Calverton, Nottingham NG14 6FZ (0115 965 4946). *Location:* off A6097. Moor Lane is one mile south east of Oxton roundabout, course one mile south east of Calverton. Parkland course set in an orchard with new and mature trees, four ponds, well drained. 18 holes, 6262 yards. S.S.S. 71. Floodlit driving range. *Green Fees:* information not available. *Eating facilities:* fully licensed, bar food, and function rooms available every day. *Visitors:* welcome, weekdays and weekends off peak, seven day booking in advance for non-members. Dress code in operation. *Society Meetings:* weekdays and off peak weekends. Professional: Mr Paul Drew (0115 965 2129). Secretary: Bill Turner (0115 965 2565).*

EAST LEAKE. **Rushcliffe Golf Club,** Stocking Lane, East Leake, Near Loughborough LE12 5RL (01509 852959). *Location:* on A60 signposted eight miles south of Nottingham. Wooded hills on edge of the Wolds. 18 holes, 6013 yards, 5800 metres. S.S.S. 70. Practice ground. *Green Fees:* information not available. *Eating facilities*: full catering except Mondays when bar snacks only. *Visitors:* welcome with reservation, weekends without a member between 9.30am to 11am and 3pm to 4.30pm. *Society Meetings:* catered for Mondays, Wednesdays, Thursdays and Fridays strictly by prior booking. Professional: Chris Hall (01509 852701). Secretary: C. Bee (01509 852959).
e-mail: secretary@rushcliffegolfclub.com
website: www.rushcliffegolfclub.com

EDWALTON. **Edwalton Golf Courses,** Wellin Lane, Edwalton, Nottingham NG12 4AS (0115 923 4775). *Location:* follow Nottingham ring road, course signposted from roundabout on ring road. Gently sloping parkland. 9 holes, 3342 yards. S.S.S. 72. Also 9 hole par 3 course. Driving range (seasonal). *Green Fees:* prices on application. *Eating facilities:* first class catering, bar open all day. *Visitors:* welcome, book in advance. Professional: Lee Rawlings (0115 923 4775). Secretary: Debbie (0115 923 5473 Mon-Fri 8.30am-12.30pm).

Ramsdale Park Golf Centre

A 'BURHILL GOLF CENTRES Ltd' course.

6500yd Seely Course. A fairly flat front nine is followed by an undulating back nine that has the reputation of being one of the best nine holes in the area.

2800yd Lee Course. An outstanding par 3 course designed to sharpen and improve a player's short game. Enables societies the opportunity to play two courses in one day.

Covered 23 bay floodlit driving range with video bay. Modern clubhouse includes well stocked shop. Society and company days a speciality.

Oxton Road, Calverton
Nottingham NG14 6NU Tel: 0115 965 5600 Fax: 0115 965 4105 View the course on: www.ramsdaleparkgc.co.uk

Nottinghamshire / ENGLAND

HUCKNALL. Leen Valley Golf Centre, Wigwam Lane, Hucknall, Nottingham NG15 7TA (0115 9642037; Fax: 0115 9642724). *Location:* 300 yards from Hucknall Railway Station (signposted). Parkland course. 18 holes, 6521 yards. S.S.S. 70. Putting green, driving range opens 2005. *Green Fees:* weekdays £11.00, weekends £17.00 (2006 fees subject to review). *Eating facilities:* "Swan" bar and restaurant. *Visitors:* always welcome. Handicap certificates not required. *Society Meetings:* always welcome. Manager/Professional: James Sawford.

KIRKBY-IN-ASHFIELD. Notts. Golf Club Ltd, Hollinwell, Kirkby-in-Ashfield, Nottingham NG17 7QR (01623 753225; Fax: 01623 753655). *Location:* three miles from Exit 27 on M1, turn off M1 then left on A611. Testing heathland championship course. 18 holes, 7098 yards. S.S.S. 75. *Green Fees:* on application. *Visitors:* welcome on production of Handicap Certificate (weekends and Bank Holidays on application only). Advisable to book beforehand. *Society Meetings:* welcome weekdays. Professional: Mike Bradley. Secretary: Brian Noble.*

LENTON LANE. Riverside Golf Centre, Trentside, Lenton Lane NG7 2SA. *Location*: A52 Nottingham to Grantham, two miles from Nottingham city centre, near Clifton Bridge. Flat course, easy to walk. 9 holes, 2000 yards. S.S.S. 31. Par 3 course. *Green Fees*: information not available. *Eating facilities*: licensed restaurant/bar. Excellent facilities. *Visitors*: welcome all week. Pay and play course, booking required. *Society Meetings*: very welcome. Professionals: Neil Thacker, Russell Meek (0115 9862179; Fax: 01159 865989). Secretary: G. Meek (0115 9862220; Fax: 01159 865989).*

LONG EATON. Trent Lock Golf Centre, Lock Lane, Sawley, Long Eaton, Nottingham NG10 2FY (0115 9464398; Fax: 0115 9461183). *Location:* Sawley/Long Eaton, two miles from M1 Junctions 24 and 25. Set in rural countryside with six lakes and River Trent. 18 holes, 6000 yards, Par 69. 9 hole Pay and Play, 2990 yards, Par 36. 23 bay floodlit driving range. *Green Fees:* information not available. *Eating facilities:* à la carte restaurant (0115 9461184), bar food, 200 seater function room. *Visitors:* welcome anytime. *Society Meetings:* all welcome. Professional: Mark Taylor. Director of Golf: E.W. McCausland (0115 9464398). *

THE APPEARANCE OF AN ASTERISK (*) AT THE END OF A CLUB OR COURSE ENTRY INDICATES THAT UP-TO-DATE INFORMATION HAS NOT BEEN SUPPLIED

MANSFIELD. Coxmoor Golf Club, Coxmoor Road, Sutton in Ashfield, Mansfield NG17 5LF (01623 559878). *Location:* exit Junction 27 M1, A611 for three miles. Testing heathland championship course. 18 holes, 6589 yards. S.S.S. 72. Practice area and nets. *Green Fees:* weekdays £40.00 per round, £55.00 per day. Golf/food packages available. *Eating facilities:* restaurant and bars. *Visitors:* welcome except weekends and Bank Holidays, pre-book through Professional. (Tuesday Ladies' Day). *Society Meetings:* catered for by prior application to Secretary. Professional: David Ridley (01623 559906). Secretary: P. Snow (01623 557359). e-mail: coxmoor@freeuk.com website: www.coxmoor.freeuk.com

MANSFIELD. Mansfield Woodhouse Golf Club, Leeming Lane North, Mansfield Woodhouse NG19 9EU (01623 23521). *Location:* Junction 27 of M1, A60 Mansfield – Warsop. Flat parkland. 9 holes, 2446 yards. S.S.S. 64. *Green Fees:* information not available. *Eating facilities:* bar snacks. *Visitors:* welcome, unrestricted – pay and play. Professional: L. Highfield Jnr. (01623 23521). Manager/Secretary: S.L. Highfield (01623 623521).*

MANSFIELD. Sherwood Forest Golf Club, Eakring Road, Mansfield NG18 3EW (01623 623327). *Location:* leave M1 at Exit 27, take signs for Mansfield, proceed via Southwell Road and Oak Tree Lane - course is located one mile east on Eakring Road. Traditional heathland course with an abundance of heather, pines and silver birch. 18 holes, 6849 yards. S.S.S. 74. Two practice grounds. *Green Fees:* £50.00 per round, £70.00 per day. *Eating facilities:* gent's bar with snooker table, mixed lounge and dining room; full catering service every day. *Visitors:* welcome by arrangement and must be member of a recognised golf club with a Handicap. *Society Meetings:* catered for by arrangement. Professional/ Golf Manager: K. Hall (01623 627403; Fax: 01623 420412). e-mail: sherwood@forest43.freeserve.co.uk

MAPPERLEY. Mapperley Golf Club, Central Avenue, Plains Road, Mapperley NG3 6RH (0115 9556672). *Location:* B684, four miles north east of centre of Nottingham. Hilly picturesque course. 18 holes, 6335 yards. S.S.S. 70. Practice ground. *Green Fees:* weekdays £22.50 per round; weekends £27.50 per round. *Eating facilities:* bar and food all day. *Visitors:* welcome except Saturdays and Ladies' Day (Tuesdays). *Society Meetings:* catered for, please ring Professional for price. Professional: Jasen Barker (0115 9556673). Secretary: Alan Newton (0115 9556672).

PINE LODGE HOTEL www.pinelodge-hotel.co.uk
281 Nottingham Road, Mansfield, Nottinghamshire NG18 4SE

Close to Coxmoor, Hollinwell and Sherwood Forest Golf Clubs – we offer quality, value, service – and a warm welcome – in addition to the good food, car parking, garden and sauna. All bedrooms en suite – featuring r/c colour TV with Fastext and satellite stations, direct-dial phone and tea/coffee making facilities.

Tel: 01623 622308 • Fax: 01623 656819 • e-mail: enquiries@pinelodge-hotel.co.uk

NEWARK. **Newark Golf Club,** Coddington, Newark NG24 2QX (01636 626241; Fax: 01636 626497). *Location:* off the A17 Sleaford road four miles east of Newark. Parkland, wooded course. 18 holes, 6444 yards. S.S.S. 71. Practice ground. *Green Fees:* £27.00 weekdays; weekends £33.00. *Eating facilities:* full catering, bar all day. *Visitors:* welcome with reservation. Handicap Certificates will be required. Restriction at peak times Saturday and Sunday, Ladies' Day Tuesday. Snooker. Professional tuition and computer/video analysis. *Society Meetings:* welcome except Tuesdays, weekends. Professional: P. Lockley (01636 626492). Secretary: D.A. Collingwood (01636 626282).

NOTTINGHAM. **Beeston Fields Golf Club,** Old Drive, Wollaton Road, Beeston NG9 3DD (0115 925 7062). *Location:* Wollaton road off A52 Derby road, M1, Exit 25. Parkland. 18 holes, 6414 yards. S.S.S. 71. Practice ground and net available. *Green Fees:* weekdays £33.00, weekends £39.00. *Eating facilities:* available daily. *Visitors:* welcome with reservation, Tuesday and Fridays not until 2.30pm. *Society Meetings:* catered for Mondays and Wednesdays. Professional: Alun Wardle (0115 925 7062). Secretary: J. Lewis (0115 925 7062). e-mail: beestonfields@btconnect.com website: www.beestonfields.co.uk

NOTTINGHAM. **Chilwell Manor Golf Club,** Meadow Lane, Chilwell, Nottingham NG9 5AE (0115 925 8958; Fax: 0115 922 0575). *Location:* four miles from Nottingham on main Nottingham to Birmingham road. Flat parkland course. 18 holes, 6379 yards. S.S.S. 70. *Green Fees:* weekdays £30.00; weekends £35.00. *Eating facilities:* available. *Visitors:* welcome weekdays with reservation, restricted at certain busy times. *Society Meetings:* societies catered for by appointment (minimum 16). Professional: P. Wilson. Hon. Secretary: D. Shakespeare.
e-mail: chilwellmanorgolfclub@barbox.net

www.uk-golfguide.com
For full details of clubs and courses, plus convenient accommodation

NOTTINGHAM. **Cotgrave Place Golf and Country Club,** Stragglethorpe, Nottingham NG12 3HB (0115 9333344; Fax: 0115 9334567). *Location:* two minutes east of Nottingham on the A52 towards Radcliffe-on-Trent, 20 miles from M1. Lakeside and parkland course. Two courses: Open Course 18 holes, 6290 yards; Masters Course 18 holes, 5933 yards. 9 bay floodlit driving range, practice net, short game area, putting green. *Green Fees:* weekdays Open Course £25.50, Masters £23.50; weekends Open Course £30.50, Masters £28.50. *Eating facilities:* restaurant and snack bar. *Visitors:* welcome at all times, subject to reservation. Conference facilities for up to 200 people. *Society Meetings:* welcome, please telephone for packages. Professional: Robert Smith. Secretary: Mike Evans. e-mail: cotgrave@americangolf.com

NOTTINGHAM. **Nottingham City Golf Club,** Lawton Drive, Bulwell, Nottingham NG6 8BL (0115 927 8021). *Location:* exit 26 M1, at first roundabout follow signs for Bulwell. Parkland. 18 holes, 6218 yards. S.S.S. 70. Practice area. *Green Fees:* information not available. *Eating facilities:* available. *Visitors:* welcome anytime except Saturdays. *Society Meetings:* welcome by prior arrangement. Professional: C. Jepson (0115 927 2767). Secretary: Gary Chappell (07740 288 694).

NOTTINGHAM. **Oakmere Park Golf Club,** Oaks Lane, Oxton, Near Nottingham NG25 0RH (0115 965 3545; Fax: 0115 965 5628). *Location:* eight miles north east of Nottingham on A614. Parkland course. Admirals Course: 18 holes, 6612 yards, S.S.S. 72. Commanders Course: 9 holes, 6573 yards, S.S.S. 72. 20 bay floodlit driving range. *Green Fees:* Admirals Course: weekdays £20.00; weekends £26.00. Special rates for High Season (April - September) and reduced rates for twilight. Commanders Course: weekdays 9 holes £6.00; 18 holes £10.00; weekends 9 holes £8.00, 18 holes £14.00. *Eating facilities:* clubhouse bar, spike bar, restaurant and resident chef. *Visitors:* welcome at all times, phone to book. *Society Meetings:* welcome, weekends after 2.00pm require maximum notice possible. Professional/Director of Golf: Daryl St. John Jones.

Oakmere Park Golf Club
"The All Weather Course"

Admiral's Course: 18 holes, 6612 yards, SSS 72
Commander's Course: 9 holes, 6573 yards, SSS 72
◆ Full clubhouse facilities ◆ Pro Shop
◆ Practice facilities with a premier learning academy.
◆ Societies welcome ◆ Package deals available
Green Fees from £20 weekdays, £28 weekends (Admiral's);
from £6 for 9 holes weekdays (Commander's)
Professional: Daryl St John Jones
Oakmere Park Golf Club
Oaks Lane, Oxton, Nottingham NG25 0RH
Tel: 0115 965 3545 • Fax: 0115 965 5628
enquiries@oakmerepark.co.uk • www.oakmerepark.co.uk

Nottinghamshire / ENGLAND

NOTTINGHAM. Ruddington Grange Golf Club, Wilford Road, Ruddington, Nottingham NG11 6NB (0115 9214139). *Location:* M1 Junction 24 Nottingham road, A52 to Nottingham Knight island, right to Ruddington, half a mile outside Ruddington. Parkland. 18 holes, 6543 yards, 5984 metres. S.S.S. 72. *Green Fees:* information not available. *Eating facilities:* full restaurant. *Visitors:* welcome all the time but at weekends members have priority. Tee times must be booked, *Society Meetings:* welcome Monday to Friday. Professional: R. Simpson (0115 9211951). Secretary: A. Johnson.*
e-mail: info@ruddingtongrange.com
website: www.ruddingtongrange.com

NOTTINGHAM. Wollaton Park Golf Club, Lime Tree Avenue, Wollaton Park, Nottingham NG8 1BT (0115 978 7574; Fax: 0115 970 0736). *Location:* entrance off slip road from A52 Derby Road at junction A614 Nottingham Ringroad. Traditional parkland course with many mature trees; two deer herds roam the course. 18 holes, 6445 yards. S.S.S. 71. Two practice areas and pitch and putt course. *Green Fees:* weekdays £35.00/£48.00; weekends £40.00/£55.00. Special rates on application for visiting societies. *Eating facilities:* full restaurant and snack bar. *Visitors:* welcome at all times except Wednesday which is Ladies' Day. *Society Meetings:* catered for Tuesdays and Fridays. Professional: John Lower (0115 978 4834). Secretary: Avril Jamieson (0115 978 7574).*
e-mail: wollatonparkgc@aol.com

RADCLIFFE-ON-TRENT. Radcliffe-on-Trent Golf Club, Dewberry Lane, Cropwell Road, Radcliffe-on-Trent NG12 2JH (0115 9333000). *Location:* A52 from Nottingham turn right at traffic lights on Cropwell Road; 400 yards along on left hand side. Flat, wooded parkland. 18 holes, 6423 yards. S.S.S. 71. Two large practice areas. *Green Fees:* weekdays £24.00 per day, weekends £30.00 per day (reductions for members' guests). *Eating facilities:* snacks, meals and bar. *Visitors:* welcome, confirm course availability with Professional or Secretary. *Society Meetings:* catered for on Wednesdays. Professional: Craig George (Telephone & Fax: 0115 9332396). Secretary: Les Wake (0115 9333000; Fax: 0115 9116991).
e-mail: les.rotgc@talk21.com
website: www.radcliffeontrentgc.com

RETFORD. Retford Golf Club Ltd, Brecks Road, Ordsall, Retford DN22 7UA (01777 711188). *Location:* one mile south off A620 midway between Worksop and Gainsborough. Wooded parkland. 18 holes, 6409 yards. S.S.S. 72, Par 72. Practice ground. *Green Fees:* information not available. *Eating facilities:* meals available and licensed bar. *Visitors:* welcome, except Tuesday mornings. *Society Meetings:* welcome by prior arrangement. Professional: C. Morris (01777 703733). Secretary/Manager: Mrs Linda Colclough (01777 711188; Fax: 01777 710412).*
e-mail: retfordgolfclub@lineone.net

RUFFORD. Rufford Park Golf & Country Club, Rufford Lane, Rufford, Newark NG18 4SY (01623 825253; Fax: 01623 825254). *Location:* 400 yards off A614, two miles south of Ollerton roundabout. Map available on request. Scenic parkland course. 18 holes, 6343 yards. S.S.S. 70. 16-bay floodlit driving range, practice facilities. *Green Fees:* information not available. *Eating facilities:* clubhouse and restaurant with spectacular views. Large function suite and meeting rooms for up to 200 people. *Visitors:* always welcome; buggies for hire. *Society Meetings:* corporate hospitality and society days catered for. *Professionals:* James Thompson and John Vaughan. Secretary: Kay Whitehead.*
website: www.ruffordpark.co.uk

SOUTHWELL. Norwood Park Golf Course Ltd, Norwood Park, Southwell NG25 0PF (01636 816626). *Location:* half-a-mile west of Southwell, off the road to Kirklington. American style layout parkland course in beautiful grounds of stately home. Natural water features and large undulating greens. 18-acre grass practice ground. 18 holes, 6805 yards from the back tees. Par 72. *Green Fees:* from £18.00. *Eating facilities:* available. *Visitors:* always welcome. 2-4-1 welcome any day. *Society Meetings:* always welcome. Conference facilities in stately home available. Professional: Paul Thornton. Secretary: Ron Beckett. Manager: Henry Starkey.
e-mail: mail@norwoodgolf.com

SOUTHWELL. Southwell Golf Club, Southwell Racecourse, Rolleston, Newark NG25 0TS (01636 816501/813706). Flat parkland course with water features. 18 holes, 5767 yards, S.S.S. 68. Driving nets, pitching, putting green, practice area. *Green Fees*: weekdays £15.00, with member £10.00; weekends £18.00, with member £10.00. *Eating facilities*: full service all day. *Visitors*: welcome, please book in advance. 12 bedroomed Motel on site. Professional: Chris White (01636 813706). Secretary: Mike Harness (01636 821651).
e-mail: misylharness@btinternet.com

STANTON-ON-THE-WOLDS. Stanton-on-the-Wolds Golf Club, Golf Course Road, Stanton-on-the-Wolds NG12 5BH (0115 937 4885). *Location:* seven miles south of Nottingham, one mile west of main Nottingham - Melton road. Meadow land. 18 holes, 6437 yards, 5886 metres. S.S.S. 71. Practice ground. *Green Fees:* information not available. *Eating facilities:* restaurant and bar. *Visitors:* welcome by prior arrangement with Secretary, weekends with member only. *Society Meetings:* catered for by arrangement with Secretary. Professional: Nick Hernon (0115 937 2390). Secretary: Mr M. J. Hathway (0115 937 4885).

THE APPEARANCE OF AN ASTERISK (*) AT THE END OF A CLUB OR COURSE ENTRY INDICATES THAT UP-TO-DATE INFORMATION HAS NOT BEEN SUPPLIED

WORKSOP. **Bondhay Golf Club,** Bondhay Lane, Whitwell, Worksop S80 3EH (01909 723608 Fax: 01909 720226. *Location:* from Junction 30 M1, A619 signposted after three-and-a-half miles. Turn left onto Bondhay lane. Flat with bordering woodland. 18 holes, 6839 yards. S.S.S.72. Par 3 family course, floodlit driving range, putting green, buggies for hire. *Green Fees:* information not available. *Eating facilities:* full catering service available. *Visitors:* welcome. *Society Meetings:* welcome, phone for brochure. Golf Professional: M. Ramsden. Director: Helen Hardisty.*

WORKSOP. **College Pines Golf Club,** Worksop College Drive, Worksop S80 3AP (Clubhouse 01909 488785; Pro Shop: 01909 501431; Fax: 01909 481227). *Location:* situated on outskirts of town on B6034, Edwinstowe road adjacent to Worksop College. Heathland course surrounded by woodland; very well drained, with Winter play a speciality. 18 holes, 6801 yards. S.S.S. 73. Driving range and short game practice area. *Green Fees:* weekdays £13.00 per round, £9.00 with a member; weekends £19.00, £11.00 with a member. Discounts for parties of 20 plus. Subject to review. *Eating facilities:* full facilities. *Visitors:* welcome by appointment; phone for starting times. *Society Meetings:* welcome by appointment. Golf Director/Professional: Charles Snell (01909 501431).

WORKSOP. **Kilton Forest Golf Club,** Blyth Road, Worksop S81 0TL (01909 479199). *Location:* main Worksop to Blyth road, right hand side. Undulating parkland. 18 holes, 6424 yards. S.S.S. 71, Par 72. Practice and putting areas. *Green Fees:* information not available. *Eating facilities:* bar meals and restaurant area. *Visitors:* welcome, club competitions most Sundays – check with Professional. *Society Meetings:* by arrangement with Professional. Professional: Stuart Betteridge (01909 486563). Secretary: Alan Mansbridge.

WORKSOP. **Lindrick Golf Club,** Lindrick Common, Worksop S81 8BH (01909 485802). *Location*: on A57 four miles west of Worksop. M1 Junction 31 on to A57 Worksop. Heathland. 18 holes, 6612 yards, 6046 metres. S.S.S. 71. Two practice areas. *Green Fees:* £50.00 per round, £60.00 per day; winter (1 Dec–31 Mar) £40.00 per day. *Eating facilities*: dining room. *Visitors*: welcome weekdays, except Tuesday mornings. Prior booking required. *Society Meetings:* catered for weekdays. Professional: John King (01909 475820). Secretary: John Armitage (01909 475282; Fax: 01909 488685).
website: www.lindrickgolfclub.co.uk

WORKSOP. **Worksop Golf Club,** Windmill Lane, Worksop S80 2SQ (01909 477731; Fax: 01909 477732). *Location:* just off Worksop bypass (A57), take B6034 Edwinstowe immediately left; clubhouse 400 yards. Heathland with gorse, broom, birch and oak; easy walking. 18 holes, 6660 yards. S.S.S. 72. Practice ground. *Green Fees:* weekdays 18 holes £35.00, per day £48.00; weekends £48.00 (18 holes only). *Eating facilities:* dining room and bar. *Visitors:* welcome, except weekends November to March without member. Advise preliminary phone call to Professional. Snooker table. *Society Meetings:* weekdays only by arrangement with Professional. Not Bank Holidays. Professional: C. Weatherhead (01909 477732). Secretary: D.A. Dufall 01909 477731; Fax: 01909 530917).

For full details of clubs and courses, plus convenient accommodation
www.uk-golfguide.com

- 18 Hole Par 72 Championship course
- 9 Hole Par 3 family course
- Floodlit driving range

EXCELLENT WINTER COURSE - *good drainage.*
SOCIETY PACKAGES available for parties of 12 or more including weekends & Bank Holidays.
Tel: 01909 723608 - *Fax:* 01909 729226
Bondhay Lane, Whitwell, Worksop, Nottinghamshire. S80 3EH
- *www.bondhay.com* -

Visit the FHG website
www.holidayguides.com
for details of the wide choice of accommodation featured in the full range of FHG titles

Oxfordshire

ABINGDON. **Frilford Heath Golf Club,** Abingdon OX13 5NW (01865 390864; Fax: 01865 390823). *Location:* on A338 Oxford/Wantage Road seven miles south-west of Oxford, four miles west of Abingdon. Flat, wooded heathland. Red course: 18 holes, 6617 yards yellow tees, 6884 white tees. S.S.S. 71/73; Green course: 18 holes, 5763 yards yellow tees, 6006 white tees. S.S.S. 69; Blue course: 18 holes, 6379 yards yellow tees, 6728 white tees. S.S.S 71/72. Three practice areas. *Green Fees:* weekdays £55.00; weekends and Bank Holidays £70.00; after 5pm £30.00 all week. *Eating facilities:* first class restaurant and bars. *Visitors:* welcome weekdays with Handicap Certificate, phone ahead for weekends and Bank Holidays. *Society Meetings:* welcome weekdays, enquire at office. Professional: D.C. Craik (01865 390887). Secretary/Manager: S. Styles (01865 390864).
e-mail: reservations@frilfordheath.co.uk

BANBURY. **Banbury Golf Centre,** Aynho Road, Adderbury, Banbury OX17 3NT (01295 810419; Fax: 01295 810056). *Location*: 6 miles south of Banbury on B4100. M40 junction 10 or 11. Undulating wooded course with water features. Three 9 hole courses, can be played in various combinations. Red & Yellow Course, 18 holes, 6553 yards, S.S.S. 71. Yellow & Blue Course, 6599 yards, S.S.S. 71. Red & Blue course, 6706 yards, S.S.S. 72. *Green Fees*: information not available. *Eating facilities*: bar menu and 3 course meals available. *Visitors*: welcome at all times. Tuition available. *Society Meetings*: welcome at all times. Professional: Stuart Kier (01295 812880; Fax: 01295 810056). Secretary: A.M. Prestidge.*
e-mail: office@banburygolfcentre.co.uk
website: www.banburygolfcentre.co.uk

BANBURY. **Cherwell Edge Golf Club,** c/o Cherwell Edge Course, Chacombe, Banbury OX17 2EN (01295 711591). *Location:* half-a-mile off M40 at Banbury. Parkland. 18 holes, 6085 yards. S.S.S. 69 men, 69 ladies. Practice area. *Green Fees:* information on request. *Eating facilities:* restaurant and bar. *Visitors:* welcome, some time restrictions. *Society Meetings:* welcome, some time restrictions. Professional: Jason Newman (01295 711591). Manager: David Newman (01295 711591).
e-mail: enquiries@cherwelledgegolfclub.co.uk
website: www.cherwelledgegolfclub.co.uk

BANBURY. **Rye Hill Golf Course,** Milcombe, Banbury OX15 4RU (01295 721818; Fax: 01295 720089). *Location:* six miles from Junction 11 M40 at Banbury, turn off A361 and follow signs through to Milcombe. Naturally free draining course. 18 holes, 6919 yards. S.S.S 73. Practice ground, three teaching academy holes. *Green Fees:* weekdays £20.00, weekends £25.00. 9-hole rates. *Eating facilities:* spike bar and restaurant. *Visitors:* welcome, no restrictions. Booking advisable at weekends. Trolleys can always be used. *Society Meetings:* welcome; various packages available. Professional: T. Pennock.

BANBURY. **Tadmarton Heath Golf Club,** Wigginton, Banbury OX15 5HL (01608 737278; Fax: 01608 730548). *Location:* off M40 Junction 11, off A422, off B4035, five miles west of Banbury. Flat links; heathland. 18 holes, 5917 yards. S.S.S. 69. Practice area. *Green Fees:* weekdays £45.00; weekends £25.00 with a member only. *Eating facilities:* full catering and bars. *Visitors:* welcome weekdays (restrictions Thursdays); weekends with member only. Must be member of another golf club with Handicap Certificate. Hand carts available. *Society Meetings:* welcome weekdays by prior arrangement. Professional: Tom Jones (01608 730047). Secretary: J. R. Cox (01608 737278; Fax: 01608 730548).
e-mail: thgc@btinternet.com
website: www.thgc.btinternet.co.uk

BICESTER. **Bicester Golf & Country Club,** Chesterton, Near Bicester OX6 8TE (01869 241204). *Location:* five minutes from Junction 9 M40, one mile off A421, Bicester/Oxford. Two miles south-west of Bicester. Flat parkland course. 18 holes, 6013 yards. S.S.S. 70. Practice ground and putting green. *Green Fees:* information not available. *Eating facilities:* restaurant and bar meals available daily. *Visitors:* welcome at all times, telephone bookings up to four days ahead. *Society Meetings:* welcome by prior arrangement. Professional: Julian Goodman (01869 242023). Manager: Paul Fox (01869 241204).*

BURFORD. **Burford Golf Club,** Burford OX18 4JG (01993 822149). *Location:* A40 - Burford roundabout. Flat parkland with superb greens. 18 holes, 6401 yards. S.S.S. 71. *Green Fees:* £36.00 per day weekdays. *Eating facilities:* full catering. *Visitors:* welcome weekdays and weekends by arrangement with the Secretary. *Society Meetings:* catered for on application. Professional: Michael Ridge (01993 822344). Secretary: Robin Thompson (01993 822583; Fax: 01993 822801).

CHIPPING NORTON. **Chipping Norton Golf Club,** Southcombe, Chipping Norton OX7 5QH (01608 642383; Fax: 01608 645422). *Location:* Junction of A3400 and A44, 18 miles from Oxford, 20 miles from Stratford-on-Avon. Downland with lakes and trees and four Par 3s. 18 holes, 6316 yards, 5830 metres. S.S.S. 70. Practice ground and putting green. *Green Fees:* £28.00 per day. *Eating facilities:* diningroom and bars – new clubhouse. *Visitors:* welcome Monday to Friday but not Bank Holidays. *Society Meetings:* welcome Mondays to Fridays by arrangement. Professional: Neil Rowlands (01608 643356; Fax: 01608 645422). Secretary: Simon Chislett (01608 642383; Fax: 01608 645422).
website: www.chippingnortongolfclub.com

CHIPPING NORTON. **The Wychwood Golf Club,** Lyneham, Chipping Norton OX7 6QQ (01993 831841; Fax: 01993 831775). *Location:* six miles from Burford off the A361 Burford to Chipping Norton Road. Parkland, several interesting water holes. 18 holes, 6669 yards, 6099 metres. S.S.S. 72. Practice range (15 bays). *Green Fees:* weekdays £24.00 per round, £30.00 per day; weekends £28.00 per round, £37.00 per day. *Eating facilities:* bar, dining room, lounge. *Visitors:* always welcome, can book start time three days in advance. *Society Meetings:* welcome, various packages available, assistance available for starting, score cards, notice board, etc. Professional: James Fincher. Hon. Secretary: Cyril Howkins. Administrator: Susan Lakin.

DIDCOT. **Hadden Hill Golf Club,** Wallingford Road, Didcot OX11 9BJ (01235 510410). *Location:* on A4130, half-a-mile east of Didcot on the Wallingford road. Well drained parkland with superb greens - never closed for rain! 18 holes, 6563 yards. S.S.S. 71. 20-bay floodlit driving range. *Green Fees:* 18 holes - weekdays £18.00, weekends £23.00. No credit cards. *Eating facilities:* good food all day, every day. *Visitors:* telephone bookings for tee times. *Society Meetings:* very welcome weekdays only. Professional: Ian Mitchell (01235 510410). Secretary: Michael Morley (01235 510410; Fax: 01235 511260). website: www.haddenhillgolf.co.uk

DRAYTON. **Drayton Park Golf Course,** Steventon Road, Drayton, near Abingdon OX14 4LA (01235 528989; Fax: 01235 525731). *Location:* A34 Didcot turn off, through Steventon to Drayton (south of Oxford). 18 hole Par 67 golf course, 9 hole Par 3 course. Driving range. Tuition from PGA qualified professionals. *Green Fees:* weekdays £19.00; weekends £22.50. *Eating facilities:* full catering and bar facilities. Clubhouse open to visitors. *Visitors:* welcome. Clubhouse available for conferences and weddings; large function room. *Society Meetings:* welcome. Professional: M. Morbey (01235 550607). Secretary: A. Davies (01235 528989).
e-mail: draytonpark@btclick.com

FARINGDON. **Carswell Golf and Country Club,** Carswell Home Farm, Carswell, Faringdon SN7 8PU (01367 870422; Fax: 01367 870592). *Location:* just off A420 between Oxford and Swindon, near Faringdon. Parkland course with many trees and water hazards. 18 holes, 6200 yards. S.S.S. 72. 19-bay floodlit driving range, practice area with putting green.

Green Fees: weekdays £18.00, weekends £25.00. Twilight fees available, telephone for more details and prices. *Eating facilities:* clubhouse bar serving varied menu. *Visitors:* welcome, soft spikes preferred. Golf shop; club, cart and buggy hire. Clubhouse accommodation - four en suite rooms. *Society Meetings:* all welcome weekdays, please telephone for information on packages. Health Club on site, call for details. Secretary: Sarah Sample (01367 870422).

HENLEY-ON-THAMES. **Aspect Park Golf Club,** Remenham Hill, Henley-on-Thames RG9 3EH (Tel & Fax: 01491 578306). *Location:* M40 Junction 4 Exit or M4 Junction 8 Exit to Maidenhead, A4130 to Henley. Listed parkland course. 18 holes, 6595 yards, S.S.S. 72. Range, putting, pitch and putt. *Green Fees:* information not available. *Eating facilities:* bar, restaurant and function room. *Visitors:* welcome anytime except Saturday morning during medal play. Golf attire on course. Manager/Professional: Mark Abberley (01491 577562).*

HENLEY-ON-THAMES. **Badgemore Park Golf Club,** Badgemore, Henley-on-Thames RG9 4NR (01491 637300). *Location:* one mile from Henley town centre on road to Rotherfield Greys. Mature parkland course. 18 holes, 6129 yards. S.S.S. 69. Chipping green, two putting greens, practice net, bunker practice. *Visitors:* always welcome, weekends during summer after 12 noon, winter after 11am. Professional lessons available. Large car park. Accommodation on site. *Society Meetings:* welcome Wednesdays, Thursdays, Fridays. Professional: Jonathan Dunn (01491 574175). Secretary: Mr J. Connell (01491 637300; Fax: 01491 576899).

HENLEY-ON-THAMES. **Henley Golf Club,** Harpsden, Henley-on-Thames RG9 4HG (01491 575781). *Location:* from centre of Henley-Reading, one mile from Harpsden Way to clubhouse. Parkland with many trees. 18 holes, 6329 yards. S.S.S. 70. *Green Fees:* weekdays £45.00; weekends with member only £20.00. *Eating facilities:* bar snacks at all times, meals by arrangement. *Visitors:* welcome weekdays, weekends and Bank Holidays with a member only. Handicap Certificate required. *Society Meetings:* catered for Wednesdays and Thursdays. Professional: Mark Howell (01491 575710). Manager: Gary Oatham (01491 575742; Fax: 01491 412179). e-mail: manager@hunleygc.com
website: www.hunleygc.com

Badgemore Park Golf Club Badgemore, Henley-on-Thames RG9 4NR
In the heart of the Chilterns, superb challenging 18-hole mature parkland course offering a friendly welcome to all golfers. S.S.S.69, chipping green, 2 putting greens, practice nets and bunker. Visitors and Societies welcome. 19th century clubhouse with restaurant, spike bar; en suite accommodation available. PGA Professional Jonathan Dunn (01491 574175). Large car park. Ideally located close to M4 and M40.
Tel: 01491 637300 • Fax: 01491 576899 e-mail: info@badgemorepark.com
website: www.badgemorepark.com

PLEASE MENTION THE GOLF GUIDE WHEN YOU WRITE OR PHONE TO ENQUIRE ABOUT CLUBS OR ACCOMMODATION

286 Oxfordshire / ENGLAND THE GOLF GUIDE 2006

HENLEY-ON-THAMES. **Huntercombe Golf Club,** Nuffield, Henley-on-Thames RG9 5SL (01491 641207). *Location:* A4130, six miles west of Henley-on-Thames. Downland wooded course. 18 holes, 6271 yards. S.S.S. 70. Practice ground. *Green Fees:* information not available. *Eating facilities:* catering and bar facilities. *Visitors:* welcome by prior arrangement only. *Society Meetings:* Tuesdays and Thursdays by arrangement. Professional: Ian Roberts (01491 641241). Secretary: Ken McCrea (Fax: 01491 642060).

HORTON-CUM-STUDLEY. **Studley Wood Golf Club,** The Straight Mile, Horton cum Studley, Oxford OX33 1BF (01865 351144; Fax: 01865 351166). *Location:* 4 miles east of Oxford. Gently undulating mature woodland course. 18 holes, 6722 yards, S.S.S. 72. 15 bay covered driving range, Callaway Custom Fit Centre, short game academy. *Green Fees:* weekdays £38.00; weekends £48.00 after midday only. *Eating facilities:* function room, Bistro restaurant and bar. *Visitors:* welcome at all times weekdays, afternoons only at weekends, must play to Handicap standard. Tee time bookings taken four days in advance. Buggies available. *Society Meetings:* welcome any time Mondays to Thursdays, and Friday mornings. Packages from £30.00 per person. Professional: Tony Williams (01865 351122). Secretary: Annie Anderson.
e-mail: admin@swgc.co.uk
website: www.studleywoodgolf.co.uk

KIRTLINGTON. **Kirtlington Golf Club,** Lince Lane, Kirtlington OX5 3JY (01869 351133; Fax: 01869 351143). *Location:* A4095, Witney/Bicester, half a mile outside Kirtlington. Undulating, dry, open parkland course with well contoured greens. 18 holes, 6107 yards. S.S.S. 69. Covered and grassed driving range, pitching/putting. Academy 9-hole course and new fully equipped clubhouse. Conference/corporate days available. *Green Fees:* weekdays £22.00; weekends £27.00. Special rates on application. *Eating facilities:* available. *Visitors:* very welcome. *Society Meetings:* welcome. Secretary: Pamela Smith.
e-mail: info@kirtlingtongolfclub.com
website: www.kirtlingtongolfclub.com

MAPLEDURHAM. **The Club at Mapledurham,** Chazey Heath, Mapledurham, Reading RG4 7UD (01189 463353; Fax: 01189 463363). *Location:* leave Reading on A4074 towards Mapledurham, Woodcote and Wallingford, club is on the right immediately after leaving built up area. Parkland. 18 holes, 5700 yards. Par 69. Academy area. *Green Fees:* weekdays £20.00, weekends £26.00. *Eating facilities:* bar/lounge, food available. *Visitors:* welcome, no restrictions. Facilities include fully equipped gym, sauna, steam room, spa and swimming pool. *Society Meetings:* welcome. Professional: Tim Gilpin. Manager: Rob Davies.

OXFORD. **Hinksey Heights Golf Course,** South Hinksey OX1 5AB (01865 327775; Fax: 01865 736930). *Location:* on the A34 between Oxford and Abingdon. Undulating course. 18 holes, 6936 yards, 6342 metres. S.S.S. 73; driving range; indoor and outdoor practice areas. 9 hole par 3 course. *Green Fees:* information not available. *Eating facilities:* Spike Bar, bar and restaurant. *Visitors:* welcome including weekends. Contact General Manager or Professional. *Society Meetings and Company Days:* welcome including weekends with forward booking. Contact General Manager or Professional. Professional: David Bolton. General Manager: John Lidstone.*
e-mail: play@oxford-golf.co.uk
website: www.oxford-golf.co.uk

OXFORD. **North Oxford Golf Club,** Banbury Road, Oxford OX2 8EZ (01865 554415; Fax: 01865 515921). *Location:* just north of Oxford on the Banbury Road to Kidlington. Flat parkland course with tree-lined fairways - six Par 3 holes. 18 holes, 5736 yards, S.S.S. 67. Indoor driving bay in Pro shop. *Green Fees:* £25.00 per day, £18.00 per round, twilight £14.00 after 5.00pm excluding Thursday and Friday. *Eating facilities:* dining room, lounge and stud bar. *Visitors:* welcome weekdays and after 4pm weekends and Bank Holidays. *Society Meetings:* welcome, details on request. Professional: R.J. Harris (01865 553977). Manager: C Page (01865 554924; Fax: 01865 515921).
e-mail: manager@nogc.co.uk
website: www.nogc.co.uk

HUNTERCOMBE

www.huntercombegolfclub.co.uk

- Famous 1901 Willie Park Jnr design, situated on the edge of the Chilterns
- Well known for its fast and true greens & its immaculate fairways
- Plays superbly well in the summer and winter

- Just 50 minutes from London
- Full catering facilities
- Societies and green fees welcome
- Winter package offer available - see website
- Fully stocked Pro shop and practice ground on-site

01491 641207 for details and bookings
or email: office@huntercombegolfclub.co.uk

Huntercombe Golf Club
Nuffield (off A4130)
Henley-on-Thames

See also Colour Advertisement on page 25

ENGLAND / Oxfordshire

OXFORD. **Southfield Golf Club,** (home of Oxford City Golf Club, Oxford Ladies Golf Club, Oxford University Golf Club), Hill Top Road, Oxford OX4 1PF. *Location:* one mile from Rover Works, along Cowley Road, turn right into Southfield Road, then right at end of road. Hilly parkland. 18 holes, 6328 yards. S.S.S. 70. Practice ground available. *Green Fees:* £30.00 per round weekdays. *Eating facilities:* restaurant facilities available, bar open seven days. *Visitors:* welcome except weekends and Public Holidays. *Society Meetings:* welcome by arrangement (not weekends or Bank Holidays). Professional: Tony Rees (01865 244258). Admin. Secretary: Michael Blight (01865 242158).

OXFORD. **Waterstock Golf Club & Driving Range,** Thame Road, Waterstock, Oxford OX33 1HT (01844 338093; Fax: 01844 338036). *Location:* on Junction 8 and 8A, M40, at the Wheatley Service Station, five minutes from Thame and Oxford, 30 minutes from London and Birmingham. Rolling parkland with 15,500 trees. 18 holes, 6535 yards, Par 72, S.S.S 71. Practice bunkers and putting facilities, 22 bay driving range. *Green Fees:* 9 holes weekdays £10.50, weekends £13.50; 18 holes weekdays £20.00, weekends £25.00; twilight weekdays £15.00, weekends £16.00; per day £35.00 weekdays, £40.00 weekends. *Eating facilities:* full bar and restaurant. *Visitors:* no restrictions, welcome at all times. Changing rooms. *Society Meetings:* fully catered for, packages available on request. Head Professional: Paul Bryant. Secretary: Andrew Wyatt.
e-mail: wgc_oxfordgolf@btinternet.com
website: www.waterstockgolf.co.uk

OXON/BUCKINGHAMSHIRE. **Magnolia Park Golf & Country Club,** Arncott Road, Boarstall, Buckinghamshire HP18 9XX (01844 239700). *Location:* B4011 south from Bicester or north from Thame; two miles north of Oakley turn to Boarstall. Parkland and landscaped terrain with seven lakes. 18 holes. Par 72. *Green Fees*: weekdays £40.00, weekends £50.00. *Eating facilities:* Bar and dining 8am to 8pm (to 6pm during winter), function room available. *Society Meetings*: societies and corporate days welcome. Professional: Jeremy Dale.

For full details of clubs and courses, plus convenient accommodation
www.uk-golfguide.com

THAME. **The Oxfordshire Golf Club,** Rycote Lane, Milton Common, Thame OX9 2PU (01844 278300; Fax: 01844 278003). *Location:* from south Junction 7 M40, A329 to Thame. From north Junction 8 M40, A418 to Thame then A329. A combination of mounded fairways and lakes offers American-style target golf. 18 holes, 6856 yards. S.S.S. 74. 28-bay driving range, practice area. *Green Fees:* on application. *Eating facilities:* spike bar, Lakes Lounge and Oaks Restaurant offering light snacks to Continental and Japanese cuisine. Private rooms available for conferences, weddings and private dining. Luxurious changing facilities with Japanese ofuro baths. *Visitors:* welcome subject to availability, call reservations 01844 278500. Electric trolleys, pull trolleys and caddies (reserved in advance) available from well stocked Pro shop. *Society Meetings:* on application. PGA Professional: Stephen Gibson (01844 278505).
e-mail: info@theoxfordshiregolfclub.com
website: theoxfordshiregolfclub.com

WALLINGFORD. **The Springs Hotel and Golf Club,** Wallingford Road, North Stoke, Wallingford OX10 6BE (01491 836687; Fax: 01491 836877). *Location:* two miles south-west of Wallingford on the B4009. M40 Junction 6. 18 holes, 6470 yards. par 72. *Green Fees:* weekdays £29.00, weekends £35.00. *Eating facilities:* restaurant and clubhouse. *Visitors:* by arrangement. Professional: P. Ivil (01491 827310; Fax: 01491 827312).
e-mail: info@thespringshotel.com
golfclub@thespringshotel.com
website: www.thespringshotel.com

WITNEY. **Witney Lakes Golf Club,** Witney Lakes Resort, Downs Road, Witney OX29 0SY (01993 893011; Fax: 01993 778866). *Location*: two miles west of Witney town centre, turn into Downs Road. From B4095. Parkland with five large lakes. 18 holes, 6500 yards. S.S.S. 71. 22-bay floodlit covered driving range, practice area. *Green Fees:* £20.00 midweek, £25.00 weekends. *Eating facilities:* Greens Sports Bar and Greens Restaurant. *Visitors:* no restrictions. Rawles - Hairdressers. Retreat Spa and Beauty Salon. Function/ conference room; health and fitness club includes swimming pool, gymnasium and sauna. 86 bedroom hotel opening January 2006. Crèche facilities. Large well-stocked golf shop, three teaching Professionals. *Society Meetings:* all welcome. Professional: Adam Souter (01993 893011; Fax: 01993 778866). Secretary (01993 893005; Fax: 01993 778866).
e-mail: golf@witney-lakes.co.uk
website:www.witney-lakes.co.uk

THE APPEARANCE OF AN ASTERISK (*) AT THE END OF A CLUB OR COURSE ENTRY INDICATES THAT UP-TO-DATE INFORMATION HAS NOT BEEN SUPPLIED

Shropshire

BRIDGNORTH. **Bridgnorth Golf Club,** Stanley Lane, Bridgnorth WV16 4SF (01746 763315; Fax: 01746 763315). *Location:* one mile from town centre on Broseley road. Parkland, alongside River Severn. 18 holes, 6582 yards. S.S.S. 73. Practice ground. *Green Fees:* weekdays £24.00, weekends £30.00. *Eating facilities:* full catering available except Mondays. *Visitors:* welcome weekdays except Wednesday. Handicap Certificate or bona fide club membership required. *Society Meetings:* catered for Monday, Tuesday, Thursday, Friday only. Professional: Paul Hinton. Secretary: G.C. Kelsall.

BRIDGNORTH. **Chesterton Valley Golf Club,** Chesterton, Near Worfield, Bridgnorth WV15 5NX (01746 783682). *Location:* B4176 Dudley/Telford road. 18 holes, Par 71. *Green Fees:* £16.00. Visitors; no restrictions but can book 24 hours in advance. Professional/Secretary: Philip Hinton.

BRIDGNORTH. **Severn Meadows Golf Club,** Highley, Bridgnorth (01746 862212; Fax: 01746 861098). *Location:* seven miles from Bridgnorth on B4555. Eight miles from Bewdley on B4194. Signposted from village. Undulating woodland course. Severn Valley Steam Railway runs through the middle of the course, on the banks of the River Severn. 18 holes, 6388 yards. S.S.S. 70. *Green Fees:* information not available. *Eating facilities:* by arrangement. *Visitors:* welcome anytime weekdays but must book tee times at weekends. *Society Meetings:* by arrangement only. Secretary: Colin Harrison (01746 861296).*

CHURCH STRETTON. **Church Stretton Golf Club,** Trevor Hill, Church Stretton SY6 6JH (01694 722281). *Location:* one mile west of A49, adjacent to Carding Mill Valley. Set on the lower slopes of the Longmynd Hills, with wonderful springy turf and panoramic views of the surrounding country. No winter greens. 18 holes, 5020 yards. S.S.S. 65. *Green Fees:* information not available. *Eating facilities:* meals and snacks available daily, full bar facilities. *Visitors:* welcome, Saturdays not between 9am and 10.30am and 1pm to 2.30pm (Winter 12noon to 1.30pm), Sundays not before 10.30am or between 1pm and 2.30pm (Winter 12noon to 1.30pm). *Society Meetings:* welcome. Contact Hon. Secretary or Professional to pre-book. Professional: James Townsend (01694 722281; mobile: 07973 762510). Hon. Secretary John Povall (01743 860679; mobile: 07817 538080).*
e-mail: secretary@churchstrettongolfclub.co.uk
website: www.churchstrettongolfclub.co.uk

CLEOBURY MORTIMER. **Cleobury Mortimer Golf Club,** Wyre Common, Cleobury Mortimer, Near Kidderminster DY14 8HQ (01299 271112). *Location:* two miles out of Cleobury on B4201. 27 hole course comprising three loops of nine holes. Badgers Sett 3271 yards, Foxes Run 2960 yards, Deer Park 3167 yards, giving three 18 hole courses with S.S.S. 71, 70, 69. *Green Fees:* weekdays £20.00 per round (£12.50 with member), £30.00 per day; weekends £24.00 per round (£15.00 with member), £36.00 per day. *Eating facilities:* restaurant and Spike Bar. *Visitors:* welcome midweek; weekends by arrangement. Snooker room. Golf Buggies for hire £17.00 per round, trolleys £3.00 per round bookable in advance. *Society Meetings:* welcome by prior arrangement, ring for details. PGA Professional: Martin Payne (01299 271112). Director of Golf: Jon Jones. Secretary/Manager: Graham Pain (01299 271112; Fax: 01299 271468).
e-mail: enquiries@cleoburygolfclub.com
website: www.cleoburygolfclub.com

LUDLOW. **Ludlow Golf Club,** Bromfield, Ludlow SY8 2BT (01584 856285; Fax: 01584 856366). *Location:* A49 one mile north of Ludlow bypass, turn right onto the Bridgnorth road. Well signposted. Heathland course based on sandy soil providing springy fairways and superb greens. 18 holes, 6277 yards. S.S.S. 70. Practice ground. *Green Fees:* (2005) weekdays £28.00 per round, £35.00 a day; weekends £35.00 per round (reductions with member). *Eating facilities:* full catering and bar service during normal hours. *Visitors:* welcome weekdays and weekends with prior booking. *Society Meetings:* call for details. Professional/Administrator: R. Price (Pro shop: 01584 856366; Admin: 01584 856285).

MARKET DRAYTON. **Market Drayton Golf Club,** Sutton, Market Drayton TF9 2HX (01630 652266). *Location:* A41 south towards Newport, turn left at crossroads just past Tern Hill Barracks. Parkland with exceptional views. 18 holes, 6214 yards, 5702 metres. S.S.S. 71. *Green Fees:* £26.00. *Eating facilities:* bar and high class catering open all day. *Visitors:* welcome weekdays only; first tee closed daily until 9.30am and from 12.30pm to 1.30pm. Tuesday Ladies' Day. On-course bungalow (sleeps 6) available from £625.00 weekly including FREE golf. *Society Meetings:* catered for weekdays by prior arrangement. Professional: Russell Clewes (01630 656237). Secretary: David Palmer (01630 652266). Stewardess: Helen Crocket (01630 658083).
e-mail: marketdraytongc@btinternet.com

NEWPORT. **Aqualate Golf Centre,** Stafford Road, Newport TF10 9DB (01952 811699). *Location:* two miles east of Newport town centre; 400 yards from the junction with A41. Parkland course with gentle gradients and water hazards. 18 holes, 5659 yards. S.S.S. 67. 20 bay floodlit driving range, practice putting green. *Green Fees:* information not available. *Eating facilities:* coffee bar. *Visitors:* welcome at all times (pay and play), but advance booking advisable. No handicap restrictions. PGA Professional tuition available by appointment - group and/or personal lessons. Golf Club Memberships available. *Society Meetings:* welcome by prior arrangement. Hire clubs and trolleys available. Opening hours: weekdays 9.00am to 10.00pm, weekends and Bank Holidays 7.30am to 9.00pm.Professional: Kevin Short (01952 811699). Director: H. Brian Dawes (01952 811699).*

ENGLAND / Shropshire

NEWPORT. Lilleshall Hall Golf Club, Lilleshall, Near Newport TF10 9AS (01952 604776; Fax: 01952 604272). *Location:* at Lillyhurst turn north off Abbey Road, which joins Wellington Road near Lilleshall and the B4379 near Sheriffhales. Wooded parkland. 18 holes, 5813 yards. S.S.S. 68. Practice ground. *Green Fees:* information not provided. *Eating facilities:* meals served 9am to 5pm, order in advance. *Visitors:* welcome on weekdays, check with Professional for tee restrictions. *Society Meetings:* catered for by prior arrangement with Secretary. Professional: S. McKane. Secretary: A. Marklew.

OSWESTRY. Llanymynech Golf Club, Pant, Near Oswestry SY10 8LB (01691 830542). *Location:* six miles south of Oswestry on A483, turn at Cross Guns Inn, Pant. Undulating lush hilltop course with extensive views, 15 holes in Wales, three in England. 18 holes, 6047 yards. S.S.S. 69. Practice area and putting green. *Green Fees:* weekdays £20.00 per round, £30.00 per day; weekends £25.00 per round, subject to review. Half price with member. Reductions for Juniors. *Eating facilities:* restaurant and bar. *Visitors:* welcome weekdays; some weekends by prior arrangement; prior enquiry advisable. *Society Meetings:* weekdays by arrangement with Secretary. Professional: A.P. Griffiths (01691 830879). Secretary: D.R. Thomas (01691 830983). website: www.llanymynechgolfclub.co.uk

OSWESTRY. Mile End Golf Club, Mile End, Oswestry SY11 4JE (01691 671246 (bookings); Fax: 01691 670580). *Location:* signposted off A5, one mile south-east of Oswestry. Gently undulating course with water features. 18 holes, 6292 yards. S.S.S. 70. Driving range. *Green Fees:* weekdays £16.00 per round, £24.00 per day; weekends £25.00 per round, £37.00 per day. *Eating facilities:* full bar/catering available. *Visitors:* welcome at all times subject to course availability. Extensively stocked quality golf shop with all top name brands. *Society Meetings:* welcome weekdays by prior arrangement. Professional: Scott Carpenter (01691 671246). Secretary: Richard Thompson (01691 671246; Fax: 01691 670580) e-mail: info@mileendgolfclub.co.uk website: www.mileendgolfclub.co.uk

---

— FHG —

Visit the **KUPERARD** website

www.holidayguides.com

for details of the wide choice of accommodation featured in the full range of FHG titles

---

27 unique holes set in 200 acres of Shropshire's most beautiful countryside

At Cleobury Mortimer Golf Club we believe that a really enjoyable game of golf takes more than just a great golf course. We make sure that your whole experience – from the friendly welcome in the golf shop to your drinks and meal in our relaxed clubhouse – is all part of a day that you'll remember.

27 holes set out in three individual 9-hole loops, covering 200 acres of Shropshire's most beautiful countryside. Each hole is designed to a very high specification, with its own character and challenge.

A Clubhouse with excellent facilities, from a full-sized antique snooker table and spike bar, – to everything a modern club must have. Choice of refreshment and dining areas to suit all tastes – open 7 days. Golf Shop with wide range of stock from all the leading brands.

Cleobury Mortimer Golf Club
Wyre Common, Cleobury Mortimer, Shropshire DY14 8HQ
Enquiries: 01299 271112 • Fax: 01299 271468
E-mail: enquiries@cleoburygolfclub.com
www.cleoburygolfclub.com

Self-catering Holiday Cottages available on site from Spring 2006

See also Colour Advertisement on page 33

OSWESTRY. Oswestry Golf Club, Aston Park, Oswestry SY11 4JJ. *Location:* a friendly members' club four miles south-east of Oswestry on A5. Mature parkland course with many feature trees, laid out by James Braid in rolling Shropshire countryside. Well drained soils ensure excellent year-round play. 18 holes, 6038 yards. S.S.S. 69. Practice ground. *Green Fees:* information not available. *Eating facilities:* dining room and bar. *Visitors:* welcome; must be member of another club with a recognised Handicap Certificate or playing with a member. Snooker table. *Society Meetings:* societies of 16 plus welcomed Wednesdays and Fridays by arrangement with the Secretary. Smaller groups catered for by arrangement with the Professional. Professional: David Skelton (01691 610448). Secretary: Peter Turner (Tel & Fax: 01691 610535).*
e-mail: secretary@oswestrygolfclub.co.uk
website: www.oswestrygolfclub.co.uk

SHIFNAL. **Shifnal Golf Club,** Decker Hill, Shifnal TF11 8QL (Tel & Fax: 01952 460330). *Location:* one mile north east of Shifnal, one mile from A5, Junction 4 M54. Parkland course. 18 holes, 6504 yards. S.S.S. 71. *Green Fees:* £25.00 per round, £30.00 per day; weekends with member only. *Eating facilities:* full catering service. *Visitors:* welcome, phone first, not weekends or Bank Holidays. *Society Meetings:* catered for by arrangement with Secretary. Professional: J. Flanagan (01952 460457). Secretary: M.J. Vanner (Tel & Fax: 01952 460330).
e-mail: secretary@shifnalgolfclub.co.uk
website: www.shifnalgolfclub.co.uk

SHREWSBURY. **Arscott Golf Club,** Arscott, Pontesbury, Shrewsbury SY5 0XP (Tel & Fax: 01743 860114). *Location:* 10 minutes from Shrewsbury off the A488 Bishops Castle road. Set in mature parkland with stunning views of South Shropshire and Welsh Borders. 18 holes, 6158 yards. S.S.S. 69. Practice area, putting green and driving net. *Green Fees:* £20.00 weekdays; £25.00 weekends. *Eating facilities:* food and beverages available from 10.30am daily. *Visitors:* welcome at all times. Please telephone Shop to book tees. *Society Meetings:* by arrangement, please telephone. Secretary: Brian Harper (01743 860114 or 01743 860881).

SHREWSBURY. **Hawkstone Park,** Weston-under-Redcastle, Shrewsbury SY4 5UY (01939 200611; Fax: 01939 200311). *Location*: 14 miles north of Shrewsbury off A49. Hawkstone Course – parkland, 18 holes, 6491 yards (white). S.S.S. 71; Windmill Course – parkland (designed by Brian Huggett), 18 holes, 6476 yards (white). S.S.S. 71; Academy Par 3 Course – 6 holes, 741 yards. Par 18, S.S.S. 18. Target practice ground, putting green and short game area. Open all year. *Green Fees:* weekdays £34.00; weekends £44.00; please call for winter rates. Eating facilities: Terrace Room, all day bar and restaurant. *Visitors*: welcome. 66 room Hotel and Historic park. *Society Meetings:* welcome. Reservations for bookings: 01939 200611. Professional: Stuart Leech (01939 200611).*
e-mail: bookings@hawkstone.co.uk
website: www.hawkstone.co.uk

SHREWSBURY. **Shrewsbury Golf Club,** Condover, Shrewsbury SY5 7BL (01743 872976; Fax: 01743 874647). *Location:* A49 two miles south west of Shrewsbury. Parkland first 9 holes, undulating back 9 holes with fine views of Longmynd. 18 holes, 6207 yards. S.S.S. 70. Large practice ground. *Green Fees:* £27.50 per round, £30.00 per day weekdays; £32.00 per round, £38.50 per day weekends and Bank Holidays. *Eating facilities:* full facilities available seven days. *Visitors:* welcome at all times except Wednesday mornings and weekends before 10am. *Society Meetings:* welcome by arrangement. Professional: Peter Seal (01743 874581). Secretary: Mrs S.M. Kenny (01743 872977).
e-mail: info@shrewsbury-golf-club.co.uk

TELFORD. **Telford Golf and Country Club,** Great Hay Drive, Sutton Heights, Telford TF7 4DT (01952 429977; Fax: 01952 586602). *Location:* turn off A442 between Bridgnorth and Telford, two miles to M54 Junction 4. Rolling wooded parkland with water features, suspended water table greens as at Augusta. 18 holes, 6761 yards. S.S.S. 72. All-weather driving range, putting green. *Green Fees:* information not available. *Eating facilities:* clubroom, coffee bar and restaurant, lounge, Sky TV, also private rooms for Societies. *Visitors:* welcome anytime but advance booking essential. Handicap Certificates or membership of bona fide golf club essential. Leisure Centre with swimming pool, gym, etc. *Society Meetings:* by arrangement. Professional: Dan Bateman (01952 586052). Secretary: Ian Lucas (01952 429977).*

TELFORD. **The Shropshire,** Muxton, Telford TF2 8PQ (01952 677800; Fax: 01952 677622). *Location:* off Junction 4 of M54, follow signs for Muxton (signposted). Parkland course featuring many water hazards, wide, American-type fairways, and undulating well-bunkered greens. Three loops of 9 holes (Blue, Silver, Gold): 27 holes, 3286 yards, 3303 yards, 3334 yards, S.S.S. 71, 72, 72. 30 bay floodlit driving range, 12 hole short course, 18 hole putting green. *Green Fees:* information not available. *Eating facilities:* Greenkeeper Bar and Grill, Conservatory Restaurant. *Visitors:* welcome, no restrictions. Pay as you Play. 15 buggies, golf school. *Society Meetings:* very welcome, packages available. Professional: Rob Grier.*

TELFORD. **Wrekin Golf Club,** Ercall Woods, Golf Links Lane, Wellington, Telford TF6 5BX (01952 244032; Fax: 01952 252906). *Location:* from M54 Junction 7 to Wellington, turn back along Holyhead road towards Wellington for three-quarters-of-a-mile. Golf Links Lane on right hand side. Undulating parkland. 18 holes, 5570 yards. S.S.S. 67. Small practice ground. *Green Fees*: midweek £22.00 per round, £30.00 per day, weekends £30.00 per round. *Eating facilities*: restaurant and bar facilities by arrangement with Stewardess. *Visitors:* welcome except weekends and Bank Holidays when limited. *Society Meetings*: by arrangement with the Secretary. Professional: K. Housden (01952 223101). Secretary: D. Briscoe (01952 244032; Fax: 01952 252906).

ENGLAND / Shropshire

WHITCHURCH. **Macdonald Hill Valley Hotel Golf and Country Club,** Terrick Road, Whitchurch SY13 4JZ (01948 667788; Fax: 01948 667373). *Location:* signposted from Whitchurch Bypass. Magnificent Alliss/Thomas Emerald Championship Course. 18 holes, 6628 yards. Par 73. Sapphire Course 4801 yards, Par 66. *Green Fees:* information not available. *Eating facilities:* full restaurant/bars, snacks available. *Visitors:* welcome without reservation. Luxury 90 bedroom 4-star hotel; leisure facilities also available. *Society Meetings:* please contact for details. Professional: Graeme Bagnall (01948 663032). Secretary: John Pickering (01948 860425). e-mail: general.hillvalley@macdonald-hotels.co.uk website: www.hillvalleygolfclub.co.uk

WOLVERHAMPTON. **Patshull Park Hotel, Golf and Country Club,** Patshull Park, Pattingham, Near Wolverhampton WV6 7HR (01902 700100; Fax: 01902 700874). *Location:* take Junction 3 off M54, turn left on A41 back towards Wolverhampton and fork right into Albrighton. From main crossroads turn right along Cross Road, taking T-junction with A464 Wolverhampton/Shifnal Road and turning right towards Shifnal. Signposted Patshull Park Golf Course. Glorious parkland course set in landscapes by Capability Brown; John Jacobs designed course. 18 holes, 6345 yards. S.S.S. 69. Large practice area. *Green Fees:* £40.00 per 18 holes, £60.00 per 36 holes. Please pre-book. Handicap Certificates required. *Eating facilities:* Lakeside Restaurant and two bars. Earl's Bar. *Visitors:* welcome on application. 49 bedroomed hotel, country club and swimming pool, fishing lakes (80 acres). Residential Breaks. Buggies available. *Society Meetings:* corporate and society meetings welcome; special group rates and facilities. Professional: Richard Bissell (01902 700342).

WORFIELD. **Worfield Golf Club,** Roughton, Worfield, Near Bridgnorth WV15 5HE (01746 716541; Fax:01746 716302). *Location*: A454 Wolverhampton to Bridgnorth Road, three miles from Bridgnorth. Parkland course set on rolling countryside. 18 holes, 6440 yards. S.S.S. 71. Chipping area, practice area, putting greens. *Green Fees:* weekdays £20.00. weekends after 1pm £25.00. *Eating facilities*: restaurant and bar meals all day. *Visitors:* welcome. Buggies available. *Society meetings:* all welcome. Professional: Stephen Russell (01746 716541). Secretary: William Weaver (01746 716372; Fax: 01746 716302).

FHG

·K·U·P·E·R·A·R·D·

FHG Guides

publish a large range of well-known accommodation guides. We will be happy to send you details or you can use the order form at the back of this book.

The Shropshire, Telford

Somerset

BATH. **Bath Golf Club,** Sham Castle, North Road, Bath BA2 6JG (01225 425182). *Location:* off A36, one mile south-east of Bath City Centre. Hilltop, undulating downland course with views of Bath and the surrounding countryside. 18 holes, 6442 yards, 5891 metres. S.S.S. 71. *Green Fees:* information not available. *Eating facilities:* catering every day. *Visitors:* with bona fide Handicap welcome. *Society Meetings:* catered for Wednesday and Friday. Professional: Peter Hancox (Tel & Fax: 01225 466953). Managing Secretary: J. M. Galley (01225 463834; Fax: 01225 331027).*

BATH. **Entry Hill Golf Club,** Entry Hill, Bath BA2 5NA (01225 834248). *Location:* one mile south of city centre, off A367 road to Wells. Hilly parkland course with many young trees. 9 holes, 2103 yards, 1922 metres. S.S.S. 61 (18 holes). Practice net. *Green Fees:* information not available. *Visitors:* no restrictions but pre-booking up to one week in advance essential. Well equipped Pro Shop. *Society Meetings:* reduced green fees for pre-booked groups of 10 or more. Professional: T. Tapley (01225 834248). Secretary: J. Sercombe (01225 834248).

BATH. **Fosseway Golf Club and Centurion Hotel,** Charlton Lane, Midsomer Norton, Bath BA3 4BD (01761 412214; Fax: 01761 418357). *Location:* off A367 Bath to Wells/Shepton Mallet. Flat parkland course on the edge of the Mendips. 9 holes, 2304 yards. S.S.S. 65. *Green Fees:* information not available. *Eating facilities:* full à la carte restaurant, five bars with bar meals. *Visitors:* welcome except Sunday mornings and Wednesday evenings. Accommodation available, gym, sauna, steam, Jacuzzi, swimming and bowls (outdoor). *Society Meetings:* welcome. Secretary: P.J. Jordan (01761 417711). *
e-mail: centurion@centurionhotel.co.uk
website: www.centurionhotel.com

BATH. **Lansdown Golf Club,** Lansdown, Bath BA1 9BT. *Location:* M4 Junction 18, A46 towards Bath, follow signs for Lansdown Park and Ride, adjacent Bath Racecourse. Flat parkland, 800ft above sea-level, panoramic views. 18 holes, 6335 yards. S.S.S. 70. Practice ground. *Green Fees:* weekdays £23.00, weekends £28.00. *Eating facilities:* dining room for 100, snacks, lunch or dinner. *Visitors:* welcome, must have Handicap Certificate. Trolleys for hire. *Society Meetings:* welcome weekdays. Professional: Terry Mercer (01225 420242; Fax: 01225 483597). Secretary: Erica Bacon (01225 422138; Fax: 01225 339252).
e-mail: admin@lansdowngolfclub.co.uk
website: www.lansdowngolfclub.co.uk

For full details of clubs and courses, plus convenient accommodation

www.uk-golfguide.com

BATH/BRISTOL. **Farrington Golf and Country Club,** Marsh Lane, Farrington Gurney, Near Bristol BS39 6TS (01761 451596; Fax: 01761 451021). *Location:* 12 miles south of Bristol, 10 miles east of Bath (through Midsomer Norton) at the junction of the A37 and A362 roads. Wooded, undulating 27 hole complex, 6 lakes, USGA-spec greens (no temporaries), tees up to 800 square yards, irrigated. Championship Course - 18 holes, (Blue tees) 6716 yards, S.S.S. 72; (White tees) 6335 yards, S.S.S. 71; (Yellow tees) 5943 yards, S.S.S. 68; (Ladies' Red tees), 5595 yards, S.S.S 73 . Executive Course - 9 holes, 3002 yards, par 54, S.S.S. 53. Floodlit, covered driving range, 300 yard practice ground, two extensive putting greens, chipping green, three practice bunkers, video professional teaching. *Green Fees:* Championship Course £20.00 weekdays, £30.00 weekends and holidays. Special twilight offers. Executive Course (9 holes): £7.00 weekdays, £9.00 weekends. (Under review for 2006.) *Eating facilities:* Large clubhouse of character, full meals service, Sunday lunches, bars, dining room, patio and courtyard. Horizon Banqueting and Function Suite and King Charles Hall both licensed for civil weddings. *Visitors:* most welcome, 2 for 1 vouchers accepted, booking essential weekends. *Society Meetings:* special midweek packages available. PGA Professional: Jonathan Cowgill (01761 451046). Secretary: Stephen Cook. Owner: Paul Harwood. General Manager (for society and membership enquiries): Debbie Cole (01761 451596).
e-mail: info@farringtongolfclub.net
website: www.farringtongolfclub.net

BRIDGWATER. **Cannington Golf Course,** Cannington Centre For Land Based Studies, Cannington, Bridgwater TA5 2LS (01278 652394; Fax: 01278 652479). *Location:* M5 Junction 24, off A39 Bridgwater to Minehead road. Flat, with slight undulations, on parkland turf; exposed to sea breezes. 9 holes (18 tees to 9 greens), 6072 yards. S.S.S. 70. Small practice area. 10 bay floodlit driving range. *Green Fees:* weekend 9 holes £12.50, weekday 9 holes £9.50; weekend 18 holes £18.50, weekday 18 holes £14.00. *Eating facilities:* College restaurant. *Visitors:* pay and play course. *Society Meetings:* by arrangement with Professional/Course Manager. Professional/Course Manager: Ron Macrow (01278 655050; Fax: 01278 655055).

BRIDGWATER. **Enmore Park Golf Club,** Enmore, Bridgwater TA5 2AN (01278 671481). *Location:* M5 Exit 23/24, left at lights in town to Spaxton, course signposted two miles on right. Wooded parkland course on Quantock foothills. 18 holes, 6406 yards, 5910 metres. S.S.S. 71. Large practice ground. *Green Fees:* £30.00 per round, £45.00 per day weekdays; £40.00 per round weekends. *Eating facilities:* lunch and evening meal available. *Visitors:* welcome weekdays. Buggy available. *Society Meetings:* welcome by arrangement. Professional: Nigel Wixon (01278 672102; Fax: 01278 671740). Secretary: Ian Wallace (01278 672100; Fax: 01278 671740).

BRISTOL. **Mendip Spring Golf Club,** Honeyhall Lane, Congresbury, Bristol BS49 5JT (01934 852322; Fax: 01934 853021). *Location:* between Congresbury and Churchill off B3133 (A370 and A38). Fairly flat courses with a lot of water hazards. Brinsea Course: 18 holes, 6352 yards. S.S.S. 70 men, 76 ladies; Lakeside Course: 9 holes, 2260 yards, S.S.S. 65 men and ladies. 15 bay floodlit driving range, putting green. *Green Fees:* Brinsea: weekdays £26.00 – £35.00 per day, weekends £32.00. Lakeside: £9.00 for 9 holes, £18.00 per day. *Eating facilities:* full restaurant and bar facilities. *Visitors:* welcome at any time. Tuition available. Buggies available April to September. *Society Meetings:* welcome, corporate days available by arrangement. Professionals: John Blackburn and Robert Moss. Secretary: A. Melhuish.

BRISTOL. **Stockwood Vale Golf Club,** Stockwood Lane, Keynsham, Bristol BS18 2ER (0117 9866505). *Location:* one mile from Hicks Gate - Bristol Ring Road. Testing parkland course set in beautiful surroundings. 18 holes, 6031 yards. S.S.S. 69. Driving range, practice green/bunker. *Green Fees:* information not available. *Eating facilities:* licensed bar and restaurant. *Visitors:* welcome at all times, must reserve start times. *Society Meetings:* welcome weekdays, prior booking essential; packages available. Professional: Mr John Richards (0117 9866505). Secretary: Mr M. Edenborough (0117 9860509; Fax: 0117 9868974).*

BRISTOL. **Tall Pines Golf Club,** Cooks Bridle Path, Downside, Backwell, Bristol BS48 3DJ (01275 472076). *Location:* between A370 and A38 to Bristol Airport. Parkland. 18 holes, 6049 yards, 5420 metres. S.S.S. 70. Practice ground, putting green. *Green Fees:* £20.00. *Eating facilities:* fully licensed bar and restaurant. *Visitors:* welcome at all times, bookings at weekends. *Society Meetings:* welcome, weekends after 1.00pm. Professional: Alex Murray. Secretary: T. Murray (01275 472076; Fax: 01275 474869).

BURNHAM-ON-SEA. **Brean Golf Club at Brean Leisure Park,** Coast Road, Brean, TA8 2QY (Tel & Fax: 01278 752111). *Location:* leave M5 at Junction 22, follow signs to Brean Leisure Park (five miles). Flat moorland, easy access to five mile sandy beach (400 yards via path). 18 holes, 5565 yards. S.S.S. 67 (Par 69). Practice area, green and bunker. *Green Fees*: weekdays from £20.00 per round; weekends from £25.00 per round. Reduced rates with a member. *Eating facilities:* snacks at bar, meals in main restaurant. *Visitors:* welcome weekdays and after 11am weekends and Bank Holidays. Prior booking advised to Pro Shop (01278 752111). Buggy and trolleys for hire. *Society Meetings:* welcome by prior booking. Professional: David Haines.

THE APPEARANCE OF AN ASTERISK (*) AT THE END OF A CLUB OR COURSE ENTRY INDICATES THAT UP-TO-DATE INFORMATION HAS NOT BEEN SUPPLIED

Brean Golf Club

Brean Leisure Park, Coast Road, Brean, Burnham-on-Sea TA8 2QY

Tel: 01278 752111

e-mail: golf@brean.com • www.breangolfclub.co.uk

Brean Golf Club is located at Brean Leisure Park, four miles north of Burnham-on-Sea, and five miles from Junction 22 of the M5. The 18-hole, 5715 yards, Par 69 course is situated in 100 acres of meadowland. Water features come into play on many of the holes, providing formidable hazards. The course is well-drained and seldom closed. The resident PGA Professional offers a range of services including coaching and club repair, as well as a comprehensive range of golf equipment at competitive prices. Adjoining the Pro Shop are changing rooms and the Club Room. There is a fleet of luxury lodges and caravans both on site and at the adjoining Holiday Park - packages are available which include golf, accommodation and meals.

www.uk-golfguide.com

BURNHAM-ON-SEA. **Burnham and Berrow Golf Club,** St Christopher's Way, Burnham-on-Sea TA8 2PE (01278 783137; Fax: 01278 795440). *Location:* one mile north of Burnham-on-Sea. Leave M5 at Exit 22. Seaside links. 18 holes, 6393 yards. S.S.S. 71; 9 holes, 6332 yards. S.S.S. 70. *Green Fees:* £45.00 weekdays, £60.00 weekends and Bank Holidays; 9 hole course £15.00 weekdays, £18.00 weekends and Bank Holidays. *Eating facilities:* catering available daily 11am to 6pm (other meals by arrangement). *Visitors:* welcome with reservation if members of a recognised golf club and with Handicap Certificate. Dormy House accommodation, sleeps up to 8. *Society Meetings:* catered for. Professional: M. Crowther-Smith (01278 784545). Managing Secretary: Mr P. E. Ware (01278 785760). e-mail: secretary@burnhamandberrowgolfclub.co.uk website: www.burnhamandberrowgolfclub.co.uk

CHARD. **Windwhistle Golf Club Ltd,** Cricket St. Thomas, Near Chard TA20 4DG (01460 30231; Fax: 01460 30055). Established 1932. *Location:* on A30 between Chard and Crewkerne, opposite Cricket St. Thomas Wildlife Park and Warner's Hotel. Parkland course with breathtaking views. 18 holes, 6510 yards Par 73, S.S.S. 71. Driving range. Golf Shop. *Green Fees:* information not available. *Eating facilities:* bar service, snacks and cooked meals daily. *Visitors:* welcome - starting time system in operation, bookings accepted up to seven days in advance. *Society Meetings:* Golfing and non-golfing, separate suite for 40 available. Squash courts available. Professional: Paul Deeprose. Secretary: Sue Davidge. website: www.windwhistlegolf.co.uk

www.uk-golfguide.com

CLEVEDON. **Clevedon Golf Club,** Castle Road, Walton, Clevedon BS21 7AA (01275 874057; Fax: 01275 341228). *Location:* M5 Junction 20, follow signs "Portishead", turn left into Holly Lane. Spectacular scenic parkland course overlooking Bristol Channel. 18 holes, 6557 yards. S.S.S. 72. Practice area. *Green Fees:* information not available. *Eating facilities:* full catering every day. *Visitors:* welcome, please telephone Professional beforehand. Handicap Certificate essential. *Society Meetings:* welcome by prior arrangement. Professional: Robert Scanlan (01275 874704).*

FROME. **Orchardleigh Golf Club,** Frome BA11 2PH (01373 454200; Fax: 01373 454202) *Location:* A362 Frome - Radstock. Parkland. 18 holes, 6800 yards. S.S.S. 73. Three practice greens, driving range. *Green Fees:* weekdays £30.00, weekends £40.00; member's guest £15.00 and £20.00. *Eating facilities:* bar menu. Society and groups menu. *Visitors:* welcome anytime except before 11.00am Saturday and Sundays. *Society Meetings:* all very welcome, competitive rates. Professional: Ian Ridsdale (01373 454206; Fax: 01373 454202) Secretary: Trevor Atkinson.

LANGPORT near. **Long Sutton Golf Club,** Long Sutton, Near Langport TA10 9JU (01458 241017; Fax: 01458 241022). *Location:* from Podimore roundabout on A303 towards Langport turn left for Long Sutton. Gently undulating course. 18 holes, 6368 yards. S.S.S. 70. Floodlit driving range. *Green Fees:* weekdays £18.00; weekends £25.00 for 18 holes. Weekdays £10.00; weekends £12.50 for 9 holes. *Eating facilities:* bar and food. *Visitors:* welcome at all times, phone for tee reservations at weekends. Golfing breaks available. *Society Meetings:* welcome. Professional: Andrew Hayes.

When in Somerset...

...*treat yourself to a stay at the Burnham & Berrow Golf Club. Championship Links golf course and accommodation at the Dormy House from £85 per night inc. Breakfast and Green Fees. Winter rate £50 per night Sundays to Thursdays.*

e-mail: secretary@burnhamandberrowgolfclub.co.uk • www.burnhamandberrowgolfclub.co.uk

**St. Christopher's Way
Burnham on Sea TA8 2PE
Tel: 01278 785760
Fax: 01278 795440**

See also Colour Advertisement on page 19

Minehead and West Somerset Golf Club, The Warren, Minehead TA24 5SJ

Weekdays Daily: **£30**, Off Peak **£22**, Twilight **£15**, Weekend **£35**, Weekend Off-Peak **£24**, Weekly **£125**.
Trolley & equipment hire available • Membership available
Adult Annual Subscription **£425** • Country Membership (over 50 miles) **£250**
Secretary: J.E. Hoskings • Professional: Ian Read
Tel: 01643 702057 • Fax: 01643 705095 • www.mineheadgolf.co.uk

MINEHEAD. **Minehead and West Somerset Golf Club,** The Warren, Minehead TA24 5SJ (01643 702057). *Location:* beside the beach at eastern end of the town, three-quarters of a mile from town centre. Flat seaside links. 18 holes, 6153 yards. S.S.S. 70. *Green Fees:* weekdays – £35.00 daily, £25.00 off-peak, £15.00 twilight; weekends and Bank Holidays – £40.00 daily, £30.00 off-peak. Weekly rate £130.00. Subject to review for 2006. *Eating facilities:* available at clubhouse, bar open every day. *Visitors:* welcome with tee reservation at Pro shop. *Society Meetings:* welcome with tee reservations. Wide wheel trolleys only. Trolley and equipment hire available. Professional: Ian Read. Secretary: J.E. Hoskings (01643 702057; Fax: 01643 705095).
e-mail: secretary@mineheadgolf.org.uk
website: www.mineheadgolf.co.uk

SALTFORD. **Saltford Golf Club,** Golf Club Lane, Saltford, Bristol BS31 3AA (01225 873220; Fax: 01225 873525). *Location:* A4 between Bristol and Bath. Wooded parkland course. 18 holes, 6081 yards. S.S.S. 69. Practice area, chipping green. *Green Fees:* information not available. *Eating facilities:* restaurant, bar service. *Visitors:* welcome, restricted to one round of golf per day weekends and during Summer. *Society Meetings:* accepted by arrangement Mondays and Thursdays. Professional: Dudley Millensted (01225 872043). Secretary: Valerie Radnedge (01225 873513). *

SHEPTON MALLET. **The Mendip Golf Club Ltd.,** Gurney Slade, Radstock, Shepton Mallett BA3 4UT (01749 840570; Fax: 01749 841439). *Location:* three miles north of Shepton Mallet (A37). Downland, undulating course. 18 holes, 6383 yards. S.S.S. 71. Practice ground. *Green Fees:* information not available. *Eating facilities:* bar and restaurant open seven days a week. *Visitors:* welcome every day, telephone Professional to check availability. *Society Meetings:* catered for Mondays to Fridays by arrangement. Professional: Adrian Marsh (01749 840793). Secretary: Jim Scott (01749 840570; Fax: 01749 841439).*
e-mail: mendipgolfclub@lineone.net
website: www.mendipgolfclub.co.uk

SOMERTON. **Wheathill Golf Club,** Wheathill, Somerton TA11 7HG (01963 240667; Fax: 01963 240230). *Location:* On B3153 three miles west of Castle Cary. Flat parkland. 18 holes, 5339 yards. S.S.S. 66. Large practice ground and 8 hole academy course. *Green Fees:* information not available. *Eating facilities:* bar and restaurant. *Visitors:* welcome. *Society Meetings:* welcome. Professional: Andrew England. Secretary: John Goymer.

STREET. **Kingweston Golf Club,** (Millfield School), Street TA11 6PP (01458 444320). *Location:* one mile south of Butleigh Village, near Street, Somerset. Flat course - trees. 9 holes, 2307 yards. S.S.S. 61. Practice area. *Green Fees:* information not available. *Eating facilities:* pub half a mile. *Visitors:* welcome only with a member. Secretary: G.L. Frisby (01458 832068).*

TAUNTON. **Taunton Vale Golf Club,** Creech Heathfield, Taunton TA3 5EY (01823 412220; Fax: 01823 413583). *Location:* just off A361 at Junction with A38 between Junctions 24 and 25 of M5; easily accessible. Parkland. Two courses. 18 holes, 6167 yards. S.S.S. 69. 9 holes, 1943 yards. S.S.S. 31. 10 bay floodlit driving range. *Green Fees:* weekdays £20.00 for 18 holes, £10.00 for 9 holes; weekends £25.00 for 18 holes, £12.00 for 9 holes. Special daily rates and Society rates available, please enquire. *Eating facilities:* two bars with dining facilities. *Visitors:* welcome, telephone for bookings essential. *Society Meetings:* welcome by arrangement. For all the latest information see our website. Professional: Martin Keitch (01823 412880). Secretary: Joanne Wyatt (01823 412220; Fax: 01823 413583).*
e-mail: tvgc@easynet.co.uk
website: www.tauntonvalegolf.co.uk

Please mention
THE GOLF GUIDE
when you enquire about clubs or accommodation

Taunton Vale Golf Club

Taunton Vale comprises eighteen and nine hole courses set amid 156 acres of gently rolling Somerset countryside just a few minutes' drive from the county town. Taunton Vale offers excellent package deals for societies and company days. We offer a range of packages for 9, 18, 27 or 36 holes plus a choice of menu.

• Visitors Welcome •

For further information contact the club secretary on

Taunton Vale Golf Club,
Creech Heathfield,
Taunton, Somerset TA3 5EY

tel: 01823 412220 or
e-mail: tvgc@easynet.co.uk
website: www.tauntonvalegolf.co.uk

See also Colour Advertisement on page 20

TAUNTON. **Oake Manor Golf Club,** Oake, Taunton TA4 1BA (01823 461993; Fax: 01823 461995). *Location:* seven minutes' drive from Junction 26 of the M5 - take A38 towards Taunton and follow signs to Oake. Enjoyable and challenging parkland course with water features on 10 of the 18 holes. Magnificent setting with views of the Blackdown and Quantock Hills. 18 holes, 6109 yards. S.S.S 69. Driving range, practice holes. *Green Fees:* information not available. Phone (01823 461993) for Golf Reservations. *Eating facilities:* bar, restaurant, lounge. *Visitors:* welcome any day but booking tee time essential. Function rooms (seat up to 300). *Society Meetings:* by arrangement, contact Golf Manager. Golf Manager & Professional: Russell Gardner (01823 461993).*
e-mail: russell@oakemanor.com
website: www.oakemanor.com

TAUNTON. **Taunton and Pickeridge Golf Club,** Corfe, Taunton TA3 7BY (01823 421240). *Location:* four miles south of Taunton on B3170. Undulating parkland. 18 holes, 6025 yards. S.S.S. 69. Practice ground, indoor shed. *Green Fees:* £26.00/£30.00 weekdays, £37.00 weekends. *Eating facilities:* restaurant and bar. *Visitors:* welcome. *Society Meetings:* by arrangement with the Secretary. Professional: Simon Stevenson (01823 421790). Secretary: M.P.D. Walls (01823 421537; Fax: 01823 421742).
e-mail: admin@tauntongolf.co.uk

TAUNTON. **Vivary Golf Course,** Vivary Park, Taunton TA1 3JW (01823 289274). *Location:* turn into Wilton Road at side of police station. Turn left at Vivary Arms Inn. Flat parkland course with ponds and ducks. 18 holes, 4620 yards. S.S.S. 63. Practice area, tennis courts. *Green Fees:* information not available. *Eating facilities:* licensed bar and restaurant. Available for private functions. *Visitors:* always welcome. Professional: Dave Hawker (01823 333875). Secretary: Dave Pike (01823 289274).

TICKENHAM. **Tickenham Golf Club,** Clevedon Road, Tickenham BS21 6RY (01275 856626). *Location:* M5 Junction 20, signposted Nailsea on left after Tickenham. Challenging championship style contoured greens. 9 holes, 2000 yards. S.S.S. 58, Par 60. 24 bay floodlit driving range, power tees, putting green, bunkers. *Green Fees:* information not available. *Eating facilities:* 19th hole licensed bar, snacks. *Visitors:* welcome. *Society Meetings:* welcome, telephone for rates. Professionals: A. Sutcliffe, S. Jarrett, A. Smith.

WEDMORE. **Isle of Wedmore Golf Club,** Lineage, Wedmore BS28 4QT (01934 713649; Fax: 01934 713696). *Location:* from A38 Bristol/Bridgwater Road, take Wedmore Road from Lower Weare. Parkland, gently undulating fairways with magnificent views. Practice area. 18 holes, 6057 yards. S.S.S. 69. Small practice area, putting green. *Green Fees:* weekdays £22.00 per round, £32.00 per day; weekends £22.00 per round, £32.00 per day; reduced rates with member. *Eating facilities:* full bar and restaurant, upstairs function/society room. *Visitors:* always welcome. Soft spikes only. *Society Meetings:* welcome. Professional: Graham Coombe (01934 712452; Fax: 01934 713554). Manager: Andrew Edwards (01934 713649; Fax: 01934 713696).

WELLS. **Wells (Somerset) Golf Club Ltd,** East Horrington Road, Wells BA5 3DS (01749 675005). *Location:* one mile east of city centre off B3139. Parkland, wooded. 18 holes, 6018 yards. S.S.S. 69. Practice area. 12 bay floodlit driving range open to the public. *Green Fees:* weekdays £25.00 per round, £32.00 per day; weekends and Bank Holidays £32.00 per round, £40.00 per day. *Eating facilities:* restaurant and bar. *Visitors:* welcome, no play before 9.30am weekends and Public Holidays. *Society Meetings:* full packages available at all times. Professional: Adrian Bishop (01749 679059). Secretary: Christine Searle (Tel & Fax: 01749 683171).*
e-mail: secretary@wellsgolfclub99.freeserve.co.uk
website: www.wellsgolfclub.co.uk

WESTON-SUPER-MARE. **Weston-Super-Mare Golf Club,** The Clubhouse, Uphill Road North, Weston-Super-Mare BS23 4NQ (01934 626968). *Location:* M5 Junction 21 - on the sea front. Flat links course with excellent greens. 18 holes, 6251 yards. S.S.S. 70. Practice area plus nets. *Green Fees:* information not available. *Eating facilities:* full bar and catering facilities. *Visitors:* welcome weekdays and weekends. Handicap Certificate required. *Society Meetings:* catered for weekdays. Professional: Mike LaBand (Tel & Fax: 01934 633360). Secretary: (01934 626968; Fax: 01934 621360).
e-mail: wsmgolfclub@eurotelbroadband.com
website: www.westonsupermaregolfclub.com

WESTON-SUPER-MARE. **Worlebury Golf Club,** Monks Hill, Worlebury, Weston-Super-Mare BS22 9SX (01934 623214). *Location:* from M5 (Junction 21) then A370 and first exit left onto old Bristol Road to town for two miles. Turn right into Baytree Road and continue to top of Milton Hill. Hill top with extensive views of the Severn Estuary and Wales. 18 holes, 5936 yards. S.S.S. 69. Practice ground and putting green. *Green Fees:* weekdays £27.50 per day, £12.50 with a member; weekends and Bank Holidays £35.00 per day, £17.50 with a member. *Eating facilities:* bar and restaurant. *Visitors:* welcome without reservation. *Society Meetings:* catered for by arrangement. Professional: Gary Marks (01934 418473). Secretary: Mike W. Wake (01934 625789; Fax: 01934 621935).

THE APPEARANCE OF AN ASTERISK (*) AT THE END OF A CLUB OR COURSE ENTRY INDICATES THAT UP-TO-DATE INFORMATION HAS NOT BEEN SUPPLIED

WINCANTON. **Wincanton Golf Club,** The Racecourse, Wincanton BA9 8BJ (01963 34606; Fax: 01963 34668). *Location:* middle of the racecourse, half a mile from the town centre. Very flat course, testing layout; large bunkers protecting very well maintained greens. 18 holes, 6182 yards. Par 70, S.S.S. 69. Good practice facilities. Teaching/coaching on individual or group basis; hire of clubs/trolley/ buggy. *Green Fees:* information not available. *Eating facilities:* coffee shop. *Visitors:* welcome at all times. Overnight accommodation available from Oct 2005. *Society Meetings:* can be catered for if booked in advance. Professionals: Andrew England and Tony Isaacs.

www.uk-golfguide.com

YEOVIL. **Yeovil Golf Club,** Sherborne Road, Yeovil BA21 5BW (01935 422965). *Location:* on A30, one mile from town centre towards Sherborne on right before Babylon Hill. Parkland. 18 holes, 6150 yards. S.S.S. 70. 9 holes, 4891 yards. S.S.S. 65. Putting green. 20-bay floodlit range. *Green Fees:* Old course – winter (Nov - March incl.) £25.00 weekdays, £30.00 weekends and Bank Holidays; summer (April - Oct incl.) £30.00 weekdays, £40.00 weekends and Bank Holidays. 9 hole Newton course – £18.00 weekdays, £20.00 weekends and Bank Holidays. *Eating facilities:* bars and dining room with full menu every day. *Visitors*: welcome, Handicap Certificates required for 18 hole course, telephone Pro shop to check times. *Society Meetings:* welcome weekdays except Tuesdays. Professional: G. Kite (01935 473763; Fax: 01935 478605). Secretary/ Manager: G. Dodd (01935 422965; Fax: 01935 411283).

Wells (Somerset) Golf Club
East Horrington Road, Wells,
Somerset BA5 3DS
Tel: 01749 675005 Fax: 01749 683170
e-mail: secretary@wellsgolfclub99.freeserve.co.uk

- Visitors and Societies very welcome
- 18-hole Par 70 course
- 12-bay floodlit driving range open to the public
- Buggies available for hire
- Trolleys allowed all winter

www.wellsgolfclub.co.uk

See also Colour Advertisement on page 19

WESTON-SUPER-MARE GOLF CLUB
(founded 1892)

A traditional and subtle links Course designed by Alister Mckenzie, of Augusta National fame, with some of the best greens in the West.

Members and staff extend a warm welcome to visitors and societies at all times of the year.

Tel: 01934 626968 • Fax: 01934 621360

e-mail: wsmgolfclub@eurotelbroadband.com • website: www.westonsupermaregolfclub.com

PLEASE MENTION THIS GUIDE WHEN YOU WRITE OR PHONE TO ENQUIRE ABOUT CLUBS OR ACCOMMODATION

Staffordshire

BARLASTON. **Barlaston Golf Club,** Meaford Road, Stone ST15 8UX (Tel & Fax: 01782 372795). *Location:* one mile south of Barlaston off A34; between Stoke and Stone. 18 holes, 5801 yards. S.S.S. 68. *Green Fees:* information not available. *Eating facilities:* dining room and bar snacks with lounge bar. *Visitors:* welcome anytime. *Society Meetings:* welcome weekdays. Professional: Ian Rogers. Secretary: H Thompson (Tel & Fax: 01782 372867).*
e-mail: barlaston.gc@virgin.net
website: www.bgc.evelplay.net

BURTON UPON TRENT. **The Branston Golf and Country Club,** Burton Road, Branston, Burton upon Trent DE14 3DP (01283 512211; Fax: 01283 566984). *Location:* A38 Junction A5121. Flat parkland adjacent to the River Trent, spectacular 18th hole, water on 13 holes (flowing). 18 holes, 6697 yards. S.S.S. 72. 9 holes 1856 yards, S.S.S. 58. Driving range. *Green Fees:* information not available. *Eating facilities:* restaurant, bar, spikes bar, private rooms. *Visitors:* welcome, two week advance booking system in operation, restrictions weekends. Buggy hire, trolleys available. Country Club has extensive leisure facilities. *Society Meetings:* welcome midweek, special rates. Professional: Richard Odell (01283 512211; Fax: 01283 566984). Golf and Estates Manager: Graham Pyle (01283 512211; Fax: 01283 566984).*

BURTON UPON TRENT. **The Craythorne,** Craythorne Road, Stretton, Burton upon Trent DE13 0AZ (01283 564329; Fax: 01283 511908). *Location:* A38 first turning to Burton from Derby, A5121 signposted Stretton. Parkland. 18 holes, 5556 yards. S.S.S. 68. Floodlit driving range, pitch and putt course. *Green Fees:* information not available. *Eating facilities:* bars and restaurant open daily; function room. *Visitors:* welcome at all times, booking required at weekends. Special society and golfing packages. *Society Meetings:* welcome, special rates for parties over 16. Professional: Steve Hadfield (01283 533745). Managing Director: Tony Wright.*
e-mail: admin@craythorne.co.uk
website: www.craythorne.co.uk

CANNOCK. **Beau Desert Golf Club,** Rugeley Road, Hazel Slade, Cannock WS12 0PJ (01543 422626; Fax: 01543 451137). *Location:* A460 Hednesford, signposted. Fowler-designed heathland course. 18 holes, 6310 yards. S.S.S. 71. Driving Range. Practice ground. *Green Fees:* £45.00 weekdays; £55.00 weekends. *Eating facilities:* full catering and bar. *Visitors:* welcome anytime subject to availability. *Society Meetings:* catered for Monday to Thursday. Professional: Barrie Stevens (01543 422492). Secretary: John Bradbury.

CANNOCK. **Cannock Park Golf Club,** Stafford Road, Cannock WS11 2AL (01543 578850). *Location:* on the A34 Stafford Road, quarter of a mile from Cannock town centre. Parkland course, playing alongside Cannock Chase. 18 holes, 5149 yards. S.S.S. 65. *Green Fees:* £9.50 weekdays, £11.50 weekends. Phone bookings up to two weeks in advance. Reductions for Juniors. *Eating facilities:* available. *Visitors:* welcome every day. Golf shop, inside leisure centre. *Society Meetings:* welcome weekdays. Professional: David Dunk (Tel & Fax: 01543 578850). Secretary: Chris Milne (01543 571091).

CHEADLE near. **Whiston Hall Golf Club and Mansion Court Hotel,** Whiston, Near Cheadle ST10 2HZ (01538 266260). *Location:* A52 Stoke to Ashbourne road, three miles from Alton Towers. Scenic course set in beautiful countryside. 18 holes, 5784 yards. S.S.S. 69. *Green Fees:* £10.00 per round. *Eating facilities:* extensive Clubhouse Bar Menu available from 8.00am onwards. *Visitors:* welcome at any time. Golfing theme rooms for all types of golfing breaks. Snooker, fly fishing. *Society Meetings:* all welcome 7 days a week. 27 hole package and lunch, three course evening meal from £29.95 per person. Golf breaks also available from £49.95 per person. Secretary: R. Cliff.

LEEK. **Leek Golf Club,** Cheddleton Road, Birchall, Leek ST13 5RE (01538 384779). *Location:* one mile south of Leek on A520. Undulating parkland. 18 holes, 6218 yards. S.S.S. 70. *Green Fees:* weekdays £28.00; weekends and Bank Holidays £34.00. *Eating facilities:* full catering facilities 11.30am-11pm. Light refreshments from 10am. *Visitors:* welcome most times by prior arrangement. *Society Meetings:* catered for by arrangement Wednesdays only. Catering (01538 384779). PGA Professional: Paul Toyer. Secretary: David T. Brookhouse (Tel & Fax: 01538 384779).

LEEK. **Leek Westwood Golf Club,** Newcastle Road, Leek ST13 7AA (01538 398385). *Location:* A53 one and a half miles south of Leek. Moorland/parkland. 18 holes, 6207 yards. S.S.S. 70. Practice area, nets, chipping green. *Green Fees:* information not available. *Eating facilities:* full facilities. *Visitors:* welcome weekdays. *Society Meetings:* weekdays by arrangement. Professional: Darren Squire (01538 398897). Secretary: Ken Hewitt (Tel & Fax: 01538 398385; Fax: 01538 382485). Club Administrator: Carol Povey.*

LICHFIELD. **The Seedy Mill Golf Club,** Elmhurst, Near Lichfield WS13 8HE (01543 417333; Fax: 01543 418098). *Location:* just off A51 north of Lichfield. Parkland with lakes, ponds and streams. The Mill: 18 holes, 6305 yards. S.S.S. 70; The Spires: 9 holes, Par 3. 26 bay floodlit driving range. *Green Fees:* weekdays £30.00, weekends £35.00. Society and corporate packages. *Eating facilities:* full clubhouse facilities open 7.30am to 11pm. *Visitors:* welcome at all times. *Society Meetings:* welcome weekdays and weekends. Professional: Simon Joyce. Secretary: Abi Burns. General Manager: Richard Gee.

THE GOLF GUIDE 2006   ENGLAND / Staffordshire 299

LICHFIELD. **Whittington Heath Golf Club,** Tamworth Road, Lichfield WS14 9PW (01543 432317). *Location:* on A51 Tamworth-Lichfield Road. Wooded heathland. 18 holes, 6490 yards. S.S.S. 71. Practice ground. *Green Fees:* weekdays £35.00 per round, £50.00 36 holes. *Eating facilities:* meals available at all times. *Visitors:* welcome weekdays only. Handicap Certificate, EGU Card or letter of introduction required. *Society Meetings:* catered for Wednesdays and Thursdays by arrangement. Professional: Adrian Sadler (01543 432261). Secretary: Mrs J.A. Burton (01543 432317; Fax: 01543 433962). Steward: 01543 432212.
e-mail: info@whgcgolf.freeserve.co.uk

NEWCASTLE-UNDER-LYME. **Jack Barkers Keele Golf Centre,** Keele Road, Newcastle-under-Lyme ST5 5AB (01782 627596). *Location:* A525 Newcastle to Whitchurch, opposite University of Keele. Undulating parkland. 18 holes, 6396 yards, 5822 metres, S.S.S. 70. Driving range. *Green Fees:* weekdays £10.50 weekends £14.50. Juniors £6.00 weekdays, £10.50 weekends. *Eating facilities:* available. *Visitors:* welcome at all times. Hire: Buggies £10.00 per round; Clubs £6.00 per round; Trolleys £2.50 per round. *Society Meetings:* welcome by arrangement. Manager: Mr N. Worrall.

NEWCASTLE-UNDER-LYME. **Newcastle-under-Lyme Golf Club,** Whitmore Road, Newcastle-under-Lyme ST5 5AB (01782 616583). *Location:* M6 Junction 15, one mile from Newcastle-under-Lyme. Parkland. 18 holes, 6331 yards white, 6203 yards yellow. S.S.S. 71 white, 70 yellow. *Green Fees:* £25.00 for 18 holes, £35.00 for 36 holes. *Eating facilities:* restaurant and bar meals. *Visitors:* welcome. Restrictions at weekends. *Society Meetings:* Wednesdays, Thursdays and a limited number of Fridays. Contact Secretary/Manager for details. Professional: P. Symonds (01782 618526). Secretary/ Manager: Vicki Wiseman (01782 617006).

PENKRIDGE. **The Chase Golf Club,** Pottal Pool Road, Penkridge ST19 5RN (01785 712191). *Location:* M6 Junction 13, take the A449 to Wolverhampton, then left onto B5012 towards Cannock then onto Rugeley Road. Flat parkland with Links characteristics. 18 holes, 6613 yards. S.S.S. 71. 20 bay floodlit driving range and teaching academy. Putting green, bunker, and chip and run facility. *Green Fees:* information not available. *Eating facilities:* excellent clubhouse facilities. *Visitors:* please ring to book, members have priority. Fully stocked pro shop. *Society Meetings:* welcome at reduced rates. Professional: James Green. General Manager: Mark Clarke.*

RUGELEY. **Lakeside Golf Club,** Rugeley Power Station, Armitage Road, Rugeley WS15 1PR (01889 575667). *Location:* nearest town Rugeley (between Lichfield and Stafford), course over power station grounds. Flat parkland adjacent River Trent. 18 holes, 5765 yards. S.S.S. 68. *Green Fees:* £10.00 with member. *Eating facilities:* bar, lunchtime weekends and every evening. *Visitors:* must be accompanied by member. *Society Meetings:* welcome if arranged in advance. Secretary: R.D. Newman (01889 575667).

RUGELEY near. **St Thomas's Priory,** Armitage Lane, Armitage, Near Rugeley (01543 491116; Fax: 01543 492244). *Location:* one mile south-east of Rugeley on A513, opposite Ash Tree Inn. Undulating parkland. 18 holes, 5969 yards. S.S.S. 70. Practice area available. *Green Fees*: information not available. *Eating facilities*: full restaurant and bar facilities. *Visitors*: welcome weekdays, weekends, Handicap Certificates required. *Society Meetings*: by arrangement. Professional: Richard O'Hanlon (Tel & Fax: 01543 492096).

STAFFORD. **Brocton Hall Golf Club,** Brocton, Stafford ST17 0TH (01785 661901; Fax: 01785 661591). *Location:* off A34 Stafford to Cannock four miles south east of Stafford. Undulating parkland. 18 holes, 6095 yards. S.S.S. 69. *Green Fees:* information not available. *Society Meetings:* by arrangement Tuesdays and Thursdays. Professional: Nevil Bland (01785 661485). Secretary: Graham Nicholls (01785 661901).*

STAFFORD. **Ingestre Park Golf Club,** Ingestre, Near Stafford ST18 0RE (01889 270845; Fax: 01889 271434). *Location:* six miles east of Stafford, between Tixall and Great Haywood. Parkland. 18 holes, 6352 yards. S.S.S. 70. Extensive practice ground. *Green Fees:* 18 holes £27.00, £32.50 more than 18 holes weekdays. *Eating facilities:* lunch and dinner menu. *Visitors:* welcome weekdays before 3.30pm. Handicap Certificate required. Buggies available. *Society Meetings:* welcome with reservation except Wednesday. £44.50 all inclusive 27 holes package for Societies. Special winter rates on application. Professional: Danny Scullion (01889 270304). Manager: C.J. Radmore (01889 270845).

STAFFORD. **Stafford Castle Golf Club,** Newport Road, Stafford ST16 1BP (01785 223821). *Location*: M6 Junction 13 or 14, two miles from club. Parkland course. 9 holes, (18 tees). 6383 yards. S.S.S. 70, Par 71. *Green Fees*: weekdays £18.00 per day; weekends £22.00 per day. Subject to review. Special winter rates on application. *Eating facilities*: snacks and full catering available except Mondays. *Visitors*: welcome except Sunday mornings. Handicap Certificate required. *Society Meetings*: catered for by arrangement. Administrator: S. Calvert.

STOKE-ON-TRENT. **Burslem Golf Club Ltd,** Wood Farm, High Lane, Tunstall, Stoke-on-Trent ST6 7JT (01782 837006). *Location:* leave Burslem centre by Hamil Road, turn left at High Lane junction, one mile on right. Parkland. 9 holes, 5360 yards. S.S.S. 66. *Green Fees:* weekdays £16.00 per day. *Eating facilities:* meals and refreshments by arrangement except Wednesday and Sunday. *Visitors:* welcome weekdays with reservation. Bona fide golf club members only. *Society Meetings:* catered for.

THE APPEARANCE OF AN ASTERISK (*) AT THE END OF A CLUB OR COURSE ENTRY INDICATES THAT UP-TO-DATE INFORMATION HAS NOT BEEN SUPPLIED

STOKE-ON-TRENT. **Goldenhill Golf Course,** Mobberley Road, Goldenhill, Stoke-on-Trent ST6 5SS (01782 784715). *Location:* on A34 between Tunstall and Kidsgrove, north of Stoke city centre. Rolling parkland course, panoramic views of Mow Cop and Newchapple. 18 holes, 5957 yards, 5447 metres. S.S.S. 69. *Green Fees:* information not available. *Eating facilities:* fully licensed bar and cafeteria. *Visitors:* municipal course with small membership, visitors and societies always welcome.*

STOKE-ON-TRENT. **Jack Barker's Greenway Hall,** Stanley Road, Stockton Brook, Stoke-on-Trent ST9 9LJ (01782 503158). *Location:* M6 (Junction15) - A500 - A53 to Leek, right at crossroads in Stockton Brook. Countryside course with wooded areas and some beautiful scenic views. 18 holes, 5681 yards, 5194 metres. S.S.S. 67. *Green Fees:* weekdays £10.00, weekends £15.00. *Eating facilities:* meals available from 10am to 11pm. *Visitors:* welcome. *Society Meetings:* welcome, packages available on request. Manager: Stephen Degg.

STOKE-ON-TRENT. **Parkhall Golf Course,** Hulme Road, Weston Coyney, Stoke-on-Trent ST3 5BH (01782 599584). *Location:* one mile east of Longton. Tight unforgiving heathland course, great character, ideal for new golfers looking to improve their game. 18 holes, 2335 yards, 2136 metres. S.S.S. 54. Par 3. *Green Fees:* information not available. *Eating facilities:* chocolate, crisps, pop, tea and coffee. *Visitors:* all welcome. Golf clubs and trolley hire available. Seven days advance booking for weekends and Bank Holidays. *Society Meetings:* welcome. Professional: Joe Mortimore.*

STOKE-ON-TRENT. **Trentham Golf Club,** 14 Barlaston Old Road, Trentham, Stoke-on-Trent ST4 8HB (01782 642347). *Location:* off A34 travelling south of Newcastle (Staffs.). Left at Trentham Gardens onto Longton Road (A5035); right at National Westminster Bank. Open Championship Regional Qualifying course. 18 holes, 6632 yards. S.S.S. 72. Practice ground. *Green Fees*: weekdays £50.00, weekends £50.00 (Sundays after 2.30pm). Playing with member first guest £15.00, second guest £20.00. *Eating facilities*: lunches and dinners available. *Visitors*: welcome, weekends; Sunday after 2.30pm. Handicap Certificate required. *Society Meetings*: welcome by prior arrangement. Professional: S. Wilson (01782 657309). Secretary: R.N. Portas (01782 658109).

STOKE-ON-TRENT. **Trentham Park Golf Club,** Trentham Park, Trentham, Stoke-on-Trent ST4 8AE *Location:* off A34 adjoining Trentham Gardens near Junction 15 on M6. 18 holes, 6425 yards. S.S.S. 71. *Green Fees:* information not available. Visitors: welcome weekdays with reservation. *Society Meetings:* catered for Wednesdays and Fridays only. Professional: Simon Lynn (01782 642125; Fax: 01782 658800). Secretary: Trevor Berrisford (Tel & Fax: 01782 658800).
e-mail: trevor.berrisford@barbox.net
website: www.trenthamparkgolfclub.com

STONE. **Izaak Walton Golf Club,** Eccleshall Road, Cold Norton, Stone ST15 0NS (01785 760900). *Location:* on the B5026 linking Stone and Eccleshall. Testing course with many water features. 18 holes, 6298 yards. S.S.S. 72. Driving range. *Green Fees:* weekdays £18.00, weekends £22.00. *Eating facilities:* available. *Visitors:* welcome with some restrictions. *Society Meetings:* welcome with some restrictions. Contact the Secretary for information. Professional: Paul Brunt. Secretary: Mr T. T. Tyler.

STONE. **Stone Golf Club,** The Fillybrooks, Stone ST15 0NB (01785 813103). *Location:* one mile north west of Stone on the A34 adjacent to the Walton Inn. Parkland. 9 holes, 6299 yards. S.S.S. 70. *Green Fees:* weekdays £20.00. *Eating facilities:* full meals to order, snacks always available, bar. *Visitors:* welcome weekdays only, not Bank Holidays. Snooker table. *Society Meetings:* catered for by arrangement. Secretary: P.R. Farley (01785 284875).

STOURBRIDGE. **Enville Golf Club Ltd,** Highgate Common, Enville, Stourbridge DY7 5BN (01384 872074). *Location:* leave A449 at Stewpony Hotel taking Bridgnorth Road A458, fork right after Fox Inn following signs for Halfpenny Green Airport. Two flat wooded heathland courses. Highgate Course: 18 holes, 6556 yards. S.S.S 72; Lodge Course: 18 holes, 6217 yards. S.S.S. 70. *Green Fees:* information not available. *Eating facilities:* meals available. *Visitors:* welcome weekdays with Handicap Certificate, advisable to phone prior to visit. Ladies' Day Thursday; weekends with members only. *Society Meetings:* welcome except Thursdays and weekends. Party of 30 or more receives a 10% discount. Professional: S. Power (01384 872585). Secretary/Manager: J.J. Bishop (01384 872074; Fax: 01384 873996).*
e-mail: secretary@envillegolfclub.com
website: www.envillegolfclub.com

Welcome to Jack Barker's WORLD of GOLF!

GREENWAY HALL GOLF CENTRE   **KEELE GOLF CENTRE**

Greenway Hall
Weekday *Green Fees*
From only £10.00
Weekend *Green Fees*
From only £15.00

Buggy Hire *Only* £10.00 /Round
Societies Welcome from *Only* £6.50
Platinum Memberships: Play 7 Courses nationwide for 1 Annual Fee
- Phone for details. *Annual subscriptions available at all Centres!*

Keele Golf Centre
Weekday *Green Fees*
From only £10.00
Weekend *Green Fees*
From only £15.00

Stanley Road, Stockton Brook, Stoke-on-Trent. ST9 9LJ.
Tel: 01782 503 158 greenway@jackbarker.com www.jackbarker.com
Keele Road, Newcastle-Under-Lyme, Staffordshire. ST5 5AB.
Tel: 01782 627 596 keele@jackbarker.com

See also Colour Advertisement on page 34

STREETLY. **Little Aston Golf Club,** Streetly, Sutton Coldfield B74 3AN (0121-353 2066). *Location:* off A454. Parkland course. 18 holes, 6670 yards. S.S.S. 73. *Green Fees:* information not available. *Eating facilities:* dining room and bars, lunch and dinner. *Visitors:* welcome on weekdays by prior arrangement, weekends with a member. *Society Meetings:* welcome Tuesday, Wednesday and Friday. Professional: Brian Rimmer (0121-353 0330). Manager: (0121-353 2942; Fax: 0121-580 8387).*
website: littleastongolf.co.uk

TAMWORTH. **Drayton Park Golf Club,** Centenary Drive, Drayton Park, Tamworth B78 3TN (01827 251139; Fax: 01827 284035). *Location:* follow signs for Drayton Pleasure Park, adjacent drive at the top. Parkland with well defined wooded holes. 18 holes, 6473 yards. S.S.S. 71. Practice ground. *Green Fees:* information not available. *Eating facilities*: full catering facilities. *Visitors*: welcome weekdays except Wednesday mornings. *Society Meetings*: catered for Tuesdays and Thursdays, booked through Secretary. Professional: M.W. Passmore (01827 251478). Secretary: D.O. Winter (01827 251139; Fax: 01827 284035).*
website: www.draytonparkgc.co.uk

TAMWORTH. **Tamworth Golf Club,** Eagle Drive, Amington, Tamworth B77 4EG (01827 709303; Fax: 01827 709304). *Location:* Junction 10 M42 Tamworth, A5, towards Amington. Parkland course used by NAPGC for Juniors' and Ladies' Championships. 18 holes, 6488 yards. Par 73 S.S.S. 72. Practice driving ground, putting green. *Green Fees:* information not available. *Eating facilities:* lounge bar with catering. *Visitors:* welcome. *Society Meetings:* contact pro shop for information. Professional: Wayne Alcock (01827 709303). Secretary: Mrs J.P. Cornall.*

UTTOXETER. **Manor Golf Club,** Leese Hill, Kingstone, Uttoxeter ST14 8QT (01889 563234). *Location*: A518, Uttoxeter to Stafford road, 3 miles from Uttoxeter. Grassland course. 18 holes, 6008 yards. S.S.S. 69. Practice range and putting green. *Green Fees*: weekdays £15.00; weekends £25.00. *Eating facilities*: bar meals available Monday to Friday from 12pm till 4pm, Saturday and Sunday from 11am to 4pm. *Visitors*: welcome every day, please book in advance for Saturdays and Sundays. Tuition available. *Society Meetings*: welcome Monday to Friday, please call for rates. Course Manager: Ant Foulds.
e-mail: ant-foulds@bigfoot.com

UTTOXETER. **Uttoxeter Golf Club,** Wood Lane, Uttoxeter ST14 8JR (01889 566552; Fax: 01889 567501). *Location:* approximately half a mile past the main entrance to the racecourse. Undulating parkland, very picturesque scenery. 18 holes, 5801 yards. S.S.S. 69. Practice area and putting green. *Green Fees:* weekdays £24.00 per day, weekends and Bank Holidays £30.00 per day. *Eating facilities:* bar, clubhouse dining room. *Visitors:* welcome except on days of "major" competitions. A starting sheet operates at weekends. Buggies and trolleys available for hire. *Society Meetings:* welcome by arrangement (maximum 60). but not at weekends or on Bank Holidays. Professional: Mr Adam McCandless (01889 564884; Fax: 01889 556552). Secretary: Roger Harvey (Tel & Fax: 01889 566552).

WOLSTANTON. **Wolstanton Golf Club,** Dimsdale Old Hall, Hassam Parade, Wolstanton, Newcastle ST5 9DR (01782 622413; Fax: 01782 622718). *Location:* one mile north of Newcastle, turn right off A34 (Dimsdale Parade), first right (Hassam Parade) then right again 75 yards. Flat parkland. 18 holes, 5533 yards. S.S.S. 68. *Green Fees:* information not available. *Eating facilities:* full catering service and bar. *Visitors:* welcome weekdays; weekends only as member's guest. Trolleys available. *Society Meetings:* catered for by arrangement. Professional: Simon Arnold (Tel & Fax: 01782 622718). Secretary: Valerie Keenan (01782 622413; Fax: 01782 622413).

Uttoxeter Golf Club
welcomes societies and visitors

One of the best kept secrets in the country.
A beautiful course with stunning views
across Staffordshire and Derbyshire.

Club Secretary: 01889 566552
Club Professional: 01889 564884

See also Colour Advertisement on page 33

Wolstanton Golf Club Dimsdale Old Hall, Hassam Parade,
Wolstanton, Newcastle ST5 9DR • Tel: 01782 622413 • Fax: 01782 622718
Flat parkland with six Par 3 holes, making it a good test for golfers of all handicaps. 18 holes, 5533 yards. S.S.S. 68. Visitors welcome weekdays; weekends only as member's guest.
OFFICE: 01782 622413 • PROFESSIONAL: 01782 622718
e-mail: admin@wolstantongolfclub.com • www.tonysdot.com/wgc

Suffolk

ALDEBURGH. **Aldeburgh Golf Club,** Saxmundham Road, Aldeburgh IP15 5PE (01728 452890). *Location:* A12 north from Ipswich; turn right on A1094 to Aldeburgh. Heathland course, abundance of dense gorse, many challenging Par 4s, no Par 5s. 18 holes, 6349 yards. S.S.S. 71; also 9 holes, 2114 yards. S.S.S. 32. *Green Fees:* weekdays £50.00 per day, £40.00 after 12 noon; weekends £60.00 per day, £40.00 after 12 noon. *Eating facilities:* lunches by arrangement. *Visitors:* welcome by arrangement, to play on 18-hole course must have club Handicap Certificate. No three or four balls allowed. *Society Meetings:* by arrangement. Professional: K.R. Preston (01728 453309). Secretary: 01728 452890; Fax: 01728 452937).

BECCLES. **Beccles Golf Club,** The Common, Beccles NR34 9BX (01502 712244). *Location:* A146 Beccles by-pass, to town centre at Safeway roundabout, left over level crossing. Flat commonland. 9 holes, 5558 yards, 5084 metres. S.S.S. 67. *Green Fees:* weekdays £7.00 (with member £5.00); weekends and Bank Holidays £10.00 (with member £5.00). Twilight fee (after 4pm) £5.00. *Eating facilities:* bar snacks available. *Visitors:* welcome anytime. *Society Meetings:* catered for by prior arrangement. Secretary: Alan Ereira (01502 712244).

BUNGAY. **Bungay and Waveney Valley Golf Club,** Outney Common, Bungay NR35 1DS (01986 892337; Fax: 01986 892222). *Location:* a quarter mile from town centre and alongside A143. Flat, heath-type course. 18 holes, 6050 yards. S.S.S. 69. *Green Fees:* £26.00 18 holes, £36.00 day, £16.00 county card. Subject to alteration for 2006. *Eating facilities:* available everyday. *Visitors:* welcome weekdays, weekends with member only. Must telephone (01986 892337) prior to a visit to book a tee time. *Society Meetings:* by arrangement with Secretary. Professional: Andrew Collison (01986 892337; Fax: 01986 892222). Secretary: John Lunniss (01986 892337; Fax: 01986 892222).

BURY ST EDMUNDS. **Bury St Edmunds Golf Club,** Tut Hill, Bury St Edmunds IP28 6LG. *Location:* B1106 just off A14. Flat parkland. 18 holes, 6675 yards. S.S.S. 72; 9 holes, 2217 yards. S.S.S. 31. Practice facilities. *Green Fees:* weekdays £35.00 per day on 18-hole course; two rounds on 9 hole course £13.00 weekdays, £16.00 weekends. *Eating facilities:* available. *Visitors:* welcome Monday to Friday on both courses; weekends on 9 hole course only. *Society Meetings:* catered for. Professional: Mark Jillings (01284 755978). Secretary: John Taylor (01284 755979; Fax: 01284 763288). e-mail: info@burygolf.co.uk

BURY ST EDMUNDS. **Flempton Golf Club,** Flempton, Bury St Edmunds IP28 6EQ (01284 728291). *Location:* follow A1101 from Bury St Edmunds towards Mildenhall for about four miles, course on right. 9 holes, 6240 yards. S.S.S. 70. *Green Fees:* £30.00 per round, £35.00 per day. *Eating facilities:* by arrangement. *Visitors:* welcome, except Bank Holidays. By prior arrangement and must produce Handicap Certificate. Professional: Chris Aldred (01284 728291). Secretary: M.S. Clark.

BURY ST EDMUNDS. **The Swallow Suffolk Hotel Golf and Country Club,** Fornham St Genevieve, Bury St Edmunds IP28 6JQ (01284 706777; Fax: 01284 706721). *Location:* Exit A14 at Bury St Edmunds West and travel north on B1106 for approx. 2 miles. Mature parkland, testing water hazards. Putting green and practice ground. 18 hole Genevieve course 6350 yards. S.S.S. 71. *Green Fees:* information not available. *Eating facilities:* Bars and restaurant; residential packages available. *Visitors:* welcome, booking advised. Club, buggy and trolley hire. Indoor pool, with spa sauna and steam room. 41 bedroom en suite hotel. Conference facilities. *Society Meetings:* society packages available. Professional: Stephen Hall. Secretary: Peter Thorpe.*
e-mail: thelodge@the-suffolk.co.uk
website: www.the-suffolk.co.uk

DISS. **Diss Golf Club,** Stuston Common, Diss IP21 4AA (01379 641025). *Location:* B1077 off A140, half-a-mile from Diss railway station, one mile from town centre. The course complete with its natural hazards provides a good test of golf. 18 holes, 6206 yards. S.S.S. 69. Par 70. New 15 bay driving range one mile from clubhouse adjacent to 15th hole. *Green Fees:* information not available. *Eating facilities:* are excellent. *Visitors:* welcome weekends with a member. *Society Meetings:* Golf Societies and groups welcome, contact the Secretary for further details. There is a well stocked shop and lessons are available from the Professional. Membership available, contact the Secretary for details. Professional: Nigel Taylor (01379 644399). Secretary: Mr Chris Wellstead (01379 641025; Fax: 01379 644586). Steward: J.W. Mackrell (01379 642847). *
e-mail: sec.dissgolf@virgin.net
www.club-noticeboard.co.uk/diss

FELIXSTOWE. **Felixstowe Ferry Golf Club,** Ferry Road, Felixstowe IP11 9RY (01394 286834). *Location:* one mile from town centre, follow signs to Golf Club. Seaside links course. 18 holes, 6269 yards. S.S.S. 70. Also a 9 hole course, 2986 yards. S.S.S. 69. Practice Area. *Green Fees:* weekdays £35.00 per day; £25.00 per round. *Eating facilities:* diningroom and bar. *Visitors:* welcome weekdays, but advisable to check first; weekends must play with member. Handicap Certificates required. Two self catering flats available, free golf included in charges. *Society Meetings:* catered for weekdays only. Professional: Ian MacPherson (01394 283975). Secretary: Richard Tibbs (01394 286834).

THE GOLF GUIDE 2006   ENGLAND / Suffolk

FRAMLINGHAM. **Cretingham Golf Club,** Swans Lane, Cretingham, Woodbridge IP13 7BA (01728 685275). *Location:* off A1120, signposted to Cretingham, 10 miles north of Ipswich. Wooded inland course, challenging water holes. 18 holes, 4966 yards. Par 68. Practice 9 hole course. *Green Fees:* weekdays 9 holes £10.00, 18 holes £16.00; weekends and Bank Holidays 9 holes £10.00, 18 holes £18.00. *Eating facilities:* restaurant and fully licensed bar. *Visitors:* always welcome, no restrictions. Please book in advance. Tennis available. Outdoor swimming pool. Caravans welcome. Log cabins available to let. *Society Meetings:* welcome. Professional: Neil Jackson (01728 685275). Secretary: Kate Jackson.

HALESWORTH. **Halesworth Golf Club,** Bramfield Road, Halesworth IP19 9XA (01986 875567). *Location*: on A144 between Halesworth and Bramfield. 18 hole Blyth course, 6506 yards, par 72. 9 hole Valley course, 2280 yards, par 33. Practice area, putting green, 10 bay floodlit driving range. *Green Fees:* information not available. *Eating facilities*: bar and restaurant. *Visitors*: welcome. *Society Meetings*: welcome. Buggies available. Professional: Simon Harrison PGA Professional (01986 875697).*
e-mail: info@halesworthgc.co.uk
website: www.club-noticeboard.co.uk/halesworth

HAVERHILL. **Haverhill Golf Club Ltd,** Coupals Road, Haverhill CB9 7UW (Tel & Fax: 01440 761951). *Location:* Sturmer Road turn into Chalkestone Way, right into Coupals Road. Club is one mile on right. Undulating parkland with river. 18 holes, 5929 yards. S.S.S. 69. Practice ground. *Green Fees:* weekdays £30.00 per day, weekends and Bank Holidays £35.00. Half price if playing with a member. *Eating facilities:* clubhouse, snacks, hot meals, bar. *Visitors:* welcome at all times except when first tee booked for matches and societies. *Society Meetings:* welcome. Professional: Nick Duc (01440 712628; Fax: 01440 712628). Secretary: Lisa Hubbard (Tel & Fax: 01440 761951).

IPSWICH. **Fynn Valley Golf Club,** Witnesham, Ipswich IP6 9JA (01473 785267; Fax: 01473 785632). *Location:* two miles north of Ipswich on B1077. Attractive, undulating parkland along the Fynn Valley. 18 holes, 6361 yards. S.S.S. 71. 9 hole Par 3 course, 23 bay floodlit golf range (10 undercover), practice bunker and putting greens. *Green Fees:* £26.00 per round weekdays; £32.00 per round weekends (twilight discounts). *Eating facilities:* bar, terrace, gourmet restaurant. *Visitors:* welcome, members only Sunday mornings, Ladies priority Wednesday mornings. Special rates for parties of 12 or more. Two golf shops. Teaching facilities, golf buggies, trolley hire. *Society Meetings:* welcome by prior arrangement. Professionals: Danny Barton, Paul Wilby, Alex Lucas, Simon Dainty (01473 785463). Secretary: A.R. Tyrrell (01473 785267; Fax: 01473 785632).
e-mail: enquiries@fynn-valley.co.uk
website: www.fynn-valley.co.uk

IPSWICH. **Hintlesham Golf Club,** Hintlesham, Ipswich IP8 3NS (01473 652761; Fax: 01473 652750). *Location:* four miles west of Ipswich on the A1071 to Sudbury. Parkland, championship standard - Architect: Martin Hawtree. 18 holes, 6638 yards. S.S.S. 72. Full practice facilities. *Green Fees:* £36.00 weekdays, £44.00 weekends. *Eating facilities:* full catering facilities. *Visitors:* please telephone for tee off times. Accommodation available at Hintlesham Hall Hotel. *Society Meetings:* telephone enquiries welcome. We have a growing national reputation for the organisation of golf days. Professional: Alastair Spink.
website: www.hintleshamgolfclub.com

IPSWICH. **Ipswich Golf Club,** Purdis Heath, Bucklesham Road, Ipswich IP3 8UQ. *Location:* three miles east of Ipswich on Bucklesham Road. Heathland. 18 holes, 6439 yards. S.S.S. 71. 9 holes, 1930 yards. S.S.S. 59. *Green Fees:* weekdays £35.00 per round, £45.00 per day, 9 holes £10.00 per day; weekends and Bank Holidays 18 holes with a member only, 9 holes £15.00 per day. *Eating facilities:* full catering facilities available for visitors to 18 hole course only. *Visitors:* by prior arrangement for 18 hole course, and must produce Handicap Certificate or letter of introduction. No restriction for 9 hole course. *Society Meetings:* by special reservation only and on Society terms. Professional: S.J. Whymark (01473 724017). Secretary: N.M. Ellice (01473 728941).
e-mail: mail@ipswichgolfclub.com
website: www.ipswichgolfclub.com

IPSWICH. **Rushmere Golf Club,** Rushmere Heath, Woodbridge Road, Ipswich IP4 5QQ (01473 727109). *Location:* off A1214 north from Ipswich, 300 yards signposted. Heathland course. 18 holes, 6265 yards. S.S.S. 70. Practice facilities. *Green Fees:* £38.00. *Eating facilities:* full catering available. *Visitors:* welcome except 4.30-5.30pm, weekends after 2.30pm. Handicap Certificate required. *Society Meetings:* welcome. Professional: Kelvin Vince (01473 728076). Secretary: R.W.G. Tawell (01473 725648).
e-mail: rushmeregolfclub@talk21.com
website: www.club-noticeboard.co.uk/rushmere

IPSWICH/WOODBRIDGE. **Best Western Ufford Park Hotel, Golf and Leisure,** Yarmouth Road, Ufford, Woodbridge, Near Ipswich IP12 1QW (01394 383555; Fax: 01394 383582). *Location*: A12 northwards to A1152 to Melton. In Melton turn left at traffic lights, one mile on the right hand side. Challenging 120-acre parkland course. A "Top 40 British Winter Course" for the last 3 years. 18 holes, 6312 yards. S.S.S. 71. 32 bay (2 storey) Driving Range: 'American Golf and the Doctorgolf Academy'. *Green Fees:* weekdays £30.00; weekends £40.00. Special Golf Breaks available. *Eating facilities:* bar snacks, carvery and à la carte restaurant. *Visitors:* welcome anytime, need to book tee time in advance. 87 en suite bedroomed hotel. Ideal for groups; full leisure centre with pool, gym, sauna, steam room, jacuzzi etc. Beauty and hair salons. Buggies for hire, tuition breaks available. *Society Meetings:* welcome, competitive rates, details on request. PGA Head Professional. Stuart Robertson (01394 383480 (Golf Academy)). Secretary: Ray Baines (01394 382836; Fax: 01394 383582).
website: www.uffordpark.co.uk
website: www.doctorgolf.co.uk

www.uk-golfguide.com

304 Suffolk / ENGLAND   THE GOLF GUIDE 2006

LOWESTOFT. **Rookery Park Golf Club,** Beccles Road, Carlton Colville, Lowestoft NR33 8HJ (01502 509190; Fax: 01502 509191)). *Location:* A146 Beccles to Lowestoft road. Parkland. 18 holes, 6729 yards. S.S.S. 72. 9 hole Par 3 course. Practice ground. *Green Fees:* weekdays £27.50, with a member £16.50; weekends £33.00, with a member £19.50. *Eating facilities:* bar, restaurant. *Visitors:* welcome weekdays (Saturdays and Bank Holidays after 11am). Handicap Cards must be produced. *Society Meetings:* welcome. Professional: M. Elsworthy (01502 515103). Secretary/Manager: R.F. Jones (01502 509190; Fax: 01502 509191).

MILDENHALL. **Royal Worlington and Newmarket Golf Club,** Golf Links Road, Worlington, Bury St. Edmunds IP28 8SD (01638 712216; Fax: 01638 717787). *Location:* seven miles north east of Newmarket, signposted off A11 just south of Barton Mills roundabout. Inland links type course. 9 holes, 3105 yards. S.S.S. 70 (18 holes). Practice ground. *Green Fees:* weekdays £55.00 per day, £40.00 if after 2pm (12 noon in winter). *Eating facilities:* lunch and tea available with prior notice; no evening meals. *Visitors:* welcome weekdays only, Handicap Certificate or letter of introduction from home club required. Trolleys for hire. Professional: (01638 715224). Secretary: Squadron Leader K.J. Weston (Tel & Fax: 01638 717787).

NEWMARKET. **Links Golf Club,** Cambridge Road, Newmarket CB8 0TG (01638 663000; Fax: 01638 661476). *Location:* one mile south-west of Newmarket, opposite racecourse. Relatively flat parkland. 18 holes, 6582 yards. S.S.S. 72. Two practice grounds. *Green Fees:* midweek £24.00 per round, £32.00 per day; weekends and Bank Holidays £28.00 per round, £36.00 per day. *Eating facilities:* restaurant and bar. *Visitors:* welcome, not before 11.30am Sundays. Handicap Certificate required. *Society Meetings:* by arrangement. Professional: Mr John Sharkey (01638 662395). Secretary: M.L. Hartley (01638 663000; Fax: 01638 661476). website: www.club-noticeboard.co.uk/newmarket

RAYDON. **Brett Vale Golf Club,** Noakes Road, Raydon, Ipswich IP7 5LR (01473 310718). *Location:* midway between Colchester and Ipswich, just off A12 on B1070 to Hadleigh, head for Raydon Water Tower. Undulating countryside parkland course within Dedham Vale in natural valley setting. 18 holes, 5813 yards. S.S.S. 69. 5 bay outdoor Golf Academy, practice ground, putting green. *Green Fees:* weekdays £22.50, day ticket £35.00; weekends £28.00. *Eating facilities:* clubroom bar and restaurant; society/function room and bar. *Visitors:* welcome anytime. Pro shop; buggies and power trolley hire. *Society Meetings:* welcome anytime, various packages available. Secretary: John Reid (01473 310718).

SOUTHWOLD. **Southwold Golf Club,** The Common, Southwold IP18 6TB (01502 723234). *Location:* from A12 Blythburgh turn off on A1095 to Southwold. Flat common land with sea views. 9 holes, 6052 yards. S.S.S. 69. *Green Fees:* weekdays £26.00 per round, weekends £28.00 per round. Weekly tickets £75.00. Daily ticket £35.00. *Visitors:* welcome, phone for availability. *Society Meetings:* welcome, Fridays only. Professional: B.G. Allen (01502 723790). Hon. Secretary: P. Obern (01502 723248).

STOKE-BY-NAYLAND. **Stoke by Nayland Golf Club,** Keepers Lane, Leavenheath, Colchester CO6 4PZ (01206 262836; Fax: 01206 263356). *Location:* just off A134 Colchester to Sudbury on B1068 towards Stoke by Nayland. Undulating parkland with water hazards. Two courses (1) Gainsborough - 18 holes, 6516 yards. S.S.S. 71. (2) Constable - 18 holes, 6544 yards. S.S.S. 71. 20 bay covered range, practice area. *Green Fees:* information not available. *Eating facilities:* full catering and bars. *Visitors:* welcome, please ring for availability and tee bookings. *Society Meetings:* welcome weekdays, book well in advance. Seasonal packages offered. Extensive Health and Leisure Facility including gymnasium, pool, sauna, jacuzzi and spa; modern, spacious, en suite hotel rooms overlooking lake and fairways. Professional: Kevin Lovelock (01206 262769). Secretary: Peter Barfield (01206 265815). e-mail: info@stokebynaylandclub.co.uk website: www.stokebynaylandclub.co.uk

STOWMARKET. **Stowmarket Golf Club Ltd,** Lower Road, Onehouse, Stowmarket IP14 3DA (01449 736473; Fax: 01449 736826). *Location:* on B1508 from Stowmarket to Onehouse. Parkland. 18 holes, 6101 yards. S.S.S. 69. Driving range. *Green Fees:* weekdays £31.00 per round, £37.00 per day; weekends £34.00 per round, £46.00 per day. *Eating facilities:* lunches, snacks all week. *Visitors:* welcome, avoid Wednesdays. Handicap Certificate required. *Society Meetings:* catered for Thursdays and Fridays only. Professional: D. Burl (01449 736392). Secretary: G.R. West (01449 736473).

SUDBURY. **Newton Green Golf Club,** Newton Green, Sudbury CO10 0QN. *Location:* on A134 three miles east of Sudbury. Flat course. 18 holes, 5947 yards. Par 69. Practice ground. *Green Fees:* day ticket £30.00, 18 holes £22.00. *Eating facilities:* fully licensed bar, full catering facilities, separate dining room available. *Visitors:* welcome (except Sundays and Tuesdays before 12.30pm); trolleys for hire. *Society Meetings:* welcome by arrangement. PGA Professional: Tim Cooper (01787 313215). Secretary/Manager: Carole List (01787 377217). e-mail: info@newtongreengolfclub.co.uk website: www.newtongreengolfclub.co.uk

---

For full details of clubs and courses, plus convenient accommodation
www.uk-golfguide.com

ENGLAND / Suffolk

THORPENESS. **Thorpeness Golf Club and Hotel,** Thorpeness, Leiston IP16 4NH (01728 452176; Fax: 01728 453868). *Location:* leave A12 at Aldeburgh turnoff. Heathland coastal course. 18 holes, 6271 yards. S.S.S. 71. *Green Fees:* information not available. *Eating facilities:* bar, restaurant, terrace and garden. *Visitors:* welcome on application, telephone Pro shop for times. Handicap Cetificate required. Accommodation available – 30 bedrooms. Snooker room, seven tennis courts. *Society Meetings:* welcome. Professional: Frank Hill (01728 454926). Golf Manager: Charlie Langlands (01728 452176).*

WOODBRIDGE. **Seckford Golf Centre,** Seckford Hall Road, Great Bealings, Near Woodbridge IP13 6NT (01394 388000; Fax: 01394 382818). *Location:* between Martlesham and Woodbridge just off A12. Undulating parkland course maintained in excellent condition. 18 holes, 4936 yards. Par 67. Full length driving range and putting green. *Green Fees:* Please call for rates and specials. *Eating facilities:* fully licensed bar and restaurant. *Visitors:* always welcome, telephone to book your place. Buggies, trolleys, clubs and shoes available for hire. *Society Meetings:* Welcome by prior arrangement, packages available. PGA Professional: Simon Jay (Tel: 01394 446191) GASP Video analysis.
e-mail: info@seckfordgolf.co.uk
website: www.seckfordgolf.co.uk

WOODBRIDGE. **Waldringfield Golf Club,** Newbourne Road, Waldringfield, Woodbridge IP12 4PT (01473 736768). *Location:* five miles north of Ipswich, off the old A12. Easy walking, picturesque heathland course with attractive water features. 18 holes, 6079 yards. S.S.S. 69. Limited practice area available. *Green Fees:* weekdays £22.00 per round, £30.00 per day; weekends £26.00 per round, £36.00 per day. Special rates available for societies by arrangement. *Eating facilities:* full service. *Visitors:* welcome weekdays and weekends. *Society Meetings:* welcome weekdays and weekends by arrangement. Course Administrator: (01473 736417). Manager: Pat Whitham (01473 736768. Fax: 01473 736793)

WOODBRIDGE. **Woodbridge Golf Club,** Bromeswell Heath, Woodbridge IP12 2PF (01394 382038; Fax: 01394 382392). *Location:* leave A12 at Melton Roundabout. After traffic lights, follow A1152 over level crossing, fork left at roundabout. Club is 400 yards on right. Heathland. 18 holes, 6299 yards. S.S.S. 70. 9 holes, 3191 yards. S.S.S. 70. Large practice ground. *Green Fees:* information not available. *Eating facilities:* main bar, casual bar and restaurant. *Visitors:* not before 9.30am, not at weekends. Handicap Certificates mandatory on 18 hole course, no restriction on 9 hole course. Telephone call advisable. *Society Meetings:* by prior arrangement, maximum number 36. Professional: C. Elliot (01394 383213). Secretary: A. Theunissen (01394 382038; 01394 382392).*

THORPENESS SUFFOLK

ROUND OFF A PERFECT DAY

Enjoy a break on the invigorating Heritage Coast. Play the challenging, mature 18-hole seaside course designed by the legendary James Braid. Guests in the hotel can enjoy concessionary rates at Aldeburgh Golf Club, one of the top 100 courses in the British Isles. Explore the unique village of Thorpeness, Aldeburgh and Southwold. A warm welcome, comfortable en suite rooms and good food. Midweek and weekends all year.

The Hotel & Golf Club, Thorpeness, Aldeburgh, Suffolk IP16 4NH
CALL NOW FOR YOUR FREE BROCHURE
Tel 01728 452176 Fax 01728 453868 www.thorpeness.co.uk

FHG

Visit the FHG website
www.holidayguides.com
for details of the wide choice of accommodation featured in the full range of FHG titles

Surrey

BAGSHOT. **Pennyhill Park Hotel and Country Club,** London Road, Bagshot GU19 5EU (01276 471774; Fax: 01276 473217). *Location*: just off A30 at Bagshot. Wooded, hilly course. 9 holes, 2000 yards. S.S.S. 64. *Green Fees*: information not available. *Eating facilities*: Ascot Bar, St James Brasserie restaurant, Latymer à la carte restaurant, five star hotel with 123 luxury bedrooms; tennis court, outdoor heated swimming pool, clay pigeon shooting, gym etc. *Visitors*: prior booking must be made in advance. *Society Meetings*: welcome anytime. Country Club Manager: Claire Williams.*

BAGSHOT. **Windlesham Golf Club,** Grove End, Bagshot GU19 5HY. *Location:* A30 west from Sunningdale at Junction of A30 and A332 or Junction 3 from M3 and take the A322 to Bracknell then junction of A30/A332. Challenging parkland course designed by Tommy Horton - USPGA, greens and tees of highest specification. 18 holes, 6650 yards. S.S.S. 72. Practice range with three covered bays, practice hole. *Green Fees:* call for details. *Visitors:* welcome, please ring first on weekdays, weekends, Bank Holidays after 12 noon. Teaching Academy School; carts available. Professional Lee Mucklow (01276 472323). Secretary: Richard Griffiths (01276 452220; Fax: 01276 452290).

BANSTEAD. **Cuddington (Banstead) Golf Club Ltd,** Banstead Road, Banstead SM7 1RD (020 8393 0952; Fax: 020 8786 7025). *Location*: 200 yards from Banstead Railway Station. 18 holes, 6614 yards. S.S.S. 71. *Green Fees*: on application. *Visitors*: welcome with reservation. *Society Meetings*: catered for on Thursdays and some Tuesdays pm. Professional: M. Warner. Secretary: D. M. Scott.
e-mail:ds@cuddingtongc.co.uk
website: www.cuddingtongc.co.uk

BLETCHINGLEY. **Bletchingley Golf Club,** Church Lane, Bletchingley RH1 4LP (01883 744666; Fax: 01883 744284). *Location:* off A25, three miles west from Junction 6 M25. Parkland course, sand based. 18 holes, 6513 yards. S.S.S. 71. Practice ground. *Green Fees*:weekdays £35.00, weekends £48.00. *Eating facilities*: lounge/dining room, large function room, bar. *Visitors*: welcome. Carts available. *Society Meetings*: welcome. Professional: A. Dyer (01883 744848; Fax; 01883 744284). Manager: R. Borer (01883 744666; Fax: 01883 744284).
website: www.bletchingleygolf.co.uk

For full details of clubs and courses, plus convenient accommodation
www.uk-golfguide.com

CAMBERLEY. **Camberley Heath Golf Club,** Golf Drive, Portsmouth Road, Camberley GU15 1JG (01276 23258; Fax: 01276 692505). *Location*: south of the M3 on the A325 Portsmouth Road, near Frimley. Heathland and pine, designed by Harry Colt - his best, established 1913. 18 holes, 6326 yards, 5780 metres. S.S.S. 71. Practice ground. *Green Fees*: £60.00. *Eating facilities:* restaurants and Teppan Yaki (Japanese Steak Bar). *Visitors*: welcome weekdays only by prior arrangement. *Society Meetings*: welcome by prior arrangement weekdays only; various packages available. Professional: Glenn Ralph (01276 27905). Managing Director/Secretary: C.M. Kennedy (01276 23258).
e-mail: info@camberleyheathgolfclub.co.uk
website: www.camberleyheathgolfclub.co.uk

CARSHALTON. **Oaks Sports Centre Ltd,** Woodmansterne Road, Carshalton SM5 4AN (020 8643 8363; Fax: 020 8770 7303). *Location:* on the B2032 past Carshalton Beeches Station, Oaks Sports Centre signposted north of A2022, half way between A217 and A237. Open 6am, 7 days, 364 days per year. Meadowland course. 18 holes, 6054 yards. S.S.S 69. 9 holes, 1497 yards. S.S.S 28. 18 bay golf range. *Green Fees:* information not available. *Eating facilities:* bar lounge and cafeteria. *Visitors:* public course, everyone welcome. Changing rooms. Conference facilities. *Society Meetings:* by arrangement. Professional: Mr G.D. Horley. Secretary: Mr D.J. Capper.
e-mail: golf@oaks.sagehost.co.uk
website: www.oakssportscentre.co.uk

CATERHAM. **Surrey National Golf Club,** Rook Lane, Chaldon, Caterham CR3 5AA (01883 344555). *Location*: M25, Junction 7 (M23) towards Croydon. After two miles turn right into Dean Lane and then left into Rook Lane, entrance on the left. Mature landscape with stunning views of South Downs. 18 holes. 6850 yards. Par 72. *Green Fees:* call club. *Eating facilities*: bar and catering facilities available. *Visitors*: welcome weekdays at anytime and weekends after 11am. Buggies and carts available for hire. *Society Meetings*: welcome weekdays at anytime and weekends at restricted times. Professional: David Kent. General Manager: Simon Hodsdon.
e-mail: caroline@surreynational.co.uk
website: www.surreynational.co.uk

CATERHAM near. **Woldingham Golf Club,** Halliloo Valley Road, Woldingham, near Caterham CR3 7HA (01883 653501; Fax: 01883 653502). *Location:* Caterham, Junction 6 M25, 3 miles. Downland course. 18 holes. 6393 yards. S.S.S. 71. Putting greens, practice ground. *Green Fees:* please call for details. *Eating facilities:* Function suite, Spike bar. *Visitors:* welcome, not before 12 noon at weekends. *Society Meetings:* welcome Monday to Friday. "ASTAR" video studio on site. Professional: James Hillen (01883 653541).
website: www.woldingham-golfclub.co.uk

THE GOLF GUIDE 2006   ENGLAND / Surrey 307

CHERTSEY. **Barrow Hills Golf Club,** Longcross, Chertsey KT16 0DS (01344 635770). *Location:* four miles west of Chertsey, adjacent to M3 at Longcross. 18 holes, 3090 yards. S.S.S. 53. *Green Fees:* information not available. *Visitors:* only with a member. Secretary: R. Hammond (01483 234807 home).

CHERTSEY. **Laleham Golf Club,** Laleham Reach, Mixnams Lane, Chertsey KT16 8RP (01932 562188; Fax: 01932 564448). *Location:* M25 to Junction 11, follow directions to Thorpe Park, entrance opposite roundabout. Flat but interesting parkland course with water features. 18 holes, 6211 yards. S.S.S. 70. *Green Fees:* weekdays £35.00 per day, £30.00 per round; weekends £32.00 per round. *Eating facilities:* full restaurant and bar facilities. *Visitors:* welcome weekdays; weekends after 3pm in summer and 12.30pm in winter. Please phone to ensure no tee reservations. *Society Meetings:* catered for at competitive rates. Professional: Hogan Stott (01932 562877). Secretary: Mrs Pauline Kennett (01932 564211; Fax: 01932 564448).
e-mail: sec@laleham-golf.co.uk

CHESSINGTON. **Chessington Golf Centre,** Garrison Lane, Chessington KT9 2LW (020 8391 0948). *Location:* off A243, 500 yards from Chessington World of Adventure. Opposite Chessington South Station, Junction 9 M25. Parkland course. 9 holes, 1679 yards. S.S.S. 28. Covered floodlit driving range. *Green Fees:* weekdays £8.50, weekends £10.00. *Eating facilities:* bar, coffee, catering available. *Visitors:* welcome. Facilities open to public 8.00am until 10.00pm (9.00 pm Saturday and Sunday). *Society Meetings:* welcome. Professional: Mark Janes (020 8391 0948; Fax: 020 8397 2068). Secretary: Martin Bedford (020 8391 0948; Fax: 020 8397 2068).

CHESSINGTON. **Surbiton Golf Club,** Woodstock Lane, Chessington KT9 1UG (020 8398 3101; Fax: 020 8339 0992). *Location:* two miles east of Esher, off A3 at Ace of Spades roundabout. Undulating parkland. 18 holes, 6055 yards. S.S.S. 69, Par 70. Practice area. *Green Fees:* information not available. *Eating facilities:* snacks and lunches to order by reservation weekdays. *Visitors:* at weekends play with member only. *Society Meetings:* catered for Monday and Friday only. Professional: Paul Milton (020 8398 6619). Secretary: Chris Cornish (020 8398 3101).*
e-mail: surbitongolfclub@hotmail.com

CHIDDINGFOLD. **Chiddingfold Golf Club,** Petworth Road, Chiddingfold GU8 4SL (01428 685888). *Location:* Exit 10 off M25, A3 towards Portsmouth, take A283 turn off, golf course quarter-of-a-mile past Chiddingfold village. Parkland. 18 holes, 5500 yards. Par 70 S.S.S. 67. *Green Fee``s:* information not available. *Visitors:* welcome seven days, including Bank Holidays. *Society Meetings:* welcome seven days, including Bank Holidays. Professionals: Jon Wells. Manager/Secretary: Moreno Pascolini.
e-mail: chiddingfoldgolf@btconnect.com
website: www.chiddingfoldgc.co.uk

CHIDDINGFOLD. **Shillinglee Park Golf Club,** Chiddingfold, Godalming GU8 4TA (01428 708158; Fax: 01428 644391). *Location:* off A283 near Chiddingfold. Parkland. 9 holes, 5300 yards. S.S.S. 64. 6 hole pitch and putt course, ideal for learners. Well equipped Pro Shop. *Green Fees:* information not available. *Eating facilities:* excellent menu from snacks to à la carte. *Visitors:* welcome all week apart from Saturday and Thursday mornings. Advisable to book. Instruction available. *Society Meetings:* always welcome. Professional: Mark Dowdell (01428 653237). Secretary: Nikki Taylor. *

CHIPSTEAD. **Chipstead Golf Club Ltd,** How Lane, Coulsdon CR5 3LN (01737 555881; Fax: 01737 555404). *Location:* by Chipstead Station (Chipstead Valley Road). Parkland. 18 holes, 5504 yards, 5332 metres. S.S.S. 67. *Green Fees:* information not available. *Eating facilities:* full catering 7 days a week, bar. *Visitors:* welcome weekdays except Tuesday mornings. *Society Meetings:* welcome full or half days. Director of Golf: Gary Torbett (01737 554939).

COBHAM. **Silvermere Golf and Leisure Complex,** Redhill Road, Cobham KT11 1EF (01932 584300). *Location:* half a mile from Junction 10 of M25 at A3. Wooded, parkland course with water on two holes. 34 bay driving range. *Green Fees:* information not available. *Eating facilities:* £½million new lakeside clubhouse serving food all day from 7am to 9pm, bar meals, snacks and lunches. *Visitors:* welcome every day but not early weekend mornings. *Society Meetings:* welcome, contact Secretary for details. Professional: Doug McClelland PGA (01932 584348). Secretary: Pauline Devereux (01932 584306; Fax: 01932 584301).*

COULSDON. **Coulsdon Manor Hotel and Golf Centre,** Coulsdon Court Road, Coulsdon CR5 2LL (020 8668 0414; Fax: 020 8668 0342). *Location:* off J7 of M25 through Coulsdon towards Caterham B2030 turning left via Stoneyfield Road and left in Coulsdon Court Road. Parkland. 18 holes, 6037 yards. Par 70. S.S.S. 68. *Green Fees:* information not available. *Eating facilities:* Terrace bar/Orangery and Manor House Restaurant. *Visitors:* welcome, subject to availability. *Society Meetings:* welcome Mondays, Tuesdays, Thursdays and Fridays. Extensive banquet and conference facilities, 35 luxurious bedrooms, all en-suite. Professionals: Gordon Ritchie and James Leaver (020 8660 6083; Fax: 020 8668 3118). General Manager: Philip Thomas.*

COULSDON. **Woodcote Park Golf Club,** Meadow Hill, Bridle Way, Coulsdon CR5 2QQ. *Location:* south of Croydon, off A237. Parkland course. 18 holes, 6720 yards. S.S.S. 72. *Green Fees:* £45.00 per day. *Eating facilities:* meals at all times. *Visitors:* welcome with reservation. Handicap Certificate required. *Society Meetings:* up to 90 catered for, by arrangement. Professional: Wraith Grant (020 8668 1843). Secretary: A. Dawson (020 8668 2788; Fax: 020 8660 0918).
e-mail: info@woodcotepgc.com
website: www.woodcotepgc.com

THE APPEARANCE OF AN ASTERISK (*) AT THE END OF A CLUB OR COURSE ENTRY INDICATES THAT UP-TO-DATE INFORMATION HAS NOT BEEN SUPPLIED

CRANLEIGH. **The Cranleigh Golf and Leisure Club,** Barhatch Lane, Cranleigh GU6 7NG (01483 268855; Fax: 01483 267251). *Location:* Guildford A281 Horsham take Cranleigh turn-off. Interesting parkland course. 18 holes, 5644 yards. S.S.S. 67. Covered driving range, practice ground. *Green Fees:* (2005) 18 holes weekdays £30.00, weekends and Bank Holidays £33.00, day ticket weekday only £38.00. *Eating facilities:* bar, bar snacks, banqueting facilities available. *Visitors:* welcome weekdays and weekends except Thursday before 11am. Weekends subject to availability. *Society Meetings:* welcome weekdays and weekends after 11.30am. Professional: Trevor Longmuir (01483 277188). Secretary: Mike Kateley (01483 268855; Fax: 01483 267251).

CRANLEIGH. **Wildwood Country Club,** Horsham Road, Alfold, Cranleigh GU6 8JE (01403 753255; Fax: 01403 752005). *Location:* 10 miles from Guildford on the A281 to Horsham, near Cranleigh. Only 40 minutes from London on the A3. Championship parkland course with mature woodland and water hazards. An exhilarating challenge to all golfers. 27 holes, 6655 yards. S.S.S. 72. All-weather practice range and 9 hole course. *Green Fees:* weekdays 18 holes £40.00, weekends 18 holes £50.00. Discounted rates in winter. *Eating facilities:* two bars/restaurant. *Visitors:* welcome. Gymnasium. *Society Meetings:* Welcome, Corporate days organised. Accommodation available locally. Director of Golf: Phil Harrison.

CRONDALL. **Bowenhurst Golf Centre Ltd,** Mill Lane, Crondall, Near Farnham GU10 5RP (01252 851695). *Location:* public golf course, south of M3, 5 miles from exit 5 Farnham side on A287 (behind garage). Parkland course with mature trees and lakes. 3658 yards S.S.S. 60. 20 bay floodlit driving range, two practice putting greens, practice bunker. *Green Fees:* information not available. *Visitors:* welcome at any time. Pro shop. *Society Meetings:* welcome, rates on application. Professional:Adam Hart (01252 851344). Secretary: Geoffrey Corbey.*

CRONDALL. **Oak Park Golfing Complex,** Heath Lane, Crondall, Near Farnham, Surrey GU10 5PB (01252 850880; Fax: 01252 850851). *Location:* one and a half miles off A287 Farnham-Odiham road, five miles from Junctions 4, 4a and 5 of M3 motorway. Gently undulating parkland course. Woodland Course - 18 holes, 6247 yards. S.S.S. 70; Village Course - 9 holes, 3279 yards. Par 36. 16 bay covered driving range, putting green, chipping green and practice bunker. *Green Fees:* Monday - Thursday £25.50; Friday £28.50; Saturday/Sunday pm only £28.50. *Eating facilities:* Restaurant: available for private hire and special occasions. Bar snacks available. V*isitors:* welcome; must book through Professional; reserved tee system at all times. *Society Meetings:* by arrangement. Professional: Paul Archer (01252 850066; Fax: 01252 850851). Manager: Mr. Robert Brewer (01252 850850).

CROYDON. **Addington Court Golf Ltd,** Featherbed Lane, Addington, Croydon CR0 9AA (020 8657 0281; Fax: 020 8651 0282). *Location*: two miles east of Croydon. Leave B281 at Addington Village. Dry, well-drained, wooded parkland course. Four courses: Championship 5755 yards, S.S.S. 67. Falconwood 5513 yards, S.S.S. 67. Lower 9 hole course S.S.S 62. 18 hole, Par 3 course. 32-bay floodlit driving range. *Green Fees*: information not available. *Eating facilities*: restaurant, bar. *Visitors*: welcome anytime, no restrictions, public courses. *Society Meetings*: welcome. Professional: Tony Healy (020 8657 0281).*

CROYDON. **The Addington Golf Club,** 205 Shirley Church Road, Croydon CR0 5AB (020 8777 1055; Fax: 020 8777 6661). *Location:* Wickam Road, Shirley. 30 minutes from centre of London. Heath and woodland as set out by the famous J.F. Abercromby with the world renowned 13th Par 3. 18 holes, 6338 yards. S.S.S. 71. *Green Fees:* £65.00. *Eating facilities:* bar and restaurant with full snack menu. *Visitors:* welcome weekdays. *Society Meetings:* by prior arrangement. Secretary: Bob Hill (020 8777 1055).
e-mail: addingtongolf@btconnect.com
website: www.addingtongolf.com

CROYDON. **Addington Palace Golf Club,** Gravel Hill, Addington, Croydon CR0 5BB (020 8654 3061). *Location:* two miles east of Croydon Station. Undulating parkland course. 18 holes, 6339 yards. S.S.S. 70. *Green Fees:* information not available. *Eating facilities:* bar all day, catering 10am to 6.30pm. *Visitors:* welcome weekdays; at weekends and Bank Holidays must be accompanied by a member. *Society Meetings:* welcome on Mondays, Tuesdays, Wednesdays and Fridays. Professional: Roger Williams (020 8654 1786). Secretary: Mr John Bowen.
e-mail: johnb@addingtonpalacegolf.co.uk
website: www.addingtonpalacegolf.co.uk

CROYDON. **Croham Hurst Golf Club,** Croham Road, South Croydon CR2 7HJ (020 8657 2075; Fax: 020 8657 3229). *Location:* midway between Croydon and Selsdon. Parkland. 18 holes, 6290 yards. S.S.S. 70. *Green Fees:* information not available. *Eating facilities:* lunches, teas, snacks. *Visitors:* welcome with reservation on weekdays. *Society Meetings:* catered for booked one year ahead. Professional: Matthew Paget (020 8657 7705). Secretary: David Free (020 8657 5581).*
e-mail: secretary@chgc.co.uk
website: www.chgc.co.uk

CROYDON. **Selsdon Park Hotel & Golf Course,** Sanderstead, South Croydon CR2 8YA (020 8657 8811; Fax: 020 8651 6171). *Location:* three miles south of Croydon on A2022 Purley-West Wickham road. Parkland course, designed by J.H. Taylor. 18 holes, 6473 yards. S.S.S. 71. Practice ground. *Green Fees:* please call for details. *Eating facilities:* hotel bars, restaurant and grill. *Visitors:* welcome all week with pre-bookable tee-off times. Buggies. *Society Meetings:* welcome by prior arrangement. P.G.A. Professional: Malcolm Churchill (020 8657 4129). Golf Office: (020 8657 8811). Ext. 3073.*

THE GOLF GUIDE 2006 — ENGLAND / Surrey 309

CROYDON. **Shirley Park Golf Club Ltd,** 194 Addiscombe Road, Croydon CR0 7LB (020 8654 1143; Fax: 020 8654 6733). *Location:* on A232 one and a half miles from East Croydon Station. Parkland. 18 holes, 6210 yards. S.S.S. 69. Practice area. *Green Fees:* £40.00 weekdays; Saturday with a member only. Winter rate £30.00. Subject to review. *Eating facilities:* seven day catering, two bars. *Visitors:* welcome weekdays and Sunday afternoons. Trolleys and caddies if booked in advance. Reduced accommodation charges available from Croydon Park Hotel if booked through the Secretary. *Society Meetings:* welcome Mondays, Tuesdays, Thursdays and Fridays. Professional: Michael Taylor (020 8654 8767; Fax: 020 8654 6733). Secretary: Steve Murphy (020 8654 1143; Fax: 020 8654 6733).
e-mail: secretary@shirleyparkgolfclub.co.uk
website: www.shirleyparkgolfclub.co.uk

DORKING. **Betchworth Park Golf Club,** Reigate Road, Dorking RH4 1NZ (01306 882052). *Location:* on A25 half-a-mile east of Dorking on Reigate Road. Parkland course. 18 holes, 6285 yards, Par 69,. S.S.S 70. *Green Fees:* £37.00 Monday to Friday. *Eating facilities:* snacks available daily. *Visitors:* welcome, by arrangement. *Society Meetings*: welcome Mondays and Thursdays. Professional: A Tocher (01306 884334). Manager: John Holton (01306 882052; Fax: 01306 877462).

DORKING. **Dorking Golf Club,** Deepdene Avenue, Dorking RH5 4BX (01306 886917). *Location:* on A24 half-a-mile south of junction with A25. Parkland/downland. 9 holes, alternative tees second 9, 5158 yards. S.S.S. 65. *Green Fees:* weekdays £18.00, £12.00 after 2pm. *Eating facilities:* full catering. *Visitors:* weekdays only without reservation. *Society Meetings:* catered for up to 48. Professional/ Manager: A. Smeal.

DORKING. **Gatton Manor,** Standon Lane, Ockley, Near Dorking RH5 5PQ (01306 627555; Fax: 01306 627713). *Location:* to the west of the village of Ockley on the A29 between Dorking and Horsham, easy access from M25 Junction 9. 18 hole championship length course in parkland, makes good use of the many rivers and lakes to make it a picturesque but challenging course. 18 holes, 6653 yards. S.S.S. 72. Additional practice facilities. *Green Fees:* on request. *Eating facilities:* full à la carte restaurant and bar with bar meals. *Visitors:* a warm and friendly welcome anytime except Sunday mornings. Refurbished changing rooms. Hotel with 18 bedrooms all en suite, conference suites and, gym. Fishing and tennis available. *Society Meetings:* welcome weekdays only. Ideal society/corporate day venue. 7 and 5 day memberships available. Golf bookings: (01306 627555). Secretary: Patrick Kiely (01306 627555; Fax: 01306 627713).
e-mail: info@gattonmanor.co.uk

EAST HORSLEY. **Drift Golf Club,** The Drift, East Horsley KT24 5HD (01483 284641). *Location:* the club is located just off the Drift Road which runs between Ockham Road (B2039) and Forest Road, East Horsley. Picturesque woodland course set in the heart of Surrey countryside. 18 holes, 6425 yards, 5877 metres. S.S.S. 72. Golf Academy, driving range and putting green. *Green Fees:* information not available. *Eating facilities:* full bar, lounge, restaurant and bar snacks. *Visitors:* welcome Monday to Friday, and after midday at weekends. Bookings accepted up to seven days in advance. *Society Meetings:* catered for weekdays. General Manager: Liam Greasley (01483 284641).

EFFINGHAM. **Effingham Golf Club,** Guildford Road, Effingham KT24 5PZ (01372 452203; Fax: 01372 459959). *Location:* A246 between Guildford and Leatherhead. Downland course with magnificent views towards London. 18 holes, 6542 yards. S.S.S. 71. Large practice ground. *Green Fees:* weekdays £55.00 full day, £40.00 for 18 holes; weekends with a member only. *Eating facilities:* full bar and catering facilities. *Visitors:* welcome Monday-Friday. Handicap Certificate required. *Society Meetings:* welcome Wednesdays, Thursdays, Fridays. Professional: Steve Hoatson (01372 452606). Secretary: Simon Sheppard (01372 452203).

EPSOM. **Epsom Golf Club,** Longdown Lane South, Epsom KT17 4JR (01372 721666; Fax: 01372 817183). *Location:* off A240 into B288, 200 yards south of Epsom Downs Station. Downland, links-type course with fast, undulating greens. 18 holes, 5656 yards. S.S.S. 67. Par 69. Practice nets, putting green and chipping area. *Green Fees:* £24.00/£30.00 per round weekday /weekend. *Eating facilities:* bar snacks available from two bars; dining room. *Visitors:* welcome anytime except am on Tuesday, Saturday and Sunday. *Society Meetings:* always welcome with similar exceptions to visitors. Professional and Tee Reservations: R. Goudie (01372 741867).
e-mail: enquiries@epsomgolfclub.co.uk
website: www.epsomgolfclub.co.uk

EPSOM. **Horton Park Golf & Country Club,** Hook Road, Epsom KT19 8QG (020 8393 8400; Fax: 020 8394 1369). *Location:* Junction 9 of M25 four miles. Epsom Town and station five minutes car or taxi. Attractive parkland course situated within a picturesque country park with water hazards and lakes. 18 holes, 5728 yards. S.S.S. 68. *Eating facilities:* bar food, restaurant and function room. *Visitors:* welcome. *Society Meetings:* welcome weekdays and weekend afternoons. Pro shop (020 8394 2626). Professional: Martyn Hirst. General Manager: Anthony Picariello.*

GATTON MANOR
- A Warm & Friendly welcome
- A la carte restaurant and bar
- Challenging 18-hole course
- 18 bedroom hotel

Standon Lane, Ockley, Dorking, Surrey RH5 5PQ
Reception: 01306 627555 Golf Bookings: 01306 627557
Fax: 01306 627713 E-mail: golf@gattonmanor.co.uk

See also Colour Advertisement on page 26

ESHER. **Moore Place Golf Club,** Portsmouth Road, Esher KT10 9LN (01372 463533). *Location:* half a mile from Esher town centre on Portsmouth Road. Undulating parkland course with featured trees - recently lengthened. 9 holes, 2148 yards. S.S.S. 60. *Green Fees:* information not available. *Eating facilities:* bar and restaurant. *Visitors:* welcome, unrestricted. Smart casual dress; golf shoes required, hire available. *Society Meetings:* welcome anytime, 10% reduction for groups of 10 or more. Professional: Nick Gadd (01372 463533). Hon. Secretary: J. Darby (01932 880186).*
website: www.moore-place.co.uk

ESHER. **Cranfield Golf at Sandown,** More Lane, Esher KT10 8AN. *Location:* signposted from A3, centre of Sandown Park Racecourse. Three golf courses; floodlit 33-bay driving range, plus grassed area. Cranfield Golf Academy. *Green Fees:* information not available. *Eating facilities:* bar and snacks. *Visitors:* welcome. *Society Meetings:* welcome. General Manager: David Parr (01372 461234; Fax: 01372 461203).*

ESHER. **Thames Ditton and Esher Golf Club,** Portsmouth Road, Esher KT10 9AL (020 8398 1551). *Location:* "Scilly Isles" roundabout(s), Junction Kingston by-pass, A3. Wooded commonland. 9 holes played twice from different tees, 5149 yards. S.S.S. 65. Practice nets. *Green Fees:* information not available. *Eating facilities:* bar snacks, meals by arrangement. *Visitors:* welcome except Sunday mornings. Trolleys. *Society Meetings:* always welcome, phone the Professional. Professional: Rob Jones. Secretary: Allan Barry.*

FARNHAM. **Farnham Golf Club Ltd,** The Sands, Farnham GU10 1PX (01252 782109; Fax: 01252 781185). *Location:* off A31 at Seale or Runfold slip roads. Follow signs to The Sands club situated at junction of Sands Road and Blighton Lane. Mixture of wooded parkland and heathland. 18 holes, 6447 yards. S.S.S. 71. Large practice ground. *Green Fees:* weekdays £40.00 round, £45.00 day; weekends with a member £19.50 per day. May to August twilight rate £25.00 inclusive, after 5.30pm. *Eating facilities:* two bars and diningroom, full high standard catering. *Visitors:* welcome weekdays with Handicap Certificate. *Society Meetings:* welcome Wednesday to Friday by prior booking. Professional: Grahame Cowlishaw (01252 782198; Fax: 01252 781185). Secretary: Mrs J. Elliott (01252 782109; Fax: 01252 781185).

FARNHAM. **Hankley Common Golf Club,** Tilford Road, Tilford, Farnham GU10 2DD (01252 792493; Fax: 01252 795699). *Location:* off A3, right at lights at Hindhead. Off A31 (Farnham by-pass) left at lights, three miles beyond level crossing. Heathland, dry and sandy links-type course. 18 holes, 6702 yards. S.S.S. 71. Practice ground. *Green Fees:* weekdays £60.00 per round, £75.00 per day; weekends £75.00 per round after 2pm. *Eating facilities:* full range available, restaurant and two bars. *Visitors:* welcome by appointment with Secretary. Handicap Certificate required. *Society Meetings:* catered for on Tuesdays and Wednesdays. Professional: Peter Stow (01252 793761). Secretary: J.S.W. Scott (01252 792493).

GODALMING near. **Hurtmore Golf Club,** Hurtmore Road, Near Godalming GU7 2RN (01483 426492; Fax: 01483 426121). *Location:* A3 Guildford, M25 (15 minutes) A3 exit Guildford to Portsmouth. Undulating parkland with seven large lakes. 18 holes, 5530yards. S.S.S. 67 men, 68 ladies. Practice nets and putting green. *Green Fees:* information not available. *Eating facilities:* bar, restaurant. *Visitors:* welcome at all times, pay and play course with 200 members. Bookings taken by telephone. *Society Meetings:* welcome by prior booking. Professional and General Manager: Maxine Burton. *

GODALMING. **West Surrey Golf Club,** Enton Green, Godalming GU8 5AF (01483 421275). *Location:* off the A3 south of Guildford, half mile past Milford Station/crossing. Wooded parkland. 18 holes, 6482 yards. S.S.S. 71. Practice ground. *Green Fees*: on application. *Eating facilities*: bar, diningroom. *Visitors*: welcome, must be member of recognised golf club and have current Handicap Certificate. *Society Meetings*: catered for by prior arrangement. Professional: A. Tawse (01483 417278). Secretary: S. Last (01483 421275)
e-mail: office@wsgc.co.uk
website: www.wsgc.co.uk

GUILDFORD. **Bramley Golf Club,** Bramley, Near Guildford GU5 0AL (01483 892696; Fax: 01483 894673). *Location:* three miles south of Guildford on the Horsham road, A281. Parkland. 18 holes, 5882 yards. S.S.S. 68. Practice area, driving range. *Green Fees:* £40.00 per day; weekends with member only. *Eating facilities:* catering from 7:30am to 9pm, bar from 11am to 10pm. *Visitors:* welcome Monday to Friday. *Society Meetings:* by prior arrangement with the Club . Professional Shop: 01483 893685. General Manager/Director of Golf: Gary Peddie (01483 892696).

GUILDFORD. **Guildford Golf Club,** High Path Road, Merrow, Guildford GU1 2HL (01483 563941). Steward: (01483 5631842). *Location:* from Guildford take Epsom Road (A246) turn right at the third set of traffic lights. Downland course. 18 holes, 6090 yards. S.S.S. 70. Practice area. *Green Fees:* £40.00 per round, £50.00 per day weekdays; weekends with a member only. Subject to review. *Eating facilities:* snacks and restaurant service. *Visitors:* welcome weekdays, with member weekends. *Society Meetings:* catered for Tuesday to Friday. Professional: P. G. Hollington (01483 566765). Secretary: B.J. Green (01483 563941; Fax: 01483 453228).

GUILDFORD. **Merrist Wood Golf Club,** Holly Lane, Worplesdon, Guildford GU3 3PB (01483 238890; Fax: 01483 238896). *Location:* three miles from Guildford, off A323 to Aldershot. 18 holes, 6909 yards. S.S.S. 73. *Green Fees:* (2005) £30.00 per round midweek, £35.00 per round weekend (Subject to review). *Visitors:* welcome; after 11.30am at weekends. Please call for up to date specials. *Society Meetings:* welcome. Professional: Greg Brodie (01483 238897). Golf Manager: Ben Beagley.

GUILDFORD. **Puttenham Golf Club,** Heath Road, Puttenham, Guildford GU3 1AL (01483 810498; Fax: 01483 810988). *Location:* On B3000 between Farnham and Guildford, signposted off Hog's Back (A31). Wooded/heathland course. 18 holes, 6211 yards. S.S.S. 70. Practice ground. *Green Fees:* on application. *Eating facilities:* dining room, bar and 19th. *Visitors:* welcome weekdays only by prior arrangement. (Weekends playing with a member). *Society Meetings:* catered for Wednesdays, Thursdays and some Fridays. Secretary and Professional: Gary Simmons. e-mail: enquiries@puttenhamgolfclub.co.uk website: www.puttenhamgolfclub.co.uk

GUILDFORD. **Roker Park Golf Club,** Fairlands Farm, Aldershot Road, Guildford GU3 3PB (01483 236677 Fax: 01483 232324). *Location:* from A3 Guildford take A323 to Aldershot, course two miles on right. Flat parkland course. 9 holes, 3037 yards. S.S.S.72. *Green Fees:* information not available. *Eating facilities:* restaurant and bar. *Visitors:* welcome, pay and play course. *Society Meetings:* welcome weekdays only, reductions for parties over 12. Driving range, £2.70 for bucket of 60 balls, or £1.50 for 30 balls. Professional: Adrian Carter. Secretary: Mrs. C.A. Tegg (Tel & Fax: 01438 232324).*

GUILDFORD near. **Sutton Green Golf Club,** New Lane, Sutton Green, Near Guildford GU4 7QF (01483 766849). *Location:* midway between Guildford and Woking, just off A3. Easy walking parkland course, co-designed by Laura Davies, water features on nine holes. 18 holes, 6300 yards. S.S.S. 70. Practice ground. *Green Fees:* weekdays £50.00; weekends £60.00. *Eating facilities:* fully air conditioned bar and restaurant. *Visitors:* welcome midweek, weekends after 2pm. Golf buggies and carts available; changing room. *Society Meetings:* welcome midweek. Professional: Paul Tedder (01483 766849; Fax: 01483 750289). Secretary: John Buchanan (01483 747898; Fax: 01483 750289).
e-mail: admin@suttongreengc.co.uk
website: www.suttongreengc.co.uk

HINDHEAD. **The Hindhead Golf Club,** Churt Road, Hindhead GU26 6HX (01428 604614; Fax: 01428 608508). *Location:* one and a half miles north of Hindhead on A287 to Farnham. The course is played over heathland and wooded valleys. Open Championship regional qualifying venue. 18 holes,

White Tees 6356 yards, S.S.S. 70; Yellow Tees 6106 yards, S.S.S. 69. *Green Fees:* weekdays £50.00 per day. *Eating facilities:* restaurant, snack bar, summer bar and members' bar. *Visitors:* welcome with Handicap Certificate, weekends by appointment. *Society Meetings:* Wednesdays and Thursdays only. Professional: Ian Benson (01428 604458). Secretary: N. Hallam Jones.

KINGSTON-UPON-THAMES. **Coombe Hill Golf Club,** Golf Club Drive, off Coombe Lane West, Kingston KT2 7DF (020 8336 7600; Fax: 020 8336 7601). *Location:* from A3 take A238 to Kingston. Hilly and tree lined. 18 holes, 6293 yards. S.S.S. 71. *Green Fees:* information not available. *Eating facilities:* diningroom 8am to 3.30pm weekdays, bar (varying hours). *Visitors:* weekdays only, with a member weekends. *Society Meetings:* please contact Secretary. Director of Golf/Professional: Craig Defoy (020 8949 3713). Secretary: Mrs Christina Defoy.*

KINGSTON-UPON-THAMES. **Coombe Wood Golf Club,** George Road, Kingston Hill KT2 7NS (020-8942 0388). *Location:* from A3 take A308(east) or A238(west). Wooded course. 18 holes, 5300 yards. S.S.S. 66. *Green Fees:* weekdays £32.00 - £38.00, £25.00 after 5pm; weekends £35.00, afternoons only. *Eating facilities:* catering all week. *Visitors:* welcome; weekends afternoons only. *Society Meetings:* by arrangement Wednesday to Friday. Professional: P. Wright (020-8942 6764). Secretary: G. McKay (020-8942 0388: Fax: 020 8942 5665).
e-mail: cwoodgc@ukonline.co.uk
website: www.coombewoodgolf.com

KINGSWOOD. **Kingswood Golf and Country Club Ltd,** Sandy Lane, Kingswood, Tadworth KT20 6NE (01737 833316: Fax: 01737 833920). *Location:* five miles south of Sutton just off A217/Junction 8 M25. 18 holes, 6904 yards. S.S.S. 73. Large practice area. *Green Fees:* weekdays £40.00 per round; weekends £55.00 per round. *Eating facilities:* table d'hôte Monday to Friday (reservations only) and bar snacks. *Visitors:* welcome anytime, restricted times at weekends. Squash courts, snooker tables. *Society Meetings:* Corporate Golf Days catered for. Professional: Terry Sims (01737 832334). Administration: Lisa Andrews/ Elaine Labbett (01737 832188).

- Wooded course on private estate. • 18 holes, 5296 yards, 4842 metres. S.S.S. 66.
- Green fees – weekdays £35.00, £25.00 after 5pm; weekends £35.00 afternoons after 3pm.
- Catering all week. Visitors welcome. Society bookings by arrangement Wednesday to Friday.
- Superb greens and tees all year round.
- Professional: (020-8942 6764).
- Secretary: (020-8942 0388 • Fax: 020 8942 5665).

Coombe Wood Golf Club
George Road, Kingston Hill, Surrey KT2 7NS
020-8942 0388 • website: www.coombewoodgolf.com

LEATHERHEAD. Leatherhead Golf Club, Kingston Road, Leatherhead KT22 0EE (01372 843966; Fax: 01372 842241). *Location:* off Junction 9 of M25, onto A243 to Kingston. Parkland, many mature trees. 18 holes, 6203 yards. S.S.S. 70. Practice ground, putting green. *Green Fees:* weekdays £37.50 18 holes, £55.00 36 holes; weekends £37.50 one round afternoons only. *Eating facilities:* à la carte restaurant, cafe/ brasserie and lounge bar. *Visitors:* welcome, no visitors Saturday or Sunday mornings. *Society Meetings:* welcome, from 16 to 100 by reservation. Professional: Dean Mara (01372 843956). Director of Golf: Simon Norman (01372 843966).
e-mail: secretary@lgc-golf.co.uk
website: www.lgc-golf.co.uk

LEATHERHEAD. Pachesham Park Golf Centre, Oaklawn Road, Leatherhead KT22 0BT (01372 843453). *Location:* half a mile outside Leatherhead just off A244, quarter of a mile off Junction 9 M25. Undulating parkland course. 9 holes, 2806 yards. S.S.S. 67. 33 bay floodlit driving range, putting green, chipping area. *Green Fees:* weekdays £10.00 9 holes; weekends £12.00 9 holes. *Eating facilities:* fully licensed bar, restaurant. *Visitors:* welcome, bookings taken two days in advance. *Society Meetings:* welcome. Professional/Secretary: Phil Taylor.
e-mail: enquiries@pacheshamgolf.co.uk

LEATHERHEAD. Tyrrells Wood Golf Club Ltd, Leatherhead KT22 8QP (01372 376025). *Location:* south-east on A24 Leatherhead by-pass, half a mile left to Headley, then 200 yards right. Hillside, wooded course with glorious views. 18 holes, 6234 yards. S.S.S. 70. Small practice ground. *Green Fees:* information not available. *Eating facilities:* catering by arrangement with Manager. *Visitors:* no visitors Saturday or Sunday mornings. *Society Meetings:* catered for by arrangement with Manager. Professional: Simon Defoy (01372 375200). Secretary: C.G.R. Kydd (01372 376025).*

LINGFIELD. Lingfield Park Golf Club, Racecourse Road, Lingfield Park, Lingfield RH7 6PQ (01342 834602; Fax: 01342 836077). *Location:* A22 turn off at Blindley Heath, six miles from M25 Junction 6. Parkland/wooded course with streams. 18 holes, 6472 yards. S.S.S. 72. Driving range and practice ground. *Green Fees:* information not available. *Eating facilities:* lounge, dining room, spike bar.

Visitors: welcome midweek only by arrangement. Changing rooms. *Society Meetings:* catered for. Professional/ Secretary: C.K. Morley (01342 832659; Fax: 01342 836077). *

MILFORD. Milford Golf Club, Station Lane, Milford, Near Godalming GU8 5HS (01483 419200; Fax: 01483 419199). *Location:* five minutes from Guildford on the A3, follow signs to Milford train station, just this side of it. Parkland course which plays like a links in the wind, mixture of attractive water holes. 18 holes, 5960 yards. S.S.S. 68. Excellent practice facilities. *Green Fees:* information not available. *Eating facilities:* restaurant and pleasant bar area. *Visitors:* welcome at most times, must phone for reservations. *Society Meetings:* all welcome, packages available, please phone Sales Manager. Professional: Paul Creamer (01483 416291). Secretary: Richard Griffiths.*

MITCHAM. Mitcham Golf Club, Carshalton Road, Mitcham Junction CR4 4HN (020 8648 1508; Fax: 020 8648 4197). *Location:* Carshalton Road, aim for Mitcham Junction Station. Flat course. 18 holes, 5935 yards. S.S.S. 68. *Green Fees:* Monday to Friday £15.00, Seniors £11.00, weekends £20.00 and Bank Holidays £25.00, £12.00 Juniors only. Twilight rates available. *Eating facilities:* meals and snacks available. *Visitors:* welcome, book times via Professional. *Society Meetings:* catered for, book through Secretary. Professional: P. Burton (020 8640 4280). Secretary: W.J. Dutch (Tel & Fax: 020 8648 4197).
e-mail: mitchamgc@hotmail.com
website: www.mitchamgolfclub.co.uk

NEWDIGATE. Rusper Golf Club, Rusper Road, Newdigate RH5 5BX (Tel & Fax: 01293 871456). *Location:* Dorking-Horsham A24. Beare Green roundabout left to Newdigate, through Newdigate, right to Rusper, course on right. Parkland course with mature woodland and natural water features.18 holes, 6724 yards. S.S.S. 72. Driving range. *Green Fees:* please contact the club for details. *Eating facilities:* fresh food and daily specials available every day. Full bar. *Visitors:* welcome every day, times bookable in advance. No Handicaps required. Golf Shop (01293 871871). *Society Meetings:* welcome, groups up to 50, various packages. Professional: Janice Arnold. Secretary: Mrs Jill Thornhill.
e-mail: jill@ruspergolfclub.co.uk
website: www.ruspergolfclub.co.uk

Founded in 1903 Leatherhead Golf Club celebrated its centenary in 2003.

- **18 hole parkland course**
- **Practice ground**
- **Professional's shop**
- **Visitors welcome**

Kingston Road, Leatherhead KT22 0EE
Telephone (01372) 843966 • Fax: (01372) 842241
E-mail: secretary@lgc-golf.co.uk
Website: www.lgc-golf.co.uk

See also Colour Advertisement on page 25

THE GOLF GUIDE 2006   ENGLAND / Surrey

NEW MALDEN. **Malden Golf Club,** Traps Lane, New Malden KT3 4RS (020 8942 0654; Fax: 020 8336 2219). *Location:* half a mile from Malden Station - near A3, between Wimbledon and Kingston. Fairly flat parkland. 18 holes, 6295 yards. S.S.S. 70. *Green Fees:* information not available. *Eating facilities:* restaurant and bar. *Visitors:* welcome weekdays, restricted weekends and Bank Holidays. Advisable to telephone Professional. Buggies and trolleys for hire. *Society Meetings:* catered for Wednesday, Thursday and Friday. Professional: Robert Hunter (020 8942 6009). Secretary: Mrs Angela Besant (020 8942 0654; Fax: 020 8336 2219). *

OTTERSHAW. **Foxhills,** Stonehill Road, Ottershaw KT16 0EL (01932 872050; Fax: 01932 874762). *Location:* Exit 11 M25, follow signs to Woking, right at roundabout, left at next roundabout, left at junction into Stonehill Road. Parkland course (Bernard Hunt) 18 holes, 6734 yards, S.S.S. 72. Wooded course (Longcross) 18 holes, 6417 yards, S.S.S. 71. Par 3 course (9 holes). *Green Fees:* information not available. *Eating facilities:* clubhouse bar open from 7am till 8pm. Manor Restaurant: breakfast, lunch and dinner daily. Summerhouse - Brasserie style food available from 11am onwards. *Visitors:* welcome from 7.30am weekdays and after 12 noon at weekends. 38 rooms; tennis, squash, gym, swimming pools. *Society Meetings:* bookings for weekdays only. Head Professional: Richard Summerscales; Professionals: Bernard Hunt MBE, Scott Patience (01932 704465). Golf Manager: Roger Hyder.

OXTED. **Limpsfield Chart Golf Club,** Westerham Road, Limpsfield, Oxted RH8 0SL (01883 722106). *Location:* on A25 between Westerham and Oxted. Heathland, now well wooded plus heather, gorse. Second/eleventh is played over an old gravel pit, a carry of 140 yards. 9 holes – alternate tees for 18 holes, 5718 yards. S.S.S. 68. Small practice area, practice net, putting green. *Green Fees:* weekdays £20.00, evenings £12.00; weekends £22.00 with a member only. *Eating facilities:* snacks always available 11.30am to 8pm; breakfast, lunch, dinner by prior arrangement. *Visitors:* welcome weekdays, Thursdays after 3pm, weekends by appointment. *Society Meetings:* catered for by prior arrangement. Secretary: R. Smitherman (01883 723405).

OXTED. **Tandridge Golf Club,** Oxted RH8 9NQ (01883 712274; Fax: 01883 730537). *Location:* from M25 Junction 6 take A22 south to A25 east, two miles. Parkland with flat first nine and undulating second nine. 18 holes, 6250 yards. S.S.S. 70. *Green Fees:* £65.00 (Summer). *Eating facilities:* full catering facilities. *Visitors:* welcome Monday, Wednesday and Thursday only. *Society Meetings:* catered for Mondays, Wednesdays and Thursdays. Professional: Chris Evans (01883 713701). Secretary: Lt. Cdr. S.E. Kennard. e-mail: secretary@tandridgegolfclub.com website: www.tandridgegolfclub.com

Please mention THE GOLF GUIDE when you enquire about clubs or accommodation

PIRBRIGHT. **Goal Farm Golf Course,** Gole Road, Pirbright, Woking GU24 0PZ (01483 473183). *Location:* public course between Woking and Guildford, off A322. Challenging, picturesque course. 9 holes, 1273 yards. S.S.S. 48. Practice net, putting green, bunker. *Green Fees:* weekdays £5.50 9 holes, Juniors and Senior Citizens £4.50, weekends and Bank Holidays £6.00. *Eating facilities:* licensed bar and cafe. *Visitors:* welcome, restrictions Saturday and Thursday mornings (Club Competitions). Lessons available from Professional. Clubs available for hire. Professional: Peter Fuller. Secretary: Graham Williams (01483 473182).

PURLEY. **Purley Downs Golf Club,** 106 Purley Downs Road, South Croydon CR2 0RB (020 8657 8347). *Location:* three miles south of Croydon, one mile east of A235. Undulating downland course. 18 holes, 6308 yards. S.S.S. 70. Practice area, nets. *Green Fees:* information not available. *Eating facilities:* dining room, bar snacks, two bars. *Visitors:* welcome weekdays. *Society Meetings:* catered for all days except Tuesday mornings and Fridays. Professional: G. Wilson (020 8651 0819). Secretary/Manager: Mrs S.J. Burr (020 8657 8347; Fax: 020 8651 5044).*

REDHILL. **Redhill Golf Centre,** Canada Avenue, Redhill RH1 5BF (01737 770204). *Location:* in the grounds of East Surrey Hospital. Parkland. 9 holes, 1632 yards. S.S.S. 58 (18 holes); 29 (9 holes). 37 bay floodlit driving range. *Green Fees:* information not available. *Eating facilities:* available at Causeway Pub. Open 8am to 10pm; weekends 9pm. *Visitors:* welcome no restrictions. Sponsored by Golf Foundation to give free junior coaching. *Society Meetings:* welcome. Professional: James Edgar. Secretary: Steven Furlonger.*

REDHILL. **Redhill and Reigate Golf Club,** Clarence Lodge, Pendleton Road, Redhill RH1 6LB (01737 244626; Fax: 01737 242117). *Location:* one mile south of Reigate between A23 and A25 – Junction 8 M25. Flat well wooded parkland course. 18 holes, 5272 yards, 4978 metres. S.S.S. 68. Small practice area. *Green Fees:* weekdays £21.00, weekends £31.00. *Eating facilities:* available seven days a week. *Visitors:* welcome weekdays, Saturdays with booking 11am to 12.30pm, Sundays please telephone. *Society Meetings:* catered for by arrangement with Manager. Professional: Warren Pike (01737 244433). Secretary: Dot Simpson (01737 240777; Fax: 01737 242117). Manager: Mark Wileman.
e-mail: dot@rrgc.net
website: www.redhillandreigategolfclub.co.uk

REIGATE. **Reigate Heath Golf Club,** The Clubhouse, Reigate Heath, Reigate RH2 8QR (01737 242610). *Location:* south of A25 on western boundary of Reigate. Heathland. 9 holes, 5658 yards. S.S.S. 67. *Green Fees:* on application. *Eating facilities:* lunches and snacks available. *Visitors:* welcome weekdays, advisable to telephone before coming. *Society Meetings:* catered for on Thursdays. Secretary: R.J. Perkins (01737 226793; Fax: 01737 249226).
e-mail: reigateheath@surreygolf.co.uk
website: www.reigateheathgolfclub.co.uk

314 Surrey / ENGLAND   THE GOLF GUIDE 2006

REIGATE. **Reigate Hill Golf Club,** Gatton Bottom, Reigate RH2 0TU (01737 645577; Fax: 01737 642650). *Location*: J8, M25 (two minutes). Parkland. 18 holes, 6175 yards. S.S.S. 70. Practice range, practice bunker and putting green. *Green Fees:* information not available. *Eating facilities*: Extensive bar menu, spike bar, lounge bar. *Visitors*: Monday - Friday no restrictions, weekends and Bank Holidays after 12.00 pm. *Society Meetings*: welcome. Professional: Stephen Dundas (01737 646070). Operations Manager: John Holmes.

RICHMOND. **The Richmond Golf Club,** Sudbrook Park, Petersham, Richmond TW10 7AS (020 8940 1463; Fax: 020 8332 7914). *Location:* off A307 two miles south of Richmond, end of Sudbrook Lane. Parkland. 18 holes, 6100 yards. S.S.S. 70. Practice driving range. *Green Fees*: weekdays £45.00; weekends £50.00 after 3.30 pm. *Eating facilities*: lunches available Monday to Friday. *Visitors*: welcome weekdays without reservation. *Society Meetings*: welcome Mondays, Tuesdays, Thursdays and Friday mornings only by arrangement with General Manager. Professional: Steve Burridge (020 8940 7792; Fax: 020 8332 6694). General Manager: D. R. Cromie (020 8940 4351; Fax: 020 8332 7914).

RICHMOND. **Royal Mid-Surrey Golf Club,** Old Deer Park, Richmond TW9 2SB (020 8940 1894; Fax: 020 8939 0150). *Location:* entrance on A316, five minutes from Richmond station. Flat parkland, wooded course. Two 18 hole courses, Inner: 5544 yards, S.S.S. 67 men, 71 ladies; Outer: 6385 yards, S.S.S. 70. Practice ground, putting green, pitching green. *Green Fees:* weekdays £75.00 (£50.00 after 1pm and in winter). *Eating facilities:* bars and dining areas. *Visitors:* welcome weekdays only. *Society Meetings:* corporate and society golf days welcome. Professional: Philip Talbot (020 8940 0459; Fax: 020 8332 6066). Secretary: Marc Newey.

SUNNINGDALE. **Sunningdale Golf Club,** Ridgemount Road, Sunningdale, Ascot SL5 9RR (01344 621681; Fax: 01344 624154). *Location:* 350 yards west of station, off A30, 25 miles from London. Heathland, 36 holes, 2 courses. *Green Fees:* £145.00 Old Course, £110.00 New Course, £185.00 both courses. *Eating facilities:* Diningroom and three bars. *Visitors:* require introduction from Secretary of own club plus Handicap Certificate on weekdays. Fridays and weekends with member only. *Society Meetings:* accepted Tuesdays, Wednesdays and Thursdays only, by arrangement. Professional: Keith Maxwell (01344 620128). Secretary: Stephen Toon. Golf Operations for bookings (01344 298006).

SUTTON. **Banstead Downs Golf Club,** Burdon Lane, Belmont, Sutton SM2 7DD (020 8642 2284; Fax: 020 8642 5252). *Location:* A217 (10 minutes from Belmont Station). 18 holes, 6192 yards. S.S.S. 69. *Green Fees:* information not available. *Eating facilities:* lunches served at Club every day. *Visitors:* welcome Monday, Tuesday, Wednesday, Thursday with letter of introduction; on Friday, Saturday, Sunday with member. *Society Meetings:* catered for all day Thursdays. Professional: Ian Golding (020 8642 6884). General Manager: Mrs Karen Cote

TADWORTH. **Walton Heath Golf Club,** Deans Lane, Walton-on-the-Hill, Tadworth KT20 7TP (01737 812060). *Location:* Junction 8 M25, A217 towards London, B2032 towards Dorking, turning right hand side Deans Lane. Two 18 hole heathland courses. Old: 6836 yards, S.S.S. 73. New: 6613 yards, S.S.S. 72. Large putting green; indoor nets and small outdoor practice facilities. *Green Fees:* information not available. *Eating facilities:* restaurant and two bars. *Visitors:* welcome by previous arrangement, Handicap Certificate or letter of introduction required; limited play weekends. *Society Meetings:* catered for by arrangement. A variety of packages available for both summer and winter. Professional: Ken MacPherson (01737 812152). Secretary: Mike Bawden. *

VIRGINIA WATER. **Wentworth Club Ltd,** Wentworth Drive, Virginia Water GU25 4LS (01344 842201; Fax: 01344 842804). *Location:* 21 miles south-west of London, just off the A30 at junction with A329 to Ascot. M25 and M3 three miles. Wooded heathland. West course - 18 holes, 7047 yards, S.S.S. 74; East course - 18 holes, 6201 yards, S.S.S. 70; Edinburgh course - 18 holes, 7004 yards, S.S.S. 74; Executive course - 9 holes. Driving range. *Green Fees:* information not available. *Eating facilities:* dining room, ballroom, private rooms, bar. *Visitors:* welcome weekdays only by appointment. Handicap Certificates required: Ladies 32, Men 24. Accommodation available. *Society Meetings:* welcome by prior arrangement. Professional: David Rennie (01344 846306). Managing Director: Julian Small (01344 842201). Deputy General Manager: Stuart Christie (01344 846313).

WALTON-ON-THAMES. **Burhill Golf Club,** Burwood Road, Walton-on-Thames KT12 4BL. *Location:* M25 Junction 10, take A3 London turn off, A245 Weybridge, right into Seven Hills Road and again into Burwood Road. Two 18 hole parkland courses both differing in character, Old Course 6479 yards. S.S.S. 71, New Course 6940 yards, S.S.S. 72 - opened May 2001. Full irrigation on both courses. Practice area, driving range, putting green and short game practice area. *Green Fees:* weekdays £65.00 per round, £90.00 per day. Special rates November to March. *Eating facilities:* Orangery Restaurant, Captains Bar, Honours Bar, Iveagh Lounge, Barnes Wallis suite for private dining, and the exclusive Hospitality Suite for special occasions. *Visitors:* welcome Monday to Friday. *Society Meetings:* catered for Monday to Friday. Golf Days organised to suit your particular requirements. Professional: (01932 221729; Fax: 01932 252533). General Manager: David Cook (01932 227345; Fax: 01932 267159). Sales Manager: Sally Owen (01932 227345; Fax: 01932 267159).
e-mail: info@burhillgolf-club.co.uk

WARLINGHAM near. **Farleigh Court Golf Club,** Old Farleigh Road, Farleigh CR6 9PX (01883 627711; Fax: 01883 627722). *Location:* south of Croydon. Exciting course utilising two landscaped valleys with many natural features. 27 holes (18 holes members, 9 hole pay and play). 9155 yards, 8368 metres. Practice bunker, chipping green, putting green and 285 yard practice range. *Green Fees:* information not available.

Eating facilities: full catering facilities available (seven days). *Visitors:* welcome anytime after 10am weekdays or weekends on members course and anytime on 9 hole pay and play. *Society Meetings:* welcome anytime. Professional/Secretary: Scott Graham.*

WEST BYFLEET. **West Byfleet Golf Club,** Sheerwater Road, West Byfleet KT14 6AA (01932 343433). *Location:* Junction 10 M25 onto A245 – half a mile west of West Byfleet. Easy walking, woodland course. 18 holes, 6211 yards. S.S.S. 70. *Green Fees:* weekdays £50.00 per round, £75.00 per day. *Eating facilities:* lunches, bar snacks, teas and evening meals available. Catering: (01932 353525). Bar: (01932 345230). *Visitors:* welcome weekdays with reservation, weekends with member only. *Society Meetings:* catered for, advance bookings, minimum group size 20. Professional: David Regan (01932 346584). Secretary: D. Lee (01932 343433).

WEST CLANDON. **Clandon Regis Golf Club Ltd,** Epsom Road, West Clandon GU4 7TT (01483 224888; Fax: 01483 211781). *Location:* between Guildford and Leatherhead on A246. Parkland setting, fairly mature for new course, four areas of water. Course designed by David Williams. 18 holes, 6419 yards. S.S.S. 71/69. Indoor practice nets, full length driving area, putting green, chipping area. *Green Fees:* weekdays £30.00; weekends £40.00 (limited). *Eating facilities:* bar meals, restaurant available for booking. *Visitors:* welcome weekdays, weekends depending on club bookings. *Society Meetings:* welcome weekdays only. Professional: Steve Lloyd (01483 223922). General Manager: Mr Paul Napier.

WEYBRIDGE. **New Zealand Golf Club,** Woodham Lane, Woodham, Addlestone KT15 3QD (01932 345049). *Location:* junction Woodham Lane and Sheerwater Road on A245. Traditional club with secluded heathland course in heather and woodland setting. 18 holes, 6075 yards. S.S.S. 69. *Green Fees:* information not available. *Eating facilities:* lunch available Tuesdays to Fridays. *Visitors:* welcome by prior arrangement. *Society Meetings:* catered for Tuesday, Wednesday, Thursday, Friday. Professional: V.R. Elvidge. Secretary: R.A. Marrett Esq.*

WEYBRIDGE. **St George's Hill Golf Club,** Golf Club Road, St. George's Hill, Weybridge KT13 0NL (01932 847758; Fax: 01932 821564). *Location:* M25, Junction 10 take A3 towards London, turn off towards Byfleet (A245) then B374 Brooklands Road, entrance to St. George's Hill estate one mile on right. Hilly, Surrey heathland - well wooded with plentiful heather and rhododendron. 27 holes, 6513 yards. S.S.S. 71. *Green Fees:* weekdays £90.00 per round, £120.00 per day. Reduced rates in winter. Subject to review for 2006. No credit cards accepted. *Eating facilities:* dining room, two bars. *Visitors:* welcome Wednesdays, Thursdays. Fridays only by prior arrangement with Secretary's office. *Society Meetings:* catered for on Wednesdays, Thursdays and Fridays by prior arrangement. Professional: A.C. Rattue (01932 843523). Secretary: J. Robinson (01932 847758).

www.uk-golfguide.com

Wentworth Club, set in glorious countryside, offers one 9 and three 18-hole golf courses, Tennis and Health Club and a heated outdoor pool. Complementing its prestigious sporting reputation with comfortable and friendly ambience, the Club is charmingly informal. **Wentworth**

Wentworth Club, Wentworth Drive, Virginia Water, Surrey GU25 4LS
Tel: 01344 842201 • www.wentworthclub.com
See also Colour Advertisement on page 26

Runnymede
★★★★ hotel&spa
Windsor Road, Egham, Surrey TW20 0AG
Tel: 01784 436171 • Fax: 01784 436340

A privately owned 4★ hotel set on the banks of the River Thames, 5 miles from Royal Windsor and minutes from Wentworth Club, the M25 and Heathrow. The hotel features 180 bedrooms, two riverside restaurants and an extensive health and fitness spa including: indoor pool, gym, tennis courts, saunas, steam room and a deluxe day package suite.

Call reservations on 01784 220980 to make a booking.

www.runnymedehotel.com • info@runnymedehotel.com

See also Colour Advertisement on page 25

WOKING. **Chobham Golf Club,** Chobham Road, Knaphill, Woking GU21 2TZ (01276 855584; Fax: 01276 855663). *Location:* on A3046 one mile outside Chobham village, ten minutes from M3 Junction 3. Wooded parkland course. 18 holes, 5959 yards, S.S.S. 69. Practice area, putting green. *Green Fees:* information not available. *Eating facilities:* bar snacks and restaurant. *Visitors:* welcome, with prior agreement with General Manager. *Society Meetings:* welcome. Professional: Tim Coombes (01276 855748). e-mail: info@chobhamgolfclub.co.uk
website: www.chobhamgolfclub.co.uk

WOKING. **Hoebridge Golf Centre,** Old Woking Road, Old Woking GU22 8JH (01483 722611; Fax: 01483 740369). *Location*: Undulating parkland on well-draining sand, well established wooded location. Three courses: Hoebridge Course - 18 holes, Back Tees 6536 yards, Par 72, Yellow Tees 6178 yards, Par 71, Ladies 5842 yards, Par 73; Maybury Course – 18 holes, 2230 yards, Par 54; Shey Copse – 9 holes, 2294 yards, Par 33. 36 bay covered, floodlit driving range. *Green Fees:* Hoebridge: weekdays £20.00, weekends £26.00. Maybury: weekdays £8.50, weekends £10.00. Shey Copse: weekdays £10.50, weekends £11.50. *Eating facilities*: full catering and bar facilities open all day. *Visitors:* welcome. Pay-and-Play facility. Clubs for hire. *Society Meetings*: welcome weekdays by prior arrangement, various packages available. Professional: Craig Butfoy. Men's Secretary: Mike Waite. Ladies' Secretary: Elaine Watts. Centre Manager: Mike O'Connell. website: www.hoebridge.co.uk

WOKING. **Traditions Golf Course 1999,** Pyrford Road, Pyrford, Woking GU22 8UE (01932 350355; Fax: 01932 350234). *Location:* into West Byfleet and turn at traffic lights into Pyrford Road. Peter Alliss design with tree-lined holes, lakes and many streams. 18 holes. Par 71. *Green Fees:* information not available. *Eating facilities:* from 7am to 10pm (to 6pm in winter). Professional: Adam Whatford.*

WOKING. **West Hill Golf Club,** Bagshot Road, Brookwood GU24 0BH (01483 472110). *Location:* M3, Junction 3, A322 entrance adjacent railway bridge Brookwood. Heathland, wooded course. Golf World "Top 100 courses in UK" listed. 18 holes, 6368 yards. S.S.S. 70. Practice range and net. *Green Fees:* information not available. *Eating facilities:* bar snacks available, meals including dinner by prior arrangement. *Visitors:* members' guests only at weekends. Buggies, caddies by arrangement. *Society Meetings:* catered for by arrangement through the Secretary. Professional: J.C. Clements (01483 473172). Secretary: I.M. McColl (01483 474365; Fax: 01483 474252).*
e-mail: secretary@westhill-golfclub.co.uk
website: www.westhill-golfclub.co.uk

WOKING. **Windlemere Golf Club,** Windlesham Road, West End, Near Woking GU24 9QL (01276 858721). *Location:* off A322. Well designed parkland course. 9 holes, 2673 yards. S.S.S. 33. Floodlit 12-bay driving range. *Green Fees:* weekdays £11.00, Seniors £9.00; weekends £12.50, Seniors £10.50. *Eating facilities:* bar with light menu, normal clubhouse facilities. *Visitors:* always welcome, may book up to one week in advance. Snooker, pool facilities. *Society Meetings:* welcome to book. Professional: Dave Thomas. Secretary: M. Walsh (01276 858727).

WOKING. **Woking Golf Club,** Pond Road, Hook Heath, Woking GU22 0JZ (01483 760053; Fax: 01483 772441). *Location:* via Hollybank Road and Golf Club Road or Hook Heath Road and Pond Road. Traditional heathland course. 18 holes, 6340 yards. S.S.S. 70. Practice ground. *Green Fees:* information not available. *Eating facilities:* lunches and snacks available. *Visitors:* welcome but only by prior arrangement, Handicap Certificate required. *Society Meetings:* welcome by prior arrangement. Professional: C.I. Bianco (01483 769582). Secretary: G.T. Ritchie.

WOKING. **Worplesdon Golf Club,** Heath House Road, Woking. *Location:* off A322, six miles from Guildford and six miles from Junction 3 (M3). Wooded heathland course. 18 holes, 6431 yards. S.S.S. 71. *Green Fees:* £60.00 per round, £80.00 per day. *Eating facilities:* lunches served at club. *Visitors:* weekdays only. *Society meetings:* by arrangement. Professional: Jim Christine (01483 473287) Secretary: J.T. Christine (01483 472277; Fax: 01483 473303).

WOKING near. **Pyrford Golf Club 1993,** Warren Lane, Pyrford, Near Woking, GU22 8XR (01483 723555; Fax: 01483 729777). *Location:* A3 - Ripley turn off, turn next to Mitsubishi garage, continue for approximately two miles, on the right Warren Lane. Inland water links, 23 acres of water. 18 holes, 6230 yards. Par 72. Practice range, putting green. *Green Fees:* information not available. *Eating facilities:* bar snack menu available all day. *Visitors:* welcome anytime Monday to Friday and after 12 noon at weekends, tee times MUST be booked. *Society Meetings:* welcome weekdays only. Professional: Darren Brewer (01483 751070). Secretary: Ian Bartlett.*
e-mail: pyrford@americangolf.uk.com

WOLDINGHAM. **North Downs Golf Club,** Northdown Road, Woldingham, Caterham CR3 7AA (01883 652057). *Location:* Eastbourne Road roundabout at Caterham. Two miles Woldingham road. 18 holes, 5857 yards, S.S.S. 68. *Green Fees:* £30.00 per round, £40.00 per day. *Eating facilities:* full restaurant facilities. *Visitors:* welcome with Handicap Certificate Monday to Friday (Thursdays after 12 noon only). *Society Meetings:* catered for. Professional: M. Homewood (01883 653004). Secretary/Manager: D. Sinden (01883 652057).

YATELEY. **Blackwater Valley Golf Course,** Chandlers Lane, Yateley GU46 7SZ (01252 874725). *Location:* Junction 4 of M3. Into Yateley to White Lion pub roundabout, into Vicarage Road, then Vicarage Lane. Parkland course with lakes and mature trees. 9 holes. Par 34. Driving range. *Green Fees:* information not available. *Eating facilities:* From 11am to 10pm (to 8pm during winter). Professional: James Rodger.*

THE APPEARANCE OF AN ASTERISK (*) AT THE END OF A CLUB OR COURSE ENTRY INDICATES THAT UP-TO-DATE INFORMATION HAS NOT BEEN SUPPLIED

East Sussex

BATTLE. **Battle Golf Club,** Netherfield Hill, Battle TN33 0LH (Tel & Fax: 01424 775677). *Location:* A2100, just 1½ miles outside historic town of Battle. Parkland, woodland course. Panoramic views, gently undulating. 9 holes, 18 tees, 5941 yards. S.S.S 68. Practice ground. *Green Fees:* weekdays 9 holes £13.00, 18 holes £20.00; weekends 9 holes £15.00, 18 holes £22.00. Senior Citizens and Juniors welcome, special rates. *Eating facilities:* large bars, 3-course meals and bar snacks available. *Visitors:* welcome daily from 7am. Strict dress code. B&B available locally. Special rates for weekly/weekend stays with golf, for more information phone or view website. Tuition available for individuals and groups. *Society Meetings*: welcome, special rates, please telephone for details. PGA Professional: Alan Tyson (01424 777497). Club Secretary: (01424 775677). website: www.battlegolfclub.com

BEXHILL-ON-SEA. **Cooden Beach Golf Club,** Cooden Sea Road, Bexhill-on-Sea TN39 4TR (Tel & Fax: 01424 842040). *Location:* A259 Eastbourne to Hastings road, follow `Cooden Beach' sign at Little Common roundabout (one mile). Seaside course, slightly undulating. 18 holes, 6500 yards. S.S.S. 72. Practice facilities. *Green Fees:* weekdays £35.00; weekends and Bank Holidays £40.00. *Eating facilities:* catering and bar every day. *Visitors:* welcome, preferably by prior arrangement. Buggies for hire. *Society Meetings:* prior booking necessary. Professional: Jeffrey Sim (01424 843938; Fax: 01424 842040). Secretary: Keith Wiley (Tel & Fax: 01424 842040). Caterers: Steve Ede (01424 843936). e-mail: enquiries@coodenbeachgc.com
website: www.coodenbeachgc.com

BEXHILL-ON-SEA. **Highwoods Golf Club,** Ellerslie Lane, Bexhill-on-Sea TN39 4LJ (01424 212625). *Location:* off A259 north west of town. Parkland, wooded course. 18 holes, 6218 yards. S.S.S. 70. *Green Fees:* £32.00 all day, £20.00 with member. *Eating facilities:* snacks, lunches and teas always available. *Visitors:* welcome Monday to Saturday. Sunday mornings with member only. *Society Meetings:* welcome Thursdays by arrangement. Professional: M. Andrews (01424 212770). Secretary: Lawrence Dennis-Smither (01424 212625; Fax: 01424 216866).

BRIGHTON. **Brighton and Hove Golf Club,** Devil's Dyke Road, Brighton BN1 8YJ (01273 507861). *Location:* A27 Brighton bypass exit for Devil's Dyke, club 1½ miles north of A27. Downland course with sea views. 9 holes, 5704 yards. S.S.S. 68. Practice area. *Green Fees:* (18 holes) weekdays £24.00; weekends and Bank Holidays £30.00. *Eating facilities:* bar and restaurant daily, limited on Mondays. *Visitors:* welcome, phone call advisable Wednesday after 12 noon, Friday after 11am, Saturday and Sunday after 12 noon. *Society Meetings:* catered for; up to 30, eating 60. Director of Golf: Phil Bonsall (01273 556482). Shop (01273 556686).

BRIGHTON. **The Dyke Golf Club,** Devil's Dyke, Devil's Dyke Road, Brighton BN1 8YJ (01273 857296; Fax: 01273 857078). *Location:* A23 onto A27 (New Brighton By-pass) heading west to Worthing, turn off for Devil's Dyke and follow signs for same. Brighton's premier downland course. 18 holes, 6627 yards. S.S.S. 72. Practice fairway and putting green. *Green Fees:* weekdays £28.00 per round, £38.00 per day; weekends £35.00 per round. Twilight round £15.00 weekdays, £25.00 weekends. *Eating facilities:* full restaurant and bar available. *Visitors:* welcome with reservation, not before 12 noon Sundays. *Society Meetings:* catered for by appointment, £53.00 for full day inclusive of snack lunch and evening meal. Professional: Richard Arnold (01273 857260; Fax: 01273 857564). Secretary: (01273 857296; Fax: 01273 857078).
e-mail: dykegolfclub@btconnect.com

BRIGHTON. **East Brighton Golf Club,** Roedean Road, Brighton BN2 5RA (01273 604838). *Location:* one and a half miles east of Palace Pier, just off A259, behind the Marina. Undulating downland course offering superb views over the Channel. 18 holes, 6346 yards. S.S.S. 71 (white tees.) Putting green. *Green Fees:* information not available. *Eating facilities:* restaurant, diningroom, bars. *Visitors:* welcome from 9am weekdays, after 11am weekends and Bank Holidays. Handicap Certificate required. Buggy hire available. *Society Meetings:* welcome, full days golf and catering from £40.00 per person. Manager of Golf Operations: Mark Stuart-William (01273 603989). Office Manager: Max Page (01273 604838; Fax: 01273 680277).

BRIGHTON. **Hollingbury Park Golf Club,** Ditchling Road, Brighton BN1 7HS (01273 552010). *Location:* between A23 and A27. 18 holes, 6482 yards. S.S.S. 71. *Green Fees:* weekdays £15.00 per round, £22.00 per day; weekends £20.00 per round. *Visitors:* welcome. All bookings through Professional. *Society Meetings:* catered for weekdays only. Professional: Graeme Crompton (01273 500086). Secretary: (Tel & Fax: 01273 552010).

BRIGHTON. **Pyecombe Golf Club,** Clayton Hill, Pyecombe, Brighton BN45 7FF (01273 845372; Fax: 01273 843338). *Location:* four miles north of Brighton on A273 Burgess Hill Road. Downland with magnificent views. 18 holes, 6278 yards, 5790 metres. S.S.S. 70. Two practice areas. *Green Fees:* information not available. *Eating facilities:* catering/bars from 11am daily. *Visitors:* welcome, after 9.15am weekdays (11am on Tuesdays). *Society Meetings:* welcome Mondays, Wednesdays and Thursdays by prior arrangement. Professional: C. White (01273 845398; Fax: 01273 843338). Secretary: I. Bradbery (01273 845372; Fax: 01273 843338).*

East Sussex / ENGLAND   THE GOLF GUIDE 2006

BRIGHTON. **Waterhall Golf Club,** Saddlescombe Road, Brighton BN1 8YN (01273 508658). *Location:* off A27 Brighton bypass, take Devil's Dyke turn off, course on the right. Downland course. 18 holes, 5773 yards, 5328 metres. S.S.S. 68. Practice area. *Green Fees:* information not available. *Visitors:* welcome except weekends. *Society Meetings:* catered for except weekends or Bank Holidays by prior arrangement with Secretary. Professional: Graeme Crompton (01273 555529). Secretary: L.B. Allen.

CROWBOROUGH. **Crowborough Beacon Golf Club,** Beacon Road, Crowborough (01892 661511). *Location:* nine miles south of Tunbridge Wells on the A26. Heathland, superb views to the sea and South Downs (on clear days). 18 holes, 6273 yards. S.S.S. 70. *Green Fees:* £50.00 per round, £60.00 per day weekdays. *Eating facilities:* restaurant available. *Visitors:* welcome weekdays, Handicap Certificate or letter of introduction essential. Please contact either the Professional or Secretary. *Society Meetings:* bookings welcome through the Secretary's office. Professional: D.C Newnham (01892 653877). Secretary: Mrs V. Harwood (01892 661511). e-mail: secretary@cbgc.co.uk

DITCHLING. **Mid-Sussex Golf Club,** Spatham Lane, Ditchling BN6 8XJ (01273 846567; Fax: 01273 847815). *Location:* five minutes from A23, one mile east of Ditchling. Mature parkland course with superbly contoured greens and strategic bunkers. 18 holes, 6431 yards. S.S.S. 71. Practice ground, driving range and short game areas. *Green Fees:* weekdays £28.00; weekends £30.00. Twilight rates available. *Eating facilities:* full bar/restaurant facilities. *Visitors:* welcome weekdays, weekends restricted. Buggies available. *Society Meetings:* welcome weekdays only. Professional: Neil Plimmer. General Manager: Andy McNiven.

EASTBOURNE. **Eastbourne Downs Golf Club,** East Dean Road, Eastbourne BN20 8ES (01323 720827; Fax: 01323 412506). *Location*: half a mile west of Eastbourne on A259. Downland course with spectacular views to the South Downs and over the sea. 18 holes, 6601 yards. S.S.S. 72. Practice area. *Green Fees*: information not available. *Eating facilities*: two bars; restaurant open seven days a week 7.30am to 8.30pm. *Visitors:* welcome unrestricted after 9am weekdays and 11.15am weekends. Trolleys for hire. *Society Meetings*: welcome – full day with coffee, lunch and four-course dinner. Professional: Terry Marshall (01323 732264). Secretary: Tony Reeves (01323 720827; Fax: 01323 412506).*

EASTBOURNE. **Eastbourne Golfing Park,** Lottbridge Drove, Eastbourne BN23 6QJ (Tel & Fax: 01323 520400). *Location:* end of A22; half a mile south of Hampden Park and one mile north of the sea. Pleasant easy walk, a fairly short flat course but with water on seven of the nine holes it tests the accuracy of any golfer. 9 holes, 5046 yards. S.S.S. 66. 21-bay floodlit driving range. *Green Fees:* 9 holes £9.00, Senior Citizens and Juniors £8.00, 18 holes £15.00, Senior Citizens and Juniors £12.00. Weekends 9 holes £10.00, 18 holes £16.00. All day golf £18.00, Senior Citizens and Juniors £15.00, after 6pm £8.00 unlimited golf. *Eating facilities:* full bar and restaurant open to all. *Visitors:* welcome at all times. Equipment hire available. *Society Meetings:* all welcome, please ring to book. Professionals: Barrie Finch, Paul Kent and Ian Pearson. Secretary: Dawn Dunkley (Tel & Fax: 01323 520400).

EASTBOURNE. **Royal Eastbourne Golf Club,** Paradise Drive, Eastbourne BN20 8BP (01323 744045). *Location:* one mile from town centre via Meads Road and Compton Place Road. Undulating downland and parkland. Devonshire course:18 holes, 6077 yards. S.S.S. 69. Hartington course: 9 holes, 2147 yards. S.S.S. 61. *Green Fees:* information not available. *Eating facilities:* full catering. *Visitors:* welcome. Handicap Certificate required Long Course only. Cottage accommodation for four people. *Society Meetings:* catered for. Professional: Alan Harrison (Tel & Fax: 01323 736986). Secretary: (01323 744045).

For full details of clubs and courses, plus convenient accommodation
www.uk-golfguide.com

CROWBOROUGH BEACON
GOLF CLUB

This well established 18 hole heathland course, founded in 1895, stands some 800 feet above sea level and with views on clear days of the Downs, Eastbourne and the sea, it must have arguably one of the finest panoramas in Sussex. Pine and fir trees are scattered around the course and there is plenty of heather and gorse. This course will test your accuracy rather than length off the tee!

Crowborough Beacon Golf Club, Beacon Road, Crowborough, East Sussex TN6 1UJ
Tel: 01892 661511   Fax: 01892 667339
e-mail: secretary@cbgc.co.uk
www.crowboroughbeacongolfclub.co.uk

See also Colour Advertisement on page 26

ENGLAND / East Sussex

EASTBOURNE. Willingdon Golf Club, Southdown Road, Willingdon, Eastbourne BN20 9AA (01323 410983). *Location:* north of Eastbourne, one mile from station, just off A22 at traffic lights (signposted). Downland course of particular beauty. 18 holes, 6113 yards, 5589 metres. S.S.S. 69. Practice ground and nets. *Green Fees:* weekdays £20.00 per round winter, £25.00 per round summer. *Eating facilities:* diningroom, lounge and casual bar. *Visitors:* welcome weekdays with Handicap after 9am. Buggies and trolleys available. *Society Meetings:* welcome, book well in advance. Professional: Troy Moore (01323 410984; Fax: 01323 411510). Secretary: Mrs Jacqueline Packham (01323 410981; Fax: 01323 411510).

EAST GRINSTEAD. Sweetwoods Park Golf Club, Cowden, Edenbridge TN8 7JN (01342 850729; Fax: 01342 850866). *Location:* directly off the A264 at Holtye, 5 miles east of East Grinstead. Wooded, parkland course with many water features. 18 holes, 5285-6610 yards, S.S.S. 69-72, Par 72. Practice ground, driving range and carts provided. *Green Fees:* information not available. *Visitors:* welcome anytime, no restrictions, can book up to 7 days in advance. Chalet accommodation available from September 2005. *Society Meetings:* welcome Monday to Friday and Saturday pm. Professional: Paul Lyons (01342 850729). Secretary: Daniel Howe (01342 850942).
website: www.sweetwoodspark.com

FOREST ROW. Royal Ashdown Forest Golf Club (Old Course) Chapel Lane, Forest Row, Near East Grinstead RH18 5LR (01342 822018; Fax: 01342 825211). *Location:* three miles south of East Grinstead to Forest Row. Take B2110 to Tunbridge Wells in the middle of village (left at second mini-roundabout) then take fourth turning on right into Chapel Lane, turn sharp left at top of Chapel Lane then bear right through golf course to Clubhouse. Undulating heathland. 18 holes, 6477 yards. S.S.S. 71. Selected to host regional qualifier for 2004 & 2005 Open Championship. *Green Fees:* weekdays £50.00 per round, £70.00 per day; weekends £70.00 per round. *Eating facilities:* lunch and tea, bar snacks. *Visitors:* welcome by prior arrangement. *Society Meetings:* welcome on Wednesday, Thursday and Friday; prior reservation essential. Steward: (01342 823014). Professional: M. Landsborough (01342 822247) Secretary: D. Neave (01342 822018; Fax: 01342 825211).
e-mail: ashdownoffice@btopenworld.com
website: www.royalashdown.co.uk

FOREST ROW. Royal Ashdown Forest Golf Club (West Course) Chapel Lane, Forest Row, Near East Grinstead RH18 5LR (01342 824866; Fax: 01342 825211). *Location:* four miles south of East Grinstead to Forest Row. Take B2110 to Tunbridge Wells in the middle of village (left at second mini-roundabout) then take fourth turning on right into Chapel Lane, turn sharp left at top of Chapel Lane then bear right through golf course to Clubhouse. 5606 yards, S.S.S. 67, a shorter, but not easier, version of the Old Course with, according to the late Henry Longhurst, "one of the finest par fours in the South of England" as its closing hole. *Green Fees:* weekdays £25.00 per round, £35.00 per day; weekends £29.00 per round, £41.00 per day. *Eating facilities:* Full dining facilities and bar snacks available all day. *Visitors and Societies:* welcome by prior arrangement. Professional: M. Landsborough (01342 822247).

HAILSHAM near. Wellshurst Golf and Country Club, North Street, Hellingly, Near Hailsham BN27 4EE (01435 813636; Fax: 01435 812444). *Location:* two miles from the A22 roundabout at Hailsham on the A267. Parkland course. 18 holes, 5771 yards, S.S.S. 68. 16 bay driving range with two bunker bays. *Green Fees:* 18 holes weekdays £18.00, weekends £22.00. *Eating facilities:* bar and restaurant open 7 days a week. *Visitors:* no restrictions, pay as you play course; advisable to book at weekends. Leisure club, conference/wedding suite. *Society Meetings:* all welcome at any time, good rates. Professional: Mark Jarvis (01435 813456). Secretary: M. Adams.

HASTINGS. TEN 66 Golf Club Ltd, Beauport Park, Battle Road, St. Leonards-on-Sea TN37 7RP (01424 854245; Clubhouse functions 01424 851165). *Location:* A2100 between Hastings and Battle, in the heart of 1066 Country in an Area of Outstanding Natural Beauty. Scenic, tree-lined undulating parkland course said to be among the best in Southern England and a very good test for all handicaps. 18 holes, 6180 yards. S.S.S. 70, 9 hole par 3 short course, 14 bay driving range. *Green Fees:* information not available. *Eating facilities:* clubhouse; hotel, restaurant and bar. *Visitors:* unrestricted. Professional coaching; indoor teaching facilities; Golf Educational Packages. Riding Stables and other activities available at adjacent Beauport Park Country House. *Society Meetings:* welcome; special rates available on request for societies/Corporate Days and for group or family membership. Managing Director: Deborah Mahon.*
e-mail: info@ten66golfclub.com
website: www.ten66golfclub.com

Beauport Park Hotel
01424 851222

This fine three-star country house hotel, standing in 33 acres of its own grounds, offers old-fashioned personal service from resident directors, Kenneth Melsom and Stephen Bayes. All bedrooms are very well equipped, and all are en suite. The hotel has a heated indoor & outdoor pool, gym, sauna & steamroom, tennis courts, croquet, a putting green, French boules, outdoor chess and country walks, while squash, golf, riding can all be enjoyed nearby. Country House Bargain Breaks available all year. Open all year.

Battle Road, Hastings TN38 8EA   AA ETC ★★★

THE APPEARANCE OF AN ASTERISK (*) AT THE END OF A CLUB OR COURSE ENTRY INDICATES THAT UP-TO-DATE INFORMATION HAS NOT BEEN SUPPLIED

HEATHFIELD. **Horam Park Golf Course,** Chiddingly Road, Horam, near Heathfield TN21 0JJ (01435 813477, Fax: 01435 813677). *Location*: 13 miles north of Eastbourne, seven miles east of Uckfield. Follow signs to Heathfield and turn right onto the Eastbourne Road A267, go through Horam village, club on right hand side. A delightful parkland course with wooded areas and several lakes and ponds. 9 holes (18 tees), 6128 yards, S.S.S. 69. Floodlit driving range, Par 3 5 hole course, large putting green. *Green Fees*: information not available. *Eating facilities*: restaurant and bar facilities open seven days a week, also spike bar. *Visitors*: all facilities at Horam Park are open to the general public with no restrictions, everybody welcome. Golf tuition available from PGA Pros seven days a week. *Society Meetings*: welcome seven days a week. Professional: Giles Velvick (01435 813477). Secretary: Angie Briggs.*

HOVE. **West Hove Golf Club Ltd,** Church Farm, Hangleton, Hove BN3 8AN (01273 419738; Fax: 01273 439988). *Location:* A27 adjacent to Brighton bypass, take Hangleton Interchange exit. Downland course overlooking the sea. 18 holes, 6216 yards. S.S.S. 70. Practice range, driving range, putting green. *Green Fees:* weekdays £25.00; weekends £30.00. *Eating facilities:* bar and catering all day. *Visitors:* welcome. Phone Professional for tee times. *Society Meetings:* welcome, phone for prices. Professional: D. Cook (01273 413494). Secretary: Megan Bibby (01273 419738; Fax: 01273 439988). e-mail: info@westhovegolf.co.uk
website: www.westhovegolfclub.info

LEWES. **Lewes Golf Club,** Chapel Hill, Lewes BN7 2BB (01273 473245). *Location:* east of town centre from A27 and A26. Downland course with spectacular views of Sussex countryside. 18 holes, 6220 yards. S.S.S. 70. Practice ground, practice putting green. *Green Fees:* £30.00 per round, £42.00 per day weekdays; £30.00 weekends. *Eating facilities:* hot and cold food available from 10am seven days a week, bar open from 11am. *Visitors:* welcome, no green fees after 2pm Tuesdays (Summer months) or before 2pm (11am Winter) at weekends. *Society Meetings:* welcome, special rates available. Professional: Paul Dobson (01273 483823). Secretary: Joan Raffety (Tel & Fax: 01273 483474).

NEWHAVEN. **Peacehaven Golf Club,** The Clubhouse, Brighton Road, Newhaven BN9 9UH (01273 514049). *Location:* one mile from Newhaven on the right hand side of A259 towards Brighton. Downland course, short but challenging. 9 holes, 5488 yards. S.S.S. 66. *Green Fees:* weekdays £16.00 18 holes, £10.00 9 holes; weekends £22.00 18 holes, £14.00 9 holes. *Eating facilities:* snacks, meals, full bar. *Visitors:* welcome but not before 11am weekends. *Society Meetings:* welcome except weekends, from £22.00 including lunch. Professional: Alan Tyson (01273 512602). Manager: Dawn Corke (01273 512571).

ROTHERFIELD. **Dewlands Manor Golf Course,** Dewlands Manor, Rotherfield TN6 3JN (01892 852266; Fax: 01892 853015). *Location:* three quarters of a mile south of village of Rotherfield, just off B2101. Challenging undulating course on second highest point of Sussex. Very high quality greens with fine bents and fescue. No mats or temporary greens used. 9 holes, 3186 yards (18 - 6372 yards). Par 72. Practice hole. *Green Fees:* information not available. *Eating facilities:* bar lunches/snacks on request. *Visitors:* welcome at all times by telephone booking. Tee times set at 15 minute intervals (optional). Handicap not required. Dress and etiquette a prerequisite. Indoor teaching with computer analysis. Buggies, trolleys for hire. *Society Meetings:* welcome. Professional: Nick Godin. Course Director: Trevor Robins (01892 852266).

RYE. **Rye Golf Club,** Camber, Rye TN31 7QS (01797 225241/225460). *Location:* A259 from Rye, take Camber road to coast. Seaside links. Old Course: 18 holes, 6308 yards. S.S.S. 71. Jubilee Course: 9 holes, 6118 yards. S.S.S. 71. *Green Fees:* information not available. *Eating facilities:* lunch and tea only. Bars. *Visitors:* welcome, only on introduction by a member. Dormy house accommodation available – contact I. Rayson (01797 227882). *Society Meetings:* very limited. Professional: Michael Lee (01797 225218). Secretary: J.A.L. Smith (01797 225241; Fax: 01797 225460).

www.uk-golfguide.com

Behind the Georgian facade of the White Hart lies an historic Tudor building which has been substantially extended to create a lively county town hotel.

◆ *53 bedrooms, all en suite with colour TV, telephone, tea-making. Some rooms have views of the Downs; some with disabled access.*

◆ *Wide range of meals and snacks available daily - à la carte, carvery, bar meals, light snacks, teas and coffees.*

◆ *Leisure Centre and Health Spa with heated indoor pool, fully equipped gym, sauna, aerobics studio, beauty clinic etc.*

**White Hart Hotel, High Street, Lewes BN7 1XE • Tel: 01273 476694
Fax: 01273 476695 • info@whitehartlewes.co.uk • www.whitehartlewes.co.uk**

See also Colour Advertisement on page 26

SEAFORD. **Seaford Golf Club,** East Blatchington, Seaford BN25 2JD (01323 892442; Fax: 01323 894113). *Location:* turn inland at War Memorial in Seaford, follow the road for one and a quarter miles. Downland course with magnificent views over Seaford Head and The Channel. 18 holes, 6233 yards, 5700 metres. S.S.S. 70. Practice ground. *Green Fees:* information not available. *Eating facilities:* bar and dining room open all day. Dormy House, 10 twin bedded rooms with en suite facilities. *Visitors:* welcome weekdays other than Tuesdays. Telephone first. *Society Meetings:* catered for Wednesdays and Thursdays. Professional: David Mills (01323 894160). Secretary: Philip Court (01323 892442; Fax: 01323 894113).
website: www.seafordgolfclub.co.uk

SEAFORD. **Seaford Head Golf Club,** Southdown Road, Seaford BN25 4HR (01323 894843). *Location:* midway between Eastbourne and Brighton on A259, signposted on entering Seaford. Downland course along cliff edge with view of "Seven Sisters". 18 holes, 5848 yards. S.S.S. 68. *Green Fees:* information not available. *Eating facilities:* bar snacks and catering for Society Meetings. *Visitors:* welcome. *Society Meetings:* welcome, bookings with Professional. Professional: F. Morley (01323 890139). Secretary: J. Wass (01323 894843).

SEDLESCOMBE. **Sedlescombe Golf Club,** Kent Street, Near Battle, TN33 0SD (01424 871700). Home of The James Andrews School of Golf. *Location:* 1066 Country, five miles north of Hastings on the A21, three miles from Battle. Gently undulating parkland course, 18 holes, 6269 yards. S.S.S. 70. 24 bay floodlit driving range, four practice putting greens, academy hole and bunkers. Residential golf school with 2,3 and 5 day intensive courses for all ages and abilities. Five PGA Professionals. Facilities include indoor video and computer analysis centre, on-site hotel, golf shop and tennis courts. *Green Fees:* information not available. *Eating facilities:* bar and restaurant open seven days. *Visitors:* Course open to public. *Society Meetings:* welcome. Head Professional: James Andrews (01424 871700). Club Secretary (01424 871700). Golf School (01424 871717). *
website: www.golfschool.co.uk

UCKFIELD. **East Sussex National Golf Club,** Little Horsted, Uckfield TN22 5ES (01825 880088; Fax: 01825 880066). *Location:* off the A22 Eastbourne road following the Uckfield by-pass, 30 minutes from Gatwick. American style, wooded, bent grasses. Two Championship courses; 1: 18 holes, 6760 yards. S.S.S. 72; 2: 18 holes, 6638 yards. S.S.S. 72. 3 hole teaching academy, driving range. *Green Fees:* information not available. *Eating facilities:* full restaurant facilities. *Visitors:* welcome anytime. Luxury country house hotel accommodation at Horsted Place situated on the West Course. To complement the complex, a new hotel development is scheduled for completion in spring 2006. The development will provide a 104 bedroom, 4 star hotel together with a state of the art health suite. General Manager: Derek Howe, M.Inst.GCM.
e-mail: golf@eastsussexnational.co.uk
website: www.eastsussexnational.co.uk

UCKFIELD. **Piltdown Golf Club,** Piltdown, Uckfield TN22 3XB (01825 722033; Fax: 01825 724192). *Location:* one mile west of Maresfield off A272, signposted. Undulating gorse and heather. 18 holes, 6076 yards. S.S.S. 69. Practice ground, putting green. *Green Fees:* £32.00 per round, £42.00 per day. Reductions after 1.30pm and 4pm. County cards £25.00 per round. *Eating facilities:* bar, full catering – please telephone to book. *Visitors:* welcome but must bring Handicap Certificate or letter of introduction from own club Secretary. Some time restrictions. No visitors before 9.15am. Jacket and tie obligatory in lounge and diningroom. Smart dress on course. *Society Meetings:* catered for by prior arrangement. Professional: Jason Partridge (01825 722389). Hon. Secretary: P.A. de Pinna (01825 722033).
e-mail: piltdowngolf@lineone.net
website: www.piltdowngolfclub.com

WADHURST. **Dale Hill Golf Club,** Ticehurst, Wadhurst TN5 7DQ (01580 201090 Fax: 01580 201249). *Location:* on B2087, one mile off A21 to west of Flimwell, 50 miles south of London, 16 miles north of Hastings. Open front nine and wooded back nine. 18 holes, 5856 yards. S.S.S. 68. Ian Woosnam Course (buggy only), 18 holes, 6512 yards. S.S.S. 72. Designed by Ian Woosnam to championship standards. Practice area and green, driving range. *Green Fees:* midweek £25.00 18 holes, £40.00 per day; weekends £35.00 18 holes. Twilight round mid-week £15.00, weekends £20.00. Ian Woosnam Course £55.00 weekdays; £65.00 weekends. Twilight round Monday to Fridays £27.50, weekends £32.50. *Eating facilities:* bar and brasserie. *Visitors:* welcome after 7.30am. 35 room luxury hotel, gym and swimming pool. Conference facilities. Buggies, trolleys. *Society Meetings:* catered for by prior arrangement. Secretary: (01580 201800).
e-mail: info@dalehill.co.uk
website: www.dalehill.co.uk

For full details of clubs and courses, plus convenient accommodation

www.uk-golfguide.com

West Sussex

ALBOURNE. **Singing Hills Golf Course Ltd,** Albourne BN6 9EB (01273 835353; Fax: 01273 835444). *Location:* on the B2117 just off the A23. Gently undulating parkland course with spectacular views of the South Downs. 3 x 9 hole courses. S.S.S. 70. 15 bay driving range, putting green. *Green Fees:* information not available. *Eating facilities:* Pavilion Restaurant, large bar. *Visitors:* welcome, no restrictions. *Society Meetings:* welcome, variety of golf and food packages for minimum 12 players. Professional: Wallace Street. Secretary: Donald Weston.*

ANGMERING. **Ham Manor Golf Club Ltd,** Angmering BN16 4JE (01903 775653). *Location:* on A259 between Worthing and Littlehampton. Flat parkland course. 18 holes, 6216 yards. S.S.S. 70. *Green Fees:* information not available. *Eating facilities:* lunches served at club except on Mondays. *Visitors:* welcome with reservation. Handicap Certificate required. *Society Meetings:* catered for thursdays only. Professional: Simon Buckley (01903 783732). Secretary: Roy Brown (01903 783288).

BILLINGSHURST. **Foxbridge Golf Club,** Foxbridge Lane, Plaistow Road, Kirdford, Billingshurst RH14 0LB (Tel & Fax: 01403 753303). *Location:* B2133, A281 Guildford to Horsham Road. Parkland course with eight lakes. 9 holes, 6236 yards. S.S.S. 70. Practice ground. *Green Fees:* weekdays 9 holes £12.00 and 18 holes £20.00; weekends 9 holes £14.00 and 18 holes £25.00. *Eating facilities:* restaurant and bar. *Visitors:* welcome, must pre-book tee times at least one day in advance. Strict dress code. Buggies and carts available. *Society Meetings:* welcome Mondays, Tuesdays and Wednesdays only. Professional: S. Hall. Secretary: Paul Clark (Tel & Fax: 01403 753303).

BOGNOR REGIS. **Bognor Regis Golf Club,** Downview Road, Felpham, Bognor Regis PO22 8JD (01243 865867; Fax: 01243 860719). *Location:* turn north at traffic lights on A259 at Felpham village. Flat parkland, many dogleg holes and water hazards. 18 holes, 6238 yards. S.S.S. 70. Practice area. *Green Fees:* information not available. *Eating facilities:* bar open every day; hot and cold snacks available weekdays, light snacks available weekends. *Visitors:* welcome weekdays (Ladies' Day Tuesday), weekends only with a member. Handicap Certificate required. *Society Meetings:* welcome by arrangement (minimum 16). Professional: Stephen Bassil (01243 865209). Secretary: (01243 821929; Fax: 01243 860719).*
website: www.bognorgolfclub.co.uk

BURGESS HILL. **The Burgess Hill Golf Academy,** Cuckfield Road, Burgess Hill RH15 8RE (01444 258585; Fax: 01444 247318). *Location:* on the B2036 north of Burgess Hill, on the Burgess Hill to Cuckfield road. An excellent short course in undulating wooded, parkland setting. 9 holes, 1250 yards. Par 3. 28 bay floodlit driving range, practice area, PGA teaching academy, Pro shop. *Green Fees*: information not available. *Eating facilities:* bar and restaurant. *Visitors*: welcome, open from 8am to 9pm. Professional/Secretary: Mark Collins (01444 258585; Fax: 01444 247318).*

CHICHESTER. **Chichester Golf Club,** Hunston Village, Chichester PO20 1AX (01243 533833). *Location:* take B2145 south of Chichester, on left hand side after Hunston Village. 45 hole golf complex. Cathedral Course 18 holes, 6442 yards, Par 72; Tower Course 18 holes, 6109 yards, Par 69. Separate family golf centre: Par 3, 829 yards short course, mini golf, Golf Academy with video analysis and 27-bay floodlit driving range including new automated power tee system. *Green Fees:* weekdays Tower £16.50, Cathedral £22.00; weekends Tower £19.50, Cathedral £30.00. *Eating facilities:* fully licensed clubhouse, bar and farmhouse cooking. *Visitors:* welcome anytime. *Society Meetings:* welcome, catered for by prior arrangement. Well stocked golf shops. Head Professional: Richard Kirby (01243 528999). Proprietor: Richard Haygarth (01243 536666; Fax: 01243 539922).
e-mail: enquiries@chichestergolf.com
website: www.chichestergolf.com

CHICHESTER. **The Goodwood Club,** Kennel Hill, Goodwood, Chichester PO18 0PN. *Location:* one mile north of Chichester at east end of Chichester Bypass (A27). Undulating downland. 18 holes, 6897 yards. S.S.S. 72. Practice ground, nets, putting greens. *Green Fees:* information not available. *Eating facilities:* full catering and bar. *Visitors:* welcome, must show Handicap Certificate. *Society Meetings:* all welcome on Wednesdays and Thursdays only. Professional: Damon Allard (01243 755135). Secretary: (01243 755130; Fax: 01243 755135).*
e-mail: golf@goodwood.co.uk

CHICHESTER. **Marriott Goodwood Park Hotel & Country Club,** Goodwood, Chichester PO18 0QB (01243 520117; Fax: 0870 400 7325). *Location:* set amidst the 12,000 acre Goodwood Estate, ancestral home of the Dukes of Richmond, yet only three miles from Chichester. Parkland championship course designed by Donald Steel and built in 1988. 6650-yards, Par 72. Tuition programmes available; fourteen bay golf range (eight covered); short game practice area; putting green; pro shop; trolleys, buggies and clubs for hire. *Green Fees:* from £12.00 per round, 7 days. *Eating facilities:* full facilities available. *Visitors:* welcome, no restrictions. *Society Meetings:* welcome. Professional: Christian Fogden.

Please mention
THE GOLF GUIDE
when you enquire about clubs or accommodation

CHICHESTER. **Selsey Golf Club,** Golf Links Lane, Selsey, Chichester PO20 9DR (01243 602203). *Location:* B2145, seven miles south of Chichester. Flat course. 9 holes playing 18, 5532 yards. S.S.S. 68. *Green Fees:* information not available. *Eating facilities:* lunches and snacks served in club. *Visitors:* welcome with bona fide Handicap Certificate or playing with a member. *Society Meetings:* small societies catered for weekdays only. Professional: P. Grindley (01243 608936). Secretary: P. Carter (01243 608935; Fax: 01243 607101).
e-mail: secretary@selseygolfclub.com
website: www.selseygolfclub.co.uk

COWDRAY PARK **Cowdray Park Golf Club,** Midhurst GU29 0BB (01730 813599; Fax: 01730 815900). *Location:* one mile east of Midhurst on A272 between Midhurst and Petworth. A testing parkland course with scenic views of the Downs and polo fields and Cowdray ruins. 18 holes, 6265 yards. S.S.S. 70. Driving range and Par 3 Academy. *Green Fees:* from £40.00 weekdays and weekends. *Eating facilities:* restaurant and bar snacks. *Visitors:* welcome. Dormy house. *Society Meetings:* catered for. Professional: Richard J. Gough. Secretary: Paul Fairminer.
e-mail: cowdray-golf@lineone.net
website: www.cowdraygolf.co.uk

CRAWLEY. **Copthorne Golf Club,** Borers Arms Road, Copthorne, Crawley RH10 3LL (01342 712033). *Location:* off Exit 10 M23, one mile on A264 towards East Grinstead. Flat wooded course. 18 holes, 6505 yards. S.S.S. 71. Practice area. *Green Fees:* weekdays £36.00 per round, £44.00 per day; weekends £38.00 after 1pm. Half fees if playing with member. *Eating facilities:* catering all day, bar. *Visitors:* welcome weekdays without reservation, after 1pm weekends. *Society Meetings:* welcome with advance bookings. Professional: Joe Burrell (01342 712405). Secretary: J. Pyne (01342 712508; Fax: 01342 717682).

CRAWLEY. **Cottesmore Golf and Country Club,** Buchan Hill, Pease Pottage, Crawley RH11 9AT (01293 528256; Fax: 01293 522819). *Location:* one mile west of Junction 11 off M23 on road through Pease Pottage. Two mature golf courses set in 247 acres of rolling Sussex countryside. The fairways are lined with rhododendrons, silver birch, oak and chestnut trees. Four holes over lakes. Griffin Course 18 holes, 6248 yards. S.S.S. 70, par 71. Phoenix Course 18 holes, 5514 yards. S.S.S. 66, par 69. Practice ground, putting greens. *Green Fees:* information not available. *Eating facilities:* restaurant, coffee shop, two bars. *Visitors:* welcome. Health Club including indoor heated pool, tennis courts and gymnasium; en suite accommodation (21 rooms) also available. Trolleys and buggies available. *Society Meetings:* welcome, advance bookings required. Professional: Calum Callan (01293 861777; Fax: 01293 522819). General Manager: (01293 528256).

CRAWLEY. **Ifield Golf and Country Club,** Rusper Road, Ifield, Crawley RH11 0LN (01293 520222). *Location:* outskirts of Crawley near A23 to Gossops Green. Undulating parkland. 18 holes, 6314 yards. S.S.S. 70. Practice ground. *Green Fees:* £32.00 per round, £45.00 per day weekdays; weekends with a member only. *Eating facilities:* fully licensed bar, à la carte restaurant. *Visitors:* welcome, please telephone. Trolley and Buggies for hire. *Society Meetings:* welcome. Professional/Golf Manager: Jon Earl (01293 523088/01293 520222; Fax: 01293 612973).

CRAWLEY. **Pease Pottage Golf Centre,** Horsham Road, Pease Pottage, Crawley (01293 521706; Fax: 01293 521706). *Location:* M23 Junction 11, Pease Pottage, James King Pub. Wooded areas surrounding golf course. 9 holes, 1864 yards. S.S.S. 60, Par 4/3. *Green Fees:* weekdays £8.50; weekends £11.00 for 18 holes. Senior Citizens £5.00. *Eating facilities:* restaurant, coffee shop. *Visitors:* welcome, no restrictions. Two PGA Professionals available for tuition. New Golf Superstore. Full on site repair service. *Society Meetings:* welcome. Professional: David Blair (01293 521706). Secretary: Natalie Leszczar.

CRAWLEY. **Tilgate Forest Golf Centre,** Titmus Drive, Tilgate, Crawley RH10 5EU (01293 530103). *Location:* Crawley, five minutes from Junction 11 M23. Wooded parkland. 18 holes, 6167 yards, 5643 metres. Par 72. 35 bay floodlit driving range. Par 3 course. *Green Fees:* weekdays £16.00, weekends £22.00. *Eating facilities:* restaurant and bar. *Visitors:* welcome at all times but there is a booking system in operation. *Society Meetings:* welcome, phone for details. Professional: Sean Trussell (01293 530103; Fax: 01293 523478).

CUCKFIELD. **Cuckfield Golf Centre,** Staplefield Road, Cuckfield RH17 5HY (01444 459999). *Location:* one mile north west of Cuckfield village. Undulating open parkland course with outstanding views in an Area of Outstanding Natural Beauty. 9 holes, 2700 yards. Par 37. Putting green. *Green Fees:* weekdays £8.00; weekends £9.00; £1.00 discount Juniors and Senior Citizens. *Eating facilities:* snacks and licensed bar available. *Visitors:* always welcome. Pay and play - no Handicap Certificate required. Hire clubs and trolleys, 6 golf carts £10.00 9 holes, £18.00 18 holes, please phone for availability. New teaching academy and practice facilities available. *Society Meetings*: always welcome. Professional: Robert Dickman. Secretary: Mrs L. Dickman.
e-mail: lucy@cuckfieldgolf.co.uk
website: www.cuckfieldgolf.co.uk

EAST GRINSTEAD. **Chartham Park,** Felcourt Road, Felcourt, East Grinstead RH19 2JT (01342 870340; Fax: 01342 870719). *Location:* Felcourt Road off A22 on north side of East Grinstead. Parkland. 18 holes, 6680 yards. S.S.S. 72. Driving range, putting green. *Green Fees:* information not available. *Eating facilities:* restaurant, light snacks and bar all day. *Visitors:* pre-booking required. Golf carts and trolleys can be hired. *Society Meetings:* by prior arrangement. Professional: David Hobbs. General Manager: David Reeves.

www.uk-golfguide.com

West Sussex / ENGLAND

EAST GRINSTEAD. **Holtye Golf Club,** Holtye Common, Cowden, Near Edenbridge TN8 7ED (01342 850635). *Location:* four miles east of East Grinstead on A264, seven miles west of Tunbridge Wells. Undulating forest course; alternate tees. 9 holes, 5325 yards. S.S.S. 66. Large practice ground. *Green Fees:* weekdays £16.00; weekends £20.00. *Eating facilities:* available every lunchtime, some evenings in summer season. *Visitors:* welcome, restrictions Wednesday, Thursday and weekend mornings. *Society Meetings:* catered for. Professional: Kevin Hinton (01342 850635). Secretary: Mrs D. M. Botham (01342 850576).

EFFINGHAM. **Effingham Park Golf Club,** West Park Road, Copthorne RH10 8AL (01342 716528). *Location:* Junction 10 M23, two miles east on A264. Parkland (wooded), large lake in play over four holes. 9 holes, 1815 yards. S.S.S. 57 (18 holes). *Green Fees:* 9 holes £10.00, 18 holes £15.00. *Eating facilities:* club bar and restaurant. *Visitors:* welcome, restricted Tuesday evenings, Wednesday and Thursday mornings. Five star Hotel on site and leisure club. *Society Meetings:* catered for anytime weekdays, weekends after 12 noon. Club Professional: Mark Root. Secretary: Ian McRobbie.

HASSOCKS. **Hassocks Golf Club,** London Road, Hassocks BN6 9NA . *Location:* on the A273 between Burgess Hill and Hassocks. Gently undulating pay and play course. 18 holes, 5703 yards, 5215 metres. S.S.S. 67. Driving range, irons only. *Green Fees:* weekdays £17.00; weekends £23.00, early morning/twilight rates available on application. *Eating facilities:* restaurant, bar, stud bar. *Visitors:* welcome anytime. Buggy for hire, £20.00. *Society Meetings:* welcome. Professional: Charles Ledger (01273 846990). Manager: Jaki Brown (01273 846630; Fax: 01273 846070).
e-mail: hgc@hassocksgolfclub.co.uk
website: www.hassocksgolfclub.co.uk

HAYWARDS HEATH. **Haywards Heath Golf Club,** High Beech Lane, Haywards Heath RH16 1SL (01444 414457). *Location:* two miles north of Haywards Heath. Parkland. 18 holes, 6216 yards. S.S.S. 70. Practice areas. *Green Fees:* weekdays £27.00 per round, £38.00 for 36 holes; weekends and Bank Holidays £37.00 for 18 holes, £42.00 for over 18 holes. Packages for societies. *Eating facilities:* bar and catering both provided. *Visitors:* welcome, by arrangement, phone Professional; Handicap Certificate required. *Society Meetings:* catered for Wednesdays and Thursdays by arrangement with the Secretary. Professional: M.P. Henning (01444 414866). Secretary: G.K. Honeysett.

HORSHAM. **Horsham Golf and Fitness,** Worthing Road, Horsham RH13 0AX (01403 271525; Fax: 01403 274528). *Location:* A24 Horsham bypass (southwest roundabout), 200 yards towards Horsham. Parkland with several water features. 9 holes, 4122 yards. S.S.S. 60. Driving range. *Green Fees:* information not available. *Eating facilities:* restaurant/bar open all day. *Visitors:* welcome at all times. Large well stocked shop, fitness suite on site. *Society Meetings:* welcome with booking. Professional: Alex Paterson. Secretary: Elaine Purton.*

HORSHAM. **Mannings Heath Golf Club,** "Fullers", Hammerpond Road, Mannings Heath, Near Horsham RH13 6PG (01403 210228; Fax: 01403 270974). *Location:* off J11 M23, three miles south of Horsham off A281. Undulating wooded course with featured streams. Waterfall: 18 holes, 6378 yards (White tees). S.S.S. 70; Kingfisher Course: 18 holes, 6217 yards. S.S.S. 70. Driving range, two practice putting greens, chipping green. *Green Fees:* information not available. *Eating facilities:* luxurious clubhouse "Fullers", full bar, restaurant and spike bar facilities. *Visitors:* welcome, may book 14 days in advance (by phone). Conference/meeting facilities. *Society Meetings:* welcome at all times, full/half day. Professional: Clive Tucker. Operations Manager: Jon Pleydell.
e-mail: enquiries@manningsheath.com
website: www.manningsheath.com

HORSHAM near. **Slinfold Park Golf and Country Club,** Stane Street (A29), Slinfold, Near Horsham RG13 7RE (01403 791154; Fax: 01403 791465). *Location:* situated on the A29, four miles west of Horsham with good road links to the M23 and East/West on the A272. A gently undulating parkland course with many interesting water features and mature trees. 18 Hole Championship Course, 6418 yards. 9 Hole course. S.S.S. 71. 19 bay floodlit driving range. *Green Fees:* information not available. *Eating facilities:* purpose built clubhouse with restaurant and bar. *Visitors:* welcome subject to tee time availability. Reservations can be made up to seven days in advance. No handicap required. *Society Meetings:* welcome weekdays, minimum group size 10; call for society pack. Professional: Alistair Cardwell (01403 791555). Secretary: Stewart Judd (01403 791154).

LINDFIELD. **Paxhill Park,** East Mascalls Lane, Lindfield RH16 2QN (01444 484467; Fax: 01444 482709). *Location:* take Lewes Road out of Lindfield village one mile then left. Parkland with water and River Ouse. 18 holes, 6200 yards. S.S.S. 70. Practice ground, putting green. *Green Fees:* weekdays £17.00; weekends £22.00. *Eating facilities:* restaurant and bar. *Visitors:* welcome daily. Trolleys. *Society Meetings:* welcome every day. Professional: (01444 484000). Secretary: J.D. Bowen.

LITTLEHAMPTON. **Littlehampton Golf Club,** 170 Rope Walk, Riverside West, Littlehampton BN17 5DL (01903 717170; Fax: 01903 726629). *Location:* leave A259 one mile west of Littlehampton at sign. Seaside links. 18 holes, 6244 yards. S.S.S. 70. *Green Fees:* information not available. *Eating facilities:* restaurant and two bars. *Visitors:* welcome weekdays, weekends after 1.00pm, but phone prior to arrival. *Society Meetings:* societies only, minimum number 12. Professional: Stuart Fallow (01903 717170 ext 225). Secretary: Steven Graham.
e-mail: lgc@talk21.com
website: www.littlehamptongolf.co.uk

FHG Guides

ENGLAND / West Sussex

PETWORTH. **Petworth Golf Course,** "Osiers Farm", London Road, Petworth GU28 9LX (Tel & Fax: 01798 344097; mobile: 07932 163941). Open all year round. *Location*: 2 miles north of Petworth on A283, heading northbound towards Guildford. Undulating natural farmland course, plenty of hedges and ditches. 18 holes, 6191 yards, S.S.S. 71. Nets and course practice holes. *Green Fees*: £13.00 weekdays and weekends, £20 per day. *Eating Facilities*: clubhouse catering for up to 80 people. *Visitors*: welcome anytime, B&B on site. Tuition available. *Society Meetings*: welcome, rates from £14.00 to £40.00. Professional: Steve Hall (01798 873487). Manager: Andy Long (01798 344097). Secretary: Paul Shaw (01730 826640).

PULBOROUGH. **West Sussex Golf Club,** Golf Club Lane, Wiggonholt, Pulborough RH20 2EN (01798 872563). *Location*: between Storrington and Pulborough on the A283. Heathland. 18 holes, 6264 yards. S.S.S. 70. *Green Fees*: £65.00 for 18 holes, £80.00 for 36 holes. Subject to review. Driving range. *Eating facilities*: lunch and tea daily, bars. *Visitors*: welcome by prior arrangement (not Fridays and weekends). No three or four balls. *Society Meetings*: catered for Wednesdays and Thursdays. Professional: T. Packham (01798 872426). Secretary: C.P. Simpson (01798 872563; Fax: 01798 872033). e-mail: secretary@westsussexgolf.co.uk
website: www.westsussexgolf.co.uk

RUSTINGTON. **Rustington Golf Centre,** Golfers Lane, Angmering BN16 4NB (01903 850790; Fax: 01903 850982). *Location:* on A259 at Rustington, near Littlehampton. 18 holes, 5735 yards, S.S.S. 70. 9 hole Par 3 course, three hole academy course, putting green, 30 bay floodlit driving range (11 automated). *Green Fees:* information not available. *Eating facilities:* coffee shop and licensed bar. *Visitors:* welcome at all times. Scott Cranfield Golf Academy available for tuition of all standards. *Society Meetings:* societies and corporate days welcome by appointment. Centre Manager/ Secretary: Gary Salt (01903 850790; Fax: 01903 850982).

WEST CHILTINGTON. **West Chiltington Golf Club,** Broadford Bridge Road, West Chiltington RH20 2YA (01798 813574; Fax: 01798 812631). *Location:* A29 Bognor from London Road, left at Adversane village B2132 then signposted. Gently undulating parkland with spectacular views of South Downs. 18 holes, 6389 yards. S.S.S. 69. 9 holes, 1360 yard short course ideal for beginners. 13 bay driving range. *Green Fees:* information not available. *Eating facilities:* bar and restaurant open all day every day. *Visitors:* always welcome, smart dress. Tee times may be booked through Pro Shop (01798 812115). *Society Meetings:* welcome, apply to Secretary. Secretary: Debbie Haines. General Manager: Geoffrey Cotton. *
website: www.westchiltgolf.co.uk

WORTHING. **Hill Barn Golf Club,** Hill Barn Lane, Worthing BN14 9QF (01903 237301). *Location:* signposted on the roundabout at the top of Broadwater, Worthing on the A27. Downland course with a few trees but generally fairly open. 18 holes, 6229 yards. S.S.S. 70. Small practice area (balls not provided) and putting green. *Green Fees:* weekdays £16.50. weekends £19.50; twilight rates: weekdays £11.00. weekends £14.00. *Eating facilities:* clubhouse and bar. *Visitors:* welcome, no restrictions or Handicap required. *Society Meetings:* welcome. Manager: Larry Chambers (01903 237301).
e-mail: info@hillbarngolf.com

WORTHING. **Worthing Golf Club,** Links Road, Worthing BN14 9QZ (01903 260801; Fax: 01903 694664). *Location:* on A27 250 yards east of junction with A24 (Offington Roundabout). Two downland courses. Lower course: 18 holes, 6530 yards. S.S.S. 71. Upper course: 5243 yards. S.S.S. 65. *Green Fees:* weekdays £40.00 per day; weekends and Bank Holidays £50.00 per day & £40.00 per round. *Eating facilities:* dining room, lounge and bar. *Visitors:* welcome, check in advance with Secretary. No visitors at weekends (for golf) during G.M.T. *Society Meetings:* catered for by arrangement. Professional: Stephen Rolley (01903 260718; Fax: 01903 694613). Secretary: Ian Evans (01903 260801; Fax: 01903 694664).

Centrally located betwen Horsham and Worthing, with stunning views of the South Downs, West Chiltington has so much more to offer than the average golf club.
• 27 holes, large putting green, covered driving range. • Green fees weekdays £19, weekends £23.50. • Modern, attractive clubhouse; bar and restaurant. •
Friendly and co-operative staff • Society packages available

West Chiltington Golf Club *We shall be delighted to tailor a day for you. Ring for more details or visit our website.*
Broadford Bridge Road, West Chiltington, West Sussex RH20 2YA • Tel: 01798 813574 • Fax: 01798 812631 • www.westchiltgolf.co.uk

---

PLEASE NOTE

All the information regarding Golf Clubs in this guide is given in good faith in the belief that it is correct. However, the publishers cannot guarantee the facts given in these pages, neither are they responsible for changes in ownership or facilities, such as green fees, that may take place after the date of going to press. Readers should always satisfy themselves that the facilities they require are available and that the terms, if quoted, still apply.

Tyne & Wear

BIRTLEY. **Birtley Golf Club,** Birtley Lane, Birtley DH3 2LR(0191-410-2207). *Location:* just off old Durham road and main A1. Parkland. 9 holes, 5660 yards. S.S.S. 67. *Green Fees:* information not available. *Eating facilities:* bar open only after 7.30pm, snacks available. *Visitors:* welcome weekdays; weekends and Bank Holidays with a member only. *Society Meetings:* welcome, must be pre-booked. Secretary: G. Barras (0191 410 2207). e-mail: secbirtleygc@aol.com

CHOPWELL. **Garesfield Golf Club,** Chopwell NE17 7AP (Tel & Fax: 01207 561309; Bar/Catering 01207 561278). *Location:* leave A694 at Rowlands Gill, follow signposts for Chopwell, approximately three miles. Turn left at Bute Arms; golf course is one mile up road on left. Undulating wooded parkland 18 holes, 6403 yards. par 72. Practice ground, nets and putting green. *Green Fees:* weekdays £28.00 per day, £22.00 per round; weekends: details on request. *Eating facilities:* full catering except Mondays. *Visitors:* welcome weekdays; weekends and Bank Holidays after 4.30pm. Buggies available £16.00 per round. *Society Meetings:* welcome. Group rates (min. 12, max. 24 on Sundays at 10.30am): £30.00 per round. Professional: D. Race (01207 563082). Secretary: Mrs J. Barclay. (Tel & Fax: 01207 561309).

EAST BOLDON. **Boldon Golf Club Ltd,** Dipe Lane, East Boldon NE36 0PQ (0191-536 4182). *Location:* near Sunderland, approximately one mile from roundabout at junction of A19 and A184 highways. Fairly flat parkland. 18 holes, 6348 yards. S.S.S. 70. *Green Fees:* weekdays £20.00, with a member £14.00; weekends £24.00, with a member £16.00. *Eating facilities:* bar snacks and restaurant. *Visitors:* welcome, not between 9am and 10am, 12.30pm and 1.30pm or 4.30pm and 6pm. Not before 3.30pm at weekends. *Society Meetings:* catered for. Professional: Phipps Golf (0191-536 5835; Fax: 0191-537 2270). Secretary: R.W. Benton (0191-536 5360; Fax: 0191-537 2270). e-mail: info@boldongolfclub.co.uk

GATESHEAD. **Heworth Golf Club,** Gingling Gate, Heworth, Gateshead. *Location:* A1 (M) south east boundary of Gateshead. Flat wooded course. 18 holes, 6422 yards. S.S.S. 71. Practice area. *Green Fees:* £20.00 per day. *Eating facilities:* diningroom, two bars. *Visitors:* weekdays up to 4pm, no visitors Saturdays; but after 10am on Sundays. *Society Meetings:* welcome mid-week only up to 4pm. Professional: A. Marshall (0191-438 4223). Secretary: G. Holbrow (0191-469 9832).

THE APPEARANCE OF AN ASTERISK (*) AT THE END OF A CLUB OR COURSE ENTRY INDICATES THAT UP-TO-DATE INFORMATION HAS NOT BEEN SUPPLIED

GATESHEAD. **Ravensworth Golf Club Ltd,** 'Angel View', Longbank, Gateshead NE9 7NE (0191-487 6014). *Location:* two miles south of Gateshead town centre, near A1 (Angel of the North). Parkland course. 18 holes, 5825 yards. S.S.S. 69. *Green Fees:* 1st April to 30th September: Monday to Friday £23.00 (£16.00 with a member), weekends and Bank Holidays £30.00 (£23.00 with a member). 1st October to 31st March: Monday to Friday £18.00 (£13.00 with a member), weekends and Bank Holidays £23.00 (£18.00 with a member). Subject to review. *Eating facilities:* meals served with reasonable notice (not Mondays). *Visitors:* welcome, weekends very restricted. *Society Meetings:* catered for. Secretary: John Jackson (0191-416 9454).

HEDDON ON THE WALL. **Close House Country Club,** Heddon on the Wall, Newcastle upon Tyne NE15 0HT (01661 852255). *Location:* 10 miles west of Newcastle off A69 to Wylam. A picturesque parkland/part wooded course set in the Tyne Valley. 18 holes, 5380 yards. S.S.S. 68. Golf packages available for visiting parties. *Green Fees:* available on request. *Eating facilities:* catering facilities available for visiting parties and also casual visitors.. *Visitors:* Visiting parties and casual visitors welcome with restricted times on weekends, preliminary phone calls advisable. Golf Operations Manager: John Glendinning (01661 852953; Fax: 01661 853322). e-mail: john.glendinning@closehouse.co.uk website: www.closehouse.co.uk

HETTON-LE-HOLE. **Elemore Golf Course,** Elemore Lane, Hetton-Le-Hole (0191-517 3057; Fax: 0191 517 3054). *Location:* follow signs to Easington Lane, located off A1068, following signs to Elemore/Pittington. Flat meadowland Public Pay & Play golf course. 18 holes, 5947 yards. S.S.S. 69. Practice area. *Green Fees:* information not available. *Eating facilities:* clubhouse with bar/lounge serving snacks and meals. *Visitors:* welcome, no restrictions. Buggy Hire £12.00 per round. *Society Meetings:* welcome throughout the year. Contact Course Manager for advance bookings (14 days' notice required). Professional: To be arranged. Course Manager: Barbara Blenkinsop. *

HOUGHTON-LE-SPRING. **Houghton-le-Spring Golf Club,** Copt Hill, Houghton-le-Spring DH5 8LU (0191 5841198). *Location:* off A690 Durham Road, take Houghton to Seaham road, course is situated at the top of Copt Hill bank. Testing hillside course. 18 holes, 6416 yards, 5867 metres. S.S.S. 71. *Green Fees:* information not available. *Eating facilities:* available most days, bar open every day. *Visitors:* welcome most days but not on competition days (Sundays). *Society Meetings:* catered for by arrangement. Professional: K. Gow (0191 5847421). Secretary: N. Wales (0191 5841198).

THE GOLF GUIDE 2006　　　ENGLAND / Tyne & Wear 327

NEWCASTLE UPON TYNE. **City of Newcastle Golf Club,** Three Mile Bridge, Gosforth, Newcastle upon Tyne NE3 2DR (0191-285 1775; Fax: 0191-284 0700). *Location:* B1318 three miles north of city. Flat parkland. 18 holes, 6528 yards. S.S.S. 71. *Green Fees:* weekdays £28.00, £34.00 per day; weekends and Bank Holidays £35.00. Discount for parties over 12. *Eating facilities:* bar, meals. *Visitors:* welcome without reservation, restricted times Fridays. *Society Meetings:* very welcome. Professional: S. McKenna (0191-285 5481; Fax: 0191-284 0700). Club Manager: A.J. Matthew (0191-285 1775; Fax: 0191-284 0700). e-mail: info@cityofnewcastlegolfclub.com website: www.cityofnewcastlegolfclub.com

NEWCASTLE UPON TYNE. **Gosforth Golf Club,** Broadway East, Gosforth, Newcastle upon Tyne NE3 5ER (0191-285 6710). *Location:* three miles north of Newcastle near Great North Road, B1318. Parkland with stream. 18 holes, 6024 yards. S.S.S. 69. *Green Fees:* information not available. *Visitors:* welcome weekdays and weekends. *Society Meetings:* catered for by arrangement with the Secretary, including some weekends and Bank Holidays. Professional: G. Garland (0191-285 0553). Secretary: Brian Pluse (0191-285 3495; Fax: 0191-284 6274).*
e-mail: gosforth.golf@virgin.net
website: www.gosforthgolfclub.co.uk

NEWCASTLE UPON TYNE. **Hobson Golf Club,** Hobson, Burnopfield, Newcastle upon Tyne NE16 6BZ (01207 271605). *Location:* on Newcastle to Consett road. Fairly flat, well designed course. 18 holes, 6403 yards, 5854 metres. S.S.S. 71. Practice area. *Green Fees:* information not available. *Eating facilities:* bar, lounge and restaurant. *Visitors:* no restrictions; booking system at weekends. Strict dress code in operation. *Society Meetings:* by prior arrangement with Professional (all bookings). Professional: J.W. Ord (01207 271605). Secretary: P. Taylor.

NEWCASTLE UPON TYNE. **Newcastle United Golf Club,** 60 Ponteland Road, Cowgate, Newcastle upon Tyne NE3 3JW (0191-286 9998). *Location:* two miles west of city centre in direction of airport. Moorland. 18 holes, 6617 yards, 6048 metres. S.S.S. 72. Practice area. *Green Fees:* information not available. *Eating facilities:* bar meals available. *Visitors:* no restrictions midweek, welcome weekends if no competitions. Book through the golf shop or see our website. *Society Meetings:* welcome, book through Secretary. Golf Shop: (0191-286 9998). Secretary: S. Darbyshire.*.
website: www.nugc.co.uk

NEWCASTLE UPON TYNE. **The Northumberland Golf Club Ltd,** High Gosforth Park, Newcastle upon Tyne NE3 5HT (0191-236 2498). *Location:* off A1. 18 holes, 6680 yards. S.S.S. 72. *Green Fees:* £40.00 per round weekdays, £50.00 weekends. *Visitors:* club members are most welcome but should contact Secretary to avoid disappointment. *Society Meetings:* small groups can now be catered for on Mondays and at weekends. Secretary: Jamie Forteath (0191-236 2498; Fax: 0191-236 2036).
website: www.thenorthumberlandgolfclubltd.co.uk

NEWCASTLE UPON TYNE. **Parklands Golf Club,** High Gosforth Park, Newcastle upon Tyne NE3 5HQ (0191-236 4867). *Location:* three miles north of centre of Newcastle, off the A1 follow signs for Gosforth Park. Parkland. 18 holes, 6013 yards, 5742 metres. S.S.S. 69. 9 holes pitch and putt, 45 bay floodlit driving range. *Green Fees:* weekdays £17.00; weekends £20.00. *Eating facilities:* restaurant and bar. *Visitors:* welcome, no restrictions. *Society Meetings:* catered for. General Manager: D. King (0191-236 4480). Secretary: Brian Woof (0191-236 4480).

NEWCASTLE UPON TYNE. **Tyneside Golf Club Ltd,** Westfield Lane, Ryton NE40 3QE (0191-413 2742; Fax: 0191-413 0199). *Location:* seven miles west of Newcastle upon Tyne, off B6317 in Ryton Village. Parkland, hilly with water hazards. Large practice area. 18 holes, 6009 yards, 5477 metres. S.S.S. 69. Practice field. *Green Fees:* weekdays £30.00; weekends negotiable. *Eating facilities:* full catering. *Visitors:* bona fide golfers welcome by arrangement with the Secretary. *Society Meetings:* weekdays by arrangement with Secretary; possibly Sunday afternoons. Professional: Geoff Dixon (0191-413 1600). Secretary: Ed Stephenson (0191-413 2742).

NEWCASTLE UPON TYNE. **Westerhope Golf Club,** Whorlton Grange, Westerhope, Newcastle-upon-Tyne NE5 1PP (0191-286 9125). *Location:* Stamfordham Road, Westerhope, near Jingling Gate Public House. Parkland/wooded. 18 holes, 6444 yards. S.S.S. 71. Two practice areas. *Green Fees:* £22.00 per round. *Eating facilities:* lunches and high teas. *Visitors:* welcome weekdays, weekends and Bank Holidays with a member only. *Society Meetings:* welcome weekdays. Professional: N. Brown (0191-286 0594). Secretary: B. Bell (0191-286 7636).

NEWCASTLE UPON TYNE. **Whickham Golf Club Ltd,** Hollinside Park, Fellside Road, Whickham, Newcastle upon Tyne NE16 5BA (0191-488 7309). *Location:* five miles south-west of Newcastle upon Tyne, turn off A1 at sign for Whickham. In Whickham take road signposted to Burnopfield (ie Fellside Road) and proceed to golf club. Parkland course - undulating with attractive panoramic views. 18 holes, 6500 yards. Par 71. Practice grounds and putting green. *Green Fees:* information not available. *Eating facilities:* lunches, teas, evening meals available by prior order, bar snacks all day. *Visitors:* welcome except Saturdays and Sundays without reservation. Smart casual wear on course and in clubhouse. *Society Meetings:* welcome by arrangement. Professional: Andrew Hall (0191-488 8591). Hon. Secretary: Mrs J. Miller (0191-488 1576; Fax: 0191-488 1577).

THE APPEARANCE OF AN ASTERISK (*) AT THE END OF A CLUB OR COURSE ENTRY INDICATES THAT UP-TO-DATE INFORMATION HAS NOT BEEN SUPPLIED

RYTON. **Ryton Golf Club,** Dr. Stanners, Clara Vale, Ryton NE40 3TD (0191-413 3737). *Location:* off A695 eight miles west of Newcastle at Crawcrook to Clara Vale. Flat parkland, wooded, running alongside River Tyne. 18 holes, 6042 yards, 5499 metres. S.S.S. 69. Practice area. *Green Fees:* weekdays £18.00 per round, £22.00 per day; weekends £22.00 per round by arrangement, £12.00 per round with member. *Eating facilities:* available by arrangement with Steward. *Visitors:* welcome weekdays, weekends with member or by prior arrangement. *Society Meetings:* catered for by arrangement with Secretary. Secretary: R. E. John (0191-413 3253; Fax: 0191-413 1642).

SHIREMOOR. **Backworth Golf Club,** The Hall, Backworth, Shiremoor NE27 0AH (Course Information Service: 0191-268 9131; Club Steward: 0191-268 1048). *Location:* A191 Newcastle to Whitley Bay; at Shiremoor crossroads turn left one mile. Flat parkland, part wooded. 9 holes, 5800 yards. S.S.S. 68. Putting/chipping area. *Green Fees:* information not available. *Eating facilities:* dinner booked in advance; bar meals/snacks. *Visitors:* welcome by arrangement but not Tuesday (Ladies' Day), not Saturday until 5.30pm (Summer), not Sunday mornings. *Society Meetings:* welcome by prior arrangement only. Secretary: G.M. Sales (0191 268 8815); e-mail: backworth.miners@virgin.net

SOUTH SHIELDS. **South Shields Golf Club Ltd,** Cleadon Hills, South Shields NE34 8EG (0191-456 0475). *Location:* near A19 and A1 M, Cleadon Chimney prominent landmark. 18 holes, 6174 yards, 5729 metres. S.S.S. 70. Excellent greens, heathland/links, practice area. *Green Fees:* weekdays £22.00, weekends and Bank Holidays £27.00. *Eating facilities:* meals available at all times, bar. *Visitors:* welcome at all times without reservation. *Society Meetings:* catered for by arrangement. Professional: G. Jones. (0191-456 0110). Secretary: R. Stanness (0191-456 8942).

SOUTH SHIELDS. **Whitburn Golf Club Ltd,** Lizard Lane, South Shields NE34 7AF (0191-529 2144). *Location:* between Sunderland and South Shields adjoining Coast Road. Parkland. 18 holes, 5944 yards, S.S.S. 68. *Green Fees:* weekdays £22.00, with a member £12.00; weekends and Bank Holidays £27.00, with a member £17.00. *Eating facilities:* available. *Visitors:* welcome except on Sunday when competitions being held and restricted Tuesdays (Ladies' Day). *Society Meetings:* catered for on weekdays by prior reservations. Professional: (0191-529 4210). Secretary: Mr A. Atkinson (0191-529 4944).

TYNEMOUTH. **Tynemouth Golf Club Ltd,** Spital Dene, Tynemouth NE30 2ER (0191 257 4578). *Location:* on A695. 18 holes, 6359 yards. S.S.S. 70. *Green Fees:* £22.50 per round, £25.50 per day. *Eating facilities:* lunches and high teas served at club. *Visitors:* welcome Monday to Friday after 9.30am. Tuesday is Ladies Day. *Society Meetings:* welcome weekdays by prior arrangement. Professional: John McKenna. Secretary: T.J. Scott.

SUNDERLAND. **Wearside Golf Club,** Cox Green, Sunderland SR4 9JT (0191-534 2518). *Location:* on south bank of River Wear, one mile west of A19. From A19 exit for A183, direction Chester-le-Street, at 100 yards turn right, signposted Offerton/Cox Green, then left at T junction, down hill over humped bridge. Parkland, bordered on north by River Wear, deep wooded gully traverses course. 18 holes, 6323 yards. S.S.S. 70. 4 holes Par 3 field and separate practice field. *Green Fees:* information not available. *Eating facilities:* full catering and bar service (sandwiches only on Mondays). *Visitors:* welcome most times, telephone Professional for information. *Society Meetings:* by advance application. Professional: Doug Brolls (0191-534 4269). Secretary: M. Gowland (0191-534 2518).*

WALLSEND. **Wallsend Golf Club,** Rheydt Avenue, Wallsend NE28 8SU. *Location:* western boundary. Parkland. 18 holes, 5935 yards. S.S.S. 68. Driving range. *Green Fees:* weekdays £15.50; weekends £18.50. *Eating facilities:* meals available on request. *Visitors:* restricted weekends - not before 12.30pm April to October. *Society Meetings:* weekdays only. Professional: K. Phillips (0191-262 4231). Secretary: D. Souter (0191-262 1973).

WASHINGTON. **George Washington Golf and Country Club,** Stone Cellar Road, Washington NE37 1PH (0191-402 9988). *Location:* Washington New Town, one mile from A1M Junction A194. Parkland course with many tree-lined fairways. 18 holes, 6604 yards, 6038 metres. S.S.S. 72. 21 bay floodlit driving range, 9 hole Par 3 course. *Green Fees:* Monday to Thursday £25.00; Friday to Sunday £30.00. *Eating facilities:* fully licensed hotel on site. *Visitors:* welcome by arrangement. Special rates for visiting parties of over 12 midweek. Hotel with 103 bedrooms. *Society Meetings:* society/corporate golf days catered for. Professional/Golf Manager: Graeme Robinson (0191-417 8346).
website: graeme.amanda@btopenworld.com

WHITLEY BAY. **Whitley Bay Golf Club,** Claremont Road, Whitley Bay NE26 3UF (0191-252 0180). *Location:* north side of town. Simulated links. 18 holes, 6529 yards. S.S.S. 71. *Green Fees:* weekdays £30.00 per round, £40.00 per day; weekends £35.00. Reductions for visiting societies. *Eating facilities:* full catering every day. *Visitors:* welcome with reservation weekdays, weekends only with member. *Society Meetings:* catered for by arrangement with Secretary. Professional: G. Shipley (0191-252 5688). Secretary: Mr Harry Hanover (0191-252 0180).

For full details of clubs and courses, plus convenient accommodation
www.uk-golfguide.com

Warwickshire

ATHERSTONE. **Atherstone Golf Club,** The Outwoods, Coleshill Road, Atherstone CV9 2RL (01827 713110). *Location:* off Coleshill Road, Atherstone, five miles north of Nuneaton and seven miles south of Tamworth. Undulating parkland. 18 holes, 6006 yards. S.S.S. 71. *Green Fees:* £25.00 per day/round Tuesday to Friday, £12.00 with a member; Saturdays with member only. *Eating facilities:* bar and dining room. *Visitors:* welcome weekdays without reservation, Saturdays with member only, not Sundays. Ladies' Day Wednesday. *Society Meetings:* 12 and above by prior arrangement with Secretary. Secretary: V.A. Walton (01827 892568).

BERKSWELL. **Nailcote Hall Golf Club,** Nailcote Lane, Berkswell CV7 7DE (02476 466174; Fax: 02476 470720). Parkland setting. Cromwell Course - 9 holes, 1037 yards. *Green Fees:* information not available. *Eating facilities*: two restaurants and two bars. *Visitors:* welcome. Host venue to the "British Professional Short Course Championship". Accommodation in hotel and leisure club facilities. Professional: Sid Mouland.*

BIDFORD. **Bidford Grange Golf Club,** Stratford Road, Bidford B50 4LY (01789 490319; Fax: 01789 490998). *Location:* 6 miles west of Stratford-upon-Avon on the B439. American links course with a variety of water holes. 18 holes, 7233 yards. S.S.S. 74. Driving range and putting green. *Green Fees:* information not available. *Eating facilities:* Spikes Bar and restaurant. *Visitors:* welcome any day, after 9am. On-site Hotel. *Society Meetings:* please call for details or view website. Secretary: Daniel Broadhurst.*
e-mail: enquiries@bidfordgrange.com
website: www.bidfordgrange.com

BRAILES. **Brailes Golf Club Ltd,** Sutton Lane, Lower Brailes, Banbury OX15 5BB (01608 685633; Fax: 01608 685205). *Location:* M40 Exit 11 Banbury, 10 miles west on B4035; A3400 Shipston on Stour, four miles east on B4035. Parkland/meadowland course. 18 holes, 6311 yards. S.S.S. 70. Practice ground. *Green Fees:* weekdays £25.00 per round, £35.00 per day, twilight (times vary) £12.00 per round; weekends £35.00 per round, twilight (times vary) £18.00 per round. *Eating facilities:* modern clubhouse; bar (10.30am to 11pm) and restaurant (10am to 9pm) facilities. *Visitors:* welcome subject to availability. Tuition; buggies and trolleys for hire. *Society Meetings:* welcome subject to availability, from £28.00pp. Professional: Alistair Brown (01608 685633). Secretary: R.A.S. Malir (01608 685336).
e-mail: office@brailes-golf-club.co.uk
website: www.brailes-golf-club.co.uk

COVENTRY. **City of Coventry Brandon Wood Golf Course,** Brandon Lane, Wolston, Near Coventry CV8 3GQ (024 7654 3141). *Location:* six miles south of Coventry off southbound carriageway A45. Parkland on banks of River Avon. 18 holes, 6521 yards. S.S.S. 71. Floodlit driving range. *Green Fees:* £11.75 weekdays; £15.75 weekends and Bank Holidays. Subject to review. *Eating facilities:* bar and restaurant. *Visitors:* welcome anytime, unrestricted, bookings available up to seven days in advance, telephone Pro shop. *Society Meetings:* phone Pro shop for details. Professional/Secretary: Chris Gledhill (024 7654 3141). Stewardess: Paula Howson (024 7654 3133).

COVENTRY. **Marriott Forest of Arden Hotel & Country Club,** Maxstoke Lane, Meriden, Coventry CV7 7HR (0870 400 7272; Fax: 0870 400 7372). *Location:* take Junction 6 from M42, follow A45 to Coventry. After one mile turn left into Shepherds Lane, hotel is one and a half miles on left. Parkland and greenside water hazards. Home to the British Masters 2003. Two courses. The Arden - 7213 yards. S.S.S. 73; The Aylesford - 5801 yards. S.S.S. 68. Floodlit golf academy. *Green Fees:* information not available. *Eating facilities:* bars and restaurants available. *Visitors:* welcome seven days subject to tee-time availability. 214-bedroom four star hotel with extensive conference and luxurious leisure facilities. *Society Meetings:* enquiries welcome. Professional: Philip Hoye (0958 632170). Director of Golf: Stephen Follett.

HENLEY-IN-ARDEN. **Henley Golf and Country Club,** Birmingham Road, Henley-in-Arden B95 5QA (01564 793715; Fax: 01564 795754). *Location:* two miles from M40 Junction 16; 20 minutes from Birmingham, Solihull, Stratford-upon-Avon and Warwick. Parkland, with lovely countryside views. 18 holes, 6933 yards. S.S.S. 73. 9-hole Par 3 course. Practice range. *Green Fees:* information not available. *Eating facilities:* bar lounge menu, Brasserie. *Visitors:* no restrictions, but must book in advance. Smart casual dress required, no denim. *Society Meetings:* very welcome. Professional: Neale Hyde.
e-mail: enquiries@henleygcc.co.uk

KENILWORTH. **Kenilworth Golf Club Ltd,** Crewe Lane, Kenilworth CV8 2EA (01926 854296; Fax: 01926 864453). *Location:* A429 Coventry to Kenilworth adjacent to A46 Coventry to Warwick Road. Parkland and wooded course. 18 holes, 6400 yards. S.S.S. 71. Practice ground and 6 hole Par 3 course. *Green Fees:* £35.00 weekdays; £45.00 weekends and Bank Holidays. *Eating facilities:* diningroom, bar snacks, bar. *Visitors:* must be members of another club with official Handicap Certificate. *Society Meetings:* groups (under 20 in number) weekdays, Societies (over 20) Wednesday only. Professional: S. Yates (01926 512732). Secretary: J.H. McTavish (01926 858517; Fax: 01926 864453).

www.uk-golfguide.com

Warwickshire / ENGLAND

LEAMINGTON SPA. **Leamington and County Golf Club,** Golf Lane, Whitnash, Leamington Spa (01926 420298). *Location:* three and a half miles from M40 south of town centre of Royal Leamington Spa. 18 holes, 6418 yards, 5869 metres. S.S.S. 72. *Green Fees:* weekdays £35.00 per round, £45.00 per day; weekends £40.00 per round. *Eating facilities:* luncheons, teas, evening meals and snacks. *Visitors:* welcome without reservation. *Society Meetings:* catered for. Professional: J. Mellor (01926 428014). Secretary: David M. Beck (01926 425961).

LEAMINGTON SPA. **Newbold Comyn Golf Club,** Newbold Terrace East, Leamington Spa CV32 4EW (01926 421157). *Location:* signposted off Willes Road. Parkland, front 9 hilly, back 9 flat. 18 holes, 6315 yards. S.S.S. 70. Practice area. *Green Fees:* weekdays £8.60 per 18 holes; weekends £12.70 per 18 holes. *Eating facilities:* Newbold Arms on site. *Visitors:* welcome, unrestricted, but please book. Leisure centre on site. *Society Meetings:* catered for, book through Professional. Professional: Ricky Carvell (01926 421157). Secretary: C.V. Baker (01926 887220).

MERIDEN. **Stonebridge,** Somers Road, Meriden CV7 7PL (01676 522442; Fax: 01676 522447). *Location:* two minutes from N.E.C., M42 Junction 6, just off the A45. Parkland. 18 holes, 6240 yards. S.S.S. 70. 21 bay floodlit driving range. *Green Fees:* information not available *Eating facilities:* Spike Bar 8am to 8pm, restaurant Wednesday to Saturday evenings, Sunday lunch. *Visitors:* welcome, nine day advance booking facility for tee-times. Coarse and trout fisheries on site. Conference and private function suite available. *Society Meetings:* welcome weekdays, packages available. Professional : Emma Clifford (01676 522442; Fax: 01676 522447).*

NORTH WARWICKSHIRE. **Purley Chase Golf Club,** Ridge Lane, Near Nuneaton CV10 0RB (024 7639 3118; Fax: 024 7639 8015). *Location:* three miles off A5 between Atherstone and Nuneaton. Slightly undulating parkland. 18 holes, 6772 yards. S.S.S. 72. Conference and corporate. *Green Fees:* information not available. *Eating facilities:* restaurant. *Visitors:* welcome. *Society Meetings:* welcome, weekdays only. Special rates. Professional: Gary Carver (024 7639 5348). Secretary: Linda Jackson (024 7639 3118; Fax: 024 7639 8015).*

NUNEATON. **Bramcote Waters Golf Course,** Bazzard Road, Bramcote, Nuneaton CV11 6QJ (01455 220807). *Location:* approximately five miles from Nuneaton, off B4114. Undulating parkland. 9 holes, 2491 yards. S.S.S. 64. *Green Fees:* weekdays £8.00 9 holes, £14.00 18 holes; weekends £9.00 9 holes, £15.00 18 holes. Reductions for Juniors. *Visitors:* always welcome, pay and play or book up to one week in advance. *Society Meetings:* welcome. Professional: Nic Gilks. Secretary: S. Britain.

NUNEATON. **Nuneaton Golf Club,** Golf Drive, Whitestone, Nuneaton CV11 6QF (024 7638 3281). *Location:* Nuneaton Road, B4112 cross with two small roundabouts, Lutterworth Road. Wooded course. 18 holes, 6429 yards. S.S.S. 71. Practice ground. *Green Fees:* information not available. *Eating facilities:* catering available except Mondays; bar open usual hours. *Visitors:* welcome weekdays. *Society Meetings:* welcome - special days Wednesdays. Professional: Mr John Salter (024 7634 0201). Secretary: Mr P. Smith (024 7634 7810; Fax: 024 7632 7563).*

NUNEATON. **Oakridge Golf Club,** Arley Lane, Ansley Village, Nuneaton CV10 9PH (01676 541389; Fax: 01676 542709). *Location:* on outskirts of Nuneaton, approximately 15 minutes from town centre, 20 minutes from Coventry and 25 minutes from Tamworth. Woodland; undulating fairways with many water hazards. 18 holes, 6242 yards. S.S.S. 70. Practice area, Pro shop, putting green. *Green Fees:* information not available. *Eating facilities:* à la carte restaurant, bar meals, lounge bar. *Visitors:* welcome. Snooker room. *Society Meetings:* welcome weekdays (Monday - Friday). Golf Shop: Tony Harper Golf (01676 540542). Secretary (Admin. and Society Bookings): Mrs S. Lovric; Mr K. Clegg (Golf Section Secretary).

RUGBY. **Rugby Golf Club,** Clifton Road, Rugby CV21 3RD (01788 544637). *Location:* one mile from Rugby town centre on the Clifton road. Parkland course. 18 holes, 5457 yards. S.S.S. 67. Practice ground. *Green Fees:* weekdays £20.00 per round, £25.00 per day, £13.00 with member; weekends with member only, £15.00. *Eating facilities:* bar open daily, dining - contact Steward (01788 544637). *Visitors:* welcome weekdays; weekends and Bank Holidays only with a member. Ladies' Day Wednesday. Snooker room. Carts for hire. *Society Meetings:* welcome if pre-booked. Professional: David Quinn (01788 575134). Secretary: Ken Clark (Tel & Fax: 01788 542306).

RUGBY near. **Whitefields Golf Club,** London Road, Thurlaston, Near Rugby CV23 9LD (01788 815555; Fax: 01788 817777). *Location:* A45 near Rugby where it meets the M45. Undulating parkland course, with water feature. Not hilly. Backdrops onto Draycote Water to the south. 18 holes, 6223 yards. S.S.S. 70, Par 71. 16 bay floodlit driving range. *Green Fees:* information not available. *Eating facilities:* restaurant, spike bar, 19th hole. *Visitors:* welcome. Accommodation available in 50 en suite bedrooms all with SkyTV. Five conference rooms available. Golf Shop (01788 815555; Fax: 01788 817777). *Society Meetings:* welcome. Special rates and packages available. Secretary: Brian Coleman (01788 815555; Fax: 01788 817777). *

PLEASE MENTION THE GOLF GUIDE WHEN YOU WRITE OR PHONE TO ENQUIRE ABOUT CLUBS OR ACCOMMODATION

ENGLAND / Warwickshire

STONELEIGH. **Stoneleigh Deer Park Golf Club,** The Old Deer Park, Coventry Road, Stoneleigh CV8 3DR (024 7663 9991; Fax: 024 7651 1533). *Location:* A46 Stoneleigh Village, close to N.A.C. Stoneleigh. Parkland. 18 holes, 6056 yards. S.S.S. 69. 9 hole par 3 course; putting green and practice area. *Green Fees:* Monday to Thursday £20.00, Friday £22.00, weekends and Bank Holidays £30.00. *Eating facilities:* bar and restaurant with full catering. *Visitors:* welcome midweek, restrictions at weekends. *Society Meetings:* welcome midweek, restrictions at weekend. Professionals: Matt McGuire and Sarah Perkins (024 7663 9912). Secretary: Cherry Reay.

STRATFORD-UPON-AVON. **Ingon Manor Hotel & Golf Club,** Ingon Lane, Snitterfield, Stratford-upon-Avon CV37 0QE (01789 731938). *Location:* Junction 15 of M40, A46 to Stratford, then signposted 'Ingon Manor'. Undulating greens with stunning views across Welcombe Hills. 18 holes, 6554 yards. Par 72. Large practice area, putting green, driving range. *Green Fees:* information not available. *Eating facilities:* available daily. Professional: Paul Taylor.*
e-mail: info@ingonmanor.co.uk
website: www.ingonmanor.co.uk

STRATFORD-UPON-AVON. **Menzies Welcombe Hotel and Golf Course,** Warwick Road, Stratford-upon-Avon CV37 0NR (01789 295252; Fax: 01789 414666). *Location:* exit M40 at Junction 15, follow signs to Stratford. Club is on A439 after five miles. Or take A439 out of town and club is on left after one mile. Undulating parkland with mature trees, lakes and waterfall. 18 holes, 6288 yards. S.S.S. 70. Practice area and putting green. *Green Fees:* telephone for prices. *Eating facilities:* clubhouse with Atrium Brasserie and private function suites *Visitors:* welcome, please telephone for starting times. Hotel on site, four star facilities. *Society Meetings:* welcome. Please contact Corporate Golf Office (01789 295252; Fax: 01789 266336)

STRATFORD-UPON-AVON. **Stratford-on-Avon Golf Club,** Tiddington Road, Stratford-upon-Avon CV37 7BA (01789 205749). *Location:* half a mile from town on B4086. Flat parkland. 18 holes, 6374 yards. S.S.S. 71. *Green Fees:* information not available. *Eating facilities:* full catering/bar service. *Visitors:* welcome any time subject to domestic commitments. *Society Meetings:* catered for Tuesdays and Thursdays. Professional: D. Sutherland (01789 205677). Secretary: C.J. Hughes (01789 205749).*

WARWICK. **Warwick Golf Club,** Warwick Golf Centre, Racecourse, Warwick CV34 6HW (01925 494316). *Location:* off M40, from A41/A46 junction, travel half a mile towards Warwick, turn right into racecourse. Flat parkland course. 9 holes, 2682 yards. S.S.S. 66. Driving range (floodlit). *Green Fees:* information not available. *Eating facilities:* bar open 7 to 10.30pm weekdays, no catering. *Visitors:* welcome any time except Sunday mornings. *Society Meetings:* accepted, must book in advance. Professional: P. Sharp (01926 491284). Secretary: R. Dunkley.*

WARWICK. **The Warwickshire,** Leek Wootton, Near Warwick CV35 7QT (01926 409409; Fax: 01926 497911). *Location:* on B4115, just off A46, five minutes from M40 Junction 15. Parkland and woodland courses with many attractive holes over water. North/West Course: 18 holes, 7407 yards. S.S.S. 74. South/East Course: 18 holes, 7157 yards. S.S.S. 74. 9-hole Par 3 course, driving range, practice and putting greens. *Green Fees:* information not available. *Eating facilities:* bar and restaurant. *Visitors:* welcome at all times. Conference facilities available. *Society Meetings:* Golf Days arranged for groups from 12 to 300. Professional: M. Dulson (01926 409409). General Manager: Steve Dixon (01926 409409; Fax: 01926 408409). *

Draycote Hotel & Whitefields Golf Course

A challenging course for all handicaps overlooking the spectacular Draycote Water Country Park.
Dine and stay at the stylish Draycote Hotel, half and full day, corporate and non-golfer packages available.

• parkland course • all year round natural drainage
• floodlit driving range • practice bunker and chipping area • 18 hole putting green
Societies, corporate golf days and visitors welcome.
London Road, Thurlaston, Near Rugby, Warwickshire CV23 9LF
Tel: 01788 521 800 • Fax: 01788 521 695
www.draycotehotel.co.uk • mail@draycotehotel.co.uk

See also Colour Advertisement on page 34

For full details of clubs and courses, plus convenient accommodation
www.uk-golfguide.com

West Midlands

BIRMINGHAM. **Brandhall Golf Club,** Heron Road, Oldbury, Warley B68 8AQ (0121-552 2195). *Location:* Wolverhampton Road A4123 off Junction 2 M5; right at Hen and Chickens Junction. Wooded course, elevated tees. 18 holes, 5833 yards. S.S.S. 68. *Green Fees:* information not available. Senior Citizens cards. *Visitors:* welcome, ring course for details. Tuition available, buggies (summer only) for hire. *Society Meetings:* welcome by prior arrangement. Professional: Carl Yates.*

BIRMINGHAM. **Cocks Moors Woods Golf Club,** Alcester Road South, Kings Heath, Birmingham B14 4ER (0121-464 3584; Fax: 0121 441 1305). *Location:* A435 Alcester Road, three and a half miles from M42 Junction 3. Undulating woodland course, many meandering streams. 18 holes, 5769 yards, Par 69. S.S.S. 68. *Green Fees:* £13.00 (subject to review 2006). *Eating facilities:* adjacent to leisure centre offering excellent bar and catering facilities. *Visitors:* welcome at all times. Full range of leisure facilities within complex. *Society Meetings:* welcome during quiet times, please telephone. Professional: Steve Ellis. Secretary: D. W. Wincott (0121-777 7837).

BIRMINGHAM. **Edgbaston Golf Club Ltd,** Church Road, Edgbaston, Birmingham B15 3TB (0121-454 1736; Fax: 0121-454 2395). *Location*: from Birmingham City Centre take A38 (Bristol Road). After one mile and at third set of traffic lights turn right into Priory Road, at end of which turn into Church Road; the club entrance is 80m on the left. Undulating parkland course set in the grounds of historic Edgbaston Hall, which is now the club house. Course designed by H.S. Colt in 1935. Ancient trees, sloping fairways and a large lake contribute to the challenge and enjoyment of the course which is also a conservation area. 18 holes, 6106 yards. S.S.S. 69, Par 69. Practice area. *Green Fees*: weekdays £45.00, weekends £55.00 (summer); weekdays £30.00 (winter). *Eating facilities:* fully licensed, lunches, teas daily and bar meals daily; other meals by prior arrangement. *Visitors:* welcome subject to some restrictions on starting times, and the production of Handicap Certificate. Facilities for business meetings/seminars; snooker rooms; fully stocked shop, offering tuition, organisation of competitions, prizes, clinics. *Society Meetings*: welcome by arrangement with General Manager. Professional: Jamie Cundy (0121-454 3226; Fax: 0121-454 2395). General Manager: Adam Grint (0121-454 1736). e-mail: secretary@edgbastongc.co.uk website: www.edgbastongc.co.uk

BIRMINGHAM. **Fulford Heath Golf Club Ltd,** Tanners Green Lane, Wythall, Birmingham B47 6BH (01564 822806). *Location:* one mile from Alcester Road, via Tanners Green Lane. Parkland with two lakes and River Cole. 18 holes, 6179 yards. S.S.S. 70. Practice ground. *Green Fees:* weekdays £35.00 (Societies £30.00). Subject to review. *Eating facilities:* available. *Visitors:* welcome weekdays, not at weekends and Bank Holidays. Buggies for hire. *Society Meetings:* catered for on application. Professional: R. Dunbar (01564 822930). Secretary: Mrs M. Tuckett (01564 824758; Fax: 01564 822629).

BIRMINGHAM. **Gay Hill Golf Club,** Hollywood Lane, Hollywood, Birmingham B47 5PP (0121-430 8544; Fax: 0121 436 7796). *Location:* M42 Junction 3, three miles. Parkland course. 18 holes, 6406 yards. S.S.S. 72. Practice area. *Green Fees:* information not available. *Eating facilities:* available. *Visitors:* welcome all week. *Society Meetings:* catered for by arrangement Thursdays. Professional: Andrew Potter (0121-474 6001). Secretary: Mrs Julie Morris (0121-430 8544).

BIRMINGHAM. **Great Barr Golf Club,** Chapel Lane, Great Barr, Birmingham B43 7BA (0121-357 1232). *Location:* six miles north-west of Birmingham M6 Junction 7. Parkland. 18 holes, 6523 yards. S.S.S. 72. *Green Fees:* information not available. *Eating facilities:* meals served, order in advance. *Visitors:* welcome weekdays, restricted at weekends. Weekends maximum handicap 18. Handicap Certificate required. *Society Meetings:* Packages available. Professional: R. Spragg (0121-357 5270). Secretary: D. Smith (0121-358 4376).

BIRMINGHAM. **Handsworth Golf Club,** 11 Sunningdale Close, Handsworth Wood, Birmingham B20 1NP (0121-554 0599). *Location:* M5 Junction 1. A41 left at first lights, left at next set of lights, second left, second left/M6 Junction 7. A34 Birmingham Road, Old Walsall Road, Vernon Avenue, Westover Road, Craythorne Avenue. Parkland course. 18 holes, 6272 yards, 5733 metres. S.S.S. 70. Large practice area and putting green. *Green Fees*: information not available. *Eating facilities*: bar snacks to à la carte menu in restaurant. *Visitors:* welcome weekdays with Handicap Certificate. *Society Meetings*: catered for by arrangement with Secretary. Special packages available. Professional: L. Bashford (0121-523 3594). Secretary: P.S. Hodnett (0121-554 3387; Fax: 0121-554 6144).

BIRMINGHAM. **Harborne Golf Club,** 40 Tennal Road, Harborne, Birmingham B32 2JE (0121-427 1728). *Location:* A4123, A456, B4124 three miles west Birmingham city centre. Undulating parkland/moorland. 18 holes, 6210 yards. S.S.S. 70. *Green Fees:* weekdays £30.00. *Eating facilities:* bar and dining area daily. *Visitors:* welcome except weekends and Bank Holidays. Trolleys for hire. *Society Meetings:* welcome with pre-booking. Special rates for parties comprising over 20 players. Professional: Paul Johnson (0121-427 3512). Secretary: Garry Tozer (0121-427 3058).

www.uk-golfguide.com

THE GOLF GUIDE 2006   ENGLAND / West Midlands 333

BIRMINGHAM. **Harborne (Church Farm) Golf Club,** Vicarage Road, Harborne, Birmingham B17 0SN (0121-427 1204; Fax: 0121-428 3126). *Location:* signposted from Harborne Centre. Parkland, brooks a special feature on five holes. 9 holes, 2441 yards. S.S.S. 64. *Green Fees:* information not available. *Eating facilities:* canteen serves hot and cold snacks. *Visitors:* welcome anytime - phone call required as a booking system is in operation. *Society Meetings:* by arrangement with the Professional. Professional: Paul Johnson. Secretary: William Flanagan (0121-427 1204; Fax: 0121-428 3126).

BIRMINGHAM. **Hatchford Brook Golf Club,** Coventry Road, Sheldon, Birmingham B26 3PY (0121-743 9821; Fax: 0121 743 3420). *Location:* on A45 three miles from Junction 6 of M42, next to Birmingham International Airport. Parkland course with wide fairways and large greens. 18 holes, 6137 yards. S.S.S. 69. Large practice area. *Green Fees:* £12.00; special rates for Senior Citizens, unemployed and Link Card holders. *Eating facilities:* restaurant and bar in clubhouse. *Visitors:* welcome with some restrictions. *Society Meetings:* contact Professional. Professional: Mark Hampton (0121 743 9821). Secretary: Ian Thomson (0121 742 6643).

BIRMINGHAM. **Hilltop Public Golf Course,** Park Lane, Handsworth, Birmingham B21 8LJ (0121-554 4463; Fax: 0121-515 2842). *Location:* Two miles from M5 J1, turn into Park Lane opposite West Bromwich Albion football ground. Wide fairways. 18 holes, 6254 yards. S.S.S. 70. *Green Fees:* 18 holes weekdays £11.00; 18 holes weekends £13.00. *Eating facilities:* café serving drinks and hot meals. Licensed bar. *Visitors:* welcome, phone to book a starting time. Municipal course. *Society Meetings:* bookings available through Professional. Professional/Secretary: Kevin Highfield.

BIRMINGHAM. **Kings Norton Golf Club Ltd.,** Brockhill Lane, Weatheroak, Alvechurch, Birmingham B48 7ED (01564 826706; Fax: 01564 826955). *Location:* M42 Junction 3, A435 to Birmingham, sign on left to Weatheroak, follow for one mile, over first crossroads. Club on right hand side. Parkland course. 27 holes, 7000 yards. S.S.S. 72, plus 12 hole par 3 course and 22 acre practice field. *Green Fees:* information not available. *Eating facilities:* excellent restaurant and bar snacks available. *Visitors:* welcome weekdays only, weekends with member. *Society Meetings:* catered for weekdays only; minimum number 20. Buggies available. Professional: Kevin Hayward (01564 822635). Manager: Terry Webb (01564 826789). *
e-mail: info@kingsnortongolfclub.co.uk
website: www.kingsnortongolfclub.co.uk

BIRMINGHAM. **Maxstoke Park Golf Club,** Castle Lane, Coleshill, Birmingham B46 2RD (01675 462158). *Location:* three miles north east of Coleshill on B4114, turn right for Maxstoke. Parkland with trees and lakes. Water-filled moat surrounding Maxstoke Castle. 18 holes, 6442 yards, S.S.S. 71. Two practice areas. *Green Fees:* £30.00 per round, £40.00 per day. *Eating facilities:* restaurant and bar. *Visitors:* welcome weekdays only, weekends with member. Handicap Certificate required. *Society Meetings:* catered for Tuesdays/Thursdays. Professional: N. McEwan (01675 464915). Secretary: A. J. Brown (01675 466743; Fax: 01675 466185).

BIRMINGHAM. **Moseley Golf Club,** Springfield Road, Kings Heath, Birmingham B14 7DX (0121-444 2115). *Location:* from M42 take A435 north to Kings Heath, turn right into Wheelers Lane (A4040), left into Barn Lane crossing Addison Road into Springfield Road where the club is on the right hand side. Rolling parkland course with major water feature. 18 holes, 6300 yards. S.S.S. 70. Practice area. *Green Fees:* £30.00. *Eating facilities:* dining room and bar. *Visitors:* welcome midweek only by prior arrangement. Handicap Certificates required. *Society Meetings:* welcome Wednesdays and Fridays, minimum of 12 players. Professional: Martin Griffin (0121-444 2063). General Manager: Janet Hey (0121-444 4957; Fax: 0121-441 4662).

BIRMINGHAM. **North Worcestershire Golf Club,** Frankley Beeches Road, Northfield, Birmingham B31 5LP (0121-475 1026). *Location:* A38 from Birmingham City Centre. Parkland, established inland course. 18 holes, 5959 yards. S.S.S. 68. *Green Fees:* information not available. *Eating facilities:* catering facilities on request, normal bar opening hours. *Visitors:* welcome weekdays. *Society Meetings:* catered for Tuesdays and Thursdays. Professional: I.F. Clark (0121-475 5721). Secretary: D. Wilson (0121-475 1047; Fax: 0121-476 8681).

BIRMINGHAM near. **Rose Hill Golf Club,** Rose Hill, Rednal, Near Birmingham B45 8RR. *Location:* Lickey Hills Country Park, Junction 1 M42, Junction 4 M5. Established 1921, parkland, semi flat course. 18 holes, 5890 yards. S.S.S. 68. *Green Fees:* Weekdays 9 holes - £6.00, 18 holes £10.00. Weekends 9 holes, £7.00, 18 holes £12.00. *Eating facilities:* no bars, restaurant all day. *Visitors:* welcome with prior bookings only via Professional. Old Rose and Crown Hotel on course. *Society Meetings:* welcome with prior booking via Professional. Professional: Mark Toombs (0121-453 3159). Secretary: A Cushing (07976 793698; Fax: 0121-250 1719).

KINGS NORTON GOLF CLUB LTD Brockhill Lane, Weatheroak, Alvechurch, Birmingham B48 7ED
website: www.kingsnortongolfclub.co.uk • e-mail: info@kingsnortongolfclub.co.uk
Tel: 01564 826706 • Fax: 01564 826955
27 holes of championship golf set in 240 acres of parkland. SSS 72, 7000 yards, plus further 9 holes, par 36, 3000 yards and 12 hole short course. Ideal for visitors and societies. Dining facilities to seat up to 200. Only 3 minutes from M42 Junction 3.

COVENTRY. **Ansty Golf Centre,** Brinklow Road, Ansty, Coventry CV7 9JH (024 7662 1341; Fax: 024 7660 2568). *Location:* half a mile from Junction 2 M6 and parallel to the M69 is the B4065 signposted to Ansty. Parkland. 18 holes, 6150 yards. S.S.S. 69, Par 71. 9 hole par 3 course. Driving range. *Green Fees:* weekdays £10.00, weekends £16.00. Golf day package £12.00 weekdays, £18.00 weekends. *Eating facilities:* available 7 days a week; fully licensed restaurant with family room. *Visitors:* always welcome. Fully stocked Golf Shop, teaching academy, open 7 days regardless of weather, driving range, putting green, practice area. *Society Meetings:* welcome. Individual parties, corporate golf days and society golf days tailored to individual requirements. Professional: Mark Goodwin (024 7662 1341; Fax: 024 7660 2568). Secretary: K. Smith (Tel & Fax: 024 7660 2671).

COVENTRY. **Coventry Golf Club,** St. Martins Road, Finham Park, Coventry CV3 6RJ (024 7641 4152; Fax: 024 7669 0131). *Location:* south Coventry off A45, one mile along B4113. Gently undulating parkland course designed by Vardon/Hawtree, an exciting challenge to all golfers. 18 holes, 6601 yards. S.S.S. 73. Practice ground. *Green Fees:* information not available. *Eating facilities:* full catering in lounge bar, restaurant (maximum 120). *Visitors:* welcome weekdays. Fully stocked shop. *Society Meetings:* welcome Wednesdays and Thursdays by prior arrangement with Secretary's Office. Handicap Certificates required. Group bookings accepted two years in advance. Professional: P. Weaver (024 7641 1298). Secretary: Anne Smith (024 7641 4152).

COVENTRY. **Coventry Hearsall Golf Club,** Beechwood Avenue, Coventry CV5 6DF (024 7671 3470; Fax: 024 7669 1534). *Location:* off A45 south of Coventry, one mile south of city centre. Flat parkland, easy walking. 18 holes, 6005 yards. S.S.S. 69, Par 70. *Green Fees:* weekdays £35.00, weekends £40.00. *Eating facilities:* restaurant open six days a week; closed Mondays but snack meals offered. *Visitors:* welcome weekdays, special request at weekends. Pull carts for hire. *Society Meetings:* welcome, must book in advance with Secretary. Professional: Michael Tarn (024 7671 3156). Secretary: Anthony Richards (024 7671 3470; Fax: 024 7669 1534).

COVENTRY. **Marconi Golf Club,** Copsewood, Coventry (024 7656 3339). *Location:* three miles from centre of Coventry on A427/A428 road to Rugby, Lutterworth. 9 holes, 6048 yards. S.S.S. 71. *Green Fees:* weekdays guests £8.00 per round, £15.00 per day; visitors £15.00 per round, £20.00 per day. Sundays guests £10.00 per round, visitors £20.00 per round. *Visitors:* welcome except Saturdays, weekdays after 2.30pm Tuesday and Friday or Sunday mornings. Secretary: R.E.C. Jones (024 7645 2793).

COVENTRY. **Marriott Forest of Arden Hotel & Country Club,** Maxstoke Lane, Meriden, Coventry CV7 7HR (0870 400 7272; Fax: 0870 400 7372). *Location:* take Junction 6 from M42, follow A45 to Coventry. After one mile turn left into Shepherds Lane, hotel is one and a half miles on left. Parkland and greenside water hazards. Home to the British Masters 2003. Two courses. The Arden - 7213 yards. S.S.S. 73; The Aylesford - 5801 yards. S.S.S. 68. Floodlit golf academy. *Green Fees:* information not available. *Eating facilities:* bars and restaurants available. *Visitors:* welcome seven days subject to tee-time availability. 214-bedroom four star hotel with extensive conference and luxurious leisure facilities. *Society Meetings:* enquiries welcome. Professional: Philip Hoye (0958 632170). Director of Golf: Stephen Follett.*

COVENTRY. **North Warwickshire Golf Club Ltd,** Hampton Lane, Meriden, Warwickshire CV7 7LL (01676 522915; Fax: 01676 523004). *Location:* on B4102, one mile from Stonebridge on A45, approximately midway between Birmingham and Coventry. Parkland. 9 holes, 6352 yards. S.S.S. 71. Small practice ground. *Green Fees:* £22.00 weekdays; weekends with member only. *Eating facilities:* snack lunch, meals by prior arrangement. *Visitors:* welcome weekdays without reservation except Thursdays, weekends by invitation. *Society Meetings:* catered for by prior arrangement, limited numbers. Professional: Andrew Bownes (01676 522259). Secretary: Mrs A. Dicks (01676 522915; Fax: 01676 523004).

COVENTRY. **Windmill Village Hotel and Golf Club,** Birmingham Road, Allesley, Coventry CV5 9AL (024 7640 4041; Fax: 024 7640 4042). *Location:* A45 westbound, west of Coventry. Rolling parkland with water features. 18 holes, 5213 yards. S.S.S. 66. Course record 63 Pro, 66 Amateur. *Green Fees:* information not available. *Eating facilities:* food and drinks available all day. *Visitors:* welcome with booking. 4-star standard 100 bedroomed hotel with leisure centre; conferences, weddings catered for. *Society Meetings:* welcome, special rates available. Professional: Robert Hunter. Managers: Marci Hartland and Brian Brodie.*

CORPORATE GOLF DAY PACKAGE
- Coffee and biscuits on arrival
- One hour golf clinic with PGA Pro
- 9-Hole Texas Scramble competition
- Light Lunch
- 18-Hole Stableford with players videoed off the first tee
- Two-course evening meal
- Video analysis playback and presentation

£40.00 *per person Min. 8 people Monday – Friday* **£48.00** *per person Min. 8 people Weekends and Bank Holidays*

Brinklow Road, Ansty, Coventry CV7 9JL
Tel: 024 7662 1341 or 024 7660 2568
1 mile from Junction 2, M6 and M69
COURSE ALWAYS OPEN REGARDLESS OF WEATHER

See also Colour Advertisement on page 35

ENGLAND / West Midlands

DUDLEY. **Dudley Golf Club Ltd,** Turners Hill, Rowley Regis, Warley (01384 233877). *Location:* one mile south of Dudley town centre on Oakham Road. 18 holes, 5730 yards. S.S.S. 68. *Green Fees:* weekdays £25.00 per day. Weekends only with member. *Eating facilities:* full catering facilities available. *Visitors:* welcome but only with a member at weekends. *Society Meetings:* by prior arrangement. Professional: Guy Dean (01384 254020). Secretary: M. B. Pritchard (01384 233877). e-mail: secretary@dudleygolfclub.com

DUDLEY. **Himley Hall Golf Centre,** Log Cabin, Himley Park, Himley Road, Dudley DY3 4DF (01902 895207). *Location:* just off A449 at Himley near Dudley. Parkland. Pay and Play course. 9 holes, 3145 yards. S.S.S. 35 for 9 holes. Practice ground, pitch and putt. *Green Fees:* Summer £8.00 for 9 holes, £12.00 for 18 holes. Winter £7.50 for 9 holes, £10.50 for 18 holes. Juniors and Senior Citizens reduced rate. *Eating facilities:* hot and cold snacks. *Visitors:* welcome weekdays, weekends with booking. *Society Meetings:* mid-week only. Professional: M. Sparrow (01902 895207). Secretary: M. Harris (01384 831932).

DUDLEY. **Sedgley Golf Centre,** Sandyfields Road, Sedgley, Dudley DY3 3DL (01902 880503). *Location:* half a mile from Sedgley town centre near Cotwall End Valley Nature Reserve, just off the A463. Undulating contours and mature trees with extensive views over surrounding countryside. 9 holes, 3147 yards. S.S.S. 71 (18 holes). Covered and floodlit golf range. *Green Fees:* £7.50 9 holes, £10.00 18 holes. Reductions weekdays for Juniors and Senior Citizens. *Eating facilities:* hot and cold snacks available on request. *Visitors:* pay and play course throughout the week, booking advisable at weekends. *Society Meetings:* weekdays preferred by prior arrangement. Professional: Garry Mercer (01902 880503). Secretary: J.A. Cox (01902 672452).

DUDLEY. **Swindon Ridge Driving Range, Shop and Golf Club,** Bridgnorth Road, Swindon, Dudley DY3 4PU (01902 896765). *Location:* B4176 Bridgnorth/Dudley Road, three miles from Himley A449. Wooded. 18 holes, 6026 yards. S.S.S. 69. 27 bays *Green Fees:* information not available. *Eating facilities:* restaurant/bar. *Visitors:* welcome at all times. *Society Meetings:* welcome. Professional: Phil Lester (01902 896191). Shop Manager: Russel Powers. Secretary: Rosemary Pope (01902 897031).*

DUDLEY near. **Swindon Golf Club,** Bridgnorth Road, Swindon, Near Dudley DY3 4PU (01902 897031). *Location:* B4176 Dudley/Bridgnorth Road, three miles from A449 at Himley. Woodland and parkland course with exceptional views. 18 holes - 6121 yards. S.S.S. (18) 70. *Green Fees:* £22.00 per round, £32.00 per day weekdays; £32.00 per round, £42.00 per day weekends and Bank Holidays. *Eating facilities:* fully licensed bar and restaurant. *Visitors:* always welcome, booking required. Buggies available. Fishing. *Society Meetings:* by arrangement weekdays only. General Manager: S.T. Edwin (01902 897031; Fax: 01902 326219).

HALESOWEN. **Halesowen Golf Club,** The Leasowes, Leasowes Lane, Halesowen B62 8QF (Tel & Fax: 0121-501 3606). *Location:* exit Junction 3 M5, A456 (Kidderminster) two miles, Halesowen town centre one mile. Parkland course in the Midlands with a Grade 1 Listed clubhouse and park. 18 holes, 5754 yards. S.S.S. 69. *Green Fees:* weekdays £26.00 per round, £31.00 per day; weekends by special arrangement. *Eating facilities:* available every day. *Visitors:* welcome weekdays. *Society Meetings:* by arrangement with Secretary. Professional: Jon Nicholas (Tel & Fax: 0121-503 0593). Secretary: Peter Crumpton (Tel & Fax: 0121-501 3606).

A Course Fit 'Fore' Champions

SWINDON GOLF CLUB, near Dudley in the West Midlands provides golfers with the one thing that makes the sport so great – a challenge. For at Swindon the course is littered with holes, bunkers and obstacles to test the talents of the greatest players.

Almost all holes are surrounded by ferns, pines and firs.

The feature hole is the 5th, a boomerang of a Par 5 flanked on both sides by towering firs. Swindon wants golfers from all over to try the course, and the experience of playing on a course with so many features will improve any player 100%.

The clubhouse has a friendly and relaxed atmosphere and you will find a selection of great food to satisfy any appetite, a snooker table and a great atmosphere. For more information telephone or visit the course.

SWINDON GOLF CLUB, BRIDGNORTH ROAD, SWINDON, DUDLEY, WEST MIDLANDS DY3 4PU
TEL: 01902 897031/895226 • FAX: 01902 326219 • www.swindongolfclub.co.uk

See also Colour Advertisement on page 34

Halesowen Golf Club, The Leasowes, Halesowen B62 8QF

The Club, which has been established for over 90 years, has an 18 hole course set in the only Grade I Listed Park in the Midlands, with excellent panoramic views of Worcestershire, and is always in excellent condition. Visitors fees £26 per round, £31 daily. Food available all day, except Mondays. Well stocked shop. Playing membership of over 500 but visitors and new members are always welcome. Places available.

Arrangements with the Secretary on 0121 501 3606, or Professional 0121 503 0593

REDNAL. **Lickey Hills Golf Club,** Rose Hill, Rednal, Birmingham B45 8RR (0121-453 3159; 0121-457 8779). *Location:* Three miles from M42 J1 or M5 J4 at the bottom of Rose Hill on Lickey Hills Country Park. Picturesque course with dramatic slopes and banks of pine trees. 18 holes, 5866 yards. S.S.S. 68. *Green Fees:* information not available. *Eating facilities:* cafe at clubhouse. *Visitors:* welcome. Professional: Mark Toombs.*

SOLIHULL. **Copt Heath Golf Club,** 1220 Warwick Road, Knowle, Solihull B93 9LN (01564 772650). *Location*: on A4141 half-a-mile south of Junction 5 with M42. Flat parkland. 18 holes, 6517 yards. S.S.S. 71. Full practice facilities available. *Green Fees*: weekdays £40.00. Weekends and Public Holidays must be introduced by a member. *Eating facilities:* lunch and evening meal available except Mondays. *Visitors:* no restrictions weekdays. *Society Meetings:* by arrangement with Secretary. Professional: Brian Barton. Secretary: Clive Hadley.
e-mail: golf@copt-heath.co.uk
website: www.coptheathgolf.co.uk

SOLIHULL. **Ladbrook Park Golf Club Ltd,** Poolhead Lane, Tanworth-in-Arden, Solihull B94 5ED (01564 742220). *Location:* south from Junction 3 M42. Parkland, gently undulating. 18 holes, 6427 yards. S.S.S. 71. Practice ground. *Green Fees:* weekdays £30.00 18 holes, £45.00 36 holes; weekends with a member only. *Eating facilities:* excellent dining. *Visitors:* welcome weekdays, prior telephone call suggested. Weekends with member only. *Society Meetings:* catered for by prior arrangement with the Secretary. Professional: Richard Mountford (01564 742581). Seccretary: Mrs S.E. Burrows (01564 742264; Fax: 01564 742909).

SOLIHULL. **Olton Golf Club Ltd,** Mirfield Road, Solihull B91 1JH (0121-705 1083; Fax: 0121-711 2010). *Location:* approximately two miles off Junction 5 (M42), A41 - Birmingham. Parkland. 18 holes, 6229 yards, 5694 metres. S.S.S. 71. *Green Fees:* from £35.00 weekdays. Discounts for large groups. *Eating facilities:* by arrangement. *Visitors:* welcome weekdays only except Wednesdays. *Society Meetings:* catered for by arrangement. Professional: C. Haynes (0121-705 7296). Hon. Secretary: Rob Weatherley (0121-704 1936; Fax: 0121-711 2010).

SOLIHULL. **Robin Hood Golf Club,** St. Bernards Road, Solihull B92 7DJ (0121-706 0159). *Location:* eight miles south of Birmingham, off A41 Birmingham to Warwick road. Flat parkland. 18 holes, 6635 yards, 6067 metres. S.S.S. 72. *Green Fees:* £30.00 weekdays. *Eating facilities:* by prior arrangement with Steward (0121-706 5010). *Visitors:* welcome weekdays only subject to limitations. Arrange with Secretary or Professional. *Society Meetings:* catered for by prior booking. Professional: A.R. Harvey (0121-706 0806). Secretary: Miss J.S. Evans (0121 706 0061; Fax: 0121-700 7502).
e-mail: robin.hood.golf.club@dial.pipex.com

SOLIHULL. **Shirley Golf Club,** Stratford Road, Monkspath, Solihull B90 4EW (0121-744 6001; Fax: 0121-746 5645). *Location:* (A3400), Junction 4 M42, towards Birmingham. Parkland. 18 holes, 6507 yards. S.S.S. 71. Practice ground, putting area. *Green Fees:* £30.00 per round, £40.00 per day. *Eating facilities:* bar and restaurant. *Visitors:* welcome weekdays without reservation, must have Handicap. Trolleys available. *Society Meetings:* welcome by arrangement. Professional: Stuart Bottrill (Tel & Fax: 0121-746 5646). General Manager: Steve Wilkins (0121-744 6001; Fax: 0121-746 5645)
e-mail: shirleygolfclub@btclick.com

SOLIHULL. **Tidbury Green Golf Club,** Tilehouse Lane, Shirley, Solihull B90 1HP (01564 824460). *Location:* two miles from Shirley and three miles off the M42. To play over numerous ponds, lakes and the River Coal. 18 holes, 4792 yards, 4382 metres. S.S.S. 64. 15 bay driving range. *Green Fees:* information not available. *Eating facilities:* excellent bar and restaurant facilities. *Visitors:* welcome, no restrictions. Facilities for fishing, crazy golf. *Society Meetings:* catered for. Professional: Ray Thompson. Secretary: L.M. Broadhurst.*

SOLIHULL. **West Midlands Golf Club,** Marsh House Farm Lane, Barston, Solihull B92 0LB (01675 444 890). *Location:* located between Birmingham and Coventry, five minutes from National Exhibition Centre, Junction 4 of M6, Junction 6 of M42. Take A452 towards Leamington and Warwick (Balsall Common) turn right to Barston and right again into Marsh House Farm Lane. USGA Golf Course over rolling parkland with island green. Putting green, open driving range, practice green. 18 holes, 6624 yards. S.S.S. 72. *Green Fees:* weekdays £17.50, weekends £25.00. *Eating facilities:* spike bar serving light meals and à la carte restaurant. *Visitors:* welcome. *Society Meetings:* please call for information, we will tailor a package to suit your needs. Secretary: Ron Guthrie.
e-mail: westmidlandsgc@aol.com
website: www.wmgc.co.uk

SOLIHULL. **Widney Manor Golf Club,** Saintbury Drive (off Widney Lane), Widney Manor, Solihull B91 3SZ (0121-704 0704; Fax: 0121-704 7999). *Location:* exit M42 Junction 4 and follow signs for Shirley, then Monkspath. A challenging course for golfers of all abilities, set in parkland with mature oaks and water hazards. 18 holes, 5500 yards. 14-bay covered driving range. *Green Fees:* information not available. *Eating facilities:* normal bar hours, catering facilities available all day. *Visitors:* welcome at all times with advance booking available. Casual but smart dress code. *Society Meetings:* welcome any day. Tailor-made to suit the customer. Professional Tim Atkinson. Secretary: Ron Guthrie.*
website: www.wmgc.co.uk

THE APPEARANCE OF AN ASTERISK (*) AT THE END OF A CLUB OR COURSE ENTRY INDICATES THAT UP-TO-DATE INFORMATION HAS NOT BEEN SUPPLIED

ENGLAND / West Midlands

STOURBRIDGE. Stourbridge Golf Club, Worcester Lane, Pedmore, Stourbridge DY8 2RB (01384 395566). *Location:* situated between Hagley and Stourbridge on Worcester road. Parkland. 18 holes, 6231 yards. S.S.S. 70. Small practice ground. *Green Fees:* weekdays £30.00; weekends with a member only £14.00. *Eating facilities:* bar meals available, lunch, dinner. *Visitors:* welcome weekdays, weekends with member. *Society Meetings:* catered for. Professional: Mark Male (01384 393129). Secretary: Mrs M.A. Betts (01384 395566; Fax: 01384 444660).
e-mail: secretary@stourbridge-golf-club.co.uk
website: www.stourbridge-golf-club.co.uk

SUTTON COLDFIELD. Aston Wood Golf Club, Blake Street, Little Aston, Sutton Coldfield B74 4EU (0121-580 7803; Fax: 0121-353 0354). *Location:* situated on Blake Street off A5127 Lichfield to Sutton Coldfield Road. Gently rolling Allis-Clark designed course with many water hazards.18 holes, 6480 yards. S.S.S. 71. Practice area, bunker and green. *Green Fees:* information not available. *Eating facilities:* superb restaurant and bars open daily 7.30am-11pm. *Visitors:* weekdays only. Buggies. *Society Meetings:* corporate and societies welcome. Excellent packages available. Superb functions and conference facilities. Professional: Simon Smith (0121-580 7800). General Manager: Ken Heathcote (0121-580 7803).*

SUTTON COLDFIELD. Boldmere Golf Club, Monmouth Drive, Sutton Coldfield B73 6JL (0121-354 3379; Fax: 0121-355 4534). *Location:* off A452 (Chester road North), next to Sutton Park on Monmouth Drive. Flat parkland, wooded. 18 holes, 4463 yards. S.S.S. 62. Practice net and putting area. Shorter, lush course ideal for those who prefer a less exhaustive round of golf. *Green Fees:* information not available. *Eating facilities:* cafe in clubhouse. *Visitors:* welcome, Link Card system in operation. *Society Meetings:* welcome at quiet times, to be arranged with the Professional. Professional: Trevor Short (0121-354 3379; Fax: 0121-354 4534). Secretary: Roy Leeson (0121-354 3379; Fax: 0121-354 4534).*
e-mail: boldmeregolfclub@hotmail.com

SUTTON COLDFIELD. Moor Hall Golf Club Ltd, Moor Hall Drive, Sutton Coldfield B75 6LN (0121-308 6130). *Location:* one mile east of Sutton Coldfield, A446. Parkland. 18 holes, 6293 yards. S.S.S. 70. Practice area. *Green Fees:* £40.00 per round, £55.00 day ticket. *Eating facilities:* available weekdays. *Visitors:* welcome weekdays only (not Thursday mornings). 4-star Moor Hall Hotel on golf estate (independently owned). *Society Meetings:* catered for. Professional: Cameron Clark (0121-308 5106). Secretary: D.J. Etheridge (0121-308 6130).

SUTTON COLDFIELD. Pype Hayes Golf Club, Eachelhurst Road, Walmley, Sutton Coldfield B76 8EP (0121-351 1014). *Location:* off the A38 Kingsbury Road, one and a half miles from Junction 9 M42. Flat wooded course with small greens, four demanding Par 3's. 18 holes, 5996 yards. S.S.S. 69. *Green Fees:* information not available. *Eating facilities:* cafeteria. *Visitors:* welcome but must book via telephone. *Society Meetings:* welcome but must book via telephone. Professional: Joe Kelly. Secretary: L. Brogan (0121-773 2958).*

SUTTON COLDFIELD. Sutton Coldfield Golf Club, Thornhill Road, Streetly, Sutton Coldfield B74 3ER (0121-353 9633; Fax: 0121-353 5503). *Location:* situated in Sutton Park, one mile off A452, seven miles from centre of Birmingham. Natural heathland. 18 holes, 6549 yards. S.S.S. 71. *Green Fees:* weekdays £30.00 per round, £40.00 all day; weekends £40.00 per round. *Eating facilities:* by arrangement with Chef (0121-353 2014). *Visitors:* welcome without reservation but please ring Professional to check availability. Handicap Certificate required. *Society Meetings:* Special arrangements for societies by arrangement with Secretary. Professional: J.K. Hayes (0121-580 7878). Secretary: R.G. Mitchell (0121-353 9633; Fax: 0121-353 5503).

SUTTON COLDFIELD. Walmley Golf Club, Brooks Road, Wylde Green, Sutton Coldfield B72 1HR (0121-373 0029; Fax: 0121-377 7272). *Location:* Birmingham/Sutton Coldfield main road, turn right at Green Hill Road. Flat parkland. 18 holes, 6585 yards. S.S.S. 72. Practice ground. *Green Fees:* weekdays £30.00, £12.50 with a member. 10% reductions for 30 or more players. *Eating facilities:* lunch and evening meals available. *Visitors:* welcome weekdays only. *Society Meetings:* catered for Wednesdays, Thursdays and some Fridays only. Professional: Chris Wicketts (0121-373 0029 Ext.3). Secretary: Peter Clarke (0121-373 0029 Ext.1).
e-mail: walmleygolfclub@aol.com

ASTON WOOD GOLF CLUB
**Blake Street, Little Aston,
Sutton Coldfield B74 4EU
Tel: 0121 580 7800 • Fax: 0121 353 0354**

An 18-hole championship course designed by Peter Alliss and Clive Clarke, constructed to USPGA standard, with well-placed bunkers, water features and fine, undulating greens. Aston Wood is easily accessible from Birmingham and the rest of the country (M6, M6 Toll, M40 and M42), and combines high standards of service with a friendly, comfortable atmosphere. Visitors welcome weekdays.

enquiries@astonwoodgolfclub.co.uk
www.astonwoodgolfclub.co.uk

See also Colour Advertisement on page 35

WALSALL. **Bloxwich Golf Club (1988) Ltd,** 136 Stafford Road, Bloxwich, Walsall WS3 3PQ (01922 476593; Fax: 01922 493449). *Location:* off main Walsall-Cannock road (A34). Semi parkland. 18 holes, 6257 yards. S.S.S. 71. *Green Fees:* information not available. *Eating facilities:* available. *Visitors:* welcome with or without reservation except weekends and Bank Holidays. *Society Meetings:* catered for midweek, reduced rates for 20 or more. Professional: R.J. Dance (01922 476889; Fax: 01922 493449). Secretary/Manager: D.A. Frost (01922 476593; Fax: 01922 493449).*

WALSALL. **Calderfields Golf Club Ltd,** Aldridge Road, Walsall WS4 2JS (01922 632243; Fax: 01922 640540). *Location:* A454 between Aldridge and Walsall, Junction 10 M6. Parkland, water hazards. 18 holes, 6509 yards, S.S.S. 73. 27 bay floodlit driving range, practice bunkers, putting green. *Green Fees:* midweek £15.00, weekends and Bank Holidays £18.00 (subject to review for 2006.) *Eating facilities:* Lake View restaurant and bar. New function suite for all occasions, seating for 150. *Visitors:* welcome at all times. *Society Meetings:* packages available 7 days a week, subject to availability. Booking Tee Time (01922 632243). Society Director: B. Kemp (07947 620680). website: www.calderfieldsgolf.com

WALSALL. **Druids Heath Golf Club,** Stonnall Road, Aldridge, Walsall WS9 8JZ (01922 455595; Fax: 01922 452887). *Location:* off A452 near Little Aston – Aldridge. Testing undulating heathland course. 18 holes, 6661 yards. S.S.S. 73. Practice ground and net. *Green Fees:* £34.00 weekdays; £42.00 weekends after 2pm. *Eating facilities:* dining room and bar snacks. *Visitors:* welcome by prior arrangement. *Society Meetings:* catered for by prior arrangement. Professional: Glenn Williams (01922 459523). Secretary: K.I Taylor.

WALSALL. **Walsall Golf Club,** The Broadway, Walsall WS1 3EY (01922 613512; Fax: 01922 616460). *Location:* one and a half miles from M6/M5 junction. Wooded course. 18 holes, 6259 yards. S.S.S. 71. *Green Fees:* on application. *Eating facilities:* all facilities available. *Visitors:* welcome weekdays only. *Society Meetings:* catered for. Professional: R. Lambert (01922 626766). Secretary: H. J. Durkin (01922 613512).

WARLEY. **Warley Woods Golf Club,** The Pavillion, Lightwoods Hill, Smethwick B67 5EO (0121-429 2440; Fax: 0121-434 4430). *Location:* Hagley Road. Adjacent to Warley Woods. Warley water tower at top of course. Parkland course. 9 holes, 2686 yards. S.S.S. 66. *Green Fees:* information not available. *Eating facilities:* cafe. *Visitors:* welcome, advised to book in advance as this is a very busy club. *Society Meetings:* welcome during quiet times, telephone Professional for details. Professional: David Ashington (0121-429 2440; Fax: 0121-434 4430). Secretary: Alan Woolridge (0121-686 2619; Fax: 0121-241 3451).*

WEST BROMWICH. **Dartmouth Golf Club,** Vale Street, West Bromwich B71 4DW (0121-588 2131). *Location:* one mile from West Bromwich town centre. All Saints Way A4031, turn right at McDonalds and follow signposts. Part flat, part undulating course, a good test for all categories. 9 holes, 6036 yards. S.S.S. 70. Practice area, putting green. *Green Fees:* 18 holes £25.00, 9 holes £10.00; with a member 18 holes £12.00, 9 holes £8.00. *Eating facilities:* bar snacks always available, meals by prior arrangement. *Visitors:* welcome weekdays, weekends with a member only. *Society Meetings:* welcome by prior arrangement. Secretary: Mr C.F. Wade (0121-532 4070).

WEST BROMWICH. **Sandwell Park Golf Club Ltd,** Birmingham Road, West Bromwich B71 4JJ (0121-553 4637; Fax: 0121-525 1651). *Location*: on A41 to Birmingham 200 yards from Junction 1 M5, turn left under footbridge. Wooded, heathland course. 18 holes, 6468 yards. S.S.S. 73. Two practice areas, chipping green. *Green Fees*: information not available. *Eating facilities*: full restaurant facilities and two bars. *Visitors*: welcome weekdays, weekend and Bank Holidays with a member only. Handicap Certificate required. *Society Meetings*: by prior arrangement with the Secretary. Professional: Nigel Wylie (0121-553 4384). Secretary: D.A. Paterson (0121-553 4637). website: www.sandwellparkgolfclub.co.uk

WISHAW. **The De Vere Belfry,** Wishaw B76 9PR (01675 470301; Fax: 01675 470178). *Location:* leave M42 at Junction 9 and follow signs for Lichfield, The Belfry is on A446. Parkland courses. The Brabazon - 18 holes, 7118 yards. S.S.S. 74. PGA National - 18 holes, 7053 yards. S.S.S. 72. The Derby - 18 holes, 6009 yards. S.S.S. 69. PGA National Golf Academy, 34 bay driving range, putting green. *Green Fees:* information not available. *Eating facilities:* use of hotel facilities including a selection of bars and restaurants. *Visitors:* welcome. 324 bedroomed four-star hotel, 21 conference rooms, leisure club, indoor heated pool, sauna, solarium, hairdressing salon, beauty rooms, Aqua Spa, gymnasium. two squash courts, snooker room, pool tables, outdoor tennis courts and jogging trail. Bel Air Night Club situated within hotel grounds. Buggies, carts and caddies available. *Society Meetings:* always welcome subject to availablity. Professional: Simon Wordsworth (01675 470301).
e-mail: enquiries@thebelfry.com
website: www.thebelfry.com

WOLVERHAMPTON. **Oxley Park Golf Club Ltd,** Stafford Road, Bushbury, Wolverhampton WV10 6DE. *Location:* one and a half miles M54/A449 junction. One and a half miles Wolverhampton town centre. Undulating parkland. 18 holes, 6226 yards. S.S.S. 71. *Green Fees:* £31.00 per round, £36.00 per day. *Eating facilities:* available daily except Monday. *Visitors:* welcome weekdays, weekends by arrangement with Professional. *Society Meetings:* preferred day Wednesday; for alternatives please contact Secretary. Professional: Leslie Burlison (01902 425445). Secretary: (01902 773989; Fax: 01902 773981).

ENGLAND / West Midlands

WOLVERHAMPTON. Penn Golf Club Ltd, Penn Common, Penn, Wolverhampton WV4 5JN (01902 341142). *Location:* two miles south west of Wolverhampton, off A449. Heathland. 18 holes, 6487 yards. S.S.S. 72. *Green Fees:* £28.00 per round, £33.00 per day. *Eating facilities:* full catering and bar facilities. *Visitors:* welcome weekdays. *Society Meetings:* catered for. Professional: D Ashton (01902 330472). Club Administrator: Mrs A Rafferty (01902 341142).

WOLVERHAMPTON. Perton Park Golf Club, Wrottesley Park Road, Perton, Wolverhampton WV6 7HL (01902 380103). *Location:* just off the A454 Bridgnorth Road or A41 Wolverhampton to Newport road. Flat meadowland. 18 holes, 6520 yards, S.S.S. 71. Driving range, putting green, bowling greens. *Green Fees:* from £16.00 per round. *Eating facilities:* available, also bar. *Visitors:* always welcome, booking times available. Buggies and trolleys for hire. *Society Meetings:* catered for. General Manager: S.T. Edwin (01902 380073; Fax: 01902 326219).

WOLVERHAMPTON. The South Staffordshire Golf Club, Danescourt Road, Tettenhall, Wolverhampton WV6 9BQ (01902 751065). *Location:* A41 out of Wolverhampton (approximately three miles). Parkland. 18 holes, 6513 yards. S.S.S. 71. Practice area (approximately 10 acres). Driving range. *Green Fees:* £42.00 weekdays, £57.00 weekends. *Eating facilities:* snacks, buffets, three-course dinners available 12 hours per day. Steward: Hugh Campbell (01902 756401). *Visitors:* welcome weekdays except Tuesdays. No mobile phones around grounds, or on the course. *Society Meetings:* by arrangement through reservations - Sue Lebeau. Teaching Professional: Shaun Ball. Club Manager: W. R. Benton (01902 751065; Fax: 01902 751159). e-mail: manager@southstaffsgc.co.uk website: http://.southstaffsgc.co.uk

WOLVERHAMPTON. Wergs Golf Club, Keepers Lane, Tettenhall, Wolverhampton WV6 8UA (01902 742225; Fax: 01902 744748). *Location:* from centre of Wolverhampton, take A41 (to Newport), after two and a half miles turn right, half a mile on right. Open parkland. 18 holes, 6949 yards. S.S.S. 73. 20 acre practice area. *Green Fees:* weekdays £15.00; weekends and Bank Holidays £20.00. Senior Citizens and Juniors £12.50 weekdays, £17.00 weekends and Bank Holidays. *Eating facilities:* full catering and bar facilities. *Visitors:* always welcome. Membership available. *Society Meetings:* welcome anytime during week, after 10am at weekends. Secretary: Mrs G. Parsons. e-mail: wergs.golfclub@btinternet.com

---

FHG

K·U·P·E·R·A·R·D

FHG Guides

publish a large range of well-known accommodation guides. We will be happy to send you details or you can use the order form at the back of this book.

SANDWELL PARK GOLF CLUB
Birmingham Road, West Bromwich, West Midlands B71 4JJ

This well established and prestigious private members club creates the complete golfing experience for those who appreciate tradition and excellence in quality surroundings. Visitors, corporate parties and societies will receive a warm welcome. Monday to Friday throughout the year.

* Please apply to Manager on 0121 553 4637 * www.sandwellparkgolfclub.co.uk *

Founded in 1990 the club boasts a flourishing membership and friendly staff. Our inland links-style 18-hole course offers a challenge to all golfers with some long and testing holes finished off with pacy yet accommodating greens. An 18-bay floodlit driving range offers you the chance to hit some balls with putting and chipping greens adding the finishing touches to your game. Green fees and membership rates are among the most attractive in the region with a variety of additional benefits. We always welcome new members with 5 day, 7 day, corporate, and family memberships available. Our clubhouse offers some of the best catering around in convivial surroundings that make your 'après golf' debate that much more enjoyable.

PERTON PARK GOLF CLUB
Wrottesley Park Road, Perton, Wolverhampton WV6 7HL
Tel/Fax: 01902 380073/380103
website: www.pertongolfclub.co.uk

See also Colour Advertisement on page 35

Wiltshire

BRADFORD-ON-AVON. **Cumberwell Park Golf Club,** Bradford-on-Avon BA15 2PQ (01225 863322; Fax: 01225 868160). *Location*: on A363 between Bath and Bradford-on-Avon, close to J17 and J18 off M4. Recognised as one of the top courses in the west country, encompassing 315 acres of parkland, enhanced by nine lakes, 34 acres of forest and streams. 27 holes (3 x 9), 6723 yards (18 holes), S.S.S. 72. Practice greens, 10 acre driving range. *Green Fees:* weekdays £26.00 per round, weekends and Bank Holidays £32.00 per round. *Eating facilities*: private dining rooms and spikes bar. *Visitors*: always welcome; accommodation can be arranged nearby. *Society Meetings*: packages including catering available from £24.00 winter, from £35.00 summer. Golf days tailored to individual requirements. Professional: John Jacobs. e-mail: enquiries@cumberwellpark.com website: www.cumberwellpark.com

CALNE. **Bowood Golf and Country Club,** Derry Hill, Calne SN11 9PQ (01249 822228; Fax: 01249 822218). *Location*: A4 between Marlborough and Chippenham, signposted off M4 Junction 17. Grade I listed, Capability Brown landscaped, parkland. 18 holes, 7317, 6890, 6566: 6027 yards. S.S.S. 74, 71: 75. Ladies 6015 yards, S.S.S. 75. Three academy holes, floodlit driving range, two putting greens. *Green Fees:* weekdays £41.00 per round, weekends £43.00 per round. Special rates available in winter and summer evenings. *Eating facilities*: public restaurant, private dining for up to 200. *Visitors*: welcome at all times except before 12 noon at weekends, bookings required. Four (double/twin) bedroomed house in centre of course, large clubhouse extension for banqueting, conferences, weddings, etc. Buggies, trolleys and clubs for hire; fully stocked Pro shop. *Society Meetings:* welcome, special packages available. Head Golf Professional: Max Taylor. Proprietor: The Marquis of Lansdowne.

www.uk-golfguide.com

CASTLE COMBE. **The Manor House Golf Club at Castle Combe,** Castle Combe SN14 7JW (01249 782982; Fax: 01249 782992). *Location:* on the B4039 midway between M4 Junction 17 and 18. Parkland course situated in a series of wooded valleys in an Area of Outstanding Natural Beauty. 18 holes, 6286 yards. S.S.S. 71. Practice range. *Green Fees:* information not available. *Eating facilities:* full restaurant and bar facilities. *Visitors:* welcome by prior arrangement provided they have a club Handicap Certificate. The luxurious Manor House Hotel (four red stars) adjoins the course offering exceptional accommodation and an award-winning restaurant. *Society Meetings:* welcome by prior arrangement. Professional: Peter Green (01249 782982; Fax: 01249 782992. General Manager: Paul Hinton (01249 782982; Fax: 01249 782992).*

CHIPPENHAM. **Chippenham Golf Club,** Malmesbury Road, Chippenham SN15 5LT (01249 652040). *Location:* A350 one mile from Chippenham, two miles from M4 (Junction 17). Parkland. 18 holes, 5570 yards. S.S.S. 67. *Green Fees:* weekdays £22.00, weekends £27.00. *Eating facilities:* snacks and evening à la carte (not Mondays). *Visitors:* welcome, prior arrangement necessary. *Society Meetings:* catered for Mondays, Tuesdays, Thursdays and Fridays only. Premier Travel Inn overlooking first fairway. Professional: Bill Creamer (01249 655519). Secretary: B. Cook (01249 652040).

CHIPPENHAM. **Monkton Park Golf Club,** Monkton Park, Chippenham SN15 3PE (Tel & Fax: 01249 653928). *Location:* centre of Chippenham, two miles from M4 Junction 17. Parkland Par 3 course. Probably the best Par 3 course in the south west of England. 9 holes, 1000 yards. S.S.S. 27. Crazy golf. *Green Fees:* from £5.50. *Eating facilities:* kiosk. *Visitors:* always welcome 364 days of the year! Golf clubs available. *Society Meetings:* welcome. Secretary: Mrs W. Claridge website: www.pitchandputtgolf.com

QUEENWOOD GOLF LODGE
Your own private residence in the heart of Bowood Golf Course
• Set in the heart of Bowood's superb Championship Golf Course
• Beautiful secluded Georgian Lodge where you and your friends are the only guests
• Packages include:
    Golf • Tea & Cake on arrival • Full English breakfast
    Gourmet dinner party • Beautiful luxury accommodation
• Signposted from M4 Junction 17.

BOWOOD
GOLF & COUNTRY CLUB

Derry Hill, Calne, Wiltshire SN11 9PQ • Tel: 01249 822228
www.bowood.org • e-mail: golfclub@bowood.org

See also Colour Advertisement on page 20

CORSHAM. **Kingsdown Golf Club,** Corsham SN13 8BS (01225 742530). *Location:* five miles east of Bath. Heathland. 18 holes, 6445 yards, 5891 metres. S.S.S. 71. *Green Fees:* information not available. *Eating facilities:* lounge bar and diningroom. *Visitors:* welcome except at weekends and Bank Holidays and must have current Handicap Certificate. *Society Meetings:* catered for by arrangement. Professional: Andrew Butler (01225 742634). Secretary: Jim Elliott (01225 743472).*

CRICKLADE. **Cricklade Hotel & Country Club,** Common Hill, Cricklade SN6 6HA (01793 750751; Fax: 01793 751767). *Location*: A419 8 miles north of Swindon, B4040 out of Cricklade town by half a mile. Undulating course set around hotel. 9 holes, 1830 yards. S.S.S. 58 (18 holes). *Green Fees:* information not available. *Eating facilities*: full à la carte restaurant and bar with snacks available. *Visitors*: guests of hotel welcome at all times, tee times must be booked at weekends. Weekends members and hotel guests only. 46-room hotel on site. *Society Meetings*: on application. Professional: Ian Bolt. Secretary: Colin Withers. Hotel General Manager: Paul Butler. e-mail: reception@cricklahotel.fsnet.co.uk website: www.cricklahotel.co.uk

DEVIZES. **Erlestoke Sands Golf Club,** Erlestoke, Near Devizes SN10 5UB (Fax: 01380 831284). *Location:* six miles east of Westbury on B3098. Downland course, on two levels, spectacular 7th hole, 170 yards Par 3, with green 100ft below, one of the finest short holes in the West Country. 18 holes, 6406 yards. S.S.S. 71, Par 73. Large practice ground. *Green Fees:* information not available. *Eating facilities:* full catering service, lounge, bar and diningroom. *Visitors:* welcome, booking advisable (01380 830300). *Society Meetings:* catered for by prior arrangement (01380 831069). Professional: Michael Walters (01380 831027). Office: M. Pugsley (01380 831069).*

DEVIZES. **North Wilts Golf Club,** Bishop's Cannings, Devizes SN10 2LP (01380 860257). *Location:* one and a half miles from A4 east of Calne. Four miles from Devizes. Downland, undulating course with spectacular views. 18 holes, 6414 yards. S.S.S. 71. Practice ground. *Green Fees:* information not available. *Eating facilities:* full catering service. *Visitors:* welcome, except on medal days. *Society Meetings:* catered for by prior arrangement. Professional: Graham Laing (01380 860330; Fax: 01380 860061). Secretary: Mrs Trish Stephenson (01380 860627; Fax: 01380 860877).*

HIGHWORTH. **Highworth Community Golf Centre,** Swindon Road, Highworth SN6 7SJ. *Location:* on A361 just south of the town. Undulating parkland. 9 holes, 3120 yards, 2851 metres. Par 35. 9 hole pitch and putt, 4 hole practice course. *Green Fees:* £12.00. *Eating facilities:* vending machines. *Visitors:* municipal course, no restrictions. *Society Meetings:* welcome any day. Professional: Barry Sandry (01793 766014). Secretary: Steve Kearley.

HIGHWORTH. **Wrag Barn Golf and Country Club,** Shrivenham Road, Highworth, Swindon SN6 7QQ (01793 861327; Fax: 01793 861325). *Location:* just six miles off the M4. Undulating, set in beautiful Wiltshire countryside, three lakes and moat around 17th green. 18 holes, 6633 yards. S.S.S. 72. 11 bay driving range, practice area. *Green Fees:* weekdays £32.00; weekends £38.00. *Eating facilities:* spike bar. restaurant, function rooms. *Visitors:* welcome weekdays and after 12 noon weekends. Buggies and trolleys for hire. *Society Meetings:* welcome any weekday. Professional: Barry Loughrey (01793 766027; Fax: 01793 861325). Secretary: M. Betteridge (01793 861327; Fax: 01793 861325).

MARLBOROUGH. **Marlborough Golf Club,** The Common, Marlborough SN8 1DU (01672 512147; Fax: 01672 513164). *Location:* about one mile north of Marlborough town centre on A346 towards Swindon. Seven miles south of J15 of the M4. Downland with panoramic views into the Og Valley and over the Marlborough Downs. 18 holes, 6514 yards, 5952 metres. S.S.S. 71, Par 72. Large practice ground and putting green. *Green Fees:* weekdays £28.00 per round, £38.00 per day; weekends £35.00 per round (after 4.00pm £17.00), £50.00 per day. *Eating facilities:* full restaurant facility, plus bar snacks open all day. *Visitors:* welcome generally, but it is best to telephone in advance; some restrictions at weekends. *Society Meetings:* discounted rates and packages available. Essential to book in advance. Professional: Simon Amor (01672 512493; Fax: 01672 513164). General Manager: J.A.D. Sullivan (01672 512147; Fax: 01672 513164). e-mail: contactus@marlboroughgolfclub.co.uk

---

WRAG BARN Golf & Country Club
Shrivenham Road, Highworth, Swindon, Wiltshire SN6 7QQ
Telephone: 01793 861327 • Fax: 01793 861325
Professional Shop: 01793 766027

Challenging Par 72 of 6633 yards. Friendly and welcoming. Corporate, Conference and Society Days a speciality. Golf clinic, scoring analysis, full conference facilities on request.

"THE PERFECT GOLF SOCIETY VENUE" Traditional style clubhouse with the views, locker rooms and the Spike Bar open all day for food and drink. Our Banbury and Bellingham Suite facilities offer an unrivalled combination of superb food and the perfect setting adaptable for any style of event. Our location is perfect. The Thames Valley is just 6 miles north of Swindon and only ten minutes from Junction 15 of the M4.

Set in the Vale of the White Horse, the views of the Wiltshire Countryside around the course are truly superb. For a successful and memorable occasion plan your next golf day at Wrag Barn Golf Club.

See also Colour Advertisement on page 20

SALISBURY. **Hamptworth Golf and Country Club,** Hamptworth Road, Hamptworth, Near Landford SP5 2DU (01794 390155; Fax: 01794 390022). *Location:* off A36 Salisbury to Southampton Road, turning off B3079. Parkland, wooded course with river running through. 18 holes, 6516 yards, 5957 metres. S.S.S. 71. Driving range, open to the public. *Green Fees:* information not available. *Eating facilities:* new clubhouse with full catering and bar. *Visitors:* welcome, must have tee reservation and Handicap Certificate. Buggies. *Society Meetings:* welcome. Professional: M. White.*

SALISBURY. **High Post Golf Club Ltd,** Great Durnford, Salisbury SP4 6AT (01722 782356; Fax: 01722 782674). *Location:* midway between Salisbury and Amesbury on A345. Downland and blackthorn. 18 holes, 6305 yards. S.S.S. 70. Large practice ground. *Green Fees:* £32.00 per round, £40.00 per day midweek; £42.00 per round, £50.00 per day weekends. *Eating facilities:* full catering and bars available. *Visitors:* welcome weekdays no restrictions, weekends and Bank Holidays require Handicap Certificate. *Society Meetings:* catered for weekdays only. Professional: Tony Isaacs (01722 782219). Manager: Peter Hickling (01722 782356).

SALISBURY. **Rushmore Golf Club,** Tollard Royal, Salisbury SP5 5QB (01725 516326). *Location:* off the B3081 between Tollard Royal and Sixpenny Handley. Parkland and wooded course. 18 holes, 6131 yards. S.S.S. 70. Covered driving range and large practice area. *Green Fees:* from £22.50. *Eating facilities:* Spike Bar plus restaurant, home cooked food seven days a week. *Visitors:* welcome any time. *Society Meetings:* welcome by prior arrangement. Professional: Sean McDonagh.

SALISBURY. **Salisbury and South Wilts Golf Club,** Netherhampton, Salisbury SP2 8PR (01722 742131). *Location:* on A3094, two miles from Salisbury, Wilton, opposite Netherhampton village. Parkland. 27 holes, 6528 yards. S.S.S. 71. Practice ground; 3-hole academy course. *Green Fees:* weekdays £26.00 per round, weekends and Bank Holidays £40.00 per round. *Eating facilities:* full catering service and bar. *Visitors:* welcome without reservation at all times, but preliminary phone call advised. *Society Meetings:* catered for by prior arrangement. Professional: Geraldine Teschner (Tel & Fax: 01722 742929). General Manager: Pat Clash (01722 742645; Fax: 01722 742676).
e-mail: mail@salisburygolf.co.uk
website: www.sswgc.com

SHRIVENHAM. **Shrivenham Park Golf Club,** Penny Hooks Lane, Near Swindon SN6 8EX (01793 783853/4). *Location:* M4 Exit 15. Follow signs to Shrivenham, go through village, golf club on left. A delightful parkland course in excellent condition. 18 holes, 5713 yards. S.S.S 69. Practice area. *Green Fees:* Monday to Thursday £16.00, Friday to Sunday £21.00. *Eating facilities:* restaurant and bar open seven days a week, families welcome. *Visitors:* open to all, Handicaps not required. *Society Meetings:* packages available. Professional: Richard Jefferies. Director of Golf: Stuart Ash (01793 783853).

SWINDON. **Broome Manor Golf Complex,** Pipers Way, Swindon SN3 1RG (01793 495761; Fax: 01793 433255 (Manager)). *Location:* two miles from Junction 15, M4 (follow signs to Swindon Town Centre then follow signs for "Golf Complex"). Wooded parkland. Two courses, 18 holes, 6283 yards, Par 71, S.S.S. 70. 9 holes, 5380 yards, Par 66, S.S.S. 66. 32 bay floodlit covered driving range. *Green Fees:* £12.00 for 9 holes, £25.00 for 18 holes, subject to review. *Eating facilities:* spike bar, conference facilities, restaurant. *Visitors:* welcome, no restrictions, booking essential for 18 hole course. *Society Meetings:* catered for weekdays Professional: Barry Sandry (01793 491911; Fax 01793 433255). Manager: Dave Buckingham (01793 495761; Fax: 01793 433255).

SWINDON. **Ogbourne Downs Golf Club,** Ogbourne St. George, Marlborough SN8 1TB (01672 841287). *Location:* A346, four miles south of Junction 15 (M4), three miles north of Marlborough. Downland course with extensive views. 18 holes, 6363 yards. S.S.S. 70. Practice area, baskets of practice balls for hire. *Green Fees:* weekdays £25.00; weekends £35.00. *Eating facilities:* full catering and bar service. *Visitors:* welcome weekdays, phone Professional at weekends for starting times. Buggy hire. *Society Meetings:* welcome, packages available. Professional: Andrew Kirk (01672 841287). Office: (01672 841327).

SWINDON. **The Wiltshire Golf and Country Club,** Wootton Bassett, Swindon SN4 7PB (01793 849999). *Location:* through Wootton Bassett, head for Calne A3102, one mile on left hand side out of town. Parkland course with water features designed by Peter Alliss and Clive Clark. 18 holes, 6519 yards. S.S.S. 72. Practice area, putting green. Covered driving range. 9 hole course opening late 2006, 3300 yards. *Green Fees:* £28.00 per round weekdays, £40.00 per round weekends. *Eating facilities:* bars and restaurant. *Visitors:* welcome, booking advised. Club, buggy and trolley hire. Indoor pool with spa, sauna and steam room. Hotel with 58 en suite bedrooms. *Society Meetings:* conference and residential packages available. Professional: Richard Lawless.
e-mail: theclub@the-wiltshire.co.uk
website: www.the-wiltshire.co.uk

TIDWORTH. **Tidworth Garrison Golf Club,** Bulford Road, Tidworth SP9 7AF (Tel & Fax: 01980 842301). *Location:* A338 Salisbury to Marlborough Road, golf course off Bulford Road. Undulating downland course. 18 holes, 6320 yards. S.S.S. 70. Practice driving area, chipping and putting greens. *Green Fees:* £34.00 per round/day, reductions when playing with member. *Eating facilities:* full bar and catering facilities except for Mondays (sandwiches only). *Visitors:* welcome at all times, except Friday mornings and normally after 2pm at weekends and Bank Holidays. *Society Meetings:* catered for Tuesdays and Thursdays. Professional: Terry Gosden (Tel & Fax: 01980 842393).
e-mail: tidworth@garrison-golfclub.fsnet.co.uk
website: www.tidworthgolfclub.co.uk

TROWBRIDGE. **Bradford-on-Avon Golf Course Ltd,** Avon Close, Trowbridge Road, Bradford-on-Avon, Trowbridge BA15 1JJ (Tel & Fax: 01225 752180). *Location*: M4, exit at Bath then take road to Bradford-on-Avon into centre, turn right on Trowbridge Road for half a mile, signpost for golf course on left. Parkland river bank course, mature trees, lakes. 9 holes Pay & Play course. *Green Fees*: information not available. *Visitors*: welcome. *Society Meetings*: welcome, please telephone for arrangements. Professional/Secretary: Richard Hussey (Tel & Fax: 01225 752180).*

UPAVON. **Upavon Golf Club,** Douglas Avenue, Upavon SN9 6BQ (01980 630787; Fax: 01980 635419). *Location*: off A342 Upavon to Andover Road, one-and-a-half miles out of Upavon. Undulating chalk downland course. 18 holes, 6402 yards. S.S.S. 71. Two practice areas. *Green Fees*: weekdays £26.00 per day, £80.00 four ball; weekends £36.00 per round, reductions when playing with a member. *Eating facilities:* bar and catering every day (restricted hours in winter). *Visitors:* visitors and societies welcome at Wiltshire's friendliest club. All County Cards and 2-fore-1 accepted. Daily course information line: 08712 300 800. Professional: Richard Blake (01980 630281). Secretary: Les Mitchell (01980 630787; Fax: 01980 635419). e-mail: play@upavongolfclub.co.uk
website: www.upavongolfclub.co.uk

WARMINSTER. **West Wilts Golf Club,** Elm Hill, Warminster BA12 0AU (Office: 01985 213133; Fax: 01985 219809; Bar: 01985 212702). *Location:* one mile off the A350 north of Warminster sign posted to the town centre. Established 1891. Chalk downland course 200 metres above sea level, designed by J.H. Taylor. 18 holes, 5754 yards. S.S.S. 68. Practice ground, and indoor net available. *Green Fees:* weekdays £25.00 per round, £30.00 per day; weekends £30.00 per round, £40.00 per day. *Eating facilities:* full catering. *Visitors:* welcome, except Saturdays, must produce a Handicap Certificate. *Society Meetings:* Wednesdays only, package details on request. Professional: Rob Morris (Tel & Fax: 01985 212110). Secretary: Geoff Morgan. House Manager: Sandra Frankle (01985 212702). e-mail: westwiltsgolf@btconnect.com
website: www.westwiltsgolfclub.co.uk

WESTBURY near. **Thoulstone Park Golf Club,** Chapmanslade, Near Westbury BA13 4AQ (01373 832825; Fax: 01373 832821). *Location:* A36 between Warminster and Westbury. Parkland course with trees and two lakes. 18 holes, 6300 yards. S.S.S. 70. Driving range, practice putting green. *Green Fees:* information not available. *Eating facilities:* Spikes Bar, function rooms. *Visitors:* welcome weekdays, weekends after 11.30am. *Society Meetings:* welcome weekdays, very attractive packages available. Professional: Tony Isaac (01373 832808; Fax: 01373 832821). Secretary: Mrs Jean Pearce.*

High Post Golf Club

Peter Allis rates High Post so highly he once said he would include the par 4 ninth hole on his 'Dream 18'. In the 1997 Golf Monthly described the course as a 'hidden gem'.

High Post has hosted the South West Amateur Championship in 1998, the prestigious Carris Trophy in 1999, the Wiltshire County Championship on countless occasions and more recently, the Girls' British Open Amateur Championship.

If further proof were needed of High Post's pedigree, how about some of the past winners/participants of the High Post Open, including Andrew Sherbourne, David Howell, Zane Scotland and Justin Rose, all of whom are now established stars in the world of professional golf.

High Post's great strength is its all year round playability. The free-draining chalk downland enables golfers to enjoy summer greens and tees even in the depth of winter.

High Post, Salisbury, Wiltshire SP4 6AT Tel: 01722 782219 • Fax: 01722 782674
e-mail: secretary@highpostgolfclub.co.uk • website: www.highpostgolfclub.co.uk

---

West Wilts Golf Club Elm Hill, Warminster BA12 0AU • www.westwiltsgolfclub.co.uk

A chalk, downland course 200 metres above sea level. 18 holes, 5754 yards. S.S.S. 68. Facilities include a practice ground and a full catering service. Visitors are welcome except on Saturdays and must have a Handicap Certificate. Societies are catered for on Wednesdays to Fridays only, package details available on request.
Professional: Rob Morris • Secretary: Geoff Morgan • House Manager: Sandra Frankle

Tel: 01985 213133
Fax: 01985 219809

---

www.uk-golfguide.com

Worcestershire

BEWDLEY. **Little Lakes Golf Club,** Lye Head, Bewdley, Worcester DY12 2UZ (01299 266385; Fax: 01299 266398). *Location:* take Lye Head turn - off A456, three miles west of Bewdley. Parkland course with superb views, wonderful walks, undulating. 18 holes, 6298 yards. S.S.S. 70. Practice ground. *Green Fees:* weekdays £19.00; weekends £24.00. *Eating facilities:* bars, restaurant, cafe. *Visitors:* welcome most days by prior arrangement. Buggies available £18 per round. *Society Meetings:* welcome by prior arrangement. All-day package £37.50 includes breakfast, lunch, three-course carvery plus two rounds of golf. Professional: Mark Laing. Secretary: Mrs J. Dean (01562 741704).

BEWDLEY. **Wharton Park Golf Club,** Longbank, Bewdley DY12 2QW (01299 405222; Fax: 01299 405121). *Location:* A456 from Kidderminster, top of Bewdley by-pass. Championship course with woods and parkland. 18 holes, 6603 yards. S.S.S. 71, Par 72. Practice range. *Green Fees:* weekdays £30.00 for 18 holes, £40.00 per day; weekends £35.00 for 18 holes. *Eating facilities:* full facilities available including "Franco's" Restaurant open Wednesday, Thursday, Friday and Saturday evenings, plus Sunday lunchtimes. *Visitors:* welcome weekdays, after 2pm weekends. Functions/Conferences catered for. *Society Meetings:* welcome weekdays, limited at weekends. Ring for details. Professional: Angus Hoare (01299 405163). Secretary: (01299 405222).

BLACKWELL. **Blackwell Golf Club,** Blackwell, Near Bromsgrove B60 1PY (0121-445 1994). *Location:* approximately 10 miles south of Birmingham and three miles east of Bromsgrove. Parkland. 18 holes, 6230 yards. S.S.S. 71. *Green Fees:* weekdays only £60.00 per round, £70.00 per day. *Eating facilities:* bar snacks at all times, meals by arrangement. *Visitors:* welcome by arrangement. *Society Meetings:* catered for by arrangement through Secretary. Professional: Nigel Blake (0121-445 3113). Secretary: J.T. Mead (0121-445 1994; Fax: 0121-445 4911).
e-mail: info@blackwellgolfclub.com
website: www.blackwellgolfclub.com

BLAKEDOWN. **Churchill and Blakedown Golf Club,** Churchill Lane, Blakedown, Near Kidderminster DY10 3NB (01562 700018). *Location:* off A456 Birmingham/Kidderminster road at Blakedown. Undulating parkland, partially wooded course. 9 holes, 6488 yards. S.S.S. 71. *Green Fees:* £25.00, £10.00 with a member. *Eating facilities:* snacks and full meals except Monday. *Visitors:* welcome weekdays, weekends with member only. Handicap Certificate required. *Society Meetings:* weekdays only by arrangement through the Secretary. (Catering: 01562 700200). Secretary: P. Bailey (01562 700018).

BRANSFORD. **Bransford Golf Club,** Bank House Hotel, Golf and Country Club, Bransford, Worcester WR6 5JD (Tel & Fax: 01886 833545). *Location:* From Junction 7 M5 follow signs to Malvern, Ross then pick up signs to Hereford A4103, Hotel is approx. 2 miles on left of small traffic island. 'Florida' style golf course, flat, 14 lakes, island greens, dog legs, etc. 18 holes, 6204 yards. S.S.S. 71. 20 bay driving range and short game practice area. *Green Fees:* information not available. *Eating facilities:* hotel and clubhouse bars. *Visitors:* welcome, not before 9.30am. Smart golf attire. Accommodation in 70 bedroomed hotel, golf breaks available. *Society Meetings:* welcome, special packages available. Professional: Scott Fordyce (01886 833621). Golf Manager: Margaret Robert (Tel & Fax:01886 833545).*
e-mail: info@bransfordgolfclub.co.uk
website: www.bankhousehotel.co.uk

BROMSGROVE. **Bromsgrove Golf Centre,** Stratford Road, Bromsgrove B60 1LD (01527 575886; Course Reception 01527 570505; Conference and Restaurant 01527 579179). *Location:* easily located on the junction of the A38 and A448, one mile from Bromsgrove town centre. Just five minutes' drive from juctions 4 and 5 of the M5 and Junction 1 of the M42 (exit west bound only). Gently undulating parkland course, large contoured greens with superb views over Worcestershire. 18 holes, 5969 yards. S.S.S. 68. 35 bay floodlit driving range, large multilevel putting green. *Green Fees:* information not available. *Eating facilities:* friendly clubhouse with full bar and restaurant facilities available to non members. *Visitors:* most welcome. Tee times bookable up to seven days in advance. Golf shoes or similar, with socks, collared shirts, tailored trousers/shorts. Wide range of tuition available with resident PGA Professionals (Tuition Fees list available). New "Teaching Studio" complete with state of the art computerised video systems. *Society Meetings:* welcome by prior arrangement, packages available on request. Head Professional: Graeme Long. Assistant Professional: Danny Wall. Secretary: David Went.*
e-mail: enquiries@bromsgrovegolfcentre.com
website: www.bromsgrovegolfcentre.com

BROMYARD. **Sapey Golf Club,** Upper Sapey, Worcester WR6 6XT (01886 853288). *Location:* situated six miles north of Bromyard on B4203. Parkland course with water features, outstanding views over Malvern Hills. The Rowan: 18 holes, 5935 yards. S.S.S. 68. The Oaks: 9-holes, 1203 yards. Practice, putting green. *Green Fees:* The Rowan – weekdays £20.00; weekends £25.00. The Oaks – weekdays £5.00. weekends £6.00. *Eating facilities:* bar and restaurant meals available seven days a week. *Visitors:* always welcome. Buggies, power trolleys, trolleys for hire. Fully stocked Pro Shop with PGA tuition available for all, including Junior coaching under the Golf Foundation Scheme. *Society Meetings:* always welcome. Professional: Chris Knowles (01886 853288). Secretary: Lynn Stevenson (01886 853506; Fax: 01886 853485).
e-mail: anybody@sapeygolf.co.uk
website: www.sapeygolf.co.uk

www.uk-golfguide.com

ENGLAND / Worcestershire

DROITWICH. **Droitwich Golf and Country Club Ltd,** Westford House, Ford Lane, Droitwich WR9 0BQ. *Location:* between Junction 5 of M5 and Droitwich just off A38. Parkland, undulating, wooded. 18 holes, 5976 yards. S.S.S. 69. Practice area. *Green Fees:* information not available. *Eating facilities:* full catering and bar facilities available. *Visitors:* welcome without reservation Mondays to Fridays (Ladies Day Tuesday, tee closed to 12 noon), weekends with member only. *Society Meetings:* catered for Wednesdays or Fridays, £26.00 per player. Professional: Mr C.S. Thompson (01905 770207). Secretary: Mike Ashton (01905 774344; Fax: 01905 797290).*

DROITWICH near. **Ombersley Golf Club,** Bishops Wood Road, Lineholt, Ombersley, Near Droitwich WR9 0LE (01905 620747; Fax: 01905 620047). *Location:* from A449, two and a half miles north of Ombersley, take A4025 then first left. High, though gently undulating course enjoying panoramic views over Severn Valley. 18 holes, 6139 yards. S.S.S. 69. Covered driving range, chipping green and bunker, putting green. *Green Fees:* information not available. *Eating facilities:* bar facilities, snacks and meals available. *Visitors:* all visitors welcome, bookable seven days in advance. Eight buggies, cart rental available. *Society Meetings:* welcome by arrangement – we specialise in corporate golf. Professional/General Manager: Graham Glenister.*

DROITWICH SPA. **Gaudet Luce Golf Club,** Middle Lane, Hadzor, Droitwich Spa WR9 7JR (Tel: 01905 796375; Fax: 01905 797245). *Location:* Junction 5 or 6 off M5, Droitwich Spa, located just off Tagwell Road. Undulating parkland course with a mixture of long and short holes offering a demanding challenge for all golfers. 18 holes, 5887 yards. S.S.S. 69. Par 3, 9 hole Academy Course, 12 bay Driving Range. *Green Fees:* Monday - Thursday £20.00, Friday, Saturday & Sunday £25.00. *Eating facilities:* full clubhouse facilities including restaurant, lounge and bar. *Visitors:* welcome most days (essential to phone the Pro Shop before visit). Fully stocked Pro Shop with PGA tuition available for all, including Junior coaching under the Young Masters Golf. *Society Meetings:* welcome most weekdays by prior arrangement with Pro Shop. Professional: Russell Adams.
e-mail: info@gaudet-luce.co.uk
website: www.gaudet-luce.co.uk

EVESHAM. **Evesham Golf Club,** Craycombe Links, Fladbury Cross, Pershore WR10 2QS (01386 860395). *Location:* M5 at Junction 6, A4538 and A44 to Evesham approximately 10 miles then towards Worcester for about three miles. Meadowland, tree-lined fairways. 9 holes (18 tees), 6415 yards, 5866 metres. S.S.S. 71. Practice area. *Green Fees:* information not available. *Eating facilities:* diningroom and bar. *Visitors:* must be members of a recognised club and have a certified Handicap. Tuesday Ladies' Day, play is not possible in summer until after 3.15pm approx. *Society Meetings:* catered for by prior arrangement. Professional: Dan Cummins (01386 861144). Secretary: John Dale.*

HAGLEY. **Hagley Golf and Country Club,** Wassell Grove, Hagley DY9 9JW (01562 883701; Fax: 01562 887518). *Location:* A456 Birmingham to Kidderminster Road. Wooded undulating course with many testing holes. 18 holes, 6553 yards. S.S.S. 72. Practice ground. *Green Fees:* £29.00 per round, £34.00 per day weekdays; weekends with a member. *Eating facilities:* full à la carte restaurant and bars. *Visitors:* welcome to play Monday to Friday, weekends with a member only. Buggies available. *Society Meetings:* welcome weekdays by prior arrangement. Professional: Iain Clark (01562 883852). Secretary: Graham F. Yardley.

KIDDERMINSTER. **Habberley Golf Club,** Habberley, Kidderminster DY11 5RF. *Location:* north west side of Kidderminster. Hilly parkland course. 9 holes, 5401 yards. S.S.S. 68. *Green Fees:* weekdays £10.00 (winter), £15.00 (summer). *Eating facilities:* food and bar available. *Visitors:* welcome weekdays, without reservation; weekends with member only. *Society Meetings:* welcome, on application. Group rate £10.00 per person. Secretary: B. Blakeway (01562 745756).

KIDDERMINSTER. **Kidderminster Golf Club,** Russell Road, Kidderminster DY10 3HT (01562 822303; Fax: 01562 827866). *Location:* signposted off A449 Worcester–Wolverhampton Road. Wooded parkland course. 18 holes, 6422 yards. S.S.S. 71. Practice ground. *Green Fees:* £35.00 per round or day weekdays. *Eating facilities:* bar and restaurant available. *Visitors:* welcome weekdays only if bona fide member of another club, weekends if guest of member. Snooker room with bar. *Society Meetings:* Thursdays; small parties catered for other weekdays. Professional: (01562 740090). Secretary: Alan Biggs (01562 822303; Fax: 01562 827866).
e-mail: info@kiddigolf.com
website: www.kidderminstergolfclub.com

KIDDERMINSTER. **Wyre Forest Golf Club,** Zortech Avenue, Kidderminster DY11 7EX (01299 822682; Fax: 01299 879433). *Location:* from Kidderminster to Stourport-on-Severn on the A451. Flat inland links type course. Full practice facilities. 18 holes, 57901 yards. S.S.S. 68. *Green Fees:* weekdays £15.00, weekends £20.00. *Eating facilities:* clubhouse bar open until 9pm daily. *Visitors:* can book 6 days in advance. Must book at weekends. *Society Meetings:* catered for. Packages start from £18.50 including golf and two-course meal. Professional/General Manager: C. Botterill.
e-mail: c.botterill@wyreforestgolf.com

MALVERN WELLS. **The Worcestershire Golf Club,** Wood Farm, Malvern Wells WR14 4PP (01684 575992; Fax: 01684 893334). *Location:* two miles south of Great Malvern, near junction of A449 and B4209. Exceptionally scenic - Malvern Hills and Vale of Evesham. 18 holes, 6500 yards. S.S.S. 72. *Green Fees:* weekdays £36.00 per day; weekends £40.00 per day. *Eating facilities:* available. *Visitors:* visitors unaccompanied by a member must provide a current Handicap Certificate. Weekends after 10am. *Society Meetings:* catered for Mondays, Thursdays and Fridays only on application. Professional: R. Lewis (Tel & Fax: 01684 564428). Secretary/Manager: Mrs J.P. Howe (01684 575992; Fax: 01684 893334).
e-mail: secretary@theworcestershiregolfclub.co.uk

PERSHORE. **The Vale Golf Club,** Hill Furze Road, Bishampton, Near Pershore WR10 2LZ (01386 462781; Fax: 01386 462597). *Location:* off the A44 road, between Evesham and Pershore at Fladbury crossroads. Feature lakes and wooded surrounds. Two courses: The Lenches, 9 holes, 2628 to 2918 yards. S.S.S 66 to 68; The International Championship Course, 18 holes, 6663 to 7174 yards. S.S.S. 72/74. Driving range. *Green Fees:* information not available. *Eating facilities:* Vale restaurant, spike bar, Sir William Lyons Suite. *Visitors:* welcome. *Society Meetings:* corporate and society days welcome. Professional: Paul Edgcombe (01386 462520; Fax: 01386 462660). General Manager: Rob Griffiths.*
e-mail: vale-sales@crown-golf.co.uk

REDDITCH. **Pitcheroak Golf Course,** Plymouth Road, Redditch B97 4PB (01527 541043). Location: 500 yards from bus/train stations. Hilly parkland course very tricky, lots of trees and bunker. 9 holes (18 tees), 4561 yards. S.S.S. 62. Practice grounds, nets, putting green. *Green Fees:* information not available. *Eating facilities:* bar and cafeteria facilities open all day. *Visitors:* welcome any time, municipal course. Changing rooms (ladies and gents). *Society Meetings:* welcome. Professional: D. Stewart (01527 541054). Secretary: Ray Barnett (01386 743370). *

REDDITCH. **Redditch Golf Club,** Lower Grinsty, Green Lane, Callow Hill, Redditch B97 5PJ (01527 543079; Fax: 01527 547413). *Location:* three miles west of Redditch town centre, off Redditch to Bromsgrove road (A448), or Astwood Bank to Redditch (A441), take Windmill Drive, look for Callow Hill signs. First 9 holes parkland, second 9 holes wooded. White - 18 holes, 6671 yards. S.S.S. 72; Yellow - 18 holes, 6285 yards. S.S.S. 70. Two practice areas. *Green Fees:* 18 holes £35.00, 27 holes £40.00, 36 holes £45.00;£5.00pp discount for parties of 20+. Weekends £15.00 with member only. *Eating facilities:* restaurant and bar with bar snacks except Mondays. *Visitors:* welcome, weekends with member. *Society Meetings:* catered for by arrangement. Professional: David Down (01527 546372). Secretary: T.J. Sheldon (01527 543079; Fax 01527 547413).
website: www.redditchgolfclub.com

REDDITCH. **Redditch Kingfisher Golf Club,** Pitcheroak Golf Course, Plymouth Road, Redditch B97 4PB (01527 541043). *Location:* just up from the station. Hilly parkland course. 9 holes, 4561 yards. S.S.S. 62. Practice, nets, putting green. *Green Fees:* information not available. *Eating facilities:* full catering and bar facilities. *Visitors:* welcome at all times. Showers/changing rooms. *Society Meetings:* welcome at all times. Professional: Mr David Stewart (01527 541054). Secretary: Ray Barnett.*

TENBURY WELLS. **Cadmore Lodge Golf and Country Club,** Berrington Green, Tenbury Wells WR15 8TQ (01584 810044). *Location:* two miles south of Tenbury Wells, just off A4112 to Leominster. Parkland with lake and streams in constant play. *Green Fees:* information not available. *Eating facilities:* hotel bar and restaurant. *Visitors:* welcome, no restrictions. Hotel with AA Rosette restaurant and 14 en suite bedrooms. *Society Meetings:* welcome. Secretary: R.V. Farr (01584 810306 home).

WORCESTER. **Perdiswell Park Golf Club,** Bilford Road, Worcester WR3 8DX (01905 754668). *Location:* 600 yards from a A38, north of the city centre. A testing 18 hole parkland course with many natural features. *Green Fees:* information not available. *Eating facilities:* food available. *Visitors:* welcome at any time, but advised to phone first. *Society Meetings:* welcome. PGA Professional: Mark Woodward (01905 754668). Secretary: Richard Gardner (01905 452399; Fax: 01905 453133).

WORCESTER. **Ravenmeadow Golf Club,** Hindlip Lane, Claines, Worcester WR3 8SA (01905 757525; Fax: 01905 458876). *Location:* Junction 6 (M5 motorway) A449, leave at Blackpole exit; at main road turn right then first left into Hindlip Lane, entrance is half-mile on the left. Gently undulating course, with greens and tees to USGA standards; Barbourne Brook meanders through the course. 10 holes (18 tees). 5352 yards, S.S.S. 66. Excellent practice facilities: driving range, 9 hole pitch and putt, adults and children's practice greens, chipping green. *Green Fees:* weekdays 9 holes £9.00, 18 holes £13.00; weekends 9 holes £11.00, 18 holes £16.00. Monday - Over 50s 9 holes £5.00, 18 holes £7.00. Wednesday Ladies' Day 9 holes £5.00, 18 holes £7.00. *Eating facilities:* Bar open 7 days, food available from 11am. *Visitors*: always welcome, telephone to reserve tee times. *Society Meetings*: welcome every day. Telephone (01905 458876) for special rates. Professional: Mark Slater (PGA) (01905 756665). Manager: Tony Senter (01905 458876; Fax: 01905 458876).

WORCESTER. **Tolladine Golf Club,** The Fairway, Tolladine Road, Worcester WR4 9BA (01905 21074). *Location*: M5, Exit 6. Warndon turn-off, one mile. Tolladine Road, opposite Virgin Tavern. Hilly course. 9 holes, 5630 yards (for 18 holes). S.S.S. 67. *Green Fees:* information not available. *Eating facilities:* bar (limited opening). *Visitors:* welcome. *Society Meetings*: welcome. Secretary: Mr D. Turner (01905 354039).*

WORCESTER. **Worcester Golf and Country Club,** Boughton Park, Worcester WR2 4EZ (01905 422555). *Location*: one-and-a-quarter miles west of city on A4103 (to Hereford). Parkland with lakes and specimen trees. 18 holes, 6251 yards. S.S.S. 70. Practice areas. *Green Fees:* information not available. *Eating facilities:* full catering available. *Visitors:* welcome weekdays, telephone Professional. Handicap Certificate required. *Society Meetings:* welcome, telephone Secretary. Professional: Colin Colenso (01905 422044). Secretary: Mr P. Tredwell (01905 422555).*

For full details of clubs and courses, plus convenient accommodation

www.uk-golfguide.com

East Yorkshire

BEVERLEY. **Beverley and East Riding Golf Club,** Westwood, Beverley HU17 8RG (01482 867190). *Location:* one mile west of Beverley on Walkington Road. Common pastureland, undulating course with 18 distinctively different holes. 18 holes, 6127 yards. S.S.S. 69. *Green Fees:* £17.00 weekdays, £24.00 weekends and Bank Holidays. *Eating facilities:* bar snacks available 11.30am until 2pm, evening meals by arrangement. *Visitors:* welcome any time. Cart and club hire. *Society Meetings:* welcome weekdays by prior arrangement. Professional: Alex Ashby (01482 869519). Secretary: Mike Drew (Tel & Fax: 01482 868757).

BEVERLEY. **Cherry Burton Golf Club,** Leconfield Lane, Cherry Burton, Beverley HU17 7RB (Tel & Fax: 01964 550924). *Location*: off the B1248 3 miles north of Beverley. Parkland course with lakes. 9 holes, 6480 yards, S.S.S 72. Driving range, putting green. *Green Fees*: information not available. *Eating facilities*: licensed bar, snacks, sandwiches. *Visitors*: welcome. Pro shop, tuition, golf academy. *Society Meetings*: welcome, please telephone. Professional: John Gray (01964 550924; Fax: 01964 550924). Secretary: James Walmsley (Tel & Fax: 01964 550924).
website: www.cherryburtongolfclub.co.uk

BRIDLINGTON. **Bridlington Golf Club,** Belvedere Road, Bridlington YO15 3NA (01262 606367). *Location:* A165 main Hull to Bridlington Road. Flat parkland course with sea views, excellent greens with ponds, ditches, bunkers and trees. 18 holes, 6638 yards. S.S.S. 72. Practice area. *Green Fees:* weekdays £24.00 per round, £30.00 per day; weekends and Bank Holidays £36.00 per round or day. Subject to review. Parties over 12 in number 10% discount per player. *Eating facilities:* food available, bar meals and full menu/usual bar hours. *Visitors:* welcome most days but limited on Wednesdays/ Sundays. Advisable to book in advance. *Society Meetings:* catered for. Professional: A.R.A. Howarth (01262 674721). Secretary: C.B. Rhodes (01262 606367).
e-mail: enquiries@bridlingtongolfclub.co.uk
website: www.bridlingtongolfclub.co.uk

BRIDLINGTON. **The Bridlington Links,** Flamborough Road, Marton, Bridlington YO15 1DW (01262 401584; Fax: 01262 401702). *Location:* on the B1255 between Bridlington and Flamborough. Links course on clifftop with spectacular views over Bridlington Bay. 18 holes, 6719 yards. S.S.S. 72. 9-hole course (seven par 3s and two par 4s). Driving range and Golf Academy. Golf schools weekly during Summer. *Green Fees:* information not available. *Eating facilities:* bar, function suite, and restaurant. *Visitors:* welcome at all times, no restrictions. *Society Meetings:* very welcome anytime, society packages available. Professional: Steve Raybould.*
website: www.bridlington-links.co.uk

BRIDLINGTON. **Flamborough Head Golf Club,** Lighthouse Road, Flamborough, Bridlington YO15 1AR (01262 850333; Fax: 01262 850417). *Location:* situated five miles north-east of Bridlington on the Flamborough headland. Links type course. 18 holes, 6189 yards. S.S.S. 69, Par 71. *Green Fees:* £23.00 per day weekdays, £30.00 per day weekends and Bank Holidays. *Eating facilities:* available; seafood a speciality in season. *Visitors:* welcome, limited Sunday and Wednesday mornings. *Society Meetings:* catered for, apply to Secretary at the above address.

BROUGH. **Brough Golf Club,** Cave Road, Brough HU15 1HB (01482 667291; Fax: 01482 669873). *Location:* 10 miles west of Hull off A63. Parkland. 18 holes, 6075 yards. S.S.S. 69 (white tees). Practice facilities. *Green Fees:* on application. *Eating facilities:* full restaurant and bar snack menu available on request. *Visitors:* welcome Mondays, Tuesdays, Thursdays and Fridays after 9.30am. *Society Meetings:* on application. Director of Golf: G. Townhill (01482 667291).
e-mail: gt@brough-golfclub.co.uk
website: www.brough-golfclub.co.uk

BROUGH. **Cave Castle Golf Club,** South Cave, Brough HU15 2EU (01430 421286; Fax: 01430 421118). *Location:* minutes from M62/A63. Undulating parkland course in 150 acres. 18 holes, 6524 yards. S.S.S. 72. *Green Fees:* £18.00 per round, £25.00 per day weekdays; £25.00 per round, £30.00 per day weekends. *Eating facilities:* licensed clubhouse. *Visitors:* welcome anytime weekdays, after 11am weekends. Must have valid Handicap Certificate. Idyllic setting, superb hotel with 70 en suite bedrooms, restaurant, lounge bar, leisure complex. Golf break packages include unlimited golf, bed, breakfast, lunch and evening meal plus use of leisure complex. *Society Meetings:* Golf society packages also available. Professional: Stephen MacKinder (01430 421286). Golf administrator: Jane Simpson (01430 421286).

CONISTON. **Ganstead Park Golf Club,** Longdales Lane, Coniston, Near Hull HU11 4LB (Tel & Fax: 01482 817754). *Location:* A165 to Bridlington, five miles from Hull City Centre. Easy walking parkland course with lakes. 18 holes, 6801 yards. S.S.S. 71 yellow, 73 white, 73 red. Nets, chipping area, putting green. *Green Fees:* weekdays £20.00 per round, £26.00 per day; weekends £28.00. With member £12.00 weekdays, £13.00 weekends. Special rates for parties. *Eating facilities:* full facilities. *Visitors:* welcome, restrictions Wednesday and Sunday mornings. *Society Meetings:* welcome; apply to Secretary or Professional. Professional: Mike Smee (01482 811121). Secretary: Geoff Drewery (Tel & Fax: 01482 817754).
e-mail: secretary@gansteadpark.co.uk
website: www.gansteadpark.co.uk

East Yorkshire / ENGLAND

COTTINGHAM. Hessle Golf Club, Westfield Road, Raywell, Cottingham HU16 5YL (01482 659187). *Location:* three miles south west of Cottingham. Parkland. 18 holes, 6291 yards, S.S.S. 70. Two practice areas. *Green Fees:* information not available. *Eating facilities:* snack lunches Tuesday to Sunday, set lunches by arrangement. *Visitors:* mid-week unrestricted except Tuesdays 9am - 1pm. Weekend visitors may play after 11.30am at Professional's discretion. *Society Meetings:* catered for weekdays only by arrangement. Professional: G. Fieldsend (01482 650190). Secretary: Derrick Pettit (01482 650171; Fax: 01482 652679).*

DRIFFIELD. Driffield Golf Club, Sunderlandwick, Beverley Road, Driffield YO25 9AD (01377 253116; Fax: 01377 240599). *Location:* from Driffield A164 to Beverley 300 yards from main roundabout on right. Mature parkland course within the attractive Sunderlandwick Estate. 18 holes, 6215 yards. S.S.S. 70. Two practice areas, practice green and two practice putting greens. *Green Fees:* Summer (1st April to 31st October): weekdays £26.00 per round, £35.00 per day; weekends £35.00 per round, £45.00 per day. Winter: weekdays £15.00 per round, £20.00 per day; weekends £20.00 per round, £25.00 per day. *Eating facilities:* full catering and bar service. *Visitors:* welcome by arrangement with Secretary. Limit of 24 players weekends and Bank Holidays. 18 holes only tee 10/11am. *Society Meetings:* welcome by prior arrangement. Professional: Kenton Wright (01377 241224). Secretary: John R. Nicholson.

HORNSEA. Hainsworth Park Golf Club, Brandesburton, Near Driffield YO25 8RT (01964 542362). *Location:* eight miles north east of Beverley, just off A165 road to Bridlington, at the Brandesburton roundabout. Easy going, well drained parkland course with mature trees. 18 holes, 6362 yards. S.S.S. 71, Par 71. Practice area. *Green Fees:* weekdays £20.00 - £24.00; weekends £24.00 - £29.00, subject to confirmation. *Eating facilities:* bar and full catering. *Visitors:* welcome anytime, please phone. Hotel accommodation. *Society Meetings:* welcome. Professional: P. Binnington (Tel & Fax: 01964 542362). Secretary: R. Hounsfield (Tel & Fax: 01964 542362).

HORNSEA. Hornsea Golf Club, Rolston Road, Hornsea HU18 1XG (Tel & Fax: 01964 532020). *Location:* follow signs for Hornsea Freeport – Golf Course 200 yards past Freeport. Flat parkland. 18 holes, 6661 yards. S.S.S. 72. Practice area. *Green Fees*: information not available. *Eating facilities:* available every day. *Visitors:* welcome, please ring Professional for a time. Ladies' Day Tuesdays. Snooker room. *Society Meetings*: welcome by prior arrangement with the Secretary. Professional: S. Wright (01964 534989). Secretary: Mr David Crossley (Tel & Fax: 01964 532020).*

HOWDEN. Boothferry Golf Club, Spaldington Lane, Howden, Near Goole DN14 7NG (01430 430364). *Location:* two and a half miles from Junction 37 of the M62 on the B1228 road between Howden and Bubwith. Flat meadowland, with natural dykes and ponds. 18 holes, 6651 yards. S.S.S. 72. Large practice area. *Green Fees:* information not available. *Eating facilities:* restaurant and bar facilities available. *Visitors:* welcome at all times. No jeans, trainers or collarless shirts. *Society Meetings:* all Golf Societies and individual parties welcome with prior booking through the Professional. Professional: James Major (01430 430364; Fax: 01430 430567).*

HULL. Cottingham Parks Golf & Country Club, Woodhill Way, Cottingham HU16 5RZ (01482 846030; Fax: 01482 845932). *Location:* from the Humber Bridge to Beverley road, take the B1233 turnoff at the Skidby roundabout to Cottingham Golf Club turnoff. Mature parkland with several water hazards. 18 holes, 6459 yards. S.S.S. 71. Two tier driving range. *Green Fees:* information not available. *Eating facilities:* bar snacks and full dining room menu available. *Visitors:* welcome. *Society Meetings:* welcome with restrictions at weekends. Special packages available. Conference and social functions catered for; full leisure facilities including gym, 20 metre pool, steam room and jacuzzi. Professional: Chris Gray (01482 842394). Administrative Office: 01482 846030; Fax: 01482 845932.*

HULL. Hull Golf Club (1921) Ltd, The Hall, 27 Packman Lane, Kirk Ella, Hull HU10 7TJ. *Location:* five miles west of Hull. Parkland and wooded. 18 holes, 6242 yards. S.S.S. 70. *Green Fees:* information not available. *Eating facilities:* available. *Visitors:* welcome weekdays except Wednesday. *Society Meetings:* by prior arrangement. Professional: David Jagger (01482 653074). Office Manager: Mrs C. Toffolo (Tel & Fax: 01482 658919).*

HULL. Springhead Park Golf Club, Willerby Road, Hull HU5 5JE (01482 614968 - Ticket Office). *Location:* off the M62/M18 onto the A63. Parkland surrounded by many trees, some undulating fairways, three ponds and many ditches around course. 18 holes, 6102 yards, 5680 metres. S.S.S. 71. Two practice areas. *Green Fees:* information not available. *Eating facilities:* mobile sandwich bar on course, restaurant meals for club members and societies. *Visitors:* welcome by booking only, some restrictions. Tuition and club hire available. *Society Meetings:* welcome. Secretary: Mrs J. Garforth (01482 656958 - Home, or phone clubhouse number 01482 656309). *

Please mention **THE GOLF GUIDE** when you enquire about clubs or accommodation

---

For full details of clubs and courses, plus convenient accommodation
www.uk-golfguide.com

ENGLAND / East Yorkshire

HULL. **Sutton Park Golf Club,** Saltshouse Road, Hull HU8 9HF (01482 374242). *Location:* A63, north ring road, Sutton Road, Leads Road, Robson Way. Flat parkland course. 18 holes, 6251 yards. S.S.S. 70. Practice area and nearby driving range. *Green Fees:* information not available. *Eating facilities:* restaurant/bar. *Visitors:* welcome, no restrictions. *Society Meetings:* welcome, bookings via Secretary. Professional: To be appointed. Secretary: Philip Webster (Tel & Fax: 01482 701428).

KILNWICK PERCY. **Kilnwick Percy Golf Club,** Kilnwick Percy, Pocklington YO42 1UF (01759 303090). *Location:* one mile east of Pocklington off B1246. Scenic, undulating parkland course on the edge of the wolds above Pocklington. 18 individually designed holes, 6218 yards. S.S.S. 70. *Green Fees:* weekdays £18.00 per round, £25.00 per day; weekends and Bank Holidays £20.00 per round, £28.00 per day. *Eating facilities:* bar snacks available all day; evening meals by prior arrangement for 10 or more golfers. *Visitors:* welcome. Buggy, trolley and club hire; professional tuition available. Accommodation locally at discounted rates for golf club visitors. *Society Meetings*: special packages, tailored to your requirements. Manager: Mr Jonathan Dixon (01759 303090).

WITHERNSEA. **Withernsea Golf Club,** Chestnut Avenue, Withernsea HU19 2PG (01964 612078 or 612258). *Location:* 25 miles north-east of Hull on main road into Withernsea (signposted). Flat course. 9 holes, 6207 yards. S.S.S. 70. *Green Fees:* information not available. *Eating facilities:* bar and meals available (except Monday). *Visitors:* welcome weekdays, weekends after 1.00pm Sunday. *Society Meetings:* by arrangement. Special rates available. Administrator: John Boasman (01964 612078)*

For full details of clubs and courses, plus convenient accommodation
www.uk-golfguide.com

HAINSWORTH PARK GOLF CLUB

18-hole parkland course located 6 miles east of Beverley
just off A165 to Bridlington.

Weekdays £20-£24 • Weekends/Bank Holidays £24-£29

Catering available. Societies welcome by arrangement.
Accommodation at Burton Lodge Hotel on the course.

For *Golf* Telephone: 01964 542362

Hotel Telephone 01964 542847; Fax: 01964 544771

Burton Lodge Hotel, Brandesburton, Driffield, East Yorkshire YO25 8RT

AA ★★

See also Colour Advertisement on page 40

Hull Golf Club

Hull Golf Club is a picturesque parkland course, designed by James Braid over 100 years ago. It offers a good challenge to golfers of all abilities, followed by a well-stocked bar and excellent catering in the fine Grade II Listed clubhouse. A warm welcome is extended to societies and visitors. Contact the Professional to discuss your requirements.

Packman Lane, Kirk Ella, Hull HU10 7TJ
Tel: 01482 658919
www.hullgolfclub.com

North Yorkshire

ALDWARK. **Aldwark Manor Golf Club,** Aldwark, Alne, York YO61 1UF (01347 838353; Fax: 01347 833991). *Location:* in village of Aldwark, five miles south-east of Boroughbridge off A1 and 12 miles north-west of York off A19. Easy walking parkland with water hazards. 18 holes, 6187 yards. S.S.S. 70. Practice ground, putting green, practice bunker. *Green Fees:* weekdays £25.00 per round, £35.00 per day; weekends and Bank Holidays £30.00 per round, £40.00 per day. *Eating facilities:* two restaurants and two bars. *Visitors:* always welcome weekdays, restricted weekends. 60 bedroomed hotel on the course. *Society Meetings:* societies and corporate meetings always welcome, restricted weekends. Manager: Geoff Platt (01347 838353; Fax: 01347 833991).

BARNOLDSWICK. **Ghyll Golf Club,** Ghyll Brow, Barnoldswick, Colne, Lancs BB9 6JH (01282 842466). *Location:* M65 to Colne. A56 towards Skipton. 1 mile past Earby B6252 to Barnoldswick. Parkland course. 9 holes, 5706 yards, 5213 metres. S.S.S. 68. *Green Fees:* weekdays £15.00 per day (£10.00 with a member), weekends £20.00 per day (£15 with a member). *Eating facilities:* bar, evening only. *Visitors:* welcome except Sundays and some Saturdays. *Society Meetings:* catered for by arrangement. Secretary: John L. Gill (01524 412958).

BEDALE. **Bedale Golf Club,** Leyburn Road, Bedale DL8 1EZ. *Location*: from A1 take A684 at Leeming Bar to Bedale; club is situated 400 yards out of town on the Leyburn Road. Undulating parkland with tree-lined fairways and water hazards. 18 holes, 6610 yards. S.S.S. 72. Practice facilities, fully stocked golf shop, lessons available. *Green Fees*: £27.50 per round, £35.00 per day weekdays; £38.50 per round, £44.00 per day weekends. *Eating facilities*: bar and catering always available. *Visitors*: welcome weekdays and weekends. *Society Meetings*: catered for weekdays by prior arrangement, limited availability on some Saturday afternoons; tailor-made packages and discounts available. Professional: Tony Johnson (01677 422443). Secretary Mrs Glenys Brown (01677 422451; Fax: 01677 427143). e-mail: bedalegolfclub@aol.com website: www.bedalegolfclub.com

BENTHAM. **Bentham Golf Club,** Robin Lane, Bentham, Near Lancaster LA2 7AG (01524 262455). *Location:* B6480 north-east of Lancaster towards Settle. Parkland with magnificent views. 18 holes, 6075 yards. *Green Fees:* £26.00 weekdays; £30.00 weekends. *Eating facilities:* hot and cold snacks and meals available. *Visitors:* welcome all week. *Society Meetings:* welcome–contact Secretary. Secretary: John Mann (01524 262470).

BROTTON. **Hunley Hall Golf Club & Hotel,** Brotton, Saltburn TS12 2QQ (01287 676216); Fax: 01287 678250). *Location:* off A174 at St. Margarets Way in Brotton. Signposted through housing estate, approximately half-a-mile to club. Picturesque 27 hole coastal courses adjacent to Heritage Coast. Morgan's Course 18 holes, 6918 yards, 6320 metres, S.S.S. 73. Millennium Course, 18 holes, 6510 yards, S.S.S. 68. Floodlit driving range, large practice and chipping area. *Green Fees:* weekdays £25.00 per day, weekends and Bank Holidays £35.00 per day. Discounts for parties and guests staying at the hotel. *Eating facilities:* excellent facilities including two restaurants, lounge bar, spike bar, golfers' bar; quality food served daily 8am to 9.30pm. *Visitors:* always welcome. Two Star Hotel offering en suite rooms, etc. Club hire, buggy hire and tuition available. *Society Meetings:* welcome Monday to Saturday, packages available. Golfing Holidays and golf schools available. Professional: Andrew Brook (Tel & Fax: 01287 677444). Secretary: Liz Lillie (01287 676216; Fax: 01287 678250).
e-mail: enquiries@hunleyhall.co.uk
website: www.hunleyhall.co.uk

CATTERICK. **Catterick Golf Club,** Leyburn Road, Catterick Garrison, Catterick DL9 3QE (01748 833401). *Location:* six miles south-west Scotch Corner, A1 turn off to Catterick Garrison. Undulating parkland/moorland with spectacular views. 18 holes, 6329 yards, S.S.S. 71. Practice ground. *Green Fees:* information not available. *Eating facilities:* bar and restaurant. *Visitors:* welcome without reservation. *Society Meetings:* catered for by appointment only. Professional: Andy Marshall (01748 833671). Secretary: Grant McDonnell (Tel & Fax: 01748 833268).*

THE BUCK INN ETC/AA ★

Delightful Country Inn overlooking cricket green in quiet Wensleydale village. Relax in our comfortable en suite bedrooms, enjoy superb home cooked food and drink from our selection of five real ales. Six fine Courses - Bedale, Masham, Ripon, Catterick Richmond and Romanby - within 20 minutes' drive.

GOLFING BREAKS AVAILABLE

Thornton Watlass, Near Bedale,
Ripon, North Yorkshire HG4 4AH

Tel: (01677) 422461   Fax: (01677) 422447
website: www.SmoothHound.co.uk/hotels/buckinn.html

See also Colour Advertisement on page 41

ENGLAND / North Yorkshire

EASINGWOLD. Easingwold Golf Club, Stillington Road, Easingwold, York YO61 3ET (01347 821486; Fax: 01347 822474). *Location:* 12 miles north of York, course one mile along Stillington Road. Flat, wooded parkland established 1930. 18 holes, 6717 yards, 6142 metres, S.S.S. 73. Practice ground. *Green Fees:* weekdays £28.00 per round, £35.00 per day; weekends and Bank Holidays £35.00. £15.00 playing with a member, £15.00 1st November to 31st March. *Eating facilities:* available. *Visitors:* welcome weekdays only, prior booking essential, contact Secretary. *Society Meetings:* weekdays only, prior booking essential, contact Secretary. Professional: John Hughes (01347 821964). Secretary: D.B. Stockley (Tel & Fax: 01347 822474).
e-mail: brian@easingwold-golf-club.fsnet.co.uk
website: www.easingwold-golf-club.co.uk

FILEY. Filey Golf Club, The Clubhouse, West Avenue, Filey YO14 9BQ (01723 513293; Fax: 01723 514952). *Location:* one mile south of town centre. Links, parkland course. 18 holes, 6112 yards. S.S.S. 69. 9 holes, 1513 yards, Par 30. Two practice grounds. *Green Fees:* information not available. *Eating facilities:* full dining and bar facilities. *Visitors:* welcome, no restrictions. *Society Meetings:* welcome by arrangement with the Secretary. Professional: Gary Hutchinson (01723 513134). Secretary: Davina Willis (01723 513293; Fax: 01723 514952).*

HARROGATE. Crimple Valley Golf Club, Hookstone Wood Road, Harrogate HG2 8PN (01423 883485; Fax: 01423 881018). *Location:* one mile south from town centre. Turn off A61 at Nidd Vale Garage on to Hookstone Road, signposted to right. Gently sloping fairways in rural setting. 9 holes, 2500 yards. S.S.S. 33. *Green Fees:* weekdays 9 holes £7.00, 18 holes £11.00, £15.00 per day; weekends 9 holes £8.00, 18 holes £12.00. *Eating facilities:* licensed bar, lunches available except Sunday. *Visitors:* welcome at all times. *Society Meetings:* special rates available. Club Proprietor: Kate Johnson.

HARROGATE. Harrogate Golf Club Ltd, Forest Lane Head, Harrogate HG2 7TF (01423 863158). *Location:* two miles from Harrogate on the A59 Harrogate/Knaresborough Road. Parkland, wooded. 18 holes, 6241 yards, 5706 metres. S.S.S. 70. Large practice ground, covered net. *Green Fees:* weekdays £30.00 per round, £36.00 per day, weekends £40.00 per round/per day. *Eating facilities:* chef catering and bar menu, lounge and casual spike bars. *Visitors:* welcome subject to club events. Society Meetings: catered for weekdays except Tuesdays. Parties of 12 or more welcome. Professional: P. Johnson (01423 862547). Secretary: Mr Peter Banks (01423 862999). Caterer: (01423 860278).
e-mail: secretary@harrogate-gc.co.uk
website: www.harrogate-gc.co.uk

THE APPEARANCE OF AN ASTERISK (*) AT THE END OF A CLUB OR COURSE ENTRY INDICATES THAT UP-TO-DATE INFORMATION HAS NOT BEEN SUPPLIED

HARROGATE. Oakdale Golf Club, Oakdale Glen, Harrogate HG1 2LN (01423 502806). *Location:* five minutes from Harrogate town centre, off Ripon road into Kent Road, follow signs. Parkland, with featured stream. 18 holes, 6456 yards. S.S.S. 71. Practice ground. *Green Fees:* weekdays £38.00 per round, £45.00 per day; weekends £55.00 per round. *Eating facilities:* first class restaurant, bar. *Visitors:* welcome at all times, Tuesday Ladies' Day. *Society Meetings:* welcome weekdays by arrangement. Professional: Clive Dell (01423 560510). Secretary: (01423 567162; Fax: 01423 536030).

HARROGATE. Pannal Golf Club, Follifoot Road, Pannal, Harrogate HG3 1ES (01423 872628; Fax: 01423 870043). *Location*: two miles south of Harrogate A61 (Leeds Road). 18 holes, 6622 yards. S.S.S. 72. Large practice ground with driving range facility. *Green Fees*: weekdays £45.00 per round, £60.00 per day; weekends and Bank Holidays £60.00 per round. *Eating facilities*: lunch available daily, dinner by arrangement. *Visitors*: welcome Monday to Friday, enquiry advised. *Society Meetings*: catered for Monday, Tuesday (pm only), Wednesday, Thursday and Friday. Professional: Mr D. Padgett (01423 872620). Secretary: R.V. Braddon (01423 872628; Fax: 01423 870043).
e-mail: secretary@pannalgc.co.uk
website: www.pannalgc.co.uk

HARROGATE. Rudding Park Golf, Harrogate HG3 1JH (01423 872100; Fax: 01423 873011). *Location*: lies just off the A658 linking the A61 from Leeds to the A59 York Road. Parkland course designed to USGA specifications. 18 holes, 6883 yards, Par 72. 18 bay floodlit driving range with four Professionals. *Green Fees:* Winter (November 1st until March 31st: Mondays to Thursdays £17.50, Fridays to Sundays £21.50. Summer (April 1st until October 31st): Mondays to Thursdays £30.00, Fridays to Sundays £36.00. *Eating facilities*: clubhouse bar open all day, every day; spike bar. *Visitors*: welcome at all times, must have a Handicap Certificate. Shop and buggies available all year round, with all-year-weather buggy tracks; caddies on request. Hotel on site with 4 Red Stars and AA 2 Rosette restaurant. *Society Meetings*: society and corporate days welcome. Professional: Mark Moore (01423 873400).
e-mail: golf.admin@ruddingpark.com
website: www.ruddingpark.com

KIRKBYMOORSIDE. Kirkbymoorside Golf Club, Manor Vale, Kirkbymoorside, York YO62 6EG (01751 431525). *Location*. on A170 through Kirkbymoorside. Undulating parkland. 18 holes, 6207 yards, 5676 metres. S.S.S. 69. Practice area, putting green. *Green Fees:* weekdays £22.00 per round, £28.00 per day; weekends and Bank Holidays £32.00 . Reduced fees in winter. *Eating facilities:* available every day. *Visitors:* welcome after 9am, not during weekend Medal competitions. *Society Meetings:* catered for by arrangement with Rose Rivis, Club Administrator. Professional: J. Hinchliffe (01751 430402). Secretary: R.J. Butler (Fax: 01751 433190).

KNARESBOROUGH. **Knaresborough Golf Club,** Boroughbridge Road, Knaresborough HG5 0QQ (01423 863219). *Location:* one-and-a-half miles from town centre, direction A1 Boroughbridge. Wooded parkland. 18 holes, 6354 yards. S.S.S.70. Large practice area. *Green Fees:* 2006 under review. Please contact Secretary for further details. *Eating facilities:* full catering. *Visitors:* welcome but not before 9.30am weekdays and 2pm weekends and Bank Holidays. *Society Meetings:* welcome by prior arrangement. Professional: Gary J. Vickers (01423 864865). Secretary: C. Hill. (01423 862690).

MALTON. **Malton and Norton Golf Club,** Welham Park, Malton YO17 9QE (01653 692959). *Location:* off A64 to Malton between York and Scarborough. One mile south on Welham road turn right at Norton level crossing. 27 holes - Longest 18: 6456 yards. S.S.S. 71. Medal Course: 6141 yards. S.S.S. 69 (Club). Practice ground. *Green Fees:* weekdays £27.00; weekends and Bank Holidays £32.00. *Eating facilities:* full bar and catering available. *Visitors:* welcome without reservation except club match days, and saturdays unless with member. *Society Meetings:* catered for by arrangement with Secretary. Professional: S. Robinson (01653 693882). Secretary: E. Harrison (01653 697912).
e-mail: maltonandnorton@btconnect.com

MIDDLESBROUGH. **Middlesbrough Golf Club,** Brass Castle Lane, Marton, Middlesbrough TS8 9EE (01642 311515; Fax: 01642 319607). *Location:* five miles south of Middlesbrough west of the A172. Parkland course. 18 holes, 6255 yards. S.S.S./Par 70. Practice facilities available. *Green Fees:* weekdays £17.00/£37.00 per day; weekends £22.00/£42.00 per day. *Eating facilities:* lunches, teas and dinners. *Visitors:* welcome when tee not booked. Venue of the North of England Open Amateur Youth Golf Championship. Conference facilities. *Society Meetings:* welcome Mondays, Wednesdays, Thursdays and Fridays. Professional: Don Jones (01642 311766). Secretary: P. M. Jackson (01642 311515).

NORTHALLERTON. **Romanby Golf Course,** Yafforth Road, Northallerton DL7 0PE. *Location:* west of Northallerton on the B6271 Richmond Road. Parkland course with formidable "Great Lake Complex" on the 2nd, 11th and 12th. 18 holes, 6663 yards. 12 bay floodlit driving range. *Green Fees:* on application. *Visitors:* always welcome, best to telephone for tee times. *Society Meetings:* golf parties a speciality. Bookings telephone (01609 778855; Fax: 01609 779084).
e-mail: mark@romanby.com
website: www.romanbygolf.com

REDCAR. **Cleveland Golf Club,** Majuba Road, Redcar TS10 5BJ. *Location:* on entering town via A1042 or A1085 follow signs to Esplanade, course runs adjacent to beach on north side of town. Flat seaside links course, easy walking. Championship course: 18 holes, 6696 yards. S.S.S. 72. Oldest golf course in Yorkshire, founded 1887. *Green Fees:* information not available. *Eating facilities:* full catering at all times. *Visitors:* welcome anytime subject to availability. *Society Meetings:* welcome by prior arrangement, special rates available. Professional: Craig Donaldson (01642 483462). Secretary: J.A. Moran (Tel & Fax: 01642 471798)
e-mail: secretary@clevelandgolfclub.co.uk
website: www.clevelandgolfclub.co.uk

REDCAR. **Wilton Golf Club,** Wilton, Redcar TS10 4QY (01642 465265). *Location:* eight miles east of Middlesbrough (A174), four miles west of Redcar. Parkland course, partly wooded. 18 holes, 6276 yards. S.S.S. 69. Small practice area. *Green Fees:* weekdays £25.00 per day; Sundays and Bank Holidays £30.00 per day. *Eating facilities:* lunches, including Sundays; evening meals by arrangement, lounge bar and 19th bar. *Visitors:* welcome except Saturdays; weekdays and Sundays not before 10am. Tuesdays ladies playing in competitions have priority. *Society Meetings:* by arrangement on Mondays, Wednesdays, Thursdays, Fridays and Sundays. Please contact the Club Secretary. Special rates for parties over 20. Professional: Miss P.D. Smillie (01642 452730). Secretary: Ray Douglas (01642 465265).
e-mail: secretary@wiltongolfclub.co.uk
website: www.wiltongolfclub.co.uk

RICHMOND. **Richmond (Yorkshire) Golf Club,** Bend Hagg, Richmond DL10 5EX (01748 825319). *Location:* Scotch Corner (A1). Wooded, parkland, some hills. 18 holes, 5704 yards. S.S.S. 69. Par 71. *Green Fees:* midweek £24.00 per day, £22.00 per round; weekends £30.00 per day, £25 per round.

Great golf - all year round!

A day at Romanby offers more than just great golf - it's a day to remember.

Set in 200 acres of tranquil parkland nestled between the Yorkshire Dales and the Hambleton Hills, with attractive lakes and rivers presenting excellent water hazards, Romanby provides a challenging but fair test for all categories of golfer.

ROMANBY
GOLF & COUNTRY CLUB
Yafforth Road, Northallerton, North Yorks
www.romanby.com

Championship Standard
Prestigious Clubhouse
Well stocked Golf Shop
Par-3 Academy Course
Floodlit Driving Range

We're golf society specialists, focused on providing a superb day out, and we're ready and waiting to make you welcome. To book your day at Romanby, call Grant on **01609 778855**

See also Colour Advertisement on page 40

THE GOLF GUIDE 2006   ENGLAND / North Yorkshire   353

Eating facilities: bar and catering. *Visitors:* welcome but not before 3.30pm Sundays. Pro Shop. *Society Meetings:* catered for, book with Professional. Professional: Paul Jackson (01748 822457). Secretary: B.D. Aston (01748 823231).

RIPON. **Masham Golf Club,** Burnholme, Swinton Road, Masham, Ripon HG4 4HT (01765 689379). *Location:* nine miles north of Ripon just off A6108. Parkland, River Burn flows through course and is featured in several holes. 9 holes, 6068 yards. S.S.S. 69. *Green Fees:* 18 holes £17.00, £20.00 per day. *Eating facilities:* mainly mid-day catering, bar all day. *Visitors:* welcome Mon-Fri, not weekends or Bank Holidays. *Society Meetings:* by arrangement with Secretary. Secretary: J McGee (Office: 01765 689148)

RIPON. **Ripon City Golf Club,** Palace Road, Ripon HG4 3HH (01765 603640). *Location:* one mile north of Ripon on A6108 (Masham). Undulating parkland with magnificent views over Ure Valley, city of Ripon, Hambleton Hills. 18 holes, 6084 yards. S.S.S. White 69, Yellow 68. Nearby golf range. *Green Fees:* information not available. *Eating facilities:* available every day. *Visitors:* welcome (not Saturdays). *Society Meetings:* welcome. Professional: S.T. Davis (01765 600411). Secretary: C.J. Webb (01765 603640).*

SCARBOROUGH. **Ganton Golf Club Ltd,** Ganton, Near Scarborough YO12 4PA (01944 710329; Fax: 01944 710922). *Location:* on A64, nine miles west of Scarborough. Heathland/links course. 18 holes, 6734 yards. S.S.S. 73. *Green Fees*: weekdays £68.00 per round or day; weekends and Bank Holidays £78.00 per round or day. Subject to review. *Eating facilities*: available. *Visitors*: welcome by prior arrangement. *Society Meetings:* catered for with reservation. Professional: Gary Brown. Secretary: Major R.G. Woolsey (01944 710329).
e-mail: secretary@gantongolfclub.com
website: www.gantongolfclub.com

SCARBOROUGH. **Scarborough North Cliff Golf Club,** North Cliff Avenue, Scarborough YO12 6PP (01723 360786; Fax: 01723 362134). *Location:* two miles north of Scarborough on coastal road to Whitby. Mainly parkland course with a clifftop start and finish; views of North Bay and Castle. 18 holes, 6425 yards. S.S.S. 71. Practice ground, chipping green, putting green. *Green Fees:* on application. *Eating facilities:* available. *Visitors:* welcome (restrictions on competition days, not allowed Sundays before 10.30am.). Must be members of golf club. Electric trolleys, carts available. *Society Meetings:* catered for, parties from 8 to 40. Prior booking through Secretary. Professional: S.N. Deller (01723 365920). Secretary: Mrs J H Lloyd (01723 355397).

SCARBOROUGH. **Scarborough South Cliff Golf Club Ltd,** Deepdale Avenue, Scarborough YO11 2UE (01723 360522). *Location:* one mile south of Scarborough off Filey road. Parkland and clifftop with panoramic sea views. 18 holes, 6405 yards. S.S.S. 71 (white tees), 69 (yellow tees). Practice ground. *Green Fees:* information not available. *Eating facilities:* dining room, bar; full catering facilities. *Visitors:* welcome when course available. *Society Meetings:* catered for by prior arrangement. Professional: T. Skingle (01723 365150). Secretary: David Roberts (Tel & Fax: 01723 374737).

SELBY. **Selby Golf Club,** Mill Lane, Brayton Barff, Selby YO8 9LD (01757 228622). *Location:* off A64 Selby bypass. Links-type course, very well drained. 18 holes, 6374 yards. S.S.S. 71. Practice ground. *Green Fees:* information not available. *Eating facilities:* restaurant and bar. *Visitors:* welcome weekdays. Snooker tables. *Society Meetings:* welcome Wednesday to Friday. Professional: Nick Ludwell (01757 228785). Secretary: Neil Proctor.*

SETTLE. **Settle Golf Club,** Buck Haw Brow, Giggleswick, Settle BD24 0DH (Tel & Fax: 01729 825288). *Location:* one mile north of Settle on B6480. Moorland. 9 holes, 6200 yards. S.S.S. 72. *Green Fees:* £15.00. *Eating facilities:* bar only on Sundays. *Visitors:* welcome, restrictions Sundays. *Society Meetings:* welcome with prior notice. Secretary: J. Ketchell (01729 823727).

SKIPTON. **Skipton Golf Club Ltd,** Short Lee Lane, Skipton BD23 3LF (01756 793922). *Location:* one and a half miles northwest of Skipton town centre on A65. Undulating, with panoramic views, some water hazards. 18 holes, 6090 yards. S.S.S. 69. Practice ground. *Green Fees:* weekdays £26.00; weekends £30.00. *Eating facilities:* full bar and catering daily. *Visitors:* welcome at all times, some restrictions weekends and Tuesdays. *Society Meetings:* welcome by prior arrangement. Special package rates. Professional: P. Robinson (01756 793257). Business Manager: Karen Chapman (01756 795657; Fax: 01756 796665).

STOCKTON-ON-TEES. **Teesside Golf Club,** Acklam Road, Thornaby, Stockton-on-Tees TS17 7JS (01642 676249; Fax: 01642 676252). *Location:* A19 - A1130 to Thornaby, 0.7 miles on right hand side. Flat parkland. 18 holes, 6535 yards. S.S.S. 71. Practice ground, putting green. *Green Fees:* weekdays £26.00, weekends £30.00. *Eating facilities:* catering except Mondays, bar 11am to 11pm. *Visitors:* welcome midweek up to 4.30pm, weekends after 11am by arrangement. *Society Meetings:* Monday - Friday. Special rates and conditions for parties and guests. Professional: K.W. Hall (01642 673822). Secretary: M. Fleming (01642 616516).
e-mail: teessidegolfclub@btconnect.com
website: www.teessidegolfclub.com

STUTTON. **Cocksford Golf Club,** Stutton, Tadcaster LS24 9NG (Tel & Fax: 01937 834253). *Location:* from A64 at Tadcaster to Stutton. Meadowland course in picturesque valley with Cock Beck running through. 18 holes, 5501 yards. S.S.S. 70. Practice facilities. *Green Fees:* information not available. *Eating facilities:* Cocksford Bar. *Visitors:* no restrictions apart from competitions - telephone prior to visit. *Society Meetings:* welcome by prior arrangement. Professional: Graham Thompson. Secretary: Sarah Watkinson.*

TADCASTER. **Scarthingwell Golf Course,** Scarthingwell, Tadcaster LS24 9PF (01937 557878; Fax: 01937 557909). *Location*: 4 miles south of Tadcaster on the A162 Tadcaster/Ferrybridge Road approximately 3 miles from A1. Parkland Course. 18 holes, 6642 yards. S.S.S.72. *Green Fees*: information not available. *Eating facilities*: licenced clubhouse facilities and snooker table, restaurant. *Visitors*: welcome every day except before 2pm on Saturdays. *Society Meetings*: welcome, packages and special rates available. Professional: Steve Footman (01937 557864). Secretary: Kathryn Pick (01937 557878).

THIRSK. **Thirsk and Northallerton Golf Club,** Thornton-le-Street, Thirsk YO7 4AB (01845 522170). *Location:* on Northallerton Road (A168), two miles from Thirsk. Flat parkland with excellent views of Hambleton Hills. 18 holes, 6530 yards. S.S.S. 71. Practice ground. *Green Fees:* on application. *Eating facilities:* catering and bar. *Visitors:* welcome, phone before arrival. Trolleys, buggies for hire. *Society Meetings:* welcome. Handicaps required. Professional: Robert Garner (01845 526216). Manager: S. C. Owram (01845 525115).e-mail: secretary@tngc.co.uk
website: www.tngc.co.uk

WHITBY. **Whitby Golf Club,** Sandsend Road, Low Straggleton, Whitby YO21 3SR (01947 602768). *Location:* on the A174, one mile from Whitby. Picturesque coastal course on cliff tops, three holes over ravines. 18 holes, 5963 yards. S.S.S. 68. *Green Fees:* £30.00 weekends, £22.00 midweek. *Eating facilities:* dining room and bar. *Visitors:* welcome, parties over 12 by prior reservation, all must be bona fide golfers. *Society Meetings:* catered for by prior arrangement. Professional: Tony Mason (01947 602719). Office: (Tel & Fax: 01947 600660).

YORK. **Forest of Galtres Golf Club,** Moorlands Road, Skelton, York YO32 2RF (01904 766198; Fax: 01904 769400). *Location:* two miles from the northern section of the ring road around the historic city of York. Parkland course, designed by Simon Gidman. 18 holes, 6534 yards. S.S.S. 71. Covered driving range and practice ground. *Green Fees:* weekdays £20.00 per round, £25.00 all day; weekends and Bank Holidays £27.00 per round, £32.00 all day. Midweek Specials starting from £27.00 including food. *Eating facilities:* full facilities available. *Visitors:* welcome any day. *Society Meetings:* welcome but must be pre-booked with Secretary, No Societies on Saturdays. Professional: Phil Bradley P.G.A. (Tel & Fax: 01904 766198). Secretary: Mrs Sue Procter (Tel & Fax: 01904 769400).
website: www.forestofgaltres.co.uk

For full details of clubs and courses, plus convenient accommodation

www.uk-golfguide.com

YORK. **Forest Park Golf Club,** Stockton on Forest, York YO32 9UW (01904 400425). *Location:* one and a half miles from east end of York bypass, follow signs for Stockton on Forest. Flat parkland course with trees and stream running through. 18 holes, 6600 yards. S.S.S. 71; 9 holes, 3186 yards. S.S.S. 70 (twice round). Open air driving range and 8 bay driving range, practice area. *Green Fees:* weekdays £10.00 for 9 holes, £23.00 per round, £30.00 per day; weekends £12.00 for 9 holes, £30.00 per round, £40.00 per day. Subject to annual review. Special party and package rates; quotation on request. *Eating facilities:* full bar and golf club catering facilities. *Visitors:* welcome mid week, limited availability weekends. *Society Meetings:* welcome by prior arrangement. Professional: Mark Winterburn (01904 400425). Secretary: Nicola Crossley (01904 400688). e-mail: admin@forestparkgolfclub.co.uk
website: www.forestparkgolfclub.co.uk

YORK. **Fulford (York) Golf Club Ltd,** Heslington Lane, York YO10 5DY *Location:* A19 (Selby) from city, turn left to Heslington (signposted to University). Heathland. 18 holes, 6775 yards. S.S.S. 72. Practice ground. *Green Fees:* weekdays £50.00 per round, £65.00 per day; weekends £65.00. *Eating facilities:* lounge, diningroom and bar. *Visitors:* welcome Monday to Friday, prior reservation recommended. Snooker table. *Society Meetings:* Monday to Friday by arrangement with Manager. Professional: Martin Brown (01904 412882). General Manager: Linda Gurnell (01904 413579; Fax: 01904 416918).
e-mail: info@fulfordgolfclub.co.uk

YORK. **Heworth Golf Club,** Muncaster House, Muncastergate, York YO31 9JY (01904 426156). *Location:* one and a half miles east of City Centre on A1036 Malton/Scarborough road. Parkland, easy walking. 12 holes, 6105 yards, 5635 metres. S.S.S. 69. Practice ground. *Green Fees:* weekdays £15.00 per round, £20.00 per day; weekends and Bank Holidays £20.00 per round, £25.00 per day. All-in rates for parties (coffee, 9 holes, soup and sandwiches, 18 holes, evening meal) £27.50. *Eating facilities:* bar (snacks), dining room. *Visitors:* generally welcome, advisable to telephone Professional in advance. Carts for hire. *Society Meetings:* by written arrangement with Professional. Professional: Stephen Burdett (Tel & Fax: 01904 422389). Secretary: Richard Hunt (Tel & Fax: 01904 426156).

YORK. **The Oaks Golf Club,** Aughton Common, Aughton, York YO42 4PW (01757 288577; Fax: 01757 288232). *Location:* on the B1228 one mile north of Bubwith village. Wooded course with seven lakes that come into play. 18 holes, 6743 yards, 6035 metres. S.S.S. 72. Practice ground. *Green Fees:* £25.00 per round, £35.00 per day. *Eating facilities:* lounge bar, normal meals, à la carte restaurant. *Visitors:* welcome weekdays. Accommodation available, for details telephone (01757 288577). *Society Meetings:* on application. Professionals: Graham Walker, Lysa Jones. Secretary: Sheila Nutt. e-mail: sheila@theoaksgolfclub.co.uk
website: www.theoaksgolfclub.co.uk

YORK. **Pike Hills Golf Club,** Tadcaster Road, Askham Bryan, York YO23 3UW (01904 706566). *Location:* four miles from York on Tadcaster Road (A64), left hand side going east. Flat parkland surrounding wildlife reserve. 18 holes, 6146 yards. S.S.S. 70. *Green Fees:* £26.00 per round, £32.00 per day. *Eating facilities:* restaurant and bar facilities. *Visitors:* welcome except weekends or Bank Holidays. *Society Meetings:* welcome by arrangement. Professional: Ian Gradwell (01904 708756). Secretary: L. Hargrave (Tel & Fax: 01904 700797).

YORK. **The York Golf Club,** Lords Moor Lane, Strensall, York YO32 5XF (01904 490304). *Location:* two miles north of York ring road (A1237). Wooded heathland. 18 holes, 6301 yards. S.S.S. 70. Practice ground; Professional shop. *Green Fees:* information not available. *Eating facilities:* full catering. *Visitors:* welcome weekdays, but advisable to ring before visiting. *Society Meetings:* catered for weekdays and Sundays. Professional: A.P. Hoyles (01904 490304). Secretary: Mike Wells (01904 491840; Fax: 01904 491852).

Orillia House
89 The Village, Stockton on Forest, YORK YO32 9UP   ETC ♦♦♦♦
Tel: 01904 400600 • Fax: 01904 400101 • E-mail: info@orilliahouse.co.uk • www.orilliahouse.co.uk

A warm welcome awaits at **ORILLIA HOUSE**, 3 miles NE of York, one mile from A64. This 17th century house has been restored to offer a high standard of comfort with modern facilities, yet retains all its original charm and character. All rooms have private facilities, colour TV and tea/coffee making. Private car park. Our local pub serves excellent evening meals. Bed and Breakfast from £25. Telephone for our brochure. **Proprietors: Mr & Mrs G.Hudson**

The Oaks Golf Club & Spa
Aughton Common, Aughton, York YO42 4PW

- Excellent golf, food and drink served in a warm, friendly environment.
- Visit the Spa for a very special treat.
- Stay in beautiful accommodation.
  - Superb practice and teaching facilities incorporating Golf Monthly Top 25 UK Coach Graham Walker's:

Walker's Golf Academy
Tel: 01757 288577 • Fax: 01757 288232
www.theoaksgolfclub.co.uk • www.walkersgolfacademy.co.uk

GOLF MONTHLY TOP 25 COACH

See also Colour Advertisement on page 40

FHG
K·U·P·E·R·A·R·D

Other specialised FHG Guides
Published annually: available in all good bookshops or direct from the publisher.

Recommended **COUNTRY INNS & PUBS** OF BRITAIN £7.99
Recommended **COUNTRY HOTELS** OF BRITAIN £7.99
Recommended **SHORT BREAK HOLIDAYS** IN BRITAIN £7.99
The bestselling **PETS WELCOME!** £8.99

FHG Guides • Abbey Mill Business Centre, Seedhill, Paisley, Renfrewshire PA1 1TJ
Tel: 0141-887 0428 • Fax: 0141-889 7204
e-mail: admin@fhguides.co.uk
www.holidayguides.com

South Yorkshire

BARNSLEY. **Barnsley Golf Club,** Wakefield Road, Staincross, Barnsley S75 6JZ (01226 382856). *Location:* A61 three miles north of Barnsley, five miles south of Wakefield. Parkland course. 18 holes, 6048 yards, 5529 metres. S.S.S. 69. *Green Fees:* information not available. *Eating facilities:* full catering and licensing facilities every day except Monday and Tuesday. *Visitors:* welcome, no restrictions; booking through Professional. Professional: S. Wyke (01226 380358). Secretary: Brian Caunt (01226 382856).

BARNSLEY. **Sandhill Golf Club,** Middlecliffe Lane, Little Houghton, Barnsley S72 0HW (Tel & Fax: 01226 753444). *Location:* 6 miles east of Barnsley, off A635. 18 holes, 6250 yards. S.S.S. 70. *Green Fees*: on request. *Eating facilities*: licensed bar providing tea, coffee, biscuits and meals at various prices. *Visitors*: welcome. Buggies available. *Society Meetings*: welcome with various packages on request. Winter Society Specials available. Secretary: Mrs V. Wistow. e-mail: vwistow@sandhillgolfclub.co.uk
bookings@sandhillgolfclub.co.uk
website: www.sandhillgolfclub.co.uk

BARNSLEY. **Silkstone Golf Club,** Field Head, Elmhirst Lane, Silkstone, Barnsley S75 4LD (01226 790328). *Location:* one mile from Junction 37 (M1) along A628 (the road to Manchester). Parkland/downland course. 18 holes, 6069 yards. S.S.S. 70. Practice ground. *Green Fees:* on application. *Eating facilities:* full catering facilities and bar. *Visitors:* welcome weekdays, Ladies' Day Tuesdays, with a member only at weekends and Bank Holidays. Caddie cart and buggy hire. *Society Meetings:* by arrangement. Professional: Kevin Guy (01226 790128). Secretary: A. Butcher (01226 790328).

www.uk-golfguide.com

DONCASTER. **Bawtry Golf Club,** Cross Lane, Austerfield, Doncaster DN10 6RF (Tel & Fax: 01302 710841). *Location:* two miles from Bawtry on the A614. Parkland. 18 holes, 6900 yards. S.S.S. 73. 10 bay floodlit golf range, practice ground. *Green Fees:* Midweek £15.00, Weekend £20.00. *Eating facilities:* bar snacks and full restaurant. *Visitors:* welcome without reservation. Trolley and cart hire; buggies. *Society Meetings:* welcome, special package rates. Professional: Darran Roberts (01302 710841). Office: (01302 711409). Catering: 01302 711755).

DONCASTER. **Crookhill Park (Municipal) Golf Club,** Carr Lane, Conisborough, Doncaster DN12 2AH (01709 862979). *Location:* off A630 Doncaster–Rotherham Road turn on A6094 (opposite castle) then one mile. 18 holes, 5846 yards. Parkland, special feature hole 11 (index 1) – approach to green over small wall to elevated green. S.S.S. 68. Practice area. *Green Fees:* information not available. *Eating facilities:* buffet lunches at club. *Visitors:* welcome pre-book with Professional if specific time is required. Professional: Richard Swaine (01709 862979). Hon. Secretary: T.A. Cusack (01709 862974).*

DONCASTER. **Doncaster Golf Club,** Bawtry Road, Doncaster DN4 7PD (01302 868316). *Location:* four miles south of Doncaster town centre on the A638. Wooded, heathland course. 18 holes, 6244 yards. S.S.S. 70. Practice area, putting green. *Green Fees:* £32.00 per round, £36.00 per day. *Eating facilities:* all day catering Monday to Saturday, up to 4pm Sundays. *Visitors:* welcome weekdays, Wednesday Ladies' Day; restricted tee times at weekends and Bank Holidays. *Society Meetings:* by arrangement, contact Secretary. Professional: G. Bailey (01302 868404). Secretary: G.J. Needham (01302 865632; Fax: 01302 865994).
e-mail: doncastergolf@aol.com
website: www.doncastergolfclub.org.uk

Sandhill Golf Club
Weekend Society Specials Available

18 hole golf course. Societies welcome with various packages on request. Licensed club house providing tea, coffee, biscuits and meals at various prices.
**Middlecliffe Lane,
Little Houghton, Barnsley S72 0HW
Tel: 01226 753444
www.sandhillgolfclub.co.uk**
e-mail enquiries:
**vwistow@sandhillgolfclub.co.uk
bookings@sandhillgolfclub.co.uk**

See also Colour Advertisement on page 41

THE GOLF GUIDE 2006   ENGLAND / South Yorkshire   357

DONCASTER. **Doncaster Town Moor Golf Club,** Bawtry Road, Belle Vue, Doncaster DN4 5HU (01302 533167). *Location:* clubhouse approximately 300 yards from racecourse roundabout travelling south towards Bawtry, same entrance as Doncaster Rovers Football Club. Flat parkland/lowland heath, centre of Doncaster racecourse. 18 holes, 5650 yards, S.S.S. 69. *Green Fees:* weekdays £12.00, with a member, £20.00 without a member, weekends £14.00 with a member, £22.00 without a member. 2005 rates, subject to review. Special rates for societies. *Eating facilities:* restaurant and bar meals. *Visitors:* welcome by arrangement. *Society Meetings:* catered for by arrangement with Professional. Discount package available. Professional: Steve Shaw (01302 535286). Secretary: S. Whitehouse (01302 533778).

DONCASTER. **Hickleton Golf Club,** Lidgett Lane, Hickleton, Near Doncaster DN5 7BE (01709 896081; Fax: 01709 896083). *Location:* from Junction 37 A1(M) six miles on A635 to Barnsley, in Hickleton village turn right to Thurnscoe, 500 yards on right. Undulating parkland. 18 holes, 6434 yards, S.S.S. 71. Practice ground. *Green Fees:* weekdays £25.00; weekends and Bank Holidays £30.00. Winter and Summer packages available. *Eating facilities:* available seven days a week. *Visitors:* welcome by arrangement, restricted times at weekends. Buggies by arrangement with Professional. *Society Meetings:* welcome by arrangement. Professional: Paul Audsley (Tel & Fax: 01709 888436). Manager: John Little (01709 896081; Fax: 01709 896083). e-mail: hickleton@hickletongolfclub.freeserve.co.uk website: www.hickletongc.co.uk

DONCASTER. **Owston Hall Hotel & Golf Club, (The Robin Hood Golf Course)** Owston Hall, Owston, Askern, Doncaster DN6 9JF (01302 722231; Fax: 01302 728885). *Location:* 7 miles north of Doncaster on the A19 from Doncaster to Askern, take the B1220 and turn right through the stone gates. Championship venue on the PGA Euro Pro Tour schedule. Parkland with mature trees. 18 holes, 6937 yards. S.S.S. 72. Putting Green, Practice ground. *Green Fees:* weekdays £20.00; weekends £28.00. *Eating facilities:* bar lunches and full evening menu. *Visitors:* welcome, booking at weekends recommended. Function and conference rooms. Hotel with 49 de luxe bedrooms; gym. *Society Meetings:* packages available – please phone for brochure. Dress code applies – locker changing and shower facilities. Lessons available. Professional: Jason Laszkowicz (01302 722231; Fax: 01302 728885). Secretary: Gerry Briggs (01302 722800). e-mail: reservations@owstonhall.com
          proshop@owstonhall.com
website: www.owstonhall.com

DONCASTER. **Serlby Park Golf Club,** Serlby, Doncaster DN10 6BA (01777 818268). *Location:* between Bawtry and Blyth. Parkland, wooded course. 9 holes, 5300 yards. S.S.S. 66. *Green Fees:* information not available. *Eating facilities:* catering and bar. *Visitors:* welcome only if playing with member. *Society Meetings:* some visiting parties allowed, please contact the Secretary prior to 1st January for bookings the following year. Secretary: Mr K.J. Crook (01302 742280). *

DONCASTER. **Thorne Golf Club,** Kirton Lane, Thorne, Near Doncaster DN8 5RJ (01405 812084; Fax: 01405 741899). *Location:* M18 Junction 5, onto M180, take first junction onto A614 Thorne, follow signposts. Flat parkland with three ponds. 18 holes, 5366 yards. S.S.S. 66. Practice ground and putting green. *Green Fees:* weekdays £10.00 18 holes; weekends and Bank Holidays £11.00 18 holes; twilight £7.00 18 holes. *Eating facilities:* snacks and meals available. *Visitors:* welcome, no restrictions. *Society Meetings:* welcome, please book in advance. Secretary/ Professional: Edward Highfield. Proprietor: Richard Highfield.
e-mail: caroline@highfield9813.freeserve.co.uk

DONCASTER. **Thornhurst Park Golf Course,** Holme Lane, Owston, Doncaster DN5 0LR (01302 337799). *Location:* 10 minutes from centre of Doncaster through Bentley on A19 to Selby. Flat, parkland course with excellent countryside views. 18 holes, 6490 yards. S.S.S. 71. Practice area, putting green. *Green Fees:* weekdays 18 holes £12.00; weekends 18 holes £14.00. 9 holes: weekdays £7.00, weekends £8.00. *Eating facilities:* restaurant, lounge bar, function room. *Visitors:* welcome every day, members have priority between 8am and 9am. *Society Meetings:* welcome any day. Professional: Kevin M. Pearce. Secretary: Dave Trent.

DONCASTER. **Wheatley Golf Club,** Armthorpe Road, Doncaster DN2 5QB (01302 831655). *Location:* follow East Coast route alongside Racecourse boundary to water tower at first crossroads. Flat parkland, water hazards between 10th and 18th holes. 18 holes, 6209 yards, S.S.S. 70 (yellow markers); 6405 yards, S.S.S. 71 (white markers). Practice area and putting green. *Green Fees:* weekdays £27.00 per round, £33.00 per day; weekends £38.00 per round. *Eating facilities:* restaurant and bars. *Visitors:* welcome if member of another club. *Society Meetings:* catered for weekdays only on written application. Professional: S. Fox (01302 834085). Secretary: Mr T. Roberts (01302 831655).

ROTHERHAM. **Grange Park Golf Club,** Upper Wortley Road, Kimberworth Park, Rotherham S61 2SJ (01709 558884). Municipal golf course, private clubhouse. *Location:* A629 from Rotherham, easy access from M1. Parkland. 18 holes, 6353 yards. S.S.S. 71. Practice ground, driving range. *Green Fees:* information not available. *Eating facilities:* licensed bar and full catering. *Visitors:* welcome without restriction. *Society Meetings:* contact Professional in first instance. Professional: Eric Clark (01709 559497). Secretary: Roy Charity (01709 583400 home, 01709 558884 club). *

For full details of clubs and courses, plus convenient accommodation
www.uk-golfguide.com

ROTHERHAM. **Phoenix Golf Club,** Phoenix Sports and Social Club, Pavilion Lane, Brinsworth, Rotherham S60 5PA (Tel & Fax: 01709 363788). *Location:* M1 (J34) Tinsley roundabout, Bawtry Road, Pavilion Lane one mile on left. 18 holes, 6181 yards. S.S.S. 70. Practice area, 20 bay driving range. *Green Fees:* information not available. *Eating facilities:* snacks or full meals. *Visitors:* welcome anytime. *Society Meetings:* welcome weekdays only. Professional: M. Roberts (01709 382624). Secretary: I. Gregory (Tel & Fax: 01709 363788).

ROTHERHAM. **Rotherham Golf Club Ltd,** Thrybergh Park, Doncaster Road, Thrybergh, Rotherham S65 4NU (01709 850466). *Location:* three and a half miles east of Rotherham on A630. Wooded parkland. 18 holes, 6234 yards, 5701 metres. S.S.S. 70. Practice ground. *Green Fees:* information not available. *Eating facilities:* full catering, bar and restaurant. *Visitors:* welcome all day with limitations. *Society Meetings:* catered for weekdays only except Wednesdays. Professional: Simon Thornhill (01709 850480). Manager: Mrs C. Davison (01709 859500; Fax: 01709 859517).*

ROTHERHAM. **Roundwood Golf Club,** Green Lane, Rawmarsh, Rotherham S62 6LA (01709 826134). *Location:* half a mile from the A633. Flat course, easy walking. 18 holes, 5568 yards, S.S.S. 67. *Green Fees:* information not available. *Eating facilities:* bar open seven days a week, food available Fridays and Saturdays. *Visitors:* welcome midweek and Sunday afternoons. *Society Meetings:* welcome weekdays and Sunday afternoons. Secretary: G. Billups (01709 525208).*

ROTHERHAM. **Sitwell Park Golf Club,** Shrogswood Road, Rotherham S60 4BY (01709 700799; Fax: 01709 703637). *Location:* A631 off M18, Bramley turn off to Rotherham thence to Sheffield, Exit 33 off M1, follow A631 to Bawtry. Undulating parkland. 18 holes, 6229 yards. Par 71. Practice ground. *Green Fees:* weekdays £26.00 per round, £34.00 per day; Sundays and Bank Holidays £32.00 per round, £40.00 per day. Parties of 30 or more players 10% discount. *Eating facilities:* restaurant and bar. *Visitors:* welcome with reservation, Saturdays only with member, Sundays after 11.30am. Carts available. *Society Meetings:* catered for if pre-arranged with Secretary. Not Saturdays; Sundays after 11.30am only. Professional: N. Taylor (01709 540961). Secretary: Geoff Hardy (01709 541046; Fax: 01709 703637).

ROTHERHAM. **Wath Golf Club,** Abdy, Rawmarsh, Rotherham S62 7SJ (01709 872149). *Location:* A633 from Rotherham, through Rawmarsh, taking B6090 towards Wentworth, right along B6089 taking signed road to Clubhouse 300 yards on right. Flat parkland course with small greens, dykes and two ponds. 18 holes, 6123 yards. S.S.S. 70. Limited practice area. *Green Fees:* £24.00 per round, £29.00 per day. Golf/meal package £33.00/£38.00. *Eating facilities:* lounge bar and dining area with seating for up to 100 people. *Visitors:* weekdays only. *Society Meetings:* welcome weekdays only by prior arrangement. Professional: Chris Bassett. Secretary: M. Godfrey (01709 878609; Fax: 01709 877097).

SHEFFIELD. **Abbeydale Golf Club,** Twentywell Rise off, Twentywell Lane, Dore, Sheffield S17 4QA (0114 2360763; Fax: 0114 2360762). *Location:* A621 five miles south of Sheffield. Parkland. 18 holes, 6241 yards. S.S.S. 70. Practice ground. *Green Fees:* weekdays £30.00; weekends and Bank Holidays £40.00. *Eating facilities:* restaurant and bar meals. *Visitors:* welcome by arrangement. Starting time restrictions April-October. *Society Meetings:* catered for by arrangement. Professional: N. Perry (0114 2365633). Secretary: Mr G.L. Lord (0114 2360763; Fax: 0114 2360762).

SHEFFIELD. **Beauchief Golf Club,** Abbey Lane, Beauchief, Sheffield S8 0DB (0114 236 7274). *Location:* near the junction with A621 Abbeydale Road 5 miles SW of Sheffield. Access from J33 or J29 via outer ring road. 'Pay and Play' parkland course with some hilly holes. 18 holes, 5452 yards,. S.S.S. 66. Practice area. *Green Fees:* information not available. *Eating facilities:* cafe/bar, open daily from 11am to dusk. *Visitors:* welcome weekdays and after 10am at weekend. *Society Meetings:* welcome weekdays and after 10am weekend, contact Mr. N. Lutey, Sheffield International Venues (01142 797451) Professional: M. Trippett (01142 367274). Secretary: Mrs B. Fryer (0114 236 5628).

SHEFFIELD. **Birley Wood Golf Club,** Birley Lane, Sheffield S12 3BP (0114 264 7262). *Location:* Junction 30 M1 then A616 to Sheffield. Undulating meadowland course with good views. Fairway Course: 18 holes, 5734 yards. Par 69, S.S.S. 68. Short Birley Course: 18 holes, 4906 yards. Par 66. S.S.S. 65. Practice field near course. Membership available. *Green Fees:* information not available. *Eating facilities:* restaurant and bar meals at adjacent Fairway Inn. *Visitors:* welcome anytime. *Society Meetings:* contact Mr N. Luety (0114 279 7451). Secretary: P. Renshaw (0114 265 3784).*

SHEFFIELD. **Concord Park Municipal Golf Course,** Shiregreen Lane, Shiregreen, Sheffield S5 6AE (0114 2577378). *Location:* M1 Junctions 34/35, one and a half miles north of junctions. Parkland, hilly, good views. 18 holes, 4872 yards, S.S.S. 64, Par 67. Driving range; buggies available. *Green Fees:* information not available. *Eating facilities:* available in new clubhouse. *Visitors:* welcome any time; busy Saturday and Sunday mornings. *Society Meetings:* welcome. Professional: W. Allcroft (0114 2577378). Secretary: P.J. Wilson (0114 2347792).*

SHEFFIELD. **Dore and Totley Golf Club,** The Clubhouse, Bradway Road, Bradway, Sheffield S17 4QR (0114 236 0492; Fax: 0114 235 3436). *Location:* leave M1 at Junction 33. Flat, easy walking parkland course. 18 holes, 6256 yards. S.S.S. 70. *Green Fees:* information not available. *Eating facilities:* bar catering facilities available except Mondays. *Visitors:* welcome. After 10am Tuesdays and Thursday; afternoons only Wednesdays and Sundays. No visitors on Saturdays. Handicap Certificates may be requested. *Society Meetings:* welcome by arrangement. Special all day price; catering by arrangement with Stewardess. Professional: Gregg Roberts (Tel & Fax: 0114 236 6844). Secretary: J. Johnson (0114 2369872).*

SHEFFIELD. **Hallamshire Golf Club Ltd,** Sandygate, Sheffield S10 4LA (0114 230 1007; Fax: 0114 230 2153). *Location:* A57 out of Sheffield, four miles out of city then fork left for Lodge Moor. Undulating moorland course, not suitable for beginners. 18 holes, 6359 yards, 5815 metres. S.S.S. 71. *Green Fees:* information not available. *Eating facilities:* dining room/verandah, two bars. *Visitors:* welcome weekdays by arrangement, some weekends. Dress code. Snooker table. *Society Meetings:* catered for by arrangement with Secretary. Professional: Geoffrey Tickell (0114 230 5222). Secretary: George Kirkpatrick (0114 230 2153; Fax: 0114 230 5413).*

SHEFFIELD. **Hallowes Golf Club,** Hallowes Lane, Dronfield, Near Sheffield S18 1UR (01246 411196; Fax: 01246 413753). *Location:* six miles south of Sheffield on old A61 (not bypass to Chesterfield). Moorland/parkland. 18 holes, 6342 yards. S.S.S. 71. Large practice area and short game facility. *Green Fees:* weekdays £35.00 per round, £40.00 per day. *Eating facilities:* bars, dining room. *Visitors:* weekdays only, no visitors at weekends and Bank Holidays except with members. *Society Meetings:* EGU registered societies welcome. special reduced packages available. Professional: Philip Dunn (01246 411196). Secretary: T. Marshall (01246 413734).

SHEFFIELD. **Hillsborough Golf Club Ltd,** Worrall Road, Sheffield S6 4BE (0114 234 9151 – Office; 0114 229 4103 – Steward). *Location:* three miles from city centre. Worrall Road via Middlewood Road, Dykes Hall Road. Undulating wooded parkland and heath. 18 holes, 6035 yards. S.S.S. 70. Practice field. *Green Fees:* weekdays £30.00, weekends and Bank Holidays £35.00. *Eating facilities:* snacks available; lunches, teas, evening meals by arrangement (not Fridays). *Visitors:* welcome weekdays, weekends with a member only. *Society Meetings:* catered for by arrangement with Professional. Professional: Lewis Horsman (0114 229 4100). Secretary: G.F. Smalley (0114 234 9151).

SHEFFIELD. **Lees Hall Golf Club Ltd,** Hemsworth Road, Norton, Sheffield S8 8LL (0114 255 4402). *Location:* three miles south of Sheffield, between A61 and A6102 ring road. Undulating parkland with extensive views over Sheffield. 18 holes, 6171 yards. S.S.S. 70. *Green Fees:* information not available. *Eating facilities:* available daily. *Visitors:* welcome, except Saturday and Sunday before 10.30am. *Society Meetings:* by arrangement only. Professional: Simon Berry (0114-250 7868). Secretary: R.W. Balloch (0114 255 2900). e-mail: secretary@leeshallgolfclub.co.uk

SHEFFIELD. **Rother Valley Golf Centre,** Mansfield Road, Wales Bar, Sheffield S26 5PQ (0114 2473000; Fax: 0114 2476000). *Location:* centrally situated between Sheffield, Rotherham, and Chesterfield. Two miles from Junction 31 of M1, signposted. Parkland with water features. Island green at 7th hole and monster par 5 18th hole. Floodlit driving range and 9 hole pitch and putt course. Jack Barker golf school. 18 holes, 6602 yards. S.S.S. 72. *Green Fees:* Monday to Thursday £13.50; Fridays: £15.00; weekends £18.00. *Eating facilities:* Bar open 9am to 10.30pm. *Visitors:* welcome. *Society Meetings:* welcome including weekends. Phone for special offers. General Manager: Maureen Goodman.

SHEFFIELD. **Stocksbridge and District Golf Club Ltd,** 30 Royd Lane, Deepcar, Sheffield S36 2RZ (0114 2882003). *Location:* 10 miles from Sheffield on A616 heading towards Manchester. Moorland course. 18 holes, 5200 yards. S.S.S. 65. Practice ground. *Green Fees:* weekdays £17.00 per round (unaccompanied), £21.00 per day; weekends £30.00. Visiting parties £25.00 – 18 holes, soup and sandwiches, 18 holes, dinner. *Eating facilities:* dining room and bars available. *Visitors:* welcome weekdays, restrictions weekends. *Society Meetings:* catered for during the week. Professional: Roger Broad (0114 2882779). Secretary: Dennis Haley (0114 2882003).

SHEFFIELD. **Tankersley Park Golf Club Ltd,** High Green, Sheffield S30 4LG (0114 2468247; Fax: 0114 2457818). *Location:* M1 north to Junction 35a, A616, golf club on right. M1 south Junction 36, A61 Sheffield, left on A616, golf club on left. Parkland/wooded. 18 holes, 6212 yards. S.S.S. 70. Practice area and practice green. *Green Fees:* £27.00 per round, £36.00 per day. 10% discount for parties of 20 or more players. *Eating facilities*: sandwiches, bar and evening meals. *Visitors*: welcome weekdays without reservation but not before 3pm weekends. *Society Meetings*: catered for by prior arrangement with Secretary. Professional: I. Kirk (Tel & Fax: 0114 2455583). Secretary: A. Brownhill (0114 2468247).

SHEFFIELD. **Tinsley Park Golf Club (Municipal),** High Hazels Park, Darnall, Sheffield S9 4PE (0114 2448974). *Location:* three miles from Junction 33 M1, exit – A6102. Wooded course. 18 holes, 6096 yards. S.S.S. 69. Practice facilities. *Green Fees:* information not available. *Eating facilities:* cafe; meals if ordered from Stewardess (07787 335747). *Visitors:* welcome without restriction, times booked through Professional up to 8 days in advance. *Society Meetings:* book through Sheffield International Venues (0114 223 3815). Professional: Mr Wayne Yellott (0114 203 7435). Secretary: Derek Bower (0114 269 0562; mobile: 07789 274503).

SHEFFIELD. **Wortley Golf Club,** Hermit Hill Lane, Wortley, Sheffield S35 7DF (0114 288 8469; Fax: 0114 288 8488). *Location:* leave M1 Junction 36 or 35A - A616 or A61 to A629 leading to Wortley Village, through village turn right. Parkland. 18 holes, 6035 yards, 5520 metres. S.S.S. 69. Practice ground. *Green Fees:* weekdays £27.00 per round, weekends £35.00 per round. *Eating facilities:* order in advance, limited on Mondays. *Visitors:* welcome, no restrictions. Golf buggy, trolley and club hire available. *Society Meetings:* welcome, must pre-book. Professional: Ian Kirk (0114 288 6490). Administrator: Carol Hill (0114 288 8469). e-mail: Wortley.golfclub@btconnect.com

WORKSOP. **Lindrick Golf Club,** Lindrick Common, Worksop S81 8BH (01909 485802). *Location*: on A57 four miles west of Worksop. M1 Junction 31 on to A57 Worksop. Heathland. 18 holes, 6612 yards, 6046 metres. S.S.S. 71. Two practice areas. *Green Fees:* information not available. *Eating facilities*: dining room. *Visitors:* welcome weekdays, except Tuesday mornings. Prior booking required. *Society Meetings:* catered for weekdays. Professional: John King (01909 475820). Secretary: John Armitage (01909 475282; Fax: 01909 488685).*
website: www.lindrickgolf.com

West Yorkshire

BINGLEY. **Bingley (St Ives) Golf Club,** The Golf Clubhouse, Harden, Bingley BD16 1AT (01274 562436; Fax: 01274 511788). *Location:* A650 Keighley/Bradford Road. Parkland/moorland. 18 holes, 6480 yards. S.S.S. 71. Practice ground. *Green Fees:* weekdays £26.00; weekends and Bank Holidays £30.00. *Eating facilities:* daily. *Visitors:* welcome weekdays, limited availability weekends. *Society Meetings:* welcome, book through Professional. Professional: R.K. Firth (01274 562506). Manager: Ray Adams (01274 562436; Tel & Fax: 01274 511788).

BRADFORD. **Baildon Golf Club,** Moorgate, Baildon, Shipley BD17 5PP (01274 584266). *Location:* five miles north-west of Bradford via Shipley. Hilly, moorland course. 18 holes, 6225 yards. S.S.S. 70. *Green Fees:* information not available. *Eating facilities:* catering except Mondays. Bar and separate dining room. *Visitors:* welcome, restricted at weekends and Tuesdays. *Society Meetings:* welcome weekdays only, by written application. Professional: R. Masters (01274 595162). Secretary: John Cooley.

BRADFORD. **Bradford Moor Golf Club,** Scarr Hall, Pollard Lane, Bradford BD2 4RW (01274 771716). *Location:* A658 two miles from top of M606. Moorland, undulating course. 9 holes, 5854 yards. S.S.S. 68. *Green Fees:* weekdays before 4pm, £12.00 (with a member £9.00); weekends with a member only (£9.00). *Eating facilities:* available by appointment only. *Visitors:* welcome weekdays. *Society Meetings:* welcome weekdays. Secretary: Chris Bedford (01274 771693).

Visit the **FHG** website
www.holidayguides.com
for details of the wide choice of accommodation featured in the full range of FHG titles

---

BRADFORD. **Clayton Golf Club,** Thornton View Road, Clayton, Bradford BD14 6JX (01274 880047). *Location:* two miles south west of Bradford, via Thornton Road, then Listerhills Road. Parkland course. 9 holes, 6200 yards. S.S.S. 72. *Green Fees:* 18 holes £15.00. *Eating facilities:* diningroom – meals and snacks daily; evening meals by arrangement; two bars. *Visitors:* welcome at all times except before 4.00pm on Sundays. Snooker room. *Society Meetings:* catered for by arrangement. Secretary: D.A. Smith (01274 572311).

BRADFORD. **East Bierley Golf Club,** South View Road, East Bierley, Bradford BD4 6PP (01274 683666). *Location:* situated about three miles east of Bradford on the Wakefield/Heckmondwike Road. Turn off at Bierley Bar and down South View Road. Parkland course. 9 holes, 4308 metres. S.S.S. 63. *Green Fees:* information not available. *Eating facilities:* lunchtime and evening catering (except Tuesdays). *Visitors:* welcome, not Sundays or Mondays after 4pm. Secretary: Mr R.J. Welch (01274 683666). Hon. Secretary: R.J. Welch. Steward: (01274 680450).

BRADFORD. **Headley Golf Club,** Headley Lane, Thornton, Bradford BD13 3LX (01274 833481). *Location:* five miles west of Bradford. Undulating parkland, excellent views. 9 holes, 4914 yards. S.S.S. 65. *Green Fees:* information not available. *Eating facilities:* dining room and bar. *Visitors:* weekdays only. *Society Meetings:* welcome weekdays, special packages available. Hon. Secretary: A. Goodman (01274 833481). *

BRADFORD. **The Manor Golf Club,** Bradford Road, Drighlington, Bradford BD11 1AB (0113 2852644). *Location:* between Leeds and Bradford, just off M62 Junction 27. Undulating parkland/meadowland, features six lakes. 18 holes, 6506 yards, 5947 metres. S.S.S 71, Par 72. 20 bay floodlit driving range, 6 hole Par 3 course. *Green Fees:* midweek £16.00 per round, weekend £20.00 per round - after 2.30pm £16.00. *Eating facilities:* clubhouse. *Visitors:* welcome at all times but prior enquiry advised. *Society Meetings:* welcome with reservation. Director of Golf/Professional: Graham Thompson.

BINGLEY ST IVES
GOLF CLUB

The Clubhouse, Harden, Bingley BD16 1AT
Superb course and facilities with magnificent views of the Aire valley.
Visitors welcome, special package rates all year round.

Contact
Pro: 01274 562506
Manager:
01274 562436
for details

e-mail: bingleyst-ives@harden.freeserve.co.uk
www.bingleystivesgc.co.uk

See also Colour Advertisement on page 42

THE GOLF GUIDE 2006   ENGLAND / West Yorkshire

BRADFORD. **Northcliffe Golf Club,** High Bank Lane, Shipley BD18 4LJ (01274 584085). *Location:* three miles west of Bradford on A650; turn left at roundabout Junction of A650/A657. Undulating woodland parkland with feature holes. 18 holes, 6104 yards. S.S.S. 70. *Green Fees:* weekdays £25.00; weekends and Bank Holidays £30.00. *Eating facilities:* bars 11am to 11pm, food 11.30am to 9.00pm summer months. No catering or bar facilities Mondays, except Bank Holidays. *Visitors:* Monday to Friday, Saturday after 4.30pm, Sunday all day. Wide wheel/electric trolleys for hire. *Society Meetings:* welcome, packages available. Professional: M. Hillas (01274 587193). Hon. Secretary: I. Collins (01274 596731; Fax: 01274 584148).

BRADFORD. **Queensbury Golf Club,** Brighouse Road, Queensbury, Bradford BD13 1QF (01274 882155). *Location:* M62 Junction 25, A644 to Brighouse, Hipperholme and Queensbury. Wooded course. 9 holes, 5024 yards. S.S.S. 65. *Green Fees:* weekdays £15.00, weekends and Bank Holidays £30.00. *Eating facilities:* lunches, teas except Monday. Bar available. *Visitors:* welcome any day, must have Handicap. No parties at weekends. *Society Meetings:* by arrangement. Professional: D. Delaney (01274 816864). Secretary: B. Cox (01274 882155).

BRADFORD. **Shipley Golf Club,** Beckfoot Lane, Cottingley Bridge, Bingley BD16 1LX (01274 568652; Fax: 01274 567739). *Location:* off A650 at Cottingley Bridge, Bradford six miles, Bingley one mile. Flat parkland. 18 holes, 6235 yards. S.S.S. 70. Practice area and net putting green. *Green Fees:* weekdays £37.00 per day; weekends and Bank Holidays £42.00 per day, subject to change. Winter rates by arrangement. *Eating facilities:* available. *Visitors:* welcome by arrangement with Golf Manager; not Tuesdays or Saturdays. *Society Meetings:* catered for by arrangement with Golf Manager. Packages available. Professional/Golf Manager: R. Parry (01274 563674; Fax: 01274 567739). Manager/Secretary: Mrs M.J. Bryan (01274 568652; Fax: 01274 567739).

BRADFORD. **South Bradford Golf Club,** Pearson Road, Odsal, Bradford BD6 1BH (01274 679195 Club; 01274 690643 Office). *Location:* follow signs for Odsal Stadium, roundabout at Stadium turn left and first left again, road leads down to clubhouse. Parkland type course with some hilly sections. 9 holes, 6004 yards. S.S.S. 69. Practice ground. *Green Fees:* information not available. *Eating facilities:* bar meals available except Mondays. *Visitors:* welcome; not before 3.30pm on weekends and Bank Holidays. *Society Meetings:* welcome – must apply in writing. Professional: Mr Paul Cooke (01274 673346). Secretary: Mr B. Broadbent (01274 679195).

BRADFORD. **West Bowling Golf Club Ltd,** Newall Hall, Rooley Lane, Bradford BD5 8LB (01274 393207; Fax: 01274 393207). *Location:* junction of M606 (off M62) and Bradford ring road (east). Parkland. 18 holes, 5779 yards. S.S.S. 68. Practice facilities. *Green Fees:* weekdays £20.00; weekends £30.00 (restricted). *Eating facilities:* full dining except Mondays. *Visitors:* welcome Wednesday, Thursday and Friday, contact Professional or Secretary. Carts for hire. Snooker. *Society Meetings:* by arrangement as above. Steward: (01274 724449). Professional: Ian A. Marshall (01274 728036). Secretary: (Tel & Fax: 01274 393207).

BRADFORD. **West Bradford Golf Club Ltd,** Chellow Grange Road, Haworth Road, Bradford BD9 6NP. *Location:* three miles west of city centre off B6144 Haworth Road. Easy walking, undulating, wooded parkland course. 18 holes, 5723 yards. S.S.S. 68, Par 69. *Green Fees:* £25.00. Package deals for parties and societies from £15.00 (unlimited golf). Happy hour weekends after 4pm – reduced green fee. *Eating facilities:* available every day except Monday. *Visitors:* welcome, except Saturdays before 4pm. *Society Meetings:* welcome by arrangement. Professional: Nigel M. Barber (01274 542102). Secretary: I.P. Milnes (01274 542767; Fax: 01274 482079).

BRIGHOUSE. **Castlefields Golf Club,** Rastrick Common, Rastrick, Brighouse HD6 3HL. *Location:* one mile out of Brighouse on A643. Parkland course, founded 1903. 6 holes, 2406 yards. S.S.S. 50, Par 54. *Green Fees:* information not available. *Eating facilities:* Globe Inn 200 yards away. *Visitors:* welcome at all times but must be accompanied by a member. *Society Meetings:* contact Secretary for details. Secretary: B. V. Knights (01484 718898).

BRIGHOUSE. **Crow Nest Park Golf Club,** Coach Road, Hove Edge, Brighouse HD6 2LN (01484 401121). *Location:* Bradford Road out of Brighouse, left at Ritz Ballroom, right after one mile. Gently undulating parkland. 9 holes, 6020 yards. S.S.S. 69. Floodlit driving range with power tees and swingcam. *Green Fees:* 9 holes £12.00, 18 holes £24.00. *Eating facilities:* food available from 11.30am till 3pm and then from 5.30pm till 9.30pm, bar open from 11am until 11pm. *Visitors:* welcome but tees must be booked in advance with Professional. *Society Meetings:* welcome by prior arrangement. Professional: Paul Everitt. Secretary: (01484 401121). Clubhouse: (01484 401152).
e-mail: crownest@btconnect.com
website: www.crownestgolf.co.uk

BRIGHOUSE. **Willow Valley Golf and Country Club,** Highmoor Lane, off Walton Lane, Clifton, Brighouse HD6 4JB (01274 878624). *Location:* Junction 25 off M62 to Brighouse A644, right at roundabout A643, two miles on right. American-style island greens, undulating fairway, water. 18 holes, 7025 yards. S.S.S. 72. 9 hole course. 18 bay covered range. New 18 hole Pine Valley course due to open 2005. *Green Fees:* Monday to Friday £25.00; Saturday and Sunday £35.00. 9-hole course from £7.50. *Eating facilities:* fully licensed bar and catering. *Visitors:* always welcome. *Society meetings:* welcome, please contact the Sales Manager Helen Butterfield.
website: www.wvgc.co.uk

www.uk-golfguide.com

CLECKHEATON. Cleckheaton and District Golf Club Ltd, Bradford Road, Cleckheaton BD19 6BU (01274 851266; Fax: 01274 871382). *Location:* four miles south of Bradford on A638, 200 yards from Junction 26 M62. Parkland course. 18 holes, 5706 yards. Par 70, S.S.S. 68. Practice area. *Green Fees:* weekdays (May - October) £30.00 per round, £35.00 per day; weekends and Bank Holidays £39.00. *Eating facilities:* available except Mondays. *Visitors:* welcome except Saturdays, suggest prior enquiry. *Society Meetings:* catered for by prior arrangement with Secretary except Saturdays. Professional: Mike Ingham (01274 851267). Secretary: R. H. Green. (01274 851266; Fax: 01274 871382).
e-mail: info@cleckheatongolf.co.uk

DEWSBURY. **Hanging Heaton Golf Club,** White Cross Road, Dewsbury WF12 7DT (01924 461606; Fax; 01924 430100). *Location:* one mile from town centre on main A653 Dewsbury to Leeds road. 9 holes, 5836 yards (for 18 holes). S.S.S. 68. *Green Fees:* information not available. *Eating facilities:* available. *Visitors:* welcome without reservation, except weekends. *Society Meetings:* catered for by arrangement with Secretary. Professional: G. Moore (01924 467077). Secretary: Ken Wood (01924 430100).*

ELLAND. **Elland Golf Club,** Hammerstone Leach Lane, Elland HX5 0TA (01422 372505). *Location:* M62 Junction 24 exit off roundabout for Blackley, one mile. Parkland. 9 holes, 5498 yards. S.S.S. 67. *Green Fees:* weekdays £18.00; weekends £30.00. *Eating facilities:* meals/bar snacks except Mondays. *Visitors:* welcome weekdays except Thursdays. *Society Meetings:* by arrangement. Professional: N. Krzywicki (01422 374886). Secretary: R. F. Winterbottom (01422 379174).

GUISELEY. **Bradford Golf Club,** Hawksworth Lane, Guiseley, Leeds LS20 8NP (01943 875570). *Location:* Shipley to Ilkley road, left at top of Hollins Hill, one mile up Hawksworth Lane. Moorland/parkland. 18 holes, 6259 yards. S.S.S. 71. *Green Fees:* £33.00 per round, £40.00 per day. Discounts available for parties over 20. *Eating facilities:* every day, preferably by prior arrangement. *Visitors:* welcome, phone Professional for availability, not on weekends without prior arrangement. *Society Meetings:* catered for on weekdays (except Tuesdays) by prior arrangement. Professional: Sydney Weldon (01943 873719). Secretary: Mr T. Eagle (01943 875570).

HALIFAX. **Halifax Bradley Hall Golf Club,** Holywell Green, Halifax HX4 9AN (01422 374108). *Location:* three miles south of Halifax on B6112. Undulating moorland. 18 holes, 6138 yards. S.S.S. 70. Practice ground. *Green Fees:* weekdays £25.00 per round, weekends £30.00 per round; limited tee times available at '4 to play 3 to pay'. Reservations only (01422 370231). *Eating facilities:* full catering by arrangement except Mondays, seven day bar. *Visitors:* welcome. Snooker. *Society Meetings:* welcome with prior reservation weekdays. Handicap Certificate. Professional: P. Wood (01422 370231). Secretary: M. Dredge (01422 374108).

HALIFAX. **The Halifax Golf Club Ltd,** Union Lane, Ogden, Halifax HX2 8XR (01422 244171; Fax: 01422 241459). *Location:* four miles out of Halifax, A629 towards Keighley. Moorland. 18 holes, 6037 yards. S.S.S. 70. *Green Fees:* weekdays £25.00 per round, £30.00 per day; weekends £30.00 per round, £35.00 per day. *Eating facilities:* luncheons and dinners served. Good restaurant facilities. *Visitors:* welcome most days by arrangement (not Saturdays). *Society Meetings:* catered for by arrangement: £20.00 - £40.00. Professional: Michael Allison (01422 240047)

HALIFAX. **Lightcliffe Golf Club,** Knowle Top Road, Lightcliffe, Halifax HX3 8RG (01422 202459). *Location:* three miles east of Halifax on A58 (main Halifax to Leeds road). Parkland. 9 holes, 5388 metres. S.S.S. 68. *Green Fees:* information not available. *Eating facilities:* bar snacks and meals (except Mondays). *Visitors:* welcome without reservation but must confirm with Professional. Not Wednesdays. *Society Meetings:* catered for. Professional: Ron Tickle (01422 202459). Secretary: Rod Crampton (01484 384066).

HALIFAX. **Ryburn Golf Club,** The Shaw, Norland, Sowerby Bridge, Near Halifax HX6 3QP (01422 831355). *Location:* Halifax to Sowerby Bridge, turn left on station road, turn right up hill, right towards Hobbit Inn (signposted), left after cottages. Demanding, hilly, windy course. 9 holes, 5127 yards. S.S.S. 65. *Green Fees:* information not available. *Eating facilities:* good catering facilities and bar. *Visitors:* welcome weekdays, weekends by prior arrangement. *Society Meetings:* welcome by prior arrangement. Secretary: Jack Hoyle (01422 843070 home).

Bradford (Hawksworth) Golf Club

Hawksworth Lane, Guiseley LS20 8NP

Set in peaceful and tranquil countryside near the picturesque village of Hawksworth, this undulating parkland course enjoys magnificent views over the Yorkshire moors. The spacious greens make this a fair test of golf which must be treated with respect.

Traditional-style clubhouse with two well-stocked bars and excellent catering facilities. Special packages for individuals and golfing parties. No visitors on Saturdays; by prior arrangement on Sundays and Bank Holidays.

Enquiries to the Manager: 01943 875570

See also Colour Advertisement on page 43

HALIFAX. **West End Golf Club (Halifax) Ltd,** Paddock Lane, Highroad Well, Halifax HX2 0NT (01422 341878). *Location:* two miles west of town centre. Parkland. 18 holes, 5937 yards. S.S.S. 68 (White markers). *Green Fees:* weekdays £29.00 per round, £34.00 per day; weekends and Bank Holidays £34.00 per round, £39.00 per day. Subject to review. *Eating facilities:* full bar and catering except Mondays. *Visitors:* welcome except Saturdays - please check with Professional. No visiting parties on Saturdays. *Society Meetings:* catered for by arrangement with Secretary. Professional: David Rishworth (01422 341878). Secretary: G. Gower (Tel & Fax: 01422 341878).
e-mail: westendgc@btinternet.com

HEBDEN BRIDGE. **Hebden Bridge Golf Club,** Wadsworth, Hebden Bridge HX7 8PH (01422 842896). *Location:* one mile upwards past Birchcliffe Centre. Moorland with superb Pennine views. 9 holes, 5242 yards. S.S.S. 67. *Green Fees:* weekdays £12.00; weekends £15.00. 50% reduction for Juniors or if playing with member. Subject to review. *Eating facilities:* bar and dining room facilities, private functions catered for. *Visitors:* welcome, please check first at weekends. *Society Meetings:* welcome midweek only except by special arrangement. Steward: Mr Alan Platten (01422 842896).

HUDDERSFIELD. **Bradley Park Municipal Golf Course,** Off Bradley Road, Huddersfield HD2 1PZ (01484 223772). *Location:* M62 Junction 25, follow Huddersfield signs then A6107. Parkland course, rolling hills with panoramic views. 18 holes, 6220 yards. S.S.S. 70. Floodlit driving range, 9 hole Par 3 course. *Green Fees:* information not available. *Eating facilities:* full catering. *Visitors:* welcome, no restrictions. No block bookings for parties at weekends, only telephone bookings to the Professional for individuals. *Society Meetings:* all welcome, book through Professional. Professional: P.E. Reilly. Secretary: K. Blackwell (01484 223772; Fax: 01484 451613).*

HUDDERSFIELD. **Crosland Heath Golf Club Ltd,** Felks Stile Road, Crosland Hill, Huddersfield HD4 7AF (01484 653216). *Location:* 3 miles from town centre off A62 Oldham road. Flat heathland with extensive views. 18 holes, 6087 yards. Par 71. Practice facilities. *Green Fees:* on application. *Eating facilities:* full catering except Mondays. *Visitors:* welcome, suggest prior enquiry. *Society Meetings:* catered for by arrangement. Professional: (01484 653877). General Manager: (01484 653216; Fax: 01484 461079).
e-mail: golf@croslandheath.wanadoo.co.uk
website: www.croslandheath.co.uk

HUDDERSFIELD. **Huddersfield Golf Club,** Fixby Hall, Lightridge Road, Fixby, Huddersfield HD2 2EP (01484 426203; Fax: 01484 424623). *Location:* M62 Junction 24; A643 from Cedar Court Hotel; turn right first traffic lights by Sun Inn. Parkland course. 18 holes, 6399 yards. S.S.S. 71. Practice ground. *Green Fees:* weekdays £37.00 for 18 holes, £47.00 for 27/36 holes; weekends and Public Holidays £47.00 for 18 holes, £57.00 for 27/36 holes. £15.00 playing with a member. *Eating facilities:* available. *Visitors:* always welcome, reservation advised but not essential. Tuesday Ladies' Day; no visitors Saturdays. Snooker. *Society and Company Days:* catered for except weekends, well appointed private rooms. Catering to suit all occasions. Professional: P. Carman (01484 426463). Office Manager: Mrs D. Lockett (01484 426203). General Manager: Mrs S. Dennis (01484 426203).
e-mail: secretary@huddersfield-golf.co.uk
website: www.huddersfield-golf.co.uk

HUDDERSFIELD. **Longley Park Golf Club,** Maple Street (off Somerset Road), Aspley, Huddersfield HD5 9AX (01484 426932). *Location:* one mile town centre, Wakefield side. 9 holes, 5212 yards. S.S.S. 66. *Green Fees:* £16.00 weekdays; £20.00 weekends and Bank Holidays. *Eating facilities:* available. *Visitors:* welcome Mondays, Tuesdays and Fridays, other times by previous arrangement only. *Society Meetings:* welcome by previous arrangement with Secretary. Professional: Nick Leeming (01484 422304). Secretary: D. Palliser.

Crosland Heath Golf Club
Crosland Heath, Huddersfield, West Yorkshire HD4 7AF

Designed by the renowned Dr Alister Mackenzie, before he moved on to design Royal Melbourne and then Augusta, with Bobby Jones, Crosland Heath has matured into one of the finest examples of heathland excellence, where shot making is amply rewarded. At nearly 900ft above sea level, this challenging course has easy walking, and players have fabulous views on all sides. Coupled with practice, pro shop, catering and clubhouse facilities, this makes Crosland Heath an ideal venue for a visiting party, where you are assured of a friendly welcome.

Please contact the Secretary for package details.

Tel: 01484 653216 • Fax: 01484 461079
e-mail: golf@croslandheath.wanadoo.co.uk

See also Colour Advertisement on page 42

THE APPEARANCE OF AN ASTERISK (*) AT THE END OF A CLUB OR COURSE ENTRY INDICATES THAT UP-TO-DATE INFORMATION HAS NOT BEEN SUPPLIED

HUDDERSFIELD. Marsden Golf Club, Hemplow, Marsden, Huddersfield HD7 6NN (01484 844253). *Location:* eight miles west of Huddersfield off A62 from Huddersfield to Manchester. Moorland. 9 holes, 5702 yards. S.S.S. 68. *Green Fees:* weekdays £15.00 per round; with member £7.00; weekends £12.00 with members only; Bank Holidays £20.00 with member £12.00 (Includes 3rd party liability ins). *Eating facilities:* lunches and snacks available except Tuesdays. *Visitors:* welcome weekdays, with a member only weekends. *Society Meetings:* catered for by arrangement. Society package from £18.00 for day golf and evening meal. Professional: Rob Johnson (01484 843300). Secretary: S. J. Boustead (01457 874158).

HUDDERSFIELD. Meltham Golf Club, Thick Hollins Hall, Meltham, Huddersfield HD9 4DQ (Tel & Fax: 01484 850227). *Location:* half mile east of Meltham, six miles south west of Huddersfield (B6107). Gently sloping course in wooded valley. 18 holes, 6390 yards, 5832 metres. S.S.S. 70. Restricted practice area. *Green Fees:* weekdays £28.00 per round, £33.00 per day; weekends and Bank Holidays £33.00 per round, £38.00 per day. 2005 rates, subject to review. *Eating facilities:* lunches, dinners (with reservation), bar meals available. *Visitors:* welcome weekdays and Sundays without reservation, not Saturdays. *Society Meetings:* catered for by arrangement. Professional: P. Davies (01484 851521). Secretary: G.W. Hopwood.
website: www.meltham-golf.co.uk

HUDDERSFIELD. Woodsome Hall Golf Club, Woodsome Hall, Fenay Bridge, Huddersfield HD8 0LQ (01484 602739). *Location:* A629 five miles from Huddersfield. Parkland and wooded course. 18 holes, 6096 yards. S.S.S. 69. Practice ground. *Green Fees:* information not available. *Eating facilities:* bar snacks and dining available; new casual bar open. *Visitors:* welcome Mondays, Wednesdays, Thursdays and Fridays, limited on Sundays by application. *Society Meetings:* welcome by arrangement, jacket and tie in public rooms. Professional: M. Higginbottom (01484 602034). Hon Secretary: R.B. Shaw (01484 602739; Fax: 01484 608260). Managing Secretary: Mrs T.J. Mee (01484 602739).*

ILKLEY. **Ben Rhydding Golf Club,** High Wood, Ben Rhydding, Ilkley LS29 8SB (01943 608759). *Location:* one mile south-east of Ilkley town centre via Ben Rhydding Road or Wheatley Lane. Turn up Wheatley Grove and keep going on and up left.Moorside parkland course with fine panoramic views over Wharfedale and surrounding moors. 9 holes, 4611 yards (18 holes). S.S.S. 63. *Green Fees:* weekdays £15.00, with member £7.50; weekends £20.00, with member £10.00. *Society Meetings:* by prior arrangement. Secretary: Steve Brown (01943 865749).

ILKLEY. **Bracken Ghyll Golf Club,** Skipton Road, Addingham, Ilkley LS29 0SL (01943 831207; Fax: 01943 839453). *Location:* situated between Ilkley and Skipton on the A65, signposted just after roundabout indicating Silsden and Keighley. Parkland course in rolling dales countryside. 18 holes, 5600 yards, S.S.S. 67. Indoor nets, practice fairway and putting green. *Green Fees:* weekdays £20.00, weekends £24.00. *Eating facilities:* fully licensed bar, lunches served seven days a week in season. *Visitors:* welcome at all times outside competitions weekends and Tuesday and Thursday mornings. Telephone bookings accepted. *Society Meetings:* welcome, brochure on application. Secretary: Mrs Gunilla Vriesendorp.
e-mail: office@brackenghyll.fsnet.co.uk
website: www.brackenghyll.co.uk

ILKLEY. **Ilkley Golf Club,** Nesfield Road, Ilkley LS29 0BE (01943 607277). *Location:* 15 miles north of Bradford. Flat course. 18 holes, 6262 yards. S.S.S. 70. *Green Fees:* weekdays £42.00; weekends £50.00. Subject to review. *Eating facilities:* by arrangement. *Visitors:* welcome by arrangement. *Society Meetings:* catered for by arrangement. Professional: J.L. Hammond (01943 607463). Secretary: Peter G. Richardson (01943 600214; Fax: 01943 816130).
e-mail: honsec@ilkleygolfclub.co.uk
website: www.ilkleygolfclub.co.uk

KEIGHLEY. **Branshaw Golf Club,** Branshaw Moor, Oakworth, Keighley BD22 7ES (01535 643235). *Location:* on B6143, two miles from town centre. Moorland with extensive views. 18 holes, 5858 yards. S.S.S. 69. *Green Fees:* information not available. *Eating facilities:* full catering except Mondays. *Visitors:* welcome anytime by prior arrangement. *Society Meetings:* catered for weekdays only. Professional: Simon Jowitt (01535 647441). Secretary: Mr T. O'Hara (01535 643235).*

KEIGHLEY. **Keighley Golf Club,** Howden Park, Utley, Keighley BD20 6DH (01535 604778). *Location:* one mile west of Keighley towards Utley on B6143. Parkland. 18 holes, 6141 yards. S.S.S. 70. Practice ground and green. *Green Fees:* weekdays 18 holes £34.00, 27 holes £42.00; weekends and Bank Holidays 18 holes £38.00, 27 holes £46.00 per day. Full package for 16 or over, from £35.00 to £48.00. *Eating facilities:* full catering and bar facilities available. *Visitors:* welcome by prior arrangement. Tuesday Ladies' Day. *Society Meetings:* catered for by arrangement. Professional: Andy Rhodes. Secretary: Cameron Dawson (Fax: 01535 604778).
e-mail: manager@keighleygolfclub.com
website: www.keighleygolfclub.com

KEIGHLEY. **Riddlesden Golf Club,** Howden Rough, Riddlesden, Keighley BD20 5QN (01535 602148). *Location:* A650 Keighley-Bradford road, left into Bar Lane, left on Scott Lane, which leads on to Scott Lane West and Elam Wood Road, approximately two miles. Moorland, with spectacular 3 par 3s in "Best Extraordinary Golf Holes Book". 18 holes, 4295 yards. S.S.S. 61. *Green Fees:* weekdays £15.00; weekends £20.00. *Eating facilities:* catering available during bar hours. *Visitors:* welcome except between 10am–2pm Saturdays and before 2pm Sundays. *Society Meetings:* catered for by prior arrangement. Secretary: Mrs J. R. Bottomley (01274 551848).

www.uk-golfguide.com

KEIGHLEY. **Silsden Golf Club,** Brunthwaite Lane, Brunthwaite, Silsden, Near Keighley BD20 0ND (01535 652998). *Location:* five miles north of Keighley. Undulating downland with extensive views. 18 holes, 5062 yards. S.S.S. 64. Practice area and putting green. *Green Fees:* information not available. *Eating facilities:* licensed bar, full catering available except Mondays. *Visitors & Society Meetings:* Welcome anytime by prior arrangement with the office (01535 652998).*

KNOTTINGLEY. **Ferrybridge Golf Club,** PO Box 39, Stranglands Lane, Knottingley WF11 8SQ. *Location:* off the A1 at Ferrybridge and quarter of a mile towards Castleford on the B6136. Undulating land. 9 holes, 6047/6076 yards. S.S.S. 69. Architect: George Barton. Practice ground. *Green Fees:* information not available. *Visitors:* welcome by prior booking. *Society Meetings:* by prior arrangement with Secretary. Secretary: Mr T.D. Ellis (01977 884165).*

LEEDS. **Alwoodley Golf Club,** Wigton Lane, Alwoodley, Leeds LS17 8SA (0113 2681680). *Location:* five miles north of Leeds on A61 (Leeds to Harrogate). 18 holes, 6666 yards. S.S.S. 72. *Green Fees:* £65.00 weekdays; £80.00 weekends. *Eating facilities:* available. *Visitors:* welcome by arrangement. *Society Meetings:* catered for by arrangement. Professional: J.R. Green (0113 2689603). Secretary: Mrs J Slater (Fax: 0113 2939458).
website: www.alwoodley.co.uk

LEEDS. **Calverley Golf Club,** Woodhall Lane, Pudsey, Leeds LS28 5QY (0113 256 9244; Fax: 0113 256 4362). *Location:* off Leeds outer ring road, signposted Pudsey. Take Bradford turn off, turn right at next roundabout onto Woodhall Lane. Parkland course. 18 holes, 5590 yards. S.S.S. 67. New 9 holes opening Spring 2005. Practice ground, putting green. *Green Fees:* weekdays £13.00, with a member £9.00; weekends £16.00, with a member £12.00. Juniors £7.00. *Eating facilities:* full bar and catering facilities available. *Visitors:* very welcome, booking advisable. Members only weekends till 1pm. Buggies. Tuition available. *Society Meetings:* welcome by prior arrangement. Professional: Neil Wendel-Jones (0113 256 9244; Fax: 0113 256 4362). Hon. Secretary: Phil Dyson (0113 256 9244; Fax: 0113 256 4362).

LEEDS. **Cookridge Hall Golf Club,** Cookridge Lane, Leeds LS16 7NL (0113 2300641; Fax: 0113 2030198). *Location:* five miles to north of Leeds, two miles from Leeds and Bradford Airport on Cookridge Lane. Heavily mounded American parkland course. Designed by Karl Litten who designed The Emirates Golf Course in Dubai and The Warwickshire in the West Midlands. 18 holes, 6779 yards, 6000 metres. S.S.S. 72. 20 bay driving range with floodlights. *Green Fees:* from £23.00. *Eating facilities:* clubhouse with full bar and restaurant. *Visitors:* very welcome, weekends after 2pm tee times can be reserved 7 days in advance, subject to availability. Academy and lessons. *Society Meetings:* all welcome with appropriate advance booking. For information please contact sales office.
e-mail: elaine@cookridgehall.co.uk
website: www.cookridgehall.co.uk

LEEDS. **Garforth Golf Club Ltd,** Long Lane, Garforth, Leeds LS25 2DS (0113 286 3308). *Location:* six miles east of Leeds on A63, then turn left on to A642. Flat parkland. 18 holes, 6306 yards. S.S.S. 70. Practice area. *Green Fees:* weekdays £36.00 per round, £42.00 per day. *Eating facilities:* available. *Visitors:* welcome, but not before 9.30am or between 12 noon and 2pm (1.30pm Tuesdays and Thursdays). Weekend as member's guest only. *Society Meetings:* catered for. Professional: K. Findlater (0113 286 2063). Managing Secretary: Neil Douglas (Tel & Fax: 0113 286 3308).

LEEDS. **Gotts Park Municipal Golf Club,** Gotts House, Gotts Park, Armley Ridge Road, Leeds LS12 2QX (0113 231 0492). *Location:* two miles west of city centre off A647 Stanningley Road. Undulating parkland. 18 holes, 4319 yards. S.S.S. 64. Putting green and practice area. *Green Fees:* information not available. *Eating facilities:* cafe, bar facilities evenings/weekends only. *Visitors:* welcome, tee reserved Sundays 7am to 10am for members. Secretary: Maurice Gill (0113 256 2994).

LEEDS. **Headingley Golf Club,** Back Church Lane, Adel, Leeds LS16 8DW (0113 2673052). *Location:* leave Leeds/Otley road (A660) at Church Lane, Adel about five miles from city centre. 18 holes, 6608 yards. S.S.S. 72. *Green Fees:* £36.00 per round, £45.00 per day weekdays, £45.00 per round or day weekends and Bank Holidays. *Eating facilities:* full catering and bar facilities. *Visitors:* members of other golf clubs welcome, preferably with prior reservation. Two snooker tables. *Society Meetings:* catered for by arrangement. Professional: N.M. Harvey (0113 2675100). Secretary: (0113 2679573; Fax: 0113 2817334). Manager: J.R. Burns (0113 2679573).

THE APPEARANCE OF AN ASTERISK (*) AT THE END OF A CLUB OR COURSE ENTRY INDICATES THAT UP-TO-DATE INFORMATION HAS NOT BEEN SUPPLIED

CALVERLEY GOLF CLUB Woodhall Lane, Pudsey, Leeds LS28 5QY
Halfway between Leeds and Bradford, Calverley's 18-hole course at 5590 yards and Par 68 poses its own unique challenge in the form of tight fairways and target greens. Visitors and societies are welcome at this friendly club with society packages from as little as £15.
For more information call 0113 256 9244
See also Colour Advertisement on page 41

LEEDS. Horsforth Golf Club Ltd, Layton Rise, Horsforth, Leeds LS18 5EX (0113 258 6819; Fax: 0113 258 9336). *Location:* midway between Leeds and Bradford, close to the Leeds and Bradford Airport. Easily accessible from the Leeds outer ring road and the main Bradford to Harrogate road. White tees 6219 yards, Yellow tees 5879, Ladies tees 5435 yards. Par 71. *Green Fees:* weekdays £26.00 per round, £32.00 per day; weekends (limited) £36.00 per day. *Eating facilities:* Bar sevice available from 11.30am to 11pm. Catering ranges from coffees, breakfast, light or full lunches; buffet and formal evening meals. No smoking in dining room or lounge bar. *Visitors:* welcome, must comply with dress code. *Society Meetings:* welcome. Professionals: Dean Stokes & Simon Booth (0113 258 5200) Steward: C. Taylor (0113 258 1703). Secretary: Mrs L. Harrison (0113 258 6819). e-mail: secretary@horsforthgolfclubltd.co.uk website: www.horsforthgolfclubltd.co.uk

LEEDS. Howley Hall Golf Club, Scotchman Lane, Morley, Leeds LS27 0NX (01924 350107; Fax: 01924 350104). *Location:* turn off the A650 Bradford/Wakefield road at the Halfway House Public House, take the B6123 towards Batley – the course is on the left. Parkland. 18 holes, 6346 yards, S.S.S. 70. Practice ground. *Green Fees:* weekdays £30.00 per round, £36.00 per day; weekends £40.00. *Eating facilities:* dining room and bar snacks available. *Visitors:* welcome. *Society Meetings:* welcome by reservation. Professional: Gary Watkinson (01924 350102). Secretary/ Manager: David Jones (01924 350100; Fax: 01924 350104).
e-mail: office@howleyhall.co.uk

LEEDS. Leeds Golf Club, Cobble Hall, Elmete Lane, Leeds LS8 2LJ (0113 2658775). *Location:* Leeds ring road to A58, turn left if from east, right if from west, fork right at dual carriageway, turn right after 250 yards. 18 holes, 6078 yards. S.S.S. 69. *Green Fees:* £35.00 per day, £30.00 per round weekdays only; weekends only with a member. Subject to review. Golf packages available with restrictions. *Eating facilities:* full catering, all day bar. *Visitors:* welcome. *Society Meetings:* very welcome. Some limited society days available on Sundays. Professional: Simon Longster (0113 2658786). Secretary: Stephen Clarkson (0113 2659203; Fax: 0113 2323369).

LEEDS. Leeds Golf Centre, Wike Ridge Lane, Shadwell, Leeds LS17 9JW (0113 288 6000; Fax: 0113 288 6185). *Location*: from Leeds city centre take A61 Harrogate road, cross A6120 outer ring road, continue for one mile, turn right at lights into Wigton Lane. After one mile turn left at T-junction into Wike Ridge Lane; golf course is on left. Set in magnificent rolling Yorkshire countryside. Wike Ridge course: 18 holes, 6354 yards. S.S.S. 70. Oaks course: 12 holes, 1610 yards. Par 36. 19-bay driving range, chipping green, putting green. *Green Fees:* information not available. *Eating facilities:* restaurant, bar and function room. *Visitors:* welcome any time. Tuition for individuals and groups. *Society Meetings:* welcome any time; special offers available throughout the year. Head Professional: Mark Pinkett, Professionals: Graham Bradley, Chris Marshall. General Manager: Adam Frontal-Gay.*
e-mail: info@leedsgolfcentre.com
website: www.leedsgolfcentre.com

LEEDS. Middleton Park (Municipal) Golf Club, Ring Road, Beeston, Middleton, Leeds LS10 3TN (0113 270 0449). *Location:* ring road to Middleton off A653 (Water Tower). Parkland, wooded course. 18 holes, 5036 yards. S.S.S. 66. Practice ground. *Green Fees:* information not available. *Visitors:* welcome weekdays, contact the Professional for bookings. *Society Meetings:* contact the Professional. Professional: J. Pape (0113 270 9506). Secretary: Mrs Lynn Ratcliffe (0113 277 7715).*
e-mail: lynn@ratcliffel.fsnet.co.uk

LEEDS. Moor Allerton Golf Club, Coal Road, Wike, Leeds LS17 9NH (0113 2661154; Fax: 0113 2371124). *Location:* off the A61, 6 miles from Leeds city centre. Undulating parkland, PGA European Tour championship course designed by Robert Trent Jones Senior. 27 holes - three loops of 9 holes. Any combination playable. 6 bay driving range, practice ground. *Green Fees:* information not available. *Eating facilities:* full restaurant facilities plus snack bar. *Visitors:* welcome but must pre-book via Professional Shop. No visitors Sundays. Banqueting facilities for 200 people; conference/room hire for groups of all sizes. *Society Meetings:* welcome by prior arrangement via club office. Professional: Richard Lane (0113 2665209) Office: (0113 2661154; Fax: 0113 2371124).*
e-mail: info@magc.co.uk
website: www.magc.co.uk

LEEDS. Moortown Golf Club, Harrogate Road, Alwoodley, Leeds LS17 7DB (0113 2686521; Fax: 0113 2680986). *Location:* five miles north of Leeds centre, A61 Leeds to Harrogate road. 18 holes, 6453 yards. S.S.S. 72. Large practice field. *Green Fees:* weekdays £65.00 per round/day, weekends and Bank Holidays £75.00 per round/day. *Eating facilities:* lunches every day, evening meals Tuesday to Saturday. *Visitors:* welcome weekdays, some tee-off time restrictions. *Society Meetings:* catered for. Professional:M. Heggie (0113 2683636). Secretary: J.L. Hall (0113 2686521).

LEEDS. Oulton Park, Rothwell Lane, Rothwell, Leeds LS26 8EX (0113 282 3152; Fax: 0113 282 6290). *Location:* M62 - Rothwell turn off, Junction 30; left at second roundabout. Parkland course built by Dave Thomas, many bunkers. 27 holes, 22 bay driving range, putting green. *Green Fees:* information not available. *Eating facilities:* restaurant and bar. *Visitors:* welcome, no restrictions; advance booking (five days) available. Dress code on course. *Society Meetings:* welcome except weekends. Professional: Steve Gromett. Manager: Allan Cooper.*

LEEDS. Rawdon Golf and Lawn Tennis Club, Buckstone Drive, Micklefield Lane, Rawdon, Leeds LS19 6BD (0113-250 6040). *Location:* eight miles north of Leeds on A65, left at Rawdon traffic lights on to Mickiefield Lane. Undulating parkland, with trees a special feature. 9 holes (18 tees), 5964 yards. S.S.S. 69. *Green Fees:* information not available. *Eating facilities:* meals and bar snacks except Mondays. *Visitors:* welcome. Facilities for tennis, visitors welcome. *Society Meetings:* catered for on application to Secretary. Secretary: John Lawson (01943 872430).

THE GOLF GUIDE 2006 — ENGLAND / West Yorkshire

LEEDS. **Roundhay Golf Club,** Park Lane, Leeds LS8 2EJ (0113 2662695). *Location:* four miles north of Leeds city centre, leave A58 to Wetherby at Oakwood. Wooded parkland. 9 holes, 5322 yards. S.S.S. 65. Practice ground. *Green Fees:* on application. *Eating facilities:* bar for members and guests, restaurant in evenings. *Visitors:* welcome without reservation. *Society Meetings:* arrangements with Leeds City Council. Professional: J. Pape (0113 2661686). Hon. Secretary: R.H. McLauchlan (0113 2664225).

LEEDS. **Sand Moor Golf Club,** Alwoodley Lane, Leeds LS17 7DJ (0113 2681685). *Location:* five miles north of Leeds off A61. Moorland, overlooking picturesque Wharfedale. 18 holes, 6414 yards, 5862 metres. S.S.S. 71. *Green Fees:* information on request. *Eating facilities:* lunches daily, evening meals by arrangement. *Visitors:* welcome most weekdays and Sundays by arrangement. *Society Meetings:* catered for by arrangement. Professional: Frank Houlgate (0113 2683925). Secretary: Ian Kerr (0113 2685180; Fax: 0113 2661105).

LEEDS. **Scarcroft Golf Club,** Syke Lane, Leeds LS14 3BQ (0113 289 2263). *Location:* A58 Wetherby road; turn left at Bracken Fox Public House, Scarcroft village seven miles north of Leeds. Undulating parkland. 18 holes, 6426 yards. S.S.S. 71. Practice ground. *Green Fees:* information not avilable. *Eating facilities:* bar and restaurant except Mondays. *Visitors:* casuals after 9.30am. *Society Meetings:* accepted Mondays to Fridays April to October. Must have official Handicaps. Party rates for groups of 20 or more. Professional: Darren Tear (0113 289 2780). General Manager: Darren Tear (0113 289 2311).

LEEDS. **South Leeds Golf Club,** Parkside Links, Gipsy Lane, Leeds LS11 5TU (0113 270 0479). *Location:* M62 and M1 within five minutes' drive, Leeds City Centre 5 minutes' drive. Parkland course with undulating fairways. 18 holes, 5769 yards. S.S.S. 69. Practice ground and net. *Green Fees:* £18.00 weekdays; £32.00 weekends and Bank Holidays (rates may change). *Eating facilities:* full catering except Mondays; bar. *Visitors:* welcome weekdays. *Society Meetings:* catered for by prior arrangement. Professional: Laurie Turner (0113 270 2598). Secretary: B. Clayton (0113 277 1676).

LEEDS. **Temple Newsam Golf Club,** Temple Newsam, Leeds LS15 0NL (0113 264 5624). *Location:* easily reached by public transport from City (to Temple Newsam or Halton). Two 18 hole courses. No. 1 Course 6448 yards. S.S.S. 71. No. 2 Course 5731 yards. S.S.S. 70. *Green Fees:* information not available. *Eating facilities:* cafe open six days a week 7.30am till 4.00pm weekends, 10.00am till 4.00pm midweek. *Visitors:* welcome without reservation, except that parties must book in advance. *Society Meetings:* catered for. Professional: A. Swain (0113 264 1464). Secretary: G. Gower.*

MIRFIELD. **Dewsbury District Golf Club,** The Pinnacle, Sands Lane, Mirfield WF14 8HJ (01924 491928). *Location:* turn off A644 opposite Swan Inn, two miles west of Dewsbury. Undulating moorland/parkland with panoramic views over surrounding countryside. 18 holes, 6360 yards. S.S.S. 71. Practice field, putting green. *Green Fees:* weekdays £20.00 per round, £25.00 per day; weekends £15.00 after 3pm. Subject to review. *Eating facilities:* bar and restaurant (catering every day). *Visitors:* welcome without reservation weekdays, weekends with member only before 3pm. *Society Meetings:* welcome by prior arrangement. Parties over 12: day £22.50 per person. Professional: N.P. Hirst (01924 496030). General Manager: Ray Dando (01924 492399). e-mail: dewsbury.golf@btopenworld.com

OTLEY. **Otley Golf Club,** West Busk Lane, Otley LS21 3NG (01943 465329). *Location:* off main Bradford to Otley road. Parkland with magnificent views across Wharfedale. 18 holes, 6237 yards. S.S.S. 70. Large practice ground. *Green Fees:* weekdays £32.00 for 18 or 27 holes, £38.00 for two rounds; weekends £38.00 for 18 or 27 holes, £45.00 for two rounds. *Eating facilities:* large dining rooms. *Visitors:* welcome except Tuesday mornings and Saturdays. Trolleys and clubs for hire. *Society Meetings:* catered for by arrangement; special facilities for company days. Professional: Steven Tomkinson (01943 465329 ext. 203; Fax: 01943 463403). Secretary/Manager: Peter J. Clarke (01943 465329 ext 202; Fax: 01943 850387).

OUTLANE. **Outlane Golf Club,** Slack Lane, off New Hey Road, Outlane, Near Huddersfield HD3 3FQ (01422 374762; Fax: 01422 311789). *Location:* from Huddersfield (A640) through Outlane Village, entrance on left just after bus terminus. Semi-moorland course, part wooded. Offers panoramic views and is challenge to the amateur. 18 holes, 6100 yards. S.S.S. 69. Practice areas and nets available. *Green Fees:* £19.00 mid week; £29.00 weekends and Bank Holidays. Reduced rates playing with member and after 1pm Sundays. *Eating facilities:* full catering available except Mondays. *Visitors:* welcome except Saturdays; Sundays by arrangement. Carts available. *Society Meetings:* welcome with reservation. Professional: D.M. Chapman (01422 374762; Fax: 01422 311789). Secretary: P. Jackson (Tel & Fax: 01422 311789). Stewardess: Mrs C.E. Hirst.

PONTEFRACT. **Pontefract and District Golf Club,** Park Lane, Pontefract WF8 4QS (01977 792241). *Location:* M62 Exit 32, one mile from Pontefract on B6134. Parkland. 18 holes, 6227 yards. S.S.S. 70. Practice ground. *Green Fees:* weekdays £25.00 per round, £30.00 per day; weekends £32.00. *Eating facilities:* available all week. *Visitors:* welcome. *Society Meetings:* catered for Mondays, Tuesdays, Thursdays and Fridays by arrangement. Professional: Nick J. Newman (01977 706806). Manager: (01977 792241). e-mail: manager@pdgc.co.uk
website: www.pdgc.co.uk

THE APPEARANCE OF AN ASTERISK (*) AT THE END OF A CLUB OR COURSE ENTRY INDICATES THAT UP-TO-DATE INFORMATION HAS NOT BEEN SUPPLIED

PONTEFRACT near. **Mid-Yorkshire Golf Club,** Havercroft Lane, Darrington, Near Pontefract (01977 704522; Fax: 01977 600823). *Location*: 300 yards from A1 at Darrington half-mile south of A1/M62 interchange. Undulating with established woodland and lakes. 18 holes, 6424 yards. Par 72. 23 bay floodlit driving range, tee to green irrigation, 18 greens played all year round. *Green Fees:* information not available. *Eating facilities:* two bars with private functions catered for. *Visitors:* welcome weekdays, afternoons only at weekends. Buggies available. *Society Meetings:* welcome weekdays. Professional: Mike Hessay (01977 600844). website: www.midyorkshiregolfclub.com

PUDSEY. **Fulneck Golf Club Ltd,** Fulneck, Pudsey LS28 8NT (0113 2565191). *Location:* between Leeds and Bradford. Undulating wooded parkland course. 9 holes, 5456 yards. S.S.S. 67. *Green Fees:* information not available. *Society Meetings:* catered for by arrangement. Secretary: Mrs P.A. Warburton (0113 2562606).*

PUDSEY. **Woodhall Hills Golf Club Ltd,** Woodhall Road, Calverley, Pudsey, Leeds LS28 5UN (0113 256 4771). *Location:* signposted Calverley from A647 Leeds to Bradford Road, quarter of a mile beyond Calverley Golf Club. Parkland course. 18 holes, 6184 yards. S.S.S. 70. *Green Fees:* weekdays £24.00 per round, £29.00 per day. Sundays/Bank Holidays £29.00 per round, £34.00 per day. *Eating facilities:* available daily except Mondays. *Visitors:* welcome without reservation. *Society Meetings:* catered for by previous arrangement. Golf Manager/Professional: W. Lockett (0113 256 2857). Club Office: (0113 255 4594)

SHIPLEY. **Marriott Hollins Hall Hotel & Country Club,** Hollins Hill, Baildon, Shipley BD17 7QW (01274 534212). Home to the PGA European Professional Tour. *Location:* North/South Leeds Ring Road, take A65 Skipton Road, then A6038 (towards Shipley), entrance on right. Superb championship heathland course in the beautiful Yorkshire Dales. 18 holes. Par 71. *Green Fees:* information not available. *Eating facilities:* available all day. *Visitors:* welcome. Trolley, buggy and shoe hire.*

TODMORDEN. **Todmorden Golf Club,** Rive Rocks, Cross Stone Road, Todmorden OL14 8RD (01706 812986). *Location:* A646 Halifax Road, half a mile left Cross Stone Road, half a mile, bear left at top. Moorland. 9 holes, 5902 yards. S.S.S. 68. *Green Fees:* weekdays £15.00; weekends and Bank Holidays £20.00. Packages (18 or 27 holes from £25.00) available Monday, Tuesday, Wednesday and Sunday, includes coffee and biscuits on arrival, soup and sandwiches, evening meal. *Eating facilities:* available, order in advance. *Visitors:* welcome without reservation, but advisable to phone beforehand. Thursday is Ladies' Day. *Society Meetings:* welcome, please phone for course availability.

WAKEFIELD. **City of Wakefield Golf Club,** Lupset Park, Horbury Road, Wakefield WF2 8QS (01924 360282). *Location:* one mile from city centre, two miles from M1 Junctions 39/40. Undulating partially wooded parkland. 18 holes, 6319 yards, 5760 metres. S.S.S. 70. *Green Fees:* on application. *Eating facilities:* full or snack catering, bar available. *Visitors:* weekdays ball chute operates, weekends booked times only. *Society Meetings:* by arrangement with Stewardess (01924 367242). Secretary: (01924 367442).

WAKEFIELD. **Lofthouse Hill Golf Club,** Wakefield Road, Wakefield WF3 3LR (Tel & Fax: 01924 823703). *Location*: A61 between Leeds and Wakefield. Parkland course. 18 holes, 5933 yards, S.S.S. 68. *Green Fees*: £12.00. Buggies £12.00. *Eating facilities*: food available all day in bar. *Visitors*: welcome, please telephone. Teaching professional. *Society Meetings:* welcome, see website. Professional: Derek Johnson (Tel & Fax: 01924 823703). Secretary: David Nicklin.
website: www.lofthousehillgolfclub.co.uk

WAKEFIELD. **Low Laithes Golf Club Ltd,** Parkmill Lane, Flushdyke, Ossett, Wakefield WF5 9AP (01924 266067). *Location:* one mile from Junction 40 M1, or along A638 Dewsbury to Wakefield road. Parkland, undulating. 18 holes, 6456 yards. S.S.S. 71. Practice area. *Green Fees:* Monday - Friday £22.00 per round, £25.00 per day. *Eating facilities:* bar and catering. *Visitors:* welcome weekdays after 9.30am to 12.30 and after 1.30pm. *Society Meetings:* by arrangement, not weekends or Bank Holidays - 27 holes and catering. Professional: Paul Browning (01924 274667). Secretary: Paul Browning (Tel & Fax: 01924 266067).

WAKEFIELD. **Normanton Golf Club,** Hatfeild Hall. Aberford Road, Stanley WF3 4JP (01924 377943; Fax: 01924 200777). *Location:* M62 Junction 30, A642 toward Wakefield. Parkland course. Practice area. 18 holes, 6191 yards, 5662 metres. S.S.S. 70. *Green Fees:* £26.00 per round. *Visitors:* welcome weekdays. Saturday limited access. *Society Meetings:* welcome during the week. Restricted at weekend. Professional: Gary Pritchard (01924 200900). General Manager (01924 377943).

WAKEFIELD. **Painthorpe House Golf and Country Club,** Painthorpe Lane, Crigglestone, Wakefield WF4 5AZ (01924 255083; Fax: 01924 252022). *Location:* half a mile from Junction 39 M1. Undulating parkland. 9 holes, 4548 yards. S.S.S. 62. *Green Fees:* weekdays £7.00, weekends £8.00. *Eating facilities:* four bars, extensive catering for private functions. Two ballrooms (one holding 450, the other 60), Saturday dinner dances. *Visitors:* welcome, by appointment if parties, after 1.30pm on a Sunday. Bowling green. *Society Meetings:* by arrangement. Secretary: T. Mead (01924 254737).

For full details of clubs and courses, plus convenient accommodation
www.uk-golfguide.com

WAKEFIELD. **Wakefield Golf Club,** Woodthorpe Lane, Sandal, Wakefield WF2 6JH (01924 258778; Fax: 01924 242752). *Location:* leave M1 at Junction 39, golf club off Barnsley Road. Parkland. 18 holes, 6653 yards. S.S.S. 72. *Green Fees:* weekdays £32.00 per round, £37.00 per day, with a member £15.00 per day; weekends and Bank Holidays £40.00, with a member £20.00. *Eating facilities:* full catering available. *Visitors:* visiting parties by arrangement Wednesdays, Thursdays and Fridays. *Society Meetings:* welcome, catered for by arrangement. Professional: I.M. Wright. Secretary: Mrs E. Newton (01924 258778).

WAKEFIELD. **Woolley Park Golf Club,** New Road, Woolley, Wakefield WF4 2JS (01226 380144; Fax: 01226 390295; 01226 382209 (Office)). *Location:* half a mile from A61 half way between Barnsley and Wakefield. Parkland course. 18 holes, 6636 yards (white tees), S.S.S. 72. Practice area, putting green. *Green Fees:* weekdays £18.50; weekends £25.00. *Eating facilities:* food available all day every day, bar. *Visitors:* welcome all week, weekend bookings from Thursday only. Tuition available. *Society Meetings:* welcome, please telephone for details. Professional: Jon Baldwin (01226 380144; Fax: 01226 390295). Secretary: David Rowbottom (01226 382209; Fax: 01226 390295). website: www.woolleyparkgolfclub.co.uk

WETHERBY. **Wetherby Golf Club,** Linton Lane, Linton, Wetherby LS22 4JF (01937 582527; Fax: 01937 581915). *Location:* three quarters of a mile west of A1 roundabout. Parkland course adjoining River Wharfe. 18 holes, 6213 yards. S.S.S. 70. Practice ground. *Green Fees:* weekdays £30.00 per round, £40.00 per day; weekends £44.00 per round/day. *Eating facilities:* available seven days a week. *Visitors:* welcome, advisable to phone first. *Society Meetings:* catered for weekdays except Tuesday mornings. Professional: Mark Daubney (01937 580089 ext. 22). Golf Club Manager: Barry Groves (01937 580089 ext. 20).

THE APPEARANCE OF AN ASTERISK (*) AT THE END OF A CLUB OR COURSE ENTRY INDICATES THAT UP-TO-DATE INFORMATION HAS NOT BEEN SUPPLIED

MID YORKSHIRE GOLF CLUB

Ideally situated where the Yorkshires meet
Easily accessible all routes. M62 J33 – A1 south ½ mile
Established in 1993, incorporating existing mature woodland.
Links style golf course, 18 holes Par 72, 6424 yards.
Superb clubhouse with function room.
23-bay floodlit driving range. Buggies available.

www.midyorkshiregolfclub.com

Havercroft Lane, Darrington, Pontefract WF8 3BP
Tel: 01977 704522 • Fax: 01977 600823

See also Colour Advertisement on page 42

Hollins Hall Marriott Hotel and Country Club

The 18 hole Championship Golf Course, and host to the Sky TV – PGA Europrotour Championships, provides a great test for golfers of all abilities.
At 6671yards, Hollins Hall is a challenging course, the best defence being the huge undulating greens and well positioned bunkering. The signature hole 14th, called 'viaduct', is a tricky par four providing a masterpiece in tactical design, with the 19th century viaduct providing a fantastic backdrop.
The greens and tees are built to USGA standards providing exceptional drainage and quality surfaces.
The Marriott Hollins Hall is a fantastic Championship Golf Venue for golfing groups.
Hollins Hall Marriott Hotel and Country Club
Hollins Hill, Baildon, Shipley, Bradford, West Yorkshire BD17 7QW
Tel: 01274 530 053 • Fax: 01274 534 251 • www.marriott.com

SCOTLAND Counties

- SHETLAND ISLANDS
- WESTERN ISLES
- HIGHLAND
- MORAY
- ABERDEENSHIRE
- ABERDEEN CITY
- PERTH AND KINROSS
- ANGUS
- DUNDEE CITY
- ARGYLL AND BUTE
- STIRLING
- FIFE
- E. LOTHIAN
- NORTH AYRSHIRE
- S. LANARKSHIRE
- BORDERS
- EAST AYRSHIRE
- SOUTH AYRSHIRE
- DUMFRIES AND GALLOWAY

1. Inverclyde
2. West Dunbartonshire
3. Renfrewshire
4. East Renfrewshire
5. City of Glasgow
6. East Dunbartonshire
7. North Lanarkshire
8. Falkirk
9. Clackmannanshire
10. West Lothian
11. City of Edinburgh
12. Midlothian

Golf in Scotland
Where to Play, Where to Stay

In 2005 the Open Championship returned to the home of Golf – St Andrews. The tournament saw the return of Tiger Woods to the top spot in golf and the retirement of arguably the greatest player ever, Jack Nicklaus. It was a reminder of just how important the country of Scotland has been to the game of golf.

Visitors to Scotland are fortunate in being able to choose from one of the widest variety of top class courses anywhere in the world. With such prestigious courses as St Andrews, Turnberry, Gleneagles, and Carnoustie, along with a huge variety of family-friendly courses, golfers in Scotland are truly spoilt for choice.

Remember that golf in Scotland need not be just a summer sport. A round on a crisp, clear Highland morning can be magical at any time of the year.

A book which readers of **The Golf Guide** may find of interest is *'The Wee Yellow Book'*. This publication, produced by Les Starkings as a 'hobby' over 18 years ago, contains details of Open Competitions throughout Scotland, giving golfers a chance to plan their season and visit new courses playing in tournaments ranging from Scratch Opens, Senior Opens, Mixed Foursomes, Ladies and Junior Opens etc.

Making use of **The Golf Guide** to give you information on the course including contact details etc, you can decide which courses you would like to visit and check the *'Wee Yellow Book'* to see when a suitable tournament is being run.

'The Wee Yellow Book' is available from most clubs, or in case of difficulty contact:
The Star-King Press, 31 Curriehill Castle Drive, Balerno, Edinburgh EH14 5TA
Tel & Fax: 0131 451 5782
e-mail: lstarkings@btinternet.com or **les@weeyellowbook.com**

In recent years the Scottish *'Wee Yellow Book'* has been joined by a *'Wee Blue Book'* for Northern England.

Royal Dornoch Golf Club

Links

Handicaps
Memberships
Bookings
Till & Stock Control
Accounts

14 Skaethorn Road, Havana Lock
Glasgow G20 0TQ • Tel: 0141 945 5501

www.linksgolf.co.uk

See also Colour Advertisement on page 56

golf breaks

carnoustie st andrews
islay campbeltown
isle of man
cork

for reservations and useful information:
0141 305 5006
golf@scotiatravel.com • www.scotiatravel.com

scotiagolf

Visit the FHG website
www.holidayguides.com
for details of the wide choice of accommodation featured in the full range of FHG titles

Aberdeenshire, Banff & Moray

ABERDEEN. **Aberdeen City Golf, Auchmill Golf Club,** Provost Rust Drive, Aberdeen AB2 7FQ (01224 714577). *Location:* approximately four miles from city centre, beside Bucksburn area. Parkland, wooded course. 18 holes, 5391 metres. Practice area. Putting area. *Green Fees:* information not available. *Visitors:* welcome anytime. Starter: (01224 714577).*
website: www.aberdeencity.gov.uk/leisure

ABERDEEN. **Aberdeen City Golf, Balnagask Golf Course,** St Fitticks Road, Aberdeen. (01224 876407). *Location:* on coast beside Girdleness Lighthouse between Aberdeen Harbour and Nigg Bay, south side of city. Seaside links. 18 holes, 5541 metres. 9-hole pitch and putt. *Green Fees:* information not available. *Visitors:* welcome. Starter: (01224 876407).*
website: www.aberdeencity.gov.uk/leisure

ABERDEEN. **Aberdeen City Golf, Hazlehead Golf Course,** Hazlehead Avenue, Aberdeen AB9 1XJ (01224 321830). *Location:* situated on west edge of city, four miles from city centre. From A944 into Aberdeen turn off into Groats Road. Two courses - 18 holes, 5690 metres; 18 holes, 5270 metres. 9 hole course, 2531 metres. *Green Fees:* information not available. *Eating facilities:* restaurant adjoining park. *Visitors:* welcome. Professional: Tel (01224 317336). Starter: (01224 321830).*
website: www.aberdeencity.gov.uk/leisure

ABERDEEN. **Aberdeen City Golf, King's Links Golf Course,** Golf Road, Aberdeen (01224 632269). *Location:* behind the Pittodrie Stadium, on the King's Links, by the beach. Seaside links. 6-hole, 1273 yards. 18-hole, 6296 yards, S.S.S 71. *Green Fees:* weekdays adult £11.25 junior £4.75 per round; weekends adult £11.25, junior £4.75 per round. *Visitors:* welcome at all times. Starter: (01224 632269).
website: www.aberdeencity.gov.uk/leisure

ABERDEEN. **Bon Accord Golf Club,** 19 Golf Road, Aberdeen AB24 5QB (01224 633464). *Location:* next to Pittodrie Stadium at Aberdeen beach. Seaside links. 18 holes, 6300 yards. S.S.S. 69. *Green Fees:* information not available. *Eating facilities:* meals on request. *Visitors:* welcome; please call starters box (01224 632269) for information regarding booking of tee times and green fees. *Society Meetings:* bookings in advance. Secretary: J. A. Morrison.

ABERDEEN. **Caledonian Golf Club,** 20 Golf Road, Aberdeen AB24 5QB (01224 632443). *Location:* 50 yards to right of Richard Donald Stand/Pittodrie Football Club. Seaside links. 18 holes, 6437 yards. S.S.S. 69. 6 hole course; driving range nearby. *Green Fees:* information not available. *Eating facilities:* clubhouse snacks and meals. *Visitors:* welcome. Entertainment is provided in clubrooms on Saturdays for members and their guests. Secretary: R. Petrie.

Visitors' Package
5 days unlimited golf £50
- Auchmill Golf Course
- Balnagask Golf Courses
- Hazlehead Golf Courses
- King's Links Golf Courses

Aberdeen City Golf

"Pay & Play" option also available

SPECIAL OFFER

01224 814772
for further info or e-mail
golf@aberdeen.gov.uk

See also Colour Advertisement on page 63

ABERDEEN. **Deeside Golf Club,** Golf Road, Bieldside, Aberdeen AB15 9DL (01224 869457). *Location:* A93 from Aberdeen to Braemar. Wooded parkland. 18 holes, 6264 yards. S.S.S. 70. Also 9 hole course, 5042 yards. S.S.S. 68. Practice ground. *Green Fees:* information not available. *Eating facilities:* full catering and bar facilities. *Visitors:* welcome weekdays up to 4pm, weekends after 4pm. *Society Meetings:* by arrangement. Professional: F.J. Coutts (01224 861041). Managing Secretary: D. P. Pern (Tel & Fax: 01224 869457).
e-mail: admin@deesidegolfclub.com
website: www.deesidegolfclub.com

THE APPEARANCE OF AN ASTERISK (*) AT THE END OF A CLUB OR COURSE ENTRY INDICATES THAT UP-TO-DATE INFORMATION HAS NOT BEEN SUPPLIED

ABERDEEN. **Murcar Golf Club,** Bridge of Don, Aberdeen AB23 8BD (01224 704354). *Location:* A90 Aberdeen - Fraserburgh Road, 5 miles north of Aberdeen city centre. Championship seaside links. 18 holes, 6314 yards. S.S.S. 72; Strabathie 9-hole course, 5369 yards. S.S.S 66. Practice ground. *Green Fees:* Murcar, weekdays £55.00 per round, £75.00 per day; weekends £65.00 per round, £85.00 per day after 11am Sundays. Strabathie, weekdays £12.00 per 9 holes, £24.00 per day; weekends £20.00 per 9 holes, £40.00 per day. *Eating facilities:* dining room/bars. *Visitors:* welcome by advance booking. Hand trolleys for hire. *Society Meetings:* catered for by advance booking. Secretary/Manager: Barbara Rogerson (Tel & Fax: 01224 704354). Professional: Gary Forbes (Tel & Fax: 01224 704370). e-mail: golf@murcar.co.uk website: www.murcar.co.uk.

ABERDEEN. **Nigg Bay Golf Club,** St Fitticks Road, Torry, Aberdeen AB1 3QT (01224 871286; Fax: 01224 873418). *Location:* junction of Victoria Road and St Fitticks Road. Seaside links, hills and hidden holes. 18 holes, 5986 yards, 5472 metres. S.S.S. 69. 9 hole pitch and putt. *Green Fees:* information not available. *Eating facilities:* full catering. *Visitors:* welcome anytime (Municipal course); golfers welcome in clubhouse after playing. Secretary: Alan Fraser.

ABERDEEN. **Northern Golf Club** 22 Golf Road, Aberdeen AB24 5QB (01224 636440; Fax: 01224 622679). *Location:* Golf Road, opposite Pittodrie Stadium. 18 holes, 5731 metres. S.S.S. 70. 6 hole course, 1251 metres; driving range next door. *Green Fees:* information not available. *Visitors:* welcome, book in person on the day of play. Public bookings restricted on Saturdays for club matches. *Society Meetings:* all welcome by writing to Aberdeen District Council (14 days notice). Professional: Mr B. Davidson (01224 641577). Secretary: Alfred Garner (Tel & Fax: 01224 622679). Steward: (01224 636440).

ABERDEEN. **Royal Aberdeen Golf Club,** Links Road, Balgownie, Bridge of Don AB23 8AT (01224 702571; Fax: 01224 826591). *Location:* on A92 Aberdeen/Fraserburgh Road, cross Bridge of Don, second right. Seaside links. Two Courses - Championship (Balgownie): 18 holes, 6985 yards, 5828 metres. S.S.S. 72; Silverburn: 18 holes, 4021 yards, 3717 metres. S.S.S. 61. Practice putting green. *Green Fees:* weekdays £80.00 per round, £120.00 per day; weekends £95.00 per round. *Eating facilities:* Old Bar, main lounge and dining room - jacket and tie. *Visitors:* welcome weekdays 10am to 11.30am and 2pm to 3.30pm, weekends after 3.30pm. Letter of introduction or Handicap Certificate required. Hire carts. *Society Meetings:* welcome. Professional/ Director of Golf: Ronnie MacAskill (01224 702221; Fax: 01224 826591). Exe. Secretary: Sandra Nicolson.

ABERDEEN. **Tarland Golf Club,** Aberdeen Road, Tarland, Aboyne AB34 4TB (Tel & Fax: 013398 81000). *Location:* six miles north of Aboyne on A93, 30 miles west of Aberdeen on B9119. Difficult upland course in picturesque scenery. 9 holes, 5816 yards for 18 holes, S.S.S. 68. Small practice area. *Green* *Fees:* weekdays £16.00 per day; weekends £21.00. Weekly tickets £80.00, fortnightly tickets £130.00. *Eating facilities:* catering available, bar 11am to midnight. *Visitors:* welcome without reservation but phone call advisable due to club competitions at weekends. *Society Meetings:* catered for with prior reservation at all times. Secretary: Mrs V. Ward (013398 81000) Apr-Oct.

ABOYNE. **Aboyne Golf Club,** Formaston Park, Aboyne AB34 5HP (013398 86328). *Location:* A93, 30 miles west of Aberdeen. Part parkland, part hilly with lovely views. 18 holes, 5944 yards. S.S.S. 69. Practice ground. *Green Fees:* weekdays £22.00 per round, £30.00 per day; weekends £25.00 per round, £35.00 per day. *Eating facilities:* full restaurant and bar facilities. *Visitors:* welcome without reservation. *Society Meetings:* by arrangement with Secretary. Professional: Steven Moir. (013398 86328). Secretary: (013398 87078; Fax: 013398 87592). e-mail: aboynegolfclub@btconnect.com website: www.aboynegolfclub.co.uk

ALFORD. **Alford Golf Club,** Montgarrie Road, Alford AB33 8AE (Tel & Fax: 019755 62178; Fax: 019755 64910). *Location:* A944, 26 miles west of Aberdeen. Flat, parkland course. 18 holes, 5483 yards. S.S.S. 66. Practice area. *Green Fees:* £20.00 per round, £25.00 per day weekdays; £25.00 per round, £30.00 per day weekends. Subject to review. *Eating facilities:* catering 9am-9pm; bar services. *Visitors:* always welcome; call club to book tee, weekends very busy. Changing rooms and showers. Buggy Hire available. *Society Meetings:* welcome by prior arrangement. Secretary: Irene Currie. e-mail: info@alford-golf-club.co.uk website: www.golf.alford.co.uk

AUCHENBLAE. **Auchenblae Golf Course,** Auchenblae Parks Committee, Linwood, Auchenblae AB30 1WQ. *Location:* nine miles south of Stonehaven, off A90, two miles west of Fordoun. Parkland. 9 holes, 4434 yards SSS 61. *Green Fees:* £12.00 (concessions). *Eating facilities:* shop open April to October. *Visitors:* welcome. Telephone Pavilion (01561 320002) for details of club nights and current information. Trolleys for hire. *Society Meetings:* welcome. Treasurer: J.M. Thomson (01561 320245).

BALLATER. **Ballater Golf Club,** Victoria Road, Ballater AB35 5QX (013397 55567). *Location:* A93, 42 miles west of Aberdeen and 62 miles from Perth. Flat picturesque parkland course close to Balmoral Castle. 18 holes, 5638 yards. S.S.S. 67. Practice ground, putting. *Green Fees:* information not available. *Eating facilities*: full catering and refreshments April to October. *Visitors:* all welcome, booking well in advance is advisable. Tennis, bowling. *Society Meetings:* all welcome, book well in advance. Professional: Bill Yule (013397 55658). Secretaries: Mrs Irene Pirie, Mrs Jennifer Smith (013397 55567). e-mail: sec@ballatergolfclub.co.uk website: www.ballatergolfclub.co.uk

Inchmarlo Royal Deeside
Inchmarlo Royal Deeside, Banchory

Ponds, meandering burns and even dry stone walls, combine with the more traditional bunkers to test the skill of even the most accomplished player, at the same time rewarding the accuracy of the short game expert. The Laird's Course opened for play in July 2001 and at 6218 yards, this championship standard par 71 course is already one of Scotland's most sought after golfing venues, complementing the existing nine-hole course and the Centre's other facilities, including tuition from a team of PGA professionals.

Catering for all age groups, the Golf Professional's shop is stocked with all the latest in golf equipment and fashions.
Cuisine of the highest standard is available in our various bars and restaurant, and a warm and friendly welcome is assured.

Classic Golf Course design, stunning scenery, excellent facilities....
The Laird's at Inchmarlo Royal Deeside is ready for the challenge - are you?

For further details contact:
Tel: 01330 826422 (Pro-shop) or 01330 826424 (Membership/Groups)
e-mail: info@inchmarlo.com • www.inchmarlo.com

BALMEDIE. **East Aberdeenshire Golf Centre,** Millden, Balmedie AB23 8YY (01358 742111; Fax: 01358 742123). Location: 3 miles from the Aberdeen Exhibition Centre, on left side of road before you reach Balmedie, on the Peterhead/Fraserburgh road. Parkland course. 18 holes, 6276 yards, S.S.S. 71. 16 bay floodlit driving range, practice chipping green, 5 hole Par 3 course. Green Fees: information not available. Eating facilities: bar, restaurant, function room, all with public house licence. Visitors: welcome any time, no jeans on course please. Society Meetings: welcome, midweek rate includes tea/coffee, bacon roll, 18 holes, two-course meal plus five free buggies. Professional: Ian Bratton (01358 742111). Secretary: Sandra Watson (01358 742111).*
e-mail: info@eagolf.com
website: www.eagolf.com

BANCHORY. **Banchory Golf Club,** Kinneskie Road, Banchory AB31 5TA (01330 822365; Fax: 01330 822491). Location: 100 yards off the A93 Aberdeen to Braemar Road. Flat parkland course, several holes on the banks of the River Dee. 18 holes, 5781 yards. S.S.S. 68. Practice ground and putting green. Green Fees: £22.00 per round, £30.00 per day. 7 month season ticket £290.00, 12 monthly season ticket £330.00. Eating facilities: attractive lounge and dining room. Visitors: welcome any time, restrictions on Tuesdays and weekends. Society Meetings: welcome except Tuesdays and weekends. Professional: David Naylor (Tel & Fax: 01330 822447). Secretary: William Crighton (01330 822365; Fax: 01330 822491).
e-mail: info@banchorygolfclub.co.uk
website: www.banchorygolfclub.co.uk

BANCHORY. **Inchmarlo Golf Centre,** Glassel Road, Inchmarlo AB31 4BQ (Tel & Fax: 01330 826424). Location: half a mile from A93 Aberdeen-Braemar road, 25 minutes from Aberdeen city centre. 9-hole course: beautiful but tricky parkland course, 4300 yards, S.S.S. 62, Par 64. 18 hole championship Laird's Course, 6218 yards, Par 71, S.S.S. 71. 30-bay floodlit driving range. Green Fees: information not available. Eating facilities: restaurant, function/ conference room, choice of bars. Visitors: very welcome any time, advisable to book in advance. Society Meetings: welcome all year by prior arrangement. Secretary: Andrew Shinie.*
e-mail: secretary@inchmarlo.com
Info@inchmarlo.com website: www.inchmarlo.com

BANCHORY. **Lumphanan Golf Club,** Main Road, Lumphanan, Banchory AB31 4PW (01339 883480). Location: on the road between Torphins and Lumphanan about 10 miles from Banchory. Hilly, quiet, village course. 9 holes, 3718 yards, S.S.S 62. Course re-designed in 2000. Green Fees: information not available. Eating facilities: clubhouse/bar open weekends and some evenings; food weekends only. Visitors: welcome - no need to book. Society Meetings: outings welcome by arrangement with Secretary. Secretary: Pamela Thorn (01339 883589).*
e-mail: lumphanan.golf.club@lineone.net
website: www.lineone.net/~lumphanan.golf.club

BANFF. **Duff House Royal Golf Club,** The Barnyards, Banff AB45 3SX (01261 812062; Fax: 01261 812224). Location: two minutes from town centre, A97, A98. Level parkland. 18 holes, 6161 yards. S.S.S. 70. Practice putting area. Green Fees: information not available. Eating facilities: lounge bar and full catering service. Visitors: welcome weekdays after 9.30am, restrictions at weekends but times available. Pro shop. Society Meetings: catered for by prior arrangement. Professional: R.S. Strachan (01261 812075). Secretary: H. Liebnitz (01261 812062).
e-mail: duff_house_royal@btinternet.com

BRAEMAR. **Braemar Golf Club,** Cluniebank Road, Braemar AB35 5XX (013397 41618). Location: about one mile from centre of the village, signposted opposite Fife Arms Hotel. Flat parkland, highest 18 hole course in Scotland, course split in two by River Clunie. 18 holes, 5030 yards. S.S.S. 64. Green Fees: weekdays £20.00 per round, £26.00 per day; weekends £23.00 per round, £28.00 per day. Weekly ticket £80.00. Special rates for parties of more than 10. Eating facilities: full bar and catering facilities. Visitors: No restrictions on visitors but advisable to 'phone in advance' for weekends. Society Meetings: welcome - book through Secretary. Secretary: Colin McIntosh (013397 41595).
e-mail: colinmcintosh4@virgin.net

THE APPEARANCE OF AN ASTERISK (*) AT THE END OF A CLUB OR COURSE ENTRY INDICATES THAT UP-TO-DATE INFORMATION HAS NOT BEEN SUPPLIED

DUFF HOUSE ROYAL
GOLF CLUB
THE BARNYARDS, BANFF AB45 3SX
OFFICE: 01261 812062 PRO SHOP: 01261 812075
e-mail: duff_house_royal@btinternet.com

* 18-HOLE PARKLAND COURSE * PRACTICE PUTTING AREA
* GOLF SHOP * PGA PROFESSIONAL * PUTTING GREEN
* LOUNGE BAR * CATERING FACILITIES
* OPEN DAYS * CHANGING FACILITIES

VISITORS AND SOCIETIES CATERED FOR

See also Colour Advertisement on page 63

DOUGLAS ARMS HOTEL

Set in the heart of Royal Deeside, this Victorian Coaching Inn is only two minutes' walk from the golf course. All bedrooms are en suite and have recently been refurbished. B&B £40 single, £60 for twin.

22 High Street, Banchory AB31 5SR
Tel: 01330 822547 • Fax: 01330 825989
e-mail: douglasarmshotel@aol.com
www.douglasarms.co.uk

Banchory Lodge Hotel

Banchory, Kincardineshire AB31 5HS
Tel: 01330 822625 Fax: 01330 825019
e-mail: enquiries@banchorylodge.co.uk
www.banchorylodge.co.uk

AA/RAC
★★★
Les Routiers
Gold Key
Award

Built as a coaching inn in the 16th century and graduating into an elegant Georgian manor house, Banchory Lodge stands in lovely wooded surroundings beside the River Dee, world-famous for its salmon. It is natural, therefore, that angling enthusiasts are attracted by its hospitable atmosphere, to say nothing of its high standards of service, cuisine and accommodation. Log fires, fresh flowers, traditional furnishings and original paintings add to the air of tranquillity. The best of fresh local produce features on the imaginative menus presented in the spacious dining room. There is also ample scope for sport, with two local golf courses, driving range, tennis, putting and bowls nearby as well as numerous forest walks and nature trails and over forty NTS properties in the vicinity.

The Burnett Arms Hotel

25 High Street, Banchory, Aberdeenshire AB31 5TD
Tel: 01330 824944 • Fax: 01330 825553

Situated in the centre of Banchory on Royal Deeside. "The Burnett" is an old coaching inn, fully modernised yet retaining its warm atmosphere of old. With over 20 golf courses within 45 minutes by car, the hotel is ideally situated for golf outings wishing to play on more than one course. The hotel has 16 en suite rooms with 10 channel TV, tea/coffee, hairdryer. Drying room and storage available for clubs. Two bars cater for all tastes, serving bar lunches and suppers. High teas and dinners available in the restaurant.

Special rates for golfers available on request
AMPLE PARKING • DOGS/PETS WELCOME • CREDIT CARDS ACCEPTED

See also Colour Advertisement on page 64

~ *The Royal British Legion Scotland* ~
RAVENSWOOD RESIDENTIAL CLUB
Ramsay Road, Banchory AB31 5TS
Secretary: 01330 822347
www.banchorylegion.com

Extends a warm welcome to Legion members and guests. Single and Double rooms available. Usual Club activities and entertainment.
Bed and Breakfast from £22.

PLEASE MENTION THE GOLF GUIDE WHEN YOU WRITE OR PHONE TO ENQUIRE ABOUT CLUBS OR ACCOMMODATION

BUCKIE. **Buckpool Golf Club (Buckie),** Barhill Road, Buckie AB56 1DU (Tel & Fax: 01542 832236). *Location:* turn off A98 signposted Buckpool. Links course with superlative view over Moray Firth. 18 holes, 6097 yards. S.S.S. 69. Putting green and net area. *Green Fees:* weekdays £18.00 per round, £23.00 per day, Senior Citizens £15.00 per round, £20.00 per day; weekends £23.00 per round, £28.00 per day, Senior Citizens £20.00 per round, £25.00 per day. Reductions during winter months and for Juniors, discounts for parties. *Eating facilities:* full catering daily, normal bar hours. *Visitors:* no restrictions except when there are scheduled competitions and visiting parties; advisable to telephone first. Two changing rooms with showers, etc; snooker, pool and squash. *Society Meetings:* welcome by prior arrangement. Club Administrator: Mrs Moira Robertson. Secretary: Miss Myra Coull (Tel & Fax: 01542 832236).

BUCKIE. **Strathlene Golf Club,** Portessie, Buckie AB56 2DJ (01542 831798). *Location:* equidistant between Aberdeen and Inverness. Raised links course which follows the natural contours of the land. 18 holes, 5996 yards. S.S.S 69. Practice facilities. 3 Hole Pitch and Putt, Driving Range. *Green Fees:* weekdays £20.00 per day, weekends £24.00 per day. *Eating facilities:* summer catering and all-day bar. *Visitors:* prior booking advised; avoid Saturday and Sunday mornings. Locker room. *Society Meetings:* booking required. Secretary: George Jappy (01542 831798).

BUCKSBURN. **Craibstone Golf Centre,** Craibstone Estate, Bucksburn AB21 9YA (01224 716777; Fax: 01224 711298). *Location:* on A96 5 miles north of Aberdeen turn left at Craibstone Roundabout (private access) through Estate to T-junction, left then first right. Parkland course. 18 holes S.S.S. 67. *Green Fees:* information not available. *Eating facilities:* available, also bar. *Visitors:* welcome. Accommodation on site. *Society Meetings:* welcome - please telephone for details. Secretary: Susan May (01224 711195). *

CRUDEN BAY. **Cruden Bay Golf Club,** Aulton Road, Cruden Bay, Peterhead AB42 0NN (01779 812285). *Location:* seven miles south of Peterhead, 23 miles north east of Aberdeen, just off A92. Traditional seaside links with magnificent views near Bay of Cruden. 18 holes, 6395 yards. S.S.S. 72; 9 holes, 2553 yards. S.S.S. 65. Covered driving range. *Green Fees:* information not available. *Eating facilities:* full bar and catering facilities. *Visitors:* welcome but restricted at weekends, telephone for details. *Society Meetings:* welcome weekdays only. Professional: Robbie Stewart (Tel & Fax: 01779 812414). Secretary: Mrs Rosemary Pittendrigh (01779 812285; Fax: 01779 812945).

CULLEN. **Cullen Golf Club,** The Links, Cullen AB56 4WB (01542 840685). *Location:* off A98 midway between Aberdeen and Inverness, on Moray Firth coast. Seaside links with elevated section, natural rock landscaping and sandy beach coming into play at several holes. 18 holes, 4597 yards. S.S.S. 62. Putting green and net area. *Green Fees:* weekdays £16.00 per round, £24.00 per day; weekends £21.00 per round, £28.00 per day. Winter Greens weekdays £8.00 per round, £10.00 per day; weekends £12.00 per round, £14.00 per day. Junior rates, weekly and fortnightly rates available with prices on request. All prices subject to review. *Eating facilities:* catering and bar facilities. *Visitors:* welcome, may be restrictions Wednesdays and Saturdays (club competitions). *Society Meetings:* catered for. e-mail: cullengolfclub@btinternet.com

DUFFTOWN. **Dufftown Golf Club,** Tomintoul Road, Dufftown AB55 4BS (Tel & Fax: 01340 820325). *Location:* on B9009 Dufftown to Tomintoul Road, one mile from Dufftown. Moorland/ Parkland course, partially hilly. 18 holes, 5308 yards. S.S.S. 67. Practice and putting facilities. *Green Fees:* £15.00 per round. Weekly (five day) ticket £60.00. Reductions for parties of 12 or more. Juniors half price. *Eating facilities:* available by arrangement. *Visitors:* welcome at all times. Tee reserved at some times Tuesdays, Wednesdays and Sundays . Please phone for details. Trolleys and clubs for hire, advance notice. *Society Meetings:* welcome by arrangement. Administrator: Marion Swann (Tel & Fax 01340 820325).

ELGIN. **Elgin Golf Club,** Hardhillock, Birnie Road, Elgin IV30 8SX (01343 542338; Fax: 01343 542341). *Location:* half a mile south of Elgin town centre just off A941 Rothes Road; on Birnie Road. Undulating parkland on sandy subsoil, many tree-lined fairways. 18 holes, 6411 yards. S.S.S. 71. Driving range, practice ground and net. *Green Fees:* £30.00 per round, £40.00 per day (seven days). *Eating facilities:* bar and catering every day. *Visitors:* welcome, arrangement through Professional is advisable. *Society Meetings:* by arrangement with Professional. Professional: Kevin Stables (Tel & Fax: 01343 542884). Secretary: David F. Black (01343 542338). website: www.elgingolfclub.com

ELGIN. **Hopeman Golf Club,** Hopeman, Elgin IV30 5YA (01343 830578). *Location:* 7 miles north-east of Elgin on B9012. Seaside links, with spectacular 12th hole. 18 holes, 5624 yards. S.S.S. 67. *Green Fees:* weekdays £18.00 per round, £23.00 per day; weekends £23.00 per round, £28.00 per day. Juniors half price. Senior Citizens: weekdays £16.00 per round, £18.00 per day; weekends £18.00 per round, £23.00 per day. Generous discounts for parties of ten or more *Eating facilities:* bar, catering. *Visitors:* welcome, some restrictions on tee times at weekends. Trolleys and golf buggy for hire. *Society Meetings:* welcome by arrangement. Secretary: Jim Fraser (01343 830578; Fax: 01343 830152). e-mail: hopemangc@aol.com
website: www.hopemangc.co.uk

THE APPEARANCE OF AN ASTERISK (*) AT THE END OF A CLUB OR COURSE ENTRY INDICATES THAT UP-TO-DATE INFORMATION HAS NOT BEEN SUPPLIED

SCOTLAND / Aberdeen, Banff & Moray

ELLON. McDonald-Ellon Golf Club, Hospital Road, Ellon AB41 9AW (01358 720576). *Location:* A90 from Aberdeen to Ellon. One mile down A948, on left. Flat parkland with trees and stream. 18 holes, 5986 yards. S.S.S. 70. Putting green and practice nets. *Green Fees:* on application. *Eating facilities:* full catering and bar facilities all week. *Visitors:* welcome at all times weekdays, after 10am and booking advisable at weekends. *Society Meetings:* must book in advance. Professional: Ronnie Urquhart (01358 722891). Secretary: Graham Gerrard (01358 720576). e-mail: mcdonald.golf@virgin.net

FOCHABERS. Garmouth & Kingston Golf Club, Spey Street, Garmouth, Fochabers IV32 7NJ (Tel & Fax: 01343 870388). *Location:* three miles north from A96 at Mosstodloch crossroads. Flat parkland/part links. 18 holes, 5935 yards. S.S.S. 69. Practice net. *Green Fees:* weekdays £20.00 per round, £25.00 per day, half price for Senior Citizens; weekends £25.00 per round or day. Reductions for parties over 10. *Eating facilities:* catering available on request. *Visitors:* very welcome except 4pm to 7pm Tuesdays (Ladies) and during club competitions (evenings). *Society Meetings:* welcome by arrangement with Admin. Assistant. Admin. Assistant: I. Fraser (01343 870388).

FORRES. Forres Golf Club, Muiryshade, Forres IV36 2RD (Tel & Fax: 01309 672250). *Location:* one mile south from clock tower in town centre; 26 miles east of Inverness on A96. Parkland - feature hole 16th. 18 holes, 6236 yards. S.S.S. 70. Practice ground and putting green. *Green Fees:* £26.00 per round, £34.00 per day. *Eating facilities:* bar and catering all day every day. *Visitors:* welcome - booking system in operation by Professional. Buggies/Trolleys for hire. *Society Meetings:* welcome. Professional: S. Aird (Tel & Fax: 01309 672250). Secretary: (01309 672949; Fax: 01309 672261).

FORRES. Kinloss Country Golf Course, Kinloss, Forres IV36 2UB (01343 850585). *Location*: 4 miles east of Forres on B9089. Parkland courses. Two 9 hole courses, Course 1 - 2535 yards, Course 2 - 2939 yards. Putting green, driving net. *Green Fees*: information not available. *Eating facilities*: hot and cold drinks, confectionery available. *Visitors*: welcome everyday, pay-as-you-play. Trolleys, clubs and buggies for hire. *Society Meetings*: discounts for large parties. Corporate outings catered for. Secretary: Sylvia Verner (01343 850242 or 01343 850585). *

---

18 holes Par 69 • Parkland • 5780 yards • 2005 Green Fees: Weekday £17, Weekend £22

Craibstone Golf Centre • Bucksburn, Aberdeen AB21 9YA

Opened in 2000, the Craibstone Golf Centre offers great facilities to all levels of golfer, and is only 5 minutes from the airport and 10 minutes from the city centre. Short in length compared to most new courses, its main defences are the large sloping greens with pins that can be tucked away, making it tricky to get up and down from a missed approach shot. Excellent short game and practice area open to the public. The resident PGA Professional is always keen to help with lessons, and the shop has all the latest equipment at competitive prices. Buggy and trolley hire available. Members of the public welcome 7 days a week and catering is available for parties of any number. **e-mail: craibstonegolf@sac.co.uk • Tel: 01224 711195**

See also Colour Advertisement on page 60

The Udny Arms HOTEL
www.udny.co.uk

A charming, family-run, small hotel offering real Scottish character and charm, along with superb service. Carefully chosen furnishings, antiques and prints make each of the 26 en suite bedrooms entirely individual. Family rooms are available, as are children's menus. This is a pet-friendly hotel.
The Udny Arms has a considerable reputation for the quality of its cuisine and the cosy, friendly atmosphere of the Forvie Room and The Parlour. There are 3 Championship golf courses within 10 minutes' drive of the hotel, and special Golf Breaks are available - call or e-mail the hotel for details.

**Main Street, Newburgh, Ellon AB41 6BL
Tel: 01358 789444 • Fax: 01358 789012
e-mail: enquiry@udny.demon.co.uk**

FHG
For full details of clubs and courses, plus convenient accommodation
www.uk-golfguide.com

FRASERBURGH. **Fraserburgh Golf Club,** Philorth, Fraserburgh AB43 8TL (01346 516616). *Location:* turn right at roundabout on entry to town from Aberdeen then first right. Splendid true seaside links. 18 holes, 6308 yards. S.S.S. 71. Additional 9 hole Rosehill Family Course 2400 yards. Practice area. *Green Fees:* to be arranged, single round, day tickets, weekly and monthly tickets available. *Eating facilities:* full bar and catering facilities. *Visitors:* welcome, some restrictions weekends. *Society Meetings:* welcome, book in advance. Tel (01346 516616).

GRANTOWN-ON-SPEY. **Craggan Golf Club,** Grantown-on-Spey PH26 3NT (01479 873283; Fax: 01479 872325). *Location:* situated beside the A95, one mile south of Grantown-on-Spey. Parkland course. 18 holes, 2005 yards. *Green Fees:* information not available. *Eating facilities:* snacks and soft drinks available. *Visitors:* welcome at all times. Secretary: Fergus Laing (01479 873283).*
e-mail: fhglaing@btopenworld.com
website: www.cragganforleisure.co.uk

HUNTLY. **Huntly Golf Club,** Cooper Park, Huntly AB54 4SH (01466 792643). *Location:* north side of Huntly, 38 miles from Aberdeen on A96. Open parkland course between The Rivers Deveron and Bogie. 18 holes, 5399 yards. S.S.S. 66. Practice area. *Green Fees:* information not available. *Eating facilities:* full catering by arrangement, lounge bar. *Visitors:* welcome, no restriction except Wednesday and Thursday evenings. Carts for hire. *Society Meetings:* by arrangement with Secretary, maximum of 40. Special package deal Mon - Fri. Administrator: Alan Donald (01466 792643).

INSCH. **Insch Golf Club,** Golf Terrace, Insch AB52 6JY (Tel & Fax: 01464 820363). *Location:* A96 27 miles from Aberdeen. Parkland - trees, water hazards. 18 holes, 5350 yards. S.S.S. 67. *Green Fees:* £16.00 per round/day, all week (Monday to Friday), £20.00 (Saturday and Sunday). *Eating facilities:* bar and catering available. *Visitors:* welcome except Mondays from 4.30pm, Tuesdays from 5pm and Wednesdays from 3.30pm. *Society Meetings:* welcome. Administrator: Jill Townsend.

Fraserburgh Golf Club FOUNDED 1779

Fraserburgh boasts a 27-hole complex with excellent practice facilities. **CORBIEHILL**, the 18-hole course, is 6308 yards (Par 70) of largely unspoiled traditional Scottish links. Its main features are the tricky Par 3s together with a handful of short but very interesting Par 4s. When visiting Fraserburgh, take some time out at the third tee – the view itself is worth the trip. **ROSEHILL**, the 2400 yard 9-hole course is essentially parkland. Although short in yards, it plays its length and has two superb finishing holes.

Philorth, Fraserburgh AB43 8TL
01346 516616
See also Colour Advertisement on page 63

Carriages Hotel 1-3 Commercial Road, Insch, Aberdeenshire AB52 6JN
Tel: 01464 820604 • Fax: 01464 821408
E-mail: reservations@carriageshotel.com

A good mix of peaceful accommodation, some at ground level separate from the main building, and friendly country atmosphere with delicious food cooked to perfection by our resident Chef and served by our friendly, helpful staff.

Local golf course, open countryside next to hotel, railway station close by, easy access by train from Aberdeen, Aberdeen Airport and Inverness. Bar, Restaurant, small function room, large function room suitable for weddings, birthdays and other special occasions. Sky and Fox Children's TV.

18 Rooms, 12 en suite: £30 single, £60 twin, £60 double, £70 Executive Double Room and £80 Family Room

www.carriageshotel.com
See also Colour Advertisement on page 62

FHG
For full details of clubs and courses, plus convenient accommodation
www.uk-golfguide.com

INVERALLOCHY. **Inverallochy Golf Club,** Whitelink, Inverallochy, Fraserburgh AB43 8XY (01346 582000). *Location:* three miles south of Fraserburgh. Seaside links course. 18 holes, 5431 yards. S.S.S. 66. *Green Fees:* £15.00 weekdays, £20.00 Saturdays. *Eating facilities:* full catering/ fully licensed, advance booking required. *Visitors:* welcome, apply in writing. *Society Meetings:* welcome, apply in writing. Secretary: George Young.

INVERURIE. **Inverurie Golf Club,** Davah Wood, Inverurie AB51 5JB (01467 624080; Fax: 01467 672869). *Location:* off A96 Blackhall roundabout, at next roundabout, approx. 300 yards, turn right. Parkland with three tree-lined (wood holes). 18 holes, 5483 yards. S.S.S. 67. Practice ground. *Green Fees*: weekdays £20.00 per round, £24.00 per day; weekends £24.00 per round, £30.00 per day. *Eating facilities*: full catering, bar and lounge area. *Visitors*: welcome, phone 01467 672863. *Society Meetings*: catered for. Professional: John Logue (01467 672863). Secretary: Arthur Angus (01467 672860; Fax: 01467 672869).

KEITH. **Keith Golf Club,** Mar Court, Fife Keith, Keith AB55 5DF (01542 882469; Fax: 01542 888176). *Location:* leave A96 on B9014 take first right. Parkland, open, panoramic views. 18 holes, 5800 yards, 5300 metres. S.S.S. 68. Small practice area and putting green. *Green Fees:* information not available. *Eating facilities:* catering available by arrangement, normal bar hours. *Visitors:* welcome anytime, advisable to telephone in advance during playing season. *Society Meetings:* all welcome, applications to Outings Convener Mr A. Hunter. e-mail: Secretary@keithgolfclub.org.uk website: www.keithgolfclub.org.uk

KEMNAY. **Kemnay Golf Club,** Monymusk Road, Kemnay AB51 5RA (01467 642225). *Location:* from A96 main Aberdeen/Inverness road. Take B994 signposted Kemnay and pass through village of Kemnay to find golf course on left hand side on leaving village. Flat wooded parkland. 18 holes, 6342 yards, 5398 metres. S.S.S. 71. *Green Fees:* weekdays £20.00 per round, £26.00 per day; weekends £24.00 per round, £30.00 per day. *Eating facilities:* bar and full catering. *Visitors:* welcome at all times except during club competitions/matches; phone club shop to book tee time. *Society Meetings:* welcome by arrangement. Professional: R. McDonald (01467 642225). Secretary: Y. Moir (Tel & Fax: 01467 643746). Club Shop: (01467 642225). Administrator: (Tel & Fax: 01467 643746).

KINTORE. **Kintore Golf Club,** Balbithan Road, Kintore, Inverurie AB51 0UR (01467 632631). *Location:* off A96 12 miles north of Aberdeen. Undulating moorland course. 18 holes, 5323 yards. S.S.S. 66. *Green Fees:* information not available. *Eating facilities:* available all day during the season, by arrangement at other times. *Visitors:* welcome daily except Mondays, Wednesdays and Fridays between 4pm and 7pm. Trolleys and buggies for hire during season. *Society Meetings:* welcome by appointment. Secretary: C. Lindsay.*

LOSSIEMOUTH. **Moray Golf Club,** Stotfield Road, Lossiemouth IV31 6QS (01343 812018; Fax: 01343 815102). *Location*: five miles from Elgin on A941, 40 miles from Inverness A96 Links course. Old Course 18 holes, 6697 yards. S.S.S. 73. New Course 18 holes, 6008 yards. S.S.S. 69. Practice ground, putting green. *Green Fees*: Old Course per round - £40.00 weekdays, £50.00 weekends; New Course per round - £30.00 weekdays, £35.00 weekends. Rates for playing a round on both courses £55.00 weekdays, £65.00 weekends. Discounts through local hotel and for parties of 12 or more. *Eating facilities*: bar plus full catering. *Visitors*: welcome every day. Secretary will advise on availability. Carts, caddies. *Society Meetings*: welcome by arrangement with Secretary. Professional: Alastair Thomson (01343 813330). Secretary: S. Crane (01343 812018; Fax: 01343 815102). e-mail: secretary@moraygolf.co.uk website: www.moraygolf.co.uk

MACDUFF. **Royal Tarlair Golf Club,** Buchan Street, Macduff AB44 1TA (01261 832897). *Location:* A98 Fraserburgh to Inverness road. Seaside cliff top course, beautiful seascapes, 13th feature hole. 18 holes, 5866 yards, 5373 metres. S.S.S. 68. *Green Fees:* £15.00 per round weekdays, day ticket £20.00; £18.00 per round weekends and public holidays, £22.00 per day ticket. *Eating facilities:* full catering and bar available. *Visitors:* very welcome. *Society Meetings:* welcome, bookings through Secretary.

The Moray Golf Club
founded 1889

There are 36 individual reasons to play golf at Moray - and every one is designed for enjoyment!

Moray Golf Club at Lossiemouth offers two traditional Scottish golf links 18-hole courses - Moray Old and Moray New. Like the Old Course at the "Home of Golf", St Andrews, the courses start and finish within the town boundaries.

www.moraygolf.co.uk

Stotfield Road, Lossiemouth IV31 6QS
Tel: 01343 812018 • Fax: 01343 815102 • e-mail: secretary@moraygolf.co.uk

See also Colour Advertisement on page 62

NAIRN. **The Nairn Golf Club,** Seabank Road, Nairn IV12 4HB (01667 453208; Fax: 01667 456328). *Location:* Nairn West Shore, on the southern shore of the Moray Firth, 16 miles east of Inverness on A96. Hosted "Amateur" Championship in 1994. Traditional Scottish links championship course, hosted 37th Walker Cup in 1999. Championship Course - 18 holes, 6705 yards. S.S.S. 73 (blue tees); Medal Course 18 holes, 6430 yards. S.S.S 72 (white tees); 9 holes (Newton Course), 1918 yards. Practice area. *Green Fees:* £75.00 per round. £105.00 per day. *Eating facilities:* full catering facilities and two bars available. *Visitors:* welcome subject to availability, restrictions at weekends - 8am to 11.00am and from 12 noon to 2.30pm for members only. Full size snooker table. *Society Meetings:* welcome subject to availability. Professional: Robin P. Fyfe (01667 452787). Secretary: David Corstorphine (01667 453208; Fax: 01667 456328). Catering Manager: (01667 452103). e-mail: bookings@nairngolfclub.co.uk website: www.nairngolfclub.co.uk

NEWBURGH. **Newburgh-on-Ythan Golf Club,** Beach Road, Newburgh (01358 789058). *Location:* 14 miles north of Aberdeen off A92. Seaside links course. 18 holes, 6162 yards. S.S.S. 71. Practice area. Driving bays. *Green Fees:* weekdays £25.00 per round, £30.00 per day; weekends £30.00, per round, £35.00 per day, subject to review. Special rates for parties. *Eating facilities:* full catering available; bar. *Visitors:* very welcome by prior arrangement, except Saturday mornings. Administrator: Heather Marr (01358 789084; Fax: 01358 788104). e-mail: secretary@newburgh-on-ythan.co.uk website: www.newburgh-on-ythan.co.uk

NEWMACHAR. **Newmachar Golf Club,** Swailend, Newmachar AB21 7UU (01651 863002). *Location:* two and a half miles north of Dyce on A947. Two courses – Hawkshill: Championship standard wooded parkland course with ponds being main feature. 18 holes, 6659 yards. S.S.S. 74; Swailend: undulating parkland course. 18 holes, 6388 yards. S.S.S. 71. 12 bay driving range, practice bunker and putting green. *Green Fees:* from £20.00. *Eating facilities:* fully licensed clubhouse with restaurant. *Visitors:* welcome by prior arrangement. Handicap Certificate required. *Society Meetings:* welcome by prior arrangement. Head Professional: Gordon Simpson (01651 863222). Secretary: Sam Wade (01651 863002; Fax: 01651 863055).

For full details of clubs and courses, plus convenient accommodation www.uk-golfguide.com

OLDMELDRUM. **Oldmeldrum Golf Club,** Kirk Brae, Oldmeldrum, Inverurie AB51 0DJ (01651 872648). *Location:* 17 miles north-west of Aberdeen on A947 to Banff. First on right entering from Aberdeen direction. Undulating parkland with tree-lined fairways and water features. 18 holes, 5988 yards, 5479 metres. S.S.S. 69. Practice area. *Green Fees:* information not available. *Eating facilities:* fully licensed bar, full catering. *Visitors:* welcome, advisable to phone first. Professional's Shop: (01651 873555) for tee reservations. *Society Meetings:* catered for by arrangement. Professional: Hamish Love (01651 873555). Secretary: John Page.*

PETERCULTER. **Peterculter Golf Club,** Oldtown, Burnside Road, Peterculter, Aberdeen AB14 0LN (01224 735245; Fax: 01224 735580). *Location:* from North Deeside Road (A93) at west end of Peterculter travel southwards, following signs for club. Scenic, undulating course, bounded by River Dee, excellent views of hills to west. 18 holes, Medal 6207 yards, Forward Tees 6000 yards, S.S.S. Medal 69, Forward Tees 68. Small practice/teaching area. *Green Fees:* information not available. *Eating facilities:* dining room, lounge bar. *Visitors:* welcome except weekdays 3.30pm to 6pm. *Society Meetings:* welcome Tuesdays to Fridays. Not Public/local holidays. Professional: Dean Vannet (01224 734994). Secretary: Robert Burnett. e-mail: info@petercultergolfclub.co.uk website: www.petercultergolfclub.co.uk

PETERHEAD. **Longside Golf Club,** West End, Longside, Peterhead AB42 7XJ (01779 821558; Fax: 01779 821564). *Location*: take A950 west from Peterhead towards Mintlaw. Wooded course with river. 18 holes, 5225 yards, S.S.S 66. *Green Fees*: information not available. *Eating facilities*: full bar and catering facilities. *Visitors*: always welcome - no visitors before 10.30am on Sunday. *Society Meetings*: welcome, £24.00 Monday to Saturday, £26.00 Sunday, booking forms available from club. Secretary: Mrs Kathleen Allan (01771 622424).*

PETERHEAD. **Peterhead Golf Club,** Riverside Drive, Peterhead AB42 1LT (01779 472149; Fax: 01779 480725). *Location:* north end of town off Blackhouse Terrace at mouth of River Ugie. Seaside links – can be affected by variable wind conditions. Old Course – 18 holes, 6173 yards. S.S.S. 71; New Course – 9 holes, 2228 yards. Par 62 for 4456 yards. Practice area. *Green Fees:* weekdays £30.00 per round, day ticket £40.00, 9 holes £14.00; weekends £38.00 per round, £48.00 per day. *Eating facilities:* snacks, meals, full bar facilities. *Visitors:* welcome anytime except some restrictions on a Saturday. Phone call advised. *Society Meetings:* welcome by arrangement. Handicap Certificate may be asked for. Secretary: D.G. Wood (Tel & Fax: 01779 480725).

A family-run hotel situated in the coastal village of Newburgh, 15 minutes' drive north of Aberdeen and 5 minutes' walk from the 18-hole Newburgh-on-Ythan Golf Course.
• Scottish breakfasts • Extensive Lunch and Supper menus
• Snacks available all day • En suite accommodation.
info@ythanhotel.com • www.ythanhotel.com

**YTHAN HOTEL
MAIN STREET
NEWBURGH
AB41 6BP
01358 789257**

PORTLETHEN. **Portlethen Golf Club,** Badentoy Road, Portlethen, Aberdeen AB12 4YA (01224 781090). *Location:* five miles south of Aberdeen on main Stonehaven Road. Rolling parkland. 18 holes, 6670 yards. S.S.S. 72. Large practice area. *Green Fees:* information not available. *Eating facilities:* bar and restaurant. *Visitors:* welcome, no visitors Saturdays, Sundays also difficult in summer. Golf buggies for hire. Snooker. *Society Meetings:* welcome weekdays by arrangement. Professional: Muriel Thomson (01224 782571). Bar/catering: 01224 782575.*

ROSEHEARTY. **Rosehearty Golf Club,** C/o Masons Arms Hotel, 1 Castle Street, Rosehearty, Fraserburgh AB43 4JP (01346 571250). *Location:* east of Rosehearty on Fraserburgh Road. Seaside links. 9 holes, 2197 yards. S.S.S. 62. Driving range and golf shop. *Green Fees:* information not available. *Eating facilities:* Masons Arms Hotel adjacent to course. *Visitors:* always welcome. *Society Meetings:* welcome by prior arrangement. Lessons available. Teaching facilities across road from Masons Arms Hotel. Professional: Scott Hornal. Secretary: Alan Watt (01346 571250).

ROTHES. **Rothes Golf Club,** Blackhall, Rothes, Aberlour AB38 7AN (01340 831443). *Location:* south west of Rothes, off A941 Elgin to Craigellachie road. A parkland course with fine views over the River Spey. 9 holes, 2486 yards (4972 yards), 2273 metres (4546 metres). S.S.S. 64. Practice net. *Green Fees:* information not available. *Eating facilities:* licensed bar open summer evenings and weekends, catering for parties by arrangement. *Visitors:* always welcome, tee reserved for Ladies 5pm to 7.30pm Tuesdays, and 5pm to 6.30pm Mondays for Juniors. *Society Meetings:* welcome, contact Secretary. Secretary: J.A. Eddie (01340 831617).*

SPEY BAY. **Golf Spey Bay**, Spey Bay Hotel, Spey Bay, Fochabers IV32 7PJ (01343 820424 all enquiries). *Location:* halfway between Inverness and Aberdeen, at the mouth of River Spey. Traditional 18-hole championship links. Special characteristics being small greens and tight, gorse-lined fairways with superb scenic views over the Moray Firth. 6230 yards. S.S.S. 70. Driving range, practice area and putting green. *Green Fees:* information not available. Buggy and trolley hire available. *Eating facilities:* The on-site three star hotel offers Bed and Breakfast, snacks, lunch and dinner. *Visitors:* all visitors welcome all year round. *Society Meetings:* catered for by prior arrangement. Special golf breaks tailor-made to suit individual requirements. All enquiries contact The Spey Bay Hotel.
e-mail: info@speybay.com
website: www.speybay.com

Please mention
THE GOLF GUIDE
when you enquire about clubs or accommodation

Newmachar Golf Club
~ Hawkshill Course ~

Designed by Dave Thomas and Peter Alliss, Hawkshill is a challenging 6700yd, Par 72, SSS 74 course. The natural features of the pine and birch woodlands have been retained and now line the narrow fairways and surround the well-bunkered greens. Water hazards also feature on 7 holes, making Hawkshill a unique experience for golfers of all standards and one of the most demanding courses in Scotland.

Other facilities at Newmachar include Swailend 18-hole course, a floodlit driving range, two putting greens, bunkers and a pitching green. A team of PGA Professionals offer a full range of teaching packages. On an elevated site the Clubhouse enjoys spectacular views, and golfers can celebrate sinking that final putt in the lounge bar or dining room.

Newmachar Golf Club,
Swailend, Newmachar, Aberdeenshire AB21 7UU
Tel: 01651 863002 ~ Fax: 01651 863055
website: www.newmachargolfclub.co.uk
e-mail: info@newmachargolfclub.co.uk

See also Colour Advertisement on page 64

STONEHAVEN. **Stonehaven Golf Club,** Cowie, Stonehaven AB39 3RH (01569 762124; Fax: 01569 765973). *Location:* A92, one mile north of town signposted at mini roundabout near Leisure Centre. Parkland course on cliffs overlooking North Sea with some challenging holes over natural gullies. 18 holes, 5128 yards. S.S.S. 65. Limited practice area. *Green Fees:* weekdays: £18.00 per round, £24.00 per day; weekends: £25.00 per round, £30.00 per day. *Eating facilities:* full catering including bar lunches. *Visitors:* welcome, but advised to reserve tee time in advance, restricted Saturdays after 4pm. *Society Meetings:* catered for except for Saturday. Secretary/Manager: W.A. Donald.
e-mail: stonehaven.golfclub@virgin.net

TORPHINS. **Torphins Golf Club,** Bog Road, Torphins, Banchory AB31 4JU (013398 82115). *Location:* through village towards Lumphanan, club signposted to right. Parkland with lovely views to Highlands. 9 holes, 4738 yards (18 holes). S.S.S. 64. *Green Fees:* £13.00 weekdays; £14.00 weekends. £7.00 for 9 holes. Juniors half price, after 6.30pm £6.00. *Eating facilities:* light refreshments at weekends, unlicensed. *Visitors:* welcome at weekends; on medal days by arrangement. *Society Meetings:* welcome; at weekends by arrangement. Secretary: Stuart MacGregor (013398 82402).

TURRIFF. **Turriff Golf Club,** Rosehall, Turriff AB53 4HD (01888 562982; Fax: 01888 568050). *Location:* A947 signposted on south side of Turriff. Wooded parkland course. 18 holes, 6095 yards. S.S.S. 70. Practice area, putting green. *Green Fees:* weekdays £21.00 per round, £25.00 per day; weekends £25.00 per round, £31.00 per day. *Eating facilities:* bar and restaurant. *Visitors:* no visitors before 10am weekends, selected times on Medal days. Tee reservation by contacting Professional – during the week up to four days in advance, weekends up to two days in advance. *Society Meetings:* by arrangement with Secretary. Professional Shop: Tel & Fax: 01888 563025. Secretary: W Steve Duguid (01888 562982; Fax: 01888 568050). Administrator: Grace Stephen
e-mail: grace@turriffgolf.sol.co.uk
website: www.turriffgolfclub.com

WESTHILL. **Westhill Golf Club,** Westhill Heights, Westhill, Aberdeenshire AB32 6RY (01224 742567; Fax: 01224 749124). *Location:* six miles from Aberdeen on A944. Parkland course. 18 holes, 5849 yards. S.S.S. 69. Practice ground. *Green Fees:* weekdays £14.00 per round, £20.00 per day; Sundays and Public Holidays £20.00 per round, £25.00 per day (subject to review). Special packages available on request. *Eating facilities:* lounge bar and dining area. *Visitors:* welcome except Saturdays. *Society Meetings:* welcome per visitors' times by arrangement. Professional: George Bruce (01224 740159).

Stonehaven Golf Club
Where visitors have been welcomed for more than 100 years.

One mile north of town, signposted at mini roundabout near open-air pool
• Parkland course on cliffs overlooking North Sea with some challenging holes over natural gullies. • 18 holes, 5128 yards. S.S.S. 65.
• Full catering including bar lunches (not Mondays). • Visitors welcome, but advised to reserve tee time in advance, restricted Saturdays after 4pm.

**Tel: 01569 762124 • Fax: 01569 765973
e-mail: stonehaven.golfclub@virgin.net**

See also Colour Advertisement on page 60

Visit the FHG website
www.holidayguides.com
for details of the wide choice of accommodation featured in the full range of FHG titles

Argyll & Bute

CAMPBELTOWN. **Machrihanish Golf Club,** Machrihanish, by Campbeltown PA28 6PT (01586 810213). *Location:* five miles west of Campbeltown on B843 road. Championship standard natural links course. 18 holes, 6225 yards. S.S.S. 71. Also 9 holes, 2395 yards. Practice area. *Green Fees:* Sunday to Fridays £40.00 per round, £60.00 per day; Saturdays £50.00 per round, £75.00 per day. Advance booking necessary. Subject to review. *Eating facilities:* full catering and bar facilities. *Visitors:* welcome, some restrictions on competition days. Open competitions in summer. Special Flight/Golf packages available through Loganair, Glasgow Airport, Paisley. *Society Meetings:* as visitors. Professional: Ken Campbell (01586 810277; Fax: 01586 810221). Secretary: Mrs Anna Anderson (01586 810213).

CARRADALE. **Carradale Golf Club,** Carradale, By Campbeltown PA28 6RY. *Location:* 15 miles north of Campbeltown on B842. Seaside course, short but demanding, unbelievable views. 9 holes. Medal Tees – 2358 yards out, 2336 yards in; Yellow Tees – 1999 yards. S.S.S. 64 (18 holes). *Green Fees:* £12.00 per day; £60.00 per week. Country Membership £89.50 per annum (may take part in competitions). *Eating facilities:* Carradale Hotel at first tee, Ashbank Hotel 100 yards. Dunvalanree close by. Network centre one mile (open Easter to October for midday meals and snacks). Glen Bar and Restaurant one-and-a-half miles. *Visitors:* all welcome, no restrictions. *Society Meetings:* welcome, would be advisable to book tee-off times. Secretary: Dr R.J. Abernethy (01583 431321).

DALMALLY. **Dalmally Golf Club,** C/o Old Sawmill, Dalmally PA33 1AE (01866 822708). *Location:* alongside the A85, two miles west of Dalmally. Flat parkland course bounded by the River Orchy and surrounded by mountains. 9 holes, 2264 yards. S.S.S. 63. *Green Fees:* £12.00. *Eating facilities:* bar and snacks by arrangement. *Visitors:* welcome at all times. Clubs and carts by arrangement. *Society Meetings:* all welcome by arrangement. Secretary: Ms C. Brown (01866 822708).

DUNOON. **Blairmore and Strone Golf Club,** High Road, Strone, by Dunoon PA23 8TH (01369 840676). *Location:* take A880, five miles north of Dunoon and first left after leaving Kilmun. A Braid designed course set above the Clyde with spectacular views, mixture of hill and flatter parkland. 9 holes, 2112 yards, 1933 metres. S.S.S. 62. *Green Fees:* weekdays and weekends, £10.00. *Eating facilities:* bar facilities Saturdays. *Visitors:* welcome but some restrictions on competition days. *Society Meetings:* welcome, apply through Secretary. Secretary: Mrs J.C. Fleming (01369 860307).

THE APPEARANCE OF AN ASTERISK (*) AT THE END OF A CLUB OR COURSE ENTRY INDICATES THAT UP-TO-DATE INFORMATION HAS NOT BEEN SUPPLIED

WHITE HART Hotel
Campbeltown, Argyll PA28 6AN
Tel: 01586 552440 • Fax: 01586 554972
e-mail: whitehartotel@amserve.net • www.whiteh.com

The White Hart is the nearest golfing hotel to Machrihanish Golf Club. If you are planning a visit to Machrihanish or Campbeltown, then the White Hart is the perfect base for your visit. While staying with us you are entitled to discounted green fees at Machrihanish. Other golf packages available.

19 stylish bedrooms, all en suite, with TV, telephone, computer outlet, and tea/coffee making facilities. Taste of Kintyre Restaurant and informal Conservatory Bistro provide a superb dining experience. Situated in the main street of Campbeltown, an ideal base for exploring the Mull of Kintyre.

See also Colour Advertisement on page 65

PLEASE MENTION THIS GUIDE WHEN YOU WRITE OR PHONE TO ENQUIRE ABOUT CLUBS OR ACCOMMODATION

DUNOON. **Cowal Golf Club,** Ardenslate Road, Kirn, Dunoon PA23 8LT (01369 705673). *Location:* quarter mile off A815 at Kirn (north-east boundary of Dunoon). Rising wooded parkland with superb views over Firth of Clyde. 18 holes, 6063 yards. S.S.S. 70. Practice area. *Green Fees:* weekdays £18.00 per round, £25.00 per day; weekends £22.00 per round, £35.00 per day (prices may be subject to increase). *Eating facilities:* full service available. *Visitors:* welcome weekdays, possible restrictions weekends. Separate visitor changing/shower facilities. Local hotels offer golf holidays – apply to Secretary for details. *Society Meetings:* welcome, special rates available. Professional: R.D. Weir (01369 702395). Secretary: Alan Douglas (Tel & Fax: 01369 705673). e-mail: secretary@cowalgolfclub.com
website: www.cowalgolfclub.com

DUNOON. **Innellan Golf Club,** Innellan, By Dunoon PA23 (01369 830242). *Location:* south of Dunoon to Innellan Pierhead, then follow signposts. Parkland course in elevated position overlooking Firth of Clyde. 9 holes, 2343 yards. S.S.S. 64. *Green Fees:* £12.00 per round, £9.00 for 9 holes. 25% discount for parties. *Eating facilities:* snack/bar; food by arrangement. *Visitors:* welcome, except Monday evenings, Ladies welcome Thursday evenings. *Society Meetings:* welcome by arrangement. Secretary: Andrew Wilson (01369 702573).

INVERARAY. **Inveraray Golf Club,** c/o The Secretary, Inveraray. *Location:* on the A83 Campbeltown road, one mile west of Inveraray, signposted. Testing course, wooded with natural trees, oak, birch, etc. Flat, some water hazards. 9 holes, 2814 yards. S.S.S. 68. *Green Fees:* weekdays and weekends £15.00 per day/round; Juniors £5.00. *Eating facilities:* none at course but good choice locally. *Visitors:* very few restrictions weekdays, occasionally at weekends. *Society Meetings:* welcome by prior arrangement through Calum Morrison (01499 302079).

ISLE OF BUTE. **Bute Golf Club,** c/o St. Ninians, 32 Marine Place, Ardbeg, Rothesay PA20 0LF (01700 502158). *Location:* six miles from Rothesay on the A845, situated on shores of Stravanan Bay. Flat seaside links in beautiful setting. 9 holes, 2497 yards, 2284 metres. S.S.S. 64 (18 holes). *Green Fees:* £10.00 adults, £5.00 Juniors. *Visitors:* welcome any day, Saturdays after 11.30am. *Society Meetings:* catered for by arrangement. Secretary: Frazer Robinson (01700 502158).
e-mail: info@butegolfclub.com
website: www.butegolfclub.com

LOCHGILPHEAD. **Lochgilphead Golf Club,** Blarbuie Road, Lochgilphead PA31 8LE (01546 602340). *Location:* close to Argyll and Bute Hospital, Lochgilphead. Signposted from town centre. Parkland. 9 holes, 4518 yards. S.S.S. 63. *Green Fees:* £15.00. *Eating facilities:* limited snacks available at weekends. *Visitors:* welcome but some restriction on competition days. *Society Meetings:* welcome by arrangement. Secretary: Mr R. Foyle (01546 510383).

OBAN. **Glencruitten Golf Club,** Glencruitten Road, Oban PA34 4PU (01631 562868). *Location:* one mile from town centre. Hilly parkland. 18 holes, 4452 yards. S.S.S. 63. Practice area. Putting green. *Green Fees:* weekdays £25.00, weekends £30.00 per day. *Eating facilities:* full catering and bar facilities. *Visitors:* very welcome. *Society Meetings:* welcome. Shop: (01631 564115). Secretary: A.G. Brown (01631 564604).
e-mail: enquiries@obangolf.com
website: www.obangolf.com

Please mention
THE GOLF GUIDE
when you enquire about
clubs or accommodation

COWAL GOLF CLUB, DUNOON

For a perfect golf day out, seven days a week • **BETTER RATES FOR 2005**

Call Secretary Allan Douglas on 01369 705673 (Tel/Fax)

e-mail: secretary@cowalgolfclub.com • www.cowalgolfclub.com

Tel: 01369 702907 • Fax: 01369 706266
e-mail: mike@westendhotel.com

Situated on the traffic-free West Bay, with private parking,
the West End enjoys magnificent views of the Clyde Estuary,
yet is only minutes' walk from the town centre.

• All rooms have en suite facilities • Varied menus • Licensed bar
• Live entertainment most weekends • Games room

*Golf Breaks are our speciality, with 3 courses within a
15 minute drive. Experience the breathtaking scenery
from the 18-hole Cowal championship course.*

West End Hotel
West Bay, Dunoon PA23 7HU
www.westendhotel.com

**3-day Golf Breaks including DB&B
and green fees from £150**

See also Colour Advertisement on page 65

SCOTLAND / Argyll & Bute

OBAN. **Isle of Seil Golf Club,** Balvicar, Isle of Seil. *Location*: turn off the A816 Oban - Lochgilphead Road at Kilninver onto the B844, follow B844, cross the Atlantic Bridge onto Seil, then on to Balvicar. Partly on shore of Balvicar Bay, partly on reclaimed quarry land. 9 holes, 2141 yards, Par 31. *Green Fees*: £10.00 per day. *Visitors*: welcome all day, every day. *Society Meetings*: by arrangement. Secretary: Mr B.R. Mitchell (01852 300348).

ROTHESAY. **Port Bannatyne Golf Club,** Bannatyne Mains Road, Port Bannatyne (01700 504544). *Location*: two miles north of Rothesay (ferry terminal). Hill course overlooking bays and sea lochs. 13 holes, 5085 yards, S.S.S. 65. *Green Fees*: weekdays £12.00 per round, £17.00 per day; weekends £18.00 per round, £22.00 per day. *Eating facilities*: can be arranged in new clubhouse. *Visitors*: welcome – almost unrestricted. *Society Meetings*: very welcome. Secretary: Mrs B.K. Burnett (01700 505142).

ROTHESAY. **Rothesay Golf Club,** Canada Hill, Rothesay PA20 9HN. *Location:* Beautiful island in the Firth of Clyde, frequent ferries from Wemyss Bay, 35 miles south-west of Glasgow, and from Colintraive in mainland Argyll. One of Scotland's most scenic island courses, designed by James Braid and Ben Sayers. 18 holes, 5456 yards. S.S.S. 67. Practice area. *Green Fees:* information not available. *Eating facilities:* full catering and bar facilities. *Visitors:* welcome, but prior booking at weekends through Professional. *Society Meetings:* welcome by arrangement. PGA Professional: James M. Dougal (Tel & Fax: 01700 503554). Hon. Secretary: D.W.W. Craig.* website: www.rothesaygolfclub.com

SOUTHEND. **Dunaverty Golf Club,** Southend, Campbeltown PA28 6RN (Tel & Fax: 01586 830677). *Location:* about 10 miles south of Campbeltown on B842. Scenic seaside course with great views to Ireland and Mull of Kintyre. 18 holes, 4799 yards. S.S.S. 63. Small practice ground. *Green Fees:* information not available. *Eating facilities:* snacks, teas/coffees, meals by arrangement; no bar. *Visitors:* welcome, phone if visiting at weekends. Limited equipment hire. *Society Meetings:* welcome, phone or write to N. Hind for bookings. Steward: N. Hind.

TARBERT. **Tarbert Golf Club,** Kilberry Road, Tarbert PA29 6XX (01880 820565). *Location:* approximately one mile south of Tarbert on B8024. Hilly wooded parkland. 9 holes, 4460 yards. S.S.S. 63. *Green Fees:* £12.00 per day. *Eating facilities:* licensed clubhouse, open weekends. *Visitors:* welcome at all times. *Society Meetings:* by arrangement. Secretary: Peter Cupples (01546 606896).

TAYNUILT. **Taynuilt Golf Club,** Taynuilt PA35 1JE (01866 822429). *Location:* 12 miles from Oban on A85, quarter of a mile, through the village, from the main road. Situated in a scenic and majestic location, surrounded by mountains and overlooking picturesque Loch Etive. Dominated by Ben Cruachan at 3695 feet, the challenging 9 hole course of undulating parkland was founded in 1987 and officially opened by Michael Bonallack of the R&A in 1991. 9 Holes, 4510 yards. S.S.S.63. Gents, 67 Ladies. *Green Fees:* £15.00. *Eating facilities:* not available - two hotels and a tearoom nearby. *Visitors:* welcome most days, some restrictions Tuesdays and Sundays. Toilet facilities available. *Society Meetings:* welcome. Secretary: Mike J.P. Urwin (01866 833341). e-mail: michael.urwin67@which.net

TIGHNABRUAICH. **Kyles Of Bute Golf Club,** Kames, Tighnabruaich PA21 2BA. *Location:* access from Dunoon and Strachur. Clubhouse by Kames Farm, turn south off B8000 Kames to Millhouse road. Hillside course with magnificent views. 9 holes, 4778 yards. S.S.S. 64. *Green Fees:* weekdays £10.00 per day; weekends £10.00. *Eating facilities:* no bar. *Visitors:* welcome, except Sunday mornings. *Society Meetings:* by special arrangement. Secretary: Dr Jeremy Thomson (01700 811603).1

Beautiful island in the Firth of Clyde. Frequent ferries from Wemyss Bay, 35 miles south west of Glasgow, and from Colintraive on mainland Argyll. One of Scotland's most scenic island courses, designed by Ben Sayers and James Braid. 18 holes. 5456 yards. SSS 67. Practice area. Green Fees: on request. Winter rates from 1st November to 31st March. Full catering and bar facilities. Visitors very welcome, but at weekends by prior arrangement.
All bookings: PGA Professional James M. Dougal (Tel & Fax 01700 503554)

ROTHESAY GOLF CLUB
Canada Hill, Isle of Bute PA20 9HN • www.rothesaygolfclub.com

---

TAYNUILT GOLF CLUB - TAYNUILT, ARGYLL TEL: 01866 822429

Situated in a scenic and majestic location, Taynuilt Golf Course is surrounded by mountains and overlooks the picturesque Loch Etive. Dominated by Ben Cruachan at 3695 feet, the challenging 9-hole course of undulating parkland was founded in 1987 and officially opened by Michael Bonallack of the R&A in 1991.
www.taynuiltgolfclub.co.uk

Ayrshire & Arran

AYR. **Belleisle Golf Course,** Doonfoot Road, Ayr KA7 4DU (01292 441258). *Location:* follow main road south through Ayr. Gently sloping parkland course with fine mature trees. 18 holes, 6477 yards. S.S.S. 72. Practice area. *Green Fees:* information not available. *Eating facilities:* hotel and bars with catering. *Visitors:* no restrictions but booking in advance advisable. Juniors under 17 must have handicap of 12 or under. *Society Meetings:* catered for, groups up to 40; groups over 40 by special application. Professional: David Gemmell (Tel & Fax: 01292 441314). Starter: Alan Thomson (01292 441258; Fax: 01292 442632).*

AYR. **Dalmilling Golf Course,** Westwood Avenue, Ayr KA8 0QR (01292 263893; Fax: 01292 610543). *Location:* A77, on north-east boundary, one mile from town centre. Parkland. 18 holes, 5724 yards. S.S.S. 68. Putting green. *Green Fees:* weekdays £13.00 per round, £20.00 per day; weekends £16.00 per round, £25.00 per day. *Eating facilities:* snacks/lunches/high teas, table licence. *Visitors:* welcome, not before 9.30am weekends, telephone to ensure availability. *Society Meetings:* welcome by arrangement. Professional: Philip Cheyney. Secretary: Stewart Graham (01292 262468).

AYR. **Seafield Golf Course,** Doonfoot Road, Ayr KA7 4DU (01292 441258). *Location:* follow main road south through Ayr. Parkland and links, gently sloping. 18 holes, 5498 yards. S.S.S. 66. *Green Fees:* information not available. *Eating facilities:* hotel and bars with catering. *Visitors:* welcome, no restrictions but booking in advance advisable. *Society Meetings:* catered for, groups up to 40; groups over 40 by special application. Professional: David Gemmell (Tel & Fax: 01292 441314). Starter: Alan Thomson (01292 441258; Fax: 01292 442632).*

BEITH. **Beith Golf Club,** Threepwood Road, Beith KA15 2JR (01505 503166). *Location:* first left off Beith bypass road travelling south. Hilly parkland course with trees and gorse. 18 holes, 5616 yards. S.S.S. 68. *Green Fees:* available on request. *Eating facilities:* snacks and meals available, bar open 9am to 11pm. *Visitors:* welcome. Restrictions as follows: Tuesday 4.30pm to 6.30pm. Saturday 7am to 2pm. Sunday 1pm to 2.30pm. *Society Meetings:* welcome by prior arrangement. Secretary: Margaret Murphy (Tel & Fax: 01505 506814).

DAILLY. **Brunston Castle Golf Course,** Dailly, Girvan KA26 9GD (01465 811471). *Location:* 18 hole championship course in most scenic part of Ayrshire, five miles north of Girvan on B471, five miles from Turnberry. *Green Fees*: 18 holes weekdays £30.00 per round; weekends £35.00 per round. Open 8am to 11pm (summer). Driving range. Full PGA tuition by Professional, full practice facilities. *Eating facilities:* full bar and restaurant facilities. *Visitors:* welcome. 16-seater minibus and trailer available. On-line booking available.
e-mail: golf@brunstoncastle.co.uk
website: www.brunstoncastle.co.uk

GALSTON. **Loudoun Gowf Club,** Galston KA4 8PA (01563 820551). *Location:* five miles east of Kilmarnock on A71. Fairly flat parkland. 18 holes, 6005 yards. S.S.S. 69. Green Fees: £25.00 per round, £35.00 per day weekdays. *Eating facilities:* full catering and bar. *Visitors:* welcome weekdays only. Trolleys and buggies available for hire. *Society Meetings:* welcome by arrangement. Secretary: (01563 821993; Fax: 01563 820011).

GIRVAN. **Girvan Golf Course,** 40 Golf Course Road, Girvan, KA26 9HW (01465 714346). *Location:* A77 from Glasgow, through Ayr, on coast road to Stranraer, off A77 north of Harbour. 8 holes seaside, 10 holes parkland. 18 holes, 5064 yards. S.S.S. 64. Practice area. *Green Fees:* information not available. *Eating facilities:* full catering available in clubhouse. *Visitors:* welcome, no restrictions except when course closed for local competitions (approximately 4 per year). *Society Meetings:* welcome, book through Starter. Secretary: W.B. Tait.

IRVINE. **Glasgow Golf Club,** Gailes, Irvine KA11 5AE (01294 311258; Fax: 01294 279366). *Location:* eight miles from Kilmarnock, two miles south of Irvine, four miles north of Troon. Championship links course with heather lined fairways. 18 holes, 6535 yards. S.S.S. 72, Par 71. Practice ground. *Green Fees:* weekdays £55.00 per round, £70.00 per day; Saturday and Sunday afternoons £60.00. Subject to review. *Eating facilities:* full catering and bar facilities. *Visitors:* welcome weekdays 8.30am-4.30pm, weekend afternoons. Prior booking recommended through the Secretary. Caddy cars/buggies for hire, caddies by arrangement. *Society Meetings:* by application to Club Secretary. Professional: Jack Steven (01294 311561). Secretary: D.W. Deas (0141-942 2011; Fax: 0141-942 0770).
e-mail: secretary@glasgow-golf.com
website: www.glasgowgailes-golf.com

PLEASE MENTION THIS GUIDE WHEN YOU ENQUIRE ABOUT CLUBS OR ACCOMMODATION

IRVINE. **The Irvine Golf Club,** Bogside, Irvine KA12 8SN (01294 275979). *Location:* through Irvine going towards Kilwinning, turn left at Ravenspark Academy. Flat links course. 18 holes, 6408 yards. S.S.S. 72. Practice ground. *Green Fees:* information not available. *Eating facilities:* dining room and bars. *Visitors:* welcome, after 3pm weekends. *Society Meetings:* welcome. Professional: J. McKinnon (01294 275626). Secretary: W.J. McMahon (01294 275979).

IRVINE. **Irvine Ravenspark Golf Club,** 13 Kidsneuk Lane, Irvine KA12 8SR (01294 271293). *Location:* on A78 between Irvine and Kilwinning at Irvine Royal Academy. Flat parkland course. 18 holes, 6453 yards. S.S.S. 71. *Green Fees:* see website for latest. *Eating facilities:* diningroom, bar. *Visitors:* welcome, except on Saturdays before 2.30pm March to October. No jeans or training shoes allowed in the clubhouse. *Society Meetings:* welcome, by arrangement weekends. Professional: P. Bond (01294 276467). Secretary: S. Howie (01294 553904). Steward: J. McVay (01294 271293).*
e-mail: secretary@irgc.co.uk
website: www.irgc.co.uk

IRVINE. **Thistle Hotel, Roseholm Golf Course**, 46 Annick Road, Irvine KA11 4LD (Hotel Tel: 0870 3339156; Fax: 0870 3339256). *Location:* course is situated on the grounds of the Thistle Hotel, Irvine. Flat parkland. 9-holes, 1277 yards. *Green Fees:* information not available. Golf free to hotel guests. Club hire for hotel guests. *Eating facilities:* lunches, snacks, tea and coffee served in the hotel bar. *Visitors:* welcome all year.*
e-mail: irvine@thistle.co.uk
website: www.thistlehotels.com/irvine

IRVINE. **Western Gailes Golf Club,** Gailes, By Irvine KA11 5AE (01294 311649; Fax: 01294 312312). *Location:* three miles north of Troon. Seaside links. 18 holes, 6639 yards, 6179 (yellow tees). S.S.S. 74. Par 71. Limited practice facilities. *Green Fees:* weekdays £95.00 per round, £140.00 per day, both include lunch; Sunday after 2.00pm £100.00 per round (lunch not included). *Eating facilities:* full bar and catering facilities. *Visitors:* welcome Mondays, Wednesdays and Fridays and Sunday afternoons, advance booking required, telephone Reservations Department, Lyn or Vicky (01294 311649). Caddies and caddy cars available for hire. *Society Meetings:* welcome by arrangement with Secretary. Secretary: Ian F. Sproule.
e-mail: enquiries@westerngailes.com

KILBIRNIE. **Kilbirnie Place Golf Club,** Largs Road, Kilbirnie KA25 7AT (01505 683398). *Location:* on main Kilbirnie to Largs Road, left hand side just outside town boundary. Parkland. 18 holes, 5116 yards. S.S.S. 67. *Green Fees:* information not available. *Eating facilities:* catering and bar. *Visitors:* welcome weekdays and Sundays only, no visiting parties Saturdays. Secretary: C. McGurk (01505 684444/683398).

KILMARNOCK. **Annanhill Golf Club,** Irvine Road, Kilmarnock KA1 2RT (01563 521644). *Location:* between Kilmarnock and Crosshouse on road to Irvine. Parkland course with excellent views and tree-lined fairways. 18 holes, 6285 yards. S.S.S. 70. Practice area. *Green Fees:* prices on request to Starter on (01563 521512). *Eating facilities:* full catering available on application. *Visitors:* no parties Saturdays, but welcome Sundays and weekdays by reservation. *Society Meetings:* catered for. Secretary: Thomas C. Denham (01563 521644).

KILMARNOCK. **Caprington Golf Club,** Ayr Road, Kilmarnock (01563 523702). Parkland/wooded course. 18 holes, 5810 yards. S.S.S. 68. *Green Fees:* information not available. *Eating facilities:* available. *Visitors:* welcome except Saturdays. *Society Meetings:* all welcome. Secretary: Gordon Bray (01563 520566).*

For full details of clubs and courses, plus convenient accommodation

www.uk-golfguide.com

THISTLE HOTELS
more than just accommodating

Just 10 minutes' transfer from Prestwick International Airport and 25 miles from Glasgow City Centre. Easy access to many world famous courses in Ayrshire including Royal Troon, host to the 133rd Open Championship. The hotel offers guests a high standard of service and comfort, with 128 large bedrooms, a choice of restaurants, a unique lagoon pool with jacuzzi and games room. On-site executive 9-hole Par 3 golf course.

Thistle Irvine, 46 Annick Road, Irvine, Ayrshire KA11 4LD
tel: 0870 333 9156 • e-mail: reservations.irvine@thistle.co.uk

2-day Golf Packages start from £150.00 • Golf Club memberships available.

LARGS. **Largs Golf Club,** Irvine Road, Largs KA30 8EU (01475 674681). *Location:* A78, south end of Largs town (opposite Marina). Parkland/woodland with scenic views over Cumbraes and Isle of Arran. 18 holes, 6115 yards. S.S.S. 71. *Green Fees:* £33.00 per round, £45.00 per day. *Eating facilities:* full catering and bar. *Visitors:* welcome, tee can be reserved one day ahead of play. Carts, caddies by arrangement. *Society Meetings:* catered for Tuesdays and Thursdays only by prior arrangement. Professional: Kenneth Docherty PGA (01475 686192). Secretary: Jim Callaghan (Tel & Fax: 01475 673594). e-mail: secretary@largsgolfclub.co.uk website: www.largsgolfclub.co.uk

LARGS. **Routenburn Golf Club,** Routenburn, Largs KA30 9AH (01475 673230). Hilly moorland course. 18 holes, 5765 yards. S.S.S. 67. *Green Fees:* information not available. *Eating facilities:* lunches at club except Thursdays, order in advance. *Visitors:* welcome with reservation. *Society Meetings:* catered for on application to club. Professional: Greig McQueen (01475 687240). Secretary: Mr R.B. Connal.

www.uk-golfguide.com

LARGS. **sportscotland National Centre: Inverclyde, Golf Training Facility,** Burnside Road, Largs KA30 8RW (01475 674666). *Location:* 40 minutes from Glasgow and Prestwick airports. Parkland, links, training bunkers. 6 hole practice area plus driving bays. *Green Fees:* information not available. *Eating facilities:* cafeteria, dining room, accommodation and bar. *Visitors:* one and two day ladies' and mixed beginners' courses, booking essential. Professionals: Kenny Docherty, Gordon Sherry, Campbell Donaldson. Assistant Pro: Derek Watters. Admin. Co-ordinator: Sandra Samuel. Manager: Angela Liddel.

MAUCHLINE. **Ballochmyle Golf Club,** Mauchline KA5 6LE (01290 550469; Fax: 01290 553657). *Location:* on B705 off A76, one mile south of Mauchline. Wooded parkland course. 18 holes, 5990 yards. S.S.S. 69. *Green Fees:* £30.00 per day weekdays; £35.00 per day weekends. *Eating facilities:* all day bar opening from 1st April until 30th September, snacks and meals available during bar hours. *Visitors:* welcome every day except Saturdays. Dress regulations both on and off the course must be adhered to. Two full size snooker tables. *Society Meetings:* all welcome to a total of 30 per party. Secretary: R. Leslie Crawford (01290 550469).

LARGS GOLF CLUB
IRVINE ROAD, LARGS KA30 8EU

- £30 per round, £40 day ticket Monday - Friday
- Fourball deals available
- Package deals for 12 or more golfers
- Contact the Secretary for details

Largs Golf Club is a long-established private club with a superb 18 hole parkland course, situated in front of Kelburn Castle, one mile south of Largs town centre. From the clubhouse and course there are magnificent views across the Firth of Clyde towards the Cumbraes, Bute and the mountains of Arran.

The course is enduringly popular with visitors, who return regularly year after year. The well balanced layout offers an interesting and challenging experience to golfers across the broad spectrum of enthusiasm and ability.

Secretary/Treasurer: **JIM CALLAGHAN**
Tel/Fax: 01475 673594 • E-mail: secretary@largsgolfclub.co.uk • www.largsgolfclub.co.uk

See also Colour Advertisement on page 65

sportscotland
National Centre Inverclyde
Golf Practice Facility

Our course, boasting six holes, eight driving bays and clubgolf coaching bays, has been in operation since 1984 and has a fantastic outlook across the Firth of Clyde to the Isles of Cumbrae and Bute and over the hills of Arran.

The practice facility is primarily used for members and as a clubgolf training centre, providing coach education courses, however, many other user groups can access the centre, by booking the facility, on an hourly/daily basis.

The centre can also organise tailor made tuition packages for parties of 4 or more, including accommodation and meals. If individual lessons are for you, we can contact our local Professionals, who will gladly help you improve your game.

Burnside Road,
Largs
KA30 8RW

Email: in.enquiries@sportscotland.org.uk
Web: www.nationalcentreinverclyde.org.uk
Tel: 0845 126 0664

See also Colour Advertisement on page 66

SCOTLAND / Ayrshire & Arran

MAYBOLE. **Maybole Golf Course,** Memorial Park, Kirkoswald Road, Maybole KA19 7DX (01292 612000). *Location:* A77 from Glasgow, on main Girvan road at Maybole. Hilly parkland. 9 holes, 2635 yards. S.S.S. 33. *Green Fees:* information not available. *Visitors:* welcome. *Society Meetings:* welcome. Secretary: A. Ferguson. Starter (01655 889770).*

MUIRKIRK. **Muirkirk Golf Club,** "Southside", Furnace Road, Muirkirk KA18 3RE. *Location:* 10 miles off A74 on A70 to Ayr. Picturesque country scenery, the course nestles amongst heather clad hills. 9 holes, 5380 yards. S.S.S. 67. *Green Fees:* day ticket £10.00 adults, £4.00 Juniors. *Eating facilities:* can be accommodated. Secretary: Robert Bradford (01290 660184).

NEW CUMNOCK. **New Cumnock Golf Club,** Lochhill, New Cumnock KA18 4BQ (01290 338848). *Location:* A76, one mile west of New Cummock. Parkland, protected area for wildlife birds, next to loch. 9 holes, 5176 yards (18). S.S.S. 66. *Green Fees:* information not available. *Eating facilities:* Lochside House Hotel sits on the edge of the course. *Visitors:* welcome at all times except Sunday up to 4pm for competitions. Clubhouse. *Society Meetings:* welcome. Secretary: John McGinn (01290 338041).*

PATNA. **Doon Valley Golf Club,** Hillside, Patna KA6 7JT (01292 531607). *Location:* 10 miles south of Ayr on the A713 Ayr to Castle Douglas road. Undulating hillside parkland course. 9 holes, 5859 yards, 5402 metres. S.S.S. 70. *Green Fees:* £10.00 per round, £15.00 per day. *Eating facilities:* bar open weekdays 7pm to 11pm, weekends 12 noon to 12 midnight. *Visitors:* welcome anytime weekdays, weekends by arrangement. *Society Meetings:* welcome, groups of more than six must apply for tee off times. Secretary: Hugh Johnstone MBE (01292 550411).

PRESTWICK. **Prestwick Golf Club,** Links Road, Prestwick KA9 1QG (01292 477404). *Location:* one mile from Prestwick airport, 40 minutes by car from Turnberry Hotel, 10 minutes from Troon, 15 minutes from Ayr. 18 holes, 6544 yards. S.S.S. 73. *Green Fees:* weekdays £100.00 per round, £150.00 per day; Sundays (limited times) £150 per round. Subject to review. *Eating facilities:* dining room (male only: prior booking required) open from 12.30pm to 2.30pm. Cardinal Room (light lunches) open to ladies and gentlemen from 10.00am until 3.30pm. *Visitors:* welcome with reservation. *Society Meetings:* catered for. Professional: D. A. Fleming. Secretary: I.T. Bunch (01292 477404; Fax: 01292 477255). e-mail: secretary@prestwickgc.co.uk
website: www.prestwickgc.co.uk

PRESTWICK. **Prestwick St Cuthbert Golf Club,** East Road, Prestwick KA9 2SX (01292 477101; Fax: 01292 671730). *Location:* south-east area of Prestwick near A77 Whitletts roundabout, follow signs for Heathfield and Prestwick Airport. Flat, some trees; semi-parkland. 18 holes, 6470 yards, 6063 metres. S.S.S. 71. Limited practice area. *Green Fees:* information not available. *Eating facilities:* bar and restaurant. *Visitors:* welcome except weekends unless introduced by and playing with member. *Society Meetings:* catered for. Secretary: J.C. Rutherford (01292 477101).*

PRESTWICK. **Prestwick St Nicholas Golf Club,** Grangemuir Road, Prestwick KA9 1SN (01292 477608; Fax: 01292 473900). *Location:* Grangemuir Road is half a mile from town centre on Prestwick to Ayr Road. Traditional links course enjoying wonderful panoramic views across Firth of Clyde to island of Arran. 18 holes, 5952 yards, 5441 metres. S.S.S. 69. *Green Fees:* weekdays £45.00 per round, weekend £50.00 per round. Weekday day ticket £60.00. *Eating facilities:* full service. *Visitors:* welcome most weekdays and Sunday afternoons. *Society Meetings:* welcome by arrangement. Secretary: T.D.M. Hepburn (01292 477608; Fax: 01292 473900).
e-mail: secretary@prestwickstnicholas.com
website: www.prestwickstnicholas.com

SKELMORLIE. **Skelmorlie Golf Club,** Beithglass Road, Skelmorlie PA17 5ES (01475 520152). *Location:* two/three miles from Wemyss Bay Pier. Hillside, moorland course. 18 holes, 5013 yards. S.S.S. 65. *Green Fees:* information not available. *Eating facilities:* bar 11am to 11 pm, some catering. *Visitors:* welcome except Saturdays before 4pm. *Society Meetings:* welcome by arrangement. Parties at discounted "all-in" rate. Secretary: Mrs A. Fahey (01475 520774).*

STEVENSTON. **Ardeer Golf Club,** Greenhead, Stevenston KA20 4JX (01294 464542). *Location:* north of Ayr, six miles from Irvine New Town, off A78. Parkland course lined with trees incorporating water on several holes. 18 holes, 6409 yards. S.S.S. 71. *Green Fees:* on application. *Eating facilities:* restaurant and bars. *Visitors:* welcome except Saturdays. *Society Meetings:* all parties holding Handicap Certificates welcome except Saturdays. Starter: Paul Forbes (01294 601327). Secretary: Peter Watson (Tel & Fax: 01294 465316).

STEVENSTON. **Moorpark Golf Club,** Auchenharvie Golf Complex, Moorpark Road West, Stevenston KA20 3HU. *Location:* on the A738 Stevenston/Saltcoats; five miles from Irvine, 20 miles from Glasgow. Flat parkland course with water feature incorporated into two holes. 18 holes, 5203 yards. S.S.S. 66. 18 bay floodlit driving range. *Green Fees:* information not available. *Eating facilities:* privately owned lounge bar within complex open to public, bar meals, functions, snacks available (01294 469051). *Visitors:* welcome, restrictions when there are club competitions. *Society Meetings:* all welcome. The course is situated right next door to Sandylands Caravan Park and there are plenty of other golf courses to play all within easy reach. Secretary: R. Paterson (01294 602493).

For full details of clubs and courses, plus convenient accommodation
www.uk-golfguide.com

TROON. **Kilmarnock (Barassie) Golf Club,** 29 Hillhouse Road, Barassie, Troon KA10 6SY (01292 313920; Fax: 01292 318300). *Location:* two miles north of Troon. Links course. 27 holes: Barassie Links 18 holes, 6484 yards. S.S.S. 74; Hillhouse 9 holes, 2888 yards, par 34. Practice ground. *Green Fees:* £65.00 per day Monday to Friday, £70.00 per round Saturday and Sunday. 2005 rates, subject to review. *Eating facilities:* coffee, lunches, snacks, high teas. *Visitors:* welcome Mondays, Tuesdays, Thursdays and Friday afternoons; limited visitors Wednesdays; Saturdays after 3pm, Sundays after 2pm. All visitors must adhere to club dress code — no denim, trainers, etc. *Society Meetings:* catered for Tuesdays and Thursdays. Professional: Gregor Howie (Tel & Fax: 01292 311322). Secretary: Donald D. Wilson (01292 313920/311077).
e-mail: golfkbgc@lineone.net
website: www.kbgc.co.uk

TROON. **Troon Municipal Golf Courses,** Harling Drive, Troon (01292 312464). *Location:* adjacent to railway station, one mile off the Ayr-Glasgow road. Three 18 hole courses. Lochgreen 6820 yards. S.S.S. 73. Darley 6360 yards. S.S.S. 72. Fullarton 4870 yards. S.S.S. 63. *Green Fees:* information not available. *Eating facilities:* hot snacks, 8am - 6pm. Bar snacks and lunches, evening meals bookings only. *Visitors:* catered for. Broad wheeled trolleys only. *Society Meetings:* catered for. Caterer: John Darge. Professional: Gordon McKinley. Advance booking should be made in writing to Starter's Office, Troon Municipal Golf Courses, Harling Drive, Troon, Ayrshire (Fax: 01292 312578). Special short breaks and day tickets available, for details telephone 01292 616270.*

TROON. **Royal Troon Golf Club,** Craigend Road, Troon KA10 6EP (01292 311555; Fax: 01292 318204). *Location:* three miles from A77 (Glasgow/Ayr trunk road). Old Course (Championship) 18 holes, 6493 metres, 7101 yards. S.S.S. 74. Portland Course 18 holes, 5751 metres, 6289 yards. S.S.S. 71. *Green Fees:* on request. *Eating facilities:* full restaurant service available, including bar snacks. *Visitors:* Mondays, Tuesdays and Thursdays between 9.30 and 11.00am and 14.30 and 16.00pm. Letter of introduction from own club and Handicap Certificate required (maximum: male 20; Ladies 30). Golfers under 18 years play on the Portland Course. *Society Meetings:* parties in excess of 24 not accepted. Professional: Brian Anderson (01292 313281). Secretary/Manager: J.W. Chandler (01292 311555; Fax: 01292 318204).
e-mail: bookings@royaltroon.com
website: www.royaltroon.com

THE APPEARANCE OF AN ASTERISK (*) AT THE END OF A CLUB OR COURSE ENTRY INDICATES THAT UP-TO-DATE INFORMATION HAS NOT BEEN SUPPLIED

modern luxury

play the legend

excitement.
anticipation.
inspiration.
and that's just the view.

Pause for a moment. Breathe in that fresh sea air. Then look around you. It could only be Turnberry.

Let us reserve your stay. Call **01655 331 000**
Best rates, guaranteed at westin.com/turnberry

THE WESTIN TURNBERRY RESORT
SCOTLAND

See also Colour Advertisement on page 66

TURNBERRY. **The Westin Turnberry Resort,** Maidens Road, Turnberry KA26 9LT (01655 331000; Fax: 01655 331706). *Location:* on main A77 between Maybole and Girvan. Two Championship Links Courses, Ailsa (host to British Open) 18 holes, 6976 yards. S.S.S. 72; The Kintyre, 6827 yards. S.S.S. 72, and The Arran (9 holes). The Colin Montgomerie Links Golf Academy, putting greens. *Green Fees:* From £60 non-residents. *Eating facilities:* clubhouse, restaurant and bar. *Visitors:* written requests only. Accommodation at The Westin Turnberry Resort, 221 Bedrooms. *Society Meetings:* written requests only. Director of Golf: Paul Burley (01655 334000; Fax: 01655 331069). Golf Sales Manager: E.C. Bowman (01655 334198).

WEST KILBRIDE. **The West Kilbride Golf Club,** 33-35 Fullerton Drive, Seamill, West Kilbride KA23 9HT (01294 823911; Fax: 01294 829573). *Location:* midway between Largs (to north) and Ardrossan (south) on A78. Seaside links course with magnificent views to Isle of Arran and Cumbraes across Firth of Clyde. 18 holes, 6452 yards, 5898 metres. S.S.S. 71. Practice area, putting greens. *Green Fees:* on application. *Eating facilities:* bar, lounge, dining room. *Visitors:* welcome weekdays only. Caddy cars for hire. *Society Meetings:* catered for Tuesdays and Thursdays. Handicap Certificates required. Professional: Graham Ross (01294 823042). Secretary: Hamish Armour (01294 823911).

THE ISLAND OF ARRAN

BLACKWATERFOOT. **Shiskine Golf and Tennis Club,** Blackwaterfoot, Shiskine KA27 8HA (Tel: 01770 860226. Fax: 01770 860205). *Location:* off B880 at Blackwaterfoot. Seaside links with outstanding views. 12 holes, 2990 yards. S.S.S. 42. Putting green, nets. *Green Fees:* weekdays £15.00 per round, £25.00 per day; weekends £19.00 per round, £30.00 per day. Special rates: Week £90.00, Fortnight £130.00. Subject to review. Maximum of two rounds per day. *Eating facilities:* tearoom, snacks, lunches, high teas, dinner. *Visitors:* welcome, preferably with Club Handicap. July and August are very busy so prefer visitors September to June. Tennis and bowls. Shop open Easter–October. *Society Meetings:* only if pre-booked with Match Secretary. Proof of Handicap required. Club Manager: Fiona M. Crawford. e-mail: info@shiskinegolf.com website: www.shiskinegolf.com

BRODICK. **Brodick Golf Club,** Brodick KA27 8DL (Tel & Fax: 01770 302349). *Location:* one mile north of pier. Flat seaside course. 18 holes, 4736 yards. S.S.S. 64. Practice area. *Green Fees:* information not available. *Eating facilities:* bar snacks available. *Visitors:* welcome without restriction. *Society Meetings:* welcome with reservation by letter. Professional: P.S. McCalla (01770 302513). Secretary: Douglas Robertson (Tel & Fax: 01770 302349).

CORRIE. **Corrie Golf Club,** Sannox, Corrie KA27 8JD (01770 810223). *Location:* seven miles north of Brodick. Short 9 hole course, full of character and very picturesque with some magnificent views. 9 holes, 1948 yards. S.S.S. 61. *Green Fees:* £14.00 per day ticket; twilight ticket £7.00. *Eating facilities:* meals available 9am to 6pm April to October. *Visitors:* welcome, course closed Saturday afternoons, Ladies medal first Thursday of every month. *Society Meetings:* catered for by arrangement (maximum number 12). Secretary: J. Milesi (01770 850247).

LAMLASH. **Lamlash Golf Club,** Lamlash KA27 8JU (Tel & Fax: 01770 600296). *Location:* A841, three miles south of Brodick Pier ferry terminal. Undulating heathland course. 18 holes, 4640 yards. S.S.S. 64. *Green Fees:* weekdays £20.00 per day; weekends £25.00. After 4pm any day £15.00 per round. Reductions for Senior Citizens. Rates subject to review. *Eating facilities:* catering, lounge bar. *Visitors:* welcome, no restrictions. Pro shop: (01770 600196). Carts/buggies for hire. *Society Meetings:* welcome, book in advance by letter. Secretary: J. Henderson (01770 600272). Starter: (01779 600196). website: www.lamlashgolfclub.co.uk

LOCHRANZA. **Lochranza Golf,** Isle of Arran KA27 8HL (01770 830273; Fax: 01770 830600). *Location:* Lochranza village. A special 'pay & play' golf course in spectacular setting with extensive wildlife. Very interesting challenging design, fun for everyone, shaped for 'game improvement'. Lower handicaps may play medal tees. 18 holes from 18 tees to 12 greens (six double,six single), 5470 yards, 5033 metres. Par 70. *Green Fees:* £16.00 per round every day. *Visitors:* welcome daily May to October inclusive. Proprietor: Ian M. Robertson. e-mail: office@lochgolf.demon.co.uk website: www.lochranzagolf.com

MACHRIE. **Machrie Bay Golf Course,** Machrie, Near Brodick KA27 8DZ (01770 840329). *Location:* on A841, three and a half miles north of Blackwaterfoot. Flat seaside course. 9 holes, 2200 yards. S.S.S. 32. Putting green and small practice area. *Green Fees:* information not available. *Eating facilities:* tea room, snacks/meals; no licence. *Visitors:* welcome anytime. *Society Meetings:* by arrangement. Secretary: R. Waine (01770 860380).*

WHITING BAY. **Whiting Bay Golf Club,** Golf Course Road, Whiting Bay, Brodick KA27 8QT (01770 700487). *Location:* eight miles south of Brodick. Undulating parkland. 18 holes, 4405 yards. S.S.S. 63. Practice net. *Green Fees:* information not available. *Eating facilities:* catering and bar. *Visitors:* welcome anytime. Clubhouse, shower, snooker and pool rooms; buggies and caddy cars for hire. *Society Meetings:* by prior booking. Secretary: Margaret Auld (01770 820208).

FHG

Visit the KUPERARD website
www.holidayguides.com
for details of the wide choice of accommodation featured in the full range of FHG titles

---

THE APPEARANCE OF AN ASTERISK (*) AT THE END OF A CLUB OR COURSE ENTRY INDICATES THAT UP-TO-DATE INFORMATION HAS NOT BEEN SUPPLIED

Borders

ASHKIRK. **Woll Golf Course,** New Woll Estate, Selkirk TD7 4PE (01750 32711). *Location:* through the village of Ashkirk, just off the A7 and only an hour from Edinburgh, Newcastle and Carlisle. Challenging course in natural parkland setting of outstanding beauty incorporating the Woll Burn and other water features. Flat course. 18 holes, 6051 yards, S.S.S. 69. *Green Fees:* £24.00 (subject to review). *Eating facilities:* full clubhouse facilities available; bar, restaurant and function suite all year round. *Visitors:* most welcome at all times. Luxury self-catering accommodation available on the course.
e-mail: wollgolf@btinternet.com
website: www.wollgolf.co.uk

COLDSTREAM. **Hirsel Golf Club,** Kelso Road, Coldstream TD12 4NJ (01890 882678; Fax: 01890 882233). *Location:* A697 west end of Coldstream. Parkland. 18 holes, 6111 yards, 5570 metres. S.S.S. 70. Practice ground. *Green Fees:* information not available. *Eating facilities:* full catering all year. Snack catering November to mid-March. *Visitors:* welcome, no restrictions; groups of over 10 players must book in advance. Two person golf carts for hire (6). *Society Meetings:* catered for by arrangement.

DUNS. **Duns Golf Club,** Hardens Road, Duns TD11 3NR (01361 882194). *Location:* about one mile west of Duns just off A6105, signposted Longformacus. Upland, undulating course with view south to Cheviot Hills. A burn runs through the course and is the main hazard. 18 holes, 6209 yards, S.S.S. 70. Practice ground. New driving range 2 miles from golf course. *Green Fees:* weekdays £25.00 per round, £30.00 per day; weekends £28.00 per round, £34.00 per day. Children £7.00 per round. Reductions 1st November to 15th March. *Eating facilities:* lounge bar open weekdays and weekends, light snacks and full catering available. *Visitors:* welcome at all times except during club competitions, visitors must tee off before 4pm Mondays, Tuesdays and Wednesdays. *Society Meetings:* welcome, booking through Clubhouse (01361 882194). Secretary: Alex Preston (01361 883599).

EYEMOUTH. **Eyemouth Golf Club,** Gunsgreenhill, Eyemouth TD14 5SF (018907 50004). *Location:* eight miles north of Berwick-on-Tweed, one mile off the A1. Superb cliff-top course with spectacular sea views. Play the Par 3 - 6th hole over a vast gully, with crashing waves below. Recently voted "Britain's most extraordinary Golf Hole'. 18 holes, 6520 yards, Par 72. Practice area. *Green Fees:* weekdays £22.00 per round, £30.00 per day; weekends £27.00 per round, £35.00 per day. Winter £15.00 per round or day, 7 days. *Eating facilities:* full catering facilities with the `Bay View' restaurant specializing in local sea food. *Visitors:* very welcome, phone Professional for booking. Games room, changing rooms, showers. *Society Meetings:* golfing groups and society packages very welcome. Professional: Paul Terras (018907 50004). Secretary: Mrs M. Gibson (018907 50551).

GALASHIELS. **Galashiels Golf Club,** Ladhope Recreation Ground, Galashiels TD1 2NJ (01896 753724). *Location:* north end of town, quarter of a mile off A7 on Ladhope Drive. Parkland with hill connecting two halves. 18 holes, 5185 yards. Par 67. Practice area. *Green Fees*: information not available. Package deals available for parties on application to the Visitors Contact. *Eating facilities*: catering midweek by arrangement only. *Visitors*: welcome anytime, booking essential for weekends. Ladies' night Tuesday 5pm to 7.30pm. *Society Meetings*: catered for. Contact: Secretary (01896 753724).*

GALASHIELS. **Torwoodlee Golf Club,** Edinburgh Road, Galashiels TD1 2NE (01896 752260). *Location:* leave Galashiels on A7 for Edinburgh. Entrance to course one mile on left. Parkland with wooded greens alongside river and splendid par 5. Designed by Willie Park/John Garner. 18 holes, 6021 yards. S.S.S 70. *Green Fees:* weekdays £26.00 per round, £36.00 per day; weekends £32.00 per round, £42.00 per day. (2005 rates) *Eating facilities:* bar, dining room. *Visitors:* welcome except 8.30 to 9.30, 12.30 to 13.30 weekdays or 07.30 to 10.15, 12.15 to 15.00 and 16.15 to 17.00 Saturdays. Showers available. *Society Meetings:* bookings required in advance, packages available. Secretary: A. Owenson (01896 752260).
e-mail: thesecretary@torwoodleegolfclub.org.uk
website: www.torwoodleegolfclub.org.uk

---

18 holes, 6021 yards, par 69, SSS 70
• lunch • dinner • club bar • bar snacks
• tea and coffee • cart hire
• trolley hire • changing room

Situated just one mile north of Galashiels on the A7

Visitors welcome daily
Voted "The Most Visitor Friendly Golf Club" 2001

Torwoodlee GOLF CLUB
Edinburgh Road, Galashiels TD1 2NE • Tel & Fax: **01896 752260**
e-mail: thesecretary@torwoodleegolfclub.org.uk • web: www.torwoodleegolfclub.org.uk

See also Colour Advertisement on page 66

HAWICK. **Hawick Golf Club,** Vertish Hill, Hawick TD9 9JY (01450 372293). *Location:* north along A7 from Carlisle or south on A7 from Edinburgh. Course situated half a mile south-west of town. Hill course with spectacular views. 18 holes, 5929 yards, 5422 metres. S.S.S. 69. Restricted practice area. *Green Fees:* information not available. *Eating facilities:* full bar and catering daily. *Visitors:* welcome Saturdays and after 10am Sundays. *Society Meetings:* catered for, advisable to book in advance. Secretary: J. Reilly (01450 375594).

HAWICK. **Minto Golf Club,** Denholm, Hawick TD9 8SH (01450 870220). *Location:* five miles north-east of Hawick leaving A698 at Denholm village. Parkland, trees. Course alterations for year 2000. 18 holes, 5542 yards, 4992 metres. S.S.S. 67. Practice area. *Green Fees:* information not available. *Eating facilities:* full facilities, except Thursday. *Visitors:* welcome, with prior booking. *Society Meetings:* accepted with Handicap Certificate (weekends difficult). Secretary: John Simpson.

INNERLEITHEN. **Innerleithen Golf Club,** Leithen Water, Leithen Road, Innerleithen EH44 6NL (01896 830951). *Location:* 25 miles south of Edinburgh, six miles south of Peebles, off A72 less than one mile from main street. Attractive 9 hole course set in valley with lovely views of surrounding hills, easy walking but challenging. 9 holes, 3033 yards, 2773 metres. S.S.S. 69. Practice ground. *Green Fees:* information not available. *Eating facilities:* by prior arrangement. *Visitors:* welcome without reservation, though parties should book. *Society Meetings:* catered for by arrangement, limit 40. Secretary: Norman Smith (01896 830050).*

JEDBURGH. **Jedburgh Golf Club,** Dunion Road, Jedburgh TD8 6TA (01835 863587). *Location:* one mile south of Jedburgh on Dunion Road to Hawick. Undulating course with trees. 9 holes, 5650 yards. S.S.S. 67. Currently extending to beautiful 18 hole layout due to open summer 2006. *Green Fees:* £22.00 per day. *Eating facilities:* bar and catering facilities available 11am to 11pm Wednesday to Sunday or by prior arrangement. *Visitors:* welcome. Buggy, trolley hire. *Society Meetings:* group discount on application. All enquiries please telephone 01835 863587.

KELSO. **Kelso Golf Club,** Berrymoss, Kelso TD5 7SL (01573 223009). *Location:* one mile north-east of town within Kelso Racecourse. Flat parkland within racecourse. 18 holes, 6066 yards. S.S.S. 69. Practice ground. *Green Fees:* information not available. *Eating facilities:* light catering Mondays and Tuesdays, full catering other days. *Visitors:* welcome without reservation. *Society Meetings:* welcome with reservation. Secretary: Donald R. Jack (01573 223009; 01573 223175 after 7pm).*

www.uk-golfguide.com

Minto Golf Club
"A Gem of a Golf Course in one of the most beautiful corners of Scotland"

Located in the village of Minto, near Denholm, 6 miles east of Hawick on the A698. All information regarding green fees, tee-booking and available dates for visiting parties will be given by telephone and confirmed in writing.

Tel: 01450 870 220 • *Denholm, Hawick TD9 8SH*

See also Colour Advertisement on page 67

Situated at the gateway to the Scottish Borders, Jedburgh Golf Club is a must for any golfers to the area. Established in 1892, the parkland/moorland layout was designed by former Open Champion, Willie Park of Musselburgh.

The Dunion Course is currently in the process of being extended from 9-holes to 18 holes, with a projected opening date of Spring 2006. It will undoubtedly prove to be a real gem and a challenge to golfers of all standards. This, allied to stunning views of the surrounding countryside, will ensure that Jedburgh Golf Club will attract visitors from all corners.

Jedburgh Golf Club

5650 yards ✦ Bar Open 11am - 11pm ✦ Green fees £22 per day ✦ Buggy & trolley hire (no club hire)

Dunion Road, Jedburgh TD8 6TA • All enquiries please phone 01835 863587 •

See also Colour Advertisement on page 67

KELSO. **The Roxburghe Golf Club,** The Roxburghe Hotel, Heiton, by Kelso TD5 8JZ (01573 450333; Fax: 01573 450611). *Location:* eight miles east of Jedburgh on the A698, three miles south of Kelso. Parkland, woodland course with water set in 200 acres alongside the River Teviot; designed by Dave Thomas to USPGA specifications. The Championship Course is home to the Scottish Seniors Open. 18 holes, 7111 yards. Chipping area, putting green, practice ground. *Green Fees:* £60.00, day ticket £80.00 subject to review. It is advisable to pre-book tee times. *Eating facilities:* spike bar, fine dining. *Visitors:* welcome at all times, Handicap Certificate required. *Society Meetings:* welcome by prior arrangement. Accommodation available; tuition, clay pigeon shooting. The course is owned by the Duke and Duchess of Roxburghe. Professional: Craig Montgomerie. General Manager: William Kirby. e-mail: hotel@roxburghe.net website: www.roxburghe.net

LAUDER. **Lauder Golf Club,** Galashiels Road, Lauder TD2 6PA (01578 722240). *Location:* off A68, 28 miles south of Edinburgh. Undulating course, originally designed by W. Park of Musselburgh, on Lauder Hill. 9 holes, 6049 yards. S.S.S. 69. Practice ground. *Green Fees:* £12.50 anyday. *Eating facilities:* none — good Hotels in Lauder. *Visitors:* individuals, groups and parties welcome. Telephone to book your tee time. Secretary: D. Dickson (01578 722526).

MELROSE. **Melrose Golf Club,** Dingleton Road, Melrose (01896 822855). *Location:* 4 miles west of Galashiels, less than one hour from Edinburgh. Tree-lined parkland course situated beneath Eildon Hills. 9 holes, 5562 yards, 5075 metres. S.S.S. 68. *Green Fees:* £20.00 per round/day. Juniors £10.00. *Eating facilities:* bar open at given times, catering on request for larger parties. *Visitors:* welcome anytime when no competitions taking place, Ladies have priority on Tuesdays; Juniors have priority on Wednesday mornings during school holidays. Locker room, shower. *Society Meetings:* welcome by arrangement. Secretary: Alex McCue (01896 752571).

NEWCASTLETON. **Newcastleton Golf Club,** Holm Hill, Newcastleton TD9 0QD. *Location:* midway between Carlisle 25 miles and Hawick 21 miles; off A7 at Canonbie. Hilly course with picturesque views, first three holes uphill. 9 holes, 5483 yards. S.S.S. 70. *Green Fees:* weekdays £10.00; weekends £10.00. Weekly ticket £35.00. *Eating facilities:* can be arranged. *Visitors:* welcome, no restrictions except competition days. *Society Meetings:* welcome. Secretary: G.A. Wilson (013873 75608).

PEEBLES. **Macdonald Cardrona Hotel, Golf and Country Club,** Cardrona, Peebles EH45 6LZ (01896 831971; Fax: 01896 831166). *Location:* from Edinburgh take 'Bridges' road to Cameron Toll; turn right at roundabout; heading to Penicuik take A703 to Peebles, turn left to Innerleithen. Club situated 3 miles out of Peebles. Flat parkland/woodland championship standard course. 18 holes, 6856 yards. S.S.S. 72. Putting/practice area. *Green Fees:* information not available. *Eating facilities:* Spikes Bar. *Visitors:* welcome at any time. *Society Meetings:* welcome at any time, special rates on request. 100-bedroom de luxe hotel on site. Secretary: David Mackinnon (01896 831144; Fax: 01896 831166).* e-mail: cardrona@macdonald-hotels.co.uk website: www.macdonald-hotels.co.uk

PEEBLES. **Peebles Golf Club,** Kirkland Street, Peebles EH45 8EU (01721 720197). *Location:* 51 miles from Glasgow, off A72 at west side of town, 23 miles from Edinburgh. Undulating parkland with panoramic views. 18 holes, 6137 yards. S.S.S. 70. *Green Fees:* weekdays £38.00 per round, £50.00 per day; weekends £44.00 per round, £60.00 per day. Generous discounts for society bookings. *Eating facilities:* full catering daily. *Visitors:* welcome subject to tee availability. Golf buggy hire April to September. *Society Meetings:* catered for subject to prior booking, groups of up to 40 persons catered for. Secretary: Hugh Gilmore.

ST BOSWELLS. **St Boswells Golf Club,** Braeheads, St Boswells, Melrose TD6 0DE (01835 823527). *Location:* quarter of a mile off trunk route A68 at St. Boswells Green. Flat attractive scenery along the banks of the River Tweed. 9 holes, 5250 yards. S.S.S. 66. *Green Fees:* £20.00, £12.00 for 9 holes (subject to review). *Visitors:* no visitors after 4pm on a weekday and when competitions are being held. Secretary: J.G. Phillips (01835 823527).

SELKIRK. **Selkirk Golf Club,** The Hill, Selkirk TD7 4NW (01750 20621). *Location:* one mile south of Selkirk on A7 road. Heather covered hill course, superb views of Border valleys. 9 holes, 5620 yards. S.S.S. 68. *Green Fees:* £20.00 for 18 holes, £10.00 for 9 holes. *Eating facilities:* bar, open evenings. *Visitors:* welcome morning and afternoon weekdays, weekends booking needed. *Society Meetings:* welcome. Secretary: J. M. Hay (01750 20621, 01750 20857 pm).

WEST LINTON. **Rutherford Castle Golf Club,** West Linton EH46 7AS (Tel & Fax: 01968 661233). *Location:* A702 ten miles south of Edinburgh City Bypass. Undulating parkland course at the foot of the Pentland Hills. 18 holes, 6525 yards, 5872 metres. S.S.S. 71. *Green Fees:* information not available. *Eating facilities:* limited facilities but can be expanded for societies by advance notice. *Visitors:* no restrictions. *Society Meetings:* all welcome, booking form available on application in writing, package available for ten or more. Buggy and trolley hire. Contact: (01968 661233).* e-mail: info@ruth-castlegc.co.uk website: www.ruth-castlegc.co.uk

WEST LINTON. **West Linton Golf Club,** West Linton EH46 7HN (01968 660463). *Location:* A702 road 17 miles south west of Edinburgh. Scenic moorland course. 18 holes, 6132 yards, 5607 metres. S.S.S. 70. Two practice areas. *Green Fees:* weekdays £25.00 per round, £40.00 per day; weekends £40.00 per round (group discounts available). Weekly ticket (Mon-Fri) £85.00. Season ticket (10 rounds) £125.00. Fees subject to review. *Eating facilities:* lunches, bar snacks, high teas, morning coffee, bar. *Visitors:* welcome at all times except on Medal days and weekends before 1pm. Buggy and carts for hire. *Society Meetings:* catered for weekdays. Professional: I. Wright (01968 660256). Secretary: J.S. Macnab (01968 660970).

SCOTLAND / Borders

- 30 bedrooms (single, twin, double, triple and family) en suite; also a four-poster for that touch of luxury
- B&B from £35pppn
- Bar lounge, a relaxing environment for light meals and refreshments which are served all day, every day, 12-9pm
- Open all year
- 20 golf courses within 45 minutes' drive

www.georgeandabbotsford.co.uk
enquiries@georgeandabbotsford.co.uk

GEORGE & ABBOTSFORD HOTEL

George & Abbotsford Hotel, High Street, Melrose, Scottish Borders TD6 9PD
Tel: 01896 822308 • Fax: 01896 823363

See also Colour Advertisement on page 67

Golf Around Scotland is a well established, Scottish-based golf tour company specialising in golf tours, golf short breaks and golf vacations – all in Scotland. Our expert knowledge of Scottish golf courses and accommodation providers means that we are able to deliver tailor-made vacations and tours to suit all budgets and group sizes. Call us today **01350 727059**

www.golfaroundscotland.com

THINK OF IT!!
- think of a golfing tour in Scotland, the USA, Asia or Africa
- everything provided for your leisure • clubs, trolleys, buggies, accommodation, transport • no lugging bags around
- your own guided escort • intelligence on each course

Don't just dream! Do it!
GLOBAL GOLF TOURS • tee up at www.ggtours.org

HEATHERLIE HOUSE HOTEL

A warm welcome awaits you at this elegant Victorian Mansion situated in the heart of the Scottish Borders. Quietly located in wooded grounds.

Comfortably furnished bedrooms, (8 en suite), with colour TV, tea/coffee making, direct dial telephones. Extensive menu, wine list and selection of Malts.

- 21 golf courses in the region, including new championship courses; The Roxburghe at Kelso and and Cardrona at Peebles. Special golfers' packages available in conjunction with the 'Freedom of the Fairways' passport.

Heatherlie Park, Selkirk TD7 5AL
Tel: 01750 721200 • Fax: 01750 720005
enquiries@heatherlie-house.co.uk
www.heatherlie-house.co.uk

See also Colour Advertisement on page 67

PLEASE MENTION THE GOLF GUIDE WHEN YOU WRITE OR PHONE TO ENQUIRE ABOUT CLUBS OR ACCOMMODATION

Dumfries & Galloway

ANNAN. **Powfoot Golf Club,** Cummertrees, Annan DG12 5QE (Tel & Fax: 01461 700276). *Location*: three miles from Annan on the B724, turnoff in the village of Cummertrees. Semi-links course on Solway shore with outstanding views. 18 holes, 6255 yards (white). S.S.S. 71. Two practice grounds. *Green Fees*: information not available. *Eating facilities*: morning coffee, lunches and teas in clubhouse - ordering in advance essential for large parties. Steward (01461 700227). *Visitors*: welcome weekdays 9am till 11am, 1pm till 4pm. Saturday 11am to 11.30am, 2.30pm to 5.00pm. Sundays 10.30am to 11.15am, 1pm to 3.30pm. All bookings through the office. *Society Meetings*: as per visitors. Office Manager: Claire McDairmant (Tel & Fax: 01461 700276).
e-mail: par71@powfootgolfclub.fsnet.co.uk

CASTLE DOUGLAS. **Castle Douglas Golf Club,** Abercromby Road, Castle Douglas (01556 502801). *Location:* half a mile from town centre on A713 Castle Douglas to Ayr Road. Parkland. 9 holes, 5388 yards. S.S.S. 66. *Green Fees:* £15 per person per day. *Eating facilities:* catering during summer season. *Visitors:* welcome without reservation, except Tuesdays or Thursdays after 4pm and competition days. *Society Meetings:* by arrangement. Secretary: James Greenfield (01556 502509).

DALBEATTIE. **Colvend Golf Club,** Sandyhills, Colvend, By Dalbeattie DG5 4PY (01556 630398). *Location:* six miles from Dalbeattie on the A710, Solway Coast road, between Dalbeattie and Dumfries. Picturesque course on the Solway Coast with superb views over Galloway Hills and the Solway Firth. 18 holes visitors' tees, 4929 yards, 4519 metres. S.S.S. 66; medal tees 5250 yards 4813 metres. S.S.S. 67. *Green Fees:* £25.00. Juniors £10.00. *Eating facilities:* modern clubhouse with full changing, catering and bar facilities. *Visitors:* all welcome. Buggies available. *Society Meetings:* welcome by booking through the club. Secretary: (01556 630398).

DALBEATTIE. **Dalbeattie Golf Club,** c/o The Secretary, 19 Maxwell Park, Dalbeattie DG5 4LR (Tel & Fax: 01556 610666; mobile: 07702 849945). Clubhouse (01556 611421 – not always manned). *Location:* signed off the B794 Haugh of Urr Road on the outskirts of Dalbeattie. Slightly undulating parkland course. 9 holes, 5710 yards (18 holes). S.S.S. 68. *Green Fees:* £16.00. *Eating facilities:* bar and food available. *Visitors*: very welcome anytime and should club competitions be in progress, every effort will be made to accommodate them. *Society Meetings:* all welcome. Contact Secretary for further information regarding tee times, accommodation, restaurants, etc. Secretary: Bryan C. Moor (Tel & Fax: 01556 610666; mobile: 07702 849945).
e-mail: ocm@associates-ltd.fsnet.co.uk
website: www.dalbeattiegc.co.uk

DUMFRIES. **Crichton Golf Club,** Bankend Road, Dumfries DG1 4TH (01387 247894). *Location: directly* opposite Dumfries and Galloway Royal Infirmary, one mile outside Dumfries on Bankend Road. Wooded parkland. 9 holes, 5952 yards. S.S.S. 69. *Green Fees:* information not available. *Visitors:* welcome, restrictions depending on club competitions, Thursdays last tee off time 1pm. *Society Meetings:* on application to the Administrator. Match Secretary: Lee Sterritt.

DUMFRIES. **Dumfries and County Golf Club,** Nunfield, Edinburgh Road, Dumfries DG1 1JX (01387 253585). *Location:* one mile north-east town centre on A701. 18 holes, 5918 yards. S.S.S. 69. Limited practice facilities. *Green Fees:* information not available. *Eating facilities:* restaurant and bar snacks. *Visitors:* welcome except on competition days. *Society Meetings:* by arrangement with Club Professional. Professional: S.J. Syme (Tel & Fax: 01387 268918). Secretary: B.R.M. Duguid (Tel & Fax: 01387 253585).*
e-mail: dumfriesc@aol.com
website: www.dumfriesandcounty-gc.fsnet.co.uk

DUMFRIES. **Dumfries and Galloway Golf Club,** 2 Laurieston Avenue, Dumfries DG2 7NY (01387 253582). *Location:* one mile from Dumfries on Castle Douglas road, A780. Parkland course. 18 holes, 6309 yards. S.S.S. 71 (under revision). Practice area. Putting green. *Green Fees:* weekdays £25.00 per round, £27.00 per day; weekends £30.00 per round, £33.00 per day (under review.) *Eating facilities:* full catering during bar hours. *Visitors:* welcome, except on competition days. Ladies' Day Tuesday. *Society Meetings:* catered for weekdays, except Tuesdays or Saturdays. Professional: Joe Fergusson (01387 256902; Fax: 01387 276297). Secretary: Alasdair T. Millar (Tel & Fax: 01387 263848).
e-mail: info@dandggolfclub.co.uk
website: www.dandggolfclub.co.uk

DUMFRIES. **The Pines Golf Centre,** Lockerbie Road, Dumfries DG1 3PF (Tel & Fax: 01387 247444). *Location:* beside A75 Dumfries bypass off Lockerbie Road roundabout. Mixed park and heathland with mature trees and water features. 18 holes, 5940 yards. S.S.S.68. 20 bay driving range with video teaching facility. Short game practice area and large undulating putting green. *Green Fees:* information not available. *Eating facilities:* bar with meals. *Visitors:* welcome. *Society Meetings:* welcome. Professionals: Brian Gemmell and Bruce Gray. *

DUMFRIES. **Southerness Golf Club,** Southerness, Kirkbean, Dumfries DG2 8AZ (01387 880677; Fax: 01387 880644). *Location:* 16 miles south west of Dumfries on A710 (Solway Coast Road). Natural challenging Championship links, designed by MacKenzie Ross, with panoramic views of Solway Firth and Galloway hills. Hosted British Ladies' Amateur 1989 and British Youths' 1990. Scottish

Amateur 1995. Scottish Amateur Stroke-play 2002. 18 holes, 6566 yards. S.S.S. 73. Practice ground. *Green Fees:* information not available. *Eating facilities:* full bar and catering facilities. *Visitors:* welcome every day other than 9 days when there are Open Competitions, other golf club members only with Handicap Certificates. Trolley hire. *Society Meetings:* welcome by prior arrangement. Secretary: I.A. Robin.*

GATEHOUSE OF FLEET. **Cally Palace Hotel,** Gatehouse of Fleet DG7 2DL. (01557 814341; Fax: 01557 814522). *Location*: one and a half hours drive from M6 and A74, nearest large town - Dumfries. Parkland. 18 holes, 6062 yards. Par 70. Course is restricted to hotel residents and those of sister hotels - North West Castle Hotel, Stranraer & Kirroughtree Country House Hotel in Newton Stewart. *Visitors/ Society Meetings*: course open only to hotel residents and those of sister hotels, North West Castle, Stranraer, and Kirroughtree Country House, Newton Stewart. *Eating facilities*: conservatory bar for snacks and dining room lunch.*

THE APPEARANCE OF AN ASTERISK (*) AT THE END OF A CLUB OR COURSE ENTRY INDICATES THAT UP-TO-DATE INFORMATION HAS NOT BEEN SUPPLIED

GATEHOUSE OF FLEET. **Gatehouse of Fleet Golf Club,** Laurieston Road, Gatehouse of Fleet, Castle Douglas (01557 814766). *Location:* quarter of a mile north of Gatehouse – Laurieston road. Sloping and wooded course with magnificent views of hills and over Fleet Bay. Very well drained; rarely closed. 9 holes, 2521 yards. S.S.S. 66. Practice net. *Green Fees:* £15.00 per day (£8.00 for Juniors) all year round – no limit on amount of golf played. Membership available £130 per year. 2005 rates, subject to review. *Visitors:* welcome at all times except Sunday mornings before 11.30am. *Society Meetings:* all welcome.

GRETNA. **Gretna Golf Club,** "Kirtle View", Gretna DG16 5HD (01461 338464). *Location:* south side of A75, one mile from A74. Scenic parkland course. 9 holes, 3215 yards, S.S.S. 72. *Green Fees:* information not available. *Visitors:* welcome, no restrictions. *Society Meetings:* welcome on application.*

KIPPFORD. **Craigieknowes Golf Club,** Barnbarroch Farm, Kippford, Dalbeattie (01556 620244). *Location:* half a mile from Kippford on side road from A710, three miles from Dalbeattie. Parkland course with lots of rocks. 9 holes, Par 3, 1391 yards. S.S.S. 54. Putting green. *Green Fees:* information not available. *Eating facilities:* tearoom. *Visitors:* welcome, no restrictions on times of play. Car park, club hire. *Society Meetings:* welcome by arrangement. Secretary: Mr D. Roan.

• HETLAND HALL HOTEL •
Golf in Dumfries & Galloway

Hetland Hall Hotel is a magnificent country house hotel set in 18 acres of parkland. We are within striking distance of around 30 golf clubs and other local attractions in Dumfries & Galloway, making us an ideal base for your golfing break. 30 en suite bedrooms and full leisure facilities including indoor heated pool, sauna, steam room, beauty room, toning tables, and, for those of you looking for some golfing practice, we have a 9-hole pitch 'n' putt!!

Tel: 01387 840201 • Fax: 01387 840211
www.hetlandhallhotel.co.uk
e-mail: info@hetlandhallhotel.co.uk
Carrutherstown, Dumfries DG1 4JX
A member of Best Western Hotels
The leading chain of Independent Hotels in the World

See also Colour Advertisement on page 68

The Summerhill Course, Dumfries & Galloway Golf Club's championship 18-hole layout (6309 yards, Par 70) has magnificent views over the hills to the north of Dumfries. The course is maintained in excellent condition, and is a very good test of golf. Visitors are welcome on most days (limited times on competition days), and an on-line booking system is available.

• Well-stocked Pro Shop • Practice facilities
• Full catering service • Dining Room • Bar • Visitors' Locker Room
Secretary: Alasdair T. Miller (Tel/Fax: 01387 263848)

Dumfries & Galloway Golf Club, Laurieston Avenue, Dumfries DG2 7NY
info@dandggolfclub.co.uk • www.dandggolfclub.co.uk

See also Colour Advertisement on page 68

KIRKCUDBRIGHT. **Brighouse Bay Golf Club and Driving Range,** Borgue, Kirkcudbright DG6 4TS (Tel & Fax: 01557 870509). *Location:* 6 miles south-west of Kirkcudbright off the B727. Beautifully situated, free-draining coastal course with glorious clifftop views. With four tees on each hole it combines natural coastal undulations with several water hazards making an exceptional test of golf, whatever your ability, playable all year. 18 holes, 6602 yards. S.S.S.73. Carts, club and trolley hire, driving range, short game area, changing and shower facilities. New 9 hole course now open. *Green Fees:* information not available. *Eating facilities:* full range of bar and catering facilities in bistro, lounge bar and function suite. *Visitors:* welcome at all times by prior arrangement, sensible dress at all times. Award-winning holiday park adjacent with accommodation and leisure facilities available all year. *Society Meetings:* welcome, inclusive golf packages now available, book in advance.*
website: www.brighousebay-golfclub.co.uk

KIRKCUDBRIGHT. **Kirkcudbright Golf Club,** Stirling Crescent, Kirkcudbright DG6 4EZ (01557 330314). *Location:* signposted near centre of town. Hilly parkland. 18 holes, 5896 yards. S.S.S. 69. Carts available. *Green Fees:* £20.00 per round. *Eating facilities:* coffee, lunch, evening meal, usual bar hours. *Visitors:* welcome most days with phone call for availability; Tuesday Ladies' Day, Wednesday Men's. *Society Meetings:* welcome, advance bookings. Secretary: Dave MacKenzie.
website: www.kirkcudbrightgolf.co.uk

LANGHOLM. **Langholm Golf Club,** Whitaside, Langholm DG13 0JS (013873 81247). *Location:* on A7 Carlisle-Edinburgh road. Turn off at market place in centre of town. Hillside course with stunning views over the town and down towards the "Lakes". 9 holes, 6180 yards. S.S.S. 70. Practice ground. *Green Fees:* £10.00; £5.00 playing with a member. *Eating facilities:* on request, bar open weekends. *Visitors:* welcome without reservation; restrictions

Saturday 9am to 9.45am, 1pm to 2pm and 4pm to 5pm, Sunday 9am to 10am (Competition times). *Society Meetings:* apply in writing to Secretary. Secretary: W. Goodfellow (013873 81408/81247).

LOCHMABEN. **Lochmaben Golf Club,** Castlehillgate, Lochmaben, Lockerbie DG11 1QF (01387 810552). *Location:* Lockerbie four miles, Dumfries eight miles on A709 road. Attractive parkland course surrounding the Kirk Loch, excellent views on this well-maintained course. 18 holes, 5933 yards. S.S.S. 70. Practice area. *Green Fees:* weekdays £24.00 per round, £30.00 per day; weekends £30.00 per round, £35.00 per day (Saturdays only). *Eating facilities:* full catering and bar. *Visitors:* welcome, bookings advisable (01387 810552). Caddy car and buggy hire. *Society Meetings:* welcome. Secretary: J.M. Dickie (01387 810552).
website: www.lochmabengolf.co.uk

LOCKERBIE. **Hoddom Castle Golf Course,** Hoddom, Lockerbie DG11 1AS (01576 300251). *Location:* A74, Junction 19 Ecclefechan. Follow signs to Hoddon Castle or A75 Annan, B723 and follow signs to Hoddon Castle. Parkland, partially wooded, bounded on two sides by River Annan. 9 holes, 2274 metres. S.S.S. 33. *Green Fees:* weekdays £10.00 per day; weekends £12.00 per day. *Eating facilities:* bar. *Visitors:* welcome anytime.

LOCKERBIE. **Lockerbie Golf Club,** Corrie Road, Lockerbie DG11 2ND (Tel & Fax: 01576 203363). *Location:* leave M74, proceed to town centre and follow signs. Parkland featuring pond which is in play on three holes – fair test of golf for all standards of golfers. 18 holes, 5614 yards. S.S.S. 67. Small practice area. *Green Fees:* weekdays £20.00 per round, weekends £24.00 per round, Juniors £4.00. *Eating facilities:* catering available 8am–8pm, bar 11am–11pm. *Visitors:* welcome, restricted on Sundays. Caddy cars and buggies available. *Society Meetings:* welcome by arrangement. Secretary: Jim Thomson (Tel & Fax: 01576 203363).

LOCKERBIE GOLF CLUB
founded 1889
A74 to Lockerbie • take Corrie Road • 500 yards on right.
Tel/Fax: 01576 203263

Parkland featuring the only pond hole in the area which is in play on 3 holes.
18 holes • 5614 yards • SSS 67 • Practice area, putting green.
Green Fees: per round – weekdays £20, weekends £24. Juniors £4.
Eating Facilities: catering 8am-8pm • Bar 11am-11pm.
Society Meetings: welcome by arrangement.
Secretary: Mr Thomson

THE MOFFAT GOLF CLUB
Moorland course designed by Ben Sayers of North Berwick

A fine, traditional Scottish moorland course with a welcoming clubhouse, making it an ideal venue for a day or weekend trip. Visitors are offered full use of the bar and catering facilities, and there are visitors' changing rooms/showers, and a games room.
Situated in the rolling hills of the southern uplands, Moffat is one hour from Glasgow, and one-and-a-half hours from Edinburgh.
Leave A74 (M) at Junction 15 and follow A701.

1884

Special packages available for midweek and weekend parties of 8 or more.
Moffat Golf Club, Coatshill, Moffat, Dumfriesshire DG10 9SB
Tel: 01683 220020 • **Fax: 01683 221802**
e-mail: bookings@moffatgolfclub.co.uk • www.moffatgolfclub.co.uk

See also Colour Advertisement on page 68

SCOTLAND / Dumfries & Galloway

MOFFAT. **The Moffat Golf Club,** Coatshill, Moffat DG10 9SB (Tel: 01683 220020; Fax: 01683 221802). *Location:* leave M74 at Beattock. Take A701 for Moffat, club signposted one mile on left. Scenic moorland course with tree plantations. 18 holes, 5259 yards. S.S.S. 67. Putting green and practice net. *Green Fees:* weekdays £19.50 per round, £25.00 per day; weekends and Bank Holidays £28.00 per round, £34.00 per day. Juniors (up to 18) £10 per round/day. Subject to review. Special Packages available to parties of 8 or more: £26.50 to £32.00 weekdays; £35.00 to £42.50 weekends – two rounds of golf, coffee/biscuits on arrival, soup and rolls lunchtime, and evening meal. *Eating facilities:* bar meals served, bar open 11am to 10pm; dining room. *Visitors:* welcome daily including weekends. Booking advisable. Games room (two full-size snooker tables, pool table, darts, TV area). Trolleys and clubs for hire. *Society Meetings:* welcome, make reservations with Clubmaster. Secretary: Jim Mein (01683 220020). Clubmaster: Toby Downer.
e-mail: bookings@moffatgolfclub.co.uk
website: www.moffatgolfclub.co.uk

NEW GALLOWAY. **New Galloway Golf Club,** New Galloway, Castle Douglas DG7 3RN (Tel & Fax: 01644 450685). *Location:* one mile off A713 Castle Douglas to Ayr road. Scenic with fine turf. 9 holes, 5006 yards. S.S.S. 67. *Green Fees:* £18.00 per day, subject to review. *Eating facilities:* bar. *Visitors:* very welcome without reservation. Accommodation and meals available in village. *Society Meetings:* by arrangement with Secretary. Secretary: N.E. White (Tel & Fax: 01644 450685).

NEWTON STEWART. **Newton Stewart Golf Club,** Kirroughtree Avenue, Newton Stewart DG8 6PF (01671 402172). *Location:* outskirts of Newton Stewart off the A75, Euroroute to Ireland. Parkland course set amidst Galloway Hills with pine forest backdrop, views from most tees have to be seen to be believed. 18 holes, 5840 yards. S.S.S. 70. Practice area. *Green Fees:* weekdays £24.00 per round, £32.00 per day; weekends and Bank Holidays £27.00 per round, £37.00 per day; weekly £115.00. Discounts for groups. *Eating facilities:* bar meals, lunches and high teas. *Visitors:* welcome all year round after 9.45am. Phone call in advance advisable. Caddy cars and buggies available. *Society Meetings:* all welcome, booking required.

NEWTON STEWART. **Wigtownshire County Golf Club,** Mains of Park, Glenluce, Newton Stewart DG8 0NN (Tel & Fax: 01581 300420). *Location:* A75 two miles west Glenluce, eight miles east Stranraer. Seaside links. 18 holes, 5907 yards, 5405 metres. S.S.S. 68. Four and a half acre practice area. *Green Fees:* weekdays £23.00 per round, £30.00 per day; weekends £25.00 per round, £32.00 per day. Half price for under 18s. Discounts for parties of 10 and over. *Eating facilities:* available all year round. *Visitors:* unrestricted except Wednesday evenings and competitions. Hand trolleys. *Society Meetings:* catered for but should pre-book. Secretary: Mr R. McKnight (01581 300532).
e-mail: enquiries@wigtownshirecountygolfclub.com
website: www.wigtownshirecountygolfclub.com

FHG

Other specialised FHG Guides

Published annually: available in all good bookshops or direct from the publisher.

Recommended **COUNTRY INNS & PUBS** OF BRITAIN £7.99

Recommended **COUNTRY HOTELS** OF BRITAIN £7.99

Recommended **SHORT BREAK HOLIDAYS** IN BRITAIN £7.99

The bestselling **PETS WELCOME!** £8.99

FHG Guides • Abbey Mill Business Centre, Seedhill, Paisley, Renfrewshire PA1 1TJ
Tel: 0141-887 0428 • Fax: 0141-889 7204
e-mail: admin@fhguides.co.uk
www.holidayguides.com

Torrs Warren
Country House Hotel

Comfortable, family-run hotel, set in its own grounds, with ample parking and beer garden. Situated in south western Scotland, just 6 miles from Portpatrick. Ideally placed for exploring beautiful countryside, secluded coves, rugged cliffs, enchanted forests and long sandy beaches.

Dunskey, Portpatrick, Stranraer and Glenluce Golf Courses all within 10 minutes' drive, Newton Stewart Golf Club 25 minutes.

Bed & Breakfast from £33 double/twin room. £42 single.
Dinner, Bed & Breakfast from £49 (double/twin room)

Torrs Warren Country House Hotel
Stoneykirk, Stranraer, Scotland DG9 9DH
Tel: 01776 830204
Fax: 01776 830298
e-mail: TorrsWarren@hotmail.com
www.torrswarrenhotel.co.uk
See also Colour Advertisement on page 69

PORTPATRICK. **Lagganmore Golf Club & Hotel,** Lagganmore, Portpatrick DG9 9AB (Tel & Fax: 01776 810499). Two miles outside Portpatrick, six miles from Stranraer. 18 holes parkland heath course, 5698 yards. S.S.S. 68. Par 69. *Green Fees:* information not available. *Eating facilities:* bar food and beverages served all day. *Visitors:* welcome, packages available for parties, to include dinner, bed and breakfast and unlimited golf, from £40.00 per person per night. Hotel on site, all rooms en suite. Buggie hire available. *Society Meetings:* welcome, telephone (01776 810499).
website: www.lagganmoregolf.co.uk

PORTPATRICK. **Portpatrick Golf Club,** Clubhouse, Golf Course Road, Portpatrick DG9 8TB (01776 810273; Fax: 01776 810811). *Location:* A77 to Stranraer, follow signs to Portpatrick; A75 fork left one and a half miles after Glenluce bypass, follow signs to Portpatrick. Enter village, fork right at war memorial, then 300 yards on right. Cliff top links-type course. "Dunskey" 18 holes, 5913 yards. S.S.S. 69; "Dinvin" 9 holes, 1346 yards. S.S.S. 27. Practice ground. *Green Fees:* weekdays £30.00 per round, £40.00 per day; weekends £35.00 per round, £45.00 per day. Winter rates apply November to mid-March. *Eating facilities:* available all year round except Mondays. *Visitors:* advisable to book in advance (members times). Handicap Certificate required for Dunskey Course. *Society Meetings:* catered for by prior arrangement. Secretary: J. McPhail (01776 810273; Fax: 01776 810811).
e-mail: enquiries@portpatrickgolfclub.com
website: www.portpatrickgolfclub.com

PORT WILLIAM. **St Medan Golf Club,** Monreith, Port William, Newton Stewart DG8 8NJ (01988 700358). *Location:* on A747, three miles south of Port William. Seaside links course with panoramic views of Mull of Galloway and Isle of Man - Scotland's most southerly course. 9 holes, 4552 yards. S.S.S. 63. Practice driving net and green. *Green Fees:* 9 holes £10.00, 18 holes £15.00, day £24.00; weekly £50.00. *Eating facilities:* available (also bar), summer only. *Visitors:* welcome without reservation. Telephone clubhouse for further information.

SANQUHAR. **Sanquhar Golf Club,** Euchan Course, Barr Road, Sanquhar DG4 6JZ (01659 50577). *Location*: situated quarter-of-a-mile from A76 Dumfries-Kilmarnock trunk road. Undulating parkland with views across the town. Practice areas/net. 9 holes, 5144 metres. S.S.S. 68. *Green Fees*: weekdays £10.00 per day; weekends £12.00 per day. Subject to review. *Eating facilities*: bar available if requested in advance. Visitors: welcome without reservation. Licensed clubhouse with full-size snooker table. *Society Meetings*: Golf package including catering for parties of 12 and over £25.00 per person.

STRANRAER. **Stranraer Golf Club,** Creachmore, Leswalt, Stranraer DG9 0LF (01776 870245; Fax: 01776 870445). *Location:* three miles from Stranraer on the Kirkcolm Road (A718). Parkland, seaside – the last course James Braid designed. 18 holes, 6308 yards. S.S.S. 72. Practice area and putting green. *Green Fees:* weekdays £25.00 per round, £36.00 per day; weekends £30.00 per round, £40.00 per day. 27 holes: weekdays £31.00; weekends £36.00. Fees subject to review. *Eating facilities:* full catering all day, lounge bar overlooks course. *Visitors:* weekdays 9.15am to 12.30pm then 1.30 to 5pm; weekends 9.30am to 11.45am then 1.45pm to 5pm. Pull trolleys and golf carts available for hire. *Society Meetings:* all welcome with prior arrangement. Secretary: Bryce C. Kelly (01776 870245; Fax: 01776 870445).
e-mail: stranraergolf@btclick.com
website: www.stranraergolfclub.net

THORNHILL. **Thornhill Golf Club,** Blacknest, Thornhill DG3 5DW (01848 330546) *Location:* 14 miles north of Dumfries on A76, 1 mile east of village. Parkland/open moorland. 18 holes, 6085 yards. S.S.S. 70. Practice ground (two areas). *Green Fees:* information not available. *Eating facilities:* catering available, bar facility. *Visitors:* welcome without reservation, but please contact the club steward to ensure tee times are available. Buggies. *Society Meetings:* welcome, contact Alex Hillier (01848 331779).*
e-mail: thornhillgc@fsmail.net

WIGTOWN. **Wigtown and Bladnoch Golf Club,** Lightlands Terrace, Wigtown, Newton Stewart DG8 9DY (01988 403354). *Location:* 200 yards from square in Wigtown. Parkland course. 9 holes, 5400 yards. S.S.S. 67. Practice bays. *Green Fees:* £17.00 for 18 holes, £9.00 for 9 holes; Senior Citizens £12.00 (9 or 18 holes), £22.00 per day; Juniors £8.00 (9 or 18 holes). Five day ticket £52.00. *Visitors:* welcome most days, tee reserved for open competitions occasional weekends. No prior booking necessary. *Society Meetings:* welcome by arrangement.

The Waterfront is a stylish new hotel, furnished to a very high specification and situated opposite the picturesque harbour of Portpatrick. With eight en suite bedrooms and an elegant restaurant serving a delicious selection of dishes and wines, The Waterfront is perfectly located for that Golfing Break, with Portpatrick (Dunskey) and Lagganmore Golf Clubs being within one mile and Stranraer Golf Club within 8 miles. Individual or Group Golfing packages at favourable rates available on request. 'We look forward to welcoming you".

Prices from £35 pppn (en suite, sharing).

The Waterfront Hotel & Bistro North Crescent, Portpatrick DG9 8SX
Telephone 01776 810800 • Fax 01776 810850
e-mail: WaterfrontHotel@aol.com • website: www.waterfronthotel.co.uk

The Lagganmore Hotel and Golf Club
Lagganmore, Portpatrick DG9 9AB

Special packages combining golf, dinner, a full Scottish breakfast and accommodation: two nights £120, three nights £150.

Situated just ten yards from the first tee, The Lagganmore Hotel combines traditional Scottish cuisine with comfortable, attractively furnished accommodation. The popular lounge bar remains open all day, serving lunches and suppers.

The Lagganmore course provides a great test for every golfer, combining natural valleys and contours with streams and water features. Our feature hole, the Par 5 7th, is the best in South West Scotland. **Tel: 01776 810499 or 01776 810262**

info@lagganmoregolf.co.uk • www.lagganmoregolf.co.uk

See also Colour Advertisement on page 70

Portpatrick Dunskey Golf Club
Tel: 01776 810273 • Fax: 01776 810811   Portpatrick, Stranraer DG9 8TB
enquiries@portpatrickgolfclub.com
www.portpatrickgolfclub.com

Two clifftop links courses:
Dunskey 18 holes • Dinvin 9 holes
Handicap Certificate required • Visitors advised to book in advance • Winter rates apply November to Mid-March • Eating facilities available all year except Mondays.

See also Colour Advertisement on page 69

Thornhill Golf Club
Blacknest, Thornhill, Dumfriesshire DG3 5DW
Tel: 01848 330546

Visit this scenic course set in the midst of the Southern Uplands, a mixture of heathland and parkland with stunning panoramic views. SSS 70, Par 71.

• Green fees on application • Full catering and bar facilities available
• Group Bookings: contact: Alex Hillier • 01848 331779

See also Colour Advertisement on page 68

Dunbartonshire

ALEXANDRIA. **Vale of Leven Golf Club,** Northfield Road, Bonhill, Alexandria G83 9ET (01389 752351). *Location:* A82 to Dumbarton, follow signs at roundabout at Dumbarton for Bonhill then club signs. Parkland with splendid views of Loch Lomond. 18 holes, 5277 yards. S.S.S. 67. *Green Fees:* weekdays £20.00 per round, £30.00 per day; weekends £25.00 per round, £37.50 per day. Weekly ticket (Monday to Friday) £70.00. *Eating facilities:* catering and bar available. *Visitors:* welcome all year round. Full changing and locker facilities. Shop: Barry Campbell. *Society Meetings:* on application. Club Administrator: Richard Barclay (01389 752351). e-mail: rbarclay@valegc.com
website: www.valegc.com

CARDROSS. **Cardross Golf Club,** Main Road, Cardross G82 5LB (01389 841213). *Location:* on A814 west of Dumbarton. Championship parkland course. 18 holes, 6469 yards. S.S.S. 72. Practice ground. *Green Fees:* weekdays £30.00 per round, £45.00 day ticket. *Eating facilities:* lunches/bar snacks available. *Visitors:* weekdays only (by phoning Professional to book time). *Society Meetings:* catered for weekdays by arrangement. Professional: Robert Farrell (01389 841350). Secretary: Iain T. Waugh (01389 841754; Fax: 01389 842162).
e-mail: golf@cardross.com
website: www.cardross.com

CLYDEBANK. **Clydebank and District Golf Club,** Glasgow Road, Hardgate, Clydebank G81 5QY (01389 873289). *Location:* Hardgate village. Off A82 10 miles west of Glasgow (off Great Western Road). 18 holes, 5832 yards, 5325 metres. S.S.S. 68. *Green Fees:* information not available. *Eating facilities:* catering as required. *Visitors:* welcome weekdays only. Professional: Alan Waugh (01389 383835). Secretary: Mrs K. Stoddart (01389 383831; Fax: 01389 383831 by request).*

CLYDEBANK. **Clydebank Municipal Golf Course,** Overtoun Road, Clydebank G81 3RE (0141-952 6372). *Location:* one mile west of Clydebank centre off Duntocher Road. Parkland course - one of the best Par 3s in Scotland. 18 holes, 5349 yards. S.S.S. 66. *Green Fees:* on application to Secretary. *Eating facilities:* tearoom. *Visitors:* municipal course, tee closed Saturdays 7.30am till 10.00am and 11.00am to 3.00pm. *Society Meetings:* contact District Council. Secretary: District Council (01389 738762).

THE APPEARANCE OF AN ASTERISK (*) AT THE END OF A CLUB OR COURSE ENTRY INDICATES THAT UP-TO-DATE INFORMATION HAS NOT BEEN SUPPLIED

Inchmurrin Island Self-Catering Holidays

Inchmurrin Island, Loch Lomond G63 0JY
Tel: 01389 850245 • Fax: 01389 850513

Inchmurrin is the largest island on Loch Lomond and offers a unique experience. Three self-catering apartments, sleeping from four to six persons, and a detached cedar clad cottage sleeping eight, are available. A ferry service is provided for guests, and jetties are available for customers with their own boats. Come and stay and have the freedom to roam and explore anywhere on the island. Ferry service available direct to Loch Lomond championship golf course - no need to queue in traffic. Also new public course at ferry terminal.

e-mail: scotts@inchmurrin-lochlomond.com • www.inchmurrin-lochlomond.com

www.uk-golfguide.com

DUMBARTON. **Dumbarton Golf Club,** Broadmeadow, Dumbarton G82 2BQ (01389 732830; Fax: 01389 765995). *Location:* off A82, one mile from town centre. Flat parkland. 18 holes, 6017 yards. S.S.S. 69. Practice area. *Green Fees:* £30.00 weekdays. *Eating facilities:* catering and bar available. *Visitors:* welcome weekdays not Saturday, Sunday or Bank Holidays. No jeans or shellsuits on course or in clubhouse. *Society Meetings:* all welcome with prior bookings through Secretary. Secretary: D.M. Mitchell.

HELENSBURGH. **Helensburgh Golf Club,** 25 East Abercromby Street, Helensburgh G84 9HZ (01436 674173; Fax: 01436 671170). *Location*: A82 from Dumbarton. Moorland course with panoramic views across Loch Lomond and The Clyde Estuary. 18 holes, 6104 yards. S.S.S. 69 Practice area and putting green. *Green Fees*: £30.00 per round, £40.00 per day weekdays. Winter conditions £15.00 per day. *Eating facilities*: full catering and bar. *Visitors*: welcome weekdays only, dress in recognised golfing attire, no denims or trainers. Clubs for hire. *Society Meetings*: welcome by arrangement. Professional: David Fotheringham (Tel & Fax: 01436 675505). Secretary: Kim Print (01436 674173; Fax: 01436 671170).

KIRKINTILLOCH. **Kirkintilloch Golf Club,** Campsie Road, Kirkintilloch G66 1RN (0141-776 1256). *Location:* from Glasgow to Bishopbriggs, then straight on to Kirkintilloch. Undulating, parkland course. 18 holes, 5860 yards. S.S.S. 69. Par 70. Putting green and practice areas. *Green Fees:* on application. *Eating facilities:* dining room and bar. *Visitors:* must be introduced by a member. *Society Meetings:* catered for Monday to Friday, information from Secretary including catering. Secretary: C. A. Harris (0141-775 2387).

LENZIE. **Lenzie Golf Club,** 19 Crosshill Road, Lenzie, Glasgow G66 5DA (0141-776 1535; Fax: 0141-777 7748). *Location:* two miles from A90 Junction to Kirkintilloch. Parkland. 18 holes, 5982 yards. S.S.S. 69. Practice ground. *Green Fees:* information not available. *Eating facilities:* bar and catering facilities available. *Visitors:* welcome any day except weekends. Carts for hire. Private room available for meetings or dinners. *Society Meetings:* welcome. Professional: James McCallum (Tel & Fax: 0141-777 7748). Secretary: Scott M. Davidson (Tel & Fax: 0141-812 3018).*
website: www.lenziegolfclub.com

Visit the FHG website
www.holidayguides.com
for details of the wide choice of accommodation featured in the full range of FHG titles

PLEASE NOTE
All the information regarding Golf Clubs in this guide is given in good faith in the belief that it is correct. However, the publishers cannot guarantee the facts given in these pages, neither are they responsible for changes in ownership or facilities, such as green fees, that may take place after the date of going to press. Readers should always satisfy themselves that the facilities they require are available and that the terms, if quoted, still apply.

Dundee & Angus

ARBROATH. **Arbroath Golf Course,** Elliot, By Arbroath DD11 2PE (Tel & Fax: 01241 875837). *Location*: off Dundee Road. Seaside links course. 18 holes, 6185 yards. S.S.S 70. Practice area, new putting green. *Green Fees*: information not available. *Eating facilities*: full catering and bar facility. *Visitors*: welcome. *Society Meetings*: all welcome. Professional: L. Ewart (Tel & Fax: 01241 875837). Secretary: Scott Milne (01382 229111).*

ARBROATH near. **Letham Grange Golf Course,** Colliston, By Arbroath DD11 4RL (01241 890377; Fax: 01241 890725). *Location:* follow brown Scottish Tourist Board signs for Letham Grange from Arbroath. Two courses – Old Course is a blend of tree-lined parkland and open rolling fairways; water plays a major role which makes the course both scenic and dramatic. Glens Course is slightly shorter and without water hazards, offers golfers a more relaxed and less arduous round; however, it could be deceptive! 36 holes, Old 6968 yards, Glen's 5528 yards. S.S.S. Old 73, Glen's 68. Very large practice area, practice putting green, practice chipping green. *Green Fees:* information not available. *Eating facilities:* golfers' bar and restaurant. *Visitors:* welcome, except reserved members' tee off times. Four star Hotel on site. Trolley, club and buggy hire, PGA Professional group tuition available. *Society Meetings:* all most welcome. Golf shop (01241 890377 or 01241 890373).*

BARRY. **Panmure Golf Club,** Burnside Road, Barry, By Carnoustie DD7 7RT (01241 853120). *Location:* two miles west of Carnoustie on A930, signposted from the Barry village bypass. Championship links. 18 holes, 6330 yards. S.S.S. 70. Driving range, practice area. *Green Fees:* £50 per round, £65 per day. *Eating facilities:* full catering seven days a week. *Visitors:* welcome daily except Tuesday and Saturday mornings. Buggy hire. Putting Simulator. *Society Meetings:* restricted but welcome. Professional: Neil Mackintosh. Managing Secretary: Charles Philip (01241 855120).
e-mail: secretary@panmuregolfclub.co.uk
www.panmuregolfclub.co.uk

BRECHIN. **Brechin Golf and Squash Club,** Trinity, By Brechin DD9 7PD (01356 622383). *Location*: Trinity Village, one mile north of Brechin just off A90. Rolling parkland course with glorious views of Grampian Mountains. 18 holes, 6096 yards. S.S.S. 70. Practice ground. *Green Fees*: weekdays £25.00 per round, £33.00 per day; weekends £30.00 per round, £40.00 per day. Mid week package for parties of eight or more £35.00. for two rounds of golf and all catering. Subject to review. *Eating facilities*: excellent catering available at all times; large bar. *Visitors*: very welcome seven days. Buggies, carts, club hire. Two squash courts. *Society Meetings*: catered for, reservations in advance. Professional: Stephen Rennie (01356 625270).
e-mail: brechingolfclub@btconnect.com
website: www.brechingolfclub.co.uk

CARNOUSTIE. **Carnoustie Golf Links,** Links Parade, Carnoustie DD7 7JE (01241 853789; Fax: 01241 852720). *Location:* 12 miles east of Dundee. Three 18-hole courses. Championship Course 6941 yards. S.S.S. 75; Burnside Course 6028 yards. S.S.S. 70; Buddon Links 5420 yards. S.S.S. 66. Golf trolleys permitted. *Green Fees:* Championship Course £105.00 per round; Burnside Course £32.00 per round; Buddon Links Course £27.00 per round. Subject to review. Juvenile rates available. Three course combination ticket £120.00. *Eating facilities:* catering facilities can be arranged with the local golf clubs. *Visitors:* welcome, times must be booked. Handicap Certificates required for play on Championship Course. *Society Meetings:* catered for by arrangement. Professional: Colin Sinclair. Course Manager: John Philp. General Manager: G.Duncan. Golf Services Manager: Colin McLeod.

DUNDEE. **Ballumbie Castle Golf Club,** 3 Old Quarry Road, Off Ballumbie Road, Dundee DD4 0SY (01382 730026; Fax: 01382 730008). *Location:* one and a half miles north of Claypotts Junction, less than 2 miles from Dundee city centre. Parkland/heathland course. 18 holes, 6127 yards, S.S.S. 70. 22 bay driving range, putting green, chipping green. *Green Fees*: information not available. *Eating facilities*: clubhouse facilities with menu and full bar. Public house licence. *Visitors*: welcome. Tuition available at driving range. *Society Meetings*: welcome, please telephone for details. Professional: Lee Sutherland (01382 770028).*
e-mail: ballumbie2000@yahoo.com
website: www.ballumbie.golf.com

DUNDEE. **Caird Park Golf Club,** Mains Loan, Dundee DD4 9BX (01382 453606). *Location:* northern edge of city, off Kingsway. Wooded parkland. 18 holes, 6273 yards, 5740 metres. S.S.S. 70. Practice range on course. *Green Fees:* information available from Starter 01382 438871. *Eating facilities:* at clubhouse. *Visitors:* welcome, must book in advance to ensure game. *Society Meetings:* see Dundee District Council, Parks Department. Professional: Jackie Black (01382 459438). Secretary: Greg Martin (01382 864029).*

DUNDEE. **Camperdown Golf Club,** Camperdown House, Camperdown Park, Dundee DD2 4TF (01382 623398). *Location:* two miles north-west of city, enter at Kingsway/Coupar Angus road junction. Wooded parkland. 18 holes, 6561 yards. S.S.S. 72, Par 71. *Green Fees:* information not available. *Eating facilities:* must be booked in advance. *Visitors:* welcome, bookable all week, contact Art and Recreation Division, Leisure Centre, Dundee. *Society Meetings:* by arrangement, catered for once booked by Parks Dept. for date and times. Professional: Roddy Brown (01382 623398). Secretary: Isobel Finegan (01382 623398).

SCOTLAND / Dundee & Angus

DUNDEE. **Downfield Golf Club,** Turnberry Avenue, Dundee DD2 3QP (01382 825595; Fax: 01382 813111). *Location*: follow tourist signs from the main A90 Kingsway for Downfield Golf Course. Wooded, parkland course. 18 holes, 6802 yards, 6266 metres. S.S.S. 73. Large practice area. *Green Fees*: information not available. *Eating facilities*: full catering and bar seven days. *Visitors*: welcome weekdays 9.30am to 11.15am and 2.15pm to 3.30pm, Sunday after 2pm only, pre-booking essential. Carts for hire. Professional: Kenny Hutton (01382 889246). Secretary: Margaret Stewart (01382 825595; Fax: 01382 813111).

DUNDEE. **Piperdam Golf and Leisure Resort,** Foulis, Dundee DD2 5LP (01382 581374; Fax: 01382 581102). *Location:* off A923 Coupar Angus road. Parkland course, 18 holes, 6500 yards. S.S.S. 72.12 bay driving range. *Green Fees:* information not available. *Eating facilities:* restaurant and bar. *Visitors:* welcome. No restrictions. Leisure Centre and Spa. Two and three bedroom lodges. *Society Meetings:* welcome. Packages available. Director: Murdie Smith. e-mail: piper.dam@virgin.net
website: www.piperdam.com

EDZELL. **Edzell Golf Club,** High Street, Edzell DD9 7TF (01356 647283; Fax: 01356 648094). *Location:* travelling north from Dundee on A90, take B966 north of Brechin by-pass, continue 3.5 miles to village of Edzell. Parkland course with tree-lined fairways at the entrance to the Angus Glens and in the foothills of the Grampians. "Golfers who are visiting the Angus area cannot afford to miss what is one of Scotland's true hidden gems" Golf Monthly, 1999. 18 holes, 6367 yards. S.S.S. 71. 9-hole West Water Course 4114 yards, S.S.S. 61. 300 yard driving range, chipping area and putting green. *Green Fees:* weekdays £28.00 per round, £38.00 per day; weekends £34.00 per round, £48.00 per day. West Water Course; Monday to Sunday £10.00 per 9 holes, £15.00 per 18 holes. *Eating facilities:* dining room, lounge and bar. *Visitors:* welcome, apply to Secretary. *Society Meetings:* welcome apply to Secretary. Professional: Alistair J. Webster (01356 648462). Secretary: Ian G. Farquhar (01356 647283). Caterer: Neil Jack (01356 648235).
e-mail: awebsterpro@aol.com
secretary@edzellgolfclub.net
website: www.edzellgolfclub.net

FORFAR. **Forfar Golf Club,** Cunninghill, Arbroath Road, Forfar DD8 2RL (01307 463773). *Location:* one mile from Forfar on A932 to Arbroath. Undulating wooded heathland Tom Morris/James Braid designed course. 18 holes, 6066 yards. S.S.S. 70. *Green Fees:* Monday to Friday and Sunday £24.00 per round, £30.00 per day. Saturday £24.00 afternoon round. *Eating facilities:* available. *Visitors:* welcome. *Society Meetings:* catered for. Professional: Peter McNiven (01307 465683). Secretary: David Crompton (01307 463773; Fax: 01307 468495).

KIRRIEMUIR. **Kirriemuir Golf Club Ltd,** Northmuir, Kirriemuir DD8 4LN (01575 573317; Fax: 01575 574608). *Location:* 20 miles north-west of Carnoustie and six miles north-west of Forfar on A926 and A928, just on edge of Kirriemuir, north of town centre. Parkland and heathland course with stunning views of Angus Glens. 18 holes, 5510 yards, 5038 metres. S.S.S. 67. Putting green, practice ground. *Green Fees:* information not available. *Eating facilities:* full catering and bar facilities. *Visitors:* welcome weekdays; at weekends by arrangement. *Society Meetings:* by prior arrangement. Special golf/catering packages available. Professional: Karyn Dallas (01575 573317; Fax: 01575 574608).

MONIFIETH. **Broughty Golf Club,** 6 Princes Street, Monifieth, Dundee DD5 4AW (01382 532147). Starter (01382 532767). *Location:* eight miles east of Dundee, in village of Monifieth. Seaside links, some fairways fringed with trees. Medal Course: 18 holes, 6655 yards. S.S.S. 72. Ashludie Course: 18 holes, 5123 yards. S.S.S. 65. Practice area. *Green Fees:* information not available. *Eating facilities:* full catering, no catering Tuesdays or Thursdays. *Visitors:* no visitors before 2pm on Saturdays or before 10am Sundays. All tee times must be booked through Starter's Box. *Society Meetings:* by arrangement. Professional: Mr I. McLeod. Secretary: Peter Flynn.*

www.uk-golfguide.com

EDZELL GOLF CLUB
Midway between Dundee and Aberdeen.
"Golfers who are visiting the Angus area cannot afford to miss what is one of Scotland's true hidden gems" – *Golf Monthly, June 1999.*
Secretary: 01356 647283; Professional: 01356 648462
website: www.edzellgolfclub.net

THE APPEARANCE OF AN ASTERISK (*) AT THE END OF A CLUB OR COURSE ENTRY INDICATES THAT UP-TO-DATE INFORMATION HAS NOT BEEN SUPPLIED

MONIFIETH. **Monifieth Golf Links,** Princes Street, Monifieth, Angus DD5 4AW (01382 532767). *Location:* seven miles east of Dundee, Monifieth High Street. Seaside links. Medal Course 18 holes, 6657 yards. S.S.S. 72; Ashludie Course 18 holes, 5123 yards. S.S.S. 64. Practice facilities. *Green Fees:* information not available. *Eating facilities:* clubs and Hotel. *Visitors:* welcome after 9.30am Monday to Friday; Saturdays after 2pm; Sundays after 10am. *Society Meetings:* parties over 12, must provide club Handicap Certificates. Buggies for hire. Professional: Ian McLeod (01382 532945). Managing Secretary: S. Fyffe (01382 535553; Fax: 01382 535816).*
e-mail: monifiethgolf@freeuk.com
website: www.monifiethgolf.co.uk

MONTROSE. **Royal Montrose Golf Club,** Dorward Road, Montrose DD10 8SW (01674 672376). *Location:* A92 north from Dundee. Private club playing over the Montrose courses. 18 holes, 6533 yards. S.S.S. 72. *Green Fees:* information not available. *Eating facilities:* available. *Visitors:* apply Montrose Golf Links Ltd. *Society Meetings:* apply Montrose Golf Links Ltd. Professional: Jason Boyd. Secretary: J.D. Sykes (01674 672376)

MONTROSE. **Montrose Golf Links Ltd,** Traill Drive, Montrose DD10 8SW (01674 672932). *Location:* A92 runs from Dundee to Aberdeen, through Montrose. Links Medal Course 6544 yards. Par 71. S.S.S. 72. Broomfield Course 4830 yards. Par 66. S.S.S. 63. *Green Fees:* Medal: weekdays £40.00 per round, £50.00 per day, Juniors £18.00 per round, £28.00 per day; weekends £44.00 per round, £58.00 per day, Juniors £20.00 per round, £30.00 per day. Broomfield: Monday to Friday £18.00 per round, Juniors £6.00 per round; weekends £20.00 per round, Juniors £6.00. Composite day fees and special rates on request. Group discounts available. Green fees subject to review. *Eating facilities:* catering facilities available by arrangement in golf clubs. *Visitors:* very welcome; no restrictions midweek, visitors allowed on Medal Course between 2.44pm and 3.38pm on Saturdays and after 10am on Sundays. Handicap Certificates required on Medal Course. *Society Meetings:* welcome by arrangement. Temporary membership available at the following clubs: Caledonia Golf Club (01674 672313); Mercantile Golf Club (01674 672408); Royal Montrose (01674 672376). Professional: Jason J. Boyd. Secretary: Mrs Margaret Stewart (01674 672932; Fax: 01674 671800).
e-mail: secretary@montroselinks.co.uk
website: www.montroselinks.co.uk

Located four miles from Carnoustie and ½ hour from St Andrews. Two courses offer golf for all levels with the Medal being used as an Open Championship Qualifier. These beautiful links courses also feature tree-lined fairways in many places.

Medal Course £39 Monday to Friday and £49 at weekends; Ashludie Course £19 Monday to Friday and £23 at weekends; a package includes a round of golf on each course, coffee, bacon rolls, soup and sandwiches, and high tea at the day's end **all for £59!**

For bookings call the Links Secretary on
01382 532767
The Starter's Box, Monifieth Links,
Princes Street, Monifieth DD5 4AW
monifiethgolf@freeuk.com

The hidden gem in Angus
Monifieth Golf Links

See also Colour Advertisement on page 70

MONTROSE GOLF LINKS LIMITED
MONTROSE GOLF COURSES

Medal Course (Par 71, SSS 72) • Broomfield Course (Par 66, SSS 63)
Medal course ranked fifth oldest in the world.
Open Championship Final Qualifying Course 1999 & 2007

Individual Round and Day Tickets available on both courses: All Visitors and Parties Welcome. Group Discounts offered. Special Packages available including catering and in conjunction with local hotels.

Enquiries to: **Mrs M. Stewart, Secretary, Montrose Golf Links Limited, Traill Drive, Montrose, Angus DD10 8SW**
Telephone: (01674) 672932 • Fax: (01674) 671800
e-mail: Secretary@montroselinks.co.uk • www.montroselinks.co.uk

See also Colour Advertisement on page 70

Edinburgh & Lothians

ABERLADY. **Craigielaw Golf Club,** Aberlady EH32 0PY (01875 870800; Fax: 01875 870620). *Location:* half mile west of Aberlady on A198. Links course. 18 holes, 6601 yards, S.S.S. 71, Par 71. Golf Academy and short course. *Green Fees:* information not available. *Eating facilities:* full catering all day; restaurant open to public. *Visitors:* welcome anytime except competition days; advisable to book in advance. Club and buggy hire. *Society Meetings:* society and group bookings welcome. *
website: www.craigielawgolfclub.com

ABERLADY. **Kilspindie Golf Club,** The Clubhouse, Aberlady, East Lothian EH32 0QD (Tel & Fax: 01875 870358). *Location:* A198 North Berwick Road (off A1 East of Edinburgh). Club's access road sign posted at east end of Aberlady, overlooking nature reserve and Aberlady Bay. Traditional Scottish links course. 18 holes, 5480 yards, S.S.S. 66, Par 69. *Green Fees:* weekdays £29.50 per round, £47.50 per day; Saturdays and Sundays £38.00 per round, £57.50 per day. *Eating facilities:* dining room with full catering and licensed bars with snack menu. *Visitors:* welcome booking advisable. *Society Meetings:* welcome, prior booking essential (01875 870358 or e-mail). Professional: Graham Sked (Tel & Fax: 01875 870695). General Manager: P.B. Casely (01875 870358).
e-mail: kilspindie@btconnect.com
website: www.golfeastlothian.com

ABERLADY. **Luffness New Golf Club,** Aberlady EH32 0QA (01620 843336; Fax: 01620 842933). *Location:* A198 - 17 miles east of Edinburgh. One mile from Gullane. Links course, 18 holes, 6122 yards. S.S.S. 70. *Green Fees:* £60.00 per round, £85.00 per day. *Eating facilities:* dining room except Mondays. *Visitors:* weekdays only (require introduction). *Society Meetings:* by prior arrangement. Secretary: Group Captain A.G. Yeates (01620 843336; Fax: 01620 842933).
e-mail: secretary@luffnessnew.com
website: www.luffnessgolf.com

BATHGATE. **Bathgate Golf Club,** Edinburgh Road, Bathgate EH48 1BA (01506 652232; Fax: 01506 636775). *Location:* three miles from M8, 400 yards east of George Square, the town centre and railway station. Flat course. 18 holes, 6328 yards. S.S.S. 71. Practice area. *Green Fees:* weekdays £20.00 per round, £25.00 per day; weekends £25.00 per round, £35.00 per day. *Eating facilities:* dining room facilities open all week. *Visitors:* welcome without reservation except on Competition days at weekends. Handicap Certificates preferred. Electric buggies available. *Society Meetings:* welcome, numbers limited at weekends. Professional: Sandy Strachan (01506 630553). Secretary: W. Allan Osborne (01506 630505; Fax: 01506 636775).

BO'NESS. **West Lothian Golf Club,** Airngath Hill, By Linlithgow EH49 7RH (01506 826030; Fax: 01506 826462). *Location:* situated midway between Linlithgow and Bo'ness. Undulating parkland course with panoramic views over River Forth beyond Stirling to below the Bridges. 18 holes, 6249 yards. S.S.S. 71. Practice ground. *Green Fees:* information not available. *Eating facilities:* bar and catering service. *Visitors:* welcome, advisable to phone weekends. Trolleys and buggies. *Society Meetings:* welcome by arrangement. Professional: Ian Taylor (01506 825060). Secretary: Ian Osborough.*

BONNYRIGG. **Broomieknowe Golf Club Ltd,** 36 Golf Course Road, Bonnyrigg EH19 2HZ (0131-663 9317; Fax: 0131-663 2152). *Location:* south of Edinburgh, A6094 from Dalkeith. Flat parkland course. 18 holes, 6150 yards. S.S.S. 70. Practice ground. *Green Fees:* weekdays £23.00 per round, £36.00 per day; £27.00 per round at weekends. *Eating facilities:* meals and snacks. *Visitors:* welcome Monday to Friday 9.30am to 4pm, weekends by prior arrangement. *Society Meetings:* welcome weekdays by arrangement. Professional: Mark Patchett (0131-660 2035). Secretary: John D. Fisher (0131-663 9317; Fax: 0131-663 2152).
e-mail: administrator@broomieknowe.com
website: www.broomieknowe.com

DALKEITH. **Newbattle Golf Club Ltd,** Abbey Road, Dalkeith EH22 3AD (0131-663 2123). *Location:* approximately seven miles south-east of Edinburgh A7 to Eskbank Toll (Newbattle exit). Parkland, wooded course. 18 holes, 6012 yards, 5498 metres. S.S.S. 69. Small practice area. *Green Fees:* £20.00 per round, £30.00 per day. Package deals available. *Eating facilities:* full catering available on request. *Visitors:* weekdays 9.30am to 4.00pm. Limited numbers Sunday afternoons. No jeans/trainers on course or in clubhouse. *Society Meetings:* welcome. Professional: S. McDonald (0131-660 1631). Secretary: H.G. Stanners (0131-663 1819).

DUNBAR. **Dunbar Golf Club,** East Links, Dunbar EH42 1LL (01368 862317; Fax: 01368 865202). *Location:* on coast half a mile east of Dunbar. Seaside links, used for final qualifying 1992 and 2002 Open Championship. 18 holes, 6404 yards, 5855 metres. S.S.S. 71. *Green Fees:* weekdays £43.00 per round, £58.00 per day; weekends £53.00 per round, £75.00 per day. Subject to review. *Eating facilities:* full catering facilities. *Visitors:* no visitors on Thursdays or before 9.30am and between 12.30pm and 2pm weekdays; or before 10am and between 12 noon and 2pm weekends. *Society Meetings:* welcome. Professional: Jacky Montgomery (01368 862086). Secretary: Liz Thom (01368 862317; Fax: 01368 865202).
e-mail: secretary@dunbargolfclub.sol.co.uk
website: www.dunbar-golfclub.co.uk

DUNBAR. **Winterfield Golf Club,** St. Margarets, North Road, Dunbar EH42 1AU (01368 862280). Seaside course. 18 holes, 4686 metres. S.S.S. 65. *Green Fees:* weekdays £16.00 per round, £23.00 day ticket; weekends £19.00 per round, £30.00 day ticket. *Eating facilities:* Full catering and bar facilities. *Visitors:* welcome without reservation or restriction. Secure changing facilities. *Society Meetings*: welcome without reservation. The Pro Shop: (01368 863562). Professional: Kevin Phillips (01368 863562) Vice Captain: W. G. Kerr; Captain: A. P. Coull (01368 862280).

EDINBURGH. **Baberton Golf Club,** 50 Baberton Avenue, Juniper Green, Edinburgh EH14 5DU (0131-453 4911). *Location:* five miles west of Edinburgh on the A70. 18 holes, 6123 yards. S.S.S. 70. *Green Fees:* weekdays £27.00 per round, £37.00 per day; weekends £30.00 per round. *Eating facilities:* by arrangement (phone Andrew Grieve (0131-453 4911). *Visitors:* welcome by arrangement with Secretary. *Society Meetings:* catered for. Professional: K. Kelly (Tel & Fax: 0131-453 3555). Club Manager: B.M. Flockhart (0131-453 4911; Fax: 0131-453 4678).

EDINBURGH. **Braid Hills Golf Course,** Braid Hills Approach, Morningside, Edinburgh EH10 6JY *Location:* Braid Hills on south side of Edinburgh. Two 18 hole courses. No.1: 5880 yards. S.S.S. 68. No.2: 4495 yards. S.S.S. 64. *Green Fees:* information not available. *Visitors:* welcome. Public courses, clubs on hire. Braids United Golf Club, Edinburgh Thistle Golf Club, Edinburgh Western Golf Club and Harrison Golf Club all have clubhouses at Braid Hills and welcome visitors. No Sunday golf on No.1 Course. Sunday catering available on request. Managed by Edinburgh Leisure.*

EDINBURGH. **Bruntsfield Links Golfing Society Ltd,** The Clubhouse, 32 Barnton Avenue, Edinburgh EH4 6JH (0131-336 2006). *Location:* off A90 at Davidson's Mains. Mature parkland course with magnificent views to north over Firth of Forth and to the west. 18 holes, 6407 yards. S.S.S. 71. Excellent practice facilities. *Green Fees:* weekdays £50.00 per round, £70.00 per day; weekends £55.00 per round, £75.00 per day. *Eating facilities:* morning coffee, lunches, dinner by arrangement. *Visitors:* welcome - telephone Professional to arrange times. *Society Meetings:* catered for by arrangement. Professional: Brian MacKenzie (0131-336 4050). Secretary: Cdr D.M. Sandford (0131-336 1479; Fax: 0131-336 5538). e-mail: secretary@bruntsfield.sol.co.uk

EDINBURGH. **Carrick Knowe Golf Course.** *Location:* situated on the west side of the city on Glendevon Park. Undulating parkland course which has recently undergone a major remodelling. 18 holes, 6150 yards. S.S.S. 69. *Green Fees:* information not available. *Visitors:* welcome. Managed by Edinburgh Leisure. *

EDINBURGH. **City of Edinburgh Golf Club,** Edinburgh Leisure, 141 London Road, Edinburgh EH7 6AE. *Location:* Club plays over the following pay and play courses - Carrick Knowe: 18 holes, 6150 yards. S.S.S. 69; Braids No.1: 18 holes, 5692 yards. S.S.S. 67; Princes Course: 9 holes, 3800 yards. Par 60; Portobello: 9 holes, 4816 yards. S.S.S. 64; Silverknowes: 18 holes, 6198 yards. S.S.S. 69; Craigentinny: 18 holes, 5413 yards. S.S.S. 66. *Green Fees:* from £9.00, membership from £15.00. *Visitors:* welcome all year round. Secretary: Alasdair Dunlop (0131-652 2178).
www.edinburghleisure.co.uk/webpages/golf.php

EDINBURGH. **Craigentinny Golf Course.** *Location*: Situated on the east side of the city on Fillyside Road. Undulating parkland course. 18 holes, 5413 yards. S.S.S. 66. *Green Fees*: information not available. *Visitors*: welcome. Managed by Edinburgh Leisure.*

EDINBURGH. **Craigmillar Park Golf Club,** 1 Observatory Road, Edinburgh EH9 3HG (0131-667 2837). *Location:* A702 from City Centre on Mayfield Road, right at King's Buildings. Parkland. 18 holes, 5851 yards, S.S.S. 69. *Green Fees:* information not available. *Eating facilities:* lunches, snacks, high teas and dinners. *Visitors:* welcome weekdays only before 4pm and on Sunday after 2.30pm. *Society Meetings:* catered for by previous arrangement. Professional: S. Gourlay (0131-667 2850). Secretary: B. Knowles (0131-667 0047). *

EDINBURGH. **Duddingston Golf Club Ltd,** Duddingston Road West, Edinburgh EH15 3QD (0131-661 1005). *Location:* adjacent to A1 Willowbrae Road, turn right at Duddingston crossroads then one mile on Duddingston Road West. Undulating parkland with stream. 18 holes, 6487 yards. S.S.S. 72. *Green Fees:* weekdays only £29.00 per round, £39.00 per day. *Eating facilities:* full catering and bar facilities. *Visitors:* welcome weekdays only. *Society Meetings:* by arrangement (rates on request). Professional: Alistair McLean (0131-661 4301). General Manager: (0131-661 7688). e-mail: generalmanager@duddingston-golf-club.com

EDINBURGH. **Kingsknowe Golf Club,** 326 Lanark Road, Edinburgh EH14 2JD (0131-441 1144). *Location:* on the western boundary of Edinburgh with easy access from the City Bypass (Calder Junction). The Clubhouse is located on the A70 Lanark Road. Parkland course. 18 holes, 5979 yards, 5466 metres. S.S.S. 69. Practice area. *Green Fees:* weekdays £23.00 per round, £30.00 per day; weekends £35.00 per round (after 3pm). *Eating facilities:* lounge bar, snacks and meals available. *Visitors:* welcome Monday to Friday, also weekends subject to availability. *Society Meetings:* catered for. Professional: Chris Morris (0131-441 4030). Secretary/Manager: L.I. Fairlie (0131-441 1145).

For full details of clubs and courses, plus convenient accommodation
www.uk-golfguide.com

EDINBURGH. **Liberton Golf Club,** 297 Gilmerton Road, Edinburgh EH16 5UJ (0131-664 3009; Fax: 0131-666 0853). *Location:* Corporation transport to Lodge Gate, buses 3 and 8 from Edinburgh. By car on A7 (Visitors' car park). Parkland, rolling. 18 holes, 5170 yards, 4730 metres. S.S.S. 65. *Green Fees:* information not available. *Eating facilities:* full catering and bar service. *Visitors:* phone professional. *Society Meetings:* catered for by arrangememt except weekends. Professional: I. Seath (0131-664 1056). General Manager: A. McMillan (0131-664 3009).
e-mail: info@libertongc.co.uk
website: www.libertongc.co.uk

EDINBURGH. **Lothianburn Golf Club,** 106a Biggar Road, Edinburgh EH10 7DU (0131 445 2206). *Location:* south on the A702 approximately four miles from city centre or easily reached from Edinburgh bypass road coming off at Lothianburn junction. Hill course close to Pentland Hills. 18 holes, 5662 yards. S.S.S. 69. Practice ground. *Green Fees*: £18.50 per round weekdays; £24.50 weekends. *Eating facilities*: normal bar hours, no hot food on Wednesdays. *Visitors*: welcome mid-week, weekends restricted. *Society Meetings*: catered for by prior arrangement with the Secretary. Professional: Kurt Mungall (0131-445 2288). Secretary: W.F.A. Jardine (0131-445 5067).
website: www.lothianburngc.co.uk

EDINBURGH. **Melville Golf Centre, Golf Course, Range and Shop,** Lasswade, Near Edinburgh EH18 1AN (0131-663 8038; Fax: 0131-654 0814). *Location:* three minutes from Edinburgh City Bypass (signposted), on A7. Short but challenging parkland course with large tees and greens, lying in the Esk Valley with panoramic views. 9 holes, 2265 yards, 2070 metres. Par 66. S.S.S. 62. Built to USPGA standard. Floodlit range, 9-hole pay and play course, 4-hole practice/short game area, bunker and putting green. *Green Fees:* weekdays 9 holes £10.00, 18 holes £18.00; weekends 9 holes £12.00, 18 holes £22.00. Concessions available. *Eating facilities:* vended hot and cold drinks and rolls available. *Visitors:* welcome at all times. 24 hour bookings available, full club equipment and shoe hire, PGA tuition. Golf shop; fully stocked ladies, gents, and juniors. Tuition available. A Junior Golf Foundation Starter Centre. *Society Meetings:* welcome, advance bookings arranged. Professional: Gary Carter. Contact Mr & Mrs MacFarlane (0131-663 8038 course; Fax: 0131-654 0814).
e-mail: golf@melvillegolf.co.uk
website: www.melvillegolf.co.uk

www.uk-golfguide.com

Edinburgh Golf

Braid Hills

Set in the historic city of Edinburgh, we have six top quality courses to challenge every standard of golfer.

We pride ourselves in providing the best golf experience within an exciting atmosphere of this beautiful 'Festival' city.

From a parkland 9 hole course to some of the most scenic and challenging golf to be found anywhere. Prices from £13.

'With the exception of the Old Course at St. Andrews, Braid Hills No. 1 is probably the best public course in Scotland." (Business A.M.).

- *Braid Hills No.1* A true gem. A test where the golf and the City merge into a breathtaking experience. Recently noted as "the best public course outside St Andrews". Book your time on **0131 447 6666**

- *Silverknowes.* An 18-hole parkland course with panoramas over the Firth of Forth. **0131 336 3843**

- *Carricknowe.* Set in the heart of Edinburgh, this 18-hole course is a challenge for beginners and pros alike. **0131 337 1096**

- *Portobello.* A wee jewel. 9 holes of pure fun, or 18 if you have a bit more time on your hands. **0131 669 4361**

- *Princes.* A short but testing 9 hole course. Ideal for children and beginners. **0131 447 3568**

- *Craigentinny.* Set within the historic Calton Hill monuments and Arthur's Seat, this 18-hole parkland course, with its mix of tricky Par 3s and challenging Par 4s, is a rewarding challenge for all. Try your hand on **0131 554 7501**.

Club and trolley hire is available at all our courses.

For any queries **e-mail:** golf@edinburghleisure.co.uk or call the Golf Team on **0131 650 1001**

Edinburgh Leisure

See also Colour Advertisement on page 71

EDINBURGH. **Merchants Of Edinburgh Golf Club,** 10 Craighill Gardens, Edinburgh EH10 5PY (0131-447 1219; Fax: 0131-446 9833). *Location:* car park Glenlockhart Road, Edinburgh EH10. Hilly, parkland. 18 holes, 4889 yards. S.S.S. 64. *Green Fees:* £18 per round; £28 per day. *Eating facilities:* full catering available daily. *Visitors:* welcome weekdays, weekends by arrangement. *Society Meetings:* catered for except weekends. Professional: N.E.M. Colquhoun (0131 447 8709). Administrator: John Elvin (0131 447 1219). e-mail: admin@merchantsgolf.com website: www.merchantsgolf.com website: www.melvillegolf.co.uk

EDINBURGH. **Mortonhall Golf Club,** 231 Braid Road, Edinburgh EH10 6PB. *Location:* take A702 south from City to Morningside traffic lights, up Braid Road one mile, course on left. Moorland course with scenic views. 18 holes, 6502 yards. S.S.S. 72. *Green Fees:* £35.00 per round, £50.00 per day. *Eating facilities:* lunch and bar snacks available. *Visitors:* welcome with introduction. *Society Meetings:* catered for (not at weekends). Professional: Malcolm Leighton. Club Manager: Bernadette M. Giefer (0131-447 6974).

EDINBURGH. **Murrayfield Golf Club Ltd,** 43 Murrayfield Road, Edinburgh EH12 6EU (0131-337 3478; Fax: 0131-313 0721). *Location:* Corstorphine Road, two miles west of city centre. Parkland on east side of Corstorphine Hill. 18 holes, 5794 yards. S.S.S. 69. Practice area, net and putting green. *Green Fees:* weekdays £35.00 per round, £40.00 per day. *Eating facilities:* lunch each day, snacks in casual bar, also full bar facilities. *Visitors:* welcome playing with member or by prior arrangement only. No visitors weekends. *Society Meetings:* catered for by prior arrangement. Professional: K. Stevenson (Tel & Fax: 0131-337 3479). Club Manager: Mrs M.K. Thomson (0131-337 3478; Fax: 0131-313 0721).

EDINBURGH. **Portobello Golf Course,** Stanley Street, Portobello, Edinburgh EH15 1JJ (0131-669 4361). *Location:* on A1 at Milton Road East. Parkland course. 9 holes, 2400 yards, 2167 metres. S.S.S. 32. *Green Fees:* £5.50 per round (9 holes) weekdays; £6.50 per round (9 holes) weekends. Reductions for Juniors and Senior Citizens. *Visitors:* welcome. *Society Meetings:* not catered for. Managed by Edinburgh Leisure.

EDINBURGH. **Prestonfield Golf Club,** 6 Priestfield Road North, Edinburgh EH16 5HS (Tel & Fax: 0131-667 9665;). *Location:* off Dalkeith Road, near Royal Commonwealth Pool on A7. Parkland. 18 holes, 6207 yards. S.S.S. 70, Par 70. Practice area. *Green Fees:* weekdays and weekends £28.00 per round, £38.00 per day. *Eating facilities:* full catering. *Visitors:* welcome weekdays. Petrol buggies available. *Society Meetings:* welcome weekdays. Professional: Gavin Cook (0131-667 8597). General Manager: John I. Archibald e-mail: generalmanager@prestonfieldgolfclub.org website: www.prestonfieldgolfclub.com

EDINBURGH. **Princes Golf Course,** Braid Hills Road, Edinburgh EH16 6NS (0131-447 3568). *Location:* Braid Hills on south side of Edinburgh. 9-hole course, ideal for beginners, children and families. Managed by Edinburgh Leisure. *

EDINBURGH. **Ratho Park Golf Club Ltd,** Ratho, Edinburgh EH28 8NX (0131-335 0069). *Location:* west side of Edinburgh near Airport, access from A71 or A8. Flat parkland course of outstanding natural beauty. 18 holes, 5960 yards. S.S.S. 68. *Green Fees:* weekdays £27.00 per round, £37.00 per day; weekends £37.00 per round. *Eating facilities:* full catering available. *Visitors:* very welcome, please telephone Professional in advance. *Society Meetings:* welcome Monday – Friday, up to 40, subject to availability. Professional: Alan Pate (0131-333 1406). Secretary/Manager: Craig R Innes (0131-335 0068). e-mail: secretary.rpgc@btconnect.com website: www.rathoparkgolfclub.com

EDINBURGH. **Ravelston Golf Club Ltd,** 24 Ravelston Dykes Road, Blackhall, Edinburgh EH4 3NZ (Tel & Fax: 0131-315 2486). *Location:* A90 Queensferry Road (leading to Forth Road Bridge). Left at traffic lights by Blackhall junction to Strachan Road, cross Craigcrook Road, clubhouse on right. Parkland course. 9 holes, 2600 yards, 2377 metres. S.S.S. 66. *Green Fees:* £18.00 weekdays. Subject to review. Eating facilities; tea, coffee, soft drinks and light snacks. *Visitors:* welcome during quiet periods weekdays only. *Society Meetings:* permitted by special application only. Secretary: Jim Lowrie.

Mortonhall Golf Club

Founded in 1892, this is the oldest course on which golf is still played in the city of Edinburgh. It is one of outstanding scenic beauty, emerging from a narrow valley to an open area bounded by a wood on the south and the Braid Hills in the north. At 6502 yards, it is the longest course in the city, and at 600ft above sea level, the wind can make it a formidable challenge.

The well appointed clubhouse contains many interesting photographs and golfing memorabilia. *Bar and catering facilities available.*

Vistors are welcome to play this picturesque and challenging course.

231 Braid Road, Edinburgh EH10 6PB
Tel: 0131 447 6974 • • Fax: 0131 447 8712
www.mortonhallgc.co.uk • • clubhouse@mortonhallgc.co.uk

See also Colour Advertisement on page 71

EDINBURGH. **Royal Burgess Golfing Society of Edinburgh,** 181 Whitehouse Road, Barnton, Edinburgh EH4 6BU. *Location:* A90 to Forth Road Bridge, behind Barnton Hotel. Parkland. 18 holes, 6494 yards. S.S.S. 71. *Green Fees:* information not available. *Eating facilities:* snacks and lunches available. *Visitors:* welcome weekdays. *Society Meetings:* catered for Tuesdays, Thursdays and Fridays. Professional: Steven Brian (0131-339 6474). Secretary: Graeme Seeley (0131-339 2075; Fax: 0131-339 3712).*
e-mail: secretary@royalburgess.co.uk
website: www.royalburgess.co.uk

EDINBURGH: **Silverknowes Golf Course,** Silverknowes, Parkway, Edinburgh EH4 5ET (0131-336 5359). *Location:* nearest main road Queensferry Road; signs Davidson Mains, Silverknowes. Parkland, flat. 18 holes, 6216 yards. S.S.S. 71. *Green Fees:* information not available. *Eating facilities:* catering available on request. Managed by Edinburgh Leisure.*

EDINBURGH. **Swanston Golf Club,** 111 Swanston Road, Edinburgh EH10 7DS (0131-445 2239). *Location:* five miles from centre of Edinburgh, west of Biggar Road (A702) on the lower slopes of the Pentland Hills. Parkland course. 18 holes, 5024 yards. S.S.S. 66. *Green Fees:* weekdays £15.00 per round, £20.00 day ticket; weekends £17.50 per round, £30.00 day ticket. *Eating facilities:* full catering facilities. *Visitors:* welcome without reservation weekdays, weekends restricted. *Society Meetings:* catered for. Golf carts available. Secretary: Rab Knowles (0131 445 2239).

EDINBURGH. **Torphin Hill Golf Club,** Torphin Road, Edinburgh EH13 0PG (0131-441 4061). *Location:* south west of Colinton Village at terminus of No. 10 bus. Holes 5 to 15 on plateau with outstanding views of Edinburgh. 18 holes, 5285 yards. Par 68. Practice area. *Green Fees:* weekdays £15.00 per round; weekends £20.00 per round (subject to review.) *Eating facilities:* dining room and bar snacks. *Visitors:* welcome without reservation except on Competition Days. *Society Meetings:* catered for except Tuesday. Reduced rates for parties over 20. Professional: Jamie Browne (0131-441 4061). Secretary: Willie McCathie (0131-441 1100; Fax: 0131 441 7166).
e-mail: torphinhillgc@btconnect.com

EDINBURGH. **Turnhouse Golf Club,** Lennie Park, 154 Turnhouse Road, Edinburgh EH12 0AD (0131-339 1014). *Location:* towards RAF Turnhouse on west side. James Braid designed course. 18 holes, 6153 yards. S.S.S. 70. Par 69. *Green Fees:* weekdays £25.00 per round, £30.00 per day; weekends £38.00 per round. *Eating facilities:* full service. *Visitors:* welcome, contact Professional. *Society Meetings:* welcome by prior arrangement with Secretary. Professional: John Murray (0131-339 7701); Secretary: David Cullum (07792 399069).
e-mail: secretary@turnhousegc.com
website: www.turnhousegc.com

FAULDHOUSE. **Greenburn Golf Club,** 6 Greenburn Road, Fauldhouse EH47 9HJ (01501 770292). *Location:* four miles south of Junctions 4 and 5 of M8 motorway. Undulating course, a mixture of moorland and parkland settings. 18 holes, 6055 yards. S.S.S. 70. Practice area. *Green Fees:* weekdays £19.00 per round, £25.00 per day. Weekends £25.00 per round, £32.00 per day. *Eating facilities:* catering available all week. *Visitors:* welcome. *Society Meetings:* welcome by arrangement with Administrator. Professional: Scott Catlin (01501 771187). Club Administrator: Kevin Johnston.

GULLANE. **Gullane Golf Club,** West Links Road, Gullane EH31 2BB (01620 842255; Fax: 01620 842327). *Location:* 18 miles east of Edinburgh on A198 Edinburgh to North Berwick Road. Links. Three 18 hole courses. No. 1 - (Medal) 6466 yards, 5913 metres. S.S.S. 72; (FWD) 6077 yards, 5557 metres. S.S.S 70. No. 2 - 6244 yards, 5710 metres. S.S.S. 71. No. 3 - 5252 yards, 4775 metres. S.S.S. 66. Practice, driving range. *Green Fees:* weekdays: No. 1 course £80.00 per round, £100.00 per day; No. 2 course £32.00 per round, £43.00 per day; No. 3 course £20.00 per round, £26.00 per day; weekends No. 1 £95.00 per round, No. 2 £38.00 per round, £52.00 per day, No. 3 £26.00 per round, £35.00 per day (prices increase on 1st March 2006). Weekly and combination rates available. *Visitors*: welcome. *Society Meetings:* catered for. Professional: Alasdair Good (01620 843111; Fax: 01620 843090). Secretary: Nigel Watt (01620 842255; Fax: 01620 842327). Starters: (01620 843115).
e-mail: bookings@gullanegolfclub.com
website: www.gullanegolfclub.com

GULLANE. **The Honourable Company Of Edinburgh Golfers,** Muirfield, Gullane EH31 2EG (01620 842123; Fax: 01620 842977). *Location:* 20 miles from Edinburgh along the coast road to North Berwick. Championship links course. 18 holes, 6601 yards. S.S.S. 73. *Green Fees:* £120.00 18 holes, £150.00 36 holes. *Eating facilities:* morning coffee, lunches and afternoon teas if ordered in advance. *Visitors:* welcome Tuesdays and Thursdays, maximum Handicap 18 for men, 20 for ladies. Secretary: ANG Brown.
e-mail: hceg@muirfield.org.uk

HADDINGTON. **Castle Park Golf Club,** Gifford EH41 4PL (01620 810733; Fax: 01620 810691). *Location:* B6369 from Haddington to Gifford, Castle Park is 2 miles south of Gifford, well signposted. Originally 9 holes, now extended to 18 (opened in 2002) combines a unique test of golf with stunning views. 6121 yards (white), 5848 yards (yellow), S.S.S. 70. 7 bay driving range, 6 hole putting green and practice bunker. *Green Fees:* from £15.00. *Eating facilities:* bar with full catering available. *Visitors:* welcome. Buggies available for hire. *Society Meetings:* welcome. Professional: Derek Small (01368 862872; mobile: 07968 209167). Secretary: Stephen Fortune.

HADDINGTON. **Haddington Golf Club,** Amisfield Park, Haddington EH41 4PT (01620 822727). *Location:* three-quarters of a mile from A1, 17 miles east of Edinburgh. Wooded parkland, slightly undulating. 18 holes, 6335 yards. S.S.S. 71, Par 71. Practice area. *Green Fees:* midweek £20 per round, £30 per day; weekends £30 per round, £40 per day. *Eating facilities:* two bars and dining room. *Visitors:* welcome, midweek no restrictions, weekends permitted 10am-12 noon, 2-4pm. *Society Meetings:* packages available on request. Professional: J. Sandilands (01620 822727). Club Manager: K. Nicholson (01620 823627; Fax: 01620 826580). e-mail: info@haddingtongolfclub.co.uk
website: www.haddingtongolf.co.uk

HADDINGTON near. **Gifford Golf Club,** Edinburgh Road, Gifford, Near Haddington EH41 4JE (0162-810 591). *Location:* quarter of a mile west of village. Undulating parkland with burn crossing the course. 9 holes, 6050 yards. S.S.S. 69. *Green Fees:* weekdays £18.00 per round, day ticket £25.00; weekends £20 per round, day ticket £30; 9 holes £12.00 weekdays, £14 weekends; Juniors (under 18s) £5.00. *Visitors:* closed all day first Sunday in the month. Secretary: G. MacColl (01620 810267). Starter (01620 810 591).

KIRKNEWTON. **Marriott Dalmahoy Hotel and Country Club,** Kirknewton, Midlothian EH27 8EB (Hotel 0131-333 1845; Fax: 0131-335 3203). *Location:* seven miles west of Edinburgh on A71. Parkland courses. East Course: (Championship) host to many major tournaments, 18 holes, 7044 yards. S.S.S. 72. West Course: with a finish around the Gogar Burn that will test your nerve. 18 holes, 5185 yards. S.S.S. 66. Driving range, extensive practice area. *Green Fees:* information not available. *Eating facilities:* The Long Weekend Restaurant and Club Bar in Country Club, restaurant and bars in Hotel also. *Visitors:* welcome 7 days. Hotel accommodation. Golf buggies, trolleys and clubs for hire. Country Club facilities include swimming pool, two outdoor tennis courts, sauna, steam room, spa, gymnasium, fitness and aerobics studio. *Society Meetings:* welcome weekdays only. Director of Golf: Iain Burns (0131-335 8010). Secretary: Mrs Jennifer Bryans (0131-335 8010).*

LASSWADE. **Kings Acre Golf Course and Academy,** Lasswade, EH18 1AU (0131 663 3456; Fax: 0131 663 7076). *Location:* A720 Edinburgh City Bypass. Lasswade is two minutes from City Bypass. Parkland course with matured woodland and large contoured greens, set in picturesque countryside close to Edinburgh City Bypass. 18 holes (pay and play), 6013 yards. S.S.S. 68. State of the art practice facility. *Green Fees:* weekdays £23.00; weekends £32.00. *Eating facilities:* spike bar, fully licensed restaurant. *Visitors:* all visitors welcome all year (no restrictions), accommodation available on site. PGA tuition, buggy and club hire. *Society Meetings:* all welcome. Director of Golf: Alan Murdoch. Secretary: Lizzie King.
e-mail: info@kings-acregolf.com
website: www.kings-acregolf.com

LINLITHGOW. **Bridgend & District Golf Club,** Willowdean, Bridgend, Linlithgow EH49 6NW (01506 834140; Fax: 01506 834706). *Location:* between Winchburgh and Linlithgow, signposted on main road. 9 holes, 5480 yards, S.S.S. 67. *Green Fees:* £12.00 weekdays, £14.00 weekends. *Eating facilities:* catering every day, bar facilities all week. *Visitors:* welcome any time. Buggies for hire. Secretary: George Green.

LINLITHGOW. **Linlithgow Golf Club,** Braehead, Linlithgow EH49 6QF (01506 844356; Fax: 01506 842764). *Location:* M8, M9, 20 miles west of Edinburgh, west end of Linlithgow - fork left. Parkland and wooded course with panoramic views. 18 holes, 5729 yards, 5239 metres. S.S.S. 68. Practice area. *Green Fees:* weekdays £25.00 per round, £35.00 per day; Sunday £30.00 per round, £40.00 per day. *Eating facilities:* full catering available, bar open every day. *Visitors:* welcome except Saturdays. *Society Meetings:* welcome by arrangement with Secretary. Professional: Steven Rosie (01506 844356). Secretary: W.S. Christie (01506 842585).

LIVINGSTON. **Deer Park Golf & Country Club,** Golf Course Road, Carmondeans, Livingston EH54 8AB (01506 446699; Fax: 01506 435608). *Location:* off M8 Junction 3 onto Deer Park roundabout. Parkland course, first 9 holes flat, back 9 holes hilly. 18 holes, 6688 yards. S.S.S. 72. *Green Fees:* information not available. *Eating facilities:* four bars, catering seven days. *Visitors:* welcome. Snooker, ten pin bowling. *Society Meetings:* catered for. Professional: Brian Dunbar. *

LIVINGSTON. **Pumpherston Golf Club,** Drumshoreland Road, Pumpherston, Livingston EH53 0LQ (01506 432869). *Location:* one mile east of Livingston, one and a half miles south of M8. Challenging parkland course, recently redeveloped. 18 holes, 6006 yards, 5492 metres. Par 70, S.S.S. 69. Practice area with pitching and bunker facilities, putting green, designed particularly for juniors. *Green Fees:* on application. *Eating facilities:* new clubhouse with bar, dining room and entertainment facilities; junior lounge. *Visitors:* welcome. *Society Meetings:* Mondays to Thursdays, maximum number 30. Professional: R. Fyvie (01506 433337). Secretary: G. C. Walker (01506 882904).

GIFFORD GOLF CLUB

Established 1904

Tel: 01620 810267
or: 01620 810591 (for tee time reservations)
Gifford Golf Club, Edinburgh Road Gifford EH41 4JE

"An enjoyable golf course to play and set in beautiful surroundings" - *Bernard Gallacher, Ryder Cup Captain.*

One of the oldest courses in East Lothian, bequeathed to the villagers in 1904 by the Marquis of Tweeddale. Golf has been played on the course since the 1880s. Full catering facilities and accommodation can be arranged.

LONGNIDDRY. **Longniddry Golf Club Ltd,** Links Road, Longniddry EH32 0NL (01875 852141; Fax: 01875 853371). *Location:* at the foot of Links Road in Longniddry village. Mainly parkland course with links features. Superb views over the Firth to Edinburgh and Fife. 18 holes, 6260 yards, 5690 metres. S.S.S. 70. Practice area, putting green, nets. *Green Fees:* weekdays £37.50 per round, £55.00 per day; weekends £48.00 per round. Subject to review. *Eating facilities:* catering available seven days, two bars and dining room. *Visitors:* welcome daily, though limited availability at weekends; advance booking recommended. *Society Meetings:* welcome Monday to Friday with Handicap Certificates. Professional: John Gray (01875 852228). Secretary: Bob Gunning (01875 852141)
e-mail: secretary@longniddrygolfclub.co.uk
website: www.longniddrygolfclub.co.uk

MUSSELBURGH. **Musselburgh Golf Club,** Monktonhall, Musselburgh EH21 6SA (0131-665 2005). *Location:* from the A1 end of the Edinburgh City bypass, on B6415 to Musselburgh. Wooded parkland, rivers. 18 holes, 6725 yards. S.S.S. 73. *Green Fees:* on application. *Eating facilities:* catering available. *Visitors:* welcome with reservation. *Society Meetings:* catered for. Professional: F. Mann (0131-665 7055).
e-mail: secretary@themusselburghgolfclub.com

MUSSELBURGH. **Musselburgh Old Course Golf Club,** 10 Balcarres Road, Musselburgh EH21 7SD (0131-665 6981). *Location*: A199 road at Musselburgh racecourse one-and-a-half miles east of town centre. Seaside links course. 9 holes, 2887 yards. S.S.S. 69. Large practice area. *Green Fees*: £9.00 9 holes. *Eating facilities*: available. *Visitors*: welcome. Starter (0131-665 5438). Secretary: L. Freedman (0131 665 6981).
e-mail: mocgc@breathemail.net
website: www.musselburgholdlinks.co.uk

NORTH BERWICK. **Glen Golf Club,** East Links, Tantallon Terrace, North Berwick EH39 4LE (01620 892726; Fax: 01620 895447). *Location:* one mile east of town centre, off A198. Seaside links with magnificent panoramic views. 18 holes, 6243 yards. S.S.S. 70. Practice ground, putting green. *Green Fees:* 2006 (Centenary Year) - midweek £35.00, weekend £48.00. *Eating facilities:* full facilities available. *Visitors:* welcome anytime, no restrictions. Pro Shop. Trolleys and caddies available. *Society Meetings:* welcome, advance booking required. Secretary: Mr Kevin Fish (01620 892726; Fax: 01620 895447). Starter: (01620 892726).
website: www.glengolfclub.co.uk

NORTH BERWICK. **The North Berwick Golf Club,** New Clubhouse, Beach Road, North Berwick EH39 4BB (01620 895040; Fax: 01620 893274). Location: 24 miles east of Edinburgh, A1 to Meadowmill roundabout then A198 to North Berwick. Seaside links. 18 holes, 6420 yards. S.S.S. 72. Practice ground. *Green Fees:* weekdays £55.00 per round, £75.00 per day; weekends £75.00 per round. *Eating facilities:* diningroom and bar. *Visitors:* welcome from 10am, book ahead Saturdays – restricted when there are club fixtures. Lounge and changing rooms available. *Society Meetings:* catered for by arrangement. Professional: D. Huish (01620 893233). Secretary: J.W.G Douglass (01620 895040). Advance Bookings: (01620 892135).

THE APPEARANCE OF AN ASTERISK (*) AT THE END OF A CLUB OR COURSE ENTRY INDICATES THAT UP-TO-DATE INFORMATION HAS NOT BEEN SUPPLIED

CRAIGESK GUEST HOUSE
10 Albert Terrace, Musselburgh EH21 7LR
Victorian terraced house overlooking racecourse, golf course and sea and near all other East Lothian golf courses. Double, single and family bedrooms, all with washbasins, colour TV, radio alarms and tea/coffee facilities. Children and pets welcome. Private parking. B&B from £18.00. Further details on request. **Miss A. R. Mitchell**
Tel: 0131 665 3344 or 3170 • Fax: 0131 665 3344

The Macdonald Marine Hotel & Spa has just undergone a multi-million pound refurbishment returning the hotel to its former glory! This Victorian building is located at the heart of East Lothian's golfing coast.
The hotel overlooks the North Berwick Championship Golf Course as well as the Firth of Forth.
The well proportioned public areas and many of the bedrooms enjoy the spectacular view.
With the addition of a magnificent Spa and an 18-metre pool, the hotel will be the natural choice for golf and leisure guests. The Craigleith Restaurant offers a mix of Scottish and International cuisine, whilst the Links Bar and Sea View Lounge serves a range of light meals throughout the day.

MACDONALD
Marine Hotel & Spa
North Berwick

Please call 0870 400 8129 for an introductory offer.
Cromwell Road, North Berwick EH39 4LZ
www.macdonaldhotels.co.uk/marine

416 Edinburgh & Lothians / SCOTLAND

PENICUIK. **Glencorse Golf Club,** Milton Bridge, Penicuik EH26 0RD (01968 677177). *Location:* A701 nine miles south of Edinburgh on Peebles Road. Parkland course with stream affecting 10 holes. 18 holes, 5217 yards. S.S.S. 66. *Green Fees:* weekdays £25.00 per round, £32.00 per day; weekends £32.00 per round. Package deals available. *Eating facilities:* all day catering and bar. *Visitors:* welcome at all times subject to Club Competitions. *Society Meetings:* catered for Mondays to Fridays and Sunday afternoons. Professional: Cliffe Jones (01968 676481). Secretary: Bill Oliver (01968 677189; Fax: 01968 674399).

PRESTONPANS. **Royal Musselburgh Golf Club,** Prestongrange House, Prestonpans EH32 9RP (Tel & Fax: 01875 810276). *Location:* B1361 North Berwick Road, Prestonpans. Fairly flat parkland, wooded course. 18 holes, 6254 yards. S.S.S. 70. *Green Fees:* weekdays £28.00 per round, £38.00 per day; weekends £38.00 per round. *Eating facilities:* available seven days a week. *Visitors:* welcome. *Society Meetings:* welcome by arrangement with the Management Secretary. Professional: John Henderson (Tel & Fax: 01875 810139). Management Secretary: Thos. H. Hardie (Tel & Fax: 01875 810276). Competition Secretary: J. Hanratty (01875 819000).
e-mail: royalmusselburgh@btinternet.com
website: www.royalmusselburgh.co.uk

SOUTH QUEENSFERRY. **Dundas Parks Golf Club,** Dundas Estate, South Queensferry, West Lothian EH30 9SS. *Location:* five miles west of Edinburgh, on South Queensferry to Kirkliston road on right of A8000. Parkland course in open countryside. 9 holes (x 2), 6024 yards, 5510 metres. S.S.S. 70. Small practice area. *Eating facilities:* no bar or food facilities. *Visitors:* welcome with member, or by prior arrangement with Club Administrator. *Society Meetings:* by prior arrangement with Club Administrator. Club Administrator: Christine Wood (0131-319 1347).

UPHALL. **Uphall Golf Club,** Uphall, West Lothian EH52 6JT (01506 856404; Fax: 01506 855358). *Location:* eight miles west of Edinburgh Airport on the A89 Edinburgh to Glasgow road. Established parkland course. 18 holes, S.S.S. 67. *Green Fees:* information not available. *Eating facilities:* hot and cold snacks, lunches, high teas and bars, à la carte available Saturday evenings. *Visitors:* welcome weekdays without reservation. A booking through the Professional is required at weekends. *Society Meetings:* catered for. Professional: Gordon Law (01506 855553). Club Administrator: Mima O'Connor: (01506 856404; Fax: 01506 855358). Secretary: J. Little (01506 856404).
e-mail: uphallgolfclub@businessunmetered.com

WEST CALDER. **Harburn Golf Club,** Harburn, West Calder EH55 8RS (01506 871256). *Location:* two miles south of West Calder on B7008. Parkland course. 18 holes, 6125 yards. S.S.S. 70. Practice ground. *Green Fees:* Monday to Thursday £25.00 per round, £30.00 per day; Friday £30.00 per round, £35.00 per day; weekends £35.00 per round, £40.00 per day. *Eating facilities:* full catering and bar service available. *Visitors:* welcome any time, no restrictions. *Society Meetings:* special terms on request. Professional: S.J. Mills (01506 871582). Secretary: J. McLinden (01506 871131; Fax: 01506 870286).
e-mail: info@harburngolfclub.co.uk
website: www.harburngolfclub.co.uk

WHITBURN. **Polkemmet Golf Course,** Polkemmet Country Park, Whitburn, West Lothian (01501 743905). *Location:* off B7066, one mile west of Whitburn. Inland course set within old private estate, mature varied woodland with belts of rhododendrons. 9 holes, 2946 metres. Par 37. 15 bay floodlit driving range. *Green Fees:* weekdays (summer) £5.40 per round, concessions £4.00; weekends and Public Holidays (summer) £6.35 per round, concessions £4.75. *Eating facilities:* Not functioning at present. *Visitors:* welcome. Public course. Facilities include bowling green, picnic areas, etc. Caddy cart hire £1.15. Secretary: West Lothian Council, Countryside Section, Property Services, Development and Environmental Services, Lammermuir House, Livingston.

WHITEKIRK. **Whitekirk Golf & Country Club,** Whitekirk, Near North Berwick EH39 5PR (01620 870300; Fax: 01620 870330). *Location*: East of North Berwick, off the main A1 Edinburgh - Berwick upon Tweed road, on the A198. Heathland, wooded, lakes, commanding views over East Lothian. 18 holes, 6526 yards. S.S.S. 72. *Green Fees*: information not available. *Eating facilities*: lunches, dinners, bar snacks. *Visitors*: welcome, no restrictions. Golf academy; buggies and carts available. *Society Meetings*: welcome seven days, special rates available. Professional: Paul Wardell (01620 870300; Fax: 01620 870330) Secretary: David Brodie (01620 870300; Fax: 01620 870330).
e-mail: countryclub@whitekirk.com
website: www.whitekirk.com

WINCHBURGH. **Niddry Castle Golf Club,** Castle Road, Winchburgh EH52 6RQ (01506 891097). *Location:* 10 miles west of Edinburgh on A803 between Kirkliston and Linlithgow. Wooded, natural parkland. 18 holes, 5514 yards. S.S.S. 69. Practice net. *Green Fees:* information not available. *Eating facilities:* full catering; bar. *Visitors:* welcome weekdays before 4.30pm, weekends on competition days after 3.30pm. *Society Meetings:* by arrangement. Secretary: G. McLeod.

GLENCORSE GOLF CLUB MILTON BRIDGE, PENICUIK EH26 0RD

Picturesque 18 hole parkland course of 5217 yards, SSS 66. Green fees £25 per round on weekdays and £32 at weekends and public holidays. A day ticket £32. Packages available on request. Outings welcome Monday to Thursday and Sunday afternoons. **Professional: Cliff Jones 01968 676481**

Please contact: W. Oliver (*Secretary*) • Tel: 01968 677189 Fax: 01968 674399

Fife

ABERDOUR. **Aberdour Golf Club,** Seaside Place, Aberdour KY3 0TX (01383 860080; Fax:01383 860050 *Location:* take Shore Road from centre of village. Parkland course situated along the shoreline of the River Forth. 18 holes, 5460 yards. S.S.S. 66. *Green Fees:* information not available. *Eating facilities:* full catering. *Visitors:* welcome. *Society Meetings:* catered for on weekdays and Sundays. On Sundays, maximum size of group 24. Professional: David Gemmell (01383 860256). Secretary. (01383 860080; Fax: 01383 860050).*

ANSTRUTHER. **Anstruther Golf Club,** Marsfield, Shore Road, Anstruther KY10 3DZ (01333 310956). *Location:* nine miles south of St Andrews, west side of Anstruther. Seaside links course. 9 holes, 4532 yards. S.S.S. 63. *Green Fees:* 9 holes weekdays £10.00; weekends £12.00. 18 holes: weekdays £16.00, weekends £18.00. *Eating facilities:* lounge bar and dining room. *Visitors:* welcome except during club competitions. *Society Meetings:* welcome except Saturdays and competition days. Secretary: S. Gardner (01333 310956)

BURNTISLAND. **Burntisland Golf House Club,** Dodhead, Burntisland KY3 9LQ (01592 874093). *Location:* Rossend Castle, near Kirkcaldy. Parkland with some hills. 18 holes, 5965 yards. S.S.S. 70. Practice ground and net. *Green Fees:* information not available. *Eating facilities:* all day bar and catering. *Visitors:* all parties catered for. Changing room. *Society Meetings:* welcome with advance bookings. Professional: P. Wytrazek (01592 872116). Manager: Wendy Taylor (01592 874093).*

www.uk-golfguide.com

CARDENDEN. **Auchterderran Golf Club,** Woodend Road, Cardenden KY5 0NH (01592 721579). *Location:* six miles north of Kirkcaldy. Flat course. 9 holes, 5252 yards. S.S.S. 66. *Green Fees*: weekdays £8.00 per round, weekends £10.00 per round. Concessionary ticket available. *Eating facilities:* clubhouse bar facilities, meals available on request, snacks available most times. *Visitors*: all welcome, Saturdays and some Sundays members' competitions held from 7am to 11am and 1pm to 3pm. *Society Meetings:* welcome. Secretary: Charles Taylor (01592 720080).

COLINSBURGH. **Charleton Golf Club,** Colinsburgh Golf Ltd, Charleton, Colinsburgh KY9 1HG (01333 340505; Fax: 01333 340583). *Location:* B942, Colinsburgh (near Elie). Parkland course. 18 holes, 6216 yards, 5684 metres. S.S.S. 72. Driving range, bunker practice area, putting green. *Green Fees:* information not available. *Eating facilities:* fully licensed clubhouse with restaurant. *Visitors:* all welcome, pay as you play, no restrictions, please book. Carts, buggies. *Society Meetings:* all welcome. Professional: George Finlayson. Secretary: Peter Griffiths.*

COWDENBEATH. **Cowdenbeath Golf Club,** Seco Place, Cowdenbeath KY4 8PD (01383 511918). *Location:* just off the A92 after Dunfermline. Parkland course. 18 holes, 6201 yards. S.S.S. 70. Practice ground and putting green. *Green Fees:* information not available. *Eating facilities:* full catering in new clubhouse. *Visitors:* welcome at any time. *Society Meetings:* booking available through Fife Council. Secretary: Graham Inglis.*

COWDENBEATH. **Dora Golf Course,** Cowdenbeath KY4 8PD (01383 513079). Parkland course, 18 holes. Par 70. *Green Fees:* information not available. *Eating facilities:* bar and catering available.

Scotland's Premier Pay-As-You-Play Golf Course

Set in stunning parkland, 15 minutes from St Andrews, with spectacular views of the Firth of Forth.

- 18 holes, Par 72 • 9-hole pitch and putt
- Driving range
- Clubhouse with restaurant and bar.

www.charleton.co.uk

Charleton Golf Course
Colinsburgh, Fife KY9 1HG
Tel: 01333 340505 • Fax: 01333 340583
e-mail: clubhouse@charleton.co.uk

See also Colour Advertisement on page 71

Fife / SCOTLAND

CRAIL. **Crail Golfing Society,** Balcomie Clubhouse, Fifeness, Crail KY10 3XN (01333 450686; Fax: 01333 450416). Instituted 1786. *Location:* eleven miles south-east of St Andrews on A917. Traditional links courses. Balcomie Links: 18 holes, 5922 yards. S.S.S. 70. Par 69. Craighead Links: 18 holes, 6728 yards. S.S.S. 74. Par 72. Practice ground. *Green Fees:* weekdays £40.00 per round, £55.00 per day; weekends and Public Holidays £50.00 per round, £65.00 per day. *Eating facilities:* quality catering and bar. *Visitors:* welcome. *Society Meetings:* advance booking available for parties. Professional: Graeme Lennie (01333 450960). Secretary: (01333 450686; Fax: 01333 450416).

CUPAR. **Cupar Golf Club,** Hilltarvit, Cupar KY15 5JT (01334 653549). *Location:* near cemetery on Ceres Road. Hillside/parkland course. 9 holes, 5153 yards. S.S.S. 66. Practice putting green. *Green Fees:* weekdays £15.00; Sundays £15.00. Weekly £50.00. Family per day £30.00. *Eating facilities:* full catering/bar. *Visitors:* welcome, except Saturdays. *Society Meetings:* by arrangement with Secretary. Secretary: John M. Houston (01334 653549). e-mail: cuparge@fsmail.net
website: www.cupargolfclub.co.uk

CUPAR. **Elmwood,** Stratheden, Near Cupar KY15 5RS (01334 658780; Fax: 01334 658781). *Location:* signposted from both A91 and A914, one mile west of Cupar, nine miles from St Andrews. Gently undulating parkland. 18 holes, 5951 yards. S.S.S 68. *Green Fees:* weekdays £19.00 per round, £28.50 per day; weekends: £23.00 per round, £32.50 per day, concessions for Seniors and Juniors. *Eating facilities:* full catering and bar. New lounge. *Visitors:* welcome anytime. Trolleys and buggies available. New indoor Golf Swing Analysis Studio. *Society Meetings:* welcome, advance bookings and special rates. Golf Administrator: Sharif Sulaiman.
e-mail: clubhouse@elmwood.ac.uk
website: www.elmwoodgc.co.uk

DUNFERMLINE. **Canmore Golf Club,** Venture Fair, Dunfermline (01383 724969). *Location:* one mile north of town centre on A823. Parkland, undulating. 18 holes, 5347 yards. S.S.S. 66. *Green Fees:* weekdays £19.00 per round, £25.00 per day; weekends £25.00 per round, £32.00 per day (including golfer's insurance). *Eating facilities:* full catering and bar. *Visitors:* welcome weekdays, limited Sundays. *Society Meetings:* we welcome visiting societies with prior reservation (not on Saturdays). Professional: Daryn Cochrane (01383 728416). Secretary: Andrew Watson (01383 724969).

DUNFERMLINE. **Dunfermline Golf Club,** Pitfirrane, Crossford, By Dunfermline KY12 8QW (01383 723534). *Location:* two miles west of Dunfermline on A994 to Kincardine Bridge. Undulating parkland. 18 holes, 6121 yards, 5597 metres. S.S.S. 70. Practice area. *Green Fees:* £27.00 per round, £38.00 per day weekdays; £35.00 per round Sundays. *Eating facilities:* full catering, bar snacks available. *Visitors:* welcome 9.30am to 4pm weekdays and Sunday. Must have official Club Handicap. *Society Meetings:* accepted weekdays and Sunday by prior arrangement. Professional: Chris Nugent (01383 729061). Secretary: Robert De Rose (01383 723534).

DUNFERMLINE. **Forrester Park Resort,** Pitdinnie, Cairneyhill KY12 8RF (01383 880505; Fax: 01383 882505). Parkland course with gentle undulations and lots of water features. 300m driving range, practice bunkers, greens and putting green. *Green Fees:* weekday £35.00, weekend £45.00. *Eating facilities:* Acanthus 5 star à la carte restaurant and bar/bistro. New members area, sports bar, X Golf. *Visitors:* welcome, no restrictions. *Society Meetings:* always welcome. Tuition, golfshop, showers available. Professional: Colin Gillies. Secretary: Robert Forrester. e-mail: forresterpark@aol.com
website: www.forresterparkresort.com

DUNFERMLINE. **Pitreavie (Dunfermline) Golf Club,** Queensferry Road, Dunfermline KY11 8PR (Tel & Fax: 01383 722591). *Location*: M90 Edinburgh/Perth, leave at Junction 2 for Dunfermline. Undulating parkland with views across Firth of Forth. 18 holes, 6008 yards. S.S.S. 69. Practice ground. *Green Fees:* information not available. *Eating facilities:* full catering and bar facilities. *Visitors:* welcome. Please phone the Professional in advance, must have recognised Golf Union Handicap. Trolleys and carts available. *Society Meetings*: catered for, must be booked through Secretary. Professional: Paul Brookes (01383 723151). Secretary: Eddie Comerford (01383 722591).

Advance bookings
01333 450686
www.crailgolfingsociety.co.uk

The World's 7th Oldest Golfing Society (1786)
invites you to experience

Golf at Crail

Spectacular location - sea views from every hole
Balcomie Links 5922 yards • SSS70 • Par 69
Classic Links Course
Craighead Links 6728 yards • SSS 74 • Par 72
USGA Spec Greens
**Crail Golfing Society, Balcomie Clubhouse,
Fifeness, Crail, Fife KY10 3XN**

See also Colour Advertisement on page 72

THE GOLF GUIDE 2006 SCOTLAND / Fife

DUNFERMLINE. **Saline Golf Club,** Kinneddar Hill, Saline KY12 9LT (01383 852591). *Location:* turn off M90 at Junction 4, 7 miles along B914 to Dollar. Hillside parkland course. 9 holes, 5302 yards. S.S.S. 66. Practice net, putting green. *Green Fees:* information not available. *Eating facilities:* bar snacks; meals by prior arrangement. *Visitors:* welcome, except Saturdays and certain Sundays. *Society Meetings:* catered for midweek or Sundays; maximum 24. Secretary: P. Bridson (01383 851040).*

ELIE. **Earlsferry Thistle Golf Club,** Melon Park, Elie (01333 330301). *Location:* A917 golf course signs in Elie. Seaside links. 18 holes, 6250 yards. S.S.S. 70. *Green Fees:* set by Elie Golf House Club, on application. *Visitors:* welcome weekdays. The course belongs to Elie Golf House Club, also played by Earlsferry Thistle.*

ELIE. **Golf House Club,** Elie KY9 1AS (01333 330301; Fax: 01333 330895). *Location:* 10 miles south of St Andrews on A917. Links course. 18 holes, 6273 yards. S.S.S. 70. *Green Fees:* (2005) weekdays £50.00 per round, £70.00 per day; weekends £60.00 per round, £80.00 per day. Subject to review. *Eating facilities:* lunches, teas, etc. *Visitors:* welcome with reservation. Elie Sports Centre nearby with leisure facilities and cafeteria. *Society Meetings:* catered for except at weekends. Professional: Ian Muir (01333 330955). Secretary: Graham Scott (01333 330301; Fax: 01333 330895).

FALKLAND. **Falkland Golf Club,** The Myre, Falkland KY15 7AA (01337 857404). *Location:* entrance on A912, 12 miles from Kirkcaldy – approximately 20 minutes from St. Andrews. Lies at the foot of East Lomond Hills. Flat meadowland, beautiful views. 9 holes, 4988 yards, 4560 metres. S.S.S. 65 for 18 holes. *Green Fees:* information not available. *Eating facilities:* by arrangement. *Visitors:* welcome. *Society Meetings:* must book in advance. Secretary: Mrs L. Henry.*

GLENROTHES. **Glenrothes Golf Club,** Golf Course Road, Glenrothes KY6 2LA (01592 758686). *Location:* at the western end of town, near airfield. Parkland, wide fairways, with burn crossing four fairways on back nine holes. 18 holes, 6444 yards, 5984 metres. S.S.S. 71. *Green Fees:* information not available. *Eating facilities:* full catering service and bar. Temporary day membership of club available to visitors. *Visitors:* welcome, some restrictions weekends. *Society Meetings:* welcome, advance booking, numbers 12-40. Hon. Secretary: Claire Dawson (01592 754561).*
website: www.glenrothesgolf.org.uk

KINCARDINE. **Tulliallan Golf Club,** Alloa Road, Kincardine on Forth, by Alloa FK10 4BB (01259 730396). *Location:* on A908 five miles east of Alloa, one mile north of Kincardine Bridge. Parkland, slightly wooded, burn winds through the course. 18 holes, 6000 yards. S.S.S. 69. Practice ground. *Green Fees:* information not available. *Eating facilities:* dining room, bar 11am to 11pm. *Society Meetings:* catered for by phoning Pro shop. Professional: Steve Kelly (Tel & Fax: 01259 730730). Secretary: D. Berry (01259 730396).

KINGHORN. **Kinghorn Municipal Golf Club,** MacDuff Crescent, Kinghorn KY3 9RE (01592 890345). *Location:* bus stop at course, railway station three minutes away. Semi links course with hills. 18 holes, 5166 yards, S.S.S. 66. *Green Fees:* information not available. *Eating facilities:* meals at clubhouse on request, local hotels. *Visitors:* welcome at any time; no large parties on Saturdays. *Society Meetings:* catered for by arrangement. Secretary: Gordon Tulloch (01592 891008). Starter: (01592 890978).

KIRKCALDY. **Dunnikier Park Golf Club,** Dunnikier Way, Kirkcaldy KY1 3LP (01592 261599 (Clubhouse); 01592 642541 (Secretary)). *Location:* one mile off A92 on the B981 north side of Kirkcaldy. Municipal parkland course, not hilly. 18 holes, 6601 yards, 6036 metres. S.S.S. 72. Practice ground. *Green Fees:* weekdays £11.50 per round, £18.00 per day; weekends £15.50 per round, £22.00 per day. Concessions for over 60s. *Eating facilities:* full bar and catering facilities. *Visitors:* welcome, no restrictions. *Society Meetings:* welcome by arrangement with Secretary (min. 12, max. 30). Professional: Gregor Whyte (01592 642121). Secretary: Raymond Johnston (01592 261599).

KIRKCALDY. **Kirkcaldy Golf Club,** Balwearie Road, Kirkcaldy KY2 5LT (01592 260370). *Location*: west end of town adjacent to Beveridge Park. Challenging parkland layout in rural setting with views across Firth of Forth. 18 holes, 6004 yards. S.S.S. 69 – Par 71. Practice ground. *Green Fees*: weekdays £24.00 per round, £30.00 per day; weekends £30.00 per round, £38.00 per day. *Eating facilities*: bar and full catering facilities. Magnificent clubhouse. *Visitors:* welcome except Saturdays, restricted Tuesdays. Professional's shop. Trolleys for hire. *Society Meetings*: welcome but please phone or write in advance. Professional: Anthony Caira (01592 203258). Secretary: Andrew Wood (01592 205240).

LADYBANK. **Ladybank Golf Club,** Annsmuir, Ladybank KY15 7RA (01337 830814). *Location:* on A92 off A91, 15 miles St. Andrews. Wooded heathland. 18 holes, 6641 yards. S.S.S. 72. Practice ground. *Green Fees:* weekdays £45.00 per round, £60.00 per day; weekends £55.00 very limited. *Eating facilities:* full catering facilities and bar. *Visitors:* welcome without reservation. Party bookings by arrangement with Secretary. *Society Meetings:* by arrangement. Professional: Sandy Smith (Tel & Fax: 01337 830725). Secretary: Fraser McCuskey (01337 830814; Fax: 01337 831505).

LESLIE. **Leslie Golf Club,** Balsillie Laws, Leslie, Glenrothes KY6 3EZ (01592 620040). Parkland with small stream running through some fairways. 9 holes, 4940 yards. S.S.S. 65. *Green Fees:* information not available. *Eating facilities:* bar open all day. *Visitors:* always welcome, some restrictions on competition days.

www.uk-golfguide.com

420 Fife / SCOTLAND THE GOLF GUIDE 2006

LEUCHARS. **St Michaels Golf Club,** Gallowhill, Leuchars KY16 0DX (01334 839365; Fax: 01334 838666). *Location:* quarter of a mile outside Leuchars on A919 towards Dundee. Undulating parkland course surrounded by plantations. 18 holes, 5802 yards. S.S.S. 68. *Green Fees:* information not available. *Eating facilities:* bar and catering available. *Visitors:* welcome anytime but not before 12 noon Sundays. Changing rooms and showers. Trolley hire. *Society Meetings:* by prior arrangement. A booking fee is payable before confirmation of reservation. Secretary: Mr Spong (Tel & Fax: 01334 838666).*

LEVEN. **Leven Golfing Society,** PO Box 14609, Links Road, Leven KY8 4HS (01333 426096; Fax: 01333 424229). *Location:* 14 miles south west of St Andrews. Championship Links course used for national and international events, including open qualifying. 18 holes, 6500 yards. S.S.S. 70. *Green Fees:* weekdays £37.00 per round, £50.00 per day; weekends £45.00 per round, £60.00 per day. *Eating facilities:* full catering available. *Visitors:* welcome except Saturdays. *Society Meetings:* by arrangement, please contact the Secretary, Links Joint Committee, Promenade, Leven KY8 4HS (01333 428859). Secretary: Verne Greger (Tel & Fax: 01333 424229).

LEVEN. **Leven Thistle Golf Club,** Balfour Street, Leven KY8 4JF (01333 426333; Fax: 01333 439910). *Location:* 10 miles south west of St. Andrews. Top championship links used for national and international events including Open qualifying. 18 holes, 6434 yards. S.S.S. 70. *Green Fees:* weekdays £30.00 per round, £40.00 per day; weekends £35.00 per round, £50.00 per day. *Eating facilities:* full catering available, two bars, function hall. *Visitors:* welcome without reservation, except Saturdays. *Society Meetings:* for group bookings contact Leven Links Joint Committee, Promenade, Leven, Fife KY8 4HS (01333 428859). Secretary: J. Scott. Links Secretary: Mr R. Bissett.

LEVEN. **Scoonie Golf Club,** North Links, Leven KY8 4SP (01333 307007). *Location:* nearest town Leven on coastal road to St Andrews. Flat, typical seaside bunkers. 18 holes, 4979 metres. S.S.S. 65. *Green Fees:* information not available. *Eating facilities:* full catering available, bar open normal hours. *Visitors:* welcome anytime. *Society Meetings:* welcome by bookings except Saturdays. Secretary: S. Kuczerepa (01333 307007; Fax: 01333 307008).*

LOCHGELLY. **Lochgelly Golf Club,** Cartmore Road, Lochgelly (01592 780174). *Location:* take M90 to Junction 4 Halbeath Interchange, follow signs. Parkland. 18 holes, 5491 yards, 5063 metres. S.S.S. 67. *Green Fees:* weekdays £19.00 per round, £29.00 per day; weekends £25.00 per round, £35.00 per day. *Eating facilities:* catering available. *Visitors:* welcome, no restrictions weekdays, weekends parties limited to 24. Professional: Martin Goldie (01592 782589). Secretary: R.F. Stuart (01383 512238).

LUNDIN LINKS. **Lundin Golf Club,** Golf Road, Lundin Links KY8 6BA (01333 320202). *Location:* three miles east of Leven, 12 miles SW of St Andrews. Seaside links. 18 holes, 6371 yards. S.S.S. 71. Practice ground. *Green Fees:* £42.00 per round, £50.00 per day weekdays; Saturdays and Sundays after 2.30pm £50.00 per round. *Eating facilities:* bar and dining room. *Visitors:* welcome Monday/Thursday 9am to 3.30pm; Friday 9am to 3pm; Saturdays no visitors before 2.30pm; limited Sunday golf available. Professional: David K. Webster (01333 320051). Secretary: A.J. McDonald (01333 320202). e-mail: secretary@lundingolfclub.co.uk
website: www.lundingolfclub.co.uk

LUNDIN LINKS. **Lundin Ladies Golf Club,** Woodielea Road, Lundin Links KY8 6AR (01333 320832). *Location:* at Lundin Links on A915, turn into road opposite Royal Bank of Scotland. Excellent parkland course, with famous standing stones. 9 holes, 2365 yards. S.S.S. 68. Putting green. *Green Fees:* Winter Rates: weekdays £5.00 9 holes, £8.00 18 holes; weekends £6.00 9 holes, £10.00 18 holes. Summer Rates: weekdays £7.50 9 holes, £14.00 18 holes; weekends £8.50 9 holes, £16.00 18 holes; member's guest £5.00; reductions for Juniors; family tickets available. *Eating facilities:* tea making facilities only. *Visitors:* welcome, restricted tee times on Wednesdays during season. Starter (01333 320022). Clubhouse: (01333 320832).

MARKINCH. **Balbirnie Park Golf Club,** The Clubhouse, Balbirnie Park, Markinch, Glenrothes KY7 6NR (01592 612095; Fax: 01592 612383). *Location:* outside Markinch near the A92. Wooded parkland course. 18 holes, 6212 yards. S.S.S. 70. *Green Fees:* information not available. *Eating facilities:* snacks, lunch, high tea and full meals available during clubhouse hours. *Visitors:* no restrictions at present other than maximum number of 24 at weekends and no visitors before 10am weekends. *Society Meetings:* welcome. Professional: Craig Donnelly (Tel & Fax: 01592 752006). Club Administrator: Steve Oliver (01592 612095; Fax: 01592 612383). Starter: (01592 752006).*
e-mail: craigfdonnelly@aol.com
website: www.balbirniegolf.co.uk.

For full details of clubs and courses, plus convenient accommodation
www.uk-golfguide.com

THE APPEARANCE OF AN ASTERISK (*) AT THE END OF A CLUB OR COURSE ENTRY INDICATES THAT UP-TO-DATE INFORMATION HAS NOT BEEN SUPPLIED

Leven Links, The Promenade, Leven, Fife KY8 4HS
Tel/Fax: 01333 428859
e-mail: secretary@leven-links.com

Leven Links, in part one of the oldest pieces of golfing ground in the world, is a true seaside links course. It has hosted many national and international events and is used as a final qualifying course for the Open Championship when it is held at St Andrews. The strength of Leven Links lies in its fine variety of links-type holes combined with large greens; turning into the prevailing west wind at the 13th leaves the golfer with a lot of work to do before reaching one of the finest finishing holes in golf.

See also Colour Advertisement on page 72

The Lundin Links Hotel

GOLFING PACKAGES ARE OUR SPECIALITY

The perfect location for a golfing break only minutes from the famous 'Old Course' at St Andrews, and with over 40 top courses all within an hour's drive. Only 9 miles from St Andrews and 45 minutes from Edinburgh. 21 superb en suite bedrooms, with top cuisine and traditional bars.

Ring now for brochure and Golfing Breaks
The Lundin Links Hotel
Lundin Links, Fife KY8 6AP Scotland
Tel: 01333 320207 Fax: 01333 320930
e-mail: info@lundin-links-hotel.co.uk
www.lundin-links-hotel.co.uk

See also Colour Advertisement on page 73

Balbirnie Park Golf Club
Balbirnie Park, Markinch, Glenrothes KY7 6NR
Tel: 01592 612095 • Fax: 01592 612383

Balbirnie Park is a fine example of the best in traditional parkland design – the natural contours being the inspiration behind the layout. With a par of 71 and measuring 6200 yards from the Gents' Back Tees, it is a good challenge for golfers of all abilities.

It is immediately apparent to any visitor that the course is blessed with a truly superb and picturesque site, situated in the heart of the magnificent Balbirnie Park. The park has the finest collection of rhododendrons and azaleas adjacent to the golf course. Visitors and parties always welcome. Individual packages arranged. Excellent cuisine. Well stocked golf shop.

e-mail: craigfdonnelly@aol.com • www.balbirniegolf.co.uk

FHG Guides publish a large range of well-known accommodation guides. We will be happy to send you details or you can use the order form at the back of this book.

ST ANDREWS. **Old Course,** St Andrews KY16 9SF (01334 466666; Fax: 01334 466664). *Location:* go into St Andrews on the A91, follow signs to West Sands. Approximately 50 miles from Edinburgh. Public links. 18 holes, 6609 yards, 6004 metres. S.S.S. 72. 44 bay driving range, practice facilities. *Green Fees:* High Season £115.00, Shoulder Season £80.00, Low Season £56.00. *Eating facilities:* Links Clubhouse with full facilities; there is a buggy shuttle run from the clubhouse to the Old Course. *Visitors:* Handicap Certificate required. Handicap limit 24 or less (Men), 36 or less (Ladies). Trolleys allowed after 12 noon from May to September.

ST ANDREWS. **Balgove Course,** St Andrews Links Trust, St Andrews KY16 9SF (01334 466666; Fax: 01334 466664). *Location:* A91 to St Andrews, turning is on the left just before the town. Public 9 hole beginners' course, 1520 yards. S.S.S. 60 (18 holes). *Green Fees:* information not available. *Eating facilities:* adjacent Eden Clubhouse with full facilities. Children's room. *Visitors:* welcome with or without reservation. Trolleys £3.00 per round. *Society Meetings:* welcome.*

ST ANDREWS. **Drumoig Hotel and Golf Resort,** Drumoig, Leuchars, St Andrews KY16 0BE (01382 541800; Fax: 01382 542211). *Location:* on A92 (St Andrews to Dundee), four miles south of Dundee. Natural free draining, rolling countryside over sandy based ground featuring spectacular water holes. Unusual quarry greens and views of St Andrews Bay and Carnoustie. 18 holes, 6835 yards. S.S.S 72. Driving Range. *Green Fees*: weekdays £31.00, weekends £36.00. Subject to review. Reduced rates for parties of 10 or more. *Eating facilities:* bar and restaurants. *Visitors*: welcome. 29 bedroom hotel, all en suite (5 executive suites). *Society Meetings*: welcome.

ST ANDREWS. **The Duke's Course,** Craigton, St Andrews KY16 8NS (01334 474371; Fax: 01334 479456). *Location:* 2½ miles from town centre, signposted on A91. Inland championship tree-lined course with undulating fairways and American-style greens. 18 holes, 7271 yards. S.S.S. 75. Grassed driving range, putting and short game area. *Green Fees:* information not available. *Eating facilities*: restaurant and bar; private dining room. *Visitors:* welcome, no restrictions. Trolley and buggy hire; club and shoe hire. *Society Meetings:* please call for details of packages. Professional: Ron Walker. Secretary: Steve Toon.*
e-mail: reservations@oldcoursehotel.co.uk
website: www.oldcoursehotel.co.uk

ST ANDREWS. **Eden Course,** St Andrews Links Trust, Pilmour House, St Andrews KY16 9SF (01334 466666; Fax: 01334 466664). *Location:* A91 main road into St Andrews, turning is left just before the town; approximately 50 miles from Edinburgh. Public links. 18 holes, 6195 yards. S.S.S. 70. 44 bay driving range. Practice facilities. *Green Fees:* High Season £33.00, Shoulder Season £23.00, Low Season £16.00. *Eating facilities:* Eden Clubhouse, lounge bar, dining room (seats 60) children's room. *Visitors:* welcome with or without reservation. Trolleys £3.00 per round. *Society Meetings:* always welcome.

ST ANDREWS. **Jubilee Course,** St Andrews Links Trust, Pilmour House, St Andrews KY16 9SF (01334 466666; Fax: 01334 466664). *Location:* go into St Andrews on the A91, follow signs to West Sands; approximately 50 miles from Edinburgh. Public links. 18 holes, 6742 yards. S.S.S. 73. 44 bay driving range, practice facilities available. *Green Fees:* High Season £55.00, Shoulder Season £39.00, Low Season £27.00. *Eating facilities:* Links Clubhouse, dining room (seats 60). *Visitors:* always welcome. Trolleys £3.00 per round. *Society Meetings:* welcome.

ST ANDREWS. **New Course,** St Andrews Links Trust, Pilmour House, St Andrews KY16 9SF (01334 466666; Fax: 01334 466664). *Location:* go into St Andrews on the A91, follow signs to West Sands; approximately 50 miles from Edinburgh. Public links course. 18 holes, 6604 yards. S.S.S. 72. 44 bay driving range, practice ground. *Green Fees:* High Season £55.00, Shoulder Season £39.00, Low Season £27.00. *Eating facilities:* Links Clubhouse, dining room (seats 60). *Visitors:* welcome. Buggies may be hired, trolleys are £3.00 per round. *Society Meetings:* welcome.

ST ANDREWS. **Strathtyrum Course,** St Andrews Links Trust, Pilmour House, St Andrews KY16 9SF (01334 466666; Fax: 01334 466664). *Location:* A91 main road into St Andrews, turning is on the left just before the town. Approximately 50 miles from Edinburgh. Public links course, 18 holes, 5620 yards. S.S.S. 65. 44 bay driving range, practice ground. *Green Fees:* High Season £22.00, Shoulder Season £16.00, Low Season £11.00. *Eating facilities:* Eden Clubhouse with full facilities. Children's room. *Visitors:* welcome. Buggies may be hired, trolleys are £3.00 per round. *Society Meetings:* welcome.

TAYPORT. **Scotscraig Golf Club,** Tayport DD6 9DZ (01382 552515; Fax: 01382 553130). *Location:* ten miles north of St Andrews. Links/parkland. 18 holes, 6550 yards. S.S.S. 72. *Green Fees:* information not available. *Eating facilities:* lunches and high teas. *Visitors:* welcome on weekdays or weekends by prior arrangement. *Society Meetings:* catered for subject to approval. Company Days available. Professional: John Kelly (01382 552855). Secretary: B.D. Liddle (01382 552515).

THORNTON. **Thornton Golf Club,** Station Road, Thornton KY1 4DW (01592 771111 office, 771173 starter). *Location:* southeast Fife located off A92, midway between Glenrothes and Kirkcaldy. Easily walked parkland course bounded by River Ore. Renowned for condition of greens. 18 holes, 6170 yards, 5695 metres. S.S.S. 69. Practice area, chipping and putting areas. *Green Fees:* weekdays £20.00 per round, £30.00 per day; weekends £30.00 per round, £40.00 per day. Parties of 18 or more get one free place. *Eating facilities:* full catering service and bar. *Visitors:* very welcome, restricted weekends before 10am and between 12 noon and 2.30pm. Recently built clubhouse; trolleys for hire. *Society Meetings:* catered for. Secretary: W.D. Rae.

Macdonald Rusacks Hotel, St Andrews

Guests who have stayed at Rusacks include golfing and rock and roll legends. Originally opened in 1887, it has been stylishly remodelled on a golfing theme to take advantage of its prestigious location and eye-catching views over the 18th green of the Old Course.

- Golf packages available
- 68 en suite bedrooms
- Old Course Restaurant

MACDONALD HOTELS

For Reservations or information
0870 400 8128

Pilmour Links, St Andrews, Fife KY16 9JQ
www.macdonaldhotels.co.uk/rusacks
general@macdonald-hotels.co.uk

See also Colour Advertisement on page 72

Scotscraig Golf Club
Golf Road, Tayport DD6 9DZ • 01382 552515

Situated on the Tay Estuary, 10 miles north of St Andrews. With fine links turf, smooth fast greens, whin bushes and rolling fairways, this is a demanding and interesting test of golf for all levels of player.

Special Golf Packages available for parties of 12+
Meals, snacks and refreshments served daily
Well-Stocked Shop with resident PGA Professional

Pro Shop: 01382 552855
e-mail: scotscraig@scottishgolf.com
www.scotscraiggolfclub.com

OPEN QUALIFYING COURSE

See also Colour Advertisement on page 72

Discover the Perfect Location

Discover Drumoig by St Andrews

- 3 Star Hotel

Summer & Winter Packages now available

Summer – 1st April to 31st October
2 nights' dinner, bed & breakfast with
2 rounds of golf from £170 per person.

Winter – 1st November to 31st March
2 nights as above from £135 per person.

Summer or Winter
1 night's dinner, bed & breakfast with 2 rounds of golf £100.

Packages tailored to suit your requirements

(All prices based on two people sharing a twin/double room)

- 18 hole championship golf course
- Parties & Societies most welcome

Golf per round
Summer midweek £25 / Weekend £30
Winter midweek £18 / Weekend £21

Drumoig Hotel Golf Resort, Drumoig, Leuchars, St Andrews, Fife KY16 0BE
Tel: 01382 541800 • Fax: 01382 542211
www.drumoigleisure.com • e-mail: drumoig@sol.co.uk

Glasgow & District

BISHOPBRIGGS. **The Bishopbriggs Golf Club,** Brackenbrae Road, Bishopbriggs G64 2DX (0141-772 1810). *Location:* quarter mile from Bishopbriggs Cross off Glasgow-Kirkintilloch road. Fairly flat parkland course. 18 holes, 6414 yards. S.S.S. 71. *Green Fees:* on application. *Eating facilities:* full service always available. *Visitors:* weekends/Public Holidays with member only, other times apply to Secretary. *Society Meetings:* catered for Monday to Friday, application to committee at least one month in advance. Secretary: Andrew Smith (0141-772 8938).

CUMBERNAULD. **Palacerigg Golf Club,** Palacerigg Country Park, Cumbernauld, Near Glasgow G67 2BY (01236 734969). *Location:* Cumbernauld off A80 between Glasgow and Stirling, Palacerigg Road, three miles south of Cumbernauld. Wooded parkland with good views to Campsie Hills, designed by Henry Cotton. 18 holes, 6444 yards, 5894 metres. S.S.S. 71. Practice area. *Green Fees:* weekdays £8.00; weekends £10.00. Full membership available contact Secretary. *Eating facilities:* full catering facilities. *Visitors:* welcome, advance booking recommended for individual rounds. *Society Meetings:* welcome weekdays, full days golf and catering £27.00. Other packages available contact Secretary or club steward. Starter: John Murphy (Tel & Fax: 01236 721461). Secretary: David S.A. Cooper (01236 734969; Fax: 01236 721461).
e-mail: palacerigg-golfclub@lineone.net
website: www.palaceriggolfclub.co.uk

CUMBERNAULD. **The Westerwood Hotel, Golf and Country Club,** Westerwood, Cumbernauld G68 0EW (01236 457171; Fax: 01236 860730). *Location*: between Glasgow and Stirling, off A80 towards Dullatur. Parkland, rolling American style; designed by Seve Ballesteros and Dave Thomas. 18 holes, 6616 yards. S.S.S. 72. *Green Fees*: weekdays £29.50, weekends £32.00. *Eating facilities*: full catering facilities. *Visitors*: welcome at all times, no restrictions. Advance booking of tee times recommended. 100 bedroom Hotel, full leisure facilities and indoor pool. *Society Meetings*: welcome by arrangement, packages available, including corporate membership. Professional and Club Manager: Alan Tait (Tel & Fax: 01236 725281). e-mail: alantait@morton-hotels.com

GLASGOW. **Alexandra Golf Club,** Alexandra Park, Alexandra Parade, Glasgow G31 8SE (0141-556 1294). *Location:* M8 off ramp to Alexandra Parade. Wooded Parkland, very hilly. 9 holes, 1965 yards, S.S.S. 35. Practice area. *Green Fees:* available on request. *Visitors:* welcome at all times. Blind Club and Unemployed club use this course. Room available for functions, to book phone 0141-770 0519 (24 hours notice is required). Bowling greens are available from Easter to September. Professional: Paul West (0141-556 1294). Secretary: G. Campbell (0141-556 1294).

GLASGOW. **Balmore Golf Club,** Balmore, Torrance G64 4AW (01360 620240; Fax: 01360 622742). *Location:* A803 then A807 from Glasgow. Parkland. 18 holes, 5530 yards. S.S.S. 67. Practice area. *Green Fees:* weekdays £30.00 per round, £40.00 day ticket. *Eating facilities:* catering and bar facilities. *Visitors:* welcome. *Society Meetings:* welcome Monday to Friday only. Professional: Kevin Craggs (01360 620123). Secretary: C. Campbell (01360 620284).

GLASGOW. **Bearsden Golf Club,** Thorn Road, Bearsden G61 4BP. *Location:* seven miles north-west of Glasgow. Parkland. 9 holes, 6014 yards. S.S.S. 69. *Green Fees:* information not available. *Visitors:* welcome, but must be accompanied by member. Secretary: Iain Inglis (0141 586 5300).

GLASGOW. **Blairbeth Golf Club,** Fernbrae Avenue, Rutherglen, Glasgow G73 4SF (0141-634 3355). *Location:* two miles south of Rutherglen off Burnside Road. Parkland. 18 holes, 5518 yards. S.S.S. 68. *Green Fees:* on application. *Eating Facilities:* available. *Visitors:* welcome weekdays only. *Society Meetings:* on application. Hon. Secretary/Treasurer: John Bell (0141-634 3325).
e-mail: golf@blairbethgc.fsnet.co.uk
website: www.blairbeth.com

GLASGOW. **Bonnyton Golf Club,** Eaglesham, Glasgow G76 0QA (01355 302645; Fax: 01355 303151). *Location:* B764. Moorland course. 18 holes, 6252 yards. S.S.S. 71. *Green Fees:* £45.00 per day. *Eating facilities:* full diningroom and snack facilities. *Visitors:* welcome except weekends. Professional: Kendal McWade (01355 302256). Secretary: A. Hughes (01355 302781).

GLASGOW. **Bothwell Castle Golf Club,** Uddingston Road, Bothwell G71 8TD (01698 853177; Fax: 01698 854052). *Location:* adjacent to M74, three miles north of Hamilton. Flat parkland course. 18 holes, 6230 yards. S.S.S. 70. Golf clubs and caddy cars for hire. Practice ground. *Green Fees:* £24.00 per round, £32.00 per day. (Playing times must be booked with Professional). *Eating facilities:* full catering and bar. *Visitors:* welcome weekdays 9.30am to 10.30am and 2pm to 3pm only. *Society Meetings:* catered for, courtesy granted by application on Tuesdays only. Professional: A. McCloskey (01698 852052). Secretary: David McNaught (Tel & Fax: 01698 854052).

For full details of clubs and courses, plus convenient accommodation
www.uk-golfguide.com

THE GOLF GUIDE 2006   SCOTLAND / Glasgow & District   425

GLASGOW. **Buchanan Castle Golf Club,** Buchanan Estate, Drymen, Glasgow G63 0HY (01360 660307). *Location:* A811, one mile beyond Croftamie village. Flat parkland course. 18 holes, 6052 yards. S.S.S. 69. 9 hole putting area. *Green Fees:* weekdays £38.00 per round , £48.00 per day; weekends £48.00 per round. *Eating facilities:* full catering and bar available. *Visitors:* welcome except Tuesday and Saturday mornings. *Society Meetings:* welcome Thursdays and Fridays only. Professional: Keith Baxter (01360 660330). Secretary: David Begbie (01360 660307; Fax: 01360 870382).
e-mail: buchanancastle@sol.co.uk
website: www.buchanancastlegolfclub.com

GLASGOW. **Cambuslang Golf Club,** 30 Westburn Drive, Cambuslang (0141-641 3130). *Location:* half a mile north of Cambuslang main street. Parkland. 9 holes, 6146 yards. S.S.S. 69. *Green Fees:* information not available. *Eating facilities:* bar snacks, lunches, evening meals. *Visitors:* welcome if introduced by a member. *Society Meetings:* by arrangement. Secretary: R.M. Dunlop.*

GLASGOW. **Cathcart Castle Golf Club,** Mearns Road, Clarkston, Glasgow G76 7YL (0141-638 0082). *Location:* one and a half miles from Clarkston Toll. Undulating parkland course. 18 holes, 5832 yards. S.S.S. 69. *Green Fees:* information not available. *Eating facilities:* full catering available, lounge bar. *Visitors:* welcome weekdays by prior arrangement. *Society Meetings:* weekdays by application. Professional: Stephen Duncan (0141-638 3436). Secretary: I.G. Sutherland (0141-638 9449).*

GLASGOW. **Cathkin Braes Golf Club,** Cathkin Road, Rutherglen, Glasgow G73 4SE (0141-634 6605). Moorland course. 18 holes, 6208 yards. S.S.S. 71. Practice ground. *Green Fees:* £33.00 per round. *Eating facilities:* available. *Visitors:* welcome Monday to Friday by prior arrangement. *Society Meetings:* catered for. Professional: Stephen Bree (0141-634 0650). Secretary/Treasurer: David Moir.
e-mail: golf@cathkinbraes.freesave.co.uk
website: www.cathkinbraesgolfclub.co.uk

GLASGOW. **Cawder Golf Club,** Cadder Road, Bishopbriggs, Glasgow G64 3QD (0141-761 1280; Fax: 0141-761 1285). *Location:* A803 north of city. Parkland. Cawder: 18 holes, 6305 yards, 5737 metres. S.S.S. 71. Keir: 18 holes, 5891 yards, 5373 metres. S.S.S. 68. Practice area. *Green Fees:* information not available. *Eating facilities:* lunches, high teas, dinners available. *Visitors:* welcome when playing with member. *Society Meetings:* catered for mid-week. Professional: Ken Stevely (0141-772 7102). Secretary: (0141-761 1281).*
e-mail: secretary@cawdergolfclub.org.uk
website: www.cawdergolfclub.org.uk

GLASGOW. **Clober Golf Club,** Craigton Road, Milngavie G62 7HP (0141-956 1685). *Location:* five minutes from Milngavie centre, seven miles from Glasgow city centre. Parkland course. 18 holes, 4963 yards. S.S.S. 65. *Green Fees:* weekdays £22.00 per round. *Eating facilities:* morning coffee, lunches, high teas. *Visitors:* welcome Monday to Thursday before 4pm, some Fridays also before 4pm; not at weekends unless introduced by a member. *Society Meetings:* catered for. Professional: J. McFadyen. (0141-956 6963; Fax: 0141-955 1416). Secretary: Brian Davidson (0141-956 1685).
e-mail: clobergolfclub@btopenworld.com
website: www.clober.co.uk

GLASGOW. **Cowglen Golf Club,** 301 Barrhead Road, Glasgow G43 1AU (0141-632 0556). *Location:* south-west Glasgow, follow M77 from Glasgow taking Pollok turnoff, turn left at traffic lights. Course half mile on right. Undulating parkland course. 18 holes, 6079 yards, 5559 metres. S.S.S. 69. Extensive practice facilities available. *Green Fees:* information not available. *Eating facilities:* full catering facilities available. *Visitors:* welcome if arranged beforehand with Secretary. Lockers and showers available. *Society Meetings:* restricted numbers, apply to Secretary. Professional: Simon Payne (0141-649 9401). Secretary: Ronald J.G. Jamieson, C.A. (Tel & Fax: 01505 503000).*
e-mail: r.jamiesonaccountants@fsmail.net

GLASGOW. **Crow Wood Golf Club,** Garnkirk House, Cumbernauld Road, Muirhead G69 9JF (0141-779 2011). *Location:* on A80 on Stirling Road, six miles north east of Glasgow. Wooded parkland. 18 holes, 6160 yards. S.S.S. 70. Practice area. *Green Fees:* weekdays £23.00 per round, £34.00 per day (incl. third-party insurance). *Eating facilities:* fully licensed, snacks or full meals served all day. *Visitors:* welcome Monday to Friday except Bank Holidays and only by arrangement with Secretary. *Society Meetings:* catered for as visitors. Professional: Brian Moffat (0141-779 1943). Secretary: F.M. Davidson (0141-779 4954).

GLASGOW. **Douglas Park Golf Club,** Hillfoot, Bearsden, Glasgow G61 2TJ (0141-942 2220). *Location:* adjacent to railway station, Hillfoot, Bearsden, off Milngavie Road. Undulating parkland course. 18 holes, 5962 yards. S.S.S. 69. *Green Fees:* £23.00 per round, £31.00 per day. *Eating facilities:* full service available, usual licensing hours. *Visitors:* must be introduced and play with member. *Society Meetings:* Wednesdays and Thursdays on application to Secretary. Professional: David B. Scott (0141-942 1482). Secretary: J.G. Fergusson (Tel & Fax: 0141-942 0985).

GLASGOW. **Dullatur Golf Club,** 1A Glen Douglas Drive, Cumbernauld G68 0DW (01236 723230; Fax: 01236 727271). *Location:* 12 miles east of Glasgow - leave A80 for Dullatur then off third roundabout (Craigmarloch). Moorland, rolling courses. Two courses Antonine, 5205 yards and Carrickstone, 5673 yards. 36 holes, S.S.S. 70. *Green Fees:* information not available. *Eating facilities:* full catering facilities. *Visitors:* welcome. Smart casual dress required in clubhouse. Full leisure centre. *Society Meetings:* welcome, book through Secretary. Professional: Duncan Sinclair (01236 723230; Fax: 01236 727271). Secretary: Graeme Campbell. *

Glasgow & District / SCOTLAND

GLASGOW. East Kilbride Golf Club, Chapelside Road, Nerston, East Kilbride G74 4PH (013552 20913). *Location:* Glasgow Road exit from East Kilbride. Parkland course with variable topography. 18 holes, 6419 yards. S.S.S. 71. *Green Fees:* weekdays £25.00 per round, £35.00 per day. *Eating facilities:* full bar and catering facilities seven days per week. *Visitors:* welcome weekdays only. *Society Meetings:* catered for weekdays only. Professional: Paul McKay (01355 222192). Secretary: W.G. Gray (01355 247728).

GLASGOW. The East Renfrewshire Golf Club, Pilmuir, Newton Mearns, Glasgow G77 6RT (01355 500256). *Location:* off M77, on A77, one and a half miles south of Newton Mearns. Moorland course with plantations of evergreen trees. 18 holes, 6097 yards, 5577 metres. S.S.S. 70. Practice ground. *Green Fees:* weekdays £40.00 per round, £50.00 per day. *Eating facilities:* by prior arrangement with club caterer. *Visitors:* welcome except Saturdays but always by prior arrangement with Professional. *Society Meetings:* welcomed weekdays on prior application. Professional: Stewart Russell (01355 500256). Secretary: Graham Tennant (01355 500256; Fax: 01355 500323).
e-mail: secretary@eastrengolfclub.co.uk
website: www.eastrengolfclub.co.uk

GLASGOW. Eastwood Golf Club, Muirshield, Loganswell, Newton Mearns, Glasgow G77 6RX (01355 500261). *Location:* on A77 road to Kilmarnock two miles south of Newton Mearns. Moorland course. 18 holes, 6071 yards. S.S.S. 70. Par 70. Practice area. *Green Fees:* weekdays £30.00 per round, £40.00 per day. *Eating facilities:* snacks or full meals available. *Visitors:* welcome weekdays on application to Secretary. *Visiting parties:* welcomed on prior application. Professional: I.J. Darroch (01355 500285). Secretary: I.M. Brown (01355 500280).

GLASGOW. Esporta (Dougalston Golf Club), Strathblane Road, Milngavie, Glasgow G62 8HA (0141-955 2404; Fax: 0141-955 2406). *Location:* A81 half a mile from Milngavie. Parkland course set in woodland estate. 18 holes, 6040 yards. S.S.S. 70, par 71. Practice ground, putting green, practice nets. *Green Fees:* weekdays £25.00, weekends £35.00. Subject to review for 2006. *Eating facilities:* restaurant, sports bar and leisure facilities. *Visitors:* welcome weekdays 8am to 4.30pm. Buggies available. *Society Meetings:* welcome weekdays. Weekends subject to availability. Other facilities include 25 metre swimming pool, along with a health suite, aerobic studios, air-conditioning fitness area, gymnasium, indoor - outdoor tennis, Sports Bar and banqueting facilities. Professional: Craig Everett (0141-955 2404; Fax: 0141-955 2406). Secretary: Hilda Everett (0141-955 2434; Fax: 0141-955 2406).

GLASGOW. Glasgow Golf Club, Killermont, Bearsden, Glasgow G61 2TW (0141-942 1713). *Location:* taking Maryhill Road out of Glasgow turn right at Killermont Avenue, half a mile before Canniesburn Toll and then turn immediately right again. Tree-lined parkland. 18 holes, 5977 yards. S.S.S. 69, Par 70. *Green Fees:* on application. *Eating facilities:* bar and dining room. *Visitors:* only if introduced by member; no visitors at weekends. *Society Meetings:* by application to Club Secretary. Professional: Jack Steven (0141-942 8507). Secretary: D.W. Deas (0141-942 2011; Fax: 0141-942 0770).
e-mail: secretary@glasgow-golf.com

GLASGOW. Haggs Castle Golf Club, Dumbreck Road, Dumbreck, Glasgow G41 4SN (0141-427 0480). *Location:* off Junction 1 of M77 from Glasgow. Flat, tree-lined course. 18 holes, 6426 yards. S.S.S. 71. Practice area and putting green. *Green Fees:* weekdays £40.00 per round, £50.00 per day. Weekends, members only. *Eating facilities:* full catering available. *Visitors:* welcome except weekends; must book through Professional. Handicap Certificate required. Golf shoes must be worn. *Society Meetings:* by arrangement through Secretary. Professional: C. Elliott (0141-427 3355). Secretary/Manager: Alan Williams (Tel & Fax: 0141-427 1157).

GLASGOW. Hayston Golf Club, Campsie Road, Kirkintilloch, Glasgow G66 1RN (0141-776 1244). *Location:* 10 miles north-east of Glasgow and one mile north of Kirkintilloch. Parkland course with tree-lined fairways. 18 holes, 6042 yards. S.S.S. 70. Practice area. *Green Fees:* information not available. *Eating facilities:* lunches, dinners, bar snacks. *Society Meetings:* Tuesdays, Wednesdays and Thursdays on application to Secretary, max 240. Professional: Steve Barnett (0141-775 0882). Secretary: J.V. Carmichael (0141-775 0723;Fax: 0141-776 9030).*
e-mail: secretary@haystongolf.com
website: www.haystongolf.com

GLASGOW. Hilton Park Golf Club, Stockiemuir Road, Milngavie, Glasgow G62 7HB (0141-956 4657). *Location:* on A809. Moorland courses. Allander course: 18 holes, 5487 yards. S.S.S. 67. Hilton course: 18 holes, 6054 yards. S.S.S. 70. Practice area. *Green Fees:* £25.00 per round, £35.00 per day. *Eating facilities:* full catering and bar. *Visitors:* on application to the Secretary (not at weekends). *Society Meetings:* as visitors. Professional: W. McCondichie (0141-956 5125). Secretary: Mrs J.A. Dawson (0141-956 4657/5124).

GLASGOW. Kirkhill Golf Club, Greenlees Road, Cambuslang, Glasgow G72 8YN (0141-641 3083). *Location:* between Rutherglen and East Kilbride adjacent to A749, three miles from East Kilbride. Slightly hilly parkland course. 18 holes, 6030 yards. S.S.S. 70. Practice area. *Green Fees:* information not available. *Eating facilities:* dining room and bar. *Visitors:* welcome weekdays only. *Society Meetings:* welcome weekdays only. Hon. Professional: D. Williamson (0141-641 7972). Hon. Secretary: Carol Downes (Tel & Fax: 0141-641 8499).
e-mail: secretary@kirkhillgolfclub.org.uk
website: www.kirkhillgolfclub.org.uk

GLASGOW. Knightswood Golf Club, Lincoln Avenue, Glasgow G13 3DN (0141-959 6358). *Location:* west along Great Western Road, turn left into Lincoln Avenue. Flat parkland course. 9 holes, 2792 yards. S.S.S. 67. *Green Fees:* £3.60 for 9 holes. Passport to Recreation holders £1.80 weekdays until 3.30pm. Subject to review. *Visitors:* tee reserved for

THE GOLF GUIDE 2006 SCOTLAND / Glasgow & District 427

Club Wednesdays and Fridays 8am to 9am and 10am to 11am, otherwise no restrictions. 24 hours' notice required. Ladies' and gents' changing areas. *Society Meetings:* welcome, as for visitors. Secretary: James Lavery (0141-954 8614).

GLASGOW. **Lethamhill Golf Course,** 1240 Cumbernauld Road, Glasgow G33 1AH (0141-770 6220; Fax: 0141-770 0520). *Location:* 100 yards off M8 Junction 12. Parkland, many holes with views of Hogganfield Loch. 18 holes, 5836 yards. S.S.S. 68. 18 holes pitch and putt course. *Green Fees:* information not available. *Visitors:* welcome at all times - this is a public course, 24 hour in advance booking system. Ladies and gents changing. *Society Meetings:* contact Golf Professional G. Taggart (0141-770 7135).*

GLASGOW. **Linn Park Golf Club,** Simshill Road, Glasgow G44 5EP (0141-633 0377). *Location:* five miles south of city centre near Carmunnock Road, near Croftfoot roundabout. Parkland. 18 holes, 5005 yards. S.S.S. 66. *Green Fees:* information not available. *Visitors:* welcome, 24 hours notice required. *Society Meetings:* all welcome. Secretary: T. Dunn (0141-633 0377).

GLASGOW. **Littlehill Golf Club,** Auchinairn Road, Bishopbriggs, Glasgow G64 1UT. *Location:* from Glasgow on A803, turn off for Stobhill Hospital. Flat, parkland. 18 holes, 6364 yards. S.S.S. 70. Small practice area. *Green Fees:* information not available. *Eating facilities:* canteen open five days weekly in season, three outwith. *Visitors:* welcome without reservation - pay and play. *Society Meetings:* no restrictions. Professional: Kevin Hughes (0141-762 3998). Secretary: W. Burke. *

GLASGOW. **Milngavie Golf Club,** Laighpark, Milngavie, Glasgow G62 8EP (0141-956 1619; Fax: 0141-956 4252). *Location:* situated off Glasgow to Drymen road approximately one mile past Stockiemuir Service Station, turn right at signpost. Moorland course. 18 holes, 5818 yards. S.S.S. 68. *Green Fees:* on application. *Eating facilities:* catering available. *Visitors:* welcome when introduced by member or by prior arrangement with the Secretary. *Society Meetings:* catered for. Secretary: S. Woods.*

GLASGOW. **Pollok Golf Club,** 90 Barrhead Road, Glasgow G43 1BG (0141-632 1080; Fax: 0141-649 1398). *Location:* Junction 2 M77. Wooded parkland. 18 holes, 6358 yards. S.S.S. 70. *Green Fees:* £50.00 per round. *Eating facilities:* dining room and bar. *Visitors:* welcome with reservation by letter or telephone to Secretary. No visitors Saturday or Sunday. *Society Meetings:* catered for by letter. Secretary: Ian Cumming (0141-632 4351; Fax: 0141-649 1398).

GLASGOW. **Rouken Glen Golf Centre,** Stewarton Road, Thornliebank, Glasgow G46 7UZ (0141-638 7044 or 0141-620 0826). *Location:* on Stewarton Road at Rouken Glen Park, only 250 yards from the A726. Parkland with wooded features, designed by James Braid. 18 holes, 4800 yards. S.S.S. 63 (Par 64). 15-bay floodlit driving range. *Green Fees:* information not available. *Eating facilities:* catering and bar facilities available. *Visitors:* welcome all week. Shop, club hire, etc. *Society Meetings:* bookings taken. Professional: (0141-638 7044). Secretary: Christine Cosh (0141-632 6816).*

GLASGOW. **Sandyhills Golf Club,** 223 Sandyhills Road, Glasgow G32 9NA (0141-778 1179). *Location:* three miles east from centre of Glasgow. Parkland. 18 holes, 6253 yards. S.S.S. 71. *Green Fees:* information not available. *Eating facilities:* full catering facilities available. *Visitors:* welcome when introduced by a member. *Society Meetings:* welcome by prior arrangement. Secretary: C.J. Wilson C.A. (01698 282062; Fax: 01698 425840).

GLASGOW. **Whitecraigs Golf Club,** 72 Ayr Road, Giffnock, Glasgow G46 6SW (0141-639 4530; Fax: 0141-616 3648). *Location:* on A77 south of city, two miles from Eastwoodmains roundabout. Parkland course. 18 holes, 6013 yards. S.S.S. 70. *Green Fees:* £40.00 per round, £50.00 per day (includes food). *Eating facilities:* restaurant and lounge bar. *Visitors:* welcome mid week, letter of introduction required. *Society Meetings:* catered for Wednesday only. Professional: Alastair Forrow (0141-639 2140). Secretary: Alan Keith (0141-639 4530).

GLASGOW. **Williamwood Golf Club,** Clarkston Road, Glasgow G44 3YR (0141-637 1783; Fax: 0141-637 6688). *Location:* behind service station on Clarkston Road. Attractive parkland course designed by James Braid. 18 holes, 5878 yards. S.S.S. 69. Practice area and putting. *Green Fees:* information not available. *Eating facilities:* meals must be ordered. *Visitors:* welcome by arrangement with Secretary or Professional. *Society Meetings:* weekdays only by arrangement. Professional: Stewart G. Marshall (0141-637 2715; Fax: 0141-637 2600). Secretary: R.J. Templeton (0141-637 1783; Fax: 0141-571 0166).*

GLASGOW. **Windyhill Golf Club,** Baljaffray Road, Bearsden, Glasgow G61 4QQ (0141-942 2349; Fax: 0141-942 5874). *Location:* one mile north from Bearsden Cross. Undulating parkland course. 18 holes, 6254 yards. S.S.S. 70. Practice area. *Green Fees:* £35.00; weekends £6.00 with member only. *Eating facilities:* full catering and bar. *Visitors:* welcome weekdays only. *Society Meetings:* welcome weekdays by arrangement. Professional: Christopher Duffy (0141-942 7157; Fax: 0141-942 5874). Secretary: James M. Young (0141-942 2349; Fax: 0141-942 5874).

KILSYTH. **Kilsyth Lennox Golf Club,** Tak-Ma-Doon Road, Kilsyth, Glasgow G65 0RS (01236 824115). *Location:* 12 miles from Glasgow on A80. Parkland/moorland, undulating ground with superb views across central Scotland. 18 holes, 5912 yards. S.S.S. 70. *Green Fees:* information not available. *Eating facilities:* new clubhouse. *Visitors:* welcome weekdays up to 5.00pm, Saturdays after 5.00pm, not Sundays. *Society Meetings:* welcome, details on application. Professional: R. Abercrombie. Secretary: A.G. Stevenson (01236 823213).*

Highlands (North)

BONAR BRIDGE. **Bonar Bridge-Ardgay Golf Club,** Market Stance, Migdale Road, Bonar Bridge IV24 3EJ (01863 766199). *Location:* off the A9, driving north cross Bonar Bridge, straight up hill for half a mile. Wooded heathland. 9 holes, 5284 yards. S.S.S. 65. *Green Fees:* £15.00 per day (2005). Subject to review. *Eating facilities:* limited catering available May to September. *Visitors:* always welcome. *Society Meetings:* limited to weekdays. Joint Secretary: John Reid (01863 766750).
e-mail: bonarardgaygolf@aol.com

BRORA. **Brora Golf Club,** 43 Golf Road, Brora KW9 6QS (+44 (0)1408 621417; Fax: +44 (0)1408 622157). *Location:* 52 miles north of Inverness on A9 trunk road. Traditional links course designed by James Braid. 18 holes, 6110 yards. S.S.S. 70. Practice ground available. *Green Fees:* weekdays £32.00 per round, £37.00 per day; weekends £37.00 per round, £42.00 per day. *Eating facilities:* full catering, bar facilities April to October. *Visitors:* welcome anytime except on tournament days, advisable to book tee times in season. Welcome to participate in open events (Certificate of Handicap required). Carts, caddies, etc available. *Society Meetings:* by arrangement with Secretary. Secretary: Tony Gill (01408 621417; Fax: 01408 622157).
e-mail: secretary@broragolf.co.uk

DORNOCH. **Royal Dornoch Golf Club,** Golf Road, Dornoch IV25 3LW (01862 810219; Fax: 01862 810792). *Location:* one mile from A9 between Tain and Golspie. Seaside links. Championship Course and Struie Course. Championship: 18 holes, 6514 yards, 5958 metres. S.S.S. 73; Struie: 18 holes, 6276 yards, 5793 metres. S.S.S. 70. Practice area. *Green Fees:* Championship Course: weekdays £72.00 per round, weekends £82.00 per round. Struie Course: £29.00 per round, £47.00 day ticket. Combination Day Ticket (one round each course) £85.00 weekdays, £95.00 weekends. All green fees are subject to alteration. *Eating facilities:* available. *Visitors:* welcome, no major restrictions other than competitions – bookings can be heavy. Saturdays members only until late afternoon. Handicap Certificates – Men 24, Ladies 35. *Society Meetings:* must be arranged through the Secretary. Professional: A. Skinner (01862 810902; Fax; 01862 811095). Secretary: J.S. Duncan (01862 810219; Fax: 01862 810792).
e-mail: bookings@royaldornoch.com
website: www.royaldornoch.com

www.uk-golfguide.com

Royal Marine Hotel & Leisure Club

Golf Road, Brora, Sutherland KW9 6QS
Telephone: (01408) 621252 • Fax: (01408) 621181
e-mail: info@highlandescape.com
website: www.highlandescapehotels.com

Play traditional links golf and stay in a traditional Highland hotel. Adjacent to James Braid's 18-hole Brora Links, the Royal Marine Hotel combines the ambience of a bygone era with the facilities and comforts expected by the modern traveller. Choice of three restaurants and two bars. Indoor swimming pool and leisure club. AA rosette for food. A warm welcome awaits you. Luxury apartments overlooking golf course available to let.

AA ★★★

See also Colour Advertisement on page 73

Ideally situated in 4.5 acres of grounds and gardens, a few minutes' walk from the famous Royal Dornoch Golf Course.
* 29 bedrooms, all en suite, with colour TV and tea/coffee making.
* A la carte Restaurant • Bar meals available
* Golf on Royal Dornoch and other local courses can be arranged, as well as loch and river fishing.
* Children and dogs welcome.

THE BURGHFIELD HOUSE HOTEL, DORNOCH IV25 3HN
TEL: 01862 810212 • FAX: 01862 810404
burghfield@cali.co.uk • www.burghfieldhouse.com

See also Colour Advertisement on page 73

THE ROYAL DORNOCH GOLF CLUB

The Championship Course, Royal Dornoch, is rated by Golf Digest Magazine 5th in the World's top courses outside the USA. It is a classic links, providing both pleasure to the eye and a challenge to the golfer's skills. Links golf, some would argue, is the truest form of golf. Dornoch is considered the finest northerly course in the world, and offers a delicious feeling of getting away from it all.

On the Championship and the Struie Course, Royal Dornoch aims to provide traditional "links golf" of the highest quality. Golfers and their friends will be made welcome to enjoy "Highland Hospitality" in an informal relaxed style in the clubhouse where they may partake of fine Scottish beverages and food.

Green Fees 2005:
Championship Course
£72 weekdays   £82 weekends
Struie Course
£29 per round   £47 per day
Combination day ticket
(one round each course)
£85 weekdays   £95 weekends
Verification of maximum Handicap
24 men, 35 ladies – required

Tel Reservations: 01862 810219 ext 185
Fax: 01862 810792
bookings@royaldornoch.com
www.royaldornoch.com
GOLF ROAD, DORNOCH,
SUTHERLAND IV25 3LW

DORNOCH. **The Carnegie Golf Club at Skibo Castle,** Skibo Castle, Dornoch (01862 894600; Fax: 01862 894601). *Location:* off A9 between Tain and Dornoch. Links course, built on peninsula, naturally contoured; Donald Steel designed. 18 holes, 6671 yards. S.S.S. 72. Practice facilities. *Green Fees:* information not available. *Eating facilities:* bar, luncheon table. *Visitors:* by prior arrangement, write or telephone only. Private members club, daily golf membership available, must be booked in advance. *Society Meetings:* welcome. Accommodation available, charges on request. Golf Secretary: Sharon Stewart. Professional: David Thomson (01862 881260).*
e-mail: sharon.stewart@carnegieclubs.com

DURNESS. **Durness Golf Club,** Balnakiel, Durness. *Location:* 57 miles northwest of Lairg on A838. Links course with final hole played over deep gully. 9 greens, 18 tees, 5555 yards. S.S.S 69. *Green Fees:* £15.00 per day. Weekly ticket £50.00. *Eating facilities:* snacks available 12-5pm June to September. *Visitors:* welcome without reservation, only restriction on Sunday mornings. *Society Meetings:* by arrangement. Secretary: Lucy MacKay (01971 511364).

GOLSPIE. **Golspie Golf Club,** Ferry Road, Golspie KW10 6ST (01408 633266; Fax: 01408 633393). *Location:* 53 miles on A9 north of Inverness. Fairly flat course, seaside links and wooded. 18 holes, 5990 yards. S.S.S. 68. Practice area available. *Green Fees:* £25.00 per round, £40.00 per day (7 days). *Eating facilities:* bar and catering service, available during season. *Visitors:* welcome, no restrictions except on competition days. Carts, caddies must be booked in advance. *Society Meetings:* welcome by prior arrangement, packages available. Golf Shop.
e-mail: info@golspie-golf-club.co.uk
website: www.golspie-golf-club.co.uk

GRANTOWN-ON-SPEY. **Grantown-on-Spey Golf Club,** The Clubhouse, Golf Course Road, Grantown-on-Spey PH26 3HY (01479 872079; Fax: 01479 873725). *Location:* turn off main road opposite police station. Parkland and woodland. 18 holes, 5710 yards, S.S.S. 68, Par 70. Practice ground and putting green. *Green Fees:* weekdays £25.00 per round, £30.00 per day; weekends £30.00 per round, £35.00 per day. Evening round £15.00. 50% reduction for under 18s. *Eating facilities:* full bar and catering facilities. *Visitors:* welcome, members have priority before 10am weekends. Shop. *Society Meetings:* welcome except before 10am weekends. Secretary: James Macpherson (01479 872079/ 873154; Fax: 01479 873725).
e-mail: secretary@grantownonspeygolfclub.co.uk
website: www.grantownonspeygolfclub.co.uk

HELMSDALE. **Helmsdale Golf Club,** Golf Road, Helmsdale KW8 6JA. *Location:* on A9, 28 miles north of Dornoch, follow signs for Melvich. undulating parkland/moorland course. 9 holes, 3720 yards. S.S.S. 61 (2 x 9 holes). *Green Fees:* information not available. Life membership now available, contact Secretary. *Visitors:* welcome at all times. *Society Meetings:* welcome by appointment. Secretary: Ronald Sutherland (01431 821063). *

LYBSTER. **Lybster Golf Club,** Main Street, Lybster. *Location:* 14 miles south from Wick on A9, half-way down village street. One of smallest courses in Scotland, heathland/parkland. 9 holes, 1929 yards. S.S.S. 61. *Green Fees:* £10.00 per round/day (adults); £5.00 per round/day (juniors). *Eating facilities:* at nearby hotels in village. *Visitors:* welcome anytime. *Society Meetings:* welcome anytime. Full membership available. Secretary: Alex Calder.
website: www.lybstergolfclub.co.uk

REAY. **Reay Golf Club,** Clubhouse, Reay, By Thurso KW14 7RE (01847 811288). *Location:* 12 miles west of nearest main town of Thurso. Most northerly 18 hole seaside links. 18 holes, 5831 yards. S.S.S. 69. *Green Fees:* £20.00 per day, £60.00 per week. Rates available for fortnight – information from Secretary. *Eating facilities:* restricted: bar open 12-3pm, 8-11pm daily July/August. *Visitors:* welcome anytime, restricted during competitions. *Society Meetings:* welcome, advance bookings via Secretary. Captain: Graeme Dunnett. Secretary: Bill McIntosh (01847 811288).
e-mail: info@reaygolfclub.co.uk
website: www.reaygolfclub.co.uk
www.caithnessgolfweek.co.uk
www.scottishopengolf.co.uk

THURSO. **Thurso Golf Club,** Newlands of Geise, By Thurso, KW14 7XF (01847 893807). *Location:* two miles from Railway Station, on road to Reay via Westfield. Flat parkland with newly planted trees. 18 holes, 5828 yards, 5290 metres. S.S.S. 69. *Green Fees:* £20.00 per day weekdays and weekends. *Eating facilities:* snacks available in the bar during the day June to August. *Visitors:* welcome, no restrictions. *Society Meetings:* welcome, notice required. Secretary: R.M. Black (01847 892575).

WICK. **Wick Golf Club,** Reiss, By Wick KW1 4RW (01955 602726). *Location:* three miles north of Wick on A9. Seaside links course. 18 holes, 6123 yards. S.S.S. 71. Practice area. *Green Fees:* £20.00 per day. *Eating facilities:* licensed; snacks available. *Visitors:* welcome. *Society Meetings:* catered for. Secretary: D.D. Slearer (01955 602935).

www.uk-golfguide.com

Highlands (Mid)

ALNESS. **Alness Golf Club,** Ardross Road, Alness IV17 0QA (01349 883877). *Location:* 20 miles from Inverness; turn into Alness from A9 (north). Beautiful surroundings with views over Cromarty Firth and Alness River. 18 holes, 4886 yards. S.S.S. 64. Practice green available. *Green Fees:* £22.00 per round weekdays, £25.00 per day weekdays, £25.00 per round weekends, £27.00 per day weekends, £50.00 weekly ticket. *Eating facilities:* licensed bar with hot meals available. *Visitors:* welcome all week. Changing rooms, hot showers; clubs and trolleys for hire. PGA Pro Shop, lessons available. *Society Meetings:* welcome with advance notice. Secretary: Alan Black (01349 883877).

FORTROSE. **Fortrose and Rosemarkie Golf Club,** Ness Road East, Fortrose IV10 8SE (01381 620529; Fax: 01381 621328). *Location:* on the Black Isle. A9 north from Inverness, across Kessock Bridge, through Munlochy, follow signs to Fortrose. Good links course, sea both sides. 18 holes, 5875 yards. S.S.S. 69. Practice area available Summer. *Green Fees:* information not available. *Eating facilities:* catering available. *Visitors:* welcome without reservation. *Society Meetings:* catered for.*
e-mail: enquiries@fortrosegolfclub.co.uk
website: www.fortrosegolfclub.co.uk

GAIRLOCH. **Gairloch Golf Club,** Gairloch IV21 2BE (01445 712 407). *Location:* 75 miles west of Inverness on the A832. Seaside links with superb views. 9 holes, 4108 yards. S.S.S. 62 over 18 holes. Practice net. *Green Fees:* £16.00 per round, £20.00 per day, £60.00 per week. Juniors £10.00 per day, £35.00 per week. Subject to review. *Eating facilities:* licensed bar and light refreshments available. *Visitors:* welcome anytime but must be regular golfers. Tee times must be booked during the summer season – call clubhouse for details. *Society Meetings:* welcome, no restrictions. Secretary: B. Jeffrey (01445 731 680).
e-mail: secretary@gairlochgc.freeserve.co.uk
website: www.gairlochgolfclub.com

INVERGORDON. **Invergordon Golf Club,** King George Street, Invergordon IV18 0BD (01349 852715). *Location:* A9 (B817), two miles, west side of town. Relatively flat, parkland. 18 holes, over 6020 yards. S.S.S. 69. Practice area. *Green Fees:* £25.00 per round, £30.00 per day ticket. *Eating facilities:* bar, bar snacks - normal licensing hours. *Visitors:* welcome without restrictions other than club competition times. Locker rooms. Club/caddy carts for hire. *Society Meetings:* welcome by prior arrangement. Clubhouse Manager: J. Ross (01349 852715).

LOCHCARRON. **Lochcarron Golf Club,** Lochcarron, Ross-shire IV54 8YU. *Location:* one mile east of Lochcarron village by A896. Seaside course, combined parkland and shore. Interesting opening hole. A short course but great accuracy required. 9 holes with some alternative tees for second nine. 3575 yards (18 holes). S.S.S. 60. *Green Fees:* £12.00 per day; £50.00 per week. Juniors (under 16 years old) half price. *Eating facilities:* snacks and refreshments available in clubhouse. *Visitors:* welcome anytime except Saturdays between 2pm and 5pm. Bookings not required. Clubs for hire. *Society Meetings:* welcome. Secretary: Peter White (01520 722206).

MUIR OF ORD. **The Muir of Ord Golf Club,** Great North Road, Muir of Ord IV6 7SX (01463 870825; Fax: 01463 871867). *Location:* 15 miles north of Inverness beside A862, 12 miles north of Inverness on A832. Heathland, moorland course, excellent greens. 18 holes, 5559 yards. S.S.S. 68. Practice area. *Green Fees:* weekdays £18.00 per round, £22.00 per day; weekends £25.00 per round, £30.00 per day. Discounts of £1.00 per player if more than 14 players in party; weekends by appointment. *Eating facilities:* lounge bar (snacks all day), meals weekends or by appointment. *Visitors:* welcome weekdays outwith competition times, weekends by appointment. Trolleys available; buggy hire. *Society Meetings:* welcome. Shop (01463 871311). Secretary/Administrator: Mrs J. Gibson (01463 870825).

FORTROSE & ROSEMARKIE GOLF CLUB
NESS ROAD EAST, FORTROSE, ROSS-SHIRE IV10 8SE
Tel: 01381 620529 • Fax: 01381 621328
e-mail: secretary@fortrosegolfclub.co.uk • www.fortrosegolfclub.co.uk

This James Braid designed links has been acclaimed by golf writers as "a gem of a course" and "perhaps the brightest jewel in the Highlands' golfing crown".

Small deceptive greens and strategically placed bunkers, as well as sea alongside eight holes and gorse waiting to devour the wayward shot inland, all add up to a greater golfing experience than many a longer course. This private club, established in 1888, gives a warm welcome to visitors in the knowledge that they will almost certainly wish to come back. A big off-course attraction is the bottle-nosed dolphins in the Firth in the view of the golfers. 15 miles north of Inverness – take the A832 off A9 North. Green fees £25 per round weekdays, £30 per round weekends. Buggy hire, practice area, putting green, golf shop, catering and bar.

See also Colour Advertisement on page 75

Highlands (Mid) / SCOTLAND

PORTMAHOMACK. Tarbat Golf Club, Tarbatness Road, Portmahomack, Tain IV20 1YB. *Location:* 10 miles east of Tain. B9165 off A9. Seaside links course with scenic views. 9 holes, 5082 yards. S.S.S. 65. Practice area. *Green Fees:* £15 per day. *Eating facilities:* catering April-October, light snacks; local hotels. *Visitors:* welcome, some restrictions Saturdays. *Society Meetings:* welcome, please telephone Secretary. Secretary: Christina Ince (01862 871486).

STRATHPEFFER. **Strathpeffer Spa Golf Club,** Strathpeffer IV14 9AS (01997 421219 or 01997 421011). *Location:* 20 minutes north of Inverness by A9, 5 miles west of Dingwall, quarter of a mile north of Strathpeffer Square (signposted). Upland course, panoramic views of moorland and mountain; water hazards at 3rd, 10th and 11th. 18 holes, 4956 yards. S.S.S. 66. Small practice area and putting green. *Green Fees:* £20.00 per round, £25.00 per day Juniors £10.00 per round, £12.00 per day. Discounts for groups of over 10. *Eating facilities:* bar and catering available seven days a week. *Visitors:* welcome without reservation, but check weekends and competition days. Club, buggy and trolley hire. *Society Meetings:* catered for by arrangement. Clubhouse (Bookings): 01997 421219.
e-mail: mail@strathpeffergolf.co.uk
website: www.strathpeffergolf.co.uk

TAIN. Tain Golf Club, Chapel Road, Tain IV19 1JE (01862 892314; Fax: 01862 892099). *Location:* off A9, 34 miles north of Inverness. Travelling north, turn right in middle of High Street - Golf Club one mile. Traditional links course designed by Old Tom Morris. 18 holes, 6404 yards. S.S.S. 71. All practice facilities available. *Green Fees:* weekdays £36.00 per round, £44.00 per day; weekends £44.00 per round, £50.00 per day. Discounts for parties of 12 or more. All green fees are subject to alteration. *Eating facilities:* full catering, licensed. *Visitors:* welcome anytime except when competitions are being held. Electric buggy, trolley, club hire and shop. *Society Meetings:* catered for. Secretary: Mrs Joanna Bell.
e-mail: info@tain-golfclub.co.uk
website: www.tain-golfclub.co.uk

ULLAPOOL. **Ullapool Golf Club,** North Road, Ullapool IV26 2TH (01854 613323; Fax: 01854 613133). *Location:* situated at the northern outskirts of the village. Parkland seaside course. 18 tees, 9 holes, 5338 yards, S.S.S. 66. 3 hole practice course, bunker, nets. *Green Fees:* £18.00 per day adults, £9.00 per day juniors. *Eating facilities:* catering/bar only available at open competitions and club events. *Visitors:* welcome except during competitions. *Society Meetings:* welcome, group rates by negotiation. Secretary: A. Paterson.
e-mail: info@ullapool-golf.co.uk
website: www.ullapool-golf.co.uk

Strathpeffer Spa Golf Club

Founded in 1888, this is arguably the most scenic course in the North of Scotland, with the drive on the first hole from tee to green featuring the longest drop on any course in the country. Visitors are welcome without reservation (although it is advisable to check in advance). Bar and catering is available daily. Clubs, trolleys and golf buggies are available for hire.

18 holes £18.00 • day ticket £23.00
Special terms for groups • 18 holes, Par 64

Golf Course Road, Strathpeffer, Ross-shire IV14 9AS
01997 421011 or 421219 • www.strathpeffergolf.co.uk
e-mail: mail@strathpeffergolf.co.uk

See also Colour Advertisement on page 75

Visit the FHG website
www.holidayguides.com
for details of the wide choice of accommodation featured in the full range of FHG titles

Highlands (South)

ARISAIG. **Traigh Golf Course,** Traigh, Arisaig PH39 4NT (01687 450 337). *Location:* on A830 Fort William to Mallaig Road, 3 miles north of Arisaig. Seaside links, close to sandy beaches on the beautiful Morar coast. 9 holes, 2456 yards. S.S.S 65. Practice green. *Green Fees:* information not available. *Eating facilities:* unlicensed, soft drinks and confectionery only. *Visitors:* welcome at all times. Clubs may be hired. *Society Meetings:* by arrangement. Manager: Bill Henderson (01687 450337/450645).
website: www.traighgolf.co.uk

BEAULY by. **Aigas Golf Course,** By Beauly IV4 7AD (01463 782942 or 782423). *Location:* A831, five miles from Beauly village. Challenging 9 hole course uniquely set in beautiful Strathglass beside the River Beauly. 9 holes, 2439 yards, S.S.S. 63 (2 x 9 holes). *Green Fees:* information not available.*

BOAT OF GARTEN. **Boat of Garten Golf and Tennis Club,** Boat of Garten PH24 3BQ (01479 831282; Fax: 01479 831523). *Location:* A9 six miles north east of Aviemore. Wooded course with birch tree-lined fairways, very scenic, overlooking Cairngorm Mountains. 18 holes, 5876 yards, 5373 metres. S.S.S. 69. Practice net. *Green Fees:* weekdays £30.00 per round, £35.00 per day; weekends £40.00 per round, £45.00 per day. Subject to review. *Eating facilities:* catering facilities open 9.30am to 8.00pm, bar open 11am to 11pm daily. *Visitors:* welcome 9.30am to 5.30pm. Two tennis courts. *Society Meetings:* welcome. Professional Shop: J. Ingram (01479 831282; Fax: 01479 831523). Secretary: (01479 831282; Fax: 01479 831523).
e-mail: boatgolf@enterprise.net
website: www.boatgolf.com

CARRBRIDGE. **Carrbridge Golf Club,** Inverness Road, Carrbridge PH23 3AU (01479 841623). *Location:* off A9, 27 miles south of Inverness. Moorland/parkland. 9 holes, 5402 yards. S.S.S. 68 Par 71. *Green Fees:* April-September £20.00 weekdays; £22.00 weekends. Reduced rates Juniors and evenings. *Eating facilities:* snacks, coffee and light lunches. Clubhouse open April to October only. *Visitors:* welcome, course closed Sunday mornings for members only. *Society Meetings:* welcome. Secretary: 084441 41415 (lo-call).
website: www.carrbridgegolf.com

CAWDOR CASTLE. **Cawdor Castle Golf Course,** Cawdor Castle, Nairn IV12 5RD (01667 404401; Fax: 01667 404674). *Location:* situated between Inverness and Nairn on the B9090 off A96. Parkland. 9 holes, 1303 yards. S.S.S. 32. *Green Fees:* £8.00 (2005). Subject to review. *Eating facilities:* licensed restaurant in Castle, snack bar in grounds. *Visitors:* welcome every day from 1st May to second Sunday in October, 10am to 5pm.
e-mail: info@cawdorcastle.com
website: www.cawdorcastle.com

FORT AUGUSTUS. **Fort Augustus Golf Club,** Markethill, Fort Augustus (01320 366660). *Location:* half-a-mile south of village on A82. Moorland course, tree lined to north, heather covered hills to the south. 9 holes (18 tees), 5379 yards. S.S.S. 67. *Green Fees:* £12.00 per round, £15.00 per day. *Eating facilities:* lounge bar. *Visitors:* welcome anytime except Saturday afternoons from 1.30pm to 5pm. Clubs and caddy cars for hire. *Society Meetings:* welcome, please book in advance. Secretary: Alex Barnett (01320 366259).

FORT WILLIAM. **Fort William Golf Club,** Torlundy, Fort William PH33 6SN (01397 704464). *Location:* north from Fort William, approx. 3 miles through town. Parkland course. 18 holes, 6217 yards, S.S.S 71. Practice area. *Green Fees:* £22.00 per round, £30.00 per day. *Eating facilities:* snacks available from the bar. *Visitors:* welcome all week except Saturday and Sunday between 8am and 11am. *Society Meetings:* welcome, discount available for parties of more than 15. Secretary: Miss Rosemary MacIntyre.

INVERNESS. **Inverness Golf Club,** The Clubhouse, Culcabock Road, Inverness IV2 3XQ (01463 233422). *Location:* one mile south of town centre. Parkland course. 18 holes, 6256 yards. S.S.S. 70. Two practice grounds. *Green Fees:* £33.00 per round, £42.00 per day. Weekly, fortnightly and monthly tickets by arrangement. *Eating facilities:* sandwiches, lunches, high teas and dinners served at club. *Visitors:* welcome except Saturdays from 25th March to 20th October. *Society Meetings:* catered for, pre-booking essential. Caterer: (01463 233259). Professional: A.P. Thomson (01463 231989). Club Manager: J.S. Thomson (01463 239882; Fax: 01463 240616).
e-mail: igc@freeuk.com
website: www.invernessgolfclub.co.uk

INVERNESS. **Loch Ness Golf Course,** Castle Heather, Inverness IV2 6AA (01463 713335; Fax: 01463 712695). *Location:* on the outskirts of Inverness, heading west along new Ring Road. Parkland course with panoramic views over Inverness and Moray Firth. Loch Ness Golf Course - 18 holes, 6493 yards (yellow), 6772 yards (white). S.S.S. 70 yellow, 72 white. *Green Fees:* weekdays £25.00 per day; weekends £30.00 per day. *Eating facilities:* lounge bar, members lounge, full catering facilities. *Visitors:* welcome. Buggies, carts and caddies available. *Society Meetings:* most welcome by prior arrangement. Professional: Martin Piggot (01463 713334). Secretary: Neil D. Hampton (01463 713335; Fax: 01463 712695).
e-mail: info@golflochness.com
website: www.golflochness.com

www.uk-golfguide.com

434 Highlands (South) / SCOTLAND — THE GOLF GUIDE 2006

INVERNESS. **Torvean Golf Club,** Glenurquhart Road, Inverness (Starter: 01463 711434). *Location:* A82 towards Fort William, approximately one mile from town centre. Parkland course. 18 holes, 5754 yards, S.S.S. 69. *Green Fees:* weekdays £22.00 (Adults), £7.50 (Juniors); weekends £24.50 (Adults), £9.50 (Juniors). *Eating facilities:* all day catering provided year round. *Visitors:* booking preferred, especially at weekends (01463 711434; Fax 01463 711417 – Starters Office). Clubs and trolleys for hire. *Society Meetings:* discounts for parties over 10. Club Manager: Susan Smith.
e-mail: info@torveangolfclub.com

KINGUSSIE. **Kingussie Golf Club,** Gynack Road, Kingussie PH21 1LR (01540 661600). *Location:* half a mile from Kingussie High Street, turning at Duke of Gordon. Hill type course. 18 holes, 5615 yards. S.S.S. 68. *Green Fees:* weekdays £22.00 per round, £27.00 per day; weekends £24.00 per round, £30.00 per day. Juniors £10.00. Weekly (seven days) £70.00. Subject to review. *Eating facilities:* bar and excellent catering. *Visitors:* welcome, certain times reserved for members at weekends. Caravan site. *Society Meetings:* welcome at all times, book in advance. Secretary: Bill Baird (01540 661600).
e-mail: sec@kingussie-golf.co.uk
website: www.kingussie-golf.co.uk

NAIRN. **Nairn Dunbar Golf Club,** Lochloy Road, Nairn IV12 5AE (01667 452741; Fax: 01667 456897). *Location:* off A96, at east end of town. Championship links. 18 holes, 6765 yards. S.S.S. 74. *Green Fees:* information not available. *Eating facilities:* new spacious clubhouse with full catering and visitors facilities. *Visitors:* welcome, also groups. Secretary: Mr Scott Falconer (01667 452741; Fax: 01667 456897). Professional: David Torrance. (01667 453964).*
e-mail: secretary@nairndunbar.com
website: www.nairndunbar.com

NETHYBRIDGE. **Abernethy Golf Club,** Nethybridge PH25 3EB (01479 821305). *Location:* 10 miles from Aviemore lying on the B970 between Boat of Garten and Grantown-on-Spey. Delightful nine hole course close to pine woods and with commanding view of the valley of the River Spey. 9 holes, 5068 yards. S.S.S. 66. *Green Fees:* weekdays £16.00, weekend £18.00. Late weekdays £10.00, late weekend £12.00. Juniors half price. *Eating facilities:* clubhouse is unlicensed but there are full catering facilities available. *Visitors:* welcome subject to short restrictions when club competitions being held. *Society Meetings:* by arrangement with the Secretary. Secretary: Mrs Janette McCool.
e-mail: info@abernethygolfclub.com
website: www.abernethygolfclub.com

NEWTONMORE. **Newtonmore Golf Club,** Golf Course Road, Newtonmore PH20 1AT (01540 673878; Fax: 01540 670147). *Location:* turn off A9 at Newtonmore, course in centre of village, 45 miles south of Inverness. Mainly flat course set by River Spey amidst beautiful scenery. 18 holes, 6029 yards. S.S.S. 69. Practice green. *Green Fees:* weekdays £20.00 per round, £30.00 per day; weekends £25.00 per round, £35.00 per day. Subject to review. Special midweek breaks available, apply Secretary. *Eating facilities:* full catering (except Tuesdays) and bar facilities. *Visitors:* welcome by appointment with Secretary. Locker and shower facilities. *Society Meetings:* all welcome. Professional: Robert Henderson (01540 673611). Secretary: Charles Bisset (01540 673878; Fax: 01540 670147).

SPEAN BRIDGE. **Spean Bridge Golf Club,** Station Road, Spean Bridge PH34 4EU. *Location:* on main A82, eight miles north of Fort William. Wooded course set on the hillside, full view of Nevis Range ski slopes and Ben Nevis. 9 holes, 2271 yards. S.S.S. 63. *Green Fees:* £12.00 day ticket. *Eating facilities:* Hotel nearby. *Visitors:* welcome, tees reserved Sundays 12 noon to 4pm. *Society Meetings:* all welcome. Secretary: K. Dalziel (07710 105478).

NAIRN DUNBAR GOLF CLUB
LOCHLOY ROAD, NAIRN IV12 5AE
TEL: **01667 452741**
FAX: **01667 456897**
secretary@nairndunbar.com
www.nairndunbar.com

Situated on the shores of the Moray Firth, this is a highly rated Scottish links Championship course, renowned for its excellent condition and friendly welcome for visitors. Described by Peter Alliss as "one of Scotland's hidden gems"

Clubhouse with comfortable lounge bars, dining room, extensive locker room facilities with visitors' room and showers • Patio area with BBQ • Pro Shop

---

FHG
For full details of clubs and courses, plus convenient accommodation
www.uk-golfguide.com

The Open of 2006

The Spey Valley Championship Golf Course is due to open in May 2006. Set in some of the most breathtaking scenery in the Highlands, if not the world, it's predicted to be one of Scotland's leading golf venues and destined to be in the top 5 rankings.

The spectacular course has been designed by one of Europe's leading golf architects, Dave Thomas, who has been designing courses worldwide for over 30 years. It will be kept by the former green keeper at Royal Dornoch, Bob Mackay.

The 7177 yard undulating golf course is a must-play for both amateur and professional golfers alike. As well as having the scenic backdrop of the Cairngorm mountains and the river Spey running alongside it, the course also has the longest hole in Scotland at 641 yards.

Located at Dalfaber, Aviemore, just 30 minutes south of Inverness, it's the latest in leisure activities available at the Macdonald Aviemore Highland Resort.

Be the first to receive information, updates and offers on the golf course and the resort, by emailing us at golf@ahresort.co.uk.

MACDONALD
AVIEMORE
HIGHLAND
RESORT

www.AviemoreHighlandResort.com

See also Colour Advertisement on page 57

Lanarkshire

AIRDRIE. **Airdrie Golf Club,** Glenmavis Road, Airdrie ML6 0PQ (01236 762195). *Location:* one mile north of Airdrie Cross. 18 holes, 6004 yards. S.S.S. 68. *Green Fees:* information not available. *Eating facilities:* available. *Visitors:* welcome only on application to the Secretary. Professional: S. McLean (01236 754360). Secretary: W. Campbell.

AIRDRIE. **Easter Moffat Golf Club,** Plains, Airdrie ML6 8NP (01236 842878; Fax: 01236 842904). *Location:* three miles east of Airdrie on old Edinburgh Road. 18 holes, 6221 yards. S.S.S. 70. Practice ground. *Green Fees:* £22.00 per round, £33.00 per day. *Eating facilities:* bar and dining room. *Visitors:* welcome except weekends. *Society Meetings:* welcome. Professional: Graham King (01236 843015). Secretary: Gordon Miller (01236 620972). Further information including course planner is available on our website. website: www.eastermoffat.com

BELLSHILL. **Bellshill Golf Club,** Community Road, Orbiston, Bellshill ML4 2RZ (01698 745124). *Location:* Bellshill to Motherwell road, turn right. Parkland course. 18 holes, 5852 yards. S.S.S. 69. *Green Fees:* May to October, midweek £26.00 per round, £32.00 per day, juniors (accompanied by adult) £5.00 per round; weekends and Public Holidays £32.00 per round, £42.00 per day, juniors (with adult) £10.00. November to March £12.00 per round. Half price rates for students. Midweek packages for visiting parties of 8 or more: two rounds of golf plus coffee, soup and rolls, and high tea £42.00; one round of golf plus coffee and a meal £27.00. All prices subject to review. *Eating facilities:* by prior arrangement with Clubmaster. *Visitors:* welcome, parties by prior application (not competition days or Sundays). *Society Meetings:* by prior arrangement with Administrator (Alex Smith) or Secretary. Secretary: Tom McLaughlin.

BIGGAR. **Biggar Golf Club,** Broughton Road, Biggar ML12 6HA (01899 220618 (Clubhouse)). *Location:* from Edinburgh A702, from Glasgow A74 or M8, turn off at Newhouse. Flat, scenic parkland course. 18 holes, 5416 yards. S.S.S. 66. *Green Fees:* information not available. *Eating facilities:* all day licence, full catering, snacks only on Tuesdays. *Visitors:* unrestricted, casual dress – no jeans. All weather tennis courts and caravan park. Buggies and carts available. *Society Meetings:* welcome, early reservation essential. Secretary: Tom Rodger. Tee Reservations: (01899 220319). *

CARLUKE. **Carluke Golf Club,** Maudslie Road, Hallcraig, Carluke ML8 5HG (01555 771070). *Location:* Carluke Cross, go west along Clyde Street for two miles. Parkland course. 18 holes, 5800 yards. S.S.S. 68. Practice Area. *Green Fees:* information not available. *Eating facilities:* available. *Visitors:* till 4pm weekdays, no visitors weekends. Tuition. *Society Meetings:* by written application to the Secretary, restriction on numbers. Professional: Craig Ronald (01555 751053). Administration: Tom Fraser (01555 770574).

CARNWATH. **Carnwath Golf Club,** 1 Main Street, Carnwath ML11 8JX (01555 840251; Fax: 01555 841070). *Location:* on main Ayr/Edinburgh Road. Fairly hilly inland course. 18 holes, 5953 yards. S.S.S. 69. *Green Fees:* weekdays £18.00 per round, £30.00 per two rounds; Sundays £24.00 per round, £36.00 per two rounds. Subject to review. *Eating facilities:* lounge bar and dining room daily. *Visitors:* welcome. Not Saturdays or after 4pm weekdays. Sunday with prior booking. *Society Meetings:* catered for by prior arrangement. Secretary: Mrs L. McPate (01555 840251).
e-mail: enquiriescarnwathgolfclub1907@hotmail.co.uk

COATBRIDGE. **Drumpellier Golf Club,** Drumpellier Avenue, Coatbridge ML5 1RX (01236 424139). *Location:* one mile from town centre. Parkland, wooded. 18 holes, 6227 yards. S.S.S. 70. Practice area. *Green Fees:* £30.00 per round, £40.00 per day weekdays. *Eating facilities:* available seven days. *Visitors:* welcome daily except weekends. *Society Meetings:* catered for by arrangement. Professional: Jamie Carver. Secretary: J.M. Craig (01236 424139; Fax: 01236 428723).
website: www.drumpellier.com

DOUGLAS WATER. **Douglas Water Golf Club,** Ayr Road, Rigside, Lanark (01555 880361). *Location:* five miles south of Lanark on A70, Junction 11 from M74. Hilly course, small greens, undulating fairways. 9 holes, 2947 yards, 2694 metres. S.S.S. 69. *Green Fees:* information not provided. *Visitors:* welcome any time, except Saturdays because of competitions. *Society Meetings:* contact Secretary. Secretary: D. Hogg (01698 882432).

EAST KILBRIDE. **Torrance House Golf Club,** Calderglen Country Park, Strathaven Road, East Kilbride G75 0QZ (013552 49720). *Location:* East Kilbride boundary on main Strathaven road. Parkland. 18 holes, 6423 yards. S.S.S. 71. Practice area. *Green Fees:* information not available. *Eating facilities:* private clubhouse. *Visitors:* welcome midweek only. *Society Meetings:* details on request. Secretary: M.D. McKerlie (013552 49720). Booking Office: (01355 248638).*

GARTCOSH. **Mount Ellen Golf Club,** Johnstone Road, Gartcosh, Glasgow G69 8EY (01236 872277; Fax: 01236 872249). *Location:* approximately six miles north-east of Glasgow, near old Gartcosh steelworks. Parkland. 18 holes, 5525 yards. S.S.S. 66. *Green Fees:* information not available. *Eating facilities:* bar and full catering service. *Visitors:* welcome weekdays from 9am to 4pm, no weekend visitors. Buggies and carts available for hire. *Society Meetings:* weekdays by arrangement with Secretary. Professional: I. Bilsborough (01236 872632). Secretary: T. Reilly (0141 779 1896).

SCOTLAND / Lanarkshire

HAMILTON. **Hamilton Golf Club,** Riccarton, Ferniegair, Hamilton ML3 7UE (01698 282872). *Location:* off M74 Hamilton turn-off, one and a half miles up Larkhall road. Parkland course. 18 holes, 6500 yards. S.S.S. 71. *Green Fees:* £35.00 per round, day ticket £45.00. *Eating facilities:* meals must be ordered. *Visitors:* by arrangement, please contact Secretary. *Society Meetings:* visitors by arrangement, contact Secretary. Professional: Derek Wright (01698 282872). Secretary: Graham Chapman (01698 282872; Fax: 01698 204650).

HAMILTON. **Strathclyde Park Golf Club,** Motehill, Hamilton ML3 6BY (01698 429350). *Location:* Hamilton/Motherwell exit off M74 to roundabout second exit East Kilbride, to new roundabout second exit, to third roundabout third exit straight ahead, to golf course passing ice rink on left hand side. Wooded parkland course surrounded by race course on one side and nature reserve on other. 9 holes, 3128 yards. S.S.S. 70. Large practice area, putting green and driving range (24 bays). *Green Fees:* weekdays £3.80, Juniors/Senior Citizens £1.90; weekends & public holidays £4.40, Juniors/Senior Citizens £2.20. (Subject to review). *Eating facilities:* bar within complex. *Visitors:* welcome, same day booking system in operation. Course opens 7am Summer, 8am Winter. *Society Meetings:* welcome by arrangement through management (01698 429350). Professional: W. Walker. Secretary: K. Will (01698 429350).

LANARK. **Kames Golf Club,** Eastend, Cleghorn ML11 8NR (01555 870015; Fax: 01555 870022). *Location:* situated on the A721 between Carluke and Carnwath. Home of the championship Mouse Valley Golf Course, 18 holes, 6300 yards. S.S.S. 72, and the delightful Kames Course, 9-holes, 2500 yards par 33 (extending to 18 holes summer 2006.) *Green Fees:* Mouse Valley 18 hole course £17.00 weekdays, £20.00 weekends; Kames course, £9.00 weekdays, £11.00 weekends. *Eating facilities:* full bar and catering. *Visitors:* welcome. *Society Meetings:* all welcome, weekend bookings taken. e-mail: info@kames-golf-club.com website: www.kames-golf-club.com

LANARK **Lanark Golf Club,** The Moor, Whitelees Road, Lanark ML11 7RX (01555 663219). *Location:* off A73. Tough moorland course. 18 holes, 6306 yards. S.S.S. 71. Also 9-hole course. Two practice grounds. *Green Fees:* weekdays £35.00 per round, £45.00 per day. 2004 prices, subject to review. *Eating facilities:* full catering and bar. *Visitors:* welcome daily until 4pm, no visitors weekends. *Society Meetings:* groups of 8/40 and over catered for Monday to Friday. Professional: Alan White (01555 661456). Secretary: G.H. Cuthill.

LANARK. **Mouse Valley Golf Course,** East End, Cleghorn, Lanark ML11 (01555 870015; Fax: 01555 870022). *Location:* 5 miles from Carluke on A721 Peebles Road. Pay as you play. Links style course, inland undulating terrain. Mouse Water (river) runs through the course. Two courses - Mouse Valley 18 holes, 6376 yards, Par 70 and Kames course - 9 holes, 2538 yards, Par 33 Practice ground. *Green Fees:* information not available. *Eating facilities:* full bar and catering. *Visitors:* welcome, no restrictions. *Society Meetings:* welcome at all times. Company days. Contact: (01555 870015).*

LARKHALL. **Larkhall Golf Club,** Burnhead Road, Larkhall ML9 3AA (01698 889597). *Location:* on A74, close to M74. Parkland. 9 holes, 6432 yards. S.S.S. 70. *Green Fees:* information not available. *Eating facilities:* bar, lunch only on Saturdays. *Visitors:* welcome, but check beforehand; not Saturdays. Secretary: Malcolm Mallinson; Booking Office (01698 881113).

LEADHILLS. **Leadhills Golf Club,** Leadhills, Biggar ML12 6AR (01659 74356). *Location:* seven miles south of Abington on B797. This short but testing course is the highest in Scotland. 9 holes, 2177 yards. S.S.S. 64. *Green Fees:* information not available. *Eating facilities:* hotel nearby. *Visitors:* welcome any time. *Society Meetings:* welcome. Secretary: Nigel Davies (01659 74356).*

LESMAHAGOW. **Hollandbush Golf Club,** Acretophead, Lesmahagow ML11 0JS (01555 893484). *Location:* off M74 (Junction 9). Golf course is between Lesmahagow and Coalburn. 18 holes, 6246 yards. S.S.S. 70. Practice area. *Green Fees:* information not available. *Eating facilities:* meals at club. *Visitors:* welcome without restriction. *Society Meetings:* catered for. Starter's Office (01555 893646). Secretary: Robert Lynch (01555 893484). *

MOTHERWELL. **Colville Park Golf Club,** Jerviston Estate, Merry Street, Motherwell ML1 4UG (01698 263017; Fax: 01698 230418). *Location:* one mile from town centre and train station (Merry Street, Motherwell). Parkland, wooded first six holes. 18 holes, 6301 yards. S.S.S. 71. *Green Fees:* information not available. *Eating facilities:* full facilities. *Visitors:* welcome between 11am and 3pm Mondays to Thursdays only. Advance booking not required. *Society Meetings:* by prior written arrangement, weekdays only. £27.00 day ticket. Professional Shop (01698 265779). Secretary: Leslie Innes (01698 262808).*

MOTHERWELL. **Dalziel Park Golf & Country Club,** 100 Hagen Drive, Motherwell ML1 5RZ (01698 862862; Fax: 01698 862863). *Location*: four miles from Motherwell with good access to M74 and M8 at Junction 6. Midway between Glasgow and Edinburgh. Wooded Parkland. 18 holes, 6300 yards. S.S.S. 70. 15 bay floodlit driving range and extensive dry and outdoor sports facilities. *Green Fees*: information not available. *Eating facilities*: restaurant, bars and lounges. 10 bedrooms, conference facilities and all functions catered for in Country Club. *Visitors*: all welcome, only restricted on Saturday morning (during Men's medal day). *Society Meetings*: welcome at all times. Secretary: Ian Donnachie (01698 862862: Fax: 01698 862863).*

www.uk-golfguide.com

SHOTTS. **Shotts Golf Club,** Blairhead, Benhar Road, Shotts ML7 5BJ (01501 822658). *Location:* off M8 at Junction 5, one and a half miles south. Semi-flat moorland/wooded course. 18 holes, 6204 yards. S.S.S. 70. Practice area, professional tuition. *Green Fees:* £20.00 per round, £28.00 per day. *Eating facilities:* full catering and bar service. *Visitors:* welcome anytime except Saturdays, Sundays (prior booking needed) or Public Holidays. *Society Meetings:* weekdays only (not Public Holidays) by arrangement. Professional: John Strachan (01501 822658). Secretary: George Stoddart (01501 825868).

STRATHAVEN. **Strathaven Golf Club,** Overton Avenue, Glasgow Road, Strathaven ML10 6NR. *Location:* on A726 on outskirts of town. 18 holes, 6226 yards. S.S.S. 71. *Green Fees:* please contact Secretary for information. *Eating facilities:* full catering and bar. *Visitors:* welcome weekdays, casual visitors before 4pm; party bookings Tuesdays only by prior arrangement. Professional: Stuart Kerr (01357 521812). Secretary: A.W. Wallace (01357 520421).

UDDINGSTON. **Calderbraes Golf Club,** 57 Roundknowe Road, Uddingston G71 7TS (01698 813425). *Location:* at end of M74, overlooking Calderpark Zoo. 9 holes, 3425 yards. S.S.S. 67. *Green Fees:* day ticket £13.00. *Eating facilities:* catering available at all times. *Visitors:* welcome weekdays only; must be off course by 5pm. *Society Meetings:* welcome, contact Secretary. Secretary: S. McGuigan.

WISHAW. **Wishaw Golf Club,** 55 Cleland Road, Wishaw ML2 7PH (01698 372869). *Location:* 400 yards from Wishaw Main Street at West Cross. Tree-lined parkland course. 18 holes, 5999 yards. S.S.S. 69. Practice area. *Green Fees:* weekdays £24.00 per round, Sundays £29.00 per round. Day tickets available. *Eating facilities:* full catering, two bars, and dining room. *Visitors:* welcome before 4pm weekdays, after 10.30am Sundays, no visitors Saturdays. *Society Meetings:* by application. Professional: Stuart Adair (01698 358247). General Manager: James W. Douglas (01698 357480). e-mail: jwdouglas@btconnect.com

Ideally situated halfway between Edinburgh and Glasgow, with easy access from the M8, this 18-hole moorland course provides a challenge for all standards of golfers. Visitors should beware the notorious 4th hole, 'The Devil's Elbow', which has ruined the cards of many aspiring hopefuls. A refurbished clubhouse provides a warm and friendly welcome, with catering and bar facilities.

See also Colour Advertisement on page 75

Shotts Golf Club
Blairhead, Shotts ML7 5BJ
Clubhouse: 01501 820431
Pro Shop: 01501 822658
e-mail: info@shottsgolfclub.co.uk
www.shottsgolfclub.co.uk

Wishaw Golf Club (est.1897) 18-hole parkland course designed by James Braid.
• Tree-lined fairways, tricky par 3s and a testing last 5 holes require concentration and a strong finish to test the 69 SSS. • The clubhouse has been totally refurbished with new bar, lounge, dining room, locker room and Pro Shop. • Catering is to a very high standard, and includes an à la carte menu, all at very favourable prices. **Tel: Pro Shop 01698 358247 or 357480 for society bookings.**
55 Cleland Road, Wishaw ML2 7PH

PLEASE NOTE

All the information regarding Golf Clubs in this guide is given in good faith in the belief that it is correct. However, the publishers cannot guarantee the facts given in these pages, neither are they responsible for changes in ownership or facilities, such as green fees, that may take place after the date of going to press. Readers should always satisfy themselves that the facilities they require are available and that the terms, if quoted, still apply.

Perth & Kinross

ABERFELDY. **Aberfeldy Golf Club,** Taybridge Road, Aberfeldy PH15 2BH (01887 820535). *Location:* A9 from Ballinluig. Scenic riverside course. 18 holes, 5283 yards. S.S.S. 66, Par 68. *Green Fees:* information not available. *Eating facilities:* high teas, lunches, etc. *Visitors:* welcome anytime. Buggy and trolley hire. *Society Meetings:* catered for. Secretary: (01887 820535).

ALYTH. **Glenisla Golf Centre,** Pitcrocknie, Alyth PH11 8JJ (01828 632445; Fax: 01828 633749). *Location:* five miles east of Blairgowrie on the B954. Parkland, with undulating, rolling fairways, and featuring over 40 bunkers and 5 water hazards. 'One of Scotland's favourite courses' (Insider Business Magazine Top 500 Survey, March 2001). 18 holes, 6402 yards. S.S.S. 71. *Green Fees:* information not available. *Eating facilities:* superbly appointed, fully licensed clubhouse with panoramic bar and restaurant overlooking the course. *Visitors:* always welcome. Conference and Function facilities and on site B&B and self-catering cottages available. *Society Meetings:* always welcome. Golf Administrator: Ewan Wilson.*
e-mail: info@golf-glenisla.co.uk
website: www.golf-glenisla.co.uk

AUCHTERARDER. **Auchterarder Golf Club,** Orchil Road, Auchterarder PH3 1LS (Tel & Fax: 01764 662804). *Location:* off A9 to southwest of town, next to Gleneagles. Flat parkland, part wooded. 18 holes, 5778 yards. S.S.S. 68. Small practice area. *Green Fees:* weekdays £24.00 per round, £35.00 per day; weekends £29.00 per round, £45.00 per day; weekdays weekly ticket (one round per day) £85.00.

Eating facilities: lounge, dining room, bar. *Visitors:* welcome without reservation except major competition days. *Society Meetings:* welcome, must book 3 months in advance. Professional: Gavin Baxter (01764 663711). Secretary: W.M. Campbell (01764 662804; Fax: 01764 664423).
e-mail: secretary@auchterardergolf.co.uk

For full details of clubs and courses, plus convenient accommodation
www.uk-golfguide.com

LANDS OF LOYAL HOTEL
Alyth, Perthshire PH11 8JQ • Telephone: 01828 633151 • Fax: 01828 633313
e-mail: info@landsofloyal.com • website: www.landsofloyal.com

Set on a hillside overlooking the Vale of Strathmore lies this impressive Victorian Mansion. Our highly acclaimed restaurant makes full use of local fish and game in a style both traditional and imaginative. For the country sportsman, fishing and shooting are available, with salmon and trout fishing in the loch and river. Pheasant and grouse shooting, wild fowling and deer stalking also available as the seasons permit. The hotel makes an ideal base for the ambitious golfer with 30 courses within an hour's drive. ***Full colour brochure and tariff available on request.***

See also Colour Advertisement on page 76

AUCHTERARDER GOLF CLUB
Secretary: W M Campbell, The Clubhouse, Orchil Road, Auchterarder PH3 1LS
Secretary: Tel 01764 662804 • Fax: 01764 664423 • Pro: Tel/Fax: 01764 663711
e-mail: secretary@auchterardergolf.co.uk • www.auchterardergolf.co.uk

Monday - Friday Round £24, Day £35
Saturday - Sunday Round £29, Day £45

This is a flat parkland course that is part woodland, with fine examples of pine, larch and birch. Just a few minutes from its famous neighbour Gleneagles, but with a character of its own. At just 5,707 yards, it is relatively short, although a mix of tricky doglegs and heavily guarded greens make it a course to remember.

AUCHTERARDER. Gleneagles Hotel Golf Courses, Auchterarder PH3 1NF (Golf Office: 01764 694469; Fax: 01764 694383). *Location:* 20 miles south of Perth, 20 miles north of Stirling. Gleneagles offers two moorland 18 hole courses and a third parkland/moorland course. King's Course: 6125 yards par 68; Queen's Course: 5660 yards par 68; PGA Centenary Course: 18 holes, 6141 yards S.S.S. 72 and a 9 hole course, The Wee Course: 1481 yards par 27. *Green Fees:* on request. *Eating facilities:* at The Dormy Clubhouse (Bar & Restaurant) and The Gleneagles Hotel. *Visitors:* welcome. Professional: Russell Smith. Hotel General Manager: Patrick Elsmie (01764 662231). Golf Contact: (01764 694469; Fax: 01764 662134).

BLAIR ATHOLL. Blair Atholl Golf Club, Blair Atholl, Pitlochry PH18 5TG (01796 481407; Fax: 01796 481751). *Location:* off A9 Perth/Inverness Road, down Invertilt Road. Flat parkland. 9 holes, 5816 yards, 5322 metres. S.S.S. 68. *Green Fees:* weekdays £18.00 per day, weekends £20.00 per day, weekly ticket £110.00. All rates include insurance. *Eating facilities:* meals/bar. *Visitors:* welcome at all times. Carts and clubs available. *Society Meetings:* by arrangement with Secretary. Secretary: D.A. Boon.

BLAIRGOWRIE. The Alyth Golf Club, Pitcrocknie, Alyth, Blairgowrie PH11 8HF (01828 632268; Fax: 01828 633491). *Location:* five miles from Blairgowrie on B954. Parkland/heathland course with interesting dog leg Par 4 5th played to a plateau green with out-of-bounds on right. 18 holes, 6205 yards, 5676 metres. S.S.S. 71. Large practice area. *Green Fees:* information not available. *Eating facilities:* all day catering and bar. *Visitors:* welcome, phone 01828 632411 six days ahead. *Society Meetings:* welcome, prior booking essential. Professional: Tom Melville (01828 632411). Secretary: Jim Docherty (01828 632268; Fax: 01828 633491).
e-mail: enquiries@alythgolf.co.uk
website: www.alythgolfclub.co.uk

BLAIRGOWRIE. Blairgowrie Golf Club, Golf Course Road, Rosemount, Blairgowrie PH10 6LG (01250 872622; Fax: 01250 875451). *Location:* take A923 out of Perth, turn right at "Rosemount" sign. Gently undulating heathland. Rosemount Course: 18 holes, 6590 yards. S.S.S. 72. Lansdowne Course: 18 holes, 6834 yards. S.S.S. 74. Wee Course: 9 holes, 4704 yards. S.S.S. 63. Two practice grounds. *Green Fees:* on application. *Eating facilities:* full catering available. *Visitors:* welcome by appointment. Handicap Certificate required. *Society Meetings:* catered for by application to Office. Professional: Charles Dernie (01250 873116). Secretary/Manager: David Swarbrick (01250 872622).
e-mail: office@theblairgowriegolfclub.co.uk
website: www.theblairgowriegolfclub.co.uk

BLAIRGOWRIE. Dalmunzie Golf Course, Spittal O' Glenshee, Blairgowrie PH10 7QG (01250 885226). *Location:* A93 Blairgowrie to Braemar road, left at Spittal O' Glenshee. A small well-kept hill course amid glorious scenery. 9 holes, 2099 yards. *Green Fees:* £13.00 per day. Under 8 free, 8–16 half price (we like young golfers). *Eating facilities:* restaurant facilities at Dalmunzie Hotel. Bar. *Visitors:* welcome without reservation. Self-catering cottages available. *Society Meetings:* catered for. Secretary: Simon Winton.

BLAIRGOWRIE. Strathmore Golf Centre, Leroch, Alyth, Blairgowrie (01828 633322; Fax: 01828 633533). *Location:* one mile south of Alyth off A926 Blairgowrie to Kirriemuir road. Rolling parkland course with magnificent views over the valley of Strathmore. Two courses - Rannaleroch Course: 18 holes, 6454 yards, 5901 metres. Par 72. S.S.S. 72; Leitfie Links Course: 9 holes, 1719 yards, 1572 metres. Par 29. S.S.S. 29. Driving range adjacent. *Green Fees:* information not available. *Eating facilities:* friendly clubhouse with bar and restaurant. *Visitors:* always welcome. *Society Meetings:* always welcome.
e-mail: enquiries@strathmoregolf.com
website: www.strathmoregolf.com

CALLANDER. Callander Golf Club, Aveland Road, Callander FK17 8EN (01877 330090; Fax: 01877 330062). *Location*: M9 Stirling, Junction 10 Crianlarich exit to A84 to Callander. Parkland, partly wooded, with panoramic views. 18 holes, 5185 yards. S.S.S. 65. Small practice ground and putting green. *Green Fees*: from £20.00. P.O.A. *Eating facilities*: bar snacks, lunches, high teas, dinners by arrangement. *Visitors*: welcome, no restrictions. Handicap Certificate required Wednesdays and Sundays. *Society Meetings*: welcome, book in advance. Professional: A. Martin (01877 330975). Secretary: Mrs Sandra Smart (01877 330090; Fax: 01877 330062).
e-mail: callandergc@nextcall.net
website: www.callandergolfclub.co.uk

CRIEFF. Comrie Golf Club, Laggan Braes, Comrie PH6 2LR (01764 670055). *Location:* six miles west of Crieff on A85 at east end of village. Parkland, wooded course with two long and tricky Par 3 holes (3rd and 5th) and well guarded Par 5 (6th). 9 holes, 6040 yards. S.S.S. 70. *Green Fees:* weekdays £16.00 per round, £20.00 per day, weekends £20.00 per round, £25.00 per day. Special rates for parties. *Eating facilities:* light refreshments and meals during summer months. *Visitors:* welcome at all times. Club Medals - Monday 1pm and 4.30pm, Ladies Tuesdays 1pm. *Society Meetings:* always welcome. Secretary: Robert K. Burns (01764 670055).
e-mail: enquiries@comriegolf.co.uk

Nine challenging holes set on a privately owned 6000 acre estate in spectacular and beautiful scenery. The course has been owned and maintained by the Winton Family for over 50 years, alongside Dalmunzie Highland Cottages. Why not come to stay, and enjoy carefree golf in spectacular surroundings? Send for details to Simon Winton.

DALMUNZIE GOLF COURSE www.dalmunziecottages.com
SPITTAL OF GLENSHEE, BLAIRGOWRIE, PERTHSHIRE PH10 7QE TEL: 01250 885226

THE GLENEAGLES HOTEL

At Gleneagles, golf is a game where everyone wins. If you're playing well and rising to the challenges of some of the finest holes in the world, the round becomes a dream. Slice a shot here, miss a green there, and, well, you've always got the stunning scenery to take in or the Dormy Clubhouse Bar and Restaurant to look forward to.

The PGA Centenary Course, designed by Jack Nicklaus, is an American/Scottish layout with many water hazards, elevated tees and raised contoured greens, and is the selected venue for the Ryder Cup 2014.

The King's and Queen's are courses deserving of their regal titles, providing everything a golfer could possibly ask for, and the relaxed clubhouse, with its luxury locker rooms and superb golf shop, also serves great food and drink.

THE GLENEAGLES HOTEL
Auchterarder, Perthshire PH3 1NF
Just one hour from Edinburgh/Glasgow

Tel: 01764 662231
Fax: 01764 662134
www.gleneagles.com

See also Colour Advertisement on page 59

One of the Treasures of Scottish Golf, Blairgowrie Golf Club offers two eighteen hole championship courses and a classic 9 hole course. The Rosemount Course ranks among the very best of all the great inland courses in the British Isles. Alongside Rosemount, the Lansdowne Course, designed by Peter Alliss and Dave Thomas, is a testing 18 holes with a more modern layout and tighter fairways. Within striking distance of Carnoustie, St Andrews and Gleneagles, Blairgowrie is ideally situated in the heart of beautiful Perthshire.

1889

The Blairgowrie Golf Club, Rosemount, Blairgowrie, Perthshire PH10 6LG
T: 01250 872622, F: 01250 875451, E: office@theblairgowriegolfclub.co.uk, W: www.theblairgowriegolfclub.co.uk

See also Colour Advertisement on page 76

Relax and enjoy a meal after your round of golf.
The Red House Hotel menu is served in our Restaurant & Conservatory from 12 noon to 9.30pm. Stay in one of our 20 en suite rooms, and play some of the finest golf courses in Scotland which are only a 15-minute drive away. Also within the Red House Hotel we can provide Snooker, Squash, Sauna and Gymnasium.

STATION ROAD, COUPAR ANGUS
PERTHSHIRE PH13 9AL
Tel: 01828 628500 • Fax: 01828 628574
e-mail: stay@red-house-hotel.co.uk • www.red-house-hotel.co.uk

See also Colour Advertisement on page 77

CRIEFF
HYDRO
Scotland's leading leisure hotel welcomes all levels of golfer to the new **Culcrieff Golf Course** at Crieff Hydro Ltd. Opened in 2002, the course enjoys panoramic views over the Strathearn valley.

18 holes • Par 66 • SSS 64 • 4876 yards
6 hole pitch and putt • 8-bay driving range
Licensed clubhouse with restaurant facilities
Weekday ticket £20 • Weekend ticket £25

Reservations necessary for groups and Perthshire Green Card holders.

For further enquiries and brochure contact Andrew Devine

Crieff Hydro Hotel
Crieff PH7 3LQ • 01764 651615
enquiries@crieffhydro.com
www.crieffhydro.com

See also Colour Advertisement on page 77

CRIEFF. **Crieff Golf Club,** Ferntower, Perth Road, Crieff PH7 3LR (01764 652397; Fax: 01764 655096). *Location*: A85 north-east outskirts of Crieff. Ferntower Course - 18 holes, 6402 yards. S.S.S. 72. Dornock Course - 9 holes, 2386 yards. S.S.S. 63. Two practice areas. *Green Fees*: information not available. *Eating facilities*: full restaurant facilities by arrangement (phone 01764 652397) and bar snacks. *Visitors*: welcome with reservation, prior arrangement advisable by phone. *Society Meetings*: book by phone (01764 652909) and confirm in writing. Professional: David Murchie (01764 652909; Fax: 01764 655096). Managing/Secretary: J.S. Miller

CRIEFF. **Culcrieff Golf Club,** Ferntower Road, Crieff PH7 3LQ (01764 651615; Fax: 01764 653087). *Location*: set high in the Strathearn Valley. A85 from Perth, A822 from Stirling. Parkland course. 18 holes, 4876 yards, S.S.S. 64, Par 66. 8-bay driving range, practice green, 6-hole pitch and putt course. *Green Fees*: information not available. *Eating facilities*: licensed clubhouse with restaurant. *Visitors*: welcome. *Society Meetings*: welcome with advance reservation. Contact Andrew Devine for details.*
e-mail: enquiries@crieffhydro.com
website: www.crieffhydro.com.

CRIEFF. **Foulford Inn Golf Course,** Foulford Inn, by Crieff PH7 3LN (Tel & Fax: 01764 652407). *Location*: 5 miles north of Crieff on the A822 in the direction of Dunkeld. Upland course with water hazards. 9 holes, 916 yards, S.S.S. 27. *Green Fees*: £5.00 per round, £7.00 per day. *Eating facilities*: bar/restaurant. *Visitors*: welcome anytime, accommodation available in Inn. Course free to residents. *Society Meetings*: welcome, on application. Secretary: B.A. Beaumont.
e-mail: foulford@btconnect.com
website: www.foulfordinn.co.uk

CRIEFF. **Muthill Golf Club,** Peat Road, Muthill, Crieff PH5 2DA (01764 681523; Fax: 01764 681557). *Location:* two miles from Crieff at entrance to Muthill. Parkland course with magnificent views. 9 holes, 4700 yards. S.S.S. 63. *Green Fees:* weekdays £17.00 per day; weekends £21.00 per day. Fees subject to review. *Eating facilities:* full meals service available. *Visitors:* no restrictions except after 5pm Wednesday and Thursdays (club competitions). Trolleys available. *Society Meetings:* welcome. Secretary: Jacq Scott (01764 681523; Fax: 01764 681557).
e-mail: muthillgolfclub@lineone.net

DUNBLANE. **Dunblane New Golf Club,** Perth Road, Dunblane FK15 0LJ (01786 821521; Fax: 01786 821522). *Location:* two miles off main road M9 at Fourways Roundabout. Parkland/undulating. 18 holes, 5936 yards, S.S.S. 69. *Green Fees:* £25.00 per round, £35.00 per day. *Eating facilities:* available seven days a week. *Visitors:* welcome, 9.30am-12 noon, 2.30pm-4pm. *Society Meetings:* catered for weekdays only except Tuesdays. Professional: R.M. Jamieson (01786 821521; Fax: 01786 821522). Secretary: Roddy Morrison (01786 821527; Fax: 01786 825066).

DUNKELD. **Dunkeld and Birnam Golf Club,** Fungarth, Dunkeld PH8 0HU (01350 727524; Fax: 01350 728660). *Location:* one mile north of Dunkeld on the A923. Heathland course with panoramic views. 18 holes, 5508 yards. S.S.S. 67. Practice area. *Green Fees:* on application. *Eating facilities:* bar and full catering facilities. *Visitors:* welcome; buggies available. *Society Meetings:* catered for. Secretary: Richard Barrance (01350 727524; Fax: 01350 728660).
e-mail: secretary-dunkeld@tiscali.co.uk

DUNNING. **Dunning Golf Club,** Rollo Park, Station Road, Dunning PH2 0QX (01764 684747). *Location:* 10 miles south-west of Perth, two miles from A9. Parkland, gently undulating. 9 holes, 4885 yards. S.S.S. 63. Small practice area. *Green Fees:* £16.00 per round for 18 holes. *Eating facilities:* tea/ coffee, soft drinks, snacks. Meals can be arranged with the Dunning Hotel at a 10% discount on production of a visitor's ticket. *Visitors:* welcome, no restrictions apart from club competitions. *Society Meetings:* welcome weekdays and most Sundays. Secretary: A. D. Cantlay (01738 812844).

DUNNING. **Whitemoss Golf Club,** Whitemoss Road, Dunning PH2 0GX (01738 730300; Fax: 01738 730490). *Location:* 10 miles south-west of Perth, two miles from A9. Parkland course. 18 holes, 5968 yards, S.S.S. 69. Practice range, chipping bunkers, practice net and putting green. *Green Fees:* information not available. *Eating facilities:* New clubhouse with restaurant and bar. *Visitors:* welcome all the time, on medal days after 10am. *Society Meetings:* Welcome, after 10am on medal days. Tuition on request. Shower facilities. Secretary: Victor Westwood (01738 730300). *

SCOTLAND / Perth & Kinross

KENMORE. Kenmore Golf Course, Mains of Taymouth, Kenmore, Aberfeldy PH15 2HN (01887 830226; Fax: 01887 829059). *Location:* west off A9 at Ballinluig on A827, six and a half miles west of Aberfeldy through village of Kenmore on RHS. Testing well kept course on natural undulating terrain, lovely scenery and first class facilities. 9 holes, 6052 yards, 5600 metres. S.S.S. 70. Practice facilities, putting green. *Green Fees:* weekdays 9 holes £13.00, 18 holes £17.00; weekends 9 holes £15.00, 18 holes £19.00. Weekly Ticket £50.00. *Eating facilities:* full bar and restaurant facilities in pleasant surroundings. *Visitors:* welcome anytime. Cottages to let (self-catering included). Pro shop; club and trolley hire; changing and shower facilities. *Society Meetings:* all welcome, please book. Secretary: Robin Menzies. e-mail: golf@taymouth.co.uk
website: www.taymouth.co.uk

KENMORE. Taymouth Castle Golf Course, Kenmore, by Aberfeldy PH15 2NT (01887 830228). *Location:* six miles west of Aberfeldy. Parkland set in scenic mountain terrain. 18 holes, 6066 yards. S.S.S. 69. Practice area. *Green Fees:* information not available. *Eating facilities:* restaurant and bar. *Visitors:* welcome, tee reservations necessary (phone or letter). Tuition available, motorised buggies. *Society Meetings:* catered for by previous arrangement only. PGA Professional: Gavin Dott (01887 830228).*

KILLIN. **Killin Golf Club,** Killin FK21 8TX (01567 820312). *Location:* west end of Loch Tay. Hilly parkland amongst beautiful scenery. 9 holes, 2510 yards. S.S.S. 65. Small practice area includes bunker and net. *Green Fees:* £18.00 per round, £24.00 per day. Subject to review. *Eating facilities:* available all day. *Visitors:* welcome. *Society Meetings:* catered for by arrangement. Secretary: Revd Ralph Taylor (0141 578 1139; Mobile: 0771 374 1578).

KINNESSWOOD. **Bishopshire Golf Club,** Kinnesswood, By Kinross KY13 9HX. *Location:* take road to Glenrothes from M90, three miles. Course has panoramic views overlooking Loch Leven. 10 holes, 4830 yards, 2268 metres. S.S.S. 64. *Green Fees:* information not available. *Eating facilities:* by arrangement or available at the hotel 400 yards away. *Visitors:* welcome, no restrictions. *Society Meetings:* by arrangement. Secretary: John Proudfoot (01592 780203).

Visit the **FHG** website
www.holidayguides.com
for details of the wide choice of accommodation featured in the full range of FHG titles

---

Royal Dunkeld Hotel

The Royal Dunkeld, a former coaching inn, is now a modern, comfortable hotel. All bedrooms have en suite facilities, colour TV, radio, hospitality tray, hairdryer, trouser press and direct-dial telephone. Located in some of the most beautiful countryside in Britain, Dunkeld is an ideal base for touring and for sporting activities such as golf, salmon fishing and trout fishing.

Atholl Street, Dunkeld, Perthshire PH8 0AR
Tel: 01350 727322 • Fax: 01350 728989 • www.royaldunkeld.co.uk

See also Colour Advertisement on page 76

Killin, Perthshire FK21 8TX
Tel: 01567 820312
e-mail: booking@killingolfclub.co.uk
www.killingolfclub.co.uk

"A Hidden Gem"

A picturesque 9-hole course set in the beautiful scenery of the Perthshire Highlands. Food is served all day, with a bar menu available from 11am. Package deals with catering for groups of 8 or more. With a river sweeping past the first fairway, playing golf in the midst of such breathtaking scenery is a unique experience.

Buggies, trolleys and clubs for hire

See also Colour Advertisement on page 76

KINROSS. **Green Hotel Golf Courses,** Green Hotel, The Muirs, Kinross KY13 8AS (01577 863467). *Location:* turn left in Kinross off M90 Junction 6, course 500 yards on right. Parkland. Two courses: Blue 18 holes, 6438 yards, 5888 metres. S.S.S. 71; Red 18 holes, 6256 yards, 5717 metres. S.S.S. 73. Practice ground. *Green Fees:* weekdays £22.00 per round, £35.00 per day; weekends £33.00 per round, £45.00 per day - subject to change. Preferred rates and tee times to Green Hotel residents. *Eating facilities:* in clubhouse. *Visitors:* welcome anytime. Hotel facilities. *Society Meetings:* welcome by arrangement. Professional: Stewart Geraghty (01577 865125). Secretary: Eileen Gray (01577 863407; Fax: 01577 863180).
e-mail: golfing@green-hotel.com

MILNATHORT. **Milnathort Golf Club Ltd,** South Street, Milnathort KY13 9XA (01577 864069). *Location*: one mile north of Kinross, M90 Junction 6 (north) or Junction 7 (south). Undulating inland course with lush fairways and excellent greens, with the addition of extra trees around the margins along with current plantations. Strategically placed copses of trees require acurate tee shots. The course is being made more interesting by the addition of extra tees/greens for some holes. 9 holes, 5973 yards. S.S.S. 69. Practice ground/green. *Green Fees*: weekdays £14.00 per round, £20.00 per day; weekends £16.00 per round, £22.00 per day. 9 hole sundowner ticket £8.00 weekends, £7.00 weekdays (subject to review). *Eating facilities*: full bar available, catering by arrangement. *Visitors*: welcome but suggest you phone. Dress code. *Society Meetings:* must be booked in advance. Secretary: via Club House.

PERTH. **Craigie Hill Golf Club (1982) Ltd,** Cherrybank, Perth PH2 0NE (01738 624377). *Location:* at west end of town, easy access from M90 and A9. Hilly course with panoramic view of Perth and surrounding hills. 18 holes, 5386 yards. S.S.S. 67. Practice ground and putting green. *Green Fees:* weekdays £20.00 per round, £30.00 per day; Sundays £30.00 per day. Visitors with member £7.00, Juniors (weekdays) £3.00 per round. *Eating facilities:* full catering and bar. *Visitors:* welcome Mondays to Fridays; Sundays by arrangement. *Society Meetings:* catered for by written application in first instance. Professional: Kris Esson (01738 622644). Secretary: Andrew Tunnicliffe (Tel & Fax: 01738 620829).

PERTH. **King James VI Golf Club,** Moncreiffe Island, Perth PH2 8NR (01738 625170). *Location:* situated on Island in River Tay, access by Footbridge alongside railway from Tay Street, Perth. Flat parkland course, surrounded by River Tay. 18 holes, 6038 yards. S.S.S. 69. Practice nets. *Green Fees:* weekdays £20.00 per round, £28.00 per day; weekends £22.00 per round, £30.00 per day. April/July/October £15.00 per round, £20.00 per day. *Eating facilities:* full catering. *Visitors:* welcome, phone for reservation, no visitors on Saturday mornings. Carts available. *Society Meetings:* catered for by prior booking. Fully stocked golf shop. Professional: Andrew Crerar (01738 632460). Secretary: (Tel & Fax: 01738 445132).
e-mail: info@kingjamesvi.co.uk
website: www.kingjamesvi.co.uk

PERTH. **North Inch Golf Course,** c/o C. Glencorse, Environment Services, Perth and Kinross Council, 35 Kinnoull Street, Perth (01738 475261). *Location:* A9 to city centre turnoff, follow Atholl Street to North Inch, course is located at Bell's Sports Centre, Hay Street. Picturesque municipal course alongside River Tay. Putting green. 18 holes, 5442 yards. S.S.S. 66. *Green Fees:* information available by calling Starter (01738 636481). *Eating facilities:* Inch Restaurant, Bell's Sports Centre.

PITLOCHRY. **Pitlochry Golf Course,** Pitlochry PH16 5QY (01796 472792). *Location:* half mile from centre of Pitlochry on A9. 18 holes, 5670 yards, S.S.S. 69. *Green Fees:* weekdays £35.00 per day, £24.00 per round; weekends £45.00 per day. £30.00 per round. Subject to review. Restricted course (1st November to 31st March). *Eating facilities:* catering and refreshments available in licensed clubhouse April to end October. *Visitors:* welcome. Caddy cars available for hire. *Society Meetings:* catered for. Phone Professional for all bookings. Professional: Mark Pirie (01796 472792). Golf Club Secretary: T.C. Leadbetter (01796 472314; Fax: 01796 473947).

ST FILLANS. **St Fillans Golf Club,** South Loch Earn Road, St Fillans, Loch Earn PH6 2NJ (01764 685312). *Location:* 13 miles west of Crieff on A85; turn off at east end of village, club 300 yards on left. A testing parkland course nestling between magnificent Perthshire mountains with one elevated tee and green. 9 holes length (18 holes), 6054 yards. S.S.S. 69. Practice facilities and putting green. *Green Fees:* information not available. *Eating facilities:* full meals and snacks available throughout the day; licensed restaurant. Golf trolleys, powered trolleys, buggy and clubs for hire. *Visitors:* welcome at all times except when matches on. *Society Meetings:* welcome with advance booking. Managing Secretary: Gordon Hibbert.*

SCONE. **Murrayshall Golf Course,** Murrayshall, Scone, By Perth PH2 7PH (01738 551171). *Location:* three miles north of Perth on A94 Coupar Angus Road. Undulating wooded parkland. 18 holes, 6043 yards. S.S.S. 72. Covered golf driving range, a second 18 hole course has been available since July 2000. *Green Fees:* information not available. *Eating facilities:* clubhouse open all day. *Visitors:* welcome, no restrictions - advance booking essential. *Society Meetings:* welcome - must pre-book. Professional: Alan Reid (01738 552784).*
website: www.murrayshall.com

STRATHTAY. **Strathtay Golf Club,** c/o Secretary, Upper Derculich, Strathtay, Pitlochry PH9 0LR. *Location:* on the right, three-quarters of a mile westwards on the minor road to Weem off the A827 Ballinluig to Grandtully. Wooded, mainly hilly course with beautiful panoramic views. 9 holes, 4082 yards. S.S.S. 61. *Green Fees:* £12.00 per day, £15.00 weekends and public holidays. *Visitors:* welcome at any time without restrictions. Changing room, toilets. *Society Meetings:* must be arranged in advance. Secretary: Ian Ramsay. (01887 840211).

SCOTLAND / Perth & Kinross

Why would you want to **stay** and **play** anywhere else

Just a short iron from our 46 bedroom hotel you'll find the first tees of our two scenic golf courses, **The Montgomery**, Par 71, 6438 yards and **The Bruce**, Par 73, 6256 yards. Both offer an enjoyable and stimulating challenge, whether you are a holiday golfer or low handicap player. And situated in Kinross we are well placed to reach some of Scotland's leading championship courses including; St Andrews, Gleneagles and Carnoustie. Call or email us today for a brochure and further details.

the green
HOTEL | LEISURE | BUSINESS | GOLF KINROSS

2 The Muirs, Kinross KY13 8AS, Scotland, Tel: +44 (0) 1577 863467, Email: reservations@green-hotel.com
www.green-hotel.com   *See also Colour Advertisement on page 77*

- Perthshire's scenic jewel
- Special off-season packages
- The golfing heart of Scotland
- Local treasures include Pitlochry, Taymouth & Rosemount
- Only 1 hour from Edinburgh

The Atholl Palace Hotel
Pitlochry, Perthshire PH16 5LY
Tel: 01796 472400 • Fax: 01796 473036
www.athollpalace.com • golf@athollpalace.com

FHG
K·U·P·E·R·A·R·D

FHG Guides publish a large range of well-known accommodation guides. We will be happy to send you details or you can use the order form at the back of this book.

Renfrewshire

BARRHEAD. **Fereneze Golf Club,** Fereneze Avenue, Barrhead, Glasgow G78 1HJ (0141-881 1519). *Location:* nine miles south west of Glasgow. Hilly moorland. 18 holes, 5962 yards. S.S.S. 70 *Green Fees:* weekdays £30.00 per round, £35.00 per day. *Eating facilities:* full catering/lounges *Visitors:* welcome by arrangement. *Society Meetings:* welcome, bookings arranged in advance. Professional: Hal Lee (0141-880 7058). Secretary: Graham McCreadie (Tel & Fax: 0141-881 7149).

BISHOPTON. **Erskine Golf Club,** Bishopton PA7 5PH (01505 862302). *Location:* club situated on south bank of the River Clyde. Leave M8 at Junction 30 onto M898 then left onto B815 (before bridge toll barriers), follow sign for Bishopton, Club approximately one mile on right. Parkland course, with breathtaking views over the river to the hills beyond. 18 holes, 6371 yards. S.S.S. 71. Putting green and practice area. *Green Fees:* £31.00 per round, £42.00 per day ticket (2004). *Eating facilities:* restaurant and bar, lunches, teas and dinners served at club. *Visitors:* welcome Monday to Friday by prior arrangement. Professional: Peter Thomson. Secretary: Donald F. McKellar.

BRIDGE OF WEIR. **Old Course Ranfurly Golf Club Ltd,** Ranfurly Place, Bridge of Weir PA11 3DE (01505 613612). *Location:* five miles west of Glasgow Airport. Moorland course. 18 holes, 6089 yards. S.S.S. 70. *Green Fees:* information not available; weekends only if introduced by and playing with a member. *Eating facilities:* dining room, lounge. *Visitors:* welcome weekdays, should contact club beforehand. Must be members of recognised golf clubs with Handicap Certificates. *Society Meetings:* on written application only. Secretary: Q.J. McClymont (Tel & Fax: 01505 613214).*
e-mail: secretary@oldranfurly.com
website: www.oldranfurly.com

BRIDGE OF WEIR. **Ranfurly Castle Golf Club Ltd,** Golf Road, Bridge of Weir PA11 3HN (01505 612609). *Location:* M8 from Glasgow exit Junction 29, A240 and A761 to Bridge of Weir. Moorland. 18 holes, 6284 yards. S.S.S. 71. Practice ground. *Green Fees:* weekdays £30.00 per round, £40.00 day ticket. *Eating facilities:* bar snacks all day; lunches, high teas, etc by arrangement. *Visitors:* welcome weekdays, at weekends only if accompanied by member. *Society Meetings:* catered for weekdays only. Professional: Tom Eckford (01505 614795; Fax: 01505 612609). Secretary: J. King (01505 612609)

THE APPEARANCE OF AN ASTERISK (*) AT THE END OF A CLUB OR COURSE ENTRY INDICATES THAT UP-TO-DATE INFORMATION HAS NOT BEEN SUPPLIED

ELDERSLIE. **Elderslie Golf Club,** 63 Main Road, Elderslie PA5 9AZ (01505 322835). *Location*: off M8 at Linwood turn-off, continue to roundabout, follow Elderslie signs A737. Club on main road. Parkland course. 18 holes, 6175 yards. S.S.S. 70. Practice area. *Green Fees*: £25.50 per round, £35.50 per day weekdays. *Eating facilities:* full meals and bar meals. *Visitors*: welcome weekdays, no visitors weekends. Caddy hire. *Society Meetings*: welcome weekdays, book through Secretary. Professional: R. Bowman (01505 320032). Secretary: Mrs A. Anderson (01505 323956; Fax: 01505 340346).
e-mail: eldersliegolfclub@btconnect.com
website: www.eldersliegolfclub.net

GOUROCK. **Gourock Golf Club,** Cowal View, Gourock PA19 1HD (01475 631001; Fax: 01475 631001). *Location:* two miles west of Gourock Station above Yacht Club. Heathland/parkland with spectacular views. 18 holes, 6512 yards. S.S.S. 72. *Green Fees:* information not available. *Eating facilities:* restaurant, full meals also bar snacks. *Visitors:* welcome Saturdays not before 4 pm. *Society Meetings:* catered for on application. Professional: James Mooney (01475 636834). Secretary: Alan D. Taylor (01475 631001).

GREENOCK. **Greenock Golf Club,** Forsyth Street, Greenock PA16 8RE (01475 720793). *Location:* one mile from town centre. Moorland course. 18 holes, 5835 yards. S.S.S. 68. *Green Fees:* information not available. *Eating facilities:* available. *Visitors:* welcome weekdays, not Saturdays. *Society Meetings:* advance booking required. Starter: Jim Duncan (01475 787236). Secretary: Eric J. Black (01475 720793).

GREENOCK. **Greenock Whinhill Golf Club,** Beith Road, Greenock PA16 9LN (01475 724694). *Location:* off Old Largs Road from Drumfrochar Road, Upper Greenock. Municipal course. Situated in hills high above Greenock, panoramic views of River Clyde and the surrounding area. 18 holes, 5504 yards. S.S.S. 68. *Green Fees:* information not available. *Visitors:* welcome except Saturdays. Secretary: Ian Shearer.

JOHNSTONE. **Cochrane Castle Golf Club,** Scott Avenue, Craigston, Johnstone PA5 0HF (01505 320146; Fax: 01505 325338). *Location:* turn left off Beith Road at Rannoch Road, second on right to end of Scott Avenue. Parkland course, fairly hilly wth excellent views to north. 18 holes, 6194 yards. S.S.S. 71. Practice area and green. *Green Fees:* weekdays £22.00 per round, £30.00 per day; weekends by introduction only. *Eating facilities:* full catering and bar. *Visitors:* welcome Monday to Friday, limited to 24. Arrangement by letter to Secretary. Trolleys. *Society Meetings:* catered for by arrangement, weekdays only. Professional: Alan J. Logan (01505 328465). Secretary: Mrs P. I. J. Quin (01505 320146).

SCOTLAND / Renfrewshire

KILMACOLM. Kilmacolm Golf Club, Porterfield Road, Kilmacolm PA13 4PD (01505 872139). *Location:* A761. Moorland course. 18 holes, 5964 yards. S.S.S. 69. Practice area. *Green Fees:* information not available. *Eating facilities:* diningroom and bar. *Visitors:* welcome on weekdays. *Society Meetings:* catered for. Professional: Iain Nicholson (01505 872695). Secretary: D.W. Tinton.*

LANGBANK. Gleddoch Golf Club, Langbank PA14 6YE (01475 540304; Fax: 01475 540201). *Location:* M8 west to Greenock/Langbank, exit B789 signposted Langbank/Houston. Parkland/moorland. 18 holes, 6357 yards. S.S.S. 71. Practice area, putting green. *Green Fees:* information not available. *Eating facilities:* bar, lounge and restaurant open all day. *Visitors:* welcome weekdays, restrictions only when competitions. Gleddoch House Hotel, 39 bedrooms plus self catering lodges. *Society Meetings:* welcome weekdays only excluding Bank Holidays. Professional: Keith Campbell (01475 540704; Fax: 01475 540201). Secretary: D.W. Tierney (01475 540304; Fax: 01475 540201). *

LOCHWINNOCH. Lochwinnoch Golf Club, Burnfoot Road, Lochwinnoch PA12 4AN (01505 842153; Fax: 01505 843668). *Location:* between Johnstone and Beith, off A737 on Largs road A760. Parkland, extremely scenic, set in quiet country village. 18 holes, 6243 yards. S.S.S. 71. Practice area. *Green Fees:* £22.00 per round, £30 per day. *Eating facilities:* licensed bar and catering every day. *Visitors:* welcome weekdays, weekends restricted. *Society Meetings;* welcome weekdays. Professional: Gerry Reilly (01505 843029). Administrator: R.J.G. Jamieson. e-mail: enquiries@lochwinnochgolf.co.uk website: www.lochwinnochgolf.co.uk

PAISLEY. Barshaw Golf Club, Barshaw Park, Glasgow Road, Paisley (0141-889 2908). *Location:* one mile from Paisley Cross travelling east towards Glasgow (Glasgow Road). Parkland course, flat/hilly. 18 holes, 5703 yards. S.S.S. 67. Putting green. *Green Fees:* information not available. *Eating facilities:* mobile van rear of clubhouse. *Visitors:* welcome anytime, must have a bag of clubs. *Society Meetings:* apply to Mr Bernard J. Forteath, Director of Environmental Services, Paisley. Secretary: W. Collins (0141-884 2533). *

PAISLEY. Paisley Golf Club, Braehead Road, Paisley PA2 8TZ (0141-884 3903). *Location:* right into Causeyside Street, Neilston Road, turn right into Glenburn, left at roundabout. Moorland course. 18 holes, 6466 yards. S.S.S. 72. Practice area. *Green Fees:* weekdays £26.00 per round, £38.00 per day. Full day golf package available. *Eating facilities:* bar snacks and full meals. *Visitors:* welcome by prior arrangement with Handicap Certificate, midweek not after 4pm and not at weekends or Public Holidays. *Society Meetings:* by arrangement with Secretary. Professional: Gordon Stewart (0141-884 4114). Club Manager: John Hillis (0141-884 3903).

PAISLEY. Ralston Golf Club, Strathmore Avenue, Ralston, Paisley PA1 3DT (0141-882 1349; Fax: 0141 883 9837). *Location:* Glasgow Road, two miles east of Paisley Cross. Parkland course. 18 holes, 6091 yards. S.S.S. 69. *Green Fees:* information not available. *Eating facilities:* dining room, bar. *Visitors:* welcome subject to course availability. *Society Meetings:* catered for on application subject to course availability. Professional: Colin Munro (0141-810 4925). Secretary: J. Pearson (0141-882 1349; Fax: 0141-883 9837). e-mail: thesecretary@ralstongolf.co.uk

PORT GLASGOW. Port Glasgow Golf Club, Devol Road, Port Glasgow PA14 5XE (01475 704181). *Location:* M8 to Newark Castle to roundabout, follow signs for Industrial Estate. Heathland with panoramic views of the Clyde and Argyll Hills. 18 holes, 5712 yards, 5224 metres. S.S.S. 68. Practice facilities. *Green Fees:* weekdays £18.00 a round, £24.00 per day; weekends £24.00 a round, £34 per day. *Eating facilities:* full catering service. *Visitors:* welcome, only by prior arrangement. *Society Meetings:* welcome by prior arrangement with Hon. Secretary (36 maximum), full catering available. Hon. Secretary: Hugh McGuiness (01475 704181).

RENFREW. Renfrew Golf Club, Blythswood Estate, Inchinnan Road, Renfrew PA4 9EG (0141-886 6692). *Location:* A8 Renfrew, turn in at Normandy Hotel. Flat parkland, wooded. 18 holes, 6818 yards, 6231 metres. S.S.S. 72. *Green Fees:* £30.00 per round, £40.00 per day. *Eating facilities:* daily restaurant facilities and bar. *Visitors:* welcome on introduction by members. Visiting parties by arrangement. *Society Meetings:* catered for on Mondays, Tuesdays and Thursdays only by written application to Secretary. Professional: Mr David Grant (0141-885 1754). Secretary: Martin Kinghorn (0141-886 6692; Fax: 0141-886 1808).

UPLAWMOOR. Caldwell Golf Club Ltd, Uplawmoor, Glasgow G78 4AU (01505 850329; Fax: 01505 850604). *Location:* five miles south of Barrhead, Glasgow on A736 Irvine Road. Parkland bounded by mature trees and a natural water hazard. 18 holes, 6335 yards, 5793 metres. S.S.S. 71. Practice area. *Green Fees:* £25.00 per round, £35.00 per day weekdays. *Eating facilities:* every day bar menu - filled rolls on Thursdays. *Visitors:* welcome weekdays only before 4.30pm, not weekends and Public Holidays (local and national). *Society Meetings:* weekdays only by prior arrangement. Professional: Stephen Forbes (Tel & Fax: 01505 850616). Secretary: H.I.F. Harper (01505 850366; Fax: 01505 850604).
e-mail: CaldwellGolfClub@aol.com
website: www.caldwellgolfclub.i8.com

www.uk-golfguide.com

THE APPEARANCE OF AN ASTERISK (*) AT THE END OF A CLUB OR COURSE ENTRY INDICATES THAT UP-TO-DATE INFORMATION HAS NOT BEEN SUPPLIED

Stirling & The Trossachs

ABERFOYLE. **Aberfoyle Golf Club,** Braeval, Aberfoyle, By Stirling FK8 3UY (01877 382493). *Location:* A81 Glasgow–Stirling. Parkland. 18 holes, 5204 yards. S.S.S. 66. *Green Fees:* information not available. *Eating facilities:* bar and catering available all day April to October; restricted service October to March. *Visitors:* welcome anytime but restrictions at weekends. Club Steward: Duncan Brown.*

ALLOA. **Alloa Golf Club,** Schawpark Golf Course, Sauchie, Alloa FK10 3AX (01259 722745 Fax: 01259 218796). *Location:* on A908 between Alloa and Tillicoultry. Parkland, tree lined fairways with spectacular views of Ochil Hills and beyond. 18 holes, 6229 yards, 5695 metres. S.S.S. 70. *Green Fees:* weekdays £26.00 per round, £36.00 per day; weekends £30.00 per round, £40.00 per day. *Eating facilities:* restaurant and lounge bar. *Visitors:* welcome. Phone to confirm booking. Guaranteed tee times can be booked. Ladies and gents changing rooms. *Society Meetings:* welcome weekdays only. Package: morning coffee, lunch, high tea, and two rounds of golf £40.00. Professional/Bookings: Bill Bennett (Tel & Fax: 01259 724476). Secretary: F. Nichols (01259 722745; Fax: 01259 218796).

ALLOA. **Braehead Golf Club,** Cambus, By Alloa FK10 2NT (01259 725766). *Location:* one mile west of Alloa on A907. Gently undulating parkland course with scenic views and a variety of challenging holes. 18 holes, 6053 yards. S.S.S. 69. Practice area. *Green Fees:* information not available. *Eating facilities:* bar/full catering available all day during Summer months; slightly restricted during Autumn/ Spring. *Visitors:* no restrictions but advisable to telephone in advance. Buggy and cart hire. *Society Meetings:* catered for with prior booking. Professional: Jamie Stevenson. Starter's Shop (01259 722078). Secretary: Mr George Nash.

ALVA. **Alva Golf Club,** Beauclerc Street, Alva FK12 5LH (01259 760431). *Location:* seven miles from Stirling on A91 Stirling to St Andrews Road - course lies at foot of Ochil Hills. Inland wooded hillside course with fast greens. 9 holes, 2423 yards, 2213 metres. S.S.S. 64. *Green Fees:* information not available. *Eating facilities:* snacks during bar hours. *Visitors:* welcome at all times. Secretary: R. McEvoy.*

BALFRON. **Balfron Golf Society,** Kepculloch Road, Balfron, By Glasgow G63 0PZ. *Location:* situated at the north end of the village on the A875, 18 miles from Glasgow and 18 miles from Stirling. Interesting, undulating upland course with splendid views. 18 holes, 5903 yards, S.S.S. 68. *Green Fees:* information not available. *Visitors:* welcome weekdays until 4pm, and at weekends, restrictions during competition days. *Society Meetings:* welcome subject to prior booking. Secretary: Brian Davidson (01360 550613). website: www.balfrongolfsociety.org.uk

DOLLAR. **Dollar Golf Club,** Brewlands House, Dollar FK14 7EA (01259 742400). *Location:* off A91 in Dollar, signposted. Hillside course without bunkers as designed by Ben Sayers in 1908. 18 holes, 5242 yards, 4796 metres. S.S.S. 66. *Green Fees:* weekdays £13.50 per round, £17.50 per day; weekends £22.00. *Eating facilities:* full catering (except Tuesdays) and bar. *Visitors:* welcome, booking in advance advisable weekends. Snooker table available. *Society Meetings:* welcome (maximum 30). Secretary: W.S. Morrison.

DOLLAR. **Muckhart Golf Club,** Muckhart, By Dollar FK14 7JH (01259 781423; Fax: 01259 781544). *Location:* off A91 east from Stirling, three miles north of Dollar. Undulating heathland. 18 holes, 6034 yards, 5523 metres. S.S.S. 70; 9 hole course, 3234 yards (medal tees), 3060 yards (casual tees), Par 35. Practice ground. *Green Fees:* information not available. *Eating facilities:* 11 am until 8.45, bar available. *Visitors:* welcome weekdays after 9.30am; weekends not before 10am or between 12 noon and 2.30pm. Trolley hire. *Society Meetings:* catered for. Professional: Keith Salmoni (Tel & Fax: 01259 781493). Club Manager: Scot Symon.

DRYMEN. **Strathendrick Golf Club,** Glasgow Road, Drymen, Glasgow G63 0AA (01360 660695). *Location:* one mile south of Drymen on A811. Undulating course, designed by Willie Fernie in 1901. 9 holes, 5116 yards. S.S.S. 64. *Green Fees:* weekdays £15.00 per 18 holes, £16.00 per day. *Visitors:* welcome 8.30am to 3.30pm weekdays only May to September. *Society Meetings:* by arrangement with Secretary. Visitors' Convener: D. McIntyre (01389 753559).

FALKIRK. **Bonnybridge Golf Club,** Larbert Road, Bonnybridge FK4 1NY (01324 812822). *Location*: five miles west of Falkirk. Parkland. 9 holes, 6132 yards. S.S.S. 70 Par 72. Practice area. *Green Fees:* weekdays £16.00 per round. With a member £6.00. *Eating facilities:* bar open lunchtimes and evenings; all day Saturday and Sunday. *Visitors*: welcome with prior permission, or accompanied by a member. *Society Meetings*: by arrangement with Hon Secretary. Secretary: J. Mullen (01324 812323).

FALKIRK. **Falkirk Golf Club,** 136 Stirling Road, Camelon, Falkirk FK2 7YP (01324 611061; Fax: 01324 639573). *Location:* one and a half miles west of town centre on A9. Parkland with streams. 18 holes, 6282 yards. S.S.S. 70. Large practice area. *Green Fees:* weekdays £20.00 per round, £30.00 per day; Sundays £30.00 per round, £40.00 per day. *Eating facilities:* full catering and bar facilities. *Visitors:* welcome Monday to Friday up to 4.00pm unaccompanied, with member only at weekends. *Society Meetings:* weekdays except Wednesdays, Sundays after 10.30am. Make arrangements with Starter (01324 612219). Professional: Stewart Craig. Secretary: John Elliott (01324 634118). e-mail: carmuirs.fgc@virgin.net

SCOTLAND / Stirling & The Trossachs

FALKIRK. **Polmont Golf Club,** Manuelrigg, Maddiston, Falkirk FK2 0LS (01324 711277; Fax: 01324 712504). *Location:* first turn to the right past Fire Brigade HQ in Maddiston. Undulating course. 9 holes, 6603 yards. S.S.S. 70. *Green Fees:* weekdays £10.00, Saturdays after 4.30pm, and Sundays £15.00. *Eating facilities:* lunches and high teas. *Visitors:* welcome without reservation, no visitors after 5pm weekdays or all day Saturday. *Society Meetings:* catered for. Secretary: John Ingram (01324 711277).

LARBERT. **Falkirk Tryst Golf Club,** 86 Burnhead Road, Stenhousemuir, Larbert FK5 4BD (01324 562415). *Location:* three miles from Falkirk (A9/A88), one mile from Larbert Station. Flat/seaside links style surface. 18 holes, 6053 yards, 5533 metres. S.S.S. 69. Practice area. *Green Fees:* information not available. *Eating facilities:* full catering - lunches, high teas, bar service. *Visitors:* welcome weekdays only except Bank and local Holidays. *Society Meetings:* catered for weekdays only except Bank and local Holidays. Professional: Mr Steven Dunsmore (01324 562091). Secretary: Mr R.C. Chalmers (01324 562054).*

LARBERT. **Glenbervie Golf Club Ltd,** Stirling Road, Larbert FK5 4SJ (01324 562983). *Location:* one mile north of Larbert on A9 Falkirk to Stirling road. Parkland course. 18 holes, 6438 yards. S.S.S. 71. Two practice areas. *Green Fees:* £30.00 per round, £40.00 per day. *Eating facilities:* lunches and high teas, bar snacks. *Visitors:* welcome weekdays until 4pm. Weekends as members' guests only. *Society Meetings:* up to 50 competitors catered for, Tuesdays and Thursdays only. Professional: Mr David Ross (01324 562725). Secretary: Ian R. Webster CA (01324 562605; Fax: 01324 551054).
e-mail: secretary@glenberviegolfclub.com

LENNOXTOWN. **Campsie Golf Club,** Crow Road, Lennoxtown, Glasgow G65 7HX (01360 310244). *Location:* on B822 Lennoxtown to Fintry. Hillside course with panoramic views. 18 holes, 5509 yards. S.S.S. 68. Practice fairway, bunker and putting green. *Green Fees:* £15.00 weekdays, £20.00 weekends. *Eating facilities:* full catering available. *Visitors:* welcome, weekdays unrestricted, weekends by prior arrangement. *Society Meetings:* catered for by arrangement. Professional: Mark Brennan (01360 310920). Club Manager: H.B. Weston.

POLMONT. **Grangemouth Golf Club,** Polmonthill, Polmont, Falkirk FK2 0YA (01324 711500). *Location:* quarter of a mile north of Junction 4 M9 motorway. Parkland course. 18 holes, 6314 yards. S.S.S. 70. Practice area. *Green Fees:* information not available. *Eating facilities:* catering and bar facilities available, open all day during season. *Visitors:* welcome, no restrictions. *Society Meetings:* welcome any day except Saturday. Professional: Greg McFarlane (01324 503840). Secretary: Jim McNairney (01324 713612) e-mail: jim.mcnairney@btinternet.com

STIRLING. **Bridge Of Allan Golf Club,** Sunnylaw, Bridge of Allan FK9 4LY (Tel & Fax: 01786 832332). *Location:* from Stirling, three miles, turn right at Bridge, keep taking the high road. Hilly course. 9 holes, 4932 yards, 4508 metres. S.S.S. 66. *Green Fees:* information not available. *Eating facilities:* by arrangement, licensed bar. *Visitors:* welcome without reservation, Saturdays after 4pm. *Society Meetings:* catered for by arrangement, phone in advance.*

STIRLING. **Brucefields Family Golf Centre,** Pirnhall Road, Bannockburn, Stirling FK7 8EH (01786 818184; Fax: 01786 817770). *Location:* half-a-mile from M9 and M80 interchange on A91. Parkland. 9 holes, 5025 yards. S.S.S. 66, Par 68; 9 hole par 3 course; driving range; putting green. *Green Fees:* information not available. *Eating facilities:* Fairways Cafe Bar and Restaurant. *Visitors:* welcome. *Society Meetings:* welcome. Corporate Membership and packages available. Club Manager: Paul Hamilton. Secretary: Christine Frost.*

STIRLING. **Stirling Golf Club,** Queen's Road, Stirling FK8 3AA (01786 464098; Fax: 01786 460090). *Location:* one mile from town centre, rail and bus stations; two miles from Junction 10 M9. Rolling parkland course. 18 holes, 6400 yards. S.S.S. 71. Practice area. *Green Fees:* £30.00 per round; £45.00 per day. *Eating facilities:* full bar and catering. *Visitors:* visiting parties welcome midweek. Casual visitors may reserve tee times only at weekends. *Society Meetings:* welcome. Professional: Ian Collins (01786 471490). Secretary: Alan Rankin (01786 464098; Fax: 01786 460090).

STIRLING. **Tillicoultry Golf Club,** Alva Road, Tillicoultry FK12 6BL (01259 750124). *Location:* on A91, nine miles east of Stirling. Parkland at foot of Ochil Hills. 9 holes, 5358 yards, 4904 metres. S.S.S. 67. *Green Fees:* weekdays £12.00 per round, £13.00 after 4pm; weekends £17.00 per round. *Eating facilities:* clubhouse bar, bar lunches. *Visitors:* welcome at all times outwith competitions. No children under 15 weekends until 4pm. *Society Meetings:* welcome by booking through Club Manager. Club Manager: (01259 750124).

FHG

Visit the **KUPERARD** website

www.holidayguides.com

for details of the wide choice of accommodation featured in the full range of FHG titles

---

PLEASE MENTION THE GOLF GUIDE WHEN YOU WRITE OR PHONE TO ENQUIRE ABOUT CLUBS OR ACCOMMODATION

Scottish Islands

COLONSAY

ISLE OF COLONSAY. **Colonsay Golf Club,** Machrins, Isle of Colonsay PA61 7YP. *Location:* two miles from ferry terminal. Traditional links course, reputedly 200 years old, natural, challenging and fun course. The 10th green has one of the best views in golf. 18 holes, 4775 yards. S.S.S. 72. *Green Fees:* information not available. *Eating facilities:* none on course, bar/ cafe/shop two miles away. *Visitors:* always welcome. *Society Meetings:* always welcome. Secretary: Donald MacAllister (01951 200307; Fax: 01951 200232).*
e-mail: donald@macallister4666.fslife.co.uk

CUMBRAE

MILLPORT. **Millport Golf Club,** Golf Road, Millport KA28 0HB (Tel & Fax: 01475 530306). *Location:* Caledonian McBrayne car ferry Largs slip to Cumbrae slip (seven minutes). Millport town four miles. On hill overlooking Firth of Clyde over Bute and Arran to Mull of Kintyre. Heathland with panoramic views. 18 holes, 5828 yards. S.S.S. 69. Large practice area. *Green Fees:* weekdays from £20.00 ; weekends and Bank Holidays from £26.00. *Eating facilities:* full à la carte and bar menu. *Visitors:* welcome without reservation. Tee reservations available for parties. Well stocked Professional's shop. Starter's telephone (01475 530305). *Society Meetings:* catered for. Special open amateur competition, Cumbrae Cup. Professional: (01475 530305). Secretary: Mrs Janette Frazer (Tel & Fax: 01475 530306).
e-mail: secretary@millportgolfclub.co.uk
website: www.millportgolfclub.co.uk

GIGHA

ISLE OF GIGHA. **Isle of Gigha Golf Club,** The Croft, Isle of Gigha PA41 7AA (01583 505287). *Location:* by ferry from Tayinloan to Gigha, course half a mile north from Post Office. Seaside course with scenic views looking over the Sound of Gigha and the Kintyre coast. 9 holes, 5042 yards (18 holes). S.S.S. 65. *Green Fees:* £12.50 per round. Phone for special rates. *Eating facilities:* available at Gigha Hotel. *Visitors:* always welcome. *Society Meetings:* welcome. Secretary: John Bannatyne (01583 505242).

HARRIS

SCARISTA. **Harris Golf Club,** Scarista, Isle of Harris. *Location:* 10 miles south of Tarbert, 50 miles south of Stornoway. Seaside links course on machair land, in an Area of Outstanding Natural Beauty. 9 holes, 2432 yards. S.S.S. 64 (18 holes). Practice area. *Green Fees:* information not available. *Visitors:* welcome, no restrictions. Secretary: John MacLean (01859 550226).

ISLAY

PORT ELLEN. **Islay Golf Club,** 25 Charlotte Street, Port Ellen PA42 7DQ (01496 300094; Fax: 01496 302117). *Location:* five miles north of Port Ellen. Championship course. 18 holes, 6235 yards, 5695 metres. S.S.S. 70. Practice area. *Green Fees:* arranged by Machrie Hotel. *Eating facilities:* full range at adjoining Machrie Hotel. *Visitors:* welcome anytime. Trolleys, caddies by arrangement. *Society Meetings:* all welcome.*

PORT ELLEN. **Machrie Golf Club,** The Machrie Hotel and Golf Links, Port Ellen PA42 7AN (01496 302310; Fax: 01496 302404). *Location:* adjacent Airport. Classic links. 18 holes, 6226 yards. S.S.S. 70. *Green Fees:* information not available. *Eating facilities:* full service in hotel. *Visitors:* welcome any day without reservation. *Society Meetings:* any number catered for. Golf packages available. Manager: Ian Brown.*
e-mail: machrie@machrie.com
website: www.machrie.com

LEWIS

STORNOWAY. **Stornoway Golf Club,** Lady Lever Park, Stornoway, Isle of Lewis HS2 0XP (01851 70 2240). *Location:* close proximity to town of Stornoway, in grounds of Lews Castle. Hilly parkland course with good views. 18 holes, 5252 yards. S.S.S. 67. *Green Fees:* £15.00 per round, £20.00 per day. Weekly tickets available - no Sunday golf. *Eating facilities:* light bar snacks available. *Visitors:* welcome. Car ferry daily (except Sunday) from Ullapool. Air services daily from Glasgow, Inverness and Edinburgh. *Society Meetings:* welcome, book through Secretary. Secretary: K.W. Galloway (01851 702240).
e-mail: admin@stornowaygolfclub.co.uk
website: www.stornowaygolfclub.co.uk

MULL

CRAIGNURE. **Craignure Golf Club,** Scallastle, Craignure PA65 6AY (01680 300402). *Location:* one mile from Oban/Mull main ferry terminal. Links course - first layout 1895, superb natural setting. 9 holes, 18 tees, 5351 yards. S.S.S. 66. Small practice area. *Green Fees:* information not available. *Eating facilities:* three-quarters-of-a-mile from MacGregor's Road House and Craignure Inn. *Visitors:* always welcome, except for Club inter-match days - please phone for details. Clubs, trolleys for hire, balls for sale. *Society Meetings:* welcome, discounts available. Secretary: Pat Van Niekerk (01688 302517). *

TOBERMORY. **Tobermory Golf Club,** Tobermory PA75 6PG. *Location:* situated on the cliffs above the town to the north west. Panoramic views of Sound of Mull; beautifully maintained and challenging course. 9 holes, 4921 yards, 4362 metres. S.S.S. 64. Practice ground. *Green Fees:* £15.00 per day, Juniors (under 18) £7.00 per day. *Eating facilities:* Club licence. Catering April–Oct. Green Fee ticket includes temporary membership. *Visitors:* unrestricted except for some competition days. Membership available, contact Secretary. Club and trolley hire available. *Society Meetings:* welcome. Secretary: Mr John Weir (01688 302338; Fax: 01688 302140).
e-mail: secretary@tobermorygolfclub.com
website: www.tobermorygolfclub.com

ORKNEY

KIRKWALL. **Orkney Golf Club,** Grainbank, Kirkwall KW15 1RD (01856 872457). *Location:* half-a-mile west of Kirkwall. Parkland with good views over Kirkwall Bay and North Isles. 18 holes, 5411 yards, 4964 metres. S.S.S. 67. Practice area. *Green Fees:* information not available. *Eating facilities:* bar lunches during summer months. *Visitors:* welcome at all times, restrictions only during competitions. *Society Meetings:* welcome, booking advised. Secretary: Andrew Bonner (01856 741317).
website: www.orkneygolfclub.co.uk

STROMNESS. **Stromness Golf Club Ltd,** Ness, Stromness KW16 3DU (01856 850772). *Location:* situated at south end of town. Seaside course bordering Hoy Sound. 18 holes, 4762 yards. S.S.S 63. *Green Fees:* £20.00 per day. *Eating facilities:* clubhouse with full facilities. *Visitors:* welcome, no restrictions. Bowling and tennis. *Society Meetings:* welcome by arrangement through Secretary. Secretary: G.A. Bevan (01856 850885).
website: www.stromnessgc.co.uk

WESTRAY. **Westray Golf Club,** Westray, Orkney Islands KW17 2DH (01857 677373). *Location:* half a mile from Pierowall Village. Seaside links course. 9 holes, 2316 yards, 2084 metres. S.S.S. 33. *Green Fees:* information not available. *Visitors:* welcome anytime. Secretary: Mr John Cable (01857 677287).*

SHETLAND

LERWICK. **Shetland Golf Club,** Dale Gott, Shetland ZE2 9SB (01595 840369). *Location:* four miles north of Lerwick on the A970. Parkland. 18 holes, 5562 yards. Par 68. S.S.S 68. Practice nets, chipping green and putting green. Driving range three miles away. *Green Fees:* £20.00 a day. *Eating facilities:* bar with sandwiches and snacks at lunchtimes, evenings and weekends. *Visitors:* welcome, no restrictions except on club competition days. Club and trolley hire available. Changing rooms, showers. *Society Meetings:* in writing by letter or e-mail. Secretary: A. Henderson.
e-mail: shetlandgolfclub@btopenworld.com

WHALSAY. **Whalsay Golf Club,** Skaw Taing, Whalsay ZE2 9AL (01806 566259). *Location:* five miles from Symbister ferry terminal - ferries run from Laxo to Symbister. Seaside course with wonderful scenery and birdlife in abundance - Britain's most northerly 18 holes. 18 holes, 6140 yards. S.S.S. 69. Changing rooms. *Green Fees:* £15.00 per round (2005). *Eating facilities:* lunch/dinner available by arrangement. *Visitors:* welcome. Saturday/Sunday competitions, check before travelling. Secretary: Charles Hutchison (01806 566450) and Harry Sandison (01806 566481).

For full details of clubs and courses, plus convenient accommodation
www.uk-golfguide.com

SKYE

SCONSER. **Isle of Skye Golf Club,** Sconser IV48 8TD (01478 650414). *Location:* on A87 halfway between Broadford and Portree, 20 miles from Skye Bridge. Seaside course with spectacular views to Isle of Raasay and North Skye. 9 holes (18 tees), 4677 yards, 4277 metres. S.S.S. 64. *Green Fees:* information not available. *Eating facilities*: tearoom serving light snacks. *Visitors:* welcome at all times. Changing and toilet facilities, trolleys and clubs for hire, small shop. *Society Meetings:* welcome. Secretary: I. Macmillan (01478 650414).*
e-mail: Isleofskye.golfclub@btinternet.com
website: www.uk-golf.com/clubs/isleofskye

SKEABOST BRIDGE. **Skeabost Golf Club,** Skeabost House Hotel, Skeabost Bridge IV51 9NP (01470 532202; Fax: 01470 532454). *Location:* A850 Portree to Dunvegan Road. Woodland course. 9 holes, 3114 yards. S.S.S. 59 (for 18 holes). *Green Fees:* information not available. *Eating facilities:* lunch, evening meals in hotel; bar food in public bar. *Visitors:* welcome, under 13s must be accompanied by an adult. *Society Meetings:* accepted. Club Captain: D. Sutherland. Secretary: D.J. Matheson.
e-mail: reception@skeabostcountryhouse.com

SOUTH UIST

LOCHBOISDALE. **Askernish Golf Club,** Askernish, Lochboisdale. *Location:* off South Uist main road B888. Seaside, undulating, designed by Tom Morris Senior 1891. 9 holes, 18 tees, 5042 yards. S.S.S. 68. *Green Fees:* information not available. *Visitors:* welcome. Secretary: Neil Elliot (01878 700298).*
e-mail: askernish.golf.club@cwcom.net

TIREE

SCARINISH. **Vaul Golf Club,** Scarinish, Isle of Tiree PA77 6XH. *Location:* two miles from Scarinish and half a mile from Lodge Hotel, ferry from Oban four hours and plane from Glasgow 45 minutes. Links course with crystal white beaches to north and south with beautiful views on all sides. 9 holes, 5674 yards (18 holes). S.S.S. 68 (18 holes). *Green Fees:* information not available. *Visitors:* welcome, no restrictions. Enquiries and fees to R. Omand, Royal Bank of Scotland, Scarinish. Secretary: Mrs S. Sweeney (01879 220729).*

Each year FHG GUIDES produce a large range of attractive holiday accommodation guides for all kinds of holiday opportunities throughout Britain.
They are great value for money and are available in most bookshops and larger newsagents at the following prices.

FHG
KUPERARD

Coast & Country Holidays	Britain's Best Holidays	Bed & Breakfast Stops	Golf Guide	Country Inns & Pubs of Britain	Short Break Holidays in Britain
£7.99	£6.99	£7.99	£9.99	£7.99	£7.99

Country Hotels of Britain	Pets Welcome!	Caravan & Camping Holidays	Self-Catering Holidays in Britain	Children Welcome!	Pets Welcome!
£7.99	£8.99	£6.99	£7.99	£7.99	£8.99

Holiday & Accommodation Guides

THE GOLF GUIDE 2006   WALES   453

Golf in Wales
Where to Play, Where to Stay

Golf Tee-Time Service

Golf Tee-Time Service offers the complete range of golfing services. From tee-time bookings, Brittany Ferries golf breaks in France/Northern Spain, Golf breaks in Wales and Portugal, through to large corporate golf days. Please phone **01822 618181** for more information on any of our services or visit **www.golfteetimeservice.co.uk** (e-mail info@golfteetimeservice.co.uk).

- **Tournaments:** For competitive golf with a friendly atmosphere played on superb courses. We have a tournament programme.
- **Corporate Management:** A total solution-why waste time, money and precious resources organising your golf day.
- **Tee-Time Booking:** We specialise in organising pre-reserved tee-times in Portugal, Spain, France, Mallorca, UK and Ireland.
- **UK Specials:** Offering superb value for short breaks at some great locations.
- **World-Wide Golf:** Golf holidays in Madeira, Barbados, Bermuda, USA and other exotic locations.
- **Brittany Ferries Golf Desk 0870-9021818.** We manage the Brittany Ferries Golf Desk and can offer superb golf in France.
- **Greens of Southern Wales 0870-600608.** Golf breaks in Wales.
- **Golf in Portugal 01822-610035.** Golf breaks in Portugal.

Monmouth Golf Club, South Wales

www.uk-golfguide.com

Anglesey & Gwynedd

ABERDOVEY. **Aberdovey Golf Club,** Aberdovey LL35 0RT (01654 767493; Fax: 01654 767027). *Location:* west end of Aberdovey on A493, adjacent to railway station. Seaside links, easy walking. 18 holes, 6445 yards, 5893 metres. S.S.S. 71. Practice ground, limited. *Green Fees*: weekdays from £30.00 per round; weekends from £35.00 per round, subject to review. Concessions for parties over 12 and for guests at local hotels. *Eating facilities*: restaurant, bar and lounge. *Visitors*: welcome on production of Handicap Certificate, restrictions some weekends. *Society Meetings*: catered for by prior arrangement (not August or Bank Holidays). Professional: John Davies (01654 767602). Secretary: J.M. Griffiths (01654 767493; Fax: 01654 767027). website: www..aberdoveygolf.co.uk

ABERSOCH. **Clwb Golff Abersoch,** Golf Road, Abersoch LL53 7EY (01758 712622; Fax: 01758 712777). *Location:* A55 to Bangor, coast road to Abersoch. Parkland and seaside links course. 18 holes, 5671 yards. S.S.S. 68, Par 69. Practice area, putting green. *Green Fees:* from £22.50 per round. *Eating facilities:* full catering and bar service. *Visitors:* welcome, Ladies' day Thursdays, Gents' competition day Sundays. Handicap Certificate required. Shop. Buggies, carts. *Society Meetings:* welcome by prior arrangement. Professional/Manager: Alan Drosinos Jones (01758 712622; Fax: 01758 712777).*
e-mail: pro@abersochgolf.co.uk
website: www.abersochgolf.co.uk

ANGLESEY. **Baron Hill Golf Club Ltd,** Beaumaris, Anglesey LL58 8YW (01248 810231). *Location:* turn left on approach to Beaumaris from Menai Bridge on A545. Moorland course with panoramic view of Snowdonia and Menai Straits. 9 holes, 5570 metres. S.S.S. 69. *Green Fees:* £16.00, £10.00 with a member. *Eating facilities:* comprehensive menu (closed Mondays). *Visitors:* welcome, competitions most Sundays, Ladies' Day on Tuesday mornings. *Society Meetings:* welcome by prior arrangement - special rates and packages available. Secretary: Alwyn Pleming.

ANGLESEY. **Bull Bay Golf Club Ltd,** Bull Bay, Amlwch, Isle of Anglesey LL68 9RY (01407 830213). *Location:* one mile west of Amlwch on A5025 coastal road towards Cemaes Bay and Holyhead. Coastal heathland championship course; Wales' northernmost golf course. 18 holes, 6217 yards. S.S.S. 70. Practice ground and putting green. *Green Fees:* £25.00 per day weekdays; £30.00 per day weekends and Bank Holidays. Discount for parties of 12 and over. *Eating facilities:* bar snacks, dining room; limited facilities on Mondays. *Visitors:* welcome, competitions permitting; advance bookings advised. Snooker and pool. *Society Meetings:* welcome, booking essential. Professional: John Burns (01407 831188). Secretary/Manager: (01407 830960; Fax: 01407 832612).

ANGLESEY. **Penrhyn Golf Complex,** Llanddaniel - Fâb LL60 6NN (01248 421150). *Location:* A5 turn off at Star Crossroads taking Llanddaniel road. Follow Brown Tourism signs from the village. Parkland with some small hills. 9 holes, Par 3. 14 bay covered and floodlit driving range and putting area. *Green Fees:* £3.50. Pay as you play course. Special rates weekdays 10am - 5pm for 18 holes. *Visitors*: no restrictions. Professional: Paul Lovell (Visiting). Owner: Mr W.R. Carter.

BALA. **Bala Golf Club,** Penlan, Bala LL23 7YD (01678 520359; Fax: 01678 521361). *Location:* turn right before coming to Bala Lake on the main Bala-Dolgellau road. Upland course with superb views in the Snowdonia National Park. 10 holes, 4970 yards, 4512 metres. S.S.S. 64. *Green Fees:* £15.00 weekdays, £20.00 weekends. *Eating facilities:* bar with snacks available. *Visitors:* welcome all year, some restrictions Bank Holidays and weekends. Snooker table and small golf shop. *Society Meetings:* very welcome by prior arrangement. Professional: Tony Davies (visiting). Secretary: G. Rhys Jones.
e-mail: balagolfclub@onetel.com

BANGOR. **St Deiniol Golf Club,** Penybryn, Bangor LL57 1PX (01248 353098; Fax: 01248 370792). *Location:* at A5/A55 Junction 11 intersection, follow A5122 for one mile to eastern outskirts of Bangor. Parkland course with magnificent views. 18 holes, 5654 yards, 5068 metres. S.S.S. 67. *Green Fees:* (2005) weekdays £19.00, weekends and Public Holidays £23.00. *Eating facilities:* two bars; full catering Mondays excepted. *Visitors:* welcome without reservation, restrictions at weekends. *Society Meetings:* welcome by prior arrangement. Secretary: Bob Thomas M.B.E.
e-mail: secretary@stdeiniol.fsbusiness.co.uk
website: www.st-deiniol.co.uk

Clwb Golff Y Bala • Bala Golf Club *Upland course with spectacular views*
SOCIETIES ARE ASSURED OF A VERY WARM WELSH WELCOME
Green Fees: £15 Weekdays, £20 Weekends
(Generous reductions for parties)
2 FOR 1 VOUCHERS ACCEPTED.
Contact: Mr G. R. Jones on
Tel: 01678 520359 • Fax: 01678 521361
e-mail: balagolfclub@onetel.com

Aberdovey Golf Club
Tel: 01654 767210 (Club)

Clubhouse (1998) now complements famous championship links.

On site accommodation available.

Telephone Secretary John Griffiths (01654 767493) for party concessions and hotel discounts.

Aberdovey, Gwynedd LL35 0RT
www.aberdoveygolf.co.uk

TREFEDDIAN HOTEL
ABERDOVEY

FOR MORE INFORMATION OR A COLOUR BROCHURE CONTACT US

01654 767213
WWW.TREFWALES.COM

- LIFT TO ALL FLOORS
- FAMILY OWNED AND MANAGED
- NEAR ABERDOVEY GOLF CLUB
- INDOOR AND OUTDOOR PLAY AREAS

R *elax in our stylish en suite bedrooms with spectacular sea views and balconies*

E *njoy the spacious lounges with views over Cardigan Bay from sumptuous sofas and dine in our award-winning dining room*

L *eisure facilities include indoor heated swimming pool, tennis court, putting green, snooker room and beauty salon*

A *n idyllic location, minutes away from golden sandy beaches or the many mountains and lakes of Snowdonia*

X *perience it!*

AND ESCAPE...

CLWB GOLFF ABERSOCH
Golf Road, Abersoch, Gwynedd LL53 7EY
www.abersochgolf.co.uk
18 Hole picturesque Links and Parkland Course with panoramic views
* Par 69 * SSS 68 * Yardage 5671 *
SOCIETIES AND VISITORS WELCOME
Full Bar and catering facilities.   Open 7 days a week.
Green Fees: 18-hole round from £22.50
Special Rates for Societies and Corporate Days.
Tel: 01758 712622 (Secretary) • 01758 712636 (Office) • Fax: 01758 712777

See also Colour Advertisement on page 45

BEAUMARIS. **The Princes' Course,** Henllys Hall, Beaumaris, Anglesey LL58 8HU (01248 811717; Fax: 01248 811511). *Location*: quarter of a mile through Beaumaris town centre. Parkland course. 18 holes, 6062 yards, S.S.S. 70. Practice ground. *Green Fees:* information not available. *Visitors*: welcome, please telephone beforehand. Tuition from PGA Professionals available. Professionals: Peter Maton/ David Gadsby (01248 811717; Fax: 01248 811511). Director of Golf: Peter Maton.
e-mail: henllys@HPBsite.com

BRYNTEG. **Storws Wen Golf Club,** Brynteg LL78 8JY (01248 852673). *Location*: one-and-three-quarter miles along the B5108 from Benllech to Brynteg. Parkland course with a stream, three lakes and spectacular views. 9 holes, 5002 yards. S.S.S. 64. *Green Fees:* information not available. *Eating facilitie*s: clubhouse with full facilities. *Visitors*: always welcome. *Society Meeting*s: welcome, terms on request. General Manager: R. Hooper. *

CAERNARFON. **Royal Town of Caernarfon Golf Club,** Aberforeshore, Llanfaglan, Caernarfon LL54 5RP (01286 678359; Fax: 01286 672535). *Location:* less than a mile from the historic Royal town of Caernarfon. Parkland course in superb sea and mountain setting. 18 holes, 5941 yards. S.S.S. 68. *Green Fees:* Summer – Monday £15.00 per round, Tuesday to Friday £25.00 per round, £29.00 per day, Saturday £32.00, Sunday £27.00. *Eating facilities:* excellent catering and bar facilities, except Mondays. *Visitors:* welcome with no restrictions except Saturdays, please contact Professional to reserve tee time. Tuition, shop. *Society Meetings:* welcome, subject to pre-arranged bookings. Professional: Aled Owen (01286 678359).

CRICCIETH. **Criccieth Golf Club,** Ednyfed Hill, Criccieth LL52 0PH (01766 522154). *Location:* in High Street (A497) turn right past Memorial Hall, keep going up lane to Club. 18 holes, 5755 yards. S.S.S. 68. *Green Fees:* £20.00 per day. *Eating facilities:* light meals available April to September. *Visitors:* welcome without reservation. *Society Meetings:* catered for with prior reservation. Secretary: M.G. Hamilton (01766 522697).

DOLGELLAU. **Dolgellau Golf Club,** Pencefn Road, Dolgellau LL40 2ES (01341 422603). *Location:* half-a-mile from town centre. Parkland with panoramic views. 9 holes and alternate tees, 4671 yards. S.S.S. 63. Practice facility. *Green Fees:* information not available. *Eating facilities:* catering facilities available. *Visitors:* welcome without reservation. *Society Meetings:* catered for. Special packages available. Secretary: Richard Stockdale (01341 422603).
website: www.dolgellaugolfclub.com

FFESTINIOG. **Clwb Golff Ffestiniog,** Y Cefn, Ffestiniog LL41 4LG (01766 762637). *Location:* located on B4391, one mile from Ffestiniog village. Upland course. 9 holes, 4570 yards. S.S.S. 66. *Green Fees:* weekdays £10.00, weekends £10.00. *Visitors:* welcome at any time, some restrictions mainly at weekends during club competitions. *Society Meetings:* by prior arrangement. Secretary: Andrew Roberts (Tel & Fax: 01766 831829).
e-mail: ffestinioggolf@aol.com

HARLECH. **Royal St David's Golf Club,** Harlech LL46 2UB (01766 780203). *Location:* A496 lower Harlech road. Championship links course. 18 holes, 6591 yards. S.S.S. 73. Large practice ground. *Green Fees:* weekdays £42.00 per round; weekends £52.00 per round (subject to review); reduced rates in winter months. *Eating facilities:* full catering and bar facilities available. *Visitors:* must be members of bona fide golf clubs with Handicap - booking essential. *Society Meetings:* catered for by prior arrangement. Professional: John Barnett (01766 780857). Secretary: D.L. Morkill (01766 780361; Fax: 01766 781110).
e-mail: secretary@royalstdavids.co.uk
website: www.royalstdavids.co.uk

LLANFAIRFECHAN. **Llanfairfechan Golf Club,** Llannerch Road, Llanfairfechan LL33 0EB (01248 680144). *Location:* signposted off old A55, 300 yards west of traffic lights. Hillside parkland. 9 holes, 3119 yards. S.S.S. 57. *Green Fees:* information not available. *Eating facilities:* no eating facilities, bar open weekends and weekday evenings. *Visitors:* welcome anytime except Sundays. *Society Meetings:* by arrangement, weekdays only in Summer. Secretary: M.J. Charlesworth (01248 680524).*

CRICCIETH GOLF CLUB
Ednyfed Hill, Criccieth LL52 0SB
Green Fees: £20 per day
Parties welcome by prior arrangement
Clubhouse: 01766 522154
Treasurer: 01766 523385

Local and Country Membership available

A pleasant undulating 18-hole course on a hilltop with magnificent views.

WALES / Anglesey & Gwynedd

LLANGEFNI. Llangefni Public Golf Course, Clai Road (B5111), Llangefni, Isle of Anglesey LL77 8YQ. Parkland course, eight Par 3s, one Par 4. 9 holes, 1467 yards, 1342 metres. Practice net. *Green Fees:* information not available. *Eating facilities:* light refreshments only. *Visitors:* welcome at all times, no restrictions. Fully stocked Discount Golf Shop. Professional: Paul Lovell (01248 722193).*

MORFA BYCHAN. Porthmadog Golf Club, Morfa Bychan, Porthmadog LL49 9UU (Tel & Fax: 01766 514124). *Location:* turn in Porthmadog High Street at Woolworths towards Black Rock Sands, club on left hand side of road one mile west. Part parkland, part seaside links. 18 holes, 6322 yards. S.S.S. 71. Two practice grounds. *Green Fees:* per round £28.00 weekdays, £35.00 weekends and Bank Holidays; £35.00 and £42.00 for day tickets. Discounts available for larger parties. *Eating facilities:* lounge bar, golfers' bar and large restaurant. *Visitors:* welcome, no restrictions except for competition days. Snooker room. *Society Meetings:* catered for by prior arrangement. Bookings via Office Manager: Åse Richardson (01766 514124). Professional: Peter L. Bright (01766 513828). Club Manager: Gwilym Jones e-mail: secretary@porthmadog-golf-club.co.uk website: www.porthmadog-golf-club.co.uk

NEFYN. Nefyn and District Golf Club, Golf Road, Morfa Nefyn, Pwllheli LL53 6DA (Fax: 01758 720476). *Location:* north coast of Lleyn Peninsula, two miles west of Nefyn. Seaside course. 27 holes. Main Course - 18 holes, 6548 yards. S.S.S. 71. Practice area. *Green Fees:* Weekdays & Sundays £31.00 per round, £39.00 per day; Saturdays and Bank Holidays £37.00 per round, £48.00 per day. 10% discount for parties of 12 or more players. *Eating facilities:* full restaurant facilities and two bars. *Visitors:* welcome without reservation, except club competition days. Snooker. *Society Meetings:* catered for by arrangement with Secretary. Professional: John Froom (01758 720102). Secretary: J. B. Owens (01758 720966).

PENMAENMAWR. Penmaenmawr Golf Club, Conwy Old Road, Penmaenmawr LL34 6RD (01492 623330). *Location:* A55 expressway three miles west of Conwy. Parkland with panoramic views. 9 holes (18 tees), 5306 yards. S.S.S. 67. Two practice areas. *Green Fees:* £15.00 weekdays, £20.00 weekends. *Eating facilities:* bar and bar snacks, meals available daily except Tuesdays. *Visitors:* welcome anytime except Saturdays. *Society Meetings:* welcome by arrangement (not Saturdays). Secretary: Mrs J. Dryhurst Jones (01492 623330).

PWLLHELI. LLyn Golf, Pen-y-Berth, Penrhos, Pwllheli LL53 7HG (01758 701200). *Location*: off A499 between Pwllheli and Abersoch. New 9-hole pay and play course. 1782 yards, Par 3 and 4. 14-bay driving range, bunker practice area. *Green Fees:* information not available. *Eating facilities:* refreshments available. *Visitors*: welcome. Open daily. Clubs for hire. *Society Meetings:* welcome.*
website: www.pen-y-berth.co.uk

PWLLHELI. Pwllheli Golf Club, Golf Road, Pwllheli LL53 5PS (01758 701644). *Location:* A499 from Caernarvon (20 miles). Parkland/seaside links. 18 holes, 6108 yards. S.S.S. 70. Two practice areas and putting green. *Green Fees:* information not available. *Eating facilities:* two large lounge bars and diningroom. Steward: (01758 701633). *Visitors:* welcome without reservation. Pro shop. *Society Meetings:* welcome. Professional: S. Pilkington (01758 612520). General Manager: Mrs Michele Nash (01758 701644).*
e-mail: admin@pwllheligolfclub.co.uk
website: www.pwllheligolfclub.co.uk

Please mention THE GOLF GUIDE when you enquire about clubs or accommodation

---

TAL-Y-BONT, NEAR BARMOUTH LL43 2BQ
Tel: 01341 247269 • Fax: 01341 242639

Our holiday park home is ideally situated for the discerning golfer as we are just 15 minutes by car from the championship course of Royal St Davids in Harlech. Other courses for consideration are picturesque Dolgellau and Aberdovey to the south with Porthmadog and delightful Nefyn to the north.

e-mail: info@islawrffordd.co.uk • website: www.islawrffordd.co.uk

---

GWESTY NANHORON ARMS HOTEL

'On the spectacular Lleyn Peninsula'

Ffordd Dewi Sant,
Nefyn, Pwllheli,
Gwynedd LL53 6EA
Telephone 01758 720203

The Nanhoron Arms Hotel provides the perfect base for your stay whether for business, holiday or sporting event.

The Bedrooms 19 en suite (bath or shower) including family rooms, suites, doubles and singles. Colour TV, hairdryer, tea & coffee facilities. Latest Z-beds and baby cots are available

Lounge Bar & Family Room Well stocked Lounge Bar. Original bar meals together with old favourites. Special children's menu and play area for younger guests.

Restaurant St David's Restaurant offers breakfast, lunch or dinner, truly "An Experience of Good Taste"

Activities Golf, pony trekking, clay shooting & walking

★ **Just 1½ miles from Nefyn Golf Club** ★

Anglesey & Gwynedd / WALES

RHOSNEIGR. **The Anglesey Golf Club Ltd,** Station Road, Rhosneigr, Anglesey LL64 5QX (Tel & Fax: 01407 811202; Club House 01407 810219). *Location*: turn south off A55 signposted Rhosneigr, Aberffraw. In about three miles turn right at Llanfaelog church about one mile from course. Flat links course with sand dunes and heathland. 18 holes, 6300 yards. S.S.S. 71. *Green Fees*: please phone for current prices. *Eating facilities*: catering facilities available all day. *Visitors*: welcome, advanced booking advisable. Dress smart casual. *Society Meetings*: club societies welcome from £10.00 per person. Professional tuition. Contact Matthew Parry for further details (01407 811202).*
e-mail: info@theangleseygolfclub.com
website: www.theangleseygolfclub.com

TREARDDUR BAY. **Holyhead Golf Club,** Trearddur Bay, Anglesey LL65 2YL (Tel & Fax: 01407 763279). *Location:* A55 to Holyhead, turn left at roundabout on B4545 for 1 mile, left for Trearddur Bay. Heathland, heavy gorse cover, superb sea views. Course designed by James Braid. 18 holes, 6058 yards. S.S.S. 70. *Green Fees:* information not available. *Eating facilities:* restaurant/bar. *Visitors:* welcome. *Society Meetings:* catered for weekdays. Dormy House accommodation available for up to 14. Professional: Steve Elliot (01407 762022). Secretary/Manager: John Williams.*
e-mail: MgrSec@aol.com
website: www.holyheadgolfclub.co.uk

The Anglesey Golf Club Ltd

SOCIETIES WELCOME
• **GREEN FEES** •

Phone Club for latest rates.
Society Packages available from £10 per person, ring for details, excellent winter links.
• Bar Meals and Restaurant • Membership available, no joining fee. • Fully-stocked Pro Shop
• Professional tuition • Ideal stopover for parties going to or coming from Ireland.

Contact Matthew Parry for further details – 01407 811202
www.angleseygolfclub.co.uk • info@angleseygolfclub.co.uk

FHG
·K·U·P·E·R·A·R·D·

FHG Guides
publish a large range of well-known accommodation guides. We will be happy to send you details or you can use the order form at the back of this book.

For full details of clubs and courses, plus convenient accommodation

www.uk-golfguide.com

North Wales

ABERGELE. **Abergele Golf Club,** Tan-y-Gopa Road, Abergele, Conwy LL22 8DS (01745 824034; Fax: 01745 824772). *Location:* A55 from Chester. Below Gwrych Castle, Abergele. Parkland in scenic setting. 18 holes, 6256 yards. S.S.S. 70. USGA greens. Practice ground and indoor practice nets. *Green Fees:* £30.00 weekdays; £35.00 weekends and Bank Holidays. For special party rates (12 or more) contact Secretary. *Eating facilities:* restaurant and bar. *Visitors:* welcome, avoid Tuesdays (Ladies' Day) and Saturdays difficult due to club competitions. Buggy hire available, trolleys. *Society Meetings:* visiting party packages available. Professional: Iain R. Runcie (Tel & Fax: 01745 823813). Secretary: Chris Langdon (01745 824034; Fax: 01745 824772). website: www.abergelegolfclub.co.uk

BETWS-Y-COED. **Betws-y-Coed Golf Club,** The Clubhouse, Betws-y-Coed LL24 0AL (01690 710556). *Location:* take Railway Museum Road in centre of the village. Parkland, flat scenic course on valley floor of River Conwy. 9 holes, 18 tees, 4998 yards. S.S.S. 63. *Green Fees:* information not available. *Eating facilities:* bar open from 12 noon onwards. *Visitors:* no restrictions provided there are no club competitions. *Society Meetings:* welcome. Secretary: P. Rowley.*
e-mail: info@golf-betws-y-coed.co.uk
website: www.golf-betws-y-coed.co.uk

BODELWYDDAN. **Kinmel Park Golf Complex,** Abergele Road, Bodelwyddan LL18 5SR (01745 833548). *Location:* Junction 25 off A55 Expressway at the famous White Marble church. Flat parkland course. 9 holes, 1550 yards. S.S.S. 58. 25 bay undercover and floodlit driving range. Practice chipping and putting green. *Green Fees:* Pay and Play course £4.00 weekdays, £5.00 weekends. Subject to review. *Visitors:* welcome. Golf lessons available. *Society Meetings:* Welcome, special rates. Professional: Rhodri Lloyd Jones. Director: Mrs Fetherstonhaugh.

CHESTER near. **Northop Country Park Golf Club,** Northop, Near Chester CH7 6WA (01352 840440; Fax: 01352 840445). *Location:* travel west on M56, follow signs for North Wales. A494/A55 for Northop. Parkland course set amongst 300 year old oak trees, designed by John Jacobs. 18 holes, 6735 yards, 6128 metres. S.S.S. 74. Practice range and academy. *Green Fees:* information not available. *Eating facilities:* clubroom for snacks, club restaurant for full meals. *Visitors:* welcome. St David's Park Hotel only five minutes away for accommodation. *Society Meetings:* welcome depending on availability. Professional: Matthew Pritchard. Director of Golf: Neil Sweeney.*

CHIRK. **Chirk Golf Club,** Chirk, Near Wrexham LL14 5AD (01691 774407; Fax: 01691 773878). *Location:* just off A5 towards Llangollen. Generally flat course. 18 holes, 6541 yards. S.S.S. 72. 9 hole Par 3 course, 15 bay driving range. *Green Fees:* from £14.00. *Eating facilities:* bar and restaurant. *Visitors:* welcome seven days a week. *Society Meetings:* all welcome. Professional: M. Maddison (01691 774407).

COLWYN. **Old Colwyn Golf Club,** The Clubhouse, Woodland Avenue, Old Colwyn LL29 9NL (01492 515581). *Location:* signposted at main Abergele road, Old Colwyn. Parkland. 9 holes (x 2), 5263 yards. S.S.S. 68. Practice area. *Green Fees:* information not available. *Eating facilities:* bar and meals by arrangement. *Visitors:* welcome except Saturday afternoons or Wednesday evenings. *Society Meetings:* welcome by arrangement with Secretary. Secretary: D.A. Jones. *

THE APPEARANCE OF AN ASTERISK (*) AT THE END OF A CLUB OR COURSE ENTRY INDICATES THAT UP-TO-DATE INFORMATION HAS NOT BEEN SUPPLIED

CLWB GOLFF BETWS-Y-COED GOLF CLUB

"The Jewel of the Nines"

Situated in the heart of the Snowdonia National Park you will find something special. Visitors and societies always welcome. Packages available.

Contact Secretary: Pat Rowley
01690 710556
e-mail: info@golf-betws-y-coed.co.uk • web: www.golf-betws-y-coed.co.uk

See also Colour Advertisement on page 47

CONWY. **Conwy (Caernarvonshire) Golf Club,** Morfa, Conwy LL32 8ER (01492 593400). *Location:* follow signs for Conwy Marina off A55. Seaside links. 18 holes, 6647 yards. S.S.S. 72. Practice facilities. *Green Fees:* Winter package (coffee on arrival, 18 holes plus meal) - weekdays £29.00, weekends £32.00; Summer (April to October) - weekdays £44.00 per day, £36.00 per round, weekends and Bank Holidays £48.00 per day, £40.00 per round. *Eating facilities:* available daily April to October. *Visitors:* welcome with reservation, restrictions at weekends. *Society Meetings:* catered for on application to Secretary. Professional: Peter Lees (Tel & Fax: 01492 593225). Secretary: Mr D.L. Brown (01492 592423; Fax: 01492 593363). e-mail: secretary@conwygolfclub.co.uk website: www.conwygolfclub.co.uk

DENBIGH. **Denbigh Golf Club,** Henllan Road, Denbigh LL16 5AA (01745 816669. Fax: 01745 814888). *Location:* one mile from Denbigh town centre on the B5382 road. Parkland with excellent views. 18 holes, 5712 yards. S.S.S. 68. *Green Fees:* weekdays from £20.50, weekends from £27.50. Subject to review. *Eating facilities:* catering daily, bar. *Visitors:* welcome. *Society Meetings:* by arrangement. Professional: M.D. Jones (01745 814159). Secretary: Christine Hewitt. e-mail: denbighgolfclub@aol.com website: www.denbighgolfclub.co.uk

DENBIGH near. **Bryn Morfydd Hotel Golf Club,** Llanrhaeadr, Near Denbigh LL16 4NP (01745 589090; Fax: 01745 589093). *Location:* off A525 between Denbigh and Ruthin. Mature parkland course overlooking the Vale of Clwyd. Two courses. The Duchess Course - 9 holes, 1146 yards. Par 27; The Duke's Course - 18 holes, 5685 yards. S.S.S. 67, Par 70. Practice area. *Green Fees:* information not available. *Eating facilities:* courses attached to three star Hotel, two restaurants, two bars, clubhouse. *Visitors:* welcome by arrangement. Hotel accommodation - 25 rooms en suite. *Society Meetings:* welcome by arrangement all year. Secretary/Director of Golf: C. Henderson. Proprietor: D. & S. Frith.

CAERLYR HALL HOTEL

Conwy Old Road, Dwygyfylchi, Conwy,
North Wales LL34 6SW
Tel: 01492 623518 Fax: 01492 622070

Charming country house hotel set in a natural amphitheatre with sea and mountain views, all rooms are en suite and well equipped.
Excellent cuisine, fine wines and a characterful bar await you.

Enjoy playing at any of the eight courses within a five mile radius or the eight others within easy travelling distance.

Proprietors: Dorothy & Peter Warner   WTB ★★★ Hotel
www.caerlyrhallhotel.co.uk

See also Colour Advertisement on page 49

18-hole parkland course offering a challenging round of golf, combined with superb panoramic views along the Vale of Clwyd to the coast.

Visitors and Societies welcome
Packages start from £20.50

Denbigh Golf Club
Henllan Road, Denbigh,
North Wales LL16 5AA
Secretary: 01745 816669
denbighgolfclub@aol.com
www.denbighgolfclub.co.uk

HOLYWELL GOLF CLUB
Brynford, Holywell, North Wales CH8 8LQ

The course lies on a plateau in the village of Brynford a mile-and-a-half outside Holywell.
Its position is renowned for invigorating fresh air and views of the Clwydian range and Snowdonia.
18 hole course.
Golf clubs, Societies and Visitors welcome.
For further details contact the Secretary.

6th green – 165 yards par 3

Tel/Fax: 01352 713937 • Professional (Tel: 01352 710040)

CLWB GOLF TREFFYNON • ESTABLISHED 1906 • HON SECRETARY BOB FIDDAMAN

See also Colour Advertisement on page 47

FLINT. **Flint Golf Club,** Cornist Park, Flint CH6 5HJ (01352 732327). *Location:* A548 coast road, one mile from town centre. Hilly parkland. 9 holes, 5927 yards. S.S.S. 69. Practice area. *Green Fees:* £12.00 per day. *Eating facilities:* full bar and catering 11am to 11pm. *Visitors:* welcome except Sundays. *Society Meetings:* welcome by arrangement. Secretary: Mr Geoff Hughes (01352 735245).

HAWARDEN. **Hawarden Golf Club,** Groomsdale Lane, Hawarden CH5 3EH (01244 531447. Fax: 01244 536901). *Location:* A55, left at Ewloe interchange, follow Hawarden signs. Undulating parkland. 18 holes, 5842 yards, 5340 metres. S.S.S. 69, Par 69. *Green Fees:* information not available. *Eating facilities:* full bar and catering. *Visitors:* welcome by arrangement. Some restrictions Wednesday (Ladies' Day). *Society Meetings:* catered for by prior arrangement. Summer and Winter packages available. Professional: Alex Rowlands (01244 520809). Secretary: Malcolm Coppack. *

HOLYWELL. **Holywell Golf Club,** Brynford, Near Holywell CH8 8LQ (01352 713937). *Location:* turn off A55 at Springfield Hotel onto A5026, turn left at traffic lights, up hill for one and a half miles, turn right at crossroads. Flat natural terrain, links type course, a good test of golf. 18 holes, 6100 yards. S.S.S. 70. *Green Fees:* weekdays £20.00, weekends and Bank Holidays £25.00. Special rates between November and March. *Eating facilities:* full bar facilities and catering. *Visitors:* welcome weekdays without reservation; Bank Holidays and weekends by prior arrangement with Secretary. Snooker table. *Society Meetings:* by prior arrangement with Secretary. Professional: Matthew Parsley (01352 710040). Hon Secretary: Bob Fiddaman (Tel & Fax: 01352 713937). e-mail: holywell_golf_club@lineone.net

HOLYWELL **Kinsale Golf Course,** Llanerchymor, Holywell CH8 9DX (01745 561080; Fax: 01745 561079). *Location:* A55 expressway, Holywell to A548; opposite White Ship Abakham Textiles. Magnificent view over Dee Estuary towards the Wirral. 9 holes, 5944 yards. S.S.S. 69. Driving range. *Green Fees:* information not available. *Eating facilities:* snacks in clubhouse, bar and restaurant at Kinsale Hall Hotel. *Visitors:* always welcome; pay as you play course. *Society Meetings:* welcome seven days. Director of Golf/Professional/Secretary: Alan Norwood.*

NORTH WALES GOLF CLUB
West Shore, Llandudno LL30 2DZ

Join us at the North Wales
• *Par 71* •

Enjoy the infinite variety of this true links championship course with its natural beauty, undulating fairways and slick greens.

• Visitors and societies welcome •
• No entrance fee payable for membership •
• Full and Country Membership available •
(Country Membership mileage restriction now 50 miles)
• Full catering facilities available •
• Golf Shop Golf Professional •
• Buggies, trolleys and clubs for hire •

e-mail: golf@nwgc.freeserve.co.uk
website: www.northwalesgolfclub.co.uk
SEE ALSO COLOUR ADVERTISEMENT ON PAGE 48

Office: 01492 875325 • Pro: 01492 876878

LLANDUDNO. **North Wales Golf Club Ltd,** 72 Bryniau Road, West Shore, Llandudno LL30 2DZ. *Location:* two miles off the A55 expressway on the A470 Junction. Seaside links with wonderful views of Conwy estuary and mountains. 18 holes, 6287 yards, S.S.S. 71. Practice ground. *Green Fees:* information not available. *Eating facilities:* full bar and catering facilities. *Visitors:* welcome after 9.30am weekdays, 10.30am weekends. Buggies, carts and clubs for hire. *Society Meetings:* catered for by arrangement. Professional: R.A. Bradbury (01492 876878; Fax: 01492 872420). General Manager: Gren Jones (01492 875325; Fax: 01492 873355).
e-mail: golf@nwgc.freeserve.co.uk
website: www.northwalesgolfclub.co.uk

The Imperial Hotel

Ideally situated overlooking Llandudno Bay. Convenient for Maesdu, North Wales and Conwy Golf Clubs. Award-winning restaurant, two bars. Use of leisure facilities during stay including 45' heated indoor pool.

The Promenade, Llandudno LL30 1AP • Tel: 01492 877466 • Fax: 01492 878043
e-mail: imphotel@btinternet.com • www.theimperial.co.uk

See also Colour Advertisement on page 48

LLANDUDNO. **Llandudno Golf Club (Maesdu) Ltd,** Hospital Road, Llandudno LL30 1HU (Tel & Fax: 01492 876450). *Location*: Llandudno General Hospital. A55 and then A470. Parkland. 18 holes, 6545 yards. S.S.S. 72. Practice ground. *Green Fees*: weekdays £25.00 per round, £30.00 per day; weekends and Bank Holidays £35.00 per round/day. *Eating facilities*: full catering, bar (large) available. *Visitors*: welcome, must book. Buggies, electric trolleys for hire. *Society Meetings*: must be booked. Professional: S. Boulden (01492 875195). Secretary: George Dean (01492 876450)
e-mail: secretary@maesdugolfclub.co.uk
website: www.maesdugolfclub.co.uk

LLANDUDNO. **Rhos-on-Sea Residential Golf Club**, Penrhyn Bay, Llandudno LL30 3PU (01492 549100). *Location:* A55 to Colwyn Bay follow signs to Rhos-on-Sea, one mile past Rhos-on-Sea on coast road in Penrhyn Bay. Flat seaside parkland course. 18 holes, 6064 yards. S.S.S. 69. *Green Fees:* information not available. *Eating facilities:* bar meals 12-2pm, teas, coffees, snacks available all day. Evening meals by arrangement. Licensed bar open 11a -3pm lunch, 5.30pm-11pm evenings; Sundays 12-2pm lunch, 7pm-10.30pm evenings. *Visitors:* all welcome any time, prior booking required particularly weekends. 18 bedrooms, two snooker tables, TV lounge. One £100 jackpot fruit machine. Trolley hire available. *Society Meetings:* all welcome. Professional: Mike Macara (01492 548115). Secretary: John Leigh (01492 549100).*

LLANGOLLEN. **Vale of Llangollen Golf Club Ltd.,** The Clubhouse, Llangollen LL20 7PR (Tel & Fax: 01978 860906). *Location:* one and a half miles east of town on the A5. Course is set on the valley floor bordered by the River Dee. 18 holes, 6656 yards, 6086 metres. S.S.S. 73. Practice ground. *Green Fees:* weekdays £30.00 per round, £40.00 per day, weekends £35.00 per round, £45.00 per day. Subject to review. *Eating facilities:* full catering service. *Visitors:* welcome any day subject to availability, handicap certificate essential. *Society Meetings:* welcome. Professional: David Vaughan (01978 860906). Secretary: Tel & Fax: 01978 860906.

MOLD. **Mold Golf Club,** Cilcain Road, Pantymwyn, Mold CH7 5EH (01352 741513; Fax: 01352 741517). *Location:* 14 miles west of Chester. Take A55 from Chester for Mold. Follow Pantymwyn signs from Mold. Uplands course offering extensive views of Cheshire, Liverpool, Peak District. 18 holes, 5628 yards. S.S.S. 67. Practice ground and practice green. *Green Fees:* information not available. *Eating facilities:* extensive restaurant and bar facilities. *Visitors:* welcome by prior arrangement. Tee bookings advised at weekends. Trolley hire. *Society Meetings:* welcome, subject to tee availability. Professional: Mark Jordan (01352 740318) (Lessons by appointment). Secretary: C. Mills (01352 741513; Fax: 01352 741517).*
e-mail: info@moldgolfclub.co.uk).

MOLD. **Padeswood and Buckley Golf Club,** The Caia, Station Lane, Padeswood, Near Mold CH7 4JD (01244 550537). *Location*: A5118 Chester - Mold, one mile west of Castle Cement Works, half a mile off main road. Flat parkland; river, lakes. 18 holes, 6042 yards. S.S.S. 69. Practice ground. *Green Fees:* information not available. *Eating facilities:* bar all day every day, catering daily. *Visitors:* welcome except on Sundays. Buggies, carts for hire; two snooker tables. *Society Meetings:* welcome, enquiries through Secretary; packages available. Professional: David Ashton (01244 543636). Secretary: J.M. Conway (01244 550537).*

For full details of clubs and courses, plus convenient accommodation

www.uk-golfguide.com

Prestatyn Golf Club

◆ *Seaside links Championship course, host to* WGU *Championships and many other national events.*

◆ *18 holes, 6564 yards, 5959 metres. S.S.S. 72.*

◆ *Visitors and societies welcome.*

◆ *Quote ref GG8 and get £1 off your green fee.*

◆ *Full bar and catering service.*

◆ *Hire of buggy, trolley and clubs available.*

Marine Road East, Prestatyn LL19 7HS
Tel: 01745 854320
www.prestatyngc.co.uk ◆ e-mail: prestatyngcmanager@freenet.co.uk

See also Colour Advertisement on page 49

THE APPEARANCE OF AN ASTERISK (*) AT THE END OF A CLUB OR COURSE ENTRY INDICATES THAT UP-TO-DATE INFORMATION HAS NOT BEEN SUPPLIED

PADESWOOD. **Old Padeswood Golf Club Ltd,** Station Road, Padeswood, Near Mold CH7 4JD (01244 547701). *Location:* off A5118 Chester to Mold road, eight miles from Chester and three miles from Mold. Situated in the beautiful Alyn Valley - nine holes flat parkland, nine holes slightly undulating. 18 holes, 6668 yards, 6079 metres. S.S.S. 72/Ladies 73. Practice ground. *Green Fees:* weekdays £25.00, with member £13.00; weekends £30.00, with member £15.00. *Eating facilities:* diningroom, bar meals - two bars. *Visitors:* welcome anytime subject to tee availability. *Society Meetings:* welcome, written applications or telephone John Whitfield on (01244 547701). Professional: Tony Davies (01244 547401). Co-Secretary: Mrs B. Jones (01244 550414; Fax: 01244 545082). Hon. Secretary: Mr B. Slater (01244 816573; Fax: 01244 545082).
e-mail: oldpad@par72.fsbusiness.co.uk
website: www.oldpadeswoodgolfclub.co.uk

PRESTATYN. **Prestatyn Golf Club**, Marine Road East, Prestatyn LL19 7HS (01745 854320). *Location*: A548, on approaching Prestatyn from Chester direction turn right at sign for Pontins Holiday Village and follow club sign. Seaside links Championship course. 18 holes, 6564 yards, 5959 metres. S.S.S. 72. Practice areas. *Green Fees:* £25.00 weekdays; £30.00 Sundays and Bank Holidays. *Eating facilities*: full catering available, bar. *Visitors*: welcome. *Society Meetings*: special "all-in" arrangement for 27 holes. Professional: D. Ames (01745 854320). Manager: J.R. Williams (Tel & Fax: 01745 854320).
e-mail: **prestatyngcmanager@freenet.co.uk**
www.prestatyngc.co.uk   www.ukgolfer.org

PRESTATYN. **St Melyd Golf Club,** The Paddock, Meliden Road, Prestatyn LL19 8NB (01745 854405; Fax: 01745 856908). *Location:* on main Prestatyn to Rhuddlan road, just outside Meliden. Parkland course with tight fairways and varied greens, set twixt the hills and the sea. 9 holes, 5811 yards. S.S.S. 68. *Green Fees:* information not available. 2 fore 1 available on green fees. *Eating facilities:* full range of catering facilities except Tuesdays which is by arrangement. *Visitors:* welcome without reservation but advise phone call first in summer season. Restriction Saturdays Competition Day; Thursdays Ladies' Day. Snooker room. *Society Meetings:* catered for by arrangement with Secretary (various golf packages). Golf coaching available from PGA Professional: Andrew Barnett. Administrator: Jean McCormick.
e-mail: info@stmelydgolf.co.uk
website: www.stmelydgolf.co.uk

RHYL. **Rhyl Golf Club,** Coast Road, Rhyl LL18 3RE (01745 353171; Fax: 01745 360007). *Location:* situated alongside A548, the Rhyl/ Prestatyn coast road. Flat links. 9 or 18 holes, 6220 yards. S.S.S. 70. Practice ground. *Green Fees:* information not available. *Eating facilities:* dining room, catering and bar snacks available. *Visitors:* always welcome; some restrictions when club competitions in play. Trolleys for hire. Buggies available. *Society Meetings:* society specials available, maximum 60; discounts for 10 or more. Professional: John Stubbs Secretary: Tim Metcalfe (01745 353171).*
e-mail: rhylgolfclub@hotmail.com
website: www.rhylgolfclub.com

RHUDDLAN. **Rhuddlan Golf Club,** Meliden Road, Rhuddlan LL18 6LB (01745 590217). *Location*: leave A55 at St Asaph for Rhuddlan, clubhouse 100m from roundabout at Prestatyn end of Rhuddlan. Gently undulating, parkland course with natural hazards; set amid splendid scenery with fine views of the Clwydian Hills. 18 holes, White 6473 yards. S.S.S. 71; Yellow 6291 yards, S.S.S. 70; Ladies 5768 yards, Par 70. Extensive practice ground. *Green Fees*: £25.00 to £30.00. *Eating facilities*: full restaurant facilities daily. *Visitors*: welcome at all times when course demand permits. Sundays with member only. No denim. Snooker table. *Society Meetings:* weekdays only, maximum 50. Professional: Andrew Carr (01745 590898). Secretary: Martin C.Jones (01745 590217; Fax: 01745 590472).
e-mail: secretary@rhuddlangolfclub.co.uk
website: www.rhuddlangolfclub.co.uk

RHUDDLAN GOLF CLUB FOUNDED 1930
Meliden Road, Rhuddlan, Denbighshire LL18 6LB
Tel: 01745 590217 (Secretary) • 01745 590898 (Pro)
Fax: 01745 590472 • e-mail: secretary@rhuddlangolfclub.co.uk
website: www.rhuddlangolfclub.co.uk

Our gently undulating and scenic parkland course is only 20 miles from Chester and less than an hour's drive from Holyhead. We offer a warm welcome, a championship quality course, and full bar and restaurant facilities. Please telephone the Secretary for our club brochure giving details of golfing breaks, our many open competitions and good local hotels.

• **18 holes, parkland course • Length 6473 yards • Par 70, SSS 71 • Green Fees £25 to £30**
• **Societies must book • Secretary Mr Martin C. Jones • Professional Mr A. Carr**

See also Colour Advertisement on page 49

PLEASE MENTION THE GOLF GUIDE WHEN YOU WRITE OR PHONE TO ENQUIRE ABOUT CLUBS OR ACCOMMODATION

RUTHIN. Ruthin Pwllglas Golf Club, Pwllglas, Near Ruthin LL15 2PE (01824 702296). *Location:* Corwen Road (A494), two miles south of Ruthin. Hilly parkland. 10 holes, 5418 yards. S.S.S. 66. Practice area. *Green Fees:* weekdays £16.00, weekends and Bank Holidays £22.00. *Eating facilities:* Bar. Secretary can arrange catering for visiting parties. *Visitors:* welcome without reservation, phone call advisable in high season and at weekends. *Society Meetings:* catered for. Hon. Secretary: Eric Owen (01824 702383 after 6pm)

WREXHAM. **Moss Valley Golf Club,** Moss Road, Wrexham LL11 6HA (Tel & Fax: 01978 720518). Private members' club. *Location:* off A541 from Wrexham roundabout. Parkland course meandering through wooded valley. 9/18 holes (twin tees on every hole), 2531 yards. S.S.S. 67. *Green Fees:* information not available. *Visitors:* welcome, booking required at weekend. *Society Meetings:* contact in advance. Manager/Secretary: John Parry.*
e-mail: info@mossvalleygolf.com
website: www.mossvalleygolf.com

THE APPEARANCE OF AN ASTERISK (*) AT THE END OF A CLUB OR COURSE ENTRY INDICATES THAT UP-TO-DATE INFORMATION HAS NOT BEEN SUPPLIED

WREXHAM. **Plassey Golf Course,** Eyton, Wrexham LL13 0SP (01978 780020; Fax: 01978 781397). *Location:* 4 miles south-east of Wrexham. Take B5426 and follow brown "Tourist Attraction" signs to "Plassey" from A483 Wrexham by-pass. Undulating parkland course. 9 holes, 4961 yards, Par 66. Practice area, driving net, pitch and putt. *Green Fees:* April to September – midweek £9.00 9 holes, £15.00 18 holes; weekends £10.00 9 holes, £16.00 18 holes. October to March – midweek £6.50 9 holes, £9.00 18 holes; weekends £7.50 9 holes, £12.50 18 holes. *Visitors:* most welcome. Please book start times at weekends. Full bar and catering facilities. Golf course is part of Plassey Leisure Park which includes shops, boutiques, craft centre, brewery, garden centre, blacksmith and award-winning Caravan & Campsite. *Society Meetings:* most welcome (please book start times at weekends). Proprietor/Professional: Simon Ward (PGA Qualified).
website: www.plasseygolf.co.uk

WREXHAM. **Wrexham Golf Club,** Holt Road, Wrexham LL13 9SB (01978 351476; Fax: 01978 364268). *Location*: A543 north east of Wrexham. 18 holes, 6263 yards. S.S.S. 70. Practice facilities. *Green Fees*: weekdays £30.00; weekends £35.00. *Eating facilities*: daily. *Visitors*: welcome, subject to competitions and Society bookings. *Society Meetings*: catered for Monday, Wednesday, Thursday and Fridays only. Professional: P. Williams (01978 351476). Secretary: Jim Johnson (01978 364268).

MOSS VALLEY GOLF CLUB
Moss Road, Moss, Wrexham LL11 6HA • Tel & Fax: 01978 720518

Established in the late 1980s the 9 hole course was designed by Golf Architects in a beautiful parkland setting just 5 minutes' drive from the centre of Wrexham. The scenery can be compared with any part of North Wales and some of the views from the course are quite breathtaking. Every hole is different in character, providing a good test of golf for both beginners and the experienced. Various categories of membership are available and the club actively encourages youngsters to become involved in the club. 9/18 holes. Twin tees on every hole.

website: www.mossvalleygolf.com
e-mail: info@mossvalleygolf.com

See also Colour Advertisement on page 48

Visit the FHG website
www.holidayguides.com
for details of the wide choice of accommodation featured in the full range of FHG titles

Carmarthenshire

AMMANFORD. **Glynhir Golf Club,** Glynhir Road, Llandybie, Ammanford SA18 2TF (Tel & Fax: 01269 851365). *Location:* seven miles from end of M4, between Ammanford and Llandybie on the A483. Turn right up Glynhir Road and proceed for about two miles. Undulating wooded parkland course. 18 holes, 6010 yards. S.S.S. 70. *Green Fees:* Summer weekdays £18.00, weekends £24.00, Winter weekdays £12.00, weekends £17.00. *Eating facilities:* full catering available. *Visitors:* welcome. *Society Meetings:* welcome anytime by prior arrangement with the Secretaries (special rates available). Professional: Richard Herbert (01269 851010). Joint Secretaries: D. Joshua, B. Jenkins (01269 851365).
e-mail: glynhir.golfclub@virgin.net
website: http://freespace.virgin.net/glynhir.golfclub

CARMARTHEN. **Carmarthen Golf Club,** Blaenycoed Road, Carmarthen SA33 6EH (01267 281588). *Location:* four miles north-west of town. Undulating heathland - a good test of golf. 18 holes, 6210 yards. S.S.S. 71. Large practice ground. *Green Fees:* weekdays £20.00, weekends £25.00. *Eating facilities:* catering every day, limited Wednesdays. *Visitors:* welcome with proof of Handicap, telephone call advisable at weekends. *Society Meetings:* by arrangement. Professional: Jon Hartley (01267 281493). Secretary: John Morgan (01267 281588).
e-mail: carmarthengolfc@aol.com
website: www.carmarthengolfclub.com

CARMARTHEN. **Derllys Court Golf Club,** Llysonnen Road, Carmarthen SA33 5DT (Tel. & Fax: 01267 211575). *Location:* three miles west of Carmarthen on A40, signposted. Gently undulating parkland. 18 holes, 5650 yards. Practice area. *Green Fees*: information not available. *Eating facilities:* bar/lounge and restaurant. *Visitors:* welcome at all times. *Society Meetings:* welcome by prior arrangement. Secretary: Rhian Walters.
e-mail: derllys@hotmail.com
website: www.derllyscourtgolfclub.co.uk

KIDWELLY/LLANELLI. **Glyn Abbey Golf Club,** Trimsaren, Kidwelly SA17 4LB (01554 810278; Fax: 01554 810889). *Location*: five miles north west of Llanelli on the B4317 between Trimsaran and Carway. Parkland course with spectacular views, Hawtree design, mature woodland. 18 holes, 6173 yards, Par 70. S.S.S. 70. *Green Fees*: £15.00 midweek, £20.00 weekends. *Eating facilities*: fully licensed clubhouse and restaurant. *Visitors*: welcome at all times with no restrictions. Advisable to phone ahead and book. *Society Meetings*: always very welcome by prior arrangement. Professional: Darren Griffiths. Managing Director: Martin Lane (01554 810304).
e-mail: course-enquiries@glynabbey.co.uk
website: www.glynabbey.co.uk

FHG

K·U·P·E·R·A·R·D

Other specialised
FHG Guides
Published annually: available in all good bookshops or direct from the publisher.

Recommended **COUNTRY INNS & PUBS** OF BRITAIN £7.99

Recommended **COUNTRY HOTELS** OF BRITAIN £7.99

Recommended **SHORT BREAK HOLIDAYS** IN BRITAIN £7.99

The bestselling **PETS WELCOME!** £8.99

FHG Guides • Abbey Mill Business Centre, Seedhill, Paisley, Renfrewshire PAI ITJ
Tel: 0141-887 0428 • Fax: 0141-889 7204
e-mail: admin@fhguides.co.uk
www.holidayguides.com

466 Carmarthenshire / WALES — THE GOLF GUIDE 2006

LLANDYSUL. **Saron Golf Course,** Penwern, Saron, Llandysul SA44 5EL (01559 370705). *Location*: midway between Carmarthen and Newcastle Emlyn on the A484. Parkland course in the Teifi Valley set in 50 acres. 9 holes 18 tees. 9 holes 2091 yards, 18 holes 4412 yards. *Green Fees*: 9 holes £8.00, under 15s £5.00, 18 holes £11.00, under 15s £6.00. *Visitors*: welcome at all times. Three cottages on course, sleeping six/ four/two. *Society Meetings*: welcome. Secretary: Mrs M.B.L. Searle (01559 370705). e-mail: c9mbl@sarongolf.freeserve.co.uk
website: www.saron-golf.com

LLANELLI. **Ashburnham Golf Club,** Cliffe Terrace, Burry Port SA16 0HN (01554 832466). *Location:* south side of A484, four miles west of Llanelli. Seaside links with Championship status. 18 holes. S.S.S. 73. Practice area. *Green Fees:*£27.50 - £40.00. *Eating facilities:* catering except Mondays, two bars. *Visitors:* welcome, starting times available from the Secretary. Handicap Certificates. Carts. *Society Meetings:* by arrangement with Secretary. Professional: Robert A. Ryder (01554 833846). Secretary: D.K. Williams (01554 832269).

ASHBURNHAM GOLF CLUB

FOUNDED 1894
Cliff Terrace,
Burry Port, West Wales SA16 0HN
Tel: 01554 832269   Pro: 01554 833846

One of the classic Welsh links courses, Ashburnham has hosted many important tournaments. Overlooking Carmarthen Bay, the course has its first two and final two holes inland, near the clubhouse. Full catering facilities, club and trolley hire.
18 holes • Par 72
Green Fees £27.50 – £40.00

See also Colour Advertisement on page 50

The Diplomat Hotel Felinfoel Road, Aelybryn, Llanelli SA15 3PJ
Tel: 01554 756156 • Fax: 01554 751649 • AA/WTB ★★★
The Diplomat Hotel offers a rare combination of charm and character, with excellent well appointed facilities to ensure your comfort. Explore the Gower Peninsula and the breathtaking West Wales coastline. Salmon & trout fishing, horse riding, golf, and motor racing at Pembrey are all within reach.
e-mail: reservations@diplomat-hotel-wales.com • www.diplomat-hotel-wales.com

---

FHG

Visit the FHG website
www.holidayguides.com
for details of the wide choice of accommodation featured in the full range of FHG titles

---

PLEASE NOTE

All the information regarding Golf Clubs in this guide is given in good faith in the belief that it is correct. However, the publishers cannot guarantee the facts given in these pages, neither are they responsible for changes in ownership or facilities, such as green fees, that may take place after the date of going to press. Readers should always satisfy themselves that the facilities they require are available and that the terms, if quoted, still apply.

Ceredigion

ABERYSTWYTH. **Aberystwyth Golf Club,** Brynymor Road, Aberystwyth SY23 2HY (01970 615104; Fax: 01970 626622). *Location:* north end of Promenade, access near to cliff railway. Undulating meadowland designed by Harry Vardon. 18 holes, white - 6119 yards. S.S.S. 71. Practice ground. *Green Fees:* information not available. *Eating facilities:* restaurant and bar. *Visitors:* welcome at all times, pre-booking helpful. *Society Meetings:* welcome, Special Deals available. Professional: (01970 625301). Secretary: (01970 615104).*

BORTH. **Borth and Ynyslas Golf Club Ltd,** Borth, Ceredigion SY24 5JS (Tel & Fax: 01970 871202). *Location:* A487 Machynlleth to Aberystwyth, turn off to Borth. Gently undulating links. 18 holes, 6116 yards. S.S.S. 70 men, 72 ladies. Practice ground. *Green Fees:* information not available. *Eating facilities:* clubhouse with full catering and bar. *Visitors:* welcome at all times. *Society Meetings:* by prior arrangement with the Secretary, special rates available. Professional: J.G. Lewis (01970 871557). Secretary: G.J. Pritchard (01970 871202).*
e-mail: secretary@borthgolf.co.uk

For full details of clubs and courses, plus convenient accommodation

www.uk-golfguide.com

Aberystwyth Golf Club
Brynymor Road, Aberystwyth SY23 2HY

Set above the picturesque town of Aberystwyth, this championship 18-hole course was designed by Harry Vardon and was formed in 1911. It provides both exciting and challenging golf for all players, as well as offering the most picturesque and panoramic views of Cardigan Bay and the mountains of Snowdonia. It is also the ideal venue for Corporate and Society golf days and provides flexible packages to suit individual requirements.

Our resident PGA Golf Professional is on hand to assist with your golfing needs. Our friendly bar and clubhouse is managed by our resident Steward, and our restaurant caters for a variety of palates, from simple bar snacks to à la carte.

You will be sure of a friendly welcome at Aberystwyth Golf Club.

Tel: 01970 615104
e-mail: aberystwythgolf@talk21.com
www.aberystwythgolfclub.com

468 Ceredigion / WALES   THE GOLF GUIDE 2006

CARDIGAN. Cardigan Golf Club, Gwbert-on-Sea, Cardigan SA43 1PR (01239 612035). *Location*: three miles from Cardigan. Seaside links course. 18 holes, 6687 yards. S.S.S. 73. *Green Fees*: weekdays £27.50, weekends and Bank Holidays £32.50. *Eating facilities*: catering and bar facilities available. *Visitors*: welcome. Tee reserved for members 1pm–2pm. *Society Meetings*: very welcome. Reductions on application. Professional: Mr Colin Parsons (01239 615359). Secretary: Mr J. Jones (Tel & Fax: 01239 621775).
e-mail: golf@cardigan.fsnet.co.uk
website: www.cardigangolf.co.uk

LAMPETER. Cilgwyn Golf Club, Llangybi, Lampeter SA48 8NN (01570 493286). *Location:* five miles north-east of Lampeter, off A485 Tregaron Road at Llangybi. Flat parkland course with natural hazards. 9 holes, 5309 yards, S.S.S. 66. Large practice ground and putting green. *Green Fees:* weekdays £12.00, weekends £17.00. *Eating facilities:* full bar and snacks. *Visitors:* welcome without restrictions – please telephone at weekends April to September. Trolley hire, pool table, TV. Caravan parking and golf for Caravan Club members. *Society Meetings:* welcome Wednesdays and Fridays by prior arrangement. Package deals for parties of six or more. Secretary: J.D. Morgan (01570 423226).

LLANDYSUL. Cwmrhydneuadd Golf Club, Pentregat, Llandysul SA44 6HD (01239 654933). *Location:* follow the Aberystwyth to Cardigan A487 trunk road to the village of Pentregat, then follow signs to golf club. Parkland course set in picturesque, secluded valley, surrounded by wooded hills. Includes three small lakes. 9 holes, 4061 yards. S.S.S. 62. *Green Fees*: information not available. *Eating facilities:* club house; home-made snacks, meals. *Visitors:* welcome, no restrictions. *Society Meetings*: welcome. Secretary: J. Curry (01559 362253).*

LLANRHYSTYD. Penrhos Golf and Country Club, Llanrhystyd SY23 5AY (01974 202999; Fax: 01974 202100). *Location:* nine miles south of Aberystwyth on A487. Parkland and meadowland with lakes and panoramic views of the Welsh countryside. 18 holes, 6641 yards. S.S.S. 73. Practice ground, 9 holes Par 3, Par 4. *Green Fees:* from £15.00. *Eating facilities:* bar meals and à la carte restaurant. *Visitors:* welcome at all times. Accommodation in en suite hotel on site and mobile homes, full leisure facilities. *Society Meetings:* welcome all week by appointment. Professional: Paul Diamond. Secretary: R. Rees-Evans.
e-mail: info@penrhosgolf.co.uk
website: www.penrhosgolf.co.uk

Cardigan Golf Club
One of the finest golf complexes in West Wales, this is a fine championship course, with outstanding views from every hole. It is a mixture of links and meadowland, with exceptional drainage making it playable all year round.

◆ Relaxed, friendly atmosphere
◆ Clubhouse with well-equipped changing rooms
◆ Three squash courts with spectator gallery
◆ Restaurant and comprehensive bar snack menu

Visitors and societies welcome every day by prior arrangement
golf@cardigan.fsnet.co.uk • www.cardigangolf.co.uk

**CARDIGAN GOLF CLUB
GWBERT-ON-SEA
CARDIGAN SA43 1PR
TEL & FAX: 01239 621775**

FHG

FHG Guides publish a large range of well-known accommodation guides. We will be happy to send you details or you can use the order form at the back of this book.

·K·U·P·E·R·A·R·D·

**PLEASE MENTION THE GOLF GUIDE WHEN YOU WRITE
OR PHONE TO ENQUIRE ABOUT CLUBS OR ACCOMMODATION**

Pembrokeshire

FISHGUARD/HAVERFORDWEST. **Priskilly Forest Golf Club,** Castlemorris, Haverfordwest SA62 5EH (Tel & Fax: 01348 840276). *Location*: A40 Haverfordwest to Fishguard road, left turn at Letterston B4331 towards Mathry. Picturesque undulating parkland surrounded by rhododendrons, etc – a challenging course. 9 holes, 5874 yards. S.S.S. 69. Practice net and ground, trolleys and buggy for hire. *Green Fees*: £14.00 for 9 holes, £20.00 for 18 holes, £24.00 per day. Special winter rates/packages available. *Eating facilities*: licensed bar, light refreshments. *Visitors*: a warm welcome is assured. Accommodation with golf inclusive packages on site in 4-Star country house. Buggies for hire £15.00 for 18 holes. *Society Meetings*: welcome. Secretary: P. Evans.
e-mail: jevans@priskilly-forest.co.uk
website: www.priskilly-golfclub.co.uk

HAVERFORDWEST. **Haverfordwest Golf Club,** Arnolds Down, Haverfordwest SA61 2XQ (01437 763565). *Location:* one mile east of town on A40 trunk road. A parkland course set in Pembrokeshire National Park – challenging but easy walking. 18 holes, 5986 yards. S.S.S. 69. Practice area and putting green. *Green Fees:* information not available. *Eating facilities:* dining room, bar snacks 11am to 9pm. *Visitors:* welcome. *Society Meetings:* welcome by arrangement. Professional: Alex Pile (01437 768409). Secretary: Mike Le Clair (01437 764523; Fax: 01437 764143).*

MILFORD HAVEN. **Dawn till Dusk Golf Club,** Furze Hill Farm, Rosemarket, Milford Haven SA73 1JY (01437 890281). *Location*: from Haverfordwest Bypass take A4076 as far as Johnston, turn left, signposted Rosemarket, one and a quarter miles to crossroads, turn right, one mile on left side of road. Flat parkland course. 9 holes (18 tees), 6373 yards, S.S.S. 71. Putting green, bunkers. *Green Fees*: 9 holes £5.00, 18 holes £8.00. *Visitors*: welcome at all times. *Society Meetings*: welcome, rates negotiable for larger groups. Grass airstrip available, by prior arrangement. website: www.dawntilldusk.co.uk

MILFORD HAVEN. **Milford Haven Golf Club Ltd,** Woodbine House, Clay Lane, Hubberston, Milford Haven SA72 3RX (01646 697762). *Location:* one mile west of Milford Haven on Dale Road. Parkland overlooking magnificent harbour. 18 holes, 6035 yards. S.S.S. 70. Practice area. *Green Fees:* information not available. *Eating facilities:* bar and restaurant facilities. *Visitors:* welcome at all times, please ring Pro shop to check availability. *Society Meetings:* welcome, special rates available. Professional: Martin Stimson (Tel & Fax: 01646 697762). Secretary: Mr W.S. Brown. Administrator: Mr C. Pugh (01646 697822).*
e-mail: cerithmhgc@aol.com
website: www.mhgc.co.uk

NEWPORT. **Newport (Pembs) Golf Club Ltd,** The Golf Club, Golf Course Road, Newport SA42 ONR (01239 820244; Fax: 01239 820085). *Location:* two miles off A487 Cardigan-Fishguard at Newport, Pembrokeshire. Flat seaside links course with breathtaking views over the mountains and bay. 9 holes, 6003 yards. S.S.S. 69. Driving range. *Green Fees:* please phone the clubhouse for current rate. *Eating facilities:* full catering and bar facilities available. *Visitors:* welcome, tee times must be booked and Handicap Certificate may be required; Pro shop and buggy hire. Self-catering accommodation available in adjoining clubhouse. *Society Meetings:* welcome by arrangement, please phone Amanda Payne (01239 820244). Professional: Julian Noott PGA (01239 820244). Operations Manager: Amanda Payne (01239 820244; Fax: 01239 820085).
e-mail: newportgc@lineone.net

THE APPEARANCE OF AN ASTERISK (*) AT THE END OF A CLUB OR COURSE ENTRY INDICATES THAT UP-TO-DATE INFORMATION HAS NOT BEEN SUPPLIED

Haverfordwest Golf Club
Arnoldstown, Haverfordwest, Pembrokeshire SA61 2XQ

Set near the Pembrokeshire National Park and boasting magnificent views of the Preseli Hills, Haverfordwest Golf Club offers a real challenge to golfers of all abilities. Easily reachable on the A40 one mile east of Haverfordwest, this course is located in majestic parkland, and despite being an easy walk, there are a few holes that test the golfer's skill. The clubhouse, built in 1994, has excellent facilities including locker rooms, lounge, bars and full catering facilities, with a wide selection of home-cooked cuisine.

• Club founded 1904 • 18 holes • Parkland • 5986 yards • Par 70
• Societies welcome by arrangement • Green Fee Visitors Welcome • Special Winter Rate Packages
Contact: Alex Pile or Mike Le Clair on 01437 768409 or 01437 764523 • Fax: 01437 764143

See also Colour Advertisement on page 51

TENBY GOLF CLUB
Est 1888
The Burrows, Tenby, Pembrokeshire SA70 7NP

Telephone/Fax: 01834 842978/844447
e-mail: tenbygolfclub@uku.co.uk
website: www.tenbygolf.co.uk

Visiting Golfers and Societies are welcome to play the oldest affiliated course in Wales

Ranked 84th in Golf Monthly Magazine's UK Top 120 Courses

See also Colour Advertisement on page 51

PEMBROKE. **South Pembrokeshire Golf Club,** Military Road, Pennar, Pembroke Dock SA72 6SE (01646 682442/621453). *Location:* on hilltop overlooking Pembroke Dock and The Haven. Parkland rapidly maturing. 18 holes, 6100 yards. S.S.S. 69. Practice facilities. Green Fees: weekdays £18.00, weekends £24.00. Eating facilities: bar, please book for food. Visitors: welcome except during club competitions, please telephone. Society Meetings: welcome by arrangement. PGA Professional: J. Tilson. Secretary: J. Gettings.

ST DAVIDS. **St Davids City Golf Club,** Whitesands Bay, St Davids SA62 6QY (01437 721751). *Location:* follow signs to Whitesands Bay, on Fishguard Road out of St Davids, for two miles. Car park is situated on crossroads with club sign at entrance. If you reach the beach you've gone too far! Seaside links course with spectacular panoramic views over Whitesands Bay and St David's Head. 9 holes, 6117 yards. S.S.S. 70. *Green Fees:* weekdays £17.00 per round, weekends and Bank Holidays £20.00 per round. *Visitors:* welcome at all times but please check at weekends and Bank Holidays; Ladies' Day Friday afternoons, Seniors' Day Thursday afternoon. *Society Meetings:* welcome, book with Secretary. Secretary: James Wilcox (01437 721751).

TENBY. **Tenby Golf Club,** The Burrows, Tenby SA70 7NP *Location:* on A478, near Tenby Railway Station. Seaside links, Championship course, oldest in Wales. 18 holes, 6224 yards. S.S.S. 71. Practice ground. *Green Fees:* information not available. *Eating facilities:* complete dining facilities; licensed bar. *Visitors:* always welcome, subject to club competitions. Handicap Certificate required. Billiards rooms. *Society Meetings:* catered for by advance booking. Professional: Mark Hawkey PGA (01834 844447). Secretary: D. Hancock (Tel & Fax: 01834 842978).
e-mail: tenbygolfclub@uku.co.uk
website: www.tenbygolf.co.uk

TENBY. **Trefloyne Golf Club,** Trefloyne Park, Penally, Tenby SA70 7RG (01834 842165). *Location:* on edge of village of Penally, just off A4139 Tenby/Pembroke road, about one mile from Tenby. Men's course - 18 holes, 6635 yards, 6068 metres, S.S.S. yellow tees 72, white 73, Par 71. Ladies' course - 18 holes, 5764 yards, 5271 metres, S.S.S. 73, Par 73. Practice ground. *Green Fees:* weekdays £26.00, weekends £30.00. Special group rates available. *Eating facilities:* full restaurant and bar service, with breakfast and snack menu. *Visitors:* always welcome. Full equipment hire, clubs, trolleys and motorised buggies. Club Professional: Christine Burton PGA, Pro Shop: (01834 845639). Course Manager: Sarah Beynon. Club Secretary: Tony Hopkins.
website: www.trefloyne.com

Visit the FHG website
www.holidayguides.com
for details of the wide choice of accommodation featured in the full range of FHG titles

---

THE APPEARANCE OF AN ASTERISK (*) AT THE END OF A CLUB OR COURSE ENTRY INDICATES THAT UP-TO-DATE INFORMATION HAS NOT BEEN SUPPLIED

Powys

BRECON. **Brecon Golf Club,** Newton Park, Brecon LD3 8PA (01874 622004). *Location:* A40 west of town, half a mile from town centre. Flat parkland course. 9 holes, 5476 yards. S.S.S. 67, Par 68. *Green Fees:* weekdays £12.00, weekends and Bank Holidays £15.00. *Eating facilities:* bars and catering available. *Visitors:* welcome, some restriction Sundays when prior arrangement advisable. *Society Meetings:* by arrangement. Secretary: T. J. Richards. (01874 622004).

BUILTH WELLS. **Builth Wells Golf Club,** Golf Club Road, Builth Wells LD2 3NF (01982 553296). *Location*: off A483, on outskirts of town on Llandovery Road. Parkland, easy walking. 18 holes. S.S.S. 66. Practice area. Host to the 2005 PGA Welsh Young Professionals Championship. *Green Fees*: £21.00 per round, £27.00 per day weekdays; £25.00 per round, £30.00 per day weekends and Bank Holidays. Three-day ticket £55.00, Five-day ticket £90.00, – prices subject to change. *Eating facilities*: catering all day, two bars. *Visitors*: welcome. *Society Meetings*: welcome, Handicap Certificate required. Professional/Secretary: Simon Edwards (01982 553296; Fax: 01982 551064).
e-mail: info@builthwellsgolf.co.uk
website: www.builthwellsgolf.co.uk

THE APPEARANCE OF AN ASTERISK (*) AT THE END OF A CLUB OR COURSE ENTRY INDICATES THAT UP-TO-DATE INFORMATION HAS NOT BEEN SUPPLIED

CRADOC. **Cradoc Golf Club,** Penoyre Park, Cradoc, Brecon LD3 9LP (01874 623658; Fax: 01874 611711). *Location:* about two miles north of the market town of Brecon, off B4520 Upper Chapel Road (signposted) past Brecon Cathedral. Attractive parkland course adjoining the Brecon Beacons National Park, scenic views. 18 holes, 6188 yards. S.S.S. 71. (off back tees) 12-bay floodlit driving range. Host of 1982 Welsh Stroke Play Championships. Home of the Coors Champion of Champions Tournament. Host to 2003 PGA Mid Wales Open. *Green Fees:* weekdays £26.00 per day, weekends and Bank Holidays £32.00 per day. *Eating facilities:* full catering facilities daily except Mondays. *Visitors:* welcome daily but restricted on Sundays. Electric trolley/buggy hire. *Society Meetings:* welcome any day; prior arrangement advised especially for Sundays. Special packages available. Professional: R.W. Davies (01874 625524). Secretary: Mrs E.G. Price (01874 623658).
e-mail: secretary@cradoc.co.uk
website: www.cradoc.co.uk

CRICKHOWELL. **Old Rectory Hotel and Golf Club,** Llangattock, Crickhowell NP8 1PH (01873 810373). *Location:* A40 to Crickhowell. Course is on a hill with spectacular views. 9 holes, 2878 yards. S.S.S. 54. *Green Fees:* information not available. *Eating facilities:* restaurant, bar meals, two bars. *Visitors:* welcome at all times, no restrictions. Accommodation available in 20 en suite bedrooms. *Society Meetings:* welcome. Secretary: G. Crawford.*

KNIGHTON. **Knighton Golf Club,** Ffrydd Wood, Knighton LD7 1DG (01547 528646). *Location:* on the A488 to Llandrindod Wells, signposted. Undulating wooded hill course with spectacular views. 9 holes, 5362 yards. S.S.S. 66. *Green Fees:* weekdays £10.00; weekends £12.00. *Eating facilities:* bar, meals available; contact Steward (01547 528646). *Visitors:* welcome, no visitors before 4.30pm on Sundays. *Society Meetings:* catered for by prior arrangement. Secretary: Mr D. B. Williams (01547 528046).

2006 GREEN FEES
• £21.00 per round, £27.00 per day weekdays •
• £25.00 per round, £30.00 per day weekends and Bank Holidays •
• Three-day ticket £55.00, Five-day ticket £90.00 •
Prices are subject to increase

The Club House
Golf Club Road, Builth Wells, Powys LD2 3NF
Tel: 01982 553296
Fax: 01982 551064
www.builthwellsgolf.co.uk
e-mail: info@builthwellsgolf.co.uk

Builth Wells Golf Club
See also Colour Advertisement on page 51

LLANDRINDOD WELLS. Llandrindod Wells Golf Club, The Clubhouse, Llandrindod Wells LD1 5NY (01597 823873). *Location:* signposted off A483 at south east of town. An 'Inland Links' course set in the rolling hills of mid Wales and patrolled by Red Kites and Buzzards. 18 holes, Men 5759 yards white, 5543 yards yellow, Par 69. Ladies 5143 yards, Par 72. Floodlit driving range. *Green Fees:* weekdays £21.00 per round, £30.00 per day; weekends and Bank Holidays £26.00 per round, £34.00 per day. Five day ticket £95.00; seven day ticket £125.00. Year 2005 prices. Winter packages 1st November to 31st March. *Eating facilities:* full catering daily except Tuesdays when bar snacks only available, two bars. *Visitors:* welcome at all times, no restrictions. Buggy, trolley hire. *Society Meetings:* welcome any day, booking essential. Golf Shop: (01597 822247). Secretary: (Tel & Fax: 01597 823873).
e-mail: secretary@lwgc.co.uk
website: www.lwgc.co.uk

LLANIDLOES. St Idloes Golf Club, Penrallt, Llanidloes SY18 6LG (01686 412559). *Location:* signposted from the town. Take road to Trefeglwys from Llanidloes for one mile, turn left at sharp bend before house. Heathland and elevated course. 9 holes, 5510 yards. S.S.S. 66. Practice putting area. *Green Fees:* information not available. *Eating facilities:* by arrangement for large group, please phone first. *Visitors:* welcome anytime except Sunday mornings or special competitions. *Society Meetings:* welcome, packages available. Please ring the clubhouse.

MACHYNLLETH. Machynlleth Golf Club, Felingerrig, Machynlleth SY20 8UH (01654 702000). *Location*: A489 from Newtown, left hand turn before the speed restriction sign on entering Machynlleth. Undulating moorland course. 9 holes, 5726 yards, 5285 metres. S.S.S. 68. Small practice area. *Green Fees*: £15.00 per day. *Eating facilities*: bar. *Visitors*: welcome except during competition days. *Society Meetings*: welcome.

NEWTOWN. St Giles Golf Club, Pool Road, Newtown SY16 3AJ (01686 625844). *Location:* convenient to town centre, quarter-of-a-mile north east on A483 from Newtown. Challenging riverside course. 9 holes, 6012 yards. S.S.S. 70. *Green Fees:* weekdays £13.50 per day, weekends and Bank Holidays £16.00 per day. *Visitors:* welcome, with reservation Saturday afternoons and Sunday mornings. 2-Fore-1 welcome. *Society Meetings:* catered for.

RHOSGOCH. Rhosgoch Golf Club, Rhosgoch, Near Hay-on-Wye, Builth Wells LD2 3JY (01497 851251). *Location:* 6 miles north west of Hay-on-Wye, half-a-mile south east of the B4594. Parkland course in beautiful picturesque valley. 9 holes, 4955 yards, Par 68. S.S.S. 66. *Green Fees:* information not available. *Eating facilities:* bar/restaurant meals. *Visitors:* welcome anytime. *Society Meetings:* welcome weekdays and Saturdays. Club Steward: Andrew Davies. Secretary: Chris Dance.

WELSHPOOL. Welsh Border Golf Club, Bulthy Farm, Middletown, Welshpool SY21 8ER (01743 884247). *Location:* situated off the A458. Parkland course. 9 holes (x2), 6114 yards. S.S.S. 69. Driving range. *Green Fees:* information not available. *Eating facilities:* lunchtime only unless otherwise arranged. *Visitors:* welcome, but tee times must be booked. *Society Meetings:* welcome by prior arrangement. Secretary: Keith Farr (0796 653 0042).

WELSHPOOL. Welshpool Golf Club, Y Golfa, Golfa Hill, Welshpool SY21 9AQ (01938 850249). *Location:* A458 out of Welshpool, approximately three and a half to four miles on right. Rather hilly but spectacular views. 18 holes, 5708 yards. S.S.S. 69. *Green Fees:* weekdays £15.50 all year; weekends and Bank Holidays £15.50 1st November to 31st March, £25.50 1st April to 31st October. *Eating facilities:* open most of the day for food and drink. *Visitors:* welcome, some weekend restrictions. Buggies now available. *Society Meetings:* welcome by arrangement, contact Don Lewis. Professional: Bob Barlow. Secretary: Don Lewis.

Llandrindod Wells Golf Club

The Clubhouse
Llandrindod Wells
Powys LD1 5NY
Tel/Fax 01597 823873
e-mail: secretary@lwgc.co.uk
www.lwgc.co.uk

Winner - Welsh Golf Club of the Year 2004
Host for Welsh Golfing Union Handicap Championship.

Established in 1905 this 'Inland Links' course offers breathtaking views over the beautiful Mid Wales mountains. Every one of the 18 holes has a different character, with natural undulating fairways that offer a 'links type' golfing experience.
Please contact us for details of our golfing breaks, open competitions and local hotels.

18 holes, par 69
Full Bar and Catering
Floodlit Driving Range
Buggies Available
Society Packages

VISITORS AND SOCIETIES MOST WELCOME

MACHYNLLETH GOLF CLUB *Ffordd Drenewydd, Machynlleth SY20 8UH*
Undulating meadowland course • 9 holes, 5726 yards, 5285 metres. S.S.S. 68.
Small practice area • Visitors welcome except during competition days.
Society Meetings welcome • Bar meals available
in clubhouse all year round.
Tel: 01654 702000

South Wales

ABERDARE. **Aberdare Golf Club,** Abernant, Aberdare CF44 0RY (01685 871188; Fax: 01685 872797). *Location:* half a mile from town centre. Mountain course with parkland features and view of whole Cynon Valley. 18 holes, 5875 yards. S.S.S. 69. *Green Fees:* weekdays £17.00, (with member £10.00); weekends and Bank Holidays £21.00, (with member £12.00). *Eating facilities:* bar, lounge and dining room. *Visitors:* welcome without reservation weekdays (see Professional). Saturdays and Sundays by prior arrangement with Secretary. Handicap Certificates required. Snooker room, and changing room. *Society Meetings:* catered for by prior arrangement with Secretary. Professional: A. Palmer (01685 878735). Secretary: Tony Mears (01685 872797).

ABERGAVENNY. **Monmouthshire Golf Club,** Llanfoist, Abergavenny NP7 9HE. *Location:* two miles from A465 on Llanfoist – Llanellen Road (B4269). Parkland with scenic mountain views. 18 holes, 5806 yards. S.S.S. 70. Practice ground. *Green Fees:* information not available. *Eating facilities:* bar snacks available, evening meals by arrangement. *Visitors:* welcome. Proof of membership of recognised golf club required. *Society Meetings:* catered for. Professional: Brian Edwards (Tel & Fax: 01873 852532). Secretary: R.F. Bradley (01873 852606; Fax: 01873 850470).*
website: www.monmouthshiregolfclub.co.uk

ABERGAVENNY. **Wernddu Golf Club,** Old Ross Road, Abergavenny NP7 8NG (01873 856223; Fax: 01873 852177). *Location:* one and a half miles east of Abergavenny on B4521 (off A465). Sloping, well drained site with pond hazards on four holes and magnificent views. 18 holes, 5413 yards. S.S.S. 67. 24- bay covered floodlit driving range, 9 hole pitch and putt, practice putting and bunker area. *Green Fees:* £15.00. *Eating facilities:* lounge bar, light snacks. *Visitors:* welcome. *Society Meetings:* welcome. Professional: Tina Tetley (Ladies European Tour) (01873 856223; Fax: 01873 852177). Secretary: Lyn Turvey (01495 308161).
e-mail: info@wernddu-golf-club.co.uk
website: www.wernddu-golf-club.co.uk

BARGOED. **Bargoed Golf Club,** Heolddu, Bargoed CF81 9GF (01443 830143). *Location:* A469 to Bargoed town centre - Moorland Road. Flat mountain top course. 18 holes, 6210 yards. S.S.S. 70. Practice area, nets, etc. *Green Fees:* £15.00. *Eating facilities:* full catering and bar. *Visitors:* welcome, only with member at weekends, no other restrictions. *Society Meetings:* catered for weekdays only by prior arrangement. Professional: C Easton (01443 836179).

The Monmouthshire Golf Club
Founded 1892
A superb example of a mature parkland course, popular with golfers of all ages and abilities.

♦ Comfortable lounge and dining area ♦ Friendly clubhouse
♦ Separate non-smoking bar ♦ Pro Shop with top-brand equipment ♦ Expert tuition: practice area and indoor academy ♦ Societies and visitors welcome by prior arrangement.

Please telephone R.F. Bradley 01873 852606; Fax: 01873 850470
Llanfoist, Abergavenny, Monmouthshire NP7 9HE
www.monmouthshiregolfclub.co.uk

See also Colour Advertisement on page 54

Wernddu Golf Club
Open to all visitors
18 Hole Golf Course • Driving Range
Snacks • Bar
Ring for Special Society Packages

Old Ross Road, Abergavenny, Monmouthshire NP7 8NG
Tel: 01873 856223 • Fax: 01873 852177
e-mail: info@wernddu-golf-club.co.uk
www.wernddu-golf-club.co.uk

See also Colour Advertisement on page 55

BARRY. **Brynhill (Barry) Golf Club,** Port Road East, Colcot, Barry CF62 8PN (01446 720277). *Location:* leave M4 at Junction 33 (A4232), follow signs for Barry and Cardiff (Wales) Airport onto the A4050. Club on right of road, just before a roundabout. Challenging, undulating meadowland course. 18 holes, 6352 yards. S.S.S. 71. Par 72. *Green Fees:* Mondays to Saturdays £25.00, with member £15.00. *Eating facilities:* Glyn, our caterer, extends a warm welcome, and will provide lunches between 12 noon and 2pm, and dinner from 5pm. Your order prior to playing is requested. *Visitors:* welcome, except Sundays; must produce membership card and Handicap Certificate. *Society Meetings:* by arrangement with Secretary – no Sundays, must be members of a golf club. Competitive rates available. Professional: Duncan Prior (01446 720277). Joint Administrators: Rita Cook and Susan Clarke (01446 720277; Fax: 01446 740422). e-mail: enquiries@brynhillgolfclub.co.uk
website: www.brynhillgolfclub.co.uk

BARRY. **RAF St Athan Golf Club,** Clive Road, St Athan CF62 4JD (01446 751043). *Location:* eight miles from Barry, turn right through St. Athan Village. Parkland. 9 holes, 6452 yards. S.S.S. 72. Practice area and nets. *Green Fees:* information not available. *Eating facilities:* available. *Visitors:* welcome except Sundays, telephone for information. *Society Meetings:* apply through the Secretary. Secretary: P.F. Woodhouse (01446 751043; Fax: 01446 751862).

BARRY. **St Andrews Major Golf Club,** Coldbrook Road East, Near Cadoxton, Barry CF6 3BB (01446 722227; Fax: 01446 748953). *Location:* off Barry Docks Link Road, Junction 33 M4. Flat parkland course with excellent greens, full 18 holes, 5500 yards, Par 69. 12-bay floodlit driving range open 7.30am to 9.30am. *Green Fees:* £16.00 adults, £13.00 Junior/Senior. Full membership packages available to cater for all needs. *Eating facilities:* restaurant and snacks; full bar facilities, specialise in large functions up to 150 people, weddings, birthdays etc. *Visitors:* welcome anytime, but advisable to ring for bookings (especially at weekends). *Society Meetings:* we specialise in society meetings, special packages available on request. Contact Andrew Edmunds.
e-mail: standrewsmajor@hotmail.com
website: www.standrewsmajorgolfclub.co.uk

BLACKWOOD. **Blackwood Golf Club,** Cwmgelli, Blackwood NP12 1EL (01495 222121/223152). *Location:* quarter of a mile north of Blackwood on A4048. 9 holes, 5350 yards. S.S.S. 67. *Green Fees:* information not available. *Visitors:* welcome weekdays only. *Society Meetings:* by arrangement. Secretary: I. E. Power (01495 222121 or 223152).*

BRIDGEND. **Coed-y-Mwstwr Golf Club,** The Clubhouse, Coychurch, Bridgend (01656 862121; Fax: 01656 864934). *Location*: Junction 35 M4, A473 towards Bridgend. Turn right into Coychurch. Parkland, south facing. 12 holes, 6144 yards. S.S.S.70. Practice nets, putting green and chipping area. *Green Fees:* information not available. *Eating facilities*: bar meals and snacks. *Visitors*: members' guests only on Saturdays. *Society Meetings*: by prior arrangement. Secretary: Jim North (Tel & Fax: 01656 864934).*
website: www.coed-y-mwstwr.co.uk

CAERLEON. **Caerleon Public Golf Course,** The Broadway, Caerleon, Newport NP6 1AY (01633 420342). *Location:* three miles off M4 at turnoff for Caerleon. Flat parkland. 9 holes, 3000 yards. S.S.S. 34 yellow, 35 white. Driving range, putting green. *Green Fees:* information not available. *Eating facilities:* bar, light meals (kitchen facilities) available all day. *Visitors:* welcome, must have a booking to tee off. *Society Meetings:* welcome. PGA Teaching Professional: Mark Phillips. Secretary: P. Inker (01633 667249).*

CAERPHILLY. **Caerphilly Golf Club,** Pencapel, Mountain Road, Caerphilly CF83 1HJ (029 2088 3481). *Location:* seven miles north of Cardiff on A469, 250 yards south of both railway and bus stations. Situated opposite Magistrates' Court. Mountainside course with undulating features and wooded areas. 18 holes, 5728 yards (white tees). S.S.S. 69. Limited practice facilities. *Green Fees:* on request. *Eating facilities:* member' and guests' bar, ladies' lounge, mixed lounge and dining room. *Visitors:* welcome weekdays (not Bank Holidays); weekends with member only. *Society Meetings:* most welcome; society packages on request. Professional: James Lee (029 2086 9104). Secretary: Alun Sedgmore (029 2086 3441).*
e-mail: secretary@caerphillygolfclub.com
website: www.caerphillygolfclub.com

CAERPHILLY. **Castell Heights Golf Club,** Blaengwynlais, Caerphilly CF83 1NG (029 2088 6686). *Location:* 5 minutes from Junction 32 on M4. Flat parkland, many trees. 9 holes, 2688 yards. *Green Fees:* information not available. *Eating facilities:* snacks, lunches and afternoon tea available. *Visitors:* welcome anytime, only members can book times. Secretary: Gareth Richards (029 2086 1128; Fax: 029 2086 9030).

CAERPHILLY. **Mountain Lakes Golf Club,** Blaengwynlais, Caerphilly CF83 1NG (029 2086 1128). *Location:* take exit 32, M4. Last exit of roundabout "Tongwynlais", right at Lewis Arms, past Castell Coch, three miles up road on left. Part parkland, part wooded, undulating. 20 water hazards, large penncross greens. 18 holes, 6500 yards. S.S.S. 73. *Green Fees:* information not available. *Visitors:* welcome at all times but must have registered Handicap. *Society Meetings:* welcome at all times but must book. Professional: Sion Bebb (029 2088 6666). Director of Golf: P. Page (029 2086 1128; Fax 029 2086 9030).*

CAERPHILLY. **Ridgeway Golf Club,** Thornhill, Caerphilly CF83 1LY (029 2088 2255). *Location:* driving out of Cardiff towards Caerphilly over Caerphilly mountains, take first left after Traveller's Pub. Mountain course but not too steep. 9 holes, 2314 yards. S.S.S. 64. Driving range. *Green Fees:* information not available. *Eating facilities:* bar with snacks available. *Visitors:* welcome but must be member of recognised golf club. *Society Meetings:* weekdays only by arrangement. Professionals: P. Johnson/S. Bowen. Secretary: R. Jones.*
e-mail: rojazzy@yahoo.co.uk

COED Y MWSTWR Golf Club
The Clubhouse, Coychurch, Bridgend CF35 6AF
Tel/Fax: 01656 864934   www.coed-y-mwstwr.co.uk

A beautiful parkland course in the middle of South Wales, with easy access from the M4. There are views across the Ogwr valley from all holes, and the club can provide meals and beverages. The par of 69 provides a fair test for golfers of all standards. Visitors (with handicap certificates) are very welcome, and memberships are currently available. Please contact the Manager on 01656 864934 for further details.

See also Colour Advertisement on page 53

COED-Y-MWSTWR HOTEL
Coychurch, Bridgend, Vale of Glamorgan CF35 6AF

Perched on a Welsh hillside overlooking the picturesque Vale of Glamorgan, Coed-y-Mwstwr, "Whispering Trees", provides a cosy and secluded hideaway. Luxurious bedrooms with all modern amenities and a host of thoughtful extras. Elegant restaurant with food prepared by award-winning chefs. Enjoy a round of complimentary golf, take advantage of our heated swimming pool, Leisure Club with fully equipped gym, sauna and steamroom. An oasis of calm in a changing world, where you are always greeted with a warm Welsh welcome and assured of friendly, courteous and professional attention. *Voted top AA Hotel for Courtesy and Care. AA Award Winning Cuisine*

Tel: 01656 860621 • Fax: 01656 863122   **AA** ★★★★

e-mail: reservations@coed-y-mwstwr.com • www.coed-y-mwstwr.com

See also Colour Advertisement on page 53

Caerphilly Golf Club
Established 1905

Societies and Guests always welcome. Membership available

Secretary: 029 208 63441
Professional: 029 208 69104

www.caerphillygolfclub.com
secretary@caerphillygolfclub.com

Visit the FHG website
www.holidayguides.com
for details of the wide choice of accommodation featured in the full range of FHG titles

South Wales / WALES — THE GOLF GUIDE 2006

CAERPHILLY. **Virginia Park Golf Club,** Virginia Park, Caerphilly CF83 3SW (029 2086 3919). *Location:* off Pontygwindy Road, near Caerphilly recreation centre. Flat parkland, Easy walking but challenging. 9 holes, 4661 yards, S.S.S. 63. 20 bay covered, floodlit, driving range. Practice putting green. *Green Fees:* on application. *Eating facilities:* catering available every day. *Visitors:* welcome but must observe dress code. Function room. *Society Meetings:* Telephone bookings. Professional: Joel Hill. Members' Secretary: Carol Lewis (029 2086 7891). *

CARDIFF. **Cardiff Golf Club,** Sherborne Avenue, Cyncoed, Cardiff (029 2075 3320). *Location:* two miles north of city centre or M4, A48 or A48M from east to Pentwyn exit on Eastern Avenue, and take Pentwyn Industrial Road to top of hill at Cyncoed Village, turn left at Spar shop into Sherborne Avenue. Undulating parkland, all greens bunkered. 18 holes. S.S.S. 70. *Green Fees:* £40.00. *Eating facilities:* catering and bars available from 11am every day. *Visitors:* welcome; Saturdays must play with a member. Snooker. *Society Meetings:* by arrangement - dining facility for up to 130 people. Professional: Terry Hanson (029 2075 4772). Secretary: Kenvyn Newling (029 2075 3320; Fax: 029 2068 0011).

CARDIFF. **Cottrell Park Golf Club,** St Nicholas, Cardiff CF5 6JY (01446 781781; Fax: 01446 781187). *Location:* four miles west of Cardiff on A48 main road. Two parkland courses. Driving range (20 bays) - clubhouse. Two courses: Mackintosh - 18 holes, 6397 yards. S.S.S. 72; Button - 18 holes, 6156 yards. S.S.S. 70. *Green Fees:* on application. *Eating facilities:* all day. *Visitors:* welcome anytime. Professional: Rhodri Donovan.
e-mail: sales@golfwithus.com
website: www.golfwithus.com

CARDIFF. **Creigiau Golf Club,** Llantwit Road, Creigiau, Cardiff CF15 9NN (029 2089 0263). *Location:* seven miles north-west of Cardiff, two miles off A4199, M4 Junction 34 two miles. 18 holes, 6063 yards. S.S.S. 70 (Par 71). Limited practice facilities. *Green Fees:* £35.00 per day. *Eating facilities:* bars and full catering available. *Visitors:* welcome weekdays except Tuesdays, prior phone call requested; weekends with members only. Must hold Handicap Certificate. *Society Meetings:* catered for by prior arrangement (maximum 40). Professional: Ian Luntz (029 2089 0263). Secretary: (029 2089 0263; Fax: 029 2089 0706). Caterer: (029 2089 0263).

CARDIFF. **Llanishen Golf Club,** Heol Hir, Cardiff CF14 9UD (Tel & Fax: 029 2075 5078; Steward: 029 2075 2205). *Location:* five miles north of Cardiff city centre, one mile north of Llanishen village. Wooded undulating course with spectacular views. 18 holes, 5338 yards, 4881 metres. S.S.S. 67, Par 68. *Green Fees:* £32.00. Special rates for County Cards or visitors playing with member weekdays except Bank Holidays. *Eating facilities:* full bar and catering except Mondays. New clubhouse opened April 1995. *Visitors:* welcome weekdays; weekends only with member. Handicap Certificate required. *Society Meetings:* catered for Thursday and Friday, on written application. Visitors must be bona fide members of a golf club. Professional: Adrian Jones (029 2075 5076). General Manager: Anne Gregory (Tel & Fax: 029 2075 5078).

CARDIFF. **Peterstone Lakes Golf Club & Hotel,** Peterstone, Wentloog, Cardiff CF3 2TN (01633 680009; Fax: 01633 680563). *Location:* in between Newport and Cardiff off the A48 at Castleton. Parkland/links course bordering the Bristol Channel. 18 holes, 6555 yards. S.S.S. 72. Indoor teaching academy. *Eating facilities:* lounge bar, Fairways Restaurant, Crystal Suite. *Visitors:* welcome, strongly recommend telephone enquiry for a tee time. *Society Meetings:* welcome. Professional: Paul Glynn (01633 680075; Fax: 01633 680563). Manager: Peter Millar.

CARDIFF. **Radyr Golf Club,** Drysgol Road, Radyr, Cardiff CF15 8BS (029 2084 2408). *Location:* Junction 32 M4, A470 to Merthyr Tydfil, first exit. Parkland course. 18 holes, 6015 yards. S.S.S. 70. *Green Fees:* £40.50. Special rates for societies over 20 people. *Eating facilities:* snacks, lunches and evening meals (029 2084 2735). *Visitors:* welcome. *Society Meetings:* catered for Wednesdays, Thursdays and Fridays only. Professional: Simon Swales (029 2084 2476; Fax: 029 2084 3914). Club Manager: Alan M. Edwards (029 2084 2408; Fax: 029 2084 3914).
e-mail: manager@radyrgolf.co.uk

CARDIFF. **St Mellons Golf Club,** St Mellons, Cardiff CF3 2XS (01633 680408; Fax: 01633 681219). *Location:* Junctions 28 and 30 of M4 to A48 between Cardiff and Newport. 70 year old parkland course. 18 holes, 6225 yards. S.S.S. 70. *Green Fees:* telephone for special rates. *Visitors:* welcome weekdays only. *Society Meetings:* catered for on written or telephone application. Professional: Barry Thomas (01633 680101). Secretary: R.H. Boyce (01633 680408; Fax: 01633 681219).

CARDIFF. **Wenvoe Castle Golf Club,** Wenvoe, Near Cardiff CF5 6BE (029 2059 1094; Fax: 029 2059 4371). *Location:* exit Junction 33 M4, follow signs for Cardiff Airport. Parkland course founded in 1936, fairly open layout with hilly front 9, hosted first PGA Welsh Classic. 18 holes, 6458 yards. S.S.S. 71. Practice areas. *Green Fees:* information not available. *Eating facilities:* bar snacks and restaurant meals. *Visitors:* welcome weekdays only. *Society Meetings:* catered for weekdays only, parties of 16 or more. Professional: Jason D. Harris (029 2059 3649). Secretary: Nicola Sims (Tel & Fax: 029 2059 4371).*
e-mail: enquiries@wenvoecastlegolfclub.com
website: www.wenvoecastlegolfclub.com

CARDIFF. **Whitchurch (Cardiff) Golf Club,** Pantmawr Road, Whitchurch, Cardiff CF14 7TD (029 2062 0985). *Location:* three miles north west of Cardiff on A470, 600 metres Junction 32 M4. Parkland, undulating and easy walking with panoramic views of Cardiff. A championship course with Ian Woosnam holding course record of 62. 18 holes, 6258 yards. S.S.S. 71. Practice facilities. *Green Fees:* £40.00 per day weekdays; £45.00 per day weekends and Bank Holidays. *Eating facilities:* restaurant and bars. *Visitors:* welcome please phone first. Trolleys for hire. *Society Meetings:* catered for by arrangement with Club Manager. Professional: Rhys Davies (029 2061 4660). Club Manager: Graham Perrott (029 2062 0985; Fax: 029 2052 9860).
e-mail: secretary@whitchurchcardiffgolfclub.com

Cottrell Park Golf Club
St Nicholas, Cardiff CF5 6JY

- Accommodation available in association with local providers
- Full Welsh Breakfast
- 18 holes on one of Cottrell's Championship golf courses.

Set in the heart of beautiful Vale of Glamorgan parkland, Cottrell Park offers the perfect Golf Break Destination

We can build the perfect Golf Getaway for you!

Mini Golf Breaks starting from £46 per person!

Cottrell Park is easily accessible from J33 of the M4 and only 15 minutes' drive from the centre of Cardiff.

www.golfwithus.com • Tel: 01446 781781 • Fax: 01446 781187 • sales@golfwithus.com

---

St Mellons Golf Club
St Mellons, Cardiff CF3 2XS
Tel: 01633 680101 • Fax: 01633 681219

First opened in 1936, St Mellons is a lovely parkland course on the eastern edge of the bustling capital city of Cardiff. Since the course was opened, some of the world's finest players have played it including Lyle, Barnes, Torrance, James, Darcy and Antonio Garrido, who held the touring Professionals' course record for many years.

Visitors are very welcome at St Mellons, which is just 15 minutes' drive from the highly rated Celtic Manor, just off Junctions 28 and 30 of the M4 and 35 minutes from the Second Severn Crossing.

See also Colour Advertisement on page 52

Wenvoe Castle Golf Club
Founded 1936

**Wenvoe
Cardiff CF5 6BE
Tel/Fax: 029 2059 4371**
enquiries@wenvoecastlegolfclub.com
www.wenvoecastlegolfclub.com

- Exit Junction 33 M4, follow signs for Cardiff Airport.
- Parkland course founded in 1936, fairly open layout with hilly front 9, hosted first PGA Welsh Classic. Practice areas.
- 18 holes, 6458 yards. S.S.S. 71.
- Bar snacks and restaurant meals.
- Visitors welcome weekdays only.
- Society Meetings catered for weekdays only, parties of 16 or more

See also Colour Advertisement on page 54

FHG

Visit the **FHG KUPERARD** website

www.holidayguides.com

for details of the wide choice of accommodation featured in the full range of FHG titles

CHEPSTOW. **Dewstow Golf Club,** Caerwent, Monmouthshire NP26 5AH (01291 430444; Fax: 01291 425816). *Location*: off A48 at Caerwent, between Chepstow and Newport, five miles from the Old Severn Bridge. Two 18-hole parkland courses, special features include Totem pole, Ekki bridge, 26-bay golf range. The Valley Course - Par 72, 6100 yards, The Park Course - 6200 yards. *Green Fees*: information not available. *Eating facilities*: restaurant, function rooms and bar snacks available all day. *Visitors*: welcome at all times. Trolley and buggy hire in season. *Society Meetings*: Society and corporate days are our speciality. Bookings and information: Hayley Battle (01291 430444). Professional: Jonathan Skuse PGA. Golf Secretary: Dave Bradbury.*
e-mail: info@dewstow.com
website: www.dewstow.com

CHEPSTOW. **Marriott St Pierre Hotel and Country Club,** St Pierre Park, Chepstow, Monmouthshire NP16 6YA (01291 635205; Fax: 01291 629975). *Location*: Junction 2 of M48, A466 Chepstow, A48 Caerwent. 400 acres of beautiful parkland, some of the rarest and oldest trees in Britain. Old Course: 18 holes, 6818 yards. S.S.S. 73 off white, 71 off yellow, 75 Ladies. Mathern Course: 18 holes, 5762 yards, S.S.S. 68. 13-bay driving range with computerised tuition facilities. *Green Fees:* Please call for details. *Eating facilities:* Trophy Bar serves light bites during day, Long Weekend Cafe Bar, private suites for groups. *Visitors*: welcome, book 10 days in advance for weekdays and 48 hours in advance for weekends. *Society Meetings:* weekdays only except when resident in hotel which has 148 bedrooms all en suite, conference rooms and extensive leisure facilities. Director of Golf: Ben Laing.

CHEPSTOW. **Shirenewton Golf Club,** Shirenewton, Chepstow NP16 6RL (01291 641642). *Location:* A48, three miles west of Chepstow, north two and three-quarter miles Shirenewton. Undulating parkland with wonderful views. 18 holes, 6607 yards. S.S.S. 72. *Green Fees:* information not available. *Eating facilities:* dining, function room, bar snacks. *Visitors:* welcome anytime but must book. *Society Meetings:* welcome but must book. Secretary: Christine Leather.*

CWMBRAN. **Greenmeadow Golf and Country Club,** Treherbert Road, Croesyceiliog, Cwmbran NP44 2BZ (01633 869321; Fax: 01633 868430). *Location:* M4 Junction 26 north on A4042, turn right at brown tourist sign for Golf Course and Driving Range. Next to Gwent Crematorium. Parkland course with undulating fairways, mature woodlands, strategically positioned lakes and bunkers. 18 holes, 6200 yards. S.S.S. 71. 26 bay floodlit driving range (8am to 10pm), putting green, six all-weather tennis courts. *Green Fees:* please phone for details and prices as there are many different packages and options. *Eating facilities:* lounge bar, patio coffee lounge and restaurant. Private function room available if required. *Visitors:* welcome, telephone golf shop for tee time. *Society Meetings:* always welcome, bookings via our golf shop. Package deals with meals available. Professional: Dave Woodman (01633 862626). Secretary: P.J. Richardson (Fax: 01633 868430).

CWMBRAN. **Llanyrafon Golf Course,** Llanfrechfa Way, Cwmbran NP44 8HT (01633 874636). *Location*: M4 Junction 26, A4042 to Cwmbran. Flat, parkland, wooded, river enclosed course. 9 holes, 1283 yards. Practice nets, putting green. *Green Fees*: information not available. *Visitors*: always welcome. Tuition available. Professional Golf Shop. Professional: David Woodman (01633 874636).

DINAS POWIS. **Dinas Powis Golf Club,** Golf House, Highwalls Road, Dinas Powis CF64 4AJ *Location:* M4 Cardiff, Junction Cardiff West, thereafter signposted Dinas Powis, Penarth and Barry. Mostly parkland, a challenging course. 18 holes, 5532 yards. S.S.S. 67. *Green Fees:* information not available. *Eating facilities:* diningroom/bar snacks. *Visitors:* welcome weekdays, weekends by arrangement. Separate function room with bar available for bookings. *Society Meetings:* call for details. Professional: G. Bennett (029 2051 3682); Secretary: C. Miller (Tel & Fax: 029 2051 2727); Club (029 2051 2157).

GLYNNEATH. **Glynneath Golf Club,** 'Penygraig', Pontneathvaughan, Near Glynneath SA11 5UH (01639 720452). *Location:* A465 trunk road to Glynneath onto B4242 to Pontneathvaughan, one and a half miles. Picturesque course overlooking Vale of Neath, in Brecon Beacons National Park, reasonably flat, half woodland, half parkland. 18 holes - white tees 6122 yards. S.S.S. 71. *Green Fees*: weekdays £16.00; weekends £22.00. (2005 fees, subject to revision.) *Visitors*: welcome, trolleys and buggies available; catering; snooker. *Society Meetings:* welcome weekdays and weekends, only by arrangement. Professional: Shane McMenamin (01639 720872). Secretary: T.A. Roberts (01639 720452).

HENGOED. **Bryn Meadows Golf Club,** Maesycwmmer, Near Hengoed CF82 7SN (01495 225590; Fax: 01495 228272). *Location:* just off A472 near Blackwood, 15 minutes to M4 Junction 28. Parkland course, spectacular views, new challenge from every tee. 18 holes, 6100 yards. Par 72. *Green Fees:* Monday to Thursday £17.00, Friday £20.00, weekends £25.00. Discounts for societies. *Eating facilities:* à la carte restaurant, bar snacks, etc. *Visitors:* welcome weekdays, weekends by prior arrangement only. Award-winning hotel and leisure club. Buggy hire. *Society Meetings:* welcome weekdays, weekends by prior arrangement. For all golf enquiries please contact: Bruce Hunter (01495 221905/225590). website: www.brynmeadows.com

---

CASTLE VIEW HOTEL
16 Bridge Street, Chepstow NP6 5EZ
Tel: 01291 620349 Fax: 01291 627397
e-mail: taciliaok@aol.com
website: www.hotelschepstow.co.uk

........*Three miles to the 1st tee at St Pierre*
Small luxury hotel opposite Chepstow Castle and car park. Golf enthusiasts welcome.
• Comfortable fully equipped bedrooms • High standard of cooking • Short break holiday terms available
"We aim to offer you comfort, good food and a friendly welcome"

DEWSTOW GOLF • CLUB

Golf at its best, supported by facilities designed for your sheer enjoyment

- Two golf courses – Valley Course and Park Course
- Golf Academy with 26-bay floodlit covered driving range, coffee shop and golf shop.
- Clubhouse with lounge, bars and restaurant open every day
- Function rooms for meetings, conferences and training.
- Societies welcome weekdays; weekends by arrangement

Dewstow Golf Club, Caerwent, Monmouthshire NP26 5AH
Tel: 01291 430444 • Fax: 01291 425816
e-mail: info@dewstow.com
website: www.dewstow.com

BRYN MEADOWS

Golf & Country Hotel

Maesycwmmer, Near Ystrad Mynach, Caerphilly, South Wales CF82 7SN

Located in the heart of the beautiful Rhymney Valley, just 25 minutes' drive from Cardiff City Centre and 15 minutes from the M4 Junction 28
The tree-lined, mature, parkland course offers a new challenge from every tee, with receptive greens, lush fairways and water features.

Golf Break Packages
2 nights DB&B + 2 rounds golf from £117.50pp

Tel: 01495 225590 • Fax: 01495 228272
www.brynmeadows.com

See also Colour Advertisement on page 52

The Beaufort Hotel

Chepstow, South Wales NP16 5EP

The Beaufort Hotel is ideal for St Pierre, Rolls of Monmouth and Celtic Manor Golf Clubs. A family run hotel with friendly, cheerful staff. Popular bar at pub prices and an award-winning restaurant. We can cater for all your requirements.

Tel: 01291 622497 • Fax: 01291 627389
E-mail: info@thebeauforthotel.co.uk • www.beauforthotelchepstow.com

See also Colour Advertisement on page 52

480 South Wales / WALES — THE GOLF GUIDE 2006

HENSOL. **The Vale Hotel, Golf and Spa Resort,** Hensol Park, Hensol, Near Cardiff CF72 8JY (01443 667800). *Location:* set in over 600 acres of beautiful countryside yet only three minutes from Junction 34 of M4, 15 minutes from Cardiff city centre and International airport. Home to the Welsh PGA. 2 Championship standard courses - Lake Course, 6438 yards, and Wales National Course, 7413 yards, Par 73, water features, greens to USGA standard. 16 bay driving range, short play area. *Green Fees:* information not available. *Eating facilities*: superb eating facilities in the clubhouse and AA Rosette Mediterranean restaurant. *Visitors:* welcome - Handicap Certificate required. Coaching available using latest video technology; pro shop. Spike and lounge bar. Buggy and trolley hire. *Society Meetings:* welcome, corporate days with full management service. Accommodation available in four-star hotel. website: www.valehotel.com

LLANWERN. **Llanwern Golf Club (Est 1929),** Llanwern Village, Newport NP18 2DY (Tel & Fax: 01633 412 029). *Location:* four miles east of Newport city centre, one mile from M4 Junction 24. Mature parkland course in a picturesque village setting, established in 1929. 18 holes, 6177 yards, S.S.S. 69 Men; 5214 yards, S.S.S. 71 Ladies. Extensive practice facilities. *Green Fees:* on application; various summer and winter packages. ≈ *Eating facilities:* full catering and bar. *Visitors:* welcome Monday to Friday and by arrangement on Saturday (no Sundays). Bookings: (01633 412029). Professional: (01633 413233).

MAESTEG. **Maesteg Golf Club,** Mount Pleasant, Neath Road, Maesteg CF34 9PR (01656 732037). *Location:* half a mile out of Maesteg town centre on the Port Talbot road (B4282). Reasonably flat hilltop course with scenic views over wooded hills and valleys down to Swansea Bay. 18 holes, 5929 yards. S.S.S. 69. Practice area and putting green. *Green Fees:* information not available. *Eating facilities:* meals available in restaurant overlooking the course, bar meals and snacks throughout the day. *Visitors:* welcome without reservation, groups of more than 12 by arrangement. *Society Meetings:* catered for weekdays only by arrangement. Secretary: Ian McBride (01656 734106).*

MERTHYR TYDFIL. **Merthyr Tydfil Golf Club,** Cloth Hall Lane, Cefn Coed, Merthyr Tydfil CF48 2NU (01685 723308). *Location:* off A470 Merthyr Tydfil to Brecon Road. Mountain top course in Brecon Beacons National Park area with outstanding views. 18 holes, 5625 yards. S.S.S. 68. *Green Fees:* £10.00 weekdays; £15.00 weekends. *Eating facilities:* available by prior arrangement. *Visitors:* welcome anytime except competition days (usually Sundays). *Society Meetings:* catered for by prior arrangement. Secretary: Vivian Price.

MERTHYR TYDFIL. **Morlais Castle Golf Club,** Pant, Dowlais, Merthyr Tydfil CF48 2UY (01685 722822). *Location:* near "Heads of Valley Road", Dowlais roundabout, follow signs for Brecon Mountain Railway. Very pleasant moorland course with excellent views. 18 holes, 6320 yards, 5744 metres. S.S.S. 71. Practice area. *Green Fees:* weekdays £16.00 per day, £10.00 with member; weekends £20.00, £16.00 with a member. *Eating facilities:* clubhouse redeveloped, now offers excellent eating facilities; lounge, bars and restaurant. *Visitors:* welcome, weekends by prior arrangement with/or by application to the Secretary. *Society Meetings:* please contact Secretary. Professional: Mr H. Jarrett (Tel & Fax: 01685 388700). Secretary: Mr Meurig Price.

MONMOUTH. **Monmouth Golf Club,** Leasbrook Lane, Monmouth NP25 3SN (01600 712212). *Location:* outskirts of town on Monmouth - Ross-on-Wye dual carriageway, left turn 100 yards from roundabout; signposted. Undulating parkland, very scenic. 18 holes, 5700 yards. S.S.S. 69. Practice area, putting green. *Green Fees:* weekdays £21.00 per round, £28.00 per day; £15.00 with member; weekends and Bank Holidays £25.00 per round. £32.00 per day, £19.00 with member; Juniors £10.00 at all times. *Eating facilities:* bar snacks, dining room facilities daily. *Visitors:* welcome at all times. Trolley and buggy hire. *Society Meetings:* contact the Secretary in advance. Secretary: Mr Peter Tully (01600 712212; Fax: 01600 772399).
e-mail: sec.mongc@barbox.net
website: www.monmouthgolfclub.co.uk

Monmouth Golf Club is situated on the A40, half a mile north of the town. It was extended to an 18-hole course in 1992, when a new clubhouse was opened, offering a most comfortable location for a drink or a meal, with magnificent views of the course and the surrounding countryside. Monmouth certainly has every justification for its claim to be one of the prettiest courses in Wales, and is renowned for the warm welcome offered to its guests.

Standing on high ground above the town, the undulating parkland course plays 5698 yards off white tees, 5507 off yellow, and 5118 off red (ladies). Each aptly named hole offers a different challenge. The 8th (Cresta Run) was recently included in "Britain's 100 most extraordinary golf holes" which also nominated Monmouth as having the best value green fees in the country.

As you leave the clubhouse you become aware of the tranquillity of the verdant surroundings, mature trees, wild flowers and an abundance of wildlife.

Monmouth Golf Club
Leasbrook Lane, Monmouth NP25 3SN
Tel/Fax: 01600 772399
sec.mongc@barbox.net
Pro Shop: 01600 712212

Visit the Monmouth Golf Club- you will not be disappointed.

See also Colour Advertisement on page 54

THE GOLF GUIDE 2006 WALES / South Wales

MONMOUTH. **The Rolls of Monmouth Golf Club**, The Hendre, Monmouth NP25 5HG (01600 715353; Fax: 01600 713115). *Location:* B4233 old Monmouth/ Abergavenny road. Arboretum wooded, hilly parkland course on private estate. 18 holes, 6283 yards. S.S.S. 71. Practice area, putting green. *Green Fees:* weekdays £38.00; weekends £42.00. Monday Special £35.00. Subject to review. *Eating facilities:* bar and catering facilities seven days a week. *Visitors:* welcome any day. Buggies and trolleys for hire. *Society Meetings:* welcome on any day including weekends. Secretary: Mrs Sandra Orton.

MOUNTAIN ASH. **Mountain Ash Golf Club,** Cefn Pennar, Mountain Ash CF45 4DT (01443 472265). *Location:* A470 Pontypridd to Aberdare road, approximately 10 miles from Pontypridd, four miles north of Abercynon. Partly wooded course. 18 holes, 5553 yards. S.S.S. 67. *Green Fees:* weekdays £20.00, £12.00 with member, weekends and Bank Holidays £20.00 only with member. *Eating facilities:* catering at club. *Visitors:* welcome anytime without reservation. *Society Meetings:* catered for, special rates by arrangement. Professional: D. Clark (01443 488770). Secretary: Geoffrey Matthews (01443 479459).

NANTYGLO. **West Monmouthshire Golf Club,** Pond Road, Nantyglo, Brynmawr NP23 4QT (01495 310233). *Location:* Heads of the Valleys Road to Brynmawr, roundabout to Nantyglo, signposted. Mountain and heathland course. Now recognised as the highest golf course in Great Britain. 18 holes, 6118 yards. S.S.S. 69. *Green Fees:* information not available. *Eating facilities:* 24 hours notice required. *Visitors:* welcome. *Society Meetings:* welcome. Special package for parties – details on request. Secretary: S.E. Williams (01495 310233).

NEATH. **Earlswood Golf Club,** Jersey Marine, Neath SA10 6JP (01792 321578). *Location:* half a mile southeast of Jersey Marine village, take B4290 turning off A483 then first right. Scenic, gently undulating course. 18 holes, 5174 yards. S.S.S. 68. *Green Fees:* information not available. *Visitors:* pay as you play course, all visitors welcome. *Society Meetings:* by arrangement.*

NEATH. **Neath Golf Club,** Cadoxton, Neath SA10 8AH (01639 643615). *Location:* two miles from Neath town centre. Mountain course, gentle slopes. 18 holes, 6492 yards. S.S.S. 72. *Green Fees:* weekdays £21.00, £13.00 with member; weekends with member only £13.00. Special rates October to March £11.00. *Eating facilities:* full catering facilities Tuesday to Sunday. *Visitors:* welcome weekdays only, Tuesdays Ladies' Day. *Society Meetings:* welcome by arrangement with Secretary. Professional: R.M. Bennett (01639 633693). Secretary: D.R. Thomas (01639 632759). e-mail: manager@neathgolfclub.com website: www.neathgolfclub.com

NEATH. **Swansea Bay Golf Club,** Jersey Marine, Neath SA10 6JP (01792 812198). *Location:* exit 42 off M4. At 1st roundabout, take B4290 turning off A483 then first right. Seaside links. 18 holes, 6605 yards. S.S.S. 72. *Green Fees:* weekdays £18.00; weekends and Bank Holidays £25.00. *Eating facilities:* bar/catering available every day from 11.00am; dinners by arrangement. *Visitors:* welcome without reservation. *Society Meetings:* by arrangement. Professional: M. Day (01792 816159). Secretary: Mrs D. Goatcher (01792 814153).

NELSON. **Whitehall Golf Club,** The Pavilion, Nelson, Treharris CF46 6ST (01443 740245). *Location:* 15 miles north of Cardiff, take A4054 off A470. Hillside course with pleasant views. 9 holes (x2), 5666 yards. S.S.S. 68. *Green Fees:* Monday to Friday £10.00, with or without a member. Saturdays £12.00 with or without a member, but Captain's permission must be requested. Sundays/Bank Holidays by arrangement with Hon Secretary. *Eating facilities:* available, contact Steward for cooked meals. *Visitors:* welcome weekdays, weekends with members. *Society Meetings:* by prior arrangement with Secretary. Secretary: P.M. Wilde. (01443 451357).

NEWPORT. **The Celtic Manor Resort,** Coldra Woods, Newport NP18 1HQ (Resort Enquiries 01633 413000; Fax: 01633 410269). *Location:* 90 minutes from London, off Junction 24 of the M4 motorway, five minutes from new Severn Bridge. The Resort is the home of The PGA Wales Open and the venue for the Ryder Cup in 2010. Three very different and challenging Trent Jones championship courses. Scenic Wentwood Hills, Par 72; Roman Road, Par 69 - voted best inland course in Wales; Coldra Woods, Par 59, a venue for PGA short course championships. The Golf School offers comprehensive practice and coaching, two tier, floodlit driving range, 3 coaching bays with A-star video graphics, practice range, award-winning Pro Shop and short play areas. *Green Fees:* information not available. *Eating facilities:* superb dining facilities at the Clubhouse. *Visitors:* welcome. Meeting and banqueting rooms available. *Society Meetings:* welcome. Full event management service for Corporate Golf Days. Accommodation available at 400 bedroom hotel. Director of Golf Operations: Chris Baron. Secretary: Shane Wesson. Golf Sales (for tee-off times): 01633 410263.*

NEWPORT. **Newport Golf Club,** Great Oak, Rogerstone, Newport NP10 9FX (01633 892643; Fax: 01633 896676). *Location:* M4 Junction 27, take B4591 to RISCA, one and a half miles on right. Rolling parkland. 18 holes, white tees 6460 yards, S.S.S. 71 yellow tees 6190 yards. S.S.S. 70. Two practice areas. *Green Fees:* information not available. *Eating facilities:* full dining facilities at club. *Visitors:* welcome Saturdays with members only, welcome other days; advisable to ring in advance. *Society Meetings:* welcome weekdays except Tuesdays, book only through Secretary. Professional: Paul Mayo (01633 893271). Secretary: Colin Duffield (01633 892643; Fax: 01633 896676).

www.uk-golfguide.com

NEWPORT. **Parc Golf Club.** Church Lane, Coedkernew, Newport NP10 8TU (01633 680933; Fax: 01633 681011). *Location:* Junction 28 M4, then A48 three miles from Newport. Flat parkland course. 18 holes, 5512 yards, S.S.S. 69. Golf range, putting machine and putting green. *Green Fees:* information not available. *Eating facilities:* bar, conservatory, function room (can cater for 120). *Visitors:* always welcome, must pre-book. Golf days arranged, weddings, exhibitions, etc. *Society Meetings:* all catered for, minimum 12. Professional: Gareth Edwards (01633 680933). Secretary: M.V. Cleary. Manager: C. Hicks*.
e-mail: enquiries@parcgolf.co.uk
website: www.parcgolf.co.uk

NEWPORT. **Tredegar Park Golf Club Ltd,** Parc-Y-Bryn, Rogerstone, Newport NP10 9TG (01633 894433). *Location:* north of M4 between Junctions 26 and 27. Newly opened parkland course. 18 holes, 6400 yards, 5850 metres. S.S.S. 72. Practice area. *Green Fees:* information not available. *Eating facilities:* restaurant and bar. *Visitors:* welcome, must be member of affiliated club. *Society Meetings:* groups of 16 and over catered for. Professional: Lee Pagett (01633 894517). General Manager: Ken Buse (01633 894433; Fax: 01633 897152).

OAKDALE. **Oakdale Golf Course,** Llwynon Lane, Oakdale NP12 0NF (01495 220044). Parkland course, 9 holes. 18 bay floodlit driving range. *Green Fees:* information not available. *Eating facilities:* licensed bar, snacks. Full-sized snooker tables. *Visitors:* welcome. *Society Meetings:* welcome.*

PENARTH. **Glamorganshire Golf Club,** Lavernock Road, Penarth CF64 5UP (Tel & Fax: 029 2070 1185). *Location:* five miles west Cardiff, one mile west Penarth Centre. Parkland course overlooking Bristol Channel. 18 holes, 6150 yards, S.S.S. 70. Practice area. *Green Fees:* information not available. *Eating facilities:* full restaurant and bar snacks, Men's bar and mixed lounge bar. *Visitors:* welcome providing no competitions in progress and/or Societies on course. Telephone call recommended. All visitors must possess current Handicap Certificate. *Society Meetings:* applications to Secretary/Manager. Reductions for parties exceeding 20. Professional: Mr A.K. Smith (029 2070 7401). Secretary/Manager: B.M. Williams (029 2070 1185).*

PENCOED. **St Mary's Golf Club,** St Mary's Hill, Pencoed CF35 5EA (01656 861100; Fax: 01656 863400). *Location:* Junction 35 of M4 and take third exit at roundabout, follow A473, take road signposted Felindre for about 300 yards, we are on left. Parkland course. 18 holes, 5291 yards. S.S.S. 66. Kingfisher 12 hole Public Course, practice area, driving range. *Green Fees:* information not available. *Eating facilities:* restaurant, three bars. *Visitors:* welcome weekdays 9am to 4pm; weekends 1pm to 4pm. 24 bedroom hotel. *Society Meetings:* welcome weekdays, restricted times at weekends. Society Secretary: Leighton Janes (01656 860280).

PONTYPOOL. **Pontypool Golf Club,** Lasgarn Lane, Trevethin, Pontypool NP4 8TR (01495 763655). *Location:* Pontypool A4042 to St. Cadoc's Church, Trevethin. Undulating hillside course, with mountain turf and fine views. 18 holes, yellow tees 5838 yards. S.S.S. 69. Practice area, Indoor teaching academy. *Green Fees:* weekdays £20.00, weekends £24.00. *Eating facilities:* `diningroom and bar snacks. *Visitors:* welcome, must have Handicap Certificates. *Society Meetings:* catered for by arrangement. Professional: Jim Howard (01495 755544). Secretary: Les Dodd (01495 763655).
e-mail: pontypoolgolf@btconnect.com
website: www.pontypoolgolf.co.uk

PONTYPOOL. **Woodlake Park Golf and Country Club,** Glascoed, Pontypool NP4 0TE (01291 673933; Fax: 01291 673811). *Location:* three miles from Usk overlooking Llandegfedd Reservoir. Undulating parkland with superb greens built to USGA specification. 18 holes, 6400 yards. S.S.S. 72. *Green Fees:* weekdays £22.50; weekends £30.00 (summer); weekdays £15.00, weekends £18.00 (winter). *Eating facilities:* spikes bar, lounge bar. *Visitors:* welcome, no restrictions. Function room for 130, private diningroom for up to 36 adjacent to Spikes Bar. *Society Meetings:* welcome, must pre-book, can cater for up to 100. Professional: Leon Lancey. Secretary: D. Hawker.

PONTYPRIDD. **Pontypridd Golf Club,** Ty Gwyn Road, Pontypridd CF37 4DJ (01443 402359). *Location:* east side of town, off A470, 12 miles from Cardiff. Wooded mountain course. 18 holes, 5881 yards, 5378 metres. S.S.S. 68. *Green Fees:* information not available. *Eating facilities:* bar, restaurant (restaurant closed Thursdays, snacks available). *Visitors:* welcome weekdays, Ladies' Day Tuesdays; weekends with member only. Must be member of recognised golf club in possession of Handicap Certificate. *Society Meetings:* catered for weekdays with prior reservation. Professional: Wade Walters (01443 491210). Secretary: Vikki Hooley (01443 409904; Fax: 01443 491622).*

PORTHCAWL **Grove Golf Club Ltd.,** South Cornelly, Porthcawl, Mid Glamorgan CF33 4RP (01656 788771. Fax: 01656 788414). *Location:* near the Glamorgan Heritage Coast at Porthcawl on A4229 two minutes from Junction 37 off M4. Parkland course with spectacular views. 18 holes, 6128 yards, S.S.S. 69. *Green Fees:* information not provided. *Eating facilities:* Full restaurant and bar snacks from 8am daily. *Visitors:* welcome every day, bookings advisable. *Society Meetings:* welcome by arrangement. A variety of packages available. Secretary: Mr Mike Thomas (01656 788771).

THE APPEARANCE OF AN ASTERISK (*) AT THE END OF A CLUB OR COURSE ENTRY INDICATES THAT UP-TO-DATE INFORMATION HAS NOT BEEN SUPPLIED

WALES / South Wales

PORTHCAWL. **Pyle and Kenfig Golf Club,** Waun-y-Mer, Kenfig, Bridgend CF33 4PU (01656 783093; Fax: 01656 772822). *Location:* one mile off M4 at Junction 37, follow Porthcawl signs. Undulating dune and downland course. 18 holes, 6776 yards (white tees). S.S.S. 73. Five practice holes, practice range. *Green Fees:* £45.00, £65.00 Sundays. *Eating facilities:* full catering facilities. *Visitors:* welcome weekdays and Sundays. *Society Meetings:* welcome by arrangement. Professional: Robert Evans (Tel & Fax: 01656 772446). Secretary: David Fellowes (01656 783093; Fax: 01656 772822).
e-mail: secretary@pandkgolfclub.co.uk
website: www.pandkgolfclub.co.uk

PORTHCAWL. **Royal Porthcawl Golf Club,** Rest Bay, Porthcawl CF36 3UW (01656 782251; Fax: 01656 771687). *Location:* Junction 37 M4, head towards Porthcawl (three miles), club located at Rest Bay. Links course. 18 holes, 6697 yards. S.S.S. 74. 27-acre practice area. *Green Fees:* weekdays £80.00 per round, £120.00 per day; weekends £100.00 per round, Sunday pm only unless residents. *Eating facilities:* full catering and bars. *Visitors:* accepted Monday afternoons, Tuesdays, Thursdays and Fridays; limited weekend availability. Dormy House – six single rooms (£45.00 B&B), three twin rooms (£80.00 B&B). *Society Meetings:* welcome. Professional: Peter Evans (01656 773702). Secretary: John Dinsdale.

PORT TALBOT. **Corus (Port Talbot),** Groes Fields, Margam, Port Talbot SA13 2NF (01639 871111 Ext. 3368). *Location:* Margam Park exit from M4. Flat course. 12 holes, 5020 yards. S.S.S. 64. *Green Fees:* information not available. *Eating facilities:* bar meals available if ordered in advance. *Visitors:* welcome midweek, weekends by arrangement with Secretary. Secretary: David Wilkinson (01639 793194).*

PORT TALBOT. **Lakeside Golf Club,** Water Street, Margam, Port Talbot SA13 2PA (01639 899959). *Location:* Junction 38 of M4 Port Talbot, Margam Country Park. Flat parkland course. 18 holes, 4390 yards, S.S.S. 63. 20 bay driving range. *Green Fees:* information not available. *Eating facilities:* bar meals, restaurant. *Visitors:* welcome. *Society Meetings:* welcome. Professional: Matthew Wootten (01639 888400). Secretary: Brian Channell. *

RAGLAN. **Raglan Parc Golf Club,** Parc Lodge, Raglan NP15 2ER (01291 690077; Fax: 01291 690075). *Location:* near junction A40 and A449. 18 holes, 6604 yards, Par 73. *Green Fees:* weekdays £19.00, weekends £26.00. *Visitors:* welcome. *Society Meetings:* welcome; packages available. Professional: Chris Murphy.
e-mail: golf@raglanparc.freeserve.co.uk
website: www.raglanparc.co.uk

GREEN ACRE PUBLIC HOUSE & MOTEL

Mike and Sue welcome you to their 17 bedroom motel, with all rooms en suite. Facilities include seasonal use of indoor swimming pool (check for availablity), squash court, Sky TV in all rooms, and bar meals served 12-2pm and 6.30-9.45pm, à la carte from 6.30-9.45pm; Sunday lunch available.
£34 single room per night, £44 double room per night.
Weekend Specials Fri/Sat or Sat/Sun £65 single or double;
Fri/Sat/Sun £95 single or double.
All prices inclusive of breakfast and VAT.

111 Heol Fach, North Cornelly, Near Bridgend, South Wales CF33 4LH
Tel: 01656 743041/744707 • Fax: 01656 744208

See also Colour Advertisement on page 53

RAGLAN PARC GOLF CLUB

A challenging 6604 yard Par 73 parkland course in historic surroundings, combined with a friendly and welcoming club atmosphere.
Beginners and experienced golfers welcome.

Professional – Chris Murphy. For further details about membership or visitor and society bookings, please contact:

RAGLAN PARC GOLF CLUB, PARC LODGE,
RAGLAN, MONMOUTHSHIRE NP15 2ER
TELEPHONE: 01291 690077 • FAX: 01291 690075
e-mail: golf@raglanparc.freeserve.co.uk
www.raglanparc.co.uk

Society & Group Packages Available

RHONDDA. **Rhondda Golf Club,** Golf House, Penrhys, Ferndale, Rhondda CF43 3PW (01443 433204). *Location:* on the Penrhys road joining Rhondda Fach and Rhondda Fawr. Mountain course. 18 holes, 6206 yards. S.S.S. 70. *Green Fees:* details on request. *Eating facilities:* all facilities daily except Mondays during winter months. *Visitors:* welcome. please telephone regarding availablilty. Handicap Certificate required. *Society Meetings:* welcome, please telephone for availability. Handicap Certificate required. Golf Shop: (01443 441385). Secretary: Paula Norman (01443 441384).
e-mail: rhonddagolf@aol.com

RHYMNEY. **Tredegar and Rhymney Golf Club,** Cwmtysswg, Rhymney NP2 3BQ (01685 840743). *Location:* A4048 Rhymney, Heads of the Valley road. Very scenic mountain course, lots of hazards. 18 holes, 6120 yards. S.S.S. 67. *Green Fees:* information not available. *Eating facilities:* bar snacks, meals by prior arrangement. *Visitors:* welcome at all times except Sunday mornings. *Society Meetings:* welcome at all times except Sunday mornings. Special rates. Secretary: Will Price (07761 005184). e-mail: golfclub@tredegarandrhymney.fsnet.co.uk

SOUTHERNDOWN. **Southerndown Golf Club,** Ogmore by Sea, Bridgend CF32 0QP (01656 880476; Fax: 01656 880317). *Location:* three miles from Bridgend on the Ogmore Road. Downland links overlooking Bristol Channel. 18 holes, 6449 yards. S.S.S. 72. Practice area. *Green Fees:* £45.00 weekdays; £65.00 weekends. *Eating facilities:* full dining room and bar facilities. *Visitors:* welcome any time except competition days (check with Secretary). Handicap Certificate required. *Society Meetings:* catered for by arrangement with Secretary. Special rates dependent on number. Professional: D. McMonagle (01656 881112). Secretary: (01656 881111). e-mail: southerndowngolf@btconnect.com

SWANSEA. **Allt-y-Graban Golf Club,** Allt-y-Graban Road, Pontlliw, Swansea SA4 1DT (01792 885757). *Location:* two miles from Junction 47 M4 turn left off A48 towards Pontarddulais, half mile past Glamorgan Arms. Parkland course. 9 holes, 4486 yards. S.S.S. 63. *Green Fees:* information not available. *Eating facilities:* full club house facilities including licensed bar and meals. *Visitors:* welcome. Secretary: S. Holston.*

SWANSEA. **Clyne Golf Club,** 120 Owls Lodge Lane, The Mayals, Swansea SA3 5DP (01792 401989; Fax: 01792 401078). *Location:* west of Swansea, right off Mumbles Road, signposted. Moorland course with extensive sea views. 18 holes, 6334 yards. S.S.S. 72. Large practice area, indoor and outdoor driving range and chipping and putting green. *Green Fees:* weekdays £26.00; weekends £32.00. Winter offer - £20.00 including two course meal. *Eating facilities:* full catering facilities, fully licensed. *Visitors:* welcome except during competition days - check with Secretary. *Society Meetings:* welcome by application. Professional: Jonathan Clewett (01792 402094). Manager: Ray Thompson.
e-mail: clynegolfclub@supanet.com
website: www.clynegolfclub.com

SWANSEA. **Fairwood Park Golf Club Ltd,** Blackhills Lane, Upper Killay, Swansea SA2 7JN (01792 297849). *Location:* A4118 road - follow signs to "Sketty" and "Killay"; road to club opposite Swansea Airport. Parkland Championship course twice hosted the Welsh PGA. 18 holes, 6650 yards. S.S.S. 73. Practice facilities available. *Green Fees:* £20.00 weekdays; £25.00 Fridays and weekends. *Eating facilities:* every day all day full range, from bar snacks to three-course meals in restaurant, two licensed bars. *Visitors:* always welcome. *Society Meetings:* always welcome. Professional: Gary Hughes (Tel & Fax: 01792 299194). Secretary: Mrs C.J. Beer (01792 297849).
e-mail: info@fairwoodpark.com
website: www.fairwoodpark.com

SWANSEA. **Gower Golf Club,** Cefn Goleu, Three Crosses, Swansea (01792 872480). *Location:* Junction 47 follow signs to Gowerton. Signposted in Gowerton and Three Crosses. Rolling parkland course. 18 holes, 6441 yards. S.S.S. 72. Practice facilities. *Green Fees:* information not available. *Eating facilities:* licensed bar, full catering facilities. *Visitors:* welcome, members start times 10am to 11am. 4 star Wales Tourist Board accommodation available for visitors. Bookings via Pro Shop (01792 879905). Tuition area. *Society Meetings:* welcome, packages arranged. Professional: Alan Williamson.*

SWANSEA. **Gowerton Golf Centre,** Victoria Road, Gowerton, Swansea SA4 3AB (01792 875188; Fax: 01792 874288). Flat wooded course with rivers and bunkers. 9 holes, 1000 yards, S.S.S. 27. *Green Fees:* information not available. *Eating facilities*: Diner, hot and cold meals provided. *Visitors*: open to the public. Lessons available. *Society Meetings*: welcome, group discounts. Professional: Mike Hobbs. Secretary: Steve Bromham.
e-mail: stevenbromham@beeb.net
website: www.gowertongolf-range.com

SWANSEA. **Inco Golf Club,** Clydach, Swansea SA6 5QR (01792 841257. *Location:* easily accessible from M4. Two minutes from Junction 24 on A4067 towards Pontardawe. A flat easy-walking parkland course bordered by the meandering River Tawe. 18 holes, 6064 yards. S.S.S 69. *Green Fees:* weekdays £18.00, weekends £23.00. *Eating facilities:* full catering facilities. *Visitors:* welcome at all times. *Society Meetings:* welcome, group discounts. Secretary: D.E. Jones (01792 842929).

SWANSEA. **Langland Bay Golf Club,** Langland Bay Road, Langland, Swansea SA3 4QR (01792 361721). *Location:* M4 Junction 42, A483 Swansea, A4067 to Mumbles, followed by Langland Bay. Parkland/seaside course. 18 holes, 5857 yards. S.S.F. 70. *Green Fees:* information not available. *Eating facilities:* full catering and refreshment service provided; limited on Mondays (01792 366023). *Visitors:* welcome best to check for availability. *Society Meetings:* parties over 12 are required to book in advance. Professional: Mark Evans (01792 366186). Secretary: Mrs Lynne Coleman (01792 361721; Fax: 01792 361082).*
e-mail: info@langlandbaygolfclub.com
website: www.langlandbaygolfclub.com

WALES / South Wales

SWANSEA. **Morriston Golf Club,** 160 Clasemont Road, Morriston, Swansea SA6 6AJ (01792 771079). *Location:* off Junction 46 M4, turn first left and follow road for one mile, clubhouse on left hand side of road. Parkland course, rather difficult. 18 holes, 5755 yards. S.S.S. 68. Practice area. *Green Fees:* information not available. *Eating facilities:* restaurant and three bars. *Visitors:* welcome most days on application. Trolleys for hire. *Society Meetings:* welcome. Professional: M. Govier (01792 772335). Secretary: K.J. Hackford (Tel & Fax: 01792 796528).*

SWANSEA. **Palleg Golf Club,** Lower Cwmtwrch, Swansea SA9 2QQ (01639 842193). *Location:* off A4067 (A4068) north of Swansea 14 miles, 25 miles Brecon. Meadowland course. 18 holes, 5902 yards . S.S.S. 70. *Green Fees:* weekdays £12.00, weekends £15.00. *Eating facilities:* to be arranged with steward. *Visitors:* welcome through week, check with Secretary for weekends. *Society Meetings:* welcome if arranged. Secretary: Mr C. Percival.

SWANSEA. **Pennard Golf Club,** 2 Southgate Road, Southgate, Swansea SA3 2BT (01792 233131; Fax: 01792 234797). *Location:* eight miles west of Swansea A4067, B4436. Seaside links. 18 holes, 6267 yards. S.S.S. 72, Par 71. Practice areas. *Green Fees:* weekdays £40.00, weekends and Bank Holidays £50.00. *Eating facilities:* dining room and two bars. *Visitors:* welcome at any time. Snooker room. *Society Meetings:* by arrangement. Professional: M.V. Bennett (01792 233451). Secretary: E.M. Howell (01792 233131). e-mail: sec@pennardgolfclub.com website: www.pennardgolfclub.com

SWANSEA. **Pontardawe Golf Club,** Cefn Llan, Pontardawe, Swansea SA8 4SH (01792 863118). *Location:* four miles north of M4 Junction 45 on A4067 Swansea-Brecon road. Wooded course. 18 holes, 6038 yards. S.S.S. 70. *Green Fees:* £20.00. *Eating facilities:* restaurant open daily except Mondays. *Visitors:* welcome, weekends by prior arrangement only. Handicap Certificate required. *Society Meetings:* catered for by application/ appointment, parties of 20 or more - £16.00 per person for 18 holes. Professional: G. Hopkins (Tel & Fax: 01792 830977). Secretary: Keith Davey. Administrator: Mrs M. Griffiths (01792 863118; Fax: 01792 830041).

TALBOT GREEN. **Llantrisant and Pontyclun Golf Club,** Talbot Green, Pontyclun CF72 8AL (01443 222148). *Location:* 10 miles north of Cardiff, two miles north of Junction 34 M4. Parkland. 18 holes, 5418 yards. S.S.S. 66. *Green Fees:* weekdays £20.00. Societies £17.50. *Eating facilities:* available. *Visitors:* welcome weekdays. *Society Meetings:* catered for by arrangement. Professionals: Andrew Bowen (01443 228169). Manager: Mike Hennessey (01443 224601). e-mail: golf@lpgc.wanadoo.co.uk

USK. **Alice Springs Golf Club,** Kemeys Commander, Usk NP15 1JY (Fax: 01873 881075). *Location*: three miles north of Usk on B4598. Undulating parkland course with beautiful views across the Usk Valley. Monnow Course: 18 holes, 6185 yards. S.S.S. 72. Usk Course: 18 holes, 6041 yards. S.S.S. 69. Driving range. *Green Fees*: £17.00 to £25.00. Buggies (30) available, from £12.00 per buggy. *Eating facilities:* restaurant facilities all day; function room. *Visitors:* welcome at all times; telephone for tee time. *Society Meetings*: catered for, special packages available. Professional: (01873 880914). Managing Director: David Rowlands (01873 880708; Fax: 01873 881075).

FHG

Other specialised FHG Guides

Published annually: available in all good bookshops or direct from the publisher.

K·U·P·E·R·A·R·D

Recommended **COUNTRY INNS & PUBS** OF BRITAIN £7.99

Recommended **COUNTRY HOTELS** OF BRITAIN £7.99

Recommended **SHORT BREAK HOLIDAYS** IN BRITAIN £7.99

The bestselling **PETS WELCOME!** £8.99

FHG Guides • Abbey Mill Business Centre, Seedhill, Paisley, Renfrewshire PA1 1TJ
Tel: 0141-887 0428 • Fax: 0141-889 7204
e-mail: admin@fhguides.co.uk
www.holidayguides.com

Ratings You Can Trust

ENGLAND

The *English Tourism Council* (now *VisitBritain*) has joined with the *AA* and *RAC* to create an easily understood quality rating for serviced accommodation, giving a clear guide of what to expect.

HOTELS are given a rating from One to Five *Stars* – the more Stars, the higher the quality and the greater the range of facilities and level of services provided.

GUEST ACCOMMODATION, which includes guest houses, bed and breakfasts, inns and farmhouses, is rated from One to Five *Diamonds*. Progressively higher levels of quality and customer care must be provided for each one of the One to Five Diamond ratings.

HOLIDAY PARKS, TOURING PARKS and CAMPING PARKS are now also assessed using *Stars*. Standards of quality range from a One Star (acceptable) to a Five Star (exceptional) park.

Look out also for the new SELF-CATERING Star ratings. The more *Stars* (from One to Five) awarded to an establishment, the higher the levels of quality you can expect. Establishments at higher rating levels also have to meet some additional requirements for facilities.

VisitBritain has launched a new *Quality Accredited Agency Standard*. Agencies who are awarded the Quality Accredited Agency marque by VisitBritain are recognised as offering good customer service and peace of mind, following an assement of their office polices, practices and procedures.

SCOTLAND

Star Quality Grades will reflect the most important aspects of a visit, such as the warmth of welcome, efficiency and friendliness of service, the quality of the food and the cleanliness and condition of the furnishings, fittings and decor.

THE MORE STARS,

THE HIGHER THE STANDARDS.

The description, such as Hotel, Guest House, Bed and Breakfast, Lodge, Holiday Park, Self-catering etc tells you the type of property and style of operation.

WALES

Places which score highly will have an especially welcoming atmosphere and pleasing ambience, high levels of comfort and guest care, and attractive surroundings enhanced by thoughtful design and attention to detail

STAR QUALITY GUIDE FOR

HOTELS, GUEST HOUSES AND FARMHOUSES
SELF-CATERING ACCOMMODATION
(Cottages, Apartments, Houses)
CARAVAN HOLIDAY HOME PARKS
(Holiday Parks, Touring Parks, Camping Parks)

★★★★★ Exceptional quality
★★★★ Excellent Quality
★★★ Very good quality
★★ Good quality
★ Fair to good quality

In England, Scotland and Wales, all graded properties are inspected annually by Tourist Authority trained Assessors.

THE GOLF GUIDE 2006　　　　　　　　　　　　　　　　IRELAND 487

Golf in Ireland
Where to Play, Where to Stay

Your Plan - Your Future

NDP

EU Programme
for Peace and Reconciliation

Funded by the European Union under the Programme for
Peace and Reconciliation 2000-2004 (Peace 11),
and part-financed by the Irish Government under
the National Development Plan

Tailor-Made Holidays in Ireland and Scotland for Groups and Individuals

Specialists in Golf & Sightseeing Holidays

Saoire Fáilte
The best of Ireland north and west

- Driver Guide / Coaching Services / Self-Drive
- Extended / Short Breaks
- Guaranteed Golf Starts and Non-Golfer Sightseeing
- All types of accommodation

The Errigal Suite, Donegal Airport, Carrickfinn,
Kincasslagh, Co Donegal, Ireland
Tel: 00353 74 95 48891 • Fax: 00353 74 95 48928
e-mail: info@saoirefailte.com　　www.saoirefailte.com

6th green at Doonbeg Golf Club, Co Clare

Northern Ireland

Four scenic miles from
Royal Portrush

Ireland's Golf Hotel
of the Year 2003

Bushmills, Co. Antrim, N. Ireland BT578QG
Tel +44 (0)28 2073 3000 mail@bushmillsinn.com
[See also Colour Advertisement on page 79]

the bushmills inn
HOTEL

www.bushmillsinn.com

ANTRIM

ANTRIM. **Massereene Golf Club,** 51 Lough Road, Antrim BT41 4DQ (028 9442 9293). *Location:* one mile S.W. of town, 3 miles from Aldergrove Airport, situated alongside the shores of Lough Neagh. 18 holes, 6602 yards. S.S.S. 72. *Green Fees:* information not available. *Eating facilities:* full catering facilities 12 noon till 9pm. *Visitors:* welcome. *Society Meetings:* catered for. Professional: Jim Smyth (028 9446 4074). Secretary: Mrs Stephanie Greene (028 9442 8096). *

BALLYCASTLE. **Ballycastle Golf Club,** Cushendall Road, Ballycastle BT64 6QP (028 2076 2536). *Location:* approximately 40 miles along the coast road west of Larne Harbour. Seaside links/undulating. 18 holes, 5744 yards, 5228 metres. S.S.S. 69. *Green Fees:* weekdays £20.00 (with member £10.00); weekends and Public Holidays £30.00 (with member £15.00). Subject to review. *Eating facilities:* catering available (Tel: 028 2076 9500). *Visitors:* welcome weekdays and afternoons at weekends. *Society Meetings:* by arrangement. Professional: I. McLaughlin (028 2076 2506). Hon. Secretary: B.J. Dillon (028 2076 2536; Fax: 028 2076 9909).
e-mail: info@ballycastlegolfclub.com
website: www.ballycastlegolfclub.com

BALLYCLARE. **Ballyclare Golf Club,** 25 Springvale Road, Ballyclare BT39 9JW (028 9332 2696/9334 2352). *Location:* one and a half miles north of Ballyclare. Parkland, lakes and river. 18 holes, 6289 yards. S.S.S. 71. Practice ground. *Green Fees:* weekdays £22.00, with member £11.00; weekends £28.00, with member £14.00. *Eating facilities:* catering available. *Visitors:* welcome weekdays except Thursday. *Society Meetings:* catered for. Special rates for 15 plus. Professional: Colin Lyttle (028 9332 4541). Secretary Manager: Michael Stone (028 9332 2696).

BALLYCLARE. **Greenacres Golf Club,** 153 Ballyrobert Road, Ballyclare BT39 9RT (028 9335 4111; Fax: 028 9335 4166). *Location:* three miles from Corrs Corner on B56. Parkland course, 18 holes. Par 71. S.S.S. 68. Floodlit driving range. *Green Fees:* information not available. *Eating facilities*: bar and catering available.*

BALLYMENA. **Ballymena Golf Club,** 128 Raceview Road, Ballymena BT42 4HY (028 2586 1207). *Location:* two miles north east of town on A42. Flat/parkland/heathland. 18 holes, 5299 metres. S.S.S. 67. *Green Fees:* information not available. *Eating facilities:* restaurant and bar snacks. *Visitors:* welcome at all times, except Tuesdays and Saturdays. *Society Meetings:* catered for except Tuesdays and Saturdays.. Professional: Ken Revie (028 2586 1652). Secretary: George Small (Tel & Fax: 028 2586 1487).*

BALLYMENA. **Galgorm Castle Golf Club,** Galgorm Castle, Ballymena BT42 1HL (028 2564 6161; Fax: 028 2565 1151). *Location:* one mile south of Ballymena on A42 to Galgorm village. Mature parkland course in the grounds of one of Ireland's most historic castles. 18 holes, 6736 yards, S.S.S. 72. Driving range, practice area. *Green Fees:* £26.00 weekdays, £32.00 weekends and Bank Holidays. *Eating facilities:* full restaurant and bar. *Visitors:* welcome. Accommodation and tuition available. Fully equipped golf shop, hire facilities including buggies with GPS satellite navigation. *Society Meetings:* welcome, special rates available. Professional: Phil Collins (028 2564 6161; Fax: 028 2565 1151). Secretary: Barbara McGeown (028 2565 0210).
e-mail: golf@galgormcastle.com
website: www.galgormcastle.com

www.uk-golfguide.com

BALLYMONEY. **Gracehill Golf Club,** 141 Ballinlea Road, Stranocum, Ballymoney BT53 8PX (028 2075 1209; Fax: 028 2075 1074). *Location:* Ballymoney; International Airport (40 minutes). Parkland. Opened May 1995 with American-style water hazards. 18 holes, 6525 yards. S.S.S. 73. Practice area. Driving range scheduled to open 2004/2005, adjacent to course. *Green Fees:* Monday to Friday £20.00, Saturday/Sunday £25.00. *Eating facilities:* restaurant/bar. *Visitors:* telephone for tee time. *Society Meetings:* all welcome. Secretary/Manager: M. McClure. website: www.gracehillgolfclub.co.uk

BELFAST. **Castlereagh Hills Golf Club,** Upper Braniel Road, Castlereagh, Belfast BT5 7TX (028 9044 8477). *Location:* two miles from city centre, east Belfast. Parkland. 18 holes. 5398 metres. S.S.S. 68. Practice area and putting green. *Green Fees:* information not available. *Eating facilities:* Saturdays only. *Visitors:* welcome, no restrictions. Club hire *Society Meetings:* all welcome. Professional: K. Gray (028 9044 8477). Secretary: A. Carson (028 9065 9653).

BELFAST. **Cliftonville Golf Club,** 44 Westland Road, Belfast BT14 6NH (028 9074 4158). Parkland with rivers bisecting three fairways. 9 holes, 6210 yards, 5672 metres. S.S.S. 70. Practice fairway and nets. *Green Fees:* weekdays £14.00, with member £10.00; Sunday £16.00, with member £11.00. *Eating facilities:* bars, catering on request. *Visitors:* no visitors after 5pm weekdays, until 6pm on Saturdays, and until 1.30 pm Sundays. *Society Meetings:* very welcome, especially by arrangement. Professional: Peter Hannah. Hon. Secretary: E. Lusty O.B.E (028 9074 6595).

BELFAST. **Dunmurry Golf Club,** 91 Dunmurry Lane, Dunmurry, Belfast BT17 9JS (028 9061 0834; Fax: 028 9060 2540). *Location:* off M1 at Dunmurry, to village, turn left past Tesco, one and a half miles on right. Parkland, partially wooded. 18 holes, 6080 yards. S.S.S. 69. Practice area. *Green Fees:* weekdays £27.00; Sundays £37.00. Subject to review. *Eating facilities:* restaurant (not Mondays) and bar. *Visitors:* welcome by arrangement; not Fridays (Ladies' Day) and not Saturdays. Trolleys available. *Society Meetings:* welcome by written application; 20 or more £23.00. Professional: John Dolan (028 9062 1314; Fax: 028 9060 2540). Golf Manager: Tony Cassidy (028 9061 0834; Fax: 028 9060 2540).

THE APPEARANCE OF AN ASTERISK (*) AT THE END OF A CLUB OR COURSE ENTRY INDICATES THAT UP-TO-DATE INFORMATION HAS NOT BEEN SUPPLIED

BELFAST. **Fortwilliam Golf Club,** Downview Avenue, Belfast BT15 4EZ (028 9077 6798). *Location:* one mile Fortwilliam Junction M2. Parkland. 18 holes, 6030 yards. S.S.S. 69. *Green Fees:* weekdays £22.00; weekends £29.00. *Eating facilities:* excellent catering and bar. *Visitors:* welcome every day except Saturdays. *Society Meetings:* catered for Tuesdays and Thursdays, special rates available. Golf cart available - £20.00 per round. Professional: Peter Hanna (Tel & Fax: 028 9077 0980). Secretary: M. Purdy (028 9037 0770; Fax: 028 9078 1891).

BELFAST. **Malone Golf Club,** 240 Upper Malone Road, Dunmurry, Belfast BT17 9LB (028 9061 2758; Fax: 028 9043 1394). *Location:* five miles south of Belfast city centre, opposite Lady Dixon Park. Parkland, wooded course with large lake. 18 holes, 6706 yards. S.S.S. 72. 9 holes, 6320 yards. S.S.S. 70 (9 holes x 2). Practice ground, putting green. *Green Fees:* Weekdays £55.00 per day, weekends £60.00 per day. *Eating facilities:* bar, bar snacks and restaurant. *Visitors:* welcome weekdays except Tuesdays (Ladies' Day); time sheet on weekends. Dress code observed on course and in clubhouse. Golf carts for hire. *Society Meetings:* welcome by arrangement Mondays and Thursdays. Professional: Michael McGee (Tel & Fax: 028 9061 4917). Manager: J.N.S. Agate (028 9061 2758; Fax: 028 9043 1394).

CARRICKFERGUS. **Carrickfergus Golf Club,** 35 North Road, Carrickfergus BT38 8LP (028 9336 3713; Fax: 028 9336 3023). *Location:* North Road, one mile from main shore road. Fairly flat parkland course, partially wooded. 18 holes, 5768 yards. S.S.S. 68. *Green Fees:* information not provided. *Eating facilities:* full catering and bar facilities. *Visitors:* welcome except on Friday afternoons and weekends. *Society Meetings:* catered for on weekdays but not after 1pm on Fridays. PGA Professional: G. Mercer PGA (028 9336 3713; Fax: 028 9336 3023). Secretary: Mr I. McLean (028 9336 3713; Fax: 028 9336 3023).

CARRICKFERGUS. **Greenisland Golf Club,** 156 Upper Road, Greenisland, Carrickfergus BT38 8RW (028 9086 2236). *Location:* situated at the foot of Knockagh Hill and on the edge of Carrickfergus town, one of the best features is the scenic view over Belfast Lough. Parkland course. 9 holes, 5624 metres. S.S.S. 69. *Green Fees:* information not available. *Eating facilities:* lunch and evening meals available, bar snacks. *Visitors:* welcome; Saturdays not before 5.30pm. *Society Meetings:* welcome by prior arrangement. Hon. Secretary: W.J. McLaughlin.*

Galgorm Castle Golf & Country Club

Galgorm Castle, Galgorm Road, Ballymena, Co. Antrim, Northern Ireland BT42 1HL
A mature parkland course in the grounds of one of Ireland's most historic castles.
Visitors always welcome • Tel: 028 2564 6161 • Fax: 028 2565 1151
Website: www.galgormcastle.com • e-mail: golf@galgormcastle.com

CARRICKFERGUS. **Whitehead Golf Club,** McCrea's Brae, Whitehead, Carrickfergus BT38 9NZ (028 9337 0822). *Location:* Whitehead, 15 miles from Belfast, 10 miles from Larne. 18 holes, 6050 yards. S.S.S. 69, par 70. *Green Fees:* weekdays £16.00, £12.00 with a member; weekends with member only. *Eating facilities:* by arrangement with Caterer. *Visitors:* welcome Monday to Friday, weekends with a member only. *Society Meetings:* by prior arrangement. Professional: C. Farr (028 9337 0821. Secretary/Manager: (028 9337 0820 9am - 5pm; Fax: 028 9337 0825). Caterer (028 9337 0823).

CUSHENDALL. **Cushendall Golf Club,** 21 Shore Road, Cushendall BT44 0NG (028 2177 1318). *Location:* 25 miles north on Antrim coast road from Larne Harbour. Seaside wooded course; river comes into play in seven out of nine holes. 9 holes, 4384 metres. S.S.S. 63. *Green Fees:* weekdays £13.00 per day, weekends and Bank Holidays £18.00; £5.00 concession if playing with member. *Eating facilities:* normal bar hours, bar snacks, full catering by arrangement. *Visitors:* welcome without reservation, avoid Wednesday afternoons, Thursday Ladies' Day, time sheet in operation at weekends. *Society Meetings:* welcome. Hon. Secretary: Shaun McLaughlin (028 2175 8366).

LARNE. **Larne Golf Club,** 54 Ferris Bay Road, Islandmagee, Larne BT40 3RT (028 9338 2228; Fax: 028 9338 2088). *Location:* six miles north of Whitehead on Browns Bay Road. Part links, part parkland. 9 holes, 18 tee boxes, 6288 yards. S.S.S. 70. Practice ground. *Green Fees:* information not available. *Eating facilities:* bar, restaurant. *Visitors:* welcome Mondays to Thursdays, and Sundays. Snooker table. *Society Meetings:* welcome on application (not Friday or Saturday). 10% reduction for societies of 20 or more. Secretary: R.I. Johnston.

LARNE. **Cairndhu Golf Club Ltd,** 192 Coast Road, Ballygally, Larne BT40 2QG (Tel & Fax: 028 2858 3324). *Location:* three miles north of Larne on the famous Antrim Coast road leading to the Glens of Antrim. Parkland course with stunning views. 18 holes, 5611 metres. S.S.S. 69. Practice area, driving range. *Green Fees:* information not available. *Eating facilities:* restaurant and bar. *Visitors:* welcome except Saturdays. *Society Meetings:* welcome. Professional: Bob Walker (Tel & Fax: 028 2858 3324). General Manager: Michael Corsar.*

LISBURN. **Lisburn Golf Club,** Blaris Lodge, 68 Eglantine Road, Lisburn BT27 5RQ (028 9267 7216; Fax: 028 9260 3608). *Location:* three miles south of Lisburn on A1. Parkland. 18 holes, 6647 yards. S.S.S. 72. Practice area. *Green Fees:* information not available. *Eating facilities:* bar and restaurant. *Visitors:* welcome weekdays, Tuesdays Ladies have preference. Saturday after 5.30pm only, Sundays with member only. Snooker room. *Society Meetings:* Mondays and Thursdays only. Professional: S. Hamill (028 9267 7217). Manager: G.E. McVeigh (028 9267 7216).*
e-mail: lisburngolfclub@aol.com

MAZE. **Down Royal Park Golf Course,** 6 Dunygarton Road, Maze BT27 5RT (Tel & Fax: 028 9262 1339). *Location:* Belfast–Hillsborough road. Lisburn–Moira road. Heathland. 18 holes, 6824 metres. S.S.S. 72. *Green Fees:* information not available. *Eating facilities:* available. *Visitors:* G.U.I. dress code applies. Budget accommodation available. *Society Meetings:* all welcome.

NEWTOWNABBEY. **Ballyearl Golf and Leisure Centre,** 585 Doagh Road, Newtownabbey BT36 8RZ (028 9084 8287; Fax: 028 9084 4896). *Location:* eight miles north of Belfast, 15 miles south of Larne. From Belfast follow signs to Larne via M2 (A8), turn right to Mossley approximately one miles from Corrs Corner Pub. Ballyearl is one mile on left. Parkland. 9 holes, 2402 yards, 2196 metres. Par 3. 27 bay covered floodlit driving range, outdoor grass teeing area. *Green Fees:* information not available. *Eating facilities:* snacks available in Squash Club bar. *Visitors:* no restrictions – pay and play. Squash courts, hi-tech fitness suite and arts theatre. Golf lessons available by appointment, golf equipment tailored to individual requirements and can be tested on driving range. Professional: Richard Johnston (028 9084 0899).*

PORTBALLINTRAE. **Bushfoot Golf Club,** 50 Bushfoot Road, Portballintrae BT57 8RR (028 2073 1317; Fax: 028 2073 1852). *Location:* off Ballaghmore Road, Portballintrae. Seaside links course. 9 holes, 6075 yards. S.S.S 67. *Green Fees:* weekdays £16.00; weekends £20.00. *Eating facilities:* full dining room, bars. *Visitors:* welcome, restrictions weekends July to September. *Society Meetings:* all welcome weekdays. Secretary/ Manager: J. Knox Thompson.

PORTRUSH. **Rathmore Golf Club,** Bushmills Road, Portrush BT56 8JG (028 7082 2285). *Location:* north east coast - six miles from Coleraine, beside roundabout on road to Bushmills. Royal Portrush Golf Club (valley links). Flat seaside links. 18 holes, 6304 yards. S.S.S. 70. *Green Fees:* information not available. *Eating facilities:* bar but no eating facilities. *Visitors:* Saturday and Sunday 1.30 to 2.30pm, Monday to Friday no restrictions except Tuesday after 11am September to March and Thursday from 4-6pm May to August. *Society Meetings:* must register at Royal Portrush Golf Club and pay green fees before commencement of play. Professional: Gary McNeill (R.P.G.C.) (028 7082 2311). Secretary: Derek Ross Williamson (Tel & Fax: 028 7082 2996).

THE APPEARANCE OF AN ASTERISK (*) AT THE END OF A CLUB OR COURSE ENTRY INDICATES THAT UP-TO-DATE INFORMATION HAS NOT BEEN SUPPLIED

PORTRUSH. **Royal Portrush Golf Club,** Dunluce Road, Portrush BT56 8JQ (028 7082 2311). *Location:* one mile from Portrush on the main Portrush/Bushmills Road. Dunluce Course-natural seaside links. 18 holes, 6845 yards. S.S.S. 73. Valley Course - flat seaside links. 18 holes, 6304 yards. S.S.S 71. Two practice grounds. *Green Fees:* Dunluce £95.00 weekdays, £110.00 weekends; Valley £32.50 weekdays, £37.50 weekends. *Eating facilities:* three bars, restaurant with snacks and à la carte. *Visitors:* Dunluce Course: must contact Secretary prior to visit. Restrictions Monday, Wednesday and Friday afternoons and Saturday and Sunday mornings. Valley Course: welcome weekdays, plus limited tee times at weekends. *Society Meetings:* accepted with prior bookings. Professional: Gary McNeill (028 7082 3335). Secretary: Miss W. Erskine (028 7082 2311; Fax: 028 7082 3139).
e-mail: info@royalportrushgolfclub.com

TEMPLEPATRICK. **Hilton Templepatrick Golf Club,** Paradise Walk, Castle Upton Estate, Templepatrick BT39 0DD (02894 435542; Fax: 02894 435511). *Location*: 5 miles from Belfast International Airport, 15 miles from Belfast city centre. Parkland course - USGA greens. 18 holes, 7010 yards. S.S.S. 71. Driving range and putting green. *Green Fees*: £45.00. Discounts for groups over 12. *Eating facilities*: à la carte Restaurant and Bar Brasserie in 4 star hotel. *Visitors*: welcome. 129 bedroomed hotel, Livingwell Health Club, Tuition package. *Society Meetings*: welcome, no restrictions. Professionals: Eamonn Logue/Lynn McCool (02894 435542; Fax: 02894 435511). Director of Golf: Lynn McCool (02894 435510).
e-mail: lynn.mccool@hilton.com

Hilton Templepatrick Hotel & Country Club

Relax with a Golf and Leisure Break

From as little as £150 sterling per person why not spend time golfing on one of Northern Ireland's finest parkland courses?

- Enjoy 2 rounds of golf
- 2 nights bed and breakfast with dinner on the first night of your stay (3 course table d'hote)

Not a golfer? Then exchange the golf for beauty treatments or master the game under the experienced eye of our PGA professional.

An oasis of peace and tranquility Hilton Templepatrick Hotel & Country Club is the perfect destination for a relaxing break. Set in 220 acres of the Castle Upton estate in County Antrim, we have a range of facilities that will find favour with the active and relaxed alike. The hotels 18 hole championship golf course meanders for over 7000 yards and will test the abilities of even the finest golfer. Make free use of LivingWell health club with its fantastic gym, 18 metre indoor swimming pool with sauna, steam room, solarium and spa. Relax in the stylish Treffners restaurant for dinner or reflect on your day in Kinahans bar brasserie.

To make your booking call **028 9443 5544** for this special deal.

Hilton Templepatrick Hotel & Country Club, Hilton Templepatrick, Castle Upton Estate, Templepatrick, BT39 0DD
Fax: **028 9443 5509** hilton.co.uk/templepatrick

Terms and conditions - Subject to availability and seasonal change.
Prices are per person for two nights, based on two people sharing a twin/double room. Terms and conditions apply.

FHG

Visit the KUPERARD website
www.holidayguides.com
for details of the wide choice of accommodation featured in the full range of FHG titles

ARMAGH

ARMAGH. **County Armagh Golf Club,** 7 Newry Road, Armagh BT60 1EN (028 3752 2501). *Location:* Armagh/Newry road. Parkland course. 18 holes, 6212 yards. S.S.S. 69. Practice area available. *Green Fees:* £15.00 weekdays, £20.00 weekends. November to February (incl.) reduction of £1.00. *Eating facilities:* diningroom/bar meals Tuesdays to Sundays, bar facilities daily. *Visitors:* welcome by arrangement. Not Saturdays or Thursdays. Carts and buggies. *Society Meetings:* welcome by arrangement except Saturdays or Thursdays. Professional: Alan Rankin (Tel & Fax: 028 3752 5864). Secretary: June McParland (Tel & Fax: 028 3752 5861).

CRAIGAVON. **Craigavon Golf and Ski Club,** Turmoyra Lane, Lurgan, Craigavon (028 3832 6606; Fax: 028 3834 7272). *Location:* half a mile from motorway, one mile from town centre, adjacent to ski slope. Parkland/wooded. 18 holes, 5901 meters. S.S.S. 72. 9 hole Par 3. 12 hole pitch and putt. Driving range. *Green Fees:* information not available. *Eating facilities:* full restaurant facilities. *Visitors:* always welcome. Modern clubhouse, showers and lockers. *Society Meetings:* welcome - book beforehand. Professional: S.Dickson.

CRAIGAVON. **Edenmore Golf and Country Club,** Edenmore House, 70 Drumnabreeze Road, Magheralin, Craigavon BT67 0RH (028 9261 9241; Fax: 028 9261 3310). *Location*: take main road for Lurgan, coming off M1 at Moira Exit. Signposted from village of Magheralin on main Moira – Lurgan Road. Undulating, parkland course with panoramic views. Well drained. 18 holes, 6244 yards. S.S.S. 70. Practice facilities, putting green. *Green Fees*: information not available. *Eating facilities:* Bailies restaurant. *Visitors:* Edenmore is a friendly, welcoming club. Visitors at all times except Saturdays before 3pm. Tuition on request. *Society Meetings:* welcome. Ring to book. Secretary: Kenneth Logan (028 9261 1310; Fax: 028 9261 3310).*
e-mail: info@edenmore.com
website: www.edenmore.com

CULLYHANNA. **Ashfield Golf Club,** Freeduff Road, Cullyhanna, Newry (028 3086 8180; Fax: 028 3086 8611). *Location:* A29 road, from Newry to Crossmaglen, 15 miles distance. Parkland course, lake, water hazard, bunkers. 18 holes, 5616 yards. S.S.S. 67. Par 69. Driving range. *Green Fees:* information not available. *Eating facilities:* licensed restaurant. *Visitors:* welcome at all times except before 11am on Sundays. *Society Meetings:* welcome, special rates available. Professional: Paddy Gribben. Secretary: Seamus McNulty.*

LURGAN. **Lurgan Golf Club,** The Demesne, Lurgan, Craigavon BT67 9BN (028 3832 2087; Fax: 028 3831 6166). *Location:* one mile from motorway, half a mile from town centre. Parkland. 18 holes, 5895 metres. S.S.S. 69. Small practice area, putting green. *Green Fees:* weekdays £17.00; weekends £22.00. Reductions if playing with a member. Students £14.00, under 18s £6.00. *Eating facilities:* restaurant and lounge bar. Caterer: (028 3832 2087). *Visitors:* welcome Monday to Friday, and Sundays after 3pm. *Society Meetings:* welcome as per visitors. Professional: Des Paul (028 3832 1068). Secretary: Muriel Sharpe (028 3832 2087; Fax: 028 3831 6166).

PORTADOWN. **Portadown Golf Club,** 192 Gilford Road, Portadown BT63 5LF (028 3835 5356). *Location:* on main Gilford Road out of Portadown. Parkland. 18 holes, 5649 metres. S.S.S. 69 off white tees; 68 off green tees, 72 off red tees. *Green Fees:* information not available. *Eating facilities:* Contact caterer on 028 3835 2214. *Visitors:* welcome at all times except Tuesdays and Saturdays. Squash, indoor bowling and snooker. *Society Meetings:* catered for by booking. Professional: Paul Stevenson (028 3833 4655). Secretary: Mrs Lily Holloway (028 3835 5356).*

TANDRAGEE. **Tandragee Golf Club,** Markethill Road, Tandragee, Craigavon BT62 2ER (028 3884 1272; Fax: 028 3884 0664). *Location*: approximately five miles from Portadown on road to Newry and Dublin. Hilly parkland and wooded. 18 holes, 5754 metres. S.S.S. 70, Par 71. Practice ground and net. *Green Fees*: information not available. *Eating facilities*: full catering except Mondays; two lounges. *Visitors*: welcome all days except Thursdays (Ladies' Day) and Saturdays (competition day). Carts and buggies available. *Society Meetings:* welcome by arrangement. Professional: D. Keenan (028 3884 1761). Administrative Assistant: Mrs Ashley Stewart.
e-mail: office@tandragee.co.uk
website: www.tandragee.co.uk

Co. DOWN

ARDGLASS. **Ardglass Golf Club,** 4 Castle Place, Ardglass BT30 7TP (028 4484 1219; Fax: 028 4484 1841). *Location:* nearest town – Downpatrick. Situated on the coast 30 miles due south of Belfast. Seaside links. 18 holes, White markers - 6231 yards. S.S.S. 70, Par 70. *Green Fees:* information not available. *Eating facilities:* bar and dining room. *Visitors:* welcome all week. *Society Meetings:* welcome except Saturdays, advance booking necessary. Professional: Philip Farrell (028 4484 1022). Club Manager: Miss Deborah Polly (028 4484 1219; Fax: 028 4484 1841).*
e-mail: info@ardglassgolfclub.com
website: www.ardglassgolfclub.com

THE APPEARANCE OF AN ASTERISK (*) AT THE END OF A CLUB OR COURSE ENTRY INDICATES THAT UP-TO-DATE INFORMATION HAS NOT BEEN SUPPLIED

BALLYNAHINCH. **Spa Golf Club,** 20 Grove Road, Ballynahinch BT24 8PN (028 9756 2365; Fax: 028 9756 4158). *Location:* Ballynahinch half mile, 11 miles south of Belfast. Parkland, wooded course with panoramic views. 18 holes, 6469 yards. S.S.S. 72. Practice area. *Green Fees:* weekdays £18.00; weekends £28.00. *Eating facilities:* bar snacks/ restaurant service. *Visitors:* welcome except Saturdays. *Society Meetings:* welcome, discount for large parties. Secretary: T.G. Magee (028 9756 2365).

BANBRIDGE. **Banbridge Golf Club,** Huntly Road, Banbridge BT32 3UR. *Location:* half-a-mile from town centre on the Huntly Road. Parkland. 18 holes, 5590 yards. S.S.S. 67. Practice ground. *Green Fees:* weekdays £17.00, with a member £10.00; weekends £22.00, with a member £12.00. Societies £14.00 weekdays, £17.00 Sundays. *Eating facilities:* full catering and bar facilities. *Visitors:* welcome, restrictions on Ladies' Day (Tuesdays) and men's competition day (Saturdays). *Society Meetings:* catered for; arrange with Secretary/Manager: Mr J. McKeown (028 4066 2211).
e-mail: info@banbridge-golf.freeserve.co.uk

BANGOR. **Bangor Golf Club,** Broadway, Bangor BT20 4RH (028 9127 0922; Fax: 028 9145 3394). *Location:* one mile from town centre off Donaghadee Road. Parkland. 18 holes, 6424 yards. S.S.S. 71. Practice facilities. *Green Fees:* information not available. *Eating facilities:* lunches and evening meals. *Visitors:* welcome except Saturdays; Tuesday is Ladies' Day. Trolleys. *Society Meetings:* advance booking necessary. Professional: Michael Bannon (028 9146 2164).
e-mail: bangorgolfclubni@btconnect.com
website: www.bangorgolfclubni.co.uk

BANGOR. **Blackwood Golf Centre,** 150 Crawfordsburn Road, Bangor BT19 1GB (028 9185 2706). *Location:* west of Bangor. Two 18-hole courses. Driving range. *Green Fees:* information not available. *Visitors:* welcome.*

BANGOR. **Carnalea Golf Club,** Station Road, Bangor BT19 1EZ (028 9146 5004). *Location:* one minute walk from Carnalea Railway Station. Seaside parkland. 18 holes, 5574 yards. S.S.S. 67. *Green Fees:* information not available. *Eating facilities:* full restaurant and two bars. *Visitors:* welcome without reservation. *Society Meetings:* catered for. Golf Shop (028 9127 0122). Professional: Tom Loughran (028 9127 0122). Secretary: G. Steele (028 9127 0368; Fax: 028 9127 3989).*

BANGOR. **Helen's Bay Golf Club,** Golf Road, Helen's Bay, Bangor BT19 1TL (028 9185 2815). *Location:* A2 from Belfast - 9 miles. Parkland. 9 holes, 5161 metres. S.S.S. 67. *Green Fees:* £18.00 to £20.00. *Eating facilities:* available - full restaurant, bar and lounge bar (028 9185 2816). *Visitors:* welcome Sunday, Monday, Wednesday and Friday; Tuesday is Ladies' Day. *Society Meetings:* catered for by prior booking confirmed by the Secretary Manager (maximum 40). Secretary Manager: (Tel: 028 9185 2815; Fax: 028 9185 2660).

BELFAST. **Balmoral Golf Club Ltd,** 518 Lisburn Road, Belfast BT9 6GX (028 9038 1514). *Location:* M1 from Belfast exit Balmoral, turn right at lights Lisburn Road, quarter mile on left beside Kings Hall or two/three miles south of Belfast on main Lisburn Road next to Kings Hall. A flat undulating course with 30 plus bunkers and a stream to contend with. Excellent greens, approached by tree-lined fairways. 18 holes, 6034 metres. S.S.S. 70 Medal, 69 regular. Practice ground and nets. *Green Fees:* information not available. *Eating facilities:* restaurant, lunch, dinner, snacks à la carte, two bars. *Visitors:* welcome except Saturdays; restricted on Sundays. *Society Meetings:* Mondays, Thursdays and Sunday afternoons. Professional: Geoff Bleakley (028 9066 7747). Chief Executive: Terry Graham (028 9038 1514; Fax: 028 9066 6759).

BELFAST. **Belvoir Park Golf Club,** 73/75 Church Road, Newtownbreda, Belfast BT8 7AN (028 9049 1693; Fax: 028 9064 6113). *Location:* three miles from city centre, Saintfield Road. Parkland, well wooded. 18 holes, 6501 yards, 5943 metres. S.S.S. 71. Practice area. *Green Fees:* information not available. *Eating facilities:* full catering and bar. *Visitors:* welcome except Saturday. *Society Meetings:* by prior booking only. Director of Golf: M. Kelly (028 9064 6714). Secretary: Ann Vaughan (028 9049 1693).*

BELFAST. **Knock Golf Club,** Summerfield, Dundonald, Belfast BT16 2QX (028 9048 2249; Fax: 028 9048 7277). *Location:* Upper Newtownards Road in east of the city of Belfast. Parkland with huge trees, large bunkers and a stream running through the course. 18 holes, 6435 yards. S.S.S. 71. Practice ground. *Green Fees:* information not available. *Eating facilities:* full catering and bar facilities available. *Visitors:* welcome except Saturday but it is advisable to ring Professional first. Trolleys available. *Society Meetings:* catered for Mondays and Thursdays. Advance booking required. Professional: G. Fairweather (028 9048 3825). Secretary/Manager: Mrs A. Armstrong (028 9048 3251).

BELFAST. **Ormeau Golf Club,** 50 Park Road, Belfast BT7 2FX (028 9064 0700; Fax: 028 9064 6250). *Location:* Belfast south/east; Ravenhill Road. Flat, parkland wooded course. 9 holes, 2783 yards, 2542 metres. S.S.S. 67. *Green Fees:* information not available. *Eating facilities:* bars and restaurant. *Visitors:* welcome, restrictions on Tuesdays and Saturdays. Snooker. *Society Meetings:* welcome most days. Shop Manager: B. Wilson (028 90 640999). Manager: W. Lynn (028 9064 0700). Caterer: (028 9064 1999).

BELFAST. **Shandon Park Golf Club,** 73 Shandon Park, Belfast BT5 6NY (028 9079 3730). Parkland. 18 holes, 5714 metres. S.S.S. 70. *Green Fees:* information not available. *Eating facilities:* restaurant facilities, bar snacks. *Visitors:* welcome except Saturdays subject to advance clearance by Professional. *Society Meetings:* Mondays and Fridays only. Professional: Barry Wilson (028 9079 7859). Secretary/Manager: Mr David Jenkins (028 9040 1856; Fax: 028 9040 2773). *

DONAGHADEE. **Donaghadee Golf Club,** 84 Warren Road, Donaghadee BT21 0PQ (028 9188 8697). *Location:* five miles south of Bangor on main coast road. Part links and inland park with scenic views over Copeland Islands and Scottish coast. 18 holes, 6000 yards, 5561 metres. Par 71, S.S.S. 69. Practice ground and putting green. *Green Fees:* information not available. *Eating facilities:* full catering available, seven days in summer, Tuesday to Sunday in winter. *Visitors:* welcome on any weekday and Sundays; Members only on Saturdays. Ladies welcome on Tuesdays. Juveniles must be accompanied by an adult. Pro shop. Club and trolley hire. Lessons available by prior arrangement. *Society Meetings:* welcome any day except Saturday. Special rates available. Professional: Gordon Drew (028 9188 2392). General Manager: Michael Corsar (028 9188 3624; Fax: 028 9188 8891)*
e-mail: deegolf@freenet.co.uk.

DOWNPATRICK. **Bright Castle Golf Club,** 14 Coniamstown Road, Bright, Downpatrick BT30 8LU (028 4484 1319). *Location:* turn right off the main B176, signposted to Bright/Minerstown. Bright Castle is an 18 hole mature woodland course featuring 4 formidable par 5s - your driving accuracy will be tested to the limit on the sloping, densely tree-lined fairways. 6645 yards. SSS 73. *Green Fees:* Weekends £15.00, Weekdays £12.00. *Eating facilities:* Restaurant and bar available. *Visitors:* Welcome. *Society Meetings:* Welcome, must book in advance. Secretary: Thomas Johnston (028 4482 8428).
e-mail: bright.castle@virgin.net

DOWNPATRICK. **Downpatrick Golf Club,** 43 Saul Road, Downpatrick BT30 6PA (028 4461 5947; Fax: 028 4461 7502). *Location:* one and a half miles from town centre, south-east direction. Parkland, challenging upland course. 18 holes, 6120 yards. S.S.S. 69. Practice area and putting area. *Green Fees:* information not available. *Eating facilities:* two lounges and diningroom. Catering: (028 4461 5244). *Visitors:* welcome, but advisable to make arrangements in advance for weekends. Snooker room. *Society Meetings:* welcome by prior arrangement. Professional: Robert Hutton (028 4461 5167). Finance Manager/ Administrator: Barbara-Ann Hitchens.*

HOLYWOOD. **Holywood Golf Club,** Nuns Walk, Demesne Road, Holywood BT18 9LE (028 9042 3135/2138; Fax: 028 9042 5040). Parkland. 18 holes, 5430 yards. S.S.S. 68. *Green Fees:* information not available. *Eating facilities:* bars and restaurant. *Visitors:* welcome, Thursday is Ladies' Day. *Society Meetings:* welcome Mondays, Tuesdays, Wednesdays and Fridays and between 8am and 9am Sundays. Professional: Paul Gray (028 9042 5503; Fax: 028 9042 5040). Secretary: (028 9042 3135; Fax: 028 9042 5040).*

HOLYWOOD. **The Royal Belfast Golf Club,** Station Road, Craigavad BT18 0BP (028 9042 8165; Fax: 028 9042 1404). *Location:* two miles past Holywood, off main Belfast to Bangor Road. Mainly parkland, bordering shores of Belfast Lough. 18 holes, 5961 yards. S.S.S. 69. Practice ground. *Green Fees:* information not available. *Eating facilities:* full catering and bar facilities. *Visitors:* with letter of introduction and by arrangement only. *Society Meetings:* by arrangement. Professional: C. Spence (028 9042 8586). Secretary/Manager: Mrs S.H. Morrison (028 9042 8165).*

KILKEEL. **Kilkeel Golf Club,** Mourne Park, Kilkeel BT34 4LB (028 4176 5095; Fax: 028 4176 5579). *Location:* Kilkeel to Newry road approximately three miles from Kilkeel. Parkland situated at the foot of Mourne Mountains. 18 holes, 6615 metres. S.S.S. 72. Practice area available. *Green Fees:* weekdays £20.00, weekends £25.00. *Eating facilities:* restaurant and bar. *Visitors:* welcome, club competitions on Tuesday, Thursday and Saturday. Booking for Saturday late afternoons and Sundays. *Society Meetings:* catered for by prior arrangement.

KILLYLEAGH. **Ringdufferin Golf Course,** 36 Ringdufferin Road, Toye, Killyleagh BT30 9PH (Tel & Fax: 028 4482 8812). *Location*: 2 miles north of Killyleagh on Comber Road. Drumlin course. 18 holes, 5113 yards, 4641 metres, S.S.S. 66. Practice facilities. *Green Fees*: information not available. *Eating facilities*: licensed restaurant. *Visitors*: welcome at all times. *Society Meetings*: welcome. Secretary: Helen Lindsay (Tel & Fax: 028 4482 8812).*

DONAGHADEE GOLF CLUB • 028 9188 3624
84 Warren Road, Donaghadee, Co. Down BT21 0PQ

Located 5 miles south of Bangor on A2 on coast road. A part links and part inland course with lovely views to the Scottish coast. Well-appointed clubhouse. Visitors welcome weekdays and Sundays. Club hire and trolleys available. Special rates for Societies.

18 holes, 5561 metres, Par 71, S.S.S. 69

e-mail: deegolf@freenet.co.uk
General Manager: Mr Michael Corsar 028 9188 3624
Professional: Gordon Drew 028 9188 2392

KNOCKBRACKEN. **Mount Ober Golf and Country Club,** 24 Ballymaconaghy Road, Knockbracken, Belfast BT8 6SB (028 9079 5666; Fax: 028 9070 5862). *Location:* 15 minutes from centre of Belfast; Saintfield Road, Cairnshill Road, Four Winds Roundabout. Parkland on undulating ground. 18 holes, 5615 yards, S.S.S. 66. Golf academy, floodlit driving range. *Green Fees:* Monday - Friday £16.00, Sundays £18.00. *Eating facilities:* full catering and bar service at all times; excellent restaurant. *Visitors:* welcome anytime, except Saturdays before 3pm. *Society Meetings:* welcome except Saturdays before 3pm. Professional: Wesley Ramsay (028 9070 1648; Fax: 028 9070 5862). Secretary: Ena Williams (028 9040 1811; Fax: 028 9070 5862).
e-mail: mt.ober@ukonline.co.uk

NEWCASTLE. **Royal County Down Golf Club,** Newcastle BT33 0AN. *Location:* adjacent to north side of Newcastle, approach from town centre. Championship Course: 18 holes, 7181 yards, S.S.S. 74. Annesley Links Course: 18 holes, 4681 yards. S.S.S. 66. *Green Fees:* information not available. *Eating facilities:* light lunches and bar, weekdays only. *Visitors:* welcome with prior reservation. *Society Meetings:* catered for. Professional: Kevan J. Whitson (028 4372 2419). Secretary: J.H. Laidler (028 4372 3314; Fax: 028 4372 6281).
website: www.royalcountydown.org

NEWTOWNARDS. **Clandeboye Golf Club,** Tower Road, Conlig, Newtownards BT23 3PN (028 9127 1767). *Location:* Conlig village off A21 between Bangor and Newtownards. Wooded, undulating parkland/heathland. Two courses: Dufferin – 18 holes, 6559 yards, S.S.S. 71; blue tees - 6742 yards, S.S.S. 72. Ava – 18 holes, 5755 yards, S.S.S. 68. Practice ground. Host to the Irish Seniors 2001; N.I. Masters, won by Darren Clarke. *Green Fees:* information not available. *Eating facilities:* full catering and bar. *Visitors:* welcome weekdays; no play before 3pm Saturdays, before 10.30am Sundays. Visitors changing facility. *Society Meetings:* welcome weekdays except Thursdays. Professional: Peter Gregory (028 9127 1750). General Manager: J. W. Thomson (028 9127 1767; Fax: 028 9147 3711).

NEWTOWNARDS. **Kirkistown Castle Golf Club,** 142 Main Road, Cloughey, Newtownards (028 4277 1233). *Location:* approximately 45 minutes from Belfast, 16 miles from Newtownards on the A2. 18 holes, Par 69, S.S.S. 70. *Green Fees:* £25.00 weekdays; £30.00 weekends and Public Holidays. Tourists 10% discount in approved accommodation. *Eating facilities:* full catering and snacks. *Visitors:* welcome. *Society Meetings:* outings welcome by arrangement. Secretary/ Manager: Rosemary Coulter (028 4277 1233). Professional: Richard Whitford (028 9177 1004). Caterer: Marion Smyth (028 4277 2395; Fax: 028 4277 1699).
e-mail: kirkistown@supanet.com
website: www.linksgolfkirkistown.com

NEWTOWNARDS. **Mahee Island Golf Club,** Mahee Island, Comber, Newtownards BT23 6ET (028 9754 1234). *Location:* Comber/Killyleagh Road. After half a mile turn left signposted Ardmillan/Mahee Island. Keep left for six miles to course. Parkland course set on an island with magnificent views over Strangford Lough. 9 holes, 5822 yards, 5108 metres. S.S.S. 70. Par 71 over 18 holes. Putting green and pitching area. *Green Fees:* weekdays £12.00; weekends £17.00. *Eating facilities:* Sunday, Monday, Wednesday and Saturday, other times by arrangement with caterer (07968 449932). *Visitors:* welcome, restricted Saturdays until 5pm. *Society Meetings:* welcome, by prior arrangement. Professional: (Shop) Colin Macaw (028 9754 1234). Secretary: Mervyn Marshall (028 9145 7385).

NEWTOWNARDS. **Scrabo Golf Club,** 233 Scrabo Road, Newtownards BT23 4SL (028 9181 2355). *Location:* approximately 10 miles from Belfast off main Belfast to Newtownards dual carriageway, follow signs to Scrabo Country Park. Upland course. 18 holes, 5699 metres. S.S.S. 71. Practice area. *Green Fees:* information not available. *Eating facilities:* full catering (closed Mondays). *Visitors:* welcome except Saturdays and avoid Wednesdays 4.30pm to 6.30pm. *Society Meetings:* over 12 players, welcome. Professional: Paul McCrystal (028 9181 7848) General Manager: Bill Brown (028 9181 2355; Fax: 028 9182 2919).

WARRENPOINT. **Warrenpoint Golf Club,** Lower Dromore Road, Warrenpoint BT34 3LN (028 4175 3695; Fax: 028 4175 2918). *Location:* five miles south of Newry on coast road. Parkland. 18 holes, 5700 metres. S.S.S. 70. Practice ground. *Green Fees:* Weekdays £22.00, Weekends £28.00. *Eating facilities:* full catering and bar facilities. *Visitors:* welcome Sunday, Monday, Thursday, Friday. Snooker facilities available. *Society Meetings:* catered for by prior arrangement. Professional: Nigel Shaw (Tel & Fax: 028 4175 2371). Secretary: Marian Trainor.

For full details of clubs and courses, plus convenient accommodation
www.uk-golfguide.com

THE APPEARANCE OF AN ASTERISK (*) AT THE END OF A CLUB OR COURSE ENTRY INDICATES THAT UP-TO-DATE INFORMATION HAS NOT BEEN SUPPLIED

FERMANAGH

ENNISKILLEN. **Castle Hume Golf Club,** Belleek Road, Enniskillen BT93 7ED (028 6632 7077; Fax: 028 6632 7076). *Location:* on A46 Belleek/Donegal Road, just a few minutes' drive from Enniskillen. Fast emerging as one of the best golfing facilities the North has to offer, this Championship Course provides golfers of all skill levels with a very enjoyable yet testing challenge. Hosted the Ulster PGA Championship 1996, 1997, 1998, 2003, 2004 & 2005. 18 holes, 5932 metres. Floodlit driving range. *Green Fees:* on application, Reduced rates for societies and groups. *Eating facilities*: excellent hospitality in the bar and restaurant. *Visitors*: welcome. Fully stocked Pro Shop. *Society Meetings:* welcome. Resident PGA Professional: Shaun Donnelly. Visit our website for Open Days and Open Week.
website: www.castlehumegolf.com

ENNISKILLEN. **Enniskillen Golf Club,** Castlecoole, Enniskillen BT74 6HZ (028 6632 5250). *Location:* off Enniskillen to Tempo Road on outskirts of town. Scenic parkland course with views of market town of Enniskillen on front nine, many mature trees on back nine. 18 holes, 6189 yards. S.S.S. 69. *Green Fees:* information not available. Reduction if playing with member. *Eating facilities:* bar snacks daily, full catering by arrangement. *Visitors:* welcome at all times; some restriction on Tuesdays (Ladies' Day) and weekends. *Society Meetings:* welcome at all times, special rates available. Hon. Secretary: Russell Ferguson (028 6632 5250).*

LONDONDERRY

CASTLEROCK. **Castlerock Golf Club,** 65 Circular Road, Castlerock, Coleraine BT51 4TJ (028 7084 8314). *Location:* A2, six miles west of Coleraine. Seaside links, stream in play at four holes. 18 holes, 6687 yards, S.S.S. 72. 9 holes, 2457 metres. S.S.S. 67. Practice area. *Green Fees:* weekdays £50.00 per round, weekends and Bank Holidays £70.00. Subject to review. *Eating facilities:* full restaurant facilities, two bars. *Visitors:* welcome weekdays Monday to Friday and weekends by arrangement. *Society Meetings:* welcome Monday to Friday. Professional: Ian Blair (028 7084 9424). Secretary: Mark Steen (028 7084 8314; Fax: 028 7084 9440).*

COLERAINE. **Brown Trout Golf and Country Club,** 209 Agivey Road, Aghadowey, Near Coleraine BT51 4AD (028 7086 8209; Fax: 028 7086 8878). *Location:* on A54 between Kilrea and Coleraine. Parkland course, heavily wooded, crossing water seven times in nine holes. 9 holes, 2755 metres. S.S.S. 68. *Green Fees:* information not available. *Eating facilities:* à la carte restaurant, bar snacks, barbecues. *Visitors:* always welcome. 15 new luxurious en suite bedrooms and four new five-star cottages available. *Society* *Meetings:* welcome. Professional: Ken Revie. Secretary/ Manager: Bill O'Hara. *
e-mail: bill@browntroutinn.com
website: www.browntroutinn.com

LIMAVADY. **Benone Golf Course,** 53 Benone Avenue, Benone, Limavady BT49 0LQ (028 7775 0555). *Location:* situated on the A2 coast road, 12 miles from Limavady. Parkland course. 9 holes, 1458 yards, 1334 metres. S.S.S. 27. Practice range, putting green. *Green Fees:* information not available. *Eating facilities:* coffee shop open July/ August, restaurant and bars within one mile. *Visitors:* welcome. Club hire available. *Society Meetings:* welcome. Secretary: M. Clark (028 7775 0555; Fax: 028 7775 0919).

LIMAVADY. **Roe Park Golf Club,** Radisson SAS Roe Park Hotel and Golf Resort, Roe Park, Limavady BT49 9LB (028 7772 2222; Fax: 028 7772 2313). *Location:* on main A2 Londonderry-Limavady road, 16 miles from Londonderry and one mile from Limavady. (028 777 60105). Parkland. 18 holes, 6318 yards. S.S.S. 69. Floodlit driving range; putting green; equipment hire. *Green Fees:* information not available. *Eating facilities:* Coach House Brasserie. *Visitors:* welcome with some restrictions at weekend. *Society Meetings:* welcome; society packages available. Accommodation on site. Professional: Seamus Duffy. Secretary: Don Brockerton.*

LONDONDERRY. **Foyle International Golf Centre,** 12 Alder Road, Londonderry BT48 8DB (028 7135 2222; Fax: 028 7135 3967). *Location:* one-and-a-half miles from Foyle Bridge heading towards Moville, Co Donegal. Parkland Championship standard Par 72, notable holes with water coming into play are third Par 3, 10th and 11th. 18 holes, 6678 yard, 6164 metres. S.S.S. 71, Par 71. 9 hole course, Par 3. Indoor floodlit driving range, putting greens. *Green Fees:* weekdays £14.00; weekends £17.00. 10% discount for groups over 12. *Eating facilities:* Pitchers Wine Bar and Restaurant within club house. *Visitors:* welcome anyday, anytime. Buggies, carts, caddies available. Golf academy with video analysis teaching system. *Society Meetings:* welcome. Professional: Kieran McLaughlin. Secretary: Margaret Lapsley.
e-mail: mail@foylegolf.club24.co.uk
website: www.foylegolfcentre.co.uk

MAGHERAFELT. **Moyola Park Golf Club,** 15 Curran Road, Castledawson, Magherafelt BT45 8DG (028 7946 8468; Fax: 028 7946 8626). *Location:* 35 miles north of Belfast on M2; off middle of Main Street, Castledawson. Attractive, spacious mature parkland. 18 holes, 6519 yards. S.S.S. 71. Practice ground, putting green. *Green Fees:* information not available. *Eating facilities:* bars and restaurant. *Visitors:* welcome with prior notice. *Society Meetings:* welcome with prior notice. Professional: Bob Cockcroft (028 7946 8830). Secretary/Manager: Tony McGuire.

Please mention THE GOLF GUIDE when you enquire about clubs or accommodation

PORTSTEWART. **Portstewart Golf Club,** Strand Road, Portstewart, BT55 7PG (028 7083 2015; Fax: 028 7083 4097). *Location:* north from Coleraine. Coastal links. No 1 Strand - 18 holes, 6784 yards, S.S.S. 73. No 2 Riverside - 9 holes, 2622 yards. No 3 Old - 18 holes, 4733 yards, S.S.S. 64. Practice area. *Green Fees:* information not available. *Eating facilities:* meals available - advance orders; no catering on Mondays. *Visitors:* welcome Mondays to Fridays; limited Wednesdays. Prior booking essential on Strand. Enquire about special rates for parties. *Society Meetings:* catered for by arrangement. Professional: Alan Hunter (Tel & Fax: 028 7083 2601). Secretary: Michael Moss (028 7083 2015; Fax: 028 7083 4097).*
e-mail: michael@portstewartgc.co.uk.

PREHEN. **City of Derry Golf Club,** 49 Victoria Road, Prehen BT47 2PU (028 7134 6369). *Location:* three miles from city centre on the road to Strabane - follow the River Foyle. Parkland, wooded. 18 holes, 5877 metres. S.S.S. 71, Par 71. Also 9 hole (Dunhugh) course, 4305 metres. Par 66. Practice area. *Green Fees:* please contact Secretary's office. *Eating facilities:* catering and bar facilities available. *Visitors:* welcome on weekdays up to 4.30pm, weekends please contact Professional. Convenient for hotels and guest houses. *Society Meetings:* welcome, please contact Manager's Office. Professional: Mr Michael Doherty (028 7131 1496). Hon. Secretary: Mr G. Mills (028 7134 6369). Secretary: Noreen Allen (028 7134 6369).*

TYRONE

COOKSTOWN. **Killymoon Golf Club,** 200 Killymoon Road, Cookstown BT80 8TW (Tel & Fax: 028 8676 3762). *Location:* private road off A29. Signposted at Dungannon end of town opposite Drum Road. Mainly flat parkland. 18 holes, 6202 yards. S.S.S. 69. Practice ground. *Green Fees:* Mondays £15.00 (excluding Bank Holidays); Tuesdays to Fridays £21.00; weekends and Bank Holidays £26.00. *Eating facilities:* full catering at club (large groups please book). *Visitors:* welcome, after 4pm Saturdays, Thursday is Ladies' Day. Booking essential. *Society Meetings:* welcome. Booking essential. Professional: Gary Chambers (Tel & Fax: 028 8676 3460); Secretary: Tony McCann (Tel & Fax: 028 8676 3762). General Manager: Norman Weir (028 8676 3762).

DUNGANNON. **Dungannon Golf Club,** 34 Springfield Lane, Dungannon BT70 1QX (028 8772 2098; Fax: 028 8772 7338). *Location:* a short distance from Dungannon along Donaghmore Road. Flat first 9, hilly second 9. Parkland course with some water hazards newly positioned. 18 holes, 6155 yards (white markers.) S.S.S. 69. *Green Fees:* weekdays £20.00; weekends and Bank Holidays £25.00. As a guest of a member £14.00 weekdays, £16.00 weekends and Bank Holidays. *Eating facilities:* bar snacks and licensed restaurant. *Visitors:* always welcome but please telephone first; precluded by timesheets at weekends, Ladies' Day Tuesdays. *Society Meetings:* welcome by prior arrangement; apply in writing. Professional: Vivian Teague. Secretary: S.T. Hughes.

FINTONA. **Fintona Golf Club,** 1 Kiln Street, Ecclesville Demesne, Fintona BT78 2BJ (Tel & Fax: 028 8284 1480). *Location:* eight miles south of Omagh, county town of Tyrone. An attractive parkland course, its main features being a trout stream; rated one of the top nine hole courses in the Province. 9 holes, 5765 metres. S.S.S. 70. Putting green. *Green Fees:* information not available. *Eating facilities:* bar snacks, meals on request. *Visitors:* welcome weekdays, weekends by arrangement. *Society Meetings:* welcome weekdays, book in advance. *

NEWTOWNSTEWART. **Newtownstewart Golf Club,** 38 Golf Course Road, Newtownstewart, Omagh BT78 4HU (028 8166 1466; Fax: 028 8166 2506). *Location:* signposted from Strabane Road (A57) at Newtownstewart, two miles west of Newtownstewart on B84. Parkland and wooded course. 18 holes, 5320 metres. S.S.S. 69. Practice ground. *Green Fees:* weekdays £17.00; weekends and Bank Holidays £25.00. *Eating facilities:* available. *Visitors:* welcome at all times. Accommodation available in chalets beside clubhouse. Buggies available. *Society Meetings:* all welcome. Special packages available. Golf Shop: (028 8166 2242; Fax: 028 8166 2506). Secretary: Mrs Diane Cook (028 8166 1466; Fax: 028 8166 2506).
e-mail: newtown.stewart@lineone.net
website: www.globalgolf.com/newtownstewart

OMAGH. **Omagh Golf Club,** 83a Dublin Road, Omagh BT78 1HQ (Tel & Fax: 028 8224 3160). *Location:* one mile from Omagh town centre on Belfast/Dublin Road. Parkland. 18 holes, 5638 metres. S.S.S. 70. *Green Fees:* information not available. *Eating facilities:* snacks and bar facilities. *Visitors:* welcome any day except Tuesday and Saturday. *Society Meetings:* welcome. Hon. Secretary: Joseph A. McElholm. Secretary: Florence E.A. Caldwell (Tel & Fax: 028 8224 3160).*

STRABANE. **Strabane Golf Club,** 33 Ballycolman Road, Strabane BT82 9PH (028 7138 2271/2007; Fax: 028 7188 6471). *Location:* A5 half mile from Strabane towards Omagh. Parkland. 18 holes, 5610 metres. S.S.S. 69. *Green Fees:* information not available. *Eating facilities:* two bars, catering by arrangement. *Visitors:* welcome, except Saturdays. Practice putting green and chipping area. *Society Meetings:* by arrangement. Secretary: Gerry Glover (028 7138 2007).*

For full details of clubs and courses, plus convenient accommodation
www.uk-golfguide.com

Republic of Ireland

COUNTY CARLOW

BORRIS. **Borris Golf Club,** Deer Park, Carlow (059 9773310; Fax: 059 9773750). Scenic parkland course with tree lined fairways and modern sandbased greens. 10 holes, 5680 yards, S.S.S. 69. Practice area and putting green. *Green Fees*: 25.00 euros. *Eating facilities*: bar meals available. *Visitors*: welcome weekdays by prior arrangement, restrictions Thursdays and weekends. *Society Meetings*: welcome by prior arrangement. Secretary: Nollaig Lucas (059 9773310; Fax: 059 9773750).

CARLOW. **Carlow Golf Club**, Deer Park, Carlow (0503 31695; Fax: 0503 40065). *Location*: N9 2.5 miles north of Carlow town. Parkland, undulating, sandy sub-soil. 18 holes, 5974 metres. S.S.S. 71. Practice ground. New 9 hole golf course. *Green Fees*: information not provided. *Eating facilities*: bar and restaurant. *Visitors*: always welcome, weekends difficult, pre-booking advisable. Carts, caddies and club hire. *Society Meetings*: must be pre-booked with Secretary. Professional: Andrew Gilbert (0503 41745; Fax: 0503 40065). General Manager: Donard MacSweeney (0503 31695; Fax: 0503 40065).
e-mail: carlowgolfclub@eircom.net
website: www.carlowgolfclub.com

COUNTY CAVAN

BALLYCONNELL. **Slieve Russell Hotel & Golf Club,** Ballyconnel (049 952 5090; Fax: 049 952 6640). Mature parkland European tour Championship course on 350 acres. 18 holes, 7053 yards, 6412 metres. Driving range and practice ground. *Green Fees*: information not available. *Eating facilities*: Summit Bar and restaurant. *Visitors*: welcome everyday, pre-booking essential. Limited availablity on Saturdays. 4 Star Hotel on site. *Society Meetings*: welcome, please contact for details. Professional: Liam McCool. Golf Director: Ivan Hewson (049 952 6458; Fax: 049 952 6640).*
e-mail: slieve-golf-club@quinn-hotels.com
e-mail: hewsoni@quinn-hotels.com

BELTURBET. **Belturbet Golf Club,** Erne Hill, Belturbet (00 353 49 9522287). *Location:* quarter-of-a-mile from Belturbet town centre on main N3 Cavan-Dublin road. Parkland with elevated greens. 9 holes, 5204 yards. S.S.S. 65. Practice area and putting green. *Green Fees: 20 euros. Eating facilities:* clubhouse and bar; catering available. *Visitors:* welcome at all times. *Society Meetings:* welcome at all times. Club/trolley hire. Various classes of Membership available, including distance/overseas. All enquiries to 00 353 49 9522287.

BLACKLION. **Blacklion Golf Club,** Toam, Blacklion, via Sligo (071 985 3024). *Location:* Blacklion/Belcoo on Enniskillen to Sligo Road. Flat parkland, wooded copses, lake partially in play, scenic. 9 holes, 6175 yards, 5614 metres. S.S.S. 69. *Green Fees:* information not available. *Eating facilities:* full catering available. *Visitors:* welcome. Course surrounded on four holes by Loch McNean. Safe swimming in lake. Scenic hill walks. *Society Meetings:* by arrangement. Hon. Secretary: Pat Gallery.*

CAVAN. **County Cavan Golf Club,** Aranmore House, Drumelis, Cavan (049 4331283). *Location:* on Killeshandra road from Cavan. Parkland course. 18 holes, 5634 metres. S.S.S 69. Practice area, driving range. *Green Fees:* information not available. *Eating facilities:* full catering facilities including bar snacks. *Visitors:* welcome; limited availablility on Wednesdays and weekends. *Society Meetings:* on application to Professional. Professional: Bill Nobel (049 4331388). Hon. Secretary: Jim McCorry (Tel & Fax: 049 4331641).
e-mail: cavangc@iol.ie

COUNTY CLARE

CLONLARA. **Clonlara Golf and Leisure,** Clonlara (061 354141; Fax: 061 354143). *Location:* 7 miles from Limerick on Corbally to Killaloe road. Parkland. 12 holes. S.S.S.67. *Green Fees:* information not available. *Eating facilities:* fully licensed bar with bar food. *Visitors:* welcome. *Society Meetings:* welcome. No walkers, caddies, or children under 14 allowed on the course. Tennis courts, sauna, children's play area, crazy golf. Self-catering apartments available. Secretary: Ms A. O'Grady (061 354141; Fax: 061 354143).*
e-mail: tmcmahon@circom.net

DOONBEG. **Doonbeg Golf Club,** Doonbeg (353 65 9055246; Fax: 353 65 9055247). *Location*: The highly acclaimed Doonbeg Golf Club is situated between two of Ireland's greatest Links courses - Ballybunion and Lahinch. Designed by Greg Norman and host of the 2002 Palmer Cup matches, it is set along 1.5 miles of crescent-shaped beach encircling Doughmore Bay, providing magnificent views. Links course. 18 holes, 6885 yards, par 72. Practice green, putting green. *Green Fees*: information not available. *Eating facilities:* restaurant. *Visitors:* welcome. On site accommodation expected 2006.*
e-mail: links@doonbeggolfclub.com

ENNIS. **Ennis Golf Club,** Drumbiggle, Ennis (065 6824074; Fax: 065 6841848). *Location:* half a mile from Ennis town centre. Parkland course set in rolling hills with five challenging Par 3s. 18 holes, 6150 yards, 5592 metres. Par 71. *Green Fees:* 35 euros.

Groups rates on request. *Eating facilities:* full catering facilities and bar. *Visitors:* Monday, Thursday, Saturday with some restrictions Tuesday and Wednesday. New Club House. Carts, clubs and caddies available. *Society Meetings:* welcome; 30 euros. Club Manager: Pat McCarthy (065 6824074; Fax: 065 6841848).
e-mail: info@ennisgolfclub.com
website: www.ennisgolfclub.com

ENNIS. **Woodstock Golf and Country Club,** Shanaway Road, Ennis (00353 656 829463; Fax: 00353 656 820304). *Location:* from Ennis town take Lahinch Road, 18 miles Shannon Airport. Parkland course. 18 holes, 5879 metres. S.S.S. 71. *Green Fees:* information not available. *Eating facilities:* bar food served daily, The Tenth Tee Bar, G/B's Restaurant (065 44430). *Visitors:* welcome at all times, telephone in advance advisable at weekends. Hotel on site. *Society Meetings:* all welcome, special rates available. Secretary: Seamie Kelly (+ 353 65 682 9463; Fax: + 353 65 682 0804).*
e-mail: woodstock.ennis@eircom.net
website: www.woodstockgolfclub.com

KILKEE. **Kilkee Golf Club,** East End, Kilkee (065 9056048; Fax: 065 9056977). *Location:* right on seafront at end of promenade. Seaside course with many cliff top tees and greens. 18 holes, 5960 metres. S.S.S. 71. *Green Fees:* 30 euros. *Eating facilities:* fully licensed restaurant and bar. *Visitors:* very welcome every day. Golf shop. *Society Meetings:* Society outings welcome, special reduced rates. Secretary/Manager: Michael Culligan (065 9056048; Fax: 065 9056977).
e-mail: kilkeegolfclub@eircom.net
website: www.kilkeegolfclub.ie

KILRUSH. **Kilrush Golf Club,** Kilrush (065 905 1138; Fax: 065 905 2633). *Location:* On main Ennis/Kilrush Road - 1km from Kilrush. Parkland course. 18 holes, 5960 yards. S.S.S. 70. *Green Fees:* information not available. *Eating facilities:* full bar and catering facilities. *Visitors:* always welcome - please book in advance. *Society Meetings:* welcome. Professional: Sean O'Connor. Secretary/Manager: Denis F. Nagle (087 623 7557).*

LAHINCH. **Lahinch Golf Club,** Lahinch (065 7081003). *Location:* 32 miles north west of Shannon Airport, 200 yards from Lahinch Village on Lisconner Road. Links course. Old Course - 18 holes, 6950 yards. S.S.S. 74; Castle Course - 18 holes, 5594 yards. S.S.S. 67. *Green Fees:* information not available. *Eating facilities:* bar and restaurant. *Visitors:* welcome. *Society Meetings:* catered for by arrangement. Professional: Robert McCavery (065 7081003). Secretary: Alan Reardon (065 7081003; Fax: 065 7081592). *
e-mail: info@lahinchgolf.com

MILTOWN MALBAY. **Spanish Point Golf Club,** Spanish Point, Miltown Malbay (065-708 4198). *Location*: two miles south of Miltown Malbay at Spanish Point Beach. Links course. 9 holes, 2312 metres, S.S.S. 63. Practice facilities. *Green Fees*: £25.00 weekdays, £30.00 weekends and Bank Holidays. *Eating facilities*: bar snacks. *Visitors*: welcome at all times, not before noon on Sundays. *Society Meetings*: welcome weekdays excluding July and August. Secretary: David Fitzgerald (086-812 5742).
e-mail: david@spanish-point.com
e-mail: dkfitzgerald@tinet.ie
website: www.spanishpointgolf.com

NEWMARKET-ON-FERGUS. **Dromoland Golf & Country Club,** Newmarket-on-Fergus (061 368444; Fax: 061 368498). *Location:* part of the Dromoland Castle Estate, 10 minutes' drive from Shannon Airport. 400 acres of wooded parkland, with the River Rine flowing through. Course designed by Ron Kirby and Joe Carr. 18 holes, 6850 yards. *Green Fees:* information not available. *Eating facilities:* available. *Visitors*: welcome. *Society Meetings:* welcome.*
e-mail: golf@dromoland.ie
website: www.dromoland.ie

SHANNON. **Shannon Golf Club,** Shannon (061 471849; Fax: 061 471507). *Location:* from Limerick take Airport road, course is 200 yards past Airport. Parkland. 18 holes, 6271 yards. S.S.S. 72. Practice area, club hire, buggy hire. *Green Fees:* information not available. *Eating facilities:* full bar and catering services. *Visitors:* welcome with prior booking. *Society Meetings:* welcome. Professional: Artie Pyke (061 471551). General Manager: Michael Corry. *

Gregans Castle Hotel
Ballyvaughan, Co. Clare
Tel: 065 707 7005 • Fax: 065 707 7111
e-mail: stay@gregans.ie • www.gregans.ie

Gregans Castle is a family-run Country Hotel with breathtaking views across The Burren and Galway Bay. Award-winning gardens and the rural setting ensure peaceful harmony. Bedrooms have every comfort; Superior Rooms and Suites are especially recommended. The hotel is only 16 miles from Lahinch Golf Course, and there are many other activities in the area, such as hillwalking, botany and historic ruins. Other local courses: *Gort, Galway Bay, Doonbeg, Woodstock, Dromoland*

AA ★★★

See also Colour Advertisement on page 81

COUNTY CORK

BANDON. **Bandon Golf Club,** Castlebernard, Bandon (023 41111; Fax: 023 44690). *Location:* one mile west of Bandon town centre. Undulating parkland course with scenic views of West Cork. 18 holes, 6421 yards, 5780 metres. S.S.S. 70. Practice ground. *Green Fees:* weekdays 40 euros, weekends 45 euros. *Eating facilities:* available, menu at bar. *Visitors:* welcome, restriction at weekends. Clubs, buggies and carts for hire. *Society Meetings:* welcome except Wednesdays and Sundays. Professional: Paddy O'Boyle (023 42224; Fax: 023 44690). Secretary: Mr John McGinley. e-mail: bandongolfclub@eircom.net

BANTRY. **Bantry Bay Golf Club,** Bantry, West Cork (353 (0) 27 50579/53773/53790; Fax: 353 (0) 27 53790). *Location:* approximately 1 mile from Bantry on N71 Killarney road. Clifftop parkland championship course to USGA standards. 18 holes, 6700 yards, 6100 metres. S.S.S. 72. *Green Fees:* 35 euros to 50 euros. *Eating facilities:* full bar and restaurant open all year. *Visitors:* welcome, with restrictions at weekend. Trolley, buggy and club hire. *Society Meetings:* rates on request. Secretary: John O'Sullivan. e-mail: info@bantrygolf.com
website: www.bantrygolf.com

CARRIGALINE. **Fernhill Golf & Country Club,** Carrigaline (00 353 (0)21 4372226; Fax: 00 353 (0)21 437 1011). *Location:* 20 minutes from Cork city and Airport, 10 minutes from Ringaskiddy Ferry Port. From city/airport follow sign to Ringaskiddy Ferry Port until roundabout with sign for Carrigaline - take Ringaskiddy exit, 2nd right, club is on left on this road. Parkland course. 18 holes, 6340 yards, S.S.S. 67. *Green Fees:* early bird 16 euros, weekdays 20 euros, weekends 30 euros. *Eating facilities:* fully licensed clubhouse, bar and restaurant, barbecue area. *Visitors:* always welcome. Booking advised at weekends. 40 bedroom hotel on site, plus 10 holiday homes, tennis court, indoor pool and sauna. Pro shop. Golf packages available. *Society Meetings:* always welcome. Booking advised at weekends. General Manager: Mr Alan Bowes.
e-mail: info@fernhillcountryclub.com
website: www.fernhillcountryclub.com

CARRIGTWOHILL. **Fota Island Golf Club,** Carrigtwohill (021 4883700; Fax: 021 4883713). *Location:* take N25 east from Cork City (9 miles), turn off for Fota and Cobh. Gently undulating parkland bordered by mature woodland, very traditional in design. Championship course, venue for the 2001 and 2002 Murphy's Irish Open. Voted 'Golf Course of the Year' 2002 by the Irish Golf Tour Operators. 18 holes, 6927 yards, S.S.S. 71. Practice range and putting green. *Green Fees:* from 62 euros to 98 euros. *Eating facilities:* restaurant and bar. *Visitors:* welcome everyday, telephone or e-mail for tee times. Metal spikes not allowed. Buggies, carts and caddies available. *Society Meetings:* welcome everyday, but limited availability on weekends. Professional: Kevin Morris (021 4883710; Fax: 021 4883713).
e-mail: reservations@fotaisland.ie
website: www.fotaisland.ie

CASTLETOWNBERE. **Berehaven Golf Club and Amenity Park,** Filane, Castletownbere, Beara (027 70700). *Location:* on main Castletownbere - Glengarriff Road, three miles from Castletownbere. Scenic course overlooking Bantry Bay. 9 holes, 2598 metres, S.S.S. 65. *Green Fees:* information not available. *Eating facilities:* bar and restaurant. *Visitors:* welcome at all times. Tennis, crazy golf, sauna, caravan park. Club hire available. *Society Meetings:* welcome by appointment, special rates. Hon. Secretary: J. J. McLaughlin (027 70700).

CHARLEVILLE. **Charleville Golf Club,** Charleville (063 81257; Fax: 063 81274). *Location:* Two kilometres west of Charleville town which is on main Cork/Limerick road. Parkland, heavily wooded. 27 holes. 18 holes 6430 yards. S.S.S. 70. 9 holes 6902 yards S.S.S. 73. Two practice areas. *Green Fees:* information not available. *Eating facilities:* full eating facilities and bar. *Visitors:* welcome, weekends by appointment. *Society Meetings:* welcome. Special rates apply. Professional: David Keating (063 81257). Hon Secretary: James A. Murphy.*
e-mail: charlevillegolf@eircom.net
website: www.charlevillegolf.com

www.uk-golfguide.com

Fernhill Golf & Country Club lies just 10km from the city of Cork, beautifully situated overlooking the scenic Owenabue Valley near the south coast. It is close to the ferry terminal at Ringaskiddy, offering the first and last opportunity for a game for those visiting Ireland by ferry. It offers a good challenge to players of all handicaps.

18-hole Parkland course • Visitors welcome.
40 rooms en suite • 10 holiday homes on site
Indoor swimming pool, sauna and tennis court

Fernhill Golf & Country Club, Carrigaline, Co. Cork, Ireland
Tel: 353 21 4372226 • Fax: 353 21 4371011
e-Mail: fernhill@iol.ie • www.fernhillcountryclub.com

COBH. **Cobh Golf Club,** Ballywilliam, Cobh (021-481 2399; Fax: 021-481 2615). Parkland course. 9 holes, 5006 yards, 4576 metres, S.S.S. 64. *Green Fees:* information not available. *Eating facilities:* available. *Visitors:* welcome mid week, restricted weekends and Tuesdays (Ladies' Day). Hon. Secretary: David Sloane (021-4812882).*

DONERAILE. **Doneraile Golf Club,** Doneraile (022 24137). *Location:* three-and-a-half miles off main Cork/Limerick Road. Parkland, mature trees. 9 holes, 5768 yards. S.S.S.67. *Green Fees:* information not available. *Eating facilities:* by request. *Visitors:* welcome weekdays. *Society Meetings:* welcome Saturdays and weekdays. Secretary: Jimmy O'Leary (022 24379).*

DOUGLAS. **Douglas Golf Club,** Douglas (021 4891086; Fax: 021 4895297). *Location:* Douglas is on the main road from Cork to ferry port at Ringaskiddy, three miles south of Cork City. Beautifully maintained flat parkland course – the views from the Clubhouse are some of the most panoramic in the country. 18 holes, 6669 yards, 5972 metres. S.S.S. 71. Practice ground. *Green Fees:* 50 euros all week. Groups of 20 or more 45 euros. Subject to review. *Eating facilities:* full restaurant and bar available from 11am. *Visitors:* Monday, Wednesday, Thursday, Friday (mornings preferably); Saturday and Sunday after 2pm. Advisable to check in advance. *Society Meetings:* welcome but bookings should be made by end of April each year. Professional: Gary Nicholson (021 4362055). Secretary/Manager: Ronan Burke (021 4895297; Fax:021 4367200).

FERMOY. **Fermoy Golf Club,** Corrin, Fermoy (025 32694; Fax: 025 33072). *Location:* 2km from Dublin to Cork main route. Parkland, wooded course. 18 holes, 5847 metres. S.S.S. 68. Practice ground. *Green Fees:* information not available. *Eating facilities:* full bar and restaurant. *Visitors:* welcome, Mondays very limited, weekends by reservation. Caddies. *Society Meetings:* welcome, booking essential. Professional: Brian Moriarty (025 31472; Fax: 025 33072). Secretary: Kathleen Murphy.*
e-mail: fermoygolfclub@eircom.net

GLENGARRIFF. **Glengarriff Golf Club,** Glengarriff (027 63150). Parkland course. 9 holes, Par 33. *Green Fees:* information not available. *Eating facilities:* light snacks available in the clubhouse. *Visitors:* welcome at all times. *Society Meetings:* welcome. Secretary: Noreen Deasy (027 50315). *

KINSALE. **Kinsale Golf Club,** Farrangalway, Kinsale (021 4774722; Fax: 021 4773114). *Location:* beautifully situated in meadowland and parkland. Two courses. 18 holes and 9 holes. *Green Fees:* information not available. *Eating facilities:* full bar and catering. *Visitors:* welcome. *
e-mail: office@kinsalegolf.com
website: www.kinsalegolf.com

Cork Golf Club was founded in 1888 and designed in 1927 by Alister MacKenzie. It has matured to become one of the finest courses in the country. Many Amateur and Professional championships have been hosted here. The course is always in immaculate condition and playable all year round.

For further information regarding green fees, please contact Matt Sands, General Manager, at:

CORK GOLF CLUB
Little Island, Co. Cork, Ireland
Tel: 00 353 21 4353451 • Fax: 00 353 21 4353410
e-mail: corkgolfclub@eircom.net
www.corkgolfclub.ie

KINSALE. **Old Head Golf Links,** Kinsale (+353 (0) 21 4778444; Fax: +353 (0) 214778022). *Location:* from Cork Airport follow R600 from Cork to Kinsale on to Old Head. 15 minutes south, signposted. Spectacular links course at an elevation of 100-200 ft. Practice ground, putting green, chipping green. 18 holes, 7300 yards. S.S.S. 72. *Green Fees:* information not available. *Eating facilities:* full bar and restaurant facilities. *Visitors:* no restrictions. *Society Meetings:* welcome subject to availability, Special rates available for groups over 24. Course closed November to March. Golf Operations: Danny Brasil. General Manager: Jim O'Brien.*

LITTLE ISLAND. **Cork Golf Club,** Little Island (021 4353451; Fax: 021 4353410). *Location:* five miles east of Cork City N25, signposted. Parkland, very scenic championship course. 18 holes, 6065 metres. S.S.S. 72, 70. Practice ground. *Green Fees:* 80.00-90.00 euros (2005 rates). *Eating facilities:* full catering facilities, bar. *Visitors:* welcome Mondays, Tuesdays, Wednesdays and Fridays except 12.30 to 2pm; Thursdays, weekends ring in advance. *Society Meetings:* catered for, arrange with General Manager. Professional: Peter Hickey (021 4353421). General Manager: Matt Sands (021 4353451; Fax: 021 4353410).
e-mail: corkgolfclub@eircom.net
website: www.corkgolfclub.ie

THE APPEARANCE OF AN ASTERISK (*) AT THE END OF A CLUB OR COURSE ENTRY INDICATES THAT UP-TO-DATE INFORMATION HAS NOT BEEN SUPPLIED

LITTLE ISLAND. **Harbour Point Golf Club,** Clash Road, Little Island (021 4353094; Fax: 021 4354408). *Location:* follow signs for Rosslare from Cork City and then take exit for Little Island (approx 6 miles from city). Parkland course by banks of River Lee. 18 holes, 6163 metres. S.S.S. 72. 21 bay floodlit driving range. *Green Fees:* information not available. *Eating facilities:* full bar and catering facilities. *Visitors:* welcome anytime, please book tee times. Carts, buggies and caddies for hire. Fully stocked golf store. *Society Meetings:* very welcome, special rates available. Professional: Morgan O'Donovan. General Manager: Aylmer Barrett (021 4353094; Fax: 021 4354408).*
e-mail: hpoint@iol.ie
website: www.harbourpointgolfclub.com

MACROOM. **Macroom Golf Club,** Lackaduv, Macroom. (026 41072; Fax: 026 41391). *Location:* through castle gates at town centre. Parkland. 18 holes, 5574 metres. S.S.S. 70. *Green Fees:* information not available. *Eating facilities:* full catering with restaurant and bar. *Visitors:* welcome, booking essential. *Society Meetings:* welcome March to October, booking essential. Manager: Cathal O'Sullivan.*

MALLOW. **Mallow Golf Club,** Ballyellis, Mallow (022 21145; Fax: 022 42501). *Location*: one mile from town, east, on the Killavullen road. Parkland course. 18 holes, 5960 metres, S.S.S.72. *Green Fees:* weekdays 35 euros, weekends and public holidays 40 euros. *Eating facilities*: available. *Visitors*: welcome Monday to Friday, restrictions on weekends and public holidays, please check for details. *Society Meetings*: welcome, please telephone for details. Professional: Sean Conway (022 43424). Secretary/ Manager: David Curtin (022 21145; Fax: 022 42501).
e-mail: golfmall@gofree.indigo.ie

MIDLETON. **East Cork Golf Club,** Gortacrue, Midleton (021 631687; Fax: 021 613695). *Location:* two miles off main Waterford to Cork road. Exit at Midleton 13 miles west of Cork city. Parkland course. 18 hole, 5491 yards. S.S.S. 67. Driving range. *Green Fees:* information not available. *Visitors:* welcome all year round. *Society Meetings:* special rates available. Professional: Don MacFarlane (021 633667). Secretary: Maurice Maloney. *

MITCHELSTOWN. **Mitchelstown Golf Club,** Limerick Road, Gurrane, Mitchelstown (025 24072). *Location:* one kilometre from Mitchelstown (main Dublin/Cork route). Flat parkland. 18 holes, 6008 metres. S.S.S. 70. Practice area. *Green Fees:* information not available. *Eating facilities:* bar food evenings/weekends. *Visitors:* welcome. Caddie car hire. *Society Meetings:* welcome. Secretary: D. Stapleton. (025 24072).*

MONKSTOWN. **Monkstown Golf Club,** Parkgarriff, Monkstown (021 4841376; Fax: 021 4841722). *Location:* 7 miles from Cork city, just 10 minutes' drive from the Cork/Swansea Ferry. Demanding parkland course for golfers of all levels and the greens have been noted for being amongst the best in the country. 18 holes, 5640 metres. S.S.S. 69. Practice ground. *Green Fees:* Monday to Thursday: 40 euros (day), Friday to Sunday 47 euros (day). *Eating facilities:* full bar and restaurant available. *Visitors:* welcome, avoid Tuesday (Ladies' Day) and Bank Holiday Mondays. Phone at weekends. *Society Meetings:* welcome with restrictions. General Manager/Secretary: Hilary Madden.*
e-mail: office@monkstowngolfclub.com
website: www.monkstowngolfclub.com

MUSKERRY. **Muskerry Golf Club,** Carrigrohane (021 4385297; Fax: 021 4516760). *Location:* seven and a half miles north west of Cork City, one and a half miles from Blarney. Parkland/wooded, two rivers. 18 holes, 5785 metres. S.S.S. 71. *Green Fees:* weekdays 35 euros; weekends 40 euros if available. *Eating facilities:* available. *Visitors:* welcome; Monday and Tuesday all day, Wednesday up to 10.30am, Thursday after 1.30pm and Friday up to 3.30pm; weekends as available. Members' hour weekdays 12.30pm to 1.30pm. *Society Meetings:* welcome; 32 euros weekdays, 37 euros weekends. Professional: W.M. Lehane (021 4381445). Manager: Hugo Gallagher (021 4385297; Fax: 021 4516860).

OVENS. **Lee Valley Golf Club,** Clashanure, Ovens (Tel & Fax: 00 353 (0)21 7331721). *Location:* eight miles from Cork on N22, turn right at Dan Sheehans. Parkland. 18 hole championship golf course designed by Ryder Cup star Christy O'Connor Jnr. 6725 yards. Par 72. 15 bay floodlit, indoor driving range, outdoor practice facilities. *Green Fees:* on application. *Eating facilities:* bar and full restaurant. *Visitors:* welcome. Club shop; club hire, caddy car hire and caddies and buggies available. *Society Meetings*: welcome. Corporate days. Lee Valley Bus available to cater for all your transport needs. Proprietor: Jerry Keohege.*
e-mail: leevalleygolfclub@eircom.net
website: www.leevalleygcc.ie

SCHULL. **Coosheen Golf Club,** Coosheen, Schull (028 28182). *Location:* one mile from Schull. Seaside parkland. 9 holes, 2023 metres. S.S.S. 58. Club hire, trolley hire. *Green Fees:* information not available. *Eating facilities:* seasonal bar and daily lunches. *Visitors:* welcome. *Society Meetings:* welcome. Secretary: A. Good or Donal Morgan. *

YOUGHAL. **Youghal Golf Club,** Knockaverry, Youghal (024 92787; Fax: 024 92641). *Location:* N25 main road from Rosslare to Cork. Seaside course with panoramic views of Youghal Bay/Blackwater Estuary. 18 holes, 5626 metres. S.S.S. 69. *Green Fees:* information not available. *Eating facilities:* full bar and restaurant facilities. *Visitors:* welcome mid-week, phone re weekends and Wednesdays (Ladies' Day). *Society Meetings:* welcome, please phone. Special rates available. Professional: Liam Burns (024 92590). Secretary: Margaret O'Sullivan.*

Please mention THE GOLF GUIDE when you enquire about clubs or accommodation

COUNTY DONEGAL

BALLYLIFFIN. **Ballyliffin Golf Club,** Ballyliffin, Inishowen. (00 353 74 93 76119; Fax: 00 353 74 93 76672). *Location:* Carndonagh from Derry, Buncrana from Letterkenny. Traditional links. Glashedy; 18 holes, 7250 yards. S.S.S. 72. Old Links; 18 holes, 6612 yards. S.S.S. 71. Practice ground and three practice holes. *Green Fees:* 60-70 euros, or check website. *Eating facilities:* bar and restaurant. *Visitors:* welcome, booking advisable. *Society Meetings:* concessions for groups of 16 and over. Manager: John Farren (00 353 74 93 76119; Fax: 00 353 74 93 76672). Professional: John Dolan.
e-mail: info@ballyliffingolfclub.com
website: www.ballyliffingolfclub.com

BUNCRANA. **Buncrana Golf Club,** Ballymacarry, Buncrana (07493 20749). *Location:* on entry to Buncrana town take first left after Inishowen Gateway Hotel. Links course. 9 holes, 4310 yards, S.S.S. 62. *Green Fees:* Men 13 euros, Ladies 8 euros, Juveniles 5 euros. *Visitors:* welcome Monday to Friday, weekends by prior arrangement. *Society Meetings:* welcome. Professional: J. Doherty (07493 62279). Secretary: Francis McGrory (07493 20749).

BUNCRANA. **North West Golf Club,** Lisfannon, Buncrana (07493 61027; Fax: 07493 63284). *Location:* eight miles north west of Derry, one mile Buncrana - main Derry/Buncrana Road. Traditional links course, established 1891 founder member of G.U.I. 18 holes, 5968 yards. S.S.S. 70. Putting green. *Green Fees:* weekdays 25 euros; weekends 30 euros. Society rates on request. *Eating facilities:* full bar and restaurant; bar snacks. *Visitors:* welcome anytime, phone in advance for weekends and Wednesdays. Caddies, carts available. *Society Meetings:* all welcome, booking essential. Professional: Seamus McBriarty (07493 61715). Hon. Secretary: Michael Jordan.

BUNDORAN. **Bundoran Golf Club,** Bundoran (071 9841302; Fax: 071 9842014). *Location:* 22 miles north of Sligo on edge of Bundoran Town. Parkland, seaside; not wooded. 18 holes, 5688 metres. S.S.S. 70. Practice ground. *Green Fees:* information not available. *Eating facilities:* soup, tea, coffee and sandwiches in bar. *Visitors:* anytime with due notice but preferably Monday to Thursday. Buggies and carts. *Society Meetings:* very welcome with due notice. Professional: David T. Robinson (071 9841302). Secretary: John McGagh. *

DONEGAL. **Donegal Golf Club,** Murvagh, Laghey (074 9734054; Fax: 074 9734377). *Location:* N15 off main Donegal/Ballyshannon Road. Seaside links course, Murvagh Peninsula. 18 holes, 6874 yards, 6249 metres. S.S.S. 73. Practice area. *Green Fees:* information not available. *Eating facilities:* restaurant and bar. *Visitors:* welcome, restrictions weekends and Mondays. Buggies, carts available, caddies on request. Administrator: (074 9734054; Fax: 074 9734377).*
e-mail: info@donegal-golfclub.ie

Ballyliffin Golf Club

Green Fee Rate 2006

Glashedy	
Midweek	€70.00
Societies: (16+)	€65.00
Winter (1st Nov 05-31 Mar 06)	€45.00
Weekend	€80.00
Societies: (16+)	€75.00
Winter (1st Nov 05-31 Mar 06)	€55.00
Old Links	
Midweek	€60.00
Societies: (16+)	€55.00
Winter (1st Nov 05-31 Mar 06)	€30.00
Weekend	€65.00
Societies: (16+)	€60.00
Winter (1st Nov 05-31 Mar 06)	€35.00

Play & Stay Special
2 Nights B&B, 1 Evening Meal & 2 rounds of Golf.
One round **Old Links** and one round **Glashedy Links**
April 11-Oct 31 Mid-Wk €215, W-end €250
Nov 1-Mar 31 Mid-Wk €150, W-end €175

**Ballyliffin
Inishowen
Co. Donegal**
Tel: 00 353 74 93 76119
e-mail: info@ballyliffingolfclub.com
www.ballyliffingolfclub.com

INISHOWEN GATEWAY HOTEL

RAILWAY ROAD, BUNCRANA, INISHOWEN, CO. DONEGAL
TEL: (00353) 74 93 61144
FAX: (00353) 74 93 62278

Elegant Hotel with 79 luxurious bedrooms, situated on the sandy shores of Lough Swilly. Close to Ballyliffin and North West Golf Clubs; ideal location for links golf enthusiasts. Gateway Health and Fitness Club with pool, steam, sauna, spa bath and gym on site. Fabulous Health and Beauty Spa now open for relaxing treatments. Groups and societies welcome.

website: www.inishowengateway.com
e-mail: info@inishowengateway.com

DOWNINGS **Rosapenna Hotel & Golf Links,** Rosapenna, Downings (074 915 5301; Fax: 074 915 5128). *Location:* 25 miles from Letterkenny. Links course, designed by Old Tom Morris. 18 holes, 6271 yards, 5735 metres. S.S.S. 71. New 18 holes opened June 2003. *Green Fees:* Old Tom Morris 50 euros per day; Sandy Hills Links 75 euros per day. *Eating facilities:* available at hotel. *Visitors:* welcome all times. Four star Hotel on course. *Society Meetings:* welcome, must have Club Handicap. Secretary: John Sweeney. Hotel and Course Manager: Frank T. Casey.

DUNFANAGHY. **Dunfanaghy Golf Club,** Kill, Dunfanaghy, Letterkenny (074 9136335; Fax: 074 9136684). *Location:* on main Letterkenny-Dunfanaghy Road N56. Seaside links course overlooking Sheephaven Bay and overshadowed by Horn Head. 18 holes, 5000 metres. S.S.S. 66. Practice net. *Green Fees:* weekdays 32 euros, weekends 37 euros. Subject to review. *Eating facilities:* bar snacks - soup, tea and sandwiches. *Visitors:* welcome weekends or most days. Time sheet in operation at weekends. Buggies, carts and caddies by request. *Society Meetings:* all welcome. Club Secretary: Sandra McGinley (074 9136335). Hon Secretary: Sam Sterritt. e-mail: dunfanaghygolf@eircom.net

KINCASSLAGH. **Cruit Island Golf Club,** Cruit Island, Kincasslagh (074 9543296). *Location:* five miles north of Dunglue, turn off opposite Daniel O'Donnell's Viking House Hotel, three miles to the clubhouse. Seaside links with 9 holes, spectacular views hugging ragged coastline. 9 holes, 4860 metres. S.S.S. 66. Practice green. *Green Fees:* information not available. *Eating facilities:* full menu available if pre-booked. *Visitors:* welcome all year. Secretary: Dermot Devenney (074 9548872).*

LETTERKENNY. **Letterkenny Golf Club,** Barnhill, Letterkenny (074 21150). *Location:* Off Ramelton Road out of Letterkenny. Parkland/wooded course by the river. Practice area, putting green. 18 holes, 6239 yards. S.S.S. 71. *Green Fees:* information not available. *Eating facilities:* bar snacks; full à la carte menu available. *Visitors:* always welcome. *Society Meetings:* special reduced rates available, phone for details. Secretary: Barry Ramsey (074 24491).*

PORTNOO. **Narin and Portnoo Golf Club,** Narin, Portnoo (074 9545112; Fax: 074 9545994). *Location:* 6 miles north of Ardara adjacent to Blue Flag beach. Links course. 18 holes, 5396 metres. *Green Fees:* weekdays 30 euros, weekends 35 euros. *Eating facilities:* soup and sandwiches. *Visitors:* welcome Monday to Saturday, and after mid-day on Sundays, please ring or e-mail for a tee time. *Society Meetings:* very welcome with special rates. Secretary: Willie Quinn.
e-mail: narinportnoo@eircom.net
website: www.narinportnoogolfclub.ie

PORTSALON. **Portsalon Golf Club,** Portsalon, Fanad (074 9159459; Fax: 074 9159919). *Location:* 22 miles north of Letterkenny via Ramelton. Milford, Kerrykeel to Portsalon. Seaside links. 18 holes, white markers 6185 metres. S.S.S. 72, par 72. *Green Fees:* weekdays 40 euros; weekends and Bank Holidays 45 euros. Subject to review. Phone for special rates. *Eating facilities:* diningroom and bar in clubhouse. *Visitors:* phone in advance. *Society Meetings:* welcome weekdays and some weekends, must book in advance - contact Cathal. Secretary: Peter Doherty (074 9159459; Fax: 074 9159919).

RATHMULLAN. **Otway Golf Club,** Saltpans, Rathmullan (074 9158319). *Location*: from Rathmullan take road to Portsalon, course is two miles out on right. Seaside links course. 9 holes, 4234 yards. S.S.S. 64. *Green Fees*: information not provided. *Eating facilities*: bar. *Visitors:* always welcome. *Society Meetings*: by arrangement. Secretary: Kevin Toland (074 9151665).
e-mail: tolandkevin@eircom.net.

REDCASTLE. **Redcastle Golf Club,** Redcastle (074 9382073; Fax: 074 9382214). *Location:* 4 miles from Moville on Londonderry Road. Parkland. 9 holes, 6152 yards, 5700 metres. S.S.S. 69. *Green Fees:* information not available. *Eating facilities:* Redcastle Hotel. *Visitors:* Always welcome. *Society Meetings:* special group rates if pre-booked. 35 bedroom 3 star hotel. Secretary: Mark Wilson.*

THE APPEARANCE OF AN ASTERISK (*) AT THE END OF A CLUB OR COURSE ENTRY INDICATES THAT UP-TO-DATE INFORMATION HAS NOT BEEN SUPPLIED

For full details of clubs and courses, plus convenient accommodation
www.uk-golfguide.com

ROSAPENNA HOTEL & GOLF LINKS
Where the Water meets the Wild

DOWNINGS, CO DONEGAL
TEL: +353 (0)74 55301 FAX: +353 (0)74 55128
e-mail: rosapenna@eircom.net • www.rosapenna.ie

A unique experience awaits you at Rosapenna Hotel & Golf Links, where four-star luxury nestles amidst the rolling Donegal landscape. Tranquil lounges and elegant dining areas overlook the bay, and a choice of bedrooms, including standard, de luxe with sea views, and spacious junior suites, provide the comforts and style one would expect from a hotel with such history. This is a haven of tranquillity where you can recharge after a day on the links or simply escape from the pressures of modern-day living.

Links course, designed by old Tom Morris • 18 holes 6271 yards, SSS 71
• New 18 hole Sandy Hills Links Course designed by Pat Ruddy due to open June 2003
• Visitors welcome at all times • Golfers welcome with Club Handicaps.

See also Colour Advertisement on page 84

The Silver Tassie Hotel

The Silver Tassie Hotel nestles in the beautiful 'Hills of Donegal' near the heritage town of Ramelton, and just 5 minutes' drive from a championship golf course. Unwind in comfort and style in our luxurious bedrooms, all en suite, with multi-channel TV and tea/coffee making facilities. The hotel has a great reputation for food, served in both the oak-panelled restaurant and the lively bar and lounge. The bustling town of Letterkenny is only five minutes away, and is an ideal base to explore Donegal and the spectacular Glenveagh National Park.

Silver Tassie Hotel
Ramelton Road, Letterkenny, Co. Donegal
Tel: 074 9125619 • Fax: 074 9124473
info@theblaneygroup.com
www.theblaneygroup.com

Milford Inn Hotel

Situated 10 miles from Letterkenny, this luxurious family hotel is ideally placed for exploring Donegal's rugged Atlantic coast. Relax in luxury and style in a choice of en suite bedrooms, all with satellite TV and tea/coffee making facilities. Carvery lunches are available, as well as an extensive bar menu, while 'The Arches' Restaurant offers both à la carte and table d'hôte menus. There is live entertainment every weekend and most nights during the holiday season, and a hair and beauty salon offering a variety of specialist treatments. Local attractions include a choice of golf courses, fishing and horse riding.

Milford Inn Hotel
Milford, Co. Donegal
Tel: 074 9153313 • Fax: 074 9153388
milfordinnhotel@eircom.net
www.milfordinnhotel.com

Blaney group

Visit the FHG website
www.holidayguides.com
for details of the wide choice of accommodation featured in the full range of FHG titles

K·U·P·E·R·A·R·D

COUNTY DUBLIN

BALBRIGGAN. **Balbriggan Golf Club**, Blackhall, Balbriggan (8412173; Fax: 8413927). *Location:* quarter of a mile south of Balbriggan on main Belfast/Dublin Road. Parkland course with fine views of Cooley Peninsula and Mourne Mountains. 18 holes, 5922 metres. S.S.S. 71. *Green Fees:* information not available. *Eating facilities:* full restaurant facilities and bar. *Visitors:* welcome, Tuesday Ladies' Day, Saturdays and Sundays not good as club competitions take place. *Society Meetings:* catered for Mondays, Wednesdays, Thursdays and Fridays. Secretary: Michael O'Halloran (8412229).*

BALCARRICK. **Donabate Golf Club,** Balcarrick, Dublin (8434346; Fax: 8434488). *Location*: 5 miles north of Dublin Airport. Tree-lined parkland course, water in 9 holes. All sand based greens. 27 holes, 6085 metres. S.S.S. 73. Practice area including pitching and putting green. *Green Fees:* information not available. *Eating facilities*: full catering and bar facilities. *Visitors*: welcome every day. Must book in advance. Tuition available. Buggy hire. New ultra-modern clubhouse opened in 2003, with panoramic views of the course. *Society Meetings*: welcome every day, some restrictions at weekends. Professional: Hugh Jackson (8436346; Fax: 8434488). Golf Administrator: Brian May (8436346; Fax: 8434488).*
e-mail: brian@donabategolfclub.com
info@donabategolfclub.com
website: www.donabategolfclub.com

BALLYBOUGHAL. **Hollywood Lakes Golf Club,** Ballyboughal (8433407; Fax: 8433002). *Location*: 15 minutes north of Dublin Airport via N1 and the R129 to Ballyboughal, right at 'T' junction then two miles on right. Parkland course with water features on 11 holes. 18 holes, 5763 metres, S.S.S. 71. Practice ground, putting greens. *Green Fees:* weekdays 35 euros, weekends and Bank Holidays 45 euros. *Eating facilities*: bar and restaurant. *Visitors*: welcome, not before 1pm at weekends, not after 4pm Wednesday. *Society Meetings*: welcome, rates negotiable. Secretary: Sid Baldwin PGA (8433407; Fax: 8433002).

BRITTAS. **Slade Valley Golf Club,** Lynch Park, Brittas (01-458 2183; Fax: 01-458 2784). *Location*: signposted from Saggart Village (approx. 4 miles). Parkland course with spectacular views over Dublin City. 18 holes, 5960 yards, 5457 metres, Par 69, S.S.S. 68. Putting green, driving net. *Green Fees*: information not provided. *Eating facilities*: bar/restaurant. *Visitors*: welcome weekdays. Professional available for lessons. *Society Meetings*: welcome weekdays - rates negotiable. Professional: John Dignam. Secretary: Dermot Clancy.

BRITTAS. **South County Golf Club,** Lisheen Road, Brittas (01 458 2965; Fax: 01 458 2842). *Location*: on the Blessington road, 7 miles from the M50 and 30 minutes from Dublin city centre. Parkland course. 18 holes, 7007 yards. S.S.S. 72. *Green Fees:* information not available. *Eating facilities:* clubhouse with catering. *Visitors*: welcome. Fully stocked Pro shop. *Society Meetings:* welcome.*
e-mail: info@southcountygolf.ie
website: www.southcountygolf.com

CASTLEKNOCK. **Luttrellstown Castle Golf and Country Club,** Castleknock, Dublin 15 (353 1 8089988; Fax: 353 1 8089989). *Location:* six miles from Dublin City. 18 holes Championship parkland course with magnificent lakes and well manicured greens. 18 holes, 7091 yards, 6384 metres. S.S.S. 72. Practice ground. *Green Fees:* information not available. *Eating facilities:* restaurant and bar. *Visitors:* some tee times reserved for members, please phone in advance. Accommodation available at Luttrellston Castle and in stable yard apartments. *Society Meetings:* welcome subject to availability. Professional: Edward Doyle.*

For full details of clubs and courses, plus convenient accommodation
www.uk-golfguide.com

Donabate Golf Club
Balcarrick, Donabate, Co. Dublin

A challenging 27-hole, mature tree lined parkland course only fifteen minutes drive north of Dublin airport, just off the M1 motorway. The greens, built to USGA standards, have the reputation as being amongst the best in the country. A relatively flat course where good course management is required, water comes into play on 8 holes. Ultra modern clubhouse with top-class facilities that are second to none. Excellent hotels, guest houses and restaurants nearby.
Food available all day, pro-shop, golf clinics, buggies for hire.
Tel: 353 1 843 6346
Fax: 353 1 843 4488
e-mail: info@donabategolfclub.com
web: www.donabategolfclub.com

See also Colour Advertisement on page 88

DONABATE. **Balcarrick Golf Club,** Corballis, Donabate (8436957; Fax: 8436228). *Location:* from Dublin take the M1 motorway north past Dublin Airport and Swords and take the first exit signposted Donabate/Skerries/Lusk; turn right in the village of Donabate, travel 1.5km and turn right again, Balcarrick is 1km on the right hand side. Parkland course. 18 holes, 6191 metres. Par 72. *Green Fees:* information not available. *Eating facilities:* full catering and bar facilities available. *Visitors:* welcome, please telephone Professional for time sheet details. *Society Meetings:* welcome. Professional: Stephen Rayfus (8434034).*

DONABATE. **Beaverstown Golf Club,** Donabate (00 353 1 843 6439/843 6721; Fax: 00 353 1 843 5059). *Location:* on the shores of Rogerstown Estuary in North Dublin, 6km north of Dublin Airport. Attractive course set in 140 acres of lush parkland, with orchards bordering the tees and fairways. Water comes into play on 12 holes. 18 holes, 5972 metres. S.S.S. 72, Par 72. Practice facilities. *Green Fees:* Monday to Friday 48 euros, Saturdays and Sundays 58 euros, weekdays early bird 25 euros. *Eating facilities:* bar, catering. *Visitors:* welcome. Please contact Club Manager in advance. Ladies' Day Tuesday. *Society Meetings:* welcome most Saturdays.
e-mail: manager@beaverstown.com
website: www.beaverstown.com

DONABATE. **Corballis Golf Links,** Donabate (8436583). *Location:* main Dublin to Belfast Road. Links course. 18 holes, 4971 yards. S.S.S. 64. Putting green. *Green Fees:* information not available. *Eating facilities:* snack food. *Visitors:* welcome anytime. Carts available. *Society Meetings:* welcome. Manager: Austin Levins.*

DONABATE. **The Island Golf Club,** Corballis, Donabate (00 353 (01)1 8436205; Fax: 00 353 (01)1 8436860). *Location:* 15 minute drive from Dublin Airport, across the estuary from the village of Malahide. Links course with challenging greens. 18 holes, 6206 metres, S.S.S. 73, Par 71. *Green Fees:* 110 euros per round, early bird 80 euros 8.30am to 9.30am. *Visitors:* warmly welcomed.
e-mail: info@theislandgolfclub.com
website: www.theislandgolfclub.com

THE ISLAND
Golf Club
Tel: +353 (0)1843 6205
Fax: +353 (0)1843 6860
Established 1890
Corballis, Donabate, Co. Dublin, Ireland

OPEN QUALIFYING COURSE FOR 2005-2010

For sheer awe – the kind inspired by 25 foot-high dunes, vaguely lunar crevasses running through the terrain and challenging greens – the best choice is The Island Golf Club. This classic championship links course is less than 15 minutes from Dublin airport, yet the members have kept it a great secret since 1890. It is one of the best courses in Ireland and is definitely the best golf course you have never heard of.
Par 71, SSS 73, 6,857 yds. €110 (£75 approx) visitor green fee. All visitors ensured of warm and friendly welcome.

THE APPEARANCE OF AN ASTERISK (*) AT THE END OF A CLUB OR COURSE ENTRY INDICATES THAT UP-TO-DATE INFORMATION HAS NOT BEEN SUPPLIED

In a very short space of time, **The South County Golf Club** has established itself as one of Dublin's 'must play' venues. The combination of a challenging course, exquisite cuisine, panoramic views, and close proximity to Dublin and the M50 have made it a real favourite.

The South County Golf Club
Lisheen Road, Brittas Village, Co. Dublin
Tel: +353 1 458 2965 • Fax: +353 1 458 2842
e-mail: info@southcountygolf.ie
www.southcountygolf.com

The split-level design clubhouse has a spacious reception area, well appointed changing facilities and an excellent Pro Shop. On the upper level, which has spectacular views of the 'Seat of Kings', are a bar, function room, restaurant and terrace. Immediately adjacent are four acres of practice area including a driving range and putting green. Society Packages available - details on request.

DUBLIN. **Deer Park Hotel and Golf Courses,** Howth, Co. Dublin (832 2624; Fax: 839 2405). *Location:* Deer Park Hotel, nine miles east of the city centre. Parkland with panoramic sea views. 18 holes, 6830 yards, Par 77; two 9 hole courses each (3100 yards and 3370 yards) Par 3, and 12-hole Par 36. Pitch and putt. *Green Fees:* information not available. *Eating facilities:* full à la carte restaurant, bistro and bar; meal bookings required at weekends. *Visitors:* welcome at all times, Sunday mornings expect delays. 80 bedroomed hotel, swimming pool, special golf holidays available. Clubs and carts for hire. *Society Meetings:* welcome. Hotel: (832 2624; Fax: 839 2405). Golf Shop: (839 8777).*
e-mail: sales@deerpark.iol.ie
website: www.deerpark-hotel.ie

DUBLIN. **Dublin City Golf Club,** Ballinascorney (01451 6430/2082; 01459 8445). *Location:* take Exit 12 off M50, head west and turn left along R114 at The Old Mill pub, course is two miles further on. Gently sloping parkland. 18 holes, 5800 yards. S.S.S. 69. *Green Fees:* information not available. *Eating facilities:* excellent clubhouse facilities. *Visitors:* welcome, phone in advance. *Society Meetings:* welcome 7 days. Buggy, club and trolley hire. Secretary: Francis Bagnall.*
e-mail: info@dublincitygolf.com
website: www.dublincitygolf.com

DUBLIN. **Edmondstown Golf Club,** Edmondstown Road, Rathfarnham, Dublin 16 (493 2461; Fax: 493 3152). *Location*: south west suburbs of Dublin city. Parkland. 18 holes, 6011 metres. S.S.S. 73 Par 71. Practice facilities available. *Green Fees:* weekdays 55.00 euros, weekends and Bank Holidays 65.00 euros. *Eating facilities*: bar and restaurant. *Society Meetings:* welcome. Professional: Gareth McShea (494 1049). Secretary: Selwyn S. Davies (493 1082).*
e-mail: info@edmondstowngolfclub.ie
website: www.edmondstowngolfclub.ie

DUBLIN. **Elm Park Golf and Sports Club,** Nutley House, Donnybrook, Dublin 4 (2693438; Fax: 2694505). *Location:* between R.T.E. and St. Vincent's Hospital. Flat parkland course. 18 holes, 5929 yards, 5422 metres. S.S.S. 68. *Green Fees:* information not available. *Eating facilities:* full bar and dining facilities. *Visitors:* welcome but must telephone to arrange times with Professional. *Society Meetings:* by special arrangement. Professional: S. Green (2692650). Secretary: A. McCormack. *

DUBLIN. **The Royal Dublin Golf Club,** North Bull Island Nature Reserve, Dollymount, Dublin 3 (8336346). *Location:* three and a half miles north east of city centre on coast road to Howth. Seaside links. 18 holes, 6309 metres. S.S.S. 73, Par 72 Championship course. 18 holes, 6002 metres, S.S.S. 71 Medal course. Large practice ground. *Green Fees:* 120 euros. *Eating facilities:* grill room, restaurant, two bars. *Visitors:* Monday, Tuesday, Thursday, Friday, Saturday from 4pm in Summer and Sunday 10.30am to 12 noon. Carts, buggies and caddies by arrangement. *Society Meetings:* catered for, written application must be made. Senior Professional: Christy O'Connor Snr (8339833). Professional: Leonard Owens (8336477). Secretary: John Lambe (8336346); Fax: 353 1 8336504). e-mail: info@theroyaldublingolfclub.com
website: www.theroyaldublingolfclub.com

DUN LAOGHAIRE. **Dun Laoghaire Golf Club,** Eglinton Park, Tivoli Road, Dun Laoghaire (280 3916; Fax: 280 4868). *Location:* half a mile from town centre and ferry port. Parkland. 18 holes, 5313 metres. S.S.S. 68. *Green Fees:* 55.00 euros. *Eating facilities:* full bar and restaurant facilities. *Visitors:* welcome by prior arrangement Saturdays. Local accommodation available. *Society Meetings:* welcome by prior arrangement. Professional: Vincent Carey (280 1694). General Manager: Dermot Murphy (280 3916; Fax: 280 4868).
e-mail: dlgc@iol.ie

KILLINEY. **Killiney Golf Club,** Ballinclea Road, Killiney (Tel. & Fax: 01 2852823). *Location:* south Dunlaoghaire. Parkland. 9 holes, 5655 metres. S.S.S. 70. *Green Fees:* information not available. *Eating facilities:* snacks available. *Visitors:* welcome with restrictions. Professional: P. O'Boyle. Secretary: M.F. Walsh.*

KILSALLAGHAN. **Corrstown Golf Club,** Corrstown, Kilsallaghan (01 864 0533/4; Fax: 01 864 0534). *Location*: 10 minutes north of Dublin Airport. Parkland course. 27 holes. Practice green and nets. *Green Fees:* weekdays 50 euros, weekends 60 euros. *Eating facilities:* full bar and restaurant. *Visitors:* welcome Monday to Friday; Saturday and Sunday when available. *Society Meetings*: outings welcome. Professional: Pat Gittens (01 864 3322; Fax: 01 864 0537). Office: (01 864 0533; Fax: 01 864 0537).
e-mail: info@corrstowngolfclub.com
website: www.corrstowngolfclub.com

FHG Guides publish a large range of well-known accommodation guides. We will be happy to send you details or you can use the order form at the back of this book.

Deer Park Hotel & Golf Courses

Deer Park Hotel incorporates Ireland's largest golf complex, with four courses to choose from, ranging from a testing 12-hole par 36 course to a par 72, 6830 yard 18 hole course.

Deer Park is just 9 miles from Dublin City and Airport. The hillside location offers spectacular views of Dublin Bay and the Northeastern coastline. 80 superb en suite rooms, 17m swimming pool complex and all weather tennis courts, bar, bistro and the elegant "Four Earls" Restaurant.

Deer Park Hotel & Golf Courses, Howth, Co. Dublin
Tel: (01) 832 2264 • Fax: (01) 839 2405
e-mail: sales@deerpark.iol.ie • www.deerpark-hotel.ie

★★★
AA / Bord Failte

The Royal Dublin Golf Club
DOLLYMOUNT, DUBLIN 3, IRELAND

Situated 3½ miles north-east of the city centre on the coast road to Howth. Seaside links. 18 hole Championship Links: Championship 6309 metres. SSS 73; Medal Course 6002 metres, SSS 71. Grill room, restaurant, bars. Visitors welcome; Society meetings catered for.

Clubhouse: 833 7153 • Secretary/Manager: 833 6346
Professional: 833 6477 • Caterer: 833 3370 • Fax: 353-1-833 6504
e-mail: info@theroyaldublingolfclub.com • www.theroyaldublingolfclub.com

Fáilte Ireland • Les Routiers Ireland • RAC • Irish Hotels Federation

THE RED BANK
Restaurant & Guesthouse
5-7 Church Street, Skerries, Co. Dublin
Tel: +353 1 8490439 • Fax: +353 1 8491598
e-mail: info@redbank.ie • www.redbank.ie

The area around this fine Bed & Breakfast, located in the sea fishing village of Skerries, just 18 miles north of Dublin, is particularly rich in golf clubs, with as many as 25 championship courses just a short drive away. Three of our links courses, situated right on the sea, are rated as belonging to the Top 100 Golf Courses in the World. So why not try some real *'Gourmet Golf'*.

• *Fantastic Offer!* • *Gourmet Golf Package*
Have dinner at the award-winning Redbank with one night accommodation and full Irish breakfast the following morning. Then on to a round of links golf at Corballis Golf Course – all for only €125.00pp.

See also Colour Advertisement on page 385

There's no mistaking the authentic charm of the Lucan Spa Hotel. From the unique copper tower on the roof to the cheerful familiarity of the staff, there's nothing quite like it. Situated on the Road to the West (N4), in close proximity to the M50, this elegant hotel offers guests comfort and convenience in a rural setting.
The exceptionally well appointed en suite rooms are equipped to 3* standard. Guests may choose to dine in The Earl Bistro or the award-winning Honora D Restaurant. This an ideal location for many events, especially as it is in close proximity (five miles) to the venue of the 2006 Ryder Cup at The K Club.

LUCAN SPA HOTEL

AA
★★★

Special Offer on round of golf at The K Club available to residents • Carton House Golf Club, Hermitage Golf Club and the Liffey Valley Golf Club are nearby

The Lucan Spa Hotel, Lucan, Co Dublin
Tel: +353 (0)1 628 0494
Fax: +353 (0)1 628 0841
info@lucanspahotel.ie • www.lucanspahotel.ie

MALAHIDE. **Malahide Golf Club,** Beechwood, The Grange, Malahide (8461611; Fax: 8461270) *Location:* 15 minutes from Dublin city, 7 miles from Dublin Airport. Parkland. 27 holes, 6066 metres. S.S.S. 71. Practice area, Proshop. *Green Fees:* weekdays 55 euros, weekends 90 euros; Group rates available. *Eating facilities:* top class restaurant and bar. *Visitors:* welcome, must book in advance. *Society Meetings:* society outings welcome. Professional: John Murray (8460002; Fax: 8461270). Secretary: P. J. Smyth. e-mail: malgc@clubi.ie

PORTMARNOCK. **Portmarnock Hotel & Golf Links,** Strand Road, Portmarnock (8461800; Fax: 8461077). *Location:* 8 miles north east of Dublin, 15 minutes from Dublin Airport. Seaside links designed by Bernhard Langer. 18 holes, 6223 metres. S.S.S. 73. Pitching area with bunker and putting green. *Green Fees:* information not available. *Eating facilities:* two restaurants and three bars. *Visitors:* no restrictions. Four star deluxe hotel, 103 bedrooms and conference facilities. *Society Meetings:* group rates and corporate packages available on request. Golf Director: Moira Cassidy.
e-mail: golfres@portmarnock.com
website: www.portmarnock.com

RATHCOOLE. **Beech Park Golf Club,** Johnstown, Rathcoole (4580522; Fax: 4588365). Gently undulating parkland course. 18 holes, 5762 metres. S.S.S. 70. *Green Fees:* 38 euros per round. *Eating facilities:* bar and restaurant. *Visitors:* welcome Monday-Friday. *Society Meetings:* welcome Monday, Thursday, Friday. General Manager: Paul Muldowney.
e-mail: info@beechpark.ie
website: www.beechpark.ie

RATHFARNHAM. **Stackstown Golf Club,** Kellystown Road, Rathfarnham, Dublin 16 (01-494 2338; Fax: 01-493 3934). *Location:* one mile from Exit 13 on M50 towards Rathfarnham. Parkland course situated on slopes of Dublin mountains. Home club of Padraig Harrington. 18 holes, 6152 yards, S.S.S. 70. Practice fairway, putting green, driving nets. *Green Fees:* weekdays 35 euros, weekends 45 euros. *Eating facilities:* full catering and bar facilities. *Visitors:* welcome everyday except Tuesday (Ladies' Day), Wednesday afternoons, Saturday and Sunday subject to availability. Professional tuition available. Fully stocked shop, buggies, clubs, trolley for hire. *Society Meetings:* welcome Monday, Thursday, Friday and Sunday, special rates available. Professional: Michael Kavanagh (01-494 4561; Fax: 01-493 3934). General Manager: Larry Clarke (01 494 1993; Fax: 01-493 3934).
e-mail: stackstowngc@eircom.net
website: www.stackstowngolfclub.com

ST MARGARET'S. **The Open Golf Centre,** Newtown House, St Margarets (8640324; Fax: 8341400). *Location:* 2km from Dublin Airport, adjacent to N2 (Derry road). Inviting parkland course, three lakes feature prominently. 27 holes, 9500 yards. S.S.S. 69/31. 20 bay driving range. *Green Fees:* information not available. *Eating facilities:* coffee shop. *Visitors:* welcome everyday. Teaching auditorium. *Society Meetings:* welcome. Professional: R. Machin (8640324; Fax: 8341400). Secretary: R. Yates (8640324 Fax: 8341400).*

ST MARGARET'S. **St Margaret's Golf and Country Club,** St Margaret's, Dublin (8640400; Fax: 8640289). *Location:* 10 minutes from Dublin Airport and 25 minutes from Dublin city centre. Parkland, championship course, ultra-modern design by Craddock and Ruddy. 18 holes, 6629 yards. S.S.S. 73. Putting and practice areas. *Green Fees:* information not available. *Eating facilities:* full bar and restaurant facilities. *Visitors:* welcome at all times. Cobra Golf Academy. *Society Meetings:* welcome. Professional: David O'Sullivan*
e-mail: cscanlon@stmargaretsgolf.com
website: www.stmargaretsgolf.com

SKERRIES. **Skerries Golf Club,** Hacketstown, Skerries (01 8491567: Fax: 01 8491591). *Location:* east of Dublin/Belfast road, approximately six miles. Parkland course close to sea with undulating fairways. 18 holes, 6081 metres. Par 73. Practice ground. *Green Fees:* weekdays 50 euros; weekends 60 euros. *Eating facilities:* restaurant, snack bar, bar, lounge. *Visitors:* welcome Mondays, Thursdays, Fridays; weekends by arrangement. *Society Meetings:* welcome. Professional: Jimmy Kinsella (01 8490925). General Manager: Billy Meehan (01 8491567; Fax: 01 8491591).

Malahide Golf Club

Set on Dublin's golden North Coast in the beautiful seaside resort of Malahide, this superb 27-hole course is one of Ireland's oldest golf clubs, established in 1892. The Eddie Hackett design offers a challenge for all on a course in play all year through.

Each hole presents its own test with trees and water a frequent feature. Located close to Dublin City and Airport.

The fine clubhouse, with a panoramic view across to the Dublin Mountains, has full catering facilities.

Our motto is "a light heart and cheerful spirit", play, dine and relax with friends in this charming venue. Societies are always welcome.

Beechwood • The Grange • Malahide • Co. Dublin
Tel: (01) 846 1611 • Fax: (01) 846 1270
e-mail: manager@malahidegolfclub.ie
www.malahidegolfclub.ie

See also Colour Advertisement on page 84

SUTTON. **Howth Golf Club,** St. Fintan's, Carrickbrack Road, Sutton, Dublin 13 (8323055; Fax: 8321793). *Location:* one and a half miles from Sutton Cross on city side of Hill of Howth. Moorland course with scenic views of Dublin Bay. 18 holes, 5672 metres. S.S.S. 69. Practice ground. *Green Fees:* 50 euros. *Eating facilities:* restaurant facilities every day from midday. *Visitors:* welcome weekdays except Wednesdays and Thursdays. Carts. *Society Meetings:* bookings accepted by arrangement with Club Manager. Reduced rates for large groups. Professional: John McGuirk (8392617). Club Manager: Paul Kennedy.
e-mail: secretary@howthgolfclub.ie
website: www.howthgolfclub.ie

SWORDS. **Swords Open Golf Course,** Balheary Avenue, Swords (Tel & Fax: 01 8409819). *Location*: three miles west of Swords. Parkland. Broadmeadow river divides course. No climbing, flat course. 18 holes, 5631 metres. S.S.S. 69. Putting green. *Green Fees*: weekdays 18 euros, weekends 25 euros. *Eating facilities:* coffee shop. *Visitors:* any time, very welcome. *Society Meetings:* very welcome. Secretary: Orla McGuinness.
e-mail: info@swordsopengolfcourse.com
website: www.swordsopengolfcourse.com

COUNTY GALWAY

ANNAGHVANE. **Connemara Isles Golf Club,** Annaghvane, Lettermore (091 572498). *Location:* Take the coast road from Galway City, at Casla (Costello) take the first right after the Texaco Station. Continue on that road for four and a half miles until you pass "An Hooker Bar" (on a bend). The golf course is 500 metres ahead. Seaside links Championship course. *Green Fees:* contact club for details. *Visitors:* always welcome. *Society Meetings:* welcome. Manager Anthony Lynch.*

ATHENRY. **Athenry Golf Club,** Palmerstown, Oran More (091 794466; Fax: 091 794971). *Location:* 8 miles from Galway city. Parkland. 18 holes, 5687 metres. Par 70, S.S.S. 70. Practice ground. *Green Fees:* midweek Monday to Thursday 35 euros per day, weekend Friday to Sunday 40 euros per round. *Eating facilities:* full bar and catering. *Visitors:* welcome except Sunday. Deals available with local hotels. Club hire and tuition. *Society Meetings:* welcome. Pro shop (091 790599). Professional: R. Ryan. Secretary/Manager: Padraig Flattery.
e-mail: athenrygc@eircom.net
website: www.athenrygolfclub.net

BALLINASLOE. **Ballinasloe Golf Club,** Rossgloss, Ballinasloe (0905 42126; Fax: 0905 42538). *Location*: 2 miles from Ballinasloe town on Portumna side. Ballinasloe on main Dublin-Galway Road, two hours from Dublin. Mature parkland course. 18 holes, 5865 metres, Par 72. Practice area, putting green. *Green Fees:* information not available. *Eating facilities*: full bar and catering facilities. Buggy and cart hire. *Society Meetings*: welcome Monday-Saturday. Secretary: Dr Conor Corr (0905 42126).*
e-mail: ballinasloegolfclub@eircom.net
website: www.ballinasloegolfclub.com

CLIFDEN. **Connemara Golf Club,** Ballyconneely, Near Clifden (095 23502/23602; Fax: 095 23662). *Location:* from Clifden to Ballyconneely, 4 miles on the right. Seaside links Championship course. 27 holes, 6611 metres. S.S.S. 73. 220 yard Par 3 13th is feature hole. Practice fairway, putting green and driving net. *Green Fees:* April 45 euros, May 50 euros, June/July/August 60 euros, Sept 50 euros, Oct 45 euros, Nov-Mar 35 euros. *Eating facilities:* full restaurant and bar facilities. *Visitors:* always welcome. Fully equipped Pro Shop. *Society Meetings:* groups of 20 or more welcome. Professional: Hugh O'Neill. Secretary: Richard Flaherty.
e-mail: links@iol.ie
website: www.connemaragolflinks.com

Connemara Golf Club
Ballyconneely, Clifden, Co. Galway
Tel: 095 23502/23602 • Fax: 095 23662
e-mail: links@iol.ie
website: www.connemaragolflinks.com

Opened in 1973, the links course is bounded on three sides by the Atlantic Ocean, with, on the inland side, superb views of the Twelve Bens.
27 holes • practice range • pitching green • putting green
Green Fees: weekdays 50 euros, weekends 55 euros
Clubs, caddie cars, golf carts and caddies for hire.

See also Colour Advertisement on page 88

Enjoy unrivalled personal service in the warmth of Galway's only 5-Star Hotel. The hotel has its own unique 9-hole double green Par 72 parkland course, with rolling hills, lakes and fabulous views of Lough Corrib.
Glenlo Abbey Hotel, Bushypark, Galway
Tel: +353 (0)91 526666 • Fax: 353 (0)91 527800
e-mail: info@glenloabbey.ie • www.glenlo.com

GORT. **Gort Golf Club,** Kilmacduagh Road, Gort (091 632244; Fax: 091 632387). *Location:* 20 minutes Galway Airport, 40 minutes Shannon Airport, 60 minutes Knock Airport, on edge of world-famous Burren, overlooking Coole Lake. Undulating parkland. 18 holes, 5974 metres. S.S.S.71. *Green Fees:* weekdays 25 euros, weekends 30 euros. *Eating facilities:* full bar and restaurant. *Visitors:* welcome all year, restrictions on Sundays. *Society Meetings:* welcome with prior booking. Time Sheet in operation every day. Administrator: Pauline Faithfull (091 632244). Designer: Christy O'Connor Jnr.
e-mail: info@gortgolf.com
website: www.gortgolf.com

LOUGHREA. **Loughrea Golf Club,** Craigue, Loughrea (091 841049). *Location:* one and a half miles north east of town, on New Inn Road. Parkland, undulating, with beautiful views of town and Slieve Aughty Mountains in background. 18 holes, 5261 yards. Par 67. Practice area. *Green Fees:* information not available. *Eating facilities:* tea, coffee, sandwiches at bar. New clubhouse with full catering under construction. *Visitors:* welcome weekdays and weekends with advance booking. *Society Meetings:* welcome, please telephone. Secretary: Vinny Ryan.*

ORANMORE **Galway Bay Golf and Country Club Hotel,** Renville, Oranmore (091 790500; Fax: 091 790510). *Location:* seven miles from Galway City, through Oranmore Village. Parkland by the sea, many water hazards with the Atlantic Ocean surrounding on three sides. 18 holes, 7144 yards, 6533 metres. S.S.S. 73. Putting green, chipping green, practice area, indoor practice bays academy. *Green Fees:* information not provided. *Eating facilities:* restaurant, spike bar, cocktail bar. *Visitors:* welcome daily. *Society Meetings:* welcome daily, reduced rates for groups. Professional: Eugene O'Connor (091 790503). Director of Golf: Anne Hanley (091 790503).
e-mail: maryhawkins@galwaybaygolfresort.com
website: www.gbay-golf.com

OUGHTERARD. **Oughterard Golf Club,** Gortreevagh, Oughterard (091 552131; Fax: 091 552733). *Location:* 15 miles west of Galway City on N59 to Connemara. Parkland, newly re-modelled with Greens to USPGA Standards. 18 holes, 5876 metres. S.S.S. 70. Practice area and putting green. *Green Fees:* information not available. *Eating facilities:* full dining facilities during daylight hours. *Visitors:* welcome. *Society Meetings:* welcome, for further information contact Pro Shop. (091 557352). Administration Office (091 557354).
e-mail: oughterardgc@eircom.net
website: www.oughterardgolf.com

SALTHILL. **Galway Golf Club,** Blackrock, Salthill (091 522033; Fax: 091 529783) *Location:* three miles west of Galway city. Parkland. 18 holes, 5832 metres. S.S.S. 71. *Green Fees:* 50 euros weekdays, 60 euros weekends. *Eating facilities:* full bar and catering facilities. *Visitors:* welcome, avoid Tuesdays and weekends. *Society Meetings:* all welcome. Professional: Don Wallace (091 523038) Secretary: Padraic Fahy (091 522033; Fax: 091 529783).

COUNTY KERRY

BALLYBUNION. **Ballybunion Golf Club,** Sandhill Road, Ballybunion (068 27146; Fax: 068 27387). *Location:* 20 miles from Tralee, 10 miles from Listowel. Links course established 1893, ranked in top ten in world. Two courses - Old and Cashen. 36 holes, 6800 yards. S.S.S. 71. *Green Fees:* 2005 - Old Course 135 euros per round, Cashen Course 95 euros per round, both courses same day 160 euros. Subject to review. *Eating facilities:* full bar and catering facilities. *Visitors:* welcome weekdays, some weekends; telephone bookings in advance. Carts and caddies for hire. *Society Meetings:* catered for. Professional: Brian O'Callaghan. Secretary: Jim McKenna.

BALLYFERRITER. **Ceann Sibeal (Dingle) Golf Club,** Ballyferriter (066 915 6255; Fax: 066 915 6409). *Location:* turn right quarter of a mile after Ballyferriter, 40 miles Tralee, 10 miles Dingle. Traditional links, most westerly golf course in Europe. 18 holes, 6696 yards. S.S.S. 70. Practice ground. *Green Fees:* information not available. *Eating facilities:* full bar and dining room. *Visitors:* welcome at all times, book in advance. *Society Meetings:* all welcome. Secretary: Steve Fahy (066 9156255; Fax: 066 9156409).
e-mail: dinglegc@iol.ie

CASTLEGREGORY. **Castlegregory Golf Club,** Stradbally, Castlegregory (066 7139444). *Location*: main Tralee Conor pass Dingle Road. Scenic links course with water features. 9 holes, 5264 metres, S.S.S. 67. Putting green. *Green Fees:* information not provided. *Eating facilities*: tea and snacks available. *Visitors:* welcome at all times. *Society Meetings*: welcome, 28 euros per person.

GLENBEIGH. **Dooks Golf Links,** Glenbeigh (066 9768205; Fax: 066 9768476). *Location:* on the N70 between Killorglin and Glenbeigh. Links course. 18 holes, 6401 yards. Par 71, S.S.S. 70. Putting green. *Green Fees*: 70 euros. *Eating facilities*: bar and restaurant. *Visitors:* welcome Monday to Saturday. *Society Meetings:* welcome with advance booking. Secretary /Manager: Declan Mangan.
e-mail: office@dooks.com
website: www.dooks.com

KENMARE. **Ring of Kerry Golf and Country Club,** Templenoe, Kenmare (00 353 6442000; Fax: 00 353 6442533). *Location*: take the N70 Ring of Kerry road from Kenmare. Club is three miles on right. Parkland/links course. 18 holes, 6869 yards. S.S.S. 73. Driving range, putting green. *Green Fees:* 80 euros. Special group, society and ad hoc rates on application. *Eating facilities:* full bar and à la carte restaurant with terrace overlooking 17th/18th holes and sea. *Visitors*: welcome anytime. Must pre-book at weekends. Some restrictions throughout the year. Tuition available. Clubhouse can be hired for private and corporate functions. *Society Meetings:* welcome anytime with advance notice, contact club for details. Professional Adrian Whitehead. General Manager: Ed Edwards.
e-mail: reservations@ringofkerrygolf.com
    generalmanager@ringofkerrygolf.com
website: www.ringofkerrygolf.com

KENMARE. **Kenmare Golf Club,** Kenmare (064 41291; Fax: 064 42061). *Location:* turn left at top of Main Street in town, on main Cork/Kilgarvan Road. Partly links, partly parkland surrounded by some breathtaking views. 18 holes, 6083 yards. S.S.S. 69. Putting green, driving net. *Green Fees:* Monday to Saturday 45.00 euros; Sunday 55 euros. *Eating facilities:* snacks in bar only. *Visitors:* welcome at all times, enquire for weekends. Always ring in advance for booking. Club hire, pull-cart hire. *Society Meetings:* welcome, must book well in advance and deposit required. Secretary: Donna Harrington. Manager: Simon Duffield.

KILLARNEY. **Beaufort Golf Club,** Churchtown, Beaufort, Killarney (064 44440; Fax: 064 44752). *Location:* seven miles west of Killarney town, just off the N72. Parkland course in unique setting surrounded by the Kerry Mountains. 18 holes, 6587 yards, 6023 metres. S.S.S. 72. Practice facilities. *Green Fees:* 50 euros weekdays, 60 euros weekends. *Eating facilities:* large bar and full food menu. *Visitors:* welcome seven days except 1pm to 2pm, but please pre-book. Electric buggies, carts, caddies by appointment. *Society Meetings:* welcome. Special rates available on request. Secretary: Colm Kelly (064 44404).
e-mail: beaufortgc@eircom.net
website: www.beaufortgolfclub.com

Céad mile Fáilte

DINGLE GOLF LINKS
CEANN SIBÉAL

Experience the Magic! 6,696 yards, Par 72 Traditional Championship Links. Each hole on this magnificent links is carved from the natural landscape of one of the most unspoiled parts of Europe, with hazards laid down long before the game of golf was dreamt of, including a winding "burn" that twists and turns through the entire course. As you play, the whole panorama of the Dingle Peninsula is revealed - hidden bays with small fishing villages, glorious hills and mountains and the Blasket Islands out in the wild Atlantic. This area abounds in archaeological treasures, wild flora and fauna, arts and crafts and ancient Gaelic culture. The Irish language is still spoken here. Thank you for visiting us !

Dingle Golf Club, Ceann Sibéal, Ballyferriter, Dingle, Co Kerry, Ireland
Tel +353 66 915 62 55 • Fax +353 66 915 64 09
e-mail: dinglegc@iol.ie • www.dinglelinks.com

Europe's most westerly Golf Course

See also Colour Advertisement on page 89

Beaufort
GOLF COURSE
KILLARNEY

18 HOLE PARKLAND CHAMPIONSHIP GOLF COURSE – PAR 71

★ Stone built clubhouse offers a traditional and warm atmosphere
★ Societies, Groups and Visitors welcome 7 days
★ Electric buggies, trolleys, clubs and caddies for hire
★ Golf Professional ★ Golf shop
★ Bar food and snacks all day

Killarney:10km • Kerry Airport: 20km • Cork Airport: 90km

Tel: 00353 64 44440 • Fax: 00353 64 44752
e-mail: beaufortgc@eircom.net
www.beaufortgolfclub.com

CHURCHTOWN • BEAUFORT • KILLARNEY • Co KERRY

KILLARNEY. **Dunloe Golf Club,** Gap of Dunloe, Kilarney (00353 64 44578). *Location:* 10 minutes from Killarney town. Take N72 (main Killarney/Killorglin Road); first left after passing Hotel Europe. Outstanding parkland layout with beautiful views of Killarney's lakes and mountains. 9 holes. Par 34. *Green Fees:* information not available. *Eating facilities:* snack bar from 8am to 9pm (from 10am in winter). Professional: Kieran P. Crehan. *
e-mail: dunloegc@gofree.indigo.ie

KILLARNEY. **Killarney Golf and Fishing Club,** Mahony's Point, Killarney (64 31034; Fax: 64 33065). *Location:* Killarney town, two miles west on Ring of Kerry road. Undulating parkland courses - lakeside. Mahony's Point: 18 holes, 6152 metres. S.S.S. 72. Killeen: 18 holes, 6474 metres. S.S.S. 73. Lackabane Course, 18 holes, 6410 metres. Practice area. *Green Fees:* information on request. *Eating facilities:* available all day. *Visitors:* welcome at all times, reservations in advance, Handicap Certificate required. *Society Meetings:* welcome. Professional: T. Coveney (64 31615). Secretary: T. Prendergast.
e-mail: reservations@killarney-golf.com
website: www.killarney-golf.com

KILLARNEY. **Ross Golf Club,** Ross Road, Killarney (064-31125; Fax: 064-31860). *Location*: from town centre follow signs to Muckross House, take first right on Muckross Road to Ross Castle and Ross Golf Club. Parkland, wooded course. 9 holes, 6450 yards, S.S.S. 73. Practice area and putting green. *Green Fees*: information not available. *Eating facilities*: full bar and snack bar serving soup and sandwiches. *Vistors*: welcome. PGA tuition and accommodation can be arranged. *Society Meetings*: welcome, special rates available. Professional & Secretary: Alan O'Meara (064 31125; Fax: 064 31860). *
e-mail: info@rossgolfclub.com
website: www.rossgolfclub.com

KILLORGLIN. **Killorglin Golf Club,** Stealroe, Killorglin (066 9761979; Fax: 066 9761437). *Location:* just 20 minutes from Killarney and from Kerry Airport, three kilometres from the bridge at Killorglin on N70 road to the county town of Tralee. Parkland course overlooking Dingle Bay. 18 holes, 6464 yards. S.S.S. 71. *Green Fees:* weekdays 30 euros; weekends 35 euros, 9 holes 20 euros. Group rates available on request. *Eating facilities:* bar and restaurant facilities all day. *Visitors:* always welcome, booking necessary at weekends. Accommodation can be arranged; all major credit cards accepted. *Society Meetings:* all welcome, rates on request. Manager: Billy Dodd.
e-mail: kilgolf@iol.ie
website: www.killorglingolf.ie

SNEEM. **Parknasilla Golf Club,** Parknasilla, Sneem (064 45195; Fax: 064 45323). *Location:* on the Ring of Kerry route, two miles east of Sneem Village. Hilly seaside course, wooded. 12 holes, 5284 metres. S.S.S. 67. Practice ground. *Green Fees:* 35 euros; guests staying at the Great Southern Hotel 20 euros. *Eating facilities:* available at Great Southern Hotel, 10 minutes' walk. *Visitors:* welcome, no restrictions. Caddy cars available. *Society Meetings:* contact 064 45195. Secretary/Manager: Maurice Walsh (064 45233).

TRALEE. **The Kerries Golf Club,** Kerries East, Tralee (667 122112; Fax: 667 120085). *Location*: one mile from Tralee town. Parkland, overlooking Tralee Bay. 9 holes. S.S.S. 68. *Green Fees:* information not available. *Eating facilities:* snacks and wine bar. *Visitors:* welcome daily except Sundays 8am-12.30 pm. *Society Meetings:* welcome. Secretary: Helen Barrett.*

TRALEE. **Tralee Golf Club,** West Barrow, Ardfert, Tralee (066 7136379; Fax: 066 7136008). *Location:* Tralee to Barrow via the Spa and Churchill. Seaside links. 18 holes, 6975 yards, S.S.S. 73. *Green Fees:* 160 euros. *Eating facilities:* bar and restaurant. *Visitors:* welcome except Wednesdays of June, July and August. Other months Wednesdays 7.30-10.30pm, Saturdays 10.00am-1.30pm, no visitors on Sundays or Bank Holidays. General Manager: Anthony Byrne.
e-mail: info@traleegolfclub.com
e-mail: reservations@traleegolfclub.com
website: www.traleegolfclub.com

WATERVILLE. **Waterville Golf Links,** Waterville (066 947 4102; Fax: 066 947 4482). *Location:* 55 miles from Killarney and Tralee, halfway round the Ring of Kerry. Links course, established in 1889 - Awards: Golf Monthly Top 5 British Isles, Golf Digest Top 100 World, Golf Digest No.1 Ireland, Golf Magazine - Best International Resorts. 7309 yards. S.S.S. 74. *Green Fees:* (2005) 150 euros pp; early/late 105 euros pp. (2006 rates on request). *Eating facilities:* bar and restaurant facilities available. *Visitors:* welcome every day. *Society Meetings:* welcome every day. Carts and caddies available on request. Secretary/ Manager: Noel Cronin (066 947 4102; Fax: 066 947 4482).
e-mail: wvgolf@iol.ie
website: www.watervillegolflinks.ie

THE APPEARANCE OF AN ASTERISK (*) AT THE END OF A CLUB OR COURSE ENTRY INDICATES THAT UP-TO-DATE INFORMATION HAS NOT BEEN SUPPLIED

FHG
please mention THE GOLF GUIDE when you enquire about clubs or accommodation

KUPERARD

KILLARNEY
Golf & Fishing Club
Mahony's Point, Killarney, Co. Kerry

Ireland's Golfing Mecca
for over 100 years.
3 Magnificent Lakeside Courses.
For Reservations
Phone: 00 353 64 31034
Fax: 00 353 64 33065
e-mail: reservations@killarney-golf.com
www.killarney-golf.com

Individual & Group rates available on request

See also Colour Advertisement on page 89

Darby O'Gills
❖ Country House Hotel ❖
Lissivigeen, Mallow Road, Killarney, Co Kerry, Ireland

Traditional Irish food with full à la carte menu, extensive wine list and 2 licensed bars. Evening music and live session throughout the weekends. Information on all golf courses within the area. Tour arrangements and collections organised. Conveniently located for Cork and Kerry courses. Tea/coffee, direct dial telephones, colour television, all rooms en suite.

Tel: 064 34168/30016 • Fax: 064 36794
e-mail: darbyogill@eircom.net • www.darbyogillskillarney.com

See also Colour Advertisement on page 89

Waterville Golf Links, Waterville, Co Kerry
Tel: 066-9474102
Fax: 066-9474482
wvgolf@iol.ie
www.watervillegolflinks.ie

Location: 55 miles from Killarney and Tralee, half way round the Ring of Kerry. Links Course established in 1889.
Awards: Golf Monthly Top 5 British Isles, Golf Digest Top 100 World, Golf Digest No.1 Ireland, Golf Magazine - Best International Resorts.
7309 yards - SSS 74. Green Fees 2006: 150 euros per person. Early/Late Green Fees: 105 euros per person. Visitors welcome every day. Bar and Restaurant facilities available, carts and caddies available on request. Secretary/Manager: Noel Cronin.

Heaven Sent

WATERVILLE
Golf Links

See also Colour Advertisement on page 89

FHG
Visit the KUPERARD website
www.holidayguides.com
for details of the wide choice of accommodation featured in the full range of FHG titles

COUNTY KILDARE

CARBURY. **Highfield Golf Course,** Carbury (Tel & Fax: 046 9731021). *Location*: 10km from N4, nearest major town is Edenderry. Flat parkland course set in quiet countryside. 18 holes, 6292 yards, 5720 metres, S.S.S. 70. Open air driving range, pitch and putt green, bunkers. *Green Fees*:information not available. *Eating facilities*: full bar and restaurant. *Visitors*: welcome, not before noon on Sundays. Tuition available. *Society Meetings*: welcome. Secretary: Damien Cullen.*
e-mail: highfieldgolf@eircom.ie
website: www.highfield-golf.ie

CURRAGH. **The Curragh Golf Club,** Curragh, Newbridge (045 441238; Fax: 045 442476). *Location:* three miles south of Newbridge. Hilly parkland course. 18 holes, 6035 metres. S.S.S. 71. Practice ground. *Green Fees:* information not available. *Eating facilities:* bar and restaurant. *Visitors:* restricted, please check in advance for course availability. *Society Meetings:* by appointment. Professional: Gerry Burke (045 441896). Secretary: Ann Culleton (045 441714; Fax: 045 442476).*
e-mail: curraghgolf@eircom.net

DONADEA. **Knockanally Golf and Country Club,** Donadea, North Kildare (Tel & Fax: 045 869322). *Location:* three miles off N4 between Enfield and Kilcock. Parkland, home of the Irish International Professional Championship. 18 holes, 6495 yards. S.S.S. 72. *Green Fees:* weekdays 35.00 euros, weekends 45.00 euros. *Eating facilities:* bar and restaurant. *Visitors:* welcome, no restrictions. *Society Meetings:* by arrangement. Professional: Martin Darcy (045 869322). Secretary: Noel A. Lyons (045 869322).*

KILKEA. **Kilkea Castle Hotel & Golf Club,** Kilkea, Castledermot (00353 503 45555). *Location:* southbound on N7, onto M9, then N78 to Athy. Before entering Athy look for Ford garage on right. Kilkea is signposted on the left. 18 holes. Par 70. *Green Fees:* information not available. *Eating facilities:* available all day. Award-winning restaurant.*
e-mail: kilkeagolf@eircom.net

KILL. **Killeen Golf Club,** Kill (045 86603; Fax: 045 875881). *Location:* South from Dublin on N7, turn right at Kill village. Parkland course with abundant wildlife. 18 holes, 6732 yards. S.S.S. 72. *Green Fees:* please call for information. *Eating facilities:* restaurant and bar. *Visitors:* welcome. *Society Meetings:* welcome. For bookings contact Manager: Maurice Kelly.*
e-mail: admin@killeengc.ie
website: www.killeengolf.com

NAAS. **Craddockstown Golf Club,** Blessington Road, Naas (045 897610; Fax: 045 896968). *Location:* off the southbound N7 turn left before Naas and take Blessington road, club one mile on right. Parkland and easy walking, built 1994 with sand-based greens and ample challenges to the best of golfers. 18 holes, 6200 yards, 5645 metres. S.S.S. 69. Practice area. *Green Fees:* information not available. *Eating facilities:* full catering service available. *Visitors:* weekdays with restrictions at weekend and Bank Holidays. *Society Meetings*: welcome. Contact club office.*

NAAS. **Naas Golf Club,** Kerdiffstown, Naas (045 897509; Fax: 045 896109). *Location:* turn left at traffic lights on N7 from Dublin and on right, one-and-a-half miles up that road. Parkland. 18 holes,6232 yards. S.S.S. 69. Practice ground. Public driving range within 200 metres. *Green Fees:* information not available. *Eating facilities:* 10.30am-11.00pm. *Visitors*: welcome on Mondays, Wednesdays, Fridays and Saturday afternoons. Contact club in advance. Dress code applies. *Society Meetings*: contact club office to book. Manager: John Coughlan (045 874644).*

NAAS. **Woodlands Golf Club,** Coill Dubh, Cooleragh (045 860777; Fax: 045 860988). *Location:* From Naas, main Road to Sallins on to Clane village, left onto prosperous village, on to public house (Dagwelds) then turn right one mile ahead. Parkland, wooded with seven lakes. 18 holes. Putting green plus 9 hole pitch & putt course. *Green Fees:* information not available. *Visitors:* welcome except Saturday pm and Sunday am. Always phone in advance. *Society Meetings:* always welcome, rates depend on number playing. Secretary: Criostoir MacBradaigh (01-6298013; Fax: 01-6298041).*
e-mail: woodlandsgolf@eircom.net

The Straffan Court Hotel

- 43 en suite bedrooms, including family rooms (some wheelchair accessible).
- Oscar's Restaurant – renowned for its exquisite cuisine and excellent value.
- Live entertainment • Conference and Wedding facilities • Free car parking
- Complimentary Courtesy Bus to bring you to and from the hotel.

Quality Accommodation, tranquil setting, fine cuisine and friendly staff.
Straffan Court Hotel, Straffan Road, Maynooth, Co. Kildare
Tel: +353 (0) 1 6285002 • Fax: +353 (0) 1 6289781 • www.straffancourthotel.com

County Kildare

Nowhere else has so many great courses

Sensational golf courses, legendary race courses and delicious main courses, historic buildings and gardens, breathtaking scenery and the warmest of Irish welcomes.

Welcome to County Kildare.

FOR FURTHER INFORMATION
County Kildare Fáilte
38 South Main Street, Naas,
County Kildare, Ireland

Tel: + 353 45 898888,
Fax: + 353 45 898887,
Email: info@rydercupcounty.com
www.visitkildare.ie
www.rydercupcounty.com

The Ryder Cup County

Check out the County Kildare Quality Golf Passport at www.rydercupcounty.com

REPUBLIC OF IRELAND

SALLINS. **Bodenstown Golf Club,** Sallins (045 897096). *Location:* Naas dual carriageway, turn right at Kill. 36 holes. S.S.S. 72. Practice green. *Green Fees:* 20 euros. *Eating facilities:* full catering and bar. *Visitors:* welcome, no restrictions. *Society Meetings:* please telephone. Secretary: Bernadette Curtin (045 897096).

STRAFFAN. **Castlewarden Golf and Country Club,** Castlewarden, Straffan (3531 4589254; Fax: 3531 4588972). *Location:* on the N7 Dublin to Naas road, take the second right after Blackchurch Inn. Parkland. 18 holes, 6690 yards. S.S.S. 71. Practice area and putting green. *Green Fees:* information not available. *Eating facilities:* full catering and bar. *Visitors:* welcome, booking advisable. *Society Meetings:* welcome. Professional: Brian O'Brien (3531 4588219). Secretary: Fiona Kane (3531 4589838).*
e-mail: castlewarden@clubi.ie
website: www.castlewardengolfclub.com

STRAFFAN. **The K Club,** Straffan, Co. Kildare (6017300; Fax: 6017399). *Location:* N7 south of Dublin to Kill, turn right, five miles from Junction. Signposted. Parkland course with trees, lakes, River Liffey – absolute Championship course. 18 holes, 7178 yards. S.S.S.76. Driving range. *Green Fees:* information not available. *Eating facilities:* Legends Restaurant and Bar, The Arnold Palmer Room, Snack Bar and Members' Restaurant. *Visitors:* members' hours Winter 11am to 1pm; Summer 1.30pm to 3.30pm weekdays. Golf shop, trolleys, clubs and shoe hire. The Kildare Hotel (within complex) AA 5 Red Star; 69 bedrooms. Professional: John McHenry (6017321; Fax: 6017399). Director of Golf: Paul Crowe.*
e-mail: golf@kclub.ie
website: www.kclub.ie

FHG Guides 2006

October Edition

- Recommended COUNTRY HOTELS
- Recommended COUNTRY INNS & PUBS
- BED & BREAKFAST STOPS • CHILDREN WELCOME!
- The Original FHG Guide to COAST & COUNTRY HOLIDAYS
- CARAVAN & CAMPING HOLIDAYS, England, Scotland, Wales & Ireland
- BRITAIN'S BEST HOLIDAYS
- THE GOLF GUIDE Where to Play / Where to Stay
- PETS WELCOME!
- Recommended SHORT BREAK HOLIDAYS in Britain
- SELF CATERING HOLIDAYS in Britain

April Edition

Available from bookshops or larger newsagents

FHG Guides LTD
Abbey Mill Business Centre,
Seedhill, Paisley PA1 1TJ
www.holidayguides.com

www.uk-golfguide.com

The finest club in Ireland

At the K Club we pride ourselves on the style and comfort we afford our guests. Nestled amid lush green woodlands, just 17 miles from Dublin, The K Club is the most rewarding place to stay. Already acclaimed as one of the finest in the world, this magnificent 5 star Hotel offers you the highest standards of accommodation and service, without losing the elegance and unique charm of an Irish country house.

For incredible relaxation, guests can enjoy our extensive facilities including the K Spa, where with its mix of the very best treatments from around the world you can be lavishly pampered. Or indulge in any of the quality leisure activities available including our two championship golf courses, both designed by Arnold Palmer.

Be it for business or pleasure, at The K Club you can expect the warmest of welcomes in the most luxurious of surroundings.

For further information and reservations:
Hotel Tel: 353 (0)1 601 7200 Fax: 353 (0)1 601 7299
Golf Tel: 353 (0)1 601 7300 Fax: (0)1601 7399
e-mail: golf@kclub.ie e-mail: sales@kclub.ie
The K Club, Straffan, Co. Kildare, Ireland.
Home of The European Open and The Ryder Cup 2006

COUNTY KILKENNY

CALLAN. **Callan Golf Club,** Geraldine, Callan (056 25136/25949; Fax: 056 55155). *Location:* One mile from Callan on the Knocktopher Road. Parkland course with many water features. 18 holes, 6400 yards. S.S.S. 70. Practice area. *Green Fees*: 25 euros weekdays; 30 euros Saturday and Sunday. *Eating facilities*: food available all day, bar. *Visitors*: welcome – best to check with Golf Shop in advance. *Society Meetings*: all welcome. Secretary/Manager: Liam Duggan (056 25136)
e-mail: info@callangolfclub.com
website: www.callangolfclub.com

CASTLECOMER. **Castlecomer Golf Club,** Drumgoole, Castlecomer (00 353 564441575; Fax: 00 353 564441139). *Location*: Main Castlecomer to Kilkenny Road. Parkland course beside the River Deen. 18 holes, 6175 metres. S.S.S. 72. Par 72. Practice ground. *Green Fees*: weekdays 35 euros, weekends 40 euros. *Eating facilities*: catering available. *Visitors*: always welcome. *Society Meetings*: welcome, society and group rates available. Secretary: Matt Dooley (00 353 567 727480).
e-mail: castlecomergolf@eircom.net
website: www.castlecomergolf.com

GOWRAN. **Gowran Park,** Gowran (056 7726699; Fax: 056 7726173). *Location*: on main Waterford–Dublin road (N9), half a mile on the Waterford side of Gowran. Parkland, part of old Annally Estate, with woodland and lakes. 18 holes, 6100 metres. S.S.S. 72 (Blue), 70 (White), 68 (Green). Putting green, practice range. *Green Fees:* 40 euros weekdays, 50 euros weekends. *Eating facilities:* full catering available. *Visitors*: welcome daily (some restrictions at weekends). *Society Meetings:* welcome daily. Rates 35-45 euros for groups of 20+. Secretary: Michael O'Sullivan.
e-mail: gowranpk@eircom.net

KILKENNY. **Kilkenny Golf Club,** Glendine, Kilkenny (056 7765400; Fax: 056 7723593). *Location:* off Castlecomer Road two kilometres from centre of city. Parkland. 18 holes, 5133 metres. S.S.S. 71. Practice area. *Green Fees:* weekdays 35 euros, weekends 40 euros. *Eating facilities*: available. *Visitors*: welcome, weekends by arrangement. *Society Meetings*: welcome, by arrangement. Professional: Jimmy Bolger (056 7761730). Secretary: Anne O'Neill (056 7765400).
e-mail: enquiries@kilkennygolfclub.com

THOMASTOWN. **Mount Juliet Golf Club,** Thomastown (056 7773064; Fax: 056 7773078). *Location:* Thomastown - on main Dublin to Waterford Road. Parkland, designed by Jack Nicklaus, home of the 1993-95 Irish Open. Home of the American Express World Golf Championship 2002 won by Tiger Woods and in 2004 won by Ernie Els. Voted Golf Course of the Year 2003. 18 holes, 7260 yards. S.S.S. 75, 73, 72. Golf academy and driving range, also Europe's first 18 hole putting course with a par of 53. *Green Fees:* 70 - 155 euros. *Eating facilities:* hotel, spike bar, President's bar, two restaurants. *Visitors:* welcome, no restrictions but please book in advance. Handicap Cards preferred. 59 bedroom de luxe Hotel. *Society Meetings:* please book in advance. Professional: Sean Cotter.

COUNTY LAOIS

ABBEYLEIX. **Abbeyleix Golf Club,** Rathmoyle, Abbeyleix (0502 31450; Fax: 0502 30108). *Location*: quarter mile outside town of Abbeyleix on Ballyroan Road. Parkland course with many water features. Practice chipping and putting green. 18 holes, 6020 yards. S.S.S. 70. *Green Fees*: weekdays 20 euros, weekends 30 euros. *Eating facilities*: bar/restaurant (by arrangement). *Visitors*: welcome weekdays, weekends after 5pm. Secretary: Malady Fogarty (0502 31546).
website: www.abbeyleixgolfclub.com

Gowran Park
Gowran, Co Kilkenny

A wonderful Jeff Howes-designed golf course set in traditional parkland of the old Annally Estate. Only 1½ hours from Dublin, this Par 71, 18-hole course provides an exciting playing experience for golfers of all abilities. Our newly developed clubhouse, with stunning views of the course, offers full restaurant and bar facilities in a relaxed atmosphere. The Golf Shop offers an excellent product range. We guarantee a warm welcome to visitors, societies and corporate groups. For full details contact Michael O'Sullivan, Secretary/Manager.

Tel: 056 77 26699 Fax: 056 77 26173
E-mail: gowranpk@eircom.net
www.gowranpark.ie

MOUNTRATH. **Mountrath Golf Club,** Knockanina, Mountrath (0502 32558 (Public) or 0502 32643 (Office) or Fax: 0502 56735). *Location:* one kilometre off Dublin/Limerick Road, turn left outside Mountrath, signposted. Undulating parkland course with river flowing through it. 18 holes, 5643 metres. S.S.S. 69. Putting green, chipping green and practice area. *Green Fees:* weekdays 20 euros, weekends 30 euros. *Eating facilities:* available everyday and by arrangement. Bar everyday. *Visitors:* welcome weekdays, and weekends after 4pm, phone beforehand. *Society Meetings:* welcome, contact office. Secretary: Dinah Kingsley.

PORTLAOISE. **The Heath Golf Club,** The Heath, Portlaoise (0502 46045; Fax: 0502 46866). *Location:* three-and-a-half miles northeast of Portlaoise, off main Dublin road. Relatively flat with furze, gorse and three lakes. 18 holes, 5736 metres. S.S.S. 71. 10 bay all-weather floodlit driving range and practice area. *Green Fees:* weekdays 18 euros, weekends 34 euros. *Eating facilities:* full bar and catering facilities available. *Visitors:* welcome at all times but advance booking required for weekends and Public Holidays. *Society Meetings:* welcome by prior arrangement. Professional: Mark O'Boyle.

PORTLAOISE. **Rathdowney Golf Club,** Rathdowney, Portlaoise (0505 46170 or Tel & Fax: 0505 46065 office). *Location*: half a mile from Rathdowney, signposted from the square. Parkland course with gentle sloping hills; good test for most golfers (second 9 holes opened June 1997). 18 holes, 5894 metres, S.S.S. 70, Par 71. *Green Fees*: weekdays 20 euros; weekends and Public Holidays 25 euros. *Eating facilities*: bar open daily (afternoon), catering by prior arrangement. *Visitors:* welcome any time during the week, Sundays after 4.30pm, Saturday mornings reserved for societies. *Society Meetings:* welcome by appointment through Hon. Secretary. Hon. Secretary: Sean Bolger. website: www.rathdowneygolf.com

www.uk-golfguide.com

COUNTY LEITRIM

BALLINAMORE. **Ballinamore Golf Club,** Ballinamore (00353 7 196 44346). *Location:* one-and-a-half miles north-west of town alongside Shannon/Erne waterway. Parkland. 9 holes, 6142 yards, 5514 metres. S.S.S.68. *Green Fees:* information not available *Eating facilities:* bar with snacks. *Visitors:* welcome with some restrictions on certain weekends. *Society Meetings:* welcome with restrictions on certain weekends. Captain: Joey Smith (2005) (00353 7196 44008). Hon. Secretary: Padraig Reynolds (2005) (00353 7196 31410).*

COUNTY LIMERICK

ABBEYFEALE. **Abbeyfeale Golf Club,** Dromtrasna Collins, Abbeyfeale (068 32033). *Location*: two miles from Abbeyfeale. Parkland. 9 holes, 4072 yards. S.S.S. 64. 20 bay indoor driving range, practice putting green. *Green Fees*: information not available. *Eating facilities*: by appointment. *Visitors*: welcome everyday. *Society Meetings*: societies/companies/ groups always welcome. Professional: (068 32033). Hon. Secretary: Conleth Dillon (068 31454). e-mail: abbeyfealegolf@eircom.net

ADARE. **Adare Manor Golf Club,** Adare (353 61 396204; Fax: 353 61 396800). *Location*: main Limerick to Killarney road, 10 miles from Limerick. Parkland course. 18 holes, 5764 yards. S.S.S. 69. Putting green, chipping area. *Green Fees*: 35 euros. *Eating facilities*: full bar and restaurant. *Visitors*: welcome all year round. Check with club for times at weekends. *Society Meetings*: societies welcome all year round. 20 euros per person for groups of 20 plus; 25 euros per person for groups of 11-19; 27.50 euros per person for 8-20; 15 euros for members. Hon. Secretary: Pat O' Brien (353 61 396204; Fax: 353 61 396800). e-mail: info@adaremanorgolfclub.com website: www.adaremanorgolfclub.com

---

Located in the picturesque village of Adare, the 4-Star Dunraven Arms Hotel offers the ambience of a country house, along with first-class service and friendly, efficient staff.
• *86 rooms incl. 24 Junior Suites and 6 Executive Suites, with antique furniture, four-poster bed, and separate dressing room and bathroom.*
• *Leisure Centre with 17m pool, steam room, gym, and massage and beauty therapy rooms.*
• *30 minutes from Shannon Airport.*
• *Two 18-hole courses in Adare incl. Adare Manor. Other courses nearby incl. Ballybunion, Lahinch, Doonbeg, Old Head and Tralee.*

The Dunraven Arms Hotel, Adare, Co Limerick
00353 61 396633 • Fax: 00353 61 396541
e-mail: reservations@dunravenhotel.com • www.dunravenhotel.com

ARDAGH. **Newcastle West Golf Club,** Ardagh (00-353-6976500; Fax: 00-353-6976511). *Location:* Off N21 roadway linking Shannon, Limerick and Killarney beyond Rathkeale. Parkland course. 18 holes, 6400 yards. S.S.S. 72. Flood-lit driving bays, practice green and bunker. *Green Fees:* information not available. *Eating facilities:* Bar and restaurant. *Visitors:* welcome except Sundays. *Society Meetings:* welcome - green fee reductions. Professional: Tom Murphy (Tel & Fax: 00-353-6976500) Secretary: Paddy Lyons (Tel & Fax: 00-353-6976500). *

BALLYNEETY. **Limerick County Golf and Country Club,** Ballyneety (061 351881; Fax: 061 351384). *Location:* five miles from Limerick City, R512 direction of Lough Gur/Kilmallock. Championship standard, parkland course with water hazards bordering 8 holes. 18 holes, 5876 metres. S.S.S. 71. Driving range, putting greens, 3 hole short game area, golf school with professional tuition. *Green Fees:* midweek 40 euros, weekend 60 euros. *Eating facilities:* excellent restaurant serving international cuisine, light snacks, lunch and dinner menus, full bar service. *Visitors:* always welcome, telephone in advance to assure tee space. Play and Stay packages available. *Society Meetings:* welcome. Professional: Donal McSweeney (061 351881). Manager: Gerry McKeon (061 351881; Fax: 061 351384).
e-mail: lcgolf@iol.ie
website: www.limerickcounty.com

CASTLETROY. **Castletroy Golf Club,** Castletroy (061 335261; Fax: 061 335373). *Location:* three miles from Limerick City on N7 (Dublin Road). Parkland with numerous trees. 18 holes, 5854 metres. S.S.S. 70. *Green Fees:* information not available. *Eating facilities:* full catering service, bar. *Visitors:* welcome all week. Tuesday is Ladies' Day - advisable to phone. Golf Shop (061 330450). *Society Meetings:* welcome Mondays, Wednesdays and Fridays, group rates available. Golf Shop: (061 330450). Secretary: Laurence Hayes (061 335753; Fax: 061 335373). General Manager: Patrick Keane.*

LIMERICK. **Limerick Golf Club,** Ballyclough, Limerick (061 414083; Fax: 061 319219). *Location*: five km from Limerick city on Fedamore Road. Parkland. 18 holes, 5932 metres. S.S.S. 71. *Green Fees:* information not provided. *Eating facilities:* full bar and dining facilities. *Visitors*: welcome Mondays, Wednesdays, Thursdays, Fridays up to 4pm. *Society Meetings*: advance booking required. Professional: Lee Harrington (061 412492). General Manager: Pat Murray (061 415146).

NEWCASTLE WEST. **Killeline Golf Club,** Newcastle West (069 61600; Fax: 069 77428). *Location:* quarter-of-a-mile off the main Limerick to Kerry road on Drumcollier road. Flat parkland. 18 holes, 7000 metres. S.S.S. 72. *Green Fees:* 35 euros weekdays, 40 euros weekends. *Eating facilities:* two bars and restaurant. *Visitors:* welcome. *Society Meetings:* welcome. Leisure facilities include swimming pool, sauna, gymnasium. 32 bedroom lodge. Secretary: Paul O'Toole. Director of Golf: Kevin Dorrian.

COUNTY LONGFORD

LONGFORD. **County Longford Golf Club,** Glack, Dublin Road, Longford (043 46310; Fax: 043 47082). *Location:* one mile from centre of town on Dublin road. 18 holes, 5766 metres. S.S.S. 71. *Green Fees:* midweek 25 euros, weekends and Bank Holidays 30 euros. *Eating facilities:* full catering and bar. *Visitors:* welcome at all times subject to availability. Buggies and carts available. *Society Meetings:* all welcome. Secretary: Mark Glancy.
e-mail: colonggolf@eircom.net

COUNTY LOUTH

ARDEE. **Ardee Golf Club,** Townparks, Ardee (041 6853227; Fax: 041 6856137). Parkland, wooded course with beautiful mature trees. 18 holes, 6348 yards, S.S.S. 71. Large practice area. *Green Fees:* information not available. *Eating facilities:* restaurant and bar. *Visitors:* welcome weekdays except Wednesdays, weekends by appointment only. Carts for hire, caddies by arrangement. *Society Meetings:* welcome Mondays to Saturdays. Professional: Scott Kirkpatrick (041 6857472). Hon Secretary: B. Healy. Secretary/ Manager: M.P. Conoulty (041 6853227; Fax: 041 6856137).*

DROGHEDA. **County Louth Golf Club,** Baltray, Drogheda (041 9881530; Fax: 041 9881531). *Location:* Drogheda, five miles north east. Championship links course. 18 holes, 7035 yards. S.S.S. 74. *Green Fees:* weekdays 120 euros; weekends 140 euros. *Eating facilities:* restaurant, coffee shop and bar. *Visitors:* welcome weekdays except Tuesdays on application, weekends restricted. Residential accommodation available for 20 persons. *Society Meetings:* on application. Professional: Paddy McGuirk (041 9881536). Secretary: Michael Delany (041 9881530; Fax: 041 9881531).

DROGHEDA. **Seapoint Golf Club,** Termonfeckin, Drogheda (041 982333; Fax: 041 982331). *Location:* Dublin–Belfast–Drogheda to Termonfeckin Road. Links course. 18 holes, 6339 metres. S.S.S. 74. Practice range and putting green. *Green Fees:* information not available. *Eating facilities:* restaurant and bar. *Visitors:* welcome at all times; members' tee times 1-2pm daily and up to 10.30am weekends. *Society Meetings:* welcome, discounts available. Trolleys and caddies available. Professional: David Carroll. Secretary: Kevin Carrie.*
e-mail: info@seapointgolfclub.com
website: www.seapointgolfclub.com

THE APPEARANCE OF AN ASTERISK (*) AT THE END OF A CLUB OR COURSE ENTRY INDICATES THAT UP-TO-DATE INFORMATION HAS NOT BEEN SUPPLIED

DUNDALK. **Dundalk Golf Club,** Blackrock, Dundalk (042 9321731; Fax: 042 9322022). *Location:* Dundalk coast road to Blackrock, two miles. Championship parkland course with tree-lined fairways. Hosted All Ireland Finals in 1997 and 2000. Attracts country's top players to Senior Scratch Cup. Hosts major PGA Pro-Am and Ladies' Home Internationals. Celebrates Centenary in 2005. 18 holes, 6776 yards, 6160 metres. S.S.S. 72 (Par 72). Six acre field practice ground. *Green Fees:* information not provided. *Eating facilities:* full restaurant and bar. *Visitors:* welcome Mondays, Wednesdays, Thursdays and Fridays, restrictions weekends and Tuesday Ladies' Day. *Society Meetings:* welcome by appointment. Professional: Leslie Walker (042 9322102). Secretary/Manager: Terry Sloane (042 9321731; Fax: 042 9322022).
e-mail: manager@dundalkgolfclub.ie
website: www.dundalkgolfclub.ie

GREENORE. **Greenore Golf Club,** Greenore (042 93 73212/73678; Fax: 042 9383898). *Location:* Dundalk/ Newry, Dundalk 15 miles, Newry 12 miles. Flat semi-links course with heathland features, pine trees, rivers, ponds – very scenic, Carlingford Mountains and Mountains of Mourne. 18 holes, 6647 yards. S.S.S. 73. *Green Fees:* weekdays 35 euros; weekends and Bank Holidays 50 euros; subject to review. *Eating facilities:* full catering and bar facilities (daylight hours). *Visitors:* always welcome, prior booking advisable. Caddies on request, trolley and golf buggy available for hire. *Society Meetings:* very welcome by prior arrangement. Professional: Robert Giles. Secretary: Linda Clarke (042 9373678).
e-mail: greenoregolfclub@eircom.net
website: www.greenoregolf.com

KILLIN. **Killin Park Golf & Country Club,** Killin, Dundalk (00353 42 9339303). *Location:* two miles west of Dundalk. Undulating parkland with mature trees. The 4th and 6th holes are surrounded by the Castletown River. 18 holes. Par 69. *Green Fees:* information not available. *Eating facilities:* available from dawn till dusk.*

COUNTY MAYO

ACHILL. **Achill Golf Club,** Keel, Achill Island (098 43456). *Location:* N59 from Westport and R319 from Mulranny to Achill. Flat seaside links in scenic setting. 9 holes, 2947 yards, 2689 metres. S.S.S. 67. *Green Fees:* information not provided. *Visitors:* welcome at all times, no restrictions. *Society Meetings:* by prior arrangement. Secretary: Sean P. Connolly.

BALLINA. **Ballina Golf Club,** Mossgrove, Shanaghy, Ballina (Tel & Fax: 096 21050). *Location:* on Bonniconlon Road. Parkland course. 18 holes, 6103 yards. S.S.S. 69. *Green Fees:* information not provided. *Eating facilities:* bar, snacks. *Visitors:* welcome every day, Sundays 11am to 1.30pm. *Society Meetings:* weekdays to 4pm, Saturdays 10am to 12 noon, Sundays 11am to 1.30pm. Secretary: Padhraig Connolly (096 21050; Fax: 096 2178).
e-mail: ballinagc@eircom.net
website: www.ballinagolfclub.com

BALLINROBE. **Ballinrobe Golf Club,** Cloonacastle, Ballinrobe (09495 41118; Fax: 09495 41889). *Location:* off N84 at Ballinrobe onto the R331 to Claremorris. Parkland course with trees and man-made lakes. 18 holes, 6354 metres. S.S.S. 73. Practice ground, driving range. *Green Fees:* information not available. *Eating facilities:* catering and bar facilities. *Visitors:* welcome at all times but is advisable to book tee times in advance. Buggies and carts available. Excellent fishing. *Society Meetings:* welcome by arrangement. Secretary/ Manager: John McMahon.*
website: www.ballinrobegolfclub.com
http:// www.iol.ie

Please mention
THE GOLF GUIDE
when you enquire about clubs or accommodation

Seapoint Golf Club
Termonfeckin, Drogheda, Co. Louth
Tel: +353 (0)41 9822333 • Fax: +353 (0)41 9822331
e-mail: info@seapointgolfclub.com
www.seapointgolfclub.com
Voted into Ireland's Top 25 Golf Courses 2003/4

Opened in 1993, Seapoint Golf Club lies by the mouth of the River Boyne, near the historic town of Drogheda which is just under one hour from Dublin.
The 260-acre course is designed to accommodate all standards of golfer – our aim is that you enjoy the challenge. Being a links course, it is playable all year. Mature trees border the course on the west, with water hazards coming into play on six of the first nine holes, and the closing holes have magnificent views of the Mountains of Mourne and the Irish Sea.
Secretary: Kevin Carrie • Professional: David Carroll

For full details of clubs and courses, plus convenient accommodation
www.uk-golfguide.com

REPUBLIC OF IRELAND

BELMULLET. **Carne Golf Links,** Belmullet (097 82292; Fax: 097 81477) *Location:* on N59 three km from centre of Belmullet town. Pure links course - feature holes 9th, 14th and 18th. 18 holes, 6119 metres. Medal S.S.S 72; Championship. S.S.S 72, Par 72. Practice ground and putting green. *Green Fees:* 55 euros per day weekdays; 55 euros per round weekends and Bank Holidays. *Eating facilities:* full restaurant and bar facilities. *Visitors:* very welcome at all times. Buggies and caddies available. *Society Meetings:* by arrangement. Secretary/Manager: James O'Hara (097 82292; Fax: 097 81477).
e-mail: carngolf@iol.ie
website: www.carnegolflinks.com

CASTLEBAR. **Castlebar Golf Club,** Rocklands, Castlebar (353 94 21649; Fax: 353 94 26088). *Location*: situated on the Galway road out of town. Championship, parkland course with abundance of water and trees. 18 holes, 6500 yards, S.S.S. 70. *Green Fees*: information not available. *Eating facilities*: full catering facilities. *Visitors*: welcome every day, except Sunday before 1.30pm. *Society Meetings*: welcome every day except Sunday. Secretary: Jim McGovern (353 87 2267936).

CLAREMORRIS. **Claremorris Golf Club,** Claremorris (094 9371527). *Location:* on N17, Galway 35 miles, Claremorris two miles, Knock airport 20 miles. Parkland/wooded course designed by Tom Craddock; numerous water hazards and excellent sand-based greens. 18 holes, 7000 yards. S.S.S. 72. Practice ground. *Green Fees:* weekdays 32 euros, weekends 40 euros. *Visitors:* welcome weekdays, weekends on request. *Society Meetings:* welcome, booking required. Admin Manager: Christina Rush (087 6441204)
e-mail: info@claremorrisgolfclub.com
website: www.claremorrisgolfclub.ie

SWINFORD. **Swinford Golf Club,** Brabazon Park, Swinford (094 92 51378). *Location:* on Kiltimagh Road beside Swinford town. Parkland. 9 holes, S.S.S. 68. Practice green and pitching area. *Green Fees:* 15 euros. *Eating facilities:* bar with catering by arrangement. *Visitors:* welcome with some restrictions. *Society Meetings:* Golf societies welcome, prices on application. Secretary: Tom Regan (087 291 3067).
e-mail: regantommy@eircom.net

WESTPORT. **Westport Golf Club,** Carrowholly, Westport (098 28262/27070; Fax: 098 27217). Parkland championship course. 18 holes. Practice area, 9 bay floodlit driving range. *Green Fees:* information not available. *Eating facilities:* bar and restaurant. *Visitors:* welcome with restrictions. *Society Meetings:* welcome. Professional: Alex Mealia. Club Administrator: Margaret Walsh. Secretary: Lorna Mathastein. Manager: Paul O'Neil.
e-mail: wpgolf@eircom.net

FHG

Other specialised
FHG Guides

Published annually: available in all good bookshops or direct from the publisher.

Recommended **COUNTRY INNS & PUBS** OF BRITAIN £7.99

Recommended **COUNTRY HOTELS** OF BRITAIN £7.99

Recommended **SHORT BREAK HOLIDAYS** IN BRITAIN £7.99

The bestselling **PETS WELCOME!** £8.99

FHG Guides • Abbey Mill Business Centre, Seedhill, Paisley, Renfrewshire PA1 1TJ
Tel: 0141-887 0428 • Fax: 0141-889 7204
e-mail: admin@fhguides.co.uk
www.holidayguides.com

PLEASE MENTION THE GOLF GUIDE WHEN YOU WRITE OR PHONE TO ENQUIRE ABOUT CLUBS OR ACCOMMODATION

Marriott
JOHNSTOWN HOUSE HOTEL & SPA ENFIELD

Set on 120 acres of stunning parkland landscape, along with its own riverside walks, this 126 bedroom luxury four star hotel is developed around a magnificent 1750s Georgian rural residence.

Located on the main Dublin to Galway Road, just 40 minutes from Dublin Airport and 45 minutes from Dublin City Centre.

Relax and enjoy a choice of dining experiences – Pavilion Restaurant, Atrium Brasserie and Coach House Bar with live music every Saturday night. Unwind after a game of golf in our 30,000 sq ft Spa and leisure facility.

Golf, fishing, horseracing and shopping are all located nearby. A courtesy car is available for free booking in the immediate locality and at reduced rates for airport transfers.

Special offers of 2 nights Bed & Breakfast and 1 Evening Meal from €150 pps.

Golf Escape – Carton House resident rates available on request

Special Group Rates available on request.

**Marriott Johnstown House Hotel & Spa
Enfield, Co. Meath
Ireland
Tel: 046 9540000**
e-mail: reservations@johnstownhouse.com
www.marriottjohnstownhouse.com

COUNTY MEATH

ASHBOURNE. **Ashbourne Golf Club**, Archerstown, Ashbourne (00 353 (0)1835 2005 or 2562). *Location:* 12 miles from Dublin, on the road to Derry. Parkland course to USGA standards. 18 holes. Par 71. *Green Fees:* information not available. *Eating facilities:* from 10am to 11pm (noon to 4pm during winter). Professional: John Dwyer.*
e-mail: ashgc@iol.ie
website: www.ashgc@iol.ie

BETTYSTOWN. **Laytown and Bettystown Golf Club**, Bettystown, Drogheda. *Location:* 25 miles north of Dublin. A traditional links golf course, a good test for any golfer, excellent conditions. 18 holes, 5697 metres. S.S.S. 72. *Green Fees:* Mondays to Thursdays 60 euros; Friday, Saturdays, Sundays 75 euros, subject to review. *Eating facilities:* full bar and catering facilities. *Visitors:* welcome but make reservation. *Society Meetings:* welcome; make reservation. Professional: Robert J. Browne (041 9828793). Secretary: Helen Finnegan (041 9827170; Fax: 041 9828506).

DUNSHAUGHLIN. **Black Bush Golf Club**, Thomastown, Dunshaughlin (01-8250021; Fax: 01-8250400). *Location*: situated on the Navan Road, Dunshaughlin. Lush fairways bordered by mature trees with sand based greens. 27 holes, played in a combination. Course A + B 6849 yards, S.S.S. 72; B + C 6434 yards, S.S.S. 70; C + A 6599 yards, S.S.S. 71. *Green Fees*: weekdays from 30 euros; weekends from 45 euros. *Visitors*: welcome weekdays, limited tee times on Saturday and Sunday, Tuesday is Ladies Day. Tuition available. *Society Meetings:* welcome, 35 euros Monday to Thursday, includes a 6.50 euros meal voucher; Friday 45 euros with meal voucher; and Saturday 50 euros with meal voucher. Professional: Shane O'Grady (01-8250793). Secretary: Michael Connellan.
e-mail: golf@blackbush.iol.ie

KELLS. **Headfort Golf Club**, Kells (046 9240146; Fax: 046 9249282). *Location:* on N3 from Dublin, bypass Navan and half-a-mile from Kells. Parkland. 18 holes x 2, 6007 metres. S.S.S. 71. Practice area. *Green Fees:* weekdays – New Course 60 euros, Old Course 45 euros; weekends – New Course 65 euros, Old Course 50 euros. *Eating facilities:* bar and full catering. *Visitors:* welcome weekdays. *Society Meetings:* welcome by prior arrangement. Professional: Brendan McGovern (Tel. & Fax: 046 9240639). Admin. Secretary: Nora Murphy (046 9282001).

KILCOCK. **Kilcock Golf Club**, Gallow, Kilcock (01 628 7592 / 628 4074). *Location:* off main Dublin to Galway motorway at Kilcock. Parkland with undulating fairways, light rough, and flat greens. Practice area. 18 holes, 5801 metres. S.S.S.71. *Green Fees:* 25 euros weekdays, 32 euros weekends. *Eating facilities:* catering available. *Visitors:* welcome but some restrictions at weekends. *Society Meetings:* welcome but must book. Secretary /Manager: Seamus Kelly.
e-mail: kilcockgolfclub@eircom.net
website: www.kilcockgolfclub.com

NAVAN. **Royal Tara Golf Club**, Bellinter, Navan (+353 46 9025244/9025508/9026868). *Location*: 25 miles north of Dublin off National Primary Route N3 - close to Hill of Tara. Parkland, private course. 27 holes. 18 hole course, 6457 yards, S.S.S. 71. 9 hole course 3184 yards, S.S.S. 35. Practice ground. *Green Fees*: 18 hole course - 35 euros weekdays, 45 euros weekends; 9 hole course - 15 euros weekdays and weekends. *Eating facilities*: full catering facilities all day every day. *Visitors*: welcome, Ladies' Day Tuesdays, please check with club in advance. Carts and caddies on request. *Society Meetings*: welcome except Tuesdays and Sundays. Professional: Mr Adam Whiston (+353 46 902 6009). Hon Secretary: Mr Damian Usher. General Manager: Larry Clarke (+353 46 902 5508; Fax: +353 46 902 6684).
e-mail: info@royaltaragolfclub.com
website: www.royaltaragolfclub.com

COUNTY MONAGHAN

CARRICKMACROSS. **Mannan Castle Golf Club,** Donaghmoyne, Carrickmacross ((42) 9663308). *Location:* 3 miles from Carrickmacross on Crossmaglen Road. Wooded parkland course. 18 holes, 6082 yards. S.S.S. 69. *Green Fees:* information not available. *Eating facilities:* full restaurant in operation. *Visitors:* welcome any day except Sunday before 4.00pm. *Society Meetings:* especially welcome, contact Sheila for details.*
e-mail: mannancastlegc@eircom.net

CARRICKMACROSS. **Nuremore Hotel & Country Club**, Carrickmacross (042 9661438). *Location:* 50 miles north of Dublin on N2. *Green Fees:* weekdays £35.00, weekends £45.00. *Eating facilities:* bar and catering facilities in hotel and clubhouse. *Visitors:* welcome at all times. Opening hours - daylight hours. All hotel facilities. Professional: Maurice Cassidy (042 967368; Fax: 042 9661853).*
e-mail: nuremore@eircom.net
website: www.nuremore-hotel.ie

PLEASE MENTION THIS GUIDE WHEN YOU ENQUIRE ABOUT CLUBS OR ACCOMMODATION

CASTLEBLAYNEY. **Castleblayney Golf Club,** Onomy, Hope Castle Estate, Castleblayney (042 9749485). *Location:* N2 road, Hope Castle Estate, 500 yards from town centre. Scenic parkland course with lakes and forest in centre of Leisure Park. 9 holes, 5345 yards. S.S.S. 66. *Green Fees:* information not available. *Eating facilities:* snacks and bar. *Visitors:* welcome at all times except during major competitions at weekends. Accommodation in Hope Castle Complex. *Society Meetings:* welcome. Secretary: Raymond Kernan (Tel & Fax: 042 9740451).*

CLONES. **Clones Golf Club,** Hilton Demesne, Clones (047 56017). *Location:* three miles from Clones on the Scotshouse Road. Parkland course. 18 holes, 5600 metres. Par 69. S.S.S. - White 69, Yellow 67. Practice area and putting green. *Green Fees:* 25 euros all week or 15 euros with a member. *Eating facilities:* full catering facilities all year round. *Visitors:* welcome at all times, advance booking necessary at weekends. Caddy cars and buggy hire available. *Society Meetings:* welcome. Hon. Secretary: Martin Taylor (049 5552354).
e-mail: clonesgolfclub@eircom.net

MONAGHAN. **Rossmore Golf Club,** Cootehill Road, Monaghan (047 81316). *Location:* 2 km from Monaghan town. Parkland. 18 holes, 5600 metres. S.S.S. 69. *Green Fees*: information not available. *Eating facilities*: available. *Visitors*: always welcome. *Society Meetings*: welcome. Professional: Gareth McShea (047 71222). Secretary: Jimmie McKenna.*

COUNTY OFFALY

BIRR. **Birr Golf Club,** "The Glenns", Birr (0509 20082; Fax: 0509 22155). *Location*: approximately two miles from Birr on the Banagher Road. Parkland/wooded, carved out of natural woodlands, with undulating fairways. The course was originally part of the Estate of the Earl of Rosse, who still lives in Birr Castle. 18 holes, 6317 yards, 5754 metres. S.S.S. 70. Driving range. *Green Fees*: 25.00 euros 7 days a week. *Eating facilities*: available; bar. *Visitors*: always welcome; some restrictions on Sundays only. *Society Meetings:* all welcome. Secretary: Mary O'Gorman.

EDENDERRY. **Edenderry Golf Club,** Kishawanny, Edenderry (0469 731072; Fax: 0469 733911). *Location*: outside Edenderry, quarter of a mile on Dublin Road then turn left after half a mile, on left hand side. Wooded course. 18 holes, S.S.S. 72. *Green Fees:* weekdays 30 euros, weekends 35 euros. *Eating facilities*: catering available. *Visitors*: welcome Monday, Tuesday, Wednesday and Friday, please telephone for booking. *Society Meetings*: welcome, please book in advance. Hon. Secretary: Noel Usher.
e-mail: enquiries@edenderrygolfclub.com
website: www.edenderrygolfclub.com

www.uk-golfguide.com

- 70 Deluxe Rooms & Suites, The Springs Leisure Club & Wellness Suites with 20m Pool, Sauna, SteamRoom, Jacuzzi, Hydrotherapy Suite, Gym & Exotic Elemis Spa Treatments.
- Discounts available for Golfing Groups of all sizes.
- Less than 90 minutes from Galway, Limerick, Shannon or the M50.
- Golf at **Birr, Roscrea, Portumna, Nenagh, Esker Hills, Tullamore, Glasson.**
- Golf from €10 (Midweek) €25 (weekend).

Check our Website for Special Offers

County Arms HOTEL

Roscrea Road, Birr, Co. Offaly
Tel: +353 (0)509 20791
Fax: +353 (0)509 21234
www.countyarmshotel.com
Completely refurbished in 2005

Visit the FHG website
www.holidayguides.com
for details of the wide choice of accommodation featured in the full range of FHG titles

OFFALY. **Castle Barna Golf Club,** Daingean (0506 53384; Fax: 0506 53077). *Location:* ten miles east of Tullamore and 8 miles south of main N6 Dublin to Galway road. Parkland with mature trees. 18 holes, 6200 yards. S.S.S. 69. *Green Fees:* weekdays 20 euros, weekends 29 euros. *Eating facilities:* meals available. *Visitors:* welcome except Sundays before noon. *Society Meetings:* welcome.

TULLAMORE. **Esker Hills Golf Club,** Tullamore (0506 55999; Fax: 0506 55021). *Location*: 3 miles from Tullamore, off the Tullamore/Clara Road (N80 Route). Parkland course with a distinct links feel. 18 holes, 6618 metres. S.S.S.71. Putting green, practice nets. *Green Fees*: information not available. *Eating facilities*: available. *Visitors*: welcome. Golf buggies available for hire at 25 euros per buggy. *Society Meetings*: welcome. Group rates on request. Secretary: Caroline Guinan (0506 55999; Fax: 0506 55021).*
e-mail: info@eskerhillsgolf.com
website: www.eskerhillsgolf.com

TULLAMORE. **Tullamore Golf Club,** Brookfield, Tullamore (0506 21439 Fax: 0506 41806). *Location:* from Dublin take N4 to Kinnegad then N6 to Kilbeggan, then N52 to Tullamore then three kilometres south of town towards Kinnity on the R421. Parkland. 18 holes, 6434 yds, 5885 metres. S.S.S. 71. Practice area. *Green Fees:* 37 euros weekdays, 48 euros weekends. 25 euros with member. *Eating facilities:* full bar and dining service, order meals before play. *Visitors:* welcome. Restrictions Tuesdays; no visitors on a Sunday, consult Secretary or Professional. Local accommodation available. *Society Meetings:* welcome, contact Secretary. Professional: Donagh McArdle (Tel & Fax: 0506 51757). Secretary: Jo Barber-Loughnane (0506 21439) or Ann Marie Cunniffe.

COUNTY ROSCOMMON

ATHLONE. **Athlone Golf Club,** Hodson Bay, Athlone (0902 92073 Fax: 0902 94080). *Location:* off the Roscommon road close to the Hodson Bay Hotel. Parkland championship standard course with mature trees and undulating fairways. 18 holes, 5854 metres. S.S.S.71. Practice ground. *Green Fees:* information not available. *Eating facilities:* restaurant and bar. *Visitors:* welcome Monday to Saturday, contact club in advance. *Society Meetings:* welcome. Professional: Martin Quinn. Administrative Secretary: I. Dockery.*

CARRICK-ON-SHANNON. **Carrick-on-Shannon Golf Club,** Woodbrook, Carrick-on-Shannon (07196 67015). *Location:* four miles west of Carrick-on-Shannon adjacent to N4. Parkland course overlooking River Shannon, a fine test of golf for low/ high handicappers. 18 holes, 5787 metres. S.S.S. 68. *Green Fees:* information not available. *Eating facilities:* full catering facilities available. *Visitors:* welcome midweek and weekends, please phone in advance. Buggy and trolley hire available. *Society Meetings:* welcome by arrangement. Secretary: Liz (07196 67015).
e-mail: ckgc3@eircom.net
website: www.carrickgolfclub.ie

THE APPEARANCE OF AN ASTERISK (*) AT THE END OF A CLUB OR COURSE ENTRY INDICATES THAT UP-TO-DATE INFORMATION HAS NOT BEEN SUPPLIED

A Christy O'Connor Jnr designed masterpiece built on unique terrain where no two holes are remotely alike. Esker Hills is located just over an hour from Dublin, Galway and Limerick, and only 45 minutes from the K Club, the 2006 Ryder Cup venue.

♦ Parkland course with excellent natural drainage and distinct links feel
♦ 18 holes, par 71.
♦ Visitors welcome daily.
♦ Golf buggies, power caddies and pull trolleys for hire.

"If you are a golfer, never, ever pass this place"
DAVID WALSHE, SUNDAY TIMES

**Esker Hills Golf Club, Tullamore, Offaly • Tel: +353 (0) 506 55999
Fax: +353 (0) 506 55021 • info@eskerhillsgolf.com • www.eskerhillsgolf.com**

www.uk-golfguide.com

ROSCOMMON. **Roscommon Golf Club,** Mote Park, Roscommon (090 6626382; Fax: 090 6626043). *Location*: half a mile south of Roscommon town. Rolling parkland, special feature 13th hole over lake Par 3. 18 holes, 6059 metres. S.S.S. 71. Practice ground, putting green. *Green Fees*. information not provided. *Eating facilities*: full bar and restaurant. *Visitors:* welcome, restrictions Sundays (competition day). Carts, caddies. *Society Meetings*: welcome. Secretary: Noreen O'Grady (090 6626382).*
e-mail: rosgolfclub@eircom.net

COUNTY SLIGO

BALLYMOTE. **Ballymote Golf Club,** Ballinascarrow, Ballymote (071 9183504/9183089). *Location:* 15 miles south of Sligo town, 12 miles west of Boyle. Undulating parkland with pleasant views. 9 holes, 2651 metres. S.S.S. 67 (for 18 holes). *Green Fees:* information not available. Trolleys available for hire 2 euros, buggies 3 euros. *Society Meetings:* please telephone John O'Connor (087 2187054).*

ENNISCRONE. **Enniscrone Golf Club,** Enniscrone (096 36297 three lines; Fax: 096 36657). *Location:* on coast road from Sligo to Ballina, about 13 km from Ballina. Championship links course - host to the Irish Close Championship 1993 - host to West of Ireland Championship 1997-1999 - host to Senior Inter Provincials 1999. 18 holes, 6857 yards. Par 73. Practice area and putting green. *Green Fees:* information not available. *Eating facilities:* bar and full catering facilities. *Visitors:* welcome, please phone beforehand. Professional: Charlie McGoldrick (096 36666). Hon. Secretary: Brian Casey (096 36414). Administrator: Anne Freeman. Secretary/ Manager: Mick Staunton. Rated number 66 in Top 100 Courses in Great Britain and Ireland - Golf World.*
e-mail: enniscronegolf@eircom.net
website: www.enniscronegolf.com

ROSSES POINT. **County Sligo Golf Club,** Rosses Point (071 9177134; Fax: 071 9177460). *Location:* 8km west of Sligo city at Rosses Point village. Championship links course which has hosted all of Ireland's major championships - rates No 24 in Golf World's 100 Best Courses. 18 holes, 6037 metres. S.S.S. 72. Large practice area. *Green Fees:* information not available. *Eating facilities:* full 80 seat restaurant, spacious lounge bar. *Visitors:* welcome seven days. No fourballs. Tuesdays Ladies' Day. Additional 9 holes Par 35. Ten electric buggies available at 40 euros per round. *Society Meetings:* welcome. Professional: Mr Jim Robinson (071 9177171; Fax: 071 9177460). Manager: Jim Ironside (071 9177134; Fax: 071 9177460). Reservations: Teresa Banks (071 9177186).*
e-mail: cosligo@iol.ie
website: www.countysligogolfclub.ie

COUNTY TIPPERARAY

CAHIR. **Cahir Park Golf Club,** Kilcommon, Cahir (052 41474; Fax: 052 42717). *Location:* half-a-mile from Cahir town on Clogheen road. Parkland. 18 holes, 5740 metres. S.S.S. 71. *Green Fees:* weekdays 25 euros, weekends 30 euros. Open Singles for men from March 17th to October 20 euros. *Eating facilities:* meals available, bar, dining room in new clubhouse. *Visitors:* welcome. Practice area. Locker rooms. Buggy available for hire.*Society Meetings:* welcome. Manager: Michael Duggan (052 41474).

CARRICK-ON-SUIR. **Carrick-on-Suir Golf Club,** Garravoone, Carrıck-on-Suir (051 640047; Fax: 051 640558). *Location:* one mile from Carrick-on-Suir on Dungarvan Road. Parkland course set against the backdrop of the Comeragh Mountains on one side and the Suir Valley on the other. 18 holes, 6061 yards. S.S.S. 70, Par 72. *Green Fees:* information not available. *Eating facilities:* full facilities, bar open 9am to 11.30pm. *Visitors:* welcome thoughout the week except during competition times on Wednesday, Tuesday and Sunday. Sean Kelly's (cyclist) home club. One buggy for hire and carts. *Society Meetings:* all welcome by prior arrangement. Secretary/Manager: Aidan Murphy (051 640047).*

CLONMEL. **Clonmel Golf Club,** Lyreanearla, Mountain Road, Clonmel (052 24050; Fax: 052 83349). *Location:* three miles up the mountain road from Clonmel town. Parkland set on the scenic slopes of the Comeragh Mountains. 18 holes, 6347 (white), 6068 (green) yards. S.S.S. 71 white, 70 green. Practice area. *Green Fees:* mid-week 25 euros, weekend 35 euros. *Eating facilities:* bar food, sit-down meals available on request. *Visitors:* always welcome but contact Secretary/ Manager re weekends. Ladies' Day Wednesdays. Golf Buggy available for hire, contact professional. *Society Meetings:* welcome, contact Secretary/ Manager for weekends. Course information (052 83344). Professional: Robert Hayes (052 24050). Secretary/ Manager: Ms Aine Myles Keating (052 24050; Fax: 052 83349).
e-mail: cgc@indigo.ie
website: www.clonmelgolfclub.com

MONARD. **Ballykisteen Golf and Country Club,** Monard, Tipperary (052 33333; Fax: 062 82587). *Location:* on the N24 20 minutes' drive from Limerick City, two miles from Tipperary town and 500 metres from Limerick Junction railway station. 4 Star rated Ramada Hotel and Suites with Leisure Centre and 18 hole Championship golf course. 6765 yards, Par 73. Driving range and practice green. *Green Fees:* fees and booking information available on website. *Eating facilities:* full restaurant and bar facilities. *Visitors:* welcome at all times. *Society Meetings:* all welcome. Bookings to John O'Dwyer (062 33333).
website: www.ballykisteenramada.com

THE APPEARANCE OF AN ASTERISK (*) AT THE END OF A CLUB OR COURSE ENTRY INDICATES THAT UP-TO-DATE INFORMATION HAS NOT BEEN SUPPLIED

TEMPLEMORE. **Templemore Golf Club,** Manna South, Templemore (0504 31400; Fax: 0504 31913). *Location:* beside N62 (South) half-a-mile from town centre. Flat parkland course, short distance between greens and tees, easy to walk. 9 holes, 5443 metres. S.S.S. 68. *Green Fees:* weekdays £15.00; weekends £20.00. (Subject to review 2006.) *Visitors:* welcome at all times, some restrictions Sundays. *Society Meetings:* welcome. Secretary: Jim Tobin (087 6882618).

THURLES. **Thurles Golf Club,** Turtulla, Thurles (0504 21983: Fax: 0504 24647). *Location:* one mile from town centre on Cork Road. Sloping parkland course. 18 holes, 6465 yards. S.S.S.71. *Green Fees:* 35 to 40 euros. *Eating facilities:* restaurant and bar. *Visitors:* welcome except Tuesday and Sunday. *Society Meetings:* welcome, special rates available. Professional: Sean Hunt. Hon. Secretary: Michael O'Sullivan (0504 24599; Fax: 0504 24647).

COUNTY WATERFORD

DUNGARVAN. **Dungarvan Golf Club,** Knocknagranagh, Dungarvan (00 353 5843310 /5841605; Fax: 00 353 5844113). *Location:* four kilometres east of Dungarvan on N25 to Waterford. Parkland course adjacent to Dungarvan Bay. 18 holes, 6785 yards, 6204 metres. S.S.S. 73. Practice ground. *Green Fees*: information not available. *Eating facilities:* Full bar and catering services by prior arrangement. *Visitors*: welcome but booking advisable. *Society Meetings*: welcome, special rates. Professional: David Hayes (00 353 5844707). Manager: Irene Howell (00 353 5843310).*
e-mail: dungarvangc@eircom.net
website: www.dungarvangolfclub.com

DUNGARVAN. **Gold Coast Golf Club,** Ballinacourty, Dungarvan (Tel & Fax: 00 353 58 44055). *Location*: 45 miles east of Cork city, 30 miles south of Waterford city, on N25, 2 miles from Dungarvan town, on the coast. Scenic and challenging course bordering the Atlantic Ocean with unrivalled panoramic views of Dungarven Bay and Comeragh Mountains. 18 holes, 6788 yards, 6171 metres. S.S.S. 72. *Green Fees*: information not available. *Eating facilities:* full hotel and leisure facilities. *Visitors*: welcome anytime. *Society Meetings*: welcome, special rates available. Secretary: Tom Considine (Tel & Fax: 00 353 58 44055).
e-mail: info@goldcoastgolfclub.com
website: www.goldcoastgolfclub.com

DUNGARVAN. **West Waterford Golf & Country Club,** Dungarvan (058 43216/41475; Fax: 058 44343). *Location*: 4km west of Dungarvan, off N25 bypass on Aglish Road. Challenging parkland course with natural water hazards, mature trees, abundant wildlife. 18 holes, 6712 yards. S.S.S. 72 blue. Large practice area and putting green. *Green Fees*: Weekdays 32 euros; Weekends and Bank Holidays 44 euros. Discounts for groups and societies. *Eating facilities:* full restaurant and catering facilities. *Visitors*: always welcome, but reservations are necessary. *Society Meetings*: always welcome, pre-booking essential. Secretary: Tom Whelan (00353 58 43216 / 41475; Fax: 00353 58 44343).
e-mail: info@westwaterfordgolf.com
website: www.westwaterfordgolf.com

DUNMORE EAST. **Dunmore East Golf Club,** Dunmore East (Tel. & Fax: 00 353 51 383151). *Location:* at the entrance to Dunmore village take first left to Strand and follow signpost to Club. Seaside parkland. 18 holes, 6070 metres. S.S.S. 70. *Green Fees:* from 25 euros. (2006 fees being reviewed). *Eating facilities:* full bar and catering facilities. *Visitors*: always welcome. Self-catering accommodation on-site. *Society Meetings:* welcome, prices on request. Distance membership available. Club Professional: Derry Kiely. Secretary: M. Skehan (Tel & Fax: 00 353 51 383151).
e-mail: dunmoregolf@eircom.net
website: www.dunmoreeastgolfclub.ie

LISMORE. **Lismore Golf Club,** Ballyin, Lismore (058 54026; Fax: 058 53338). *Location:* one kilometre north of Lismore Heritage Town, just off the N72. Undulating parkland with mature trees, course surrounded by woodlands. 9 holes, 5367 metres. S.S.S. 68. *Green Fees:* 20 euros. *Eating facilities:* tea, coffee, snacks. *Visitors:* welcome weekdays, restriction may apply on Wednesday (Ladies' Day) and weekends. *Society Meetings:* welcome except Wednesday. Secretary: Katherine Moynihan.

An island dream!... that is **Waterford Castle Hotel & Golf Club**

Waterford Castle Hotel & Golf Club is Ireland's only true island golf course resort. Detached from the mainland and the only golf course in Ireland, Europe and possibly the world to be accessed by private ferry. This privately owned 320-acre island, home of the renowned Waterford Castle Hotel, is the site for a wonderful parkland golf course. Designed by Des Smith, this 18-hole Par 72 championship golf course leads you through mature woodland and parkland. The course itself runs to 6814 yards, and covers an area of 200 acres.

Waterford Castle Hotel & Golf Club
The Island, Ballinakill, Waterford, Ireland
Tel: 00 353 51 871633 • Fax: 00 353 51 871634
e-mail: golf@waterfordcastle.com • www.waterfordcastle.com/golf

TRAMORE. **Tramore Golf Club,** Newtown Hill, Tramore (051 386170; Fax: 051 390961). *Location*: seven miles from Waterford city. Parkland. 18 holes, 5918 metres. S.S.S. 72. *Green Fees*: information not available. *Eating facilities:* full catering and bar. *Visitors*: welcome Monday to Saturday. No visitors on Sundays. *Society Meetings:* welcome on application. Professional: Derry Kiely (087 2398856). Club Manager: James Cox. *

WATERFORD. **Faithlegg Golf Club,** Faithlegg House, Waterford (051 382241; Fax: 051 382664). *Location:* 6 miles from Waterford city centre on Dunmore road; head for Cheek Point on the road past Jack Meades pub. Premier course in the south-east, a challenge to all levels of golfer, with superb views. Ranked in the top ten best new courses in Britain and Ireland by Golf World Magazine in 1993. 18 holes, 6629 yards. S.S.S. 72. Practice ground and putting green. *Green Fees:* information not available. *Eating facilities:* full bar and restaurant facilities available every day. *Visitors:* always welcome. Hotel on site. *Society Meetings:* always welcome, booking advisable. Professional: Derry Kiely (051 382241; Fax: 051 382664). Corporate and Events Manager: Tracy McDaid (051 380581). General Manager: Darragh Tighe (051 380588).*
e-mail: golf@faithlegg.com
website: www.faithlegg.com

WATERFORD. **Waterford Castle Golf Club,** The Island, Ballinakill, Waterford City (00 353 51 871633; Fax: 00 353 51 871634). *Location*: one mile east of Waterford City on the R683. A unique island course surrounded by River Suir and accessed by private ferry. Parkland course, internal water features, mature woodlands and a Swilken Bridge. 18 holes, 6814 yards, 6231 metres. S.S.S. 73. Driving range, practice ground, chipping area. *Green Fees*: information not provided. *Eating facilities*: full bar and bar food. *Visitors*: welcome, no restrictions subject to availability. Accommodation available at five star Waterford Castle Hotel with all its facilities including all weather tennis courts. Golf buggies, trolleys available. *Society Meetings*: welcome, special rates available. Director of Golf: Michael Garland (051 871633).
e-mail: directorofgolf@waterfordcastle.com
e-mail: golf@waterfordcastle.com
website: www.waterfordcastle.com

Please mention THE GOLF GUIDE when you enquire about clubs or accommodation

Each year FHG GUIDES produce a large range of attractive holiday accommodation guides for all kinds of holiday opportunities throughout Britain.
They are great value for money and are available in most bookshops and larger newsagents at the following prices.

FHG KUPERARD

Coast & Country Holidays £7.99
Britain's Best Holidays £6.99
Bed & Breakfast Stops £7.99
Golf Guide: Where to play, Where to stay £9.99
Country Inns & Pubs of Britain £7.99
Short Break Holidays in Britain £7.99
Country Hotels of Britain £7.99
Pets Welcome! £8.99
Caravan & Camping Holidays £6.99
Self-Catering Holidays in Britain £7.99
Children Welcome! £7.99
Pets Welcome! £8.99

Holiday & Accommodation Guides

COUNTY WESTMEATH

ATHLONE. **Glasson Golf and Country Club,** Glasson, Athlone (090 6485120; Fax: 090 6485444). *Location*: take the N55 from Athlone to Glasson village and turn left. Parkland course bordering Lough Ree and the Shannon – spectacular scenery and 555 yard 14th hole. 21 holes, 7120 yards. S.S.S. 74. 3 hole golf academy. *Green Fees*: information not provided. *Eating facilities*: restaurant, spike bar, snack bar and private rooms available. *Visitors*: welcome every day. *Society Meetings:* welcome, no restrictions, all facilities available. Office: Fidelma Reid (090 6485120; Fax: 090 6485444).
e-mail: info@glassongolf.ie
website: www.glassongolf.ie

MOATE. **Mount Temple Golf Club,** Mount Temple Village, Moate (09064 81841/81545; Fax: 09064 81957). *Location:* four miles off N6 Dublin/Galway road signposted to Mount Temple village. Parkland. 18 holes, 5927 metres. S.S.S. 72. Three hole practice area. *Green Fees:* weekdays 30 euros, weekends 35 euros. *Eating facilities:* Snacks and farmhouse cuisine, dinner by arrangement, wine licence, pub 100 yards. *Visitors:* welcome but possible restrictions at weekends. *Society Meetings:* welcome. Professional: David Keenan (044 44728). Secretary: Michelle Allen (090 648 1841).
e-mail: mttemple@iol.ie
website: www.mounttemplegolfclub.com

COUNTY WEXFORD

Welcome to Ashdown Park Hotel....

Ashdown Park Hotel

Where your time is our pleasure.....

★★★★

Luxurious, superbly appointed hotel, located on its own private grounds, just a three minute stroll from Gorey Town. Eighty splendid bedrooms incorporating Executive Suites, all are modern classical in style, offering the highest level of comfort, with all conveniences.

CONFERENCE & LEISURE CENTRE
THE COACH ROAD - GOREY TOWN
COUNTY WEXFORD - IRELAND
Tel: 00 353 5594 80500
Fax: 00 353 5594 80777
e-mail: info@ashdownparkhotel.com
www.ashdownparkhotel.com

ENNISCORTHY. **Enniscorthy Golf Club,** Knockmarshal, Enniscorthy (054 33191; Fax: 054 37637). *Location:* one mile from Enniscorthy town on New Ross Road. Parkland course, renowned for excellent greens. 18 holes, 6115 metres. S.S.S. 72. Practice ground. *Green Fees:* Monday to Thursday 25.00 Euro, Friday to Sunday/Public Holidays 35.00 Euro. *Eating facilities:* bar and restaurant facilities. *Visitors:* welcome. Please telephone for bookings. Golf buggies available, must be pre-booked. Carts available. *Society Meetings:* welcome, must be pre-booked. Professional: Martin Sludds (054 37600). General Manager: A. P. Colley (054 33191; Fax: 054 37637).

GOREY. **Seafield Golf and Country Club,** Ballymoney, Gorey (055 24777; Fax: 055 24837). *Location:* in the north Wexford coastal village of Ballymoney. Challenging parkland course with mature woodland and water features. 18 holes, 6814 yards, Par 72. *Green Fees:* on application: *Visitors:* welcome.*
e-mail: info@seafieldgolf.com
website: www.seafieldgolf.com

FHG

·K·U·P·E·R·A·R·D·

FHG Guides

publish a large range of well-known accommodation guides. We will be happy to send you details or you can use the order form at the back of this book.

www.uk-golfguide.com

Ireland's Ryder Cup Region

The K Club, Co. Kildare

Ireland's East Coast & Midlands region will host one of the world's most prestigious golfing events, the **Ryder Cup, in 2006**.

We invite you to come and experience the magnificent range of links, heath and parkland courses all within an hour of Ireland's Ryder Cup venue.

Want to play the K Club, Carton House & PGA National Ireland for just €300? Now you can using the Quality Golf Passport.

For your *FREE* Ryder Cup Region Golf Guide and other great golf offers log onto:

www.eastcoastmidlands.ie

East Coast and Midlands Tourism, Dublin Road, Mullingar, Co. Westmeath, Ireland
Tel: +353 (0) 44 48650 Fax: +353 (0) 44 40413
email: info@eastcoastmidlands.ie web: www.eastcoastmidlands.ie

Kildare - Laois - Longford - Louth - Meath
Offaly - Westmeath - Wicklow

Ireland   Fáilte Ireland   RYDER CUP 2006 IRELAND   East Coast & Midlands Tourism

ROSSLARE. **Rosslare Golf Club,** Rosslare Strand, Wexford (053 32203; Fax: 053 32263). *Location:* 6 miles from ferry terminal at Rosslare Harbour. 10 miles south of Wexford. Seaside links course, beside Irish Sea. Old Course – 18 holes, 6608 yards. S.S.S. 72. New Course – 12 holes, 3983 yards. S.S.S. 70. Practice ground. *Green Fees:* information not available. *Eating facilities:* available all day. *Visitors:* welcome, telephone for booking. *Society Meetings:* welcome, telephone for booking. General Manager: J.P. Hanrick (053 32203).*
e-mail: office@rosslaregolf.com

ROSSLARE HARBOUR. **St Helen's Bay Golf Resort,** St Helens Bay, Kilrane, Rosslare Harbour (053 33234; Fax: 053 32263). *Location:* six miles from ferry terminal at Rosslare Harbour, 10 miles south of Wexford. Seaside parkland and links course with several water features. 18-hole championship course, 6608 yards, S.S.S. 72. *Green Fees:* 28-42 euros. *Eating facilities:* newly refurbished fully licensed bar and restaurant. *Visitors:* always welcome with no restrictions. Advisable to book in advance, especially in high season. Self-catering cottage and B&B accommodation on site. *Society Meetings:* play and stay specialists. Meetings/conferences welcome. Secretary: Kevin Doherty.
e-mail: info@sthelensbay.com
website: www.sthelensbay.com

COUNTY WICKLOW

ARKLOW. **Coollattin Golf Club,** Shillelagh, Arklow (055 29125; Fax: 055 29930) *Location*: take N11 from Dublin to Rathnew, then travel to Rathdrum, Aughrim, Tinahely and Coollattin. Parkland with large oak trees being a special feature of the course. 18 holes, 5831 yards, par 70. S.S.S. 68. *Green Fees:* information not provided. *Eating facilities*: full bar and catering facilities. *Visitors*: by arrangement with Professional. *Society Meetings*: by arrangement with Dave Masterson. Professional: Peter Jones. Secretary: Billy Stamp (055 29938).

BALTINGLASS. **Baltinglass Golf Club,** Stratford Lodge, Baltinglass (059 6481350; Fax: 059 6482842). *Location:* just outside Baltinglass on main Dublin road (N81). Picturesque course with mature trees and breathtaking views. 18 holes, 5912 metres. Par 71. *Green Fees:* rates available on request. *Eating facilities:* bar and catering facilities available. *Visitors:* welcome. *Society Meetings:* booking now for 2006. Contact Hon. Secretary, Genevieve or Patricia at Club Office.*
e-mail: baltinglassgc@eircom.net
website: www.baltinglass.com

BLAINROE. **Blainroe Golf Club,** Blainroe (0404 68168; Fax: 0404 69369). *Location:* three miles south of Wicklow town on coast road. Parkland terrain with extensive views of the sea. 18 holes, 6175 metres, S.S.S. 72. Practice area, putting green. *Green Fees:* weekdays 53 euros; weekends 68 euros. Special rates for groups/outings. *Eating facilities:* full bar and restaurant facilities. *Visitors:* welcome Tuesday to Friday; weekends and Bank Holidays by previous booking. Carts and caddies available. *Society Meetings:* welcome. Professional: John McDonald (0404 66470). Secretary: Mr William O'Sullivan.

Glenview Hotel & Leisure Club
AA/RAC ★★★★

• 70 De luxe en suite bedrooms
• 5 ★ Leisure Centre with indoor pool
• Beauty treatments and therapies
• Award-winning Woodlands Restaurant
• Conservatory Bar
• Snooker room
• Woodland walks and gardens. Golf nearby

E-mail: sales@glenviewhotel.com
www.glenviewhotel.com

GLEN OF THE DOWNS, DELGANY, CO. WICKLOW
TEL: 00353 1287 3799

Kilrane, Rosslare Harbour Co. Wexford

Tel: (053) 33234 • Fax: (053) 32263
E-mail: info@sthelensbay.com

18 hole championship seaside parkland and links course, with several water features, 10 miles south of Wexford. Newly refurbished fully licensed bar and restaurant. Visitors always welcome with no restrictions. Society stay and play specialists. **Self-catering cottage & B&B acccommodation on site.**

www.sthelensbay.com

St Helens Bay Golf Resort

See also Colour Advertisement on page 96

Rathsallagh House Hotel & Golf Club
County Wicklow • Tel: +353 45 403112

Rathsallagh is a large 4-star Grade A country house set in peaceful parkland and surrounded by the magnificent Rathsallagh Golf Club. Dublin is less than one hour's drive away. The atmosphere is happy and relaxed, with log and turf fires, central heating throughout, and luxurious en suite bathrooms. The food is country house cooking at its best – game in season and fresh fish are specialities.

Other leisure facilities include the Brendan McDaid Golf Academy, sauna, tennis, croquet, snooker, clay pigeon shooting, archery. Fishing and horse riding can be arranged. Nearby courses include the K Club, Mount Juliet and Portmarnock.

www.rathsallaghhousehotel.com

BLESSINGTON. **Tulfarris Golf Club,** Blessington Lakes, Blessington (045 867600; Fax: 045 867565). *Location*: through Blessington village take N81, 4 miles outside town, turn left after Poulaphuca House. Parkland course built on 3 peninsulas, surrounded by Poulaphuca Lake. 18 holes, 7116 yards, S.S.S. 72. Practice range, chipping area, putting green. *Green Fees*: information not available. Tuition available. *Society Meetings*: welcome, rates available on request. Director of Golf: David Murray (045 867654).*
e-mail: golf@tulfarris.com
website: www.tulfarris.com

BRAY. **Old Conna Golf Club,** Ferndale Road, Bray (01282 6055; Fax: 01282 5611). *Location:* two miles from Bray town, 12 miles south of Dublin route N11. Parkland course set in wooded hillside terrain with panoramic views of Irish Sea and Wicklow. 18 holes, 6650 yards. S.S.S 72. *Green Fees:* on application. *Eating facilities:* full catering facilities. *Visitors:* welcome, Tuesdays Ladies' Day, semi open Wednesdays. Hire of clubs/caddy car. *Society Meetings:* society outings welcome Mondays, Thursdays and Fridays. Professional: Ciaran Carroll (01272 0022; Fax: 01282 5611). General Manager: Tom Sheridan.*

BRAY. **Woodbrook Golf Club,** Dublin Road, Bray (003531 2824799; Fax: 003531 2821950). *Location:* Bray, Co Wicklow. Flat parkland course on the cliff above Bray harbour. 18 holes, 6800 yards, S.S.S. 72. *Green Fees:* information not available. *Eating facilities:* bar/restaurant. *Visitors:* welcome Monday, Tuesday and Friday. *Society Meetings:* welcome Monday, Tuesday and Friday. Professional: Billy Kinsella (0035312 820205). Secretary: Jim Melody. *
e-mail: woodbrook@internet-ireland.ie
website: www.woodbrook.ie

BRITTAS BAY. **The European Club,** Brittas Bay, Wicklow (0404 47415). *Location:* one mile south of main Brittas Bay beach on coast road, 40 miles south of Dublin City Centre. Rolling linksland overlooking Arklow Bay, designed and owned by Pat Ruddy. Ranked No. 5 among Ireland's 30 greatest golf courses by Irish Golf Institute (1999); 24th Greatest Golf Course of the 20th Century (Golfer's Companion Jan. 2000). 18 holes, 7323 yards. S.S.S. 73. Extensive practice areas. *Green Fees:* 150 euros Apr-Oct; 80 euros Nov-Mar. *Eating facilities:* full services. *Visitors:* welcome to all golfers, advisable to book. *Society Meetings:* welcome. Secretary: Sidon Ruddy (0404 47415; Fax: 0404 47449).
e-mail: info@theeuropeanclub.com

DELGANY. **Delgany Golf Club,** Delgany (01287 4536; Fax: 01287 3977). *Location:* half an hour from Dublin city centre just off the N11 to Wexford in Delgany village. Wooded parkland course with splendid hill and sea views. 18 holes, 5473 metres. S.S.S. 69. *Green Fees:* 45 euros midweek, 55 euros weekends. *Eating facilities:* restaurant and bar food. Mondays bar snacks only. *Visitors:* particularly welcome Mondays, Thursdays and Fridays; Wednesdays before 9am and Sundays pm (check availability). Carts for hire, three motor buggies. Special packages with local hotels see website. *Society Meetings:* welcome. Professional: Gavin Kavanagh (01287 4697; Fax: 01287 3977). General Manager: Peter Ribeiro.
e-mail: delganygolf@eircom.net
website: www.delganygolfclub.com

DELGANY. **Glen of the Downs Golf Club,** Coolnaskeagh, Delgany (01287 6240; Fax: 01287 0063). *Location:* off the N11, 35 minutes from Dublin. Parkland course. 18 holes, 6443 yards. Practice area. *Green Fees:* information not available. *Eating facilities:* Pavilion with restaurant and bar. *Visitors:* welcome. Golf shop, locker rooms; clubs, buggies and caddy cars for hire. *Society Meetings:* welcome.*
e-mail: info@glenofthedowns.com
website: www.glenofthedowns.com

DUNLAVIN. **Rathsallagh Golf Club,** Dunlavin (045 403316; Fax: 045 403295). *Location:* take M7 south from Naas, exit onto M9 southbound, turn left eight miles south of Kilcullen. Set on 270 acres of mature rolling parkland of which the golf course takes up 252 acres, surrounded by thousands of trees, water on five holes. 18 holes, 6920 yards. S.S.S. 72. Practice tees, putting green, driving range. *Green Fees:* information not available. *Eating facilities:* full bar and restaurant. *Visitors:* welcome all week. Reservation essential, no handicap required. 29 bedrooms. Golf Academy. *Society Meetings:* welcome all week. Club Professional: Brendan McDaid (045 403316; Fax: 045 403295). Secretary: Joe O'Flynn (045 403316; Fax: 045 403295).*
e-mail: info@rathsallagh.com
website: www.rathsallagh.com

www.uk-golfguide.com

ENNISKERRY. **Powerscourt Golf Club,** Powerscourt Estate, Enniskerry (2046033; Fax: 2761303). *Location:* 12 miles south of Dublin city centre just off N11, south of Bray adjacent to Enniskerry village. Two parkland courses (East designed by Peter McEvoy, West by David McLay Kidd) located in Powerscourt Estate with links characteristics, exceptional tiered greens, selection of 5 tee boxes on each course. Practice range, short game practice area. *Green Fees:* 130 euros. Special rates for groups and corporates. *Eating facilities:* restaurant and bar food available, full bar facilities. *Visitors:* welcome daily. Five studio apartments (sleeping two/three per apartment) available. Buggies, carts and caddies available. Conference facilities available. Professional: Paul Thompson. Manager: Bernard Gibbons.
e-mail: maria.dome@powerscourt.net
website: www.powerscourt.ie

GREYSTONES. **Charlesland Golf and Country Club,** Greystones. *Location*: 45 minutes south of Dublin just off the N11. Charlesland boasts a magnificent location beside the sea, in the shadow of the Wicklow mountains. 18 hole parkland Championship Course 6169 metres. S.S.S. 72. Large practice area, putting green, public driving range available within 500 metres. *Green Fees*: information not available. *Eating facilities*: restaurant and bar food available. Full bar facilities. *Visitors*: welcome daily. Please make prior booking. Neat dress essential. Buggies and handcarts for hire from our well-stocked Golf Shop. 12 en suite bedrooms. Boardroom and Conference facilities. For reservations phone (01-2878200; Fax: 01-2870078). *Society Meetings*: Corporate, society and group rates available on request. For golf bookings phone (01-2874350; 01-2874360). General Manager: Patrick Bradshaw.*
e-mail: teetimes@charlesland.com
website: www.charlesland.com

GREYSTONES. **Greystones Golf Club,** Whitshed Road, Greystones (01-287 4136; Fax: 01-287 3749). Parkland course. 18 holes, 5322 metres, S.S.S. 69. Practice facilities. *Green Fees*: information not available. *Eating facilities*: full catering available. *Visitors*: welcome Monday, Tuesday, Friday and Sunday. *Society Meetings*: especially welcome, please contact the Secretary for details. Professional: Karl Holmes (01-287 5308). Secretary: Jim Melody (01-287 4136).*
e-mail: secretary@greystonesgc.com
website: www.greystonesgc.com

KILCOOLE. **Kilcoole Golf Club,** Kilcoole (01 2872066; Fax: 01 2010497). *Location:* two miles from Greystones off N11. Flat course one mile from sea. 9 holes, 5506 metres. S.S.S. 69. Practice area. *Green Fees:* 30 euros midweek, 35 euros weekends. *Eating facilities:* bar with meals available. *Visitors:* welcome, booking advisable. *Society Meetings:* welcome, special rate available. Secretary/Manager: Eddie Lonergan.

At Powerscourt you get a choice of courses.

With two of Ireland's finest golf courses and a new clubhouse located just half an hour south of Dublin, isn't it time you paid a visit to Powerscourt? Both our courses are open to visitors every day of the week, so why not find out for yourself what makes us one of the country's leading golf locations. Come and shoot a round here, it's always open season.

POWERSCOURT
GOLF CLUB

West Course   East Course

Powerscourt Estate, Enniskerry, Co. Wicklow Tel: +353 1 204 6033 Fax: +353 1 276 1303
email: golfclub@powerscourt.ie www.powerscourt.ie/golfclub

THE GOLF GUIDE 2006 REPUBLIC OF IRELAND 537

NEWTOWNMOUNTKENNEDY. **Druids Glen Golf Club,** Newtownmountkennedy (00 353 1 287 3600; Fax: 00 353 1 287 3699). *Location:* 20 miles south of Dublin. Two great championship courses: Druids Glen and Druids Heath. 18 holes, par 71. New golf academy. *Green Fees*: from 110 euros. *Eating facilities*: available. *Visitors:* welcome. Five-star Marriott hotel on site. Professional: George Henry. General Manager: Donal Flinn. Golf Director: John Kinsella.

NEWTOWNMOUNTKENNEDY. **Druids Heath Golf Club,** Newtownmountkennedy (00 353 1 281 2278; Fax: 00 353 1 281 2279). *Location:* 20 miles south of Dublin. Two great championship courses: Druids Glen and Druids Heath. 18 holes, par 71. New golf academy. *Green Fees*: from 75 euros. *Eating facilities*: available. *Visitors:* welcome. Five-star Marriott hotel on site. Professional: George Henry. General Manager: Donal Flinn. Golf Director: Barry Dowling.

Tranquil luxury and indulgent relaxation. A convivial Irish experience.

Championship Golf Resort
• Druids Glen – host to four Irish Open Championships and the Seve Trophy; Voted 'European Golf Course of the Year 2000' by Hertz International Travel Awards;
• Druids Heath scheduled to open in September 2003.
A stunning Championship golf course carved from the natural landscape of Ireland's Garden County.

Magnificent Spa and Health Club
Journey on the pathway of rediscovery to soothe the mind, nourish the soul, calm the spirit, and escape the challenges of a modern lifestyle.

thinking of you...
DRUIDS GLEN
• 20 minutes from South Dublin in County Wicklow, "The Garden of Ireland"
Marriott
HOTEL & COUNTRY CLUB

Newtownmountkennedy, Co. Wicklow, Ireland.
Tel: +353 1 2870800 Fax: +353 1 2870801
email: events.druids@marriotthotels.co.uk
www.marriotthotels.com/dubgs

For full details of clubs and courses, plus convenient accommodation
www.uk-golfguide.com

Druids Glen Golf Club

Venue for the Seve Trophy 2002
European Golf Course of the Year 2000
Home of the Irish Open 1996, '97, '98 & '99

Druids Glen Golf Club – although nestling in the beauty of the Wicklow County, this golfers' dream is only 30 minutes from Dublin City Centre.

**Newtownmountkennedy
Co. Wicklow, Ireland
Tel: 00353 1287 3600
Fax: 00353 1287 3699
e-mail: druids@indigo.ie
www.druidsglen.ie**

Geann na Draoice

The Chester Beatty Inn • Ashford • Co. Wicklow
(on main N11 40km from Dublin)

With 12 superbly appointed bedrooms and a renowned reputation for hospitality, the hotel is ideally suited for small groups. All rooms are 5* standard, with spacious en suite facilities, TV, telephone etc. A fine range of food and wine is available in the Restaurant, and the traditional Irish Bar and Lounge with open log fires offer an authentic Irish atmosphere. Wicklow is a golfers' paradise, with many courses within a short distance of the hotel, and there are many visitor attractions, as well as fishing, hillwalking and sailing.

**Tel: 0404 40206 • Fax: 0404 49003
e-mail: hotelchesterbeatty@eircom.net • www.hotelchesterbeatty.ie**

See also Colour Advertisement on page 96

RATHDRUM. **Glenmalure Golf Club,** Greenan, Rathdrum (0404 46679). *Location:* two miles west of Rathdrum - signposted. Parkland, hilly course. 18 holes, 5500 yards. S.S.S. 66. *Green Fees:* 35 euros weekends, 25 euros weekdays. *Eating facilities:* full facilities. *Visitors:* welcome, no restrictions. Self catering Scandinavian Lodges available. Buggies, carts available, caddy on notice. *Society Meetings:* welcome weekdays and Saturdays. Secretary: Kathleen Byrne (0404 46679).

REDCROSS. **Millbrook Golf Course,** Redcross (0404 41647). *Location:* in Redcross village, two miles off N11, eight miles from Wicklow. Parkland, Par 3 course. 18 holes, 2009 yards. S.S.S 55. *Green Fees:* information not available. *Eating facilities:* restaurant, takeaway, coffee bar and wine bar. Clubs for hire. River Valley Caravan and Camping park with mobile homes and houses to let; many other facilities also available.*

WICKLOW. **Wicklow Golf Club,** Dunbur Road, Wicklow. *Location:* Wicklow Town, off N11. Parkland course by the seaside. 18 holes, 5695 metres. S.S.S. 70. *Green Fees:* 40 euros. *Eating facilities:* full facilities available. *Visitors:* welcome; some restrictions Wednesday and Thursday evenings and Sunday. Caddy cars. *Society Meetings:* welcome, prior arrangement with secretary advisable. Information brochure sent on request . Professional: Darren McLoughlin (00 353 404 66122). Secretary: Joe Kelly (00353 404 67379; Fax: 00353 404 64756).

THE APPEARANCE OF AN ASTERISK (*) AT THE END OF A CLUB OR COURSE ENTRY INDICATES THAT UP-TO-DATE INFORMATION HAS NOT BEEN SUPPLIED

Wicklow Golf Club

Situated on cliffs overlooking Wicklow Bay, on the coast road to Brittas Bay, this is a challenging test of golf, each hole having its own individual features. The new clubhouse, with stunning views of the course and coastline, offers full bar, snacks, lunch and dinner facilities.

Caddy car and buggy hire • Green Fees: 40 Euros weekdays and weekends.
• Group rates available on request •

**Dunbur Road, Wicklow Town, Co Wicklow
Tel: 00353 0404 67379 • www.wicklowgolfclub.ie
e-mail: info@wicklowgolfclub.ie**

FHG

Visit the KUPERARD website
www.holidayguides.com
for details of the wide choice of accommodation featured in the full range of FHG titles

The Isle of Man

CASTLETOWN. **Castletown Golf Links,** Derbyhaven, Castletown IM9 1UA (01624 822220). *Location:* five minutes from Ronaldsway Airport and 20 minutes from Douglas. Championship links course voted in the Top 100 in the UK by 'Golf World' magazine. Host to the Duke of York Young Champions Trophy in 2003. 18 holes, 6707 yards. S.S.S. 72. *Green Fees:* information not available. *Visitors:* most welcome but must be pre-booked. *Society Meetings:* welcome, must be pre-booked. Golf Director: Debbie Barron (01624 822220; Fax: 01624 829661).
e-mail: 1sttee@manx.net
website: www.golfiom.com

DOUGLAS. **Douglas Golf Club,** Pulrose Park, Douglas IM2 1AE (01624 675952). *Location:* one mile out of Douglas near Pulrose Power Station. Parkland - 17th hole tee off 200ft above green (214 yards). 18 holes, 5982 yards. S.S.S. 69. Practice and putting area. *Green Fees:* mid-week £7.50, weekends £10.00 adult, £5.25 junior. *Visitors:* welcome, but not before 10am Sundays. Dress code in bar, no jeans. *Society Meetings:* catered for by arrangement with Pro Shop (01624 661558). Manager/Professional: Mike Vipond. Secretary: Elaine Vincent (Tel & Fax: 01624 616865).

DOUGLAS. **Pulrose Golf Course,** Pulrose Park, Douglas IM2 1AE (01624 675952). *Location:* one mile from town centre. Undulating parkland with memorable 17th hole. 18 holes, 5922 yards. S.S.S. 68. Putting and practice area. *Green Fees:* information not available. *Eating facilities:* bar; snacks available at all times. *Visitors:* welcome, not before 10am on Sundays. Dress code in bar - no jeans. *Society Meetings:* by arrangement with Professional: Mike Vipond (01624 661558).*

ONCHAN. **King Edward Bay Golf Club,** Groudle Road, Howstrake, Onchan (01624 672709). *Location:* north headland of Douglas Bay. Stunning views from Headland links course. Watered greens, excellent fairways. 18 holes, 5450 yards. S.S.S. 67. Practice area. *Green Fees:* information not available. *Eating facilities:* full catering available (except Mondays), three bars. *Visitors:* welcome without reservation but not before 9.30am Sundays. *Society Meetings:* most welcome by arrangement. Special rates. Professional: Donald Jones (01624 672709). Secretary: Cyril Kelly (01624 827726; Fax: 01624 827724).

PEEL. **Peel Golf Club,** Rheast Lane, Peel IM5 1BG (01624 842227). *Location:* outskirts of Peel on main Douglas Road. Combination of links and heathland. 18 holes, 5850 yards. S.S.S. 69. Practice ground. *Green Fees:* information not available. *Eating facilities:* full bar service and meals. *Visitors:* welcome, but check in advance for weekend availability. *Society Meetings:* catered for, check in advance. Pro Shop. Professional: Murray Crowe (01624 844232). Secretary/Manager: Michael N.D. Robinson (01624 843456).*

THE APPEARANCE OF AN ASTERISK (*) AT THE END OF A CLUB OR COURSE ENTRY INDICATES THAT UP-TO-DATE INFORMATION HAS NOT BEEN SUPPLIED

Voted in the TOP 100 in the British Isles in 2004.

"How Mother Nature intended Golf Courses"

Castletown Golf Links
Fort Island, Derbyhaven, Isle of Man
Telephone (01624) 822220
Fax (01624) 829661
e-mail: 1sttee@manx.net
www.golfiom.com

See also Colour Advertisement on page 43

PLEASE MENTION THE GOLF GUIDE WHEN YOU WRITE OR PHONE TO ENQUIRE ABOUT CLUBS OR ACCOMMODATION

Golf in THE ISLE OF MAN

PORT ERIN. Rowany Golf Club, Rowany Drive, Port Erin IM9 6LN (Tel & Fax: 01624 834072). *Location:* off the Promenade, five minutes from Port Erin. Hilly setting and meadowland. 18 holes, 5774 yards. S.S.S. 69. Practice ground. *Green Fees*: weekdays £22.00 per round, weekends £28.00 per round. *Eating facilities:* restaurant and bar meals. *Visitors:* welcome by arrangement, few restrictions. Accommodation can be arranged. *Society Meetings:* welcome. Secretary: Mr A.Q. Bashforth. General Manager: Mr C.A. Corrin (Tel & Fax: 01624 834072).

PORT ST MARY. Port St Mary Golf Club, Point Road, Port St Mary (01624 834932). *Location:* clearly signposted after entering Port St Mary. Seaside links with beautiful panoramic views. 9 holes, 2885 yards. S.S.S. 68. *Green Fees:* weekdays £10.00; weekends £15.00. Twilight or with member £9.00. 10% discount for Societies. *Eating facilities:* restaurant and bar open all day. *Visitors:* welcome at all times, only restrictions weekends between 8am to 10.30am. Handicap Certificate required. Secretary: T. M. Boyle (01624 837231; 07624 497387).

RAMSEY. Ramsey Golf Club, Brookfield, Ramsey (01624 812244; Fax: 01624 815833). *Location:* west boundary of Ramsey. Parkland. 18 holes, 5982 yards. S.S.S. 69. Practice area. *Green Fees:* weekdays £25.00; weekends: £35.00. *Eating facilities*: bar and restaurant. *Visitors:* welcome. *Society Meetings:* welcome weekdays only. Professional: Andrew Dyson (01624 814736).

SANTON. **Mount Murray Golf Club,** Mount Murray, Santon (01624 661111; Fax: 01624 661116). *Location:* three miles from Douglas on the Castletown road. Wooded parkland set on hills with panoramic views. 18 holes, 6715 yards. S.S.S. 73. 24-bay driving range, two-tier putting green. *Green Fees:* information not available. *Eating facilities:* full hotel catering, bistro, dining room, two bars. *Visitors:* welcome at any time by arrangement with the Professional. 90 bedroomed four star hotel. *Society Meetings:* welcome at any time by arrangement with the Secretary. Professional: Andrew Dyson. *

FHG Guides 2006

October Edition

- Recommended COUNTRY HOTELS
- Recommended COUNTRY INNS & PUBS
- BED & BREAKFAST STOPS • CHILDREN WELCOME!
- The Original FHG Guide to COAST & COUNTRY HOLIDAYS
- CARAVAN & CAMPING HOLIDAYS, England, Scotland, Wales & Ireland
- BRITAIN'S BEST HOLIDAYS
- THE GOLF GUIDE Where to Play / Where to Stay
- PETS WELCOME!
- Recommended SHORT BREAK HOLIDAYS in Britain
- SELF CATERING HOLIDAYS in Britain

April Edition

Available from bookshops or larger newsagents

FHG Guides LTD
Abbey Mill Business Centre,
Seedhill, Paisley PA1 1TJ
www.holidayguides.com

please mention THE GOLF GUIDE when you enquire about clubs or accommodation

The Channel Islands

ALDERNEY. **Alderney Golf Club,** Route des Carrieres, Alderney (01481 822835; Fax: 01481 823609). *Location:* one mile east of St Annes. Seaside links with sea views from every hole. 9 holes, 2528 yards. S.S.S. 65. Putting green and practice range. *Green Fees:* available on request. *Eating facilities:* friendly lounge bar with bar meals all day. *Visitors:* welcome all year, tees reserved for competitions only. *Society Meetings:* welcome by arrangement. Hon. Secretary: C.L. Cummings.

GUERNSEY. **La Grande Mare Golf Club,** Vazon Bay, Castel, Guernsey GY5 7LL (01481 253544; Fax: 01481 255194). *Location*: on west coast main road. Parkland course. 18 holes, 5112 yards. S.S.S. 67. *Green Fees:* information not provided. *Eating facilities*: full hotel facilities, restaurant, bar, leisure club. *Visitors:* welcome at most times by prior booking. La Grande Mare Hotel. Changing facilities and Pro Shop. Trolleys, clubs for hire. *Society Meetings:* welcome. Professional: Matt Groves (01481 253432; Fax: 01481 255194). Secretary: Mr Nick Graham (01481 253544; Fax: 01481 255194).

GUERNSEY. **Royal Guernsey Golf Club,** L'Ancresse, Vale, Guernsey GY3 5BY (01481 247022). *Location:* three miles north of St Peter Port. Seaside links. 18 holes, 6215 yards. S.S.S. 70. Driving range. *Green Fees:* information not available. *Eating facilities:* restaurant and bar. *Visitors:* welcome except Thursday and Saturday afternoons and Sundays unless playing with a member. Must have Handicap Certificate. Professional: Norman Wood (01481 245070). Secretary: Roy Bushby (01481 246523; Fax: 01481 243960).*

GUERNSEY. **St Pierre Park Golf Club,** Rohais, St. Peter Port, Guernsey (01481 727038; Fax: 01481 712041). *Location:* 10 minutes' drive from town centre. Wooded parkland with numerous lakes. 9 holes, 1323 yards, 1210 metres. S.S.S. 50. Driving range, putting green. *Green Fees:* information not available. *Eating facilities:* two restaurants and two bars. *Visitors:* welcome, all times bookable. Subject to rules and regulations on display. Hotel accommodation in 135 luxurious rooms and suites. Tennis. Pro Shop/Club Manager: R. Corbet. *

Discover ALDERNEY

Leave behind the 9 to 5 and the stress of modern life. Just off the south coast of England lies the Channel Island of Alderney - so close, but a world away! Stunning scenery, mild climate, golden beaches, abundant wildlife, miles of rambling or cycling, superb cuisine, genuine hospitality, duty free and, most important of all ... total relaxation. However, for those with more energy there's a great golf course and some of the best fishing in Europe.

Getting there is fast and easy with direct flights from Bournemouth, Brighton, Southampton or Jersey and Guernsey.
For a free brochure contact: Alderney Tourism, PO Box 1, Alderney GY9 3AA Tel: 01481 822333 Email: tourism@alderney.net
Please quote this publication.

The Island for Every Season

www.alderney.net
Men's Golf Open: 2-4 June
Senior Veterans Golf Open: 1-3 September

See also Colour Advertisement on page 22

ALDERNEY GOLF CLUB
Route des Carrieres, Alderney, Channel Islands
Tel: 01481 822835 Fax: 01481 823609
- 9 holes, 2528 yards. S.S.S. 365
- Putting green and practice range
- Green Fees: available on request
- Eating facilities: friendly lounge bar with bar meals all day
- Visitors welcome all year, tees reserved for competitions only
- Society Meetings welcome by arrangement
- Hon. Secretary: C.L. Cummings

~ Located one mile east of St Annes. ~
Seaside links with sea views from every hole.

JERSEY. **Jersey Recreation Grounds,** Greve d'Azette, St Clement, Jersey (01534 721938). *Location:* inner coast road near St Helier. Flat course with some water hazards. 9 holes, 2149 yards. S.S.S. 30. Practice green and putting green. *Green Fees:* information not available. Clubs available to hire. *Eating facilities:* licensed buffet. *Visitors:* welcome at all times. *Society Meetings:* welcome. Manager: H. Cooper.

JERSEY. **La Moye Golf Club,** St Brelade, Jersey JE3 8GQ (01534 743401; Fax: 01534 747289). *Location:* on road to Corbiere Lighthouse at La Moye, St Brelade. Turn right at airport crossroads, right again at crossroads traffic lights. Seaside links championship course. 18 holes, 6664 yards. S.S.S. 72. Practice ground. *Green Fees:* weekdays £55.00; weekends £60.00. *Eating facilities*: full restaurant/snack facilities, three bars. *Visitors*: weekdays 9.30 to 11am and 2 to 3.30pm, weekends 2.30pm onwards. Must have Handicap Certificate. *Society Meetings*: by prior appointment only. Professional: Mike Deeley (01534 743130; Fax: 01534 7499565). Secretary/Manager: Ian Prentice (01534 743401). Course Ranger's Office: (01534 747166).

JERSEY. **Les Mielles Golf and Country Club,** St Ouen's Bay, Jersey JE3 7FQ (01534 482787; Fax: 01534 485414). *Location:* centre of St Ouen's Bay. Set in an American styled seaside parkland course with "bent grass" greens and fairways of "dwarf rye". The 18 hole course plays 5758 yards, Par 70 gents, 5253 yards, Par 71 ladies. Other facilities include: 25 bay covered driving range, practice putting green, 75 yard short hole practice hole. *Green Fees:* please refer to our website or telephone for 2006 prices. *Eating facilities:* Rocco's on site 120 seater restaurant, Rocco's bar, BBQ and seasonal patio area. *Visitors:* always welcome, pre-booking necessary. Smart golfing attire required; no jeans. VAT Free Pro Shop, miniature golf, laser clay pigeon shooting, hire equipment available - carts, buggies, clubs. *Society Meetings:* welcome, packages available. Professionals: Wayne Osmand, Lynne Cummins and Adam Jones (ATZ) (01534 483252). Administration, Enquiries & Corporate Bookings: please call (01534 485984).
e-mail: enquire@lesmielles.co.je
website & online booking: www.lesmielles.com

JERSEY. **Les Ormes Golf & Leisure Club,** Mont à la Brune, St. Brelade JE3 8FL (01534 497000; Fax: 01534 499122). *Location:* on top of Mont à la Brune, adjacent to the airport. Attractive elevated course with beautiful coastal views. 9 hole course, 2509 yards, S.S.S. 65 white, 63 yellow. 17 bay covered driving range, practice bunkers and putting green. *Green Fees:* information not available. *Eating facilities;* restaurant and bar with terrace. *Visitors:* welcome, pre-booking advisable. Health and fitness complex, eight indoor tennis courts and LTA qualified coaches. Hair and Beauty salon on site. *Society Meetings:* welcome by arrangement. Professional: Andrew Chamberlain (01534 744464). General Manager: Mike Graham (01534 497002). Secretary: Frank Le Quesne (01534 853809).

JERSEY. **Royal Jersey Golf Club,** Grouville, Jersey JE3 9BD (01534 854416; Fax: 01534 854684). *Location:* take coast road from St Helier, head towards Gorey. Seaside links course. 18 holes, 6100 yards. S.S.S. 70. *Green Fees:* information not provided. *Eating facilities:* restaurant and bar. *Visitors:* welcome weekdays between 10am and 12 noon or 2pm to 4pm; weekends after 2.30pm. Handicap Certificate required. *Society Meetings:* welcome by prior arrangement. Professional: D Morgan (01534 852234; Fax: 01534 854684). Secretary: D.J. Attwood.

JERSEY. **Wheatlands Golf Course and Country Hotel,** Off Old Beaumont Hill, St Peter, Jersey JE3 7ED (01534 888844; Fax: 01534 69880). *Location:* Le Vieux Beaumont, which is road forking off to right by Cannon, and then first right at top of hill. Officially opened by Ian Woosnam in 1994, Jersey's only inland/parkland course; undulating setting with pond features and extensive countryside views. 9 holes (18 tees), 2767 yards, S.S.S. 54. Practice nets. *Green Fees:* weekdays £12.50 per round, weekends £14.00 per round. *Eating facilities:* "Tenth Hole Bar", "Garden Terrace" - snacks and meals. *Visitors:* always welcome. Accommodation available in 20 en suite rooms. Hire equipment available - clubs, shoes, carts; VAT free shop. Professional tuition. *Society Meetings:* welcome. Professional: Terry Le Brocq. website: www.wheatlandsjersey.com

---

▶ The Royal Jersey Golf Club ◀
Grouville, Jersey JE3 9BD
Tel: 01534 854416 • Fax: 01534 854684

- Seaside links course – 18 holes, 6100 yards, SSS 70.
- Restaurant and bar • Visitors welcome between 10am and 12 noon or 2pm to 4pm; weekends after 2.30pm.
  Handicap Certificate required. • Society meetings welcome by prior arrangement

See also Colour Advertisement on page 23

Golf in France
Where to Play, Where to Stay
Michael Gedye

Of all the overseas countries we have featured here in *The Golf Guide*, France is the only one with short-term access from Britain by car, either via ferry, rail link or the Channel Tunnel. It is feasible to motor to Spain and Portugal, possibly using a car ferry to northern Spain, but it only makes sense if you have enough time to spare. The beauty of France is that most of the holiday golf courses follow the coastline and many are within easy reach for a weekend or short golfing break. With the excellent domestic motorway network, even more southerly destinations are closer than they used to be but, as an alternative, the increasing availability of cheap flights offers a further dimension. One big advantage of taking your car, especially if it is not too overloaded to start with, is the opportunity to stock up on the wide range of regional foods and culinary specialities as well as a few cases of surprisingly affordable vintage wines.

There is a familiar feel to playing the game in France. Many courses represent the country's golfing heritage, having been laid out by British professionals in the first part of the last century. Even more recent holiday resort courses, while incorporating the latest features of international design, retain a clubhouse atmosphere that embodies the essential spirit of the game. Should you have the opportunity to play in a local club competition, remember your handicap certificate. Some aspects will be different; both sexes play in the same competition together, tees vary according to your handicap, which in France ranges up to 54 for men, and competitions are almost invariably stableford rather than strokeplay. However, whatever your score, the *apres-golf* prizegiving, often with accompanying buffet and wine, is memorable. We have recommended those courses with most holiday golf appeal, in seven national regions. You will discover fine facilities, good value and a warm welcome.

Just across the narrowest Channel crossing is the NORTH, covering the areas of Pas-de-Calais, Picardy and Normandy. Play Le Touquet, Hardelot, Wimereux or elegant Deauville for a taste of golfing history or alternatively, seek out the modern challenges of Champ de Bataille and Belle Dune.

Mirroring the West Country, Brittany in the NORTH-WEST has long been a British holiday favourite. With the Western Loire, it is part of a region of contrasts. There is the typical coastal links-style golf of Brest Iroise and St Jean de Monts or inland you can find the wooded parkland and ancient châteaux of La Freslonnière near Rennes, popular Golf de la Bretesche and Golf International Barrière La Baule, linked to its long-established resort hotels and casino.

Nobody would visit enchanting PARIS just for golf, but a number of courses are available, including the French Open challenge of Golf National and the gentle parkland of Golf des Yvelines.

WEST & CENTRE includes the châteaux country of the River Loire plus the regions of Poitou Charentes, Limousin and Auvergne. You can expect some fine golf here including the unheralded test of Les Bordes, enchanting Château des Sept Tours and the majestic slopes of Golf de Royan near the sea.

The largest area is the EAST, with Champagne-Ardennes, Lorraine, Alsace, Burgundy, Franche Compte, French Alps and the Rhone Valley. Along with the golf is a deserved reputation for cuisine and wine amid a panorama of crystal lakes and snow-capped peaks. Remember your camera and a good appetite.

The most concentrated choice of high quality golf is located in the pine-wood coastline of the SOUTH-WEST. The historic region of Aquitaine is home to truffles, foie gras and, unquestionably, the finest grand cru wines in the world around Bordeaux. Golf in France was born here at Pau exactly 150 years ago and this historic pedigree is exemplified at Biarritz du Phare (1888), Chiberta, Chantaco, La Nivelle and Hossegor. Golf is linked to neighbouring vineyards at the more recent, superbly challenging 36-holes of Golf du Médoc or Château des Vigiers. American-style layouts wind past tall local pines at Golf du Pessac, Gujan Mestras and Moliets and, a bit further south, dictate play at demanding Seignosse and Arcangues.

From Languedoc-Roussillon bordering Spain, the Mediterranean coastline curves past Provence to the glittering Côte d'Azur and Monte Carlo. This is the SOUTH, world-famous as an upmarket holiday destination and home to a good selection of courses, both old and new. Notables include Cap d'Agde, La Grande-Motte, Massane, Nîmes and Riviera plus the coastal crags of Fregate and gentler parkland of Royal Mougins. Offshore, on the island of Corsica, the Robert Trent Jones layout of Sperone offers dramatic golf above the sea.

Golf Hotel Seignosse, Bayonne

NORTH

BAYEUX. **Golf d'Omaha Beach,** Ferme St. Sauveur, 14520 Port-en-Bessin (02 31.22.12.12; Fax: 02 31.22.12.13). *Location:* from Paris, A13 towards Caen. Don't go into the city, take the ring road towards Bayeux, follow signs to Port-en-Bessin. Hilly course; 9 holes on the sea, above the cliffs and beaches that witnessed the landing of the allied forces in June 1944. 18 holes, 6216 metres. S.S.S. 70; 9 holes, 2693 metres. S.S.S. 36. Driving range, practice area, pitch and putt course. *Green Fees:* information not available. *Eating facilities:* available at the clubhouse. *Visitors:* welcome. Professional: M. Marc Eve, M. Julien Thomas. Secretary: Stephanie Cornil, Laure Tancoigne (02 31.22.12.12; Fax: 02 31.22.12.13). *

BOULOGNE. **Golf de Wimereux,** Route d'Ambleteuse, 62930 Wimereux (03 21.32.43.20). *Location:* just off motorway A16 between Calais and Boulogne, North of Wimereux on the D940, seven km north of Boulogne. Venerable Scottish-style links course with broad fairways between sea and dunes. 18 holes, 6150 metres, Par 72. Two practice grounds, putting green, training bunker. *Green Fees:* 40 euros for 18 holes, 25 euros for 9 holes; members 28 euros for 18 holes, 15 euros for 9 holes. *Eating facilities:* bar and restaurant (closed Mondays July/August). *Visitors:* welcome. Trolley and buggy hire. *Society Meetings:* welcome weekdays, special rates. Professional: Alexandre Devaux. Office: Nicolas Bouzin/ Maxime Domaine (03 21.32.43.20; Fax: 03 21.33.62.21).
e-mail: golf.wimereux@wanadoo.fr

CAEN. **Golf de Caen,** Le Vallon, 14112 Bieville Beuville (02 31.94.72.09; Fax: 02 31.47.45.30). *Location:* follow road to Guistreham car ferries, first on your right to Château de Beauregard. A hilly course, wooded. 18 holes, 6155 metres, Par 72; 9 holes, 2950 metres, Par 36. Practice area, putting green. *Green Fees:* information not available. *Eating facilities:* available except Tuesdays. Pro shop. Professional: Christian Carle (02 31.95.17.70). Secretaries: Corinne/Elizabeth (02 31.94.72.09).*

DEAUVILLE. **Golf Barrière de Deauville,** Le Mont Canisy, BP 63500, Saint-Arnoult, 14803 Deauville (02 31.14.24.24; Fax: 02 31.14.24.25). *Location:* on the south-western side of Deauville with the sea to the north. A scenic and varied course, hilly in part with fast greens. 18 holes, 5951 metres, Par 71. 9 holes, 3038 metres, Par 36. Practice ground and putting green. *Green Fees:* information not available. *Eating facilities:* bar and restaurant in clubhouse; all facilities at the adjoining Golf Hotel. *Visitors:* welcome, Handicap Certificates required. Reservations 24 hours in advance. Pro shop; cart and trolley hire. Professional: C. Hausseguy (02 31.14.24.24). Secretary: J Paul Oudin.*

DEAUVILLE. **Golf de St Gatien Deauville,** Le Mont Saint Jean, 14130 Saint Gatien des Bois (02 31.65.19.99; Fax: 02 31.65.11.24). *Location:* about eight km inland and eight km east of Deauville. An interesting course with 9 holes, sloping steeply through woodland, plenty of sand and strategic water. Three 9 hole courses Par 72 (18 holes), 3044 metres (White), 3228 metres (Red), 3035 metres (Yellow). Practice facilities, putting, bunkers. *Green Fees:* information not available. *Eating facilities:* bar and restaurant in rustic 18th century clubhouse (02 31.65.48.97). *Visitors:* welcome. Pro shop; cart, trolley and club hire. *Society Meetings:* welcome, special rates available. Three professionals. *

GRANVILLE. **Golf de Granville - Baie du Mont Saint Michel,** Route de la Plage, 50290 Breville-sur-Mer (02 33.50.23.06; Fax: 02 33.61.91.87). *Location:* near Granville, towards Coutances and Cherbourg. Seaside links. 18 holes, 5834 metres, Par 71. 9 holes, 2186 metres, Par 33. Driving range, putting green. *Green Fees:* information not available. *Eating facilities:* bar and restaurant in clubhouse. Pro shop; trolley and club hire. *Visitors:* welcome, no restrictions. Special rates for groups over 10. *
e-mail: granville@best-channel-golfs.com
www.best-channel-golfs.com/granville/acces.htm

HARDELOT. **Golf d'Hardelot "Les Dunes",** 3 Avenue du Golf, 62152 Hardelot (03 21.91.90.90; Fax: 03 21.83.24.33). *Location:* at Hardelot Plage, 15km south of Boulogne. Gently sloping dunes with attractive pine trees. 18 holes, 6031 metres, Par 73. Golf academy, practice facilities. *Green Fees:* information not available. *Eating facilities:* available. *Visitors:* welcome. Handicap Certificate required. *Society Meetings:* welcome. Professionals: Louis Maisonnave/ David Amat (06.83.34.70.62/ 06.87.45.72.27). Secretary: B. Blampain (03 21.83.73.10; Fax: 03 21.83.24.33). Director of Golf: Ken Strachan. *
e-mail: hardelot@opengolfclub.com
website: www.opengolfclub.com

HARDELOT. **Golf d'Hardelot "Les Pins",** 3 Avenue du Golf, 62152 Hardelot (02 21.83.73.10; Fax: 03.21.83.24.33). *Location:* the beach-resort of Hardelot Plage is 15 km south of Boulogne. Attractive course carved through a pine forest. 18 holes, 5926 metres, Par 73. Practice ground, putting green. *Green Fees:* information not available. *Eating facilities:* clubhouse with bar and fine restaurant. Handicap Certificate required. Pro shop; club and trolley hire. Professionals: Louis Maisonnave/David Amat (03 21.91.89.80/ 06.87.45.72.27). Secretary: B. Blampain (03 21.83.73.10; Fax: 03 21.83.24.33). Director of Golf: Ken Strachan. *
e-mail: hardelot@opengolfclub.com
website: www.opengolfclub.com

LAON. **Golf de l'Ailette,** 02860 Cerny-en-Laonnois (03.23.24.83.99). *Location:* about 12km south of Laon, autoroute A26 exit Laon. An interesting course laid out on the edge of a forest flanked by large areas of water. 18 holes, 6127 metres, Par 72. 9 holes, 1753 metres, Par 32. Practice ground, pitch and putt, putting green. *Green Fees:* information not available. *Eating facilities:* bar and restaurant. *Visitors:* welcome. Handicap required (maximum 35). *Society Meetings:* welcome, 20% to 30% discount for groups. Professional: Eric Censier. Secretaries: Miss Sylvie Dolat and Mrs Marie Christine Harant (03.23.24.83.99; Fax: 03.23.24.84.66). *

546 Golf in FRANCE

LE TOUQUET. **Golf du Touquet,** Avenue du Golf - BP41, 62520 Le Touquet (03 21.06.28.00; Fax: 03 21.06.28.01). *Location:* 20km from Boulogne, on the coast, 3km from Le Touquet centre. La Forêt Course created in 1904 set in the heart of an old pine forest - 18 holes, 5821 metres, S.S.S. 70.6, Par 71. La Mer Course, designed by Harry S. Colt (1931), is a championship links course laid out amongst wild sand dunes - 18 holes, 6275 metres. S.S.S 74.9, Par 72. Le Manoir Course is perfect for beginners - 9 holes, 2817 metres, S.S.S. 35, Par 35. Practice range and putting green. *Green Fees:* midweek from 45 euros to 79 euros; weekends from 55 euros to 99 euros. *Eating facilities:* bar and restaurant in clubhouse. *Visitors:* welcome. Maximum Handicaps: La Forêt Course 35, La Mer Course 24 Gentlemen, 28 Ladies; no Handicap required for Le Manoir Course. *Society Meetings:* welcome. Pro Shop; carts, caddies. Accommodation available in Le Manoir Hotel (3 Star) facing La Forêt course. Professionals: Didier Behin, Daphné Lesur. Manager: Gilles Grattepanche.

LILLE. **Golf de Bondues,** Château de la Vigne, BP 54, 59587 Bondues Cedex (03 20.23.20.62). *Location:* about 10km north of Lille, west of the N17. In the grounds of an 18th century chateau, the courses have well protected greens with deep bunkers and several water hazards. 18 holes, 6163 metres, Par 73. 18 holes, 6009 metres, Par 72. Driving range, putting green. *Green Fees:* information not available. *Eating facilities:* bar and restaurant in clubhouse. *Visitors:* welcome. Closed Tuesdays. Trolley hire. Lessons available. Professional: (03 20.23.13.87). Secretary: (03 20.23.20.62; Fax: 03 20.23.24.11). *
e-mail: golfdebondues@nordnet.fr

NEUBOURG. **Golf Club du Champ de Bataille,** 27110 Le Neubourg (02 32.35.03.72; Fax: 02 32.35.83.10). *Location:* south west of Rouen, about 28km north west of Evreux. A fine test of golf attractively laid out through the wooded estate of the elegant château. Par 3 holes. 18 holes, 6575 yards, 5983 metres, Par 72. Driving range, putting green. *Green Fees:* information not provided. *Eating facilities:* bar and restaurant. *Visitors:* welcome, no restrictions. Pro shop; cart, trolley and club hire. Guest rooms available in the château. New clubhouse built on the edge of the wood, independent of the Château, offering a wide range of services. *Society Meetings:* welcome. Secretary: Ingrid Thommerel.

ROUEN. **Golf du Vaudreuil,** 27100 le Vaudreuil (02 32.59.02.60; Fax: 02.32.59.43.88). *Location*: 30km south-east of Rouen, east of the RN15 and the A13, 5 km from Louviers. A flat course, designed by Hawtree in 1961 in wooded parkland. 18 holes, Par 73. Driving range, buggies, trolleys, clubs. *Green Fees:* information not available. *Eating facilities*: beautiful clubhouse with bar and restaurant. On course Hotel du Golf (Two star) offers special Hotel and Golf packages (02.32.59.02.94; Fax: 02 32.59.67.39).*

THE GOLF GUIDE 2006

SAINT-JULIEN-SUR-CALONNE. **Golf & Country Club de Saint-Julien,** B.P. 76, 14130 Pont l'Eveque, Saint-Julien-sur-Calonne (02.31.64.30.30; Fax: 02.31.64.12.43). *Location:* A13 leaving Pont l'Eveque, near Deauville (Normandy). Hilly 18 and 9 hole courses in the heart of the Pays d'Auge in Normandy. 18 hole course 6670 yards, 6065 metres, S.S.S. 72; 9 hole course 2500 yards, 2275 metres, S.S.S. 33. Driving range, putting green, bunker and approach green. *Green Fees:* information not available. *Eating facilities:* Restaurant open from 12 noon to 4pm from April to September. Bar facilities available. *Visitors:* welcome every day. *Societies:* welcome every day, special rates for groups of more than ten. Driving range, buggies, carts, caddies, trolleys available. Professional: Alain Quibeuf (02.31.64.99.58; mobile: 06.07.01.64.27). Manager: J. M. Bonnet. *

ST OMER. **Aa Saint-Omer Golf Club,** Chemin des Bois, Acquin-Westbécourt 62380 Lumbres (03.21.38.59.90; Fax: 03.21.93.02.47). *Location:* from Calais take A26 Autoroute, Junction 3 St Omer, right onto RN42 Expressway, first exit Acquin/Lumbres (30 minutes from Calais). Undulating parkland with mature trees overlooking the valley of the River Aa. La Haute Drève: 9 holes 2015 metres, Par 31; Le Val 18 holes 5979 metres, Par 73. Practice ground and putting green. *Green Fees:* information not available. *Eating facilities:* clubhouse bar and restaurant. *Visitors:* welcome all year, no restrictions. Golf and accommodation packages on request. Pro shop; trolley, buggy and club hire. Course selected by the European Tour. *Society Meetings:* welcome, special packages available. Professional: Sylvain Raout. Manager: Sandrine Grevet. *
e-mail: aa-st-omer.golf@najeti.com
website: www.aa-st-omer-golfclub.com

NORTH WEST

ANGERS. **Anjou Golf and Country Club,** Route de Cheffes, 49330 Champigne (02 41.42.01.01; Fax: 02 41.42.04.37). *Location:* about 20km north of Angers, from Paris A11, exit Durtal. Flat course with a few lakes and trees. 18 holes, 6227 metres, Par 72. Short 6 hole course, 750 metres, Par 19. Practice facilities. *Green Fees:* information not available. *Eating facilities:* "Le Prince Noir" traditional catering; "L'Auberge de Mozé" gastronomic catering. *Visitors:* welcome. Starting times must be booked in advance. Pro shop; cart, trolley and club hire; flats to rent at golf course. Professional/Director: Stephane Guguen. Secretaries: Christelle, Gaëlle, Valérie. *
e-mail: info@anjougolf.com

THE APPEARANCE OF AN ASTERISK (*) AT THE END OF A CLUB OR COURSE ENTRY INDICATES THAT UP-TO-DATE INFORMATION HAS NOT BEEN SUPPLIED

Golf in FRANCE

ANGERS. **Golf de Sablé-Solesmes,** Domaine de l'Outinière, Route de Pincé, 72300 Sablé-sur-Sarthe (02 43.95.28.78; Fax: 02 43.92.39.05). *Location:* east of the A11, exit 10 (Sablé La Flèche), about 40km north of Angers, south-east of Le Mans. Three totally different 9s - Forest and River: 18 holes, 6189 metres, Par 72; Waterfall: 9 holes, 3069 metres, Par 36, radiate from the large clubhouse. Testing and spectacular with park, woodland and lakeside holes. Driving range, putting green. *Green Fees:* information not available. *Eating facilities:* bar and restaurant in clubhouse. Pro shop; cart, trolley and club hire. Professional: Christian Blanc. Director: Yves Pironneau.

AURAY. **Golf de Baden,** Kernic, 56870 Baden (02 97.57.18.96; Fax: 02 97.57.22.05). *Location:* between the village of Baden and the sea, south of the RN 165 at Auray exit. Undulating course partly through pine woods and around lakes. 18 holes, 6112 metres, Par 72. 3 hole, 535 metres pitch and putt course. Practice area, putting green, approach green. *Green Fees:* information not available. *Eating facilities:* bar and restaurant. Pro shop; trolley and club hire; club repair. Neighbouring hotels "Le Gavrinis" and "du Loch" offer year-round golfing breaks. *Society Meetings:* welcome, special rates. Professional: J. F. Le Gall. Secretaries: Mme. Le Quilliec, Mme. Burguin. Director: Mr O. Charmont.*

AURAY. **Golf de Saint Laurent,** 56400 Ploemel, Auray (02 97.56.85.18; Fax: 02 97.56.89.99). *Location:* about 10 km west of Auray and not far from Carnac with its ancient standing stones. High quality championship course, undulating through mature trees. 18 holes, 6112 metres, Par 72. 9 hole course, 2705 metres, Par 35. Driving range. *Green Fees:* information not available. *Eating facilities:* bar and restaurant in on-course Fairway Hotel St Laurent; also on-course "Maeva" self-catering cottages available. *Visitors:* welcome. Pro shop; cart, trolley and club hire. Professionals: Mr D. Jouan and Mr A. Brien.*

BENODET. **Golf de l'Odet,** Benodet Menez Groas, Clohars-Fouesnant, 29950 Benodet (02.98.54.87.88; Fax: 02.98.54.61.40). *Location:* 12km south of Quimper, towards the sea at Benodet. An undulating partly wooded course. 18 holes, 6235 metres, Par 72. 9 holes, 1100 metres, Par 27. Driving range, putting green, pitching green, short game area. *Green Fees:* information not available. *Eating facilities:* bar, restaurant and on-site Hotel Eurogreen, whose residents have reduced green fees. *Visitors:* welcome, no restrictions but advisable to book tee times. Other accommodation nearby. Pro shop; cart, trolley and club hire. Professional: C. Olivard. Secretary: Christophe Bodere (02.98.54.87.88; Fax: 02.98.52.61.40)*

BREST. **Golf de Brest Iroise,** Parc de Loisirs de Lann Rohou, 29800 Landerneau (02 98.85.16.17; Fax: 02 98.85.19.39). *Location:* 10 miles east of Brest, three miles south of Landerneau. A tough course, open to the breeze in a beautiful natural setting. 18 holes, 5672 metres, Par 71. 9 holes, 3329 metres, Par 37. 22 bay driving range, 2 putting greens. *Green Fees:* information no available. *Eating facilities:* bar and restaurant and all facilities at the Golf Hotel d'Iroise. *Visitors:* welcome. Pro shop; cart, trolley and club hire. Golf/Hotel packages. *Society Meetings:* welcome. Professional: Philippe Le Verche. Secretary: Guylene (02 98 85 16 17).

LA BAULE. **Golf de la Bretesche,** 44780 Missillac (02 51.76.86.86; Fax: 02 40.88.36.28). *Location:* 20km and 20mm north-east of La Baule; 50km and 30mm north of Nantes on the N167. In a wooded and magnificent forest (2600 acres), large fairways and superb greens cover an area of 480 acres and borders the picturesque Chateau de la Bretesche surrounded by a vast lake. 18 holes, 6700 yards, S.S.S. 72. Practice ground, putting green, training bunker. *Green Fees:* information not available. *Eating facilities:* two bars and two restaurants. *Visitors:* welcome. Pro shop, cart, club and trolley hire. *Society Meetings:* welcome. Professional: Thierry Mathon. Manager: Fabrice Gicquiand. Secretary: Stephane Harouard/Francoise Desmarches (02 51.76.86.86; Fax: 02 40.88.36.28). *

LA BAULE. **Golf International Barrière La Baule,** 44117 St-André-des-Eaux (02.40.60.46.18; Fax: 02.40.60.41.41). *Location:* to the east of La Baule, 3 km from St André des Eaux. Three parkland courses with interesting water features. Red Course: 18 holes, 6055 metres, Par 72. Green Course: 9 hole course, 2961 metres, Par 36. Blue Course 18 hole, 6301 metres, Par 72. Golf Academy: designed by Jack Nicklaus. *Green Fees:* information not available. *Eating Facilities:* bar and restaurant. *Visitors:* welcome by reservation booked the day before. Pro shop; cart, club and trolley hire; target and putting green, approach zone, training bunker and coaching studio. *Society Meetings:* welcome by arrangement.*
e-mail: golfinterlabaule@lucienbarriere.com
website: www.lucienbarriere.com

LA ROCHE-SUR-YON. **Golf Club de la Domangère,** Route de la Rochelle, 85310 Nesmy (02 51.07.65.90; Fax: 02 51.07.65.95). *Location:* approximately 10km south of La Roche-sur-Yon west of the D747. A long and majestic course with plenty of strategic water, mature trees and bordered by the River Yon. 18 holes, 6480 metres, Par 72. 4 hole practice course, driving range, putting green. *Green Fees:* information not available. *Eating facilities:* bar, grill-room. *Visitors:* welcome. Club, cart and trolley hire. Hotel apartments. *Society Meetings:* welcome, booking required. Professional: Mr A. Stephane.*

For full details of clubs and courses, plus convenient accommodation
www.uk-golfguide.com

LORIENT. **Golf du Val Quéven,** Kerrousseau RD 6, 56530 Quéven (02 97.05.17.96; Fax: 02 97.05.19.18). *Location*: nearest main road RN165, Quéven situated between Lorient and Pont Scorff. Offering an impressive and diversified landscape built around 100 year old trees, the course is very challenging and is one of the best in western France. 18 holes, 6140 metres, Par 72. Driving range, putting green. *Green Fees*: information not available. *Eating facilities*: bar and restaurant. Visitors: welcome. Pro shop; club and trolley hire. *Society Meetings*: welcome. Professional: Mario Zimmermann (02 97.05.17.96; Fax: 02 97.05.19.18). Secretaries: Anita Le Bousseau and M. Frédéric Dellsperger (02 97.05.17.96; Fax: 02 97.05.19.18). Director: Jean Luc Leroux.

LORIENT. **Parcours Formule Golf Ploemeur Ocean,** Saint Jude-Kerham, 56270 Ploemeur (02 97.32.81.82; Fax: 02 97.32.80.90). *Location*: RN165 exit Ploemeur, towards Fort Bloque. Seaside links course, huge American style greens, water hazards. 18 holes, 6517 yards, 5957 metres, S.S.S. 72. Covered driving range. *Green Fees*: information available. *Eating facilities*: bar and restaurant. *Visitors*: welcome. Hotels in immediate surroundings. *Society Meetings*: managed by the Parcours Formule Golf. Professional: Laurent Queffelec. Manager: Jeau Luc Leroux. *

RENNES. **Golf de la Freslonnière,** 35650 Le Rheu (02 99.14.84.09; Fax: 02 99.14.94.98). *Location:* three km from Rennes towards Lorient. Woodland course with water features and banks of rhododendrons. 18 holes, 5756 metres, Par 72. Practice ground and putting green. *Green Fees:* 34 euros/46 euros. *Eating facilities:* clubhouse, restaurant and bar (closed Mondays). *Visitors:* welcome, no restrictions. Pro shop; club, cart and trolley hire. Professional: Richard Triaire. Director: Frederic Bessonneaud.
e-mail: contact@golfdelafreslonniere.com
website: www.golfdelafreslonniere.com

RENNES. **Golf de Rennes**, St. Jacques de la Lande, 35136 Rennes (02 99.30.18.18. Fax: 02 99.30.10.25). *Location:* eight km south of Rennes, off the D177 to Redon. Brittany's largest golf course is a championship course, with fast, high quality greens. The narrow fairways have players of all levels thinking carefully about their tactics. This complex has something for everyone. 18 holes, 6713 yards, Par 72. 9 holes, 2262 yards, Par 32. 9 hole pitch and putt course. *Green Fees:* High Season 49 euros, Low Season 35 euros. *Eating facilities:* bar and restaurant in clubhouse. *Visitors:* welcome, no restrictions. Pro shop; buggies; trolley and club hire. Director: Gregory Dudouit.
e-mail: golf.rennes@formule-golf.com
website: www.formule-golf.com

For full details of clubs and courses, plus convenient accommodation

www.uk-golfguide.com

ST MALO. **Saint Malo Golf Club,** Le Tronchet, 35540 Miniac Morvan (02 99.58.96.69). *Location:* 23km south of St Malo, 12km east of Dinan, south of the N176. The 27 hole golf course is set alongside the lake of Mirloup and the forest of Mesnil and harks back to the days of Robert Surcouf's hunting lands. With a slope of 133, the strategic use of water will really test the good golfers but the rough is cut short to promote faster play and accessibility to all players. 18 holes, 5936 metres, Par 72. 9 holes, 2684 metres, Par 35. Driving range and practice facilities. *Green Fees:* approx between 35 to 50 euros. *Eating facilities:* bar and restaurant on site. *Visitors:* welcome. Charming 3 star hotel on site with 29 spacious air conditioned rooms (approx 30M^2) and L'Etang restaurant for evening meal. Ask for packages. Pro shop; trolley, club car and club hire. *Society Meetings:* welcome, bookings required. Professional: Eric Chaperon. General Manager: Philip Petersson.
website: www.saintmalogolf.com

ST JEAN-DE-MONTS. **Golf Club de St Jean-de-Monts,** Avenue des Pays de la Loire, 85160 St. Jean-de-Monts (02 51.58.82.73; Fax: 02 51.59.18.32). *Location:* a partly links-style course along the seaside with pine trees and dunes. On the Atlantic coast some 60/70km south-west of Nantes. 18 holes, 5962 metres, Par 72. Short 5 hole course. Practice ground and putting greens. *Eating facilities:* clubhouse with bar and restaurant. The Hotel de la Plage in nearby Notre Dame de Monts offers golfing breaks. Pro shop; cart, club and trolley hire. *

PARIS

PARIS. **Golf de Forges-les-Bains,** Rue de General Leclerc, 91470 Forges-les-Bains (01 64.91.48.18; Fax: 01 64.91.40.52). *Location:* A10 Orleans, exit Les Ulis then towards Limours and Forges-les-Bains; 35 minutes from Paris. Parkland course with a lot of variety and suitable for all levels of golfers. 18 holes, 6207 metres, Par 72. Driving range, three holes training course. *Green Fees:* information not available. *Eating facilities:* bar and restaurant in clubhouse. *Visitors:* welcome, no restrictions but reservations preferred. Special rates for groups and societies. David Leadbetter Golf Academy on site. Pro shop; trolley and club hire. Professionals: Jean Luc Poü and Yann Yver. Secretary: Philippe Wibaux.*

PARIS. **Golf de la Vaucouleurs,** 78910 Civry-la-Forêt (01.34.87.16.04). *Location:* off the A13 at the Mantes interchange, south off the road to Houdan. Two 18 hole courses. "The River" - very varied with trees, water and hills, 6138 metres, Par 73; "The Little Valley" - a links-type course, 5553 metres, Par 70. Practice ground, putting green. *Green Fees:* information not provided. *Eating facilities:* bar and restaurant in clubhouse; also at nearby Hotel la Dousseine at Anet. Pro shop; club and trolley hire, buggy available. Professional: Pierre Girard. Secretary: (01.34.87.62.29; Fax: 01 34.87.70.09).

Golf in FRANCE

PARIS. **Golf de St Quentin-en-Yvelines,** RD 912, 78197 Trappes (01.30.50.86.40; Fax: 01.34.82.88.82). *Location:* about 20km west of Paris off the D912. A very popular public facility of 36 holes. White Course - 18 holes, 6100 metres, S.S.S. 72; Red Course - 18 holes, 5700 metres, S.S.S. 69. Also 9 hole compact course, driving range, putting green. *Green Fees:* information not available. *Eating facilities:* bar and restaurant in clubhouse. Pro shop; trolley and club hire. Professional: Jean Marc Lecuona. Secretary: Jerome Lauredi. *

PARIS. **Golf des Yvelines,** Château de la Couharde, 78940 La Queue-les-Yvelines (01 34.86.48.89; Fax: 01 34.86.50.31). *Location:* about 45km west of Paris by N12, near Montfort-l'Amaury. Built around the elegant château, with fairways cut through thick woods. 18 holes, 6344 metres, S.S.S. 72. 9 holes, 2065 metres, S.S.S. 31. Practice ground, putting green. *Green Fees:* information not available. *Eating facilities:* bar and restaurant. *Visitors:* all visitors welcome. Club and trolley hire. Professional: Jean Paul Chardonnet. Secretary: Stephane Bessette. *

PARIS. **Golf National,** 2 Avenue du Golf, 78280 Guyancourt (01 30.43.36.00; Fax: 01 30.43.85.58). *Location:* about 25km south-west of Paris off the A13/A12, six miles from Versailles. A public facility of 45 holes laid out in three courses. "The Albatross" (now the venue for the French Open) - 18 holes, 6500 metres championship course with severe water hazards and winding fairways, Par 72; "The Eagle" - 18 holes, 6000 metres, Par 72 for experienced players; "The Birdie" - 9 holes, 2100 metres beginners' course, Par 32 and driving range; "The Par" - a warm-up, practice course. Putting greens. *Eating facilities:* on-site Hotel Novotel. Two restaurants. *Visitors:* all welcome, public course. Club and trolley hire. *

WEST & CENTRE

CHEVERNY. **Golf du Château de Cheverny,** La Rousselière, 41700 Cheverny (33 (0) 2.54.79.24.70; Fax: 33 (0) 2.54.79.25.52). *Location:* to the south of Cheverny 15km south of Blois. Built over the former hunting grounds of the Château with large well-kept greens. 18 holes, 6272 metres, Par 71. 3 hole practice course, driving range, putting green. *Green Fees:* information on website. Overseas membership available. *Eating facilities:* bar and restaurant in clubhouse. *Visitors:* welcome. Pro shop; club and trolley hire, electric carts. Swimming pool by the bar. *Society Meetings:* 20% reduction on fees. Sister Club: Rolls Of Monmouth (Wales). Professional: Pierre Raguet. e-mail: contact@golf-cheverny.com website: www.golf-cheverny.com

COGNAC. **Golf du Cognac,** Saint-Brice, 16100 Cognac (05 45.32.18.17; Fax: 05 45.35.10.76). *Location:* five km east of Cognac, north of the N141 across the River Charente. Undulating fairways with views of vineyards and the river; some water hazards. 18 holes, 6142 metres, Par 72. 4 hole practice course, putting green and driving range. *Green Fees:* information not available. *Eating facilities:* clubhouse with restaurant and bar. Pro shop; cart, club and trolley hire. Professional: (05 45.32.37.60). Secretary: (05 45.32.18.17).*

LOUDUN. **Golf de Loudun-Roiffe,** Domaine St Hilaire, 86120 Roiffe (05 49.98.78.06; Fax: 05 49.98.72.57). *Location:* 15km north of Loudun towards Saumur on the D147. An attractive woodland course with a few water hazards and well guarded greens. 18 holes, 6343 metres, S.S.S. 73, Par 72. 6 hole pitch and putt course, driving range, practice green and putting green. *Green Fees:*information not available. *Eating facilities:* restaurant; bar in clubhouse. *Visitors:* welcome, no restrictions. Two-star hotel with 64 rooms and 13 self-catering apartments, seminar rooms, entertainment room. Tennis, bicycles for hire, crazy-golf, swimming pool, playground for children, marked trails. Pro shop, trolley and club hire. *Society Meetings*: welcome. Professional: Jean-Marc Warot.*
e-mail: golf-france@interpc.fr
website: www.france-in.com

ORLEANS. **"Les Bordes" Golf International,** 41220 St-Laurent Nouan (02 54.87.72.13; Fax: 02 54.87.78.61). *Location:* from Paris motorway A10 exit Meung sur Loire. Laid out on a former hunting park. 18 holes, 7041 yards, 6412 metres, Par 72. Driving range, putting green. *Green Fees:* information not available. *Eating facilities:* bar and restaurant in clubhouse. *Visitors:* welcome every day. Pro shop; carts, trolleys and clubs for hire. Accommodation on site. *

POITIERS. **Golf du Haut-Poitou,** Parc de Loisirs de St Cyr, 86130 Saint Cyr (05 49.62.53.62; Fax: 05 49.88.77.14). *Location:* 20km north of Poitiers and 15km south of Chatellerault. Undulating course with wooded hills, a lake and water hazards. Host of a Professional International Open at the end of October in 2005. 18 holes, 6590 metres, S.S.S. 75. 9 holes, 1800 metres, Par 31. Practice ground, driving range, putting and pitching greens. *Green Fees:* information not provided. *Eating facilities:* clubhouse with brasserie and bar; Restaurant (05 49.61.53.56) *Visitors:* welcome without restriction. Pro shop and equipment hire. *Society Meetings:* welcome. Professionals: Martin Guilbaud and David Maxwell. Secretaries: Catherine Marchais and Jessica Guillon (05 49.62.53.62; Fax: 05 49.88.77.14).
e-mail: contact@golfduhautpoitou.com

PLEASE MENTION THE GOLF GUIDE WHEN YOU ENQUIRE ABOUT CLUBS OR ACCOMMODATION

ROYAN. **Golf de Royan,** Maine-Gaudin, 17420 St-Palais-sur-Mer (05 46.23.16.24; Fax: 05 46.23.23.38). *Location:* on the D25 coast road, nine km north-west of Royan. An exciting course with narrow fairways undulating through tall pines. Two courses. 18 holes, 5924 metres, S.S.S. 71; 6 hole, 920 metres, S.S.S. 20. Practice ground with driving range, putting green. *Green Fees:* information not provided. *Eating facilities:* restaurant and bar in clubhouse. *Visitors:* welcome. Pro shop with equipment hire. *Society Meetings:* welcome by arrangement with the Secretary. Professionals: Gilles Delavallade and Christine Wenandy. Secretaries: Nathalie, Christelle and Valérie (05 46.23.16.24; Fax: 05 46.23.23.38). e-mail: golfderoyan@wanadoo.fr
website: www.golfderoyan.com

TOURS. **Blue Green Golf d'Ardrée,** Golf d'Ardrée Tours, 37360 Saint Antoine du Rocher (02 47.56.77.38; Fax: 02 47.56.79.96). *Location:* near Tours north, direction of le Mans, nearest town St Antoine Du Rocher. Parkland course, wooded with water and bunkers. 18 holes, 5758 metres, Par 70. Practice ground and putting green. *Green Fees:* information not available. *Eating facilities:* restaurant and bar in clubhouse. *Visitors:* welcome but it would be better to reserve the tee two or three days in advance for weekdays, and five days in advance for weekends. *Society Meetings:* welcome but reservation a month in advance please. Professional: Karl Cotteray. Secretaries: Virginie and Corinne. *

TOURS. **Golf du Château des Sept Tours,** 37330 Courcelles de Touraine (02.47.24.69.75; Fax: 02.47.24.23.74). *Location:* 30kms from Tours on the D34 between Château la Vallière and Langeais. A fairly long course but relatively flat with attractive trees and water, excellent greens. 18 holes, 6194 metres, Par 72. Practice ground and putting green. *Green Fees:* information not available. *Eating facilities:* restaurant and bistro in clubhouse. *Visitors:* 4 star Hotel, restaurant and golf club open all year. Pro shop; club and trolley hire. Professional: Pascal Petit. *

THE APPEARANCE OF AN ASTERISK (*) AT THE END OF A CLUB OR COURSE ENTRY INDICATES THAT UP-TO-DATE INFORMATION HAS NOT BEEN SUPPLIED

EAST

AIX-LES-BAINS. **Golf d'Aix-les-Bains,** Avenue du Golf, 73100 Aix-les-Bains (04 79.61.23.35). *Location:* three km south of Aix by the Lac du Bourget. An attractive parkland course on sloping land surrounded by wooded hills. 18 holes, 5519 metres. S.S.S. 70. Practice, putting green. *Green Fees:* from 43.00 to 55.00 euros. *Eating facilities:* restaurant (04.79.61.47.20). *Visitors:* welcome. Pro shop; trolley and club hire (04.79.61.31.56). Professional: (04 79.35.39.41). Secretary: (Fax: 04 79.34.06.01). e-mail: info@golf-aixlesbains.com
website: www.golf-aixlesbains.com

CHAMONIX. **Golf de Chamonix,** 35 route du Golf, Les Praz, 74400 Chamonix (04 50.53.06.28; Fax: 04 50.53.38.69). *Location:* on the N506 three km north of Chamonix. A subtle and technical course, enhanced by water obstacles and numerous bunkers. Spectacular mountain views including Mont Blanc. 18 holes, 6076 metres, S.S.S. 72. Driving range, putting green. *Green Fees:* information not available. *Eating facilities:* restaurant. *Visitors:* welcome every day with a Handicap Certificate, tee off times must be booked one day in advance. Pro shop; cart, trolley and club hire. Professional: Jean Claude Bonnaz. Director: Christophe de Carné (04 50.53.06.28; Fax: 04 50.53.38.69)*.

EVIAN. **Evian Masters Golf Club,** South Bank of Lake Geneva, 74500 Evian-les-Bains (33-(0)4.50.26.85.00; Fax: 33-(0)4.50.75.65.54). *Location:* on high ground above Evian. 8kms from Thonon, 45kms west of Geneva. Hilly fairways overlooking Lake Geneva, sloping greens guarded by deep bunkers. Evian Masters course. 18 holes, 6674 yards, 6006 metres, Par 72. Covered and uncovered practice range, two putting greens, chipping green, pitching green, training bunkers, pitch and putt. Opening May 2006: The Evian Masters Camp. *Green Fees:* information not provided. *Eating facilities:* restaurant and bar: Le Chalet du Golf. *Visitors:* welcome, Handicap 35 or course authorization. Pro shop; clubs, bags and carts. *Society Meetings:* welcome (up to 180 people). Professional: Christophe Martigniere (courses). Co-Director: Margo Perrolaz. Director: Yannic Le Hec.

GRENOBLE. **Golf International de Grenoble,** Route de Montavie, Bresson, 38320 Eybens (04 76.73.65.00; Fax: 04 76.73.65.51). *Location:* five km south of Grenoble. A long course with winding fairways, small lakes, trees - architect Robert Trent Jones Jnr. Bresson Course 18 holes, 6343 metres, Par 73; Uriage Course 9 holes, 2005 metres. Practice ground and putting green; driving range. *Green Fees:* information not available. *Eating facilities:* clubhouse and nearby hotel. *Visitors:* welcome at all times. Professional: Loic Landoas. Manager: Herve Segrais.*

Golf in FRANCE

LYON. **Golf Club de Lyon,** 38280 Villette d'Anthon (04 78.31.11.33; Fax: 04 72.02.48.27). *Location:* Lyon, Rocade Est exit Meyzieu Grand Large. Brocards - flat, wooded; Sangliers - hilly, wooded. Brocards 18 holes, 6229 metres. S.S.S. 72; Sangliers 18 holes, 6727 metres. S.S.S 72. Practice ground, putting green, training centre. *Green Fees:* information not available. *Eating facilities:* bar and restaurant in clubhouse. *Visitors:* welcome anytime. No jeans, no powered trolleys. *Society Meetings:* welcome. Pro shop; equipment hire. Professionals: Raphael Reynaud and Ludovic Henninot (04.78.31.11.33; Fax: 04.72.02.48.27). Secretary: (04.78.31.11.33; Fax: 04 72.02.48.27). *

ST JULIEN (Geneva). **Golf and Country Club de Bossey,** Chateau de Crevin, Bossey, 74160 St-Julien-en-Genevois. *Location:* just near the main road between St. Julien en Genevois and Annemasse about five miles from each of these towns. Just in France on the southern outskirts of Geneva. Challenging mountain golf with fine views. Well wooded with water hazards. 18 holes, 5952 metres, Par 71. Driving range, putting green. *Green Fees:* information not available. *Eating facilities:* bar and restaurant in chateau clubhouse. *Visitors:* welcome weekdays only, maximum of three times a year. Maximum handicap 35. No jeans allowed on course. Contact General Manager for details. Pro shop; cart, trolley and club hire. *Society Meetings:* catered for, contact General Manager. Professional: Mark Cobley (04.50.43.65.66). Secretary: (04.50.43.95.50; Fax: 04.50.95.32.57). *

SOUTH WEST

ALBI. **Golf d'Albi Lasbordes,** Chateau de Las Bordes, 81000 Albi (05.63.54.98.07; Fax: 05.63.47.21.55). *Location:* three minutes from town centre, overlooking the River Tarn and offering beautiful views towards the cathedral. A championship course with trees. 18 holes, 6155 metres, Par 72. *Green Fees:* information not available. *Eating facilities:* bar and restaurant in clubhouse. *Visitors:* welcome all year. Club and trolley hire. Professional: Olivier Doan. *

ANGLET. **Golf de Chiberta,** 104 Boulevard des Plages, 64600 Anglet (05 59.52.51.10; Fax: 05 59.63.30.56). *Location:* three km from Biarritz and from Bayonne. A well-established combination of seashore and wooded parkland. 18 holes, 5650 metres, Par 71. Driving range, putting green. *Green Fees:* information not available. *Eating facilities:* bar and restaurant in clubhouse. *Visitors:* welcome, Handicap Certificate required. Pro shop; trolley and club hire. Professional: H. Brouson, P Dufourg, C. Lecuona. Secretary: (05 59.52.51.10; Fax: 05 59.63.30.56). *

www.uk-golfguide.com

ARCACHON. **Golf de Gujan Mestras,** BP 74, Route de Sanguinet, 33470 Gujan Mestras (05 57.52.73.73; Fax: 05 56.66.10.93). *Location:* autoroute Bordeaux/Bayonne, A66 in the direction of Arcachon. A spectacular course with well located water obstacles. 18 holes, 6225 metres, Par 72. 9 holes, 2630 metres, Par 35. Practice facilities and putting green. *Green Fees:* information not available. *Eating facilities:* restaurant, clubhouse and at nearby hotel. Pro shop; equipment and trolley hire. *

BAYONNE. **Golf de Moliets,** Rue Mathieu Desbieys, 40660 Moliets (05 58.48.54.65; Fax: 05 58.48.54.88). *Location:* about 30km north of Bayonne on the Atlantic coast at Moliets. Part of a leisure seaside complex with links and wooded inland holes. 18 holes, 6164 metres, Par 72. 9 holes, 1905 metres, Par 31. Practice ground, putting green. *Green Fees:* information not provided. *Eating facilities:* bar and restaurant in clubhouse and on-site hotels. *Visitors:* welcome. Pro shop; cart, club and trolley hire; tennis. *Society Meetings:* welcome. Professionals: Franck Ducousso, Christophe Beithet. website: www.golfmoliets.com

BAYONNE. **Seignosse Golf Hotel,** Avenue du Belvedere, 40510 Seignosse (05 58.41.68.30; Fax: 05 58.41.68.31). *Location:* about 25km north of Bayonne on the D79 north of Hossegor. Very hilly, exciting and undulating course, a pleasure to look at as well as play. Ranked 21st in the top 100 European courses by 'Golf World International'. 18 holes, 6124 metres, Par 72. Practice ground. *Green Fees:* information not available. *Eating facilities:* two bars and two restaurants. *Visitors:* welcome. 3 Star Hotel. Pro shop; cart, club and trolley hire; swimming pool. *Society Meetings:* welcome. Special golf/hotel packages available 'Golf Pass Biarritz' member. Professional: F. Martin. Director: Armand Gadea. Sales Manager: Sidonie Blanc (05 58.41.68.30). e-mail: golfseignosse@wanadoo.fr website: www.golfseignosse.com

BIARRITZ. **Golf d'Arcangues,** 64200 Arcangues (05 59.43.10.56; Fax: 05 59.43.12.60). *Location:* three km south-east of Biarritz. A fine rolling test in modern but natural style. Mounded bunkers and strategic water. 18 holes, 6142 metres, Par 72. *Green Fees:* information not available. *Eating facilities:* bar and restaurant in clubhouse. *Visitors:* welcome, no restrictions. Pro shop and equipment hire. Professional: O. Leglise. Secretary: English/French Mme Sylvie Cormier; French Mme Marie-José Dabbadie. *
e-mail: golf.arcangues@wanadoo.fr

BIARRITZ. **Golf de Biarritz Le Phare,** 2 Avenue Edith Cavell, 64200 Biarritz (05 59.03.71.80). *Location:* in Biarritz, facing the ocean with cooling breezes. A historic course (1888) with fast greens, level, many bunkers. 18 holes, 5379 metres, S.S.S. 69. Practice ground, putting green. *Green Fees:* information not available. *Eating facilities:* bar and restaurant in clubhouse, the nearby Hôtel du Palais and other hotels. Pro shop; club and trolley hire. Secretary: (05 59.03.71.80; Fax: 05 59.03.26.74).
e-mail: info@golfbiarritz.com

BORDEAUX. **Golf de Bordeaux Cameyrac,** R.N. 89 Bordeaux Libourne No. 5, 33450 Cameyrac (05 56.72.96.79; Fax: 05 56.72.86.56). *Location:* 15km from Bordeaux close to the famous vineyards of St Emilion and Pomerol. Fairways run through forest, alongside ponds and vineyards. 18 holes, 5972 metres, Par 72. 9 holes, 1188 metres, Par 28. Practice ground, putting green. *Green Fees:* 18 holes 25 to 39 euros, 9 holes 12 to 15 euros. Special fees for couples and students, Green fee packages on demand. *Eating facilities:* bar and restaurant. *Visitors:* welcome every day. Pro shop; equipment hire. *Society Meetings:* welcome. Professionals: C. Bouchet, V Fructuoso.
e-mail: contact@golf-bordeaux-cameyrac.com
website: www.golf-bordeaux-cameyrac.com

BORDEAUX. **Golf du Médoc,** Chemin de Courmateau, 33290 Le Pian Médoc (05 56 70 11 90; Fax: 05 56 11 99). *Location:* 20 minutes by car from Bordeaux International Airport. Vintage golf in Bordeaux Country, 36 holes named after Medoc Wine Chateaux. The "Chateaux Course" 6316 par 71, traditional links course, host of the French Open in 1999 (PGA European Tour), host of the European Amateur Championship in 1998. The "Vignes Course" 6220m par 71 set in a typically regional landscape winding through lakes and pine trees. Practice ground, pitching and putting greens. *Green Fees:* low season 42 euros, high season 60 euros. *Eating facilities:* clubhouse with bar and quality restaurant. *Visitors:* welcome. *Society Meetings:* please contact Secretary. Professionals: Gilles Arnaud and Nicolas Besançon. General Manager; Vincent Paris
e-mail: info@golf-du-medoc.com

BORDEAUX. **Golf de Pessac,** Rue de la Princesse, 33690 Pessac (05 57.26.03.33; Fax: 05 56.36.52.89). *Location:* on the western outskirts of Bordeaux, four km from the city and close to the airport, St Jean d'Illiac road. A level course with large bunkers and some water. 27 holes providing alternative 9 hole layouts plus 9 hole practice course. 18 holes, 6040 metres. Par 72; 9 holes, 2911 metres. Par 36. Driving range, putting green. *Green Fees:* information not available. *Eating facilities:* restaurant and bar. *Visitors:* welcome at any time. *Society Meetings:* welcome. Pro shop; cart, club and trolley hire. Professionals: Ramuntcho Artola, Nagalie Gaillard. Secretary: Alain Egloff. *

CASTELJALOUX. **Golf de Casteljaloux,** Route de Mont-de-Marsan, 47700 Casteljaloux (05.53.93.51.60; Fax: 05.53.20.90.98). *Location:* situated on the D933 facing Lake Clarens on the road to Mont-de-Marsan, 15km from the exit of the motorway, 90km from Bordeaux, 170km from Toulouse. Flat and wooded on six holes, 12 holes undulating. 18 holes, 6500 yards, 5916 metres, Par 72, S.S.S. 71. Practice holes, bunkers and tees, driving range and putting green. *Green Fees:* high season weekdays 30 euros, weekends 35 euros. *Eating facilities:* bar and restaurant in clubhouse with fine views - menu from 11 euros. *Visitors:* welcome. Pro shop; club and trolley hire; 3 buggies. 15 bungalows for rent (5 doubles and 10 singles). *Society Meetings:* by arrangement. Professional: Citin Krault. Golf Manager: Denis Muller-Feuga.
e-mail: golfdecasteljaloux@wanadoo.fr
website: www.golf-casteljaloux.com

DORDOGNE. **Château des Vigiers Golf and Country Club,** 24240 Monestier (05 53.61.50.00; Fax: 05 53.61.50.20). *Location:* about an hour's drive east of Bordeaux on D936, bearing right on D18 at Ste-Foy-la-Grande. Rolling past orchards, vineyards, woods, lakes surrounding a 16th century château. 18 holes, 6003 metres. Par 72. 6 hole practice course, driving range and putting green. *Green Fees:* from 45 euros to 65 euros. *Eating facilities:* restaurant and bar. Pro shop, club, cart and trolley rental; luxury hotel. Professional: Vincent Trojani.
e-mail: reserve@vigiers.com
website: www.vigiers.com

HOSSEGOR. **Golf d'Hossegor,** Avenue du Golf, 40150 Hossegor (05 58.43.56.99; Fax: 05 58.43.98.52). *Location:* about 15km north of Bayonne just west of the A63. Fine classic test of golf over gently undulating, heavily wooded land. 18 holes, 5920 metres, Par 71. Driving range, putting green. *Eating facilities:* bar and restaurant in clubhouse. Pro shop; trolley hire. *

LACANAU-OCEAN. **Golf Hotel ★★★ 3 de Lacanau Ocean,** 33680 Lacanau Océan (05 56.03.92.98; Fax: 05 56.26.30.57). *Location:* between Lac de Lacanau and the sea, 60km west of Bordeaux. Level, within a pine and oak forest, some water hazards. 18 holes, 5900 metres, Par 72. Covered and open practice ground, putting green. *Green Fees:* information not available. *Eating facilities:* regional restaurant, snacks at clubhouse; bar. *Visitors:* welcome all year round. *Society Meetings:* welcome. Pro shop; equipment, trolley, buggy hire. Special packages with Golf–Hotel and Restaurant. Three Star Hotel, 50 rooms direct onto the course; swimming pool; cottages. (05 56.03.92.92; Fax: 05 56.26.30.57).*

LAVAUR. **Golf des Etangs de Fiac,** Brazis, 81500 Fiac (05.63.70.64.70; Fax: 05.63.75.32.91). *Location:* Toulouse to Lavaur, course is 10km after Lavaur in the direction of Castres. A technically interesting course, very green, with water hazards across natural ponds. 18 holes, 5800 metres. S.S.S. 71. *Green Fees:* information not available. *Eating facilities:* bar and restaurant open all year. *Visitors:* welcome all year. Pro shop, equipment hire. Swimming pool in season (golfers only) Lessons available. Professional: Pierre Crouzet. Secretaries: J. Phillippe and Sandie. Owner: Hilda Stevens. *

MAZAMET. **Golf de Mazamet la Barouge,** 81660 Pont de l'Arn, Mazamet (05.63.61.06.72). *Location:* three km north of Mazamet. A standard course with small wooded areas, set in magnificent surroundings. Notable for tricky and long Par 3s. 18 holes, 5953 metres. Par 70. *Green Fees:* information not available. *Eating facilities:* bar and restaurant in clubhouse. *Visitors:* welcome all year. Buggy hire. Professional: Didier Charria. *

PAU. **Pau Golf Club,** Rue du Golf, 64140 Billere (05 59.13.18.56; Fax: 05 59.13.18.57). *Location:* RN 117 Commune de Billere 5km from Pau towards Bayonne. The first course in continental Europe (1856). Flat, wooded, along the River Gave. 18 holes, 5312 metres, S.S.S. 69. Practice facilities including three practice holes. *Green Fees:* information not available. *Eating facilities:* bar and restaurant in clubhouse. *Visitors:* welcome. *Society Meetings:* by arrangement. Professional: D. Loustalet (06.08.41.16.14), Ph. Heugas (06.11.03.30.57). Secretary: Sylvie Loustalet et Nilda Bellanger (05 59.32.02.33). *

SAINT-JEAN-DE-LUZ. **Golf de la Nivelle,** Place William Sharp, 64500 Ciboure (05 59.47.19.72; Fax: 05 59.47.21.16). *Location:* two km south of Saint-Jean de Luz on the banks of the River Nivelle. Classic parkland with mature trees and harbour views. 18 holes, 5513 metres, Par 70. Practice ground, putting green. *Green Fees:* information not available. *Eating facilities:* bar and restaurant in clubhouse. *Visitors:* welcome, maximum Handicap 35. Self catering flats on golf course. Pro shop; equipment hire. *

TOULOUSE. **Maeva Latitudes Toulouse Seilh,** Route de Grenade, 31840 Seilh (05 62.13.14.14; Fax: 05 61.42.34.17). *Location:* about 12km north-west of Toulouse near the A62. "Yellow" Course of moderate difficulty, 18 holes, 4202 metres, Par 64; "Red" Course of competition standard, 18 holes, 6200 metres, Par 72. Extensive practice and training facilities. *Eating facilities:* bar and restaurant in clubhouse. Pro shop; club, cart and trolley hire. A new hotel with 175 rooms and apartments is now available on site with tennis and private swimming pool (05.62.13.14.15). *
e-mail: toulouse.golf@maeva.fr
website: www.maeva.latitudes.toulouse.com

VILLENEUVE-SUR-LOT. **Villeneuve sur Lot Golf and Country Club,** 47290 Castelnaud de Gratecambe (05. 53. 01. 60.19; Fax: 05. 53. 01. 78. 99). *Location:* on the N21 10km north of Villeneuve, between the scenic valleys of the Lot and the Dordogne. Inland course with water and many trees. 18 holes, 6322 metres, Par 72. Debutants Ecole de Golf 6 hole course. Practice ground, putting green. *Eating facilities:* the clubhouse is an 18th century manor house with brasserie/snack restaurant. Pro shop; equipment hire.
e-mail: info@vslgolf.com
website: www.vslgolf.com

SOUTH

AGDE. **Golf du Cap d'Agde,** 4 Avenue des Alizés, 34300 Cap d'Agde (04 67.26.54.40; Fax: 04 67.26.97.00). *Location:* autoroute A9 exit Agde. Seaside links. 18 holes, 6279 metres. S.S.S. 73. Practice ground; 9 hole pitch and putt, 800 metres, S.S.S. 27. *Green Fees:* information not available. *Eating facilities:* bar and restaurant in clubhouse. *Visitors:* welcome, no restrictions. Club, trolley and cart hire. Spikes on shoes forbidden. *Society Meetings:* welcome by reservation. Professionals: Jean Pierre Prieur, Franck Renard. Secretary: Myriam Delcayre.

AIX-EN-PROVENCE. **Golf International de Château L'Arc,** Domaine de Château L'Arc, 13710 Fuveau (04 42.53.28.38; Fax: 04 42.29.08.41). *Location:* about 15km south-east of Aix-en-Provence just south of the A8. A challenging course of varying terrain through trees, sloping fairways and water hazards. 18 holes, 6200 metres. S.S.S. 71. Driving range, putting green. *Green Fees:* information not available. *Eating facilities:* bar and restaurant in clubhouse. Pro shop; cart, trolley and club hire. *Visitors:* welcome, no restriction but it is necessary to make a reservation for weekends. Professional: Eric Follet. Secretary: Catherine Peter. *

AVIGNON. **Golf de Servanes,** Domaine de Servanes, 13890 Mouries (04 90.47.59.95; Fax: 04 90.47.52.58). *Location:* leave autoroute at Salon and head for Arles; leave at Avignon and head for St. Remy. Undulating course with serveral water hazards. 18 holes, 6121 metres, S.S.S. 72. Practice facilities. *Green Fees:* information not available. *Eating facilities:* available. *Visitors:* welcome, no restrictions. *Society Meetings:* welcome. Professional: Alain Brioland.*

BANDOL. **Golf de Fregate,** Route de Bandol, RD 559, 83270 St-Cyr-sur-Mer (04 34.29.38.00; Fax: 04 94.29.96.94). *Location:* about 4km from St-Cyr-sur-Mer on the road to Bandol on the right hand side. A dramatic new course in a vineyard setting overlooking the Mediterranean. 18 holes, 6209 metres. Par 72. Also 9 holes, 1500 metres, Par 29. Practice ground and two putting greens. *Green Fees:* information not available. *Eating facilities:* bar and restaurant. Also on-site hotel (four star, 133 rooms) by 18th green. Pro shop, club, cart and trolley hire.*

CANNES. **Golf Club de Cannes-Mandelieu,** Route du Golf, 06210 Mandelieu-la-Napoule (04 92.97.32.00; Fax: 04 93.49.92.90). *Location:* across the mouth of the small River Siagne, about seven km west of Cannes, south of the A8. A short, level course, third oldest and most popular in France. 18 holes, 5867 metres, Par 71. 9 holes, 2409 metres, Par 33. Practice ground, putting green. *Green Fees:* information not available. *Eating facilities:* bar and restaurant in attractive clubhouse. *Visitors:* welcome. *Society Meetings:* welcome. Director: Jean Stefan Camerini.*

For full details of clubs and courses, plus convenient accommodation
www.uk-golfguide.com

CANNES. **Golf Country Club de Cannes-Mougins,** 175 Avenue du Golf, 06250 Mougins (04 93.75.79.13; Fax: 04 93.75.27.60). *Location:* eight km north of Cannes, near the A8. A high-class private course, undulating through wooded hills. 18 holes, 6849 yards, 6263 metres, S.S.S. 72. Driving range, two putting greens, pitching green. *Green Fees:* information not available. *Eating facilities:* restaurant, bar, snacks. *Visitors:* welcome, no restrictions. Sauna. Magasin du Golf; cart, trolley and club hire. Professionals: Michel Damiano, Patrick Lemaire, Richard Sorrell (04 93.75.53.32). Secretaries: Hugues Danjou, Maryline Eynaud (04 93.75.79.13; Fax: 04 93.75.27.60). *

CANNES. **Riviera Golf Club,** Avenue des Amazones, 06210 Mandelieu (04.92.97.49.49; Fax: 04.92.97.66.57). *Location:* less than five km west of Cannes, just south of the A8, Fréjus direction. A new 18 hole course by American master Robert Trent Jones; mostly level, some hills and lakes. 18 holes, 5736 metres, Par 72. Driving range, putting green. *Green Fees:* information not available. *Eating facilities:* in clubhouse. *Visitors:* welcome, Handicap of 35 and insurance required. Professional/Manager: Y. Lecrubier. President: R.G. Boillat. *

CORSICA. **Golf de Sperone,** Domaine de Sperone, 20169 Bonifacio (04 95.73.17.13; Fax: 04 95.73.17.85). *Location:* near Bonifacio, southern point of Corsica. Another new Trent Jones creation, part on rocky maquis inland, part overlooking the Mediterranean. 18 holes, 6106 metres. S.S.S. 72. Practice facilities. *Green Fees:* information not available. *Eating facilities:* bar and restaurant with panoramic views. *Visitors*: welcome every day, please make a reservation. The golf course is closed on Thursdays from November to March and on Thursday afternoons from April to October. Pro shop, practice area, putting green, car, club and trolley hire; rented accommodation available at course. *Society Meetings*: welcome except July and August. Chairman: J.B. Casabianca. Professional: Marc Malrieu. Secretary: Céline Metier, Nafissa Bartoli. website: www.sperone.com

COTE D'AZUR. **Golf Opio-Valbonne,** Route de Roquefort Les Pins, 06650 Opio ([33] 04 93 12 00 08; Fax: [33] 04 93 12 26 00). *Location*: from Nice, A8 to Aix, out Villeneuve-Loubet, D2085, at Roquefort Les Pins, Valbonne, D204. Situated between Riviera coast and mountains, in a natural park of 530 acres. 18 holes, 5782 metres, S.S.S.73. Practice area, putting green. *Green Fees*: information not available. *Visitors*: welcome. Car, club and trolley hire. Instruction school. *
e-mail: opiovalbonne@opengolfclub.com
website: www.opengolfclub.com

THE APPEARANCE OF AN ASTERISK (*) AT THE END OF A CLUB OR COURSE ENTRY INDICATES THAT UP-TO-DATE INFORMATION HAS NOT BEEN SUPPLIED

GRASSE. **Golf de la Grande Bastide,** Chemin des Picholines, 06740 Chateauneuf de Grasse (04 93.77.70.08; Fax: 04 93.77.72.36). *Location:* autoroute A8 exit Cannes towards Mougin-Valbonne-Opio. Gently rolling, of equal challenge to all grades of player. 18 holes, 6105 metres, S.S.S. 72. Driving range, putting green. *Green Fees:* information not available. *Eating facilities:* bar and restaurant in clubhouse. *Visitors:* welcome anytime. Trolley and club hire. *Society Meetings:* welcome. Professional: S. Damiano (06.07.56.31.57). Manager: Alain Decovan.*

LES BAUX. **Golf des Baux de Provence,** Domaine de Manville, 13520 Les Baux de Provence (04 90.54.40.20; Fax: 04 90.54.40.93). *Location:* 25km from Avignon, 18km from Arles, 80km from Marseilles (Airport), the course is on the D27 between Les Baux and Maussane-les-Alpilles. Designed by the British architect Martin Hawtree, the course is set between pines, olive trees and scented lavender. 9 holes, 2842 metres. Par 36. Practice, putting green. *Green Fees:* 9 holes 34 euros, 18 holes 50 euros. *Eating facilities:* bar and restaurant in clubhouse. *Visitors:* always welcome. Hire of clubs, trolleys and golf carts. Professional: Joël Laggoune.

MARSEILLES. **Golf d'Aix Marseille,** Domaine de Riquetti, 13290 Les Milles (04 42.24.20.41; Fax: 04 42.39.97.48). *Location:* between Marseilles and Aix-en-Provence, west of the A51. A mature parkland course in a natural setting with a wealth of established trees. 18 holes, 6291 metres, Par 73. Driving range, putting green. *Green Fees:* information not available. *Eating facilities:* bar and restaurant in clubhouse. *Visitors:* welcome, closed Tuesdays. Pro shop; trolley and club hire. *

MARSEILLES. **Golf de Marseille La Salette,** Impasse des Vaudrans, Quartier de la Valentine, 13011 Marseille (04.91.27.12.16; Fax: 04.91.27.21.33). *Location:* Autoroute A50 exit La Valentine, follow the signs for "Valentine" then "Golf de la Salette". Hilly parkland course. 18 holes, 5436 metres. Par 71. *Green Fees:* information not available. *Eating facilities:* restaurant. *Visitors:* welcome. *Society Meetings:* welcome - conference and ballrooms available for seminars. Tennis courts and swimming pool. Golf school and buggy hire available. *

MONTE CARLO. **Monte Carlo Golf Club,** Route du Mont Agel, 06320 La Turbie (04 93.41.09.11/ 04 92 41 50 70: Fax: 04 93.41.09.55). *Location:* from Nice, take autoroute A8 Exit for La Turbie. Signpost at end of town, left turn for Mont Agel. Golf course entrance after 5 kms. Picturesque course with exceptional views of the Mediterranean sea and southern Alps. 18 holes, 5700 metres, Par 71. Driving range, practice, putting green. *Green Fees:* information not available. *Eating facilities:* bar and restaurant. *Visitors:* welcome, Handicap Certificate required. *Society Meetings:* welcome by prior arrangement. Professionals: F. Ruffier-Meray, J.M. Loustalan and Sophie Halsall. Secretary: C. Houtart. *

MONTPELLIER. **Golf de la Grande-Motte,** Club House du Golf, 34280 La Grande-Motte ((33) 04.67.56.05.00; Fax: (33) 04.67.29.18.84). *Location:* on the coast, east of Montpellier. Former marshland, now a 42 hole complex with fast greens, water, trees and bunkers. "The Pink Flamingos" - 18 competition class holes, 6161 metres, Par 72; "The Seagulls" - 3220 metres, Par 58; and 6 hole practice green, 560 metres, Par 19. Practice ground, putting green. *Green Fees:* information not available. *Eating facilities:* bar and restaurant in clubhouse and on-course Golf Hotel. Pro shop; trolley and cart hire. Professionals: V. Etchevers, P.H. Milhau, A. Schneider. Manager: J C. Mathieu. *

MONTPELLIER. **Golf de Massane,** Domaine de Massane, 34670 Baillargues (04.67.87.87.87; Fax: 04.67.87.87.90). *Location:* seven km from airport, 10km from Montpellier and two km from autoroute. Tough championship layout which hosts the annual Volvo Tour qualifying. Elevated greens protected by sand and water. 18 holes, 7037 metres, Par 72. 9 hole compact course. Extensive teaching school with large driving range, pitching and putting greens. *Green Fees:* information not available. *Eating facilities*: bar, snacks and restaurant in clubhouse, hotel on course. Pro shop. Leadbetter Academy. *Visitors:* welcome all year. *Society Meetings:* welcome. Professional: Nicolas Armand (04.67.87.87.91). Secretary: M. Brunet (04.67.87.87.87). *

MONTPELLIER. **Golf Hotel de Fontcaude,** Route de Lodève, Domaine de Fontcaude 34990 Juvignac (04.67. 45.90.10; Fax: 04.67.45.90.20). *Location:* at Juvignac, six km west of Montpellier. Undulating over a rolling, scrub-covered landscape, this course provides a fair and interesting challenge. Two courses: International 18 holes, 6292 metres, Par 72. Executive 9 holes, 1290 metres, Par 29. Driving range, putting green, pitching green. *Green Fees:* information not provided. *Eating facilities:* bar and restaurant in clubhouse. *Visitors:* welcome, no restrictions. Pro shop; cart, trolley and club hire. *Society Meetings:* welcome. Professional: Bruno Tancogne. Assistant Manager: Antony Bonsergent (04 67.45.90.10). Golf Club Manager: Jean Claude Lenoire.

NANS LES PINS. **Golf de la Sainte-Baume,** Domaine de Chateauneuf, 83860 Nans-les-Pins. (04.94.78.60.12; Fax: 04.94.78.63.52). *Location:* 40 kms from Marseilles, A8 exit Saint-Maximin. 45 kms from Aix-en-Provence. Wooded, undulating course. 18 holes, 6167 metres, Par 72. *Green Fees:* information not provided. *Eating facilities:* restaurant. *Visitors:* welcome. *Society Meetings:* welcome. Golf school and pro shop, buggy hire available. Accommodation available in our 4 star Domaine de Châteauneuf "Relais et Chateaux" located in the centre of the course. Managers: Alain Batteux and Marie-Pierre Puisset.

NIMES. **Golf de Nîmes-Campagne,** Route de Saint-Gilles, 30900 Nîmes (04.66.70.17.37; Fax: 04.66.70.03.14). *Location:* close to the A54, exit Nîmes Garons (Airport). A classic flat parkland course of championship calibre built around a superb clubhouse. 18 holes, 6135 metres, Par 72. Driving range, practice bunker, putting green. *Green Fees:* information not available. *Eating facilities:* bar and excellent restaurant. *Visitors:* welcome with reservation. Pro Shop; buggies and carts for hire. *Society Meetings:* welcome during weekdays with reservation, maximum 12/15 persons. Professionals: Marc Dolisie and Didier Behin. Secretary: Sandra Dombret. *

NIMES. **Golf de Nîmes Vacquerolles,** 1075 Chemin du Golf, 30900 Nimes ((33)04.66.23.33.33; Fax: (33) 04.66.23.94.94). *Location:* five minutes from Nimes, autoroute A9, exit Nimes Ouest, then Le Vigan. Running up a valley and over steeply wooded hills. 18 holes, 6260 metres, Par 73. Practice area, putting green. *Green Fees:* information not available. *Eating facilities:* bar and restaurant in clubhouse. *Visitors:* welcome. Self-catering apartments on the course. *Society Meetings:* welcome. Open Golf Club. Professionals: Eric Rossary and Emmanuel Thomas. e-mail:vacquerolles.opengolfclub@wannadoo.fr website: www.opengolfclub.com

PERPIGNAN. **Golf de St-Cyprien,** Mas d'Huston, 66750 Saint-Cyprien Plage, Perpignan (33 04.68.37.63.63; Fax: 33 04.68.37.64.64). *Location:* just south of Perpignan, a renowned course between sea and lake with the Pyrenees mountains in the background. Challenging championship course with water hazards. 18 holes, 6480 metres, Par 73. South Course - 9 holes, 2724 metres, Par 35. *Green Fees:* information not available. *Eating facilities:* bar at clubhouse. Bars, restaurants and accommodation at Le Mas d'Huston, on-course hotel. Self-catering apartments a la residence on-course also. Open all year. Pro shop, golf clinic. Professional: Patrick Lacroix. Secretary: Mandy Hogdson. *

ST RAPHAEL. **Golf de l'Estérel Latitudes,** Avenue du Golf, 83700 St Raphaèl (04 94.52.68.30; Fax: 04 94.52.68.31). *Location:* inland just a few metres north of St Raphaèl, close to Golf de Valescure. Not long but rated difficult; many trees, narrow fairways and water hazards protecting beautiful greens. 18 holes, 5921 metres, Par 71. 9 holes, 1400 metres, Par 29. Driving range, 9 hole school. *Green Fees:* information not available. *Eating facilities:* bar, clubhouse and restaurant. *Visitors:* welcome. On-site Hotel Latitudes-Valescure (discounts for residents). Pro shop; club, cart and trolley hire. *Society Meetings:* welcome, pre-booking with hotel. Professional: Hugues Gioux (04.94.44.64.65). *

ST RAPHAEL. **Golf et Tennis Club de Valescure,** BP451, Route de Golf, 83700 St Raphaèl (04 94.82.40.46; Fax: 04 94.82.41.42). *Location:* about five km east of St. Raphaèl. An established course (1895), winding attractively through the umbrella pine trees. 18 holes, 5067 metres, Par 68. Driving range, putting green. *Eating facilities:* bar and restaurant in period clubhouse and at golf hotel nearby. Pro shop; trolley and club hire.*

Please mention THE GOLF GUIDE when you enquire about clubs or accommodation

Golf in Portugal
Where to Play, Where to Stay
Michael Gedye

For many British golfers, Portugal not only presents excellent winter golf in warm remedial sunshine just a short jet hop away, but there is also the reassurance that the bulk of the holiday golf market comes from their shores. The long-standing British influence on all aspects of the game in Portugal, dating back to 1890, means the golfing resorts represent a 'home from home' and most of the visiting players will be fellow northern Europeans fleeing the winter chills.

That said, there is much to find and enjoy in this historic country, the launching point of early global exploration and discovery. Virtually all of Portugal's coastline borders the Atlantic Ocean, which not only produced the ocean navigators but also a bounteous supply of fresh fish and seafood. One of the abiding memories of Portuguese cuisine is the pungent aroma of sardines grilled under the stars, or a steaming *cataplana* of clams, prawns and smoked sausage. Try *caldo verde* (cabbage, potato and garlic sausage soup) and the rich choice of locally-made sweetmeats, which owe much to longstanding North African influence in the south. The country is not internationally famous for its wines, except of course for port, although a large quantity of both white and red is produced annually. An important reason is that the Portuguese know a good thing when they see it and consume over three-quarters of the annual output themselves. Look out for the vibrant reds of the Alentejo and Douro, Dao and Bairrada; for white, try the crisp *vinho verde* from the far north.

Nearly half of all the courses in the country lie along the southern coast of the ALGARVE, all built to cater to visiting holiday players and most in resort areas. Sheltered by inland mountains, the Algarve offers a mild winter climate and an interesting cultural mix, due to past integration from Northern Africa. Not that many years ago this was a relatively unknown rural area, somewhat isolated geographically from the north, devoted to fishing and agriculture. Then an emerging summer holiday market, attracted by the superb weather and affordable charter flights, discovered its charms. Golf soon followed, with developers realising the immense attractions of playing in warm winter sunshine. Over forty years, the number and quality of courses has grown. There are now thirty-two open for play, laid out in verdant splendour under the native cork oaks and umbrella pine, with many more to come. They stretch from Cape St Vincent in the west to the Spanish border; a rich variety of golfing choice by some of the world's finest designers. You can choose between tough championship tests and gentler, very scenic locations, but all a world away from winter golf at home.

The area around LISBON, the capital city and cultural centre of this charming country, has never been as closely associated with holiday golf. Running south through the sandy Costa Azul or north and west of the city on the Costa Estoril, no less than twenty-four courses are waiting for you. To complement the subtle charms of ageless, strategic Estoril, enjoy the more modern layouts of Penha Longa, Belas

Clube de Campo, Praia d'El Rey and Golden Eagle north-west of Lisbon. Latest arrival, in a natural dune and pine setting is Quinta da Marinha Oitavos by Arthur Hills, site of the recent Portuguese Open. Travel south across the Tagus bridge from the city and you reach the golden chain of Aroeira 1 & 2, Quinta do Peru and the toughest test of all – Robert Trent Jones' superb Troia, laid out on a windswept sandbar by the sea. Never forget to finish your round with some excellent fresh local seafood and chilled white wine – all part of the holiday golfing experience.

Although golf was first played in the NORTH, near Oporto, more than a century ago, it has taken time to grow at the same rate as in the south. This may in part be due to less predictable holiday weather, but there is much to see and do here in a region of ancient castles, unique handicrafts and cuisine, and some of the best red wines in the country, including traditional fortified port. Best golf is at Ponte de Lima, carved from wooded mountain slopes. Sub-tropical Madeira boasts two courses at volcanic altitude and now, just offshore, the island of Porto Santo has opened 27 holes by Spanish legend Severiano Ballesteros. For something different, visit the Azores, which have three highly playable courses in colourful floral settings.

Hotel Berry A Colina •• Algarve

Your host, Keith Lloyd, and his staff welcome you to this country inn hotel which specialises in all-inclusive golfing packages, winter breaks, birdwatching and summer holidays. They offer a friendly and personal service, a refreshing change from the often impersonal attitudes of larger hotels. The hotel is located in the peaceful Ludo Valley near Almancil and the Ria Formosa Natural Park. It is just 15 minutes from Faro International Airport and a short drive from many golf courses – 12 within 15 minutes' drive.

SPECIAL GOLFING PACKAGES from a weekend break to a comprehensive golf holiday. All we need to know is numbers, dates and courses – just bring your clubs and we will do the rest!

Keith Lloyd, Hotel Berry A Colina, Apartado 3761, Almancil, Algarve, Portugal
Tel/Fax: ++00351 289 395322 • www.acolina.com
See also Colour Advertisement on page 102

ALGARVE

ALBUFEIRA. **Golf de Salgados,** Apartado 2266, Vale Rebelho, 8200-917 Albufeira (00351 289 583030); Fax: 00351 289 591112). Location: from Faro on EN125, turn left for Vale de Parra. Next to a nature reserve. Level course carved from seamarsh with plenty of water hazards. 18 holes, 6080 metres. Par 72. Driving range, putting green. *Green Fees:* information not available. *Eating facilities:* bar and restaurant in clubhouse. *Visitors:* welcome. Pro shop; cart, trolley and club hire. *Society Meetings:* all welcome. Professional: John Wood. Director: Pedro Silvestre. *

ALBUFEIRA. **Sheraton Algarve Pine Cliffs Golf and Country Club,** PO Box 644, Praia da Falesia, 8200 Albufeira (289 500113; Fax: 289 500117). *Location:* seven km from Vilamoura, situated outside Olhos d'Agua. Seaside links. 9 holes, 2557 yards, 2324 metres, Par (equivalent) 67. 9 holes Par 3 course. *Green Fees:* information not available. Discounts for hotel guests. *Eating facilities:* bar, restaurant. *Visitors:* welcome, advance booking required. Golf academy, changing facilities. *Society Meetings:* all groups welcome. Professional/Golf Director: Manuel Batista. *

ALMANCIL. **San Lorenzo Golf Club,** Quinta do Lago, 8135 Almancil (00 351 289 396522; Fax: 00 351 289 396908). *Location:* 20km from Faro Airport towards west. Parkland with seaside view surrounded by wildlife and umbrella pine trees designed by Joseph Lee. 18 holes, 6238 metres. Par 72. Practice range, putting green and driving range. *Green Fees:* information not provided. *Eating facilities:* bar and restaurant. *Visitors:* welcome, please reserve 24 hours in advance before wishing to play, Handicap Certificate required - Men 28, Ladies 36. Caddies and cart rental available. Soft spikes required. Pro shop. *Society Meetings:* welcome if staying in Dona Filipa Hotel. Professional: A. Rodrigues. Golf Manager: Antonio Santos (00 351 289 396534).
website: www.donafilipa.lemeridien.com

558 Golf in PORTUGAL

ALMANCIL. **Sociedade do Golfe da Quinta do Lago,** Quinta do Lago, 8135-024 Almancil (+351 289 390700; Fax: +351 289 394013). *Location:* 15 minutes west of Faro Airport, nearest town Almancil. Gently undulating sandy site covered with umbrella pines, wild flowers and lakes. 2 courses: Quinta do Lago South and Quinta do Lago North. Both 18 holes, 7136 and 6738 yards, 6488 and 6126 metres. S.S.S. 72. Driving range. *Green Fees:* information not provided. *Eating facilities:* clubhouse bar, restaurants (9 Iron and Casa do Lago), and Buggy Bar. *Visitors:* welcome subject to availability, first starting time around 7.30am. Pro Shop and golf academy; buggies, trolleys and power caddies. *Society Meetings:* welcome subject to availability. Professional: Domingos Silva, Rogério Valente and Jason Hoyles (+351 289 394368; Fax: +351 289 394013). Golf Director: José Capela. General Manager: João Paulo Sousa.

ALMANCIL. **Vale do Lobo Golf Club,** Vale do Lobo, 8135-864 Vale do Lobo, Almancil (00 351 289 353464 Fax: 00 351 289 353003). *Location:* on the cliff edge, overlooking the sea, 15 minutes' drive west from Faro. 2 courses. "Ocean Course", 18 holes, 5815 metres. Par 72. "Royal Course", 18 holes, 6050 metres. Par 72. Coastline scenery with fairways lined with pine, eucalyptus and almond trees. *Green Fees:* Ocean Course 140.00 euros, Royal Course 150.00 euros. *Eating facilities:* clubhouse with restaurant, bar and cafe. *Visitors:* always welcome. *Society Meetings:* welcome. Teaching Professional: Steve Walker. Tour Professionals: Antonio Sobrinho, Jarmo Sandelin and Brian Davis. Golf Director: Mr Ian Church.
e-mail: golf@vdl.pt
website: www.valedolobo.com

ALVOR. **Alto Golf & Country Club,** Quinto do Alto do Poco, Apartado 1, 8501 906 Alvor - Portimao (282 460870; Fax: 282 460879). *Location:* in Alvor, overlooking the Atlantic Ocean and the Bay of Lagos. A parkland course designed by Sir Henry Cotton with gently undulating fairways and challenging sloping greens. Stunning views of the Monchique Mountains in the background. 18 holes, 6125 metres, S.S.S. 73. Driving range, putting green. *Green Fees:* information not provided. *Eating facilities:* bar and restaurant in clubhouse. *Visitors:* welcome. *Society Meetings*: groups also welcome, Handicap Certificate required. Pro shop; cart, trolley and club hire. Professional: BGLC - Bennets Golf Learning Centre. 5 Pros with all the latest computer teaching software and Explanar training aid. Resort Director: Colin Snape.
e-mail: golf@altoclub.com

BUDENS/SALEMA. **Parque da Floresta Golf and Leisure Resort,** Vale do Poco, 8650-060 Budens (+351 282 690056; Fax: +351 282 695157). *Location:* EN125, 16km west of Lagos. Located just past Budens on right. Undulating course with spectacular views; member of the Portuguese Golf Federation. 18 holes, 5670 metres. S.S.S. 72. Short game practice area, driving range, golf academy, three putting greens. *Green Fees:* information not available. *Eating facilities:* clubhouse with restaurant and bar overlooking 18th hole. *Visitors:* very welcome but advisable to book.

THE GOLF GUIDE 2006

Enquire about Special Rates. Pro shop; swimming pools, tennis court, health and beauty spa. Self-catering villas and townhouses available. *Society Meetings:* welcome, catered for by arrangement with Golf Director. PGA Professionals: Gary Silcock, Scott Catlin. Golf Director: Billy Sim. *
e-mail: b.sim@vigiasa.com OR golf@vigiasa.com
website: www.vigiasa.com

CACELA. **Quinta da Ria**, 8900-057 Vila Nova de Cacela, Algarve (351 281 950 580; Fax: 351 281 950 589). *Location:* take N125 east from Faro; after Tavira turn right at sign for Cacela Vehla and golf. Situated in the Ria Formosa Nature Reserve, a spectacular course by Rocky Roquemore, with superb views over the tidal estuary and the sea. 18 holes, 6,016 metres, Par 72. Driving range, golf academy, putting green. *Green fees:* 90 euros. *Eating facilities:* clubhouse snack bar. *Visitors:* welcome. Electric carts, pull and electric trolleys, club rental. Golf Director: Antonio Cavaco.
e-mail: qdria@mail.telepac.pt

CACELA. **Quinta de Cima**, 8900-057 Vila Nova de Cacela, Algarve (351 281 950 580; 351 281 950 589). *Location*: take N125 east from Faro; after Tavira turn right at sign for Cacela Velha and golf. Highly-rated new course by Rocky Roquemore winding past ancient olive and carob trees, with sea and mountain views. 18 holes, 6,256 metres, Par 72. Driving range, golf academy, putting green. *Green fees:* 90 euros. *Eating facilities:* clubhouse snack bar. *Visitors*: welcome. Electric carts, pull and electric trolleys, club rental. Golf Director: Antonio Cavaco.
e-mail: qdria@mail.telepac.pt

LAGOA. **Gramacho Course,** Pestana Golf and Resort, Carvoeiro, Apartado 1011, Praia do Carvoeiro, 8400-908 Lagoa (282 340900; Fax: 282 340901). *Location:* 2km south of Lagoa on the Estrada Nacional E125, follow road signs. Two superbly prepared golf courses undulating through olive groves. Gramacho - 18 hole course 6718 yards, 6107 metres. Par 72. David Leadbetter Golf Academy, practice putting and chipping greens, driving range. *Green Fees:* information not available. *Eating facilities:* restaurant, bar plus magnificent terrace. *Visitors:* welcome, check availability, year round. Carvoeiro Golf Clube luxury villa and apartments; international golf school, video swing analysis centre. Buggies and carts available. Pro Shop. Accommodation available locally (282 340900). *Society Meetings:* welcome by arrangement. Professional: Carlos Ribeiro (282 340440; Fax: 282 340901). Secretary: Rui Gago. Director of Golf: José Matias.

THE APPEARANCE OF AN ASTERISK (*) AT THE END OF A CLUB OR COURSE ENTRY INDICATES THAT UP-TO-DATE INFORMATION HAS NOT BEEN SUPPLIED

LAGOA. **Pinta Course,** Pestana Golf and Resort, Carvoeiro, Apartado 1011, Praia Do Carvoeiro, 8400-908 Lagoa (282 340900; Fax: 282 340901). *Location:* 2kms south of Lagoa on the Estrada Nacional E125, follow signs. Parkland in ancient olive groves with trees 600/700 years old. 18 holes, 6727 yards, 6152 metres. S.S.S. 71. David Leadbetter Golf Academy, buggies, trolleys, two practice putting and two chipping greens, driving range. *Green Fees:* information not available. *Eating facilities:* snack bar. *Visitors:* welcome, check availability, year round. Handicap Certificate required: men 27, ladies 35. Accommodation available locally (282 340900). Golf School, Pro shop, rental of pull trolleys, electric trolleys, clubs and buggies. *Society Meetings:* welcome anytime by arrangement. Professional: Carlos Ribeiro (282 340440; Fax: 282 340449). Secretary: Rui Gago. Director of Golf: José Matias.

LAGOS. **Boavista Golf Resort,** Apartado 62, 8601-901 Lagos (00 351 282 000111; Fax: 00 351 282 000150). Location: 500m west of 2nd roundabout on the Lagos spur (Junction 1) of the Trans-Algarve Highway (A22). Spectacular clifftop golf with stunning views. 18 holes, 6,053 metres, Par 71. Driving range, short game area, putting greens. *Green fees:* 65 euros high season; 45 euros low season. *Eating facilities:* bar and restaurant. *Visitors:* welcome, normal dress code, soft spikes; Handicap Certificate required – maximum 27 men; 34 ladies; booking essential. Carts, trolleys and clubs for rent. Golf Director: Antonio Castelo. e-mail: golf.reception@boavistagolf.com

www.uk-golfguide.com

LAGOS. **Palmares Golf,** Apartado 74, Meia Praia, Lagos (282 790500; Fax: 282 790509). *Location*: five km from centre of Lagos on main Meia Praia beach road. Five links type holes - very scenic and serene. Magnificent views over Lagos Bay. 18 holes, 5961 metres. S.S.S. 72, Par 71. Driving range, putting green, pitch and putt area. *Green Fees*: information not provided. *Eating facilities*: Palmares Restaurant serving international and Portuguese cuisine with fresh fish. Panoramic bar and veranda with spectacular views over the Bay of Lagos. *Visitors*: open to all players with Handicap Certificate all year round. Two golf shops, trolleys, buggies and golf lessons available. *Society Meetings*: always welcome at all times. Professionals: Luis Espadinha and José Dias.
e-mail: golf@palmaresgolf.com
website: www.palmaresgolf.com

PORTIMAO. **Golfe do Morgado,** Apartado 293, 8501-912 Portimao (351 282 402 150/1; Fax: 351 282 402 153). Location: from the A22, direction Portimao, take Exit 5 (Portimao/Monchique) and follow direction Monchique. After one km, turn left at 'Golf' sign. A moderately landscaped course, one of the longest in the region, with large greens, lakes and strategic bunkers. 18 holes, 6,399 metres, Par 73. Second course Golfe dos Alamos, 18 holes, 5641 metres, S.S.S. 71, due to open November 2005. Driving range, putting and chipping greens with practice bunkers. Green fees: 85 euros high season; 64 euros low season. *Eating facilities:* bar and restaurant. *Visitors:* welcome; maximum handicaps – 28 men; 36 ladies. Electric carts, trolleys, club rental. Professional: Nelson Cavalheiro. Manager: Jorge Papa.
e-mail: playgolf@golfedomorgado.com

Quinta da Ria, Cacela

PORTIMAO/PENINA. **Penina Golf Club,** Le Meridien Penina Golf Resort Hotel, PO Box 146, Penina, 8501-952 Portimao (282 420200; Fax: 282 420300). *Location:* five km from Portimao, 12km from Lagos. Long, flat course with lakes, trees and bunkers. 18 holes° (plus two 9 hole courses), 6935 yards, 6273 metres. S.S.S. 73. Also Resort Course - 9 holes, 3268 yards, 2987 metres. S.S.S. 35 and Academy Course - 9 holes, 2035 yards, 1851 metres. S.S.S. 30. Golf academy, putting greens. *Green Fees:* please check with hotel. *Eating facilities:* clubhouse and Hotel restaurants. *Visitors:* welcome, Handicap Certificate (28 for men and 36 for ladies) and soft spike shoes required to play all courses. *Society Meetings:* welcome. Professional: José Lourenco, Robin Liddle and José Marcelino. Director: Leonel Rio.
website: www.lemeridien.com

QUINTA DO LAGO. **Pinheiros Altos Golf Club,** Quinta do Lago, 8135 Almancil, Algarve (289 359910; Fax: 289 394392). *Location:* south of Almancil just east of the Quinta do Lago and San Lorenzo courses, bear left on first roundabout at Quinta do Lago. Pine trees and water hazards with fast bent grass greens and the island green 17th hole. 18 holes, 6236 metres. S.S.S. 72. Driving range areas, three putting greens, two chipping/ bunker areas. *Green Fees:* information not available. *Eating facilities:* restaurant, snack bar; drinks buggy. *Visitors:* welcome, Handicap Certificate required: Men 28, Ladies 36. Buggy compulsory. Pro shop; club hire. 'A' Star equipped Golf Academy. *Society Meetings:* on request. Professionals: Eddie Charnock, Dennis Struchtrup. Director of Golf: Brian Evans. *

VILAMOURA. **Laguna Golf Course,** Lusotur Golfes SA, 8125 - 507 Vilamoura, Algarve (00 351 289 310 180; Fax: 00 351 289 310 183). *Location:* 20 kms from Faro Airport, 25 kms from Faro. Relatively flat, open course with challenging placement of bunkers and water hazards, designed by Joseph Lee. 18 holes. 6133 metres. Par 72. Practice facilities, putting green, driving range. *Green Fees:* information not available. *Eating facilities:* restaurant and bar. *Visitors:* open to players with Handicap Certificate (max. Men 28, Ladies 36). *Society Meetings:* welcome at all times. Pro shop, equipment hire. Professionals: Abilio Coelho and Joaquim Catarino (089 380724). Bookings: (00 351 289 310 333; Fax: 00 351 289 310 349). Commercial Manager: Alice Carlota. Golf Manager: Eduardo de Sousa.*
e-mail: reservas_golfe@lusotur.pt
website: www.vilamoura.net

VILAMOURA. **Millennium Golf Course, Clube de Golfe Vilamoura,** Lusotur Golfes SA, 8125 - 507 Vilamoura, Algarve (00 351 289 310 188; Fax: 00 351 289 310 183). *Location:* 20km from Faro Airport, 25km from Faro. Narrow fairways through pine woods and natural countryside. 18 holes, 6143 metres. Par 72. Practice and putting greens, driving range. *Green Fees:* information not available. *Eating facilities:* restaurant and bar. *Visitors:* course open to all players with Handicap Certificate (max. Men 24, Ladies 28). Soft spikes only. Pro shop, hire of trolleys. Professional: Abilio Coelho and Joaquim Catarino Bookings: (00 351 289 310 333; Fax: 00 351 289 310 349). Commercial Manager: Alice Carlota. Golf Manager: Eduardo de Sousa.*
e-mail: reservas_golfe@lusotur.pt
website: www.vilamoura.net

VILAMOURA. **The Old Course, Clube de Golfe Vilamoura,** Lusotur Golfes SA, 8125 - 507 Vilamoura, Algarve (00 351 289 310 341; Fax: 00 351 289 310 321). *Location:* 20km from Faro Airport, 25km from Faro. Narrow fairways through pine woods, sea views. 18 holes, 6254 metres. Par 73. Practice and putting greens; driving range. *Green Fees:* information not available. *Eating facilities:* restaurant and bar. *Visitors:* course open to all players with Handicap Certificate (max. Men 24, Ladies 28). Soft spikes only. Pro shop, equipment hire. Professional: Joaquim Sequeira. Bookings: (00 351 289 310 333; Fax: 00 351 289 310 349). Commercial Manager: Alice Carlota. Golf Manager: Eduardo de Sousa.*
e-mail: reservas_golfe@lusotur.pt
website: www.vilamoura.net

VILAMOURA. **Pinhal Golf Course,** Lusotur Golfes SA, 8125 - 507 Vilamoura, Algarve (00 351 289 310 390; Fax: 00 351 289 310 393). *Location:* 20 kms from Faro Airport. Pine wood setting and magnificent sea views, designed by Frank Pennink and Robert Trent Jones. 18 holes, 6353 metres. Par 72. Driving range and putting green. *Green Fees:* information not provided. *Eating facilities:* bar and restaurant. *Visitors:* open to players with Handicap Certificate (max. Men 28, Ladies 36), all year round. *Society Meetings:* welcome at any time. Pro shop, equipment hire. Professionals: Manuel Pardal and Francisco Pontes. Bookings: (00 351 289 310 333; Fax: 00 351 289 310 349). Commercial Manager: Alice Carlota. Golf Manager: Maria de Jesus Beltrão.
e-mail: reservas_golfe@lusotur.pt
website: www.vilamoura.net

VILAMOURA. **Victoria Clube de Golfe,** Lusotur Golfes S.A., Apartado 970. 8126-912 Vilamoura, Algarve (00 351 289 320 100; Fax: 00 351 289 320 104). *Location*: 20 km west from Faro airport on N125. Follow signs on left for Vilamoura and golf. A new links-style championship course by Arnold Palmer, complementing the four existing courses, with indigenous carob, almond and olive trees, and many large water hazards. An excellent strategic test, with superb clubhouse and practice facilities, venue for the World Cup in November 2005. 18 holes, 6,560 metres, Par 72. Driving range, huge putting green, plus bunker and chipping areas. *Green Fees:* 150 euros (Bookings: 00 351 289 310 333; Fax: 00 351 289 310 3490. *Eating facilities:* restaurant, bar, buggy bar on course. *Visitors:* welcome; maximum handicap – men 24, ladies 28. Soft spikes only. Electric and pull trolleys, club rental. Golf Manager: Maria de Jesus Beltrao.
e-mail: reservasgolfea@vilamouragolf.com
website: www.vilamouragolf.com

www.uk-golfguide.com

VILAMOURA. **Vila Sol Beach, Golf & Country Club,** Morgadinhos, Alto do Semino, 8125 Vilamoura (289 300505/522; Fax: 289 316499). *Location*: just east of Vilamoura off the road leading down to Quarteira. An excellent natural course undulating through umbrella pines with good water hazards and superb greens. 27 holes, 6320 metres - men 5935 metres, ladies 5372 metres. Par 72, S.S.S 72. Driving range, putting green, golf academy, pro shop, trolley, club hire. *Green Fees*: information not available. *Eating facilities*: bar and restaurant in clubhouse. Pro shop; cart, trolley, buggy and club hire. *Visitors*: welcome. Handicap Certificate required. Soft spikes only. (Men 27, Ladies 35). Professional: Roel Gritter. Golf Secretary: Alexandra Piedade. *
e-mail: golfsecretary@vilasol.pt
e-mail: golfreservation@vilasol.pt

LISBON

AROEIRA. **Aroeira Golf,** Herdade da Aroeira, 2820 567 Chameca de Caparica, Aroeira, Costa Lisboa (00351 21 2979110; Fax: 00351 21 2971238). *Location*: south from Lisbon across the bridge, turn right to Costa Caparica and follow signs. This well-established course remains one of Portugal's best kept secrets. Venue of Portugal Open-European Tour 1996, 1997; Portuguese Ladies' Open 2002, 2003 and 2004. A superb test through a floral pine forest by Frank Pennink; one for purists to savour. 18 holes, 6040 metres, Par 72. Practice ground with shelters for bad/ hot weather. Aroeira 2 opened in 2000, designed by Donald Steel. *Green Fees:* (both courses) weekdays 48 euros, weekends 75 euros. *Eating facilities:* restaurant, snack bar, cocktail bar and lounge. *Visitors:* welcome, no restrictions; subject only to having a valid Handicap and availability of tees. Private apartments with 1,2 or 3 bedrooms available for rental, all facing the Golf Course. Self catering. New golf school specialising in intensive courses, indoor and outdoor facilities. Driving range. Buggies, electric trolleys and golf bags available for hire. Professionals: Joaquim Moura, Alexandre Daninos. Operations Director: Carlos Fonseca. Commercial Director: Francisco Pinto Leite. President: Pedro Silveira.
e-mail: golf.reservas@aroeira.com
website: www.aroeira.com

AZEITAO. **Quinta do Peru Golf Course,** Alameda da Serra 2, 2975-666 Quinta do Conde (+351 21 213 43 20; Fax: +351 21 213 43 21). *Location*: Cross the bridge "25 de Abril" and follow A2 motorway to Junction 3 (24km from Lisbon). Exit A2 at Junction 3 – pass through toll (portagem) then immediately exit right up slope, signs to "COINA"– then follow signs to Quinta do Peru – Golf. Fine new, American- shaped course laid out through rolling pine woods with lakes and fine views. 18 holes, 6036 metres. S.S.S. 72. Driving range, two putting greens, chipping and bunker practice area. *Green Fees*: weekends 88 euros, weekdays 58 euros. *Eating facilities*: restaurant and bar in clubhouse. *Visitors*: welcome. Pro shop, carts, trolleys, club hire. Professional: António Dantas. Manager: Pedro de Mello Breyner.
e-mail: play@golfquintadoperu.com
website: www.golfquintadoperu.com

BELAS. **Belas Clube de Campo,** Al. Aqueduto, 2605-193 Belas (21 962 6640; Fax: 21 962 6644). *Location:* make your way to the CREL (A9) from either the A1, A5, A8 or IC19. From the CREL take the exit signposted 'Belas', and after the toll, follow signs to N250. At the N250 T-junction turn right. First left over small bridge and then follow signs to Club. Very new, American-designed course built on a grand scale amongst a dramatic rolling landscape. 18 holes, 6380 metres. S.S.S. 72. Pro shop, driving range, short game area, putting green. *Green Fees*: on request. *Eating facilities*: restaurant and bar in clubhouse. *Visitors:* welcome. Carts, trolleys, club hire. Professional: Keith Barret. Director: Fernando Nunes Pedro.
e-mail: golfe@planbelas.pt
website: www.belasgolf.com

ESTORIL. **Academia de Golf Estoril Sol,** Estrada da Lagoa Azue, Quinta do Outeiro, Linho, Sintra 2710-314 (00351-21-924 04 44). *Location:* take the main Cascais-Sintra road and turn left at the village of Linho towards Lagoa Azul. 9 holes (18 tees), 1805 metres. S.S.S. 62. Purpose-built golf academy - practice facility, chipping greens, putting green. *Green Fees:* information not available. *Eating facilities:* restaurant and bar. *Visitors:* no restrictions. *Society Meetings:* welcome. Bennett's Golf Learning Centre. Golf Academy with full services. Three Professionals. Golf Director: Tony Bennett.*
e-mail: scoringzone@hotmail.com

PLEASE NOTE

All the information regarding Golf Clubs in this guide is given in good faith in the belief that it is correct. However, the publishers cannot guarantee the facts given in these pages, neither are they responsible for changes in ownership or facilities, such as green fees, that may take place after the date of going to press. Readers should always satisfy themselves that the facilities they require are available and that the terms, if quoted, still apply.

Golf in PORTUGAL

ESTORIL. **Golf Do Estoril,** Avenida Da Republica, 2765-273 Estoril (351 214 680176; Fax: 351 214 682796). *Location*: in Estoril. An undulating links course with views of the Atlantic and Sintra Mountains. 18 holes, 5238 metres. S.S.S. 69. *Green Fees:* information not available. Reductions for Estoril Palacio Hotel guests. Driving range. *Eating facilities*: Clubhouse with bar and restaurant. Professionals: Joaquim Rodrigues, Henrique Pallino, Carlos Aleixo. Director: Francisco Pinherio. *

ESTORIL. **Hotel Quinta da Marinha & Villas Golf Resort,** Quinta da Marinha, Casa 36 - 2750 Cascais (351 1 4860180; Fax: 351 1 4869032). *Location:* 3km from Cascais centre, 25km from Lisbon, near Guincho beach. Championship golf course designed by Robert Trent Jones. Open sandy course with pine trees, lakes and spectacular views over the mountains and ocean. 18 holes, 6684 yards. S.S.S. 71. Driving range, putting greens. *Green Fees:* information not available. *Eating facilities:* bar, restaurant and club house. *Visitors:* welcome. Men's Handicap 28, Ladies' Handicap 36. Club hire, trolley rental; Pro shop. Accommodation available in 42 villas or the new 200-bedroom Hotel Quinta da Marinha facing the course, with conference facilities, swimming pools, tennis courts and health centre. *Society Meetings:* not applicable. Professional: Richard Allen. Golf Director: Maria Padrela.

ESTORIL. **Penha Longa Hotel & Golf Resort,** Estrada da Lagoa Azul, Linho, 2714-511 Sintra (21.524.9031; Fax: 21.924.9024). *Location:* half an hour west of Lisbon, just north of Estoril on the main road to Sintra. Designed by Robert Trent Jones Jnr, laid out over craggy hills, wooded slopes and valleys surrounding an ancient royal palace; the 18 holes hosted the Portuguese Open in 1994 and again in 1995. 18 holes, 6910 yards, 6290 metres. S.S.S. 73. 9 holes, 2845 yards, 2588metres, S.S.S. 35. Driving range, large putting green, chipping green with two bunkers. *Green Fees:* information not available. *Eating facilities:* three bars and four restaurants. *Visitors:* welcome, Handicap Certificate required. Five star Hotel and Country Club; eight tennis courts, squash and bicycles. Golf Academy, Pro shop, cart, trolley, club and shoe hire. Sauna, jacuzzi. No jeans. Professional: Robert Judd/Antonio Dantas. Director: Andrew Glen.

ESTORIL. **Quinta da Marinha Oitavos Golfe,** Lote 64, 2750-004 Cascais (351 21 486 0606; Fax: 351 21 486 0609). *Location*: from Cascais, take the seaside coast road direction Sintra-Guincho. Entrance to golf on right about 3 km. A fine new course by Arthur Hills, set among pine woods and reforested dunes in the Sintra-Cascais Natural Park protected environment.

Superb views of sea and mountains. 18 holes, 6,379 metres, Par 71. Driving range, short game practice area, two putting greens, golf lessons. *Green Fees:* 150 euros. *Eating facilities:* bar and restaurant in modern clubhouse with regional, Italian and international menus. Also seaview deck. *Visitors:* welcome. Maximum handicap: 28 men; 36 ladies. Soft spikes. Restricted times weekends and Bank Holidays. Electric carts, manual and electric trolleys, club rental, pro shop. Professional: Philip A'Court. Golf Director: Nuno Teixeira Bastos
e-mail: oitavosgolfe@quinta-da-marinha.pt

LISBON. **Lisbon Sports Club,** Casal da Carregueira, Belas - 2745 BELAS (00 4310077). *Location:* 25 km from Lisbon. Parkland. 18 holes, 5233 metres. S.S.S. 69. *Green Fees:* information not available. *Eating facilities:* clubhouse with restaurant, bar and swimming pool, sauna. *Visitors:* welcome weekdays, Handicap Certificate required. Professional: Jose Baltazar (00 4321474). Director: Carlos Galvao (00 432 1474). *

OBIDOS. **Praia D'el Rey Golf and Country Club,** Vale de Janelas, Apartado 2, 2510 Obidos (262 905005; Fax: 262 905009). *Location:* from A8 to Obidos, take turnoff 14 to Peniche and follow EN114, turn right at course sign in Sierra D'el Rey. True links course; one of the best in Europe. 18 holes, 6467 metres. S.S.S. 72. Driving range, pitching and putting greens. *Green Fees:* information not available. *Eating facilities:* snack bar, bar, restaurant. *Visitors:* always welcome. Caddies, trolleys, equipment hire. *
e-mail: golf@praia-del-rey.com

PRAIA DE MIRAMAR. **Clube de Golf de Miramar,** Av. Sacadura Cabral, Miramar, 4405-013 Arcozelo (22 7622067; Fax: 22 7627859). *Location:* approximately 13km south of Oporto by A1, N109 direction Espinho. Flat coastal course amongst dunes alongside the beach. 9 holes, 4884 metres. S.S.S. 67. Driving range. *Green Fees*: information not provided. *Eating facilities*: clubhouse with restaurant and bar. *Visitors:* welcome, Handicap Certificate required. Hotels, restaurants and casino nearby. Pro shop. Professional: Sergio Ribeiro, Nelson Ribeiro. Secretary: Paula Sousa.

RIO MAIOR. **Quinta do Brincal Club de Golfe,** Quinta do Brincal, Arrouquelas, 2040 Rio Maior (243 908148; Fax: 243 908149). *Location:* A1 from Lisbon to Aveiras exit, follow N366, turn right to IC2, course on right at 63km. Undulating heathland with strategic sand and water. 18 holes, 6200 metres. S.S.S. 72. Driving range, putting green. *Green Fees:* information not available. *Eating facilities:* bar, restaurant. *Visitors:* always welcome. Trolley hire available. *

www.uk-golfguide.com

TROIA. **Troia Golf Club,** Troia, Carvalhal GDL (265 494112; Fax: 265 494315). *Location:* on the Troia Peninsula, 42 km south of Lisbon. From Lisbon, A2/A12 to Setubal, then follow signs for Troia to the ferry boat; in Troia follow EN243-1 to Comporta; golf course signposted. Spectacular links, 30th on list of Europe's 100 best golf courses and a superb challenge to all golfers. Designed by Robert Trent Jones Snr; host to Portuguese Open-European Tour in 1983. 18 holes, 6320 metres Par 72. Driving range, two putting greens, practice area. *Green Fees:* information not available. *Eating facilities:* clubhouse with bar/restaurant. *Visitors:* welcome, Handicap Certificate (27 men, 35 ladies). Hotel accommodation available (265 499030). Special rates for Troia Hotels guests. Pro shop, trolley and buggy rental. Director of Golf : Henrique de Sousa.*

VIMEIRO. **Vimeiro Golf Club,** Praia de Porto Novo, Termas do Vimeiro, 2560 Torres Vedras (261 980800). *Location:* situated in a wonderful cliff over the Atlantic coast, next to the beach. A level course divided by a river and sheltered by rocky cliffs. 9 holes with 18 tees, 5228 yards. S.S.S. 67. *Green Fees:* information not available. *Eating facilities:* restaurant in hotel Golf Mar, three bars. Caddies and hand trolleys available. Guests at the Hotel play for free.*

MADEIRA

FUNCHAL. **Palheiro Golf Club,** Rua Do Balancal No 29, 9060 - 414 Funchal (00 351 291 790120; Fax: 00 351 291 792456). *Location:* take Camacha turn-off from airport road, straight on under bridge, past car inspection centre (I.P.O.). Follow golf signs. A Cabell Robinson design, built on a hill top overlooking Funchal. Parkland course, amazing views with superb trees and flora. 18 holes, 6086 metres. Par 72. Driving range, putting green. *Green Fees:* Day Ticket 90 euros. *Eating facilities:* bar and restaurant – excellent international cuisine. Pro shop; cart, trolley and club hire. Casa Velha, the five-star hotel, is situated on the course. Professional: Ashley Northridge PGA.

MADEIRA. **Campo de Golfe da Madeira,** Santo Antonio da Serra, 9100 Santa Cruz (291 550100; Fax: 291 550105). *Location:* main highway to Airport (Santa Cruz) Machilo. Wooded, mountainous with view over Atlantic Ocean. 27 holes, 6082 metres. Driving range, putting and chipping green. *Green Fees:* information not available. *Eating facilities:* restaurant, snack bar, lounge bar. *Visitors:* welcome to play in tournaments except PGA Madeira Island Open (January). Pro shop; cart, trolley and club hire. Professional: Joao Sousa. Secretary: Anthony Barton (acting). *

PORTO SANTO. **Porto Santo Golfe,** Sitio das Marinhas, 9400-162 Porto Santo, P.O.Box 174 (351 291 983 777; Fax: 351 291 983 508). *Location*: Porto Santo island – 15 minutes' flight from Madeira and one hour from Lisbon. The course is 10 minutes from Porto Santo airport. Designed by Severiano Ballesteros, the course combines length and strategic water hazards with some links-style cliff top holes overlooking the sea. 18 holes, 6,434 metres, S.S.S.Par 72. Driving range, putting green, chipping green with bunkers. *Green fees:* 50 euros 18 holes. *Eating facilities:* two bars and restaurant with panoramic verandah views. Buggy bar. *Visitors:* welcome. Golf carts, electric and pull trolleys, club rental. Professional: Andrew Oliveira. Manager: Mario Silva.
e-mail: sdps@netmadeira.com

OPORTO

AMARANTE. **Amarante Golf Clube, Quinta da Deveza,** Fregim, 4600 - 593 Amarante. (+351 255 44 60 60; Fax: +351 255 44 62 02). *Location*: take A4 from Oporto heading to Vila Real, come off at Amarante Oeste, then follow signs for Fregim, the golf course is signposted from here. A true mountain course with spectacular views over surrounding peaks and valleys. 18 holes, 5035 metres. Par 68. Driving range, putting green, bunker and chipping practice area, Pro-shop, swimming pools, tennis courts. *Green Fees*: 9 Holes - 26.50 euros weekdays. 40.00 euros weekends and holidays, 18 holes 37.00 euros weekdays, 49.00 euros weekends and holidays. *Eating facilities*: restaurant and bar in clubhouse. *Visitors*: welcome. Caddies, carts, trolleys, club hire. Hotels – Casa Da Calgada (+351 255 410830; Fax: +351 255 426670); Hotel Navarras (+351 255 431 036; Fax: +351 255 432 991) Professional: João Silva.
e-mail: sgagolfeamarante@oninet.pt

ESPINHO. **Oporto Golf Club,** Paramos, 4500 Espinho (227 342008; Fax: 227 346895). *Location:* 18 miles south of Oporto, one mile south of Espinho. Seaside links, few trees, founded in 1890. 18 holes, 5556 metres. Course rating 70.2; Slope rating 127; Par 71. Practice ground. *Green Fees:* information not available. Half price for guests of Hotels mentioned below. *Eating facilities:* bar with snacks (restaurant - members only). *Visitors:* welcome Tuesdays to Fridays (closed Mondays); weekends and Bank Holidays till 10.30am. Handicap Certificate required. Beach, hotels - Hotel Solverde, Hotel Praia - Golf, casino nearby. Professional: Eduardo Maganinho (02 7313649). *

PLEASE MENTION THE GOLF GUIDE WHEN YOU WRITE OR PHONE TO ENQUIRE ABOUT CLUBS OR ACCOMMODATION

ESPOSENDE. **Golfe de Quinta da Barca,** Gemezes, Barca do Lago, 4740 476 Esposende (+351 253 966723; Fax: +351 253 969068). *Location*: 50km north of Oporto on JC 1, turn right to Esposende and before Esposende turn to Quinta da Barca. A 9 hole course but very demanding. The river, lakes, bunkers and undulating greens make it a precision test. 9 holes, 1927 metres. C.R. 62,2; S.R. 106. Driving range, putting and chipping greens, apart hotel, marina, tennis. *Green Fees*: information not available. *Eating facilities*: restaurant and bar in clubhouse. *Visitors*: welcome. Pro shop, caddies, cart, trolley, club hire. Professional: Manuel Carneiro. Director: Luis Catarino.*
e-mail: lcatarino@quintabarca.com
website: www.quintabarca.com

ESTELA. **Estela Golf Club,** Rio Alto-Estela, 4490 Povoa de Varzim (52 612700/601567; Fax: 52 612701). *Location:* 30 km north of Oporto, 24 km from the international airport. Seaside links. 18 holes, 6095 metres. S.S.S. 73. *Green Fees:* information not available. *Eating facilities:* full bar and catering facilities. *Visitors:* welcome anytime when no competitions taking place. Sopete Hotel guests entitled to special privileges. *Society Meetings:* by arrangement. Professionals: Carlos Alberto, Carlos Henrique. Secretary/Manager: Salete Correia. *

PONTE DE LIMA. **Golfe de Ponte de Lima,** Quinta de Pias, Fornelos, 4990 Ponte de Lima (258 743414; Fax: 258 743424). *Location*: one kilometre north of Ponte de Lima on EN201. Beautiful and scenic; hilly front nine. 18 holes, 6005 metres. S.S.S. 70. Driving range, Putting green, chipping and bunker practice area. *Green Fees*: information not available. *Eating facilities*: restaurant and bar in clubhouse "Beni-Golf". *Visitors*: welcome. Pro shop, caddies, cart, trolley, club hire. Professionals: Manuel Carneiro, Paulo Teixeira. Director: Manuel Farncisco de Miguel.*

VIDAGO. **Vidago Golf Club,** Vidago 5425 (276 999404; Fax: 276 907359). *Location:* mountain valley course, in spa/resort area well inland, only 25 km from Spanish border. Short 9-hole course, 1000ft high, 2678 yards. S.S.S. 63 (18 holes). *Eating facilities:* Vidago Palace Hotel.*

THE AZORES

SAO MIGUEL. **Batalha Golf Course,** Rua do Bom Jesus, Aflitos, 9545-234 Fenais da Luz, Sao Miguel-Azores (296 498559; Fax: 296 498284). *Location:* go north from Ponta Delgada in direction Faja de Cima, turn right for Aflitos before reaching Fenais da Luz. Championship course with sweeping views over large flowing greens with wide and generous fairways. Beautiful surroundings and fabulous scenery. 18 holes, 6435 metres. S.S.S. 72. Driving range, two large putting greens, chipping area. *Green Fees:* information not provided. *Eating facilities:* modern clubhouse with classic island architecture; bars and restaurant. *Visitors:* welcome. Complete range of support services. Caddies, carts, trolleys, club hire. Professional: Rui Indio. Golf Director: Luis Indio (296 498559).

SAO MIGUEL. **Furnas Golf Course,** Achada das Furnas, 9675-030 Furnas, Sao Miguel-Azores. (296 584341; Fax: 296 498284). *Location:* 40 minutes from Ponta Delgada. Designed originally by McKenzie Ross and extended by Bob Cameron. Unique style and characteristics, with fairways flanked by trees and fiendishly undulating greens. 18 holes, 6232 metres. Par 72. *Green Fees:* 47 euros. *Eating facilities:* modern clubhouse; bar, restaurant. *Visitors:* always welcome. Carts, trolleys, club hire. Professional: Rui Indio. Golf Director: Luis Indio (296 584341).

TERCEIRA. **Terceira Golf Club,** Caixa Postal 15, 9760 Praia da Vitoria, Terceira (00351 295 902444/902299; Fax: 00351 295 902445). *Location:* a few kilometres from Angra do Heroismo and Praia da Vitoria on the island of Terceira in the Azores. Landscaped course through trees and low hills, with small lakes. 18 holes, 6227 metres. S.S.S. 70. Practice facilities. *Green Fees:* on request. *Eating facilities:* available. *Visitors:* always welcome. Hotel accommodation nearby. *Society Meetings:* always welcome. Professional: Eduardo Correia. General Director: Antonio P. Camara.*

FHG

Visit the KUPERARD website

www.holidayguides.com

for details of the wide choice of accommodation featured in the full range of FHG titles

Golf in Spain
Where to Play, Where to Stay
Michael Gedye

Winter golf should not only be about frosty fairways, mud on your ball and temporary greens; about several sweaters and raingear, a howling gale and driving rain. There is another choice – an opportunity to relax in warm sunshine on winding, verdant fairways flanked by crystal lakes and twisted cork oaks, to enjoy the scented breeze off the sea and greens like undulating carpet. Just a short flight away, Spain can offer welcome relief from the ravages of winter with a wide selection of excellent golf in an exciting, colourful and historic environment. There are now more than 200 holiday resort courses around the country's Mediterranean coastline, more than in any other country outside of the United States. The majority of these have been constructed during the last twenty years, designed by some of the best architects in the game and built to the most modern specifications.

The sport in Spain used to trail far behind other more popular activities such as football and bullfighting. But times have changed; nearly a quarter of a million Spaniards now play, spurred on by the successes of Ballesteros, Olazabal and Garcia. Such domestic interest can only be good for the holiday market, with more reason to create resorts with golf in attractive Mediterranean coastal regions. The five main vacation areas – Andalucia, Catalonia, Majorca, Valencia and Murcia – already have 172 golf courses, with more under construction.

The focal point for summer sunshine, winter golf and second home/retirement purchase has been the COSTA DEL SOL, the coastal strip of southern Andalucia popularly called the 'Costa del Golf'. In recent years, the number of places to play has mushroomed, giving even more opportunity for relaxing play in the sun. With so many courses, the region has been divided into three sections. The most westerly includes the exciting new courses of Sherry Golf near Jerez and a second eighteen holes at San Roque, adding to a list that includes the regular PGA Tour venue of Montecastillo, Novo Sancti Petri, designed by Severiano Ballesteros, and the two Trent Jones' masterpieces of Sotogrande and Valderrama, site of the 1977 Ryder Cup.

ANDALUCIA CENTRAL, running from Estepona east past lively Marbella to a little past the city of Malaga, has most of the golf opportunities, probably more than you will ever play. This region has hosted two World Cups, the Ryder Cup and numerous Spanish Open championships over the years. Visit Las Brisas, Los Arqueros and La Quinta for golf of high quality; La Cala or Monte Mayor for spectacular settings. More tranquil golf awaits at Rio Real and Santa Maria; there are also many teaching academies, where you can sharpen your game, and even a course floodlit at night. East beyond Malaga lie Anoreta and Golf Almerimar in a peaceful seaside setting.

Further north is MURCIA, where Europe's foremost multi-sports resort, La Manga, popular with a number of international sports teams, is situated. Here you are offered a choice of three palm-fringed courses encircled by low hills, as well as many other sports, leisure facilities and good accommodation.

Then you reach VALENCIA, home of paella and what is arguably one of the finest public courses anywhere, the genuine links challenge of El Saler, created by Spaniard master architect, Javier Arana. Nearby you can find the varied tests of Golf Escorpion, Villamartin and demanding El Bosque.

CATALONIA covers the regions of Girona and the ever-popular coastline of the Costa Brava in Spain's northeast. Pals has two fine courses in pinewoods near the sea, complementing a choice of other fine golf in the area, some of it well established and some built more recently.

The Balearic Islands have a deserved holiday reputation, with many well developed coastal resorts. Latest arrival on the golfing scene in MAJORCA is Golf Alcanada, the creation of Robert Trent Jones Jr, which follows gently sloping land on the island's west coast, with great views out to sea and the distant Sierra Levante mountains. Elsewhere, play Santa Ponsa, Poniente and Pollensa or stay in the elegant Son Vida hotel, encircled by its own long-established golf course. There is more than enough golf on this holiday island, where warm out-of-season sunshine is tempered by the gentle sea breeze.

ANDALUCIA – CENTRAL

BENAHAVIS. **La Quinta Golf and Country Club,** Urb La Quinta, s/n 29660 Nueva, Andalucia (Marbella), Malaga (95.276.23.90; Fax: 95.276.23.99). *Location:* on main road to Ronda, 3.5km from N340 coast road. Inland hilly course. 18 holes, 5517 metres, Par 72, S.S.S. 71; also 9 hole course, 2848 metres. Par 36, S.S.S. 71. *Green Fees:* information not available. *Eating facilities:* clubhouse, restaurant. *Visitors:* welcome, please book in advance. Golf Academy, Pro-shop, table tennis, squash, sauna, swimming pool, fitness centre, therapic and static centre. *Society Meetings:* welcome. Professional: Manuel Pinero. Director: D. Marcos Lería Couderc.*

BENAHAVIS. **Monte Mayor Golf Club,** Apartado 962, 29679 Benahavis (Malaga) (952 937111; Fax: 952 937112. *Location:* in the hills between San Pedro de Alcantara and Estepona; inland from Ctra. N-340, km. 165.6. Possibly the Costa del Sol's most spectacular course, a challenging layout over mountainous terrain for the bold and accurate. 18 holes, 5652 metres, Par 71. *Green Fees:* information not available. *Eating facilities:* bar and restaurant in clubhouse. Cart hire. Pyr Hotel, Puerto Banos - very good package for golfers.*

BENALMADENA. **Golf Torrequebrada,** Edif Club de Golf, 29630 Benalmadena (95 244 27 42; Fax: 95 256 11 29). *Location:* Exit CN 340 at junction 222. Undulating terrain, lots of vegetation, superb views over Mediterranean Sea. 18 holes, 5852 metres, Par 72. Driving range. *Green Fees:* information not available *Eating facilities:* full bar and restaurant. *Visitors:* welcome at all times. Handicap Certificate required, maximum 27 men, 35 ladies. Pro shop, changing rooms. One of the Costa's favourite golf courses, has hosted two Spanish PGA Championships. Professional: Juan Jimenez. Commercial Director: Eddie MacLean.*

ESTEPONA. **Atalaya Golf & Country Club Estepona-Malaga,** Ctra de Benahavis, 29688 Estepona, Malaga (95 2882812; Fax: 95 2887897). *Location:* between Marbella and Estepona, off N340 going west, turn inland for Benahavis just past Guadalmina. Two courses Atalaya Old and New. The fairly open parkland holes are lined with eucalyptus and pine. 36 holes, 6142 metres, Par 72. Large practice ground and putting greens. *Green Fees:* information not available. *Eating facilities:* bar and restaurant in clubhouse. Pro shop; club, cart and trolley hire. Professional: (95 2882812; Fax: 95 2887897). Secretary: Maribel Martin (95 2882812/95 2882811; Fax: 95 2887897). Golf Director: Andres Sanchez.*

For full details of clubs and courses, plus convenient accommodation

www.uk-golfguide.com

ESTEPONA. Golf El Paraiso, Carretera de Cadiz-Malaga 29680 Estepona, Malaga (95.288.38.35; Fax: 95.288.58.27). *Location:* west on N340, turn right at Benavista then inland 3 km. A fine rolling parkland style course opened in 1974. The holes run over and around a hill surmounted by the El Paraiso Hotel. 18 holes, 6116 metres, Par 71. Practice ground and putting green. *Green Fees:* 1st Jan - 31st Jan; Individuals 50 euros, 2 persons and buggy 105 euros. 1st Feb - 31st May; 75 euros per person, 25 euros per buggy. 1st June - 30th Sept; special offers, phone for prices. *Eating facilities:* bar and restaurant. Pro shop; club, cart and trolley hire. Professionals: Paul Crangle and Daniel Westermark. Secretary: Colin Christison.
e-mail: info@elparaisogolfclub.com
website: www.elparaisogolfclub.com

MALAGA. **Guadalhorce Club de Golf,** Ctra de Cartama, Apartado 48, 29590 Campanillas, Malaga (952 179378; Fax: 952 179372). *Location:* east towards Malaga on N340 past airport; turn right at sugar refinery taking underpass towards Bacardi distillery. A combination of classic parkland on level land with sculptured holes with raised greens and strategic water. 18 holes, 6194 metres, Par 72. Practice ground and putting green. Also 9 short holes. *Green Fees:* information not available. *Eating facilities:* bar and restaurant in classical 19th century Andalucian manor house. Pro shop; club, buggies and trolley hire. Professional: S. Bruna. Director of Golf: G Alvarez. *

MARBELLA. **Aloha Golf Club,** Nueva Andalucia, 29660 Marbella, Malaga (952-90 70 85/86; Fax: 952-81 23 89). *Location:* 3 km inland from Puerto Banus, 8km west of Marbella. Very tight driving course with tree-lined fairways and very strategically placed lakes and streams. 18 holes, 6293 metres, S.S.S. 74 (back tees). Practice area. *Green Fees:* information not provided. *Eating facilities:* bar and restaurant (952-61 23 50). *Visitors:* basically a members' club. Pro shop; club, cart and trolley hire. Professional and Sport Director: Jose Luis Mangas (952 81 47 55; Fax: 952 81 23 89).

MARBELLA. **Golf Rio Real,** Apartado 82, 29600 Marbella (952-76 57 33; Fax: 952-77 21 40). *Location:* 5km east from Marbella on N340, situated in a very nice valley with sea views and crossed by the Rio Real Creek. A relatively gentle test of golf. Well-cared for and closely linked to the five star Rio Real Golf Hotel. 18 holes, 6166 metres, Par 72. Practice ground and putting green. *Green Fees:* information not available. *Eating facilities:* restaurant and bar. *
e-mail: golf@rioreal.com
website: www.rioreal.com

MARBELLA. **Guadalmina Club de Golf,** Urb. Guadalmina Alta, 29678 S. Pedro Alcantara, Malaga (952 883375; Fax: 952 883483). *Location:* turn right off N340 approximately 1km west of San Pedro de Alcantara. A development which now boasts 45 holes - the original South course, the North which is more open despite some strategic water, and a short 9 hole layout. North: 18 holes, 5825 metres, Par 71. South: 18 holes, 6021 metres, Par 72. Driving range and putting greens. *Green Fees:* information not available. *Eating facilities:* spike bar and restaurant.

Visitors: welcome, Handicaps 27 men, 35 ladies. Pro shop; club, cart and trolley hire. Professional: Francisco Hernandez. Secretary: Alvaro Beamonte (2883455/2883375; Fax: 2883483). *

MARBELLA. **Los Naranjos Golf Club,** Apartado 64, 29660 Nueva Andalucia, Malaga (952-81 24 28; Fax: 952-81 14 28). *Location:* turn right off N340 (going west) at Puerto Banus. Pass bullring and go over hill for 2km. The front nine holes run in a quiet undulating landscape and second nine through an orange grove giving the name to the course. 18 holes, 6038 metres, Par 72. Practice ground and putting green. *Green Fees:* Information not available *Eating facilities:* bar and restaurant in new clubhouse. Pro shop, club, cart and trolley hire. *Visitors:* Handicap Certificates required. Manager: Christer Sorensson. *

MARBELLA. **Real Club de Golf Las Brisas,** Apartadode Correos 147, Nueva Andalucia, 29660 Marbella, Malaga (952-81 08 75; Fax: 952-81 55 18). *Location:* turn right off N340 at Puerto Banus. Over hill past bullring, then right and follow signs to Hotel Del Golf. A fine course which has played host to two World Cups and numerous other major Opens. Tough, with plenty of water and fast, sloping greens. 18 holes, 6163 metres, Par 72. Practice ground and putting green. *Green Fees:* as this is a members' club, green fee playing space is limited. Check availability in advance. *Eating facilities:* bar and restaurant. Pro shop; club, cart and trolley hire.

MIJAS. **La Cala Resort,** Apdo de Correos 106, La Cala de Mijas, 29649 Mijas Costa, Malaga (34 952669000; Fax: 34 952669034). *Location:* situated between Fuengirola and Marbella, on N340 highway, turn at La Cala Village, "Cala de Mijas" 6km inland. La Cala offers elevated greens, large bunkers, playable and challenging holes and some magnificent views. 54 holes, North Course – 6187 metres, Par 73; South Course – 5966 metres, Par 72. Campo Europa - 6014metres. David Leadbetter Academy, one driving range, 6 hole Executive Par 3 course, football academy. *Green Fees:* information not available. *Eating facilities:* bars and restaurants. *Visitors:* always welcome. Pro shop. Squash and tennis. La Cala Five Star Hotel. *Society Meetings:* welcome. Golf Director: Alan Saunders (34 952669036; Fax: 34 952669034).

MIJAS. **Mijas Golf International,** Apartado 145, 29640 Fuengirola, Malaga (0034 52 47 6843; Fax: 0034 52 46 7943). *Location:* from Marbella on N340 take the Fuengirola bypass and turn left at underpass. Then drive for two km before turning right. Two excellent courses: Los Lagos - 18 holes, 6448 metres, Par 71; and Los Olivos - 18 holes, 5896 metres, Par 72. The former course is relatively open although the greens are well protected by sand and water; the latter is narrower with smaller greens, favouring finesse over power. Driving range and putting green. *Green Fees:* information not provided. *Eating facilities:* excellent food and bars. *Visitors:* welcome at anytime subject to availability. Pro shop; club, cart and trolley hire. Secretary: Felipe Perez.*
website: www.mijasgolf.org

ANDALUCIA – EAST

ALMERIA. Golf Almerimar, Urb Almerimar, 04700 El Ejido, Almeria (950-49 74 54; Fax: 950-49 72 33). *Location:* 7 km from El Ejido, which is some 35 km from Almeria on the main Malaga road. This is a well-established course in a relatively level situation, with a wealth of trees and the chance of a breeze from the sea alongside. 18 holes, 5892 metres, S.S.S. 72. Practice ground and putting green. *Green Fees:* information not available. *Eating facilities:* snack bar and restaurant. Pro shop; club, cart and trolley hire. Professional: Juan Parron. *

RINCON DE LA VICTORIA. Anoreta Golf, Avda. del Golf, s/n, 29730 Rincon de la Victoria, Malaga (952-40 40 00; Fax: 952-40 40 50). *Location:* 12 km east of Malaga at Rincon de la Victoria, only second course to be built east of Malaga. Seaside/parkland course. 18 holes, 5976 metres, Par 71. Driving range and putting green. *Green Fees:* information not available. *Eating facilities:* bar and restaurant. *Visitors:* welcome, no restrictions. Pro shop; club, cart and trolley hire.*

ANDALUCIA – WEST

CADIZ. Club de Golf Novo Sancti Petri, Urb. Novo Sancti Petri, Playa de la Barrosa, 11130 Chiclana de la Frontera, Cadiz (0034 956 49 40 05; Fax: 0034 956 49 43 50). *Location:* end of the La Barrosa road at Chiclana. 36 holes divided into two rounds, one round bordered by trees, the other with magnificent views overlooking the Atlantic Ocean. Various water hazards. Designed by Severiano Ballesteros. Round A 6097 metres, Round B 5846 metres (yellow tees), all Par 72. Practice ground and putting green. *Green Fees:* 67 euros (1 Jan -31 Oct). *Eating facilities:* bar and restaurant. *Visitors:* welcome, no restrictions.Only soft spikes to be worn. Pro shop; club, cart and trolley hire. Professionals: Chema Andrade, Pip Andrade, Daniel Kiewitz, Jeroen Dekker, Günther Winkler, Jose Lorca, Christophe Meymat, Björn Raschovsky. Secretary: Mrs Ruiz-Cortina. Director: Uwe Born. e-mail: sales@golf-novosancti.es

CADIZ. Montecastillo Hotel & Golf Resort, Ctra de Arcos, 11406 Jerez de la Frontera, Cadiz ([34] 9-56 15 12 00; Fax: [34] 9-56 15 12 09). *Location:* half a mile main road, four miles Jerez, 46 miles Sevilla. A relatively level but rolling layout with a distinct links flavour. Plenty of mounds and elevated tees, vast bunkers and water. 18 holes, 6424 metres, Par 72. Driving range and putting green. *Green Fees:* information not available. *Eating facilities:* restaurant, two coffee shops. *Visitors:* welcome. Special packages available. Tennis court, football pitches, paddle tennis courts and Montecastillo Spa, including indoor swimming pool, jacuzzi, saunas, massage rooms, gym, cafeteria and solarium. *Society Meetings:* welcome. Secretary: Immaculada Fernandez (956 151213; Fax: 956 151215). *

JEREZ. Sherry Golf Jerez, Autovia A-4, Km.642, 11407 Jerez de la Frontera, Cadiz (34 956 088 330; Fax: 34 956 088 331). *Location:* 1.5 km. from Jerez; take motorway Jerez-El Puerto de Santa Maria; access to golf after 5 minutes. An interesting course to play for golfers of all levels, with wide fairways and large greens. Also 9-hole Par 3 course. 18 holes, 6,572 metres, Par 72. Driving range, putting green, golf academy. *Green Fees:* 57 euros 18 holes. *Eating facilities:* bar, snack bar, à la carte restaurant. *Visitors:* welcome, with maximum handicap 36. Golf carts, pull trolley, club rental. Professional: Javier Romero. Manager: Emilio Lustau. e-mail: info@sherrygolf.com comercial@sherrygolf.com (groups)

SAN ROQUE. Real Club de Golf Sotogrande, Paseo del Parque, Apartado 14, 11310 Sotogrande (956 785012). *Location:* km 130 of national road N340, turn 2.5km towards sea. Well established (1964) and a major golfing landmark in Europe. Rolling slopes and strategic water are offset by cork oak, eucalyptus, palm and pine, first golf course in Europe designed by Robert Trent Jones. A demanding golfing feast. 18 holes, 6224 metres, Par 74. Also 9 hole short course. Practice ground and putting green. *Green Fees:* information not available. *Eating facilities:* cafeteria and restaurant. *Visitors:* welcome daily from 11am to 1pm. Pro shop; club, cart and trolley hire; tennis, paddle and swimming pool. Professional: Teddoro Gonzalez (345 6795722). Secretary: Fugenio Reviriego (345 6794516). *

SAN ROQUE. San Roque Club, CN 340, KM 126, 11360 San Roque, Cadiz ([34] 9-56 613030/60/90; Fax: 613013). *Location:* 3km from Sotogrande towards San Roque village. Undulating first 9 holes, wooded second 9 holes, water hazards. 18 holes, 6494 metres White markers, 6134 metres Yellow, 5588 metres Blue, 5174 metres Red. S.S.S. 74, Par 72. Two-tiered, covered range (28 bays), two pitching areas, putting greens, three practice bunkers. *Green Fees:* information not available. *Eating facilities:* Snack Bar, "El Bolero" Restaurant, "Tappan Yaki" Japanese Restaurant. *Visitors:* welcome anytime but must pre-book tee times. Pro shop, locker facilities, club rental, buggy, trolley rental, golf lessons available. Golf Director: Ian F. Martin.•

SAN ROQUE. Club de Golf Valderrama, Avda Los Cortijos, s/n, 11310 Sotogrande, Cadiz ([34] 9-56 791200; Fax: [34] 9-56 796028). *Location:* access through the main Sotogrande entrance (right of N340 going west); then 2.5 km inland. Cork oaks, rolling hills, view to the sea. Ryder Cup venue 1997 and home of the Volvo Masters. 18 holes, 6356 metres, Par 71. Practice ground and putting green. *Green Fees:* information not available. *Eating facilities:* bar and restaurant open to non members for dinner Tuesdays to Saturdays; buffet on Sundays. *Visitors:* tee off times for visitors 12 noon to 2pm, must book in advance. Handicap maximum 24 men, 32 ladies. Soft spikes on golf shoes compulsory. Pro shop. Valderrama hosted the World Golf Championships and the American Express Championships 1999/2000. *Society Meetings:* welcome by prior arrangement. Professional: Miguel Sedeno. Director General: Derek Brown. *

CATALONIA

GIRONA. **Costa Brava Golf Club,** Urb. Golf Costa Brava, "La Masia", 17246 Sta. Cristina D'Aro, Girona (972 83 70 55; Fax: 83 72 72). *Location:* from A7 highway Exit 9. 30km from Girona, five/six km from the coast. From a hilly, wooded first 9 holes with fine views, the back 9 holes slope down by the river to flatter ground. 18 holes, 5625 metres. S.S.S. 70. Putting greens and practice areas. *Green Fees:* information not provided. Special rates for groups. *Eating facilities:* restaurant, bar and snack bar. *Visitors:* welcome anytime, no restrictions. Pro shop, changing rooms. Buggies and caddy carts for hire. *Society Meetings:* welcome, discounts available. Professional: Miguel Gil Garcia (Tel & Fax: 83 50 33). Secretary: Ma. Victoria Figueras Garcia (83 71 50; Fax: 83 72 72).

GIRONA. **Club de Golf Girona,** Urbanitz. Golf Girona, 17481 Sant Julia Ramis (Girona). (00.34.972.17.16.41;Fax:00.34.972.17.16.82). *Location:* four km north of Girona town centre, near the Girona North Exit (6) of the Girona-la Jonquera Motorway (A7). An undulating course around wooded valleys and hills with three man-made lakes. 18 holes, 6100 metres. S.S.S. 72. Driving range, putting green. *Green Fees:* information not available. *Eating facilities:* bar, restaurant, golfer's menu. *Visitors:* welcome all year by arrangement. Pro shop, caddy carts for hire. *Society Meetings:* welcome by arrangement; 10% reduction. Professionals: Pepe Rowerd and Gerard Solano (972.17.00.11; Fax: 972. 17.16.82). e-mail: golfgirona@golfgirona.com

GIRONA. **Club de Golf D'Aro Mas Nou,** 17250 Playa de Aro, Costa Brava (Girona) (972 826900; Fax: 972 826906). *Location:* on the Costa Brava, between Playa de Aro and Santa Cristina, 35 km east of Girona. A scenic course with panoramic views of the Costa Brava from its situation on the Les Gavarres mountains. Trees and lakes add to the course's charm. 18 holes, 6218 metres. S.S.S. 72. 9 hole Par 3 course, practice area. *Green Fees:* information not available. *Eating facilities:* clubhouse with bar, snack bar and restaurant. Caddies. Professionals: Piter Runlus, Pedro Martinez. Secretary: Toni Hidalgo (003 4 972 826900/816727; Fax: 972 826906). Manager: Rudolf Glanzmann (003 4 972 826900). *
e-mail: golfdaromasnou@retemail.es

PALS. **Emporda Golf Club,** Ctra. Palafrugell-Torroella de Montgri, 17257 Gualta (Girona) (972 760450; Fax: 972 757100). *Location:* 40km from Girona almost on the coast, between Pals and Torroella. Combination course with dunes, lakes, wooded, flat course. 27 holes. S.S.S. 71. Large driving range, chipping area. *Green Fees:* information not available. *Eating facilities:* clubhouse, restaurant, snack bar. *Visitors:* welcome anytime, no restrictions. Swimming pool. Professional: Jordi Riera. Manager: Isidre Soria. Commercial Director: Jaume Marin. *

PALS. **Golf Platja de Pals,** Ctra. del Golf, s/n, 17256 Pals, Costa Brava (34 972 667739; Fax: 34 972 636799) *Location:* on the coast at Playa de Pals beach, eight km from Begur and 40 km east of Girona. The oldest course on the Costa Brava, requires great golfing skills as its fairways are ringed by 100-year old pine trees. 18 holes, 6222 metres. S.S.S. 72/74. Par 73. Practice course with pitching, chipping and putting green areas. *Green Fees:* 51-71 euros, depending on season. *Eating facilities:* snack bar, dining area with spectacular golfing views. Mediterranean style menu. *Visitors:* welcome. Clubs, caddy cars and golf carts can be hired. *Society Meetings:* welcome.
e-mail: comercial@golfplatjadepals.com
website: www.golfplatjadepals.com

PALS. **Golf Serres de Pals,** Pals, Girona 17256 ([972] 637 375; Fax: [972] 667 447). *Location:* motorway to Le Bisbel, 3km from Flaça take the first turn on the left and then follow the signs for Golf Serres de Pals. Three different areas with smooth hill top and pine tree forest, and fairways between lakes. 18 holes, 6882 yards, 6263 metres. S.S.S. 72. Driving range with practice areas and three Par 3 holes. *Green Fees:* information not available. *Eating facilities:* restaurant and bar. *Visitors*: always welcome. Closed Christmas Day. Shop, golf school, changing rooms etc. Hotel accommodation on site. Hire of buggies, clubs, trolleys. *Society Meetings:* always welcome. Tailor-made packages. Secretary: Pedro Garcia Ruiz.*
e-mail: info@golfserresdepals.com
website: www. golfserresdepals.com

La Costa *Golf & Beach Resort* ★★★★
...for Pals Beach
...for Pals Golf

With its magnificent location at the heart of the Costa Brava, the Hotel La Costa offers a huge range of activities on land and sea in addition to its own health and leisure facilities.

Adjoining Platja de Pals Golf, one of the best courses in Spain, 5 minutes from Serres de Pals course, and convenient for the other courses in the region, the Hotel naturally attracts golfers and their families. 50% discount on green fees at Platja de Pals and Serres de Pals.

Fine cuisine and wines, a choice of bars and restaurants, large and exotic pool and tennis make the Hotel La Costa an obvious choice for golfing holidays in Spain.

Hotel La Costa, 17256 Playa de Pals, Pals (Costa Brava), Girona, Spain
Tel: +34 972 667 740. Fax: +34 972 667 736
e-mail: info@lacostahotel.com www.lacostahotel.com

See also Colour Advertisement on page 104

MURCIA

MURCIA. **La Manga Club,** Los Belones, Cartagena, 30385 Murcia (968 175000; Fax: 968 175058). *Location:* 330 km from Cartagena, 75 km from Murcia and 100 km from Alicante airport. Access off road to Murcia Airport. A true sporting resort in all aspects, with 54 holes of palm-lined golf backed by low hills as well as tennis, squash, bowls, health club and watersports at the Mar Menor close by. Five star La Manga Club hotel on site. Three courses: North 18 holes, 5780 metres, Par 71; South 18 holes, 6361 metres, Par 72; West 18 holes, 5971 metres, Par 72. Driving range and putting green. *Green Fees:* information not available. *Eating facilities:* bar and restaurant. Pro shop; club, cart and trolley hire. *
e-mail: golf@lamangaclub.es

VALENCIA

BETERA. **Club de Golf Escorpion,** Apartado 1, 46117 Betera, Valencia (96-160 12 11; Fax: 96-169 01 87). *Location:* take the road from Valencia to Liria, turning off at San Antonio de Benageber. Go 4 km to the right in the direction of Betera. A fine private club offering parkland-style golf with a mountain backdrop. Tree-lined and interesting. 18 holes, 6319 metres, Par 72. Driving range and putting green. *Green Fees:* information not available. *Eating facilities:* bar and restaurant. Pro shop; club, cart and trolley hire. *

CHIVA. **Club de Golf El Bosque,** Carretera Godelleta, Urban. El Bosque 46370 Chiva, Valencia (96-180 8000; Fax: 96-180 8001). *Location:* take the Nacional III road (Madrid-Valencia) Exit 337, turn off for Godelleta. Wooded course, designed by Robert Trent Jones Snr. 18 holes, 6276 metres, S.S.S. 72. Driving range and putting green. *Green Fees:* information not available. *Eating facilities:* cafeteria, restaurant. *Visitors:* welcome. One, two and three bedroom flats available. Professionals: Alfonso Pinto, Ignecio Briz. *

ORIHUELA. **Campo de Golf Villamartin,** Crta Alicante Cartagena, 03189 Orihuela, Alicante (96 6765127; Fax: 96 6765158). *Location:* 7 km from Torrevieja, 3 km from the beach and 3km from the main road N332. Two courses laid out on interesting coastal sandy land with some pines. A good test of golf, open to the breeze. 18 holes, 6132 metres, Par 72; 18 holes, 5770 metres, Par 72. Driving range and putting green. *Green Fees:* information not provided. *Eating facilities:* bar, coffee shop and restaurant. *Visitors:* welcome. Pro shop; buggies and carts. *Society Meetings:* welcome, 10% discount. Professional: Emilio Rodriguez (96 6765127; Fax: 96 6765158). Secretary: Juan Miguel Buendia (96 6765051; Fax: 96 6765170).

VALENCIA. **Campo de Golf El Saler,** Parador De Turismo "El Saler", El Saler, Valencia (96 161 0384; Fax: 96 162 7366). *Location:* at 18km on the road from Nazaret to Oliva, right by the sea. One of the great Spanish tests of golf, with open links fairways and tight holes lined with umbrella pine; a public facility offering true seaside conditions. 18 holes, 6042 metres, Par 72. Driving range and putting green. *Green Fees:* information not available. *Eating facilities:* bar, restaurant and coffee shop. *Visitors:* welcome. Pro shop; club, cart and trolley and electric trolley hire.*

MAJORCA

CALA D'OR. **Club Vall D'Or Golf,** Ctra Cala d'Or a Portocolom, 07669 S'Horta (971 837068; Fax: 971 837299). *Location:* approximately 60km east of Palma on the road from Porto Colom to Cala D'Or. Undulating, winding course, with trees. 18 holes, 5824 metres. S.S.S. 71. Driving range, club hire. *Green Fees:* information not available. *Eating facilities:* clubhouse, bar and restaurant. *Visitors:* welcome with Handicap. Nearby hotels include Cala D'Or, Rocador, Rocador Playa. Professional: Antonio Gonzalez. Secretary: Barbara Denk (971 837001). *

MAGALLUF. **Golf de Poniente,** Crta. Cala Figuera S/N, 07182 Calvia (0034971 130148; Fax: 0034971 130176). *Location:* 18km west of Palma, one km from Magalluf on the Andraitx Road. The course is considered long and difficult, surrounded by trees and water, with large and fast greens. 18 holes, 6430 metres. S.S.S. 72. Driving range, putting green. *Green Fees:* information not provided. *Eating facilities:* clubhouse, restaurant and bar. *Visitors:* welcome. Nearby hotels include Son Caliu, Club Galatzo. Professionals: Paco Ruiz, Brian Salter.
e-mail: golf@ponientegolf.com
website: www.ponientegolf.com

PALMA. **Real Golf de Bendinat,** Campoamor S/N, 07181 Bendinat Calvia (971 405200; Fax: 971 700786). *Location:* five km west from Palma centre on the road between Illetas and Portals Nous. Mixed woodland, good vistas. 18 holes, 5650 metres. S.S.S. 71. Driving range, putting green. *Green Fees:* information not available. *Eating facilities:* excellent restaurant. *Visitors:* welcome, limited numbers. Please reserve tee-off times through our Fax No: (971 700786). *Society Meetings:* welcome. Professional: Ricardo Galiano (971 405450; Fax: 971 700786). Secretary: Alison Bradshaw (971 405200; Fax: 971 700786).*

THE APPEARANCE OF AN ASTERISK (*) AT THE END OF A CLUB OR COURSE ENTRY INDICATES THAT UP-TO-DATE INFORMATION HAS NOT BEEN SUPPLIED

PALMA. **Son Vida Golf,** Urb. Son Vida, 07013 Palma de Mallorca (34/971-79.12.10; Fax: 34/971.79.11.27). *Location:* three km from Palma centre, access via the Sinora Exit Son Rapina. Majorca's first course (1964) winding through trees and estate villas with lakes and gentle slopes. 18 holes, 5740 metres. S.S.S. 71. Driving range, Pro Shops, car, trolley and club rental. *Green Fees:* information not available. *Eating facilities:* snacks and lunches in the comfortable clubhouse, excellent restaurant El Pato (The Duck) overlooking 18th hole. *Visitors:* welcome, Handicap Certificate/Card required. Nearby hotels (discount on green fees) include Arabella Golf Hotel (5 stars), Hotel Son Vida (4 stars) on the course, Victoria Sol (4 stars), Palma, Bonanza Playa Illetas, Son Caliu. *Society Meetings:* welcome. Professionals: R. Maer, S. Ruiz. Secretary: Mrs Layda. Manager: Juan Alvarez. *

POLLENSA. **Golf Pollensa,** Ctra. Palma Pollensa, 07460 Pollensa (0034971 533216; Fax: 0034971 533265). *Location:* in the north of the island, 45 km from Palma Airport and 2 km from Pollensa. On the south side of a hill with smooth and beautiful undulations and sea views. 9 holes: White tees 5304 metres S.S.S. 68; Red tees 5116 metres S.S.S. 70, Par 70. Driving range, putting and pitching green. *Green Fees:* 35-60 euros. *Eating facilities:* snack bar, beautiful restaurant, excellent food, 7 days a week. *Visitors:* welcome, tee reservation recommended. Changing room. Pro shop, golf lessons, club and electric cart rental. *Society Meetings:* welcome. Professional: Carlos Insua. Director: Christina Schallock. * website: www.golfpollensa.com

PUERTO DE ALCUDIA. **Club de Golf Alcanada,** Ctra.del Faro s/n, 07410 Puerto de Alcudia, Mallorca (971 54 95 60; Fax: 971 89 75 78). *Location:* near Puerto de Alcudia. Created by Robert Trent Jones Jr, the course slopes gently down past pine, oak and olive trees with views across the sea to Alcanada island and the distant Sierra Levante mountains. 18 holes, 6,499 metres, Par 72. Driving range, pitching and putting green. *Green Fees:* information not available. *Eating facilities:* clubhouse restaurant with large terrace. *Visitors:* welcome. Electric golf carts, pull trolleys, club rental. Professional: Peter Dost. Director of Golf: Kristoff Both. e-mail: info@golf-alcanada.com

SANTA PONSA. **Santa Ponsa Golf Club One,** Santa Ponsa, 07184 Calvia (971 690211; Fax: 971 693364). *Location:* 18km on motorway from Palma to Andraitx, turn off roundabout Santa Ponsa. Gently sloping fairways with water hazards. 18 holes, 6543 metres. S.S.S. 72 men, 72 ladies. Practice range, two putting greens. *Green Fees:* 70 euros 18 holes. *Eating facilities:* restaurant and bar in clubhouse, also small bar on golf course. *Visitors:* welcome; maximum Handicaps - 28 men, 36 ladies. Guests at the hotel receive 50% reduction on green fees. Accommodation available, swimming pool, paddling pool, tennis. Hotel Golf Santa Ponsa at the golf course. Five star Hotel Vista Port Adriano near golf course. *Society Meetings:* welcome. Professionals: Diego Lopez/Mark Schmidt. Director: Jose M. Gomez. Secretary: Ana-Vanessa Doulina.

SANTA PONSA. **Santa Ponsa Golf Club Two,** Santa Ponza, Calvia (971 690211; Fax: 971 663364). *Location:* as Santa Ponza One. A very interesting and enjoyable course, it has a mixture of holes, some with very tight fairways and others with many water hazards. Designed by Jose Gancedo. 18 holes, 6053 metres. S.S.S. 73, Par 72. Practice range, putting green. *Green Fees:* on request. *Eating facilities:* as Santa Ponza One. *Visitors:* at moment only open for shareholders. *

SON SERVERA. **Son Servera Golf Club,** Costa de los Pinos, 07550 Son Servera (71 84.00.96; Fax: 71 84.01.60). *Location:* Palma - Manacor - Sant Lloreng - Son Servera. Fairly flat, narrow, seaside course, set among pine trees. 9 holes, 2978 metres. S.S.S. 72. *Green Fees:* information not available. *Eating facilities:* bar and restaurant. *Visitors:* welcome. Handicap Certificate required. Nearby hotels include Eurotel Golf Punta Roja, Flamenco, Royal Mediterranea, Gran Sol. Professional: Jaime Artiach. Secretary: Jose Colom.*

8th hole at Club de Golf Alcanada

Golf in USA
Where to Play, Where to Stay
Michael Gedye

There is much to be said for visiting the USA for golf, despite being a longer flight away. The game has its origins in Scotland back in the distant past but, since it was introduced to our transatlantic cousins, they have embraced the sport with enthusiasm. In true American fashion, in keeping with the scale of their domestic market, they have emerged as leaders in all aspects of the game. They have more players and courses than the rest of the golfing world put together. They have the largest and wealthiest professional golf tours, arguably the best players (despite Europe's recent Ryder Cup successes!) and lead the world in the manufacture of the highest quality golf equipment.

Such strength allows the average American holiday golfer to experience the full variety of topography and climate, summer or winter, without ever setting foot overseas. It has spawned a vast and highly efficient vacation golf resort industry, where the market knows what it wants and, since competition on price and facilities is fierce, is able to demand it.

Visitors from Europe can only benefit, not least because you can travel with confidence in what to expect, knowing the courses and related facilities will be of excellent quality and good value, supported by the reassurance that everyone speaks English. Golfing resorts in the USA are just that, purpose-built for the visiting holiday market. You are unlikely to need your handicap certificate; just the ability to pay and enjoy your stay.

From the broad selection of vacation areas, we have chosen three. On the eastern coast, with some of the best throughout the sunshine state of Florida, there are more than a thousand courses waiting to be played. Further up the coast are the two Carolinas, each offering a quite different ambience but equally excellent golf. Finally, west to California and fabled Palm Springs, where everything is ranked in superlatives in a truly unique desert location.

Vacation resort golf is a way of life in FLORIDA. We have chosen the elegance of Palm Beach north of Miami, central Orlando (also home to Disney World) and, by way of contrast, the western coast of the state along the Gulf of Mexico. You can test yourself at PGA National or Innisbrook or relax amongst the extensive facilities at Saddlebrook or Naples Beach.

NORTH CAROLINA forms part of American golfing history. The championship location of Pinehurst, which held the US Open last year, has been an established golfing resort for decades. It is noted for its elegant southern hospitality and the quality of its eight courses laid out under towering pines. While there, visit the PGA Hall of Fame and Golf Museum, which is close by.

SOUTH CAROLINA offers more golf than you can ever play, in two quite distinct locations. Cosmopolitan Myrtle Beach, with its lively beachfront strip of motels, fast food outlets, bargain shopping (including a number of vast golf equipment emporia) and vibrant nightlife, conceals genuine treasure inland. Here more than 110 golf courses wait for your custom, many of truly excellent quality, designed by some of the world's leading golf architects. This is the greatest concentration of pure holiday golf in the world, laid out in one long coastal strip and not to be missed. An added benefit is that all are interlinked by a computer booking system, so that your hotel can find you a tee-off time with ease. Just one aspect of the smooth, efficent, somewhat standardised American way of golf. By way of a complete change, Hilton Head Island, just a bit further down the same coast, is a peaceful world apart. Here holiday homes and low-rise hotels offer an atmosphere of relaxed upmarket isolation sprinkled with some excellent golf, often edging its Atlantic shores. Best known is Harbour Town with its red and white lighthouse by the final hole, annual venue of the USPGA Tour Heritage Classic.

A snapshot of California could well show movie stars, millionaires, endless sunshine and understated excess. This could also apply equally to PALM SPRINGS, a man-made resort location just an hour and a half east of Los Angeles. On a 25-mile strip of impossibly green acreage in the middle of the endless sand of the Mojave desert, is a totally artificial world that is pure Hollywood. Started as a weekend retreat for the rich and famous from the movie industry around the time talking pictures evolved, it has evolved into a community for the super-rich, with over 90 excellent golf courses, each created by the best in the game. Lush fairways, tall palms and many water hazards, all irrigated by a limitless underground water supply. There are 160 hotels, 600 tennis courts and only 10,000 swimming pools! Encircled by ranges of pastel-shaded mountains, with constant warm sunshine and virtually no humidity, this is the ultimate luxury golf experience – American-style.

FLORIDA

AVENTURA. **Turnberry Isle Resort & Club,** 19999 West Country Club Drive, Aventura, FL. 33180 (305) 932 6200; Fax: (305) 933 6922. North Miami Beach. This luxurious private resort and country club is the perfect spot for sports enthusiasts. Two Robert Trent Jones, Sr. championship courses keep resort guests and members in the swing. North 6323 yards, Par 70; South 7003 yards, Par 72. Full facilities.*

BOCA RATON. **Boca Raton Resort & Club,** 501 East Camino Real, Boca Raton, Florida 33431 (561-447 3000; Fax: 561-447 5294). *Location:* 22 miles from Palm Beach. Historic golf resort which combines links with the past and contemporary luxury. 36 holes: Country Club Course 6714 yards Par 72. Resort Course 6253 yards, Par 71. Full facilities. *Eating facilities:* beverage carts, snack bars and restaurants. *Green Fees:* information not available. *Visitors:* closed to public, must be a member, guest of a member or staying at the resort. Director of Golf: Bob Coman. *

BONITA SPRINGS. **Pelican's Nest Golf Club at Pelican Landing,** 4450 Pelican's Nest Drive, Bonita Springs FL (239) (947 4600). *Location:* just inside Pelican Landing, a wonderful complement to local amenities. Two, member-owned, Tom Fazio designed, private golf courses. Gator: 18 holes, 7066 yards, Par 73, Rating 74.7. slope 137. Hurricane: 18 holes, 6894 yards, Par 72, Rating 74, slope 137. *Green Fees:* information not available. *Eating facilities:* new clubhouse. *
website: www.nestgolf.com

LAKE COUNTY. **Mission Inn Golf and Tennis Resort.** *Location:* on the country side of Orlando, less than one hour from central Florida's famous attractions. Mission Inn boasts 36 holes of championship golf on two renowned courses. El Campeon: 18 holes, 6852 yards, Par 72. Las Colinas: 18 holes, 6879 yards. *Green Fees:* information not available. *Visitors:* Stay & Play golf packages available inclusive of green fees, accommodation, meals, and for green fees and accommodation only. Many other resort facilities are available for guests travelling with golf enthusiasts - tennis, hydro spa, heated outdoor pool, fitness room, bicycle trails, marina, shopping, etc. Reservations made by calling Destination Golf: 0181-891 5151. *

NAPLES. **Lely Resort,** 8202 Lely Resort Boulevard, Naples, Fl. 34113 (941) 793 2200; Fax: (941) 793 3963. 40 miles from Fort Myers. Great golf in substantial homesite development. Golf design by Jones, Player and Trevino. 54 holes Flamingo Course 7171 yards Par 72. Full facilities. *

www.uk-golfguide.com

NAPLES. **Naples Beach Hotel & Golf Club,** 851 Gulf Shore Boulevard North, Naples, Florida 37102 (941 2612222; Fax: 941 2617380). *Location:* 30 miles from S.W. Florida International Airport in Fort Myers. Beachside hotel and golf resort with much tradition. Very popular with British players. 18 holes 6642 yards Par 72. Full facilities. Golf school, driving range and full service spa. Professional: Larry Guntzer. *

ORLANDO. **Grenelefe Golf & Tennis Resort,** 3200 SR 546, Haines City, Fl. 33844 (941) 422 7511. 25 miles south-west of Disney World. A comprehensive golf and tennis resort in a rolling, wooded setting. Popular also for conventions. 54 holes: East 6802 yards, Par 72; South 6869 yards, Par 71; West 7325 yards, Par 72. Full facilities. *

ORLANDO. **The Villas of Grand Cypress One,** North Jacaranda, Orlando, FL 32836 (800/835 7377; Fax: 407/239 7219). *Location:* take I4 to Exit 68 right to SR 535 North. Superb resort complex. Four Courses: New Course 18 holes, 6773 yards Blue, 6181 yards White; North Course 9 holes, Gold 3521, Blue 3143, White 2912, Par 36; South Course 9 holes, Gold 3472 yards, Blue 3212 yards, White 2911 yards, Par 36; East Course 9 holes, Gold 3434 yards, Blue 3151 yards, White 2878 yards, Par 36. Driving Range. *Green Fees:* information not available. *Eating facilities:* The Club restaurant and Sports Bar, Black Swan Restaurant. *Visitors:* only if guests of Villas of Grand Cypress or Hyatt Regency Grand Cypress. Locker room. Academy of Golf, Equestrian Centre and racquet club. Director of Golf: Bill Rowden (407 239 1956; Fax: 407 239 1969). Secretary: Lisa Monohan (407 239 1913; Fax: 407 239 1969). *

PALM BEACH. **PGA National Golf Club,** 400 Avenue of the Champions, Palm Beach Gardens Fl 33418 (561 627 1800). 15 miles from West Palm Beach. Golf for all levels, including beginners, at a superb resort which hosted the 1983 Ryder Cup. 90 holes: Champion Course 7022 yards Par 72. Full facilities including teaching academy. *

TAMPA. **Saddlebrook Resort,** 5700 Saddlebrook Way, Wesley Chapel Tampa, Fl. 33543-4499 (813 973 1111; Fax: 813 973 4504). *Location:* 33 miles north of Tampa International Airport, take I-75 to SR54, then east one mile. 480 acres of natural countryside surrounded by tall cypress, pines, palm trees, blue lakes and rolling hills. Two courses (both designed by Arnold Palmer): Saddlebrook Course - 18 holes, 6564 yards, Par 70. Palmer Course - 18 holes, 6469 yards. S.S.S. 71. Practice green, practice range. *Green Fees:* seasonal, please enquire. *Eating facilities:* four restaurants, lounge, pool bar and sports bar. *Visitors:* welcome, open all year. Pro shop; Arnold Palmer Golf Academy; cart and club rental. *Society Meetings:* welcome. Professional: Jerry Couzynse. *

TARPON SPRINGS. **Innisbrook Hilton Resort,** 36750 US 19 N, Palm Harbor, Fl. 34684 (813 942 2000/800 456 2000). *Location:* 20 miles from Tampa International Airport. Florida's finest golf resort. The Copperhead course ranks in Florida's top five. 72 holes: Copperhead 7087 yards Par 71; Island 6999

yards Par 72. Three practice ranges. *Green Fees:* seasonal, please enquire. *Eating facilities:* seven restaurants. *Visitors:* welcome. 13 tennis courts, six pools, golf school, children's programme, fitness centre, airport shuttle. *

NORTH CAROLINA

VILLAGE OF PINEHURST. **Pinehurst Resort & Country Club,** PO Box 4000, Carolina Vista, Village of Pinehurst, North Carolina 28374 (800 487-4653). *Location:* 70 miles from Raleigh. Truly historic with great golf, an old world atmosphere and service to match. 8 courses, 24 tennis courts, croquet lawn, bowls and fitness centre. *Green Fees:* seasonal. *Eating facilities:* Carolina Dining Room, Donald Ross Grill, Mulligan's Sports Bar and Grill. *Visitors:* Pinehurst is a stay and play facility. Visitors must be a guest of the resort to play on the courses. Four practice ranges and four clubhouses. *

SOUTH CAROLINA

HILTON HEAD. **Harbour Town Golf Links,** Sea Pines Plantation, Hilton Head Island, South Carolina (803) 842 1892. Home of the Heritage Classic and a true thoroughbred regularly ranked in US top 25. 18 holes 6912 yards Par 71. Full facilities. *

HILTON HEAD. **Port Royal Golf Club,** Hilton Head Island, South Carolina (803 686 8801). Three fine courses winding past magnolia and oak to a hospitable plantation-style clubhouse. 54 holes Robber's Row 6711 yards Par 72; Planter's Row 6520 yards Par 72; Barony 6530 yards Par 72. Full facilities.*

HILTON HEAD. **Shipyard Golf Club,** Hilton Head Island, South Carolina (803 785 2402. Plenty of water hazards on these well-established tree-lined holes near the sea. 27 holes: Galleon 3364 yards; Brigantine 3352 yards; Clipper 3466 yards, all Par 36. Full facilities. *

HILTON HEAD ISLAND. **Palmetto Dunes Resort,** Hilton Head Island, South Carolina (803 785 1161). Rolling dunes and fairways make a contrast at this popular golf and vacation resort. 54 holes: Arthur Hills Course 6651 yards, Par 72; George Fazio Course 6873 yards, Par 70; Robert Trent Jones Course 6710 yards, Par 72. Full facilities. *

THE APPEARANCE OF AN ASTERISK (*) AT THE END OF A CLUB OR COURSE ENTRY INDICATES THAT UP-TO-DATE INFORMATION HAS NOT BEEN SUPPLIED

MYRTLE BEACH. **Litchfield Country Club**, PO Box 379, Pawleys Island, South Carolina 29585 (843 237 3411). *Location:* 20 miles south of Myrtle Beach. Fine plantation-style golf winding past giant oaks, cypress, marshland and strategic lakes. 18 holes 6752 yards Par 70.6/119. Driving range. *Green Fees:* information not available. *Eating facilities:* full clubhouse with grill and bar. *Visitors:* always welcome. Accommodation available; carts for hire. Professional: Bob Vanderbloemen (843 237 3411). *

MYRTLE BEACH. **Pine Lakes International Country Club,** Woodside Drive, Central Myrtle Beach, South Carolina (803 449 6459). Old fashioned service and style colour every aspect of this mature Scottish-designed golf setting. 18 holes 6709 yards Par 71. Full facilities. *

MYRTLE BEACH. **Tidewater Golf Club,** 901 Little River Neck Road, North Myrtle Beach, South Carolina 29582 (800 446 5363). *Location:* from Highway 17, take Cherry Grove Exit. Stop at end of exit ramp, turn left, turn right on to Little River Neck Road (at Harbour Gate). Two miles to Tidewater. Situated on a seaside peninsula, course designed by Ken Tomlinson. 18 holes, 7150 yards Championship, 6530 yards Blue, 6000 yards Men, 5090 yards Ladies, 4665 yards Juniors. *Green Fees:* call golf course for rates. *Eating facilities:* full facilities. *Visitors:* welcome, public course. Professional: Paul Kline. *

MYRTLE BEACH. **Wild Wing Plantation,** PO Box 51090, Myrtle Beach, South Carolina 29579 (800 736 9464; Fax: 843 347 5732). *Location:* on US Highway 501, six miles west of the Intracoastal waterway. Parkland setting. Wood Stork Course - 18 holes, 7044 yards; Hummingbird Course - 18 holes, 6853 yards; Avocet Course - 18 holes, 7127 yards; Falcon Course - 18 holes. Extensive practice facility. *Green Fees:* fees vary. *Eating facilities:* Wishbones Restaurant, Players' Pub. *Visitors:* always welcome. Wild Wing School of Golf, Golf Villas/Homes (888 398 9464). Director of Golf: Timothy P. Tilma. *

MYRTLE BEACH. **The Witch Golf Club,** Highway 544 between Conway and Myrtle Beach, South Carolina (803 448 1300). 5 miles from Myrtle Beach. A natural spellbinding course winding through dense forest and mangrove swamp. 18 holes 6702 yards Par 71. Full facilities.

PALM SPRINGS

INDIAN WELLS. **Indian Wells Golf Resort,** 44-500 Indian Wells Lane, Indian Wells (00 1 760 346 4653). 36 holes of rolling holiday golf by Ted Robinson, well-watered, manicured, a handicapper's delight. 36 holes: East 6662 yards, West 6478 yards, both Par 72. Driving range, putting green. *Green Fees:* information not available. *Eating facilities:* bar/snacks in clubhouse. Pro shop; cart and club rental. Head Professional: Joe Williams.

LA QUINTA. **La Quinta Resort & Club (Dunes),** 50-200 Avenue Vista Bonita, La Quinta, Palm Springs (00 1 619 564 7686). A fine resort course by Pete Dye with plenty of hazards. 18 holes, 6251 yards. Par 72. Driving range, putting green. *Green Fees:* information not available. *Eating facilities:* bar and restaurants in low-rise Spanish-style hotel. Pro shop; cart and club hire. Head Professional: Todd Williams.*

LA QUINTA. **La Quinta Resort & Club (Mountain),** 50-200 Avenida Vista Bonita, La Quinta, CA 92253, Palm Springs (00 1 619 564 7686; Fax: 00 1 760 564 2757). Carved into the base of the Santa Rose hills, these Pete Dye courses have been ranked in USA Top 100. 18 holes, 6303 yards. Par 72. Driving range, putting green. *Green Fees:* information not available. *Eating facilities:* bar and restaurants in low-rise Spanish-style hotel. Pro shop; car and club hire. Professional: Randy J. Duncan. *

Palm Springs, California

LA QUINTA. **PGA West Resort Course (Nicklaus),** 55-900 PGA Boulevard, La Quinta, Palm Springs (00 1 619 564 7170). One of Jack Nicklaus's best with rolling mounds, much sand and water. Accuracy is all. 18 holes, 6671 yards. Par 72. Driving range, putting green. *Green Fees:* information not available. Pro shop; cart and club hire. Head Professional: Billy Neal. *

LA QUINTA. **PGA West Resort Course (TPC Stadium),** 55-900 PGA Boulevard, La Quinta, Palm Springs (00 1 619 564 7170). Highly strategic with vast mounds and steep escarpments; a Pete Dye course almost unplayable by mere mortals. 18 holes, 6836 yards. Par 72. Driving range, putting green. *Green Fees:* information not available. *Eating facilities:* bar and restaurant in clubhouse. Pro shop; cart and club hire. Head Professional: Billy Neal. *

NORTH PALM SPRINGS. **Desert Dunes,** 19-300 Palm Drive, Palm Springs (00 1 619 251 5366). *Location:* north west of downtown, approaching the foothills. A course by Robert Trent Jones Jr. full of natural, savage beauty; a contrast to the norm, home from home for real golfers. 18 holes, 6614 yards. Par 72. Driving range, putting green. *Green Fees:* information not available. *Eating facilities:* bar and restaurant. Pro shop, cart and club hire. Head Professional: Tom Connelly. *

PALM DESERT. **Desert Falls Country Club,** 1111 Desert Falls Parkway, Palm Desert, CA (00 1 760 304 5646) Top ten rated course in greater Palm Springs area. Links style course with rolling terrain accented by palms, water and sand hazards. A Ron Fream designed course with panoramic views of the mountains on every hole. 18 holes, 7005 yards. Par 74, 6529 yards Par 72, 5250 yards (Ladies) Par 72. Large practice facility. *Green Fees:* information not available. *Eating facilities:* Restaurant, snackbar and lounge. Full service. Pro shop, club rental (Titleist) available. Head Professional: Terry Ferraro. *

PALM DESERT. **Marriott's Desert Springs Resort and Spa,** 74855 Country Club Drive, Palm Desert, Palm Springs (760 341 1756; Fax: 760 341 1828). Two excellent resort courses rich in tall palms and strategic yet ornamental water features and falls, with island greens by Ted Robinson, backed by vast 884 room hotel. 36 holes: Palms 6381 yards, Valley 6326 yards, both Par 72. Driving range, 18 hole putting course, John Jacobs teaching. *Green Fees:* information not available. *Eating facilities:* 5 restaurants and many bars. Pro shop; cart and club hire. Head Professional: Tim Skogen (760 341 1757). Assistant: Irma Garcia (760 341 6757). *

RANCHO MIRAGE. **Rancho Las Palmas Country Club,** 42-000 Bob Hope Drive, Rancho Mirage, Palm Springs (00 1 619 862 4551). A 27 hole resort complex with hotel on site. Gently rolling land with many established trees. Short and tight, now 20 years old. West/South Course 18 holes, 6128 yards. Par 70. Driving range, putting green. *Green Fees:* information not available. *Eating facilities:* bar and snacks in golf clubhouse. Hotel close by. Pro shop; cart and club hire, daily golf clinics, extensive instruction programme. Head Professional: Troy Sprister. *

RANCHO MIRAGE. **Westin Mission Hills Resort Golf Club,** 71-501 Dinah Shore Drive, Rancho Mirage, Palm Springs (760 328 3198; Fax: 760 770 4984). *Location*: five miles east of Palm Springs. Pete Dye and Gary Player have built two excellent courses here, undulating past colourful shrubs and water with a mountain backdrop. Pete Dye Resort Course, 18 holes, 6706 yards S.S.S.70. Gary Player Signature Course 18 holes, 7062 yards S.S.S.70. Magnificent 15 acre driving range, putting green. *Green Fees:* information not available. *Eating facilities:* bar and restaurants in palatial Moroccan-style clubhouse. Pro-shop, cart and club hire. Professional: Alan Deck.*

PLEASE NOTE

All the information regarding Golf Clubs in this guide is given in good faith in the belief that it is correct. However, the publishers cannot guarantee the facts given in these pages, neither are they responsible for changes in ownership or facilities, such as green fees, that may take place after the date of going to press. Readers should always satisfy themselves that the facilities they require are available and that the terms, if quoted, still apply.

www.uk-golfguide.com

Golf in South Africa
Paul Dimmock

The international golf enthusiast will find South Africa is a unique experience. Nowhere else in the world can offer the discerning and adventurous golfer such an array of challenging golf courses. The courses are surrounded by gloriously stunning panoramas which include the splendour of Table Mountain, sweeping views of the Indian Ocean, the mystique of the African bushveld and areas of beautiful lush tropical vegetation inhabited by an amazing display of wildlife. South Africa is a vibrant and emerging world golf destination, with over 400 courses. Many of the courses are championship standard and on a par with major European and North American courses. To complete the South African experience there is a full range of accommodation from luxurious 5 star hotels offering the best of international comfort and cuisine, to the game park lodge with its cultural delights. Thanks to an advantageous exchange rate the visitor from the UK will find South Africa incredible value for money.

FISH HOEK. **Clovelly Golf Club,** P.O. Box 22119, Fish Hoek 7974 (+27 21 782 1118; Fax: +27 21 782 6853). *Location*: 30 minutes drive south of Cape Town to Clovelly in the Clovelly Valley. Excellent fairways, bent grass greens - some sloping. Offers stern challenges on almost every hole. Surrounded by mountains and sand dunes. 18 holes. Men's - Par 72. 5869 metres. Ladies' - Par 73, 5156 metres. *Green Fees*: visitors R400. *Eating facilities*: clubhouse, light snacks, restaurant. *Visitors*: welcome, book in advance. Handicap not required. Luxury accommodation: Ocean View Estate - contact John or Hazel Goatley (+27 21 789 1053). Pro shop. Tennis and bowls. Club Professional: Dave Odendaal. Club Manager: Jeremy Lindquist.
e-mail: clubhouse@clovelly.co.za
website: www.clovelly.co.za

GEORGE. **Fancourt Golf and Country Club Estate,** P.O. Box 2266, Montagu Street, Blanco, George 6530 (+27 (0) 44 804 0000; Fax:+27 (0) 44 804070). *Location*: 440km south east of Cape Town on the N2 Garden Route in Blanco on the western boundary of the pretty village of George. Four 18 hole Gary Player designed championship courses including The Links - Home of the Presidents Cup 2003. Warm up area, putting and chipping green, driving range, 4-hole academy course. Member of "Great Golf Resorts of the World Association" and "Preferred Hotels & Resorts Worldwide". *Green Fees*: information not available. E*ating facilities*: clubhouse, light snacks, dining room and four restaurants. *Visitors*: exclusive private club, visiting players must be Fancourt Hotel Guests, advance booking essential. Tennis, swimming, spa. *
e-mail: golf@fancourt.co.za

MOWBRAY. **Mowbray Golf Club,** Raapenberg Road, Mowbray, P.O. Box 38003, Howard Place 7450 (+27 21 685 3018; Fax: +27 21 686 6008). *Location*: south of Cape Town, approximately 10 km or 10 minutes from airport. Parkland course. No steep hills but plenty of trees, bent grass greens, numerous water hazards. The cross-wind on 14 holes is a real test. Beautiful views of Table Mountain, Devils Peak. Host to South Africa Open on a number of occasions. 18 holes, Par 72. Men's 6054/5760 metres, Ladies' 5049 metres. *Green Fees*: R350. *Eating facilities*: clubhouse, halfway house, restaurant. *Visitors*: advance booking necessary, maximum Handicap men 24, ladies 30. Pro Shop. Professional: Greg McDonald. Manager: Dave Duncan. Secretary: Mrs Ingrid Tait.
e-mail: info@mowbraygolfclub.co.za

SOMERSET WEST. **Erinvale Country Estate and Golf Course,** Lourensford Road, Somerset West 7129 (+27 24 847 1144; Fax: +27 24 847 1901). *Location*: 40 minutes due south from central Cape Town in the heart of the winelands. Parkland, wide kikuyu fairways and bent/poa annua greens. Front nine mainly flat with elongated greens protected by water hazards, back nine on rolling high ground with spectacular views of mountains, vineyards and False Bay. Hosted 1996 World Cup of Golf and 2003, 2004 SAA Open (European Tour). Gary Player designed course. 18 holes, Par 72. Mens 5892 metres, ladies 5126 metres. *Green Fees*: 2005 R495.00, Cart R210.00, trolley R50.00, hire clubs R300.00, No caddies. *Eating facilities*: restaurant, Halfway House. *Visitors*: welcome, booking essential. certain days restricted. Maximum Handicap: men 24, ladies 36, and certificate required. Professional: Johan Piek.
e-mail: pro-shop@erinvale.com

SUN CITY. **Gary Player Country Club,** Sun City, Pilansberg, North Western Province (+27 14 557 1000; Fax: +27 14 657 3426). *Location:* 150km north west of Johannesburg. 18 holes, Par 72, rating 76. 6938 meters. The most demanding course in South Africa. Mainly flat but unique hole designs, water hazards and deceptive greens. Kikuyu fairways and bent grass greens. A variety of tees can shorten the course. Venue for Million Dollar Challenge. *Green Fees*: information not available. *Eating facilities*: clubhouse, light snacks, restaurant. *Visitors*: welcome, book in advance. Part of Sun City complex, bowls and casino.*
website: www.milliondollar.co.za/course.asp

WOODBRIDGE ISLAND. **Milnerton Golf Club,** Bridge Road, Woodbridge Island, Milnerton 7441 (+27 21 552 1047; Fax: +27 21 551 5897). *Location*: ten miles due north (Otto du Plessis Drive) from Cape Town. Only true Links course in Western Cape. Nestled between Atlantic Ocean and a lagoon, spectacular views of Table Mountain. Wind direction plays a major role, first nine downwind, second nine almost directly into the wind. 18 holes, Par 72. Men's 5721 metres, Ladies' 5022 metres. *Green Fees*: information not available. *Visitors*: welcome, book in advance. *Eating facilities*: halfway house, Maestro's Restaurant. Pro Shop. Professional: Stuart Howard. Manager: Gideon Hitchcock.*
e-mail: milgolf@intekom.co.za

WYNBERG. **Royal Cape Golf Club,** 174 Ottery Road, Wynberg 7800 (+27 21 761 6551; Fax: +27 21 797 5246). *Location*: southern suburbs of Cape Town. 15 minute drive from city centre and 15 minutes from international airport. Flat parkland course. Narrow tree-lined kikuyu fairways. Dominant Bent greens, water on six holes, 58 bunkers. Wind plays a major part on some holes. Host to the South Africa Open 11 times. The oldest golf club in South Africa. Spectacular views. 18 holes, Par 72. Men's 6121 metres, Ladies' 5288 metres. *Green Fees*: information not available. *Eating facilities*: clubhouse, light snacks and restaurant. *Visitors*: welcome, advance booking necessary. Pro Shop. Professionals: Craig Ross and Barbara Pestana.*
e-mail: manager@royalcapegolf.co.za
bookings@royalcapegolf.co.za
website: www.royalcapegolf.co.za

Golf in Dubai

Dubai is a thriving commercial centre with magnificent hotel and leisure amenities which now include unique opportunities for serious business and holiday golf. The Emirates Club, The Dubai Golf and Racing Club and the Dubai Creek Golf and Yachting Club all have unrivalled facilities for visiting golf, including the Dubai Golf Pass. Details from The Secretary, PO Box 6302, Dubai, United Arab Emirates.

DUBAI. **Dubai Creek Golf and Yacht Club,** PO Box 6302, Dubai (00971 4 2956000; Fax: 00971 4 2956044). *Location:* beside the Al Garhoud Bridge, close to the city centre and airport. Long, Venue of the Dubai desert classic in 1999 and 2000. Re-designed in 2004 by European Golf Design in association with Thomas Bjorn. Stunning golf course featuring `Creek-side' holes, man-made lakes and large sandy wastes. 6857 yards, S.S.S 72. Floodlit Par 3 course, driving range and practice facilities. *Green Fees:* information not available. *Eating facilities:* Lakeview, Legends Steakhouse, The Aquarium, QD's and the Boardwalk. *Visitors*: welcome. Golf carts (with GPS) compulsory. Hyatt Hotel, Swimming pool, gym, yacht club, proshops and marina. Director of Golf: Alan MacKenzie. Administration Manager: Shona McRae.
e-mail: dcgyc@dubaigolf.com
website: www.dubaigolf.com

DUBAI. **Emirates Golf Club,** PO Box 24040, Dubai (971-4-3473222; Fax: 971-4-3472888). *Location*: on the Dabai - Abu Dhabi Highway junction 5. Two Championship standard 18-hole, Par 72 courses. Home of the Dubai Desert Classic. Majlis Course: 7101 yards with palm-edged fairways, lakes and immaculate greens. Wadi course: 7000 yards with water hazards and bunkers. Two driving ranges (one floodlit), 3 hole Academy course, pitching/putting greens. Academy of Golf with three PGA qualified professionals. *Green Fees:* information not available. *Eating facilities:* Five star Le Classique restaurant, Spike Bar and The Terrace. *Visitors:* welcome. Tennis, squash, swimming and gym available. Golf Operations Manager: Adrian Flaherty. *
e-mail: booking@dubaigolf.com

DUBAI. **Nad Al Sheba Club,** PO Box 52872, Nad Al Sheba, Dubai (971-4-3363666; Fax: 971-4-3363717). *Location:* Nad Al Sheba Racecourse, a few kilometres from the city centre. A links-type course with undulating fairways, heavily bunkered and water comes into play on 14 holes. 18 holes, 6428 yards S.S.S. 71. Fully floodlit. Golf clinics, floodlit driving range, practice area, chipping and putting. *Green Fees:* on application. *Eating facilities:* well equipped clubhouse with licensed steak house and spike bar. *Visitors:* welcome; overseas pass available, open daily. Lessons available. Golfing attire and Handicap Certificates required. General Manager: Jerry Kilby. See website for full details.*
website: www.nadalshebaclub.com

Golf in Thailand
Where to Play, Where to Stay
Michael Gedye

When people think of Asia, and Thailand in particular, their thoughts favour the exotic, historic, colourful images of a fabled destination in the far Far East. But these days, with faster flights at ever-cheaper rates, visiting the former Kingdom of Siam takes no longer than a trip to South Africa or California. What may surprise many is that Thailand has a flourishing and rapidly expanding golf market, with over 200 courses, mostly of recent origin and true international class, and more than 300,000 domestic players. The majority of these courses, apart from those surrounding the vibrant capital city of Bangkok, have been laid out in the prime holiday areas of coastal Chonburi and Hua Hin/Cha-Am, western Kanchanaburi, northern Chiang Mai and the idyllic southern islands of Phuket and Koh Samui. Thailand is a large country, extending from the cooler, mountainous north, through the central rice-growing plains around Bangkok, to the warmer south where the Kingdom borders Malaysia. It has twice the land area of Great Britain and a similar number of people.

Already established as an important long-haul destination for Europeans in the prime winter season, the country boasts a magnificent holiday infrastructure in the aforementioned golfing areas – five-star hotels, often right by the beach, superb service, excellent transportation, and all the exotic dining one would expect in a colourful, tropical location. Thailand is famous for its myriad Bhuddist temples, the saffron-robed monks, delicate shimmering silks, local gemstones and jewellery, and a wealth of delicate handicrafts and tailored clothing. Prices are low by Western standards and this applies equally to the golf, where world-class, uncrowded courses (except Bangkok at weekends) can be played for bargain rates, with the added bonus of a charming young lady caddie to help you enjoy your round to the full. However, nobody should travel to Thailand without taking the rich opportunities for quality sightseeing and shopping to interleave with your holiday rounds.

The courses listed in this section have been divided into six regions, three within a relatively short driving distance of Bangkok, where your international flight will arrive. Two more are southern island destinations, one nudging the Andaman Sea, the other in the Gulf of Thailand. The last group are the two most northern cities, Chiang Mai and Chiang Rai. All are served by regular, short internal flights.

The more southerly of the island destinations is PHUKET, offering both popular and up-scale holidays and a choice of excellent golf, including the newly-opened Mission Hills Phuket Golf Resort & Spa with 27 holes. Best known is the 36-hole complex of Blue Canyon, carved around a former tin mine. Despite the ravages of the tsunami in 2004, none of the golf destinations, many well inland, have been affected.

Another island destination, KOH SAMUI, can now offer some of the most spectacular golf anywhere. Laid out at nearly 1,000 feet over mountain slopes with fantastic sea views, the new Santiburi Samui golf course has rich green ribbons of fairway winding and plunging past tall palms. Luxury golf as close to heaven as one may ever be.

The CENTRAL region covers the city of Bangkok and the area just to the west. A 'must stop' is the Rose Garden for delightful floral golf and a unique cultural show. There is golf further northwest near the infamous bridge over the River Kwai at Kanchanaburi and a choice of courses down the coast near Cha-Am and Hua Hin. This is a quiet area, with good hotels, pristine beaches, fresh seafood restaurants perched over the sea, and a gently relaxed ambience backed by wooded hills.

The NORTH-EASTERN region is a two hour drive from Bangkok, offering dramatic wooded mountains, sensational views and wildlife in the Khao Yai National Park and a fair choice of golf.`

Now easily reached via the super highway from Bangkok, the EASTERN region covers the south-east coastline of the Gulf of Siam. Linking the cities of Chonburi, Pattaya and Rayong, it offers the greatest selection of modern resort golf in Thailand. The rolling slopes contain fine golf courses by the best international design names, sprinkled with tall palms, vivid tropical flowers and much strategic water. Toughest tests are undoubtedly the 27 Jack Nicklaus-designed holes of Laem Chabang and the recently renamed Mountain Shadow, by Ronald Fream. There are around twenty others to play plus a wealth of international restaurants and legendary nightlife.

Tucked away in the mountainous NORTH, attractively cooler during the winter season, are the ancient cities of Chiang Mai and Chiang Rai. Plenty to see and do here, with colourful hilltribes, delicate handicrafts, elephants and also excellent golf, including Royal Chiangmai, by Peter Thomson, and Chiangmai Lamphun. The northern jewel, however, is up the road in Chiang Rai. Here Robert Trent Jones Jr's Santiburi Country Club course is right out of the top drawer – elegant, serene and manicured to perfection.

PHUKET

LAGUNA PHUKET. **Laguna Phuket Golf Club,** 34 Moo 4, Tambon Cherngtalay, Amphur Talang, Phuket 83110 (66 76-324 350; Fax: 66 76-324 351). *Location*: part of the Laguna resort complex, 20 minutes south west from Phuket airport. Pleasant, not too demanding modern resort course by Max Wexler and David Abell. Palm trees and water hazards open to the sea breeze. 18 holes, 6768 yards. Par 71. Pro shop, teaching professionals, driving range, chipping areas, putting greens. *Green Fees*: information not available. *Eating facilities*: restaurant and bar in clubhouse. *Visitors*: welcome. Club, shoe, umbrella, chair hire. *
e-mail: golf-phuket@banyantree.com

PHANG-NGA. **Thai Muang Beach Golf & Marina,** 157/12 Moo 9, Limdul Road, Tambon Thai Muang, Amphur Thai Muang, Phang-Nga 82120 (66 76 571 533/5; Fax: 66 76 571 214). *Location*: off Highway 4, 40 km (30 minutes drive) north of Phuket Airport over road bridge into Phang-Nga. Created by Dye Designs, this is the only true seaside course along the Andaman Sea. Demanding layout in a relaxed, remote setting. 18 holes, 7019 yards. Par 72. Pro shop, driving range, putting green. *Green Fees*: information not available. *Eating facilities*: restaurant and bar in clubhouse. Beach chalet accommodation available. Reservations and Information: (66 76 571 533/4; Fax: 66 76 571 214). Refreshment kiosks on course. *Visitors*: welcome. Carts, club, shoe, umbrella and chair hire. *
website: www.thaimuanggolf.com

PHUKET. **Blue Canyon Country Club,** 165 Moo 1, Thepkasattri Road, Maikaw, Thalang, Phuket 83110 (076 327440-7; Fax: 076 327449). *Location:* just 5 minutes drive south of Phuket International Airport. One of the premier golf resorts in Asia. Two dramatic 18-hole courses built around a former tin mine with some spectacular carries and kept in excellent condition. Twice venue of Johnnie Walker Classic. Clubhouse hotel overlooks course from crest of hill. Canyon Course: 18 holes, 7179 yards, Par 72. Lakes Course: 18 holes, 7129 yards, Par 72. Pro shop, Blue Canyon Golf School, driving range, putting greens. *Green Fees:* available on request. Playing rights open only to residents of clubhouse hotel and guests of members. *Eating facilities:* Canyon Restaurant, Golfers' Terrace, Lobby Lounge, Members' Lounge. *Visitors*: only by invitation or as hotel guest. Caddies, club hire.*
e-mail: reservation@bluecanyonclub.com
website: www.bluecanyonclub.com

PHUKET. **Loch Palm Golf Club Phuket,** 38 Moo 5, Vichitsongkram Road, Kathu District, Phuket 83120 (076 321 930; Fax: 076 321 927/8). *Location:* in kathu village about 7km from Phuket town and 40 minutes drive from Phuket Airport. Laid out around a large lake on the site of a former tin mine, this is a pleasant course with palm trees and encircled by wooded hills. 18 holes, 6434 yards, Par 72. Pro shop, driving range, chipping and putting green. *Green Fees:* information not available. *Eating facilities:* lakeside restaurant in temporary clubhouse. Four refreshment kiosks on course. *Visitors:* welcome. Cart, club, shoe, umbrella, chair hire. *

PHUKET. **Phuket Country Club,** 80/1 Vichitsongkram Road, Moo7, Katu District, Phuket 83120 (076 321 038; Fax: 076 321 721). *Location*: 30 minutes from Phuket Airport on main road (4020) to Patong Beach. Two very interesting and well-kept courses. (18 and 9 holes) with plenty of water hazards. Scenic, with mature flowering shrubs and palms in location of former tin mine. Surrounded by wooded hills. Old Course 18 holes, 6483 yards, Par 72. Country Club Course 9 holes, 3575 yards, S.S.S. 37. Pro shop, driving range, putting green. *Green Fees:* weekdays and weekends Baht 2,350 per round; caddie fee Baht 200 per round. *Eating facilities:* restaurant and bar terrace in clubhouse. Refreshment kiosks on course. *Visitors:* welcome. Club hire. Soft spikes only. General Manager: Mr Keat Lau.
e-mail: bookings@phuketcountryclub.com
website: www.phuketcountryclub.com

KOH SAMUI

SURATHANI. **Santiburi Samui Country Club,** 12/15 Moo 4, Tambon Maenam, Amphur Koh Samui, Surathani 84330 (66 (0) 7742 1700-8; Fax: 66 (0) 77 421 709). *Location:* on the north coast of the island near Mae Nam, a short drive from the airport. An amazing creation rising to more than 950 feet above spectacular sea views. Embraced by tall coconut palms, this is a world-class course which demands precision, kept in superb condition. 18 holes, 6,881 yards, Par 72. Driving range, golf academy, practice green, pro shop. *Green Fees:* 4,350 baht (including golf cart and caddie). *Eating facilities:* clubhouse restaurant with panoramic seaview terrace. *Visitors:* welcome. Club rental. Professional: Vuthirut Manee-in. General Manager: Surawut Wannapintu.
e-mail: proshop@santiburi.com

CENTRAL REGION

AYUTTHAYA. **Bangsai Country Club,** 77/7 Moo 3, Bangplee, Bangsai, Ayutthaya 13190 (035 371 490-7; Fax: 035 371491). *Location*: due north of Bangkok on Route 1 direction Ayutthaya. Near Bangsai follow signs to course. Superbly innovative 18 holes course offering a mixture of parkland and links-style golf in an inland setting. 18 holes, 6923 yards, Par 72. Pro shop, driving range, putting green. *Green Fees:* information not available. *Eating facilities*: clubhouse restaurant, refreshment kiosk on course. *Visitors*: welcome. Cart, club hire. *

BANGKOK. **Muang Ake Golf Club,** 52 Moo 7, Phaholyothin Road, Amphoe Muang, Pathum Thani (02 533 9335; Fax: 02 533 9345). *Location:* take Vibhavadi Rangsit Road north out of the city past Don Muang Airport. Filter left before junction with Phaholyothin Road. After 2km turn left at petrol station and then bear right at fork. Pleasant, mature course on fairly compact site with many water hazards. 18 holes, 6398 yards, Par 72. Pro shop, driving range, putting green. *Green Fees:* information not available. *Eating facilities:* restaurant and bar in clubhouse. *Visitors:* welcome. Club, shoe, umbrella hire. *

CHA-AM. **Imperial Lake View Hotel and Golf Club,** 79 Moo 4, Hubkrapong-Praburi, Highway Tambol Samphraya, Cha-Am, Petchburi 76120 (032 456233; Fax: 032 456241). *Location:* 25 minutes north up the coast road from central Hua Hin. Very imaginative and challenging 27 holes of golf by Roger Packard. Rolling mounds, large greens, lakes and palms. 18 holes, 6915 yards. Par 72 plus new 9 holes. Hotel, pro shop, putting green. *Green Fees:* information not available. *Eating facilities:* cafe and restaurant in clubhouse. Refreshment Kiosks on course. *Visitors:* welcome. Cart, club, shoe, umbrella hire. *

THE APPEARANCE OF AN ASTERISK (*) AT THE END OF A CLUB OR COURSE ENTRY INDICATES THAT UP-TO-DATE INFORMATION HAS NOT BEEN SUPPLIED

www.uk-golfguide.com

CHA AM. **Springfield Royal Country Club,** Springfield Village Golf and Spa, 193 Moo 6 Huay Sai Nua, Cha am, Petchaburi 76120 (+66 32593223; Fax: +66 3259 3260). *Location*: about 110 miles from Bangkok by new highway; 30 minutes north of central Hua Hin and 15 minutes from Springfield Beach resort. This is golf of true championship calibre, part of a planned 36 hole layout. The first course, designed by Jack Nicklaus and opened in 1993 is a great test with all the usual trademarks and one of the best maintained courses in Thailand. Venue of Thailand Open 2000 and 1993/2000 APGA qualifying schools. 18 holes, 7043 yards. Second course under construction). Driving range, pitching area, putting greens. *Green Fees:* information not available. Hearland Golf School. Lessons and clinics available. *Eating facilities:* lounge bar and coffee shop in clubhouse. Refreshment Kiosks on course. *Visitors:* welcome. Soft spikes only. 5 Star accommodation available. Director of Golf: Toni Meechai. General Manager: Lt. Col. Kittithep Krinchai. Head Professional: Michael van Amelsvoort (66 32 593 223; Fax: 66 32 593 227).*
e-mail: springfieldgolf@yahoo.com
playgolf@springfieldresort.com
website: www.springfieldresort.com

HUA-HIN. **Palm Hills Golf Resort and Country Club,** 1444 Petchakasem Highway, Cha-Am District, Petchaburi 76120 Thailand (6632 520801-9; Fax: 6632 520820). *Location:* on Petchakasem highway just 8km before Hua Hin. Links/seaside course. A most pleasant course by Max Waxler with good use of rocks and flowers to decorate holes that mostly follow the natural terrain spilling down from wooded hills behind. 18 holes (Tiff Eagle green), 6373 yards. Par 72. Pro shop, driving range, putting green. *Green Fees:* 1800 bhat. *Eating facilities:* international restaurant and executive bar lounges in clubhouse, refreshment kiosks on course. *Visitors*: welcome. Cart, club, shoe, chair hire. *

HUA HIN. **The Majestic Creek Country Club,** Ban Wangkoi, Thumbol Tabtai, Hua Hin District, Prachuap Klirikan (032-520162-6, Fax: 032-520477). *Location:* 25 minutes drive directly inland on Huay Mongkil Road from Hua Hin town, backing up to low hills. Plenty of streams and water hazards on this rolling, challenging but well-maintained course. 18 holes, 6961 yards. Par 72. Pro shop, driving range, putting green. *Green Fees:*information not available. *Eating facilities:* restaurant and bar in clubhouse. Refreshment kiosks on course. *Visitors:* welcome. Cart, club, shoe, umbrella hire. Accommodation is also provided by the Majestic Creek Country Club at the Majestic Beach Resort about 25km from the golf course, by the sea. Transport can be included. (032 520162-6; Fax: 032 520 477).*

HUA HIN. **Royal Hua Hin Golf Course,** Hua Hin District, Prachuapkirikhan (032 512 475: Fax: 032 513 038). *Location*: in the centre of Hua Hin town right by the railway station. Built in 1922 this is the oldest 'proper' golf course in the Kingdom. Historic, very natural golf running back into wooded hills offering sensational views. 18 holes, 6654 yards. Par 72. Pro shop, driving range, putting green. *Green Fees:* information not available. *Eating facilities:* restaurant and bar in clubhouse. Refreshment kiosks on course. *Visitors:* welcome. Club, shoe, umbrella hire.*

KANCHANABURI. **Mission Hills Golf Club,** 27/7 Moo 7, Tambon Pungtru, Amphur Tha Muang, Kanchanaburi (reservations: 034 644147; Fax: 034 644323). *Location:* about 126 km northwest of Bangkok from Bang Pong, take the left fork and continue 15km towards Tha Maka. At Route 3089 turn left and find course on left. No expense spared on this Jack Nicklaus designed course with waste bunkers, water hazards and mature palms. Course slopes gently away from clubhouse nestling under a wooded hill. 18 holes, 7042 yards. Par 72. Hotel, pro shop, putting green. *Green Fees:* information not available. *Eating facilities:* restaurant and bar in clubhouse. Turf roofed refreshment kiosks on course. *Visitors:* welcome. Club, shoe, umbrella, cart hire. *

KANCHANABURI. **Nichigo Resort & Country Club,** 106 Moo 4, Tambol Wangdong, Ampor Muang, Kanchanaburi 71000 (034 584000; Fax: 034 518518). *Location:* about 25km from Kanchanaburi town (150km north-west of Bangkok) on Ladya-Erawan Falls Road. 27 holes of superb resort golf on land skoping down either side of the Kwai Yai River. Gentle contours, shallow bunkers and few trees offer an attractive round against a backdrop of craggy rock outcrops. Three distinct nines - River, Lake and Mountain courses. Two 18 hole combinations, 7133 and 7260 yards, both Par 72. Hotel, pro shop, driving range, putting green. *Green Fees:* information not available. *Eating facilities:* bar and restaurant in clubhouse; drinks huts on course. *Visitors:* welcome. cart, club hire. *

NAKORN PATHOM. **The Rose Garden Aprime Resort,** Km 32, Pet Kasem Highway, Sampran, Nakorn Pathom 73110 (034 322 588-93; Fax: 034 322 775). *Location:* about one hour north-west of Bangkok on Petchakasem Road Km 32. A unique gem both to visit and to play, where the overall ambience and standards of service only enhance an interesting, mature test of golf over a level site with flowering shrubs, trees and water hazards. A genuine treat – not least from the smiling assistance of over 400 knowledgeable young lady caddies. 18 holes, 7085 yards, Par 72. Riverside hotel, pro shop, driving range, putting green. *Green Fees:* information not provided. *Eating facilities:* international restaurant in clubhouse includes sushi bar; refreshment kiosks on course. *Visitors:* welcome. Club, cart, shoe, umbrella hire.
e-mail: docs@rose-garden.com

For full details of clubs and courses, plus convenient accommodation
www.uk-golfguide.com

NORTH REGION

CHIANGMAI. **Chiangmai-Lamphun Golf Club,** San Kamphaeng-Banthi Road, Chiangmai 50130 (66 (0) 5388 0880-4; Fax: 66 (0) 5388 0888). *Location:* about half-an-hour's drive south-east of Chiangmai. Sheltered in the golden teak valley with delightful trees and many hazards. 18 holes, 6919 yards, Par 72. Golf shop, driving range, putting green. *Green Fees:* information not available. *Eating facilities:* restaurant and bar in clubhouse. *Visitors:* welcome. Cart, club, shoes and umbrella hire. *

CHIANGMAI. **Royal Chiangmai Golf Resort,** 169 Moo 5, Chiangmai-Phrao Road 26km, Maefak, Sansai, Chiangmai 50290 (053 849301-6; Fax: 053 849310). *Location:* a little north-east of Chiangmai city towards Chiangrai. Attractive course laid out in a valley surrounded by wooded hills. 18 holes, 6969 yards, Par 72. Golf shop, driving range, putting green. *Green Fees:* information not available. *Eating facilities:* restaurant and bar in clubhouse. *Visitors:* welcome. Cart, club hire. Five star 56 room hotel with swimming pool, fitness centre, massage and sauna, snooker, karaoke and function rooms. *
e-mail: rcgc@cm.ksc.co.th
e-mail:golf1@cm.ksc.co.th
website: www.royalchiangmai.co.th

CHIANG RAI. **Santiburi Country Club,** 12 Moo 3, Hoadoi-Sobpao Road, Wiangchai, Chiang Rai 57210 (0-5366 2821-6; Fax: 0-5371 7377). *Location:* take route 1020 south-east from Chiang Rai; turn left route 1152 . Follow signs to golf. A magnificent championship layout by Robert Trent Jones Jr, one of the best in the Kingdom, with rolling hills, strategic water and mountain views. Always kept in immaculate condition. 18 holes, 6,853 yards, Par 72. Driving rang, putting green, pro shop. *Green Fees:* 1,600 baht weekdays; 2,200 baht weekends. *Eating facilities:* clubhouse restaurant with open-air balcony views over the course. Refreshment shelters on course. *Visitors:* welcome. Caddies, electric cart, club and umbrella rental. General Manager: Chotiwut Gajesanandana.

CHIANG RAI. **Waterford Valley Chiangrai Golf Course & Resort,** 333 Moo 5, Tamboon Pasang, Amphur Wiangchai, Chiangrai 57210 (053 953 440; Fax: 053 953 447). *Location:* about 40 minutes' drive west from Chiang Rai. A well-established course combining holes falling steeply down from the hilltop clubhouse with more level, lake country. 18 holes, 6961 yards, Par 72. Golf shop, driving range, putting green. *Green Fees:* information not available. *Eating facilities:* clubhouse restaurant; refreshment kiosks on course. *Visitors:* welcome. Club, cart hire. *

Par 3 at Natural Park Resort, Chonburi, Thailand

N. EASTERN REGION

NAKHON RATCHASIMA. **Mission Hills Khao Yai Golf Club,** 151 Moo 5, Tambon Musi, Amphur Pakchong, Nakhon Ratchasima (reservation: 02 391 9346/8; Fax: 02 221 3736). *Location:* up Friendship Highway from Bangkok; turn to Thanaratch (Km 165) then turn right at Km 20 before Khao Yai National Park. Designed by Jack Nicklaus, this gently undulating course, part of a luxurious prestige resort, is protected by dramatic forested crags and hills. Mature trees and some water. 18 holes, 7058 yards, Par 72. Hotel, pro shop, putting green. *Green Fees:* information not provided. *Eating facilities:* coffee shop and restaurant in clubhouse. *Visitors:* welcome as hotel or member's guest. Cart, club hire.

NAKHON RATCHASIMA. **The Country Club Khao Yai,** Km 23 Thanaratch Road, Pakchong District, Nakhon Ratchasima (reservation: 02 255 3979; Fax: 02 255 2168). *Location:* take Friendship Highway from Bangkok; to Pakchong District, turn to Thanaratch Road at Km 165 to Khao Yai National Park. Open nearly five years and designed by Jack Nicklaus, there is plenty of sand and water in this demanding valley course surrounded by wooded mountain environment. 18 holes, 7102 yards, Par 72. Pro shop, putting green. *Green Fees:* information not available. *Eating facilities:* coffee shop and restauraunt in clubhouse. *Visitors:* welcome. Cart, club, shoe hire. *

EASTERN

CHANTABURI. **Soi Dao Highland Golf Club & Resort,** 153/1 Moo 2, Tambon Tabsai, Pong Nam Ron, Chantaburi 22140 (039-320 174-6; Fax: 039-320 177). *Location:* direction Chantaburi on Route 3, turn left to route 317 direction Sao Kaeo. Sign for golf on left at 42 km marker. Gently sloping course surrounded by rain forest below towering Soi Dao mountain. A great design by Dennis Griffiths; well worth the trip. 18 holes, 7,162 yards, Par 72. Driving range, putting green. *Green Fees:* 550 baht weekdays; 990 baht weekends. *Eating facilities:* clubhouse restaurant, snack shelters on course. On-site accommodation. *Visitors:* welcome, advance telephone call suggested. Caddies, cart, club, umbrella and shoe hire.

CHONBURI. **Laem Chabang International Country Club,** 106/8 Moo 4, Beung, Sriracha, Chonburi 20230 (038 372 273; Fax: 038 372275). *Location:* just 120km from Bangkok by the new highway and 30 minutes north of Pattaya. On new Chonburi-Pattaya Road 32km. Three superb nine hole loops by Jack Nicklaus - Lake, Valley and Mountain - of championship quality. Satisfying from the normal tees; tough off the back. Plenty of variety of terrain, plus strategic sand and water. Three x 9 holes, Lake 3472, Valley 3608, Mountain 3486 yards, all Par 36. Golf lodge, pro shop, driving range, putting greens. *Green Fees:* information not available. *Eating facilities:* international restaurant and coffee shop; refreshment kiosks around course. *Visitors:* welcome. Cart, club, shoe, umbrella, chair hire. Swimming pool.*

CHONBURI. **Mountain Shadow Golf Club,** 159/1 Moo 2, Saensuk-Bangpra Road, Ban Muang, Chonburi 20131 (038 393 001/18; Fax: 038 393 019). *Location:* turn left at third exit of Chonburi bypass onto route 36 (keep right onto flyover). At 6km market, turn right and follow road to course. A fine rolling natural design by Ronald Fream, spilling downhill from the clubhouse set against a wooded hill past mature mango trees and palms to several strategic lakes. 18 holes, 6807 yards, Par 72. Pro shop, driving range (irons), putting green. *Green Fees:* information not available. *Eating facilities:* restaurant and bar lounge in clubhouse; refreshment kiosks around course. *Visitors:* welcome. Carts, club, shoe hire. *

CHONBURI. **Crystal Bay Golf Club,** 502 Moo 10, Bangpra, Sriracha, Chonburi 20210 (038 349 370/80; Fax: 038 349 383). *Location:* take routes 34 and 3 from Bangkok through Chonburi (bypass). Course is on left of main road at 109km marker. Well-established 27-hole layout with much use of flowering shrubs, rocks, waterfalls as decoration. Level site with interesting but not overly demanding holes defined by palms and water. 27 holes, A 3526, B 3483, C 3480 yards, all Par 36. Pro shop, driving range, putting green. *Green Fees:* information not available. *Eating facilities:* coffee shop in clubhouse; refreshment kiosks around course. *Visitors:* welcome. Pro-shop, cart, club, shoe, umbrella, chair hire; sports club, fitness centre, Golf Lodge. *

For full details of clubs and courses, plus convenient accommodation
www.uk-golfguide.com

CHONBURI. **Noble Place Golf Resort & Country Club,** 88/8 Moo 6, Tambon Klongkiew Banbung, Chonburi 20220 (038 263458-60; Fax: 01 940 3250). *Location*: leave Bangkok on Bangna-Trad Road, then turn to by-pass 344 and after right on to 331. Club is on left after 5km. Another example of the natural style of Peter Thomson and Michael Wolveridge. Rolling slopes, gentle mounds, pot bunkers and wild grasses create a seaside feel to a palm lined 27 hole course backed by wooded hills. 27 holes - A 3500, B 3500 and C 3565 yards, all Par 72. Pro shop, driving range, putting green, sand bunker practice area. *Green Fees:* information not available. *Eating facilities:* restaurant in clubhouse. *Visitors:* welcome. Cart, club, shoe, umbrella hire. Managing Director: Ekapol Chakshuraksha. *
website: www.babadoogolf.com

CHONBURI. **Plutaluang Navy Golf Course,** Plutaluang, Sattahip, Chonburi (038 701891). *Location*: about 30km south of Pattaya towards Rayong. Take route 331 across 36 and 332, turning right under bridge at 5km, fork left, then right. Established since 1969, the course, 36 holes, is managed by the Royal Thai Navy. Well-established trees and fairly traditional design make for interesting and challenging golf on well-maintained holes in a most attractive setting. 36 holes - South 3274, East 3175, North 3374 and West 3353 yards, all Par 36. Pro shop, putting green. *Green Fees*: information not available. *Eating facilities:* restaurant in clubhouse. *Visitors:* welcome. Cart, club hire.*
e-mail: plutaluang1969@thailand.com
aree1960@hotmail.com

RAYONG. **Eastern Star Country Club,** 241/5 Moo 3, Ban Chang District, Rayong 21130 (038 630 410/7; Fax: 038 630 418). *Location*: take the Bangna-Trad highway towards Rayong and route 3 all the way to 193 km marker, 58 km south of Pattaya and 2 km short of Ban Chang. Enjoyable, gently undulating course by Robert Trent Jones Jr edged with mature palms. Sand is not too penal but some strategic water hazards. 18 holes, 7134 yards, Par 72. Pro shop, driving range, putting green. *Green Fees:* information not available. *Eating facilities:* restaurant and bar in clubhouse, refreshment kiosks on course. *Visitors:* welcome. Cart, club hire. *

RAYONG. **Rayong Green Valley Country Club,** 23 Moo 7, Banchang, Rayong 21130 (038 893 838-42, 01 940 8181, 01 940 8228; Fax: 038 893838). *Location:* club is 25 km from North Pattaya. Drive from the end of the Bang Na Expressway to Km15 on highway 36. Wonderfully natural golf created on sloping terrain by Peter Thomson and Michael Wolveridge. Low hills and lush foliage frame the links-style contouring of an interesting layout. 18 holes, Pro 7264 yards Yellow 6856 yards, Am 6835 yards, Ladies 5685 yards. Par 72. Pro shop, driving range, putting green. *Green Fees:* information not available. *Eating facilities:* international menu in clubhouse restaurant. *Visitors:* welcome. Cart, club, shoe, umbrella hire. *

SRIRACHA. **Sriracha Golf Club,** 284-285 Moo 6, Sukhumvit 7, Sriracha, Chonburi 20230 (038 338 375/8; Fax: 038 338 379). *Location:* 40km north-east of Pattaya. From Benga-Trad Highway from Bangkok, turn left onto 3241 at Sriracha, soon after Chonburi. Club on right. Host to the 1996 Thailand Open, this course designed by Gary Player follows relatively level land below the hillside clubhouse. Plenty of mature trees; watch out for the Par 3 3rd hole, 180 yards over a crocodile filled lake! 18 holes, 6227 yards, Par 72. Hotel, pro shop, driving range, putting green. *Green Fees:* information not available. *Eating facilities:* restaurant and lounge in clubhouse. *Visitors:* welcome. Cart, club, shoe hire. *

THE APPEARANCE OF AN ASTERISK (*) AT THE END OF A CLUB OR COURSE ENTRY INDICATES THAT UP-TO-DATE INFORMATION HAS NOT BEEN SUPPLIED

PLEASE NOTE

All the information regarding Golf Clubs in this guide is given in good faith in the belief that it is correct. However, the publishers cannot guarantee the facts given in these pages, neither are they responsible for changes in ownership or facilities, such as green fees, that may take place after the date of going to press. Readers should always satisfy themselves that the facilities they require are available and that the terms, if quoted, still apply.

Driving Ranges
England • Scotland • Wales • Ireland

LONDON

CHINGFORD. **Chingford Golf Range,** Waltham Way, Chingford E4 8AQ (020 8529 2409). *Location:* two miles south of Junction 26 M25. 23 bay floodlit, covered two tier driving range. *Fees:* information not provided. *Opening hours:* 8am to 10pm. Practice putting green, practice bunker; new multi-level practice mat; video, tuition available at all times. Professional: Gordon Goldie PGA (020 8529 2409)

LONDON. **Dukes Meadows Golf Club and Chiswick Bridge Golf Range,** Dukes Meadows, Great Chertsey Road, London W4 2SH (020 8995 0537; Fax: 020 8995 5326). *Location:* Next to Chiswick Bridge on A316, one mile south of the Hogarth Roundabout. Golf Range with 50 covered, floodlit bays and practice bunker. *Fees*: information not available. *Eating facilities:* bar restaurant area. *Opening hours*: weekdays from 9am to 10pm, weekends 8.30am to 10pm. Twelve PGA teaching professionals. Indoor digital tuition studio, individual group and on-course tuition. 9 hole, Par 3 course. Dress code in operation. Practice, putting green. Promenade Suite function room - catering up to 300 people. Professional: Malcolm Henbery (020 8995 0537). General Manager: Scott Margetts (020 8994 3314).*

LONDON. **Ealing Golf Range,** Rowdell Road, Northolt, Middlesex UB5 6AG (Tel & Fax: 020 8845 4967). *Location:* A40 Target roundabout, Northolt. Golf range with 35 floodlit, covered bays. Bunker. Artificial putting green. *Fees:* information not available. *Eating facilities:* bar and snack bar. *Opening hours:* 9.30am to 10pm. Five professionals, video tuition, large golf shop, repair shop. Head Professional: Paul O'Brien (Tel & Fax: 020 8845 4967).*
e-mail: pob.golf@cwco.net

NORTHOLT. **Lime Trees Park Golf Club,** Ruislip Road, Northolt UB5 6QZ (020 8845 3180). *Location:* 500 yards south of Polish War Memorial roundabout off A40, two miles inside M25. 20 bay covered, floodlit, grassed driving range. *Fees*: information not available. *Eating facilities:* two bars and bistro (bar open 11am to 11pm). *Opening Hours*: 10am to 10pm. Two PGA Professionals, 'Geoff Buddis' golf superstore, public golf course. Social club with pool and snooker; functions catered for. Professional: Neil MacDonald. Secretary: Adam Phelps (020 8842 0442; Fax: 020 8842 2097).*

NORTHOLT. **London Golf Centre,** Ruislip Road, Northolt UB5 6QZ (020 8845 3180). *Location:* 500 yards south of Polish War Memorial roundabout off A40, two miles inside M25. 20 bay covered, floodlit, grassed driving range. *Fees:* information not available. *Eating facilities:* full bar and catering facilities (bar open 11am to 11pm). *Opening Hours:* daybreak to sunset. Two PGA Professionals, golf superstore, public golf course. Social club with pool and snooker; functions catered for.*

STANMORE. **Brockley Hill Golf Park,** Brockley Hill, Stanmore HA7 4LR (020 8420 6222; Fax: 020-8420-6333). *Location:* 200 yards down on right hand side from Royal Orthopaedic Hospital, (A5). 38 bay covered floodlit driving range. *Fees*: information not available. *Eating facilities:* sandwiches and soft drinks available. *Opening hours:* Monday to Friday 8am-10pm every day. Group lessons and academy programmes available. Professionals: James Reynolds (Head), Martyn Shoulder and Andrew Stubbs. *

BEDFORDSHIRE

DUNSTABLE. **Tilsworth Golf Centre,** Dunstable Road, Tilsworth, Near Leighton Buzzard LU7 9PU (01525 210721). *Location:* two miles north of Dunstable, off A5 Tilsworth turn. 30 bay covered floodlit range. *Fees*: information not available. *Eating facilities:* restaurant and bar (extensive menu), function suite. *Opening hours:* 10am to 10pm. Large Pro shop, repairs, tuition and group lessons. 18 hole golf course open to public. *Society Meetings*: catered for; prior reservation essential. Professional: Nick Webb (01525 210721; Fax: 01525 210465).

LEIGHTON BUZZARD. **Aylesbury Vale Golf Club,** Stewkley Road, Wing, Leighton Buzzard LU7 0UJ (01525 240196). *Location:* four miles west of Leighton Buzzard between the villages of Wing and Stewkley. 9 bay covered, floodlit range.18 hole golf course, 6612 yards, Par 72. *Fees:* Midweek £19.00, Weekends before 11am £25.00, Weekends after 11am £20.00. *Eating facilities:* downstairs bar and restaurant, first floor bar and balcony. *Opening hours:* Daylight hours. Please telephone. Group and individual lessons. Professional: Terry Bunyan (07731 966 749). Secretary/Manager: Chris Wright (01525 240196).

THE APPEARANCE OF AN ASTERISK (*) AT THE END OF A CLUB OR COURSE ENTRY INDICATES THAT UP-TO-DATE INFORMATION HAS NOT BEEN SUPPLIED

BERKSHIRE

BINFIELD. **Blue Mountain Golf Centre,** Wood Lane, Binfield, Bracknell RG42 4EX (01344 300 200; Fax: 01344 360 960). *Location*: two miles from M4 near Bracknell/Wokingham. 33 bay covered floodlit range. Parkland course with numerous lakes. 18 holes, 6097 yards. S.S.S 70. *Eating facilities:* fully licensed restaurant/bar. New Blues Bar with live jazz and food. *Opening hours*: 7am - 9pm. Manager: Steve Coles (01344 300220).

MAIDENHEAD. **Bird Hills Golf Centre,** Drift Road, Hawthorn Hill, Near Maidenhead SL6 3ST (01628 771030). *Location*: on A330 Ascot to Maidenhead road. 36 covered, floodlit bays. 18 hole "pay and play" course. Professional's tuition. *Fees*: information not available. *Opening hours*: 7.30am to 10pm daily. *Eating facilities:* "Racecourse Restaurant" and Golfers Bar and terrace.*

WARGRAVE. **Hennerton Golf Club,** Crazies Hill Road, Wargrave RG10 8LT (01189 401000; Fax: 01189 401042). *Location*: halfway between Maidenhead and Reading off the A321 to Henley. Scenic course overlooking the Thames valley. 9 holes, 5460 yards. S.S.S. 67. *Visitors:* welcome. Driving range. *Eating facilities:* clubhouse with full facilities. Fully stocked Pro shop. Professional/ Manager: William Farrow (01189 404778).*

WOKINGHAM. **Downshire Golf Complex,** Easthampstead Park, Wokingham RG11 3DH (01344 302030; Fax: 01344 301020). *Location*: between Bracknell and Wokingham, off the Nine Mile Ride. 30 bay covered floodlit driving range. *Fees*: information not available. *Eating facilities:* bar and restaurant, bar snacks available. *Opening hours*: 7.30am to 10pm. Tuition, 18 hole course, 9 hole pitch and putt; golf super store. Societies welcome. Golf Manager: Paul Stanwick. e-mail: downshiregc@bracknell-forest.gov.uk website: www.bracknell-forest.gov.uk/downshiregc/

BUCKINGHAMSHIRE

AYLESBURY. **Aylesbury Golf Centre,** Hulcott Lane, Bierton, Aylesbury HP22 5GA (01296 393644). *Location*: north of Aylesbury on the A418 Leighton Buzzard road. 30 bay covered, floodlit driving range. *Fees*: information not available. *Eating facilities:* bar, bar snacks 11am to 11pm. *Opening hours*: weekdays 8am to 10pm; weekends 7am to 10pm. Professional coaching. 18 hole golf course. General Manager: Kevin Partington. Professional: A Saary.*

COLNBROOK. **Colnbrook Golf Range,** Galleymead Road, Colnbrook SL3 0EN (01753 682670). *Location*: one mile from Junction 5 M4, one mile Junction 14 M25. 27 bay floodlit, grassed range; 14 covered bays. *Fees*: information not available. *Opening hours*: 9am to 6pm. Professional: Alistair McKay. Full tuition, video assisted lessons given. *

MILTON KEYNES. **Kingfisher Country Club,** Buckingham Road, Deanshanger MK19 6DG (01908 562332; Fax: 01908 260857). *Location*: Between Milton Keynes and Buckingham on A422 opposite Shires Motel. 10 bay covered, grassed driving range. *Fees:* information not available. *Eating facilities:* full clubhouse and lodge facilities. *Opening hours:* 7.30am to 7.30pm Monday to Sunday. Professional tuition by request. Director Golf & Leisure: Major D. M. Barraclough (01908 562332; Fax: 01908 260857).*

MILTON KEYNES. **Windmill Hill Golf Centre,** Tattenhoe Lane, Bletchley, Milton Keynes MK3 7RB (01908 630660; Fax: 01908 630034; Tee reservations: 01908 631113. 7 days in advance). *Location*: M1 South Junction 14/M1 North Junction 13, A421 towards Buckingham. 23 bay covered floodlit driving range, 7 grassed bays. Two putting greens; practice area; two pool tables. *Fees*: information not available. *Eating facilities:* carvery restaurant, cafeteria, two bars, function room. *Opening hours*: 7.30am till dusk. *Society Meetings:* welcome (after 11am weekends and Bank Holidays). Three teaching Professionals, tuition, Pro shop. Professional: Colin Clingan (01908 378623; Fax: 01908 271478). Secretary: Brian Smith (Tel & Fax: 01908 366457).*

STOKE POGES. **Lanes Golfing Academy,** Stoke Road, Stoke Poges (01753 554840). *Location:* half-a-mile from Slough Railway Station in direction of Stoke Poges. 18 bay covered, floodlit driving range. Parkland course ideal for the less experienced player. 9 holes. 2400 yds. S.S.S. 62 (18 holes). *Eating facilities:* small lounge area with snack facilities. *Opening hours:* contact for details. Clubs for hire. Expert tuition available. A Golf Foundation starter centre. Professional: P. Warner (01753 554840). *

STOWE. **Silverstone Golf Club,** Silverstone Road, Stowe MK18 5LH (01280 850005; Fax: 01280 850156). *Location:* A43 Oxford-Northampton opposite Grand Prix Circuit. 11 bay covered range. *Fees:* please telephone for information. *Eating facilities:* Restaurant/bar. *Opening hours:* dawn to dusk. Tuition by teaching professional is available - group or private. Corporate packages with motor sport. Professional: Rodney Holt.

CAMBRIDGESHIRE

CAMBRIDGE. **Cambridge Golf Club,** Station Road, Longstanton, Cambridge CB4 5DR (01954 789388). *Location*: 10 minutes from city, off A14 at Bar Hill, turn right to Longstanton B1050. 9 bay floodlit driving range. Parkland course. 18 holes, 6736 yards, S.S.S. 72. 9 holes pitch and putt. *Fees*: information not available. *Eating facilities:* clubhouse. *Opening hours*: contact for details. Buggies and trolleys for hire. Society meetings catered for. Professional: Geoff Hugget.

588 DRIVING RANGES THE GOLF GUIDE 2006

HUNTINGDON. **Edrich Driving Range and Old Nene Golf and Country Club,** Muchwood Lane, Bodsey, Ramsey PE26 2XQ (01487 813519). *Location:* halfway between Ramsey and Ramsey Mereside, three quarters of a mile north of Ramsey, half a mile from Rainbow Supercentre. 24 bay driving range, 12 covered, 24 floodlit. *Fees:* information not available. *Eating facilities:* at adjoining club house, open to all. *Opening hours:* summertime, dawn to 9pm, winter to 7pm weekends. Private and group instruction arranged on 9 hole (18 tee) golf course. Coarse fishing on half acre lake and barbecues for summer months arranged. Ramsey Miniature Car Racing Club meetings at weekends. Professional: Ian Galloway. Secretary/Director: P.B. Cade.*

PETERBOROUGH. **Thorney Golf Centre,** English Drove, Thorney, Peterborough PE6 0TJ (01733 270570). *Location:* A47 Leicester to Wisbech, turn left in Thorney, first right out of village. 13 bay covered, floodlit, grassed range. Two 18 hole courses. *Fees:* information not available. *Eating facilities:* full bar and restaurant open to public. *Opening hours:* 8am to 9.30pm seven days.*

ST NEOTS. **Abbotsley Golf Hotel & Country Club,** Eynesbury, Hardwicke, St Neots PE19 4XN (01480 474000; Fax: 01480 471018). *Location:* A428 St Neots bypass to Abbotsley, south east of St Neots Junction 13 M11. 21 bay floodlit driving range, 300 yard grass driving range. Two 18 hole courses, 9 hole par 3 course. Abbotsley course is regarded by many as one of the finest golf courses in the county and combines the best of both parkland and woodland features. Excellent drainage makes it an ideal venue for all year round corporate and society days. Home of the Denise Hastings School of Golf. *Fees:* information not available. *Visitors:* welcome. 42 room hotel, gym, squash courts, beauty salon.*

CHESHIRE

ADLINGTON. **Adlington Golf Centre,** Sandy Hey Farm, Adlington, Macclesfield SK10 4NG (01625 850660). *Location:* 2 miles south of Poynton off A523, via Adlington Industrial Estate. 24 bay covered, floodlit driving range. *Fees:* Information not available. *Eating facilities:* tea and coffee available. *Opening hours:* 9am to 10.00pm Monday to Friday, 8.30am to 9.00pm weekends. 9 hole Par 3 course plus 9 hole Academy Course. Reductions for Senior Citizens/Juniors. Tuition available all the time. Professionals: Chad Goldstraw, John Watson and Dave Jeffery. Proprietor: David Moss (01625 850660).

CHESTER. **Carden Park Golf Hotel Resort and Spa,** Chester CH3 9DQ (01829 731000; Fax: 01829 731599). *Location:* on A543 east of Wrexham. Golf School. 13 bay covered driving range and short game area. *Eating facilities:* Full Clubhouse facilites and 192 bedroom four star hotel. Nicklaus Course - 7045 yards. Cheshire Course - 6653 yards. Azalea Course 9 hole, Par 3. Professional: Paul Hodgson (01829 731000).

NORTHWICH. **Hartford Golf Range,** Burrows Hill, Hartford, Northwich CW9 3AP. *Location:* off A556 Northwich, near ICI. 26 bay floodlit driving range. Golf shop. 9 hole pay as you play course now open. Professional: (01606 871162; Fax: 01606 872182).*

STOCKPORT. **Cranford Golf Centre,** Harwood Road, Heaton Mersey, Stockport SK4 3AW (0161-432 8242; Fax: 01625 827365). *Location:* five minutes from M60 and M56 motorways. 43 all-weather covered tees, fully floodlit. Two indoor bunkers, 9 hole indoor putting course. *Fees:* £3.50 per bucket (50 balls); £6.00 100 balls. No booking or membership required. School, Junior and group concessions. *Eating facilities:* drinks and snacks available. *Opening hours:* Monday to Thursday 10am to 10pm, Friday to Sunday 10am to 9.30pm. Hours may vary during Winter months and Bank Holidays. Changing rooms and golf shop. Group facilities and lessons available. Custom club fitting and repair centre now open. Professionals: Tony Murray & Matt Griffin. Director: Jeffrey S. Yates.

STYAL. **Styal Golf Driving Range and Par 3 Academy Course,** Home of Cheshire Golf Academy, Styal Golf Club, Station Road, Styal SK9 4JN (Office: 01625 530063; Golf Booking Line: 01625 531359; Pro: 01625 528910). *Location:* five minutes from Manchester Airport. Junction 5 M56, near Wilmslow. 24 bay covered floodlit range plus 12 outdoor bays and practice bunker. 10 bays on the existing range have been fitted with power tee self loading ball dispensers. *Fees:* £4.00 for 50 balls, £6.00 for 100 balls, £15.00 for 300 balls. *Eating facilities:* drinks and snacks available. *Opening hours:* 7.30am to 9.30pm midweek, 7am to 8.30pm weekends. Happy hours are from 10am-12pm and 4pm-6pm Monday to Friday and 5.30pm-7.30pm Saturday and Sunday. Cheshire Golf Academy, tuition available for beginners and established players. Range is fully carpeted with target distances and two-piece premium golf balls. Latest hi-tec teaching and practice facilities. 9 hole deluxe par 3 course, USGA spec greens, 1242 yards, par 27. Professional: Simon Forrest. Secretary: Bill Higham. Golf Director: Glynn Traynor.
e-mail: gtraynor@styalgolf.co.uk
website: www.styalgolf.co.uk

CORNWALL

NEWQUAY. **Merlin Golf Course and Driving Range,** Mawgan Porth, Newquay TR8 4DN (01841 540222). *Location:* on coast road between Newquay and Padstow, after Mawgan Porth take St. Eval Road, golf course and range on right. 6 bay covered, floodlit driving range. *Fees:* information not available. *Eating facilities:* use of the club facilities. *Opening hours:* 8am till dark. Secretary: Mr Richard Burrough.

www.uk-golfguide.com

REDRUTH. **Radnor Golf and Ski Centre,** Radnor Road, Treleigh, Redruth TR16 5EL (01209 211059). *Location*: two miles north east of Redruth, signposted from A3047 at Treleigh and North Country crossroads. Purpose-built Par 3 - interesting layout. 9 holes, 1312 yards. S.S.S. 52. Covered driving range. *Green Fees:* information not available. *Eating facilities:* coffee, tea etc. *Visitors:* welcome. Indoor ski training machine. Small touring caravan site. Professional: Gordon Wallbank

SALTASH. **China Fleet Country Club,** Saltash PL12 6LJ (01752 848668). *Location*: one mile from Tamar Bridge. Parkland course with beautiful river views. 18 holes, 6551 yards, S.S.S. 72. 28 bay floodlit driving range. *Fees:* information not available. *Eating facilities:* bars and bar meals, full restaurant facilities, coffee shop. *Visitors:* welcome, Handicap Certificate required. Other facilities include large Pro Shop, full leisure facilities and 40 apartments. *Society Meetings:* welcome, minimum number 12. Professional: Nick Cook (01752 848668 extension 460; Fax: 01752 848456). Golf Manager: Linda Goddard (01752 848668 extension 657; Fax: 01752 848456).

TRURO. **Killiow Golf Club & Driving Range,** Kea, Truro TR3 6AG (01872 270246; Fax: 01872 240915). *Location*: take A39 Truro to Falmouth Road. Turn right into club at first playing place roundabout (2½ miles). 18 hole golf course (Par 72). All weather floodlit driving range. *Opening hours:* 8am to 9pm weekdays; weekends till 6pm. *Eating facilities:* bar and restaurant. *Visitors*: only restricted by competitions – phone for availability. Secretary: John Crowson (01872 266876).

CUMBRIA

BRAMPTON. **Brampton Golf Club,** Tarn Road, Brampton CA8 1HN (016977 2000; Fax: 016977 41487). *Location:* situated one and a half miles from Brampton on the B6413 Castle Carrock Road. The town of Brampton is 8 miles to the east of Carlisle on the main A69 to Newcastle. Part of Brampton Golf Club. 6 grassed bays. *Fees:* £1.00 per bucket of balls. *Eating facilities:* use of club's bar and dining facilities. Tuition and practice facilities available. Professional: Stewart Wilkinson (016977 2000; Fax: 016977 41487). e-mail: wilkinsonwilf@aol.com
secretary@bramptongolfclub.com
website: www.bramptongolfclub.com

CARLISLE. **The Eden Golf Course,** Crosby-on-Eden, Carlisle CA6 4RA (01228 573003; Fax: 01228 818435). *Location:* M6 Junction 44, A689 to Crosby-on-Eden village. 16 bay floodlit range. *Fees:* Bucket of balls only £1.00. *Eating facilities*: modern clubhouse, Fairway restaurant. *Opening hours:* 10am to 10pm. Professional tuition. Junior school of excellence. 18 hole parkland course, tree lined fairways and numerous water hazards. *Society Meetings:* welcome. Discounts for societies, company days, etc. Professional/Manager: Steven Harrison (01228 573003).
website: www.edengolf.co.uk

DERBYSHIRE

BRAILSFORD. **Brailsford Golf Centre,** Pools Head Lane, Brailsford, Near Ashbourne DE6 3BU (01335 360096). *Location*: on the main A52 Derby to Ashbourne road, Derby 6 miles, Ashbourne 5 miles. Parkland course. 9 holes, 6219 yards (18 holes), S.S.S. 70. Practice facilities and driving range. *Green Fees*: weekdays 9 holes £10.00, 18 holes £13.50; weekends 9 holes £12.00, 18 holes £16.50. Special rates for juniors, Senior Citizens (weekdays only). *Eating facilities*: available. *Visitors*: welcome at any time except Sunday mornings. Tuition available - two teaching Professionals. *Society Meetings*: welcome except Sunday mornings. Special rates available. Professional: David McCarthy (01335 360096). Secretary: Mr K. Wilson (01332 553703).

BUXTON. **Peak Practice Golf,** Barms Farm, Fairfield, Buxton SK17 7HW (01298 74444; Fax: 01298 78692). *Location:* approximately one mile north of Buxton off A6 on right hand side. Same drive as for Barms Farm Guesthouse. 300 metre floodlit public driving range offering 20 covered bays, 12 outdoor bays, sand bunker and putting green. Top quality two-piece balls and mats used, clubs for hire. *Fees*: £3.00 for 50 balls, £5.00 for 100 balls (Discounted rates for PPG range members). *Eating facilities*: drinks and snacks available. *Opening hours*: Monday to Thursday 10am to 9pm, Friday to Sunday 10am to 6pm. Five PGA Professionals available for individual and group tuition. Societies very welcome with advance notification.
e-mail: peakpracticegolf@aol.com
website: www.peakpracticegolf.co.uk

CHESTERFIELD. **Grassmoor Golf Centre,** North Wingfield Road, Grassmoor, Chesterfield S42 5EA (01246 856044; Fax: 01246 853486). *Location*: 4 miles M1 Junction 29 or A61 near Chesterfield. 26 bay covered, floodlit range, grass landing areas and target greens. 18 hole pay as you play course. 5723yds Par 69. *Fees*: weekdays £12.00, weekends and Bank Holidays £15.00. *Eating facilities:* Bar and Restaurant open daily 8am to 10pm. *Opening hours*: seven days a week 8am to 10pm. Coaching available. Club Membership. Societies welcome, must book in advance. Discount Golf Superstore. Professional: Gary Hagues. Club Manager: Helen Hagues.
website: www.grassmoorgolf.co.uk

DEVON

BARNSTAPLE. **Portmore Golf Range,** Portmore Golf Park, Landkey Road, Barnstaple EX32 9LB (01271 378378). *Location:* one and a half miles east of Barnstaple on A361. 24 floodlit bays with bunkers and putting. 27 holes (9 hole par 3 course, and 18 hole full Barum Course). *Fees*: £2.00 for 50 balls. *Eating facilities:* full clubhouse open to all. *Opening hours:* 9am to 9pm weekdays, 8am to 9pm weekends. All facilities are pay and play; there is also a membership. 2 PGA Professionals. Steve Gould of GASP systems

ILFRACOMBE near. **Ilfracombe & Woolacombe Golf Range,** Woolacombe Road, Near Ilfracombe EX34 7HF (01271 866222). *Location*: Woolacombe Road (B3343). 12 covered bays. *Fees*: £2.00 for 50 balls. *Eating facilities*: snacks. *Opening hours*: 10am-7pm Summer, 11am-5pm Winter. Facilities include tuition and tennis. PGA Professional: David Sheppard. e-mail: DCWRanger@aol.com

DORSET

SHAFTESBURY. **Twyford Golf Range,** Twyford, Shaftesbury SP7 0JN (Tel & Fax: 01747 811356). *Location*: situated 4½ miles south of Shaftesbury between Twyford and Bedchester, 14 bay grassed range, 6 covered. 310 yards long with markers, flags and sand bunker. *Fees*: information not available. *Opening hours:* open every day dawn until dusk.

DURHAM

SEDGEFIELD. **Knotty Hill Golf Centre,** Sedgefield, Stockton-on-Tees TS21 2BB (01740 620320; Fax: 01740 622227). *Location*: A1 (M) Junction 60, one mile north of Sedgefield on A177. Indoor Golf Academy, tuition and video range, 20 bay covered, floodlit range, 14 tees open and grassed, chipping and putting greens, practice bunker, target golf. *Fees*: small baskets £2.00, large basket £3.00 (two-piece balls). *Eating facilities*: restaurant and coffee shop. *Opening hours*: 8am to 9pm. Professional tuition. Secretary: Mrs J. Reynolds (01740 620320).

ESSEX

BRAINTREE. **Towerlands Driving Range,** Panfield Road, Braintree CM7 5BJ (01376 326802; Fax: 01376 552487). *Location*: take A120 into Braintree then B1053. 6 grassed bays. *Fees*: information not available. *Eating facilities:* full bar and restaurant. *Opening hours*: 8.30am till dark. 9 hole course, professional tuition, indoor bowls, squash, full sports hall and equestrian facilities.*

CHADWELL HEATH. **Warren Park Golf Centre,** Whalebone Lane North, Chadwell Heath, Romford RM6 6SB (020 8597 1120; Fax: 020 8590 5457). *Location*: on A12 opposite "Moby Dick" public house. 37 bay covered, floodlit driving range. *Fees*: information not available. *Eating facilities:* bar and snacks; function suite. *Opening hours*: 9am to 9.45pm Monday to Friday, 9am to 8.45pm Saturday and Sunday. Warren Park is a JJB Golf Centre. Seven PGA Professionals. Fully stocked golf shop, golf club repair facilities. Two piece range balls and astroturf mats. *

COLCHESTER. **Colchester Golf Range,** Old Ipswich Road, Ardleigh, Colchester (01206 230974). *Location*: next to the Crown Inn, Old Ipswich Road. Covered, floodlit range, 12 bays. Professional tuition available. Fully stocked Pro shop and repair centre. *Fees*: information not available. *Opening hours*: weekdays 10am to 9pm, weekends 10am to 6pm. *Eating facilities:* The Crown Inn, 50 yards from golf range.

COLCHESTER. **The Essex Golf and Country Club,** Earls Colne, Colchester CO6 2NS (01787 224466; Fax: 01787 224410). *Location:* A1124 signed from A1124 and B1024. 22 bay covered floodlit driving range. Indoor bunker range. 18 hole and 9 hole courses. *Fees*: information not available. *Eating facilities:* Sports Brasserie and bar facilities. *Opening hours*: weekdays 7am to 11pm, weekends 8am to 9pm. Tuition available from 3 professional teachers. Video studio, Leisure centre - swimming pool, gym, sun beds, aerobics, beauty parlour, spa bath. Six indoor tennis courts and three all-weather outdoor courts. Full day nursery facilities. Sports injury clinic. Hairdresser. Conference and banqueting facilities. 42 bedroom hotel. Professional: Lee Cocker. Golf Secretary: David Clark.*

COLCHESTER. **Lexden Wood Golf Club,** Bakers Lane, Colchester CO3 4AU (01206 843333; Fax: 01206 854775). *Location*: one mile north west of Colchester off A133. 24 bay driving range (floodlit and covered). *Eating facilities:* home-cooked food and snacks are always available. *Fees*: information not available. *Opening hours*: weekdays 7.30am to 9pm; weekends 7am to 7.30pm. Tuition available. 9 hole Par 3 course and 18 hole main course playing over many water features. Brand new golf superstore now open. Society Meetings: welcome by appointment. Professional/Centre Director: Phil Grice.*

ILFORD. **Fairlop Waters,** Forest Road, Barkingside, Ilford IG6 3JA (020 8500 9911). *Location*: two miles north of Ilford, half a mile from A12, one and a half miles from southern end of M11. Covered, floodlit range, 36 bays. 18 hole golf course, 9 hole Par 3 course. Individual or group tuition available. *Fees*: information not available. *Opening hours*: 7am to 10pm. *Eating facilities:* bars and diner. Banqueting facilities and conferences. 38 acre sailing lake, 25 acre country park, children's play area. Professional: Paul Davies (020 8501 1881).*

MALDON. **Five Lakes Resort,** Colchester Road, Tolleshunt Knights, Maldon CM9 8HX. *Location*: eight miles from Colchester on the B1026. 10 bay grassed, covered driving range. Mats. *Fees*: information not available. Monthly season ticket available. *Eating facilities*: full catering, bar snacks. *Opening hours*: 7.30am to 10pm weekdays; 7am to 10pm weekends. Lessons given to non-members, group lessons. Professional: Gary Carter.*

THE APPEARANCE OF AN ASTERISK (*) AT THE END OF A CLUB OR COURSE ENTRY INDICATES THAT UP-TO-DATE INFORMATION HAS NOT BEEN SUPPLIED

GLOUCESTERSHIRE

BRISTOL. Europro Golf Centre, Hambrook Golf Range, Common Mead Lane, Filton Road, Bristol BS16 1QQ (0117-970 1116; Fax: 0117-970 1118). *Location*: by the side of Holiday Inn Hotel on A4174 by Junction 1 of M32. 24 bay covered, floodlit range with power tees. *Fees*: £3.25 for 50 balls approx. *Eating facilities:* coffee shop. *Opening hours*: weekdays 9am to 10pm; weekends 9am to 8pm. Astroturf putting green, bunker and chipping green. 9 PGA Professionals available for group and individual lessons. Award-winning golf shop with club repair facilities. Main Powakaddy repair centre.

CHURCHDOWN. Brickhampton Court Golf Complex, Cheltenham Road, Churchdown GL2 9QF (01452 859444; Fax: 01452 859333). *Location:* midway between Cheltenham and Gloucester on B4063 within Brickhampton Court Golf Complex. 26 bays floodlit and covered Driving Range and Ping Custom Fit Centre. Adjacent practice bunker and putting green. Part of Brickhampton Court Golf Complex which includes 18 hole, par 71 and 9 hole par 31 courses. *Fees*: information not provided. *Eating facilities*: full catering facilities at Clubhouse. *Opening hours*: weekdays 9am to 9pm; weekends 9am to 5.30pm. PGA qualified teaching staff available for group and individual lessons. Two fully stocked Pro Shops. website: www.brickhampton.co.uk

GLOUCESTER. Ramada Hotel & Resort Gloucester, Robinswood Hill, Matson Lane, Gloucester GL4 6EA (01452 525653). 12 bays covered and floodlit. *Fees:* information not available. *Opening Hours*: 10am to 8.45pm. *Eating facilities*: available. Professional instructors, private and group tuition available. Sebastian Coe Health Park, dry ski slope, 9 and 18 hole golf course, indoor swimming pool, sauna, solarium, gymnasium, 5 squash courts, two tennis courts, snooker, pool, etc.

TEWKESBURY. Sherdons Golf Centre, Tredington, Tewkesbury GL20 7PB (01684 274782; Fax: 01684 275358). 26 bays; 20 covered, 6 grassed. Floodlit. Bunker, putting, 9 hole golf course. *Fees*: information not available. *Opening Hours:* April to October inclusive 8am to 9 pm. October to March weekdays 8am to 9pm; weekends 8am to 6pm. *Eating facilities*: coffee, bar, pies and pasties. Group and individual tuition, Golf Foundation junior coaching. Professionals: Philip Clark/John Parker. Secretary: Richard Chatham.*

www.uk-golfguide.com

HAMPSHIRE

ANDOVER. The Hampshire Golf Club, Winchester Road, Goodworth, Clatford, Andover SP11 7TB (01264 357555; Fax: 01264 356606). *Location:* two minutes from the A303 on the A3057 near Andover. Beautiful countryside. Part of the Hampshire Golf Club. 10 covered bays; three practice bunkers. *Fees:* £2.00 for 60 balls. Telephone for special offers. *Opening hours:* 8am to 8pm weekdays, 7am to 8pm (or dusk) weekends. *Eating facilities:* restaurant, bar, conference rooms. Tuition available. PGA Professional: Iain Powell (01264 357555; Fax: 01264 356606).
e-mail: iainpowell@btconnect.com
  enquiry@thehampshiregolfclub.co.uk
website: thehampshiregolfclub.co.uk

BORDON near. **Kingsley Golf Club,** Main Road, Kingsley, Near Bordon GU35 9NG (01420 489478). *Location*: B3004 off A325 Farnham to Petersfield road. 9 hole course; driving range. *Fees*: information not available. Professional/Acting Secretary: G.W. Doggrell. *

CRONDALL. **Oak Park Golf Club Driving Range,** Heath Lane, Crondall, Farnham GU10 5PB (01252 850066; Fax: 01252 850851). *Location:* behind the club house at Oak Park Golf Club. 13 covered bays, (five grassed bays for members only); one bunker. *Fees:* £2.50 for 50 balls, £10.00 for 250 balls; £18.00 for 500 balls. *Opening hours:* open during daylight hours. *Eating facilities:* full clubhouse facilities. Tuition, practice area, pitching etc. Professional: Gary Murton (01252 852567)
e-mail: x.murton@ntlworld.com
  oakpark@crown-golf.uk.co.uk
website: www.crown-golf.co.uk/oakpark

ROMSEY. **Paultons Golf Centre,** Old Salisbury Road, Ower, Near Romsey SO51 6AN (023 8081 3992). *Location:* off M27 at Junction 2, A36 towards Salisbury, at first roundabout take first exit then first right at the Vine Public House. 24-bay covered floodlit driving range. *Fees*: information not available. *Eating facilities:* full bar and restaurant. *Opening hours:* 8am until 9pm. Full Professional shop and teaching facilities. 27 holes.*

SOUTHAMPTON. **Chilworth Golf Club,** Main Road, Chilworth, Southampton SO16 7JP (02380 740544). *Location*: on the A27. 22 floodlit bays, 11 grassed, covered driving range. Bunker practice. *Fees*: information not available. *Eating facilities*: bar. *Opening hours*: Monday to Friday 7.30am till 9.00pm, Saturday and Sunday 7.30am till 6.00pm. Tuition available. Professional: Garry Stubbington (02380 740544). *

FHG

For full details of clubs and courses, plus convenient accommodation
www.uk-golfguide.com

HEREFORDSHIRE

LEOMINSTER. **Grove Golf Centre,** Fordbridge, Leominster HR6 0LE (01568 610602). *Location*: adjacent to Leominster Golf Club three miles south of Leominster on A49. 18 bay floodlit driving range, four outdoor bays. 9 hole putting green, practice bunker. *Fees*: information not available. *Eating facilities*: full bar and catering facilities every day. *Visitors*: welcome anytime. *Opening hours*: 8am to 9pm. Professional: Peter Lowery (01568 615333). e-mail: info@grovegolf.co.uk
website: www.grovegolf.co.uk

ROSS-ON-WYE. **South Herefordshire Golf Club,** Twin Lakes, Upton Bishop, Ross-on-Wye HR9 7UA (01989 780535; Fax: 01989 740611). *Location:* end roundabout of M50. At Ross take B4221 to Upton Bishop. At Upton Bishop turn right half a mile. 16 bay covered, floodlit driving range. Top quality mats and two piece balls. *Green Fees*: information not available. *Eating facilities:* fully licensed bar serving snacks and full meals. Opening hours: 8.30am to last balls 8pm. 9 hole Par 3 £5.00 per round. 18 hole Par 71, S.S.S. 72 Course. £18.00 per round weekdays, £22.50 per round weekends. Fully qualified PGA Professional, club fitting centre, Pro shop. Lessons available. Director of Golf: James Leaver.*

HERTFORDSHIRE

BROXBOURNE. **The Hertfordshire Golf & Country Club,** Broxbournebury Mansion, Broxbourne EN10 7PY (01992 466666; Fax: 01992 470326). *Location*: 10 minutes north on A10 from Junction 25 of M25 take Broxbourne Exit, third left Bell Lane, over A10 right hand side. Driving range with 30 covered floodlit bays and 25 grassed bays. *Fees*: information not available. *Eating facilities:* Spike Bar, Cocktail Bar. Health club, indoor pool, indoor and outdoor tennis courts, golf academy. 18 hole "Nicklaus" design course set around a Grade II Listed country house. 18 holes 6400 yards. Professionals: Adrian Shearn and David Smith. *

ROYSTON. **Whaddon Golf Centre,** Whaddon, Royston SG8 5RX (01223 207325). *Location*: four miles north of Royston off A1198, nine miles south of Cambridge off A603. 14 bays covered, floodlit, and 9 grassed. Putting green and Par 3 9 hole course. *Fees*: £1.50 for 40 balls. £4.00 per round, £4.50 weekends. *Eating facilities:* available. *Opening hours:* 8am to 9pm daily. Video, group and individual tuition available daily. Crazy golf. Professional: Geoff Huggett (01223 207325).

WARE. **Whitehill Golf Centre,** Dane End, Ware SG12 0JS (01920 438495; Fax: 01920 438891). *Location:* turn at 'Raj Villa', High Cross four miles north of Ware. 25 bays covered, floodlit, grassed. *Fees:* information not available. *Eating facilities:* full catering facilities 8am to 6pm. *Opening hours:*

Monday to Friday 7am to 10pm, Tuesday 10am to 10pm, weekends 7am to dusk. Professional tuition, 18 hole golf course, practice bunkers, snooker. Professional: Matthew Belsham (01920 438326). Secretary: Andrew Smith.*

WATFORD. **Topgolf Game Centre,** Bushey Mill Lane, Watford WD24 7AB (01923 222045; Fax: 01923 222885). *Location*: off Junction 5 on M1. The latest in golf driving ranges. 44 heated bays with screens giving instant feedback on how far you hit each shot and a points score – thanks to a microchip inside each and every Dunlop LoCo golf ball. *Eating facilities:* Café/bar. American Golf Discount Centre and Cranfield Golf Academy. As seen on Sky Sports* Golf Extra and Tomorrow's World.
website: www.topgolf.co.uk

WELWYN GARDEN CITY. **Gosling Golf Range,** Gosling Sports Park, Stanborough Road, Welwyn Garden City AL8 6XE (01707 331056). *Location:* A1(M) Junction 4, follow signs for Welwyn Garden City. 22 bays covered floodlit driving range. *Fees:* information not available. *Opening hours:* 10am to 10pm weekdays, weekends 9am to 8pm. *Eating facilities:* extensive bar/catering within Sports Park. Resident Professional, tuition and shop. Extensive facilities with ski-ing, tennis, athletics, bowls, cycling, badminton. Health suite, etc. Brochure available.*

KENT

ASHFORD. **Ashford Great Chart Golf & Leisure Complex,** Great Chart, Ashford (01233 645858; Fax: 01233 663550). *Location*: signposted from Great Chart, Ashford. 26 bay covered floodlit, heated, carpeted driving range, 9 hole full course, 9 hole Par 3 course, practice bunkers. Floodlit beach soccer/volleyball. *Fees*: information not available. Golf £8.50 weekdays, £11.50 weekends - 9 holes main course, £4.50 par 3 course. *Eating facilities:* bar/café. *Opening hours:* 9am to 10pm 7 days a week. Tuition, video tuition, shop. Juniors and families welcome. Professional: Cameron Cowie. Secretary: Grant Kay/John Kay.*

ASHFORD. **The Homelands Bettergolf Centre,** Ashford Road, Kingsnorth, Ashford TN26 1NJ (01233 661620; Fax: 01233 720934). *Location*: take exit 10 off M20. Signed to international passenger station, at second roundabout turn left, course signposted through Kingsnorth. 14 bay covered floodlit range. 4 grassed bays. 9 hole parkland course. Practice ground; bunker, pitching, chipping and putting green. 4 hole junior academy course. *Fees*: information not available. *Eating facilities*: licensed bar and bar snacks. *Opening hours*: 8am to 8pm. Close-circuit TV Sportsview system. Accredited as a National Junior Starter Centre by the England Junior Golf Committee. Professional: Tony Bowers. Secretary: Ian S. Johnson.

THE GOLF GUIDE 2006 　　　　　　　　　　　　　　DRIVING RANGES 593

CHATHAM. **Chatham Golf Centre,** Street End Road, Chatham ME5 0BG. *Location*: five minutes' drive from Rochester Airport. Covered, floodlit range, 30 bays. Tuition available. *Fees:* information not available. *Opening hours*: 10am to 10pm. *Eating facilities:* vending area. Fully stocked Pro Shop. Competitive prices. Pro Shop: (01634 848925). Secretary: R. Burden (01634 848907).*

CHISLEHURST. **World of Golf,** A20 Sidcup Bypass, Chislehurst BR7 6RP (020 8309 0181; Fax: 020 8308 1691). *Location:* six miles from Junction 3 on M25 heading towards London on A20. 54 bay floodlit driving range, Golf School and coaching studio. Par 3 9 hole course, floodlit short game practice area, putting green and bunker, golf shop, club repair service. Adventure putting course, tennis courts, cafe/bar. JJB Sports Golf Store. *Eating facilities:* licensed cafe/bar. *Visitors:* welcome, no restrictions. *Opening hours*: 9am to 10.30pm weekdays; 8am to 10pm weekends. Head Golf Professional: David Young. Centre Manager: Colin Payne.*

DARTFORD. **Birchwood Park Golf Centre,** Birchwood Road, Wilmington, Dartford DA2 7HJ (01322 662038; Fax: 01322 667283). *Location:* Take Junction 3 off M25 onto B2173 towards Sidcup, turn right into Birchwood Road at Vauxhall Garage. 41 bay floodlit driving range. *Fees:* information not provided. *Eating facilities:* snacks and bar food always available, dining/function room also available. *Visitors:* very welcome. 18 hole course and 9 hole course available teaching professionals and extensive golf shop. Manager: Scott Morley (01322 662038; Fax: 01322 667283).

GRAVESEND. **Thamesview Golf Centre at Gravesend,** Thong Lane, Gravesend DA12 4LG (01474 335002; Fax: 01474 335004). *Location:* only one and a half miles from the A2. 30 bay floodlit, covered driving range. *Opening hours:* 9am to 10pm daily. Thamesview Golf School 9 hole Par 3 golf course, practice putting green, floodlit short game practice area, golf shop, club repair service. Head Teaching Professional: Chris Lightfoot.*

MAIDSTONE. **Maidstone Golf Centre,** Sutton Road, Langley, Maidstone ME17 3NQ (Tel & Fax: 01622 863163). *Location:* south of Maidstone on A274, first turning after Park Wood Industrial Estate. 26 covered, floodlit bays. *Fees:* information not provided. *Opening hours:* 10am to 10pm weekdays, 9.30 am to 7.30 pm weekends. PGA tuition, video coaching, putting green. Professional: Cormac McCarthy.

ORPINGTON. **Ruxley Park Golf Centre,** Sandy Lane, St Pauls Cray, Orpington BR5 3HY (01689 871490; Fax: 01689 891428). *Location:* off old A20 at Ruxley Corner. 24 bays, covered, floodlit, grassed. *Fees*: information not available. *Opening hours*: 9am to 10.30pm. *Eating facilities:* breakfast, lunch available, bar open all day. 18 hole, Par 71 golf course. *

RAMSGATE. **Manston Golf Centre,** Manston Road, Manston, Ramsgate CT12 5BE (01843 590005). *Location:* quarter of a mile east of Manston village. 20 floodlit bays, grassed and covered. New 9 hole course open to the public, 2505 yards. Par 33. *Fees:* Midweek 9 holes for £5.00, Weekends 9 holes for £7.50. *Eating facilities:* snacks, coffee, tea, etc. *Opening hours*: 8am till 9.30pm. Specialised teaching unit and short game practice area with real greens and bunkers. Absolute beginners welcome. Five PGA qualified teaching Professionals. Professional /Manager: Philip Sparks. website: www.manstongolf.com

RAMSGATE near. **Stonelees Golf Centre,** Ebbsfleet Lane, Near Ramsgate CT12 5DJ (01843 823133; Fax: 01843 850569). *Location:* near junction of A256 and B2048. 22 bay covered floodlit/carpeted range. Animated and jackpot range targets. 2 piece balls. Practice bunker, putting green and chipping area. *Fees*: 30 balls £1.30, 60 balls £2.60. Golf course club member discount. *Eating facilities:* licensed bar/restaurant. *Opening hours*: Centre - 8am to 10pm. Range - weekdays 10am to 10pm, weekends 9am to 10pm. Open every day except Christmas Day. PGA Approved teaching centre. Smart Golf simulator. Golf course members' competitions and social activities. Professional: David Bonthron. Secretary: Dr Peter Nicholson.

SITTINGBOURNE. **The Oast Golf Centre Ltd,** Church Road, Tonge, Sittingbourne ME9 9AR (01795 473527). *Location:* one mile north A2 between Faversham and Sittingbourne, take the turning to Tonge at Bapchild. 9-hole Par 3 course; 17 bay covered floodlit driving range. *Green Fees*: 9 holes £5.50, 18 holes £7.50. *Eating facilities:* sandwiches, rolls. *Visitors:* Welcome. Tuition available, golf shop. Two short mat bowls facility. *Society Meetings*: welcome. Professional: David Chambers. Secretary: Sally Chambers.
e-mail: mail@oastgolf.co.uk

SWANLEY. **Olympic Golf Range,** Beechenlea Lane, Swanley BR8 8DR (01322 615126). *Location*: Junction 3 M25, take Swanley exit then first on right. 17 covered, 8 open air bays, all floodlit. Putting green and practice bunker. *Fees*: 80 balls £3.30 peak; £2.60 off-peak. *Eating facilities:* bar, restaurant and sun terrace, all open to the public. *Opening hours*: 10am to 10pm. Extensive group tuition by PGA qualified staff. Also snooker centre, bowling green and conference rooms.

SWANLEY. **Pedham Place Golf Centre,** London Road, Swanley BR8 8PP (01322 867000; Fax: 01322 861646). *Location:* off Junction 3 of M25, A20 towards Brands Hatch. 40-bay floodlit driving range, putting green, practice facilities.18-hole and 9-hole golf courses. *Fees:* information not available. *Eating facilities:* bar; food available daily. *Opening hours:* weekdays 8am to 10pm, weekends 8am to 9pm.*
e-mail: golf@ppgc.co.uk
website: www.ppgc.co.uk

TONBRIDGE. **Hilden Golf Centre,** Rings Hill, Hildenborough, Tonbridge TN11 8LX (01732 833607; Fax: 01732 834484). *Location:* take exit off A21 for Tonbridge North/Hildenborough; take second turning right (Watts Cross Road), follow road past station to bottom of the hill, golf centre is on the left. 36 bay covered, floodlit and grassed driving range. *Fees:* information not available. *Eating facilities:* fully licensed bistro bar serving food until 9pm. *Visitors:* open to the public all day every day, memberships available. Health and leisure centre, creche (9.30am to 11.20am weekdays), French boules - Petanque. Teaching academy and large golf discount store stocking all the top brands at discount prices. *Society Meetings:* welcome. Professional: Nicky Way (01732 834404; Fax: 01732 834484). Secretary: Vicki Brett (01732 834404; Fax: 01732 834484).*

LANCASHIRE

BLACKBURN. **Blackburn Golf Centre and Driving Range,** Queens Park Playing Fields, Haslingden Road, Blackburn BB2 3HQ. *Location*: east side of Blackburn, one mile from town centre. 27 bay covered, floodlit range. Two bunkers and two greens for outdoor practice. *Fees*: information not available. *Opening hours*: 9am to 9pm weekdays; 9am to 5pm weekends. PGA Professional/Owner Mark McEvoy (01254 581996).

BLACKPOOL. **De Vere Herons' Reach Golf Club,** East Park Drive, Blackpool FY3 8LL (01253 766156; Fax: 01253 798800). Location: leave M55 at Junction 4, follow signs for Stanley Park and Victoria Hospital. Testing championship course with 10 man-made lakes - all year round play course. Herons Reach Course - 18 holes, 6461 yards, S.S.S. 72. 18 bay floodlit driving range, putting and chipping green. *Fees:* information not available. *Eating facilities:* spikes bar serving from 7am to 6pm daily, leisure bar and Cairolis open seven days. *Visitors:* welcome. Handicap Certificate required. 164 bedroomed hotel with extensive conference and banqueting facilities for up to 600 plus leisure complex. *Society Meetings:* welcome. Secretary: Mr P. Heaton. *

LEICESTERSHIRE

BOTCHESTON. **Forest Hill Golf Club,** Markfield Lane, Botcheston LE9 9FJ (01455 824800; Fax: 01455 828522). *Location*: M1 junction 22, take Leicester exit on A50, at first roundabout turn right towards Desford, 3 miles on left. 20 bay floodlit, grassed driving range. 18 hole course. *Fees*: information not available. *Eating facilities*: food available all day. *Society Meetings*: welcome Monday to Thursday. Professional: Phil Harness (01455 824800). Secretary: G.D. Hyde (01455 824800; Fax: 01455 828522). e-mail: gerry@hyde14.fsnet.co.uk

COALVILLE. **Discovery Golf & Leisure,** Ashby Road, Coalville LE67 3LG (01530 812332). *Location:* Follow the signs to Snibston Discovery Park at Coalville. 24 mat floodlit range with 18 covered bays and 6 grassed. *Eating facilities:* Licensed bar with bar food available most times. *Fees:* Very reasonable. *Opening hours:* Mon to Thurs - 12noon to 9.30pm, Fri - 12noon to 7pm, Sat & Sun - 9.30am to 7pm. Golf shop, tuition, repairs. 9 hole Par 3 golf course, Friendly and pleasant atmosphere.

LEICESTER. **Humberstone Golf Range,** Gipsy Lane, Leicester LE5 (0116 2740033; Fax: 01509 210185). *Location:* Leicester city location, opposite the Hamilton Retail Site, on ring road 5 minutes from A46, A47 and M1 link road. Part of Humberstone Golf Complex. 30 covered, floodlit and heated bays; two grassed. Automatic Power Tees, Video Bays, Multi-level mats. *Fees:* information not available. *Opening hours:* 7am to 9.30pm. *Eating facilities:* bar and restaurant. Tuition by PGA Professionals available.*

LINCOLNSHIRE

GRIMSBY. **Great Grimsby Golf Centre (incorporating Willow Park Golf Club),** Cromwell Road, Grimsby DN31 2BH (01472 250555; Fax: 01472 267447). *Location:* two miles from A180 and A46. Four-and-a-half miles from A16. Adjacent to Grimsby Leisure Centre/Auditorium. 27 bay covered, floodlit range. *Fees:* information not available. *Opening Hours*: 9am to 9.30 pm. *Society Meetings:* welcome by prior arrangement. 2500 sq ft golf superstore. All club repairs undertaken. Pay and Play and Membership available for Willow Park Golf Club. Reductions for Juniors and Seniors. European Tour Professional: Stephen Bennett. Secretary: B.J. Hoggett. *

STAMFORD. **Rutland County Golf Club,** Great Casterton, Stamford PE9 4AQ (01780 460330; Fax: 01780 460437). *Location:* on A1 two miles north of Stamford. Part of Rutland County Golf Club. 20 covered, grassed and floodlit bays; bunkers. 9 hole and 18 hole courses, chipping green, putting green. *Fees:* £2.00 per bucket of balls; two buckets for £3.00. *Opening hours:* 8am to 8pm. *Eating facilities:* restaurant and bar. Tuition available. Professional: Fred Fearn (01780 460239; Fax: 01780 460437). e-mail: info@rutlandcountygolf.freeserve.co.uk website: www.rutlandcountygolf.co.uk

WOODHALL SPA. **National Training Academy,** The Broadway, Woodhall Spa LN10 6PU (01526 351837; Fax: 01526 351817). *Location:* 19 miles South East of Lincoln. Part of Woodhall Spa Golf Club. 20 floodlit bays. *Fees:* information not available. *Opening hours:* 8.30am to 6.30pm Summer; 9am to 6.30pm Winter. *Eating facilities:* clubhouse. Grass tees and short game area available only with professional. Professional: Simon Williams (01526 351851; Fax: 01526 351817).*
e-mail: swilliams@englishgolfunion.org
booking@englishgolfunion.org
website: www.woodhallspagolf.com

GREATER MANCHESTER

KEARSLEY. **Kearsley Golf Driving Range,** Moss Lane, Kearsley, Bolton BL4 8SF (01204 575726). *Location:* Two miles north on A666 from Junction 16 on M60. Driving range, 10 covered, 15 grassed tees. Fees: £2.90 for 50 balls. *Opening hours:* weekdays 11am to 9.30pm; weekends 11am to 4pm. *Visitors:* welcome. Bar. Small 3 hole pitch and putt with practice sand bunker. Open to the public. Professional/Owner: E. Raymond Warburton PGA. 18 hole pay as you play course immediately adjacent.

ROCHDALE. **Castle Hawk Driving Range,** Chadwick Lane, Castleton, Rochdale OL11 3BY (01706 659995). *Location:* five minutes from exit 20 M62. 20 bay covered, floodlit, grassed driving range. 27 hole course. *Fees:* information not available. *Eating facilities:* restaurant available at club. *Opening hours:* 9am to 7.30pm. Professional tuition available. Professionals: Frank Accleton and Craig Bowring.*
e-mail: teeoff@castlehawk.co.uk
website: www.castlehawk.co.uk

MERSEYSIDE

MORETON. **Moreton Hills Golf Centre,** Tarran Way, Moreton, Wirral CH46 4TP (0151-677 6606; Fax: 0151-678 4359). *Location:* off Pasture Road, opposite Cadbury's factory. 30 bay covered floodlit driving range. *Fees:* information not available. *Eating facilities:* not available. *Opening hours:* 8am to 9pm. 6 hole golf course, 27 hole putting green, practice bunkers, golf shop, PGA Professionals, golf lessons in an indoor academy. *

NORTHAMPTONSHIRE

CHURCH BRAMPTON. **Brampton Heath Golf Centre,** Sandy Lane, Church Brampton, Northampton NN6 8AX (01604 843939; Fax: 01604 843885). *Location:* 2 miles north east of Kingsthorpe off A5009 (Welford Road). 18 bay covered floodlit driving range. *Fees:* information not available. *Eating facilities:* Spike bar/restaurant. *Opening hours:* Summer: weekdays 8am to 10pm. Weekends 7.30am to 9pm. Winter: 8am to 9pm. Weekends 8am to 8.30pm. Group/individual tuition available. 9 hole Par 3 academy course. Professional: Richard Hudson. Manager: Simon Lawrence (Fax: 01604 843885). *

NORTHAMPTON. **Delapre Golf Centre,** Eagle Drive, Nene Valley Way, Northampton NN4 7DU (01604 764036; Fax: 01604 706378). *Location:* two miles from Junction 15 M1 on A45 towards Wellingborough. 40 bay covered, floodlit range. 18 hole main course Par 70; 9 hole course; two Par 3 courses; pitch and putt course and putting greens. *Fees:* please visit website for information. *Eating facilities:* licensed bar and restaurant, coffee shop. *Opening hours:* 7am to 10.30pm daily. PGA qualified teaching staff available for private or group tuition; golf schools - video, etc. Professional: Greg Iron. Secretary/General Manager: Julie Howes 01604 764036.
website: www.jackbarker.com

NOTTINGHAMSHIRE

CALVERTON. **Ramsdale Park Golf Centre,** Oxton Road, Calverton NG14 6NV (01159 655600; Fax: 01159 654105). *Location:* off the A614 from Nottingham to Mansfield. 25 covered, floodlit bays; one bunker. *Fees:* £2.30 for 50 balls, £3.20 for 75 balls, £4.20 for 100 balls. *Opening hours:* 8.30am to 10pm. *Eating facilities:* full bar and catering. Tuition available. Professional: Rob Macey (01159 655600; Fax: 01159 654105).
e-mail: info@ramsdaleparkgc.co.uk

LONG EATON. **Trent Lock Golf Centre,** Lock Lane, Sawley, Long Eaton, Nottingham NG10 2FY (0115 946 4398; Fax: 0115 9461183). *Location:* 2 miles from M1 motorway Junction 24 or 25. 23 bay covered, floodlit driving range. 18-hole and 9 hole golf course. *Fees:* information not available. *Eating facilities:* à la carte restaurant, 200 capacity function suite, bar and bar food area. *Opening hours:* 8am until midnight. Professional tuition available, five PGA staff. River trips and walking available. Professional: Mark Taylor (01159 464398; Fax: 01159 461183). *

NEWARK. **Rufford Park Golf & Country Club,** Rufford Lane, Rufford, Newark (01623 825253; Fax: 01623 825254). *Location:* situated 400 yards off A614, two miles south of Ollerton Roundabout - map available on request. 16 bay floodlit driving range. 18 hole golf course. Practice greens. *Eating facilities:* large function suite and clubhouse available for social functions, restaurant with spectacular views offering a warm and genuine welcome to all who enjoy superb food. *Opening hours:* 7.30am to 9.00pm. Tuition available from both professionals. 10 buggies for hire. Corporate hospitality and Society days a speciality. Meeting rooms available. Professionals: James Thompson/John Vaughan. Secretary: Kay Whitehead.

NOTTINGHAM. **Cotgrave Place Golf and Country Club,** Cotgrave, Near Stragglethorpe, Radcliffe-on-Trent, Nottingham NG12 3HB (0115 933 3344; Fax: 0115 933 4567). *Location:* two minutes from A52 to Grantham from Nottingham city centre. 10 bay covered, floodlit range. *Fees:* information not available. *Eating facilities:* food available all day in the golf clubhouse. *Opening hours:* 8am to dusk seven days a week. Professional tuition. 36 holes of golf. Ideal for all standards. Buggies available. Golf clinics. Professional: Robert Smith (0115 933 3344; Fax: 0115 933 4567). General Manager: Mike Evans.
e-mail: cotgrave@americangolf.com

OXFORDSHIRE

DRAYTON. **Drayton Park Golf Course**, Steventon Road, Drayton, near Abingdon OX14 2RR (01235 528989). *Location:* A34 Didcot turn off, through Steventon to Drayton. 21 bay covered floodlit driving range. 18 hole Par 67 Golf Course. 9 hole Par 3 course. *Fees:* information not available. *Eating facilities:* full facilities available. *Opening hours:* 8am to 9pm. Fully qualified PGA Professional. Societies, groups and individual golfers welcome. Professional: Martin Morbey Secretary: Alan Davies.*

HORTON-CUM-STUDLEY. **Studley Wood Golf Club,** The Straight Mile, Horton-cum-Studley, Oxford OX33 1BF (01865 351122; Fax: 01865 351166). *Location:* 4 miles east of Oxford. 15 bay covered driving range. *Fees:* information not available. *Eating facilities:* full Clubhouse facilities; bar, bistro, function room. *Opening hours:* 9am to dusk. Four teaching professionals, short game academy, practice putting green. Eight target greens complete with bunkers, fully irrigated grass practice tee and target greens. Official Callaway Fitting Centre. Professional: Tony Williams. Competitions Secretary: Annie Anderson. Ladies' Competitions Secretary: Connie Brean.*
e-mail: admin@swgc.co.uk
website: www.studleywoodgolf.co.uk

OXFORD. **Oxford Golf Centre,** Binsey Lane, Botley Road, Oxford OX2 0EX (01865 721592). *Location:* within city boundary, past railway station, fourth turn on right going south. 26 bay covered floodlit driving range. *Fees:* information not available. *Eating facilities:* light refreshments. *Opening Hours:* weekdays 10am to 9pm, weekends 10am to 8pm. Two professionals, group and individual tuition available. Shop and video room. Professional: Simon Walker.*

OXFORD. **Waterstock Golf Club and Driving Range,** Thame Road, Waterstock, Oxford OX33 1HT (01844 338093). *Location:* on Junction 8 M40, one mile from Wheatley, four miles from Oxford, three miles from Thame. 22 bay covered, fully floodlit, open grassed driving range. *Fees:* 50 balls for £3.00, 100 balls for £5.00. Golf prices: 18 holes £21.00 weekdays, £26.00 weekends; 9 holes £11.50 weekdays, £14.50 weekends; day ticket £35.00 weekdays, £40 weekends; twilight £15.00 weekdays, £17.00 weekends. *Eating facilities:* full bar and catering facilities. *Opening hours:* weekdays 7.30am to 10pm, Saturdays 7am to 9pm, Sundays 7am to 8pm. Resident Professional offers tuition; large junior and adult golf academy; Pro shop with many demonstration clubs; 18-hole golf course; clubhouse with full facilities (societies and functions catered for).

Visit the **FHG** website
www.holidayguides.com
for details of the wide choice of accommodation featured in the full range of FHG titles

---

WITNEY. **Witney Lakes Golf Club,** Witney Lakes Resort, Downs Road, Witney OX29 0SY (01993 893011; Fax: 01993 778866). *Location:* two miles west of Witney town centre, turn into Downs Road. from B4095. 22-bay floodlit covered driving range. *Fees:* information not available. *Opening hours:* 7am to 9pm. *Eating facilities:* Greens Sportsbar and Greens Restaurant, Function/ Conference room. Health and fitness club includes swimming pool, gymnasium and sauna. Rawles Hairdresser, Retreat Spa, Beauty Salon, Creche facilities. Large well-stocked golf shop, 3 teaching Professionals. Head Professional: Adam Souter (01993 893011; Fax: 01993 778866). Secretary: (01993 893005; Fax: 01993 778866).
e-mail: golf@witney-lakes.co.uk
website: www.witney-lakes.co.uk

SHROPSHIRE

NEWPORT. **Aqualate Golf Centre,** Stafford Road, Newport TF10 9DB (01952 811699). *Location*: On A518 two miles east of Newport town centre and 400 yards from junction with A41. 20 floodlit bay driving range. *Fees*: 45 balls for £1.50, 90 balls for £2.50. *Opening hours*: weekdays 9.00am to 10.00pm, weekends and Bank Holidays 7.30am to 9.00pm. *Eating facilities*: coffee bar. PGA Professional tuition available by appointment - group and/or personal lessons. Golf Club Memberships available. 9 hole, 18 tee golf course - Pay and Play golf available. Visitors welcome. No handicap restrictions. Professional: Kevin Short. Director: H. Brian Dawes.

OSWESTRY. **Oswestry Golf Driving Range,** Mile End, Oswestry SY11 4JF (01691 671246; Fax: 01691 670580). *Location:* signposted "Mile End Golf Club" off A5, one mile south-east of Oswestry. 11 bay covered, floodlit driving range. *Fees:* £1.00 for 30 balls. *Eating facilities:* bar/catering available to members and green fee paying visitors who adhere to dress code. *Opening hours*: Summer: 8.00am until dusk daily; Winter: 8.00am to 8pm weekdays, 8.00am to 6pm weekends. Group bookings welcome. Many "Try before you buy" demo days. Professional tuition available, fully stocked Pro shop. Par 71 18 hole golf course. Professional: Scott Carpenter (01691 671246). Proprietor: Richard Thompson.
website: www.mileendgolfclub.co.uk

TELFORD. **The Shropshire,** Granville Park, Muxton, Telford TF2 8PQ (01952 677800; Fax: 01952 677622). *Location:* Take B5060 off M54/A5 heading for Donnington. Take third exit at Granville roundabout. 30 bay covered, floodlit driving range. *Fees*: information not available. *Eating facilities:* Greenkeeper Bar open from 8am serving food. *Opening hours*: 7am to 10pm. 27 hole golf course, 12 hole Par 3 course, 2 putting greens, retail shop. Entertainment nights, seven function suites, and conference facilities. *Society Meetings*: welcome. Professional: Andrew Holmes (07866 721956). *

SOMERSET

BRISTOL. **Mendip Spring Golf Club,** Honeyhall Lane, Congresbury, Bristol BS49 5JT (01934 852322). *Location*: between A370 and A38. 15 bay covered, floodlit driving range with a grassed area. Practice bunker and putting green. *Fees*: information not available. *Eating facilities:* none at range but restaurant/bar facilities available at the clubhouse. *Opening hours*: 7.30am to 8pm. Tuition available from our team of professionals. Buggies for hire April to September. There is also an active members' social club. Societies welcome by arrangement.

LANGPORT. **Long Sutton Golf Club,** Langport TA10 9JU (01458 241017; Fax: 01458 241022). *Location:* three miles north of A303 from Podimore roundabout on A372 to Langport and Taunton. 18 hole golf course and large practice putting green. 12 bay covered, floodlit, grassed range. *Green Fees:* 18 holes weekdays £18.00; weekends £25.00. 9 holes weekdays £10.00; weekends £12.50. *Eating facilities:* snacks in bar, restaurant. *Opening hours*: 8am till dusk. Tuition from Andrew Hayes by appointment. Secretary: T. Tulk.

TAUNTON. **Oake Manor Driving Range,** Oake Manor Golf Club and Range, Oake, Taunton TA4 1BA (01823 461993). *Location:* Junction 26 M5, take A38 to Taunton, follow signs to Oake, only seven minutes from motorway. 11 bay covered range. *Fees:* information not available. *Eating facilities:* adjacent bar/lounge, food available seven days all day long. *Opening hours*: 8am to dark. *Visitors:* welcome. 18 hole course, tuition by appointment, new golf academy and 3 practice holes; Pro shop, 4 PGA Professionals; club fitting centre - free equipment advice service and demo clubs.*
e-mail: golf@oakemanor.com
website: www.oakemanor.com

TICKENHAM. **Tickenham Golf Club,** Clevedon Road, Tickenham BS21 6RY (01275 856626). *Location:* M5 Junction 20, follow Nailsea signs, Centre on left after Tickenham village. 9 hole course, 24 bay covered, floodlit driving range. Power tees. Practice bunkers. *Fees:* 40 balls for £2.00. Members' discount half-price. *Eating facilities:* 19th hole licensed bar, hot and cold food. *Opening hours:* 8.30am to 8.30pm daily. Professionals available for tuition, group lessons, etc.

STAFFORDSHIRE

BURTON-ON-TRENT. **The Craythorne,** Craythorne Road, Stretton, Burton-on-Trent DE13 0AZ (01283 564329). *Location:* Stretton, one and a half miles north of Burton – A5121/A38 Junction. 14 bay covered floodlit driving range. *Fees*: £1.00 per bucket. *Eating facilities:* 80 cover restaurant open to public every day, two bars. *Opening Hours*: weekdays 7.30am to 10pm. *Society Meetings:* welcome, rates available. Conference and function facilities available; discounts at local hotels. Professional (PGA): Steve Hadfield. Managing Director: A.A. Wright.
website: www.craythorne.co.uk

SUFFOLK

HALESWORTH. **Halesworth Golf Club,** Bramfield Road, Halesworth IP19 9XA (01986 875567; Fax: 01986 874565). *Location:* A12, A144 to and through Bramfield, over crossroads and then first right. 13 bays floodlit (10 covered). *Fees*: basket of balls £1.00. *Opening hours:* dawn until dusk (9pm Winter months). Professional tuition and fully equipped Pro shop; 27-hole golf course, putting and chipping greens. Professional: Simon Harrison. Secretary: Mr D. Cotton.

IPSWICH. **Fynn Valley Golf Club,** Witnesham, Ipswich IP6 9JA (01473 785463; Fax: 01473 785632). *Location:* two miles due north of Ipswich on B1077. 23 bays floodlit (10 covered). Practice green and bunker. 9 hole par 3 course. 18 hole course. *Fees*: Buckets of range balls from £1.50. *Opening hours*: 9am to 9pm Monday to Friday and 8am to 6pm Saturday and Sunday. *Eating facilities:* meals available every lunchtime. Evening meals Tuesday to Saturday. *Societies:* welcome. Professional tuition, group lessons, etc. Golf shop. Golf range membership available. Professionals: Danny Barton, Paul Wilby, Alex Lucas, Simon Dainty. Secretary: A. Tyrrell.
e-mail: enquiries@fynn-valley.co.uk
website: www.fynn-valley.co.uk

WOODBRIDGE. **Seckford Golf Club,** Seckford Hall Road, Great Bealings, Near Woodbridge IP13 6NT (01394 388000; Fax: 01394 382818). *Location:* signposted from A12 near Woodbridge. 12 bay fixed mats driving range. *Fees:* information not available. *Eating facilities:* fully licensed bar and restaurant. *Opening Hours:* dawn - dusk. Golf lessons available from qualified PGA staff using GASP video analysis system as seen on Sky TV. Hire equipment available. Professionals: Simon Jay, Nic Grundtvig.

For full details of clubs and courses, plus convenient accommodation
www.uk-golfguide.com

SURREY

CARSHALTON. **Oaks Sports Centre,** Woodmansterne Road, Carshalton SM5 4AN (020 8643 8363; Fax: 020 8770 7303). Covered, grassed and floodlit bays with bunkers. 18 hole and 9 hole courses. *Fees:* £1.50 per bucket of balls. *Opening hours:* 9am to 9.30pm. *Eating facilities:* Sunday carvery, cafeteria and bar. Pay and play and membership available. PGA Professional teaching. Professional: Michael Pilkington (020 8770 7303). e-mail: golf@oaks.sagehost.co.uk
website: www.oaksportscentre.co.uk

CHESSINGTON **Chessington Golf Centre,** Garrison Lane, Chessington KT9 2LW (020 8391 0948). *Location:* off A243, 500 yards from Chessington World of Adventure. Opposite Chessington South Station, Junction 9 M25. Covered, floodlit range, 18 bays. 9 hole course. Private and group tuition available. *Fees:* information not available. *Opening hours:* 8am to 10pm. *Eating facilities:* bar and catering. Tuition, public course.

COBHAM. **Silvermere Driving Range,** Redhill Road, Cobham KT11 1EF (01932 584300; Fax: 01932 584301). *Location:* half-a-mile from Junction 10 on M25 at A3; 30 minutes from central London. Covered, floodlit range, 34 bays. Public golf course. *Fees:* information not available. *Eating facilities:* full service available. *Opening hours:* 8.30am to 9.30pm. Tuition available. Telephone bookings taken. Administrator: Claire Wheeley (01932 584300; Fax: 01932 584301).*

CROYDON. **Croydon Driving Range Ltd,** 175 Long Lane, Addiscombe, Croydon CR0 7TE (020 8656 1690; Fax: 020 8654 7859). *Location:* on A222 about two miles east of Croydon. 24 bay covered, floodlit, driving range. *Fees:* £3.50 for 56 balls, £6.50 for 112 balls. *Eating facilities:* snacks/coffee. *Opening hours:* weekdays 9am to 10pm, weekends 9am to 8pm. *Visitors:* very welcome at all times, open to the public. Lessons from 5 PGA qualified instructors, and club repairs available. Professional: Bill Woodman (020 8656 1690; Fax: 020 8654 7859).

ESHER. **Sandown Golf Centre,** More Lane, Esher KT10 8AN (01372 461234). *Location:* signposted from A3, centre of Sandown Park Racecourse. 33 bay covered floodlit driving range, plus grassed area. Three golf courses. *Fees:* on application. *Eating facilities:* bar and restaurant. *Opening hours:* 8am to 10pm weekdays; 7am to 8pm weekends. Cranfield Golf Acadamy *Visitors:* visitors and societies welcome. General Manager: David Parr (01372 461234; Fax: 01372 461203).*

GODALMING. **Broadwater Park Golf Club,** Guildford Road, Farncombe, Near Godalming GU7 3BU (01483 429955). 16 bay covered, floodlit driving range. *Fees:* information not available. *Eating facilities:* licensed bar. *Opening hours:* 8am to 10pm. Professional, tuition and 9 hole Par 3 course. Professional: Kevin Milton.*

LEATHERHEAD. **Pachesham Park Golf Centre,** Oaklawn Road, Leatherhead KT22 0BT (01372 843453). *Location:* half-a-mile outside Leatherhead, just off A244. Junction 9 M25. 33 bay covered floodlit range with Power Tees. 9 hole golf course. *Fees:* 25 balls £2.00, 50 balls £3.50, 75 balls £4.50, 125 balls £6.00. Discount range ball cards available. *Eating facilities:* available. *Opening hours:* April to October, weekdays 9am to 10pm, weekends 9am to 9pm; November to March 9am to 8pm. PGA teaching professionals. Club membership also available.

NEWDIGATE. **Rusper Golf Club and Driving Range,** Rusper Road, Newdigate RH5 5BX (01293 871871). *Location:* Dorking-Horsham A24, Beare Green roundabout, left to Newdigate, in village turn right to Rusper, club approximately one mile on right hand side. 12 bay covered driving range. 18 hole golf course. *Fees:* please contact the club. *Eating facilities:* fresh food and daily specials available every day; bar. *Opening hours:* dawn till dusk. Qualified professional tuition by arrangement; club hire. Membership available. Professional: Janice Arnold. Secretary: Mrs Jill Thornhill.
e-mail: jill@ruspergolfclub.co.uk
website: www.ruspergolfclub.co.uk

NEW MALDEN. **World of Golf at Beverley Park,** Beverley Way, New Malden KT3 4PH (020 8949 9200; Fax: 020 8336 2856). *Location:* leave the A3 northbound at B282, follow sign to A3 London, entrance on left before rejoining A3. Southbound exit A3 at A298, follow A3 London from roundabout. 60 bay floodlit, covered driving range. Golf School, two coaching studios, floodlit putting green and bunker. *Fees:* information not available. *Eating facilities:* cafe/bar. *Opening hours:* 8am to 11pm daily. JJB Golf Store, club repair service.
website: www.worldofgolf.biz

OLD WOKING. **Hoebridge Golf Centre,** Woking Road, Old Woking GU22 8JH (01483 722611; Fax: 01483 740369). *Location:* on outskirts of Woking on the Woking to Byfleet Road. 36 bay covered, floodlit range. Two 18 hole courses and 9 hole course. *Fees:* information not available. *Eating facilities:* full catering available. *Opening hours:* 8am to 11pm. Individual and group tuition. Fully equipped video bay available. *Society Meetings:* welcome. Professional: Tim Powell. Centre Manager: Patrick Dawson. *

REDHILL. **Redhill Golf Centre,** Canada Avenue, Redhill RH1 5BF (01737 770204). *Location:* in the grounds of East Surrey Hospital, one-and-a-half miles south of Redhill. 37 bay covered, floodlit driving range. 9-hole golf course (unlimited golf from £9.00). *Fees:* information not provided. *Eating facilities:* available at Causeway Pub. *Opening hours:* 8am to 10pm; weekends 9pm. Sponsored by Golf Foundation to give free junior coaching. Lessons available from PGA qualified instructor. Private and group tuition available. Repairs service. Hot and cold drinks available. *Society Meetings:* welcome. Professional: Mike Lovegrove. Secretary: Steven Furlonger.

EAST SUSSEX

HELLINGLY. **Wellshurst Golf and Country Club,** North Street, Hellingly BN27 4EE (01435 813456). *Location:* two miles from the A22 London to Eastbourne Road on A267. 16 bay covered, floodlit range. 18 hole course, two sand bunker bays. *Fees:* £2.00 per large bucket of quality two piece balls. *Eating facilities:* full bar and catering facilities available at all times. *Opening hours:* 7.30am to 9.30pm. Full leisure and conference facilities. Full professional staff for lessons, well stocked pro shop.

HORAM. **Horam Park Golf Course and Floodlit Driving Range,** Chiddingly Road, Horam TN21 0JJ (01435 813477, Fax: 01435 813677). *Location:* 13 miles north of Eastbourne, 7 miles east of Uckfield. Covered, floodlit, Astroturf range. 15 bays. Pitch and putt course, large putting green. *Fees:* £2.50 per large basket of approximately 60 balls. Call for discount times/happy hours. Golf prices 9 holes £11.00 weekdays, £11.50 weekends; 18 holes £16.50 weekdays, £18.00 weekends. Call for early bird and twilight rates. *Eating facilities:* restaurant bar and spike bar, seven days, children welcome. PGA golf Professionals, lessons and tuition available. Golf shop. Professional: Giles Velvick.

SEDLESCOMBE. **Sedlescombe Golf Club,** Kent Street, Near Battle TN33 0SD (01424 871700). *Location:* 1066 country, five miles north of Hastings on the A21, three miles from Battle. Home of The James Andrews School of Golf. 24 bay floodlit driving range, 14 covered. Residential golf school with two, three and five day intensive courses for all ages and abilities. Five PGA Professionals. Facilities include indoor video and computer analysis centre, on-site hotel, golf shop and tennis courts. *Eating facilities:* Greens bar and restaurant open seven days. *Opening hours:* 7am to 9.30pm. Group coaching and individual lessons available daily, Residential Golf School (01424 871717). Head Professional: James Andrews (01424 871701).

CHICHESTER. **Chichester Golf Club,** Hunston Village, Chichester PO20 6AX (01243 528999). *Location:* take B2145 off A27 to Selsey, golf club is on the left after Hunston Village. 27 bay covered, floodlit, grassed driving range. Two 18 hole golf courses, 9 hole Par 3 minigolf. *Fees:* information not available. *Eating facilities:* fully licensed clubhouse. *Opening hours:* 8.30am to 9.30pm. *Society Meetings:* welcome seven days a week. Video teaching academy. Membership available. Professional:John Slinger.*

CRAWLEY. **Gatwick Manor Golf Club,** Gatwick Manor Hotel, London Road, Lowfield Heath, Crawley RH10 2ST (01293 526301 (Hotel); 01293 538587 (Club)). *Location:* A23 Crawley to Gatwick Airport on London Road on right. 9 grassed tees. *Fees:* information not available. *Eating facilities:* hotel facilities at Gatwick Manor. *Opening hours:* 9am to 8.00pm seven days a week. *

CRAWLEY. **Tilgate Forest Golf Centre,** Titmus Drive, Tilgate, Crawley RH10 5EU (01293 530103; Fax: 01293 523478). 35 floodlit bays. *Fees:* £2.50 per bucket of balls. *Opening hours:* 7am to 9.15pm. *Eating facilities:* bar and restaurant. Tuition, practice area, putting green etc. Professional: Sean Trussell (01293 530103).
e-mail: tilgate@glendale-services.co.uk.

RUSTINGTON. **Rustington Golf Centre,** Golfers Lane, Angmering, BN16 4NB (01903 850790; Fax: 01903 850982). *Location:* on A259 at Rustington, between Worthing and Littlehampton. 9 holes with 18 tees, 5735 yards. Par 70. 9 hole par 3 course, 3 hole golf academy course, putting green, 30 bay floodlit driving range. Two golf academies work from the facility. *Fees:* information not provided. *Opening hours:* 8.30am - 9.00pm, 7 days a week. *Eating facilities:* coffee shop and licensed bar. *Visitors:* welcome at all times. Two golf academies available for tuition of all standards. *Society Meetings:* societies and corporate days welcome. Centre Manager: Gary Salt (01903 850790; Fax: 01903 850982).

WEST SUSSEX

BURGESS HILL. **The Burgess Hill Golf Academy,** Cuckfield Road, Burgess Hill RH15 8RE (01444 258585; Fax: 01444 247318). *Location:* on the B2036 north of Burgess Hill, on the Burgess Hill to Cuckfield road. 28 bay undercover, grassed, floodlit driving range. 9 hole short course. New practice bunker, synthetic grass tees (first in UK), Augusta style putting green. *Fees:* information not available. *Eating facilities:* Bar and restaurant. Tea and coffee. *Opening Hours:* seven days a week 8am to 9pm. Well stocked golf shop. PGA teaching academy including video tuition. Professional: Mark Collins. Secretary: (01444 258585; Fax: 01444 247318).

TYNE & WEAR

NEWCASTLE-UPON-TYNE. **Parklands,** High Gosforth Park, Newcastle-upon-Tyne NE3 5HQ (0191-236 4480). *Location:* off A1 for Gosforth Park. 45 bay covered, floodlit range. *Fees:* information not available. *Eating facilities:* bar and restaurant. *Opening hours:* 8am to 10.30pm. Professional tuition, 18 hole golf course, 9 hole pitch and putt. Societies welcome at weekends.. Ring for package details.*

www.uk-golfguide.com

WASHINGTON. **George Washington Golf and Country Club,** Stone Cellar Road, High Usworth, District 12, Washington NE37 1PH (0191 4029988; Fax: 0191 4151166). *Location:* just off A1(M), take A194 then exit A195 Washington. 21 bay covered, floodlit, grassed range. 9 hole pitch and putt. *Fees*: information not available. *Eating facilities:* Bunkers Bar – hours vary, serves snacks. Buffets etc by arrangement. Tuition available. Golf buggies. Leisure club with sauna, pool, solarium, multi gym, spa and squash. Professional: Graeme Robinson (0191 417 8346).

WARWICKSHIRE

COVENTRY. **John Reay Golf Centres,** Sandpits Lane, Keresley, Coventry CV7 8NJ (024 7633 3920). *Location:* three miles from Coventry city centre along A51 Tamworth Road. Covered, floodlit driving range. 60 bays. Golf club repair facility. Teaching professionals using latest video techniques. *Fees*: information not available. *Opening hours:* daily 9am to 10pm. *Eating facilities:* Hogan's Bar & Bistro open every day. *Visitors:* open to the public. Large Golf Shop with all the leading brands of golf equipment. Professional: John Reay (024 7633 3920/3405). website: www.johnreaygolf.com

WARWICK. **Warwick Golf Centre,** The Racecourse, Warwick CV34 6HW (01926 494316). *Location:* A46 off the M40 (middle of Warwick). 25 bay covered, floodlit range. 9 hole golf course (Par 34) open to the public. *Fees*: information not available. *Eating facilities:* bar only. *Opening hours*: driving range 10am to 9pm, 9 hole golf course 8am to 9pm. Professional tuition. Professional: Phil Sharp. Secretary: Roma Dunkley.

WEST MIDLANDS

DUDLEY near. **Swindon Ridge Golf Driving Range, Shop & Golf Club,** Bridgnorth Road, Swindon, Near Dudley DY3 4PU (01902 896191). *Location:* B4176 Bridgnorth/Dudley Road, three miles from Himley A449 Junction. 27 bay floodlit range (22 covered). *Fees*: information not available. *Opening hours:* 9am to 9.30pm weekdays, 8.30am to 6pm weekends. *Eating facilities:* licensed bar and restaurant. 18 hole private golf club on site plus 9 hole Par 3. Snooker table in bar.*

SUTTON COLDFIELD. **Lea Marston Hotel & Leisure Complex,** Haunch Lane, Lea Marston, Sutton Coldfield B76 0BY (01675 470468; Fax: 01675 470871). *Location:* From Junction 9 of M42, take A4097 towards Kingbury for just over one mile, take second right into Haunch Lane, right after 150 yards approximately. 27 floodlit bays. 9 hole Marston Lakes Par 31 and 9 hole Par 3 pay and play course. *Fees:* information not available. *Eating facilities:* Adderley Restaurant, Sportsman's Lounge Bar and Conservatories. *Visitors:* welcome. Professional tuition available. Golf simulator with 20 courses including Valderrama and the Belfry's Brabazon. Fully stocked golf shop. 83 bedroom hotel, leisure facilities including indoor swimming pool.*

WOLVERHAMPTON. **Three Hammers Golf Complex,** Old Stafford Road, Coven WV10 7PP (01902 790428). *Location:* Junction 2 M54 north on A449, one mile on right. 24 covered floodlit bays. *Fees*: information not provided. *Eating facilities:* bookings taken from 10.30am, details on (01902 791917). *Opening hours*: weekdays 9.30am to 10pm, weekends 9.30am to 9pm. 18 hole Par 3 course, two teaching Professionals.

WILTSHIRE

CALNE. **Bowood Golf & Country Club,** Derry Hill, Calne SN11 9PQ (01249 822228; Fax: 01249 822218). *Location:* located off A4 between Calne and Chippenham. Signposted from Junction 17. Part of Bowood Golf & Country Club, a championship course on the beautiful Bowood Estate. 10 covered, floodlit bays. *Fees:* £3.00 per bucket of balls (members £2.00). *Opening hours:* telephone for details. *Eating facilities:* conservatory serving lunches and snacks; bar. Tuition, academy course, putting green. Professional: Max Taylor (01249 822228; Fax: 01249 822218).
e-mail: golfclub@bowood.org
website: www.bowood.org.

SALISBURY: **Hamptworth Academy,** Hamptworth Road, Hamptworth, Near Salisbury SP5 2DU (01794 390155; Fax: 01794 390022). *Location:* halfway between Southampton and Salisbury, one mile off A36. 3 covered bays, 8 grassed bays, bunkers. 18 hole golf course, putting green. *Fees:* £2.00 for 40 balls; 10 credits for £15.00. *Opening hours:* 8am till dusk. *Eating facilities:* all-day menu in clubhouse. Tuition, available. Professional: Mark White (01794 390155; Fax: 01794 390022).
e-mail: info@hamptworthgolf.co.uk
website: www.hamptworthgolf.co.uk

SWINDON. **Broome Manor Golf Complex,** Pipers Way, Swindon SN3 1RG (01793 532403). *Location:* two miles from Junction 15 of M4, follow signs for Golf Complex. 34 bays, 27 covered, seven uncovered, floodlit range (astroturf). *Fees*: information not available. *Eating facilities:* full service available. *Opening hours*: Summer 8am to 10pm, Winter 8am to 9pm. Five PGA professionals - group and individual lessons always available. 18 hole courses, 9 hole course and nearby pitch and putt course. Restaurant available for functions and conferences.*

Please mention THE GOLF GUIDE when you enquire about clubs or accommodation

WESTBURY near. **Thoulstone Park Golf Club and Driving Range,** Chapmanslade, Near Westbury BA13 4AQ (01373 832825; Fax: 01373 832821). *Location:* three miles north-west of Warminster on A36. 20 bay covered, floodlit range. *Fees:* information not available. *Eating facilities:* Clubhouse open 11am to 3.30pm for food and 11.00am to 9.00pm for drinks. *Opening hours:* weekdays and Saturdays 8am to 9pm, Sundays 8am to 6pm. Professional available for lessons, Pro shop (8.00am to 7.30pm weekdays and Saturdays; 7.30am to 6.00pm Sundays). 18 hole course. Professional: T. Isaacs (01373 832808). *

WORCESTERSHIRE

REDDITCH. **The Abbey Hotel, Golf and Country Club,** Hither Green Lane, Dagnell End Road, Redditch B98 9BE (01527 406500; Fax: 01527 406514). *Location:* leave M42 at Junction 2, take A441 towards Redditch, at end of dual carriageway turn left still keeping on the A441, at petrol station turn left into Dagnell End Road (A4101) - hotel and golf club are approximately 600 yards on right. 12 bay range. *Fees:* information not available. *Eating facilities:* extended Bramblings Restaurant and Tawnys Bar. *Opening hours:* 7:00am until 8:30pm in summer, 7:30am until dusk in winter. Fully stocked golf shop. Golf & Leisure Complex . Professional tuition available. Professional: Rob Davies.*

WORCESTER. **Bromsgrove Golf Centre,** Stratford Road, Bromsgrove B60 1LD (01527 575886; Course Reception: 01527 570505; Conference & Restaurant 01527 579179). *Location:* easily located at the roundabout junction of the A38 and A448, one mile from Bromsgrove town centre. Five minutes' drive from Junctions 4 and 5 M5 and Junction 1 M42 (exit west bound only). 35 bay floodlit driving range, new teaching studio with state-of-the-art computerised video systems. Large multi-level putting green. *Golf and Professional Fees:* wide range of tuition available with resident P.G.A. professionals, 'on' course, video tuition etc - tuition fees list available on request. 18 hole "Pay and Play" course (Hawtree and Son design). Large fully stocked Terry Matthews Golf Shop. *Eating facilities:* clubhouse with full bar and restaurant facilities. Bar snacks or 'Daily Specials' available in spacious bar/lounge. Sky TV. *Opening hours:* weekdays 8am to 9pm, Saturdays, 7am to 9pm, Sundays 7am to 5pm (Sunday lunch 12 noon to 4pm).

WORCESTER. **Ravenmeadow Golf Club,** Hindlip Lane, Claines, Worcester WR3 8SA (01905 458876; Fax: 01905 458876). *Location:* Junction 6 M5 motorway, take A449 signed Kidderminster, leave at Blackpole exit. At main road turn right, first left into Hindlip Lane, half mile on left. Part of Ravenmeadow Golf Club. 4 grass, 4 outside mats, 10 covered tees. 5 automatic tees. Putting green, chipping green, 9 hole pitch and putt course; finest practice facilities in the country. *Fees:* £3.00 per basket of balls. *Opening hours:* 8am till dusk. *Eating facilities:* bar, snack meals. Professional: Mark Slater (01905 756665).

WORCESTER. **Worcester Golf Range,** Weir Lane, Lowerwick WR2 4AY (01905 748788/421213). *Location:* Junction 7 M5 off Malvern Road next to Lowerwick Swimming Pool. 26 bay covered, floodlit, golf range. 9 hole pitch and putt. *Fees:* information not available. *Eating facilities:* cold drinks, free coffee, confectionery and sandwiches. *Opening hours:* 9.30am to 10pm Monday - Friday, 9.30am to 6pm Saturday and Sunday. Three fully qualified PGA professionals always available for teaching. Swimming pool next door. Professional: Mark Dove.*

EAST YORKSHIRE

BEVERLEY. **Cherry Burton Golf Club,** Leconfield Lane, Cherry Burton, Beverley HU17 7RB (Tel & Fax: 01964 550924). *Location:* off the B1248 3 miles north of Beverley. 6 bay covered, grassed, floodlit driving range. One bunker. *Fees:* information not available. *Eating facilities:* licensed bar with snacks. *Opening hours:* dawn to dusk. James Calam Golf Academy. Professional: James Calam (01964 550924 or 07979 596134; Fax: 01964 550924). *
website: www.cherryburtongolfclub.co.uk

SCUNTHORPE. **Grange Park Golf Range,** Butterwick Road, Messingham, Scunthorpe DN17 3PP (01724 764478). *Location:* five miles south of Scunthorpe between Messingham and East Butterwick, four miles south of Junction 3 of M180. 20 bay covered floodlit driving range. 9 hole pay and play course on site. *Fees:* information not available. *Opening hours:* 9am to 9.30pm weekdays, 9am to 8.30pm weekends. Large Pro shop and exclusive golf ladies' wear shop. Smart Golf indoor simulator. Professional available.*

NORTH YORKSHIRE

HARROGATE. **Rudding Park Golf,** Rudding Park, Harrogate HG3 1JH (01423 872100; Fax: 01423 873011). *Location:* lies just off the A658 linking the A61 from Leeds to the A59 York Road. Parkland course designed to USGA specifications. 18 holes, 6883 yards. Par 72. 18 bay floodlit driving range with four professionals. *Fees:* £1.00 for a basket of 20 balls. *Eating facilities:* Clubhouse open all day everyday, spike bar. *Visitors:* welcome at all times, must have a Handicap Certificate. Shop and buggies available all year round with all year weather buggy tracks, caddies on request. Society and corporate days welcome. Professional: Mark Moore (01423 873400). e-mail: golf.admin@ruddingpark.com
website: www.ruddingparkgolf.com

THE APPEARANCE OF AN ASTERISK (*) AT THE END OF A CLUB OR COURSE ENTRY INDICATES THAT UP-TO-DATE INFORMATION HAS NOT BEEN SUPPLIED

602 DRIVING RANGES

THE GOLF GUIDE 2006

NORTHALLERTON. **Romanby Driving Range,** Romanby Golf Course, Yafforth Road, Northallerton DL7 0PE (01609 778855; Fax: 01609 779084). *Location:* on the North West of Northallerton, easy road access. Part of Romanby Golf Course Ltd. 12 covered, grassed, floodlit bays. Practice bunkers. Academy Course. *Fees:* information not available. *Opening hours:* 8am to 9pm; closes 6pm weekends. *Eating facilities:* Country Club open daily from 8am till 9pm; full bar and restaurant facilities. Lessons available; shop. Full disabled facilities. Professional: Tim Jenkins (01609 779990; Fax: 01609 771193).*
e-mail: info@timjenkinsgolf.co.uk
         mark@romanby.com
website: www.romanby.com

SALTBURN. **Hunley Hall Golf Club & Hotel,** Brotton, Saltburn TS12 2QQ (01287 676216; Fax: 01287 678250). *Location:* off A174 at St. Margarets Way in Brotton. Signposted through housing estate, approximately half-a-mile to club. 12 bay floodlit driving range, large practice and chipping area. Picturesque 27 hole coastal courses adjacent to Heritage Coast. *Fees:* £3.50 for 90 balls (members), £4.00 for 90 balls (non members). *Eating facilities:* excellent facilities including two restaurants, lounge bar, spike bar, golfers' bar; quality food available all day, every day. *Opening hours:* Summer - 8am to 8pm, 6pm weekends and Bank Holidays. Winter - 8am till dusk, floodlit Wednesday, Thursday and Friday to 7.30pm. Two Star Hotel on site. Club hire, buggy hire and tuition available. *Society Meetings:* welcome Monday to Saturday, packages available. Golfing Holidays available. Professional: Andrew Brook (Tel & Fax: 01287 677444). Secretary: Liz Lillie (01287 676216; Fax: 01287 678250)*.
e-mail: enquiries@hunleyhall.co.uk
e-mail: andy@asbrook-golf.fsnet.co.uk
website: www.hunleyhall.co.uk

SOUTH YORKSHIRE

DONCASTER. **Bawtry Golf Club Driving Range,** Cross Lane, Austerfield, Bawtry, Doncaster DN10 6RF (01302 710841). *Location:* A614 Doncaster to Blyth Roundabout on the A1. Adjacent to the new Robin Hood Doncaster Airport. 10 covered, grassed, floodlit bays; bunkers. *Fees:* information not available. *Opening hours:* 8am to 8pm. *Eating facilities:* full clubhouse facilities. Tuition available. Professional: Mark Cunningham (01302 710841).*
e-mail: enquiries@bawtrygolfclub.co.uk
website: www.bawtrygoldclub.co.uk

SHEFFIELD. **Concord Park Driving Range,** Concord Park Golf Club, Shiregreen, Sheffield S5 6AE (Tel & Fax: 0114 257 7378). *Location:* next to Concord Park Golf Club. 30 covered, floodlit bays; 2 bunkers. Putting green. *Fees:* information not available. *Opening hours:* 7am to 9pm. *Eating facilities:* restaurant in the clubhouse, also fully licensed bar. Tuition available. Professional: Warren Allcroft (07968 618766).*

SHEFFIELD. **Rother Valley Golf Centre,** Mansfield Road, Wales Bar, Sheffield S26 5PQ (0114 247 3000; Fax: 0114 247 6000). *Location:* Junction 31 off M1 motorway, follow signs to Rother Valley Country Park. 25 covered, floodlit bays; bunkers. *Fees:* information not available. *Opening hours:* 9am to 9pm (10pm in Summer). *Eating facilities:* bar and restaurant. Professional: Jason Ripley.*
e-mail: rother-jackbarker@btinternet.com
website: www.jackbarker.com

WEST YORKSHIRE

BRADFORD. **Shay Grange Golf Centre,** Long Lane, off Bingley Road, Bradford BD9 6RX (01274 491945). *Location:* take the A650 Bradford to Bingley road, turn left at Cottingley lights, the Centre will be found on the left after two miles. 32 bay covered, floodlit, grassed range. *Fees:* information not available. *Eating facilities:* fully licensed bar and catering facilities. *Opening hours:* weekdays 9am to 9pm, weekends and Bank Holidays 7am to 9pm. 9 hole (Par 29) course, Golf Academy, all weather putting green, sand bunker, grass short game area.Tuition. Golf clinics - Juniors, Senior Citizens, Ladies. Golf shop staffed by qualified PGA professionals. Manager: T. Grunwell.*

BRIGHOUSE. **Willow Valley Golf and Country Club,** Highmoor Lane, off Walton Lane, Clifton, Brighouse HD6 4JB (01274 878624; Fax: 01274 852805). *Location:* Junction 25 off M62 to Brighouse A644, right at roundabout A643, 2 miles on right. 24 bay, covered, floodlit, grassed driving range. 18 hole and 9 hole courses. *Fees:* information not available. *Eating facilities:* fully licensed bar and catering. Junior Golf Foundation courses and 3 hole floodlit golf course. Professional: Julian Haworth.
website: www.wvgc.co.uk

HUDDERSFIELD. **Stadium Golf Driving Range,** The Alfred Macalpine Stadium, Stadium Way, Huddersfield HD1 6PG (01484 452564; Fax: 01484 452540). *Location:* off A62 centre of Huddersfield, signposted the Macalpine Stadium. 30 bay covered, floodlit driving range, range grassed. *Fees:* information not available. *Eating facilities:* snack bar serving sandwiches, etc., licensed bar. *Opening hours:* weekdays 9am to 10pm (last balls 9.30pm). weekends 9am to 7pm (last balls 6.30pm). State of the art Panasonic split screen video lessons with PGA qualified instructors. Corporate and group evenings a speciality. Team and video golf fun for juniors to seniors and all in between. Well stocked shop with all major brands. Professional: Simon Roberts.

LEEDS. **Leeds Golf Centre,** Wike Ridge Lane, Shadwell, Leeds LS17 9JW (0113 2886000; Fax: 0113 2886185). *Location:* two miles north of Leeds between A61 and A58 at the village of Wike. 19 bay covered, floodlit range. *Fees:* basket of balls £2.80. *Eating facilities:* bar/brasserie open 8.30am to 10pm. *Opening hours:* 7am to 10pm. 3 resident teaching professionals, 18 hole championship course, 12 hole Par 3 course. Professional: Mark Pinkett. Managing Director: Graham Bradley

SCOTLAND

ABERDEEN, BANFF & MORAY

ABERDEEN. **Kings Links Golf Centre,** Golf Road, Aberdeen AB24 1RZ (01224 641577; Fax: 01224 639410). *Location:* in front of Pittodrie football stadium, 56 covered, floodlit bays on two tiers. *Fees:* £2.75 for 50 balls, £5.00 for 100 balls. Concession rate for senior citizens and under 14's. *Eating facilities:* vending drinks, vending snacks and sandwiches. *Opening hours*: 9am to 10pm weekdays, 9am to 5.30pm weekends. 5 PGA Professionals available for tuition, club repairs, advise and custom fitting service. Video academy equipped with the latest video analysis equipment. Floodlit outdoor short game area. 3000sq ft golf superstore stocking all the latest golf equipment. Beginners welcome. Director of Golf: Paul Girvan. e-mail: info@kings-links.com
website: www.kings-links.com

AYRSHIRE & ARRAN

DAILLY. **Brunston Castle Golf Course,** Dailly, Girvan KA26 9GD (01465 811471). *Location:* five miles north of Girvan on B471, five miles from Turnberry. *Fees*: information not available. Golf £30.00 weekdays, £35.00 weekends. *Eating facilities:* full bar and restaurant facilities. *Opening hours:* 8am to 11pm (Summer). 18 hole championship course in most scenic part of Ayrshire. Driving range. Full PGA tuition by Professional, full practice facilities. 16-seater minibus and trailer available.
e-mail: golf@brunstoncastle.co.uk
website: www.brunstoncastle.co.uk

DUMFRIES & GALLOWAY

GRETNA. **Gretna Golf Course,** Gretna DG16 5HD (01461 337362). *Location:* half-a-mile south west of M74 and A75 junction, half-a-mile on west side of Gretna. 14 bay covered driving range, 7 bays grassed. 9 hole golf course. *Fees:* information not available. *Eating facilities:* available. *Opening Hours:* 10am to dark. *

DUNDEE & ANGUS

DUNDEE. **Ballumbie Castle Golf Club,** 3 Old Quarry Road, Off Ballumbie Road, Dundee DD4 0SY (01382 730026; Fax: 01382 730008). *Location*: one and a half miles north of Claypotts Junction, less than 2 miles from Dundee City Centre. 22 bay floodlit driving range, putting green, chipping green. 18 hole course. *Fees*: information not available. *Eating facilities*: clubhouse facilities with menu and full bar. Public house licence. *Opening hours*: 9am to 9pm weekdays, 9am to 7pm weekends. Tuition available. *Society Meetings*: welcome, please telephone for details. Professional: Lee Sutherland (01382 770028).*
e-mail: ballumbie2000@yahoo.com
website: www.ballumbiegolf.com

EDINBURGH & LOTHIANS

EDINBURGH. **Braid Hills Shop & Golf Centre,** 91 Liberton Drive, Edinburgh EH16 6NS (0131-658 1111; Fax: 0131-672 1411). *Location:* leave Edinburgh bypass at Straiton Junction, head towards city centre, take left turn at second set of traffic lights, proceed half-a-mile along Liberton Drive. 32 bay covered, floodlit range. Short game area and 3 putting greens. *Fees:* information not available. *Opening Hours:* 10am to 9pm weekdays, 9am to 6pm weekends. Scotland's top Professionals available for group and individual tuition. S.A.S video tuition. Professionals: Ian Young, Colin Brooks, Sandy Stephen, Mark Berrie, Paul Malone, Craig Waddell.*

EDINBURGH. **Port Royal Golf Driving Range,** Eastfield Road, Ingliston, Edinburgh EH28 8TR (0131-333 4377). *Location:* situated next to Edinburgh Airport. Recently refurbished to cater for golfers of every ability. 25 covered, floodlit practice bays, 17 outside bays, double teaching studio with swing analysis software, 100 square yard Himalayan putting green, 9 hole Par 3 golf course. PGA Professionals and tuition. *Fees*: information not available. *Eating facilities:* licensed cafe/bar area, snacks served all day. *Opening hours:* 10am to 10pm summer, 10am to 9pm winter. Open all year. General Manager/Head Professional: Keith Pickard. *

THE APPEARANCE OF AN ASTERISK (*) AT THE END OF A CLUB OR COURSE ENTRY INDICATES THAT UP-TO-DATE INFORMATION HAS NOT BEEN SUPPLIED

EDINBURGH near. **Melville Golf Centre, Golf Course, Range & Shop,** Lasswade, Near Edinbugh EH18 1AN (0131-663 8038; Fax: 0131-654 0814). *Location:* south of Edinburgh, three minutes from City Bypass on A7 South (signposted). 22 floodlit, covered bays plus 12 bays. 300 yards long. *Fees:* £2.50 for 50 balls and concessions. *Eating facilities:* hot and cold vended drinks, sandwiches, crisps, etc. *Opening hours:* weekdays 9am to 10pm, weekends 9am to 8pm. Full equipment and shoe hire. Repairs. Golf shop fully stocked, ladies, gents, and juniors; professional tuition; practice bunker, putting green, 4 hole practice area, pay & play 9-hole golf course, par 66. Children under 14 must be accompanied by an adult. A Golf Foundation Starter Initiative Centre. Professional: Gary Carter. Owners Mr and Mrs MacFarlane.*
e-mail: golf@melvillegolf.co.uk
website: www.melvillegolf.co.uk

FIFE

ST ANDREWS. **St Andrews Links Trust Golf Practice Centre,** St Andrews, KY16 9SF (01334 474989; Fax: 01334 479555). *Location:* situated parallel to the Old Course, just 10 minutes' walk from the town centre. *Fees:* From £1.40 for 25 balls. *Eating facilities:* light refreshments and seated viewing area. *Opening hours*: 7am to 9pm daily from 1 May-31 August; 8am to 9pm from 1 September-30 April. Pitching, putting, bunker area using own balls. Golf club hire available. Locker rooms: (01334 474489).

GLASGOW & DISTRICT

GLASGOW. **Mearns Castle Golf Academy,** Waterfoot Road, Newton Mearns, Glasgow G77 5RR (0141 644 8200; Fax: 0141 644 1133). *Location:* near Newton Mearns. 34 covered, floodlit bays; bunkers. *Fees:* £5.50 for 100 balls, £4.50 for 75 balls, £3.50 for 50 balls, £2.00 for 25 balls. *Opening hours:* 8.30am to 10pm, last balls 8.30pm. *Eating facilities:* cafe bar. Tuition available; 9 hole pay and play course, short game facility. Memberships available.
website: www.mcgolfacademy.co.uk

UDDINGSTON. **Clydeway Golf Centre,** Blantyre Farm Road, Uddingston G71 7RR (0141-641 8899). *Location:* near Glasgow Zoo. 25 covered floodlit bays. *Fees:* information not available. Professional tuition. Group rates for parties, schools, colleges, works, offices, etc. Now incorporates Nevada Bob's golf discount superstore, target golf competition. *

HIGHLANDS

INVERNESS. **Loch Ness Golf Course,** Castle Heather, Inverness IV2 6AA (01463 713335; Fax: 01463 712695). *Location:* on the southern outskirts of Inverness, heading west along the new ring road. 20 bay covered, floodlit driving range. 18 hole, par 73 golf course. 6493 yards yellow, 6772 yards white. *Fees:* information not available. Golf: £25.00 day ticket weekdays, £30.00 weekends. *Eating facilities:* Restaurant and lounge bar. *Opening hours:* Monday to Saturday 8am to 11pm daily. *Visitors*: welcome, buggies, carts available. *Society Meetings*: welcome by prior arrangement. Professional tuition. Professional: Martin Piggot. Secretary: Neil D. Hampton.
e-mail: info@golflochness.com
website: www.golflochness.com

PERTHSHIRE

BLAIRGOWRIE. **Strathmore Golf Centre Driving Range.** Leroch, Alyth, Blairgowrie PH11 8NZ (01828 633322; Fax: 01828 633533). *Location:* one mile south of Alyth, (off the A926 Alyth-Kirriemuir Road). 10 bay floodlit driving range. *Fees:* information not available. *Eating facilities:* restaurant and bar at Clubhouse . *Opening hours:* dawn to 10pm. 18 and 9 hole courses available. General Manager: Christopher Spencer.*
e-mail: enquiries@strathmoregolf.com
website: www.strathmoregolf.com

MIDDLEBANK. **Middlebank Golf Range,** Middlebank, Errol PH2 7SX (01821 670320). *Location:* midway between Perth and Dundee on the A90. 23 bay floodlit driving range; 7 covered, 16 grassed. *Fees*: information not available. *Eating facilities:* coffee, sandwiches, etc. available. *Opening Hours:* Summer 9am to 9pm 7 days, Winter 9am to 5pm 7 days. PGA professional for tuition by appointment, and well stocked golf shop. *

SCONE. **Murrayshall Golf Range,** Murrayshall Hotel & Golf Courses, Scone PH2 7PH (01738 554804; Fax: 01738 552595). *Location:* 3 miles outside Perth (NE) off A94. 18 bay covered, floodlit driving range, 11 grassed, bunkers. Two 18 hole golf courses. *Fees*: information not available. *Eating facilities*: 4 Star Hotel and golf clubhouse on site. *Opening hours*: Daylight until 9:30pm. Video analysis tuition. Professional: Alan Reid.*
e-mail: golf@murrayshall.co.uk
website: www.murrayshall.co.uk

RENFREWSHIRE

RENFREW. **John Mulgrew Normandy Golf Centre,** Inchinnan Road, Renfrew PA4 9EG (0141-886 7477; Fax: 0141-885 0786). *Location:* take M8, then take Glasgow Airport turn-off, then take Renfrew Road one mile away. 20 bays covered, floodlit. 5 bays short game area. *Fees:*information not available. *Opening hours:* 9.30am to 9pm Mon-Fri, 9.30am to 6pm weekends (last token 30 mins before closing). *Eating facilities:* full hotel facilities. Professional, assistants, tuition anytime. Adjacent to Renfrew Golf Club. Large comprehensive stock of all leading golf equipment. Director: N. Carlin.*

WALES

ANGLESEY & GWYNEDD

ANGLESEY. **Penrhyn Golf Complex,** Llanddaniel - Fâb LL60 6NN (01248 421150). *Location:* A5 turn off at Star Crossroads taking Llanddaniel road. Follow Brown Tourism signs from the village. *Course:* 14 bay covered and floodlit driving range, 9 hole golf course. *Fees:* information not provided. *Visitors:* no restrictions. Professional: Paul Lovell (Visiting). Owner: Mr W.R. Carter.

PWLLHELI. **Llyn Golf,** Pen-y-Berth, Penrhos, Pwllheli LL53 7HG (01758 701200). *Location:* Situated off the A499 between Pwllheli and Abersoch. 14 covered floodlit bays and bunker practice area. 9-hole pay and play golf course, 1782 yards, Par 3 and 4. Hire clubs available. *Fees:* information not available. *Eating facilities:* refreshments available. *Opening hours:* open daily. *

NORTH WALES

CHESTER near. **Bannel Golf Driving Range,** Mold Road, Penymynydd, Near Chester CH4 0EN (01244 544639). *Location:* A5118 Penymynydd to Mold road, 7 miles from Chester. 10 bay covered floodlit range; three bays open. *Fees:* information not available. *Eating facilities:* light refreshments available. *Opening hours:* 10am to 9pm weekdays, 10am to 6pm weekends. 9 hole putting green, golf shop. Lessons from PGA Professional by appointment. Proprietors: L.J. & J. Povey (01244 544639).*

ST ASAPH. **North Wales Golf Driving Range and 9 hole Course,** Llannerch Park, St Asaph LL17 0BD (01745 730805;). *Location:* on the A525 between St Asaph and Trefnant, one-and-a-quarter miles from St Asaph Cathedral. 14 bay covered, floodlit driving range. *Fees*: £1.00 for 25 balls. *Eating facilities:* refreshments, hot and cold drinks, sweets, biscuits, crisps. *Opening hours:* 10am to 9pm seven days a week during Summer, early closing in Winter 5pm Friday to Monday. Lessons with non-resident Professional by arrangement. 9 hole course also on site - £4.00 pay and play. Non-membership Complex. Secretary: Stephen Mueller (07771 733651 mobile).*

THE APPEARANCE OF AN ASTERISK (*) AT THE END OF A CLUB OR COURSE ENTRY INDICATES THAT UP-TO-DATE INFORMATION HAS NOT BEEN SUPPLIED

POWYS

CRADOC. **Cradoc Golf Club,** Penoyre Park, Cradoc, Brecon LD3 9LP (01874 623658; Fax: 01874 611711). *Location*: two miles north of the market town of Brecon, off B4520 Upper Chapel Road (signposted) past Brecon Cathedral. 12-bay undercover floodlit driving range. *Fees*: Prices from 50p per basket of balls. *Eating facilities*: full catering facilities daily except Mondays. *Opening hours*: 8.00am till 8.45pm. Tuition, 18 hole golf course. Professional: R.W. Davies (01874 625524). Secretary: Mrs E.G. Price (01874 623658).
e-mail: secretary@cradoc.co.uk
website: www.cradoc.co.uk

SOUTH WALES

ABERGAVENNY. **Wernddu Golf Club,** Old Ross Road, Abergavenny NP7 8NG (01873 856223; Fax: 01873 852177). *Location:* one and a half miles east of Abergavenny on B4521 (off A465). 26 bay floodlit driving range. *Fees:* information not available. *Eating facilities:* lounge bar, bar snacks. *Visitors:* welcome. Professional tuition, 9 hole pitch and putt and 18 hole Par 67 golf course. Contact: Tina Tetley (L.E.T.).

BARRY. **South Wales Golf Range and Course,** Port Road East, Barry (Range: 01446 742434; Mobile: 07986 738744). *Location:* A4050 road Cardiff to Barry. 16 covered floodlit bays. *Fees:* information not available. *Opening hours:* weekdays 9am to 8pm; weekends 9am to 6pm. Professional tuition available from Simon Cox (three times Welsh Champion); 9-hole Par 3 course.

CAERPHILLY. **Virginia Park Golf Club,** Virginia Park, Caerphilly CF8 1LP (029 2086 7891). *Location:* off Pontygwindy Road, next to recreation centre. 20 bay covered, floodlit, grassed driving range. *Fees:* information not available. *Eating facilities:* licensed bar in clubhouse, full catering. Coffee shop in driving range. *Opening hours:* Weekdays 10.30am to 10pm. Weekends 7am to 7pm seven days a week. Professional: Richard Barter. Secretary: Carol Lewis.*

CHEPSTOW. **Dewstow Golf Club,** Caerwent, Chepstow NP26 5AH (01291 430444; Fax: 01291 425816). *Location*: Off A48 at Caerwent, between Chepstow and Newport, four miles from Severn Bridge. 26 bay floodlit, covered golf range. Two 18 hole courses. *Fees*: information not available. *Eating facilities*: restaurant, bars. *Opening hours*: on application. *Society Meetings*: welcome weekdays. Limited weekends. Professional: Jonathan Skuse. Golf Secretary:Dave Bradbury (01291 430444; Fax: 01291 425816). Booking Secretary: Hayley Battle.*

www.uk-golfguide.com

COEDKERNEW. **Parc Golf Club,** Church Lane, Coedkernew NP1 9TU (01633 680933). *Location:* Junction 28 M4, then A48 towards Cardiff. 38 bay covered, floodlit driving range. Automatic tee system installed. New 9 hole Par 3 course available. *Fees:* information not available. *Eating facilities:* excellent full facilities. *Opening Hours:* weekdays 7.30am to 10pm, weekends 7.30am to 8.30pm. Three Professionals, individual and group tuition, excellent shop. Function suite, corporate and society days organised. Weddings, seminars, private parties catered for.

CWMBRAN. **Greenmeadow Golf and Country Club,** Treherbert Road, Croesyceiliog, Cwmbran NP44 2BZ (01633 869321; Fax: 01633 868430). *Location:* M4 Junction 26 five miles north on A4042. Turn right at brown tourist sign. Golf Course & Range next to Gwent Crematorium. 26 bay covered floodlit driving range. *Fees:* please phone for details and prices as there are many different packages and options. *Eating facilities:* lounge bar, patio coffee lounge and restaurant, private function room. *Opening hours:* 8am to 10pm all year. *Visitors:* welcome. Professional tuition by appointment. Six floodlit all-weather tennis courts, 18 hole parkland golf course, putting green. Range situated with panoramic views, facing easterly. Professional: Dave Woodman (01633 862626. Fax: 01633 868430). Secretary: P. Richardson (01633 869321).*

SWANSEA. **Gowerton Golf Range,** Victoria Road, Gowerton, Swansea, SA4 3AB (01792 875188; Fax: 01792 874288). 20 covered bays, 8 grassed, all floodlit. Bunker. *Fees*: information not available. *Eating facilities*: diner, hot and cold meals available. *Opening hours:* 10am to 9pm, closed at 7pm winter weekends. Tuition available. Putting green, golf course. Professional: Mike Hobbs.
e-mail: stevenbromham@beeb.net
website: www.gowertongolfrange.com

NORTHERN IRELAND

ANTRIM

NEWTOWNABBEY. **Ballyearl Golf and Leisure Centre,** 585 Doagh Road, Newtownabbey BT36 8RZ (028 9084 0899). *Location:* from Belfast take M2 then A8 to Larne, half a mile through second roundabout following exit from motorway turn right to Mossley. Ballyearl one mile on left. 24 bay covered, floodlit range, large grassed area. *Fees:* information not available. *Eating facilities:* squash club with bar facilities. *Opening hours:* 9.30am to 9.30pm. 9 hole Par 3 course, PGA Golf Professional, tuition, fully stocked golf shop, repairs. Squash court, fitness suite, arts theatre.*

ARMAGH

CRAIGAVON. **Craigavon Golf and Ski Club,** Turmoyra Lane, Lurgan, Craigavon (028 3832 6606; Fax: 028 3834 7272). *Location:* half a mile from motorway, one mile from town centre, adjacent to ski slope. Driving range. 18-hole course, 9-hole par 3 course, 12-hole pitch and putt. *Fees:* information not available. *Eating facilities:* full restaurant facilities. *Visitors:* always welcome. Modern clubhouse, showers and lockers. *Society Meetings:* welcome - book beforehand. Professional: D. Paul. *

Co. DOWN

KNOCKBRACKEN. **Mount Ober Golf and Country Club,** 24 Ballymaconaghy Road, Knockbracken, Belfast BT8 6SB (028 9079 5666; Fax: 028 9070 5862). *Location:* outskirts of Belfast, approximately three miles from the centre along Ormeau Road to "Four Winds" public house and restaurant. 36 bays covered, floodlit, and grassed area. *Fees:* £4.00 for 100 balls, £3.00 for 70 balls, £2.00 for 35 balls. *Eating facilities:* bar open seven days a week during normal opening hours, catering available seven days a week 11am to 10pm. *Opening hours:* 10am to 11pm. Tuition available at Golf Academy by PGA professionals. Snooker and pool tables. Professional: (028 9070 1648). Secretary: (028 9079 5666).
e-mail: mt.ober@ukonline.co.uk

For full details of clubs and courses, plus convenient accommodation
www.uk-golfguide.com

Please mention THE GOLF GUIDE when you enquire about clubs or accommodation

WARRENPOINT. **Pat Trainor's Golf Academy,** Milltown Street, Burren, Warrenpoint BT34 3RJ (028 4177 3247). *Location:* six miles south of Newry, at Warrenpoint roundabout turn left for Burren: approximately one mile. Driving range - 10 covered, 20 grassed bays, all floodlit. 9 hole pitch and putt course. *Fees*: £3.50 for 50 balls, £4.00 for 80 balls. *Opening hours:* weekdays 10am to 10pm; weekends 10am to 8pm. Tuition available at all times for individuals, groups and schools. Indoor video lessons. Owner/ Professional: Pat Trainor.

REPUBLIC OF IRELAND

COUNTY CORK

CARRIGTWOHILL. **Fota Island Golf Club,** Carrigtwohill (021 4883700; Fax: 021 4883713). *Location:* take the N25 east from Cork City, turn off Carrigtwohill/Cobh exit. Follow sign for Fota (100m). Venue for the 2001 and 2002 Murphy's Irish Open. 18 hole championship course. Voted golf course of the year in 2002 by the Irish Golf Tour Operators. *Fees*: Prices from 62 to 98 euros. *Eating facilities:* full bar and restaurant. *Opening hours*: daylight only. PGA professional plus assistants available for tuition. Professional: Kevin Morris.
e-mail: reservations@fotaisland.ie
website: www.fotaisland.ie

FERMANAGH

ENNISKILLEN. **Ashwoods Golf Centre,** Sligo Road, Enniskillen (028 6632 5321; Fax: 028 6632 5874). *Location:* one and a half miles west of Enniskillen on main Sligo Road. 7 bay covered, floodlit range. *Fees:* information not available. Golf from £5.00 to £10.00. *Eating facilities:* none on site, available 300 yards away. *Opening hours:* 9am to 10pm summer, 9am to 7pm winter. Professional lessons. Professional golf shop stocking full range of clubs, clothes and all golf accessories.

COUNTY DUBLIN

FOXROCK. **Leopardstown Driving Range,** Foxrock (2895341). *Location:* five miles south of Dublin city centre situated in Leopardstown Race Course. 38 indoor, 38 outdoor floodlit bays. *Opening hours*: 9am to 10pm. *Fees*: information not available. *Eating facilities:* restaurant. Tuition available from three PGA Professionals - practice green. 18 hole golf course.Manager: Michael Hoey.*

Co. LONDONDERRY

LIMAVADY. **Roe Park Golf Club,** Radisson SAS Roe Park Resort, Roe Park, Limavady BT49 9LB (028 777 6015; Fax: 028 7772 2313). *Location:* on main A2 Londonderry-Limavady Road, 16 miles from Londonderry and one mile from Limavady. 10 covered, floodlit, astroturfed and 6 uncovered bays. 18 hole parkland course. *Fees:* information not available. *Eating facilities:* Coach Brasserie. *Opening hours:* 8am until 10pm, golf course open from 8am until 8pm. PGA Tuition available. Professional: Seamus Duffy. Secretary: Don Brockerton.*

ST MARGARET'S. **The Open Golf Centre,** Newtown House, St Margaret's (010 3531 8640324; Fax: 010 3531 8341400). *Location:* 2kms from Dublin Airport, adjacent to N2 (Derry road). 16 bay floodlit, grassed range. *Fees:* information not available. *Eating facilities:* coffee shop. *Opening hours*: 7.30am to dusk. Nine golf professionals on site, groups organised, video, lecture room and club fitting room.*

LONDONDERRY. **Foyle International Golf Centre,** 12 Alder Road, Londonderry BT48 8DB (028 71 352222; Fax: 028 71 353967). *Location*: one and a half miles from Foyle Bridge towards Moville, Co Donegal. 25 bay covered, floodlit driving range. 18 hole, par 72 course and 9 hole par 3 course. *Fees:* information not available. *Eating facilities*: Pitchers Wine Bar and Restaurant. *Opening hours*: 8.00am to 10.00pm. Tuition available. Professional indoor video analysis. Professional: Kieran McLaughlin (028 71 352222; Fax: 028 71 353967).*
e-mail: mail@foylegolf.club24.co.uk
website: www.foylegolfcentre.co.uk

THE APPEARANCE OF AN ASTERISK (*) AT THE END OF A CLUB OR COURSE ENTRY INDICATES THAT UP-TO-DATE INFORMATION HAS NOT BEEN SUPPLIED

For full details of clubs and courses, plus convenient accommodation
www.uk-golfguide.com

COUNTY MONAGHAN

CARRICKMACROSS. **Nuremore Golf Club,** Nuremore Hotel and Country Club, Carrickmacross (042 61438). *Location:* 50 miles from Dublin on N2. *Fees:* on request. *Eating facilities:* bar and catering facilities in new clubhouse and hotel. *Opening hours:* daylight hours. PGA Professional, all hotel facilities.*

COUNTY WATERFORD

DUNGARVAN. **Gold Coast Golf Club,** Ballinacourty, Dungarvan (058 44055; Fax: 058 43378). *Location:* from Waterford left of N25 two miles before Dungarvan. Parkland bordered by Atlantic. 18 holes, 6788 yards, 6171 metres. S.S.S. 72. *Green Fees:* information not available. *Eating facilities:* full hotel and leisure facilities. *Visitors:* welcome. *Society Meetings:* welcome, special rates available. Secretary: Tom Considine (Tel & Fax: 058 44055). e-mail: info@clonea.com
website: www.clonea.com

Please mention **THE GOLF GUIDE** when you enquire about clubs or accommodation

CHANNEL ISLANDS

ST OUEN'S. **Les Mielles Golf and Country Club,** St Ouen's Bay, Jersey JE3 7PQ (01534 482787; Fax: 01534 485414). *Location:* centre of St Ouen's Bay. 30 bay covered driving range. *Fees:* information available on line. *Opening hours:* dawn till dusk. *Eating facilities:* restaurant, alfresco eating, kiosk. Public golf facility. Putting green; golf shop. Professional: Wayne Osmand (01534 483699; Fax: 01534 485414). Director of Golf: J.A. Le Brun.*
website: www.lesmielles.com

PORTUGAL

ESTORIL. **Quinta da Marinha Golf Conference and Golf Resort,** Quinta da Marinha Hotel Village Resort, Casa 36, 2750 Cascais, Portugal (01 4869881/9; Fax: 4869032). *Location:* motorway to Cascais from Lisbon. Grassed driving range. *Fees:* information not available. *Eating facilities:* club restaurant and bar. Opening hours: 7.45am to 9pm. Professional tuition for driving range and lessons. Driving range also available for rental. 18-hole golf course, two putting greens. Six tennis courts and two swimming pools, conference rooms and banqueting facilities. Accommodation available in 70 villas or the new 200 bedroom Marinha Golf Hotel facing the course. Professional: Keith Ashdown. Secretary: Maria Pinto Coelho. *

FHG

Other specialised
FHG Guides
Published annually: available in all good bookshops or direct from the publisher.

Recommended **COUNTRY INNS & PUBS** OF BRITAIN £7.99

Recommended **COUNTRY HOTELS** OF BRITAIN £7.99

Recommended **SHORT BREAK HOLIDAYS** IN BRITAIN £7.99

The bestselling **PETS WELCOME!** £8.99

FHG Guides • Abbey Mill Business Centre, Seedhill, Paisley, Renfrewshire PA1 ITJ
Tel: 0141-887 0428 • Fax: 0141-889 7204
e-mail: admin@fhguides.co.uk
www.holidayguides.com

Index of Clubs and Courses

Aa Saint-Omer Golf Club ST OMER 546
Abbey Hill Golf Centre MILTON KEYNES 139
Abbey Hotel, Golf and Country Club REDDITCH 601
Abbeydale Golf Club SHEFFIELD 358
Abbeyfeale Golf Club ABBEYFEALE 521
Abbeyleix Golf Club ABBEYLEIX 520
Abbotsley Golf Club & Hotel ST NEOTS 145, 588
Aberdare Golf Club ABERDARE 473
Aberdour Golf Club ABERDOUR 417
Aberdovey Golf Club ABERDOVEY 454
Aberfeldy Golf Club ABERFELDY 439
Aberfoyle Golf Club ABERFOYLE 448
Abergele Golf Club ABERGELE 459
Abernethy Golf Club NETHYBRIDGE 434
Aberystwyth Golf Club ABERYSTWYTH 467
Aboyne Golf Club ABOYNE 374
Abridge Golf & Country Club STAPLEFORD TAWNEY 196
Academia de Golf Estoril Sol ESTORIL 561
Accrington and District Golf Club ACCRINGTON 232
Achill Golf Club ACHILL 523
Acre Gate Golf Club FLIXTON 252
Adare Manor Golf Club ADARE 521
Addington Court Golf Ltd CROYDON 308
Addington Golf Club CROYDON 308
Addington Palace Golf Club CROYDON 308
Adlington Golf Centre ADLINGTON 588
Aigas Golf Club BEAULY 433
Ailette Golf de L' LAON 545
Airdrie Golf Club AIRDRIE 436
Airlinks Golf Club HOUNSLOW 126
Aix Marseille Golf d' MARSEILLES 554
Aix-les-Bains Golf d' AIX-LES-BAINS 550
Albi Lasbordes Golf d' ALBI 551
Alcanada Club de Golf PUERTO DE ALCUDIA 571
Aldeburgh Golf Club ALDEBURGH 302
Aldenham Golf & Country Club WATFORD 218

Alder Root Golf Club WARRINGTON 152
Alderley Edge Golf Club ALDERLEY EDGE 146
Alderney Golf Club ALDERNEY 541
Aldersey Green Golf Club CHESTER 147
Aldwark Manor Golf Club ALDWARK 350
Aldwickbury Park Golf Club HARPENDEN 215
Alexandra Golf Club GLASGOW 424
Alford Golf Club ALFORD 374
Alfreton Golf Club ALFRETON 166
Alice Springs Golf Club USK 485
Allendale Golf Club ALLENDALE 273
Allerton Park Golf Club LIVERPOOL 260
Allestree Park Golf Club DERBY 167
Alloa Golf Club ALLOA 448
Allt-y-Graban Golf Club SWANSEA 484
Almerimar Golf ALMERIA 568
Alness Golf Club ALNESS 431
Alnmouth Golf Club Ltd. ALNMOUTH 273
Alnmouth Village Golf Club ALNMOUTH 273
Alnwick Golf Club ALNWICK 273
Aloha Golf MARBELLA 567
Alresford Golf Club ALRESFORD 204
Alsager Golf & Country Club ALSAGER 146
Alston Moor Golf Club ALSTON 161
Alto Golf & Country Club ALVOR 558
Alton Golf Club ALTON 204
Altrincham Golf Club ALTRINCHAM 250
Alva Golf Club ALVA 448
Alvaston Hall Golf Club NANTWICH 150
Alwoodley Golf Club LEEDS 364
Alyth Golf Club BLAIRGOWRIE 440
Amarante Golf, Quinta da Devesa AMARANTE 563
Amida Golf Course & Teaching Academy TWICKENHAM 128
Ampfield Par Three Golf & Country Club AMPFIELD 204
Andover Golf Club ANDOVER 204
Anglesey Golf Club Ltd. RHOSNEIGR 458
Anjou Golf and Country Club ANGERS 546
Annanhill Golf Club KILMARNOCK 389

WHEREVER YOU'RE PLAYING
pick up a guide map to what's best in the area
From all leading Tourist Information Centres and participating hotels & golf clubs
TOURIST PUBLICATIONS 5 Eglinton Crescent, Edinburgh EH12 5DH
Tel: 0131 225 4547   Fax: 0131 220 6789

Golf GUIDE MAPS

Anoreta Golf RINCON DE LA VICTORIA 568
Anstruther Golf Club ANSTRUTHER 417
Ansty Golf Centre COVENTRY 334
Antrobus Golf Club NORTHWICH 150
Appleby Golf Club APPLEBY 161
Aqualate Golf Centre NEWPORT 288
Aqualate Golf Centre NEWPORT 596
Aquarius Golf Club SOUTHWARK 128
Arbroath Golf Course ARBROATH 406
Arcangues Golf de BIARRITZ 551
Arcot Hall Golf Club Ltd. NEWCASTLE-UPON-TYNE 277
Ardee Golf Club ARDEE 522
Ardeer Golf Club STEVENSTON 391
Ardglass Golf Club ARDGLASS 492
Arkley Golf Club BARNET 213
Army Golf Club ALDERSHOT 204
Aroeira Golf AROEIRA 561
Arrowe Park Golf Course BIRKENHEAD 258
Arscott Golf Club SHREWSBURY 290
Ashbourne Golf Club ASHBOURNE (Derbyshire) 166
Ashbourne Golf Club ASHBOURNE (Co. Meath) 526
Ashburnham Golf Club LLANELLI 466
Ashbury Hotel OKEHAMPTON 176
Ashby Decoy Golf Club SCUNTHORPE 247
Ashfield Golf Club CULLYHANNA 492
Ashford (Kent) Golf Club ASHFORD 221
Ashford Great Chart Golf & Leisure ASHFORD 221, 592
Ashford Manor Golf Club ASHFORD 123
Ashley Wood Golf Club BLANDFORD 180
Ashridge Golf Club BERKHAMSTED 213
Ashton & Lea Golf Club Ltd. PRESTON 236
Ashton-in-Makerfield Golf Club Ltd ASHTON-IN-MAKERFIELD 250
Ashton-on-Mersey Golf Club SALE 256
Ashton-under-Lyne Golf Club ASHTON-UNDER-LYNE 250
Ashwoods Golf Centre ENNISKILLEN 607
Askernish Golf Club LOCHBOISDALE 452
Aspect Park Golf Club HENLEY-ON-THAMES 285
Aspley Guise and Woburn Sands Golf Club ASPLEY GUISE 130
Astbury Golf Club CONGLETON 148
Aston Wood Golf Club SUTTON COLDFIELD 337
Atalaya Golf & Country Club ESTEPONA 566
Athenry Golf Club ATHENRY 511
Atherstone Golf Club ATHERSTONE 329
Athlone Golf Club ATHLONE 528
Auchenblae Golf Course AUCHENBLAE 374
Auchmill Golf Club ABERDEEN 373

Auchterarder Golf Club AUCHTERARDER 439
Auchterderran Golf Club CARDENDEN 417
Austin Lodge Golf Club EYNSFORD 224
Axe Cliff Golf Club AXMOUTH 170
Aylesbury Golf Centre AYLESBURY 137, 587
Aylesbury Park Golf Club AYLESBURY 137
Aylesbury Vale Golf Club LEIGHTON BUZZARD 131, 486

Baberton Golf Club EDINBURGH 410
Backworth Golf Club SHIREMOOR 328
Bacup Golf Club BACUP 232
Baden Golf de AURAY 547
Badgemore Park Golf Club HENLEY-ON-THAMES 285
Baildon Golf Club BRADFORD 360
Bakewell Golf Club BAKEWELL 166
Bala Golf Club BALA 454
Balbirnie Park Golf Club MARKINCH 420
Balbriggan Golf Club BALBRIGGAN 506
Balcarrick Golf Club DONABATE 507
Balfron Golf Society BALFRON 448
Balgove Course ST ANDREWS 422
Ballards Gore Golf and Country Club ROCHFORD 195
Ballater Golf Club BALLATER 374
Ballina Golf Club BALLINA 523
Ballinamore Golf Club BALLINAMORE 521
Ballinasloe Golf Club BALLINASLOE 511
Ballinrobe Golf Club BALLINROBE 523
Ballochmyle Golf Club MAUCHLINE 390
Ballumbie Castle Golf Club DUNDEE 406, 603
Ballybunion Golf Club BALLYBUNION 512
Ballycastle Golf Club BALLYCASTLE 488
Ballyclare Golf Club BALLYCLARE 488
Ballyearl Golf and Leisure Centre NEWTOWNABBEY 490, 606
Ballykisteen Golf and Country Club MONARD 529
Ballyliffin Golf Club BALLYLIFFIN 503
Ballymena Golf Club BALLYMENA 488
Ballymote Golf Club BALLYMOTE 529
Balmoral Golf Club Ltd BELFAST 493
Balmore Golf Club GLASGOW 424
Balnagask Golf Course ABERDEEN 373
Baltinglass Golf Club BALTINGLASS 534
Bamburgh Castle Golf Club BAMBURGH 273
Banbridge Golf Club BANBRIDGE 493
Banbury Golf Centre BANBURY 284
Banchory Golf Club BANCHORY 376
Bandon Golf Club BANDON 500
Bangor Golf Club BANGOR 493
Bangsai Country Club AYUTTHAYA 581

Bannel Golf Driving Range CHESTER 605
Banstead Downs Golf Club SUTTON 314
Bantry Bay Golf Club BANTRY 500
Bargoed Golf Club BARGOED 473
Barkway Park Golf Club BARKWAY 213
Barlaston Golf Club BARLASTON 298
Barnard Castle Golf Club BARNARD CASTLE 184
Barnehurst Public Pay & Play Golf Course BEXLEY HEATH 123
Barnham Broom Hotel & Golf Club NORWICH 266
Barnsley Golf Club BARNSLEY 356
Baron Hill Golf Club ANGLESEY 454
Barriere de Deauville Golf DEAUVILLE 545
Barrington Saiyoke Sports Club KANCHANABURI 595
Barrow Golf Club BARROW-IN-FURNESS 161
Barrow Hills Golf Club CHERTSEY 307
Barshaw Golf Club PAISLEY 447
Barton-on-Sea Golf Club BARTON-ON-SEA 204
Basildon Golf Club BASILDON 189
Basingstoke Golf Club BASINGSTOKE 205
Batalha Golf Course SAO MIGUEL 564
Batchwood Golf and Tennis Centre ST ALBANS 217
Batchworth Park Golf Club RICKMANSWORTH 216
Bath Golf Club BATH 292
Bathgate Golf Club BATHGATE 409
Battle Golf Club BATTLE 317
Baux de Provence Golf des LES BAUX 554
Bawburgh Golf Club NORWICH 267
Bawtry Golf Club DONCASTER 356, 602
Baxenden & District Golf Club BAXENDEN 232
Beacon Park Golf Course UPHOLLAND 238
Beaconsfield Golf Club BEACONSFIELD 137
Beadlow Manor Hotel, Golf & Country Club BEADLOW 130
Beamish Park Golf Club BEAMISH 184
Bearsden Golf Club GLASGOW 424
Bearsted Golf Club MAIDSTONE 226
Bearwood Golf Club SINDLESHAM 136
Bearwood Lakes Golf Club WOKINGHAM 136
Beau Desert Golf Club CANNOCK 298

Beauchief Golf Club SHEFFIELD 358
Beaufort Golf Club KILLARNEY 513
Beaverstown Golf Club DONABATE 507
Beccles Golf Club BECCLES 302
Beckenham Place Park Golf Club BECKENHAM 221
Bedale Golf Club BEDALE 350
Bedford and County Golf Club BEDFORD 130
Bedford Golf Club BEDFORD 130
Bedfordshire Golf Club BEDFORD 130
Bedlingtonshire Golf Club BEDLINGTON 273
Beech Park Golf Club RATHCOOLE 510
Beedles Lake Golf Centre EAST GOSCOTE 239
Beeston Fields Golf Club NOTTINGHAM 281
Beith Golf Club BEITH 388
Belas Clube de Campo BELAS 561
Belfairs Golf Club LEIGH-ON-SEA 193
Belford Golf Club BELFORD 274
Belhus Park Golf Club OCKENDON 194
Belleisle Golf Course AYR 388
Bellingham Golf Club BELLINGHAM 274
Bellshill Golf Club BELLSHILL 436
Belmont Lodge and Golf BELMONT 211
Belton Park Golf Club GRANTHAM 244
Belturbet Golf Club BELTURBET 498
Belvoir Park Golf Club BELFAST 493
Ben Rhydding Golf Club ILKLEY 364
Benone Golf Course LIMAVADY 496
Bentham Golf Club BENTHAM 350
Bentley Golf Club BRENTWOOD 189
Benton Hall Golf Club WITHAM 196
Berehaven Golf Club and Amenity Park CASTLETOWNBERE 500
Berkhamsted Golf Club BERKHAMSTED 213
Berkshire Golf Club ASCOT 133
Berwick-upon-Tweed (Goswick) Golf Club BERWICK-UPON-TWEED 274
Best Western Ufford Park Hotel Golf & Leisure IPSWICH/WOODBRIDGE 303
Betchworth Park Golf Club DORKING 309
Betws-y-Coed Golf Club BETWS-Y-COED 459
Beverley and East Riding Golf Club BEVERLEY 347

WHEREVER YOU'RE PLAYING
pick up a guide map to what's best in the area
From all leading Tourist Information Centres and participating hotels & golf clubs
TOURIST PUBLICATIONS 5 Eglinton Crescent, Edinburgh EH12 5DH
Tel: 0131 225 4547   Fax: 0131 220 6789

Golf Guide Maps

Bexley Heath Golf Club BEXLEY HEATH 222
Biarritz Le Phare Golf de BIARRITZ 551
Bicester Golf & Country Club BICESTER 284
Bidford Grange Golf Club BIDFORD 329
Bidston Golf Club Ltd BIDSTON 258
Bigbury Golf Club Ltd. BIGBURY 170
Biggar Golf Club BIGGAR 436
Billingham Golf Club BILLINGHAM 184
Bingley (St. Ives) Golf Club BINGLEY 360
Birch Grove Golf Club COLCHESTER 191
Birch Hall Golf Club CHESTERFIELD 166
Birchwood Golf Club WARRINGTON 152
Birchwood Park Golf Centre DARTFORD 223, 593
Bird Hills (UK) Ltd MAIDENHEAD 134, 587
Birley Wood Golf Club SHEFFIELD 358
Birr Golf Club BIRR 527
Birstall Golf Club BIRSTALL 239
Birtley Golf Club BIRTLEY 326
Bishop Auckland Golf Club BISHOP AUCKLAND 184
Bishopbriggs Golf Club BISHOPBRIGGS 424
Bishop's Stortford Golf Club BISHOP'S STORTFORD 213
Bishopshire Golf Club KINNESSWOOD 443
Bishopswood Golf Club BASINGSTOKE 205
Blaby Golf Centre BLABY 239
Black Bush Golf Club DUNSHAUGHLIN 526
Blackburn Golf Club BLACKBURN 232
Blackburn Golf Driving Range BLACKBURN 594
Blackley Golf Club MANCHESTER 253
Blacklion Golf Club BLACKLION 498
Blackmoor Golf Club BORDON 205
Blacknest Golf & Country Club ALTON 204
Blackpool North Shore Golf Club BLACKPOOL 233
Blackpool Park Golf Club BLACKPOOL 233
Blackwater Valley Golf Course YATELY 316
Blackwell Golf Club BLACKWELL 344
Blackwell Grange Golf Club DARLINGTON 185
Blackwood Golf Centre BANGOR 493
Blackwood Golf Club BLACKWOOD 473

Blainroe Golf Club BLAINROE 534
Blair Atholl Golf Club BLAIR ATHOLL 440
Blairbeth Golf Club GLASGOW 424
Blairgowrie Golf Club BLAIRGOWRIE 440
Blairmore and Strone Golf Club DUNOON 385
Blankney Golf Club BLANKNEY 243
Bletchingley Golf Club BLETCHINGLEY 306
Bloxwich Golf Club WALSALL 338
Blue Canyon Country Club PHUKET 580
Blue Green Golf d'Ardree TOURS 550
Blue Mountain Golf Centre BINFIELD 133, 587
Blundells Hill Golf Club RAINHILL 261
Blyth Golf Club Ltd. BLYTH 274
Boat of Garten Golf and Tennis Club BOAT OF GARTEN 433
Boavista Golf Resort LAGOS 559
Boca Raton Resort & Club BOCA RATON 573
Bodenstown Golf Club SALLINS 518
Bognor Regis Golf Club BOGNOR REGIS 322
Boldmere Golf Club SUTTON COLDFIELD 337
Boldon Golf Club Ltd. EAST BOLDON 326
Bolton Golf Club Ltd. BOLTON 250
Bolton Old Links Golf Club Ltd. BOLTON 250
Bolton Open Golf Course BOLTON 233
Bon Accord Golf Club ABERDEEN 373
Bonar Bridge-Ardgay Golf Club BONAR BRIDGE 428
Bondhay Golf Club WORKSOP 283
Bondues Golf de LILLE 546
Bonnybridge Golf Club FALKIRK 448
Bonnyton Golf Club GLASGOW 424
Boothferry Golf Club HOWDEN 348
Bootle Golf Club BOOTLE 258
Bordeaux Cameyrac Golf de BORDEAUX 552
Borris Golf Club BORRIS 498
Borth and Ynyslas Golf Club Ltd BORTH 467
Bossey Golf and Country Club de ST JULIEN 551
Boston Golf Club Ltd. BOSTON 243
Boston West Golf Club BOSTON 243

WHEREVER YOU'RE PLAYING
pick up a guide map to what's best in the area
From all leading Tourist Information Centres and participating hotels & golf clubs
TOURIST PUBLICATIONS 5 Eglinton Crescent, Edinburgh EH12 5DH
Tel: 0131 225 4547 Fax: 0131 220 6789
Golf GUIDE MAPS

Bothwell Castle Golf Club GLASGOW 424
Botley Park Golf Club SOUTHAMPTON 209
Boughton Golf Club FAVERSHAM 224
Bovey Castle MORETONHAMPSTEAD 174
Bowenhurst Golf Centre Ltd FARNHAM 308
Bowood Golf and Country Club CALNE 340, 600
Bowood Park Hotel & Golf Course CAMELFORD 154
Bowring Municipal Golf Club HUYTON 260
Boxmoor Golf Club HEMEL HEMPSTEAD 215
Boyce Hill Golf Club Ltd SOUTH BENFLEET 195
Bracken Ghyll Golf Club ILKLEY 364
Brackenwood Golf Club WIRRAL 263
Brackley Golf Club SALFORD 256
Bradford Golf Club GUISELEY 362
Bradford Moor Golf Club BRADFORD 360
Bradford-On-Avon Golf Course Ltd TROWBRIDGE 343
Bradley Park Municipal Golf Course HUDDERSFIELD 363
Braehead Golf Club ALLOA 448
Braemar Golf Club BRAEMAR 376
Braeside Golf Club BECKENHAM 221
Braid Hills Golf Centre EDINBURGH 410, 603
Brailes Golf Club Ltd BRAILES 329
Brailsford Golf Club BRAILSFORD 166, 589
Braintree Golf Club BRAINTREE 189
Bramall Park Golf Club STOCKPORT 256
Bramcote Hills Golf Course BRAMCOTE 279
Bramcote Waters Golf Course NUNEATON 330
Bramhall Golf Club STOCKPORT 256
Bramley Golf Club GUILDFORD 310
Brampton Golf Club BRAMPTON 162, 589
Brampton Heath Golf Centre NORTHAMPTON 269, 595
Brampton Park Golf Club HUNTINGDON 143
Bramshaw Golf Club LYNDHURST 208
Brancepeth Castle Golf Club BRANCEPETH 184
Brandhall Golf Club BIRMINGHAM 332
Bransford Golf Club BRANSFORD 344
Branshaw Golf Club KEIGHLEY 364
Branston Golf & Country Club BURTON-UPON-TRENT 298

Braxted Park Golf Club WITHAM 196
Brayton Park Golf Club ASPATRIA 161
Brean Golf Club at Brean Leisure Park BURNHAM-ON-SEA 293
Brechin Golf and Squash Club BRECHIN 406
Brecon Golf Club BRECON 471
Breightmet Golf Club BOLTON 251
Brent Valley Golf Club HANWELL 125
Brest Iroise Golf de BREST 547
Bretesche Golf de La LA BAULE 547
Brett Vale Golf Club RAYDON 304
Brickendon Grange Golf Club HERTFORD 215
Brickhampton Court Golf Complex CHURCHDOWN 199, 591
Bridge of Allan Golf Club STIRLING 449
Bridgend & District Golf Club LINLITHGOW 414
Bridgnorth Golf Club BRIDGNORTH 288
Bridlington Golf Club BRIDLINGTON 347
Bridlington Links BRIDLINGTON 347
Bridport & West Dorset Golf Club BRIDPORT 180
Briggens House Golf Club WARE 218
Brighouse Bay Golf Club & Driving Range KIRKCUDBRIGHT 400
Bright Castle Golf Club DOWNPATRICK 494
Brighton and Hove Golf Club BRIGHTON 317
Bristol and Clifton Golf Club BRISTOL 197
Broadstone (Dorset) Golf Club BROADSTONE 180
Broadwater Park Golf Club GODALMING 598
Broadway Golf Club BROADWAY 198
Brocket Hall Golf Club WELYN GARDEN CITY 218
Brockley Hill Golf Park STANMORE 128, 586
Brocton Hall Golf Club STAFFORD 299
Brodick Golf Club BRODICK 393
Broke Hill Golf Club HALSTEAD 225
Brokenhurst Manor Golf Club BROCKENHURST 206
Bromborough Golf Club BROMBOROUGH 258
Bromley Golf Club BROMLEY 123
Bromsgrove Golf Centre BROMSGROVE 344, 601
Brookdale Golf Club Ltd. MANCHESTER 253

For full details of clubs and courses, plus convenient accommodation
www.uk-golfguide.com

Brookmans Park Golf Club HATFIELD 215
Broome Manor Golf Complex SWINDON 342, 600
Broome Park Golf club CANTERBURY 222
Broomieknowe Golf Club Ltd BONNYRIGG 409
Brora Golf Club BRORA 428
Brough Golf Club BROUGH 347
Broughty Golf Club MONIFIETH 407
Brown Trout Golf and Country Club COLERAINE 496
Brucefields Family Golf Centre Ltd STIRLING 449
Brunston Castle Golf Course DAILLY 388, 603
Bruntsfield Links Golfing Society Ltd EDINBURGH 410
Bryn Meadows Golf Club HENGOED 478
Bryn Morfydd Hotel Golf Club DENBIGH 460
Brynhill (Barry) Golf Club BARRY 473
Buchanan Castle Golf Club GLASGOW 425
Buckingham Golf Club BUCKINGHAM 138
Buckinghamshire Golf Club DENHAM 138
Buckpool Golf Club (Buckie) BUCKIE 378
Bude and North Cornwall Golf Club BUDE 153
Budock Vean Golf and Country House Hotel FALMOUTH 154
Builth Wells Golf Club BUILTH WELLS 471
Bulbury Woods Golf Club POOLE 182
Bull Bay Golf Club Ltd. ANGLESEY 454
Bullpits Golf Club BOURTON 180
Bulwell Forest Golf Club BULWELL 279
Buncrana Golf Club BUNCRANA 503
Bundoran Golf Club BUNDORAN 503
Bungay and Waveney Valley Golf Club BUNGAY 302
Bunsay Downs Golf Club MALDON 193
Burford Golf Club BURFORD 284
Burgess Hill Golf Academy BURGESS HILL 322, 599
Burgham Park Golf and Leisure Club MORPETH 276
Burghill Valley Golf Club HEREFORD 211
Burghley Park (Stamford) Golf Club STAMFORD 249
Burhill Golf Club WALTON-ON-THAMES 314
Burley Golf Club RINGWOOD 208
Burnham and Berrow Golf Club BURNHAM-ON-SEA 294
Burnham Beeches Golf Club BURNHAM 138
Burnham-on-Crouch Golf Club Ltd BURNHAM-ON-CROUCH 190
Burnley Golf Club BURNLEY 234

Burntisland Golf House Club BURNTISLAND 417
Burslem Golf Club Ltd. STOKE-ON-TRENT 299
Burstead Golf Club LITTLE BURSTEAD 193
Burton-on-Trent Golf Club BURTON-ON-TRENT 166
Bury Golf Club BURY 251
Bury St Edmunds Golf Club BURY ST EDMUNDS 302
Bush Hill Park Golf Club WINCHMORE HILL 129
Bushey Country Club BUSHEY 214
Bushey Hall Golf Club BUSHEY 214
Bushfoot Golf Club PORTBALLINTRAE 490
Bute Golf Club ISLE OF BUTE 386
Buxton and High Peak Golf Club BUXTON 166

Cadmore Lodge Golf & Country Club TENBURY WELLS 346
Caen Golf de CAEN 545
Caerleon Public Golf Course CAERLEON 473
Caerphilly Golf Club CAERPHILLY 473
Cahir Park Golf Club CAHIR 529
Caird Park Golf Club DUNDEE 406
Cairndhu Golf Club Ltd. LARNE 490
Calcot Park Golf Club READING 135
Caldecott Hall Golf Club & Hotel GREAT YARMOUTH 264
Calderbraes Golf Club UDDINGSTON 438
Calderfields Golf Club Ltd WALSALL 338
Caldwell Golf Club UPLAWMOOR 447
Caldy Golf Club Ltd CALDY 258
Caledonian Golf Club ABERDEEN 373
Callan Golf Club CALLAN 520
Callander Golf Club CALLANDER 440
Cally Palace Hotel GATEHOUSE OF FLEET 399
Calverley Golf Club LEEDS 365
Camberley Heath Golf Club CAMBERLEY 306
Cambridge Golf Club CAMBRIDGE 142, 587
Cambridge National Golf CAMBRIDGE 142
Cambridgeshire Moat House Hotel Golf Club CAMBRIDGE 142
Cambuslang Golf Club GLASGOW 425
Came Down Golf Club DORCHESTER 181
Camperdown Golf Club DUNDEE 406
Campo de Golfe da Madeira MADEIRA 563
Campsie Golf Club LENNOXTOWN 449
Cams Hall Estate Golf Club FAREHAM 206
Canford Magna Golf Club WIMBORNE 183
Canford School Golf Club WIMBORNE 183
Canmore Golf Club DUNFERMLINE 418

Cannes-Mandelieu Golf Club de CANNES 553
Cannes-Mougins Golf Country Club de CANNES 554
Cannington Golf Course BRIDGWATER 292
Cannock Park Golf Club CANNOCK 298
Canons Brook Golf Club HARLOW 192
Canterbury Golf Club CANTERBURY 222
Canwick Park Golf Club LINCOLN 245
Cap d'Agde Golf du AGDE 553
Cape Cornwall Golf and Country Club PENZANCE 158
Caprington Golf Club KILMARNOCK 389
Carden Park Hotel Golf Resort and Spa CHESTER 147, 588
Cardiff Golf Club CARDIFF 476
Cardigan Golf Club CARDIGAN 468
Cardross Golf Club CARDROSS 404
Carholme Golf Club LINCOLN 245
Carlisle Golf Club CARLISLE 162
Carlow Golf Club CARLOW 498
Carluke Golf Club CARLUKE 436
Carlyon Bay Hotel Golf Course ST AUSTELL 158
Carmarthen Golf Club CARMARTHEN 465
Carnalea Golf Club BANGOR 493
Carne Golf Links BELMULLET 524
Carnegie Golf Club at Skibo Castle DORNOCH 430
Carnoustie Golf Links CARNOUSTIE 406
Carnwath Golf Club CARNWATH 436
Carradale Golf Club CARRADALE 385
Carrbridge Golf Club CARRBRIDGE 433
Carrick Knowe Golf Course EDINBURGH 410
Carrickfergus Golf Club CARRICKFERGUS 489
Carrick-on-Shannon Golf Club CARRICK-ON-SHANNON 528
Carrick-on-Suir Golf Club CARRICK-ON-SUIR 529
Carswell Golf and Country Club FARINGDON 285
Carus Green Golf Club KENDAL 162
Carvynick Golf and Country Club NEWQUAY 156
Castelnjaloux Golf de CASTELJALOUX 552
Castell Heights Golf Club CAERPHILLY 473
Casterton Golf Course KIRKBY LONSDALE 164

Castle Barna Golf Club OFFALY 528
Castle Douglas Golf Club CASTLE DOUGLAS 398
Castle Eden Golf Club HARTLEPOOL 186
Castle Hawk Golf Club & Driving Range ROCHDALE 255, 595
Castle Hume Golf Club ENNISKILLEN 496
Castle Park Golf Club HADDINGTON 413
Castle Point Golf Club CANVEY ISLAND 190
Castle Royle Golf and Country Club READING 135
Castlebar Golf Club CASTLEBAR 524
Castleblayney Golf Club CASTLEBLAYNEY 527
Castlecomer Golf Club CASTLECOMER 520
Castlefields Golf Club BRIGHOUSE 361
Castlegregory Golf Club CASTLEGREGORY 512
Castlereagh Hills Golf Club BELFAST 489
Castlerock Golf Club CASTLEROCK 496
Castletown Golf Links CASTLETOWN 539
Castletroy Golf Club CASTLETROY 522
Castlewarden Golf & Country Club STRAFFAN 518
Cathcart Castle Golf Club GLASGOW 425
Cathkin Braes Golf Club GLASGOW 425
Catterick Golf Club CATTERICK 350
Cave Castle Golf Club BROUGH 347
Cavendish Golf Club Ltd. BUXTON 166
Cawder Golf Club GLASGOW 425
Cawdor Castle Golf Course CAWDOR CASTLE 433
Ceann Sibeal (Dingle) Golf Club BALLYFERRITER 512
Celtic Manor Resort NEWPORT 481
Central London Golf Centre WANDSWORTH 128
Chadwell Springs Golf Club WARE 218
Chalgrave Manor Golf Club TODDINGTON 132
Chamonix Golf de CHAMONIX 550
Champ de Bataille Golf Club du NEUBOURG 546
Channels Golf Club CHELMSFORD 190
Chapel-en-le-Frith Golf Club CHAPEL-EN-LE-FRITH 166
Charlesland Golf & Country CLub GREYSTONES 536
Charleton Golf Club COLINSBURGH 417

WHEREVER YOU'RE PLAYING
pick up a guide map to what's best in the area
From all leading Tourist Information Centres and participating hotels & golf clubs
TOURIST PUBLICATIONS 5 Eglinton Crescent, Edinburgh EH12 5DH
Tel: 0131 225 4547 Fax: 0131 220 6789

Golf GUIDE MAPS

Charleville Golf Club CHARLEVILLE 500
Charminster Golf Club DORCHESTER 181
Charnock Richard Golf Club CHORLEY 234
Charnwood Forest Golf Club LOUGHBOROUGH 241
Chart Hills Golf Club ASHFORD 221
Chartham Park EAST GRINSTEAD 323
Chartridge Park Golf Club CHESHAM 138
Chase Golf Club PENKRIDGE 299
Chateau de Cheverny Golf du CHEVERNY 549
Chateau des Sept Tours Golf du TOURS 550
Chateau des Vigiers Golf & Country Club DORDOGNE 552
Chateau L'Arc Golf International de AIX-EN-PROVENCE 553
Chatham Golf Centre CHATHAM 593
Cheadle Golf Club CHEADLE 146
Chedington Court Golf Club SOUTH PERROTT 182
Chelmsford Golf Club CHELMSFORD 190
Chelsfield Lakes Golf Centre ORPINGTON 227
Cherry Burton Golf Club BEVERLEY 347, 601
Cherry Lodge Golf Club BIGGIN HILL 222
Cherwell Edge Golf club BANBURY 284
Chesfield Downs Golf Club HITCHIN 216
Chesham and Ley Hill Golf Club CHESHAM 138
Cheshunt Golf Club WALTHAM CROSS 218
Chessington Golf Centre CHESSINGTON 307, 598
Chester Golf Club CHESTER 147
Chesterfield Golf Club Ltd. CHESTERFIELD 167
Chester-Le-Street Golf Club CHESTER-LE-STREET 184
Chesterton Valley Golf Club BRIDGNORTH 288
Chestfield (Whitstable) Golf Club WHITSTABLE 231
Chevin Golf Club DUFFIELD 168
Chiangmai-Lamphun Golf Club CHIANGMAI 583
Chiberta Golf de ANGLET 551
Chichester Golf Club CHICHESTER 322, 599
Chiddingfold Golf Club CHIDDINGFOLD 307
Chigwell Golf Club CHIGWELL 191
Childwall Golf Club Ltd LIVERPOOL 260
Chiltern Forest Golf Club AYLESBURY 137
Chilwell Manor Golf Club NOTTINGHAM 281
Chilworth Golf Club SOUTHAMPTON 209, 591
China Fleet Country Club SALTASH 159, 589
Chingford Golf Club CHINGFORD 123
Chingford Golf Range CHINGFORD 586
Chippenham Golf Club CHIPPENHAM 340
Chipping Norton Golf Club CHIPPING NORTON 284
Chipping Sodbury Golf Club BRISTOL 197
Chipstead Golf Club Ltd CHIPSTEAD 307
Chirk Golf Club CHIRK 459
Chislehurst Golf Club CHISLEHURST 223
Chobham Golf Club WOKING 316
Chorley Golf Club CHORLEY 234
Chorleywood Golf Club Ltd. CHORLEYWOOD 214
Chorlton-cum-Hardy Golf Club MANCHESTER 253
Chulmleigh Golf Course CHULMLEIGH 170
Church Stretton Golf Club CHURCH STRETTON 288
Churchill & Blakedown Golf Club BLAKEDOWN 344
Churston Golf Club Ltd BRIXHAM 170
Cilgwyn Golf Club LAMPETER 468
Cirencester Golf Club CIRENCESTER 200
City of Coventry Brandon Wood Golf Course COVENTRY 329
City of Derry Golf Club PREHEN 497
City of Edinburgh Golf Club EDINBURGH 410
City Of Newcastle Golf Club NEWCASTLE UPON TYNE 327
City of Wakefield Golf Club WAKEFIELD 368
Clacton-on-Sea Golf Club CLACTON-ON-SEA 191
Clandeboye Golf Club NEWTOWNARDS 495
Clandon Regis Golf Club WEST CLANDON 315
Claremorris Golf Club CLAREMORRIS 524
Clayton Golf Club BRADFORD 360
Cleckheaton and District Golf Club Ltd CLECKHEATON 362
Cleethorpes Golf Club Ltd CLEETHORPES 244
Cleeve Cloud Golf Club CHELTENHAM 198
Cleobury Mortimer Golf Club CLEOBURY MORTIMER 288
Clevedon Golf Club CLEVEDON 294
Cleveland Golf Club REDCAR 352
Cliftonville Golf Club BELFAST 489
Clitheroe Golf Club CLITHEROE 234
Clober Golf Club GLASGOW 425
Clones Golf Club CLONES 527
Clonlara Golf & Leisure CLONLARA 498
Clonmel Golf Club CLONMEL 529
Close House Country Club HEDDON ON THE WALL 326

Index of Clubs & Courses

Clovelly Golf Club FISH HOEK 577
Club at Mapledurham MAPLEDURHAM 286
Clwb Golff Abersoch ABERSOCH 454
Clwb Golff Ffestiniog FFESTINIOG 456
Clydebank & District Golf Club CLYDEBANK 404
Clydebank Municipal Golf Course CLYDEBANK 404
Clydeway Golf Centre UDDINGSTON 604
Clyne Golf Club SWANSEA 484
Cobh Golf Club COBH 501
Cobtree Manor Park Golf Club MAIDSTONE 227
Cochrane Castle Golf Club JOHNSTONE 446
Cockermouth Golf Club EMBLETON 162
Cocks Moors Woods Golf Club BIRMINGHAM 332
Cocksford Golf Club STUTTON 353
Coed-Y-Mwstwr Golf Club BRIDGEND 473
Cognac Golf du COGNAC 549
Colchester Golf Club COLCHESTER 191
Colchester Golf Range COLCHESTER 590
Cold Ashby Golf Club NORTHAMPTON 269
College Pines Golf Club WORKSOP 283
Collingtree Park Golf Course NORTHAMPTON 270
Colmworth and North Bedfordshire Golf Club COLMWORTH 131
Colnbrook Golf Range COLNBROOK 587
Colne Golf Club COLNE 234
Colne Valley Golf Club COLCHESTER 191
Colonsay Golf Club ISLE OF COLONSAY 450
Colvend Golf Club DALBEATTIE 398
Colville Park Golf Club MOTHERWELL 437
Colworth Golf Club SHARNBROOK 132
Comrie Golf Club CRIEFF 440
Concord Park Driving Range SHEFFIELD 602
Concord Park Municipal Golf Course SHEFFIELD 358
Congleton Golf Club CONGLETON 148
Connemara Golf Club CLIFDEN 511
Connemara Isles Golf Club ANNAGHVANE 511
Consett & District Golf Club CONSETT 184
Conwy (Caernarvonshire) Golf Club CONWY 460
Cooden Beach Golf Club BEXHILL-ON-SEA 317
Cookridge Hall Golf Club LEEDS 365
Coollattin Golf Club ARKLOW 534
Coombe Hill Golf Club KINGSTON-UPON-THAMES 311
Coombe Wood Golf Club KINGSTON-UPON-THAMES 311
Coosheen Golf Club SCHULL 502
Copt Heath Golf Club SOLIHULL 336
Copthorne Golf Club CRAWLEY 323
Corballis Public Golf Links DONABATE 507
Corhampton Golf Club SOUTHAMPTON 209
Cork Golf Club LITTLE ISLAND 501
Corrie Golf Club CORRIE 393
Corrstown Golf Club KILSALLAGHAN 508
Corus (Port Talbot) Golf Club PORT TALBOT 483
Cosby Golf Club COSBY 239
Costa Brava Golf Club GIRONA 569
Costessey Park Golf Course NORWICH 267
Cotgrave Place Golf & Country Club NOTTINGHAM 281, 595
Cotswold Edge Golf Club WOTTON-UNDER-EDGE 202
Cotswold Hills Golf Club Ltd CHELTENHAM 198
Cottesmore Golf & Country Club CRAWLEY 323
Cottingham Parks Golf & Country Club HULL 348
Cottrell Park Golf Club CARDIFF 476
Coulsdon Manor Hotel & Golf Centre COULSDON 307
Country Club Khao Yai NAKHON RATCHASIMA 584

Visit the FHG website
www.holidayguides.com
for details of the wide choice of accommodation featured in the full range of FHG titles

618 Index of Clubs & Courses

County Armagh Golf Club ARMAGH 492
County Cavan Golf Club CAVAN 498
County Longford Golf Club LONGFORD 522
County Louth Golf Club DROGHEDA 522
County Sligo Golf Club ROSSES POINT 529
Coventry Golf Club COVENTRY 334
Coventry Hearsall Golf Club COVENTRY 334
Cowal Golf Club DUNOON 386
Cowdenbeath Golf Club COWDENBEATH 417
Cowdray Park Golf Club COWDRAY PARK 323
Cowes Golf Club COWES 220
Cowglen Golf Club GLASGOW 425
Coxmoor Golf Club MANSFIELD 280
Craddockstown Golf Club NAAS 516
Cradoc Golf Club CRADOC 471, 605
Craggan Golf Club GRANTOWN-ON-SPEY 380
Craibstone Golf Centre BUCKSBURN 378
Craigavon Golf & Ski Centre CRAIGAVON 492, 606
Craigentinny Golf Course EDINBURGH 410
Craigie Hill Golf Club (1982) Ltd PERTH 444
Craigieknowes Golf Club DALBEATTIE 399
Craigielaw Golf Club ABERLADY 409
Craigmillar Park Golf Club EDINBURGH 410
Craignure Golf Club CRAIGNURE 451
Crail Golfing Society CRAIL 418
Crane Valley Golf Club VERWOOD 182
Cranfield Golf at Sandown ESHER 310
Cranford Golf Centre STOCKPORT 588
Cranleigh Golf & Leisure Club CRANLEIGH 308
Cray Valley Golf Club ORPINGTON 227
Craythorne (The) BURTON-ON-TRENT 298, 597
Creigiau Golf Club CARDIFF 476
Cretingham Golf Club FRAMLINGHAM 303
Crewe Golf Club Ltd CREWE 148
Crews Hill Golf Club ENFIELD 124
Criccieth Golf Club CRICCIETH 456
Crichton Golf Club DUMFRIES 398
Cricklade Hotel & Country Club CRICKLADE 341
Crieff Golf Club CRIEFF 442
Crimple Valley Golf Club HARROGATE 351
Croham Hurst Golf Club CROYDON 308
Crompton and Royton Golf Club Ltd OLDHAM 255

Crondon Park Golf Club STOCK 196
Crook Golf Club CROOK 184
Crookhill Park (Municipal) Golf Club DONCASTER 356
Crosland Heath Golf Club Ltd HUDDERSFIELD 363
Crow Nest Park Golf Club BRIGHOUSE 361
Crow Wood Golf Club GLASGOW 425
Crowborough Beacon Golf Club CROWBOROUGH 318
Croydon Driving Range Ltd CROYDON 598
Cruden Bay Golf Club PETERHEAD 378
Cruit Island Golf Club KINCASSLAGH 504
Crystal Bay Golf Club CHONBURI 584
Cuckfield Golf Course CUCKFIELD 323
Cuddington (Banstead) Golf Club Ltd BANSTEAD 306
Culcrieff Golf Club CRIEFF 442
Cullen Golf Club CULLEN 378
Cumberwell Park Golf Club BRADFORD-ON-AVON 340
Cupar Golf Club CUPAR 418
Curragh Golf Club CURRAGH 516
Cushendall Golf Club CUSHENDALL 489
Cwmrhydneuadd Golf Club LLANDYSUL 468

Dainton Park Golf Club NEWTON ABBOTT 174
Dalbeattie Golf Club DALBEATTIE 398
Dale Hill Golf Club WADHURST 321
Dalmally Golf Club DALMALLY 385
Dalmilling Golf Course AYR 388
Dalmunzie Golf Course BLAIRGOWRIE 440
Dalston Hall Golf Club CARLISLE 162
Dalziel Park Golf & Country Club MOTHERWELL 437
Darenth Valley Golf Course SEVENOAKS 229
Darlington Golf Club (Members) Ltd DARLINGTON 185
D'Aro Mas Nou Club de Golf GIRONA 569
Dartford Golf Club Ltd DARTFORD 223
Dartmouth Golf & Country Club DARTMOUTH 171
Dartmouth Golf Club WEST BROMWICH 338
Darwen Golf Club DARWEN 235
Datchet Golf Club SLOUGH 136
Davenport Golf Club POYNTON 150

WHEREVER YOU'RE PLAYING
pick up a guide map to what's best in the area
From all leading Tourist Information Centres and participating hotels & golf clubs
TOURIST PUBLICATIONS 5 Eglinton Crescent, Edinburgh EH12 5DH
Tel: 0131 225 4547 Fax: 0131 220 6789

Golf Guide Maps

Daventry & District Golf Club DAVENTRY 269
Davyhulme Park Golf Club DAVYHULME 252
Dawn Till Dusk Golf Club MILFORD HAVEN 469
De Vere Belfry WISHAW 338
De Vere Belton Woods Hotel and Country Club GRANTHAM 244
De Vere Dunston Hall NORWICH 267
De Vere Herons' Reach Golf Club BLACKPOOL 233, 594
De Vere Mottram Hall Golf Course PRESTBURY 150
De Vere Slaley Hall Hotel, Golf Resort & Spa NEWCASTLE-UPON-TYNE 277
Dean Wood Golf Club UPHOLLAND 238
Deane Golf Club BOLTON 251
Deangate Ridge Golf Club DEANGATE 224
Deanwood Park Golf Club NEWBURY 134
Deer Park Golf & Country Club LIVINGSTON 414
Deer Park Hotel & Golf Courses DUBLIN 508
Deeside Golf Club ABERDEEN 373
Delamere Forest Golf Club NORTHWICH 150
Delapre Golf Centre NORTHAMPTON 270, 595
Delgany Golf Club DELGANY 535
Denbigh Golf Club DENBIGH 460
Denham Golf Club DENHAM 138
Denton Golf Club DENTON 252
Derby Golf Club DERBY 167
Dereham Golf Club DEREHAM 264
Derllys Court Golf Club CARMARTHEN 465
Desert Dunes Golf Club NORTH PALM SPRINGS 576
Desert Falls Country Club PALM DESERT 576
Dewlands Manor Golf Course ROTHERFIELD 320
Dewsbury District Golf Club MIRFIELD 367
Dewstow Golf Club CHEPSTOW 478, 605
Dibden Golf Centre DIBDEN 206
Didsbury Golf Club Ltd MANCHESTER 253
Dinas Powis Golf Club DINAS POWIS 478
Dinsdale Spa Golf Club DARLINGTON 185
Discovery Golf & Leisure COALVILLE 594
Disley Golf Club DISLEY 148
Diss Golf Club DISS 264, 302
Dolgellau Golf Club DOLGELLAU 456
Dollar Golf Club DOLLAR 448

Domangere Golf Club de La LA ROCHE-SUR-YON 547
Donabate Golf Club BALCARRICK 506
Donaghadee Golf Club DONAGHADEE 494
Doncaster Golf Club DONCASTER 356
Doncaster Town Moor Golf Club DONCASTER 357
Donegal Golf Club DONEGAL 503
Doneraile Golf Club DONERAILE 501
Donnington Grove Country Club NEWBURY 134
Donnington Valley Hotel & Golf Club NEWBURY 134
Dooks Golf Links GLENBEIGH 512
Doon Valley Golf Club PATNA 391
Doonbeg Golf Club DOONBEG 498
Dora Golf Course COWDENBEATH 417
Dore and Totley Golf Club SHEFFIELD 358
Dorking Golf Club DORKING 309
Dorset Golf & Country Club WAREHAM 182
Douglas Golf Club DOUGLAS (Co. Cork) 501
Douglas Golf Club DOUGLAS (Isle of Man) 539
Douglas Park Golf Club GLASGOW 425
Douglas Valley Golf Club BOLTON 233
Douglas Water Golf Club DOUGLAS WATER 436
Down Royal Park Golf Course MAZE 490
Downes Crediton Golf Club CREDITON 171
Downfield Golf Club DUNDEE 407
Downpatrick Golf Club DOWNPATRICK 494
Downshire Driving Range WOKINGHAM 587
Downshire Golf Course WOKINGHAM 136
Drayton Park Golf Club TAMWORTH 301
Drayton Park Golf Course DRAYTON 285, 596
Driffield Golf Club DRIFFIELD 348
Drift Golf Club EAST HORSLEY 309
Droitwich Golf & Country Club DROITWICH 345
Dromoland Golf & Country Club NEWMARKET-ON-FERGUS 499
Druids Glen Golf club NEWTOWNMOUNTKENNEDY 537
Druids Heath Golf Club WALSALL 338
Druids Heath Golf Club NEWTOWNMOUNTKENNEDY 537
Drumoig Hotel & Golf Resort ST ANDREWS 422

PLEASE MENTION THE GOLF GUIDE WHEN YOU WRITE OR PHONE TO ENQUIRE ABOUT CLUBS OR ACCOMMODATION

Drumpellier Golf Club COATBRIDGE 436
Dubai Creek Golf and Yacht Club DUBAI 578
Dublin City Golf Club DUBLIN 508
Duddingston Golf Club Ltd EDINBURGH 410
Dudley Golf Club LIVERPOOL 260
Dudley Golf Club Ltd. DUDLEY 335
Dudmoor Farm Golf Course CHRISTCHURCH 181
Dudsbury Golf Club FERNDOWN 181
Duff House Royal Golf Club BANFF 376
Dufftown Golf Club DUFFTOWN 378
Duke's Course ST ANDREWS 422
Dukes Meadows Golf Club LONDON 126
Dukes Meadows Golf Club & Chiswick Bridge Golf Range LONDON 586
Dukinfield Golf Club DUKINFIELD 252
Dullatur Golf Club GLASGOW 425
Dulwich & Sydenham Hill Golf Club DULWICH 123
Dumbarton Golf Club DUMBARTON 405
Dumfries & Galloway Golf Club DUMFRIES 398
Dumfries and County Golf Club DUMFRIES 398
Dummer Golf Club BASINGSTOKE 205
Dun Laoghaire Golf Club DUN LAOGHAIRE 508
Dunaverty Golf Club SOUTHEND 387
Dunbar Golf Club DUNBAR 409
Dunblane New Golf Club DUNBLANE 442
Dundalk Golf Club DUNDALK 523
Dundas Parks Golf Club SOUTH QUEENSFERRY 416
Dunfanaghy Golf Club DUNFANAGHY 504
Dunfermline Golf Club DUNFERMLINE 418
Dungannon Golf Club DUNGANNON 497
Dungarvan Golf Club DUNGARVAN 530
Dunham Forest Golf & Country Club ALTRINCHAM 250
Dunham Golf Club SWAFFHAM 268
Dunkeld & Birnam Golf Club DUNKELD 442
Dunloe Golf Club KILLARNEY 514
Dunmore East Golf Club DUNMORE EAST 530
Dunmurry Golf Club BELFAST 489
Dunnerholme Golf Club ASKAM-IN-FURNESS 161
Dunnikier Park Golf Club KIRKCALDY 419
Dunning Golf Club DUNNING 442
Duns Golf Club DUNS 394
Dunscar Golf Club Ltd. BOLTON 251
Dunstable Downs Golf Club DUNSTABLE 131
Dunstanburgh Castle Golf Club EMBLETON 274

Dunwood Manor Golf Club ROMSEY 209
Durham City Golf Club DURHAM 186
Durness Golf Club DURNESS 430
Duxbury Park Golf Club (Municipal) CHORLEY 234
Dyke Golf Club BRIGHTON 317

Eagles Golf Club KINGS LYNN 266
Eaglescliffe Golf Club Ltd EAGLESCLIFFE 186
Ealing Golf Club GREENFORD 124
Ealing Golf Range LONDON 586
Earlsferry Thistle Golf Club ELIE 419
Earlswood Golf NEATH 481
Easingwold Golf Club EASINGWOLD 351
East Aberdeenshire Golf Centre BALMEDIE 376
East Berkshire Golf Club CROWTHORNE 133
East Bierley Golf Club BRADFORD 360
East Brighton Golf Club BRIGHTON 317
East Cork Golf Club MIDLETON 502
East Devon Golf Club BUDLEIGH SALTERTON 170
East Herts Golf Club Ltd BUNTINGFORD 214
East Kilbride Golf Club GLASGOW 426
East Renfrewshire Golf Club GLASGOW 426
East Sussex National Golf Club UCKFIELD 321
Eastbourne Downs Golf Club EASTBOURNE 318
Eastbourne Golfing Park EASTBOURNE 318
Easter Moffat Golf Club AIRDRIE 436
Eastern Star Country Club RAYONG 585
Eastham Lodge Golf Club EASTHAM 259
Eastwood Golf Club GLASGOW 426
Eaton (Norwich) Golf Club NORWICH 267
Eaton Golf Club CHESTER 147
Eccleston Park Golf Club RAINHILL 261
Eden Course ST ANDREWS 422
Eden Golf Course CARLISLE 162, 589
Edenbridge Golf & Country Club EDENBRIDGE 224
Edenderry Golf Club EDENDERRY 527
Edenmore Golf & Country Club CRAIGAVON 492
Edgbaston Golf Club Ltd BIRMINGHAM 332
Edmondstown Golf Club DUBLIN 508
Edrich Driving Range and Old Nene Golf & Country Club HUNTINGDON 588
Edwalton Golf Courses EDWALTON 279
Edzell Golf Club EDZELL 407
Effingham Golf Club EFFINGHAM 309
Effingham Park Golf Club EFFINGHAM 324
El Bosque Club de Golf CHIVA 570
El Paraiso Golf ESTEPONA 567

Index of Clubs & Courses

El Saler Campo de Golf VALENCIA 570
Elderslie Golf Club ELDERSLIE 446
Elemore Golf Course HETTON-LE-HOLE 326
Elfordleigh Hotel Golf & Leisure Club PLYMOUTH 176
Elgin Golf Club ELGIN 378
Elland Golf Club ELLAND 362
Ellesborough Golf Club AYLESBURY 137
Ellesmere Golf Club MANCHESTER 253
Ellesmere Port Golf Club SOUTH WIRRAL 151
Elm Park Golf and Sports Club DUBLIN 508
Elmwood CUPAR 418
Elsenham Golf Centre ELSENHAM 191
Elsham Golf Club BRIGG 243
Elstree Golf & Country Club ELSTREE 214
Eltham Warren Golf Club ELTHAM 124
Elton Furze Golf Club PETERBOROUGH 144
Ely City Golf Course Ltd. ELY 143
Emirates Golf Club DUBAI 578
Emporda Golf Club PALS 569
Enderby Golf Club ENDERBY 240
Enfield Golf Club ENFIELD 124
Enmore Park Golf Club BRIDGWATER 292
Ennis Golf Club ENNIS 498
Enniscorthy Golf Club ENNISCORTHY 532
Enniscrone Golf Club ENNISCRONE 529
Enniskillen Golf Club ENNISKILLEN 496
Entry Hill Golf Club BATH 292
Enville Golf Club Ltd STOURBRIDGE 300
Epsom Golf Club EPSOM 309
Erewash Valley Golf Club ILKESTON 168
Erinvale Country Estate & Golf Course SOMERSET WEST 577
Erlestoke Sands Golf Club DEVIZES 341
Erskine Golf Club BISHOPTON 446
Escorpion Club de Golf BETERA 570
Esker Hills Golf Club TULLAMORE 528
Esporta (Dougalston Golf Club) GLASGOW 426
Essex Golf & Country Club COLCHESTER 590
Essex Golf and Country Club COLCHESTER 192
Estela Golf Club ESTELA 564
Esterel Latitudes Golf de L' ST RAPHAEL 555
Estoril Golf Do ESTORIL 562
Etangs de Fiac Golf des LAVAUR 552

Etchinghill Golf Club ETCHINGHILL 224
European Club BRITTAS BAY 535
Europro Golf Centre BRISTOL 591
Euxton Park Golf Centre CHORLEY 234
Evesham Golf Club EVESHAM 345
Evian Masters Golf Club EVIAN 550
Exeter Golf & Country Club EXETER 172
Eyemouth Golf Club EYEMOUTH 394

Fairfield Golf and Sailing Club MANCHESTER 253
Fairhaven Golf Club Ltd. LYTHAM ST ANNES 235
Fairlop Waters ILFORD 192, 590
Fairwood Park Golf Club Ltd. SWANSEA 484
Faithlegg Golf Club WATERFORD 531
Fakenham Golf Club FAKENHAM 264
Falkirk Golf Club FALKIRK 448
Falkirk Tryst Golf Club LARBERT 449
Falkland Golf Club FALKLAND 419
Falmouth Golf Club FALMOUTH 154
Fancourt Golf & Country Club Estate GEORGE 577
Farleigh Court Golf Club WARLINGHAM 314
Farnham Golf Club Ltd FARNHAM 310
Farnham Park Pay and Play Golf Course SLOUGH 140
Farrington Golf & Country Club BATH/BRISTOL 292
Farthingstone Golf Club & Hotel TOWCESTER 272
Faversham Golf Club Ltd FAVERSHAM 225
Fawkham Valley Golf Club DARTFORD 223
Felixstowe Ferry Golf Club FELIXSTOWE 302
Feltwell Golf Club THETFORD 268
Fereneze Golf Club BARRHEAD 446
Fermoy Golf Club FERMOY 501
Ferndown Forest Golf Club FERNDOWN 181
Ferndown Golf Club FERNDOWN 181
Fernhill Golf & Country Club CARRIGALINE 500
Ferrybridge Golf Club KNOTTINGLEY 364
Filey Golf Club FILEY 351
Filton Golf Club BRISTOL 197
Finchley Golf Club Ltd. FINCHLEY 124

WHEREVER YOU'RE PLAYING
pick up a guide map to what's best in the area
From all leading Tourist Information Centres and participating hotels & golf clubs
TOURIST PUBLICATIONS 5 Eglinton Crescent, Edinburgh EH12 5DH
Tel: 0131 225 4547 Fax: 0131 220 6789

Golf GUIDE MAPS

Fingle Glen Hotel, Golf & Country Club EXETER 172
Fintona Golf Club FINTONA 497
Fishwick Hall Golf Club PRESTON 236
Five Lakes Resort MALDON 194, 590
Flackwell Heath Golf Club Ltd. HIGH WYCOMBE 138
Flamborough Head Golf Club BRIDLINGTON 347
Fleetlands Golf Club GOSPORT 207
Fleetwood Golf Club Ltd FLEETWOOD 235
Fleming Park Golf Club EASTLEIGH 206
Flempton Golf Club BURY ST EDMUNDS 302
Flint Golf Club FLINT 461
Flixton Golf Club MANCHESTER 253
Fontcaude Golf Hotel de MONTPELLIER 555
Forest Hill Golf Club BOTCHESTON 239, 594
Forest Hills Golf Club Ltd COLEFORD 200
Forest of Dean Golf Club COLEFORD 200
Forest of Galtres Golf Club YORK 354
Forest Park Golf Club YORK 354
Forest Pines Golf Club BRIGG 244
Forfar Golf Club FORFAR 407
Forges-les-Bains Golf de PARIS 548
Formby Golf Centre FORMBY 259
Formby Golf Club FORMBY 259
Formby Ladies' Golf Club FORMBY 259
Forres Golf Club FORRES 379
Forrester Park Golf and Tennis Club MALDON 194
Forrester Park Resort DUNFERMLINE 418
Fort Augustus Golf Club FORT AUGUSTUS 433
Fort William Golf Club FORT WILLIAM 433
Fortrose and Rosemarkie Golf Club FORTROSE 431
Fortwilliam Golf Club BELFAST 489
Fosseway Golf Club and Centurion Hotel BATH 292
Fota Island Golf Club CARRIGTWOHILL 500, 607
Foulford Inn Golf Course CRIEFF 442
Four Marks Golf Club FOUR MARKS 207
Foxbridge Golf Club BILLINGSHURST 322
Foxhills OTTERSHAW 313
Foyle International Golf Centre LONDONDERRY 496, 607

Fraserburgh Golf Club FRASERBURGH 380
Fregate Golf de BANDOL 553
Freshwater Bay Golf Club FRESHWATER 220
Freslonniere Golf de La RENNES 548
Frilford Heath Golf Club ABINGDON 284
Frinton Golf Club FRINTON-ON-SEA 192
Frodsham Golf Club FRODSHAM 148
Fulford (York) Golf Club Ltd. YORK 354
Fulford Heath Golf Club Ltd BIRMINGHAM 332
Fulneck Golf Club Ltd PUDSEY 368
Fulwell Golf Club HAMPTON HILL 125
Furnas Golf Course SAO MIGUEL 564
Furness Golf Club BARROW-IN-FURNESS 161
Furzeley Golf Club DENMEAD 206
Fynn Valley Golf Club IPSWICH 303, 597

Gainsborough Golf Club GAINSBOROUGH 244
Gairloch Golf Club GAIRLOCH 431
Galashiels Golf Club GALASHIELS 394
Galgorm Castle Golf Club BALLYMENA 488
Galway Bay Golf & Country Club Hotel ORANMORE 512
Galway Golf Club SALTHILL 512
Ganstead Park Golf Club CONISTON 347
Ganton Golf Club Ltd SCARBOROUGH 353
Garesfield Golf Club CHOPWELL 326
Garforth Golf Club Ltd LEEDS 365
Garmouth & Kingston Golf Club FOCHABERS 379
Gary Player Country Club SUN CITY 578
Gatehouse of Fleet Golf Club GATEHOUSE OF FLEET 399
Gathurst Golf Club WIGAN 257
Gatley Golf Club Ltd. CHEADLE 147
Gatton Manor DORKING 309
Gatwick Manor Golf Club CRAWLEY 599
Gaudet Luce Golf Club DROITWICH 345
Gay Hill Golf Club BIRMINGHAM 332
Gedney Hill Golf Course SPALDING 248
George Washington Golf & Country Club WASHINGTON 328, 600
Gerrards Cross Golf Club GERRARDS CROSS 138
Ghyll Golf Club BARNOLDSWICK 350
Gifford Golf Club HADDINGTON 414

WHEREVER YOU'RE PLAYING
pick up a guide map to what's best in the area
From all leading Tourist Information Centres and participating hotels & golf clubs
TOURIST PUBLICATIONS 5 Eglinton Crescent, Edinburgh EH12 5DH
Tel: 0131 225 4547 Fax: 0131 220 6789

Gillingham Golf Club Ltd GILLINGHAM 225
Girona Club de Golf GIRONA 569
Girton Golf Club CAMBRIDGE 142
Girvan Golf Course GIRVAN 388
Glamorganshire Golf Club PENARTH 482
Glasgow Golf Club IRVINE 388
Glasgow Golf Club GLASGOW 426
Glasson Golf & Country Club ATHLONE 532
Gleddoch Golf Club LANGBANK 447
Glen Golf Club NORTH BERWICK 415
Glen Gorse Golf Club OADBY 242
Glen of the Downs Golf Club DELGANY 535
Glenbervie Golf Club Ltd LARBERT 449
Glencorse Golf Club PENICUIK 416
Glencruitten Golf Club OBAN 386
Gleneagles Hotel Golf Courses AUCHTERARDER 440
Glengarriff Golf Club GLENGARRIFF 501
Glenisla Golf Centre ALYTH 439
Glenmalure Golf Club RATHDRUM 538
Glenrothes Golf Club GLENROTHES 419
Glossop and District Golf Club GLOSSOP 168
Gloucestershire (The) BRISTOL 197
Glyn Abbey Golf Club KIDWELLY/LLANELLI 465
Glynhir Golf Club AMMANFORD 465
Glynneath Golf Club GLYNNEATH 478
Goal Farm Golf Course PIRBRIGHT 313
Gog Magog Golf Club CAMBRIDGE 142
Gold Coast Golf Club DUNGARVAN 530, 608
Goldenhill Golf Course STOKE-ON-TRENT 300
Golf House Club ELIE 419
Golf International BARRIERE LA BAULE 547
Golf National PARIS 549
Golf Spey Bay SPEY BAY 383
Golspie Golf Club GOLSPIE 430
Goodwood Club CHICHESTER 322
Goring and Streatley Golf Club STREATLEY ON THAMES 136
Gorleston Golf Club GREAT YARMOUTH 264
Gort Golf Club GORT 512
Gosfield Lake Golf Club HALSTEAD 192
Gosforth Golf Club NEWCASTLE UPON TYNE 327
Gosport & Stokes Golf Club GOSPORT 207
Gotts Park Municipal Golf Club LEEDS 365
Gourock Golf Club GOUROCK 446
Gower Golf Club SWANSEA 484
Gowerton Golf Centre SWANSEA 484, 606
Gowran Park GOWRAN 520
Gracehill Golf Club BALLYMONEY 489
Gramacho Course LAGOA 558
Grande Bastide Golf de la GRASSE 554
Grande-Motte Golf de La MONTPELLIER 555
Grange Fell Golf Club GRANGE-OVER-SANDS 162
Grange Park Golf Club ROTHERHAM 357, 601
Grange Park Golf Club SCUNTHORPE 247
Grange Park Golf Club ST HELENS 261
Grange Park Golf Range SCUNTHORPE 615
Grangemouth Golf Club POLMONT 449
Grange-over-Sands Golf Club GRANGE-OVER-SANDS 162
Grantown-on-Spey Golf Club GRANTOWN-ON-SPEY 430
Granville-Baie du Mont Saint Michel Golf De GRANVILLE 545
Grassmoor Golf Centre CHESTERFIELD 167, 589
Great Barr Golf Club BIRMINGHAM 332
Great Grimsby Golf Centre GRIMSBY 594
Great Hadham Golf & Country Club BISHOP'S STORTFORD 213
Great Harwood Golf Club BLACKBURN 232
Great Lever and Farnworth Golf Club Ltd BOLTON 251
Great Salterns Golf Course PORTSMOUTH 208
Great Torrington Golf Club TORRINGTON 178
Great Yarmouth & Caister Golf Club GREAT YARMOUTH 265
Green Haworth Golf Club ACCRINGTON 232
Green Hotel Golf Courses KINROSS 444
Greenacres Golf Club BALLYCLARE 488
Greenburn Golf Club FAULDHOUSE 413
Greenisland Golf Club CARRICKFERGUS 489
Greenmeadow Golf and Country Club CWMBRAN 478, 606
Greenmount Golf Club BURY 252
Greenock Golf Club GREENOCK 446
Greenock Whinhill Golf Club GREENOCK 446
Greenore Golf Club GREENORE 523
Greetham Valley Golf & Country Club RUTLAND 242
Grenelefe Golf & Tennis Resort ORLANDO 574
Grenoble Golf International de GRENOBLE 550
Gretna Golf Club GRETNA 399, 603
Greystones Golf Club GREYSTONES 536
Griffin Golf Club CADDINGTON 131
Grim's Dyke Golf Club PINNER 127
Grimsby Golf Club Ltd GRIMSBY 245
Grove Golf Centre LEOMINSTER 212, 592
Grove Golf Club Ltd. PORTHCAWL 482

Guadalhorce Club de Golf MALAGA 567
Guadalmina Club de Golf MARBELLA 567
Guildford Golf Club GUILDFORD 310
Gujan Mestras Golf de ARCACHON 551
Gullane Golf Club GULLANE 413

Habberley Golf Club KIDDERMINSTER 345
Hadden Hill Golf Club DIDCOT 285
Haddington Golf Club HADDINGTON 414
Hadley Wood Golf Club BARNET 213
Haggs Castle Golf Club GLASGOW 426
Hagley Golf & Country Club HAGLEY 345
Haigh Hall Golf Club WIGAN 257
Hainault Forest Golf Club CHIGWELL 191
Hainsworth Park Golf Club HORNSEA 348
Hale Golf Club ALTRINCHAM 250
Halesowen Golf Club HALESOWEN 335
Halesworth Golf Club HALESWORTH 303, 597
Halifax Bradley Hall Golf Club HALIFAX 362
Halifax Golf Club Ltd HALIFAX 362
Hall Garth Golf & Country Club Hotel DARLINGTON 185
Hallamshire Golf Club Ltd SHEFFIELD 359
Hallowes Golf Club SHEFFIELD 359
Halstock Golf Club HALSTOCK 182
Haltwhistle Golf Course CARLISLE 274
Ham Manor Golf Club Ltd ANGMERING 322
Hamilton Golf Club HAMILTON 437
Hampshire Golf Club ANDOVER 212, 604
Hampstead Golf Club HAMPSTEAD 125
Hampton Court Palace Golf Club HAMPTON WICK 125
Hamptworth Academy SALISBURY 600
Hamptworth Golf and Country Club SALISBURY 342
Hanbury Manor Golf & Country Club WARE 218
Handsworth Golf Club BIRMINGHAM 332
Hanging Heaton Golf Club DEWSBURY 362
Hankley Common Golf Club FARNHAM 310
Hanover Golf & Country Club RAYLEIGH 194
Harborne (Church Farm) Golf Club BIRMINGHAM 332
Harborne Golf Club BIRMINGHAM 332
Harbour Point Golf Club LITTLE ISLAND 502
Harbour Town Golf Links HILTON HEAD 574
Harburn Golf Club WEST CALDER 416

Hardelot Les Dunes Golf de HARDELOT 545
Hardelot Les Pins Golf de HARDELOT 545
Harewood Downs Golf Club AMERSHAM 137
Harleyford Golf Club MARLOW 139
Harpenden Common Golf Club HARPENDEN 215
Harpenden Golf Club HARPENDEN 215
Harris Golf Club SCARISTA 450
Harrogate Golf Club Ltd HARROGATE 351
Hartford Golf Club NORTHWICH 150
Hartford Golf Range NORTHWICH 588
Hartland Forest Golf Club BIDEFORD 170
Hartlepool Golf Club Ltd HARTLEPOOL 186
Hartley Wintney Golf Club HARTLEY WINTNEY 207
Hartsbourne Golf and Country Club BUSHEY HEATH 214
Hartswood Golf Club BRENTWOOD 189
Harwich and Dovercourt Golf Club HARWICH 192
Harwood Golf Club BOLTON 251
Hassocks Golf Club HASSOCKS 324
Hatchford Brook Golf Club BIRMINGHAM 332
Hatfield London Country Club HATFIELD 215
Haut-Poitou Golf du POITIERS 549
Haverfordwest Golf Club HAVERFORDWEST 469
Haverhill Golf Club Ltd HAVERHILL 303
Hawarden Golf Club HAWARDEN 461
Hawick Golf Club HAWICK 395
Hawkhurst Golf Club HAWKHURST 225
Hawkstone Park SHREWSBURY 290
Haydock Park Golf Club NEWTON-LE-WILLOWS 261
Hayling Golf Club HAYLING ISLAND 207
Hayston Golf Club GLASGOW 426
Haywards Heath Golf Club HAYWARDS HEATH 324
Hazel Grove Golf Club STOCKPORT 256
Hazelwood Golf Club SUNBURY ON THAMES 128
Hazlehead Golf Course ABERDEEN 373
Hazlemere Golf Club HIGH WYCOMBE 139
Headfort Golf Club KELLS 526
Headingley Golf Club LEEDS 365
Headley Golf Club BRADFORD 360
Heath Golf Club PORTLAOISE 521
Heathpark Golf Club WEST DRAYTON 129

For full details of clubs and courses, plus convenient accommodation
www.uk-golfguide.com

Heaton Moor Golf Club STOCKPORT 256
Heaton Park Golf Centre MANCHESTER 254
Hebden Bridge Golf Club HEBDEN BRIDGE 363
Hedsor Golf Course WOODBURN COMMON 141
Hele Park Golf Club NEWTON ABBOT 174
Helen's Bay Golf Club BANGOR 493
Helensburgh Golf Club HELENSBURGH 405
Hellidon Lakes Golf Club DAVENTRY 269
Helmsdale Golf Club HELMSDALE 430
Helsby Golf Club HELSBY 148
Helston Golf & Leisure HELSTON 154
Hemingford Abbots Golf Club HUNTINGDON 143
Hemsted Forest Golf Club CRANBROOK 223
Henbury Golf Club BRISTOL 197
Hendon Golf Club HENDON 125
Henley Golf & Country Club HENLEY-IN-ARDEN 329
Henley Golf Club HENLEY-ON-THAMES 285
Hennerton Golf Club WARGRAVE 136, 587
Hereford Municipal Golf Course HEREFORD 211
Herefordshire Golf Club HEREFORD 211
Herne Bay Golf Club HERNE BAY 225
Hertfordshire Golf & Country Club BROXBOURNE 214, 592
Hesketh Golf Club SOUTHPORT 262
Hessle Golf Club COTTINGHAM 348
Heswall Golf Club HESWALL 259
Hever Castle Golf Club HEVER 226
Heworth Golf Club GATESHEAD 326
Heworth Golf Club YORK 354
Hexham Golf Club HEXHAM 274
Heydon Grange Golf and Country Club ROYSTON 217
Heyrose Golf Club KNUTSFORD 148
Heysham Golf Club HEYSHAM 235
Hickleton Golf Club DONCASTER 357
High Elms Golf Club FARNBOROUGH 224
High Post Golf Club Ltd SALISBURY 342
High Throston Golf Club HARTLEPOOL 186
Highbullen Hotel Golf & Country Club CHITTLEHAMHOLT 170
Highcliffe Castle Golf Club CHRISTCHURCH 181
Highfield Golf Course CARBURY 516
Highgate Golf Club HIGHGATE 125

Highwoods Golf Club BEXHILL-ON-SEA 317
Highworth Community Golf Centre HIGHWORTH 341
Hilden Golf Centre TONBRIDGE 230, 594
Hill Barn Golf Course WORTHING 325
Hillingdon Golf Club HILLINGDON 126
Hillsborough Golf Club Ltd SHEFFIELD 359
Hillside Golf Club SOUTHPORT 262
Hilltop Public Golf Course BIRMINGHAM 333
Hilton Park Golf Club GLASGOW 426
Hilton Puckrup Hall TEWKESBURY 202
Hilton Templepatrick Golf CLub TEMPLEPATRICK 491
Himley Hall Golf Centre DUDLEY 335
Hinckley Golf Club HINCKLEY 240
Hindhead Golf Club HINDHEAD 311
Hindley Hall Golf Club WIGAN 257
Hinksey Heights Golf Course OXFORD 286
Hintlesham Hall Golf Club IPSWICH 303
Hirsel Golf Club COLDSTREAM 394
Hobson Golf Club NEWCASTLE UPON TYNE 327
Hockley Golf Club WINCHESTER 210
Hoddom Castle Golf Course LOCKERBIE 400
Hoebridge Golf Centre WOKING 316, 598
Hollandbush Golf Club LESMAHAGOW 437
Hollingbury Park Golf Club BRIGHTON 317
Hollywood Lakes Golf Club BALLYBOUGHAL 506
Holme Hall Golf Club SCUNTHORPE 247
Holsworthy Golf Club HOLSWORTHY 172
Holtye Golf Club EAST GRINSTEAD 324
Holyhead Golf Club TREARDDUR BAY 458
Holywell Bay Golf Park NEWQUAY 156
Holywell Golf Club HOLYWELL 461
Holywood Golf Club HOLYWOOD 494
Homelands Bettergolf Centre ASHFORD 221, 592
Honiton Golf Club HONITON 173
Honourable Company of Edinburgh Golfers GULLANE 413
Hopeman Golf Club ELGIN 378
Horam Park Golf Course HEATHFIELD 320
Horam Park Golf Course & Floodlit Driving Range HORAM 599
Horncastle Golf Club HORNCASTLE 245
Hornsea Golf Club HORNSEA 348

WHEREVER YOU'RE PLAYING
pick up a guide map to what's best in the area

From all leading Tourist Information Centres and participating hotels & golf clubs
TOURIST PUBLICATIONS 5 Eglinton Crescent, Edinburgh EH12 5DH
Tel: 0131 225 4547 Fax: 0131 220 6789

Golf Guide Maps

Horsenden Hill Golf Club GREENFORD 124
Horsforth Golf Club Ltd LEEDS 366
Horsham Golf & Fitness HORSHAM 324
Horsley Lodge Golf Club HORSLEY 168
Horton Park Golf & Country Club EPSOM 309
Horwich Golf Club HORWICH 252
Hossegor Golf de HOSSEGOR 552
Houghton-le-Spring Golf Club
HOUGHTON-LE-SPRING 326
Houghwood ST HELENS 237
Houldsworth Golf Club Ltd. MANCHESTER 254
Hounslow Heath Municipal Golf Course
HOUNSLOW 126
Howley Hall Golf Club LEEDS 366
Howth Golf Club SUTTON 511
Hoylake Golf Club WIRRAL 263
Huddersfield Golf Club HUDDERSFIELD 363
Hull Golf Club (1921) Ltd HULL 348
Humberstone Heights Golf Club
LEICESTER 250, 607
Hunley Hall Golf Club & Hotel BROTTON 350
Hunley Hall Golf Club & Hotel SALTBURN 602
Hunstanton Golf Club HUNSTANTON 265
Huntercombe Golf Club HENLEY-ON-THAMES 286
Huntly Golf Club HUNTLY 380
Huntswood Golf Club BURNHAM 133
Hurdwick Golf Club TAVISTOCK 178
Hurlston Hall Golf Club SCARISBRICK 237
Hurst Golf Club READING 135
Hurtmore Golf Club GODALMING 310
Huyton and Prescot Golf Club Ltd HUYTON 260
Hylands Golf Complex INGATESTONE 193
Hythe Imperial Golf Club HYTHE 226

Ifield Golf and Country Club CRAWLEY 323
Ilford Golf Club ILFORD 193
Ilfracombe & Woolacombe Golf Range
ILFRACOMBE 173, 590
Ilfracombe Golf Club ILFRACOMBE 173
Ilkeston Borough Golf Club ILKESTON 168
Ilkley Golf Club ILKLEY 364
Immingham Golf Club IMMINGHAM 245
Imperial Lake View Hotel & Golf Club
CHA-AM 581
Inchmarlo Golf Centre BANCHORY 376
Inco Golf Club SWANSEA 484
Indian Wells Golf Resort INDIAN WELLS 575
Ingestre Park Golf Club STAFFORD 299
Ingol Golf Club PRESTON 236
Ingon Manor Hotel & Golf Club
STRATFORD-UPON-AVON 331

Innellan Golf Club DUNOON 386
Innerleithen Golf Club INNERLEITHEN 395
Innisbrook Hilton Resort TARPON SPRINGS 574
Insch Golf Club INSCH 380
Inverallochy Golf Club INVERALLOCHY 381
Inveraray Golf Club INVERARAY 386
Invergordon Golf Club INVERGORDON 431
Inverness Golf Club INVERNESS 433
Inverurie Golf Club INVERURIE 381
Ipswich Golf Club IPSWICH 303
Irvine Golf Club IRVINE 389
Irvine Ravenspark Golf Club IRVINE 389
Island Golf Club DONABATE 507
Islay Golf Club PORT ELLEN 450
Isle of Wedmore Golf Club WEDMORE 296
Isle of Gigha Golf Club ISLE OF GIGHA 450
Isle of Purbeck Golf Club STUDLAND 182
Isle Of Seil Golf Club OBAN 387
Isle of Skye Golf Club SCONSER 452
Isles of Scilly Golf Club ST MARY'S 160
Iver Golf Club IVER 139
Ivinghoe Golf Club LEIGHTON BUZZARD 131
Izaak Walton Golf Club STONE 300

Jack Barker's Greenway Hall Golf Club
STOKE-ON-TRENT 300
Jack Barker's Keele Golf Club
NEWCASTLE-UNDER-LYME 299
Jedburgh Golf Club JEDBURGH 395
Jersey Recreation Grounds JERSEY 542
John Mulgrew Normandy Golf Centre
RENFREW 604
John O'Gaunt Golf Club SANDY 132
John Reay Golf Centres COVENTRY 600
Jubilee Course ST ANDREWS 422

K Club STRAFFAN 518
Kames Country Club CLEGHORN 437
Kearsley Golf Driving Range KEARSLEY 595
Kedleston Park Golf Club QUARNDON 169
Keighley Golf Club KEIGHLEY 364
Keith Golf Club KEITH 381
Kelso Golf Club KELSO 395
Kemnay Golf Club KEMNAY 381
Kendal Golf Club KENDAL 164
Kendleshire Golf Club BRISTOL 197
Kenilworth Golf Club Ltd KENILWORTH 329
Kenmare Golf Club KENMARE 513
Kenmore Golf Course KENMORE 443
Kent National Golf & Country Club
BRENCHLEY 222
Kenwick Park Golf Club LOUTH 246
Kerries Golf Club TRALEE 514
Keswick Golf Club KESWICK 164
Kettering Golf Club KETTERING 269

Kibworth Golf Club LEICESTER 140
Kidderminster Golf Club KIDDERMINSTER 345
Kilbirnie Place Golf Club KILBIRNIE 389
Kilcock Golf Club KILCOCK 526
Kilcoole Golf Club KILCOOLE 536
Kilkea Castle Hotel & Golf Club KILKEA 516
Kilkee Golf Club KILKEE 499
Kilkeel Golf Club KILKEEL 494
Kilkenny Golf Club KILKENNY 520
Killarney Golf and Fishing Club KILLARNEY 514
Killeen Golf Club KILL 516
Killeline Golf Club NEWCASTLE WEST 522
Killin Golf Club KILLIN 443
Killin Park Golf & Country Club KILLIN 523
Killiney Golf Club KILLINEY 508
Killiow Golf Club & Driving Range TRURO 159, 589
Killorglin Golf Club KILLORGLIN 514
Killymoon Golf Club COOKSTOWN 497
Kilmacolm Golf Club KILMACOLM 447
Kilmarnock (Barassie) Golf Club TROON 392
Kilnwick Percy Golf Club KILNWICK PERCY 349
Kilrush Golf Club KILRUSH 499
Kilspindie Golf Club ABERLADY 409
Kilsyth Lennox Golf Club KILSYTH 427
Kilton Forest Golf Club WORKSOP 283
Kilworth Springs Golf club NORTH KILWORTH 242
King Edward Bay Golf Club ONCHAN 539
King James VI Golf Club PERTH 444
Kingfisher Country Club MILTON KEYNES 139, 587
Kinghorn Municipal Golf Club KINGHORN 419
King's Acre Golf Course & Academy LASSWADE 414
King's Hill Golf Club WEST MALLING 231
King's Links Golf Centre ABERDEEN 603
King's Links Golf Course ABERDEEN 373
King's Lynn Golf Club KING'S LYNN 266
King's Norton Golf Club Ltd. BIRMINGHAM 333
Kingsdown Golf Club CORSHAM 341
Kingsknowe Golf Club EDINBURGH 410
Kingsley Golf Club BORDON 206, 591
Kingsthorpe Golf Club NORTHAMPTON 270
Kingswood Golf & Country Club Ltd KINGSWOOD 311
Kington Golf Club KINGTON 212
Kingussie Golf Club KINGUSSIE 434
Kingweston Golf Club STREET 295
Kinloss Country Golf Course FORRES 379
Kinmel Park Golf Complex BODELWYDDAN 459
Kinsale Golf Club KINSALE 501
Kinsale Golf Course HOLYWELL 461
Kintore Golf Club KINTORE 381
Kirby Muxloe Golf Club KIRBY MUXLOE 240
Kirkby Lonsdale Golf Club KIRKBY LONSDALE 164
Kirkbymoorside Golf Club KIRKBYMOORSIDE 351
Kirkcaldy Golf Club KIRKCALDY 419
Kirkcudbright Golf Club KIRKCUDBRIGHT 400
Kirkhill Golf Club GLASGOW 426
Kirkintilloch Golf Club KIRKINTILLOCH 405
Kirkistown Castle Golf Club NEWTOWNARDS 495
Kirriemuir Golf Club Ltd. KIRRIEMUIR 407
Kirtlington Golf Club KIRTLINGTON 286
Kirton Holme Golf Club BOSTON 243
Knaresborough Golf Club KNARESBOROUGH 352
Knebworth Golf Club KNEBWORTH 216
Knighton Golf Club KNIGHTON 471
Knighton Heath Golf Club BOURNEMOUTH 180
Knights Grange Sports Complex WINSFORD 152
Knightswood Golf Club GLASGOW 426
Knock Golf Club BELFAST 493
Knockanally Golf and Country Club DONADEA 516
Knole Park Golf Club SEVENOAKS 229
Knott End Golf Club BLACKPOOL 233
Knotty Hill Golf Centre STOCKTON-ON-TEES 188, 590
Knowle Bristol Golf Club BRISTOL 197
Knutsford Golf Club KNUTSFORD 149
Kyles Of Bute Golf Club TIGHNABRUAICH 387

PLEASE MENTION THIS GUIDE WHEN YOU WRITE OR PHONE TO ENQUIRE ABOUT CLUBS OR ACCOMMODATION

La Cala Resort MIJAS 567
La Grande Mare Golf Club GUERNSEY 541
La Manga Club MURCIA 570
La Moye Golf Club JERSEY 542
La Quinta Golf and Country Club
BENAHAVIS 566
La Quinta Resort & Club (Dunes) LA
QUINTA 575
La Quinta Resort & Club (Mountain) LA
QUINTA 575
Lacanau Ocean Golf Hotel LACANAU
OCEAN 552
Ladbrook Park Golf Club Ltd SOLIHULL 336
Ladybank Golf Club LADYBANK 419
Laem Chabang International Country Club
CHONBURI 584
Lagganmore Golf Club & Hotel
PORTPATRICK 402
Laguna Golf Course VILAMOURA 560
Laguna Phuket Golf Club LAGUNA PHUKET 580
Lahinch Golf Club LAHINCH 499
Lakeside Golf Club RUGELEY 299
Lakeside Golf Club PORT TALBOT 483
Lakeside Lodge Golf Centre HUNTINGDON 143
Laleham Golf Club CHERTSEY 307
Lamberhurst Golf Club TUNBRIDGE WELLS 231
Lambourne Golf Club BURNHAM 138
Lamerwood Country Club
WHEATHAMPSTEAD 219
Lamlash Golf Club LAMLASH 393
Lanark Golf Club LANARK 437
Lancaster Golf Club Ltd LANCASTER 235
Lanes Golfing Academy STOKE POGES 141,587
Langdon Hills Golf Centre BULPHAN 190
Langholm Golf Club LANGHOLM 400
Langland Bay Golf Club SWANSEA 484
Langley Park Golf Club BECKENHAM 221
Lanhydrock Golf Club BODMIN 153
Lansdown Golf Club BATH 292
Lansil Golf Club LANCASTER 235
Largs Golf Club LARGS 390
Larkhall Golf Club LARKHALL 437
Larne Golf Club LARNE 489

Lauder Golf Club LAUDER 396
Launceston Golf Club LAUNCESTON 154
Lavender Park Golf Centre ASCOT 133
Laytown & Bettystown Golf Club
BETTYSTOWN 526
Lea Marston Hotel & Leisure Complex
SUTTON COLDFIELD 600
Leadhills Golf Club LEADHILLS 437
Leamington and County Golf Club
LEAMINGTON SPA 330
Leaside Golf Club EDMONTON 124
Leasowe Golf Club MORETON 261
Leatherhead Golf Club LEATHERHEAD 312
Lee Park Golf Club LIVERPOOL 260
Lee Valley Golf Club OVENS 502
Lee Valley Leisure Golf Course EDMONTON 124
Leeds Castle Golf Course MAIDSTONE 227
Leeds Golf Centre LEEDS 366, 602
Leeds Golf Club LEEDS 366
Leek Golf Club LEEK 298
Leek Westwood Golf Club LEEK 298
Leen Valley Golf Centre HUCKNALL 280
Lee-on-the-Solent Golf Club LEE-ON-THE-SOLENT 207
Lees Hall Golf Club Ltd SHEFFIELD 359
Leicestershire Golf Club LEICESTER 240
Leigh Golf Club WARRINGTON 152
Leighton Buzzard Golf Club LEIGHTON BUZZARD 131
Lely Resort NAPLES 573
Lenzie Golf Club LENZIE 405
Leominster Golf Club LEOMINSTER 212
Leopardstown Driving Range FOXROCK 607
Les Bordes Golf International ORLEANS 549
Les Mielles Golf and Country Club ST OUEN'S 542, 608
Les Ormes Golf & Leisure Club JERSEY 542
Leslie Golf Club LESLIE 419
Letchworth Golf Club LETCHWORTH 216
Letham Grange Golf Course ARBROATH 406
Lethamhill Golf Course GLASGOW 427
Letterkenny Golf Club LETTERKENNY 504
Leven Golfing Society LEVEN 420
Leven Thistle Golf Club LEVEN 420

WHEREVER YOU'RE PLAYING
pick up a guide map to what's best in the area
From all leading Tourist Information Centres and participating hotels & golf clubs
TOURIST PUBLICATIONS 5 Eglinton Crescent, Edinburgh EH12 5DH
Tel: 0131 225 4547 Fax: 0131 220 6789

Index of Clubs & Courses

Lewes Golf Club LEWES 320
Lexden Wood Golf Club COLCHESTER 191, 590
Leyland Golf Club Ltd LEYLAND 235
Libbaton Golf Club Ltd UMBERLEIGH 178
Liberton Golf Club EDINBURGH 411
Lickey Hills Golf Club REDNAL 336
Lightcliffe Golf Club HALIFAX 362
Lilleshall Hall Golf Club NEWPORT 289
Lilley Brook Golf Club CHELTENHAM 199
Lime Trees Park Golf Club NORTHOLT 586
Limerick County Golf & Country Club BALLYNEETY 522
Limerick Golf Club LIMERICK 522
Limpsfield Chart Golf Club OXTED 313
Lincoln Golf Club LINCOLN 246
Lincolnshire Golf Course SCUNTHORPE 247
Lindrick Golf Club WORKSOP 283, 359
Lingdale Golf Club WOODHOUSE EAVES 242
Lingfield Park Golf Club LINGFIELD 312
Links Country Park Hotel and Golf Club CROMER 264
Links Golf Club NEWMARKET 304
Linlithgow Golf Club LINLITHGOW 414
Linn Park Golf Club GLASGOW 427
Liphook Golf Club LIPHOOK 207
Lisbon Sports Club LISBON 562
Lisburn Golf Club LISBURN 490
Lismore Golf Club LISMORE 530
Litchfield Country Club MYRTLE BEACH 575
Little Aston Golf Club STREETLY 301
Little Chalfont Golf Club LITTLE CHALFONT 139
Little Hay Golf Complex HEMEL HEMPSTEAD 215
Little Lakes Golf Club BEWDLEY 344
Littlehampton Golf Club LITTLEHAMPTON 324
Littlehill Golf Club GLASGOW 427
Littlestone Golf Club NEW ROMNEY 227
Llandrindod Wells Golf Club LLANDRINDOD WELLS 472
Llandudno Golf Club (Maesdu) Ltd LLANDUDNO 462
Llanfairfechan Golf Club LLANFAIRFECHAN 456
Llangefni Public Golf Course LLANGEFNI 457
Llanishen Golf Club CARDIFF 476
Llantrisant and Pontyclun Golf Club TALBOT GREEN 485
Llanwern Golf Club LLANWERN 480
Llanymynech Golf Club OSWESTRY 289
Llanyrafon Golf Course CWMBRAN 478
Llyn Golf PWLLHELI 457, 605
Lobden Golf Club ROCHDALE 256
Loch Ness Golf Course INVERNESS 433, 604
Loch Palm Golf Club PHUKET 581
Lochcarron Golf Club LOCHCARRON 431
Lochgelly Golf Club LOCHGELLY 420
Lochgilphead Golf Club LOCHGILPHEAD 386
Lochmaben Golf Club LOCHMABEN 400
Lochranza Golf LOCHRANZA 393
Lochwinnoch Golf Club LOCHWINNOCH 447
Lockerbie Golf Club LOCKERBIE 400
Lofthouse Hill Golf Club WAKEFIELD 368
London Golf Centre NORTHOLT 586
London Golf Club ASH 221
London Scottish Golf Club LONDON 126
Long Ashton Golf Club BRISTOL 198
Long Sutton Golf Club LANGPORT 294, 597
Longcliffe Golf Club LOUGHBOROUGH 241
Longhirst Hall Golf Club MORPETH 276
Longley Park Golf Club HUDDERSFIELD 363
Longniddry Golf Club Ltd LONGNIDDRY 415
Longridge Golf Club PRESTON 237
Longside Golf Club PETERHEAD 382
Looe Golf Club LOOE 154
Los Naranjos Golf Club MARBELLA 567
Lostwithiel Hotel Golf & Country Club LOSTWITHIEL 156
Lothianburn Golf Club EDINBURGH 411
Loudoun Gowf Club GALSTON 388
Loudun-Roiffe Golf de LOUDUN 549
Loughrea Golf Club LOUGHREA 512
Loughton Golf Club LOUGHTON 193
Louth Golf Club LOUTH 246
Low Laithes Golf Club Ltd WAKEFIELD 368
Lowes Park Golf Club Ltd BURY 252
Ludlow Golf Club LUDLOW 288
Luffenham Heath Golf Club STAMFORD 242
Luffness New Golf Club ABERLADY 409
Lullingstone Park Golf Club ORPINGTON 227
Lumphanan Golf Club BANCHORY 376
Lundin Golf Club LUNDIN LINKS 420
Lundin Ladies Golf Club LUNDIN LINKS 420
Lurgan Golf Club LURGAN 492
Lutterworth Golf Club LUTTERWORTH 241

PLEASE MENTION THE GOLF GUIDE WHEN YOU WRITE OR PHONE TO ENQUIRE ABOUT CLUBS OR ACCOMMODATION

Luttrellstown Castle Golf and Country Club CASTLEKNOCK 506
Lybster Golf Club LYBSTER 430
Lydd Golf Club & Driving Range LYDD 226
Lydney Golf Club LYDNEY 200
Lyme Regis Golf Club LYME REGIS 182
Lymm Golf Club LYMM 149
Lyon Golf Club de LYON 551
Lyons Gate Golf Club DORCHESTER 189
Lytham Green Drive Golf Club LYTHAM ST. ANNES 235

Macclesfield Golf Club MACCLESFIELD 149
Macdonald Cardrona Hotel, Golf & Country Club PEEBLES 396
Macdonald Hill Valley Hotel Golf & Country Club WHITCHURCH 291
Macdonald Linden Hall MORPETH 276
Machrie Bay Golf Course MACHRIE 393
Machrie Golf Club PORT ELLEN 450
Machrihanish Golf Club CAMPBELTOWN 385
Machynlleth Golf Club MACHYNLLETH 472
Macroom Golf Club MACROOM 502
Maesteg Golf Club MAESTEG 480
Maeva Latitudes Toulouse Seilh TOULOUSE 553
Magdalene Fields Golf Club BERWICK-UPON-TWEED 274
Magnolia Park Golf & Country Club OXON/BUCKINGHAMSHIRE 286
Magpie Hall Lane Municipal Golf Club BROMLEY 222
Mahee Island Golf Club NEWTOWNARDS 495
Maidenhead Golf Club MAIDENHEAD 133
Maidstone Golf Centre MAIDSTONE 593
Majestic Creek Country Club HUA HIN 582
Malahide Golf Club MALAHIDE 510
Malden Golf Club NEW MALDEN 313
Maldon Golf Club MALDON 194
Malkins Bank Municipal Golf Course SANDBACH 151
Mallow Golf Club MALLOW 502
Malone Golf Club BELFAST 489
Malton and Norton Golf Club MALTON 352
Malton Golf ROYSTON 217
Manchester Golf Club MANCHESTER 254
Mannan Castle Golf Club CARRICKMACROSS 526
Mannings Heath Golf Club HORSHAM 324
Manor Golf Club GRIMSBY 245

Manor Golf Club UTTOXETER 301
Manor Golf Club BRADFORD 360
Manor House Golf Club at Castle Combe CASTLE COMBE 340
Manor of Groves SAWBRIDGEWORTH 217
Mansfield Woodhouse Golf Club MANSFIELD 280
Manston Golf Centre RAMSGATE 228, 593
Mapperley Golf Club MAPPERLEY 280
March Golf Club MARCH 143
Marconi Golf Club COVENTRY 334
Market Drayton Golf Club MARKET DRAYTON 288
Market Harborough Golf Club MARKET HARBOROUGH 241
Market Rasen and District Golf Club MARKET RASEN 246
Market Rasen Racecourse 9-Hole Pay & Play Course MARKET RASEN 247
Marlborough Golf Club MARLBOROUGH 341
Marple Golf Club MARPLE 255
Marriott Breadsall Priory Hotel & Country Club DERBY 167
Marriott Dalmahoy Hotel and Country Club KIRKNEWTON 414
Marriott Forest of Arden Hotel & Country Club COVENTRY 329, 334
Marriott Goodwood Park Hotel & Ctry Club CHICHESTER 322
Marriott Hollins Hall Hotel & Country Club SHIPLEY 368
Marriott Meon Valley Hotel and Country Club SHEDFIELD 210
Marriott Sprowston Manor Hotel & Country Club NORWICH 267
Marriott St Pierre Hotel & Country Club CHEPSTOW 478
Marriott Tudor Park Hotel and Country Club MAIDSTONE 227
Marriott Worsley Park Hotel & Country Club WORSLEY 257
Marriott's Desert Springs Resort & Spa PALM DESERT 576
Marsden Golf Club HUDDERSFIELD 364
Marseille la Salette Golf de MARSEILLES 554
Martin Moor Golf Club METHERINGHAM 247
Maryport Golf Club Ltd MARYPORT 164
Masham Golf Club RIPON 353
Massane Golf de MONTPELLIER 555
Massereene Golf Club ANTRIM 488

for a wide choice of holiday accommodation www.holidayguides.com

Matfen Hall Golf Club MATFEN 276
Matlock Golf Club MATLOCK 168
Mattishall Golf Club MATTISHALL 266
Maxstoke Park Golf Club BIRMINGHAM 333
Maybole Golf Course MAYBOLE 391
Maylands Golf and Country Club ROMFORD 195
Maywood Golf Club RISLEY 169
Mazamet la Barouge Golf de MAZAMET 552
McCaulay's Fitness and Golf IVYBRIDGE 173
McDonald-Ellon Golf Club ELLON 379
Mearns Castle Golf Academy NEWTON MEARNS 604
Medoc Golf du BORDEAUX 552
Mellor and Townscliffe Golf Club STOCKPORT 256
Melrose Golf Club MELROSE 396
Meltham Golf Club HUDDERSFIELD 364
Melton Mowbray Golf Club MELTON MOWBRAY 242
Melville Golf Centre, Golf Course, Range & Shop DALKEITH 411, 604
Mendip Golf Club Ltd. SHEPTON MALLET 295
Mendip Spring Golf Club BRISTOL 293, 597
Mentmore Golf and Country Club LEIGHTON BUZZARD 132
Menzies Welcombe Hotel & Golf Course STRATFORD-UPON-AVON 331
Merchants of Edinburgh Golf Club EDINBURGH 412
Mere Golf and Country Club KNUTSFORD 149
Merlin Golf Club & Driving Range NEWQUAY 156, 588
Merrist Wood Golf Club GUILDFORD 310
Mersey Valley Golf & Country Club WIDNES 152
Merthyr Tydfil Golf Club MERTHYR TYDFIL 480
Meyrick Park Golf Club BOURNEMOUTH 180
Mickleover Golf Club MICKLEOVER 169
Middlebank Golf Range MIDDLEBANK 604
Middlesbrough Golf Club MIDDLESBROUGH 352
Middlesbrough Municipal Golf Centre MIDDLESBROUGH 187

Middleton Hall Golf Club KING'S LYNN 266
Middleton Park (Municipal) Golf Club LEEDS 366
Mid-Herts Golf Club ST ALBANS 217
Mid-Kent Golf Club GRAVESEND 225
Mid-Sussex Golf Club DITCHLING 318
Mid-Yorkshire Golf Club PONTEFRACT 368
Mijas Golf International MIJAS 567
Mile End Golf Club OSWESTRY 289
Milford Golf Club MILFORD 312
Milford Haven Golf Club MILFORD HAVEN 469
Mill Green Golf Club WELWYN GARDEN CITY 219
Mill Hill Golf Club LONDON 126
Mill Ride Golf Club ASCOT 133
Millbrook Golf Club AMPTHILL 130
Millbrook Golf Course REDCROSS 538
Millport Golf Club MILLPORT 450
Milnathort Golf Club Ltd MILNATHORT 444
Milnerton Golf Club WOODBRIDGE ISLAND 578
Milngavie Golf Club GLASGOW 427
Minchinhampton Golf Club (New Courses) MINCHINHAMPTON 201
Minchinhampton Golf Club (Old Course) MINCHINHAMPTON 200
Minehead & West Somerset Golf Club MINEHEAD 295
Minto Golf Club HAWICK 395
Miramar Clube de Golf de PRAIA DE MIRAMAR 562
Mission Hills Golf Club KANCHANABURI 582
Mission Hills Khao Yai Golf Club NAKHON RATCHASIMA 584
Mission Inn Golf and Tennis Resort LAKE COUNTY 573
Mitcham Golf Club MITCHAM 312
Mitchelstown Golf Club MITCHELSTOWN 502
Mobberley Golf Club KNUTSFORD 149
Moffat Golf Club MOFFAT 401
Mold Golf Club MOLD 462
Moliets Golf de BAYONNE 551
Mollington Grange Golf CHESTER 147
Monifieth Golf Links MONIFIETH 408
Monkstown Golf Club MONKSTOWN 502

WHEREVER YOU'RE PLAYING
pick up a guide map to what's best in the area
From all leading Tourist Information Centres and participating hotels & golf clubs
TOURIST PUBLICATIONS 5 Eglinton Crescent, Edinburgh EH12 5DH
Tel: 0131 225 4547 Fax: 0131 220 6789

Golf Guide Maps

Monkton Park Golf Club CHIPPENHAM 340
Monmouth Golf Club MONMOUTH 480
Monmouthshire Golf Club ABERGAVENNY 473
Monte Carlo Golf Club MONTE CARLO 554
Monte Mayor Golf Club BENAHAVIS 566
Montecastillo Hotel & Golf Resort CADIZ 568
Montrose Golf Links Ltd MONTROSE 408
Moor Allerton Golf Club LEEDS 366
Moor Hall Golf Club Ltd SUTTON COLDFIELD 337
Moor Park Golf Club RICKMANSWORTH 216
Moore Place Golf Club ESHER 310
Moorpark Golf Club STEVENSTON 391
Moors Valley Golf Centre RINGWOOD 209
Moortown Golf Club LEEDS 366
Moray Golf Club LOSSIEMOUTH 381
Morecambe Golf Club Ltd. MORECAMBE 236
Moreton Hills Golf Centre MORETON 595
Morgado Golfe do PORTIMAO 559
Morlais Castle Golf Club MERTHYR TYDFIL 480
Morley Hayes Golf Club ILKESTON 168
Morpeth Golf Club Ltd MORPETH 276
Morriston Golf Club SWANSEA 485
Mortehoe & Woolacombe Golf Club MORTEHOE 174
Mortonhall Golf Club EDINBURGH 412
Moseley Golf Club BIRMINGHAM 333
Moss Valley Golf Club WREXHAM 464
Mossock Hall Golf Club ORMSKIRK 236
Mount Ellen Golf Club GARTCOSH 436
Mount Juliet Golf Club THOMASTOWN 520
Mount Murray Golf Club SANTON 540
Mount Ober Golf & Country Club KNOCKBRACKEN 495, 606
Mount Oswald Manor and Golf Course DURHAM 186
Mount Pleasant Golf Course HENLOW 131
Mount Temple Golf Club MOATE 532
Mountain Ash Golf Club MOUNTAIN ASH 481
Mountain Lakes Golf Club CAERPHILLY 473
Mountain Shadow Golf Club CHONBURI 584
Mountrath Golf Club MOUNTRATH 521

Mouse Valley Golf Course LANARK 437
Mowbray Golf Club MOWBRAY 577
Mowsbury Golf Club BEDFORD 130
Moyola Park Golf Club MAGHERAFELT 496
Muang Ake Golf BANGKOK 581
Muckhart Golf Club DOLLAR 448
Muir of Ord Golf Club MUIR OF ORD 431
Muirkirk Golf Club MUIRKIRK 391
Mullion Golf Club HELSTON 154
Mundesley Golf Club NORWICH 267
Murcar Golf Club ABERDEEN 374
Murrayfield Golf Club EDINBURGH 412
Murrayshall Golf Course SCONE 444, 604
Muskerry Golf Club MUSKERRY 502
Musselburgh Golf Club MUSSELBURGH 415
Musselburgh Old Course Golf Club MUSSELBURGH 415
Muswell Hill Golf Club WOOD GREEN 129
Muthill Golf Club CRIEFF 442
Mytton Fold Hotel & Golf Complex BLACKBURN 232

Naas Golf Club NAAS 516
Nad Al Sheba Club DUBAI 578
Nailcote Hall Golf Club BERKSWELL 329
Nairn Dunbar Golf Club NAIRN 434
Nairn Golf Club NAIRN 382
Naples Beach Hotel & Golf Club NAPLES 574
Narin and Portnoo Golf Club PORTNOO 504
National Golf Centre WOODHALL SPA 249
National Training Academy WOODHALL SPA 594
Naunton Downs Golf Club Ltd CHELTENHAM 199
Nazeing Golf Club NAZEING 194
Neath Golf Club NEATH 481
Nefyn and District Golf Club NEFYN 457
Nelson Golf Club NELSON 236
Nevill Golf Club TUNBRIDGE WELLS 231
New Course ST ANDREWS 422
New Cumnock Golf Club NEW CUMNOCK 391
New Forest Golf Club LYNDHURST 208
New Galloway Golf Club NEW GALLOWAY 401
New Mills Golf Club STOCKPORT 169

WHEREVER YOU'RE PLAYING
pick up a guide map to what's best in the area
From all leading Tourist Information Centres and participating hotels & golf clubs
TOURIST PUBLICATIONS 5 Eglinton Crescent, Edinburgh EH12 5DH
Tel: 0131 225 4547 Fax: 0131 220 6789

Golf
GUIDE MAPS

THE GOLF GUIDE 2006　　Index of Clubs & Courses 633

New North Manchester Golf Club Ltd MANCHESTER 254
New Zealand Golf Club WEYBRIDGE 315
Newark Golf Club NEWARK 281
Newbattle Golf Club Ltd DALKEITH 409
Newbiggin-by-the-Sea Golf Club NEWBIGGIN-BY-THE-SEA 277
Newbold Comyn Golf Club LEAMINGTON SPA 330
Newburgh-on-Ythan Golf Club NEWBURGH 382
Newbury & Crookham Golf Club NEWBURY 134
Newbury Racecourse Golf Club NEWBURY 134
Newcastle United Golf Club NEWCASTLE UPON TYNE 327
Newcastle West Golf Club ARDAGH 522
Newcastleton Golf Club NEWCASTLETON 396
Newcastle-under-Lyme Golf Club NEWCASTLE-UNDER-LYME 299
Newmachar Golf Club NEWMACHAR 382
Newport (I.O.W.) Golf Club NEWPORT 220
Newport (Pembs) Golf Club NEWPORT 469
Newport Golf Club NEWPORT 481
Newquay Golf Club NEWQUAY 156
Newton Abbot (Stover) Golf Club NEWTON ABBOT 174
Newton Green Golf Club SUDBURY 304
Newton Stewart Golf Club NEWTON STEWART 401
Newtonmore Golf Club NEWTONMORE 434
Newtownstewart Golf Club NEWTOWNSTEWART 497
Nichigo Resort & Country Club KANCHANABURI 582
Niddry Castle Golf Club WINCHBURGH 416
Nigg Bay Golf Club ABERDEEN 374
Nimes Vacquerolles Golf de NIMES 555
Nimes-Campagne Golf de NIMES 555
Nivelle Golf de La ST JEAN-DE-LUZ 553
Nizels Golf Club TONBRIDGE 231
Noble Place Golf Resort & Country Club CHONBURI 585
Norfolk Golf & Country Club REYMERSTON 268
Normanby Hall Golf Club SCUNTHORPE 247
Normanton Golf Club WAKEFIELD 368
North Berwick Golf Club NORTH BERWICK 415

North Downs Golf Club WOLDINGHAM 316
North Foreland Golf Club BROADSTAIRS 222
North Hants Golf Club FLEET 207
North Inch Golf Course PERTH 444
North Middlesex Golf Club BARNET 123
North Oxford Golf Club OXFORD 286
North Shore Hotel and Golf Club SKEGNESS 248
North Wales Golf Club Ltd LLANDUDNO 461
North Wales Golf Driving Range & 9 Hole Course ST ASAPH 605
North Warwickshire Golf Club Ltd COVENTRY 334
North Weald Golf Club EPPING 192
North West Golf Club BUNCRANA 503
North Wilts Golf Club DEVIZES 341
North Worcestershire Golf Club BIRMINGHAM 333
Northampton Golf Club NORTHAMPTON 270
Northamptonshire County Golf Club NORTHAMPTON 270
Northcliffe Golf Club BRADFORD 361
Northenden Golf Club MANCHESTER 254
Northern Golf Club ABERDEEN 374
Northop Country Park Golf Club CHESTER 459
Northumberland Golf Club Ltd NEWCASTLE UPON TYNE 327
Northwood Golf Club Ltd NORTHWOOD 127
Norton Golf Course STOCKTON-ON-TEES 188
Norwood Park Golf Course Ltd SOUTHWELL 282
Nottingham City Golf Club NOTTINGHAM 281
Notts. Golf Club Ltd. KIRKBY IN ASHFIELD 280
Novo Sancti Petri Club de Golf CADIZ 568
Nuneaton Golf Club NUNEATON 330
Nuremore Hotel & Country Club CARRICKMACROSS 526, 608

Oadby Golf Course OADBY 242
Oak Leaf Golf Complex NEWTON AYCLIFFE 187
Oak Park Golfing Complex CRONDALL 206,308
Oakdale Golf Club HARROGATE 351
Oakdale Golf Course OAKDALE 482

for a wide choice of holiday accommodation　**www.holidayguides.com**

Oake Manor Golf Club TAUNTON 296, 597
Oakland Park Golf Club CHALFONT ST GILES 138
Oakmere Park Golf Club NOTTINGHAM 281
Oakridge Golf Club NUNEATON 330
Oaks Golf Club YORK 354
Oaks Sport Centre Ltd CARSHALTON 306, 598
Oast Golf Centre Ltd. SITTINGBOURNE 230, 593
Oastpark Golf Club SNODLAND 230
Odet Golf de L' BENODET 547
Ogbourne Downs Golf Club SWINDON 342
Okehampton Golf Club OKEHAMPTON 176
Old Colwyn Golf Club COLWYN 459
Old Conna Golf Club BRAY 535
Old Course ST ANDREWS 422
Old Course Ranfurly Golf Club Ltd BRIDGE OF WEIR 446
Old Fold Manor Golf Club BARNET 123
Old Head Golf Links KINSALE 525
Old Nene Golf Club RAMSEY 144
Old Padeswood Golf Club Ltd PADESWOOD 463
Old Rectory Hotel & Golf Club CRICKHOWELL 471
Old Thorns Hotel, Golf & Country Club LIPHOOK 208
Oldham Golf Club OLDHAM 255
Oldmeldrum Golf Club OLD MELDRUM 382
Olton Golf Club Ltd. SOLIHULL 336
Olympic Golf Range SWANLEY 593
Omagh Golf Club OMAGH 497
Omaha Beach Golf de BAYEUX 545
Ombersley Golf Club DROITWICH 345
Onneley Golf Club CREWE 148
Open Golf Centre ST MARGARETS 510, 607
Opio-Valbonne Golf COTE D'AZUR 554
Oporto Golf Club ESPINHO 563
Orchardleigh Golf Club FROME 294
Orkney Golf Club KIRKWALL 451
Ormeau Golf Club BELFAST 493
Ormonde Fields Golf Club CODNOR 167
Ormskirk Golf Club ORMSKIRK 236
Orsett Golf Club ORSETT 194
Orton Meadows Golf Club PETERBOROUGH 144
Osborne Golf Club EAST COWES 220
Oswestry Golf Club OSWESTRY 290
Oswestry Golf Driving Range OSWESTRY 596
Otley Golf Club OTLEY 367
Otter Valley Golf Centre HONITON 173
Otterbourne Golf Centre WINCHESTER 210
Otway Golf Club RATHMULLAN 504
Oughterard Golf Club OUGHTERARD 512
Oulton Park LEEDS 366

Oundle Golf Club OUNDLE 271
Outlane Golf Club OUTLANE 367
Overstone Park Golf and Country Club NORTHAMPTON 270
Owston Hall Hotel & Golf Club DONCASTER 357
Oxford Golf Centre OXFORD 596
Oxfordshire Golf Club THAME 287
Oxley Park Golf Club Ltd WOLVERHAMPTON 338

Pachesham Park Golf Centre LEATHERHEAD 312, 598
Padbrook Park Golf Club CULLOMPTON 171
Padeswood & Buckley Golf Club MOLD 462
Painswick Golf Club PAINSWICK 201
Painthorpe House Golf and Country Club WAKEFIELD 368
Paisley Golf Club PAISLEY 447
Palacerigg Golf Club CUMBERNAULD 424
Palheiro Golf Club FUNCHAL 563
Palleg Golf Club SWANSEA 485
Palm Hills Golf Resort & Country Club HUA-HIN 582
Palmares Golf LAGOS 559
Palmetto Dunes Resort HILTON HEAD ISLAND 574
Panmure Golf Club BARRY 406
Pannal Golf Club HARROGATE 351
Panshanger Golf Complex WELWYN GARDEN CITY 219
Parc Golf Club NEWPORT 482
Parc Golf Club COEDKERNEW 606
Parcours Fornule Golf Ploemeur Ocean LORIENT 548
Park Golf Course WINCHESTER 210
Park Hill Golf Club LOUGHBOROUGH 241
Park Wood Golf club TATSFIELD 230
Parkhall Golf Course STOKE-ON-TRENT 300
Parklands Golf Club NEWCASTLE UPON TYNE 327, 599
Parknasilla Golf Club SNEEM 514
Parkstone Golf Club POOLE 182
Parley Court Golf Club CHRISTCHURCH 181
Parque da Floresta Golf and Leisure Resort BUDENS/SALEMA 558
Pastures Golf Club MICKLEOVER 169
Pat Trainor's Golf Academy WARRENPOINT 607
Patshull Park Hotel & Golf Club WOLVERHAMPTON 291
Pau Golf Club PAU 553
Paultons Golf Centre ROMSEY 217, 604
Pavenham Park Golf Club BEDFORD 130
Paxhill Park LINDFIELD 324

Index of Clubs & Courses

Peacehaven Golf Club NEWHAVEN 320
Peak Practice Golf BUXTON 589
Pease Pottage Golf Centre CRAWLEY 323
Pedham Palace Golf Centre SWANLEY 593
Pedham Place Golf Club SWANLEY 230
Peebles Golf Club PEEBLES 396
Peel Golf Club PEEL 539
Pelican's Nest Golf Club BONITA SPRINGS 573
Penha Longa Hotel & Golf Resort ESTORIL 561
Penina Golf Club PORTIMAO/PENINA 560
Penmaenmawr Golf Club PENMAENMAWR 457
Penn Golf Club WOLVERHAMPTON 339
Pennard Golf Club SWANSEA 485
Pennington Golf Club (Municipal) LEIGH 253
Pennyhill Park Hotel & Country Club BAGSHOT 306
Penrhos Golf and Country Club LLANRHYSTYD 468
Penrhyn Golf Complex ANGLESEY 454, 605
Penrith Golf Club PENRITH 164
Penwortham Golf Club PRESTON 237
Peover Golf Club KNUTSFORD 149
Percy Wood Golf & Country Retreat SWARLAND 278
Perdiswell Park Golf CLub WORCESTER 346
Perivale Park Golf Club GREENFORD 125
Perranporth Golf Club PERRANPORTH 158
Perton Park Golf Club WOLVERHAMPTON 339
Pessac Golf de BORDEAUX 552
Peterborough Milton Golf Club PETERBOROUGH 144
Peterculter Golf Club PETERCULTER 382
Peterhead Golf Club PETERHEAD 382
Petersfield Golf Club (New Course) PETERSFIELD 208
Petersfield Golf Club (Pay & Play Course) PETERSFIELD 208
Peterstone Lakes Golf Club & Hotel CARDIFF 476
Petworth Golf Course PETWORTH 325
PGA National Golf Club PALM BEACH 574
PGA West Resort Course (Nicklaus) LA QUINTA 576
PGA West Resort Course (TPC Stadium) LA QUINTA 576
Phoenix Golf Club ROTHERHAM 358
Phuket Country Club PHUKET 581
Pike Fold Golf Club BURY 252
Pike Hills Golf Club YORK 355
Piltdown Golf Club UCKFIELD 321
Pincents Manor Golf READING 135
Pine Lakes International Country Club MYRTLE BEACH 575
Pinehurst Resort & Country Club PINEHURST 574
Pines Golf Centre DUMFRIES 398
Pinhal Golf Course VILAMOURA 560
Pinheiros Altos Golf Club QUINTA DO LAGO 560
Pinner Hill Golf Club PINNER 127
Pinta Course LAGOA 559
Piperdam Golf & Leisure Resort DUNDEE 407
Pitcheroak Golf Course REDDITCH 346
Pitlochry Golf Course PITLOCHRY 444
Pitreavie (Dunfermline) Golf Club DUNFERMLINE 418
Plassey Golf Course WREXHAM 464
Platja de Pals Golf PALS 569
Pleasington Golf Club BLACKBURN 232
Plutaluang Navy Golf Course CHONBURI 585
Polkemmet Golf Course WHITBURN 416
Pollensa Golf POLLENSA 571
Pollok Golf Club GLASGOW 427
Polmont Golf Club FALKIRK 449
Poniente Golf de MAGALLUF 570
Pontardawe Golf Club SWANSEA 485
Ponte de Lima Golfe de PONTE DE LIMA 564
Pontefract & District Golf Club PONTEFRACT 367
Ponteland Golf Club NEWCASTLE UPON TYNE 277
Pontypool Golf Club PONTYPOOL 482
Pontypridd Golf Club PONTYPRIDD 482
Port Bannatyne Golf Club ROTHESAY 387
Port Glasgow Golf Club PORT GLASGOW 447
Port Royal Golf Club HILTON HEAD 589
Port Royal Golf Club HILTON HEAD 574
Port Royal Golf Driving Range EDINBURGH 604
Port St Mary Golf Club PORT ST MARY 540

WHEREVER YOU'RE PLAYING
pick up a guide map to what's best in the area
From all leading Tourist Information Centres and participating hotels & golf clubs
TOURIST PUBLICATIONS 5 Eglinton Crescent, Edinburgh EH12 5DH
Tel: 0131 225 4547   Fax: 0131 220 6789

Golf Guide Maps

Portadown Golf Club PORTADOWN 492
Portal Golf & Country Club TARPORLEY 151
Portal, Premier Course TARPORLEY 151
Porters Park Golf Club RADLETT 216
Porthmadog Golf Club MORFA BYCHAN 457
Portlethen Golf Club PORTLETHEN 383
Portmarnock Hotel & Golf Links PORTMARNOCK 510
Portmore Golf Park BARNSTAPLE 170, 589
Porto Santo Golfe PORTO SANTO 563
Portobello Golf Course EDINBURGH 412
Portpatrick Golf Club PORTPATRICK 402
Portsalon Golf Club PORTSALON 504
Portsmouth Golf Club (1926) PORTSMOUTH 208
Portstewart Golf Club PORTSTEWART 497
Pottergate Golf Club LINCOLN 245
Potters Bar Golf Club POTTERS BAR 216
Poult Wood Public Golf Centre TONBRIDGE 231
Poulton Park Golf Club Ltd. WARRINGTON 152
Poulton-le-Fylde Golf Club BLACKPOOL 233
Powerscourt Golf Club ENNISKERRY 536
Powfoot Golf Club ANNAN 398
Praa Sands Golf Club PENZANCE 158
Praia D'el Rey Golf & Country Club OBIDOS 562
Prenton Golf Club BIRKENHEAD 258
Prestatyn Golf Club PRESTATYN 463
Prestbury Golf Club PRESTBURY 150
Preston Golf Club PRESTON 237
Prestonfield Golf Club EDINBURGH 412
Prestwich Golf Club MANCHESTER 254
Prestwick Golf Club PRESTWICK 391
Prestwick St Cuthbert Golf Club PRESTWICK 391
Prestwick St Nicholas Golf Club PRESTWICK 391
Princes' Course BEAUMARIS 456
Prince's Golf Club SANDWICH BAY 228
Princes Golf Course EDINBURGH 412
Princes Risborough Golf Club PRINCES RISBOROUGH 140
Priors Hall Golf Club CORBY 269
Priskilly Forest Golf Club FISHGUARD/HAVERFORWEST 469

Prudhoe Golf Club PRUDHOE 277
Pryors Hayes Golf Club CHESTER 147
Pulrose Golf Course DOUGLAS 539
Pumpherston Golf Club LIVINGSTON 414
Purley Chase Golf Club NORTH HARWICKSHIRE 330
Purley Downs Golf Club PURLEY DOWNS 313
Puttenham Golf Club GUILDFORD 311
Pwllheli Golf Club PWLLHELI 457
Pyecombe Golf Club BRIGHTON 317
Pyle & Kenfig Golf Club PORTHCAWL 483
Pype Hayes Golf Club SUTTON COLDFIELD 337
Pyrford Golf Club 1993 WOKING 316

Queens Park (Bournemouth) Golf Club BOURNEMOUTH 180
Queens Park Golf Course CREWE 148
Queensbury Golf Club BRADFORD 361
Quinta da Barca Golfe de ESPOSENDE 564
Quinta da Marinha Golf Resort ESTORIL 562, 608
Quinta da Marinha Oitavos Golfe ESTORIL 562
Quinta da Ria CACELA 558
Quinta de Cima CACELA 558
Quinta do Brincal Club de Golfe RIO MAIOR 562
Quinta do Lago Sociedade do Golfe ALMANCIL 558
Quinta do Peru Golf Course AZEITAO 561

Radcliffe-on-Trent Golf Club RADCLIFFE-ON-TRENT 282
Radnor Golf and Ski Centre REDRUTH 158, 589
Radyr Golf Club CARDIFF 476
RAF Coningsby Golf Club LINCOLN 245
RAF St Athan Golf Club BARRY 473
Raglan Parc Golf Club RAGLAN 483
Ralston Golf Club PAISLEY 447
Ramada Hotel & Resort GLOUCESTER 200, 591
Ramsdale Park Golf Centre CALVERTON 279, 595
Ramsey Golf and Bowls Club HUNTINGDON 143
Ramsey Golf Club RAMSEY 540
Ramside Hall Hotel & Golf Club DURHAM 186

WHEREVER YOU'RE PLAYING
pick up a guide map to what's best in the area
From all leading Tourist Information Centres and participating hotels & golf clubs
TOURIST PUBLICATIONS 5 Eglinton Crescent, Edinburgh EH12 5DH
Tel: 0131 225 4547 Fax: 0131 220 6789

Golf GUIDE MAPS

THE GOLF GUIDE 2006   Index of Clubs & Courses 637

Rancho Las Palmas Country Club RANCHO MIRAGE 576
Ranfurly Castle Golf Club Ltd BRIDGE OF WEIR 446
Rathdowney Golf Club PORTLAOISE 521
Rathmore Golf Club PORTRUSH 490
Ratho Park Golf Club Ltd EDINBURGH 412
Rathsallagh Golf Club DUNLAVIN 535
Ravelston Golf Club Ltd EDINBURGH 412
Ravenmeadow Golf Club WORCESTER 346, 601
Ravensworth Golf Club Ltd. GATESHEAD 326
Rawdon Golf & Lawn Tennis Club LEEDS 366
Rayong Green Valley Country Club RAYONG 585
Reading Golf Club READING 135
Real Club de Golf Las Brisas MARBELLA 567
Real Club de Golf Sotogrande SAN ROQUE 568
Real Golf de Bendinat PALMA 570
Reaseheath Golf Club NANTWICH 150
Reay Golf Club REAY 430
Redbourn Golf Club REDBURN 216
Redcastle Golf Club REDCASTLE 504
Reddish Vale Golf Club STOCKPORT 257
Redditch Golf Club REDDITCH 346
Redditch Kingfisher Golf Club REDDITCH 346
Redhill and Reigate Golf Club REDHILL 313
Redhill Golf Centre REDHILL 313, 598
Redlibbets Golf Club ASH 221
Regent Park Golf Club Ltd BOLTON 251
Regiment Way Golf Centre CHELMSFORD 190
Reigate Heath Golf Club REIGATE 313
Reigate Hill Golf Club REIGATE 314
Renfrew Golf Club RENFREW 447
Renishaw Park Golf Club SHEFFIELD 169
Rennes Golf de RENNES 548
Retford Golf Club Ltd. RETFORD 282
Rhondda Golf Club RHONDDA 484
Rhosgoch Golf Club RHOSGOCH 472
Rhos-on-Sea Residential Golf Club LLANDUDNO 462
Rhuddlan Golf Club RHUDDLAN 463
Rhyl Golf Club RHYL 463
Richings Park Golf & Country Club IVER 139
Richmond Golf Club RICHMOND 314

Richmond (Yorkshire) Golf Club RICHMOND 352
Richmond Park Golf Club LONDON 126
Richmond Park Golf Club THETFORD 268
Rickmansworth Public Golf Course RICKMANSWORTH 217
Riddlesden Golf Club KEIGHLEY 364
Ridge Golf Club MAIDSTONE 227
Ridgeway Golf Club CAERPHILLY 473
Ring Of Kerry Golf & Country Club KENMARE 512
Ringdufferin Golf Course KILLYLEAGH 494
Ringway Golf Club Ltd ALTRINCHAM 250
Rio Real Golf MARBELLA 567
Ripon City Golf Club RIPON 353
Risebridge Golf Centre ROMFORD 195
Rishton Golf Club BLACKBURN 232
Riverside Golf Centre LENTON LANE 280
Riviera Golf Club CANNES 554
RNAS Culdrose Golf Club HELSTON 154
Robin Hood Golf Club SOLIHULL 336
Rochdale Golf Club ROCHDALE 256
Rochester and Cobham Park Golf Club ROCHESTER 228
Rochford Hundred Golf Club ROCHFORD 194
Rodway Hill Golf Course GLOUCESTER 200
Roe Park Golf Club LIMAVADY 496, 607
Roehampton Club Ltd. ROEHAMPTON 127
Roker Park Golf Club GUILDFORD 311
Rolls Of Monmouth Golf Club MONMOUTH 481
Romanby Golf Course NORTHALLERTON 352, 602
Romiley Golf Club Ltd STOCKPORT 257
Romney Warren Golf Club NEW ROMNEY 227
Romsey Golf Club SOUTHAMPTON 210
Rookery Park Golf Club LOWESTOFT 304
Rosapenna Hotel & Golf Links DOWNINGS 504
Roscommon Golf Club ROSCOMMON 528
Rose Garden Resort NAKORN PATHOM 582
Rose Hill Golf Club BIRMINGHAM 333
Roseberry Grange Golf Club CHESTER-LE-STREET 184
Rosehearty Golf Club ROSEHEARTY 383
Roserrow Golf & Country Club WADEBRIDGE 160
Ross Golf Club KILLARNEY 514
Rossendale Golf Club Ltd. ROSSENDALE 237

FHG

For full details of clubs and courses, plus convenient accommodation
www.uk-golfguide.com

Rosslare Golf Club ROSSLARE 534
Rossmore Golf Club MONAGHAN 527
Ross-on-Wye Golf Club ROSS-ON-WYE 212
Rothbury Golf Club ROTHBURY 277
Rother Valley Golf Centre SHEFFIELD 359, 602
Rotherham Golf Club ROTHERHAM 358
Rothes Golf Club ROTHES 383
Rothesay Golf Club ROTHESAY 387
Rothley Park Golf Club ROTHLEY 242
Rouken Glen Golf Centre GLASGOW 427
Roundhay Golf Club LEEDS 367
Roundwood Golf Club ROTHERHAM 358
Routenburn Golf Club LARGS 390
Rowany Golf Club PORT ERIN 540
Rowlands Castle Golf Club HAVANT 207
Roxburghe Golf Club KELSO 396
Royal Aberdeen Golf Club ABERDEEN 374
Royal Ascot Golf Club ASCOT 133
Royal Ashdown Forest Golf Club (Old Course) FOREST ROW 319
Royal Ashdown Forest Golf Club (West Course) FOREST ROW 319
Royal Belfast Golf Club HOLYWOOD 494
Royal Birkdale Golf Club SOUTHPORT 262
Royal Blackheath Golf Club ELTHAM 124
Royal Burgess Golfing Society of Edinburgh EDINBURGH 413
Royal Cape Golf Club WYNBERG 578
Royal Chiangmai Golf Resort CHIANGMAI 583
Royal Cinque Ports Golf Club DEAL 223
Royal County Down Golf Club NEWCASTLE 495
Royal Cromer Golf Club CROMER 264
Royal Dornoch Golf Club DORNOCH 428
Royal Dublin Golf Club DUBLIN 508
Royal Eastbourne Golf Club EASTBOURNE 318
Royal Epping Forest Golf Club CHINGFORD 123
Royal Guernsey Golf Club GUERNSEY 541
Royal Hua Hin Golf Course HUA HIN 582
Royal Jersey Golf Club JERSEY 542
Royal Liverpool Golf Club HOYLAKE 260
Royal Lytham & St Annes Golf LYTHAM ST. ANNES 236
Royal Mid-Surrey Golf Club RICHMOND 314
Royal Montrose Golf Club MONTROSE 408
Royal Musselburgh Golf Club PRESTONPANS 416
Royal North Devon Golf Club WESTWARD HO 179
Royal Norwich Golf Club NORWICH 267
Royal Porthcawl Golf Club PORTHCAWL 483
Royal Portrush Golf Club PORTRUSH 491

Royal St David's Golf Club HARLECH 456
Royal St. Georges Golf Club SANDWICH 228
Royal Tara Golf club NAVAN 526
Royal Tarlair Golf Club MACDUFF 381
Royal Town of Caernarfon Golf Club CAERNARFON 456
Royal Troon Golf Club TROON 392
Royal West Norfolk Golf Club KING'S LYNN 266
Royal Wimbledon Golf Club WIMBLEDON 129
Royal Winchester Golf Club WINCHESTER 210
Royal Worlington and Newmarket Golf Club MILDENHALL 304
Royan Golf de ROYAN 550
Royston Golf Club ROYSTON 217
Rudding Park Golf HARROGATE 351, 601
Ruddington Grange Golf Club NOTTINGHAM 282
Rufford Park Golf & Country Club RUFFORD 282, 595
Rufford Park Golf & Country Club NEWARK 595
Rugby Golf Club RUGBY 330
Ruislip Golf Club RUISLIP 127
Runcorn Golf Club RUNCORN 151
Rushcliffe Golf Club EAST LEAKE 279
Rushden Golf Club RUSHDEN 271
Rushmere Golf Club IPSWICH 303
Rushmore Golf Club SALISBURY 342
Rusper Golf Club NEWDIGATE 312, 598
Rustington Golf Centre RUSTINGTON 325, 599
Rutherford Castle Golf Club WEST LINTON 396
Ruthin Pwllglas Golf Club RUTHIN 464
Rutland County Golf Club STAMFORD 249, 594
Ruxley Park Golf Centre ORPINGTON 228, 593
Ryburn Golf Club HALIFAX 362
Ryde Golf Club RYDE 220
Rye Golf Club RYE 320
Rye Hill Golf Course BANBURY 284
Ryston Park Golf Club DOWNHAM MARKET 264
Ryton Golf Club RYTON 328

Sable-Solesmes Golf de ANGERS 547
Saddlebrook Resort TAMPA 574
Saddleworth Golf Club OLDHAM 255
Saffron Walden Golf Club SAFFRON WALDEN 195
St Andrews Links Trust Golf Practice Centre ST ANDREWS 604
St Andrews Major Golf Club BARRY 473

St Annes Old Links Golf Club LYTHAM ST ANNES 236
St Augustine's Golf Club RAMSGATE 228
St Austell Golf Club ST AUSTELL 158
Sainte-Baume Golf de la NANS-LES-PINS 555
St Bees Golf Club ST BEES 164
St Boswells Golf Club ST BOSWELLS 396
St Cleres Golf Club STANFORD LE HOPE 195
St-Cyprien Golf de PERPIGNAN 555
St Davids City Golf Club ST DAVIDS 470
St Deiniol Golf Club BANGOR 454
St Enodoc Golf Club WADEBRIDGE 160
St Fillans Golf Club ST FILLANS 444
St Gatien Deauville Golf de DEAUVILLE 545
St George's Hill Golf Club WEYBRIDGE 315
St Giles Golf Club NEWTOWN 472
St Helen's Bay Golf Resort ROSSLARE HARBOUR 534
St Idloes Golf Club LLANIDLOES 472
St Ives (Hunts) Golf Club ST IVES 145
St Jean-de-Monts Golf Club de ST JEAN-DE-MONTS 548
Saint-Julien Golf & Country Club de ST-JULIEN-SUR-CALONNE 546
St Kew Golf Club WADEBRIDGE 160
Saint Laurent Golf de AURAY 547
Saint Malo Golf Club ST MALO 548
St Margaret's Golf & Country Club ST MARGARET'S 510
St Mary's Golf Club PENCOED 482
St Medan Golf Club PORT WILLIAM 402
St Mellion Hotel Golf & Country Club SALTASH 159
St Mellons Golf Club CARDIFF 476
St Melyd Golf Club PRESTATYN 463
St Michaels Golf Club LEUCHARS 420
St Michaels Jubilee Golf Club WIDNES 152
St Neots Golf Club ST NEOTS 145
St Pierre Park Golf Club GUERNSEY 541
St Quentin-en-Yvelines Golf de PARIS 549
St Thomas's Priory RUGELEY 299
Sale Golf Club SALE 256
Salgados Golf de ALBUFEIRA 557
Saline Golf Club DUNFERMLINE 419
Salisbury & South Wilts Golf Club SALISBURY 342
Saltburn by Sea Golf Club Ltd SALTBURN BY THE SEA 187
Saltford Golf Club SALTFORD 295
San Lorenzo Golf Club ALMANCIL 557
San Roque Club SAN ROQUE 568
Sand Martins Golf Club WOKINGHAM 136
Sand Moor Golf Club LEEDS 367
Sandbach Golf Club SANDBACH 151
Sandford Springs Golf Club BASINGSTOKE 205
Sandhill Golf Club BARNSLEY 356
Sandilands Golf Club MABLETHORPE 246
Sandiway Golf Club NORTHWICH 150
Sandown Golf Centre ESHER 598
Sandwell Park Golf Club Ltd WEST BROMWICH 338
Sandy Lodge Golf Club NORTHWOOD 127
Sandyhills Golf Club GLASGOW 427
Sanquhar Golf Club SANQUHAR 402
Santa Ponsa Golf Club One SANTA PONSA 571
Santa Ponsa Golf Club Two SANTA PONSA 572
Santiburi Country Club CHIANG RAI 583
Santiburi Samui Country Club SURATHANI 581
Sapey Golf Club BROMYARD 344
Saron Golf Course LLANDYSUL 466
Saunton Golf Club SAUNTON 176
Scade Valley Golf Club BRITTAS 506
Scarborough North Cliff Golf Club SCARBOROUGH 353
Scarborough South Cliff Golf Club Ltd SCARBOROUGH 353
Scarcroft Golf Club LEEDS 367
Scarthingwell Golf Course TADCASTER 354
Scoonie Golf Club LEVEN 420
Scotscraig Golf Club TAYPORT 422
Scrabo Golf Club NEWTOWNARDS 495
Scraptoft Golf Club LEICESTER 240
Seacroft Golf Club SKEGNESS 248
Seafield Golf & Country Club GOREY 532
Seafield Golf Course AYR 388
Seaford Golf Club SEAFORD 321
Seaford Head Golf Club SEAFORD 321
Seaham Golf Club SEAHAM 187
Seahouses Golf Club SEAHOUSES 278
Seapoint Golf Club DROGHEDA 522
Searles Resort Golf Course HUNSTANTON 266
Seascale Golf Club SEASCALE 165

WHEREVER YOU'RE PLAYING
pick up a guide map to what's best in the area
From all leading Tourist Information Centres and participating hotels & golf clubs
TOURIST PUBLICATIONS 5 Eglinton Crescent, Edinburgh EH12 5DH
Tel: 0131 225 4547   Fax: 0131 220 6789

Golf GUIDE MAPS

640 Index of Clubs & Courses — THE GOLF GUIDE 2006

Seaton Carew Golf Club HARTLEPOOL 186
Seckford Golf Centre WOODBRIDGE 305, 597
Sedbergh Golf Club SEDBERGH 165
Sedgley Golf Centre DUDLEY 334
Sedlescombe Golf Club SEDLESCOMBE 321, 599
Seedy Mill Golf Club LICHFIELD 298
Seignosse Golf Hotel BAYONNE 551
Selby Golf Club SELBY 353
Selkirk Golf Club SELKIRK 396
Selsdon Park Hotel & Golf Course CROYDON 308
Selsey Golf Club CHICHESTER 323
Sene Valley Golf Club FOLKESTONE 225
Serlby Park Golf Club DONCASTER 357
Serres De Pals Golf PALS 569
Servanes Golf de AVIGNON 553
Settle Golf Club SETTLE 353
Severn Meadows Golf Club BRIDGNORTH 288
Shandon Park Golf Club BELFAST 493
Shanklin & Sandown Golf Club SANDOWN 220
Shannon Golf Club SHANNON 499
Shaw Hill Hotel Golf & Country Club CHORLEY 234
Shay Grange Golf Centre BRADFORD 602
Sheerness Golf Club SHEERNESS 229
Shendish Manor Golf Club HEMEL HEMPSTEAD 215
Sheraton Algarve Pine Cliffs Golf & Country Club ALBUFEIRA 557
Sherborne Golf Club SHERBORNE 182
Sherdley Park Municipal Golf Course ST HELENS 261
Sherdons Golf Centre TEWKESBURY 202, 591
Sheringham Golf Club SHERINGHAM 268
Sherry Golf Jerez JEREZ 568
Sherwood Forest Golf Club MANSFIELD 280
Shetland Golf Club LERWICK 451
Shifnal Golf Club SHIFNAL 290
Shillinglee Park Golf Club CHIDDINGFOLD 307
Shipley Golf Club BRADFORD 361
Shipyard Golf Club HILTON HEAD 574
Shirehampton Park Golf Club BRISTOL 198
Shirenewton Golf Club CHEPSTOW 478
Shirland Golf Club SHIRLAND 169
Shirley Golf Club SOLIHULL 336
Shirley Park Golf Club Ltd. CROYDON 309
Shiskine Golf & Tennis Club BLACKWATERFOOT 393
Shooters Hill Golf Club Ltd SHOOTERS HILL 127
Shortlands Golf Club BROMLEY 222
Shortwood Lodge Golf Club BRISTOL 198
Shotts Golf Club SHOTTS 438
Shrewsbury Golf Club SHREWSBURY 290
Shrigley Hall Hotel. Golf & Country Club POYNTON 150
Shrivenham Park Golf Club SHRIVENHAM 342
Shropshire (The) TELFORD 290, 596
Sickleholme Golf Club SHEFFIELD 169
Sidcup Golf Club (1926) Ltd. SIDCUP 230
Sidmouth Golf Club SIDMOUTH 176
Silecroft Golf Club SILECROFT 165
Silkstone Golf Club BARNSLEY 356
Silloth on Solway Golf Club SILLOTH 165
Silsden Golf Club KEIGHLEY 364
Silverdale Golf Club SILVERDALE 238
Silverknowes Golf Course EDINBURGH 413
Silvermere Golf & Leisure Complex COBHAM 307, 598
Silverstone Golf Club STOWE 141, 587
Singing Hills Golf Course Ltd ALBOURNE 322
Sittingbourne and Milton Regis SITTINGBOURNE 230
Sitwell Park Golf Club ROTHERHAM 358
Six Hills Golf Club MELTON MOWBRAY 242
Skeabost Golf Club SKEABOST BRIDGE 452
Skelmorlie Golf Club SKELMORLIE 391
Skerries Golf Club SKERRIES 510
Skipton Golf Club Ltd SKIPTON 353
Sleaford Golf Club SLEAFORD 248
Slieve Russell Hotel Golf Club BALLYCONNELL 498
Slinfold Park Golf and Country Club HORSHAM 324
Soi Dao Highland Golf Club & Resort CHANTABURI 584
Solent Meads Golf Club BOURNEMOUTH 180
Son Servera Golf Club SON SERVERA 572
Son Vida Golf PALMA 571
Sonning Golf Club READING 135
South Beds. Golf Club LUTON 132
South Bradford Golf Club BRADFORD 361

PLEASE MENTION THE GOLF GUIDE WHEN YOU WRITE OR PHONE TO ENQUIRE ABOUT CLUBS OR ACCOMMODATION

South County Golf Club BRITTAS 506
South Essex Golf & Country Club BRENTWOOD 189
South Herefordshire Golf Club ROSS-ON-WYE 212, 592
South Herts Golf Club TOTTERIDGE 128
South Kyme Golf Club SOUTH KYME 248
South Leeds Golf Club LEEDS 367
South Moor Golf Club STANLEY 187
South Pembrokeshire Golf Club PEMBROKE 470
South Shields Golf Club Ltd SOUTH SHIELDS 328
South Staffordshire Golf Club WOLVERHAMPTON 339
South Wales Golf Range and Course BARRY 605
South Winchester Golf Club WINCHESTER 210
Southampton Golf Club SOUTHAMPTON 210
Southend-on-Sea Golf Club SOUTHEND-ON-SEA 195
Southern Valley Golf Course GRAVESEND 225
Southerndown Golf Club SOUTHERNDOWN 484
Southerness Golf Club DUMFRIES 398
Southfield Golf Club OXFORD 287
Southport & Ainsdale Golf Club SOUTHPORT 262
Southport Municipal Golf Club SOUTHPORT 262
Southport Old Links Golf Club SOUTHPORT 262
Southview Golf Club SKEGNESS 248
Southwell Golf Club SOUTHWELL 282
Southwick Park Golf Club FAREHAM 206
Southwold Golf Club SOUTHWOLD 304
Southwood Golf Course FARNBOROUGH 206
Spa Golf Club BALLYNAHINCH 493
Spalding Golf Club SPALDING 248
Spanish Point Golf Club MILTON MALBAY 499
Sparkwell Golf Club PLYMOUTH 176
Spean Bridge Golf Club SPEAN BRIDGE 434
Sperone Golf de CORSICA 554

sportscotland National Centre LARGS 390
Springfield Park Golf Club ROCHDALE 256
Springfield Royal Country Club CHA-AM 582
Springhead Park Golf Club HULL 348
Springs Hotel & Golf Club WALLINGFORD 287
Springwater Golf Club CALVERTON 279
Sriracha Golf Club SRIRACHA 585
Stackstown Golf Club RATHFARNHAM 510
Staddon Heights Golf Club PLYMOUTH 176
Stadium Golf Driving Range HUDDERSFIELD 602
Stafford Castle Golf Club STAFFORD 299
Stamford (Stalybridge) Golf Club STALYBRIDGE 151
Stand Golf Club MANCHESTER 254
Standish Court Golf Club WIGAN 238
Stanedge Golf Club CHESTERFIELD 167
Stanmore Golf Club STANMORE 128
Stanton-on-the-Wolds Golf Club STANTON-ON-THE-WOLDS 282
Stapleford Abbotts Golf Club STAPLEFORD ABBOTTS 195
Staverton Park Golf Club DAVENTRY 269
Stevenage Golf Centre STEVENAGE 218
Stinchcombe Hill Golf Club DURSLEY 200
Stirling Golf Club STIRLING 449
Stock Brook Golf & Country Club BILLERICAY 189
Stockley Park Golf Club UXBRIDGE 128
Stockport Golf Club Ltd. STOCKPORT 257
Stocks TRING 218
Stocksbridge and District Golf Club Ltd SHEFFIELD 359
Stocksfield Golf Club STOCKSFIELD 278
Stockwood Park Golf Club LUTON 132
Stockwood Vale Golf Club BRISTOL 293
Stoke Albany Golf Club MARKET HARBOROUGH 269
Stoke By Nayland Golf Club STOKE BY NAYLAND 196, 304
Stoke Park Club STOKE POGES 141
Stoke Rochford Golf Club GRANTHAM 244
Stone Golf Club STONE 300
Stonebridge MERIDEN 330
Stoneham Golf Club SOUTHAMPTON 210
Stonehaven Golf Club STONEHAVEN 384
Stonelees Golf Centre RAMSGATE 228, 593

WHEREVER YOU'RE PLAYING
pick up a guide map to what's best in the area

From all leading Tourist Information Centres and participating hotels & golf clubs

TOURIST PUBLICATIONS 5 Eglinton Crescent, Edinburgh EH12 5DH
Tel: 0131 225 4547 Fax: 0131 220 6789

Golf Guide Maps

Stoneleigh Deer Park Golf Club STONELEIGH 331
Stoney Holme Municipal Golf Course CARLISLE 162
Stornoway Golf Club STORNOWAY 450
Storws Wen Golf Club BRYNTEG 456
Stourbridge Golf Club STOURBRIDGE 336
Stowe Golf Club STOWE 141
Stowmarket Golf Club Ltd STOWMARKET 304
Strabane Golf Club STRABANE 497
Stranraer Golf Club STRANRAER 402
Stratford-on-Avon Golf Club STRATFORD-UPON-AVON 331
Strathaven Golf Club STRATHAVEN 438
Strathclyde Park Golf Club HAMILTON 437
Strathendrick Golf Club DRYMEN 448
Strathlene Golf Club BUCKIE 378
Strathmore Golf Centre BLAIRGOWRIE 440, 604
Strathpeffer Spa Golf Club STRATHPEFFER 432
Strathtay Golf Club STRATHTAY 444
Strathtyrum Course ST ANDREWS 422
Strawberry Hill Golf Club TWICKENHAM 128
Stressholme Golf Club DARLINGTON 185
Stromness Golf Club Ltd STROMNESS 451
Studley Wood Golf Club HORTON-CUM-STUDLEY 286, 596
Sturminster Marshall Golf Club WIMBORNE 183
Styal Golf Club STYAL 151
Styal Golf Driving Range & Par 3 Academy Course STYAL 588
Sudbrook Moor Golf Club GRANTHAM 244
Sudbury Golf Club Ltd. WEMBLEY 129
Summerhill Golf Course HAY-ON-WYE 211
Sunbury Golf Club SHEPPERTON 127
Sundridge Park Golf Club BROMLEY 222
Sunningdale Golf Club SUNNINGDALE 314
Sunningdale Ladies Golf Club SUNNINGDALE 136
Surbiton Golf Club CHESSINGTON 307
Surrey National Golf Club CATERHAM 306
Sutton Bridge Golf Club SPALDING 248
Sutton Coldfield Golf Club SUTTON COLDFIELD 337

Sutton Green Golf Club GUILDFORD 311
Sutton Hall Golf Club SUTTON WEAVER 151
Sutton Park Golf Club HULL 349
Swaffham Golf Club SWAFFHAM 268
Swallow Suffolk Hotel Golf & Country Club BURY ST EDMUNDS 302
Swansea Bay Golf Club NEATH 481
Swanston Golf Club EDINBURGH 413
Sweetwoods Park Golf Club EAST GRINSTEAD 319
Swindon Golf Club DUDLEY 335
Swindon Ridge Driving Range Shop & Golf Club DUDLEY 335, 600
Swinford Golf Club SWINFORD 524
Swinley Forest Golf Club ASCOT 133
Swinton Park Golf Club MANCHESTER 254
Swords Open Golf Course SWORDS 511

Tadmarton Heath Golf Club BANBURY 284
Tain Golf Club TAIN 432
Tall Pines Golf Club BRISTOL 293
Tamworth Golf Club TAMWORTH 301
Tandragee Golf Club TANDRAGEE 492
Tandridge Golf Club OXTED 313
Tankersley Park Golf Club SHEFFIELD 359
Tapton Park Golf & Leisure Centre CHESTERFIELD 167
Tarbat Golf Club PORTMAHOMACK 432
Tarbert Golf Club TARBERT 387
Tarland Golf Club ABERDEEN 374
Taunton and Pickeridge Golf Club TAUNTON 296
Taunton Vale Golf Club TAUNTON 295
Tavistock Golf Club TAVISTOCK 178
Taymouth Castle Golf Course KENMORE 443
Taynuilt Golf Club TAYNUILT 387
Teesside Golf Club STOCKTON-ON-TEES 188, 353
Tehidy Park Golf Club CAMBORNE 153
Teign Valley Golf Club EXETER 172
Teignmouth Golf Club TEIGNMOUTH 178
Telford Golf & Country Club TELFORD 290
Temple Golf Club MAIDENHEAD 134
Temple Newsam Golf Club LEEDS 367
Templemore Golf Club TEMPLEMORE 530
Ten 66 Golf Club Ltd. HASTINGS 319

FHG please mention THE GOLF GUIDE when you enquire about clubs or accommodation

Tenby Golf Club TENBY 470
Tenterden Golf Club TENTERDEN 230
Terceira Golf Club TERCEIRA 564
Test Valley Golf Club BASINGSTOKE 205
Tewkesbury Park Hotel, Golf & Country Club TEWKESBURY 202
Thai Muang Beach Golf & Marina PHANG-NGA 580
Thames Ditton & Esher Golf Club ESHER 310
Thamesview Golf Centre LONDON 126
Thamesview Golf Centre GRAVESEND 593
Thetford Golf Club THETFORD 268
Theydon Bois Golf Club EPPING 192
Thirsk and Northallerton Golf Club THIRSK 354
Thistle Hotel Roseholm Golf Course IRVINE 389
Thornbury Golf Centre BRISTOL 198
Thorndon Park Golf Club Ltd. BRENTWOOD 189
Thorne Golf Club DONCASTER 357
Thorney Golf Centre PETERBOROUGH 144, 588
Thornhill Golf Club THORNHILL 402
Thornhurst Park Golf Course DONCASTER 357
Thornton Golf Club THORNTON 422
Thorpe Hall Golf Club SOUTHEND-ON-SEA 195
Thorpe Wood Golf Course PETERBOROUGH 144
Thorpeness Golf Club & Hotel THORPENESS 304
Thoulstone Park Golf Club WESTBURY 343, 601
Three Hammers Golf Complex WOLVERHAMPTON 600
Three Locks Golf Club MILTON KEYNES 140
Three Rivers Golf & Country Club CHELMSFORD 190
Thurles Golf Club THURLES 530
Thurlestone Golf Club THURLESTONE 178
Thurso Golf Club THURSO 430
Tickenham Golf Club TICKENHAM 296
Tickenham Golf Club TICKENHAM 597
Tidbury Green Golf Club SOLIHULL 336
Tidewater Golf Club MYRTLE BEACH 575
Tidworth Garrison Golf Club TIDWORTH 342

Tilgate Forest Golf Centre CRAWLEY 323, 599
Tillicoultry Golf Club STIRLING 449
Tilsworth Golf Centre DUNSTABLE 131, 486
Tinsley Park Golf Club (Municipal) SHEFFIELD 359
Tiverton Golf Club TIVERTON 178
Tobermory Golf Club TOBERMORY 451
Todmorden Golf Club TODMORDEN 368
Toft Hotel Golf Club BOURNE 243
Tolladine Golf Club WORCESTER 346
Toot Hill Golf Club ONGAR 194
Top Meadow Golf Club and Hotel UPMINSTER 196
Torphin Hill Golf Club EDINBURGH 413
Torphins Golf Club TORPHINS 384
Torquay Golf Club TORQUAY 178
Torrance House Golf Club EAST KILBRIDE 436
Torrequebrada Golf BENALMADENA 566
Torvean Golf Club INVERNESS 434
Torwoodlee Golf Club GALASHIELS 394
Touquet Golf du LE TOUQUET 546
Towerlands Golf Club BRAINTREE 189, 590
Towneley Golf Club BURNLEY 234
Traditions Golf Course 1999 WOKING 316
Traigh Golf Course ARISAIG 433
Tralee Golf Club TRALEE 514
Tramore Golf Club TRAMORE 531
Tredegar & Rhymney Golf Club RHYMNEY 484
Tredegar Park Golf Club NEWPORT 482
Trefloyne Golf Club TENBY 470
Tregenna Castle Hotel Golf & Country Club ST IVES 158
Treloy Golf Club NEWQUAY 156
Trent Lock Golf Centre LONG EATON 280, 595
Trent Park Public Golf Course LONDON 127
Trentham Golf Club STOKE-ON-TRENT 300
Trentham Park Golf Club STOKE-ON-TRENT 300
Trethorne Golf Club LAUNCESTON 154
Trevose Golf and Country Club PADSTOW 156
Troia Golf Club TROIA 563
Troon Municipal Golf Courses TROON 392
Truro Golf Club TRURO 159

Tulfarris Golf Club BLESSINGTON 535
Tullamore Golf Club TULLAMORE 528
Tulliallan Golf Club KINCARDINE 419
Tunbridge Wells Golf Club TUNBRIDGE WELLS 231
Tunshill Golf Club Ltd ROCHDALE 237
Turnberry Isle Resort & Club AVENTURA 573
Turnhouse Golf Club EDINBURGH 413
Turriff Golf Club TURRIFF 384
Turton Golf Club BOLTON 251
Twyford Golf Range SHAFTESBURY 590
Tydd St Giles Golf Centre WISBECH 145
Tylney Park Golf Club BASINGSTOKE 205
Tynedale Golf Club HEXHAM 276
Tynemouth Golf Club Ltd. TYNEMOUTH 328
Tyneside Golf Club Ltd NEWCASTLE UPON TYNE 327
Tyrrells Wood Golf Club Ltd LEATHERHEAD 312
Tytherington Club MACCLESFIELD 149

Ullapool Golf Club ULLAPOOL 432
Ullenwood Manor Golf Course CHELTENHAM 199
Ullesthorpe Court Golf Club LUTTERWORTH 241
Ulverston Golf Club Ltd ULVERSTON 165
Upavon Golf Club UPAVON 343
Upchurch River Valley Golf Courses SITTINGBOURNE 230
Uphall Golf Club UPHALL 416
Upminster Golf Club UPMINSTER 196
Upton-By-Chester Golf Club CHESTER 147
Uttoxeter Golf Club UTTOXETER 301
Uxbridge Golf Course UXBRIDGE 128

Val Queven Golf du LORIENT 548
Valderrama Club de Golf SAN ROQUE 568
Vale do Lobo Golf Club ALMANCIL 558
Vale Golf Club PERSHORE 346
Vale Hotel, Golf & Spa Resort HENSOL 480
Vale of Leven Golf Club ALEXANDRIA 404
Vale of Llangollen Golf Club Ltd LLANGOLLEN 462
Vale Royal Abbey Golf Club NORTHWICH 150
Valescure Golf et Tennis Club de ST RAPHAEL 555
Vall D'Or Golf Club CALA D'OR 570
Vaucouleurs Golf de La PARIS 548
Vaudreuil Golf du ROUEN 546
Vaul Golf Club SCARINISH 452
Ventnor Golf Club UPPER VENTNOR 220
Verulam Golf Club ST ALBANS 217
Vicars Cross Golf Club CHESTER 148

Victoria Clube de Golfe VILAMOURA 560
Vidago Golf Club VIDAGO 564
Vila Sol Beach, Golf & Country Club VILAMOURA 561
Vilamoura Clube de Golfe, Old Course VILAMOURA 560
Vilamoura, Millennium Course VILAMOURA 560
Villamartin Campo de Golf ORIHUELA 570
Villas of Grand Cypress ORLANDO 574
Villeneuve Sur Lot Golf and Country Club VILLENEUVE-SUR-LOT 553
Vimeiro Golf Club VIMEIRO 563
Virginia Park Golf Club CAERPHILLY 476, 605
Vivary Golf Course TAUNTON 296

Wakefield Golf Club WAKEFIELD 369
Waldringfield Golf Club WOODBRIDGE 305
Wallasey Golf Club WALLASEY 263
Wallsend Golf Club WALLSEND 328
Walmer and Kingsdown Golf Club DEAL 224
Walmersley Golf Club BURY 252
Walmley Golf Club SUTTON COLDFIELD 337
Walsall Golf Club WALSALL 338
Waltham Windmill Golf Club GRIMSBY 245
Walton Hall Golf Club WARRINGTON 152
Walton Heath Golf Club TADWORTH 314
Wanstead Golf Club WANSTEAD 129
Wareham Golf Club WAREHAM 183
Warkworth Golf Club WARKWORTH 278
Warley Park Golf Club BRENTWOOD 190
Warley Woods Golf Club WARLEY 338
Warren Golf Club DAWLISH 172
Warren Golf Club MALDON 194
Warren Golf Club WALLASEY 263
Warren Park Golf Centre CHADWELL HEATH 590
Warrenpoint Golf Club WARRENPOINT 495
Warrington Golf Club APPLETON 146
Warwick Golf Centre WARWICK 600
Warwick Golf Club WARWICK 331
Warwickshire (The) WARWICK 331
Waterbridge Golf Course CREDITON 171
Waterford Castle Golf Club WATERFORD 531
Waterford Valley Chiangrai Course CHIANG RAI 583
Waterhall Golf Club BRIGHTON 318
Waterlooville Golf Club PORTSMOUTH 208
Waterstock Golf Club & Driving Range OXFORD 287, 596
Waterville Golf Links WATERVILLE 514
Wath Golf Club ROTHERHAM 358
Wavendon Golf Centre MILTON KEYNES 140

Index of Clubs & Courses

Weald of Kent Golf Course HEADCORN 225
Weald Park Golf Club BRENTWOOD 190
Wearside Golf Club SUNDERLAND 328
Wellingborough Golf Club WELLINGBOROUGH 272
Wellow Golf Club ROMSEY 209
Wells (Somerset) Golf Club Ltd WELLS 296
Wellshurst Golf and Country Club HAILSHAM 319, 599
Welsh Border Golf CLub WELSHPOOL 472
Welshpool Golf Club WELSHPOOL 472
Welton Manor Golf Centre LINCOLN 246
Welwyn Garden City Golf Club Ltd WELWYN GARDEN CITY 219
Wensum Valley Hotel, Golf & Country Club NORWICH 268
Wentworth Club Ltd VIRGINIA WATER 314
Wenvoe Castle Golf Club CARDIFF 476
Wergs Golf Club WOLVERHAMPTON 339
Wernddu Golf Centre ABERGAVENNY 473, 605
Werneth Golf Club OLDHAM 255
Werneth Low Golf Club HYDE 252
Wessex Golf Centre WEYMOUTH 183
West Berkshire Golf Course NEWBURY 135
West Bowling Golf Club Ltd BRADFORD 361
West Bradford Golf Club Ltd BRADFORD 361
West Byfleet Golf Club WEST BYFLEET 315
West Chiltington Golf Club WEST CHILTINGTON 325
West Cornwall Golf Club ST IVES 159
West Derby Golf Club LIVERPOOL 260
West End Golf Club (Halifax) Ltd HALIFAX 363
West Essex Golf Club CHINGFORD 123
West Herts Golf Club WATFORD 218
West Hill Golf Club WOKING 316
West Hove Golf Club HOVE 320
West Kent Golf Club ORPINGTON 228
West Kilbride Golf Club WEST KILBRIDE 392
West Lancashire Golf Club BLUNDELLSANDS 258
West Linton Golf Club WEST LINTON 396
West Lothian Golf Club BO'NESS 409
West Malling Golf Club MAIDSTONE 227
West Middlesex Golf Club SOUTHALL 128
West Midlands Golf Club SOLIHULL 336
West Monmouthshire Golf Club NANTYGLO 481
West Surrey Golf Club GODALMING 310
West Sussex Golf Club PULBOROUGH 325
West Waterford Golf & CountryClub DUNGARVAN 530
West Wilts Golf Club WARMINSTER 343
Westerham Golf Club WESTERHAM 231
Westerhope Golf Club NEWCASTLE UPON TYNE 327
Western Gailes Golf Club IRVINE 389
Western Park Golf Club LEICESTER 241
Westerwood Hotel, Golf & Country Club CUMBERNAULD 424
Westgate and Birchington Golf Club WESTGATE ON SEA 231
Westhill Golf Club WESTHILL 384
Westhoughton Golf Club WESTHOUGHTON 257
Westin Mission Hills Resort Golf Club RANCHO MIRAGE 576
Westin Turnberry Resort TURNBERRY 392
Weston Park Golf Club NORWICH 268
Weston Turville Golf Club AYLESBURY 137
Westonbirt Golf Club TETBURY 201
Weston-Super-Mare Golf Club WESTON-SUPER-MARE 296
Westport Golf Club WESTPORT 524
Westray Golf Club WESTRAY 451
Wetherby Golf Club WETHERBY 369
Wexham Park Golf Course WEXHAM 141
Weybrook Park Golf Club BASINGSTOKE 205
Weymouth Golf Club Ltd WEYMOUTH 183
Whaddon Golf Centre ROYSTON 592
Whalley Golf Club CLITHEROE 234

Visit the FHG website
www.holidayguides.com
for details of the wide choice of accommodation featured in the full range of FHG titles

646 Index of Clubs & Courses

Whalsay Golf Club WHALSAY 451
Wharton Park Golf Club BEWDLEY 344
Wheathill Golf Club SOMERTON 295
Wheatlands Golf Course & Country Hotel JERSEY 542
Wheatley Golf Club DONCASTER 357
Whetstone Golf Club and Driving Range LEICESTER 241
Whickham Golf Club Ltd NEWCASTLE UPON TYNE 327
Whipsnade Park Golf Club DAGNALL 214
Whiston Hall Golf Club & Mansion Court Hotel CHEADLE 298
Whitburn Golf Club Ltd SOUTH SHIELDS 328
Whitby Golf Club WHITBY 354
Whitchurch (Cardiff) Golf Club CARDIFF 476
Whitecraigs Golf Club GLASGOW 427
Whitefield Golf Club WHITEFIELD 257
Whitefields Golf Club RUGBY 330
Whitehall Golf Club NELSON 481
Whitehaven Golf Club WHITEHAVEN 165
Whitehead Golf Club CARRICKFERGUS 489
Whitehill Golf Centre WARE 592
Whitehill Golf Club WARE 218
Whitekirk Golf & Country Club WHITEKIRK 416
Whiteleaf Golf Club Ltd PRINCES RISBOROUGH 140
Whitemoss Golf Club DUNNING 442
Whitewebbs Golf Club ENFIELD 124
Whiting Bay Golf Club WHITING BAY 393
Whitley Bay Golf Club WHITLEY BAY 328
Whitsand Bay Hotel Golf Club TORPOINT 159
Whitstable and Seasalter Golf Club WHITSTABLE 231
Whittaker Golf Club LITTLEBOROUGH 253
Whittington Heath Golf Club LICHFIELD 299
Whittlebury Park Golf & Country Club TOWCESTER 271
Wick Golf Club WICK 430
Wickham Park Golf Club FAREHAM 206
Wicklow Golf Club WICKLOW 538
Widnes Golf Club WIDNES 152
Widney Manor Golf Club SOLIHULL 336
Wigan Golf Club WIGAN 238

Wigtown and Bladnoch Golf Club WIGTOWN 402
Wigtownshire County Golf Club NEWTOWN STEWART 401
Wild Wing Plantation MYRTLE BEACH 575
Wildernesse Club SEVENOAKS 229
Wildwood Country Club CRANLEIGH 308
Willesley Park Golf Club ASHBY DE LA ZOUCH 239
William Wroe Municipal Golf Course TRAFFORD 257
Williamwood Golf Club GLASGOW 427
Willingdon Golf Club EASTBOURNE 319
Willow Valley Golf and Country Club BRIGHOUSE 361
Willow Valley Golf and Country Club BRIGHOUSE 602
Wilmslow Golf Club KNUTSFORD 149
Wilpshire Golf Club Ltd BLACKBURN 233
Wilton Golf Club REDCAR 352
Wiltshire Golf & Country Club SWINDON 342
Wimbledon Common Golf Club WIMBLEDON 129
Wimbledon Park Golf Club WIMBLEDON 129
Wimereux Golf de BOULOGNE 545
Wincanton Golf Club WINCANTON 297
Windermere Golf Club WINDERMERE 165
Windlemere Golf Club WOKING 316
Windlesham Golf Club BAGSHOTT 306
Windmill Hill Golf Club MILTON KEYNES 140, 587
Windmill Village Hotel and Golf Club COVENTRY 334
Windwhistle Golf Club Ltd CHARD 294
Windyhill Golf Club GLASGOW 427
Winter Hill Golf Club MAIDENHEAD 134
Winterfield Golf Club DUNBAR 410
Wirral Ladies' Golf Club Ltd BIRKENHEAD 258
Wishaw Golf Club WISHAW 438
Witch Golf Club MYRTLE BEACH 575
Withernsea Golf Club WITHERNSEA 349
Withington Golf Club. MANCHESTER 254
Witney Lakes Golf Club WITNEY 287, 596
Woburn Golf Club MILTON KEYNES 140
Wokefield Park Golf Club READING 135

www.uk-golfguide.com

THE GOLF GUIDE 2006   Index of Clubs & Courses 647

Woking Golf Club WOKING 316
Woldingham Golf Club CATERHAM 306
Woll Golf Course ASHKIRK 394
Wollaton Park Golf Club NOTTINGHAM 282
Wolstanton Golf Club WOLSTANTON 301
Woodbridge Golf Club WOODBRIDGE 305
Woodbrook Golf Club BRAY 535
Woodbury Park Golf & Country Club Ltd EXETER 172
Woodcote Park Golf Club. COULSDON 307
Woodford Golf Club WOODFORD GREEN 196
Woodhall Hills Golf Club Ltd PUDSEY 368
Woodham Golf and Country Club NEWTON AYCLIFFE 187
Woodlake Park Golf and Country Club PONTYPOOL 482
Woodlands Golf and Country Club BRISTOL 198
Woodlands Golf Club NAAS 516
Woodlands Manor Golf Club SEVENOAKS 229
Woodsome Hall Golf Club HUDDERSFIELD 364
Woodstock Golf and Country Club ENNIS 499
Woodthorpe Hall Golf Club ALFORD 243
Wooler Golf Club WOOLER 278
Woolley Park Golf Club WAKEFIELD 369
Woolston Manor Golf Club CHIGWELL 191
Woolton Golf Club LIVERPOOL 261
Worcester Golf and Country Club WORCESTER 346
Worcester Golf Range WORCESTER 601
Worcestershire Golf Club MALVERN WELLS 345

Worfield Golf Club WORFIELD 291
Workington Golf Club Ltd WORKINGTON 165
Worksop Golf Club WORKSOP 283
World of Golf CHISLEHURST 223, 593
World of Golf at Beverley Park NEW MALDEN 598
Worldham Park Golf Club ALTON 204
Worlebury Golf Club WESTON-SUPER-MARE 296
Worplesdon Golf Club WOKING 316
Worsley Golf Club ECCLES 252
Worthing Golf Club WORTHING 325
Wortley Golf Club SHEFFIELD 359
Wrag Barn Golf and Country Club HIGHWORTH 341
Wrangaton Golf Club SOUTH BRENT 178
Wrekin Golf Club TELFORD 290
Wrexham Golf Club WREXHAM 464
Wrotham Heath Golf Club SEVENOAKS 229
Wyboston Lakes Golf Course WYBOSTON 132
Wychwood Golf Club CHIPPING NORTON 285
Wychwood Park Golf Club WESTON 152
Wycombe Heights Golf Centre HIGH WYCOMBE 139
Wyke Green Golf Club ISLEWORTH 126
Wyre Forest Golf Club KIDDERMINSTER 345

Yelverton Golf Club YELVERTON 179
Yeovil Golf Club YEOVIL 297
York Golf Club YORK 355
Youghal Golf Club YOUGHAL 502
Yvelines Golf des PARIS 549

PLEASE NOTE
All the information regarding Golf Clubs in this guide is given in good faith in the belief that it is correct. However, the publishers cannot guarantee the facts given in these pages, neither are they responsible for changes in ownership or facilities, such as green fees, that may take place after the date of going to press. Readers should always satisfy themselves that the facilities they require are available and that the terms, if quoted, still apply.

FHG
K·U·P·E·R·A·R·D

FHG Guides publish a large range of well-known accommodation guides. We will be happy to send you details or you can use the order form at the back of this book.

Index of Advertisers

Aberdeen City Golf	63, 373
Aberdovey Golf Club	46, 455
Aberystwyth Golf Club	50, 467
Aldenham Golf & Country Club	28, 219
Alderley Edge Golf Club	146
Alderney Golf Club	22, 541
Alderney Tourism	22, 541
Alnwick Golf Club	273
Alsager Golf & Country Club	146
Amer Sport UK Ltd	111, 113, 119, 12
Anglesey Golf Club Ltd.	458
Ansty Golf Centre	35, 334
Ashburnham Golf Club	50, 466
Ashdown Park Hotel	96, 532
Ashton-under-Lyne Golf Club	250
Aston Wood Golf Club	35, 337
Atholl Palace Hotel	445
Auchterarder Golf Club	439
Aviemore Highland Resort	57, 435
Badgemore Park Golf Club	285
Bala Golf Club	454
Balbirnie Park Golf Club	73, 421
Ballyliffin Golf Club	503
Banchory Lodge Hotel	377
Beaufort Golf Club	92, 513
Beaufort Hotel	52, 479
Beauport Park Hotel	319
Bell Hotel	229
Berwick-upon-Tweed (Goswick)	275
Betws-y-Coed Golf Club	47, 459
Bingley (St. Ives) Golf Club	42, 360
Blackwell Grange Golf Club	185
Blairgowrie Golf Club	76, 441
Blaney Hotels	83, 505
Blankney Golf Club	243
Blue Bell	39, 275
Blyth Golf Club Ltd.	275
Bondhay Golf Club	283
Bovey Castle	13, 175
Bowood Golf and Country Club	20, 340
Bowood Park Hotel & Golf Club	Inside Front Cover, 155
Bradford Golf Club	43, 362
Brampton Golf Club	37, 163
Brean Golf Club at Brean Leisure Park	293
Brickhampton Court Golf Complex	199
Bryn Meadows Golf & Country Hotel	52, 479
Buck Inn	41, 350
Builth Wells Golf Club	51, 471
Burghfield House Hotel	73, 428
Burghill Valley Golf Club	31, 211
Burnett Arms Hotel	64, 377
Burnham and Berrow Golf Club	19, 294
Bushey Hall Golf Club	214
Bushmills Inn Hotel & Restaurant	79, 488
Caerlyr Hall Hotel	49, 460
Caerphilly Golf Club	53, 475
Calverley Golf Club	41, 365
Cambridge National Golf	28, 142
Cardigan Golf Club	50, 468
Cardrona Hotel Golf & Country Club	58, 397
Carriages Hotel	62, 380
Castle View Hotel	478
Castletown Golf Links	43, 539
Charleton Golf Club	71, 417
Charlton Kings Hotel	15, 199
Chester Beatty Inn	96, 537
Chimneys	155
Cleobury Mortimer Golf Club	33, 289
Clwb Golf Abersoch	45, 455
Cockermouth Golf Club	163
Coed Y Mwstwr Golf Club	53, 475
Coed-Y-Mwstwr Hotel	53, 475
Collingtree Park Golf Course	32, 270
Connemara Golf Club	88, 511
Coombe Wood Golf Club	311
Cork Golf Club	82, 501
Cosby Golf Club	239
Cotswold	233
Cottrell Park Golf Club	55, 477
County Arms Hotel	94, 527
Courtyard	275
Cowal Golf Club	386
Craibstone Golf Centre	60, 379
Craigesk Guest House	415
Crail Golfing Society	72, 418
Criccieth Golf Club	46, 456
Crosland Heath Golf Club Ltd	42, 363
Crowborough Beacon Golf Club	26, 318
Culcrieff Golf Club	77, 442

for a wide choice of holiday accommodation www.holidayguides.com

Index of Advertisers

Dalmunzie Golf Course	440
Darby O'Gills Country House Hotel	89, 515
Darlington Golf Club Ltd	39, 185
Dartmouth Golf & Country Club	15, 171
Deer Park Hotel & Golf Course	86, 509
Denbigh Golf Club	460
Dewstow Golf Club	54, 479
Dingle Golf Club	89, 513
Diplomat Hotel	466
Donabate Golf Club	88, 506
Donaghadee Golf Club	81, 494
Douglas Arms Hotel	377
Draycote Hotel & Whitefields Golf Course	34, 331
Druids Glen Golf Club	97, 537
Druids Glen Marriott Hotel & Country Club	97, 537
Drumoig Hotel and Golf Resort	423
Duff House Royal Golf Club	63, 376
Dumfries & Galloway Golf Club	68, 399
Dunraven Arms Hotel	92, 521
E & L Insurance	6, 110, 122
East Coast & Midlands Tourism	95, 533
Eaton Golf Club	147
Eden Golf Course	37, 163
Edinburgh Golf	71, 411
Edzell Golf Club	407
Elfordleigh Hotel Golf & Leisure	12, 177
Ely City Golf Course Ltd.	143
Esker Hills Golf Club	94, 528
Essex Golf & Country Club	193
Fernhill Golf & Country Club	82, 500
Fingal Tourism	87
Fleetwood Golf Club Ltd	235
Fortrose & Rosemarkie Golf Club	75, 431
Fraserburgh Golf Club	63, 380
GMM Golf Breaks	112
Galgorm Castle Golf Club	489
Gatton Manor Hotel, Golf & Country Club	26, 309
George & Abbotsford Hotel	67, 397
Gifford Golf Club	414
Glencorse Golf Club	416
Gleneagles Hotel Golf Courses	59, 441
Glenlo Abbey Hotel	511
Glenview Hotel	97, 534
Global Golf Tours	109, 120
Golf Around Scotland	109
Golf Guide Maps	5, Index
Golf Tee-Time Services	112, 120, 453
Gowran Park Golf Club	92, 520
Grange & Links Hotel	31, 247
Great Yarmouth & Caister Golf Club	265
Green Acre Public House & Motel	53, 483
Green Hotel	77, 445
Gregans Castle Hotel	81, 499
Grove Farm	265
Gwesty Nanhoron Arms Hotel	45, 457
Hadley Wood Golf Club	213
Hainsworth Park Golf Club	40, 349
Halesowen Golf Club	335
Harbour Holidays	10, 157
Haverfordwest Golf Club	51, 469
Heatherlie House Hotel	67, 397
Heaton Park Golf Centre	255
Hetland Hall Hotel	68, 399
High Post Golf Club Ltd	343
Hilton Puckrup Hall	17, 203
Hilton Templepatrick Hotel	80, 491
Hinckley Golf Club	240
Holywell Golf Club	47, 460
Honiton Golf Club	173
Hotel Berry A Colina	102, 557
Hull Golf Club (1921) Ltd	349
Huntercombe Golf Club	25, 286
Imperial Hotel	48, 461
Inchmarlo Golf Centre	61, 375
Inchmurrin Island	404
Ingol Golf Club	237
Inishowen Gateway Hotel	84, 503
Island Golf Club	86, 507
Islawrffordd Caravan Park	457
Jack Barker's Greenway Hall	34, 300
Jedburgh Golf Club	67, 395
K Club	Front Cover, 91, 519
Kildare Tourism	90, 517
Killarney Golf and Fishing Club	89, 515
Killin Golf Club	76, 443
Kings Norton Golf Club Ltd	333
Kirkby Lonsdale Golf Club	164

For full details of clubs and courses, plus convenient accommodation
www.uk-golfguide.com

Index of Advertisers

La Costa Golf & Beach Resort	104, 569	Nairn Dunbar Golf Club	75, 434
Lagganmore Hotel	70, 403	Newmachar Golf Club	64, 383
Lands Of Loyal Hotel	76, 439	North Wales Golf Club Ltd	48, 461
Largs Golf Club	65, 390		
Le Strange Arms Hotel	29, 265	Oakmere Park Golf Club	33, 281
Leatherhead Golf Club	25, 312	Oaks Golf Club	40, 355
Leven Links Golf Club	72, 421	Orillia House	355
Lincoln Golf Club	32, 246	Orton Meadows Golf Course	144
Linden Hall	40, 276		
Links Golf	56, 372	Parley Court Golf Club	181
Llandrindod Wells Golf Club	472	Peover Golf Club	149
Lockerbie Golf Club	400	Perranporth Golf Club	158
London Borough Of Ealing Parks		Perton Park Golf Club	35, 339
& Countryside Services	23, 125	Petwood Hotel	249
Lostwithiel Hotel Golf & Country Club		Pine Lodge Hotel	280
	11, 155	Portpatrick Golf Club	69, 403
Lucan Spa Hotel	88, 509	Powerscourt Golf Club	98, 536
Lundin Links Hotel	73, 421	Prestatyn Golf Club	49, 462
Lydd Golf Club & Driving Range	24, 226		
		Queenwood Golf Lodge	20, 340
Machynlleth Golf Club	472		
Magdalene Fields Golf Club	275	Raglan Parc Golf Club	483
Malahide Golf Club	84, 510	Ramada Hotel & Resort	16, 201
Malton Golf Club	217	Ramsdale Park Golf Centre	279
Manor & Ashbury Sport & Craft Hotels		Ramside Hall Hotel & Golf Club	186
	14, 177	Rathsallagh House Hotel & Golf Club	97, 535
Marine Hotel	70, 415	Ravenswood Residential Club	377
Marriott Hollins Hall Hotel & Country Club		Red Bank House & Restaurant	85, 509
	42, 369	Red House Hotel	77, 441
Marriott Johnstown House Hotel	93, 525	Rhuddlan Golf Club	49, 463
Merlin Golf & Country Club	11, 157	Riverdale Hall Hotel	275
Metropole Hotel	262	Romanby Golf Course	40, 352
Mid Yorkshire Golf Club	42, 369	Rosapenna Hotel & Golf Links	84, 505
Minehead & West Somerset Golf Club	294	Rothbury Golf Club	277
Minto Golf Club	67, 395	Rothesay Golf Club	64, 387
Moffat Golf Club	68, 400	Royal Dornoch Golf Club	74, 429
Monifieth Golf Links	70, 408	Royal Dublin Golf Club	88, 509
Monmouth Golf Club	54, 480	Royal Dunkeld Hotel	76, 443
Monmouthshire Golf Club	54, 473	Royal Jersey Golf Club	23, 542
Montrose Golf Links Ltd	70, 408	Royal Liverpool Golf Club	260
Moray Golf Club	62, 381	Royal Marine Hotel	73, 428
Morley Hayes Golf Club	31, 168	Royal North Devon Golf Club	179
Mortonhall Golf Club	71, 412	Runnymede Hotel & Spa	25, 315
Moss Valley Golf Club	48, 464	Rusacks Hotel	72, 423

FHG please mention The Golf Guide when you enquire about clubs or accommodation

K·U·P·E·R·A·R·D

Index of Advertisers

St Mellion Golf Breaks	10, 159
St Helens Bay Golf Resort	96, 534
St Mellons Golf Club	52, 477
Sandhill Golf Club	41, 356
Sandwell Park Golf Club	339
Saoire Failte	79, 487
Saunton Golf Club	176
Scotia Golf	112, 372
Scotscraig Golf Club	72, 423
Seahouses Golf Club	278
Seapoint Golf Club	94, 523
Searles Of Hunstanton	29, 266
Seascale Golf Club	38, 165
Seaton Carew Golf Club	38, 187
Sherdons Golf Centre	202
Shotts Golf Club	75, 438
Silverdale Golf Club	238
South County Golf Club	85, 507
sportscotland	66, 390
Stonehaven Golf Club	60, 384
Stony Holme Golf Club	163
Straffan Court Hotel	516
Strathpeffer Spa Golf Club	75, 432
Stutelea Hotel	43, 262
Swindon Golf Club	34, 335
Taunton Vale Golf Club	20, 295
Taynuilt Golf Club	387
Tenby Golf Club	51, 470
Tewkesbury Park Country Club Resort	16, 203
Thistle Hotel Irvine	65, 389
Thornbury Golf Centre	18, 198
Thornhill Golf Club	68, 403
Thorpe Wood Golf Course	144
Thorpeness Golf Club & Hotel	305
Torrs Warren Hotel	69, 402
Torwoodlee Golf Club	66, 394

Treffeddian Hotel	47, 455
Treglos Hotel	11, 157
Trethorne Golf Club	155
Trevose Golf and Country Club	11, 157
Turton Golf Club	251
Udny Arms Hotel	379
Uttoxeter Golf Club	33, 301
Walmer & Kingsdown Golf Club	24, 224
Warren Golf Club	172
Waterford Castle Golf Club	94, 530
Waterfront Hotel & Bistro	69, 403
Waterville Golf Links	89, 515
Wavendon Golf Centre	140
Wellingborough Golf Club	272
Wells (Somerset) Golf Club Ltd	19, 297
Wentworth Club Ltd	26, 315
Wenvoe Castle Golf Club	54, 477
Wernddu Golf Club	55, 473
West Chiltington Golf Club	325
West End Hotel	65, 386
West Lancashire Golf Club	259
West Wilts Golf Club	343
Westin Turnberry Resort	66, 392
Weston Turville Golf & Squash Club	24, 137
Weston-Super-Mare Golf Club	297
White Hart Hotel	65, 385
White Hart Hotel & Leisure Complex	26, 320
Whittlebury Park Golf & Country Club	271
Wicklow Golf Club	98, 538
Wishaw Golf Club	438
Withington Golf Club Ltd	255
Wolstanton Golf Club	301
Woodhall Spa National Golf Centre	249
Wrag Barn Golf and Country Club	20, 341
Wyke Green Golf Club	126
Ythan Hotel	382

FHG
K·U·P·E·R·A·R·D

Visit the FHG website
www.holidayguides.com
for details of the wide choice of accommodation featured in the full range of FHG titles

CAPE SOLUTIONS
LEISURE · SPORT · MEDICAL

With first hand experiences of all Southern Africa and its people, **CAPE SOLUTIONS** offer first class tailor made tours and holidays throughout Southern Africa.

7/8/10/12/14 DAY GOLF ESTATE TOUR

Steenberg – Erinvale – De Zalze – Arabella – Atlantic Beach – Clovelly

Visit world famous Cape Town, the stunning winelands, historic Stellenbosch and the quaint fishing village of Hermanus while staying on four magnificent golf estates, each offering top quality golf in surroundings filled with mountains, vineyards and lush vegetation. Convert to 12/14 day "Golf Estate Tour" by including a visit to Fancourt Golf and Country Estate where you can play The Links, host of 2003 President's Cup, The Outeniqua & Montagu as well as many other famous and prestige courses in the local region.

10/12/14/16 DAY GARDEN ROUTE / SHAMWARI / DURBAN / SUN CITY

Play Golf at any & as many courses as you want; Steenberg, Royal Cape, Westlake, Clovelly, Rondebosch, Mowbray, Atlantic Beach, Milnerton, Stellenbosch, Paarl, Spier, Erinvale, Pearl Valley, Arabella, Hermanus, George, Fancourt's 3 The Links, The Outeniqua & The Montagu & Pezula Club. Package includes a tour of the stunning winelands and the famous Garden Route as well as a safari at Shamwari Game Reserve or other exciting lodges in the region. We offer the very best in car hire selection, rates & service throughout South Africa with a huge selection of all types of new vehicles from 4x4 to the very basic. In addition, we can organise many exciting activities such as hot air ballooning, helicopter tours, deep sea fishing and rock and mountain climbing, white water rafting and all extreme sports.

SPECIALISING IN PROPERTY SALES, RENTALS AND HOLIDAY LETS

SA TEL/Fax: +27 21 847 0505   SA Mobile: +27 82 675 8158

E-mail: info@capesolutions.co.uk

www.capesolutions.co.uk

CULTURE SMART! GUIDES
A quick guide to customs and etiquette

·K·U·P·E·R·A·R·D·
www.KUPERARD.co.uk

CULTURE SMART! Guides are the only guides giving essential information on attitudes, beliefs and behaviour in over 30 different countries, turning ignorant tourists into informed travellers.

Suitable for short breaks, long stays or business trips. Ideal for the culturally unaware Brit. These concise guides tell you what to expect, how to behave, and how to establish a rapport with your hosts.

Covers all cultural aspects – customs, traditions, politics, history and religion.

Breaks down cultural barriers without causing offence.

'Full of fascinating tips to help you avoid embarrassing faux pas'   **The Observer**

'Culture Smart! has come to the rescue of hapless travellers'   **The Sunday Times**

'Perfect introduction to the weird, wonderful and odd quirks and customs of various countries'   **Global Travel**

CULTURE SMART! THE SMARTER WAY TO TRAVEL

Regularly featured on: **BBC WORLD**   **BBC RADIO**

**Price
£6.95 each**

·K·U·P·E·R·A·R·D·

Publishers and Distributors
59 Hutton Grove, London N12 8DS
Tel: 020 8446 2440 • Fax: 020 8446 2441 • E-mail: culturesmart@kuperard.co.uk

'Order any Culture Smart! guide via the Kuperard website and receive free postage on any quantity of guides. Visit www.kuperard.co.uk to see the full range in the series and type in the following promotional code on the payment page FHG01. Or call us on 0208 446 2440 and quote the same code' hotels - retreats – haciendas - villas - chalets - spas

chic guides

Price £16.95 each

A vividly illustrated guide to exciting destinations

The modern traveller's companion to the most exciting luxurious and alluring hotels, mountain retreats, beachside villas, spas, exciting shops and choice restaurants.

Available from all good bookshops

Stunning illustrated chapters, describe in detail the design and their intimate character and surroundings. Fact panels on each property provide suitable information on local attractions and facilities lying within easy reach.

Stylish paperback style makes this the ideal travel and coffee table guide

Alpine   Bali   Mexico   Morocco   South Africa   Thailand

·K·U·P·E·R·A·R·D·

www.KUPERARD.co.uk
Tel: 020 8446 2440 • Fax: 020 8446 2441 • E-mail: chic@kuperard.co.uk

Publishers and Distributors
59 Hutton Grove, London N12 8DS

THE GOLF GUIDE 2006　　　　　　　　　　　　　　　　　　　　655

OTHER FHG TITLES FOR 2006

FHG Guides Ltd have a large range of attractive holiday accommodation guides for all kinds of holiday opportunities throughout Britain. They also make useful gifts at any time of year. Our guides are available in most bookshops and larger newsagents but we will be happy to post you a copy direct if you have any difficulty. POST FREE for addresses in the UK. We will also post abroad but have to charge separately for post or freight.

The original
Farm Holiday Guide to COAST & COUNTRY HOLIDAYS in England, Scotland, Wales and Channel Islands. Board, Self-catering, Caravans/Camping, Activity Holidays.

BED AND BREAKFAST STOPS
Over 1000 friendly and comfortable overnight stops. Non-smoking, Disabled and Special Diets Supplements.

BRITAIN'S BEST HOLIDAYS
A quick-reference general guide for all kinds of holidays.

Recommended
SHORT BREAK HOLIDAYS in Britain
"Approved" accommodation for quality bargain breaks.

Recommended
COUNTRY HOTELS of Britain
Including Country Houses, for the discriminating.

Recommended
COUNTRY INNS & PUBS of Britain
Pubs, Inns and small hotels.

CHILDREN WELCOME!
Family Holidays and Days Out guide.
Family holidays with details of amenities for children and babies.   ☐

The FHG Guide to CARAVAN & CAMPING HOLIDAYS,
Caravans for hire, sites and holiday parks and centres.   ☐

SELF-CATERING HOLIDAYS
in Britain
Over 1000 addresses throughout for self-catering and caravans in Britain.   ☐

PETS WELCOME!
The original and unique guide for holidays for pet owners and their pets.   £8.99   ☐

Tick your choice above and send your order and payment to

**FHG Guides Ltd. Abbey Mill Business Centre
Seedhill, Paisley, Scotland PA1 1TJ
TEL: 0141- 887 0428 • FAX: 0141- 889 7204
e-mail: admin@fhguides.co.uk**

Deduct 10% for 2/3 titles or copies; 20% for 4 or more.

Send to: NAME ....

ADDRESS ....
....
....

POST CODE ....

I enclose Cheque/Postal Order for £ ....

SIGNATURE...DATE ....

Please complete the following to help us improve the service we provide.
How did you find out about our guides?:

☐ Press   ☐ Magazines   ☐ TV/Radio   ☐ Family/Friend   ☐ Other